W9-AUY-663

CANADA

Lake Superior

St. Lawrence R.

MAINE
1820

VT.
1791

N.H.

MASS.

CONN.

R.I.

Lake Michigan

Lake Huron

Lake Ontario

NEW YORK

THIRTEEN COLONIES

MINNESOTA
1858

WISCONSIN
1848

MICHIGAN
1837

Lake Erie

PENNSYLVANIA

NEW
JERSEY
1790

IOWA
1846

OHIO
1803

MASON-DIXON LINE

DELAWARE

INDIANA
1816

WEST
VIRGINIA
1863

MARYLAND

ILLINOIS
1818

THE ORIGINAL

VIRGINIA

ATLANTIC

OCEAN

MISSOURI
1821

KENTUCKY
1792

THE ORIGINAL UNITED STATES
(By Treaty with Britain, 1783)

MISSOURI
COMPROMISE
LINE   2000
36°30'N

NORTH
CAROLINA

TENNESSEE
1796

ARKANSAS
1836

Mississippi R.

SOUTH
CAROLINA

THE ORIGINAL

Territorial Growth
of the
United States

MISSISSIPPI
1817

ALABAMA
1819

GEORGIA

1820 Date of states admission to the Union

● Geographic center of population by decade

LOUISIANA
1812

(Seized from Spain,
1810, 1813)

0   150   300 Km.

0   150   300 Mi.

FLORIDA
(By Treaty with
Spain, 1819)

FLORIDA
1845

Gulf of Mexico

BAHAMAS

PUERTO RICO
(Acquired from
Spain, 1898)

VIRGIN IS.
(Acquired from
Denmark, 1916–1917)

19°N

68°W

PUERTO RICO

VIRGIN
ISLANDS

18°N

0 25 50 Km.

0   25   50 Mi.

67°W

66°W

65°W

CUBA

HAITI

DOMINICAN
REPUBLIC

CourseMate

Engaging. Trackable. Affordable.

CourseMate brings course concepts to life with interactive learning, study, and exam preparation tools that support the printed textbook. Watch student comprehension soar as your class works with both the book and the text-specific website. **History CourseMate** goes beyond the page to deliver what you need, with:

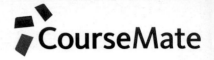

Engagement Tracker:

How do you assess your students' engagement in your course? How do you know your students have read the material or viewed the resources you've assigned? How can you tell if your students are struggling with a concept? With **CourseMate**, you can use the included Engagement Tracker to assess student preparation and engagement. Use the tracking tools to see progress for the class as a whole or for individual students. Identify students at risk early in the course. Uncover which concepts are most difficult for your class. Monitor time on task. Keep your students engaged!

Interactive eBook:

In addition to interactive teaching and learning tools, **CourseMate** includes an interactive eBook. Students can take notes, highlight, search and interact with embedded media specific to their book. Use it as a supplement to the printed text, or as a substitute—the choice is your students' with **CourseMate**.

Interactive Teaching and Learning Tools, including:

- Quizzes
- Flashcards
- Videos
- And more!

eAudio *The History Handbook* Podcasts

Carol Berkin and Betty Anderson's **eAudio *The History Handbook* Podcasts** allows students to download podcasts for each chapter of the text! Students will learn both basic and history-specific study skills such as how to read primary sources, research historical topics using print and online sources, and correctly cite sources. In addition to providing a no-nonsense guide to the skills needed in a history course, this handbook also introduces students to the type of questions historians ask and the sources they turn to for answers.

Students can purchase and download the complete eAudio handbook or any of its eighteen individual units to their computer or MP3 player from **CengageBrain.com**. Each 5-15 minute podcast addresses a separate topic designed to develop students' critical thinking and historical analysis skills.

American History Resource Center

This interactive website for American History offers students a wealth of support materials, including:

- **Thousands of live links** to trustworthy online sources
- **Hundreds of primary source materials**, from speeches and letters to legal documents, transcripts, and a variety of digitized original media
- **Online simulations** that actively introduce students to different historical periods and cultural perspectives
- **Interactive timelines** featuring embedded links to pictures of the people, places, and events that shaped particular periods
- **Extensive map resources** from Wadsworth history texts and additional sources—many of which are accompanied by assignable questions and Google Earth™ coordinates

The **American History Resource Center** is the ideal resource for student study, review, and research—and bundled access is free with this text! Ask your sales representative for more information.

Making America

Making America

A History of the United States

SIXTH EDITION

Carol Berkin
Baruch College, City University of New York

Christopher L. Miller
The University of Texas—Pan American

Robert W. Cherny
San Francisco State University

James L. Gormly
Washington and Jefferson College

WADSWORTH
CENGAGE Learning™

Australia • Brazil • Japan • Korea • Mexico • Singapore • Spain • United Kingdom • United States

WADSWORTH
CENGAGE Learning

Making America: A History of the United States, 6e

Berkin, Miller, Cherny, Gormly

Senior Publisher: Suzanne Jeans

Senior Sponsoring Editor: Ann West

Development Editor: Jan Fitter

Assistant Editor: Megan Chrisman

Senior Media Editor: Lisa Ciccolo

Senior Marketing Manager: Katherine Bates

Marketing Coordinator: Lorreen Pelletier

Marketing and Communication Director:
Talia Wise

Senior Content Project Manager:
Carol Newman

Senior Art Director: Cate Rickard Barr

Senior Print Buyer: Judy Inouye

Senior Rights Acquisition Specialist, Text:
Katie Huha

Senior Image Rights Specialist II:
Jennifer Meyer Dare

Production Service:
S4Carlisle Publishing Services

Photo Researcher: Bruce Carson

Text Designer:
Cia Boynton/Boynton Hue Studio

Cover Designer: Anthony L. Saizon

Cover Image: Benton, Thomas Hart (1889-1975)
© VAGA, NY Wheat, 1967. Oil on canvas,
20 × 21 in. (50.8 × 53.5 cm). Gift of Mr. and
Mrs. James A. Mitchell. © Copyright
VAGA, NY. Smithsonian American Art
Museum, Washington, DC, U.S.A.
Smithsonian American Art Museum,
Washington, DC/Art Resource, NY/
© T.H. Benton and R.P. Benton
Testamentary Trusts/UMB Bank Trustee/
Licensed by VAGA, New York, NY

Compositor: S4Carlisle Publishing Services

For product information and technology assistance, contact us at
Cengage Learning Customer & Sales Support, 1-800-354-9706

For permission to use material from this text or product, submit all requests
online at **www.cengage.com/permissions.**
Further permissions questions can be emailed to
permissionrequest@cengage.com.

Library of Congress Control Number: 2010931814

Student Edition:
ISBN-13: 978-0-495-90979-8
ISBN-10: 0-495-90979-3

High School Edition:
ISBN-13: 978-0-495-89964-8
ISBN-10: 0-495-89964-X

Wadsworth
20 Channel Center Street
Boston, MA 02210
USA

Cengage Learning is a leading provider of customized learning solutions
with office locations around the globe, including Singapore, the United
Kingdom, Australia, Mexico, Brazil and Japan. Locate your local office at
international.cengage.com/region

Cengage Learning products are represented in Canada by Nelson Education, Ltd.

For your course and learning solutions, visit **www.cengage.com.**

Purchase any of our products at your local college store or at our preferred online
store **www.cengagebrain.com.**

Printed in the United States of America
1 2 3 4 5 6 7 14 13 12 11 10

Brief Contents

Contents

Maps

Features

Preface

Like all history teachers, the authors of this book have heard the groans that arise from a class as students open the textbook. They see page after page of densely packed information, destined to be highlighted or underlined, memorized, and then quickly forgotten. We all agreed: There must be a better way, a way to convey the excitement, the human drama, the surprising twists and turns, the individual and collective stories of success and failure that made our American past. This complex story should be told clearly and engagingly. And "how we know," as much as "what we know," should be shared with students, so that as soon as they begin to read Chapter 1, they too are historians, playing an active role in reconstructing the past. This conviction—that a textbook can challenge students intellectually and spark their curiosity about the past as well as provide them with necessary information—has been, and remains, the guiding principle behind *Making America*.

To achieve our goal, we had to know our students. As professors in large public universities located on three of the nation's borders—the Pacific Ocean, the Atlantic, and the Rio Grande—we are keenly aware that today's classroom reflects our cultural diversity, our mix of native-born students and recent immigrants, those for whom English is a first language and those for whom it is a second or even a third tongue. Every class may include a significant number of serious-minded men and women whose formal skills lag behind their interest and enthusiasm for learning. Thus, from its first edition to its present one, we made certain that our textbook built on certain key elements. It offers a chronological, historical narrative that does not assume or demand a lot of prior knowledge about the American past. It does not rely solely on words to tell this story, for we know that people, places, and events can be brought to life through maps, paintings, photos, and cartoons as well as the written word. Our book speaks to students in a voice that strives to communicate rather than impress, sharing with them the difficult questions we seek to answer in each chapter. To help them draw their own conclusions about the causes and consequences of individual choices, public policies, political decisions, protest, and reform, we provide primary source materials on which they can build their own interpretations. Perhaps most importantly, this book offers a full array of integrated and supportive learning aids to help students at every level of preparedness comprehend what they read.

Over the years we have remained learners as well as teachers. In each edition of *Making America* we have listened to its readers, both professors and students, and made changes to improve the book. Thus, this sixth edition has eliminated elements that did not prove effective and added features that we believe will help us convey the pleasure and value of understanding the people of the past and their role in making America.

The Approach

Professors and students who have used the previous editions of *Making America* will recognize immediately that we have preserved many of its central features. We have again set the nation's complex story within an explicitly political chronology, relying on a basic and familiar structure that is nevertheless broad enough to accommodate generous attention to social, economic, and diplomatic aspects of our national history. Because our own scholarly research often focuses on the experiences of women, immigrants, African Americans, and Native Americans, we would not have been content with a framework that marginalized their history. *Making America* continues to be built on the premise that all Americans are historically active figures, playing significant roles in creating the history of our nation's development. We have also continued what is now a tradition in *Making America*, that is, providing pedagogical tools for students that allow them to master complex material and enable them to develop analytical skills.

Themes

The sixth edition continues to weave five central themes through the narrative. The first of these themes, the political development of the nation, is evident in the text's coverage of the creation and revision of the federal and local governments, the contests waged over domestic and diplomatic policies, the internal and external crises faced by the United States and its political institutions, and the history of political parties and elections.

The second theme is the diversity of a national citizenry created by both Native Americans and immigrants. To do justice to this theme, *Making America* explores not only English and European immigration during the early settling of the country but the full array of groups immigrating to the North American continent from Paleolithic times to the present. The text attends to the tensions and conflicts that arise in a diverse population, but it also examines the shared values and aspirations that define middle-class American lives.

Making America's third theme is the significance of regional subcultures and economies. This regional theme is developed for society before European colonization and for the colonial settlements of the seventeenth and eighteenth centuries. It is evident in our attention to the striking social and cultural divergences that existed between the American Southwest and the Atlantic coastal regions and between the antebellum South and North, as well as significant differences in social and economic patterns in the West.

A fourth theme is the rise and impact of large social movements, from the Great Awakening in the 1740s to the rise of youth cultures in the post–World War II generations, movements prompted by changing material conditions or by new ideas challenging the status quo.

The fifth theme is the relationship of the United States to other nations. In *Making America* we explore in depth the causes and consequences of this nation's role in world conflict and diplomacy, whether in the era of colonization of the Americas, the eighteenth-century independence movement, the removal of Indian nations from their traditional lands, the impact of the rhetoric of manifest destiny, American policies of isolationism and interventionism, or the modern role of the United States as a dominant player in world affairs. Viewing American history in a global context, we point out the parallels and the contrasts between our society and those of other nations.

Learning Features

The chapters in *Making America* provide students with essential study aids. The first page of each chapter begins with "**Behind the Stories**," a message from the author that sets the tone for that chapter. Like the book itself, "Behind the Stories" bridges the gap between reader and author and between student and historian. The author explains why the events that will unfold in the chapter continue to capture his or her personal interest. The author also conveys some of the challenges he or she faced in uncovering what happened, why it happened, and who played a critical role in making it happen. Many "Behind the Stories" messages invite readers to take up these challenges themselves. Others unveil linkages between the current and previous chapters, reminding students that decisions made in one era or time period shape choices in the next.

"Behind the Stories" is followed by a topical **outline** of the material students will encounter in the chapter.

On the second page, "**Individual Choices**" spotlights a woman or man whose experiences provide a window on the major events and themes of the chapter and whose own words, whether public or private, are part of the written record of the era relied upon by historians. Whether historical figures or lesser-known individuals, these people demonstrate the importance of individual agency, or the ability to make choices and act on them.

To help students focus on the broad questions and themes, we provide critical thinking **focus questions** at the beginning of each major chapter section. Students can use these focus questions as guideposts to prepare for reading and also as review prompts to help remember the important points to take from a section. At the end of the chapter, "**Individual Voices**" offers a primary source related to the "Individual Choices" profile at the beginning of the chapter—with thought-provoking questions and comments about that source. These primary sources allow historical figures to speak for themselves and encourage students to engage directly in historical analysis. An introduction to each source explains how the source can aid historians in understanding the era and its events.

Each chapter concludes with "**Study Tools**," which include a summary that reinforces the most important themes and information covered in the chapter; a chronology that lists key events discussed in the chapter; a restatement of the focus questions that have guided the students as they read each section; and finally, a list of the glossary terms that are highlighted as key study terms in the on-page glossary, with page numbers provided for review. These tools can help students gain a firmer understanding of the material they have just read.

Within each chapter students will encounter several distinctive features that will help them get the most out of their reading. First, *Making America* provides a unique on-page glossary that defines two types of words for students. The first type is basic vocabulary—words that might trip up some students. The glossary defines words such as "allegory," "impeach," and "dividend" and each word's historical context to assure that students understand the full meaning of a discussion. The second type of term highlighted and defined includes major historical events, people, phrases, and documents. These historical key terms are annotated with a color bullet to emphasize their importance to the historical narrative. We believe that this approach will help students simultaneously build their vocabularies and review for tests; it reflects our concern about communicating fully with student readers without sacrificing the complexity of the history we are relating.

The sixth edition also retains the popular feature "**It Matters Today**," which points out critical connections between current events and past ones. This feature includes discussion and reflection questions that challenge students to examine and evaluate these connections. We hope that these brief essays will also provide a spark for faculty and students to generate their own additional "It Matters Today" discussions on other key issues within the chapter. The new feature entitled "**In the Wider World**" introduces a global perspective on the era covered in each chapter. It reminds students that, no matter how significant or how unique to American society an event or development may be, it always exists within the context of a world in motion around it.

Finally, the illustrations in each chapter were chosen carefully to provide a visual connection to the past that is useful rather than simply decorative. The captions that accompany these illustrations analyze the subject of the painting, photograph, or artifact—and relate it to the narrative. For this edition we have selected many new illustrations to reinforce or illustrate the themes of the narrative.

New to This Edition

In this new edition we have preserved what our colleagues and their students considered the best and most useful aspects of *Making America*, including the strong narrative voice, the respect for chronology, and features such as Individual Choices, Individual Voices, and focus questions. We have replaced what was less successful, revised what could be improved, and added new elements to strengthen the book. We have also introduced a new, slightly more spacious format. Miraculously, we have achieved these goals while reducing the overall page count.

Our "In the Wider World" feature is new and reflects the recent emphasis on understanding American history within a global context. We have also introduced several new Individual Choices and Individual Voices profiles and primary sources. In addition, *Making America*'s maps have been revised to improve their clarity, geographical detail, and attractiveness. Our most significant new feature is the end-of-chapter "Study Tools," which, as described above, provides students with the tools they will need to review what they have learned and to formulate their own analysis of its significance.

We have made important changes in the text itself. Many of these changes are based on reviewer feedback, and all of them reflect our commitment to incorporating the newest scholarship and to producing a coherent narrative, rather than an oversimplified one. Perhaps the most significant change to this edition was made as part of our ongoing effort to pace the content in a way that reflects current teaching needs. The four chapters covering the period from 1865 to 1900 have been reduced to three chapters. Details about how this was accomplished—and other chapter revisions—are as follows:

Chapter 1
- New Individual Choices on Wahunsunacock (The Powhatan).
- New Individual Voices (visual source) on Powhatan's Mantle.
- New In the Wider World on migration in the South Pacific.

Chapter 2
- An added discussion reflects new scholarship on the Protestant role in establishing New France.
- New In the Wider World on Russian exploration in America.

Chapter 3
- Coverage of the Jamestown settlement has been revised and updated.
- New In the Wider World feature on religious conflict.

Chapter 4
- Added discussion of support among a minority in British politics for the colonists' position on government policies.
- A revised Behind the Stories feature focuses on regional differences and similarities.
- New In the Wider World feature on the scientific orientation of the era.

Chapter 5
- A revised Behind the Stories feature focuses on the choice of loyalties on the eve of the American Revolution.
- New In the Wider World feature on Quianlong's empire in the Far East.

Chapter 6
- New Individual Choices and Individual Voices features on Esther DeBerdt Reed and "Sentiments of an American Woman."
- New In the Wider World feature on the British in India.

Chapter 7
- Streamlined and tightened throughout.
- New Individual Choices and Individual Voices features on Gouverneur Morris.
- New In the Wider World feature on rebellions abroad.

Chapter 8
- New It Matters Today feature on the peaceful transition of power.
- New coverage of Gabriel's rebellion.
- Addition on Jefferson's attitude toward women.
- New In the Wider World feature on slave rebellion in San Domingue and the Republic of Haiti.

Chapter 9
- New emphasis on historiography in Behind the Stories.

- New coverage of Denmark Vesey's conspiracy.
- New In the Wider World feature on Luddites.

Chapter 10
- Discussion of Jackson's administration reorganized.
- New Individual Choices and Individual Voices on Martin Van Buren.
- New In the Wider World feature on the slavery debate in Britain.

Chapter 11
- New Individual Choices and Individual Voices on Elizabeth Yale Hancock.
- New In the Wider World feature on transoceanic steamers.

Chapter 12
- New In the Wider World feature on Russian imperial expansion.
- The section on the Mexican War has been moved to Chapter 13.

Chapter 13
- Coverage of the Mexican War has been moved into this chapter.
- Added explanation of the beginning of the Free Soil Party and the outcome of the 1848 election.
- Discussion of the Know-Nothings has been revised and tightened.

Chapter 14
- New In the Wider World on the Geneva Convention.
- Several new maps illustrating Civil War events.

Chapter 15
- New Individual Choices and Individual Voices features on Blanche K. Bruce.
- New In the Wider World feature on abolition around the world.

Chapters 16–18 combine and consolidate material covered in Chapters 16–19 of the fifth edition, reducing four chapters to three. In addition, the following revisions have been made:

Chapter 16 The Nation Industrializes, 1865–1900
- Chapter 16 now focuses largely on the emergence of an industrial economy, including the role of specific entrepreneurs, the rise of big business, and the roles of technology and finance.
- New Individual Choices and Individual Voices on John D. Rockefeller.
- New In the Wider World feature on cartels.
- Discussion of the economic transformation of the West (previously in a separate chapter) is now integrated into a chapter that addresses the whole national economy.

- Similarly, additional coverage of the South emphasizes economic developments, including advocacy of a New South.

Chapter 17 Life in the Gilded Age, 1865–1900
- Chapter 17 now focuses largely on new social and cultural patterns, especially urbanization, immigration, ethnic and racial relations, and changing gender roles.
- A new section has been added on changing social patterns in the New South.
- New Individual Choices and Individual Voices features on Frank Roney on the dignity of labor.
- New In the Wider World feature on racial separation in South Africa.

Chapter 18 Politics and Foreign Relations in a Rapidly Changing Nation, 1865–1902
- This chapter now focuses centrally on domestic politics and foreign relations, including the dominant role of political parties in the 1870s and 1880s, various radical and reform groups, Populism, and short-term and long-term results of the election of 1896.
- New Individual Choices and Individual Voices features on Carl Schurz.
- New In the Wider World feature on woman suffrage around the world.

Chapter 19 (formerly 20)
- New coverage added on Southern Progressivism.
- New In the Wider World feature on the scramble for last colonies.

Chapter 20 (formerly 21)
- Analysis of Wilson's decision to go to war has been revised.
- New data regarding civilian deaths in World War I.
- New In the Wider World feature on demonizing the enemy.

Chapter 21 (formerly 22)
- New Individual Voices (visual source) on sexual innuendo in movie advertising, featuring ads for films.
- New In the Wider World feature on hyperinflation in Germany.

Chapter 22 (formerly 23)
- This chapter has been significantly expanded and revised throughout.
- Text revisions include new statistics on 1929 suicide rates and the effect of the Crash on the Dow Jones average; expanded discussion of the role of installment buying; tightened and clarified discussion of banks and credit; expanded attention to the U.S. Communist Party; new analysis of the First Hundred Days; expanded coverage of labor

action in 1934; expanded coverage of the Second Hundred Days; more on cultural expression during this period.
- New It Matters Today feature discusses lessons applied in 2008–2009 to avoid another depression.

Chapter 23 (formerly 24)
- Provides new information on U.S. economic and security preparations as the Roosevelt administration responded to the conflicts in Europe and Asia.
- Provides new discussion and examples of women's role in the wartime economy.
- The ideology of fascism is featured in the new In the Wider World feature.

Chapter 24 (formerly 25)
- New Individual Choices highlights baseball great Jackie Robinson; the Individual Voice section presents two editorials from the *Sporting News* discussing race and baseball.
- Material on Latino postwar experiences has been expanded.
- Material on the origins of the Cold War has been revised and incorporates Kennan's "Long Telegram" as part of the text; an excerpt of Novikov's long telegram remains as an insert to provide a Soviet perspective.
- A new In the Wider World features an examination of Simone de Beauvoir's *The Second Sex.*

Chapter 25 (formerly 26)
- Provides expanded information on the economic changes and concerns of the 1950s, including the movement toward conglomerates.
- A new In the Wider World feature focuses on China's Great Leap Forward.

Chapter 26 (formerly 27)
- New Individual Choices and Voices features focus on Eunice Kennedy Shriver's involvement in the development of the Special Olympics.
- Provides a new discussion of student activism involved in the Students for a Democratic Society and in the Free Speech movements.
- The new In the Wider World feature spotlights the "Prague Spring."

Chapter 27 (formerly 28)
- Sections on Nixon's domestic programs and Watergate are revised and expanded.
- Discussion of environmental issues includes material on Rachel Carson and a new It Matters Today feature focuses on DDT.
- The new In the Wider World feature examines OPEC and the Oil Shock of 1973.
- A new Individual Voices highlights a Dolores Huerta speech discussing Mexican American activism.

Chapter 28 (formerly 29)
- The chapter has been reorganized and includes a new section, "New Economic and Political Alignments, 1976–1992."
- Expanded coverage of the Americans with Disabilities Act.
- A new It Matters Today explores the topic of migrant workers.
- The new In the Wider World looks at Deng Xiaoping's Economic Plan and the origins of China's economic surge.

Chapter 29 (formerly 30)
- New chapter title, "Entering a New Century, 1992–2010," reflects revised and updated coverage and focus.
- New Individual Choices examines the decisions made by Evan Williams, whose companies developed the "Blogger" and "Twitter" programs, while the new Individual Voices, "Is Google Making Us Stupid?" by Nicholas Carr, provides a guarded assessment of new technology.
- Revised coverage of the Clinton administration includes the Clinton/Mitchell role in the Northern Ireland peace process.
- The It Matters Today feature on Islamic fundamentalism is now in this chapter.
- Updated through Obama's first year and a half in office, including material on the Great Recession and the recovery plans offered by Bush and Obama, the struggle over the passage of a national healthcare plan, the Tea Party movement, and the Gulf disaster.
- The In the Wider World feature provides a snapshot of those nations currently using forms of government-run or -directed national healthcare services.

We, the authors of *Making America*, believe that this new edition will be effective in the history classroom. Please let us know what you think.

Learning and Teaching Ancillaries

The program for this edition of *Making America* includes a number of useful learning and teaching aids. These ancillaries are designed to help students get the most from the course and to provide instructors with useful course management and presentation tools.

Kelly Woestman has been involved with *Making America* through previous editions and has taken an even more substantive role in the sixth edition. We suspect that no other technology author has been so well integrated into the author team as Kelly has been with our team, and we are certain that this will add significantly to the value of these resources.

Instructor Resources

Instructor Companion Site Instructors will find here all the tools they need to teach a rich and successful U.S. history survey course. The protected teaching materials include the Instructor's Resource Manual, customizable Microsoft® PowerPoint® slides of both lecture outlines and images from the text, and JoinIn® PowerPoint® slides with clicker content. The companion website also provides instructors with access to HistoryFinder and to the Wadsworth American History Resource Center (see descriptions below). Go to www.Cengage.com/history to access this site.

PowerLecture CD-ROM with ExamView® and JoinIn® This dual-platform, all-in-one multimedia resource includes the Instructor's Resource Manual, Test Bank in Word and PDF formats, customizable Microsoft® PowerPoint® slides of both lecture outlines and images from the text, and *JoinIn*® PowerPoint® slides with clicker content. Also included is ExamView, an easy-to-use assessment and tutorial system that allows instructors to create, deliver, and customize tests in minutes.

HistoryFinder This searchable online database allows instructors to quickly and easily search and download selections from among thousands of assets, including art, photographs, maps, primary sources, and audio/video clips. Each asset downloads directly into a Microsoft® PowerPoint® slide, allowing instructors to easily create exciting PowerPoint presentations for their classrooms.

eInstructor's Resource Manual Prepared by Kelly Woestman of Pittsburg State University, this manual includes instructional objectives, chapter outlines and summaries, lecture suggestions, suggested debate and research topics, cooperative learning activities, and suggested readings and resources. Available on the instructor's companion website and from the Power-Lecture CD.

WebTutor™ on Blackboard® and WebCT® With WebTutor's text-specific, pre-formatted content and total flexibility, instructors can easily create and manage their own custom course website. WebTutor's course management tool gives instructors the ability to provide virtual office hours, post syllabi, set up threaded discussions, track student progress with the quizzing material, and much more. For students, WebTutor offers real-time access to a full array of study tools, including audio chapter summaries, practice quizzes, glossary flashcards, and weblinks.

CourseMate Cengage Learning's CourseMate brings course concepts to life with interactive learning, study, and exam preparation tools that support the printed textbook. Watch student comprehension soar as your class works with the printed textbook and the *Making America* CourseMate site with interactive teaching and learning tools and EngagementTracker, a first-of-its-kind tool that monitors student engagement in the course. Learn more at www.cengagebrain.com.

Student Resources

CourseMate For students, the *Making America* CourseMate website provides an additional source of interactive learning, study, and exam preparation outside the classroom. Students will find outlines and objectives, focus questions, flashcards, quizzes, primary source links, and video clips. The CourseMate site also includes an integrated *Making America* eBook. Students taking quizzes will be linked directly to relevant sections in the ebook for additional information. The ebook is fully searchable and students can even take notes and save them for later review. In addition, the ebook links to rich media assets such as video and MP3 chapter summaries, primary source documents with critical thinking questions, and interactive (zoomable) maps. Students can use the ebook as their primary text or as a companion multimedia support. Available at www.cengagebrain.com.

Wadsworth American History Resource Center This gives your students access to a "virtual reader" with hundreds of primary sources, including speeches, letters, legal documents and transcripts, poems, maps, simulations, timelines, and additional images that bring history to life, along with interactive assignable exercises. A map feature including Google Earth™ coordinates and exercises will aid in student comprehension of geography and use of maps. Students can compare the traditional textbook map with an aerial view of the location today. It's an ideal resource for study, review, and research. In addition to this map feature, the resource center also provides blank maps for student review and testing. Ask your sales representative for more information on how to bundle access to the HRC with your text.

cengagebrain.com Save your students time and money. Direct them to www.cengagebrain.com for choice in formats and savings and a better chance to succeed in class. Students have the freedom to purchase à la carte exactly what they need when they need it. There, students can purchase a downloadable ebook or electronic access to the American History Resource Center, the premium study tools and interactive ebook in the *Making America* CourseMate, or eAudio modules from *The History Handbook* (see below). Students can save 50 percent on the electronic textbook and can pay as little as $1.99 for an individual eChapter.

***The History Handbook,* 2e** Written by Carol Berkin of Baruch College, City University of New York, and Betty Anderson of Boston University, this book teaches students both basic and history-specific study skills such as how to take notes, get the most out of lectures and readings, read primary sources, research historical topics, and correctly cite sources. Substantially less expensive than comparable skill-building texts, *The History Handbook* also offers tips for Internet research and evaluating online sources. Additionally, students can purchase and download the **eAudio** version of *The History Handbook* or any of its eighteen individual units at www.cengagebrain .com to listen to on-the-go.

Doing History: Research and Writing in the Digital Age, 1e [ISBN: 0534619533 and 9780534619534] Prepared by Michael J. Galgano, J. Chris Arndt, and Raymond M. Hyser of James Madison University. Whether you're starting down the path as a history major, or simply looking for a straightforward and systematic guide to writing a successful paper, you'll find this text to be an indispensable handbook to historical research. This text's "soup to nuts" approach to researching and writing about history addresses every step of the process, from locating your sources and gathering information, to writing clearly and making proper use of various citation styles to avoid plagiarism. You'll also learn how to make the most of every tool available to you—especially the technology that helps you conduct the process efficiently and effectively.

Reader Program Cengage Learning publishes a number of readers, some containing exclusively primary sources, others a combination of primary and secondary sources, and many designed to guide students through the process of historical inquiry. Visit www .Cengage.com/history for a complete list of readers or ask your sales representative to recommend a reader that would work well for your specific needs.

Custom Options

Nobody knows your students like you, so why not give them a text that is tailor-fit to their needs? Cengage Learning offers custom solutions for your course—whether it's making a small modification to *Making America* to match your syllabus or combining multiple sources to create something truly unique. You can pick and choose chapters, include your own material, and add additional map exercises along with the Rand McNally Atlas (including questions developed around the maps in the atlas) to create a text that fits the way you teach. Ensure that your students get the most out of their textbook dollar by giving them exactly what they need. Contact your Cengage Learning representative to explore custom solutions for your course.

CourseReader Our new CourseReader lets you create a customized electronic reader in minutes! With our easy-to-use interface and assessment tool, you can choose exactly what your students will be assigned—simply search or browse Cengage Learning's extensive document database to preview and select your customized collection of readings.

Once you've made your choice, students will always receive the pedagogical support they need to succeed with the materials you've chosen: each source document includes a descriptive headnote that puts the reading into context, and every selection is further supported by both critical thinking and multiple-choice questions designed to reinforce key points.

Rand McNally Atlas of American History, 2e [ISBN: 0618842012 and 9780618842018] This comprehensive atlas features more than eighty maps, with new content covering global perspectives, including events in the Middle East from 1945 to 2005, as well as population trends in the United States and around the world. Additional maps document voyages of discovery; the settling of the colonies; major U.S. military engagements, including the American Revolution and World Wars I and II; and sources of immigrations, ethnic populations, and patterns of economic change.

Acknowledgments

The authors of *Making America* have benefited greatly from the critical reading of this edition of the book by instructors from across the country. We would like to thank these scholars and teachers who provided feedback for this current revision:

Tom Angle, Metropolitan Community College
Anthony Beninati, Valencia Community College
Martha Bonte, Clinton Community College,
    Eastern Iowa Community College District
Scott Buchanan, South Plains College
Thomas Clarkin, San Antonio College
Robert Cray, Montclair State University
Latangela Crossfield, Paine College
Jeffrey Davis, Bloomsburg University of
    Pennsylvania
Julian DelGaudio, Long Beach City College
Gretchen Eick, Friends University
Jennifer Fry, King's College
Michael Gabriel, Kutztown University
Leah Hagedorn, Tidewater Community College
Stephen Katz, Community College of Philadelphia
Kurt Kortenhof, Saint Paul College
Mark Kuss, Our Lady of Holy Cross College
Margaret Lowe, Bridgewater State College

Mark McCarthy, Southern New Hampshire
  University Online
Suzanne McCormack, Community College of
  Rhode Island
Todd Menzing, Saddleback College
Rebecca Montgomery, Texas State University
Bryant Morrison, South Texas College
David Parker, California State
  University–Northridge
Laura Perry, The University of Memphis
Steven Rauch, Augusta State University
Kathryn Rokitski, Old Dominion University
James Seaman, Saddleback College
Carey Shellman, Armstrong Atlantic State
  University

Carol Berkin, who is responsible for Chapters 3 through 7, wants to acknowledge the colleagues and students who suggested interesting new Individual Choices and primary sources for her chapters. She also thanks the many teachers across the country whom she met as she participated in Teaching American History grant programs for their excellent ideas about what makes a textbook useful in the classroom. She offers special thanks to Margaret Crocco and Barbara Winslow, her co-editors on a new book on teaching women's history, for the long conversations about how to make history exciting to students of all ages. As always, she thanks her children, Hannah and Matthew, for their support as she revised this book.

Christopher L. Miller, who is responsible for Chapters 1 and 2 and 8 through 14, is indebted to the community at the University of Texas—Pan American for providing the constant inspiration to innovate. Colleagues, including David Carlson, Amy M. Hay, and Kristine Wirts, were particularly helpful in identifying events to include in the In the Wider World features. Colleagues on various H-net discussion lists as always were generous with advice, guidance, and often abstruse points of information. As in each of

our collaborative projects, thanks are owed to Carol Berkin, Bob Cherny, and Jim Gormly and to Kelly Woestman.

Robert W. Cherny, who is responsible for Chapters 15 through 22, wishes to thank his students who, over the years, have provided the testing ground for much that is included in these chapters, and especially to thank his colleagues and research assistants who have helped with the previous editions and Sarah Alexander, his research assistant for this edition. Much of the revision was done while in residence as a Fulbright Scholar at the Heidelberg Center for American Studies, University of Heidelberg, and thanks are due to the faculty and staff there, especially Mischa Honeck. The staff of the Leonard Library at San Francisco State has always been most helpful. Rebecca Marshall Cherny, Sarah Cherny, and Lena Hobbs Kracht Cherny have been unfailing in their encouragement, inspiration, and support.

James L. Gormly, who is responsible for Chapters 23 through 30, would like to acknowledge the support and encouragement he received from Washington and Jefferson College. He wants to gives a special thanks to Sharon Gormly, whose support, ideas, advice, and critical eye have helped to shape and refine his chapters.

As always, this book is a collaborative effort between authors and the editorial staff of Wadsworth, Cengage Learning. We would like to thank Ann West, senior sponsoring editor; Megan Chrisman, assistant editor; Carol Newman, senior content project manager; Bruce Carson, who helped us fill this edition with remarkable illustrations, portraits, and photographs; and Charlotte Miller, who helped us improve the maps in the book. Finally, but far from least, we thank Jan Fitter, our always patient and tactful text editor, who made our prose clearer and more concise in every chapter. These talented, committed members of the publishing world encouraged us and generously assisted us every step of the way.

A Note for the Students

YOUR GUIDE TO *MAKING AMERICA*

Dear Student:

History is about people—brilliant and insane, brave and treacherous, lovable and hateful, murderers and princesses, daredevils and visionaries, rule breakers and rule makers. It has exciting events, major crises, turning points, battles, and scientific breakthroughs. We, the authors of *Making America*, believe that knowing about the past is critical for anyone who hopes to understand the present and chart the future. In this book, we want to tell you the story of America from its earliest settlement to the present and to tell it in a language and format that helps you enjoy learning that history.

This book is organized and designed to help you master your American History course. The narrative is chronological, telling the story as it happened, decade by decade or era by era. We have developed special tools to help you learn. In the following pages, we'll introduce you to the unique features of this book that will not only help you understand the complex and fascinating story of American history but also provide you the tools to "do" history yourself.

At the back of the book, you will find some additional resources. The Appendix provides an annotated, chapter-by-chapter list of suggested readings. You will also find reprinted several of the most important documents in American history: the Declaration of Independence, the Articles of Confederation, and the Constitution. Here, too, a table gives you quick access to important data on presidential elections. Finally, you will see the index, which will help you locate a subject quickly if you want to read about it. Terms that appear in the on-page glossary are bold-faced in the index.

In addition, you will find a number of useful study tools on the *Making America* Coursemate website. These include map and chronology exercises, chapter quizzes, and primary sources—all geared to help you study, do research, and take tests effectively. Here, now, is some additional advice on how to approach your learning experience.

How to Succeed in Your History Course

We know that, at first glance, a history textbook can seem overwhelming. There is so much to learn, so much to remember, so much to think about. The features of *Making America* are all designed to help you conquer your anxiety and enjoy your journey through the American past. Here are a few tips to make this a smoother trip:

- Follow all the clues the authors provide. What are the important issues raised in the Individual Choices story? How many of the key topics in the chapter outline are familiar to you—and which ones are new? Don't just pay attention to the unfamiliar material; read carefully how the authors describe those events you have encountered before. Surprises may be in store. Use the focus questions as your guide to each major section of the chapter. Don't highlight everything. Read the whole section once; then read it again to find the answers to the focus questions. They are there because they point to the most important issues in the section.

- Don't skip over unfamiliar words in the text. Use the glossary to help you understand the reading—and to increase your vocabulary. That vocabulary will come in handy if you are asked to write an exam essay.

- Use the study tools feature to test your own strengths and weaknesses as you prepare for an exam. Would your own summary of the chapter be similar to the summary the authors provide? Can you remember the context for the events that appear in the chapter chronology? Can you answer the focus questions now that you have read and taken notes on the chapter? Would you be able to identify and explain the significance of the key terms if your professor required you to do so? If not, page numbers will help you review and strengthen your command of the material.

Working with Primary Sources The Individual Voices feature at the end of each chapter lets you try your hand at doing the work of a historian. Increasingly, professors ask students to examine and analyze primary sources. This feature gives you a primary source document that we have annotated to show you what kinds of questions historians hope the source can answer. We call this process "interrogating the source," much as a detective interrogates a witness. Often the questions historians ask cannot be answered by a single source, and so we turn to other sources to help us piece together the puzzle of the past. Any public, official, or private document, any illustration or portrait, even any artifact that was created during the era we are examining is a primary source. You can find them in books, in historical societies, in libraries, and sometimes in your own attic.

In addition to those in the book, *Making America* offers you a wealth of primary sources on its website, and your professor is likely to distribute some in the class. Practice analyzing some primary sources, asking questions such as: Who was the person who created this source? Under what circumstances was it created? What prompted this person to write this document or to paint this portrait or to build this house or make this piece of clothing or this tool or weapon? Was the author a reliable witness or was he or she a participant in the event being described? Does this source agree with or contradict other sources you have found? Does it challenge the interpretations you have read in history books?

This type of analysis is not only useful for success in a history class. It will also benefit you as you read the newspaper, watch today's news on the Web or TV, or listen to the critical arguments of your own day. It will help you form your own independent judgments about the world around you.

We hope that our textbook conveys to you our own fascination with the American past and sparks your curiosity about the nation's history. We invite you to share your feedback on the book: you can reach us through Wadsworth Cengage's **Making America CourseMate website**, which you'll find initially at www .cengagebrain.com.

CAROL BERKIN, CHRIS MILLER,
BOB CHERNY, *and* JIM GORMLY

About the Authors

CAROL BERKIN

Born in Mobile, Alabama, Carol Berkin received her undergraduate degree from Barnard College and her Ph.D. from Columbia University. Her dissertation won the Bancroft Award. She is now Presidential Professor of history at Baruch College and the Graduate Center of City University of New York. She has written *Jonathan Sewall: Odyssey of an American Loyalist* (1974); *First Generations: Women in Colonial America* (1996); *A Brilliant Solution: Inventing the American Constitution* (2002); *Revolutionary Mothers: Women in the Struggle for America's Independence* (2005); and *Civil War Wives: The Lives and Times of Angelina Grimke Weld, Varina Howell Davis, and Julia Dent Grant* (2009). She has edited *Women of America: A History* (with Mary Beth Norton, 1979); *Women, War and Revolution* (with Clara M. Lovett, 1980); *Women's Voices, Women's Lives: Documents in Early American History* (with Leslie Horowitz, 1998); *Looking Forward/Looking Back: A Women's Studies Reader* (with Judith Pinch and Carole Appel, 2005); and *Clio in the Classroom: A Guide to Teaching U.S. Women's History* (with Margaret Crocco and Barbara Winslow, 2009). Professor Berkin edits *History Now,* an online journal for teachers sponsored by The Gilder Lehrman Institute of American History. She has appeared in the PBS series *Liberty! The American Revolution; Ben Franklin;* and *Alexander Hamilton;* and The History Channel's *Founding Fathers.* She has served on the Planning Committee for the U.S. Department of Education's National Assessment of Educational Progress, and chaired the CLEP Committee for Educational Testing Service. She currently serves on the Board of Trustees of The Gilder Lehrman Institute of American History and The National Council for History Education and is an elected member of the American Antiquarian Society and The Society of American Historians.

CHRISTOPHER L. MILLER

Born and raised in Portland, Oregon, Christopher L. Miller received his bachelor of science degree from Lewis and Clark College and his Ph.D. from the University of California, Santa Barbara. He is currently associate professor of history at the University of Texas—Pan American. He is the author of *Prophetic Worlds: Indians and Whites on the Columbia Plateau* (1985), which was republished (2003) as part of the Columbia Northwest Classics Series by the University of Washington Press. His articles and reviews have appeared in numerous scholarly journals and anthologies as well as standard reference works. Dr. Miller is also active in contemporary Indian affairs, having served, for example, as a participant in the American Indian Civics Project funded by the Kellogg Foundation. He has been a research fellow at the Charles Warren Center for Studies in American History at Harvard University and was the Nikolay V. Sivachev Distinguished

Chair in American History at Lemonosov Moscow State University (Russia). Professor Miller has also been active in projects designed to improve history teaching, including programs funded by the Meadows Foundation, the U.S. Department of Education, and other agencies.

ROBERT W. CHERNY

Born in Marysville, Kansas, and raised in Beatrice, Nebraska, Robert W. Cherny received his B.A. from the University of Nebraska and his M.A. and Ph.D. from Columbia University. He is professor of history at San Francisco State University. His books include *Competing Visions: A History of California* (with Richard Griswold del Castillo and Gretchen Lemke Santangelo, 2005); *American Politics in the Gilded Age, 1868–1900* (1997); *San Francisco, 1865–1932: Politics, Power, and Urban Development* (with William Issel, 1986); *A Righteous Cause: The Life of William Jennings Bryan* (1985, 1994); and *Populism, Progressivism, and the Transformation of Nebraska Politics, 1885–1915* (1981). He is co-editor of *California Women and Politics from the Gold Rush to the Great Depression* (with Mary Ann Irwin and Ann Marie Wilson, 2011) and of *American Labor and the Cold War: Unions, Politics, and Postwar Political Culture* (with William Issel and Keiran Taylor, 2004). In 2000, he and Ellen Du Bois co-edited a special issue of the *Pacific Historical Review* that surveyed woman suffrage movements in nine locations around the Pacific Rim. Most of his thirty articles in journals and anthologies have dealt with politics and labor in the late nineteenth and early twentieth centuries. He has been an NEH Fellow, Distinguished Fulbright Lecturer at Lomonosov Moscow State University (Russia), Visiting Research Scholar at the University of Melbourne (Australia), and Senior Fulbright Scholar at the Heidelberg Center for American Studies, University of Heidelberg (Germany). He has served as president of H-Net (an association of more than one hundred electronic networks for scholars in the humanities and social sciences), the Society for Historians of the Gilded Age and Progressive Era, and the Southwest Labor Studies Association; as treasurer of the Organization of American Historians; and as a member of the council of the American Historical Association, Pacific Coast Branch.

JAMES L. GORMLY

Born in Riverside, California, James L. Gormly received a B.A. from the University of Arizona and his M.A. and Ph.D. from the University of Connecticut. He is now professor of history and chair of the history department at Washington and Jefferson College. He has written *The Collapse of the Grand Alliance* (1970) and *From Potsdam to the Cold War* (1979). His articles and reviews have appeared in *Diplomatic History, The Journal of American History, The American Historical Review, The Historian, The History Teacher,* and *The Journal of Interdisciplinary History.*

Making America

1

Making a "New" World, to 1588

Behind the Stories

When we began this project with the first edition, we did not have a clear idea of where to start. Traditionally this story begins with Christopher Columbus, who accidentally stumbled upon a chain of continents that lay between Europe and Asia. This makes a convenient starting point, but is terribly misleading. As you will learn in the pages to come, Columbus discovered a world populated by ancient and sophisticated societies whose presence would prove essential to the process of European conquest and colonization of this "New World." We decided that the history of those societies before Columbus's arrival had to be included in our story.

But we also realized that it would have to range farther in space. Making America was a truly global process. For generations exotic items from China, Persia, and other mysterious places wound their way westward along the Silk Road and northward across the Sahara Desert, bringing novel luxuries into an evolving cosmopolitan marketplace. Atlantic nations like Portugal

and Spain sought to make these transactions more efficient by substituting sailing ships for camels, hoping to enhance their own importance in that marketplace. This explosion in commerce helps explain why Columbus and other adventurers of his day risked the open seas of the Atlantic. And this is why Asia and Africa, as much as Europe, were essential to the process of making America.

Yet America was equally essential in the making of the Europe, Africa, and Asia that we know today. The influx of wealth from America and the demand for labor to harness that wealth changed the face of the globe. Old unchallenged certainties fell away or were shattered by rising new intellectual traditions. In the process new states, new churches, new generations of leaders sprang up—all of which would drive American and global history onward.

This was a story that we found compelling and explains why we begin our discussion of Making America as we do. And

this thread of how the world influenced America and America has influenced the world will be woven throughout our narrative as our story unfolds.

—C.L.M.

Individual Choices
Wahunsunacock (The Powhatan)

Things were bad, and getting worse, for the people who lived along North America's eastern shore. For generations they had lived peacefully in their largely self-sufficient villages on the corn that the women grew and the game that the men hunted. Warfare was infrequent, and famine all but unknown. But around 600 years ago a long-lasting change in the weather made corn production less dependable, and the people were forced to hunt and gather more wild foods to supplement their diet. As hunters from individual villages roamed deeper and deeper into the forests looking for food, they encountered others who, like themselves, were desperate to harvest the diminishing resources. Conflicts became common.

The Algonkian-speaking Powhatan people decided that collaboration with neighbors for both defense and expansion of resources was the best solution. Though we have no written records about this process, oral testimony suggests that in around 1550, six village-based Algonkian groups whose territories occupied about 25 square miles near what is now Richmond, Virginia, formed an alliance and placed a hereditary chieftain (*weroance*)

Wahunsunacock (The Powhatan)

in charge of coordinating their mutual efforts. At about the same time a child was born in one of those villages who would become a great figure in the confederation's future. We do not know what his childhood name was, but as an adult he was called Wahunsunacock or sometimes just The Powhatan.

Throughout Wahunsunacock's life, conditions for the people got continuously worse. In addition to the bad weather, other neighboring groups had also begun to consolidate into local confederacies and brushfire conflicts were common. But what was more troubling was the increasingly frequent appearance of odd-looking strangers who arrived in ever greater numbers along their shores. Most times these strangers seemed just to be looking around, exploring the coastline and various river inlets. Other times they seemed interested in trading often wonderful things for items that the Indians traditionally traded among themselves. But sometimes they came wrapped in metal and carrying loud, deadly sticks that

3

could kill a man at a long distance; frequently they took away women and children never to be seen again. And what was worse, shortly after each time these strangers appeared, people in the villages became sick and a great many died.

When Wahunsunacock reached adulthood, he became the *weroance* of the six-village confederacy into which he had been born. He decided that, in light of worsening conditions, the limited scope of his little alliance system was not adequate to ensure the continued safety and prosperity of his people. He then made a consequential decision: his political state must either expand or die. Calling for support upon the five to six hundred fighting men who lived in the six villages, Wahunsunacock launched an effort to restructure the region's political makeup.

Over a period of twenty years or so, Wahunsunacock and his followers used a combination of diplomacy, intermarriage, and brute force to pull other little confederacies and isolated villages into a larger confederation, as depicted on Powhatan's Mantle, shown in the Individual Voices feature at the end of this chapter. By 1607, when the mysterious strangers who had unsettled life throughout Wahunsunacock's lifetime actually began to settle permanently in the region, the little six-village alliance had grown to nearly thirty villages that occupied some eight thousand square miles and could field between fifteen hundred and two thousand armed soldiers. As the strange newcomers quickly learned, their entire existence in what they called "Virginia" would depend largely on the good will of Wahunsunacock.

As remarkable as Wahunsunacock's story is, his experience was not entirely unique. Faced with changing conditions, natural ones at first and then those brought by invading Europeans, Indians throughout the Americas struggled valiantly and creatively to restructure their societies and their lives. Sometimes the effort brought success, but often at the cost of war and great sacrifice. Wahunsunacock and his contemporary visionaries succeeded in reshaping America, crafting what Europeans naively—but in this one sense quite correctly—called the New World. And in the process, they helped shape the entire Atlantic world, where the making of America would soon take center stage.

For nearly a thousand years before the Powhatans formed their confederacy, a combination of natural and human forces truly global in scope was having a profound impact throughout the Atlantic world. For example, in 632, a vibrant new religion swept out of the Arabian Peninsula to conquer much of the Mediterranean world. Eventually Europeans, who had themselves adopted a new and dynamic religion, Christianity, only a few centuries earlier, struck back in a protracted series of Crusades designed to break Islamic power. At the same time, climatic changes encouraged expansion by Viking warlords out of Scandinavia southward into the European mainland and westward all the way into North America. Together these expansive societies introduced new technologies and knowledge of distant and mysterious worlds that would engender an air of restlessness throughout Europe.

One of those mysterious worlds lay to the south of the forbidding Sahara Desert in Africa. There, as in both America and Europe, people had been dealing with changing conditions by crafting societies and economies that made the most of varying environments. When trading caravans began penetrating this region in the eighth century, they found highly developed cities that could draw on massive populations and natural resources to produce goods that were in great demand throughout the evolving Atlantic world. Like Native Americans, Africans too would be drawn into the restlessness that characterized this dynamic age.

A mere fifty or so years before the Powhatans united, Christopher Columbus, a Genoese navigator in Spain's employ, rediscovered the **Western Hemisphere** while trying to find the hidden and

4 CHAPTER 1 Making a "New" World, to 1588

distant worlds known to Islamic traders. Columbus's accident brought two historical streams together, and from that point onward, the history of each helped to form the future of both. On a global scale, this event launched a new era in human history. On a more local scale, it began a process we call *Making America*.

A WORLD OF CHANGE

★ How did environmental changes influence the development of various societies in North America during the millennia before the emergence of the Atlantic world?

★ What forces came into play in the centuries before 1500 that would launch Europeans on a program of outward exploration?

★ What factors in sub-Saharan African history helped lead to the development of the slave trade?

Christopher Columbus's accidental encounter with the Western Hemisphere came after nearly a thousand years of increasing restlessness and dramatic change that affected all of the areas surrounding the Atlantic Ocean. After **millennia** of relative isolation, the natural and human environments in America were opened to the flow of people, animals, and goods from the rest of the Atlantic world. During the centuries before 1492, Christian monarchs and church leaders conducted a series of **Crusades** to wrest control of the **Holy Land** from the **Muslims**. As armies of Crusaders pushed their way into the region, they came into contact with many desirable commodities—fine silks, exotic spices, and precious stones and metals. As word spread of the finery Muslims obtained through trade with Africa and Asia, enterprising individuals began looking for ways to profit by supplying such luxuries to European consumers. At the same time, northern European **Vikings** were extending their holdings throughout many parts of Europe and westward all the way to North America. Both Crusaders and Vikings came into contact with equally restless and vibrant societies in Africa and the Western Hemisphere, lending greater impetus to continuing exploration.

American Origins

It might be said that the process of Making America actually began about 2.5 million years ago with the onset of the Great Ice Age. During the height of the Ice Age, great sheets of ice advanced and withdrew across the world's continents. During the last ice advance, the Wisconsin glaciation, a sheet of ice more

than 8,000 feet thick covered the northern half of both Europe and North America and so much water was frozen into the glaciers that sea levels dropped as much as 450 feet. Migratory animals found vast regions closed to them by the imposing ice fields and ventured into areas exposed by the receding sea. One such region, Beringia, lay between present-day Siberia on the Asian continent and Alaska in North America (see Map 1.1). Now covered by the waters of the Bering Sea and Arctic Ocean, Beringia during the Ice Age was a dry, frigid grassland—between 70,000 and 10,000 years ago, it was a perfect grazing ground for animals such as giant bison and huge-tusked woolly mammoths. Hosts of predators, including large wolves and saber-toothed cats, followed them.

What was true for other species may also have been true for humans. Each of the indigenous peoples who continue to occupy this hemisphere has its own account of its origins, some of which involve migration while others do not. Biological evidence suggests that the majority of Native Americans did migrate here and are descended from a common genetic line (see Map 1.1). Though science paints a clear picture of this process, a great many anomalies exist. Recent archaeological finds and isolated discoveries such as

■ **Western Hemisphere** When discussing the world longitudinally (lengthwise), geographers often divide the globe into two halves (hemispheres). The **Western Hemisphere** includes North America, Mexico, Central America, and South America; the **Eastern Hemisphere** includes Europe, Asia, and Africa.

millennia The plural of *millennium*, a period of one thousand years.

■ **Crusades** Military expeditions undertaken by European Christians in the eleventh through the thirteenth centuries to recover the Holy Land from the Muslims.

■ **Holy Land** Palestine, which now is divided between Israel, Jordan, and Syria; called the Holy Land because it is the region in which the events described in the Old and New Testaments of the Bible took place; it is sacred to Christians, Jews, and Muslims.

■ **Muslims** People who practice the religion of Islam, a monotheistic faith that accepts Mohammed as the chief and last prophet of God; born ca. 570 on the Arabian Peninsula, around 610 Mohammed began having religious visions, which were recorded as the Qur'an, the sacred text that is the foundation for the Islamic religion.

■ **Vikings** Medieval Danish, Swedish, and Norwegian groups who responded to land shortages and climatic conditions in Scandinavia by taking to the sea and establishing communities in various parts of western Europe, Iceland, Greenland, and North America.

MAP 1.1 First Americans Enter the New World
Although DNA evidence indicates that all Paleo-Indians were genetically related, at least two cultural groups moved into different parts of North America between 70,000 and 40,000 years ago. The Old Cordilleran group, to the west of the Rocky Mountains, and the Clovis group, to the east, left records of their passing at numerous sites, the most prominent of which are labeled here.
Copyright © Cengage Learning

Map legend:
- Extent of land, ca. 33,000–10,500 B.C.E.
- Glaciers, ca. 15,000 B.C.E.
- Probable ancient shoreline
- Probable overland route
- Possible coastal route
- Selected Paleo-Indian site

■ **Kenniwick Man** The name given to a human skeleton discovered next to the Columbia River near Kenniwick, Washington, in 1996. The skeleton is believed to be over 9,000 years old and appears to have facial features unlike those of other ancient Indian relics.

maize Corn; the word *maize* comes from an Indian word for this plant.

that of the **Kenniwick Man** suggest that many different groups of migrating or truly indigenous people may have coexisted or succeeded each other over this 60,000-year period.

Beginning about 9,000 years ago temperatures warmed, leading to the extinction of the large Ice Age animals. As these staple meat sources disappeared,

James Chatters and Thomas McClelland.

Although some archaeologists and many Native Americans dispute the accuracy of this forensic reconstruction, many experts consider this bust of the Kenniwick Man, based on a skull discovered on the banks of the Columbia River in 1996, to be the best indication of both the deep antiquity and diversity of Native American peoples.

to different spots during different seasons of the year, following an annual round of movement from camp to camp—perhaps collecting shellfish for several weeks at the mouth of a river, then moving on to where wild strawberries were ripening, and later in the summer relocating to fields in which maturing wild onions or sunflower seeds could be harvested.

Although these ancestors of modern Native Americans believed in and celebrated the animating spirits of the plants and animals that they depended on for survival, they nonetheless engaged in large-scale environmental engineering. They used fire to clear forests of unwanted scrub and to encourage the growth of berries and other plants they found valuable. In this way they produced vegetables for themselves and also provided food for browsing animals such as deer, which increased in number while other species, less useful to people, declined. They also engaged in genetic engineering. A highly significant example comes from north-central Mexico, where, beginning perhaps 7,000 years ago, human intervention helped a wild strain of grass develop bigger seedpods with more nutritious seeds. Such intervention eventually transformed a fairly unproductive plant into an enormously nourishing and prolific food crop: **maize**.

Maize (corn), along with other engineered plants like beans, squash, and chilies, formed the basis for an agricultural revolution in North America, allowing many people to settle in larger villages for longer

people everywhere in North America abandoned big-game hunting and began to explore newly emerging local environments for new sources of food, clothing, shelter, and tools. In the forests that grew up to cover the eastern half of the continent, they developed finely polished stone tools, which they used to make functional and beautiful implements out of wood, bone, shell, and other materials. There and along the Pacific shore, people hollowed out massive tree trunks, making boats from which they could harvest food from inland waterways and from the sea. During this time domesticated dogs were introduced into North America also. With boats for river transportation and dogs to help carry loads on land, Native American people were able to make the best use of their local environments by moving around

Service Historique de la Marine, Vincennes, France/Lauros/Giraudon/The Bridgeman Art Library International.

This sixteenth-century engraving illustrates the variety, abundance, and importance of agriculture in pre-Columbian and post-contact America. The product of centuries of genetic engineering, crops like corn, squashes, and other vegetables supported large settled communities in much of North America.

It Matters Today

Native Americans Shape a New World

It may be hard to imagine why understanding the original peopling of North America and how native cultures evolved during the millennia before Columbus could possibly matter to the history of the United States or, more specifically, to how we live our lives today. Without this chapter in our history, there likely would have been no U.S. history at all. Europeans in the fifteenth century lacked the tools, the organization, the discipline, and the economic resources to conquer a true wilderness—such a feat would have been the equivalent of our establishing a successful colony on the moon today. But the environmental and genetic engineering conducted through the millennia of North American history created a hospitable environment into which European crops, animals, and people could easily transplant themselves. And while the descendants of those Europeans may often suppose that they constructed an entirely new world in North America, the fact is that they simply grafted new growth onto ancient rootstock, creating the unique hybrid that is today's America.

- Describe what you think it would take technologically, economically, and politically for the United States to establish a successful permanent colony on the moon. How would the presence of a biologically identical indigenous population change those requirements?
- In what ways are the Indian heritages of America still visible in our society today?

periods. Successful adaptation—including plant cultivation and eventually agriculture—along with population growth and the constructive use of spare time allowed some Indians in North America to build large, ornate cities. The map of ancient America is dotted with such centers. Beginning about 3,000 years ago, the Ohio and Mississippi Valleys became the home for a number of **mound builder** societies whose cities became trading and ceremonial centers that had enormous economic and social outreach. Large quantities of both practical and purely decorative artifacts from all over North America have been found at these sites. Then, about 800 years ago, midwestern mound builder sites fell into decline, and the people who

once had congregated there withdrew to separated villages or bands. No single satisfactory explanation accounts for why this happened.

Change and Restlessness in the Atlantic World

During the few centuries following the death of the prophet Mohammed in 632, Muslim Arabs, Turks, and **Moors** made major inroads into western Asia and northern Africa, eventually encroaching on Europe's southern and eastern frontiers (see Map 1.2). During these same years, Scandinavian Vikings, who controlled the northern frontiers of Europe, began expanding southward and westward. Accomplished and fearless seamen, the Vikings swept down Europe's western shore and through Russia by river to the Mediterranean. They also began colonizing Iceland and Greenland. And, according to Viking sagas, these sailors launched their first expedition to North America in the year 1000. Over the decades that followed, Vikings established several American colonies.

By about the year 1000, then, the heartland of Europe was surrounded by dynamic societies that served as conduits to a much broader world. Although Europeans resented and resisted both Viking and Islamic invasion, the newcomers brought with them

■ **mound builder** Name applied to a number of Native American societies, including the Adena, Hopewell, and Mississippian cultures, that constructed massive earthen mounds as monuments and building foundations.

■ **Moors** Natives of northern Africa who converted to Islam in the eighth century and carried the Islamic religion and culture both to southern Africa and to the Iberian Peninsula (Spain and Portugal), which they conquered in the eighth century.

Beginning in about the year 1000, two dynamic seafaring societies controlled the European continent's perimeters: various allied Islamic societies to the south and Vikings on all other sides. Both groups used innovative technologies and advanced geographical knowledge to continually expand their holdings, including holdings in North America. Their ships carried many new commodities as well as new knowledge into Europe, helping to create a restless, exploring spirit among Europeans.

MAP 1.2 Europe and Its Neighbors, ca. 1000

During medieval times, Viking and Islamic empires surrounded western Europe, and their trade routes crisscrossed the region. Copyright © Cengage Learning

In the Wider World

Polynesians Populate the Pacific

At the same time that the American populations were settling into their new environments, another great migration was taking place on the opposite side of the world. Some 6,000 years ago, from a starting point somewhere near the modern island nation of Taiwan, people in sail-rigged canoes began taking well-planned voyages toward the Philippine Islands. Setting up residence there, they continued to island hop until around 1,200 B.C.E., by which time they had established populations in a chain all the way to the Solomon Islands, east of New Guinea. From here, they continued moving eastward, setting up residence in Fiji, Samoa, and Tonga. Over the next thousand years such voyages continued until these Polynesian people occupied, in the words of anthropologist Jared Diamond, "every habitable scrap of land in the vast watery triangle of ocean whose apexes are Hawaii, New Zealand, and Easter Island." And while there is little physical evidence of their voyaging to the west coast of the Americas, it was certainly within their technical and navigational abilities, and some speculate that they may well have.

tempting new technologies, food items, and expansive knowledge. These contributions not only enriched European culture but also improved the quality of life. For example, new farming methods increased food production so much that Europe began to experience a population explosion. Soon Europeans would begin turning this new knowledge and these new tools against the people who brought them.

Iberians launched a **Reconquista**, an effort to break Islamic rule on the peninsula, and in 1096, European Christians launched the first in a series of Crusades to sweep the Muslims from the Holy Land and elsewhere. With the aid of English Crusaders, Portugal attained independence in 1147. In the Holy Land, hordes of Crusaders captured key points only to be expelled by Muslim counterattacks. The effort to dislodge Islamic forces from Jerusalem and other sacred sites came largely to an end in 1291, but the struggle continued in the Iberian Peninsula. By 1380 Portugal's King John I had united that country's various principalities under his rule. In Spain, unification took much longer, but in 1469 **Ferdinand and Isabella**, heirs to the rival thrones of Aragon and Castile, married and created a united state in Spain.

■ **Reconquista** The campaign undertaken by European Christians to recapture the Iberian Peninsula from the Moors, accomplished in 1492.

■ **Ferdinand and Isabella** Joint rulers of Spain (r. 1469–1504); their marriage in 1469 brought together the rival kingdoms of Aragon and Castile and united Spain.

Twenty-three years later, in 1492, the Spanish subdued the last Moorish stronghold on the peninsula, completing the Reconquista.

Dealings with the Vikings in the north took a somewhat different turn. Although they maintained trading contacts with North America for several hundred years, the Vikings began to retreat in the middle of the 1300s. By 1450 or so, they had withdrawn entirely from their transatlantic colonies. The most likely cause of their departure was a shift in climate. Although experts disagree about the exact timing, it appears that at some time between 1350 and 1450 a significant climatic shift called the Little Ice Age began to affect the entire world. In the Arctic and subarctic, temperatures fell, snowfall increased, and sea ice became a major hazard to navigation. This shift made it impossible for the Vikings to practice the herding, farming, and trading that supported their economy in Greenland and elsewhere. Finding themselves cut off from a vibrant North Atlantic empire, Viking settlements in the British Isles, Russia, France, and elsewhere merged with local populations.

Like Native Americans at the same time, these Viking refugees often joined with their neighbors in recognizing the value of large-scale political organization. Consolidation began in France in around 1480, when Louis XI took control of five rival provinces to create a unified kingdom. Five years later in England, Henry Tudor and the House of Lancaster defeated the rival House of York in the Wars of the Roses, ending nearly a hundred years of civil war. Tudor, now styling himself King Henry VII, cemented this victory by marrying into the rival house, wedding Elizabeth of York to finally unify the English throne. As in Spain and

Portugal, the formation of unified states in France and England opened the way to new expansive activity that would accelerate the creation of an Atlantic world.

The Complex World of Indian America

The world into which Vikings first sailed at the beginning of the second millennium and into which other Europeans would intrude half a millennium later was not some static realm stuck in the Stone Age. Native American societies were every bit as progressive, adaptable, and historically dynamic as those that would invade their homes. In fact, adaptive flexibility characterized Indian life throughout North America; the vast variety in environmental conditions that characterized the continent led to the emergence of enormous differences between various Indian groups. **Anthropologists** have tried to make the extremely complicated cultural map of North America understandable by dividing the continent into a series of culture areas—regions where the similarities among native societies were greater than the differences (see Map 1.3).

In the southeastern region of North America, peoples speaking Siouan, Caddoan, and Muskogean languages formed vibrant agricultural and urban societies with ties to exchange centers farther north as well as to traders from Mexico. At places like Natchez, fortified cities housed gigantic pyramids, and farmland radiating outward provided food for large residential populations. These were true cities and, like their counterparts in Europe and Asia, were magnets attracting ideas, technologies, and religious notions from the entire continent.

Farther north, in the region called the Eastern Woodlands, people lived in smaller villages and combined agriculture with hunting and gathering. The Iroquois, for example, lived in towns numbering three thousand or more people, changing locations only as soil fertility, firewood, and game became exhausted. Each town was made up of a group of **longhouses**, structures often 60 feet or more in length.

A tradition that may go back to the time when the Iroquois lived as nomadic hunters and gatherers dictated that men and women occupy different spheres of existence. The women's world was the world of plants, healing, nurturing, and order. The men's was the world of animals, hunting, and war. By late **pre-Columbian** times, the Iroquois had become strongly agricultural, and because plants were in the women's sphere, women occupied places of high social and economic status in Iroquois society, ruling over domestic politics. Families were matrilineal, meaning that they traced their descent through the mother's line, and matrilocal, meaning that a man left his home to move in with his wife's family upon marriage. Women distributed the rights to cultivate specific fields and controlled the harvest.

Variations on the Iroquois economic and social pattern were typical throughout the Eastern Woodlands and in the neighboring Great Plains and Southwest. Having strong ties with agriculturalists in the east, Plains groups such as the Mandans began settling on bluffs overlooking the many streams that eventually drain into the Missouri River. Living in substantial houses insulated against the cold winters, these people divided their time among hunting, crop raising, and trade. Over a five-hundred-year period, populations increased, and agricultural settlements expanded. By 1300, such villages could be found along every stream ranging southward from North Dakota into present-day Kansas.

In the Southwest, groups with strong ties to Mexico began growing corn as early as 3,200 years ago, but they continued to follow a migratory life until about 400 C.E., when they began building larger and more substantial houses and limiting their migrations. The greatest change, however, came during the eighth century, when a shift in climate made the region drier and a pattern of late-summer thunderstorms triggered dangerous and erosive flash floods.

There seem to have been two quite different responses to this change in climate. A group called the Anasazi expanded their agricultural ways, cooperating to build flood-control dams and irrigation canals. The need for cooperative labor meant forming larger communities, and between about 900 and 1300 the Anasazi built whole cities of multistory apartment houses along the high cliffs, safe from flooding but near their irrigated fields. In these densely populated towns Anasazi craft specialists manufactured goods such as pots, textiles, and baskets for the community while farmers tended fields and priests attended to the spiritual needs of the society.

Another contingent of southwestern Indians abandoned the region, moving southward into Mexico. Here they came upon the remnants of classical city-states like Teotihuacán. One of several highly developed societies of central Mexico, Teotihuacán was the largest city-state in the Western Hemisphere, with a population of nearly 200,000. However, by around

anthropologists Scholars who study human behavior and culture in the past or the present.

longhouses Communal dwellings, usually built of poles and bark and having a central hallway with family apartments on either side.

pre-Columbian Existing in the Americas before the arrival of Columbus.

MAP 1.3 Indian Culture Areas in North America

Social scientists who study Native American societies have divided them into a complex of "culture areas": regions in which cultural similarities outnumber differences between resident groups. While there is some disagreement among scholars about the exact number and extent of specific areas, this map provides a representative view of the various culture areas in North America. Copyright © Cengage Learning

the year 600, urban Mexican societies were in decline. Over the next several hundred years, migrants from southwestern North America—so-called Chichimecs or "wild tribes"—borrowed architectural and agricultural skills from the fallen societies and built new monumental cities. One of these groups, the **Aztecs**, arrived in the Valley of Mexico soon after 1200, settling on a small island in the middle of a brackish lake. From this unappealing center, a series of strong leaders used a combination of diplomacy and brutal warfare to establish a **tributary empire** that eventually ruled as many as 6 million people.

In the American Southwest, the Anasazi Indians built monumental cities of multi-story buildings housing hundreds, sometimes thousands of people. This community, called Cliff Palace on Mesa Verde in Colorado, is but one example. The name "Palace," by the way, is misleading; there was no royalty among the Anasazi, and this was a dwelling for everyday farmers and craft workers.

© Natalie Tepper/Arcaid/Corbis.

Other major changes occurred in the Southwest after 1300. During the last quarter of the thirteenth century, a long string of summer droughts and bitterly cold winters forced the Anasazi to abandon their cities. They disappeared as a people, splitting into smaller communities that eventually became the various Pueblo groups. At the same time, an entirely new population entered the region. These hunter-gatherers brought new technologies, including the bow and arrow, into the Southwest. About half of them continued to be hunter-gatherers, while the rest borrowed cultivating and home-building techniques from the Pueblos. Europeans who later entered the area called the hunter-gatherers Apaches and the settled agriculturalists Navajos.

In other regions agriculture was practiced only marginally, if at all. In areas like the Great Basin, desert conditions made agriculture too risky, and in California, the Northwest Coast, and the Intermountain Plateau (see Map 1.3), the bounty of available wild foods made it unnecessary. In these regions, hunting and gathering remained the chief occupations. For example, the Nez Perces and their neighbors living in the Plateau region occupied permanent village sites in the winter but did not stay together in a single group all year. Rather, they formed task groups—temporary villages that came together to share the labor required to harvest a particular resource—and then went their separate ways when the task was done. These task groups brought together not only people who lived in different winter villages but often people from different tribes and even different language groups. In such groups, political authority passed among those who were best qualified to supervise particular activities. If the task group was hunting, the best and most senior hunters—almost always men—exercised political authority. If the task group was gathering roots, then the best and most senior diggers—almost always women—ruled. Thus among such hunting-gathering people, political organization changed from season to season, and social status depended on what activities were most important to the group at a particular time.

As these examples illustrate, variations in daily life and social arrangements in pre-Columbian North America reflected variations in climate, soil conditions, food supplies, and cultural heritages from place to place across the vast continent. But despite the enormous size of the continent and the amazing variety of cultures spread across it, economic and social connections within and between ecological regions tied the people together in complex ways. For example, varieties of shell found only along the Northwest Pacific Coast were traded to settlements as far away as Florida, having been passed from hand to hand over thousands of miles of social and physical space.

■ **Aztecs** An Indian group living in central Mexico; the Aztecs used military force to dominate nearby tribes; their civilization was at its peak at the time of the Spanish conquest.

tributary empire An empire in which subjects rule themselves but are required to contribute goods and labor, called tribute, to an imperial government in return for protection and services.

After being separated from the rest of Africa by the formation of the Sahara Desert, the Bantu people—aided perhaps by their mastery of iron-smelting technology—expanded throughout the sub-Saharan portion of the continent. This painting, rendered by non-Bantu Bushmen, records a battle between themselves and Bantus. Note the relatively huge size and menacing quality of the Bantus compared with the retreating Bushmen, an indication of how the newly dominant group was perceived by its neighbors. Mansell/Time Life Pictures/Getty Images.

A World of Change in Africa

Like North America, Africa was home to an array of societies that developed in response to varying natural and historical conditions. But unlike contemporary Indian groups, Africans maintained continual if perhaps only sporadic contacts with societies in Europe and Asia.

In ancient times tendrils of trade tied the Mediterranean and **sub-Saharan Africa** together, but over the last five thousand years increasing desertification cut off most of Africa from the fertile areas of the Mediterranean coast. The people living south of the desert were forced to largely reinvent civilization in response to changing conditions. They abandoned the wheat and other grain crops that had predominated in earlier economies, domesticating new staples such as **millet**

sub-Saharan Africa The region of Africa south of the Sahara Desert.

millet A large family of grain grasses that produce nutritious, carbohydrate-rich seeds used for both human and animal feed.

fictive ancestor A mythical figure believed by a social group to be its founder, from whom all members are biologically descended.

and native strains of rice. They also abandoned the cattle and horses that had been common in earlier times, adopting sheep and goats, which were better suited to arid environments. Depending on immediate conditions, groups could establish large villages and live on a balance of vegetables, meat, and milk or, if necessary, shift over to a purely nomadic lifestyle following their herds.

Social organization tended to follow a similar adaptive strategy. The most common social structure was based on the belief that large geographically and linguistically related groups were descended from a common **fictive ancestor**. These larger organizations were then subdivided into smaller and smaller groups, each independent—as a modern nuclear family might be—but tied through an elaborate family tree to hundreds or even thousands of other similar groups.

The status of each group was determined by seniority in the line of descent—those descended from the oldest offspring of the common ancestor were socially and politically superior to those descended from younger branches. This fundamental hierarchy created an organizational structure that permitted large-group cooperation and management when appropriate but also permitted each small band to function independently when conditions required. Within each group, seniority also determined political and social status: the eldest descendant of the common ancestor within each group held superior power.

Sometime between two and three thousand years ago, sub-Saharan groups appear to have discovered iron smelting. Inventing a furnace shaped like a long tube that permitted both the high heat and the air draft necessary for melting iron ore, craftsmen were able to make use of abundant raw iron deposits in southern Africa to produce tools, vessels, and weapons. Often, large cities with elaborate social hierarchies grew in neighborhoods where iron and other ores were particularly abundant. These would then become centers for trade as well as political hubs, the seeds from which later kingdoms and empires would sprout.

These trading centers became particularly important when Islamic expansion brought new, outside sources for trade into the sub-Saharan world. The first mention of trade between Islamic adventurers and African communities stems from the eighth century, and it seems to have developed slowly over the next several hundred years. One catalyst of the trade growth was the introduction of the camel as a draft animal. Native to Asia and the Arabian Peninsula,

Introducing camels as draft animals made it possible for Arab and other traders to penetrate the forbidding Sahara Desert to open up a highly profitable trade with sub-Saharan states that were rich with gold, ivory, and other valuable commodities. This gold and diamond miniature (the sculpture is only about two-and-a-half inches tall) celebrates the riches that these animals carried out of Africa. Indian, Mughal period, ca. 1800. Camel: gold enamel, diamond chips, ivory. Gr. H. 2 ⅝ in. (6.7 cm.). L. 2 ¾ in. (7.0 cm.). Diam. 1 ³⁄₁₆ in. (3.0 cm.). The Metropolitan Museum of Art, New York, N.Y, U.S.A. Gift of The Shaw Foundation, Inc., 1959 (59.44.1). Photograph © 1996 The Metropolitan Museum of Art/Art Resource, New York.

camels were ideally suited for crossing the inhospitable desert, making it possible to establish regular caravan routes that linked sub-Saharan trading centers with the outside world. Increasingly after 1100, iron, gold, precious gems, and slaves were carried across the desert by Arab, Berber, and other Muslim traders, who gave African middlemen silks, spices, and other foreign goods in exchange. This trade tended to enhance the power of African elites, leading to ever larger and more elaborate states.

EXPLOITING ATLANTIC OPPORTUNITIES

★ How did the Atlantic world change as a result of efforts to exploit new discoveries leading up to and following 1492?

★ How did Native Americans and Africans respond initially to European expansion?

Dynamic forces in America, Europe, Africa, and beyond were drawing the disparate societies that occupied the Atlantic shore into a complex world of mutual experience. But this process was not automatic. Enterprising people throughout the globe seized opportunities created by the spirit of restlessness and the merging of historical streams, advancing the process and giving it peculiar shape. Generally seeking profits for themselves and advancement for their own nations, tribes, or classes, those who sought to exploit the emerging new world nonetheless had enormous impact on the lives of all who occupied it. The process of outreach and historical evolution that helped launch the American experience grew directly from these efforts at exploitation.

The Portuguese, Africa, and Plantation Slavery

The first of the European states to pull itself together was also the first to challenge Islamic dominance in both the Asian and African trade. Portugal's John I encouraged exploration by establishing a school of navigation on his kingdom's southwestern shore; the school sent numerous expeditions in search of new sources of wealth. By the 1430s, the Portuguese had discovered and taken control of islands off the western shore of Africa, and within thirty years had pushed their way to Africa itself, opening relations with the Songhai Empire.

The **Songhai Empire** was typical of the sub-Saharan trading states that emerged through Muslim contacts (see Map 1.4). As was common in the region, the Songhai state consisted of numerous smaller societies, all related through a common ancestor and organized along hierarchical lines. Society remained largely village based, with slaves at the bottom, skilled craftsmen in the middle, and a small noble class at the top. These nobles assembled in Timbuktu, a trading hub and the Songhai capital, which became a cosmopolitan center where African and Islamic influences met. Its art and architecture and the accomplishments of its scholars impressed all who ventured there. From Timbuktu, Songhai traders shipped valuable trade goods across the Sahara by means of caravans. The Portuguese, however, offered speedier shipment and higher profits by carrying trade goods directly to Europe by sea.

By the end of the fifteenth century, Portuguese navigators had gained control over the flow of prized items such as gold, ivory, and spices out of West Africa, and Portuguese colonizers were growing sugar and other crops on the newly conquered Azores and Canary Islands. From the beginning of the sixteenth

■ **Songhai Empire** A large empire in West Africa whose capital was Timbuktu; its rulers accepted Islam around the year 1000.

MAP 1.4 Sub-Saharan Africa Before Sustained European Contact

During the many centuries that followed the formation of the Sahara Desert, Bantu people expanded throughout the southern half of Africa. They and other groups established a number of powerful kingdoms, the capitals of which served as major trading centers among these kingdoms and for Islamic traders, who finally penetrated the desert after the year 750. Copyright © Cengage Learning

Legend:
- Original Bantu homeland
- Bantu migration
- Islamic settlement and influence to 1500
- Trans-Saharan trade route
- Coastal trade route

During the years before European penetration into the region, western Africa became a center for Islamic culture. Islamic scholars congregated at holy sites like the Sankoré Mosque in Timbuktu (*left*). Here they discussed Islamic law and wrote scholarly treatises like the unidentified document depicted on the right. This is one of thousands of manuscripts from Mali that are currently being restored and deciphered. Left: Photo © www.danheller.com; right: McPhoto/Blickwell/Still Pictures.

century onward, the Portuguese also became increasingly involved in slave trafficking, at first to their own plantations and then to Europe itself. By 1550, Portuguese ships were carrying African slaves throughout the world.

The Continued Quest for Asian Trade

Meanwhile, the Portuguese continued to venture outward. In 1487 Bartolomeu Dias became the first European to reach the **Cape of Good Hope** at the southern tip of Africa. Ten years later Vasco da Gama sailed around the cape and launched the Portuguese exploration of eastern Africa and the Indian Ocean.

By the end of the fifteenth century, England, Spain, and France were vying with Portugal to find the shortest, cheapest, and safest sea route between Europe and Asia. Because of its early head start, Portugal remained fairly cautious in its explorations, hugging the coast around Africa

before crossing the ocean to India. As latecomers, Spain and England could not afford to take such a conservative approach to exploration. Voyagers from those countries took advantage of borrowed technologies to expand their horizons. From China, Europeans acquired the magnetic compass, which allowed mariners to determine direction even when out of sight of land. An Arab invention, the astrolabe, allowed seafarers to calculate the positions of heavenly bodies and determine their latitude (their distance north or south of the equator). These inventions, together with improvements in steering mechanisms and hull design, made voyages much less risky.

Cape of Good Hope A point of land at the southern tip of Africa around which European mariners had to sail to reach the Indian Ocean and trade with Asia.

A number of visionary navigators longed for the opportunity to seek new routes. One, an ambitious sailor from the Italian port city of Genoa, **Christopher Columbus**, approached a number of European governments to support a voyage westward from Europe across the Atlantic to the East Indies, but found no one willing to fund him. Finally, in 1492, Ferdinand and Isabella's defeat of the Moors provided Columbus with an opportunity.

Eager to break into overseas trading, dominated in the east by the Arabs and in the south and west by the Portuguese, Ferdinand and Isabella agreed to equip three ships in exchange for a short, safe route to the Orient. On August 3, 1492, Columbus and some ninety sailors departed on the *Niña*, *Pinta*, and *Santa Maria* for the uncharted waters of the Atlantic. More than three months later, they finally made landfall. Columbus thought he had arrived at the East Indies, but in fact he had reached the islands we now call the **Bahamas**.

Over the next ten weeks, Columbus explored the mysteries of the Caribbean, making landfalls on the islands now known as Cuba and Hispaniola. He collected spices, coconuts, bits of gold, and some native captives. Columbus then returned to Spain, where he was welcomed with great celebration and rewarded with backing for three more voyages. Over the next several years, the Spanish gained a permanent foothold in the region that Columbus had discovered and became aware that the area was a world entirely new to them.

England, like Spain, was jealous of Portugal's trade monopoly, and in 1497 Henry VII commissioned another Italian mariner, Giovanni Caboto, to search for a sea route to India. John Cabot, as the English called him, succeeded in crossing the North Atlantic, arriving in the area that Vikings had colonized nearly five hundred years earlier. Shortly thereafter, another Italian, **Amerigo Vespucci**, sailing under the Spanish flag, sighted the northeastern shore of South America and sailed northward into the Caribbean in search of a passage to the East. Finally, in 1524, Giovanni da Verrazano, sailing for France, explored the Atlantic

coast of North America, charting the coastline of what later became the thirteen English mainland colonies, quite possibly becoming the first of the strangers to visit Wahunsunacock's land.

A New Transatlantic World

At first, European monarchs greeted the discovery of a new world as bad news: they wanted access to the riches of Asia, not contact with some undiscovered place. As knowledge of the New World spread, the primary goal of exploration became finding a route around or through it. Yet even before Verrazano, ambitious adventurers from western Europe began exploring the fertile fishing grounds off the northern shores of North America. By 1506, such voyages became so common that the king of Portugal placed a 10 percent tax on fish imported from North America. But these voyages did more than feed the European imagination and the continent's appetite for seafood. Europeans, even relatively poor fishermen, had many things that the Indians lacked: copper pots, jewelry, woolen blankets, and hundreds of other novelties. For their part, the Indians provided firewood, food, ivory, and furs. Apparently the trade grew quickly. By 1534, when Jacques Cartier made the first official exploration of the Canadian coast for the French government, he was approached by party after party of Indians offering to trade furs for the goods he carried. He could only conclude that many other Europeans had come before him.

The presence of explorers such as Verrazano and Cartier and of unknown numbers of anonymous fishermen and part-time traders had several effects on the native population. The Mi'kmaqs, Hurons, and other northeastern Indian groups approached the invading Europeans in friendship, eager to trade and to learn more about the strangers. In part this response was a sign of natural curiosity, but it also reflected some serious changes taking place in the native world of North America.

As we have noted, the onset of the Little Ice Age had far-reaching effects. The deteriorating climate made it more difficult for groups like Wahunsunacock's villages to depend on their corn crops for food. Forced to rely more on hunting and gathering, they had to expand their territory, and in doing so came into conflict with their neighbors. As warfare became more common, groups increasingly formed alliances for mutual defense—systems like the Powhatan Confederacy. And Indians often found it beneficial to welcome European newcomers into their midst—as trading partners bearing new tools, as allies in the evolving conflicts with neighboring Indian groups, and as powerful magicians whose **shamans** might provide explanations and remedies for the hard times that had befallen them.

■ **Christopher Columbus** (Cristoforo Colombo) Italian explorer in the service of Spain who attempted to reach Asia by sailing west from Europe, thereby arriving in America in 1492.

Bahamas A group of islands in the Atlantic Ocean east of Florida and Cuba.

■ **Amerigo Vespucci** Italian explorer of the South American coast; Europeans named America after him.

shamans People who act as a link between the visible material world and an invisible spirit world; a shaman's duties include healing, conducting religious ceremonies, and foretelling the future.

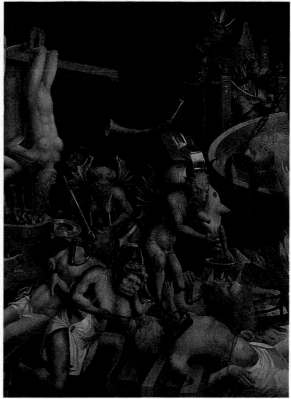

Europeans had trouble fitting American Indians into their preconceived ideas about the world. Native Americans were sometimes cast as noble savages and other times as devils. The Brazilian Indian shown in these two works illustrates the conflicting views. In one, the feather-clad Indian is shown as a wise magus paying homage to the Christ-child; in the other, an Indian devil wears the same costume while presiding over the tortures of Hell.

THE CHALLENGES OF MUTUAL DISCOVERY

★ *How did Native Americans and Europeans respond to increasing contact with each other?*

★ *What global changes occurred through the process called the Columbian Exchange?*

Europeans approached the New World with certain ideas in mind and defined what they found there in terms that reflected what they already believed. American Indians approached Europeans in the same way. Both of these groups—as well as Africans—were thrown into a new world of understanding that challenged many of their fundamental assumptions. They also exchanged material goods that affected their physical well-being profoundly.

A Meeting of Minds in America

Most Europeans had a firm sense of how the world was arranged, who occupied it, and how they had come to be where they were. The existence of America—and even more the presence there of American Indians—challenged that secure knowledge. In the first stages of mutual discovery in America, most Europeans were content mentally to reshape what they found in the New World to fit with what they expected to find. Columbus expected to find India and Indians, and he believed that was precisely what he had found. Other Europeans understood that America was a new land and that the Indians were a new people, but they attempted to fit both into the cosmic map outlined in the Bible.

Columbus's initial comments about the American Indians set the tone for many future encounters. "Of anything that they possess, if it be asked of them, they never say no," Columbus wrote; "on the contrary, they invite you to share it and show as much love as if their hearts went with it." Such writings were widely circulated in Europe and led to a perception of the Indians as noble savages, men and women free from the temptations and vanities of modern civilization. On the other hand, Amerigo Vespucci found them far from noble. "They marry as many wives as they please," he explained. "The son cohabits with mother, brother with sister, male cousin with female, and any man with the first woman he meets. . . . Beyond the fact that they have no church, no religion and are not **idolaters**, what more can I say?"

In some ways, Europeans may have been easier for American Indians to understand than the existence of American Indians was for Europeans. To Indians, the world was alive, animated by a spiritual force that was both universal and intelligent. This force took on many forms. Some of these forms were visible in the everyday world of experience, some were visible only at special times, and some were never visible. Social ties based on fictive kinship and **reciprocal trade** linked all creatures—human and nonhuman—together into a common cosmos. These connections were chronicled in myth, maintained through ritual, and graphically recorded in forms like the Powhatan Mantle. Their formation and continuity often involved the exchange of ceremonial items believed to have spiritual value. In the pre-Columbian trading world, such prized goods passed from society to society, establishing a spiritual bond between the initial givers and the eventual receivers, even though the two groups might never meet.

Europeans and European goods slipped easily into this ceremonial trading system. The trade items that the Europeans generally offered to American Indians on first contact—glass beads, mirrors, brass bells—resembled closely the items that the Indians traditionally used to establish friendly spiritual and economic relations with strangers. The perceived similarity of the trade goods offered by the Europeans led Indians to accept the newcomers as simply another new group in the complex social cosmos uniting the spiritual and material worlds.

On the other hand, Europeans perceived such items as worthless trinkets, valuing instead Indian furs and Indian land. This difference in perception became a major source of misunderstanding and conflict. To the Indians, neither the furs nor the land was of much value because by their understanding they did not "own" either. According to their beliefs, all things had innate spirits and belonged to themselves. Thus passing animal pelts along to Europeans was simply extending the social connection that had brought the furs into Indian hands in the first place. Similarly, according to Indian belief, land was seen as a living being—a mother—who feeds, clothes, and houses people as long as she receives proper respect. The idea of buying or selling land was therefore unthinkable. When Europeans offered spiritually significant objects in exchange for land on which to build, farm, or hunt, Indians perceived the offer as an effort to join an already existing relationship, and not as a contract transferring ownership.

The Columbian Exchange

Even though Europeans and American Indians saw some similarities in each other, their worlds differed greatly, sometimes in ways hidden to both groups. The natural environments of these worlds were different, and the passage of people, plants, and animals among Europe, Africa, and North America wrought profound changes in all three continents. Historians call this process the **Columbian Exchange**.

Perhaps the most tragic trade among the three continents came about as the direct and unavoidable consequence of human contact. During the period leading up to the age of exploration, many Europeans lost their lives to epidemic diseases. The Black Death of the fourteenth century, for example, wiped out over a third of Europe's population. Exposure to smallpox, measles, typhus, and other serious diseases had often had devastating results, but Europeans gradually developed resistance to infection. In contrast, the Indian peoples whom Columbus and other European explorers encountered lived in an environment in which contagious diseases were never a serious threat until the Europeans arrived. They had no **acquired immunity** to the various bacteria and viruses that Europeans carried. As a result, the new diseases spread very rapidly and were much more deadly among the native peoples than they were among Europeans.

Controversy rages over the number of Indians killed by imported European diseases. Estimates of how many people lived in America north of Mexico in 1492 run from a high of 25 million to a low of 1 million. At the moment, most scholars accept a range

idolater A person who worships symbols or objects, idol worship, a practice forbidden in the Judeo-Christian and Muslim traditions.

■ **reciprocal trade** A system of trading in which the objective is equal exchange of commodities rather than profit; Native Americans easily incorporated Europeans into this system of trade and personal connection. Europeans, however, viewed trade as a transfer of ownership without obligation.

■ **Columbian Exchange** The exchange of people, plants, and animals among Europe, Africa, and North America that occurred after Columbus's arrival in the New World.

■ **acquired immunity** Resistance or partial resistance to a disease; acquired immunity develops in a population over time as a result of exposure to harmful bacteria or viruses. Indians lacked acquired immunity to European diseases, which decimated Indian populations.

of from 3 to 10 million. Even if the most conservative estimate is correct, the raw numbers of people who died of imported diseases were enormous. Between 90 and 95 percent of the native population appears to have died of disease during the first century of contact. Although the percentage was probably lower in areas where contact was infrequent and where native populations were sparse, disease took a terrible toll as it followed the lines of kinship and trade that held native North America together.

Disease, however, did not flow in only one direction. Some diseases that originated in Africa found their way to both North America and Europe. At least one, **syphilis**, may have originated in the Western Hemisphere and migrated eastward. Less immediate but perhaps equally extreme ecological effects arose from the passage of plants among Europe, North America, and Africa. The introduction of plants into the New World extended a process that had been taking place for centuries in the Old World. Trade with Asia had carried exotic plants such as bananas, sugar cane, and rice into Africa as early as 2,300 years ago. From Africa, these plants were imported to Iberian-claimed islands such as the Canaries and eventually to America, where, along with cotton, indigo, coffee, and other imports, they would become **cash crops** on European-controlled plantations. Grains such as wheat, barley, and millet were readily transplanted to some areas in North America, as were grazing grasses and various vegetables, including turnips, spinach, and cabbage.

North American plants also traveled from west to east in the Columbian Exchange. Leading the way in economic importance was tobacco, a stimulant used widely in North America for ceremonial purposes and broadly adopted by Europeans and Africans as a recreational drug. In addition, New World vegetables helped to revolutionize world food supplies. Remarkably easy to grow, maize thrived virtually everywhere. In addition, the white potato, tomato, **manioc**, squash, and beans native to the Western Hemisphere were soon cultivated throughout the world. Animals also moved in the Columbian Exchange. Europeans brought horses, pigs, cattle, oxen, sheep, goats, and domesticated fowl to America, where their numbers soared.

The transplanting of European grain crops and domesticated animals reshaped the American landscape. Changing the contours of the land by clearing trees and undergrowth and by plowing and fencing altered the flow of water, the distribution of seeds, the nesting of birds, and the movement of native animals. Gradually, imported livestock pushed aside native species, and imported plants choked out indigenous ones.

Probably the most important and far-reaching environmental impact of the Columbian Exchange was its overall influence on human populations. Although exchanged diseases killed many millions of Indians and lesser numbers of Africans and Europeans, the transplantation of North American plants significantly expanded food production in what had been marginal areas of Europe and Africa. At the same time, the environmental changes that Europeans wrought along the Atlantic shore of North America permitted the region to support many more people than it had sustained under Indian cultivation. The overall result in Europe and Africa was a population explosion that eventually spilled over to repopulate a devastated North America.

New Worlds in Africa and America

As the Columbian Exchange redistributed plants, animals, and populations among Europe, Africa, and North America, it permanently altered the history of both hemispheres. In North America, for example, the combination of disease, environmental transformation, and immigrant population pressure changed American Indian life and culture in profound ways.

Clearly, imported disease had the most ruinous influence on the lives of Indians. Cooperative labor was required for hunting and gathering, and native groups faced extinction if disease caused a shortage of labor. Also, most societies in North America were **nonliterate** and wholesale death by disease wiped out the elders and storytellers who preserved practical, religious, and cultural knowledge, resulting in confusion and disorientation among survivors. In an effort to avert extinction, remnant groups banded together to share labor and lore. Members of formerly self-sustaining kinship groups joined together in composite villages or, in some cases, intertribal leagues or confederacies. And the devastation that European diseases wrought eased the way for the

syphilis An infectious disease usually transmitted through sexual contact; if untreated, it can lead to paralysis and death.

cash crops A crop raised in large quantities for sale rather than for local or home consumption.

manioc Also called cassava and tapioca, a root vegetable native to South America that became a staple food source throughout the tropical world after 1500.

nonliterate Lacking a system of reading and writing, relying instead on storytelling and mnemonic (memory-assisting) devices such as pictures.

The Granger Collection, New York.

Africa's Gulf of Guinea (see Map 1.5). Armed with European firearms, aggressive tribes engaged in large-scale raiding deep into the Niger and Congo river regions. These raiders captured millions of prisoners, whom they herded back to the coast and sold to Portuguese, Spanish, Dutch, and other European traders to supply labor for mines and plantations in the New World.

The most recent estimates suggest that more than 9.5 million enslaved Africans arrived in the New World between 1500 and 1800. And they were only a small portion of the total number of Africans victimized by the system. On average, between 10 and 20 percent of the slaves shipped to the Americas died in transit. Adding in the numbers who were shipped to other locations in the Eastern Hemisphere, who were kept in slavery within Africa, and who died during the raids and on the marches to the coast yields a staggering total.

deeper penetration of Europeans into North America as Indians sought alliances with the newcomers to gain new tools, new sources of information, and new military partners, pushing Indians into increasingly tangled relationships with Europeans.

The Columbian Exchange also severely disrupted life in Africa. Africa had long been a key supplier of labor in the Old World. Perhaps as many as 4 million slaves were carried across the desert by Muslim traders between 800 and the time the Portuguese redirected the trade in the sixteenth century, which introduced European technology, wealth, and ideas that fostered the development of aggressive centralized states along the **Slave Coast** on the shore of West

A New World in Europe

The discovery of America and the Columbian Exchange also had staggering repercussions on life in Europe. New economic opportunities and new ideas demanded new kinds of political and economic organization. The discovery of the New World clearly forced a new and more modern society onto Europeans.

Europe's population was already rising when potatoes, maize, and other New World crops began to revolutionize food production. Populations then began to soar despite nearly continuous wars and a flood of migration to the New World. European rulers and their advisers saw that centralized states offered the most promising device for harnessing the riches of

■ **Slave Coast** A region of coastal West Africa adjacent to the Gold Coast; it was the principal source of the slaves taken out of West Africa from the sixteenth to the early nineteenth centuries.

MAP 1.5 Western Africa and the Atlantic Slave Trade
Africa's western shore was the major source for slaves who were transported to European colonies on the Atlantic islands, the Caribbean islands, and mainland North and South America. Powerful coastal kingdoms mounted organized raids into many inland areas to capture people who were then marched to the coast for shipment to the New World. This map shows the several regions from which slaves were taken, and the approximate numbers of people exported to different destinations. Copyright © Cengage Learning

the New World while controlling ever-increasing numbers of people at home. The sons and daughters of Europe's first generation of **absolute monarchs** chose to continue the consolidation of authority begun by their parents.

As Europeans responded to social, political, and economic changes, traditional patterns of authority broke down, especially in the realm of religion. A generation of theologians who were dissatisfied with the perceived corruption and superstition they found in the medieval Catholic Church launched the period known as the **Reformation**. Known as **Protestantism**, the doctrines adopted by these reformers launched an ideology that appealed to a broad audience in the rapidly changing European world of the sixteenth century. Ever critical of entrenched authority, the new doctrines attracted lawyers, bureaucrats, merchants, and manufacturers, whose economic and political status was on the rise thanks to increased prosperity generated by

the Columbian Exchange. But many in the ruling classes also found aspects of the new theology attractive. In Germany, the Protestant challenge to Catholic authority led many local princes to question the

absolute monarch The ruler of a kingdom in which every aspect of national life—including politics, religion, the economy, and social affairs—comes under royal authority.

■ **Reformation** a religious movement beginning in the sixteenth century that began as an internal attempt to reform the Roman Catholic Church, but soon led to the breakup of the Church into competing denominations.

■ **Protestantism** The beliefs and practices of Christians who broke with the Roman Catholic Church during the Reformation; rejecting church authority and the necessity of the priesthood, Protestants accepted the Bible as the only source of revelation, salvation as God's gift to the faithful, and a direct, personal relationship with God as available to every believer.

divine right claimed by the ruler of the **Holy Roman Empire**. Similarly, **Henry VIII** of England, at one time a critic of Protestant ideas, found Protestantism convenient when he wanted to resist the authority of the pope and expand English national power.

Henry VIII, the son of Henry VII and Elizabeth of York, was the first undisputed heir to the English throne in several generations, and he was consumed with the desire to avoid renewed civil war. When his wife, Catherine of Aragon, failed to bear a son who might inherit the throne, Henry demanded in 1527 that Pope Clement VII grant him a divorce and

permission to marry someone else. Clement refused, and in desperation, Henry launched an English Reformation by seizing the Catholic Church in England, gaining complete control of it by 1535.

For Henry, the idea of unifying religious and civil authority under his personal control was appealing. He needed Protestant support in his war against the pope's authority, so he reluctantly opened the door to Protestant practices in his newly created Church of England.

After Henry's death, his very young son ascended the throne as Edward VI. In the absence of a strong king, Protestants had virtual free rein, and the pace of reform quickened. Edward, however, died after ruling for only six years, and Mary, his oldest sister, succeeded him. Married to Philip II of Spain and a devout Roman Catholic, Mary attempted to reverse the reforming trend, cruelly suppressing Protestantism by executing several hundred leading reformers. But her brutality only drove the movement underground and made it more militant. By the time her half-sister Elizabeth, who was born and raised a Protestant, inherited the crown in 1558, the Protestant underground had become powerful and highly motivated. In fact, **Elizabeth I** spent her entire half-century reign trying to reach a workable settlement with Protestant **dissenters** that would permit them free worship without endangering her control over church and state.

divine right The idea that monarchs derive their authority to rule directly from God and are accountable only to God.

Holy Roman Empire A political entity, authorized by the Catholic Church in 1356, unifying central Europe under an emperor elected by four princes and three Catholic archbishops.

■ **Henry VIII** King of England (r. 1509–1547); his desire to divorce his first wife led him to break with Catholicism and establish the Church of England.

■ **Elizabeth I** Queen of England (r. 1558–1603); she succeeded the Catholic Mary I and reestablished Protestantism in England; her reign was a time of domestic prosperity and cultural achievement.

dissenters People who do not accept the doctrines of an established or national church.

Individual Voices

Native Americans' View of the World: "Powhatan's Mantle"

Though we usually do not think of maps as "voices," they do give voice to particular views of the world held by particular people in particular places and they are designed for particular purposes. A case in point is a map referred to as Powhatan's Mantle. Though it may not have been an actual cloak worn by Wahunsunacock, experts agree that it is from that time and that place. This map depicts the alliance system constructed by Wahunsunacock during his lifetime, with him in the center and the various confederation villages, as beaded disks, surrounding him.

1 This is an example of what geographers call an "egocentric" map. What makes the map effective in symbolizing the importance of the central figure?

2 Given its location and size, what can you say about the village represented by this disk?

3 Or this one?

© Ashmolean Museum, University of Oxford, UK/The Bridgeman Art Library International.

4 Taken in its entirety, how does this map differ from what we think of as conventional maps? What might that tell us about how Wahunsunacock and his people thought about relationships in their world? How might their view differ from that of Europeans?

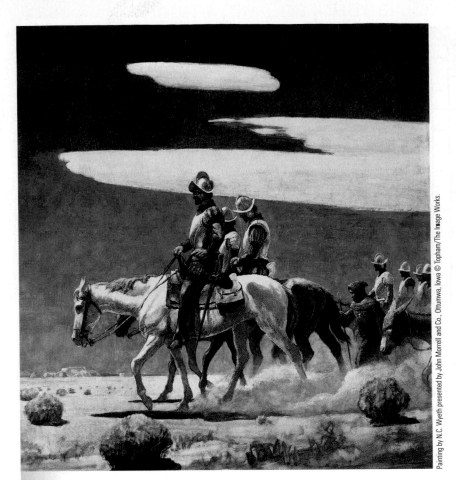

these voyages, Pánfilo de Narváez embarked on a colonizing mission to Florida in 1527. When his party became stranded, local Indians killed most of its members but took a few captives. One of these captives, Álvar Núñez Cabeza de Vaca, escaped with three others in 1534. The stories they told upon returning to Mexico led the Spanish to send Hernando de Soto to claim the Mississippi River, and he penetrated into the heart of the mound builders' territory in present-day Louisiana and Mississippi. One year later, **Francisco Vásquez de Coronado** left Mexico to look for seven cities that Cabeza de Vaca had heard glittered with gold. Coronado eventually crossed what are now the states of New Mexico, Arizona, Colorado, Oklahoma, and Kansas. These explorations were but a few of the ambitious adventures undertaken by Spanish conquistadores.

Coronado never found Cabeza de Vaca's "cities of gold," but other Spaniards did locate enormous sources of mineral wealth. Enslaving local Indians for labor, Spanish officials everywhere in the New World quickly moved to rip precious metals both out of the ground and out of what they characterized as "heathen temples." Between 1545 and 1660, Indian and later African slaves extracted over 7 million pounds of silver from Spanish-controlled areas, twice the volume of silver held by all of Europe before 1492. In the process, Spain became the richest nation in Europe, perhaps in the world.

Acting on information collected from Indians on Mexico's frontiers, in 1540 Francisco Vásquez de Coronado set out with an armed party to find seven cities of gold rumored to exist in the northern wilderness. Though the party crisscrossed much of the American Southwest, venturing as far as modern-day Kansas, they found no golden cities. Such parties, however, increased the Spaniards' knowledge of America and, through numerous encounters, increased Americans' knowledge of the new invaders in their land.

strained but peaceful relations with them. However, good relations with Indians who were subjects of the Aztec Empire also proved critical to the effort. An Indian woman whom he called Doña Marina served as his translator and cultural adviser, and with her help the conquistadores gained military support from numerous tribes of Mexican Indians who resented the Aztecs' power and their continuous demands for tribute.

The Spanish Crown supported many other exploratory ventures designed to bring new regions under Spain's control. In 1513 and again in 1521, Juan Ponce de León led expeditions to Florida. Following up on

Dreams of an English Eden

Given the stormy political and religious climate that prevailed during the sixteenth century, it is not surprising that Spain's early successes in the New World stirred up conflict with the other emerging states in Europe. To England, France, and other European countries, the massive flow of wealth made Spanish power a growing threat that had to be checked. The continuing religious controversies that accompanied the Reformation worsened the situation. Economic, religious, and political warfare was the rule throughout the century. One of the most celebrated of these early conflicts involved Spain and England.

Tension between Spain and England had been running high ever since Henry VIII had divorced his Spanish wife, Catherine of Aragon. That he quit the Catholic Church to do so and began permitting Protestant reforms in England added to the

■ **Francisco Vásquez de Coronado** Spanish soldier and explorer who led an expedition northward from Mexico in search of fabled cities of gold; his explorations gave Spain a claim to most of the American Southwest.

affront. Firmly wedded to the Catholic Church politically and religiously, Spain was aggressive in denouncing England. For his part, Henry was concerned primarily with domestic issues and steered away from direct confrontations with Spain or any of the other outraged Catholic countries.

Henry did, however, move to bring Ireland firmly under his control through colonization and land confiscation. During the years to come, England's rulers continued a systematic policy of colonization in Ireland. In the process, British authorities instituted a new set of colonial offices and encouraged generations of military adventurers, both of which would shape and advance later ventures in North America.

During the reign of Henry's younger daughter, Elizabeth, the continuing flow of New World wealth into Spain and that nation's anti-Protestant aggression led to an upturn in hostile activity. When Philip II of Spain, Elizabeth's brother-in-law and most vehement critic, sent an army of twenty thousand soldiers to root out Protestantism in the nearby **Netherlands**, the English queen began providing covert aid to the **Dutch** rebels. Elizabeth also struck at Philip's most valuable and vulnerable possession: his New World empire. In 1577 Elizabeth secretly authorized English **privateer** and explorer Francis Drake to attack Spanish ships. Drake carried out his task with enthusiasm, seizing tons of gold and silver during a three-year cruise around the world.

Elizabeth was open to virtually any venture that might vex her troublesome brother-in-law. New World colonizing efforts promised to do that and had the potential to enrich the kingdom as well. Although Elizabeth's father had confiscated and redistributed large tracts of church-owned land during his reign, farmland was becoming extremely scarce, and members of both the traditional nobility and the **gentry**—a class that was becoming increasingly important because of its investments in manufacturing and trading ventures—wanted more space for expansion. A relatively small island, England could acquire more territory only by carving it out of the New World.

Thus in 1578, Elizabeth granted Sir Humphrey Gilbert permission to settle two hundred colonists between the St. Lawrence River and the mythical land of Norumbega in what is now Newfoundland. One disaster after another plagued the effort, and Gilbert himself died at sea while trying to return to England. Thereafter, Gilbert's half-brother, **Sir Walter Raleigh**, took over the colonizing effort. This time, Elizabeth commanded Raleigh to locate farther south on the border of Spanish Florida, where an English base would facilitate raids on Philip's treasure fleets. Raleigh chose an island off the coast of present-day North Carolina. He advertised **Roanoke Island** as an

Netherlands/Holland/Dutch The first two terms, often used interchangeably, refer to the low-lying area in western Europe on the coast north of France and Belgium; the Dutch are the inhabitants of the Netherlands.

privateer A ship captain who owned his own boat, hired his own crew, and was authorized by his government to attack and capture enemy ships.

gentry The class of English landowners ranking just below the nobility.

Sir Walter Raleigh English courtier, soldier, and adventurer who attempted to establish the Virginia Colony.

■ **Roanoke Island** Island off North Carolina that Raleigh sought to colonize beginning in 1585.

"American Eden," where "the earth bringeth forth all things in abundance, as in the first Creation, without toile or labour." To honor his benefactor, he decided to call this paradise Virginia, tribute to the unwed, and thus officially virgin, queen.

In 1585 Elizabeth further angered the Spanish king by openly sending an army of six thousand troops to aid the Dutch rebels. In the meantime, Philip was supporting various Catholic plots within England, as well as in Scotland and Ireland, to subvert Elizabeth's authority and bring down the Protestant state. As tensions increased, so did English piracy. In 1586 Drake intensified his campaign, not only raiding Spanish ships at sea but attacking settlements in the Caribbean. By 1586, war between the two powers loomed.

The Decline of Spanish Power

The enormous inflow of wealth from the New World brought Spain power that no European country since the Roman Empire had enjoyed, but such rapid enrichment was a mixed blessing. Starting in Spain and radiating outward, prices began to climb as the growth of the money supply outpaced the growth of European economies. Too much money was chasing too few goods. Between 1550 and 1600, prices doubled in much of Europe, and **inflation** continued to soar for another half-century.

In addition, the social impact of the new wealth was forcing European monarchs to expand geographically and crack down domestically. As prices rose, the traditional landholding classes earned enormous profits from the sale of food and other necessities. Other groups fared less well. Artisans, laborers, and landless peasants—by far the largest class of people in Europe—found the value of their labor constantly shrinking. Throughout Europe, social unrest increased as formerly productive and respected citizens were reduced to poverty and begging. Overseas expansion seemed an inviting solution to the problem of an impoverished population. It was a safety valve that relieved a potentially dangerous source of domestic pressure while opening opportunities for enhancing national wealth through the development of colonies.

Sitting at the center of the new economy, Philip's Spain had the most to lose from rapid inflation and popular unrest. It also had the most to lose from New World expansion by any other European nation. Each New World claim asserted by England, France, or some other country represented the loss of a piece of treasure that Spain claimed as its own. Philip finally chose to confront building tensions by taking a desperate gamble: he would destroy England. This ploy, he thought, would effectively remove the Protestant threat, rid him of Elizabeth's ongoing harassment, and demonstrate to the rest of Europe that Spain intended to exercise absolute authority over the Atlantic world. In the spring of 1585, when tensions were at their peak, Philip began massing what was to be the largest marine force Europe had ever witnessed.

In 1588 Philip launched 132 warships carrying more than three thousand cannons and an invasion force of thirty thousand men. Arriving off the shores of England in July, the so-called "Invincible **Spanish Armada**" ran up against small, maneuverable British defense ships commanded by Elizabeth's skilled pirate captains. Drake and his fleet harassed the Spanish ships, preventing them from launching a successful attack. Then a storm blowing down from the North Sea scattered the Spanish fleet. Though Spanish power remained great for some time to come, the Armada disaster effectively ended Spain's near-monopoly over New World colonization.

EUROPEAN EMPIRES IN AMERICA

★ *What similarities and differences characterized Spanish, French, and Dutch patterns of empire building in North America? What role did colonists' experiences play?*

★ *How did natural environments help shape the colonial enterprises?*

In the seventeenth and eighteenth centuries, Spain, France, England, and a number of other European nations vied for control of the Americas and for domination of the transatlantic trade (see Map 2.1). For reasons explained in Chapter 3, England was somewhat delayed in its colonizing efforts, and by the time it became deeply involved in New World ventures, Spain, France, and Holland had already made major progress toward establishing empires in America. These European settlements not only affected England's colonization process profoundly, but through their interactions among themselves and with the Native Americans, they also created unique societies in North America whose presence influenced the entire course of the continent's history.

The Troubled Spanish Colonial Empire

Although the destruction of the Armada in 1588 struck a terrible blow at Spain's military power and its New World monopoly, the Spanish Empire continued to grow. By the end of the seventeenth century,

---

inflation Rising prices that occur when the supply of currency or credit grows faster than the available supply of goods and services.

■ **Spanish Armada** Fleet of warships sent by Spain in 1588 to invade England.

MAP 2.1 European and Indian Settlements in the Americas
Although Europeans were at first unsure about the implications of stumbling over a portion of the world that was new to them, they quickly came to understand the economic, political, and military potential involved in American colonization. As the colored arrows show, exploration continued into the seventeenth century as Europeans scrambled to claim individual pieces of New World real estate. Copyright © Cengage Learning

it stretched from New Mexico southward through Central America and much of South America into the Caribbean islands and northward again into Florida. Governing such a vast empire was difficult, and periodic efforts to reform the system usually failed. Two agencies in Spain, the House of Trade and the Council of the Indies, set Spanish colonial policy. In the colonies, Crown-appointed viceroys wielded military and political power in each of the four divisions of the empire. The Spanish colonies set up local governments as well; each town had a **cabildo secular**,

■ **cabildo secular** Secular municipal council that provided local government in Spain's New World empire.

a municipal council, as well as judges and other minor officials. The colonial administrators were appointed rather than elected, and most were envoys from Spain rather than native-born individuals.

Over the centuries, as the layers of bureaucracy developed, corruption and inefficiency developed as well. One major source of corruption and unrest stemmed from a persistent New World problem: the shortage of labor. The Spanish had adapted traditional institutions to address the demand for workers in mines and on plantations. In Spain, work was directed by **feudal** landlords, *encomenderos*, whose military service to the king entitled them to harness the labor of Spanish peasants. In New Spain, Indians took the place of the peasants in what was called the *encomienda* system. Under a law passed in 1512, when the Spanish first encountered an Indian group, the conquistador was required to explain to them that they were subject to the Spanish king and to the Catholic Church, offering to absorb them peacefully. Having satisfied this **requerimiento**, the *encomenderos* gained the right to use the Indians' labor for nine months each year. For his part, the *encomendero* paid a tax to the Crown for each Indian he received and agreed to teach his workers the Catholic faith, Spanish language, and a "civilized" vocation.

Despite some commitment to uplifting local Indians, the system in reality was brutally exploitative. As Bartolomé de Las Casas reported both to the Council of the Indies and to the king himself, landlords frequently overworked their Indian **serfs** and failed in their "civilizing" responsibilities. As the result of Las Casas's appeal, the *Leyes Nuevas* turned Indian relations in New Spain over to the church, and priests were assigned to enforce the laws. As Las Casas discovered, however, colonists often ignored even these slim protections.

The Dutch Enterprise

Interestingly, it was a former Spanish colony, the Netherlands, that presented one of the most serious threats to Spain's New World monopoly. The Armada disaster in 1588 had tipped the scales in favor of Dutch Protestant rebels, and the newly independent nation quickly developed a thriving commercial economy. Holland's first serious claim to American territory came in 1609, when Dutch sea captain **Henry Hudson** explored the East Coast in search of a passage eastward toward east Asia. He sailed up a large river that he hoped would lead him west to the Pacific. After realizing that he had not found the hoped-for route to the Far East, he returned to Holland and reported that the territory surrounding this river—which he named after himself—was "pleasant with Grasse & Flowers and Goodly Trees" and that the Indians were friendly. Surely, he added, profits could be made there. Hudson's employers did not share his enthusiasm for settlement; however, a fashion trend that seized Europe late in the sixteenth century provided a powerful incentive for some investment in the region. The immense popularity of the broad-brimmed beaver felt hat created a nearly insatiable demand for fur, and the experiences of early explorers and fishermen along America's North Atlantic shore indicated that a near endless supply was ripe for the trapping. Seeking to tap in on this "brown gold," the Dutch built a trading post on the Hudson River at Albany and an export station on Manhattan Island in 1614. Real Dutch efforts at New World colonization, however, did not begin until investors formed the **Dutch West India Company** in 1621.

In 1626, the company instructed official Peter Minuit to negotiate a lease for the entire island of Manhattan from the Manhates Indians, but the focus remained upriver; the company did nothing to attract settlers. By 1629, only three hundred colonists had spread themselves in a thin ribbon from Manhattan Island upriver to Albany. The situation began to change, however, when the Dutch West India Company drew up a comprehensive business plan to maximize profits and minimize dependence on local Indians for food and other support. To encourage the agricultural development necessary to support the fur industry, the company offered huge estates called **patroonships** to any company stockholder willing to bring fifty colonists to **New Netherland** at his own expense. In exchange, the patroons would enjoy near-feudal powers over their tenants. But few prosperous Dutchmen were interested in becoming New World barons. Rensselaerswyck, the estate of Kilian van Rensselaer, was the only patroonship that resembled the company's plan.

feudal Relating to a system in which landowners held broad powers over peasants or tenant farmers, providing protection in exchange for loyalty and labor.

■ *requerimiento* Spanish colonial law requiring conquistadores to inform Indians that they were subject to Spanish authority and offer to absorb them peacefully.

serfs Peasants who were bound to a particular estate but, unlike slaves, were not the personal property of the estate owner and received traditional feudal protections.

■ **Henry Hudson** Dutch ship captain and explorer who sailed up the Hudson River in 1609, giving the Netherlands a claim to the area now occupied by New York.

■ **Dutch West India Company** Dutch investment company formed in 1621 to develop colonies for the Netherlands in North America.

■ **patroonships** Huge grants of land given to any Dutch West India Company stockholder who, at his own expense, brought fifty colonists to New Netherland; the colonists became the tenants of the estate owner, or patroon.

■ **New Netherland** The colony founded by the Dutch West India Company in present-day New York; its capital was New Amsterdam on Manhattan Island.

Its location at the mouth of the Hudson River made the Dutch settlement of New Amsterdam a particularly important colonial trading center. Furs flowed down the river from Fort Orange (near modern Albany, New York), while guns, tools, and other trade goods traveled the other way. This etching (detail), based on a watercolor illustration painted around 1653, captures the city's colorful vibrancy after Peter Stuyvesant and the Dutch burghers merged their power to bring order and prosperity. The weighing beam in the foreground illustrates both the prosperity and quest for order: it was used not only to weigh the loads of goods flowing through the town, but was also used as a whipping post and gallows when necessary.

The colony's development came to rely instead on many poorer migrants who were drawn by unofficial promises of land ownership and economic betterment.

Settlers from just about anywhere were welcome in New Netherland—the colony attracted an extremely diverse population, including German and French Protestants, free and enslaved Africans, Catholics, Jews, and Muslims. In 1638 the Dutch even encouraged Swedish fur traders to create their own colony, New Sweden, within New Netherland's boundaries. Local government in such a disparate community was a persistent problem. Although the Dutch West India Company was officially in charge, day-to-day affairs were actually run by an elite group of **burghers**, men in New Amsterdam whose economic and political successes gave them significant influence. To reassert its power, the company reorganized its New World operations in 1645, appointing Peter Stuyvesant to manage all of its affairs in the Western Hemisphere. Stuyvesant immediately came into conflict with the local burghers in New Amsterdam, who in 1647 forced him to create a compromise government that gave the burghers an official voice through a council of nine appointed representatives. Six years later, Stuyvesant and the council created a municipal government modeled on those back in Holland. Despite this nod to democratic government, Stuyvesant ran company affairs with an iron hand, significantly tightening operations throughout the colony. In 1655 he even invaded and rooted out the Swedes, eliminating that source of dissension and competition.

The French Presence in America

Although France made a number of efforts to compete with Spain's New World projects during the sixteenth century, Spanish power was sufficient to prevent any major successes. For example, when a force of French Protestants established a colony in Florida in 1564, Spanish authorities sent an army to root them out. This led to increased Spanish vigilance, prompting Pedro Menéndez de Aviles to build the city of **Saint Augustine** the following year.

burghers In New Amsterdam, men who were not Dutch West India Company officials, but who governed civic affairs through their political influence.

■ **Saint Augustine** First colonial city in the present-day United States; located in Florida and founded for Spain in 1565.

It Matters Today

The Felt Hat Fad

Changes in fashion come and go, and we seldom give much thought to them as being historically significant. But the sudden popularity of felt hats in the late sixteenth century had a profound impact on not just America's history, but the history of the entire world. The flood of new wealth flowing into Europe from America permitted people of means—not just the nobility, but the landed gentry and even urban craftsmen and small business owners—to keep up with the latest fashions. Being in style became increasingly important to status-conscious merchants, manufacturers, and other beneficiaries of the New World boom. Demand for the beaver fur to make the felt became so steep that virtually the entire population of Old World beavers was wiped out, and entire industries arose in France, the Netherlands, Great Britain, and Russia to import this "brown gold" from the Americas. Fur drew Europeans up virtually every waterway in North America, leading to the founding of many of the most prominent cities in America today. It is safe to say that without this seemingly silly fashion trend, little in the United States would be as we know it today.

- Another important trade item during this era was deerskins. Research the demand for deerskins and then discuss what this tells us about socioeconomic changes during this era.
- Identify a current fashion trend and discuss its impact on global society. What differences do you think this trend will make on the future?

Unable to penetrate Spain's defenses in the south, the French concentrated their efforts farther north. In 1599, French Protestants facing an increasingly discriminatory environment at home began seeking investment opportunities in the New World. Pierre Chauvin and **Pierre Dugua de Mons** established a year-round trading post at Tadoussac, northeast of the eventual site of Quebec City. De Mons went back to France but in 1604 returned with **Samuel de Champlain**, establishing a string of settlements in what would be called **New France**. In 1608 de Mons and Champlain founded the city of Quebec and formed an enduring alliance with the Huron Indians. Two years later, King Henri IV was assassinated, setting off a wave of religious violence in France and destabilizing the French settlement in America. Over the next decade, French colonial authorities took little interest in overseas enterprises.

Finally in 1627 French minister Cardinal Richelieu chartered the **Company of New France**, awarding a group of the king's favorites licenses to establish plantations in Canada, but the venture failed to attract much interest. Frustrated by the lack of profits, Richelieu reorganized the Company of New France in 1633, dispatching Champlain, now bearing the title Lieutenant of New France, with three ships of supplies, workmen, and soldiers who, it was hoped, would breathe new life into the colony. In its new form, the company ignored the government's demands that it establish agricultural settlements and focused instead on the fur trade. Setting up posts in Quebec, Montreal, and a few more remote locations, the company became the primary outfitter of and buyer from the **coureurs de bois** and amassed huge profits by reselling the furs in Europe. After Richelieu's death in 1642, queen mother and French regent Anne of Austria acted on complaints filed by both fur trade investors and Jesuit missionaries that the Company of New France was not governing effectively. She chose to empower a new company, the **Community of Habitants of New France**,

■ **Pierre Dugua de Mons** French Protestant investor and adventurer who helped to found the French fur trade in Canada.

■ **Samuel de Champlain** French explorer who traced the St. Lawrence River inland to the Great Lakes, founded the city of Quebec, and formed the French alliance with the Huron Indians.

■ **New France** The colony established by France in what is now Canada and the Great Lakes region of the United States.

■ **Company of New France** Company established by Cardinal Richelieu to bring order to the running of France's North American enterprises.

■ **coureurs de bois** Literally, "runners of the woods"; independent French fur traders who lived among the Indians and sold furs to the French.

■ **Community of Habitants of New France** Company chartered by Anne of Austria to make operations in New France more efficient and profitable; it gave significant political power to local officials in Canada.

With permission of the Royal Ontario Museum © ROM.

Although this scene in Quebec was not painted until 1820, back streets in the old part of the city still looked very much as they had during the heyday of the French *coureurs de bois*. So did the people. Shops, like the one on the left, sold provisions and tools—often on credit—to the outward-bound runners of the woods, binding them to bring their next load of furs back to satisfy their debt. Thus, while the French Crown did little to encourage it, the fur business formed the core of Canada's woodland and urban economies.

with a monopoly on the fur trade and the privilege of granting land claims. Then, in 1647, Anne approved the formation of a council that consisted of the governor, the local director of the Jesuits, the colony's military commandant, and three elected officials. Meanwhile, the Company of New France continued technically to own the land and retained the power to appoint the governor and court officials in the colony.

Local authorities managed most of the colony's affairs until 1663, when the Crown began to intervene seriously in Canada. Having taken the functions of state into his own hands, young Louis XIV gave his finance minister, Jean-Baptiste Colbert, considerable authority over all monetary matters, including colonial enterprises. Seeking to make New France more efficient and to increase its contribution to the empire

at large, Colbert founded the **Company of the West**, modeled on the highly successful Dutch West India Company. He also revoked the land titles held by the Company of New France, putting them directly into the king's hands, and overturned the political power of the Community of Habitants, making New France a royal colony.

Although the king reaped enormous profits from the fur trade, his colonial interests ranged beyond this single source of income. In 1673 a French expedition led by Louis Joliet and Jacques Marquette set out on a systematic exploration of New France's many waterways. They discovered what appeared to be a major river, but it fell to **Robert Cavelier**, **Sieur de La Salle**, to prove the strategic and economic value of that discovery. In 1683 he and a party of French *coureurs de bois* and Indians retraced the earlier expedition and then followed the Mississippi River all the way to the Gulf of Mexico. La Salle immediately claimed the new territory for Louis XIV of France, naming it **Louisiana** in his honor. In 1698 the king sent settlers to the lower Mississippi Valley under the leadership of Pierre Le Moyne d'Iberville, who in 1699 raised Louisiana's first French fort, near present-day Biloxi, Mississippi. In 1718 French authorities built the city of New Orleans to serve as the capital of the new territory.

The acquisition of Louisiana was a major accomplishment for La Salle and for France. The newly discovered river way gave the French a rich, untapped source of furs as well as an alternative shipping route, allowing them to avoid the cold, stormy North Atlantic. Also, if an agricultural venture could be started in the new territory, it might serve as an inexpensive source of supplies to support both the fur trade in Canada and France's sugar plantations in the Caribbean. But perhaps of greatest importance was Louisiana's strategic location between Spain's claims in the Southwest and the Dutch and other colonies along the eastern seaboard. Controlling this piece of real estate gave Louis considerable leverage in international diplomacy.

■ **Company of the West** Company chartered after New France became a royal colony, designed to maximize profits to the Crown.

■ **Robert Cavelier, Sieur de La Salle** French explorer who followed the Mississippi River from present-day Illinois to the Gulf of Mexico in 1683, giving France a claim to the entire river way and adjoining territory.

■ **Louisiana** French colony south of New France; it included the entire area drained by the Mississippi River and all its tributary rivers.

In the Wider World

INDIANS AND THE EUROPEAN CHALLENGE

★ *How did changes in the natural environment affect Indian societies during the early colonial period?*

★ *How did the arrival of Europeans influence continuing adaptations by Native American groups?*

Native Americans did not sit idly by while the European powers carved out empires in North America. Some joined the newcomers, serving as advisers and companions. Others sought to use the Europeans as allies to accomplish their own economic, diplomatic, or military goals (see Map 2.2). Still others, overwhelmed by the onset of European diseases and shifting population pressures, withdrew into the interior. The changes in native America created both obstacles and opportunities, giving shape to the patterns of expansion and conflict that characterized the colonial world.

The Indian Frontier in New Spain

Indian assistance had been critical in Spain's successful campaign against the Aztecs. Groups who had been forced to pay tribute to the Aztec Empire gladly allied themselves with the Spanish in what the natives perceived as an opportunity to win their independence. Their hopes were soon dashed when the Spanish simply replaced the Aztecs as the new lords of a tributary empire.

Once Spain's New World empire was firmly rooted, Spanish expansion met little native resistance until 1598, when a particularly brutal conquistador named **Don Juan de Oñate** led a large expedition to the Rio Grande region of New Mexico. When some Pueblos resisted Oñate's efforts to impose Spanish culture and religion, the conquistador chose to make an example of **Ácoma pueblo**. It took Oñate's troops three days to subdue the settlement, but Spanish steel finally overcame Ácoma clubs and stone knives. When the battle was over, Oñate ordered eight hundred Indians executed and made slaves of the nearly seven hundred survivors, mostly women and children. In addition, each male survivor over the age of 25 had one foot chopped off to prevent his escape from slavery. Two **Hopi Indians** who had been visiting Ácoma at the time of the battle had their right hands cut off and then were sent home as examples of the price of resistance.

This blatant cruelty disgusted even the most cynical authorities in New Spain, and both the church and state stepped in. Oñate was removed, and the surviving Indians were placed under joint military and religious protection. Some members of Oñate's company remained, however, founding the town of **Santa Fe** in 1609. Others scattered to set up ranches throughout the region.

Thanks in part to Las Casas's efforts, the church played a key role in developing the colonies, especially in the stark regions along Mexico's northern frontier where there were no gold mines or profitable plantations. The Franciscan order led church efforts in New Mexico and put a peculiar stamp on

■ **Don Juan de Oñate** Spaniard who conquered New Mexico and claimed it for Spain in the 1590s.

■ **Ácoma pueblo** Indian community that resisted Spanish authority in 1598 and was subdued by the Spanish.

■ **Hopi Indians** Indians who were related to the Comanches and Shoshones and took up residence among the Pueblo Indians as agricultural town-dwellers; their name means "peaceful ones."

■ **Santa Fe** Spanish colonial town established in 1609; eventually the capital of the province of New Mexico.

MAP 2.2 Indian Economies in North America
Indian economic activities helped to shape patterns of European settlement and investment in the New World.
Regions that were primarily agricultural, like the Atlantic shoreline, lent themselves to European farming activities.
Farther north and west, however, where hunting played a more prominent role in native life, the fur trade was a
more attractive investment for European settlers. Copyright © Cengage Learning

Primary economic activity
- Agriculture
- Hunting
- Hunting-gathering
- Fishing

FOX Tribal location
Original range of bison

the pattern of Indian relations. A highly **ascetic** and disciplined order, the Franciscans were particularly offended by Pueblo religion and the Pueblo lifestyle. Indian ceremonies that involved various types of traditional religious objects smacked of idolatry to the Franciscans, and the priests embarked on a wholesale effort to destroy every vestige of the Indians' religion. The priests also interfered in the most intimate social aspects of Pueblo life, imposing foreign ideas about sexual relations and family structure, punishing most of the Pueblos' traditional practices as sinful.

After nearly a century of enduring these assaults on their most fundamental values, the Pueblos struck back. In 1680 a traditional leader named Popé led an uprising that united virtually all of the Indians in New Mexico against Spanish rule. The **Pueblo Revolt** left four hundred Spaniards dead as the rebels captured Santa Fe and drove the invaders from their land. It took almost a decade for the Spanish to regroup sufficiently to reinvade New Mexico. In 1689 troops moved back into the region and over the next several years waged a brutal war to recapture the territory.

ascetic Practicing severe abstinence or self-denial, generally in pursuit of spiritual awareness.

■ **Pueblo Revolt** Indian rebellion against Spanish authority in 1680 led by Popé; succeeded in driving the Spanish out of New Mexico for nearly a decade.

Alfred Jacob Miller based this 1837 painting of eighteenth-century mounted buffalo hunters on interviews with Shoshone Indians he met on a trip through the American West. It illustrates clearly the enormous impact the arrival of horses had on Plains Indian life. Note how few mounted men it took to drive vast numbers of animals over a cliff to their deaths. At the bottom of the cliff, women would butcher the dead animals and the meat, bones, and hides would provide food, clothing, tools, tents, and trade goods sufficient to support an entire band of Indians for some time. The arrival of the horse on the Great Plains in the late 1600s marked the beginning of 150 years of unprecedented wealth and power for the Indians in the region.

neighbors in Minnesota, who continued to farm and harvest wild rice and other crops. This continued tie, like that between the Crows and Hidatsas, increased both the hunters' and the farmers' chances for survival in an ever more hostile world: intergroup trade became the key to the welfare of all.

The buffalo also began to play an important role on the southern plains. There, groups such as the Apaches, Comanches, and Kiowas specialized in hunting the ever-increasing herds and then exchanging part of their kill for village-based products from their neighbors and kin, the Navajos, Hopis, and Pueblos. And it was in these intergroup trades that the Plains Indians acquired a new advantage in their efforts to expand their hunting economy: the horse.

One unintentional outcome of the Pueblo Revolt was the liberation of thousands of Spanish horses. The Pueblos had little use for these animals, but their trading partners, the Kiowas and Comanches, quickly adopted them. Horses could carry much larger loads than dogs and could survive on a diet of grass rather than taking a share of the meat. In less than a generation, horses became a mainstay of the buffalo-hunting cultures on the southern plains. And from there, horses spread quickly to other hunting people.

Northern plains dwellers such as the Shoshones quickly began acquiring horses from their southwestern kin. Following a northward path along the eastern flank of the Rocky Mountains, horses were passed from one group to another in the complex trading system that had come into existence in the plains region. Well adapted to grasslands and virtually free from natural predators or diseases, horses greatly increased in number. By 1730, virtually all of the plains hunting peoples had some horses and were clamoring for more.

The steady demand for horses and hunting grounds created a new dynamic on the Great Plains and set a new economy into motion (see Map 2.3). After the Spanish reconquest of New Mexico, Indians could obtain horses only through warfare and trade, and both increased significantly. Surprise raids to steal horses from neighboring Indian groups and European settlements brought both honor and wealth to those who were successful.

MAP 2.3 Intergroup Trading on the Plains Although movies portray Plains Indians as unsophisticated hunters and warriors, Native American societies in America's midsection maintained extremely complex and cosmopolitan trading networks. As this map shows, trade routes that had existed before Europeans entered the region acquired added importance in distributing the novel technologies and ideas that the newcomers brought with them. The most important of these were horses, which were passed very quickly from group to group along these trade routes. Copyright © Cengage Learning

Legend:
- Regional trading hub
- Major trading center
- Secondary center
- Major trade route
- Secondary route
- Conjectural route

Area of horse use
- 1630
- 1675
- 1710

CONQUEST AND ACCOMMODATION IN A SHARED NEW WORLD

☆ *How did settlers and American Indians adapt to changing conditions in the different regions of colonial occupation?*

Old World cultures, Native American historical dynamics, and New World environmental conditions combined to create vibrant new societies in European pioneer settlements. Despite the regulatory efforts of Spanish bureaucrats, French royal officials, and Dutch company executives, life in the colonies developed in its own peculiar ways. Entire regions in what would become the United States assumed cultural contours that would shape all future developments in each.

New Spain's Northern Frontiers

After suppressing the Pueblo Revolt during the 1690s, Spaniards began drifting back into New Mexico. Unlike areas to the south, New Mexico offered no rich deposits of gold or silver, and the climate was unsuitable for large-scale agriculture. With neither mines nor plantations to support the *encomienda* system, the basic underpinnings of the traditional ruling order never

emerged. Even so, the Spanish colonial bureaucracy followed conventional imperial procedures and made Santa Fe the official municipal center for the region. But there were no *encomenderos* to provide wealth. The church, which was channeling money to missions, and the Spanish government, which allocated both military and civic support funds, were the only major employers in the region. Those in neither church's nor state's employ had to scramble for a living.

Under Pueblo control following the revolt, the small flocks of sheep abandoned by the fleeing Spanish had grown dramatically, and sheep ranching had become a reliable way to make a living. Thus, rather than concentrating near the municipal center in Santa Fe, the population in New Mexico spread out across the land, forming two sorts of communities. South of Santa Fe, people settled on scattered ranches. Elsewhere, they gathered in small villages along streams and pooled their labor to make a living from irrigated **subsistence farming**.

---

subsistence farming Farming that produces enough food for survival but no surplus that can be sold.

Commenting on conveying indigenous ideas using European languages, Ácoma Pueblo poet Simon Ortiz observed, "a vital sense of cultural continuity [is] maintained because of Indigenous cultural consciousness." The mirror image of this process may be seen in this icon of Jesus wrought using traditional American feather-working techniques. Through such ingenious workmanship, natives indigenized foreign ideas, converting them from colonial to native expressions.

Like colonists elsewhere in Spain's New World empire, the New Mexico colonists were almost entirely male. Isolated on sheep ranches or in small villages, these men sought Indian companionship and married into local populations. These marriages gave birth not only to a new hybrid population but also to lines of kinship, trade, and authority that were in sharp contrast to the imperial ideal. For example, when Navajo or Apache raiding parties struck, ranchers and villagers turned to their Indian relatives for protection rather than to Spanish officials in Santa Fe.

Far away from the imperial economy centered in Mexico City, New Mexicans looked northward for trading opportunities. Southern Plains Indians—Apaches, Comanches, Kiowas, and their kin—needed a continuous supply of horses. They could obtain them by raiding Spanish ranches, but doing so brought reprisals by ranchers and their Indian relatives. Trade was a safer option. Facing labor shortages, New Mexicans accepted Indian slaves—especially children—in exchange for horses. Soon, these young captives became another important commodity in the already complex trading and raiding system that prevailed among the southwestern Indians and Spanish New Mexicans.

In this frontier world, unlike the rest of Spanish America, a man's social status came to depend less on his Spanish connections than on his ability to work effectively in the complicated world of kinship that prevailed in the Indian community. The people who eventually emerged as the elite class in New Mexico were those who best perfected these skills. Under their influence, Santa Fe was transformed from a traditional mission and imperial town into a cosmopolitan frontier trading center. During the next two centuries, this multiethnic elite absorbed first French and then Anglo-American newcomers while maintaining its own social, political, and economic style.

The Dutch Settlements

Few of the wealthy stockholders in the Dutch West India Company wanted to trade their lives as successful gentleman investors for a pioneering existence on a barely tamed frontier. The economy in Holland was booming, and only the most desperate or adventurous wanted to leave. But having no one to pay their way, even the few who were willing were hard-pressed to migrate to the colony.

Desperate to draw settlers, the Dutch West India Company created an alternative to patroonship, agreeing to grant a tract of land to any free man who would agree to farm it. This offer appealed to many groups in Europe who were experiencing hardship in their own countries but who, for one reason or another, were unwelcome in the colonies of their homelands. French Protestants, for example, were experiencing terrible persecution in France but were forbidden to go to Canada or Louisiana. Roman Catholics, Quakers, Jews, Muslims, and a wide variety of others also chose to migrate to New Netherland. Most of the colonists settled on small farms, called *bouweries* in Dutch, and engaged in the same agricultural pursuits they had practiced in Europe. Thus New Netherland was dotted with little settlements, each having its own language, culture, and internal economy.

Farming was the dominant activity among the emigrants, but some followed the example of the French *coureurs de bois* and went alone or in small groups into the woods to live and trade with the Indians. Called **bosch loopers**, these independent traders traveled through the forests, trading cheap brandy and rum for the Indians' furs, which they then sold for enormous profits. Although both tribal leaders and legitimate

■ **bosch loopers** Dutch term meaning "woods runners"; independent Dutch fur traders.

The French had difficulty persuading settlers to come to their New World province in Louisiana. As a result, the region's development depended on a mixture of various European refugees, native Indians, and imported Africans for labor. Alexander de Batz's 1735 painting gives us a good idea of what the population around New Orleans looked like at that time. As in neighboring New Mexico, a multiracial and multicultural society emerged in Louisiana that left a permanent legacy in the region.

Courtesy of the Peabody Museum of Archeology and Ethnology. Harvard University 41-72-10/20 T2377.

traders complained about the *bosch loopers'* illegal activities, company officials could not control them.

In fact, the Dutch West India Company was unable to control much of anything in New Netherland. The incredible diversity of the settlers no doubt contributed to this administrative impotence. For example, Dutch law and company policy dictated that the **Dutch Reform Church** was to be the colony's official and only religion. But instead of drawing everyone into one congregation, the policy had the opposite effect. As late as 1642 not a single church of any denomination had been planted. Poor leadership and unimaginative policies also contributed to the general air of disorder. Following Peter Minuit's dismissal by the company in 1631, a long line of incompetent governors ruled the colony. In the absence of any legislative assembly or other local body to help keep matters on track, for years one bad decision followed another. It took a major reorganization by the West India Company and its appointment of Peter Stuyvesant in 1645 to turn the colony around.

Life in French Louisiana

France's colony in Louisiana had many of the same qualities and faced many of the same problems as Holland's and Spain's North American possessions. Like most European settlements, Louisiana suffered from a critical shortage of labor, leading first to dependence on the Indians and eventually to the wholesale adoption of African slavery. And like all Europeans who settled in North America, Louisianans found themselves embroiled in a complicated Native American world that usually defied European understanding.

Despite the territory's strategic location, fertile soils, and fur-bearing animals, few Frenchmen showed any interest in settling there. In the first years of the colony's existence, the population consisted primarily of three groups: military men, who were generally members of the lower nobility; *coureurs de bois* from Canada looking for new and better sources of furs; and French craftsmen seeking economic independence in the New World. The men in each group had little in common with those in the other groups, and more important, none had knowledge of or interest in food production. In the absence of an agricultural establishment, the small number of settlers in Louisiana had to depend on imported food. At first, ships from France carried provisions to the colonies, but war in Europe frequently interrupted this source. In desperation, the colonists turned to the Indians.

■ **Dutch Reform Church** Calvinistic Protestant denomination; the established church in the Dutch Republic and the official church in New Netherland.

Conquest and Accommodation in a Shared New World   **47**

The **Natchez**, **Chickasaws**, and **Choctaws** were all close by and well provisioned. The Chickasaws refused to deal with the French, and the Natchez, divided into quarreling factions, were sometimes helpful and sometimes hostile. But the Choctaws, locked into a

■ **Natchez** An urban, mound-building Indian people who lived on the lower Mississippi River until they were destroyed in a war with the French in the 1720s; survivors joined the Creek Confederacy.

■ **Chickasaws** Another lower Mississippi urban, mound-building Indian people, who became a society of hunters after the change in climate and introduction of disease after 1400; they were successful in resisting French aggression throughout the colonial era.

■ **Choctaws** Like the Chickasaws, a mound-building people who became a society of hunters after 1400; they were steadfast allies of the French in wars against the Natchez and Chickasaws.

war with the Chickasaws and a tense relationship with the Natchez, found the prospect of an alliance with the French quite attractive. In the realignment process, the Choctaws helped shape France's Indian policies and expansion plans. For example, they were able to convince the French to expand onto Natchez land rather than in Choctaw territory. When the Natchez resisted French incursion, the Choctaws helped their European allies destroy the tribe. The Choctaws also assisted the French in a thirty-year-long conflict with the Chickasaws, though with less success.

Despite the Choctaw alliance, which guaranteed ample food supplies and facilitated territorial acquisitions, Louisiana remained unappealing to Frenchmen. Increasingly, settlers in Louisiana followed their Spanish neighbors' example by importing African slaves to do necessary work. By 1732, slaves made up two-thirds of the population.

Individual Voices

Bartolomé de Las Casas Argues
for the American Indians

One of the serious problems in assessing relations between Native Americans and Europeans during the period of early contact is a general lack of evidence about what participants thought about their situations and each other. Fortunately, the Spanish Crown and the Roman Catholic Church kept detailed records. The records of the debate between Juan Ginés de Sepúlveda and Bartolomé de Las Casas before the Council of Valladolid give us insight into how at least some people were thinking. We know, for example, Sepúlveda's view that Indians lacked souls and therefore could never become truly civilized Christians. We also know from Las Casas of Indians' many remarkable accomplishments, both in creating advanced civilizations of their own and in adapting to Spanish civilization. And in the following excerpt, we learn his views about the relationship between the Indians and God. Even so, despite his sympathy for the Indians, Las Casas's voice does not give us a clear insight into how the Indians themselves perceived things.

1 What, exactly, is Las Casas asserting in this sentence? How does this proposition set up the rest of his argument?

2 What does the reference to writings by Saint Thomas tell us about Las Casas's view of human nature? How does it refute Sepúlveda's claims concerning Indians?

3 Judging from this brief excerpt from Las Casas's argument, why do you suppose he won the debate? Why would the Catholic Church have chosen to endorse and publicize his views and not Sepúlveda's?

Who, therefore, except one who is irreverent toward God and contemptuous of nature, has dared to write that countless numbers of natives across the ocean are barbarous, savage, uncivilized, and slow witted when, if they are evaluated by an accurate judgment, they completely outnumber all other men? **1** This is consistent with what Saint Thomas writes: "The good which is proportionate to the common state of nature is to be found in most men and is lacking only in a few. . . . Thus it is clear that the majority of men have sufficient knowledge to guide their lives, and the few who do not have this knowledge are said to be half-witted or fools." Therefore, since barbarians of that kind, as Saint Thomas says, lack that good of the intellect which is knowledge of the truth, a good proportionate to the common condition of rational nature, it is evident that in each part of the world, or anywhere among the nations, barbarians of this sort or freaks of rational nature can only be quite rare. For since God's love of mankind is so great and it is his will to save all men, it is in accord with his wisdom that in the whole universe, which is perfect in all its parts, his supreme wisdom should shine more and more in the most perfect thing: rational nature. **2**

Again, if we believe that such a huge part of mankind is barbaric, it would follow that God's design has for the most part been ineffective, with so many thousands of men deprived of the natural light that is common to all peoples. And so there would be a great reduction in the perfection of the entire universe— something that is unacceptable and unthinkable for any Christian. **3**

Source: Bartolome de las Casas, In Defense of the Indians: The Defense of the Most Reverend Lord, Don Fray Bartolome de las Casas, of the Order of Preachers, Late Bishop of Chiapa, Against the Persecutors and Slanderers of the Peoples of the New World Discovered Across the Seas, translated, edited, and annotated by Stafford Poole (Dekalb, Northern Illinois University Press, © 1974).

Study Tools

SUMMARY

Spain's opening ventures in the Americas had been wildly successful, making the Iberian kingdom the envy of the world. Hoping to cash in on the bounty, other European nations challenged Spain's monopoly on American colonization, creating an outward explosion. Although slow to consolidate an imperial presence in North America, England was the first to confront the Spanish in force, wounding them severely. France and the Netherlands took advantage of the situation to begin building their own American empires.

For Native Americans, the entry of Europeans into their realms combined with other forces to create an air of crisis. Presented with a series of new challenges, Indians sought new ways to solve their problems and created altogether new societies. This often involved difficult choices: perhaps allying with the newcomers, resisting them, or fleeing. As different groups exercised different options, the outcome was a historically dynamic world of interaction involving all of the societies that were coming together in North America.

This dynamic interaction yielded interesting fruit. In New Spain, New France, Louisiana, New Netherland, and throughout the Great Plains, truly cosmopolitan societies emerged. Bearing cultural traits and material goods from throughout the world, these new transatlantic societies set the tone for future development in North America. As we see in Chapter 3, societies on the Atlantic coast, too, were evolving as English colonists interacted with the land and its many occupants. The outcome of such interchange, over the centuries, was the emergence of a multicultural, multiethnic, and extraordinarily rich culture—an essential element in Making America.

CHRONOLOGY
New World Colonies and Native Americans

1494	Treaty of Tordesillas
1512	Creation of the *encomienda* system
1519–1521	Hernando Cortés invades Mexico
1551	Council of Valladolid rules that American Indians are human beings with souls
1558	Elizabeth I becomes queen of England
1565	Spanish found St. Augustine in present-day Florida
1588	English defeat Spanish Armada
1598	Don Juan de Oñate destroys Ácoma pueblo
1608	French-Huron alliance
1609	Spanish found Santa Fe in present-day New Mexico
1627	Creation of Company of New France
1680	Pueblo Revolt
1683	La Salle expedition down the Mississippi River to the Gulf of Mexico
ca. 1700	Beginning of French-Choctaw alliance

FOCUS QUESTIONS

If you have mastered this chapter, you should be able to answer these questions and to explain the terms that follow the questions.

1. ☆ *Why did European rulers promote exploration and colonization in North America?*

2. ☆ *How did religious and political rivalries influence each European power's approach to New World colonization?*

3. ☆ *What similarities and differences characterized Spanish, French, and Dutch patterns of empire building in North America? What role did colonists' experiences play?*

4. ☆ *How did natural environments help shape the colonial enterprises?*

5. ☆ *How did changes in the natural environment affect Indian societies during the early colonial period?*

6. ☆ *How did the arrival of Europeans influence continuing adaptations by Native American groups?*

7. ☆ *How did settlers and American Indians adapt to changing conditions in the different regions of colonial occupation?*

Study Tools

KEY TERMS

encomendero (p. 29)

conquistadores (p. 29)

Treaty of Tordesillas (p. 31)

Hernando Cortés (p. 31)

Francisco Vásquez de Coronado (p. 32)

Roanoke Island (p. 33)

Spanish Armada (p. 34)

cabildo secular (p. 35)

requerimiento (p. 36)

Henry Hudson (p. 36)

Dutch West India Company (p. 36)

patroonships (p. 36)

New Netherland (p. 36)

Saint Augustine (p. 37)

Pierre Dugua de Mons (p. 38)

Samuel de Champlain (p. 38)

New France (p. 38)

Company of New France (p. 38)

coureurs de bois (p. 38)

Community of Habitants of New France (p. 38)

Company of the West (p. 39)

Robert Cavelier, Sieur de La Salle (p. 39)

Louisiana (p. 39)

Don Juan de Oñate (p. 40)

Ácoma pueblo (p. 40)

Hopi Indians (p. 40)

Santa Fe (p. 40)

Pueblo Revolt (p. 41)

Creek Confederacy (p. 42)

Fort Orange (p. 43)

Mohicans (p. 43)

Lakotas/Dakotas (p. 43)

bosch loopers (p. 46)

Dutch Reform Church (p. 47)

Natchez (p. 48)

Chickasaws (p. 48)

Choctaws (p. 48)

 CourseMate   Go to the History CourseMate website for primary source links, study tools, and review materials for this chapter. www.cengagebrain.com

3

Founding the English Mainland Colonies, 1585–1732

Behind the Stories

The first English settlers who landed on the shores of Virginia in 1607 were probably as nervous and frightened as a spaceship crew landing on Mars. They had come to a world of strange vegetation, exotic animals, dangerous aliens, and deadly diseases. Yet during the seventeenth century, thousands of English and European men and women chose to follow these adventurers. Like modern immigrants, they were fleeing their homelands because of poverty, religious persecution, and political conflicts. They came to North America seeking land, religious freedom, and a better life.

If we attempt to write the story of this era of colonization, whose perspective should we use? The dreams that carried English men across the Atlantic Ocean were not shared by the Africans brought to America by force. Every acre of land cleared and claimed by the settlers meant a loss of land to the Native Americans. The opportunities and responsibilities that defined women in the colonies were dramatically different than those that defined men. As a historian I have learned

that whose story we choose to tell determines what questions we feel must be answered.

Even when historians focus on the same group, their answers to key questions are often very different. Some, for example, have argued that a great expanse of ocean isolated the New World from the Old and prompted the rise of a unique American character—more practical, more ambitious, more democratic. Others, however, paint the ocean as a great waterway that created a transatlantic community of Europe, Africa, and the Americas in which ideas and values flowed as quickly as cargoes of sugar, tobacco, and slaves.

As you move through this chapter, you might find yourself asking new questions about colonial history. This would not surprise me, for my work on colonial women took me down many unexpected paths. The past is always being debated, rewritten, and rediscovered, and history, like housework, is "never done." This is what ensures that the old and often-told story of American colonization will always be, in some respect, new.

—C.B.

Chapter Outline

England and Colonization
England's First Attempts at Colonization
Turmoil and Tensions in England

Settling the Chesapeake
The Jamestown Colony
Maryland: A Catholic Refuge
Troubles on the Chesapeake
Colonial Chesapeake Life

New England: Colonies of Dissenters
The Plymouth Colony
Massachusetts Bay and Its Settlers
Government in Puritan Massachusetts
Indian Suppression
Change and Reaction in England and New England

The Pluralism of the Middle Colonies
From New Netherland to New York
Leisler's Rebellion
William Penn's Holy Experiment

Colonies of the Lower South
The Carolina Colony
Georgia, the Last Colony
INDIVIDUAL VOICES: Nathaniel Bacon: Manifesto Concerning the Troubles in Virginia, 1676

Study Tools

Individual Choices
Nathaniel Bacon

In 1674 a charismatic young Englishman named Nathaniel Bacon arrived in Virginia. He was wealthy enough to buy a large plantation near Jamestown and a large tract of land on the frontier, and he was quickly appointed to Governor William Berkeley's elite advisory council. Yet, within two years, Bacon had become the leader of a rebellion of poor farmers that almost toppled the colonial government.

Bacon could have lived out his days comfortably among the planter elite. Why, then, did he become a rebel? He had arrived in Virginia at a tense moment when the colony's backcountry farmers' dream of prosperity was threatened by drought, a drop in the price of tobacco, unfair taxing policies by Berkeley's administration, and, most frightening of all, Indian raids. When Indians attacked his own frontier farm, Bacon threw in his lot with his neighbors.

Bacon demanded that the governor raise a militia to rid the area of all Indians. The governor refused—and Bacon took matters into his own hands. He raised a vigilante army and began a war against all nearby Indians, even the peaceful tribes. The amazed and enraged governor branded Bacon a traitor. Bacon quickly struck back. Over five hundred men flocked to join "General" Bacon, and together they seized

Nathaniel Bacon

Courtesy Preservation Virginia.

control of the colony's capital. By mid-October Bacon's rebels controlled over two-thirds of Virginia. Then tragedy struck. On October 26, 1676, Nathaniel Bacon suddenly died of dysentery. Without his leadership, the revolution faltered and by the spring of 1677, it had been crushed.

For the next hundred years, the royal governors and the wealthy coastal planters dominated Virginia political life. To these elite colonists, Nathaniel Bacon symbolized a dangerous breakdown of law and order. To backcountry families, Bacon remained a frontier hero. His defense of the rebellion, "The Manifesto of the People," excerpted at the end of this chapter, made it clear that Bacon believed he was fighting for a just cause. But villain or hero, Nathaniel Bacon would not be the last colonist to fight against unfair treatment.

Religious tensions troubled the nation as well. Although the official **Church of England** that Henry VIII had created in 1531 was Protestant, a movement to "purify" the church had grown steadily in the early seventeenth century, led by Protestants who believed the church had kept too many Catholic rituals and customs. To the monarchs of the Stuart dynasty, this **Puritan** criticism smacked of treason as well as heresy, for the king was not only head of the nation but head of the Anglican Church. The mistrust between Puritan reformers and their kings grew during the reigns of James I and his son Charles I, for both men were rumored to be secretly practicing Catholicism.

The political situation was equally tense. A power struggle between the Crown and **Parliament**, which was the legislative branch of the English government, erupted into open warfare in 1642. This civil war brought together many of the threads of religious and political discontent and conflict, pitting Puritans, merchants, and members of the rising middle class against the Stuart king. A Puritan army, led by Oliver Cromwell, overthrew the monarchy and, in 1649, Cromwell took the radical step of executing Charles I. This execution established the supremacy of Parliament. Cromwell headed the new **Commonwealth** government until his death in 1658, but he proved no more popular than the former king. In 1660, the Stuart family was invited to take the throne once again. For the next twenty-five years, a period called the **Restoration**, Charles II ruled England. But when the crown passed to his brother, James II, who openly

practiced Catholicism, a second revolution began. This time, there was little bloodshed, for James wisely fled to the safety of France. His Protestant daughter Mary and her Dutch husband, William, then came to the English throne. This **Glorious Revolution** of 1688 ended almost a century of political, ideological, and economic instability. But by that time, thousands of English men and women had journeyed across the Atlantic Ocean and twelve colonies covered the mainland shores.

Settling the Chesapeake

★ What were the goals of the Virginia Company and of the Calvert family in creating their Chesapeake colonies? Did the colonies achieve these goals?

★ What events illustrate the racial, class, and religious tensions in the Chesapeake?

Fears of financial ruin had prevented any Englishman from following in Sir Walter Raleigh's footsteps. But by the beginning of the seventeenth century, English **entrepreneurs** had developed a new method of financing high-risk ventures, the **joint-stock company**. In 1603, King James I granted a charter to two such companies eager to establish colonies on mainland North America. The Plymouth Company's settlement quickly failed, for the frigid rocky coast of Maine proved uninviting and the local Indians unfriendly. It thus fell to the remaining Virginia Company to create the first successful English colony in North America.

The Jamestown Colony

The 101 men and four boys sent by the Virginia Company found themselves crammed aboard three small ships, the *Susan Constant*, the *Godspeed*, and the *Discovery*. Tempers grew short as the months at sea grew long, and trouble erupted on the *Susan Constant*. One of the troublemakers, an adventurer named John Smith, landed in the ship's brig for his role in attempting to organize a mutiny. The colonists had more to worry about than Mr. Smith's temper, however. The Spanish had proven eager to repel any European competitors from the vast territory stretching from Florida to Maine that the pope had granted them in the sixteenth century. French Huguenots seeking refuge in Florida had learned this all too well when Spanish forces brutally massacred the small band of Protestants who dared to settle there. And although the Indians had been friendly on the Caribbean Islands where the English colonists had stopped for provisions, the colonists were far from certain of the reception they would receive when they reached their destination.

■ **Church of England** The Protestant church established in the sixteenth century by King Henry VIII as England's official church; also known as the Anglican Church.

■ **Puritans** Members of the Church of England who wanted to reform its worship service and religious doctrines to make it a more thoroughly Protestant church.

■ **Parliament** The lawmaking branch of the English government, composed of the House of Lords, representing England's nobility, and the House of Commons, an elected body of untitled English citizens.

■ **Commonwealth** The republic established after the victory of Oliver Cromwell in the English civil war; the Commonwealth lasted from 1649 until the monarchy was restored in 1660.

■ **Restoration** The era following the return of monarchy to England, beginning in 1660 with King Charles II and ending in 1688 with the exile of King James II.

■ **Glorious Revolution** A term used to describe the removal of James II from the English throne and the crowning of the Protestant monarchs, William and Mary.

entrepreneur A person who organizes and manages a business enterprise that involves risk and requires initiative.

joint-stock company A business financed through the sale of shares of stock to investors; the investors share in both the profits and losses from a risky venture.

The three ships entered Chesapeake Bay five months after they had set sail (see Map 3.1). The colonists decided to establish themselves on a small peninsula that jutted out from a river they named the James, in honor of their king, calling their little foothold **Jamestown**. As they explored their surroundings and met the local Indians, the Englishmen concluded that prospects looked good for forging a peaceful and profitable relationship.

Yet even the least insightful among them should have recognized the wide chasm that separated Englishmen from Indians. To the local tribes, the land on which the colonists had set up their tents and begun to build their fortifications was not Virginia but Tsenacommacah, and it belonged to the confederation of some thirty Algonkian-speaking tribes dominated by the Powhatan chieftain Wahunsunacock, as described in Chapter 1. If the English found the Indians exotic—in their body and face paints, their relative nakedness, their religious ceremonies, and their weaponry—the Pamunkeys, Arrohatecks, and Mattoponis found the cumbersome dress and the noisy but less than effective weaponry of the new arrivals equally odd. Each viewed their own culture as superior and, for a brief period, seemed willing to tolerate the misguided beliefs and behaviors of the other. The colonists were thus convinced that they had met the instructions given them to "take great care not to offend the naturals."

MAP 3.1 Chesapeake Expansion
In Maryland and Virginia, tobacco became the staple crop, making planters who owned land in the tidewater areas quite wealthy. Barrels of dried tobacco were shipped out of the broad Chesapeake Bay, across the Atlantic to England. Increasingly, as the eighteenth century began, ships sailing into the Bay carried African slaves who did the backbreaking labor required to produce this profitable "brown gold." Copyright © Cengage Learning

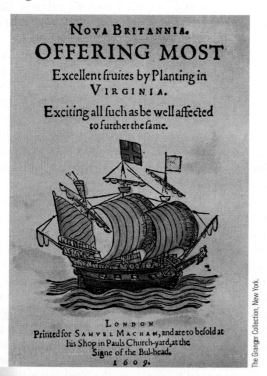

Advertisements like this one were designed to promote settlement of England's first permanent mainland colony. Recruiters hoped that the promise of economic opportunity would offset the fears of settling in a dangerous, strange, and distant land.

If the English men and boys had known what lay in store for them in the next decade, they might have sailed for home at once. For even without attacks from Indians or the Spanish, the settlers soon faced a seemingly endless series of survival challenges. The site of their encampment proved unhealthy, and one by one, colonists fell ill, suffering from typhus, malaria, or dysentery. Few of them had the skills needed to survive in what was proving to be a hostile and alien environment. Many lacked the experience or the

■ **Jamestown** First permanent English settlement in mainland America, established in 1607 by the Virginia Company and named in honor of King James I.

The early Jamestown colonists huddled inside the safety of this fort, built on the James River. More of the first groups of settlers would die from disease and starvation, however, than from attack by local Powhatan Indians.

Private Collection/Peter Newark American Pictures/The Bridgeman Art Library International.

motivation needed to clear fields, plant crops, or build fortifications. These adventurers, as one Englishman bluntly put it, "never knew what a day's labour meant."

The disease, starvation, and exposure to the elements that threatened to destroy the colony were temporarily relieved when the former troublemaker, John Smith, took command. Smith was hardly a well-liked man: he was overconfident and self-centered, full of exaggerated tales of his heroic deeds as a mercenary in exotic lands. He had narrowly escaped execution on the voyage from England. Smith did have some survival knowledge, however, and he did know how to discipline men. He established a "no work, no food" policy, and he negotiated with the Powhatans for corn and other supplies. When Smith left in 1609, the discipline and order he had established quickly collapsed. The original colonists and those who joined them the following spring remembered that winter as "the starving time." The desperate colonists burned their housing to keep warm and ate dogs, cats, mice, snakes, even shoe leather in their struggle to survive. Only sixty settlers were alive at winter's end.

The Powhatans had little sympathy for the desperate colonists. Even before Smith had departed, cooperation between the two groups had begun to disintegrate, for despite all their problems, the English exhibited a sense of superiority and entitlement that alienated Wahunsunacock and his confederacy. By 1609 tension and resentment had turned to bloodshed, and raids and counterattacks defined Anglo-Indian relationships for over a decade. Wahunsunacock made several efforts to establish peace, but English encroachments on Indian lands made any lasting truce impossible. Wahunsunacock and his successor, Opechancanough, the chief of the

Pamunkeys, recognized that dealing with the English colonists would require warfare, not words.

If the settlers were learning hard lessons in survival, the Virginia Company was learning hard lessons, too. The colony was hanging on by a thread, but the stockholders saw no profits, only their yearly expenses of passage for new colonists and supplies for old ones. The Virginia Company seemed caught in an investor's nightmare, pumping good money after bad in hopes of delaying a total collapse. Prospects seemed bleak: the only gold the colonists had found was "fool's gold," and the investors could see nothing else of economic value in the Chesapeake.

Fortunately the investors were wrong. Tobacco, a weed native to the Americas, proved to be the colony's salvation. Pipe smoking had been a steady habit in England since the mid-sixteenth century, and Englishmen were a steady market for this "brown gold." The local strain of tobacco in Virginia was too harsh for English tastes, but one of the colonists, an enterprising young planter named John Rolfe, managed to transplant a milder strain of West Indian tobacco to the colony. This success changed Rolfe's life, earning him both wealth and the admiration of his neighbors. Rolfe made a second contribution to the colony soon afterward, easing the strained Indian-white relationships by his marriage to an Indian princess, Pocahontas, who John Smith insisted had saved his life.

By 1612, the Virginia Colony's settlers were engaged in a mad race to plant and harvest as many acres of tobacco as possible. Yet the Virginia Company was unable to take full advantage of this unexpected windfall, for it had changed its policies in an effort to ease its financial burdens. In the beginning the company owned all the land but also bore all the costs of colonization. By 1618, however, the company's new policy allowed individual colonists to own land if they paid their own immigration expenses. This **head right system** granted each male colonist a deed for

■ **head right system** The grant of 50 acres of land for each settler brought over to Virginia by a colonist.

The Virginia House of Burgesses was the first representative assembly to be established in the British colonies. The legislators held their first session in a small Jamestown church, but by 1669, the tobacco planters who served in this assembly had moved into elegant quarters in the colonial capital of Williamsburg. The imposing building sent a clear message to all Virginians that government was the proper domain of gentlemen of wealth and social standing.

George Calvert, Lord Baltimore, hoped to create a refuge for English Catholics in America. But Maryland soon filled with Protestants, hoping for a new start in a new world. Conflict between colonists of the two faiths soon followed.

50 acres of land for himself and for every man, woman, or child whose voyage he financed. In this way the Virginia Company shifted the cost of populating and developing the colony to others. But the head rights also ended the company's monopoly on the suddenly valuable farmland.

Other important concessions to the colonists soon followed. The military-style discipline instituted by John Smith and continued by later leaders was abandoned. At the same time, a measure of self-government was allowed. In 1618 the company created an elected, representative lawmaking body called the **House of Burgesses**, which gave the landholders—tobacco planters—of Virginia some control over local political matters. In effect, a business enterprise had finally become a colonial society.

The Virginia Company did retain one of the colony's earliest traditions: a bad relationship with the Powhatan Indians. By 1622, the English seemed to have the upper hand, for the population had grown and tobacco had brought a measure of prosperity. As Virginia planters pressed farther inland, seizing Indian land along local rivers, the new Powhatan chief, Opechancanough, decided to strike back. On what the Christian settlers called Good Friday, he mounted a deadly attack on Jamestown, killing a quarter of the colonists in a single day. The company

responded as quickly as it could, sending weapons to the Virginians. For two years, war raged between Indians and the English. Although the bloodshed became less frequent by 1625, a final peace was not reached for a decade. By that time, disease and violence had taken its toll on the Powhatans. Once over forty thousand strong, they had dwindled to fewer than five hundred people.

The Good Friday Massacre, as the English called it, brought important changes for the colony. King James I had already begun an investigation of the Virginia Company's management record—and the colony's growing profit potential. When he learned of the renewed conflict between Indians and colonists, the king took away the company's charter and declared Virginia to be a royal possession.

If the king's advisers had tallied the cost in human life for planting this first English colony in the same manner that the company tallied expenses in pence and pounds, they would have found the outcome

■ **House of Burgesses** The elected lawmaking body of Virginia, established by the Virginia Company in 1618; the assembly first met in 1619.

In the Wider World

Religious Conflict in Europe and the Colonies

Although a wide ocean separated the English colonists from Europe, events abroad resonated in their lives. In 1618, a long and devastating war began between Catholics and Protestants that eventually involved conflict both within and among most of the major European powers. The loss of life and resources was so great in this Thirty Years' War that both Protestant and Catholic nations agreed that religious tolerance was preferable to more decades of bloodshed. The peace settlement included a call for "Christian and universal peace, and a perpetual, true and sincere amity" among the combatants. A similar religious warfare, smaller in scale but equally fierce, erupted in Maryland in 1649, and in seventeenth-century Massachusetts, Quakers and other non-Puritans were harassed, jailed, driven out of the colony, and on occasion, executed. Although Pennsylvania and Rhode Island did embrace religious toleration, "true and sincere amity" often proved no easier to establish in the New World than in the Old.

sobering. By 1624, only 1,275 of the 8,500 settlers who had arrived since 1607 remained alive. Fortunately, no other English colony would pay such a price for its creation.

Maryland: A Catholic Refuge

As Virginians spread out along the river ways of their colony, searching for good tobacco land, plans for a second Chesapeake colony were brewing in England. The man behind this project was not a merchant or entrepreneur, and profit was not his motive. George Calvert, a wealthy Catholic whom King Charles I had just made Lord Baltimore, envisioned a religious refuge in America for fellow Catholics suffering growing harassment and discrimination at home. Calvert acquired a charter from the king for a generous tract of land east and north of Chesapeake Bay. Here, he planned to establish a highly traditional society, dominated by powerful noblemen and populated by obedient tenant farmers. Thus, in the 1630s, George Calvert was a reactionary thinker with a radical vision.

Calvert died before a single colonist could be recruited for his Maryland. His oldest son, Cecilius Calvert, the second Lord Baltimore, took on the task of establishing the colony. To Calvert's surprise, few English Catholics showed any enthusiasm for the project. When the first boatload of colonists sailed up the Chesapeake Bay in 1634, most of the two hundred volunteers were young Protestants seeking a better life. Calvert wisely adopted the head right system developed by the Virginia Company to attract additional settlers. The lure of land ownership, he realized, was the key to populating Maryland.

Calvert's colony quickly developed along the same lines as neighboring Virginia. Marylanders immediately turned to planting the profitable **staple crop**, tobacco, and joined the scramble for good riverfront land. Like the Virginians, these colonists used trickery, threats, and violence to pry acres of potential farmland from resisting Indians. By midcentury, the two Chesapeake colonies could claim a modest prosperity, even though their populations grew slowly. But they could not claim a peaceful existence. The political crises that shook England during the mid-seventeenth century sent shock waves across the Atlantic Ocean to American shores. These crises intertwined with local tensions among colonists or between colonists and Indians to produce rebellions, raids, and civil wars.

Troubles on the Chesapeake

In Maryland, tensions ran high between the Catholic minority, who had political influence beyond their numbers because of Lord Baltimore's support, and the Protestant majority in the colony. But with the rise to power of the Puritan leader Oliver Cromwell, Calvert realized that his power to protect Maryland's Catholics was in jeopardy. Hoping to avoid persecution of the Catholic colonists, Calvert offered religious toleration to all Marylanders. In 1649 he issued the innovative Toleration Act, protecting all Christians from being "troubled [or] molested...in respect of his or her religion." Cromwell, however, promptly repealed the act. In 1654 Parliament took Maryland away from the Calvert family and established a Protestant assembly in the colony. As Calvert had feared, a wave of anti-Catholic persecution swept over Maryland.

Within a year, a bloody civil war was raging in Maryland. Protestant forces won the fiercely fought Battle of the Severn, but their victory proved futile when Oliver Cromwell died and the monarchy was restored. Charles II returned Maryland to the Calvert

staple crop A basic or necessary agricultural item, produced for sale or export.

family, who had always been loyal supporters of the Stuart dynasty. Despite this reversal of fortunes, Protestants in Maryland continued their struggle, organizing unsuccessful rebellions in 1659, 1676, and again in 1681. Then, in 1689, the Glorious Revolution prompted Maryland's Protestants to rally once again. Led by an unlikely looking hero, the stooped and nearly crippled minister **John Coode**, these colonists formed an army they called the Protestant Association. By 1691, Coode had persuaded the Crown to make Maryland a royal colony. The story did not end there, however. In 1715 the fourth Lord Baltimore gave up the Catholic faith and joined the Church of England. Maryland was once again returned to the Calverts.

Virginia was less affected by religious controversy than its neighbor. There, colonists were primarily Anglicans although small communities of Quakers, Puritans, and even members of the radical Dutch Labadist sect were scattered throughout Virginia. Religious differences, however, did not spark hostilities. Instead, the fault lines in Virginia society developed between the wealthy planters of the **tidewater** region and the ambitious newcomers seeking to make their fortunes in the backcountry. It was this tension that led to Bacon's Rebellion. Many of the ideas behind this failed rebellion would resurface one hundred years later during the events leading up to the Revolutionary War.

Colonial Chesapeake Life

Every aspect of life in the Chesapeake colonies, observers noted, seemed to be shaped by tobacco. Its cultivation set rhythms of work and play. Planting, tending, harvesting, and drying tobacco leaves took almost ten months of the year, beginning in late winter and ending just before Christmas. In the short period between the holiday and the start of a new planting cycle, Chesapeake planters, their families, and their servants worked frantically to catch up on other, neglected farm chores. They did repairs, sewed and mended, built new cabins and sheds, cut timber and firewood. They also compressed what meager social life they had into these winter weeks, engaging—whenever possible—in hasty courtships followed by marriage.

Because tobacco quickly exhausted the soil in which it grew, planters moved frequently to new acres on their estates or to newly acquired lands farther west. Since they rarely stayed in one place very long, planters placed little value on permanent homes or on creating permanent social institutions such as schools. Throughout the century, Chesapeake colonists sacrificed many of the familiar forms of community life to the demands of their profitable crop.

Planters needed a labor force large enough and cheap enough to ensure their profits. As long as poverty and social unrest plagued England, they found the workers they needed in their homeland. Over 175,000 young, single, and impoverished immigrants flooded the Chesapeake during the seventeenth century, their passages paid by the ship captain or the planter. In exchange for their transatlantic voyage, these **indentured servants** worked for several years in the tobacco fields without pay. Planters preferred a male work force, for they shared the general European assumption that farming was a masculine activity. As a result, these colonies had an unusual population profile: men outnumbered women in most areas of Virginia and Maryland by 3 to 1. In some areas, the ratio was a remarkable 6 to 1 until the end of the century.

For indentured servants, and often for their masters as well, life was short and brutal. They spent long, backbreaking days in the fields. Their food rations were meager, their clothing and bedding inadequate, and their shoulders frequently scarred by the master's whip. Servants wrote letters home describing their miserable existence. "People cry out day, and night," wrote one young man, who told his father that most servants would give up "any limb to be in England again."

Most servants also expressed doubts that they would survive to win their freedom. In many cases, they were correct. Disease and malnutrition took the lives of perhaps a quarter of these bound laborers. Free colonists fared little better than servants. Typhus, dysentery, and malaria killed thousands. Over one-quarter of the infants born in the Chesapeake did not live to see their first birthdays; another quarter of the population died before reaching the age of 20. Early death, the skewed ratio of men to women, and high infant mortality combined to create a **demographic disaster** that continued until the last decades of the century.

By the end of the 1600s, the labor force had become increasingly biracial. The steady supply of English workers dried up as economic conditions in England improved. At the same time, the cost of purchasing an African slave declined. During the next century, the shift from English servants to African slaves would be completed.

■ **John Coode** Leader of a rebel army, the Protestant Association, that won control of Maryland in 1691.

tidewater Low coastal land drained by tidal streams in Maryland and Virginia.

■ **indentured servants** People working out their compulsory service for a fixed period of time, usually from four to seven years; the terms were most often agreed to in exchange for passage to the colonies; a labor contract called an indenture spelled out the agreement.

demographic disaster The outcome of a high death rate and an unbalanced ratio of men to women in the Chesapeake colonies.

NEW ENGLAND: COLONIES OF DISSENTERS

★ What type of society did the Puritans create in Massachusetts?

★ What troubles confronted New England colonists, and how did they respond?

While Captain John Smith was barking orders at the settlers in Jamestown, some religious dissenters in a small English village were preparing to escape King James's wrath. These residents of Scrooby Village were people of modest means, without powerful political allies or a popular cause. But they had gone one step further than the majority of Puritans, who continued to be members of the Anglican Church despite their criticisms of it. The Scrooby villagers had left the church altogether, forming a separate sect of their own. James I despised these **separatists** and declared his intention to drive them out of England—or worse.

The Scrooby separatists took James's threats seriously. In 1611 they fled to the Netherland city of Leyden. They saw themselves as **Pilgrims** on a spiritual journey to religious freedom. The Dutch welcomed them warmly, but several Pilgrims feared that the comfortable life they had found in Holland was diminishing their devotion to God. By 1620, **William Bradford** was leading a small group of these transplanted English men and women on a second pilgrimage—to America.

The Plymouth Colony

The Leyden Pilgrims were joined by other separatists in England. Together, they set sail on an old, creaky ship called the *Mayflower*. On board, too, were a band of "strangers," outsiders to the religious sect who simply wanted passage to America. Crammed together in close and uncomfortable quarters, Pilgrims and strangers weathered a nightmare voyage of violent storms and choppy waters. After nine weeks at sea, the captain anchored the *Mayflower* at Cape Cod, almost 1,000 miles north of the original Virginia destination (see Map 3.2) on page 69. The exhausted passengers did not complain; they fell to the ground to give thanks. Once the thrill of standing on dry land had passed, however, many of them sank into depression. The early winter landscape of New England was dreary, alien, and disturbingly empty. William Bradford's own wife, Dorothy, may have committed suicide in the face of this bleak landscape.

Talk of setting sail for Virginia spread through the ranks of the ship's crew and the passengers. Mutiny was in the air. To calm the situation, Bradford negotiated an unusual contract with every man aboard the ship—Pilgrim, crew, servant, and stranger. This document, known as the **Mayflower Compact**, granted political rights to any man willing to remain and to abide by whatever laws the new colony enacted. Here was an unheard-of opportunity for poor men to participate in governing themselves. All agreed, and the new colony of Plymouth Plantations began to prepare for the long winter ahead.

In Plymouth Plantations, as in Virginia, the first winter brought sickness, hunger, and death. Half of the colonists did not survive. When a Patuxet Indian, **Squanto**, came upon the remaining men and women in the spring of 1621, he found them huddled in flimsy shelters, trapped between a menacing forest and a dangerous ocean. Squanto sympathized with their confusion and their longings for home, for he had crossed the Atlantic in 1605 aboard an English trading ship and spent several years in an alien environment. He also understood what it meant to be a survivor, for the Pilgrims had settled where his own

separatists English Protestants who chose to leave the Church of England because they believed it was corrupt.

■ **Pilgrims** A small group of separatists who left England in search of religious freedom and sailed to America on the *Mayflower* in 1620.

■ **William Bradford** The separatist who led the Pilgrims to America; he became the first governor of Plymouth Plantations.

■ **Mayflower Compact** An agreement drafted in 1620 when the Pilgrims reached America that granted political rights to all male colonists who would abide by the colony's laws.

■ **Squanto** A Patuxet Indian who taught the Pilgrims survival techniques in America and acted as translator for the colonists.

The Bible was the most cherished book, and often the only book, in a colonist's home. To safeguard this treasure, many Pilgrims stored their Bibles in hand-carved boxes like this one belonging to William Bradford. This box, once decorated with the lion and unicorn symbol of England, was politicized during the American Revolution, when the British lion was scraped off. Courtesy of the Pilgrim Hall Museum, Plymouth, Massachusetts.

village had once stood. His entire family and tribe had been wiped out by diseases carried by English traders and fishermen.

Squanto helped the colonists, teaching them how to plant corn, squash, and pumpkins. Perhaps his greatest service, however, was in helping William Bradford negotiate a peace treaty with Massasoit, leader of the local Wampanoag Indians. The combined efforts of Squanto and Massasoit saved the Plymouth Colony, and in the fall of 1621, English settlers and Indian guests sat down together in a traditional harvest celebration of thanksgiving.

Plymouth grew slowly, its colonists earning their livings by farming, fishing, and lumbering. A few Pilgrims grew wealthy by developing a fur trade with the Indians. Unlike the Jamestown settlers, the Plymouth community purchased land rather than seizing it, and they were strong allies when warfare broke out between Massasoit's people and their enemies. In fact, the colonists proved to be such ferocious fighters that they were known as Wotoroguenarge, or "Cutthroats."

Massachusetts Bay and Its Settlers

A second colony soon appeared beside Plymouth Plantations. In 1629 a group of prosperous Puritans, led by the 41-year-old lawyer and landowner **John Winthrop**, secured a charter for their Massachusetts Bay Company from King Charles I. These Puritans had grown increasingly worried about the government's policies toward dissenters. Harassment, coupled with a deepening economic depression in England, spurred them to set sail for New England. Advertising their colony as "a refuge for many who [God] means to save out of the general calamity," Winthrop and his colleagues had no trouble recruiting like-minded Puritans to migrate. As religious tensions and economic distress increased in England, Massachusetts attracted thousands of settlers. This **Great Migration** continued until Oliver Cromwell's Puritan army took control of England.

While profit motivated the Virginia colonists and a desire to worship in peace prompted the Pilgrims to sail to America, the Puritans of Massachusetts were people with a mission. They hoped to create a model Christian community, a "city upon a hill" that would persuade all English men and women that the reforms they proposed in the Anglican Church were correct. John Winthrop set out their mission in a speech to the passengers aboard the *Arabella*. "The eyes of all peoples are upon us," Winthrop warned, and, more importantly, God, too, was watching them. If they abandoned or forgot their mission, the consequences would surely include divine punishment.

This sense of mission influenced the physical as well as spiritual shape of the colony. Massachusetts colonists created tight-knit farming villages and small seaport towns in which citizens could monitor one another's behavior as well as come together in prayer. This settlement pattern fit well with the realities of New England's climate and terrain, since the short growing season and the rocky soil made large, isolated plantations based on staple crops impossible. The colonists, homesick for English villages in regions such as East Anglia, did their best to reproduce familiar architecture and placement of public buildings. The result was often a hub-and-spoke design, with houses tightly clustered around a village green or common pasture, a church beside this green, and most of the fields and farms within walking distance of the village center. This design set natural limits on the size of any village because beyond a certain point—usually measured in a winter's walk to church—a farm family was considered outside the community circle. As a town's population grew and the available farmland was farther from the village green, settlers on the outer rim of the town usually chose to create a new community for themselves. The Puritans called this process of establishing a new village "hiving off."

Massachusetts and other New England settlements that followed were societies of families. Many of the colonists arriving during the Great Migration came as members of a family. Of course, each ship carried unmarried male and female servants too, but unlike in the Chesapeake, the gender ratio in the northern colonies was never dramatically skewed. And unlike their Chesapeake counterparts, New Englanders never endured a demographic disaster. The cool temperatures and clean drinking water made the region a healthy place for Europeans, healthier than England itself. Infant mortality was low, and most children lived to marry and produce families of their own. A couple could expect to live a long life together and raise a family of five to seven children. One outcome of this longevity was a rare phenomenon in the seventeenth-century English world: grandparents.

Both Puritans and neighboring Pilgrims spoke of the family as "a little commonwealth," the building block on which the larger society was constructed. And, like the larger society, the family was a **hierarchy**. Children were to obey parents; wives were to obey husbands. "Wives," Puritan ministers preached, "are part of the House and Family, and ought to be under

> ■ **John Winthrop** One of the founders of Massachusetts Bay Colony and the colony's first governor.
> ■ **Great Migration** The movement of Puritans from England to America in the 1630s, caused by political and religious unrest in England.
> **hierarchy** A system in which people or things are ranked above one another.

a Husband's Government." A husband, however, was bound by sacred obligations to care for and be respectful toward his wife. Marriage involved many practical duties as well. Wives were expected to strive to be "notable housewives"—industrious, economical managers of resources and skilled at several crafts. They were to spin yarn, sew, cook, bake, pickle, butcher farm animals, cure meat, churn butter, and set cheeses. Husbands were expected to labor in the fields or in the shop to provide for their families.

Although obligated to be tender and loving, the husband controlled the resources of the family. This was true in all English colonies, although in the Chesapeake, a husband's early death often left the wife in charge of the family farm or shop and its profits until sons came of age. Under English law, a married woman, as a *femme couverte*, lost many of her legal rights because, in law, she came under the protection and governance of her husband. Married women could not acquire, sell, or bequeath property to another person. They could not sue or be sued or claim the use of any wages they earned. They could gain such basic legal rights only through special contracts made with their husbands. Puritan communities, however, frowned on any such arrangements. A husband also represented the family's interests in the realm of politics. No matter how wise or wealthy a woman might become, she did not have a political voice.

Government in Puritan Massachusetts

To create the "city upon a hill" the directors of the Massachusetts Bay Company needed, and expected, the full cooperation of all colonists. However, John Winthrop made it clear that the "wilderness Zion" was not intended to be an **egalitarian** society. Like most of his audience, Winthrop believed that it was natural and correct for some people to be rich and some to be poor. Other colonies denied women, children, servants, young men, and adult men without property a political voice, but Massachusetts further limited political participation. No man in Massachusetts had a full political voice unless he was an acknowledged church member, not just a churchgoer. Church membership, or **sainthood**, was granted only after a person testified to an experience of "saving grace," a moment of intense awareness of God's power and a reassuring conviction of personal salvation. Thus Massachusetts made religious qualifications as important as gender or economic status in the colony's political life.

Massachusetts differed from the Chesapeake colonies in other significant ways. The colony's government enforced biblical law as well as English civil and criminal law. This meant that the government regulated a colonist's religious beliefs and practices, style of dress, sexual conduct, and personal behavior. For example, every colonist was required to attend church and to observe the Sabbath as Puritan custom dictated. The church played a role in supervising business dealings, parent-child relationships, and marital life.

In the early decades of the colony, the Puritan sense of mission left little room for religious toleration. Colonial leaders saw no reason to welcome anyone who disagreed with their religious views. English America was large, they argued, and people of other faiths could settle elsewhere. Winthrop's government was particularly aggressive against members of a new sect called the **Quakers**, who came to Massachusetts on a mission of their own—to convert Puritans to their faith. Quakers entering the colony were beaten, imprisoned, or branded with hot irons, and thrown out. If they returned, they were hanged. Puritan leaders showed just as little tolerance toward members of their own communities who criticized or challenged the rules of the Bay Colony or the beliefs of its church. They drove out men and women they perceived to be **heretics**, or religious traitors.

Almost anyone could be labeled a heretic—even a popular Puritan minister like **Roger Williams**. Williams, the assistant minister of the Salem church, attracted a devoted following with his electrifying sermons and his impressive knowledge of scripture. But he soon attracted the attention of local authorities as well, for his sermons were highly critical of the colonial government. From his pulpit, Williams condemned political leaders for seizing Indian land, calling their tactics of intimidation and violence a "National Sinne." He also denounced laws requiring church attendance.

In 1635 John Winthrop's government banished Roger Williams from the colony. With snow thick on the ground, Williams left Salem and sought refuge with the Narragansett Indians. When spring came,

femme couverte From the French for "covered woman"; a legal term for a married woman; this legal status limited women's rights, denying them the right to sue or be sued, own or sell property, or earn wages.

egalitarian Believing in human equality.

sainthood Full membership in a Puritan church.

■ **Quakers** Members of the Society of Friends, a radical Protestant sect that believed in the equality of men and women, pacifism, and the presence of a divine "inner light" in every individual.

heretic A person who does not behave in accordance with an established attitude, doctrine, or principle, usually in religious matters.

■ **Roger Williams** Puritan minister banished from Massachusetts for criticizing its religious rules and government policies; in 1635, he founded Providence, a community based on religious freedom and the separation of church and state.

many of his Salem congregation joined him in exile. Together, in 1635, they created a community called Providence that welcomed dissenters of all kinds, including Quakers, Jews, and Baptists. Providence also attracted other Massachusetts colonists tired of the tight controls imposed on their lives by Winthrop and his colleagues. In 1644 the English government granted Williams a charter for his colony, which he eventually called Rhode Island. Within their borders, Rhode Islanders firmly established the principle of separation of church and state.

Soon after the Massachusetts authorities rid the colony of Roger Williams, a new challenge arose. In 1634 a merchant named William Hutchinson arrived in Massachusetts with his family. His wife, **Anne Hutchinson**, had received an exceptionally fine education from her father and was eloquent, witty, and well versed in scripture. In addition, she was clearly knowledgeable about the religious debates of the day. Like Williams, Hutchinson put little stock in the power of a minister or in any rules of behavior to assist an individual in the search for salvation.

Hutchinson's opinions, aired in popular meetings at her home, disturbed the Puritan authorities. That she was a woman made her outspoken defiance even more shocking. Men like John Winthrop believed that women ought to be silent in the church and had no business criticizing male authorities. A surprising number of Puritans, however, were untroubled by Hutchinson's sex. Male merchants and craftsmen who lacked political rights because they were not members of the saintly elect welcomed her attacks on the authorities. Hutchinson also attracted Puritan saints who resented the tight grip of the colonial government on their business, personal, and social lives.

In the end, none of Hutchinson's supporters could protect her against the determined opposition of the Puritan leadership. In 1637 she was arrested and brought to trial. John Winthrop and his colleagues declared her a heretic, "unfit to our society." They banished her from Massachusetts.

Many Puritans who left Massachusetts did so by choice, not because they were banished. For example, in 1636 the Reverend Thomas Hooker and his entire Newton congregation abandoned Massachusetts and resettled in the Connecticut River valley. Other Puritan congregations followed. In 1644 the Connecticut Valley towns of Hartford, Wethersfield, and Windsor united with the Saybrook settlement at the mouth of the Connecticut River to create the colony of Connecticut. In 1660 the independent New Haven community joined them. Other Bay colonists, searching for new or better lands, made their way north to what later became Maine and New Hampshire. New Hampshire settlers won a charter for their own colony in 1679, but Maine remained part of Massachusetts until it became a state in 1820.

This statue of Anne Hutchinson conveys her as a courageous and determined woman. Massachusetts Bay's Puritan officials would not have approved. They considered her a dangerous heretic who overstepped her proper place as a woman by challenging the established religious and political authorities. Like Roger Williams, Anne Hutchinson was exiled from the colony for her unorthodox views. Collection of Picture Research Consultants.

Indian Suppression

Although the Puritan colonists hoped to create a godly community, they were often motivated by greed and jealousy. Between 1636 and the 1670s, New Englanders came into conflict with one another over desirable land. They also waged particularly violent warfare against the Indians of the region.

When the Connecticut Valley towns sprang up, for example, Winthrop tried to assert Bay Colony authority over them. His motives were personal: he and his friends had expected to develop the valley area lands

■ **Anne Hutchinson** A religious leader banished from Massachusetts in 1636 because of her criticism of the colonial government and what were judged to be her heretical beliefs.

themselves someday. The Connecticut settlers ignored Winthrop's claims and blocked his attempts to prevent their independence from Massachusetts. But they could not ignore the Indians of the area, who understood clearly the threat that English settlers posed to their territories and their way of life. Sassacus, leader of the Pequots, hoped that an armed struggle would break out between Winthrop and the new Connecticut towns, destroying them both. Instead, however, the two English rivals concentrated on destroying the Pequots.

By 1636, the **Pequot War** had begun, with the Indians under attack from both Massachusetts and Connecticut armies and their Indian allies, the Narragansetts and the Mohicans. Mounting a joint effort, the colonists, under Captain John Mason, attacked the Pequot town of Mystic Village, although the village was defenseless and contained only civilians. Captain John Underhill of the Massachusetts army recorded the slaughter with obvious satisfaction: "Many [Pequots] were burnt in the fort, both men, women, and children." When the survivors tried to surrender to the Narragansetts, Puritan soldiers killed them. The brutal war did not end until all the Pequot men had been killed and the women and children sold into slavery. If the Narragansett Indians believed their alliance with Winthrop would protect them, they were mistaken. Within five years the Puritans had assassinated the Narragansett chief, an act of insurance against problems with these Indian allies.

An uneasy peace followed, despite the ongoing struggle over the land. By 1675, however, new Pilgrim demands for Indian lands had so eroded the friendship between the Plymouth colonists and the Wampanoags that Chief **Metacomet**, known to the English as King Philip, made the difficult decision to resist. Employing **guerrilla tactics**, Metacomet's early, devastating raids on white settlements terrified the colonists, but soon the casualties grew on both sides. Atrocities were committed by everyone involved in this struggle, which the English called King Philip's War. With the help of Iroquois troops sent by the

Library of Congress.

No portrait of Metacomet, or King Philip, was painted during his lifetime. In this nineteeth-century painting, Metacomet wears traditional New England Indian clothing, yet he is armed with a European musket, providing a stark reminder that even the bitterest enemies borrowed from one another's culture.

governor of New York, the colonists finally defeated the Wampanoags. The victors murdered Metacomet and impaled his head on a stick.

Indian objections to colonial expansion in New England had been silenced. Indeed, few native peoples remained to offer resistance of any sort. Several tribes had been wiped out entirely in the war, or their few survivors sold into slavery in the Caribbean. Those who escaped enslavement or death scattered to the north and the west. The victory had cost the English dearly also. More than two thousand New England colonists lost their lives as the war spread from Plymouth to nearby settlements. And the war left a legacy of hate that prompted Indian tribes west of Massachusetts to block Puritan expansion whenever possible. The costs of New England's Indian policy prompted colonial leaders in other regions to try less aggressive tactics in dealing with local Indians. For the Wampanoags, the Narragansetts, and the Pequots, however, this decision came too late.

Change and Reaction in England and New England

The rise of England's Puritan Commonwealth during the 1640s was celebrated in New England. But Cromwell's victory had unexpected consequences for "the

■ **Pequot War** Conflict in 1636 in which the colonists of Massachusetts Bay and Connecticut and their Indian allies destroyed the Pequot Indians inhabiting eastern Connecticut.

■ **Metacomet** A Wampanoag chief, known to the English as King Philip, who led the Indian resistance to colonial expansion in New England in 1675.

guerrilla tactics A method of warfare in which small bands of fighters in occupied territory harass and attack their enemies, often in surprise raids; the Indians used these tactics during King Philip's War.

city upon a hill." Many Puritans returned to England to enjoy Cromwell's success. Many of the newcomers to the colony during the rest of the century were not Puritans at all, but men and women eager to improve their fortunes. Among those Puritans who remained, religious zeal seemed to fade. Few native-born colonists petitioned for full membership, or sainthood, in their local churches as their parents had done, perhaps because of their growing involvement with commerce or because their mission seemed to have been fulfilled by Cromwell and his followers. By 1662, anxious members of the older, saintly generation approved a compromise to ensure that their sons would enjoy political rights despite their failure to recount a conversion experience. The resulting **Half-Way Covenant** kept political power in the hands of Puritans—for the moment.

Pressures from England could not be dealt with so easily, however. After the Restoration in 1660, Charles II cast a doubtful eye on a colony that sometimes ignored English civil law if it conflicted with biblical demands. In 1683 Charles insisted that the Bay Colony revise its charter to weaken the influence of biblical teachings and eliminate the stringent voting requirements. The Massachusetts government said no. With that, Charles revoked the charter. Massachusetts remained in political limbo until 1685, when James II came to the throne. Then conditions grew far worse.

In an effort to centralize administration of his growing American empire, King James decided on a massive reorganization of the mainland colonial world. He combined several of the northern colonies into one large unit under direct royal control. This megacolony, the **Dominion of New England**, included Massachusetts, Rhode Island, Connecticut, Plymouth Plantations, and the newly acquired colonies of New Jersey and New York. James expected the Dominion to increase the **patronage**, or political favors, he could provide to his loyal supporters—favors such as generous land grants or colonial administrative appointments. He also expected to increase revenues by imposing duties and taxes on colonial goods in the vast region he now controlled.

What King James did not expect was how strongly colonists resented his Dominion and the man he chose to govern it: the arrogant and greedy Sir Edmund Andros. Andros immediately offended New England Puritans by establishing the Church of England as the official religion of the new colony. Then he added insult to injury by commandeering a Puritan church in Boston for Anglican worship. Andros also alienated many non-Puritans in Massachusetts by abolishing the representative assembly there. Non-Puritan men had been struggling to be included in the assembly, not to have the assembly destroyed. Andros's high-handed tactics united Massachusetts colonists who had been at odds with each other. One sign of this cooperation surfaced when the Dominion governor imposed new taxes: saints and nonsaints alike refused to pay them.

When Boston citizens received news of the Glorious Revolution, they imprisoned Edmund Andros and shipped him back to England to stand trial as a traitor to the nation's new Protestant government. Massachusetts Puritans hoped to be rewarded for their patriotism, but although William and Mary abolished the Dominion, they chose not to restore the Bay Colony charter. In 1691 Massachusetts became a royal colony, its governor appointed by the Crown. **Suffrage**, or voting rights, was granted to all free males who met an English **property requirement**. Church membership would never again be a criterion for citizenship in the colony.

Over the course of its sixty-year history, Massachusetts had undergone many significant changes. The Puritan ideal of small, tightly knit farming communities whose members worshiped together and shared common values and goals had been replaced for many colonists by an emerging "Yankee" ideal of trade and commerce, bustling seaport cities, diverse beliefs, and a more secular, or nonreligious, orientation to daily life. This transition increased tensions in every community, especially during the difficult years of the 1680s. Those tensions contributed to one of the most dramatic events in the region's history: the Salem witch trials.

In 1692 a group of young women and girls in Salem Village began to show signs of what seventeenth-century society diagnosed as bewitchment. They fell into violent fits, contorting their bodies and showing great emotional distress. Under questioning, they named several local women, including a West Indian slave named Tituba, as their tormentors. The conviction that the devil had come to Massachusetts spread quickly, and the number of people accused of witchcraft mushroomed. Within months, more than a hundred women, men, and children were

■ **Half-Way Covenant** An agreement (1662) that gave partial membership in Puritan churches to the children of church members even if they had not had a "saving grace" experience.

Dominion of New England A megacolony created in 1686 by James II that brought Massachusetts, Plymouth Plantations, Connecticut, Rhode Island, New Jersey, and New York under the control of one royal governor; William and Mary dissolved the Dominion when they came to the throne in 1689.

patronage Jobs or favors distributed by political leadership, usually as rewards for loyalty or service.

suffrage The right to vote.

property requirement The limitation of voting rights to citizens who own certain kinds or amounts of property.

crowded into local jails, awaiting trial. Accusations, trials, and even executions—nineteen in all—continued until the new royal governor, Sir William Phips, arrived in the colony and forbade any further arrests. Phips dismissed the court that had passed judgment based on "spectral evidence"—that is, testimony by the alleged victims that they had seen the spirits of those tormenting them. In January 1693, Phips assembled a new court that acquitted the remaining prisoners.

What had prompted this terrible episode in colonial history? Seventeenth-century people throughout Europe and America widely believed that the devil and his disciples could work great harm in a community. But in part, the Salem witch trials played out a struggle between Puritan farmers of Salem Village and the town's more worldly merchants, for the accusers were often members of the farming community while the accused were often associated with commercial activities. In part, the trials reflected that despite the busy port towns and the prosperity of the older farming communities, danger continued to lurk nearby. French and Indian attacks on the border settlements were frequent and brutal, and refugees from this violence could be seen in many older towns. In the despair that followed these attacks, colonists looked for someone to blame for their losses. It was easy to conclude that hostile Indians were the agents of the devil in Massachusetts.

Martha Corey and her husband Giles were among the many Massachusetts Puritans accused of witchcraft in 1692. Although she was admired in her community before the witch-hunts began, she was nevertheless found guilty and hanged by the colonial government.

THE PLURALISM OF THE MIDDLE COLONIES

★ How did New Netherland develop under English control, and what cultural and economic tensions came to a head in Leisler's Rebellion?

★ What made William Penn's vision for Pennsylvania so distinctive?

Between the Chesapeake and New England lay the vast stretch of forest and farmland called New Netherland, a Dutch colony that was home to settlers from Holland, Sweden, Germany, and France. In the 1660s, Charles II seized the area and drove the Dutch from the Atlantic coast of North America. The English divided the conquered territory into three colonies: New York, New Jersey, and Pennsylvania. Although the region changed hands, it did not change its character: the Middle Colonies remained a multicultural, commercially oriented, and competitive society no matter whose flag flew over them.

From New Netherland to New York

By 1652, England and Holland had become bitter rivals, fighting three naval wars to decide who would control the transatlantic trade in raw materials and manufactured goods. After each war, the Dutch lost ground, and their decline made it likely that their New Netherland settlement would be abandoned.

King Charles II of England wanted New Netherland very much, and James, Duke of York (later King James II), was eager to satisfy his brother's desires. In 1664 Charles agreed to give James control of the region lying between the Connecticut and Delaware Rivers—if James could wrest it from the Dutch (see Map 3.2). The promise and the prize amounted to a declaration of war on New Netherland.

When the duke's four armed ships arrived in New Amsterdam harbor and aimed their cannons at the town, Governor Peter Stuyvesant tried to rally the local residents to resist. They refused. Life under the English, they reasoned, would probably be no worse than life under the Dutch. Perhaps it might be better. The humiliated governor surrendered the colony, and in 1664 New Netherland became New York without a shot being fired.

In many ways, James proved to be a very liberal ruler, allowing the Dutch and other European colonists to keep their lands, practice their religions, and conduct their business in their native languages. But the

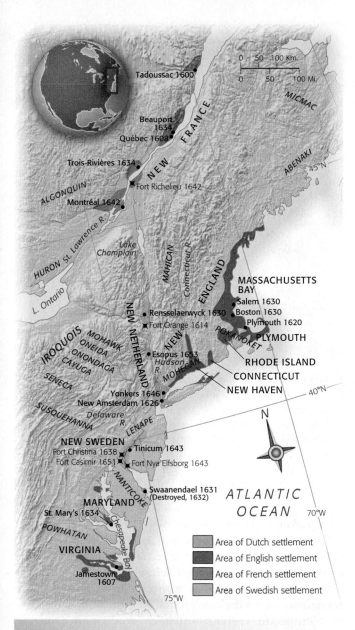

MAP 3.2 European Civilization in the Middle and North Atlantic
In the seventeenth century, several nations competed to establish a colonial foothold along the Atlantic coast of North America. Swedish and Dutch settlements separated the English colonial world of New England from its counterpart in the Chesapeake. While these European colonies hugged the coastline, Native Americans continued to dominate the lands to the west.
Copyright © Cengage Learning

duke's generosity and tolerance did not extend to taxation matters. James saw his colonists much as his brother the king saw every colonist: as a source of personal revenue. James taxed New Yorkers heavily and allowed no representative assembly that might interfere with his use of the treasury. All political offices in the new colony, high or low, went to the duke's friends, creating a patronage system that impressed even King Charles.

James's colony did not develop as he had hoped, however. Settlement did not expand to the north and east as he wished. He could not enlist the aid of influential New Yorkers in his expansion plans, even though he offered them the incentive of a representative assembly in 1682. By 1685, James—now king of England—had lost interest in the colony, abandoning his schemes for its growth and abolishing the representative assembly as well.

Leisler's Rebellion

Although James viewed New York as a failure, the colony actually grew rapidly during his rule. The population doubled between 1665 and 1685, reaching fifteen thousand the year the duke ascended to the English throne. These new settlers added to the cultural diversity that had always characterized the region. The colony became a religious refuge for French Protestants, English Quakers, and Scottish **Presbyterians**. New York's diverse community, however, did not always live in harmony. English, Dutch, and German merchants competed fiercely for control of New York City's trade and for dominance in the city's cultural life. An equally intense rivalry existed between Manhattan's merchants and Albany's fur traders. Only one thing united these competitors: a burning resentment of James's political control and the men he chose to enforce his will. Their anger increased when James created the Dominion of New England.

In 1689 news of the Glorious Revolution prompted a revolt in New York City similar to the one that shook Boston. **Jacob Leisler**, a German merchant, emerged as its leader. Although Leisler lacked the charisma and commanding presence that had allowed Nathaniel Bacon to rise to power in 1676, he was able to take control of the entire colony. When William and Mary sent a new governor to New York, Leisler refused to surrender the reins of government. This time, the abrasive, headstrong merchant found few supporters, and eventually he was forced to step down. To Leisler's surprise, he was then arrested and charged with treason. Both he and his son-in-law were tried, found guilty, and executed. As befit traitors in the seventeenth century, the two rebels were hanged, disemboweled while still alive, and then beheaded.

Presbyterians Members of a Protestant sect that eventually became the established church of Scotland but that in the seventeenth century was sometimes persecuted by Scotland's rulers.

■ **Jacob Leisler** German merchant who led a revolt in New York in 1689 against royal officials representing the Dominion of New England; he was executed as a traitor when he refused to surrender control of the colony to a governor appointed by William and Mary.

Afterward, their mutilated bodies were quartered. In death, Leisler became a hero and a martyr. Popular anger was so great that to quiet the discontent, the new governor had to permit the formation of a representative assembly. Several of the men elected to this new legislature were ardent Leislerians, and for many years New York politics remained a battleground between home rule advocates and supporters of the royal governor and the king.

William Penn's Holy Experiment

More than most dissenting sects, Quakers had paid a high price for their strongly held convictions. Members of the Society of Friends had been jailed in England and Scotland and harassed by their neighbors throughout the empire. Quaker leaders had strong motives to create a refuge for members of their beleaguered sect. In the 1670s, a group of wealthy Friends purchased New Jersey from its original **proprietors** and offered religious freedom and generous political rights to its current and future colonists, many of whom were, in fact, Puritans. The best known of these Quaker proprietors was **William Penn**, who had given up a life of privilege, luxury, and self-indulgence in Restoration society and embraced the morally demanding life of the Friends.

Penn's father, Admiral Sir William Penn, was one of England's naval heroes and a political adviser to King Charles II. The senior Penn and his son had little in common except their loyalty to the king and their willingness to provide liberal loans to support their monarch's extravagant lifestyle. Eventually, Charles rewarded the Penns' devotion. In 1681, he granted the younger Penn a charter to a huge area west of the Delaware River. This gave Penn the opportunity to create a refuge for Quakers that fully embodied their religious principles.

Penn called his new colony Pennsylvania, meaning "Penn's Woods," in memory of his father. (The southernmost section of Penn's grant, added later by Charles II, developed independently of Penn's control and in 1776 became the state of Delaware.) Like most colonial proprietors, Penn expected to profit from his charter, and he set a quitrent, or small fee, on all land purchased within his colony. But his religious devoutness ensured that he would not govern by whim. Instead, Quaker values and principles were the basis for his "holy experiment." At the heart of

William Penn was about 50 years old when this chalk drawing was done. Although Pennsylvania was famous for its religious tolerance and welcoming of non-English immigrants, Penn held many views in common with New England's Puritan leaders. He believed that government should impose and enforce a moral code, because drunkenness, luxury, gambling, and cursing were not only "sins against Nature" but "sins against Government."

the Quaker faith was the conviction that the divine spirit, or "inner light," resided in every human being. Quakers thus were expected to respect all individuals. By their plain dress and their refusal to remove their hats in the presence of their social "betters," Quakers demonstrated their belief that all men and women were equal. In keeping with their egalitarian principles, Quakers also recognized no distinctions of wealth or social status in their places of worship. At the strikingly simple Quaker meeting, or worship service, any member who felt moved to speak was welcome to participate, no matter how poor or uneducated and no matter what sex or age. Although they actively sought converts, Quakers were always tolerant of other religions.

Pennsylvania's political structure reflected this egalitarianism. All free male residents had the right to vote during Penn's lifetime, and the legislature they elected had full governing powers. Penn honored the legislature's decisions even when they disturbed or amazed him. The political quarrels that developed in Pennsylvania's assembly actually shocked Penn, but his only action was to urge political leaders not to be "so noisy, and open, in your dissatisfactions."

Penn's land policy also reflected Quaker principles. Unlike many proprietors, he wanted no politically

proprietor In colonial America, a proprietor was a wealthy Englishman who received a large grant of land in America from the king or queen in order to create a new colony.

■ **William Penn** English Quaker who founded the colony of Pennsylvania in 1681.

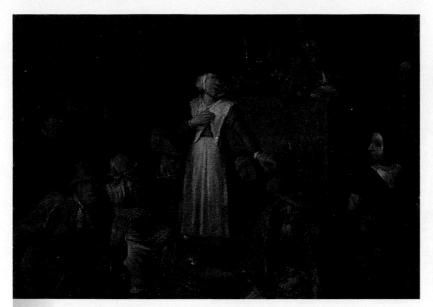

This sketch of a Quaker meeting highlights one of the most radical of Quaker practices: allowing women to speak in church. Most Protestant denominations, because of their reading of Saint Paul, enforced the rule of silence on women. But Quakers struck a blow at seventeenth-century gender notions by granting women an active ministerial role, a voice in church policy, and decision-making responsibilities on issues relating to the church and the family. "The Quaker Meeting" (detail) by Egbert Van Heemskerk. The Quaker Collection, Haverford College Library.

on their ambitions and preferred to seize land from the Indians rather than purchase it. The demand for military protection from Indians by these land-hungry farmers in the western part of the colony, similar to the demands made decades before by Nathaniel Bacon and his followers, became a major political issue and a matter of conscience for Quakers, whose religious principles included **pacifism**. Eventually many Quakers chose to resign from the colonial government rather than struggle to uphold a holy experiment their neighbors did not support.

COLONIES OF THE LOWER SOUTH

★ What type of society did the founders of Carolina hope to create? How did the colony differ from their expectations?

★ Why did philanthropists create Georgia? Why did the king support this project?

powerful landlords and no economically dependent tenant farmers. Instead, he actively promoted a society of independent, landowning farm families. Penn also insisted that all land be purchased fairly from the Indians, and he pursued a policy of peaceful coexistence between the two cultures. William Penn took an active role in making Pennsylvania a multicultural society, recruiting non-English settlers through pamphlets that stressed the religious and political freedoms and economic opportunities his colony offered. More than eight thousand immigrants poured into the colony in the first four years. Many did come from England, but Irish, Scottish, Welsh, French, Scandinavian, and German settlers came as well. To their English neighbors who did not speak German, newcomers from Germany such as the Mennonites and Amish were known as the "Pennsylvania Dutch" (*Deutsch,* meaning "German," would have been correct).

When William Penn died in 1717, he left behind a successful, dynamic colony. Philadelphia was already emerging as a great shipping and commercial center, rivaling the older seaports of Boston and New York City. But this success came at some cost to Penn's original vision and to his Quaker principles. The commercial orientation here, as in Puritan Massachusetts, attracted colonists who were more secular in their interests and objectives than the colony's founders. Many newcomers saw Penn's Indian policy as a check

In 1663 King Charles II surprised eight of his favorite supporters by granting them several million acres lying south of Virginia and stretching from the Atlantic to the Pacific Ocean. The gesture was both grand and calculated. France, Spain, Holland, and the Indian tribes that inhabited this area all laid claim to it, and Charles thought it would be wise to secure England's control of the region by colonizing it. The eight new colonial proprietors named their colony Carolina to honor the king's late father, who had lost his head to the Puritan Commonwealth (and whose name in Latin was Carolus; see Map 3.3).

The Carolina Colony

The proprietors' plan for Carolina, called the Fundamental Constitution, was similar to Lord Baltimore's medieval dream. It was an elaborate blueprint for a society of great landowners, **yeomen** (small, independent farmers), and serfs (agricultural laborers) bound to work for their landlords. Like the Calverts, however, the Carolina proprietors discovered that few English people were willing to travel three thousand miles across the ocean to become serfs. Bowing to reality, the proprietors offered the incentive of the head right system.

pacifism Opposition to war or violence of any kind.
yeoman Independent landowner entitled to suffrage.

The Lynch family, wealthy rice planters of South Carolina, built this elegant home on the banks of the North Santee River in the 1730s. The Hopsewee Plantation is a striking example of the luxury enjoyed by the small number of elite white planters whose fortunes depended on the labor of enslaved African field workers. Courtesy of the Hopsewee Plantation.

The early settlers in Carolina, many of them relocating from the Caribbean island of Barbados, made their way to the southeastern portion of the colony, drawn there by the fine natural harbor of the port city, Charles Town (later Charleston), and its fertile surroundings. Despite the dangers of the Spanish to the south in Florida and the Yamasee Indians to the southwest, Charles Town grew rapidly, becoming the most important city in the southern colonies. The early Carolinians experimented with several moneymaking activities: they traded with the Indians for deerskins and for captive victims of tribal warfare, whom the colonists sold as slaves in the Caribbean; they produced naval stores from the region's pine forests and experimented with several cash crops, such as sugar cane, tobacco, silk, cotton, ginger, and olives. The colonists' first real success turned out to be cattle raising, a skill they learned from African slaves brought into the colony by the settlers from Barbados. But by the 1680s rice cultivation became the road to riches. In 1719, Carolina's elite rice planters took control of the southern section of the colony from the original proprietors and named it South Carolina. These planters quickly became the richest English colonists on the mainland.

The northern region of Carolina did not fare as well. Bordered by the Great Dismal Swamp to the north and by smaller swamps to the south, this isolated area attracted few colonists. The land around Albemarle Sound was fertile enough, but the remaining coastline was cut off from the Atlantic by a chain of barrier islands that blocked access to oceangoing vessels. Despite all these constraints, some poor farm families and freed white indentured servants had drifted in from Virginia, searching for unclaimed land and a fresh start. They had modest success in growing tobacco and producing naval stores.

In 1729 the Albemarle colonists followed the lead of their elite neighbors around Charleston and rid themselves of proprietary rule. These North Carolinians then officially separated from the rice-rich southern section of the colony. Thus both South Carolina and North Carolina had become royal colonies.

MAP 3.3 The Settlements of the Lower South
This map shows the towns and fortifications of North Carolina, South Carolina, and Georgia, as well as the overlapping claims by the Spanish and the English to the territory south and west of Fort King George. The many Georgia forts reflect that colony's role as a buffer state between rice-rich South Carolina and the Spanish troops stationed in Florida.
Copyright © Cengage Learning

MAP 3.4 The Colonies and Their Major Cities
The creation of the English mainland colonies spanned almost 125 years, from the first settlement at Jamestown, Virginia, in 1607 to the founding of the last colony of Georgia in 1732. This map indicates the year each colony was founded, and the date in which eight of these colonies came directly under royal control. The map also locates the major colonial cities in each region.
Copyright © Cengage Learning

Georgia, the Last Colony

In 1732 **James Oglethorpe**, a wealthy English social reformer, and several of his friends requested a charter for a colony on the Florida border. Their goal was to provide a new, moral life for English men and women imprisoned for minor debts. King George II had other motives for granting the charter, however. He was anxious to create a protective buffer between the valuable rice-producing colony of South Carolina and the Spanish in Florida. The king inserted a clause in the Georgia charter requiring military service from every male settler. Thus he guaranteed that the poor men of Georgia would protect the rich men of South Carolina (see Map 3.4).

■ **James Oglethorpe** English philanthropist who established the colony of Georgia in 1732 as a refuge for debtors.

Oglethorpe and his associates added their own special restrictions on the lives of the Georgia colonists. Because they believed that poverty was the result of a weak character or, worse, of an addiction to vice, they did not think debtors could govern themselves. They forbade a representative assembly and denied the settlers a voice in selecting political leaders and military officers. In an effort to reform the character of their colonists, the trustees set other rules, including a ban on all alcoholic beverages. To ensure that these settlers worked hard, they kept individual land grants small, and they banned slavery.

Oglethorpe interviewed many imprisoned debtors, searching for members of the "deserving poor" who would benefit from Georgia. But few of these debtors met his standards. In the end, most of the colony's settlers turned out to be middle-class English immigrants and South Carolinians looking for new land. These colonists did not welcome the trustees' paternalistic attitudes, and they soon challenged all the restrictive rules and regulations in the charter. They won the right to accumulate and sell land. They introduced slave labor in defiance of the trustees. By the 1740s, illegal slave auctions were a common sight in Georgia's largest town, Savannah. By 1752, Oglethorpe and his fellow trustees had lost enthusiasm for their reform project and, with relief, returned Georgia to the king.

Individual Voices

Nathaniel Bacon: Manifesto Concerning the Troubles in Virginia, 1676

Sometimes historical figures leave behind a clear statement of the motives and goals for their actions. Nathaniel Bacon is a good example. He was not setting down this information for future generations, of course; he was issuing a ringing statement of the grievances suffered by his followers, and his audience was the governor and his allies, English authorities, and his loyal followers. "The Declaration of the People" is designed to persuade readers of the justice of the rebellion and to ensure that Bacon will be hailed as a defender of the people's rights and liberties rather than condemned as a traitor.

❶ Here Bacon declares that a just God would condone his attacks on the Indian population since they had slaughtered innocent colonists. Yet Bacon attacked peaceful Indians as well. How do Bacon's attacks on these peaceful Indian communities suggest a larger issue of racism in the colonies?

❷ In this section Bacon reminds his readers that the haughty tidewater planters came to Virginia as poor men, not as gentlemen, and are thus no better than his followers.

❸ Bacon argues that the governor and his friends have done nothing to earn the public's trust or admiration and have failed to provide basic protection for the colony's citizens. One hundred years later, American revolutionaries will make the same claim against the king and Parliament. Do you think Bacon's claims are accurate? Why or why not?

If virtue be a sin, if piety be guilt, all the principles of morality, goodness and justice be perverted, we must confess that those who are now called rebels may be in danger of those high imputations. Those loud and several bulls would affright innocents and render the defense of our brethren and the inquiry into our sad and heavy oppressions, treason. **❶** But if there be, as sure there is, a just God to appeal to; if religion and justice be a sanctuary here; if to plead the cause of the oppressed; if sincerely to aim at his Majesty's honour and do public good without any reservation or by interest; if to stand in the gap after so much blood of our dear brethren bought and sold; if after the loss of a great part of his Majesty's colony deserted and dispeopled, freely with our lives and estates to endeavour to save the remainders be treason; God Almighty judge and let guilty die. But since we cannot in our hearts find one single spot of rebellion or treason, or that we have in any manner aimed at the subverting of the settled government or attempting of the person of any either magistrate or private man, notwithstanding the several reproaches and threats of some who for sinister ends were disaffected to us and censured our innocent and honest designs, and since all people in all places where we have yet been can attest our civil, quiet, peaceable behaviour far different from that of rebellion and tumultuous persons, let truth be bold and all the world know the real foundations of pretended guilt. . . . [L]et us trace these men in authority and favour to whose hands the dispensation of the country's wealth has been committed. **❷** Let us observe the sudden rise of their estates composed with the quality in which they first entered this country, or the reputation, they have held here amongst wise and discerning men. And let us see whether their extractions and education have not been vile, and by what pretence of learning and virtue they could so soon [come] into employments of so great trust and consequence. **❸** Let us consider their sudden advancement and let us also consider whether any public work for our safety and defence or for the advancement and propagation of trade, liberal arts, or sciences is here extant in any way adequate to our vast charge. Now let us compare these things together and see what sponges have sucked up the public treasure, and whether it has not been privately contrived away by unworthy favourites and juggling parasites whose tottering fortunes have been repaired and supported at the public charge. Now if it be so, judge what greater guilt can be than to offer to pry into these and to unriddle the mysterious wiles of a powerful cabal; let all people judge what can be of more dangerous import than to suspect the so long safe proceedings of some of our grandees, and whether people may with safety open their eyes in so nice a concern.

Study Tools

SUMMARY

In 1607, the English created their first permanent colony at Jamestown. By 1732, thirteen English colonies hugged the coast of the Atlantic Ocean. Some, like Maryland, Pennsylvania, and Massachusetts, were founded as religious refuges; others were founded for profit. Four distinct regions soon emerged, based primarily on how the settlers made their livings.

Virginia and Maryland made up the Chesapeake region. Here tobacco shaped every aspect of life. Thousands of poor young Englishmen were brought over to work in the tobacco fields. They came as indentured servants, working without pay in exchange for passage to America. Few women were recruited, and the combination of an unbalanced sex ratio and frequent deaths caused by an unhealthy climate, grueling labor, and poor diet produced what historians call a "demographic disaster" in the seventeenth-century Chesapeake.

The colonies of the Lower South, the Carolinas and Georgia, were established many decades after the Chesapeake by two groups of wealthy Englishmen. Carolina's proprietors tried to create a feudal society, and Georgia's founders wanted to build a haven for debtors. In the end, however, neither goal was achieved. After experiments in cattle raising and other enterprises, the settlers of what became South Carolina focused on rice production, using African slave labor, and these

planters became the richest group in the colonies. North Carolinians were poorer, growing tobacco and farming.

Plymouth Plantations, Massachusetts, Rhode Island, Connecticut, and later New Hampshire made up the New England colonies, with their small farms and shipping and lumbering industries. Here, the earliest settlers were dissenters who sought religious freedom. In 1620, separatists known as the Pilgrims founded the first New England colony, Plymouth Plantations. Their leaders drafted a radical document known as the Mayflower Compact, which assured broad political rights to all the men on board their ship, including the crew and servants. In 1630, Massachusetts Bay was founded by Puritans who intended it to be a model Protestant community. They demanded conformity to their religious views and drove out those who challenged them, especially Quakers. When Puritans like Roger Williams and Anne Hutchinson challenged the colony's leadership and its religious practices, they too were exiled. Williams went on to found Rhode Island on the principle of separation of church and state. Other colonists left Massachusetts voluntarily and founded Connecticut. In 1691, Massachusetts was taken over by the King, and the Puritans' religious experiment ended. The anxiety produced by this political change coupled with economic tensions and dangers on the frontier contributed to the Salem witch-hunts of 1691.

CHRONOLOGY
Settling the Mainland Colonies

1585	English colonize Roanoke Island
1607	Virginia Company founds Jamestown
1619	Virginia House of Burgesses meets
1620	Pilgrims found Plymouth Plantations
1625	Charles I becomes king of England
1630	Puritans found Massachusetts Bay Colony
1634	Lord Baltimore establishes Maryland
1635	Roger Williams founds Providence
1636	Anne Hutchinson banished from Massachusetts Pequot War in New England Connecticut settled
1642–1648	English civil war
1649	Charles I executed; Cromwell and Puritans come to power in England
1655	Civil war in Maryland

1660	Restoration of English monarchy
1663	Carolina chartered
1664	New Netherland becomes New York
1675	King Philip's War in New England
1676	Bacon's Rebellion in Virginia
1681	Pennsylvania chartered
1685	James II becomes king of England
1686	Dominion of New England established
1688	Glorious Revolution in England
1689	Leisler's Rebellion in New York
1691	Massachusetts becomes royal colony
1692	Salem witch trials
1732	Georgia chartered

Study Tools

The Middle Colonies region was originally settled by the Dutch and the Swedes, but the English seized the area in 1664. New Sweden and New Netherland became New Jersey and New York. In 1681 William Penn created the colony of Pennsylvania, west of New Jersey, as a home for Quakers. Unlike the Puritans, however, he welcomed people of all faiths into his "holy experiment." The Middle Colonies, where many colonists grew wheat and exported it through the major ports of Philadelphia and New York, were noted for their diverse populations and policies of religious toleration.

Religious, economic, and political conflicts were common back in England, and it was often no more peaceful in the colonies. In Maryland, Protestants and Catholics warred with each other and in Virginia, poor backcountry farmers, led by Nathaniel Bacon, rose up against the wealthier coastal planters in 1676. The desire for land also led to bloodshed. Land-hungry colonists in Virginia and New England made war against the Indians. Finally, English policies prompted rebellions, as colonists in Boston and New York rose up to overthrow the hated Dominion of New England in 1689.

As you will see in Chapter 4, most colonists continued to think of England as "home" even as they developed their own societies and their own institutions. Some developments, like widespread African slavery, would seem to widen the differences among the colonial regions; some, like the rise of local representative government, would seem to bring them together. Slowly, however, colonists in all regions developed interests and goals that conflicted with the policies of the Mother Country. One thing was certain: great changes would take place in the eighteenth century.

FOCUS QUESTIONS

If you have mastered this chapter, you should be able to answer these questions and to explain the terms that follow the questions.

1. ☆ *What circumstances or conditions in England affected people's willingness to join England's colonizing efforts?*

2. ☆ *What were the goals of the Virginia Company and of the Calvert family in creating their Chesapeake colonies? Did the colonies achieve these goals?*

3. ☆ *What events illustrate the racial, class, and religious tensions in the Chesapeake?*

4. ☆ *What type of society did the Puritans create in Massachusetts?*

5. ☆ *What troubles confronted New England colonists, and how did they respond?*

6. ☆ *How did New Netherland develop under English control, and what cultural and economic tensions came to a head in Leisler's Rebellion?*

7. ☆ *What made William Penn's vision for Pennsylvania so distinctive?*

8. ☆ *What type of society did the founders of Carolina hope to create? How did the colony differ from their expectations?*

9. ☆ *Why did philanthropists create Georgia? Why did the king support this project?*

KEY TERMS

Church of England *(p. 56)*

Puritan *(p. 56)*

Parliament *(p. 56)*

Commonwealth *(p. 56)*

Restoration *(p. 56)*

Glorious Revolution *(p. 56)*

Jamestown *(p. 57)*

head right system *(p. 58)*

House of Burgesses *(p. 59)*

John Coode *(p. 61)*

indentured servants *(p. 61)*

Pilgrims *(p. 62)*

William Bradford *(p. 62)*

Mayflower Compact *(p. 62)*

Squanto *(p. 62)*

John Winthrop *(p. 63)*

Great Migration *(p. 63)*

Quakers *(p. 64)*

Roger Williams *(p. 64)*

Anne Hutchinson *(p. 65)*

Pequot War *(p. 66)*

Metacomet *(p. 66)*

Half-Way Covenant *(p. 67)*

Jacob Leisler *(p. 69)*

William Penn *(p. 70)*

James Oglethorpe *(p. 73)*

 CourseMate Go to the History CourseMate website for primary source links, study tools, and review materials for this chapter. www.cengagebrain.com

4

The English Colonies in the Eighteenth Century, 1689–1763

Behind the Stories

It may surprise you to know that eighteenth-century colonists did not think of themselves as Americans. They were Marylanders, or Virginians, or New Yorkers. Great technological revolutions allow us to travel across the country in five hours, watch the same television shows each evening, and text or e-mail each other in an instant from state to state. But such communications were unimaginable for Massachusetts farm women, South Carolina field workers, and Rhode Island merchants. Their world was smaller, more intimate, and if their loyalties and identifications stretched beyond their community or their colony, they were to England, not their neighboring colonists. Even within their own colony, they saw differences rather than similarities: race and religion divided them, gender separated them, and the contrast between rural life and the bustle of port cities was sharply felt.

Despite their perceived differences, these eighteenth-century colonists did have much in common. First, they lived on the margins rather than at the center of the British Empire. The seat of wealth, power, and prestige was London, not New York or Charleston. Second, the English government, not the colonists, determined the flow of trade across the Atlantic that lay at the heart of the colonial economy. Third, by midcentury, every colony had well-established, locally elected legislatures that they assumed had the right to govern them as much, or more, than Parliament did. Finally, the competition between England and its rivals, France and Spain, linked the colonists to one another, drawing them into bloody imperial wars.

For the historian, the critical task is to uncover and explain those things that divided colonists and those that united them. Only in that way can she hope to understand a world so different from her own—and from yours.

—C.B.

78

Individual Choices
Eliza Lucas

Eliza Lucas of South Carolina was only sixteen when her father surprised his neighbors by leaving her in charge of his plantations when he was called away to war. But George Lucas's confidence in his daughter's abilities was correct. Under her management, the family plantations prospered. She even introduced a new crop, **indigo**, from which a valuable blue dye was made. While most other wealthy young women focused on marriage and children, Eliza busied herself with planting, paying bills, directing overseers, and selling crops. But she also made time for traditional female tasks like attending teas, visiting the sick, and learning how to dance and play the piano. To do all this, she set herself a grueling daily schedule, beginning each day at 5:00 A.M., as described in the Individual Voices feature at the end of this chapter.

Eliza's father had encouraged many nontraditional skills in his daughter. For example, he opened his legal library to her and educated her fully on her legal rights as a single woman, or *femme sole*.

Eliza stubbornly protected the independence her father had nurtured. When she finally married it was to an old and respected friend, Charles Pinckney, a widower twice her age who was a leading lawyer and political figure in the colony. As a wife, Eliza turned her full attention to domestic concerns and to the education of her five children. She rejected the traditional notion that children were burdened by original sin and raised her family according to Rousseau's theories of the power of nurture and encouragement. The French philosopher's advice served her well: Eliza and Charles's two surviving sons grew up to be political leaders during the revolutionary struggle and her only daughter followed in Eliza's footsteps, eventually running her own plantation.

National Museum of American History, Smithsonian Institution, Behring Center.

Eliza Lucas Pinckney's Gown

indigo Shrublike plant with clusters of red or purple flowers, grown on plantations in the South; it was a primary source of blue dye in the eighteenth century.

femme sole From the French for "woman alone"; a legal term for an unmarried, widowed, or divorced woman with the legal right to own or sell property, sue or be sued, or earn wages.

Even the most casual observer of colonial society could not fail to note major regional changes and developments during the eighteenth century. A new system of slave labor was defining the Southern colonies; cities were growing dramatically in the Middle Colonies; and in New England, a Puritan world was transforming into a world of enterprising Yankees.

These differences among the regions were offset by many shared experiences. The colonists were all part of a common imperial structure as well as a sprawling transatlantic community in which goods, people, and ideas steadily flowed between England, Europe, the Americas, and Africa. Although some three thousand miles of ocean separated New Yorkers from Londoners, colonists journeyed between the two worlds, bringing news of developments in politics, changes in fashion, and popular books. Events in Europe, in England, and in the Caribbean had an impact on everything in colonial life from the religious background of new immigrants to debates over slavery in Virginia to the safety of life on the Maine frontier.

Although most Americans eagerly awaited news from an England they still called "home," few members of the English elite followed American developments closely—or at all. Most continued to think of the colonies as a dumping ground for misfits and hayseeds who would struggle to survive, or die, on a violent frontier. Members of the English Parliament viewed the colonists as a collective source of endless problems. They expected insubordinate colonial legislatures, defiant merchants who violated trade regulations, and a dangerously unstable political atmosphere in a society that gave common men an **unprecedented** voice in government. Yet it was the colonists who often suffered from decisions made by Parliament and king. England's fierce rivalries with European nations produced a long series of imperial wars that disrupted colonial life and cast a long shadow over communities from the Maine border to Georgia. In the end, England would triumph over every rival for a North American empire. The outcome of this victory would prove surprising to everyone.

unprecedented Unheard of or novel.

subsistence society A society that produces the food and supplies necessary for its survival but that does not produce a surplus for market.

absentee planter An estate owner who collects profits from farming or rent but does not live on the land or help cultivate it.

piedmont Land lying at the foot of a mountain range.

★ *What were the main regional differences in colonial commerce and what kind of economic choices did each region offer colonists?*

Although the English spoke of "the colonial trade," British America did not have a single, unified economy. Instead, four distinctive regional economies had developed on the mainland, concentrated along the Atlantic coastline and bordered on the west by the primarily **subsistence society** that was commonly found on the edge of white settlement. To the south, the sugar islands of the Caribbean made up a fifth unique regional economy. Each of these economies was shaped by environmental conditions, natural resources, English commercial policy, the available labor force, and the available technological know-how.

Regions of Commerce

The sugar-producing islands of the West Indies were the brightest jewels in the English imperial crown. Spain had first laid claim to most of these islands, but England had slowly gobbled up many of them, and thus, by the eighteenth century, the English flag flew over St. Kitts, Barbados, Nevis, Montserrat, and Jamaica. Here, English plantation owners built fabulous fortunes on the sugar that African slaves produced. While the **absentee planters** lived in luxury in England, black slaves lived—and died in staggering numbers—on the islands, working the cane fields and tending the fires that burned day and night under the sugar vats of the boiling houses where the raw sugar, or molasses, was produced.

Few mainland colonists enjoyed the wealth of this "Sugar Interest." Still, in the Lower South, planters of South Carolina and Georgia, like Eliza Lucas Pinckney, amassed considerable fortunes by growing rice in the lowlands along the Atlantic coast. By the 1730s, this American rice was feeding the people of the Mediterranean, Portugal, and Spain. By midcentury, planters were making additional profits from indigo crops. Like the sugar planters, Carolina and Georgia rice growers based their production on slave labor, but unlike the island moguls, these plantation masters never became permanently absent landowners.

Tobacco or "brown gold" continued to dominate the economy of the Chesapeake, although the high taxes placed on this crop prompted many eighteenth-century planters to diversify. They began producing wheat and other grains for export. Tobacco production shifted west to the area along the Potomac, the James River valley, and the **piedmont** foothills. The second major shift came in the labor force used in tobacco cultivation. By the eighteenth century,

Like the planters of the Caribbean, ship captains and ship owners made their fortunes from the liquid sugar, or molasses, they carried from the West Indies to the mainland colonies, England, and Africa. The sugar planters lived in luxury in England while thousands of slaves labored in the cane fields to produce the profits these men enjoyed.

African slaves had replaced indentured servants in the fields. Planters who could afford to purchase a number of slaves enjoyed a competitive advantage over their neighbors in both the old and the new tobacco areas because they had enough workers to plant and harvest bigger crops. This large-scale production kept tobacco the number one export of the mainland colonies.

Together, these two southern regions provided the bulk of the mainland's agricultural exports to Great Britain. In contrast, the New England regional economy depended far less on Britain as a market. Except in the Connecticut River valley, where tobacco was grown, the region's rocky soil made large-scale farming unfeasible for New Englanders. Instead, shipbuilding and the ambitious **carrying trade** dominated New England's economy. Colonists made great profits from an extensive shipping network that carried colonial exports across the Atlantic and to the Caribbean and distributed foreign goods and English manufactured products to the colonies. Some merchant-shippers—the slave traders of Newport, Rhode Island, for example—specialized in a certain commodity, but most were willing to carry any cargo that promised a profit. An economy based on the carrying trade made New Englanders rivals of English merchants rather than useful sources of profit for the Mother Country.

Sandwiched between the South and New England, the colonies of New York, New Jersey, Pennsylvania, and later Delaware developed their own regional economy, which combined the successes of their neighbors to the north and south. They created profits from both staple-crop farming and trade. The forests of the Pocono Mountains and upper New York were a source of wood and wood products for the shipbuilding industry, and locally harvested flaxseed was exported to Ireland for its linen industry. The central crop, however, was wheat. Fortunately for the colonists of this area, the price of wheat rose steadily during the eighteenth century. The carrying trade was equally important in this region's mixed economy. Ships carrying cargoes of grain and flour across the Atlantic and into the Caribbean crossed paths with other colonial ships bringing manufactured goods and luxury items from Europe to the region's two major port cities, New York and Philadelphia.

Not everyone in the colonies participated in the market-oriented activity, of course. In the older coastal settlements of each region, harbors and river ways provided the necessary transportation routes for the shipment of crops, goods, and supplies. But most colonies had an inland backcountry that was sparsely populated and farmed by European immigrants, ex-servants, or the families of younger sons from older communities. There, on what white settlers thought of as the frontier and Indians called the invasion line, colonists struggled to produce enough for survival. They lacked both the labor force to clear and work sufficient acreage for a marketable crop and the transport to get a crop to market. And they had no financial or political resources that might help overcome these obstacles. This belt of subsistence extended like a border from Maine to western Pennsylvania, to inland Carolina, along every region of the mainland colonies. But even these backcountry farms had a fragile link to the world of international trade, for settlers brought with them the farm tools and basic household supplies that had been manufactured in England or imported through colonial ports.

■ **carrying trade** The business of transporting goods across the Atlantic or to and from the Caribbean.

Many colonists believed that Britain's victory over France in 1763 would usher in a new era of economic growth, westward expansion, and improved cooperation between Mother Country and colonies. But these hopes for harmony and good will were quickly dashed. Less than two years after the Treaty of Paris ended the war, colonists were protesting British policy and resisting new trade regulations. In the next thirteen strife-filled years, the colonists and the British government discovered that fundamental political differences existed between them. They found that they did not agree over the meaning of representative government or the proper division of power between Parliament and the local elected assemblies. And they found themselves in conflict over major imperial policies. English officials, for example, thought it made good sense to curtail westward settlement to prevent costly Indian wars. But American colonists believed loyal citizens deserved the economic opportunity that westward settlement would provide. The British insisted that the Americans ought to help pay the costs of maintaining the empire, but the colonists believed that this was the duty of those who remained in the Mother Country. By the 1770s, Americans who had once toasted the king and his government now drank instead to liberty and resistance to tyrants. By 1775, a new choice faced the colonists: loyalty or rebellion. And colonists such as Charles Inglis seemed caught in the midst of a struggle they had never anticipated and could not avoid.

The colonists who chose to protest taxation by the British government in 1765 and 1767, or to oppose the creation of juryless courts, or to complain of the presence of troops in their towns in peacetime, did not know they were laying the groundwork for a revolution. Indeed, most of them would have been shocked at the suggestion that they were no longer loyal British patriots. Yet events between 1763 and 1776 forced these colonists to choose between two versions of patriotism—loyalty to the king or loyalty to colonial independence—and between two visions of the future—as members of a great and powerful empire or as citizens of a struggling new nation. These events also forced Indians and African American slaves to choose an alliance with the king or with the rebels, just as they forced churchmen and royal officials such as Inglis to decide if the solemn oath of allegiance they had taken to the king was binding under all circumstances.

The war for independence set neighbor against neighbor, father against son, wife against husband, and slave against master. For thousands, the outcome of this crisis of loyalty was exile from home and family. For others, it meant death or injury on the battlefield, widowhood, or life as an orphan. In 1776, however, its outcome was unclear.

VICTORY'S NEW PROBLEMS

☆ Why did Prime Minister Grenville expect the colonists to accept part of the burden of financing the British Empire in 1764?

☆ How did colonists understand their obligations to the Empire?

☆ Why were the colonists alarmed by Grenville's 1765 stamp tax?

☆ How did the colonists protest Parliament's taxation policies?

In the midst of the French and Indian War, King George II died in his bed. Loyal subjects mourned the old king and in 1760 welcomed his grandson

It Matters Today

The Right to Dissent

Charles Inglis was a man of integrity who considered himself as much an American patriot as his opponent in the pamphlet wars, Alexander Hamilton. But unlike Hamilton, Inglis believed that the protests against Parliament and the king were dangerous and unjustified and would lead to an unjust and tragic war. Throughout American history, men and women have opposed political and social choices made by the nation, including the entrance of the United States into World War I, woman suffrage, Prohibition, and the wars in Vietnam and Iraq. The right to dissent, guaranteed by the Constitution, has been a critical part of the American political tradition since the nation began. Examining how dissent has been offered and how it has been received is part of the story of all major controversial events.

- Consider your position on dissent in times of national crisis. Do you believe the government has the right to suppress dissent during times of war or major disasters? Why or why not?
- Discuss the impact modern technology has had on the ability of citizens to voice opposition and organize resistance to government policies.

In the Wider World

Quianlong's Empire

As the ruler of England, Scotland, Ireland, Wales, and vast holdings in North America and the Caribbean, King George III could boast in 1776 of ruling the most powerful empire in the world. Yet his was not the only impressive empire of the era. Far to the east, Emperor Qianlong of the Qing Dynasty ruled over three million people and 13 million square kilometers, including Tibet, Taiwan, and Mongolia. Arts and literature flourished during Qianlong's reign. The French Enlightenment philosopher Voltaire was so impressed by the efficient and well-organized Chinese imperial system that he and other European thinkers advised their own kings to copy Chinese methods of "enlightened despotism."

George III. At 22, the new monarch was hardworking but highly self-critical, and he was already showing the symptoms of an illness that produced **delusions** and severe depression. Although he was inexperienced in matters of state, George III meant to rule—even if he had to deal with politicians, whom he distrusted, and engage in politics, which he disliked. He chose **George Grenville**, a no-nonsense, practical man, to assist him. Grenville's two most pressing postwar tasks were negotiating England's victory treaty with France and designing Britain's peacetime policies.

At the peace table with France, England had the opportunity to decide what the spoils of war would be: a French Caribbean sugar island or the mainland territory of Canada. English sugar planters opposed adding a new competitor to their profitable market and so the government opted for the vast region north and west of the thirteen colonies. American colonists could not help but be pleased. With one sweep of the pen, their worst enemies had been eliminated from their borders. The treaty also held out the promise of profitable fishing off the Newfoundland coast and new farmlands in the fertile Ohio Valley. By the end of 1763, George III and his subjects could look with pride on an empire that had grown in physical size, on a nation that dominated the markets of Europe, and on a navy that ruled the seas.

Unfortunately, victory also brought new problems. First, the new English glory did not come cheaply. To win the war, William Pitt had spent vast sums of money, leaving the new king with an enormous war debt. English taxpayers, who had groaned under the wartime burden, now demanded tax relief, not tax increases. Second, the new Canadian territory posed serious governance problems because the Indians were unwilling to pledge their allegiance to the English king and the French Canadians were unwilling to abandon their traditions, their laws, or the Catholic Church.

Dealing with Indian and French Canadian Resistance

Both the Canadian tribes and Spain's former Indian allies along the southeastern borders of the English colonies felt threatened by Britain's victory. For decades, Indian diplomats had protected their lands by playing European rivals against one another, but with the elimination of France and the weakening of Spain in mainland America, this strategy was now impossible. Warfare rather than diplomacy had become their only option. When settlers from the southern colonies poured into Creek and Cherokee lands, the Cherokees mounted a full-scale, but ultimately futile, resistance along the Virginia and Carolina western settlement line. Defeated, the Cherokee leaders were forced to sign treaties opening up their lands to both English settlement and military bases.

In the Ohio Valley, Indian tribes were determined to resist not only the settlers' invasion of their homelands but also the increase in the price British traders set on tools, clothing, and liquor. Together, Senecas, Ojibwas, Potawatomis, Hurons, Ottawas, Delawares, Shawnees, and Mingoes formed an alliance known as the **Covenant Chain**. Led by the Ottawa chief **Pontiac**,

---

■ **George III** King of England (r. 1760–1820); his government's policies produced colonial discontent that led to the American Revolution in 1776.

delusion A false belief strongly held in spite of evidence to the contrary.

■ **George Grenville** British prime minister who sought to tighten controls over the colonies and to impose taxes to raise revenues.

■ **Covenant Chain** An alliance of Indian tribes established to resist colonial settlement in the Ohio Valley and Great Lakes region and to oppose British trading policies.

■ **Pontiac** Ottawa chief who led the unsuccessful resistance against British policy in 1763.

In this 1710 portrait, Tao Yec Neen Ho Gar Ton, Emperor of the Six Nations, holds a wampum belt, a woven or beaded belt that often represented treaty agreements or other diplomatic decisions. The British government courted the support of the Iroquois confederation, whose alliance of six Indian nations made them a critical force in the military and territorial rivalries between France and England in North America. Left:Private Collection/The Bridgeman Art Library International; right: The Granger Collection, New York.

the Indians mounted their attack on British forts and colonial settlements in the spring of 1763. By fall, however, their resistance had evaporated, and the Covenant Chain tribes were forced to acknowledge British control of the Ohio Valley.

The British realized that their victories did not mean a permanent peace in the West. As long as the "middle ground" between Indian and colonial populations continued to shrink, Indians would rise up against what Creeks bluntly called "people greedily grasping after the lands of red people." Settlers would then demand expensive military protection as they pushed westward. If the army did not respond, settlers were ready to take vigilante action on their own. Violence would lead to violence—unless Grenville could keep Indians and settlers at arm's length. Grenville's solution was a proclamation, issued in 1763, temporarily banning all colonial settlement west of the Appalachian Mountains.

Grenville's **Proclamation Line of 1763** (see Map 5.1) outraged colonists hoping to move west and wealthy land speculators hoping to reap a profit from their western investments. Most colonists simply ignored the Proclamation Line. Over the next decade, areas such as Kentucky began to fill with eager homesteaders, creating a wedge that divided northern from southern Indian tribes and increasing Indian anxiety about their own futures.

Because of their long tradition of anti-Catholic sentiment, American colonists also objected to Grenville's strategy of winning over Britain's new French-speaking Catholic Canadian subjects rather than strong-arming them. To balance their loss of fishing and fur-trading industries, Grenville promised the Canadians the right to preserve their religious and cultural way of life. American colonists were scandalized by this concession to the losers in the war.

Demanding More from the Colonists

Colonists were not the only ones growing discontented. In London, the king and many members of Parliament were impatient with colonial behavior and attitudes. Hadn't the colonists benefited more than anyone from the French defeat? asked George Grenville. And hadn't they contributed less than anyone to securing that victory? Such questions revealed the subtle but important rewriting of the motives and goals of the French and Indian War. Although Britain had

■ **Proclamation Line of 1763** Boundary that Britain established in the Appalachian Mountains, west of which white settlement was banned; it was intended to reduce conflict between Indians and colonists.

MAP 5.1 The Proclamation Line of 1763

Victory over the French in 1763 meant that the Ohio Valley region was now British territory. But the Indians living in this region united under a Covenant Chain to fiercely resist white settlement there. Pontiac's Rebellion led the British government to declare a moratorium on settlement west of the Proclamation Line. Colonists were outraged by this restriction. Copyright © Cengage Learning

Legend:
- European settlement before 1700
- European settlement 1700–1763
- Frontier, 1763
- Proclamation Line of 1763
- Pontiac's uprising, 1763
- **OTTOWA** Member of Covenant Chain

waged the war to win dominance in European affairs, not to benefit the colonies, Grenville now declared that the war had been fought to protect the colonists and to expand their opportunities for settlement.

This new interpretation fit well with the government's increasing sense that something had gone wrong in the economic relationship between England and its mainland colonies. Colonial cities such as Boston, Philadelphia, and New York had grown considerably, yet their growth did not make England as rich as **mercantile theory** said it should. One reason was that in every colony locally produced goods competed with English-made goods. A more important reason, however, was widespread illegal trade with Britain's rivals. In fact, to English amazement, colonials had continued to trade with the French Caribbean islands throughout the French and Indian War. In peacetime, colonists avoided paying the required **import duties** on foreign goods by bribing customs officials or landing cargoes where no customs officers were stationed.

What Grenville discovered when he examined the imperial trade books proved shocking. By the 1760s, the Crown had collected less than £2,000 in revenue from colonial trade with other nations, yet the cost of collecting these duties was over £7,000 a year. Such discoveries fueled British suspicions that the colonies were underregulated and undergoverned, not to mention ungrateful and uncooperative. When the strong doubts about colonial loyalty met the reality of British government debts and soaring expenses, something drastic could be expected to follow. And it did. In 1764 Parliament approved Grenville's dramatic reforms of colonial trade policy. Colonists greeted these new policies with shock and alarm.

Separately, each of Grenville's measures addressed a loophole in the proper relationship between Mother Country and colonies. For example, a **Currency Act** outlawed the use of paper money as legal tender in the colonies. Grenville reasoned that this would drive colonial manufacturers, who were paid with paper money, out of business and ensure that colonists bought their manufactured goods from England. But Grenville's main focus was the widespread practice of colonial smuggling.

Lawbreakers were so common, and customs officers so easily bribed, that smuggling had become an acceptable, even respectable form of commerce. To halt this illegal traffic, Grenville created the American Revenue Act. This 1764 act increased the powers of the customs officers, allowing them to use blanket warrants, called writs of assistance, to search ships and warehouses for smuggled goods. He also changed the regulations regarding key foreign imports, including sugar, wine, and coffee. This startling shift in policy, known popularly as the **Sugar Act**, revealed Grenville's practical bent. He knew that any attempt to stop the flow of French sugar into the colonies was a waste of time and resources. So he decided to make a profit for the Crown from this trade. He would lower the tax on imported sugar—but he would make sure it was collected. He would also change the way in which alleged smugglers were brought to justice. Until 1764, a colonist accused of smuggling was tried before a jury of his neighbors in a **civil court**. He expected, and usually got, a favorable verdict from his peers. Grenville now declared that anyone caught smuggling would be tried in a juryless **vice-admiralty court**, where a conviction was far more likely. Once smuggling became too costly and too risky, Grenville reasoned, American shippers would declare their cargoes of French sugar and pay the Crown for the privilege of importing them.

The Colonial Response

Grenville's reforms were spectacularly ill timed as far as Americans were concerned. The colonial economy was suffering from a postwar **depression**, brought on in part by the loss of the British army as a steady market for American supplies and of British soldiers as steady customers who paid in hard currency rather than paper money. In 1764 unemployment was high among urban artisans, dockworkers, and sailors, and colonial merchants were caught in a credit squeeze—unable to pay their debts to British merchants because their colonial customers had no cash to pay for their purchases. These colonists were not likely to cheer a Currency Act that shut off a source of money or a Sugar Act that established a new get-tough policy on foreign trade. In the eyes of many anxious colonists, the English government was turning into a greater menace than the French army had ever been.

Protests and proposals for action soon filled the pages of colonial newspapers. This concern suggested that Grenville's reforms had raised profound issues about the

---

mercantile theory The economic notion that a nation should amass wealth by exporting more than it imports; colonies are valuable in a mercantile system as a source of raw materials and as a market for manufactured goods.

import duties Taxes on imported goods.

■ **Currency Act** British law of 1764 banning the printing of paper money in the American colonies.

■ **Sugar Act** British law of 1764 that taxed sugar and other colonial imports to pay for some of Britain's expenses in protecting the colonies.

civil court Any court that hears cases regarding the rights of private citizens.

vice-admiralty court Nonjury British court in which a judge heard cases involving shipping.

depression A period of drastic economic decline, marked by decreased business activity, falling prices, and high unemployment.

rights of citizens and of the relationship between Parliament and the colonial governments—issues that needed to be resolved. The degree to which Parliament had, or ought to have, power over colonial economic and political life required serious, public pondering. Years later, with the benefit of hindsight, Massachusetts lawyer and revolutionary John Adams stressed the importance of the Sugar Act in starting America down the road to independence. "I know not why we should blush to confess," wrote Adams, "that molasses [liquid sugar] was an essential ingredient in American independence." But in 1764 colonists were far from agreement over the issue of parliamentary and local political powers. They were not even certain how to respond to the Sugar Act.

The Stamp Act

Did Grenville stop to consider the possibility of "great events" arising from his postwar policies? Probably not. He was hardly a stranger to protest and anger, for he had often heard British citizens grumble about taxes and assert their rights against the government. As he saw it, his duty was to fill the treasury, reduce the nation's staggering debt, arm its troops, and keep the royal navy afloat. The duty of loyal British citizens, he believed, was to obey the laws of their sovereign government. Grenville had no doubt that the measures he and Parliament were taking to regulate the colonies and their revenue-producing trade were constitutional. Some colonists, however, had doubts. To settle the issue, Grenville proposed another piece of legislation designed not only to raise revenue but to assert the principle of parliamentary sovereignty. The new law was called the Stamp Act.

The **Stamp Act** of 1765 was to be the first **direct tax** ever laid on the colonies by Parliament. There was nothing startling or novel about this revenue-collecting method. A stamp tax raised money by requiring the use of government "stamped paper" on certain goods or as part of the cost for certain services. It was simple and efficient, and several colonial legislatures used this method themselves. What was startling, however, was that this tax had nothing to do with foreign trade. Until 1765, Parliament had passed many acts regulating colonial trade, and if these regulations generated revenue for the Crown, the colonists did not complain. They accepted this as a form of **external taxation**. But colonists were convinced that only their local assemblies had the power to impose direct taxation like the stamp tax. Grenville's Stamp Act was a sharp break with the traditional understanding of the relationship between Mother Country and colonies, and it challenged the distribution of political power between colonial assemblies and Parliament. Did Parliament realize what it had done?

Most members of Parliament did not. They saw the Stamp Act as an efficient and modest redistribution of the burdens of the empire—and a constitutional one.

Colonists were certainly not being asked to shoulder the entire burden, since the estimated £160,000 in revenue from the stamped paper would cover only one-fifth of the cost of maintaining a British army in North America.

The new law, passed in February 1765, was set to go into effect in November. The nine-month delay was necessary, for Grenville needed time to print the stamped paper, arrange for its shipment across the Atlantic, and appoint agents to receive and distribute the stamps in each colony. News of the tax, however, crossed the ocean rapidly and was greeted with outrage and anger. Virtually every free man and woman was affected by a tax that required stamps on all legal documents, newspapers and pamphlets, playing cards and dice. Grenville was reaching into the pockets of the rich, who would need stamped paper to draw up wills and property deeds and to bring suit in court. And he was emptying the pockets of the poor, who would feel the pinch when dealing a hand of cards in a tavern or buying a printed **broadside** filled with advertising. Colonial merchants and ship captains would have to use stamped clearances for all shipments or risk the seizure of their cargoes by the royal navy. Lawyers feared the loss of clients if they had to add the cost of the stamps to their fees. Thus, with the stamp tax Grenville united northern merchants and southern planters and rural women and urban workingmen, and he riled the most articulate and argumentative of all Americans: lawyers and newspaper publishers.

The Popular Response

Many colonists proved ready to resist the new legislation. Massachusetts, whose smugglers were already choking on the new customs regulations, and whose assembly had a long history of struggle with local Crown officers, led the way. During the summer of 1765, a group of Bostonians formed a secret resistance organization called the **Sons of Liberty**. The Sons were led by the irrepressible **Samuel Adams**,

■ **Stamp Act** British law of 1765 that directly taxed a variety of items, including newspapers, playing cards, and legal documents.

direct tax A tax imposed to raise revenue rather than to regulate trade.

external taxation Revenue raised in the course of regulating trade with other nations.

broadside An advertisement, public notice, or other publication printed on one side of a large sheet of paper.

■ **Sons of Liberty** A secret organization first formed in Boston to oppose the Stamp Act.

■ **Samuel Adams** Massachusetts revolutionary leader and propagandist who organized opposition to British policies after 1764.

Left: Broadside: Massachusetts Historical Society; right: Mr. Rivington: Library of Congress.

E187

St—p! fl—p! fl—p! No:

Tuesday-Morning, December 17, 1765.

THE True-born Sons of Liberty, are desired to meet under LIBERTY-TREE, at XII oClock, THIS DAY, to hear the the public Resignation, under Oath, of ANDREW OLIVER, Esq; Distributor of Stamps for the Province of the Massachusetts-Bay.

A Resignation ? YES.

The Sons of Liberty were able to silence many who criticized them. In 1765, the Boston Sons demanded the resignation of local stamp agent Andrew Oliver (*left*). In 1774, New York's pro-British editor, James Rivington, used the illustration on the right while reporting that a New Brunswick mob had hanged him in effigy. The New York Sons promptly attacked his office, destroyed his press, and forced his paper to close.

a Harvard-educated member of a prominent Massachusetts family who preferred the company of local working men and women to the conversation of the elite. More at home in the dockside taverns than in the comfortable parlors of his relatives, Adams was a quick-witted, dynamic champion of working-class causes. He had a genius for writing propaganda and for mobilizing popular sentiment on political and community issues. Most members of the Sons of Liberty were artisans and shopkeepers, and the group's main support came from men of the city's laboring classes who had been hard hit by the postwar depression and would suffer from the stamp tax. These colonists had little influence in the legislature or with Crown officials, but they compensated by staging public demonstrations and protests to make their opinions known. By January 1765, New York City also had a Sons of Liberty organization, and by August, the Sons could be found in other cities and towns across the colonies.

Demonstrations and protests were soon mounted, and Boston led the way. On August 14, shoemaker **Ebenezer McIntosh** led a crowd to protest the appointment of the colony's stamp agent, the wealthy merchant Andrew Oliver. The crowd included a number of the city's gentlemen, disguised as workingmen. Together with the workingmen, they paraded through the city streets carrying an effigy of Oliver. The crowd then destroyed Oliver's dockside warehouse and went on to break all the windows in his home. The message was clear—and Oliver understood it well. The following day Andrew Oliver resigned as stamp agent. Boston Sons of Liberty celebrated by declaring the tree on which they hanged Oliver's effigy the "liberty tree."

But Oliver's resignation did not end the protest. Customs officers and other Crown officials living in Boston were threatened with words and worse. The chief target of abuse, however, was the wealthy merchant and political office holder **Thomas Hutchinson**, resented by many of the ambitious younger political leaders because he monopolized appointive offices in the colony's government and hated by the workingmen because of his disdain for ordinary people. Late one August evening, a large crowd surrounded Hutchinson's elegant brick mansion. Hutchinson and his family, warned of trouble, had wisely fled, escaping just before rocks began to shatter the parlor windows. By dawn, the house was in ruins, and Hutchinson's furniture, clothing, and personal library had been trashed. The attack on Hutchinson revealed that sometimes protests were not simply over British policies but over local issues and against local elites as well. It was not surprising, therefore, that prosperous merchants and shippers soon saw a potential danger in the mobilization of lower-class crowds like the Sons of Liberty. For elites like Hutchinson, crowd protest was a double-edged sword, a useful weapon that could be deadly in the wrong hands.

Ebenezer McIntosh Boston shoemaker whose workingman's organization, the South End "gang," became the core of the city's Sons of Liberty in 1765.

■ **Thomas Hutchinson** Boston merchant and judge who served as lieutenant governor and later governor of Massachusetts; Stamp Act protesters destroyed his home in 1765.

The campaign against the stamp agents spread like a brushfire across the colonies. Agents in Connecticut, Rhode Island, Maryland, and New York were mercilessly harassed. Most stamp agents resigned. When the stamps reached colonial ports in November, only the young and conservative colony of Georgia could produce anyone willing to distribute them. Colonial governors retaliated by refusing to allow any colonial ships to leave port. They hoped this disruption of trade would persuade local merchants to help end the resistance. Their strategy backfired. Violence increased as hundreds of unemployed sailors took to the streets, terrorizing customs officers and any colonists suspected of supporting the king's taxation policy.

Political Debate

While the Sons of Liberty and their supporters demonstrated in the streets, colonial political leaders were proceeding with caution. Virginia lawyer and planter **Patrick Henry** briefly stirred the passions of his colleagues in the House of Burgesses when he suggested that the Stamp Act was evidence of the king's tyranny. Not everyone agreed with him that the measure was so serious. Many did agree, however, that the heart of the matter was not stamped paper but parliamentary sovereignty versus the rights of colonial citizens. "No taxation without representation"—the principle that citizens cannot be taxed by a government unless they are represented in it—was a fundamental assumption of free white Englishmen on both sides of the Atlantic. The crucial question was, Did the House of Commons represent the colonists even though no colonist sat in the House and none voted for its members? If the answer was no, then the Stamp Act violated the colonists' most basic "rights of Englishmen."

Stating the issue in this way led to other concerns. Could colonial political leaders oppose a single law such as the Stamp Act without completely denying the authority of the government responsible for its passage? Massachusetts lawyer James Otis pondered this question when he sat down to write his *Rights of the British Colonists Asserted and Proved.* Any opposition to the Stamp Act, he decided, was ultimately a challenge to parliamentary authority over the colonies, and it would surely lead to colonial rebellion and a declaration of colonial independence. He, for one, was not prepared to become a rebel. Instead he proposed that Parliament give seats in the government to colonial representatives.

Like Otis, most political leaders shrank from denying Parliament's authority. But his suggestion that Parliament admit colonial representatives satisfied no one. A small contingent of colonial members of Parliament would have little power and was likely to find its views ignored. The only solution seemed to be to protest against the Stamp Act, demand its repeal, and

When Parliament enacted the Stamp Act of 1765, the government designed this special embossed tax stamp to be used on the items that came under the new law. These items included newspapers, most legal documents, playing cards, and dice. The Stamp Act provoked the first major protest and boycott by colonists against the Mother Country.
The Granger Collection, New York.

warn Parliament that Americans would resist further efforts to infringe on their rights and liberties.

Yet many members of the colonial legislatures felt more was needed than strong words and implicit threats. Their own authority was at stake, for if Parliament acted on its assertion that it had the right to govern the colonies directly, their powers would be diminished. These men had much to lose—status, prestige, and the many benefits that came from deciding how tax monies would be allocated. Thus, when Massachusetts put out a call for an intercolonial meeting of delegates to discuss the Stamp Act crisis, the idea was greeted with enthusiasm.

Grenville's policies appeared to be bringing about what had once seemed impossible: united political action by the colonies. Until the Stamp Act, competition among the colonial governments was far more common than cooperation. Yet in the fall of 1765 delegates from nine colonies met in New York "to consider a general and unified, dutiful, loyal and humble Representation [petition]" to the king and Parliament.

■ **Patrick Henry** Member of the Virginia House of Burgesses and American revolutionary leader noted for his oratorical skills.

The petitions this historic **Stamp Act Congress** ultimately produced were far bolder than the delegates first intended. They were powerful, tightly argued statements that conceded parliamentary authority over the colonies but denied Parliament's right to impose any direct taxes on them. "No taxes," the Congress said, "ever have been, or can be Constitutionally imposed" on the colonies "but by their respective Legislatures." Clearly Americans expected this tradition to be honored.

Repeal of the Stamp Act

Neither the protest in the streets nor the arguments of the Stamp Act Congress moved the king or Parliament to repeal the stamp tax. But economic pressure did. Thus the most powerful weapon in the colonial arsenal was a refusal to purchase English goods, for English manufacturers relied heavily on their colonial markets. On Halloween night, just one day before the stamp tax officially went into effect, two hundred New York merchants announced that they would not import any new British goods. Local artisans and laborers rallied to support this **boycott**. A mixture of patriotism and self-interest motivated both of these groups. The merchants saw the possibility of emptying warehouses bulging with unsold goods because of the postwar depression. Unemployed and underemployed artisans and laborers saw the chance to sell their own products if the supply of cheaper English-made goods dried up. The same combination of interests existed in other colonial cities, and thus the movement for a boycott, which they called nonimportation and nonconsumption, spread quickly. By the end of November, several colonial assemblies had publicly endorsed the boycott agreements signed by local merchants. Popular support widened as well.

English exporters complained bitterly of the damage done to their businesses and pressured Parliament to take colonial protest seriously. The Grenville government reluctantly conceded that enforcement of the Stamp Act had failed miserably. Even in colonies where royal officials dared to distribute the stamped paper, Americans refused to purchase it. Colonists simply ignored the hated law and continued to sue

their neighbors, sell their land, publish their newspapers, and buy their playing cards as if the stamped paper and the Stamp Act did not exist.

By winter's end, Grenville had been replaced by Lord Rockingham, and for the new prime minister the critical issue was how to repeal the Stamp Act without appearing to cave in to colonial pressure. In 1766, the government came up with a satisfactory solution. Great Britain repealed the Stamp Act but at the same time passed a **Declaratory Act**, which asserted that the colonies were "subordinate unto, and dependent upon the imperial Crown and parliament of Great Britain." Thus Parliament's right to pass legislation for and raise taxes from the North American colonies was reaffirmed as absolute.

Colonists celebrated the repeal with public outpourings of loyalty to England that were as impressive as their public protests had been. There were cannon salutes, bonfires, parades, speeches, and public toasts to the king and Rockingham. In Boston, Sons of Liberty built a pyramid and covered its three sides with patriotic poetry. In Anne Arundel County, Maryland, colonists erected a "liberty pillar" and buried "Discord" beneath it. And in a spectacular but poorly executed gesture, the Liberty Boys of Plymouth, Massachusetts, tried to move Plymouth Rock to the center of town. When the famous rock on which the Pilgrims were said to have landed split in two, half of it was carried to Liberty Pole Square, where it remained until 1834. As for the Declaratory Act, colonists greeted it with indifference. Those who commented on it at all dismissed it as a face-saving device. To a degree, they were correct. But the Declaratory Act expressed the views of powerful men in Parliament, and within a year they put it to the test.

ASSERTING AMERICAN RIGHTS

★ Why did Charles Townshend expect his revenue-raising measures to be successful?

★ What forms of resistance did the colonists use against Townshend's measures and what were the results?

By the summer of 1766, William Pitt had returned to power within George III's government. But Pitt was old and preoccupied with his failing health. A young playboy named Charles Townshend, serving as chancellor of the exchequer, rushed in to fill the leadership void. This brash young politician wasted little time foisting a new package of taxes on the colonies.

The Townshend Acts and Colonial Protest

During the Stamp Act crisis, Benjamin Franklin had assured Parliament that American colonists accepted indirect taxation through trade regulations, even if

■ **Stamp Act Congress** A meeting convened in October 1765 to call for the repeal of the Stamp Act. Delegates from nine colonies attended this first example of colonial cooperation.

■ **boycott** An organized political protest, used by the colonists to protest British taxation, in which people refuse to buy goods from a nation or group of people whose actions they oppose; also called *nonimportation*.

■ **Declaratory Act** A statement of Parliament's authority over the American colonies "in all cases whatsoever," passed on the same day as the repeal of the Stamp Act.

they violently protested a direct tax such as the Stamp Act. In 1767 Townshend decided to test this distinction by proposing new regulations on a variety of imported necessities and luxuries. But unlike any import taxes the colonies had ever seen, the **Townshend Acts** taxed products made within the British empire.

The Townshend Acts taxed glass, paper, paint, and lead products, all made in England. The acts also placed a three-penny tax on tea, considered a necessity by virtually all colonists. Townshend wanted to be certain these taxes were collected, so he ordered new customs boards in the colonies and created new vice-admiralty courts in the major port cities of Boston, Charleston, and Philadelphia to try cases of smuggling or tax evasion. In case Americans tried to harass customs officials, Townshend ordered British troops transferred from the western regions to the major colonial port cities. To help finance this military occupation of key cities, Townshend invoked the 1766 Quartering Act, a hated law requiring colonists to provide room and board; "candles, firing, bedding, cooking utensils, salt and vinegar"; and a ration of beer, cider, or rum to troops stationed in their midst. Clearly taking every precaution to avoid the embarrassment Grenville had suffered in the Stamp Act disaster, Townshend relied on the presence of uniformed soldiers—known as "redcoats" because of their scarlet jackets—to keep the peace.

When news of the new regulations reached the colonies, however, the response was immediate, determined, and well-organized resistance. Newspaper accounts indicate that the colonists were united in their opposition to the Townshend Acts and the repressive enforcement policies. Some once again angrily invoked the principle of "no taxation without representation." In Boston, Samuel Adams voiced his outrage: "Is it possible to form an idea of Slavery, more compleat, more miserable, more disgraceful than that of a people, where justice is administer'd, government exercis'd, and a standing army maintain'd at the expense of the people, and yet without the least dependence upon them?" Others worried more about the economic burden of new taxes and quartering troops than about political rights. Boston lawyer Josiah Quincy, Jr., asked readers of the *Boston Gazette*: "Is not the bread taken out of the children's mouths and given unto the Dogs?"

John Dickinson, a well-respected Pennsylvania landowner and lawyer, laid out the basic American position on imperial relations in his pamphlet *Letters from a Farmer in Pennsylvania* (1767). Direct taxation without representation violated the colonists' rights as English citizens, Dickinson declared. But by imposing any tax that did not regulate foreign trade, Parliament also violated those rights. Dickinson also considered, and rejected, the British claim that Americans were represented in the House of Commons. According to the British argument, colonists enjoyed "virtual representation" because the House of Commons represented the interests of all citizens in the empire who were not members of the nobility, whether those citizens participated directly in elections to the House or not. Like most Americans, Dickinson discounted virtual representation. What Englishmen were entitled to, he wrote, was *actual* representation by men they had elected to government to protect their interests. For qualified voters in the colonies, who enjoyed actual representation in their local assemblies, virtual representation was nothing more than a weak excuse for exclusion and exploitation. As one American quipped: "Our privileges are all virtual, our sufferings are real."

Popular resistance began when Samuel Adams set in motion a massive boycott of British goods to begin on January 1, 1768. Some colonists who worried about the growing **materialism** among their neighbors welcomed the chance for a boycott to "mow down luxury and high living." But simple economics also contributed forcefully to support for the boycott. Boston artisans remained enthusiastic about any action that stopped the flow of inexpensive English-made goods to America. Small-scale merchants who had little access to British goods were also eager to see nonimportation enforced. The large-scale merchants who had led the 1765 boycott were not enthusiastic, however. By 1767, their warehouses were no longer overflowing with unsold English stock, and the boycott might cut off their livelihoods. Many of these elite merchants delayed signing the agreements. Others did not sign at all.

Those who opposed resistance to the Townshend Acts most strongly were colonists holding Crown-appointed government offices. These fortunate few—including judges and customs men—shared their neighbors' sensitivity to abuse or exploitation by the Crown, but they had sworn to uphold the policies of the British government. Because their careers and their identities were closely tied to the authority of the Crown, they were inclined to see British policymakers as well intentioned, and they saw acceptance of British policy as a patriotic duty. Jonathan Sewall, the king's attorney general in Massachusetts, was perhaps typical of these royal officeholders.

Sewall had deep roots in his colonial community, for his family went back many generations and included lawyers, judges, merchants, and assemblymen. His closest friend was John Adams, cousin of

■ **Townshend Acts** Revenue-raising measure imposing duties, for the first time, on colonial imports from within the British empire.

materialism Excessive interest in worldly matters, especially in acquiring goods.

Samuel Adams, whose family owned a Boston brewery, was the undisputed leader of the popular protest movement in Massachusetts during the 1760s and 1770s. Adams was one of the organizers of the Sons of Liberty, a group responsible for many of the demonstrations against British policies as well as some of the violence against British officials. After the Revolution, he served as governor of Massachusetts.

Samuel Adams, and the wealthy Boston merchant and smuggler John Hancock would soon become his brother-in-law. Yet Sewall became a staunch public defender of Crown policy. In his newspaper articles he urged his neighbors to ignore the call to resistance, and he questioned the motives of the leading activists, suggesting that greed, thwarted ambition, and envy rather than high-minded principles motivated the rabble-rousers. But despite their prestige and their positions of authority, Crown officers like Sewall were no more able to prevent the boycott or slow the spread of resistance than Anglican ministers like Charles Inglis.

The 1768 boycott brought politics into the lives of women just as the Stamp Act mobilized working-class men. Women's boycott of English cloth was critically important and many women rose to the challenge, resurrecting the tedious skill of spinning yarn for cloth. Taking a bold political stance, women, including wealthy mothers and daughters, formed groups called the Daughters of Liberty and staged large public spinning bees to show support for the boycott. Wearing clothing made of "homespun" became a mark of honor and a political statement. As one male observer noted, "The ladies . . . while they vie with each other in skill and industry in their profitable employment, may vie with the men in contributing to the preservation and prosperity of their country and equally share in the honor of it." Through the boycott, politics had entered the domestic circle.

The British Humiliated

Although the Townshend Acts met with defiance in almost every colony, Massachusetts provided the greatest embarrassment for Parliament and the king. The colonial governor Francis Bernard had lost his control over local politics ever since the assembly defied him by issuing a Circular Letter to other colonies, calling for united protest against the Townshend Acts. The helpless governor could do nothing to save face except dismiss the assembly, leaving the colony without any representative government. Bernard's ability to ensure law and order eroded rapidly after this. Throughout 1768, enforcers of the boycott roamed the streets of Boston, intimidating pro-British merchants and harassing anyone wearing British-made clothing. Boston mobs of men and women openly threatened customs officials, and the Sons of Liberty protected the colony's thriving business in smuggling foreign goods and the items listed in the hated Townshend Acts. One of the town's most notorious smugglers, the flamboyant John Hancock, grew more popular with his neighbors each time he unloaded his illegal cargoes of French and Spanish wines or West Indian sugar. When customs officers seized Hancock's vessel, aptly named the *Liberty*, in June 1768, protesters beat up senior customs men, and mobs visited the homes of other royal officials. The now-desperate Governor Bernard sent an urgent plea for help to the British government.

In October 1768, four thousand troops arrived in Boston. The Crown clearly believed that the presence of one soldier for every four citizens would be enough to restore order quickly. John Adams marveled at what he considered British thickheadedness. The presence of so many young soldiers, far from home and surrounded by a hostile community, was certain to worsen the situation. Military occupation of Boston, Adams warned, made more violence inevitable. Adams was right. With time on their hands, the soldiers passed the hours courting any local women who would speak to them and pestering those who would not. They angered local dockworkers by moonlighting in the shipyards when off duty and taking jobs away from colonists by accepting lower pay. For their part, civilians taunted the sentries, insulted the soldiers, and refused the military any sign of hospitality. News of street-corner fights and tavern brawls inflamed feelings on both sides. Samuel Adams and his friends did their best to fan the flames of hatred, publishing daily accounts of both real and imaginary confrontations in which soldiers threatened the honor or endangered the safety of innocent townspeople.

The military occupation dragged on through 1769 and early 1770. On March 5, the major confrontation most people expected occurred. An angry crowd began throwing snowballs—undoubtedly laced with bricks and rocks—at British sentries guarding the customs house. The redcoats, under strict orders not to fire on civilians, issued a frantic call for help in withdrawing to safety. When Captain Thomas Preston and his men arrived to rescue the sentries, the growing crowd immediately enveloped them. How, and under whose orders, Preston's soldiers began to fire is unknown, but they killed five men and wounded eight other colonists. Four of the five victims were white laborers. The fifth, Crispus Attucks, was a free black sailor.

Massachusetts protest leaders immediately labeled the confrontation the **Boston Massacre**. Their account appeared in colonial newspapers everywhere and included a dramatic anti-British illustration engraved by silversmith Paul Revere. A jury of colonists later cleared Preston and all but two of his men of the charges against them. But nothing that was said at their trial—no sworn testimony, no lawyer's arguments—could erase the image of British brutality against British subjects.

Even before the bloodshed of March 5, Edmund Burke, a member of Parliament known for his sympathy to the colonial cause, had warned the House of Commons that the relationship between Mother Country and colonies was both desperate and tragic. "The Americans," Burke said, "have made a discovery, or think they have made one, that we mean to oppress them; we have made a discovery, or think we have made one, that they intend to rise in rebellion. We do not know how to advance; they do not know how to retreat." Burke captured well the growing American conviction of a conspiracy by Parliament to deprive the colonists of their rights and liberties. He also captured the British government's growing sense that a rebellion was being hatched. But Parliament was ready to act to ease the crisis and make a truce possible. A new minister, Frederick, Lord North, was given the reins of government, and on the very day Captain Preston's men fired on the crowd at Boston, Lord North repealed the Townshend Acts and allowed the hated Quartering Act to expire. Yet Lord North wanted to give no ground on the question of parliamentary control of the colonies. For this reason, he kept the tax on tea—to preserve a principle rather than fill the king's treasury.

Success Weakens Colonial Unity

Repeal of the Townshend Acts allowed the colonists to return to the ordinary routine of their lives. But it was not true that all tensions had vanished. Troubling ones remained—and they were largely among the

Paul Revere's engraving of the Boston Massacre appeared in newspapers the day after the confrontation between redcoats and Boston citizens. Even though Captain Preston and most of his soldiers were found innocent of wrongdoing, Revere's striking image of innocent civilians and murderous soldiers remained fixed in the popular mind. It reinforced suspicion that the British were plotting to deprive Americans of their rights and liberties.

colonists themselves. Struggling artisans and laborers now found themselves at odds with their former allies, the merchants. In fact, many elite colonists gladly abandoned the radical activism they had shown in the 1760s in favor of social conservatism. Their fear of British tyranny dimmed, but their fear of the lower classes' clamor for political power grew. The tyranny that some of them opposed seemed to them to be close to home. "Many of the poorer People," observed one supporter of expanded political participation, "deeply felt the Aristocratic Power, or rather the intolerable Tyranny of the great and opulent." The new political language in which common men justified their demands made their social superiors uneasy. Their own impassioned appeals for rights and liberties were returning to haunt some of the colonial elite.

■ **Boston Massacre** A clash between Boston citizens and British soldiers on March 5, 1770, that resulted in the deaths of five civilians and the trials of nine British soldiers.

In 1776, patriots everywhere celebrated independence by destroying local symbols of royal authority. New Yorkers, however, combined the practical with the symbolic, tearing down an imposing statue of King George III that had stood near the tip of Manhattan since 1770 and recycling its lead to make ammunition for the Revolutionary army.

"Pulling Down the Statue of George III" by William Walcott. Collection of Picture Research Consultants and Archives.

the consent of the governed, Jefferson asserted, and the people had the right to overthrow any government that tyrannized rather than protected them, that threatened rather than respected their unalienable rights.

The genius of Jefferson's Declaration was not that it contained novel ideas but that it contained ideas that were commonly accepted by most colonists. Jefferson gave voice to these beliefs, clearly and firmly. He also gave voice to the sense of abuse and injustice that had been growing in colonial society for several decades.

Declaring Loyalties

Delegates to the Second Continental Congress approved the Declaration of Independence on July 2, 1776, and made their approval public on July 4 (the text of the Declaration is reprinted in the Documents section at the end of this book). As John Adams was fond of saying, "The die had been cast," and Americans had to weigh loyalty to king against loyalty to a new nation. In the face of such a critical choice, many wavered. Throughout the war that followed the Declaration, a surprising number of colonists clung to neutrality, hoping that the breach could be resolved without their having to participate or choose sides.

Those who did commit themselves based their decisions on deeply held beliefs and personal considerations as well as fears. For some of the perhaps

150,000 active loyalists, their commitment was a matter of personal character. Reluctance to break a solemn oath of allegiance to the king or fear of the chaos and violence that were a real part of revolution could motivate a colonist to remain loyal rather than rebel. Many loyalists believed that tradition and common sense argued for acknowledging parliamentary supremacy and the king's right to rule. These colonists had an abiding respect for the structure of the British government. In addition, in their judgment, the advantages of remaining within the protective circle of Europe's most powerful nation seemed too obvious to debate, and the likelihood of swift and bloody defeat at the hands of the British army and navy too obvious to risk. Many of the men who articulated the loyalist position were members of the colonial elite. They frankly admitted their fears that a revolution would unleash the "madness of the multitude." The tyranny of the mob, they argued, was far more damaging than the tyranny of which the king stood accused.

For many colonists who chose loyalism, however, the deciding issues were economic. Holders of royal offices and merchants who depended on trade with British manufacturers found loyalty the compelling option. The loyalist ranks were also filled with colonists from the "multitude." Many small farmers in the Carolinas and tenant farmers in New York gave their support to the Crown when their political and economic foes—the great planters or the wealthy manor lords—became patriots. The choice of which side to back often hinged, therefore, on local struggles and economic conflicts rather than on beliefs about government and imperial issues.

For African Americans, the rallying call of liberty was familiar long before the Revolution began. Decades of slave resistance and rebellion demonstrated that black colonists did not need the impassioned language of a Patrick Henry to remind them of the value of freedom. Instead, many slaves viewed the Revolution as they viewed epidemics and imperial warfare: as a potential opportunity to gain their own liberty. In the same way, many free blacks saw the Revolution as a possible opportunity to win civil rights they had been denied before 1776.

African Americans had pointed out the inconsistencies of the radical position even before the Declaration of Independence. In 1773, a group of enslaved blacks in Boston petitioned the governor and the assembly for their freedom, "in behalf of all those, who . . . are held in a state of SLAVERY, within the bowels of a FREE country." Some white colonists appreciated these sentiments. In 1774, while John Adams debated the threat of political slavery for colonial Englishmen

Peter Salem (1750–1816) was an African American soldier who fought in the battle of Concord on April 19, 1775, and later in the Battle of Bunker Hill. He reenlisted in 1776 and fought once again in the battles of Saratoga and Stony Point. After the war, he returned to his home state of Massachusetts where he died in a poorhouse at the age of 66. Schomburg Center/Art Resource, New York.

in the First Continental Congress, his wife Abigail observed: "It always appeared a most iniquitous [sinful] scheme to me—to fight ourselves for what we are daily robbing and plundering from those who have as good a right to freedom as we have." Tom Paine agreed. Writing as "Humanus" in a Philadelphia newspaper, Paine urged white patriots to abolish slavery and give freed blacks western land grants.

Other patriots worried that slaves would seek their freedom by supporting the British in the war. Indeed, in 1775 the royal governor of Virginia, Lord Dunmore, expressed his intention to "arm all my own Negroes and receive all others that will come to me whom I shall declare free." Rumors of this plan horrified neighboring Maryland planters, who demanded that their governor issue arms and ammunition to protect against slave **insurrection**. Throughout the South, white communities braced themselves for a black struggle for freedom that would emerge in the midst of the colonial struggle for independence.

When Dunmore did offer freedom to "all indentured Servants, negroes or others . . . able and willing to bear Arms who escaped their masters," he was more interested in disrupting the slave-based plantation economy of his American enemies than in African American rights. Yet slaves responded, crossing into British lines in great enough numbers to create an "Ethiopian Regiment" of soldiers. These black loyalists wore a banner across their uniforms that read "Liberty to Slaves." In the southern campaigns of the long war

that followed, thousands of black men, women, and children made their way to the British lines. Once in uniform, black soldiers were usually assigned to work in road construction and other manual labor rather than participate in combat. Perhaps as many as fifty thousand slaves gained their freedom during the war as a result of either British policy or the disruptions that made escape possible.

Indians' responses to news of the war were far from uniform. At first, many considered the Revolution a family quarrel that should be avoided. The revolutionaries would have been satisfied to see Indians adopt this policy of neutrality. They knew they were unlikely to win Indian support given the legacy of border warfare and the actions of land-hungry settlers. As early as 1775, the Second Continental Congress issued a proclamation warning Indians to remain neutral. But the British, recognizing their advantage, made strong efforts to win Indian support. Indian leaders proceeded cautiously, however. When a British negotiator boasted to Flying Crow that British victory was inevitable, the Seneca chief was unimpressed. "If you are so strong, Brother, and they but as a weak Boy, why ask our assistance?" The chief was unwilling to commit his tribe based on issues that divided Crown and colonists but meant little to the welfare of his own people. "You say they are all mad, foolish, wicked, and deceitful— I say you are so and they are wise for you want us to destroy ourselves in your War and they advise us to live in Peace."

The British continued to press for Indian participation in the war, and many Indian tribes and confederations eventually decided that the Crown would better serve their interests and respect their rights than would the colonists. First, the British were much more likely than the colonists to be able to provide a steady supply of the manufactured goods and weapons the Indians relied on in the eighteenth century. Second, colonial territorial ambitions threatened the Indians along the southern and northwestern frontiers. Third, an alliance with the British offered some possibility of recouping land and trading benefits lost in the past. No uniformity emerged, however. Intertribal rivalries and Indians' concerns about the safety of their own villages often determined alignments. Even among the Iroquois, pro-British Senecas burned the crops and houses of Oneidas who had joined forces with the patriots. In the southern backcountry, fierce fighting between Indians and revolutionaries seemed a continuation of the century's

insurrection An uprising against a legitimate authority or government.

many border wars. But there, too, alignments could shift. Although the Cherokees began the war as British allies, a split developed, producing an internal civil war.

Fewer than half of the colonists threw in their lot immediately with the revolutionaries. Among those who did were people whose economic interests made independence seem worth the risk, including artisans and urban laborers as well as merchants who traded outside the British Empire, most large and some small farmers, and many members of the southern planter elite. For these Americans, it was not simply a matter of escaping unfair taxation. A release from Britain's mercantile policies, which restricted colonial trade with other nations, held out the promise of expanded trade and an end to the risks of smuggling. Sometimes the pressure for independence came from below rather than from a colony's political leadership, most notably in Virginia where many elite planters were pressed by more radical ordinary farmers to support independence or lose their positions of authority. Colonists

affected by the Great Awakening's message of egalitarianism often chose the patriot side. Americans with a conscious, articulated radical vision of society—the Tom Paines and Samuel Adamses—supported the Revolution and its promise of a republic. Many who became revolutionaries shared the hope for a better life under a government that encouraged its citizens to be virtuous and to live in simplicity.

As Americans—of English, European, Indian, and African heritage—armed themselves or fled from the violence and bloodshed they saw coming, they realized that the conflict wore two faces: this was a war for independence, but it was also a civil war. In the South, it pitted slave against master, Cherokee against Cherokee, and frontier farmer against coastal planter. In New England, it set neighbor against neighbor, forcing scores of loyalist families to flee. In some instances, children were set against parents, and wives refused to support the cause their husbands had chosen. Whatever the outcome of the struggle ahead, Americans knew that it would come at great cost.

Individual Voices

Charles Inglis Calls for Reconciliation

Charles Inglis, Anglican minister and rector of New York City's Trinity Church, was one of the few loyalists who dared take issue with Thomas Paine's dramatic and powerful call to revolution, *Common Sense*. In his 1776 pamphlet, *The True Interest of America Impartially Stated*, Inglis drew a vivid picture of the chaos, devastation, and humiliation the rebellious colonies would suffer if they broke their allegiance to their king and challenged the most powerful army and navy in the world. Inglis's fears and regrets were echoed in the private letters of loyalists everywhere, as they pleaded with friends, neighbors, and family members to resist the madness of revolution.

In many ways, Inglis and his fellow loyalists proved correct. Much American blood was spilled during the Revolution, and the long home-front war produced great devastation for revolutionaries and loyalists alike. For loyalists such as Inglis and Jonathan Sewall of Massachusetts the greatest blow was exile from their homes and often from their families. Inglis was wrong, however, about the outcome of the war: in one of the greatest military upsets of Western history, the Americans defeated the proud British empire.

1 Inglis is referring to the battles in Massachusetts at Lexington, Concord, and Bunker Hill, in April and June 1775.

2 Although revolutionaries suffered the loss of crops, homes, and livestock, it was the loyalists who, in the end, saw their estates seized by the state governments and sold to patriotic neighbors. Do you think that confiscating their lands and possessions was justified?

3 Modern nations have also established colonies and fought wars to keep them. What economic advantages do colonies provide? Can you think of non-economic reasons why colonies might be valuable?

4 If you were writing a response to Inglis's dire scenario, how would you refute his predictions of American defeat? Based on Chapters 4 and 5, what American advantages would you cite? What British disadvantages? What do you think were the most important factors in the American victory?

The blood of the slain, the weeping voice of nature cries—it is time to be reconciled, it is time to lay aside those animosities which have pushed on Britons to shed the blood of Britons; **1** it is high time that those who are connected by the endearing ties of religion, kindred and country, should resume their former friendship, and be united in the bond of mutual affection, as their interests are inseparably united. . . . By a Reconciliation with Great-Britain, Peace—that fairest offspring and gift of Heaven—will be restored. . . .

Suppose we were to revolt from Great-Britain, declare ourselves Independent, and set up a Republic of our own—what would be the consequence? I stand aghast at the prospect—my blood runs chill when I think of the calamities, the complicated evils that must ensue. . . . All our property throughout the continent would be unhinged; the greatest confusion, and most violent convulsions would take place. . . . What a horrid situation would thousands be reduced to who have taken the oath of allegiance to the King; yet contrary to their oath, as well as inclination, must be compelled to renounce that allegiance, or abandon all their property in America! **2** . . .

By a Declaration of Independency, every avenue to an accommodation with Great-Britain would be closed; the sword only could then decide the quarrel; . . .

The importance of these colonies to Britain need not be enlarged on, it is a thing so universally known. **3** The greater their importance is to her, so much the more obstinate will her struggle be not to lose them. . . . Great-Britain therefore must, for her own preservation, risk everything, and exert her whole strength, to prevent such an event from taking place. This being the case—Devastation and ruin must mark the progress of this war along the sea coast of America. Hitherto, Britain has not exerted her power. . . . But as soon as we declare for independency . . . ruthless war, with all its aggravated horrors, will ravage our once happy land. . . . Torrents of blood will be spilt, and thousands reduced to beggary and wretchedness. . . . **4**

Study Tools

SUMMARY

The British victory in the Great War for Empire produced many new problems. The British had to govern the French population in Canada and maintain security against Indians on a greatly expanded colonial frontier. They had to pay an enormous war debt but continue to finance strong and well-equipped armed forces to keep the empire they had won. To deal with these new circumstances, the English government chose to impose revenue-raising measures on the colonies.

The Sugar Act of 1764 tightened customs collections, the Stamp Act of 1765 placed a direct tax on legal documents, and the Townshend Acts of 1767 set import taxes on English products such as paint and tea. Colonists protested each of these sharp shifts in policy, for they saw Parliament's revenue-raising actions as an abuse of power. Political debate in the colonies began to focus on the possibility that the British government meant to curtail American liberties.

Crowds directed by the Sons of Liberty attacked royal officials, and in Boston five civilians died in a clash with British troops known as the Boston Massacre. But colony-wide boycotts of British goods proved to be the most effective form of protest. They led to the repeal of all three taxes.

Political activists prepared for a quick and united response to any new crises by creating organizations such as the committees of correspondence. In 1773 the British expected little American opposition to the Tea Act, but they were wrong. In Boston a group of activists dumped thousands of pounds' worth of tea into the harbor, enraging British officials, who as a punishment closed the port of Boston to all trade. This and other Intolerable Acts infuriated colonists, and they took united action in support of Massachusetts. A new colonial forum, the First Continental Congress, met in 1774 to debate the colonies' relationship to England and to issue a united protest. A Declaration of Rights and Grievances was sent to the king, but he rejected the colonists' appeal for compromise, instead declaring that "blows must decide."

After British troops fought militiamen at Lexington and Concord, the Second Continental Congress prepared for war. Tom Paine's pamphlet *Common Sense* pushed many reluctant colonists into the revolutionary camp. Not even a reasoned rebuttal of this call to revolution, such as the one written by Charles Inglis, could halt the progress toward independence. In July 1776, Congress issued the Declaration of Independence, drafted by Thomas Jefferson, which defended the colonists' right to resist a tyrannical king. In 1776 Americans faced the difficult task of choosing sides: loyalty to the Crown or revolution. African Americans and Indians had to decide whether to support one side or the other or try to remain neutral in the midst of revolution. The outcome was both a war for colonial independence and a civil war that divided families and communities across America. In Chapter 6, you will see how independence was won.

CHRONOLOGY
Loyalty or Rebellion?

1763	Treaty of Paris ends French and Indian War
	Pontiac's Rebellion
	Proclamation Line
1764	Sugar Act
1765	Stamp Act
	Sons of Liberty organized
	Stamp Act Congress
	Nonimportation of British goods
1766	Stamp Act repealed
	Declaratory Act
1767	Townshend Acts
1768	Renewed boycott of British goods
1770	Boston Massacre
	Townshend Acts repealed
1773	Tea Act and Tea Party
1774	Intolerable Acts
	First Continental Congress
	Continental Association
	Declaration of Rights and Grievances
1775	Battles of Lexington and Concord
	Second Continental Congress
	Olive Branch Petition
1776	Tom Paine's *Common Sense*
	Declaration of Independence

Study Tools

FOCUS QUESTIONS

If you have mastered this chapter, you should be able to answer these questions and to explain the terms that follow the questions.

1. ☆ *Why did Prime Minister Grenville expect the colonists to accept part of the burden of financing the British Empire in 1764?*

2. ☆ *How did colonists understand their obligations to the empire?*

3. ☆ *Why were the colonists alarmed by Grenville's 1765 stamp tax?*

4. ☆ *How did the colonists protest Parliament's taxation policies?*

5. ☆ *Why did Charles Townshend expect his revenue-raising measures to be successful?*

6. ☆ *What forms of resistance did the colonists use against Townshend's measures and what were the results?*

7. ☆ *What British policies led Americans to imagine a plot against their rights and liberties?*

8. ☆ *How did the king hope to crush resistance in Massachusetts and how did the Continental Congress respond?*

9. ☆ *What compromises were still available in 1775-1776 and how might the Revolutionary War have been avoided?*

10. ☆ *What motivated some colonists to become loyalists and others to become patriots?*

KEY TERMS

George III   *(p. 107)*

George Grenville   *(p. 107)*

Covenant Chain   *(p. 107)*

Pontiac   *(p. 107)*

Proclamation Line of 1763   *(p. 108)*

Currency Act   *(p. 110)*

Sugar Act   *(p. 110)*

Stamp Act   *(p. 111)*

Sons of Liberty   *(p. 111)*

Samuel Adams   *(p. 111)*

Thomas Hutchinson   *(p. 112)*

Patrick Henry   *(p. 113)*

Stamp Act Congress   *(p. 114)*

boycott   *(p. 114)*

Declaratory Act   *(p. 114)*

Townshend Acts   *(p. 115)*

Boston Massacre   *(p. 117)*

committees of correspondence   *(p. 119)*

Intolerable Acts   *(p. 120)*

First Continental Congress   *(p. 121)*

Battles of Lexington and Concord   *(p. 124)*

Common Sense   *(p. 124)*

republic   *(p. 125)*

Declaration of Independence   *(p. 125)*

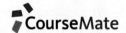 **CourseMate**   Go to the History CourseMate website for primary source links, study tools, and review materials for this chapter. www.cengagebrain.com

6 Recreating America: Independence and a New Nation, 1775-1783

Behind the Stories

Like most Americans, I have always been drawn to the stories of bravery, daring, and betrayal in the American Revolution. In part, the appeal lies in the unlikely victory of a ragtag army over the greatest military and naval force in the eighteenth-century world. In part, it is because the war marks the birth of our nation. In part, it is because the cast of characters—from the elegant young Marquis de Lafayette to the luxury-loving British general "Gentleman Johnny" Burgoyne to the fearless George Washington to the treacherous General Arnold—seem so much larger than life.

Yet if the story of the war itself captures our imagination, the complete story does not take place on the battlefield. It also takes place in Congress and Parliament where the money was raised to arm and equip the men who fought. It takes place in the homes of civilians who had to be mobilized to support or oppose this home-front war. It takes place in Paris where diplomats gathered to draft the peace treaty. And it takes place in the intellectual and social spheres—or as John Adams put it, in the hearts and minds of the participants—for the war produced revolutions in the way people thought about themselves and about others, in the way they behaved within their families and communities, and in the way they defined their rights and duties to their government.

Some of you may have ancestors who fought in the war, spied for the army, provided supplies to the soldiers, or served as diplomats or congressmen. My own ancestors were far away in Russia and Poland when the colonists waged their war for independence. Many of you may trace your roots to even more distant lands. Yet the American Revolution is the heritage of us all, for the values it defended and the rights it promised to its citizens are our legacy no matter when our families became part of the American experience.

—C.B.

132

Individual Choices
Esther de Berdt Reed

Esther de Berdt was born in London, but came to Philadelphia in 1770 as the bride of a young lawyer, Joseph Reed. She began her life as a colonial wife and mother in the midst of the crisis that would lead to the American Revolution. By 1778, her husband was the governor of the state of Pennsylvania and, though Esther had no formal political voice, she was determined to make her own contribution to the Revolution.

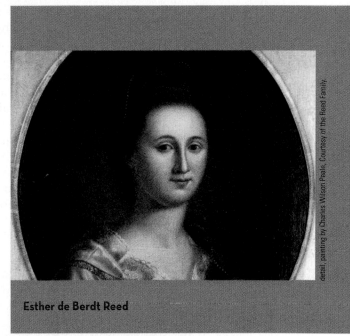

Esther de Berdt Reed

detail, painting by Charles Wilson Peale, Courtesy of the Reed Family.

Working with Ben Franklin's daughter, Sarah Bache, Esther de Berdt Reed organized the first major fund drive in American history. Together these two "daughters of liberty" mobilized some of the most prominent Philadelphia women to go door to door, collecting money for Washington's army. Over fifteen hundred people contributed $300,000 in paper money and almost $7,500 in gold and silver. Reed shared her fund-raising plan with patriot women in Maryland, New Jersey, and Virginia and they, too, collected money for the troops.

Realizing that the fund-raising campaign was a radical act for "proper women," Reed issued a bold statement entitled "Sentiments of an American Woman" that defended women's active participation in the patriot cause. Later, in this chapter's Individual Voices feature, you will be able to read part of her argument for women's entrance into the public sphere.

Reed did not live to see the full success of her plan. She died in September 1780 at the age of 34. She had shocked some Philadelphians by her actions, but many agreed with a French government representative who declared Esther de Berdt Reed "the most zealous and active" patriot the Revolution had inspired.

The war that changed Esther de Berdt Reed's life, and the lives of most colonists, began in April 1775 as a skirmish at Concord's North Bridge. Great Britain expected an easy victory over the colonial rebels, and, on paper, at least, the odds against an American victory were staggering. Great Britain could commit vast human and material resources to crush the rebellion. The well-trained and harshly disciplined British ground troops were assisted and supplied by the most powerful navy in the world, and they carried the flag of Europe's richest imperial power. Many Indian tribes, including most of the Iroquois, allied with the British, and the Crown could expect thousands of white and black loyalists to fight beside them as well.

The American resources were far less impressive. The Continental Congress had a nearly empty treasury, and the country had none of the foundries or factories needed to produce arms, ammunition, or other military supplies. The army administration was inefficient, the population was wary of professional soldiers, and the new state governments were unwilling to raise tax monies to contribute to Congress's war chest. Through most of the war, therefore, American officers and enlisted men could expect to be underpaid or not paid at all. They were likely to go into battle poorly equipped, often half-starved, and frequently dressed in rags. Unlike the British redcoats, these Americans had little military skill or formal military training. Britain's advantage was not absolute, however. The British had to transport arms, provisions, and men across thousands of miles of ocean. They risked delays, disasters, and destruction of supplies on the open seas. The Americans, on the other hand, were fighting on familiar ground, and geography gave them an additional advantage: their vast, rural society could not be easily conquered even if major colonial cities were taken or an entire region were occupied. Longstanding European rivalries gave the Americans valuable allies. Holland, France, and Spain all stood to gain from England's distress, and they willingly lent money and provided much-needed supplies to the rebellion. In 1778, when France and Spain decided to formally recognize American independence, the war suddenly expanded into a global struggle that stretched British resources thin. The support of the French navy led eventually to the defeat of the British army at Yorktown.

No matter what eighteenth-century Americans felt about the war, no matter which side they supported or what role they played, they shared the experience of extraordinary events and the need to make extraordinary choices when the war disrupted their lives. In this most personal and immediate sense, the war was as revolutionary for them as it was for the farm boys who would become, for a brief but critical moment, soldiers in the name of liberty.

American artist John Trumbull painted "The Battle of Bunker Hill" in 1786, over a decade after the bloody encounter between redcoats and American militiamen. He had not witnessed the battle and thus the painting was based on secondhand accounts and Trumbull's desire to express the patriotism of his fellow Americans. "The Battle of Bunker's Hill," John Trumbull (1756–1843), 1786. Oil on canvas, 25 5/8 x 37 5/8 in. (65.1 x 95.6 cm.). Trumbull Collection, 1832.1, Yale University Art Gallery, New Haven, Connecticut, U.S.A./Art Resource, New York.

THE FIRST TWO YEARS OF WAR

★ What were the British and American strategies in the early years of the war?

★ What decisions and constraints kept the British from achieving the quick victory many expected?

In 1775 General **Thomas Gage**, the military governor of Massachusetts and commander of the British army of occupation there, surely wished he were anywhere but Boston. The town was unsophisticated by British standards, many of its inhabitants were unfriendly, and its taverns and lodging houses bulged at the seams with complaining loyalist refugees from the countryside. Gage's army was restless, and his officers were bored. The American encampments outside the city were growing daily, filling with local farmers and artisans after the bloodshed of Lexington and Concord. These thousands of colonial **militiamen** were clearly the military enemy, yet in 1775 they were still citizens of the British Empire, not foreign invaders or foes. Gage, like his American opponents, was caught up in the dilemma of an undeclared war.

The Battle for Boston

With proper artillery, well placed on the hills surrounding the city, the Americans could have done serious damage to Gage's army of occupation. To supply the needed cannon, a New Haven druggist named **Benedict Arnold** joined forces with a Vermont farmer named Ethan Allen and, in May 1775, their troops captured Fort Ticonderoga in New York and began transporting the fort's cannon across hundreds of miles of mountains and forests to Boston. By the time the artillery reached the city, however, a bloody battle between Gage and the American militia had already taken place.

In early June, Gage had issued a proclamation declaring all armed colonists traitors, but he offered **amnesty** to any rebel who surrendered to British authorities. When the militiamen ignored the general's offer, Gage decided a show of force was necessary. On June 17, 1775, Gage's fellow officer **William Howe** led a force of twenty-four hundred soldiers against rebel-held Breed's Hill (see Map 5.3, page 122). Despite the day's oppressive heat and humidity, General Howe ordered his men to advance in full dress uniform, weighed down with wool jackets and heavy knapsacks. Howe also insisted on making a proper frontal attack on the Americans. From the top of the hill, Captain William Prescott's militiamen immediately opened fire on the unprotected redcoats. The result was a near massacre. The tables turned, however, when the Americans ran out of ammunition. Most of Prescott's men fled in confusion, and the British soldiers bayoneted the few who remained to defend their position.

Even battle-worn veterans were shocked at the carnage. The British suffered more casualties that June afternoon than they would in any other battle of the war. The Americans, who retreated to the safety of Cambridge, learned a costly lesson on the importance of an effective supply line of arms and ammunition to their fighting men. Little was gained by either side. That the battle was misnamed the **Battle of Bunker Hill** captured perfectly the confusion and the absurdity of the encounter.

Congress Creates an Army

While militiamen and redcoats turned the Boston area into a war zone, the Continental Congress took its first steps toward recruiting and supplying an army. The "regular" army that took shape was not really a national force. It was a collection of small state armies whose recruits preserved their local or regional identities. While this army was expected to follow the war wherever it led, the Continental Congress still relied on state militias to join in any battles that took place within their own borders.

Congress chose French and Indian War veteran **George Washington** to command the Continental forces. Washington wrote gloomily of the task before him. Nothing he saw when he reached Massachusetts on July 3, 1775, made him more optimistic. A carnival atmosphere seemed to prevail inside the militiamen's camps. Farm boys turned soldiers fired their muskets at random, often using their weapons to start fires or to shoot at geese flying overhead. In the confusion, they sometimes accidentally wounded or killed

---

Thomas Gage British general who was military governor of Massachusetts and commander of the army occupying Boston in 1775.

■ **militiamen** Soldiers who were not members of a regular army but ordinary citizens called out in case of an emergency.

■ **Benedict Arnold** Pharmacist turned military leader whose bravery and daring made him an American hero and a favorite of George Washington until he committed treason in 1780.

amnesty A general pardon granted by a government, especially for political offenses.

■ **William Howe** British general in command at the Battle of Bunker Hill; three years later he became commander in chief of British forces in America.

Battle of Bunker Hill British assault on American troops on Breed's Hill near Boston in June 1775; the British won the battle but suffered heavy losses.

George Washington Commander in chief of the Continental Army; he led Americans to victory in the Revolution and later became the first president of the United States.

themselves and others. "Seldom a day passes but some persons are shot by their friends," Washington noted in amazement.

The camps resembled pigsties. The stench from open latrines was terrible, and rotting animal carcasses, strewn everywhere, added to the aroma. The men were dirty and infected with lice, and most soldiers were constantly scratching, trying to relieve an itch that left them covered with scabs and raw, peeling skin. General Washington was disturbed but not surprised by what he saw. He knew that the men in these camps were country boys, away from home for the first time in their lives. The chaos they created resulted from a combination of fear, excitement, boredom, inexperience, and plain homesickness, all brewing freely under poor leadership. Despite his sympathy for these young men, Washington acted quickly to reorganize the militia units, replace incompetent officers, and tighten discipline within the camps.

The British meanwhile laid plans for the evacuation of Boston, spurred in part by the knowledge that Arnold's wagon train of cannon was nearing Massachusetts. In March 1776 a fleet arrived to carry Thomas Gage, his officers, the British army, and almost a thousand loyalist refugees north to the safety of Halifax, Nova Scotia. By this time, His Majesty's war was in the hands of General William Howe and his brother **Richard Howe**, an admiral in the royal navy. With the help of military strategists and the vast resources of the Crown, the Howes were expected to bring the rebellion to a speedy end and restore order to the colonies.

The British Strategy in 1776

General Howe thought the most effective strategy would be to locate areas with high concentrations of loyalists and mobilize them to secure the allegiance of their undecided and even rebellious neighbors. Howe and his advisers targeted two reputed centers of loyalist strength. The first—New York, New Jersey, Pennsylvania—had a legacy of social and economic conflicts, such as the revolt of the Paxton Boys, that had caused many of the region's elite families to fear that independence threatened their prosperity. But loyalism was not confined to the conservative and wealthy. Its second stronghold was among the poor settlers of the Carolina backcountry. There, decades of bitter struggle between the coastal planters and the backcountry farmers had led to the Regulator

■ **Richard Howe** British admiral who commanded British naval forces in America; he was General William Howe's brother.

Hessian troops German soldiers from the state of Hesse who were hired by Britain to fight in the American Revolution.

movement and to intense loyalist sentiment among many of the embattled westerners.

General Howe's strategy had its flaws, however. First, although many people in these two regions were loyal, their numbers were never as great as the British assumed. Second, everywhere they went, British and **Hessian troops** left behind a trail of destruction and memories of abuse that alienated many Americans who might have considered remaining loyal. Howe was not likely to win over families who saw their "cattle killed and lying about the fields and pastures . . . household furniture hacked and broken into pieces . . . wells filled up and . . . tools destroyed."

Nevertheless, in 1776 Howe launched his first major military assaults in the South and the mid-Atlantic region. In North Carolina, loyalists did turn out to fight for the Crown, but the British, directed by General Henry Clinton, failed to provide them the military support they needed. Poorly armed and badly outnumbered, Carolina loyalists were decisively defeated by the rebel militia on February 27 in the Battle of Moore's Creek. Rather than rush to their defense, the British abandoned their loyalist allies in favor of taking revenge on South Carolina. An impressive fleet of fifty ships and three thousand men sailed into Charleston harbor. But the British had unexpected bad luck. As the troops started to wade ashore, they found themselves stranded on small islands surrounded by a sudden rush of tidal waters. The Americans, meanwhile, had unexpected good luck. Working frantically to defend the harbor, they constructed a flimsy fort out of local palmetto wood. To the surprise of both sides, the cannon balls fired by British ships sank harmlessly into the absorbent, pulpy palmetto stockade. The fort—and the city of Charleston—remained standing.

Embarrassed and frustrated, the British abruptly ended the southern campaign, and General Clinton sailed north. The North and South Carolina loyalists, however, could not escape British failures. They had been denounced, mobbed, imprisoned, and sometimes tortured since 1775. Their situation grew even worse after the British withdrew.

Escape from New York

While Clinton was failing in the Carolinas, the Howe brothers were preparing a massive invasion of the mid-Atlantic region. In July 1776, Admiral Howe and General Howe sailed into New York harbor with the largest expeditionary force of the eighteenth century. With thirty thousand men, one-third of them Hessian mercenaries, this British army was larger than the peacetime population of New York City.

The Howes were not eager to demolish New York, however. Unlike most British officers, the brothers were genuinely fond of Americans, and they preferred to be agents of compromise and negotiation rather than of

MAP 6.1 The War in the North

This map details the movements of both British and American troops during the Northern Campaign, and it indicates the victories and defeats for both armies. The American attempt to capture Canada and General George Washington's effort to save New York from British occupation were failures, but Washington did manage to stage successful raids in New Jersey before retreating to safety in the winter of 1777. Discussion of Burgoyne's failed New York campaign begins on the next page. Copyright © Cengage Learning

destruction. They hoped that a spectacular show of force and a thorough humiliation of rebel commander George Washington would be enough to bring the Americans to their senses and end the rebellion.

General Washington rushed his army south from Massachusetts to defend the city, but he had few illusions that his twenty-three thousand men, many of them sick and most of them inexperienced at war, could repel the invading British forces. For a month, the Howes made no move on the city. Finally, early in the morning of August 22, 1776, the British began their advance, landing unopposed and moving toward the Brooklyn neck of Long Island (see Map 6.1). Just as Washington had feared, when fighting began five days later almost all his raw and inexperienced troops surrendered or ran. A single Maryland regiment made a heroic stand against the landing forces but was destroyed by the oncoming British. Washington, at the scene himself, might have been captured had the Howes pressed their advantage. But they withdrew, content that they had made the American commander look foolish.

Washington took advantage of the Howes' delay to bring his troops to the safety of Manhattan Island. But on September 15, a British attack again sent his army into flight. Angry and frustrated, Washington threw his hat to the ground and shouted, "Are these the men with whom I am to defend America!"

Washington's army fled north with the British in hot pursuit. In a skirmish at Harlem Heights, the American commander was relieved to see his men stand their ground and win their first combat victory. He was even more relieved by the strange failure of the British to press their advantage. When the redcoats finally engaged the Continentals again at White Plains, the Americans managed to retreat safely. Soon afterward, Washington took his army across the Hudson River to New Jersey and marched them farther west, across the Delaware River into Pennsylvania.

Winter Quarters and Winter Victories

Following European customs, General Howe established winter quarters for his troops before the cold set in. His men made their camps in the New York area and in Rhode Island that December, expecting Washington to make camp somewhere as well. But Washington, safe for the moment in Pennsylvania, was too restless to settle in just yet. Enlistment terms in his army would soon be up, and without some encouraging military success he feared few of his soldiers would reenlist. Thus Washington looked eagerly for a good target to attack—and found one. Across the Delaware, on the Jersey side, two or three thousand Hessian troops held a garrison near the town of Trenton.

On Christmas night, amid a howling blizzard, General Washington led twenty-four hundred of his men back across the river. Marching 9 miles, the Americans arrived to find the Hessians asleep. The surprised enemy surrendered immediately. Without losing a single man, Washington had captured nine hundred prisoners and many badly needed military supplies. Taking full advantage of the moment, Washington made a rousing appeal to his men to reenlist. About half of the soldiers agreed to remain.

■ **Battle of Trenton** Battle on December 26, 1776, when Washington led his troops by night across the Delaware River and captured a Hessian garrison wintering in New Jersey.

■ **John Burgoyne** British general forced to surrender his entire army at Saratoga, New York, in October 1777.

The **Battle of Trenton** was a crucial victory, but Washington enjoyed his next success even more. In early January he again crossed into New Jersey to attack the British garrison at Princeton. On the way, his advance guard ran into two British regiments. As both sides lined up for battle, Washington rode back and forth in front of his men, shouting encouragement and urging them to stand firm. His reckless behavior put him squarely in the line of fire, but it was effective. When the British turned in retreat, Washington rashly rode after them, clearly delighted to be in pursuit for once in the war.

The Trenton and Princeton victories raised the morale of the Continental Army as it settled at last into its winter quarters near Morristown, New Jersey. They also stirred popular support for the raids that many called Washington's "nine-day wonder." Of course, General Howe was still poised to march on Philadelphia when warm weather returned. And Congress still had few resources to spare for Washington's army. When Washington pleaded for supplies, Congress urged him to commandeer what he needed from civilians nearby. The general wisely refused. English high-handedness and cruelty had turned many people of the area into staunch supporters of the Revolution, and Washington had no intention of alienating them by seizing their livestock, food, or weapons.

Burgoyne's New York Campaign

In July 1777 General William Howe sailed up the Chesapeake Bay toward Philadelphia with fifteen thousand men. The Continental Congress had already fled the city, knowing that Washington could not prevent the enemy occupation, and the British had little difficulty capturing Philadelphia. The problems they did face in 1777 came not from Washington but from the poor judgment of one of their own, a flamboyant young general named **John Burgoyne**.

Burgoyne had won approval for an elaborate plan to separate New England from the rest of the American colonies. He would move his army south from Montreal, while a second army of redcoats and Iroquois, commanded by Colonel Barry St. Leger, would veer east across the Mohawk Valley from Fort Oswego. At the same time, William Howe would send a third force north from New York City. The three armies would rendezvous at Albany, effectively isolating New England and, it was assumed, giving the British a perfect opportunity to crush the rebellion.

On paper, this daring plan seemed to have every chance of success. In reality, however, it had serious flaws. First, neither Burgoyne nor the British officials in England had any knowledge of the American terrain that had to be covered. Second, they badly misjudged the Indian support St. Leger would receive.

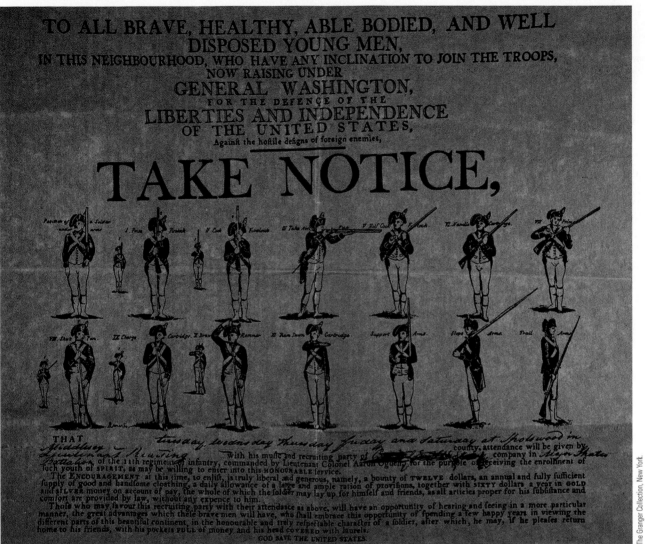

This recruiting poster for the Continental Army invites young men to join in the defense of American liberty and independence. The bounty of $12, along with "good and handsome clothing," a daily allowance of provisions, and $60 a year paid in gold, tempted many poor farm and city boys.

Third, General Howe, no longer in New York City, knew absolutely nothing of his own critical role in the plan. Blissfully unaware of these problems, Burgoyne led his army from Montreal in high spirits in June 1777 (see Map 6.1). The troops floated down Lake Champlain in canoes and flatbottom boats and easily retook Fort Ticonderoga. From Ticonderoga, the invading army continued to march toward Albany. From this point on, however, things began to go badly for Burgoyne.

In true eighteenth-century British style, Burgoyne chose to travel well rather than lightly. The thirty wagons moving slowly behind the general contained over fifty pieces of artillery for the campaign. They also contained Burgoyne's mistress, her personal wardrobe

and his, and a generous supply of champagne. But when the caravan encountered New York's swamps and gullies, movement slowed to a snail's pace. Ethan Allen and his Green Mountain Boys harassed the British as they entered Allen's home region of Vermont. A bloody, head-on battle near Bennington further slowed Burgoyne's progress. When the general's army finally reached Albany in mid-September, neither St. Leger nor Howe were in sight.

The full support St. Leger had counted on from the Iroquois had not materialized, and he met fierce resistance as he made his way to the rendezvous point. When news reached him that Benedict Arnold and an army of a thousand Americans were approaching, St. Leger simply turned around and took his exhausted men to safety at Fort Niagara. Howe, of course, had no idea that he was expected in Albany. This left John Burgoyne stranded in the heart of New York. His supplies dwindling, on September 19 he attacked the American lines, hoping to clear a path of retreat toward Canada for his army. The American general, Horatio "Granny" Gates, was neither bold nor particularly clever, but it took little daring or genius to defeat Burgoyne's weary, dispirited British soldiers. On October 17, 1777, General John Burgoyne surrendered.

News that a major British army had been defeated spread quickly on both sides of the Atlantic. It was a powerful boost to American confidence and an equally powerful blow to British self-esteem. The report also reversed the fortunes of American diplomatic efforts. Until the **Battle of Saratoga**, American appeals to the governments of Spain, France, and Holland for supplies, loans, and military support had met with only moderate success. Now, hopes ran high that France would recognize independence and join the war effort.

Winter Quarters in 1777

John Adams, who never wore a uniform, had once toasted a "short and Violent war." After Burgoyne's defeat, many Americans believed that Adams's wish was coming true. General Washington, however, did not share their optimism. French help might be coming, he pointed out, but who knew when? In the meantime, he reminded Congress, his army still needed funds and supplies. Congress ignored all his urgent requests. The result was the long and dreadful winter at Valley Forge. **Valley Forge** was 20 miles from Philadelphia, where General Howe and his army were comfortably housed for the winter. Throughout December 1777, Washington's men labored to build the huts and cabins they needed. While two officers were assigned to share quarters, a dozen enlisted men were expected to crowd into a 14-by-16-foot hut. Rations were a problem from the start. Most soldiers at Valley Forge lived entirely on a diet of fire cakes, made of flour and water baked in the coals or over the fire on a stick. Blankets were scarce, coats were rare, and firewood was

precious. An army doctor summed up conditions when he wrote: "Poor food—hard lodgings—cold weather—fatigue—nasty clothes—nasty cookery—vomit half my time—smoked out of my senses—the devil's in it—I can't endure it."

The doctor, however, did endure it. So did the soldiers he tended to daily, men such as the barefoot, half-naked, dirty young man who cried out in despair, "I am sick, my feet lame, my legs are sore, my body covered with this tormenting itch." While civilians mastered the steps of the latest dance craze, "the Burgoyne surrender," soldiers at Valley Forge traded the remains of their uniforms and sometimes their muskets for the momentary warmth and sense of well-being provided by liquor.

The enlisted men who survived the winter at Valley Forge were strangers to luxury even in peacetime. Most were from the humblest social classes: farm laborers, servants, apprentices, even former slaves. But if poverty had driven them into the army, a commitment to see the war through kept them there. The contrast between their own patriotism and the apparent indifference of the civilian population made many of these soldiers bitter. Private Joseph Plumb Martin expressed the feelings of most when he said "a kind and holy Providence" had done more to help the army while it was at Valley Forge "than did the country in whose service we were wearing away our lives by piecemeal."

These suffering soldiers did get one thing they desperately needed—professional military training. In the spring of 1778, an unlikely Prussian volunteer arrived at Valley Forge. **Baron Friedrich von Steuben** was almost 50 years old, dignified, elegantly dressed, with a dazzling gold and diamond medal always displayed on his chest. Like most foreign volunteers, many of whom plagued Washington more than they helped him, the baron claimed to be an aristocrat, to have vast military experience, and to have held high rank in a European army. In truth, he had purchased his title only a short time before fleeing his homeland in bankruptcy, and he had only been a captain in the Prussian army. He had not, however, exaggerated his talent as a military drillmaster. All spring, the baron could be seen drilling Washington's troops, alternately shouting in rage and applauding with delight. Washington had little patience with most foreign volunteers, but he considered von Steuben a most unexpected and invaluable surprise.

In the spring of 1778, Washington received the heartening news that France had formally recognized the independence of the United States. He immediately declared a day of thanks and issued brandy to each enlisted man at Valley Forge. American diplomacy had triumphed; Washington hoped the combined forces of France and America would soon bring victory as well.

■ **Battle of Saratoga** American victory in October 1777 that helped convince France to openly aid the American rebellion and turned the tide in the war.

■ **Valley Forge** Winter encampment of Washington's army in Pennsylvania in 1777–1778, where the soldiers suffered greatly from cold and hunger.

■ **Baron Friedrich von Steuben** Prussian military officer who served as Washington's drillmaster at Valley Forge, helping to turn American soldiers into a disciplined army.

Friedrich Wilhelm Augustus von Steuben, or Baron von Steuben, came to America in 1777 and served as an effective drillmaster to General George Washington's troops at Valley Forge. Because he spoke little or no English, he swore and yelled at the troops in German and French. When this proved ineffective, he instructed his French-speaking aide to deliver the curses for him in English!

DIPLOMACY ABROAD AND PROFITEERING AT HOME

★ *What strategy did Benjamin Franklin pursue to win recognition from the French?*

★ *How did the French alliance affect the war effort and wartime spending?*

Like most wars, the Revolutionary War was not confined to the battlefields. Diplomacy was essential, and American diplomats hoped to secure supplies, safe harbors for American ships, and if at all possible, formal recognition of independence and the open military assistance that would allow. British diplomats, on the other hand, worked to prevent any formal alliances between European powers and the American rebels. Both sides issued propaganda to ensure continued popular support for the war. General Burgoyne's defeat and the widening of the war into an international struggle affected popular morale in both America and Britain.

The Long Road to Formal Recognition

In 1776 England had many enemies and rivals in Europe who were only too happy to see George III expend his resources and military personnel to quell a colonial rebellion. Although these nations expected the American Revolution to fail, they were more than eager to keep the conflict going as long as possible. Before Saratoga, they preferred to keep their support for the Revolution unofficial.

The Americans hoped for more. In December 1776, Congress sent the printer-politician-scientist **Benjamin Franklin** to Paris in hopes of winning formal recognition of American independence. The charming and witty Franklin was the toast of Paris, adored by aristocrats and common people alike, but even he could not persuade the king to support the Revolution openly. Burgoyne's surrender changed everything. After Saratoga, the British government began scrambling to end a war that had turned embarrassing, and the French government began scrambling to reassess its diplomatic position. French foreign minister Charles Gravier, comte de Vergennes, suspected that the English would quickly send a peace commission to America after Burgoyne's defeat. If the American Congress agreed to a compromise ending the rebellion, France could gain nothing more. But if the French helped keep the war alive, perhaps they could recoup some of the territory and prestige lost to England in the Seven Years' War. This meant, of course, recognizing the United States and entering a war with Britain. Vergennes knew a choice had to be made—but he was not yet certain what to do.

■ **Benjamin Franklin** American writer, inventor, scientist, and diplomat instrumental in bringing about a French alliance with the United States in 1778; he later helped negotiate the treaty ending the war.

Between 1776 and 1783, Americans fought to create an independent nation. But what kind of nation would that be? Most free white Americans embraced the idea of a republic. Yet a republic could take many forms, and Americans who enjoyed a political voice disagreed on what form was best. As a consequence, the transition from independence to nationhood generated heated debate.

How should power be divided between state and national governments? How should laws be made, and by whom? Who should administer those laws? What programs and policies should the national government pursue? How could the government be designed to protect the unalienable individual rights of free white Americans? These questions had to be answered, and soon.

The Articles of Confederation, which joined the states in a "league of friendship," was the nation's first effort at republican government. It guided Americans through the last years of the war and the peace negotiations. It also organized the northwest territories and established the steps toward statehood for a territory. These were major achievements. But many political leaders believed this government was too limited in its powers to solve America's economic and social problems or set its course for the future.

In 1787 delegates to a Constitutional Convention produced a new plan of government, the Constitution. It was the result of compromises between the interests of small states and large ones, between southern and northern regional interests, and between those who sought to preserve the sovereignty of the states and those who wished to increase the power of the national government. The Constitution created a stronger national government with the power to regulate interstate and foreign trade, create a uniform currency, and impose taxes.

Antifederalists, who opposed the adoption of this new constitution, argued that it threatened the basic ideals of the Revolution, especially the commitment to local representative government. Revolutionaries such as Boston's Mercy Otis Warren and Virginia's Patrick Henry insisted that state governments were the best guarantee that republican values would survive. Others feared the new government would be dominated by the wealthiest citizens. Federalists, who supported the constitution, argued that the new government would save America from economic disaster, international scorn, and domestic unrest. Leading patriots of the 1760s and 1770s could be found on both sides of this debate, but the Federalists carried the day.

The adoption of the Constitution did not magically solve all America's problems. Tensions between northern and southern states were growing more serious. The nation was deeply divided over foreign policy and the choice of allies and enemies in Europe. And even after the Constitution was ratified, many Americans continued to believe that strong local governments protected their liberties best. Nevertheless, when President George Washington said his farewells to public life in 1796, most Americans were confident that their young nation would survive.

AMERICA'S FIRST CONSTITUTIONS

★ *What types of legislatures did the states create?*

★ *What were the major elements of the Articles of Confederation?*

★ *What problems arose in ratifying the Articles?*

The writers of state constitutions were the first to grapple with troubling but fundamental issues—in particular, the definition of citizenship and the extent of political participation. Could landless men, servants, free blacks, or apprentices enjoy a political voice? Should women with property be allowed to vote? These were exactly the kinds of questions John Adams feared might arise in any discussion of voting rights, or suffrage. They raised the specter of democracy, which he and most other revolutionary leaders considered a dangerous system. Once the question was posed, he predicted, "There will be no end of it . . . women will demand a vote, lads from twelve to twenty-one will think their rights are not enough attended to, and every man who has not a **farthing** will demand an equal voice with any other in all acts of state."

English political tradition supported Adams's view that political rights were not universal. Under English law, "rights" were, in fact, particular *privileges* that a group enjoyed because of special social circumstances—including age, sex, wealth, or family ties. In their first constitutions, several states extended these privileges to all free white men, a democratic reform but one that still set special conditions of race and sex.

The state constitutions reflected the variety of opinion on this matter of democracy within a republic. At one end of the spectrum was Pennsylvania, whose constitution abolished all property qualifications and granted the vote to all white males in the state. At the other end were states such as Maryland, whose constitution continued to link the ownership of property to voting. To hold office, a Marylander had to meet even higher standards of wealth than the voters.

While constitution writers in every state believed that the legislature was the primary branch of government, they were divided over other issues. Should there be a separate executive branch? Should the legislature

farthing A British coin worth one-fourth of a penny and thus a term used to indicate something of very little value.

have one house or two? What qualifications should be set for officeholders? Again, Pennsylvania produced the most democratic answer to this question. Pennsylvania's constitution concentrated all power to make and to administer law in a one-house, or **unicameral**, elected assembly, and it eliminated the executive office. In contrast, Maryland and the other states divided powers among a governor, or executive branch, and a **bicameral** legislature, although the legislature enjoyed the broader powers. Members of the upper house in Maryland's legislature had to meet higher property qualifications than those in the lower house, or assembly. In this manner, political leaders in this state ensured their elite citizens a secure voice in lawmaking.

Pennsylvania and Maryland represented the two ends of the democratic spectrum. The remaining states fell between these poles. The constitutions of New Hampshire, North Carolina, and Georgia followed the democratic tendencies of Pennsylvania. New York, South Carolina, and Virginia chose Maryland's more conservative or traditional approach. New Jersey and Delaware took the middle ground, with at least one surprising result. New Jersey's first constitution, written in 1776, gave the vote to "all free inhabitants" who met certain property qualifications. This requirement denied the ballot to propertyless men but granted voting rights to property-holding women. A writer in the *New York Spectator* in 1797 snidely remarked that New Jersey women "intermeddl[ing] in political affairs" made that state's politics as strange as those of the "emperor of Java [who] never employs any-but women in his embassies." Nevertheless, for thirty-one years, at least a few New Jersey women regularly exercised their right to vote.

A state's particular history often determined the type of constitution it produced. For example, coastal elites and lowland gentry had dominated the colonial governments of New Hampshire, South Carolina, Virginia, and North Carolina. These states sought to correct this injustice by ensuring representation to small farming districts in interior and frontier regions. The memory of high-handed colonial governors and elitist upper houses in the legislature led Massachusetts lawmakers to severely limit the powers of their first state government. The constitutions in all of these states reflected the strong political voice that ordinary citizens had acquired during the Revolution.

Beginning in the 1780s, however, many states revised their constitutions, increasing the power of the government. At the same time, they added safeguards they believed would prevent abuse. The 1780 Massachusetts' constitution was the model for many of these revisions, building in a system of so-called checks and balances among the legislative, judicial, and executive branches to ensure that no branch of the government could grow too powerful or overstep its assigned duties. Most of these revised constitutions restored wealth as a qualification to govern, although they did not allow

The men who drafted the New Jersey constitution took care to include a property qualification for voting but forgot to specify the sex of an eligible voter. Thus women who owned property had the right to vote from 1776 to 1807, when state lawmakers corrected the "error," arguing that "the weaker sex" was too easily manipulated by political candidates to be allowed to vote.

the wealthy to tamper with the basic individual rights of citizens. In seven states, these individual rights were safeguarded by a **bill of rights** guaranteeing freedom of speech, religion, and the press as well as the right to assemble and to petition the government.

The Articles of Confederation

There was little popular support for a powerful central government in the early years of the Revolution. Instead, as John Adams later recalled, Americans wanted "a Confederacy of States, each of which must have a separate government." When Pennsylvania's **John Dickinson** submitted a blueprint for a strong national government to the Continental Congress in July of 1776, he watched in wonder and dismay as his colleagues transformed his plan, called **Articles of Confederation**, into a government that preserved the rights and privileges of the states.

---

unicameral Having a single legislative house.

bicameral Having a legislature with two houses.

bill of rights A formal statement of essential rights and liberties under law.

■ **John Dickinson** Philadelphia lawyer and revolutionary pamphleteer who drafted the Articles of Confederation.

■ **Articles of Confederation** The first constitution of the United States; it created a central government with limited powers, and it was replaced by the Constitution in 1788.

MAP 7.1 Western Land Claims After American Independence This map shows the claims, based on colonial charters, made by several of the thirteen original states to land west of the Appalachian Mountains and in the New England region. Until this land was ceded to the federal government, new states could not be created here.
Copyright © Cengage Learning

Members of the one-house Continental Congress agreed that the new Confederation government should also be a unicameral legislature, without an executive branch or a separate judiciary. Democrats like Tom Paine and Samuel Adams praised the Articles' concentration of lawmaking, administrative, and judicial powers in the hands of an elected assembly, whereas conservatives like John Adams condemned the new government as "too democratical," lacking "any equilibrium" among the social classes.

In any case, the powers of the proposed Confederation government were severely limited. It had no authority to tax or to regulate trade or commerce. These powers remained with the state governments, reflecting the view of many Americans that the behavior of their local governments could be closely monitored. Because it had no taxing power, the Confederation had to depend on the states to finance its operations.

Dickinson's colleagues agreed that the state legislatures, not the voters themselves, should choose the

■ **proportional representation** Representation in the legislature based on the population of each state.

members of the Confederation Congress. But they did not agree on how many members each state should have. Should the states have equal representation or **proportional representation** based on population? Dickinson argued for a one-state, one-vote rule, but fellow Pennsylvanian Benjamin Franklin insisted that large states such as his own deserved more influence in the new government. This time, Dickinson's argument carried the day, and the Articles established that each state, large or small, was entitled to a single vote when the Confederation roll was called. The same jealous protection of state power also shaped the Confederation's amendment process. Any amendment required the unanimous consent of the states.

Arguments over financial issues were as fierce as those over representation and sovereignty. How was each state's share of the federal operating budget to be determined? Dickinson reasoned that a state's contribution should be based on its population, including inhabitants of every age, sex, and legal condition (free or unfree). This proposal brought southern political leaders to their feet in protest. Because their states had large, dependent slave populations, the burden of tax assessment would fall heavily on slave masters and other free white men. In the end, state assessments were based

Having a Vision for the Future

In 1791, Alexander Hamilton outlined his vision for the economic future of the United States. When Hamilton predicted that manufacturing would, and should, overtake agriculture as the basis for the American economy, he knew he would be setting himself against some of the most important people in the nation. Hamilton's *Report on Manufactures* was not adopted by Congress, but the ideas set forth in it would eventually become central to the economy of the United States. Hamilton's belief that a strong central government with broad economic powers could encourage the fledgling manufacturing industries of the new country set the stage for this country to become the economic superpower it is today.

- Presidential candidates often outline their vision for the nation's future in their inaugural addresses. Select one such inaugural address and analyze the vision it offers.
- If you had the chance to put forward your vision of the future, what priorities would you insist upon?

on the value of land, buildings, and improvements rather than on population. The Continental Congress thus shrewdly avoided any final decision on the larger question of whether slaves were property or people.

When Congress finally submitted the Articles to the states for their approval in November of 1777, the fate of the western territories proved to be the major stumbling block to **ratification**. In his draft of the Articles, Dickinson had designated the Northwest Territory as a national domain. But states with colonial charters granting them land from the Atlantic to the Pacific Oceans protested, each claiming the exclusive right to the lands beyond the Appalachian mountains (see Map 7.1). Delegates from Maryland, a state having no claim to western territory, dug in their heels, insisting that citizens of every state ought to have the right to pioneer the northwestern territories. Maryland's ultimatum—no national domain, no ratification—produced a stalemate until, at last, Virginia agreed to cede all claims to Congress. The other states with claims followed suit, and the crisis was over. In 1781 Maryland became the thirteenth and final state to ratify the Confederation government. Establishing this first national government had taken three and a half years.

CHALLENGES TO THE CONFEDERATION

★ What problems faced the Confederation?

★ What gains did nationalists expect from a stronger central government?

★ How did the Confederation establish relations with other nations?

The members of the first Confederation Congress had barely taken their seats in 1781 when Cornwallis surrendered at Yorktown and peace negotiations began

in Paris. Even the most optimistic of the Confederation leaders could see that the postwar problems of the new nation were daunting. The long home-front war had left physical, psychological, and economic scars. In New Jersey and Pennsylvania, communities were still recovering from the rape and looting by the British occupying armies. In the South, where civil war had raged, a steady stream of refugees filled the cities. In New England, the postwar depression and food shortages were made worse by an insect attack that destroyed the local wheat crops.

The postwar economic depression seemed to touch everyone's lives. Four years after the American victory, Thomas Jefferson might boast that Americans "adore [their] country, its climate, its equality, liberty, laws, people and manners." But America's unemployed sailors, debt-ridden farmers, and destitute widows and orphans would have found it difficult to share his enthusiasm.

Depression and Financial Crisis

Financial problems plagued wealthy Americans as well as poor farmers and unpaid Revolutionary War veterans. Many merchants had overextended their credit importing foreign goods after the war, while those who had once imported English goods were forced to close their shops. Land **speculators** had also borrowed too heavily in order to grab confiscated loyalist lands

ratification The act of approving or confirming a proposal.

speculator A person who buys and sells land or some other commodity in the hope of making a profit.

or portions of the Northwest Territory, and planters were hard hit when the demand for staple crops such as rice dropped dramatically after the war. By 1786 the New England fisheries were operating at only about 80 percent of their prewar level. Not surprisingly, the English did nothing to ease the plight of their former colonists. In fact, Britain banned the sale of American farm products in the West Indies and limited the American shipping there. These restrictions hit New England shipbuilding so hard that whole communities were impoverished.

The Confederation government did not create these economic problems, but it had little success in dealing with them. In fact, it was helpless to solve its own most pressing problem—debt. To finance the war, the Continental Congress had printed more than $240 million in paper money backed by "good faith" rather than by the hard currency of gold and silver. As doubts grew that the government could ever **redeem** these continentals for hard currency, their value fell rapidly. The scornful phrase "not worth a continental" indicated popular attitudes about a government that owed money to its own citizens and to allies abroad.

In 1781 the government turned to Philadelphia shipper and merchant **Robert Morris** for advice on how to raise funds. Morris, known as a financial wizard, came up with a solution: ask the states to approve federal **tariffs**, or import taxes, on certain foreign goods. The tariffs would provide desperately needed income for the Confederation and relieve the states from having to contribute funding many could scarcely afford. But even this modest plan failed. Both Virginia and Rhode Island said no, and, to add insult to injury, some states promptly passed their own tariffs on imported goods. The failure of the tariff strategy prompted one critic of the Confederation government to comment: "Thirteen wheels require a steady and powerful regulation to keep them in good order." Until Congress could act without the unanimous consent of all states, nothing could prevent the machine from becoming useless.

The Northwest Ordinances

The Confederation turned to the sale of western lands to solve its financial problems. Here at least Congress had the authority to act, for it could set policy for the settlement and governance of all national territories. In 1784, 1785, and 1787, a national land policy took shape in three **Northwest Ordinances**.

The 1784 ordinance established that five new states would be carved out of the region, each to stand on an equal footing with the older, original states. In the earliest stages of settlement, each territory would have an appointed governor. As soon as the number of eligible voters in the territory increased sufficiently, however, they could elect a representative assembly, and the territory could begin to govern itself. Once a state constitution was drafted and approved by the territory's voters, the new state could send elected representatives to the Confederation Congress. Ohio, Indiana, Illinois, Michigan, and Wisconsin would each follow this path to full statehood (see Map 7.2).

The ordinance of 1785 spelled out the terms for sale of the land. Mapmakers divided the region into five

"Alexander Hamilton" by Charles Wilson Peale. Courtesy of the Independence National Historical Park Collection.

Alexander Hamilton was a true American success story: an illegitimate son of a Scottish merchant, he immigrated from the West Indies to the mainland during his teenage years. Hamilton served as Washington's aide-de-camp, became a leader of the New York bar, and entered New York's social elite by his marriage into the Schuyler family. As the author of many of the *Federalist Papers* essays and the first secretary of the treasury, Hamilton helped shape the future of the new nation. In 1804, a political enemy, Aaron Burr, killed Hamilton in a duel.

redeem To pay a specified sum in return for something; in this case, to make good on paper money issued by the government by exchanging it for hard currency, silver or gold.

■ **Robert Morris** Pennsylvania merchant and financial expert who advised the Continental Congress during the Revolution and served as a fundraiser for the Confederation government.

■ **tariff** A tax on imported or exported goods.

■ **Northwest Ordinances** Three laws (1784, 1785, 1787) that dealt with the sale of public lands in the Northwest Territory and established a plan for the admission of new states to the Union.

MAP 7.2 Competing Claims in the West, 1783-1796

This map shows American westward settlement before 1800. Congress approved the eventual creation of five new states in the Northwest Territory, ensuring that the citizens of these states would enjoy the same political rights as those in the original thirteen states. But settlement in this region, as in the area west of Georgia, was challenged by territorial claims made by Native American tribes. As the map indicates, the issue was settled in the 1790s by military action and treaty negotiations. French and Spanish claims west of the Mississippi and in Florida would prompt diplomatic efforts at treaty negotiations.

Copyright © Cengage Learning

Map legend:
- U.S., 1783
- Spanish territory
- Area claimed by Spain, to 1796
- British territory
- Spanish fort on U.S. soil
- British fort on U.S. soil
- U.S.-Indian battle

districts and subdivided each district into townships. Each township, covering 36 square miles, was broken down in a gridlike pattern of thirty-six 640-acre plots. Congress intended to auction off these plots to individual settlers rather than to land speculators, but when the original selling price of $1 per acre in hard currency proved too high for the average farm family, Congress lowered the price and lifted the ban on sales to speculators.

The ordinance of 1787 established that sixty thousand white males were needed for a territory to apply for admission as a state. Thomas Jefferson, who drafted this ordinance, took care to protect the liberties of the settlers with a bill of rights and to ban slavery north of the Ohio River. Yet these provisions trampled on the rights of American Indians whose claims to the land were ignored.

Diplomatic Problems

The Confederation's diplomatic record was as discouraging as its financial plight. Problems with the British and the Indians arose in the West as settlers began to pour into the Northwest Territory. According to the Treaty of Paris, the British were to evacuate their western forts, but they refused to do so until the Americans honored their treaty promises to repay war debts and return confiscated property to loyalists. Instead, the British encouraged Indian resistance by selling arms and supplies to the Shawnees, Miamis, and Delawares. These tribes, and others, denied the legitimacy of the two treaties that turned over the northwest territories to the Americans.

American claims to western lands rested on the 1784 **Treaty of Fort Stanwix** and the 1785 **Hopewell Treaties**. But these treaties had not been approved by all the tribes of either area. The Shawnees and their

■ **Treaty of Fort Stanwix** 1784 treaty by which the Iroquois opened all their lands to white settlement.

■ **Hopewell Treaties** Treaties signed by 1785 in which the Choctaws, Chickasaws, and Cherokees granted American settlement rights in the Southwest.

In the Wider World

Rebellion

The last decades of the eighteenth century witnessed a number of revolutions, rebellions, and independence movements. In 1789, the year that the U.S. Constitution was ratified, French radicals stormed the Paris prison, the Bastille, setting in motion that country's revolution. In that same year, in Ireland, a coalition of Protestants and Catholics led by men such as Henry Joy McCracken and Henry Munro mounted an unsuccessful revolt to win their independence from England, while in the Portuguese colony of Brazil, colonists like Joaquim José da Silva Xavier were inspired by the American Revolution to give their lives in an attempt to win their independence. Two years later, men like Dutty Boukman would lead slaves on the French sugar island of Haiti in launching a revolt that became a decade of civil war and ended in the first independent nation in Latin America (see Chapter 8 feature, In the Wider World, page 196).

allies challenged both treaties, asking what right other tribes had to speak for them. Throughout the 1780s, the Confederation and the Indians resorted to warfare rather than negotiation, (see Map 7.2).

The Confederation preferred diplomacy to armed conflict when dealing with European powers. The new nation desperately needed trade concessions from its former Mother Country, for commercial ties with France and Holland had not developed as rapidly as some patriots had predicted. American merchants thus remained economically dependent on England as a source of manufactured goods, and on British possessions in the Caribbean for trade. Congress sent John Adams to Great Britain, but the American bargaining position was weak. Britain had no desire to end America's economic dependency.

The Confederation had problems with allies as well as with enemies. Spain, for example, was alarmed to find thousands of Americans ready to join the almost fifty thousand Americans who had moved into what would become Kentucky and Tennessee. The Spanish government, which controlled access to the Mississippi River and the port of New Orleans, responded to this threat by banning all American traffic on the river. The Confederation appointed **John Jay**, fresh from his success as a Paris peace commissioner, to negotiate with Spain on this and other issues, but Jay could make no headway.

■ **John Jay** New York lawyer and diplomat who negotiated with Great Britain and Spain on behalf of the Confederation; he later became the first chief justice of the Supreme Court and negotiated the Jay Treaty with England.

■ **Barbary pirates** Pirates along the Barbary Coast of North Africa who attacked European and American vessels engaged in Mediterranean trade.

squatter A person who settles on unoccupied land to which he or she has no legal claim.

The Confederation had no better luck in dealing with the **Barbary pirates**. For many years, the rulers of Algiers, Tunisia, Tripoli, and Morocco had taken advantage of their location along the Barbary Coast of North Africa to attack European vessels engaged in Mediterranean trade. Most European nations kept this piracy under control by paying blackmail or by providing armed escorts for their merchant ships. The Barbary pirates found a new target in the American merchant marine, for American ships were no longer protected by the royal navy. In 1785 a New England ship was captured, its cargo seized, and the crew stripped and sold into slavery. The Confederation Congress was outraged, but with no navy and no authority to create one, it could do nothing to ensure American safety in the Mediterranean.

A Farmers' Revolt

After the Revolution, the postwar economic depression weighed on backcountry farmers, and these Americans began to protest burdens they had long resented—high rents and land prices, heavy taxes, debts, oppressive legal fees, and the failure of central governments to provide protection from Indian attacks and frontier bandits. They used the language of republicanism to defend their position and to justify the occasional violence that erupted in their areas. "We fought for land & liberty," wrote one **squatter** in response to a land speculator's claim to his farm. "Who can have a better right to the land than we who have fought for it, subdued it & made it valuable?" Members of the political and economic elite, who remembered the violence of the Regulator movement and the Paxton Boys revolt, grew uneasy. When farmers in western Massachusetts began an organized protest in 1786, this uneasiness reached crisis proportions.

Western Massachusetts farmers were among those hardest hit by the postwar depression. Many were deeply in debt to creditors who held mortgages on their farms and lands. In the 1780s, these farmers looked to the state government for temporary relief, hoping that it would pass **stay laws** that would temporarily suspend creditors' rights to foreclose on lands and farm equipment. The Massachusetts assembly responded sympathetically but met stubborn resistance from the merchants and creditors who were themselves deeply in debt to foreign manufacturers. The upper house of the state legislature, with its more elite members, sided with the creditors and blocked the passage of stay laws. The Massachusetts government then shocked the farmers by raising taxes.

In 1786 hundreds of farmers revolted. They believed they were protecting their rights and their communities as true republicans must do. To their creditors, though, the farmers appeared to be dangerous rebels threatening the state with "anarchy, confusion, and total ruin." The rebels, led by men such as Revolutionary War veteran **Daniel Shays**, closed several courts and freed a number of their fellow farmers from debtors' prison.

Their actions struck a chord among desperate farmers in other New England states, and fear of a widespread uprising spurred the Massachusetts government to action. It sent a military force of six hundred to Springfield, where more than a thousand farmers, most armed with pitchforks rather than guns, had gathered to close the local courthouse. The troops let loose a cannon barrage that killed four protesters and set the remaining men to flight. Although Daniel Shays managed to escape, by February 4, 1787, the farmers' revolt was over.

Shays's Rebellion revealed the temper of the times. When the government did not respond to their needs, the farmers acted as they had been encouraged to act in the prerevolutionary years. They organized, and they protested—and when government still did not respond, they took up arms against what they considered to be injustice. Across the country, many Americans sympathized with these farmers. But just as many did not. Abigail Adams, adopting language earlier used against her husband by his loyalist opponents, condemned the leaders of the farmers' revolt as "ignorant, restless, desperadoes, without conscience or principles," who were persuading a "deluded multitude to follow their standards."

The revolt stirred up fears of slave rebellions and pitched battles between debtors and creditors, haves and have-nots. Above all, it raised doubts among influential political figures about the ability of either state governments or the Confederation to preserve the basic rule of law. To George Washington, Shays's Rebellion was also a tragedy for the reputation of the United States. When the farmers' protest began, Washington wrote to authorities in Massachusetts urging them to act fairly but decisively. "If they have real grievances," he said, the government should acknowledge them. But if not, authorities should "employ the force of government against them at once. . . . To be more exposed to the eyes of the world, and more contemptible than we already are, is hardly possible."

The Revolt of the "Better Sort"

By 1786, members of the nation's elite, or the "better sort," believed the survival of the nation was in question. Of the Confederation's limited central government, Washington predicted "the worst consequences from a half-starved, limping government, always moving upon crutches and tottering at every step." For him, for Hamilton, and for others like them who thought of themselves as **nationalists**, the solution was clear. "I do not conceive we can long exist as a nation," Washington remarked, "without having lodged somewhere a power which will pervade the whole Union in as energetic a manner as the authority of the State government extends over the several states." Here was a different form of republican government to consider.

Support for a stronger national government grew in the key states of Virginia, Massachusetts, and New York. Leaders in these states wanted to give the central government taxing powers, devise an easier amendment process, and provide some legal means to enforce national government policies that a state might oppose. They wanted a government that could establish stable diplomatic and trade relations with foreign countries. They also wanted a national government able to preserve their property and their peace of mind. Alexander Hamilton was one of the driving forces behind this movement. At Hamilton's urging, in 1786 a group of influential Virginians called for a meeting on problems of interstate trade. With the approval of the Confederation Congress, delegates met at Annapolis, Maryland. But beyond trade issues, the meeting organizers had a second agenda: to test the waters on revising the nation's constitution. Although only a third of the states participated in the Annapolis conference, nationalists were convinced that their position had substantial support. They asked Congress to call a convention in Philadelphia so that political leaders could continue to discuss interstate commerce problems—and other aspects of government reform. Some members of Congress were reluctant, but news of Shays's Rebellion tipped the balance in favor of the convention.

stay laws Laws suspending the right of creditors to foreclose on, or seize, debtors' property; they were designed to protect indebted farmers from losing their land.

■ **Daniel Shays** Revolutionary War veteran considered the leader of the farmers' uprising in western Massachusetts called Shays's Rebellion.

■ **nationalists** Americans who preferred a strong central government rather than the limited government prescribed in the Articles of Confederation.

CREATING A NEW CONSTITUTION

☆ What major compromises did the framers make in writing the new constitution?

☆ What safeguards did James Madison see in his "checks and balances" system?

Late in May 1787, George Washington called the convention to order in Philadelphia. Before him sat delegates from eleven of the thirteen states (New Hampshire's delegates did not arrive until late July), closeted behind curtained windows and locked doors in the heat and humidity of a Philadelphia summer. These secrecy precautions stemmed in large part from the delegates' ultimate purpose. Rhode Island, refusing to participate in the deliberations, accused the convention of masquerading as a discussion of interstate trade while intending to drastically revise the national government. The accusation was correct. The fifty-five prominent and prosperous delegates did expect to make significant changes in the structure of the government. This objective and the need to freely debate the compromises it would require were ample reasons to keep the deliberations secret.

Most of the men gathered in that room were lawyers, merchants, or planters—Americans of social standing though not necessarily intellectual achievement. When the absent Thomas Jefferson later referred to the convention members as "demigods," he was probably thinking of the likes of 81-year-old Benjamin Franklin, whose sparkling wit and crafty political style set him apart from his colleagues despite his advanced age; or of the articulate, brilliant Alexander Hamilton of New York, whose reputation as a financial mastermind equal to the Confederation's adviser Robert Morris was well established; or of Pennsylvania's Gouverneur Morris, who was widely admired for his intelligence as well as for his literary skills; or of **James Madison**, the prim Virginia planter who turned out to be the chief architect of a new constitution. Several notable men were absent. Jefferson, author of the Declaration of Independence, was abroad serving as ambassador to France. John Adams was representing the United States in the same capacity in London. And the two great propagandists of the Revolution, Samuel Adams and Thomas Paine,

■ James Madison Virginia planter and political theorist known as the "father of the Constitution"; he would become the fourth president of the United States.

Virginia Plan Fourteen proposals by the Virginia delegation to the Constitutional Convention for a more powerful central government giving states proportional representation in a bicameral legislature.

veto The power or right of one branch of government to reject the decisions of another branch.

were also absent, for both opposed any revision of the Articles of Confederation.

Revise or Replace?

Most of the delegates were nationalists, but they did not necessarily agree on how best to proceed. Should they revise the Articles or abandon them? Several delegates, including Alexander Hamilton himself, would present blueprints for the new government. But it was the Virginia planter and lawyer Edmund Randolph who first captured the convention's attention with his delegation's proposal, which effectively amended the Articles of Confederation out of existence.

Although Randolph introduced the **Virginia Plan** on the convention floor, James Madison was its guiding spirit. The 36-year-old Madison was no dashing figure. He was small, frail, charmless, and a hypochondriac. But he was highly respected as a scholar of philosophy and history and as an astute political theorist, and his long service as a member of the Virginia legislature and in the Confederation Congress gave him a practical understanding of politics and government. At the convention, Madison brought all his knowledge to bear on one question: What was the best form of government for a strong republic? He concluded, as John Adams had done early in the 1780s, that the fear of tyranny should not rule out a powerful national government. Any dangerous abuse of power could be avoided if internal checks and balances were built into the republican structure.

Madison's Virginia Plan embodied this conviction. It called for a government with three distinct branches—legislative, executive, and judicial—to replace the Confederation's Congress, which was performing all three functions. By dividing power in this way, Madison believed the plan could prevent an individual or group of men from wielding too much authority, especially for self-interested reasons. Madison's plan also gave Congress the power to **veto** laws passed by the state legislatures and the right to intervene directly if a state acted to interrupt "the harmony of the United States."

The delegates endorsed Madison's notion of a strong government able "to control the governed" but also "obliged to control itself." But they were in sharp disagreement over many specific issues in the Virginia Plan. The greatest controversy swirled around representation in the legislative branch—Congress—a controversy familiar to those who had helped draft the Articles of Confederation. Madison proposed a two-house or bicameral legislature. Membership in both houses would be based on proportional representation. Large states supported the plan, for representation based on population worked to their advantage. Small states objected heatedly, arguing that proportional representation would leave them helpless against a national government dominated by the large ones. Small-state delegates threw their support behind a second proposal, the **New Jersey Plan**, which also called for three branches of government and gave Congress the power to tax and to control national commerce. This plan, however, preserved an equal voice and vote for every state within a unicameral legislature.

Debate over the two plans dragged on through the steamy days of a June heat wave. Tempers flared, and at times the deadlock seemed hopeless. Threats to walk out of the convention came from both sides. Ultimately, a compromise, hammered out by a special committee, was presented by Roger Sherman of Connecticut. This **Great Compromise** proposed a two-house legislature to satisfy both sides, with proportional representation in the lower house (the House of Representatives) and equal representation in the upper house (the Senate).

The Great Compromise resolved the first major controversy at the convention but opened the door to the next one. The delegates had to decide how the representatives in each house were to be elected. A compromise also settled this issue. State legislatures would select senators, and the eligible voters of each state would directly elect their member of the House. This formula allowed the delegates to acknowledge the sovereignty of the state governments but also to accommodate the republican commitment to popular elections in a representative government.

The delegates faced one last stumbling block over representation: Which Americans were to be counted to determine a state's population? This issue remained as divisive as it had been when the Articles of Confederation were drafted. Southern delegates argue that slaves, who composed as much as one-third and sometimes more of each plantation state's residents, should be included in the population count that determined a state's seats in the House of Representatives. Northern delegates protested, declaring that slaves should be considered property. These delegates were motivated by self-interest rather than a desire for consistency, for if slaves were considered property, not people, the North would dominate the lower house.

A compromise that defied reason but made brilliant political sense settled this question. The **Three-Fifths Compromise** established that three-fifths of the slave population would be included in a state's critical headcount. A clause was then added guaranteeing that the slave trade would continue for a twenty-year

In 1867, Thomas Pritchard Rossiter painted his *Signing of the Constitution of the United States* honoring a group of statesmen that included James Madison, Alexander Hamilton, and George Washington, who presided over the Constitutional Convention. Thomas Jefferson, absent because of his duties as ambassador to France, later referred to the fifty-five delegates who crafted the Constitution as a gathering of "demigods."

"Signing of the Constitution of the United States" by Thomas Pritchard Rossiter, 1867. Gift of John Schermerhorn Jacobus, 1960. Collection of Frances Tavern® Museum, New York City.

period. Some southern leaders, especially in South Carolina, wanted this extension badly because they had lost many slaves during the Revolution. But not all slave-owners concurred. Virginia's George Mason, a slave-owner himself, spoke passionately of the harm slavery did to his region. It not only prevented white immigration to the South, Mason said, but infected the moral character of the slave master. "Every master of slaves," Mason argued, "is born a petty tyrant." Slave-owners "bring the judgment of heaven upon a country," particularly one intended as a republic.

Drafting an Acceptable Document

The Three-Fifths Compromise ended weeks of debate over representation. No other issue arose to provoke such controversy, and the delegates proceeded calmly to implement the principle of checks and balances. For example, the president, or executive, was named commander in chief of the armed forces and given primary responsibility for foreign affairs. To balance these **executive powers**, only Congress was given the right to declare war and to raise an army.

New Jersey Plan A proposal submitted by the New Jersey delegation for a government in which the states would have equal representation in a unicameral legislature.

■ **Great Compromise** A proposal calling for a bicameral legislature with equal representation for the states in one house and proportional representation in the other.

■ **Three-Fifths Compromise** An agreement to count three-fifths of a state's slave population for purposes of determining a state's representation in the House of Representatives.

executive powers Powers given to the president by the Constitution.

Congress received the critical "power of the purse," but this power to tax and to spend the revenues raised by taxation was checked in part by the president's power to veto congressional legislation. As yet another balance, Congress could override a presidential veto by the vote of a two-thirds majority. Following the same logic of distributing power, the delegates gave authority to the president to name federal court judges, but the Senate had to approve all such appointments.

Occasionally, as in the system for electing the president, the convention chose awkward or cumbersome procedures. For example, many delegates opposed direct popular election of the president. A few agreed with the elitist sentiments of George Mason, who said this "would be as unnatural . . . as it would [be] to refer a trial of colours to a blind man." Others simply doubted that the citizens of one state would be familiar enough with a candidate from a distant state to make a valid judgment. In an age of slow communication, few men besides George Washington had a truly national reputation. Should the president be chosen by state legislators who had perhaps worked in government with political leaders from outside their states? Delegates rose to object that this solution threatened too great a concentration of power in the legislators' hands. As a somewhat clumsy compromise, the delegates created the **Electoral College**, a group of special electors to be chosen by the states to vote for presidential candidates. Each state would be entitled to a number of electors equal to the number of its senators and representatives sitting in Congress, but no one serving in Congress at the time of a presidential election would be eligible to be an elector. If two presidential candidates received the same number of Electoral College votes, or if no candidate received a majority of the Electoral College votes, then the House of Representatives would choose the new president. This complex procedure honored the **discretion** of the state governments in appointing the electors but limited the power of individuals already holding office.

The long summer of conflict and compromise ended with a new plan for a national government. Would the delegates be willing to put their names to the document they had created in secrecy and by overreaching their authority? Benjamin Franklin fervently hoped so. Though sick and bedridden, Franklin was carried by friends to the convention floor, where he pleaded for unanimous support for the new government. When a weary George Washington at last declared the meetings adjourned on September 17, 1787, only a handful of delegates left without signing what the convention hoped would be the new American constitution.

RESOLVING THE CONFLICT OF VISION

☆ What were the Antifederalists' arguments against the Constitution? What were the Federalists' arguments in its favor?

☆ What was the outcome of the ratification process?

The framers of the Constitution called for special state **ratifying conventions**, with delegates chosen by voters, to discuss and then vote on the proposed change of government. The framers believed that these conventions would give citizens, including themselves, a more direct role in this important political decision, while bypassing the state legislatures, which stood to lose power under the new government and were thus likely to oppose it. The framers added to their advantage by declaring that the approval of only nine states was necessary to establish the Constitution. Reluctantly, the Confederation Congress agreed to all these terms and procedures. By the end of September 1787, Congress had passed the proposed Constitution on to the states, triggering the next round of debates over America's political future.

The Ratification Controversy

As Alexander Hamilton boasted, "The new Constitution has in favor of its success . . . [the] very great weight of influence of the persons who framed it." Hamilton was correct. Men of wealth, political experience, and frequently great persuasive powers put their skills to the task of achieving ratification. But what Hamilton did not mention was that many revolutionary heroes and political leaders opposed the Constitution with equal intensity—most notably Patrick Henry, Samuel Adams, George Mason, and George Clinton, the popular governor of New York. Boston's most effective revolutionary propagandist, Mercy Otis Warren, immediately took up her pen to attack the Constitution and even **canvassed** her neighbors to stand firm against what she called an assault on republican values. Thus the leadership on both sides of the issue was drawn from the political elite of the revolutionary generation.

The pro-Constitution forces won an early and important victory by clouding the language of the debate. They abandoned the label "nationalists," which drew attention to their belief in a strong central

■ **Electoral College** A body of electors chosen by the states to elect the president and vice president; the number of each state's electors equals the number of its senators and representatives in Congress.

discretion The power or right to act according to one's own judgment.

■ **ratifying conventions** A meeting of delegates in each state to determine whether that state would ratify the Constitution.

canvass To survey people relating to an issue.

MAP 7.3 The Federalist and Antifederalist Struggle over the Constitution
The battle over ratification of the Constitution was fierce throughout 1787 and 1788. This map shows the areas of strong antifederalism, the areas of Federalist strength, and the scattered pockets where opinion was evenly divided. The date of each state's ratification and its convention vote are also shown. Copyright © Cengage Learning

government, and chose to call themselves **Federalists**, a name originally associated with a system of strong state governments and limited national government. This shrewd tactic cheated opponents of the Constitution out of their rightful name. The pro-Constitution forces then dubbed their opponents **Antifederalists**. This label implied that their adversaries were negative thinkers and pessimists who lacked a program of their own.

Although the philosophical debate over the best form of government for a republic was an important one, voters considered other, practical factors in choosing a Federalist or Antifederalist position. Voters in states with a stable or recovering economy were likely to oppose the Constitution because the Confederation system gave their states greater independent powers. Those in small, geographically or economically disadvantaged states were likely to favor a strong central government

that could protect them from their competitive neighbors. Thus the small states of Delaware and Connecticut ratified the Constitution quickly, but in New York and Virginia ratification was hotly contested.

To some degree, Federalist and Antifederalist camps matched the divisions between the relatively urban, market-oriented communities of the Atlantic coast and the frontier or rural communities of the inland areas (see Map 7.3). For example, the backcountry of North and South Carolina and the less

■ **Federalists** Supporters of the Constitution; they desired a strong central government.

■ **Antifederalists** Opponents of the Constitution; they believed a strong central government was a threat to American liberties and rights.

This political cartoon captures the celebration that followed the ratification of the nation's new government. The shrine of liberty rests solidly upon the rock of a written constitution and written laws, guaranteeing the success of a nation made up of citizens from many different backgrounds. The sheaf of wheat symbolizes prosperity under the new constitution. The Granger Collection, New York.

Antifederalists rejected the claim that the nation was in a "critical period," facing economic and political collapse. As one New Yorker put it: "I deny that we are in immediate danger of anarchy and commotions. Nothing but the passions of wicked and ambitious men will put us in the least danger." Nevertheless, the Federalists were successful in portraying the moment as a crisis or turning point for the young republic—and in insisting that their plan for recovery was better than no plan at all.

The Antifederalists struck hard against the dangerous elitism they believed they saw in the Constitution. They portrayed the Federalists as a privileged, sophisticated minority, ready and able to tyrannize the people if their powerful national government were ratified. Be careful, one Massachusetts man warned, because "these lawyers, and men of learning, and moneyed men, that talk so finely and gloss over matters so smoothly, to make us poor illiterate people swallow down the pill, expect to get into Congress themselves." And New York Antifederalist Melancton Smith predicted that the proposed new government would lead inevitably to rule by a wealthy, unrepresentative minority. The Virginia revolutionary leader Richard Henry Lee was flabbergasted that his generation would even consider ratifying the Constitution. "'Tis really astonishing," he wrote to a New York opponent in the summer of 1788, "that the same people, who have just emerged from a long and cruel war in defense of liberty, should agree to fix an elective **despotism** upon themselves and posterity."

The Antifederalists' most convincing evidence of elitism and its potential for tyranny was that the proposed Constitution lacked a bill of rights. It contained no written guarantees of the people's right to assemble or to worship as they saw fit, and it gave no assurances of a trial by jury in civil cases or the right to bear arms. The framers believed these rights were secure because most state constitutions contained strong guarantees of them. But Antifederalists put the question to both voters and delegates: What did this glaring omission tell Americans about the framers' respect for republican ideals? The only conclusion, Antifederalists argued, was that the Constitution was a threat to republican principles of representative government, a vehicle for elite rule, and a document unconcerned with the protection of the people's individual liberties. Federalists countered by insisting that the Constitution fulfilled and could preserve the republican ideals of the Revolution far better than the Articles of Confederation had done. Their cause was put forward most convincingly by Alexander Hamilton, James Madison, and John Jay, who entered the newspaper wars over ratification in the key state of New York. Together, they produced a series of essays known today as the **Federalist Papers**. Although these 85 essays were all signed "Publius," Hamilton wrote

economically developed areas of Virginia saw little benefit in a stronger central government, especially one that might tax them. But coastal centers of trade and overseas commerce such as Boston, New York City, and Charleston were eager to see an aggressive and effective national policy regarding foreign and interstate trade. In these urban centers, artisans, shopkeepers, and even laborers joined forces with wealthy merchants and shippers to support the Constitution as they had once joined them to make the Revolution. No generalization can explain every political choice, of course. No economic or social group was unified under the Federalist or the Antifederalist banner. On the whole, however, it can be said that the Federalists were better organized, had more resources at their disposal, and campaigned more effectively than the Antifederalists.

Public debates sharply defined the political differences between the Federalists and Antifederalists.

despotism Rule by a tyrant.

■ **Federalist Papers** Essays written by Alexander Hamilton, John Jay, and James Madison in support of the Constitution.

51 of them, Madison 29, and Jay 5. Their common theme was the link between American prosperity, American liberties, and a strong central government.

The Federalist Victory

Practical politics rather than political theory seemed to influence the outcome of many of the ratifying conventions. Delaware, New Jersey, Georgia, and Connecticut—all small states—quickly approved the Constitution. In Pennsylvania, Antifederalists in the rural western regions lost control of the convention to the Federalists and thus that state also endorsed the Constitution. In the remaining states, including Massachusetts, Virginia, and New York, the two sides were more evenly matched.

Antifederalists were in the majority in the Massachusetts convention, where most of the delegates were small farmers from the western counties and more than twenty of them had participated in Shays's Rebellion. The Federalists' strategy was to make political deals with key delegates, winning over Antifederalists such as Samuel Adams and John Hancock, for example, with promises to demand the addition of a bill of rights to the Constitution. At the final count, a 19-vote margin gave the Federalists a narrow victory in Massachusetts.

After Massachusetts ratified, the fight shifted to New Hampshire. Here, too, Federalists won by a small majority. Rhode Island, true to its history of opposition to strong central authority, rejected the Constitution decisively. But Maryland and South Carolina ratified it, and the tide in favor of the new government influenced the next critical vote: that of Virginia. There, Antifederalist leaders Lee, Henry, and James Monroe focused on the absence of a bill of rights in the proposed Constitution. James Madison and George Washington directed the Federalist counterattack. In the end, the presence of Washington proved irresistible because Virginians knew that this war hero and admired colleague was certain to be the first president of the United States if the Constitution went into effect. When the vote was taken on June 25, 1788, Virginia became the tenth state to ratify the new government.

New York's battle was equally intense. Acknowledging that the absence of a bill of rights was a major political error, Federalist leaders Jay and Hamilton made a public pledge to support its inclusion. By then, however, ten states had already ratified the Constitution, and so the new government was a **fait accompli**. Realizing this, on July 26, 1788, a majority of New York delegates voted yes on ratification.

President George Washington

The election of senators and Congress members was almost complete by February 4, 1789, when presidential electors met in each state to choose the nation's

The unknown artist of "The Federal Procession in New York, 1788," captured the jubilant mood of Americans as they celebrated their new Constitution with parades, bonfires, and banquets. As the "Ship of State" float indicates, New Yorkers were particularly eager to acknowledge the role of their own Alexander Hamilton in launching the new government.

first president. Although George Washington did not seek the position, he knew the nation expected him to serve. He was hailed as the hero of the Revolution, and he looked and acted the part of the dignified, virtuous patriot. Washington became president by a unanimous vote of the Electoral College. For regional balance, New Englander John Adams was chosen vice president.

In April 1789, as Washington made his way from Virginia to his inauguration in New York City, the temporary national capital, Americans thronged to greet him with parades, sharply dressed military escorts, and choruses of church bells and cannon fire. Near Trenton, New Jersey, he passed through a triumphal arch 20 feet high, supported by thirteen pillars, and inscribed in gold with the date of the Battle of Trenton. Thousands of supporters gathered to see him take the oath of office. Yet amid the celebration, Washington and his closest advisers knew the future was uncharted and uncertain. "We are in a wilderness," Madison observed, "without a single footstep to guide us."

Washington agreed and proceeded with caution and deliberation. He labored carefully over each of his selections to the almost one thousand federal offices waiting to be filled. He took particular care in choosing the men to head four executive departments created with approval from Congress. Naming his

fait accompli An accomplished deed or fact that cannot be reversed or undone.

protégé Alexander Hamilton to the Treasury Department was probably Washington's easiest decision. He asked the Massachusetts military strategist Henry Knox to head the War Department and fellow Virginian Edmund Randolph to serve as attorney general. Washington chose another Virginian, Thomas Jefferson, to be secretary of state. Over time, the president established a pattern of meeting with this **cabinet** of advisers on a regular basis to discuss policy matters. Together, they made major decisions and, as Washington expected, expressed serious disagreements that exposed him to differing viewpoints on policy.

COMPETING VISIONS RE-EMERGE

☆ How did Alexander Hamilton's expectations for the new nation differ from those of Thomas Jefferson? What were the consequences of this conflict of vision?

☆ How did the French Revolution affect Washington's diplomatic policy?

A remarkable but, as it turned out, short-lived spirit of unity marked the early days of Washington's administration. Federalists had won the overwhelming majority of seats in the new Congress, and this success enabled them to work quickly and efficiently on matters they felt had priority. But the unity was fragile. By 1792, as the government debated foreign policy and domestic affairs, two distinct groups, voicing serious differences of opinion, began to form. Alexander Hamilton's vision for America guided one group, Thomas Jefferson's vision the other.

Unity's Achievements

In addition to creating the four executive departments that became the cabinet, the First Congress passed the **Judiciary Act of 1789**. This act established a Supreme Court, thirteen district courts, and three

protégé An individual whose welfare or career is promoted by an influential person.

■ **cabinet** A body of officials appointed by the president to run the executive departments of the government and to act as the president's advisers.

■ **Judiciary Act of 1789** Law establishing the Supreme Court and the lower federal courts; it gave the Supreme Court the right to review state laws and state court decisions to determine their constitutionality.

■ **Bill of Rights** The first ten amendments to the U.S. Constitution, added in 1791 to protect certain basic rights of American citizens.

civil liberties Fundamental individual rights such as freedom of speech and religion, protected by law against interference from the government.

circuit courts. It also empowered the Supreme Court to review the decisions of state courts and to nullify any state laws that violated either the Constitution or any treaty made by the federal government. President Washington chose John Jay to serve as first chief justice of the Supreme Court.

The First Congress also managed to break the stalemate on the tariff issue. Southern leaders had opposed a tariff because a tax on imports added to the cost of the consumer goods that southern agriculturalists had to purchase. Northeastern leaders had favored tariff legislation because such a tax, by making foreign goods more expensive, would benefit their region's merchants and manufacturers. During Washington's first term, southerner James Madison took the lead in conducting the delicate negotiations over tariffs. The result was an import tax on certain items such as rum, cocoa, and coffee.

Madison also prodded Congress to draft the promised **Bill of Rights** and helped craft the ten amendments that on December 15, 1791, were added to the Constitution. Soon after, both Rhode Island and North Carolina ratified the Constitution and joined the union. Eight of these original constitutional amendments spelled out the government's commitment to protect individual **civil liberties**. They guaranteed that the new national government could not limit free speech, interfere with religious worship, deny U.S. citizens the right to keep or bear arms, force the quartering of troops in private homes, or allow homes to be searched without proper search warrants. The amendments prohibited the government from requiring persons accused of crimes to testify against themselves, nor could it deny citizens the right to a trial by jury. The government also could not deprive a citizen of life, liberty, or property without "due process of law," or impose excessive bail, or administer "cruel and unusual punishments." The Ninth Amendment made clear that the inclusion of these protections and rights did not mean that others were excluded. The Tenth Amendment stated that any powers not given to the federal government or denied to the states belonged solely to the states or the people.

Condensed into these ten amendments was a rich history of struggle for individual rights in the face of abusive power. It was a history that recalled the illegal search and seizure of cargoes in Boston Harbor, the British government's insistence on quartering troops in New York homes, and the religious persecution of men and women who dissented from established churches both in England and in the colonies.

Hamilton and Jefferson's Differences

Alexander Hamilton was consumed by a bold dream: to transform agricultural America into a manufacturing society that rivaled Great Britain. His blueprint for achieving this goal called for protective tariffs designed to assist developing American industry rather than simply raise revenue. It also called for subsidies, or government financial support, for new enterprises and for incentives to support new industries. And it relied on strong economic and diplomatic ties with the mercantile interests of England. Hamilton's vision had great appeal in the Northeast but few advocates in the southern states. Indeed, his ambitious development program seemed to confirm Patrick Henry's worst fear that the new government would produce "a system which I have ever dreaded—subserviency of Southern to Northern Interests."

Virginia planters Thomas Jefferson and James Madison offered a different vision of the new nation: a prosperous, agrarian society. Instead of government tariffs designed to encourage American manufacturing, they advocated a national policy of **free trade** to keep consumer prices low. They did not rule out commerce and industry in the United States but believed it should remain only as "a handmaiden to agriculture." In the same fashion, Hamilton was content to see agriculture thrive as long as it did not stand in the way of commercial or industrial growth. Hamilton and men of similar vision around him spoke of themselves as true **Federalists**. Those who agreed with Jefferson and Madison identified themselves as **Republicans**.

The emergence of two political camps was certain to trouble even the men who played a role in creating them. The revolutionary generation believed that **factions**, or special-interest parties, were responsible for the corruption of English politics. John Adams seemed to speak for all these political leaders when he declared: "A division of the republic into two great parties . . . is to be dreaded as the greatest political evil." Yet as President Washington was quick to see, **sectionalism** fueled the growth of just such a division.

Hamilton's Economic Plan

As secretary of the treasury, Alexander Hamilton was expected to seek solutions to the nation's **fiscal** problems, particularly the foreign and domestic debts hanging over America's head. His proposals were the source of much of the conflict that divided Congress in the early 1790s.

In January 1790 Hamilton submitted a *Report on Public Credit* to the Congress. In it, he argued that the public debt fell into three categories, each requiring attention: (1) foreign debt, owed primarily to France; (2) state debts, incurred by the individual states to finance their war efforts; and (3) a national debt in the form of government securities (the notorious paper continentals) that had been issued to help finance the war. To establish credit, and thus to be able to borrow money and attract investors in American enterprises, Hamilton declared that the nation had to make good on all it owed.

Hamilton proposed that the federal government assume responsibility for the repayment of all three categories of debt. He insisted that continentals be redeemed for the amount shown on the certificate, regardless of what their current value might be. And he proposed that *current* holders of continentals should receive that payment regardless of how or when they had acquired them. These recommendations, and the political agenda for economic growth they revealed, raised furious debate within Congress.

Before Hamilton's *Report on Public Credit*, James Madison had been the voice of unity in Congress. Now Madison leapt to his feet to protest the treasury secretary's plan. The government's debt, both financial and moral, Madison argued, was not to the current creditors holding the continentals but to the *original* holders, many of whom were ordinary citizens and Continental soldiers who had sold these certificates to speculators at a tremendous loss during the postwar depression. The state treasuries of New York, Pennsylvania, and Maryland were three of the largest speculators, having bought up great quantities of these bonds when they were disgracefully cheap. If Hamilton's plan were adopted, Madison protested, these speculators, rather than the nation's true patriots, would reap enormous unfair profits.

Although enslaved men and women performed the work done on Madison's plantation, the Virginia planter believed that wealth acquired by productive labor was moral whereas wealth gained by the manipulation of money was corrupt. Hamilton simply sidestepped the moral issue by explaining the difficulty of identifying and locating the original holders of the continentals. Whatever the ethical merits of Madison's argument, Hamilton said, his solution was impractical. Congress supported Hamilton, but the vote reflected the growing rift between regions.

free trade Trade between nations without any protective tariffs.

■ **Federalists** Political group formed during Washington's first administration (after and distinct from those who supported the Constitution); led by Alexander Hamilton, they favored an active role for government in encouraging commercial and manufacturing growth.

■ **Republicans** Political group opposing Federalists; led by Thomas Jefferson and James Madison, they favored limited government involvement in encouraging manufacturing and the continued dominance of agriculture in the national economy.

factions A political group with shared opinions or interests.

■ **sectionalism** Competition between regional interests, for example, Southern versus Northern interests.

fiscal Relating to finances.

■ *Report on Public Credit* Hamilton's proposal, ultimately adopted, that the federal government pay debts incurred to finance the Revolution, including debts to foreign countries, continentals at face value, and debts owed by the states.

Far from silenced, Madison next led the opposition to Hamilton's proposal that the federal government assume, or take over, the states' debts. Here, Hamilton's motives were quite transparent: as a fierce nationalist, he wished to concentrate both political and economic power in the federal government at the expense of the states. He knew that creditors, who included America's wealthiest citizens, would take a particular interest in the welfare and success of any government that owed them money. By concentrating the debt in the federal government, Hamilton intended to give America's elite a clear stake in that government's success. Hamilton also knew that a sizable debt provided a compelling reason for raising revenue. By assuming the state debts, the federal government could undercut state governments' need for new taxes—and justify its own.

Congress saw the obvious **inequities** of the plan. States such as Maryland and Virginia had paid all their war debts during the 1780s. Their members protested that if the national government assumed state debts and raised taxes to repay them, responsible citizens of Maryland and Virginia would be taxed for the failure of Massachusetts or New York to honor their obligations. Although the Senate approved the assumption of state debts, members of the House strongly objected and deferred a decision. Hamilton, realizing he faced defeat, sought a behind-the-scenes compromise with Madison and his ally Jefferson, using the location of the national capital as a bargaining chip.

In 1789 the new government had made New York its temporary home until Congress could settle on a permanent site. Hamilton was willing to put the capital right in Jefferson's backyard in exchange for the Virginian's support on assumption of state debts. Southern regional pride was not the only reason Madison and Jefferson agreed to the deal. Like many good Republicans, they believed it was important to monitor the deliberations of a powerful government. In an age of slow land travel and communication, it was difficult to keep watch from a distance. New Englanders knew that "watching" from nearby meant the chance to influence the government. "The climate of the Potomac," one New Englander quipped, would prove unhealthy, if not deadly, to "northern constitutions." Nevertheless, by trading away the capital location, Hamilton ensured the success of his assumption plan.

Library of Congress.

New York City served only temporarily as the capital of the new United States. Plans were soon laid for a new capital city to be built on the banks of the Potomac River, on land donated by Virginia and Maryland. This new city would be named Washington, in honor of the hero of the Revolution and the nation's first president. Elaborate plans such as this one depicted elegant, tree-lined streets, but for many years visitors and residents alike described Washington, DC, as a dismal town of muddy streets and dreadful climate.

As the year 1791 began, Hamilton outlined another controversial proposal—a plan for chartering a national bank, modeled on the Bank of England, to serve as fiscal agent for the federal government. The bank would not be an exclusively public institution but instead would be funded by both the government and private sources in a partnership that fit nicely with Hamilton's plan to tie national prosperity to the interests of private wealth.

Once again, James Madison led the opposition. He argued that the government had neither the express right nor the **implied power** to create a national institution such as the bank. The majority of Congress did not agree, and the bill passed. But Madison's argument that the bank was unconstitutional did cause President Washington to hesitate over signing the bill into law. Turning to his advisers as usual, Washington asked both Secretary of State Jefferson and treasury secretary Hamilton to set down their views on the matter.

Like Madison, Jefferson was at that time a **strict constructionist** in his interpretation of the Constitution. On February 15, 1791, he wrote of the dangers of interpreting the government's powers broadly. "To take a single step beyond the boundaries . . . specifically drawn around the powers of Congress," he warned, "is to take possession of a boundless field of power." A **broad constructionist**, Hamilton saw no such danger

inequities Unfair circumstances or proceedings.

implied power Power that is not specifically granted to the government by the Constitution but can be viewed as necessary to carry out the governing duties that the Constitution does list.

strict constructionist A person who believes the government has only the powers specifically named in the Constitution.

broad constructionist A person who believes the government can exercise implied powers in keeping with the spirit of the Constitution.

in the bank. He based his argument on Article 1, Section 8 of the Constitution, which granted Congress the right to "make all Laws which shall be necessary and proper" to exercise its legitimate powers. Because it seemed obvious that "a bank has a natural relation to the power of collecting taxes," Hamilton believed there could be no reasonable constitutional argument against it. As he put it on February 23: "The powers contained in a constitution . . . ought to be construed liberally in advancement of the public good." Hamilton's argument persuaded the president, and the **Bank of the United States** was chartered on February 25, 1791, with stock offered for sale by July 4, 1791.

To complete his vision, Hamilton in 1792 issued his *Report on Manufactures*, a package of aggressive policies aimed to industrialize the nation—including protective tariffs and government incentives and subsidies. But this time his program was too extreme to win support in Congress. Still, the Bank of the United States, which provided much-needed working **capital** for new commercial and manufacturing enterprises, and the establishment of sound national credit, which attracted foreign capital to the new nation, had gone far toward moving the economy in the direction of Hamilton's vision.

Foreign Affairs and Deepening Divisions

In 1789, just as George Washington became the first president of the United States, the **French Revolution** began. And in the years in which Hamilton was advancing his economic programs, that revolution stirred new controversy within American politics.

On July 14, 1789, as crowds took to the streets in the name of broad social reform, Parisian radicals stormed the Bastille prison, a symbol of royal oppression, tearing down its walls and liberating its political prisoners. The crowds filling the Paris streets owed some of their political rhetoric and ideals to the American Revolution, a debt the marquis de Lafayette, who had volunteered in the American Revolution, acknowledged when he sent his old friend President Washington the key to the Bastille. Like most Americans in these early days of the French Revolution, Washington was pleased to be identified with this new struggle for the "rights of man." Briefly, enthusiasm for the French Revolution united Hamilton's Federalists and Jefferson's Republicans.

By 1793, however, American public opinion began to divide sharply on the French Revolution. Popular support faded when the revolution's most radical party, the Jacobins, executed King Louis XVI and his wife. Many shocked Americans denounced the revolution completely when the Jacobins, in their **Reign of Terror** against any who opposed their policies, began marching moderate French reformers as well as members of the nobility to the guillotine to be beheaded.

Soon, the Jacobin government vowed to bring "liberty, equality, and brotherhood" to the peoples of Europe, by force if necessary. This campaign to spread the revolution led France into war with England, Spain, Austria, and **Prussia**. At the very least, France expected the Americans to honor the terms of the treaty of 1778, which bound the United States to protect French possessions in the West Indies from enemy attack. The enemy most likely to strike was England, which suddenly made a second war between England and the United States a possibility.

American opinion on a second war with England was contradictory and complex. George Blake, a Boston lawyer and political figure, reminded his fellow citizens, "The [French] cause is half our own, and does not our policy and our honor urge us to most forcibly cherish it?" But others who continued to support the French Revolution, including Thomas Jefferson, did not want the United States to become embroiled in a European war. On the other hand, many who condemned the French Revolution were eager to use any excuse to attack the British, who still were occupying forts in the Northwest and restricting American trade in the Caribbean. Political leaders such as Hamilton who were working toward better relations with England were appalled by the French assault on other nations and by the prospect of American involvement in it.

The French, meanwhile, plotted to mobilize American support. In 1793 the new French republic sent a diplomatic minister to the United States. When Citizen **Edmond Genêt** arrived in Charleston, he wasted no time on formal matters such as presenting his **diplomatic credentials** to either the president or the secretary of state. Instead, he immediately launched a campaign to recruit Americans to the war effort. By all accounts, Genêt was charming, affable, and in the words of one observer, so humorous that he could "laugh us into the war." President Washington, however, was not amused.

> ■ **Bank of the United States** National bank, proposed by Hamilton and funded by the government and private investors, to ensure the country's financial stability.
>
> **capital** Money needed to start or sustain a commercial enterprise.
>
> ■ **French Revolution** Political rebellion against the French monarchy and aristocratic privileges; it began in 1789 and ended in 1799.
>
> ■ **Reign of Terror** The period from 1793 to 1794 in the French Revolution when thousands of people were executed as enemies of the state.
>
> **Prussia** A northern European state that became the basis for the German Empire in the late nineteenth century.
>
> ■ **Edmond Genêt** Diplomat sent by the French government to bring the United States into France's war with Britain and Spain.
>
> **diplomatic credentials** Papers certifying that a government has empowered someone to represent it to another government; procedure calls for credentials to be formally presented upon arrival.

In 1793, French revolutionaries executed both the king and the queen of France. More executions would follow in what came to be known as the years of "The Terror." In this pen and ink drawing, executioners tie the hands of King Louis XVI in preparation for his beheading on the guillotine while soldiers and citizens look on.

character. Federalist newspapers struck back, insisting that Jefferson and his followers had actively encouraged the outrageous behavior of Genêt. By the end of 1793, Jefferson had resigned from Washington's government, more convinced than ever that Hamilton and his supporters posed a serious threat to the survival of the American republic.

More Domestic Disturbances

Hamilton's Federalists agreed that the republic was in danger—from Jefferson's Republicans. By Washington's second term (he was reelected in 1792), both political groups were trying to rouse popular sentiment for their programs and policies and against those of their opponents. Just as in the prerevolutionary years, these appeals to popular opinion broadened participation in the debate over the future of the nation. In the wake of the French Revolution and British interference in the west and on the seas, organizations rose up to make demands on the government. The most troubling of these to President Washington were the **Democratic-Republican societies**.

Between 1793 and 1794, thirty-five Democratic-Republican societies were created. Made up primarily of craftsmen and men of the "lower orders," these pro-French political groups also had their share of professional men, merchants, and planters. In Philadelphia, for example, noted scientist and inventor David Rittenhouse and Alexander Dallas, secretary to the governor of Pennsylvania, were society members. In Kentucky, which had split from Virginia in 1792, local elites organized their own society, separate from the one made up of western farmers. No matter what the background of the membership, these societies shared a common agenda: to serve as a platform for expressing the public's will. They insisted that political officeholders were "the agents of the people," not their leaders, and thus should act as the people wished.

In 1794, protest turned violent. That July, a crowd in western Pennsylvania, angry about a new federal **excise** tax on the whiskey they produced, ransacked and burned the home of the federal excise inspector and then threatened to march on Pittsburgh if the tax were not repealed.

President Washington, haunted by the memory of Shays's Rebellion and worried that the radical spirit of the French Revolution was spreading throughout America, determined to crush this **Whiskey Rebellion** firmly. Calling up thirteen thousand militiamen, the president marched into the countryside to do battle with a few hundred citizens armed with rifles and pitchforks. In the face of such an overwhelming military force, the whiskey rebels abruptly dispersed.

Genêt's total disregard for formal procedures infuriated Washington. Genêt's bold attempts to provoke incidents between the United States and Spain stunned Hamilton. Even Thomas Jefferson grew uncomfortable when the Frenchman used the port of Philadelphia to transform a captured British ship into a French privateer!

On April 22, 1793, Washington decided to act. Publicly, the president issued a proclamation that declared American **neutrality** without actually using the term. While allowing Washington to avoid a formal **repudiation** of America's treaty with France, the proclamation made clear that the United States would give no military support to the French. Privately, Washington asked the French government to recall Genêt.

The Genêt affair had domestic as well as diplomatic repercussions. For the first time, George Washington came under public attack. A Republican newspaper whose editor was employed by Jefferson in the state department, questioned the president's integrity in refusing to honor the Franco-American treaty. Washington was furious with this assault on his

neutrality The policy of treating both sides in a conflict the same way and thus favoring neither.

repudiation The act of rejecting the validity or the authority of something.

■ **Democratic-Republican societies** Political organizations formed in 1793 and 1794 to demand greater responsiveness by the state and federal governments to the needs of the citizens.

excise A tax on goods or services produced and sold within the country.

■ **Whiskey Rebellion** A protest by grain farmers against the 1794 federal tax on whiskey; militia forces led by President Washington put down this Pennsylvania uprising.

In 1794, the new federal government passed an excise tax on whiskey, made from grain. Farmers in western Pennsylvania rose up in protest against what they considered an unfair assault on their livelihood. Using tactics straight out of the pre-Revolutionary War era, including tarring and feathering the "revenooer" assigned to collect the taxes, the "Whiskey Rebels" challenged the federal government's authority. President Washington assembled an army of almost thirteen thousand men to put down the Whiskey Rebellion. Critics declared the president's response excessive. Do you agree?

Washington publicly laid the blame for the western insurrection on the Democratic-Republican societies. Federalists in Congress rushed to propose a resolution condemning those groups. These societies, one Federalist declared, "arrogantly pretended sometimes to be the people and sometimes the [people's] guardians, the champions of the people." Instead, he said, they represented no one but themselves.

By 1796, the Democratic-Republican organizations had vanished from the American political scene. The president's public condemnation and Congress's censure undoubtedly damaged them. But improvements on the western borders also diminished the farmers' interest in protest organizations. In October 1795, Carolina planter Thomas Pinckney won the concession from Spain that Jay had been unable to obtain in earlier negotiations: free navigation of the Mississippi River. Pinckney's **Treaty of San Lorenzo** not only gave western farmers an outlet to ocean trade through the port of New Orleans but also ensured that Indian attacks would not be launched from Spanish-held territories.

Jay's Treaty

During Washington's second administration, the diplomatic crisis continued to worsen. England resented America's claim to neutrality, believing it helped France. The British, therefore, ignored American claims that "free ships made free goods" and began to seize American vessels trading with the French Caribbean islands. These seizures prompted new calls for war with Great Britain.

Anti-British emotion ran even higher when the governor of Canada actively encouraged Indian resistance to American settlement in the Northwest. Indian relations were dismal enough without such meddling, especially since efforts to crush the Miamis of Ohio had recently ended in two embarrassing American defeats. In February 1794, as General Anthony Wayne headed west for a third attempt against the Miamis, the Canadian governor's fiery remarks were particularly disturbing.

Anti-British sentiment showed itself in the House of Representatives, where Republicans considered restricting trade with England. Outside the government, war hysteria led mobs to attack English seamen and tar and feather Americans expressing pro-British views. What would Washington do?

Early in 1794, the president sent Chief Justice John Jay to England as his special **envoy**. Jay's mission was to produce a compromise that would prevent war. Jay, however, was pessimistic. Britain wanted to avoid war with the United States, but what would British diplomats concede to his weak nation?

Jay's negotiations did resolve some old nagging issues. In the treaty that emerged, Britain agreed to evacuate the western forts, although it did not promise

■ **Treaty of San Lorenzo** 1795 treaty negotiated by Thomas Pinckney in which Spain granted the United States the right to navigate the Mississippi River and use the port of New Orleans.

envoy A government representative charged with a special diplomatic mission.

On August 3, 1795, after an American victory in the Battle of Fallen Timbers, representatives from a number of tribes, including Wyandots, Delawares, Shawnees, Ottawas, Miamis, and Potawatomis, signed a treaty with the United States that established the "Greenville Treaty line," which marked the boundary between Indian and white territories for several years. In exchange for goods such as blankets, utensils, and domestic animals the Indians turned over a large territory that would include much of modern-day Ohio and modern-day Chicago.

Ohio Historical Society.

Although Federalists in Congress credited **Jay's Treaty** with preserving the peace, Republicans condemned it as an embarrassment and a betrayal of France. Once again, the president came under attack, and Kentucky settlers threatened rebellion, warning Washington that if he signed Jay's Treaty, "western America is gone forever—lost to the Union." The treaty finally squeaked through the Senate in the spring of 1795 with only two southern senators supporting ratification. Despite the criticism heaped upon him, Jay knew he had accomplished his mission, for American neutrality in the European war continued.

Jay's negotiations with England damaged the prestige and authority of Washington's administration. The president did far better, however, in military and diplomatic affairs in the West. In August 1794, Anthony Wayne's army defeated the northwestern Indians at the **Battle of Fallen Timbers**. Wayne then lived up to his reputation as "Mad Anthony" by rampaging through enemy villages, destroying all he could. These terror tactics helped produce the **Treaty of Greenville** in August 1795. By this treaty, the Indians ceded most of the land that later became the state of Ohio. These victories, combined with the auspicious terms of Pinckney's Treaty of San Lorenzo, won praise for the troubled president.

to end support for Indian resistance to American western settlement. Britain also granted some small trade favors to America in the West Indies. For its part, the United States agreed to see that all prewar debts owed to British merchants were at last paid. Jay, a fierce opponent of slavery, did not press for any provision to pay slaveholders for slaves lost during the Revolution. In the end, Jay knew he had given up more than he gained: he had abandoned America's demand for freedom of the seas and acknowledged the British navy's right to remove French property from any neutral ship.

■ **Jay's Treaty** Controversial 1794 treaty between the United States and Great Britain negotiated by John Jay to ensure American neutrality in the French and English war.

■ **Battle of Fallen Timbers** 1794 battle in which Kentucky riflemen defeated Indians of several tribes, helping to end Indian resistance in the Northwest.

■ **Treaty of Greenville** 1795 treaty in which the United States agreed to pay northwestern Indians about $10,000 for the land that later became the state of Ohio.

market economy An economy in which production of goods is geared to sale or profit.

partisan Taking a strong position on an issue out of loyalty to a political group or leader.

Washington's Farewell

As his second term drew to a close, George Washington made a precedent-setting decision: he would not seek a third term as president. Instead, in 1796 he would return to his beloved Virginia home, Mount Vernon, and resume the life of a gentleman planter.

When Washington retired, he left behind a nation very different from the one whose independence he had helped win and whose survival he had helped secure. The postwar economic depression was over, and the war raging in Europe had produced a steadily rising demand for American foodstuffs. More fundamentally, in the fifteen years since the Revolution, the U.S. economy had moved decisively in the direction that Alexander Hamilton had envisioned. The values and expectations of a **market economy**—with its stress on maximizing profit and the pursuit of individual economic interests—had captured the imagination and shaped the actions of many white Americans. Hamilton's policies as secretary of the treasury had both reflected and advanced a growing interest in the expansion of trade, the growth of markets, and the development of American manufacturing and industry. In its political life, the republic had been reorganized and the relationships between the states and the central government redefined. The new Constitution granted greater diplomatic and commercial powers to the federal government but protected individual citizens through the Bill of Rights. America's political leaders, though convinced that factions were dangerous to the survival of the republic, had nevertheless created and begun to work within an evolving party system.

In his Farewell Address to the public, Washington expressed his thoughts on many of these changes. Although Jefferson had viewed the president as a **partisan** Federalist, Washington spoke with feeling against parties in a republic, urging the nation to return to nonpartisan cooperation. Washington also warned America and its new leaders not to "interweave our destiny with any part of Europe" or "entangle our peace and prosperity in the toils of European ambition." An honorable country must "observe good faith and justice toward all nations," said the aging Virginian, but Americans must not let any alliance develop that draws the nation into a foreign war. The final ingredient in Washington's formula for America's success and its "permanent felicity" was the continuing virtue of its people.

Individual Voices

Gouverneur Morris Speaks as More than a Nationalist

At the constitutional convention, Pennsylvania delegate Gouverneur Morris called on his fellow political leaders to set aside local and provincial interests and, as Alexander Hamilton put it, "think continentally." But Morris urged more than a concern for national interest; he believed that the principles embodied in the constitution these men were writing would inspire people throughout the world. Morris's impassioned speech would be lost to us if delegate James Madison had not been secretly taking notes on the convention's debates. Historians of the era are fortunate that Madison disobeyed the convention rules and thus preserved Morris's vision of America as an inspiration to everyone.

① Most Americans identified themselves by their town, state, or region rather than as citizens of the United States. What events or cultural changes might have helped forge a strong national identity in the decades that followed the Constitutional Convention?

② Does Morris's tone, as described by Madison, strike you as optimistic or pessimistic? Does he seem to doubt the integrity of his fellow delegates?

> He came here as a Representative of America; he flattered himself he came here in some degree as a representative of the whole human race; for the whole human race will be affected by the proceedings of this Convention. He wished gentlemen to extend their views beyond the present moment of time, beyond the narrow limits of place from which they derive their political origin. **①** If he were to believe some of the things which he had heard, he should suppose that we were assembled to truck and bargain for our particular States. He cannot descend to think that any gentlemen are really actuated by these views. We must look forward to the effects of what we do. These alone ought to guide us. **②**
>
> *Source: James Madison, Notes on Debates in the Federal Convention of 1787.*

Study Tools

SUMMARY

After independence was declared, Americans faced the challenge of creating a new nation out of thirteen distinct states. The new nation faced enormous debt and was still surrounded by real and potential enemies, and its ability to survive seemed doubtful to many.

As colonies became states, they drafted their own constitutions. Some put in place democratic forms of government while others built in more restrictive features such as high property qualifications for officeholding. The first national government, created by the Articles of Confederation, reflected the states' desire to preserve their individual sovereignty. It also embodied the revolutionary generation's opposition to a strong centralized government. The Confederation government thus lacked basic powers: it could not raise taxes or regulate commerce. However, it negotiated the peace treaty of 1783, and it established, through three Northwest Ordinances, the process by which territories became states on an equal footing with the original states. But with limited powers, the Confederation could not resolve the nation's financial problems, deal effectively with foreign nations, or ensure social order within its borders. By the time Massachusetts farmers, hard hit by the postwar depression, rose up in revolt in Shays's Rebellion in 1786, many of the nation's elite political figures were calling for a stronger national government.

In the summer of 1787, these nationalists met in Philadelphia to consider a new constitution. The Constitution they produced, after long months of debate, steered a middle ground between a central government that was too powerful and one that was too limited. It established executive, legislative, and judicial branches, which could "check and balance" one another and thus, it was hoped, safeguard the nation from tyranny. The new government could both raise taxes and regulate commerce. After intense battles between pro-Constitution forces, known as Federalists, and their Antifederalist opponents, the new Constitution was ratified by the states in 1788.

Soon after George Washington took office as the first president, serious differences in political opinion again emerged. Alexander Hamilton's vision of a vigorous commercial and industrial nation conflicted with Thomas Jefferson's desire for an agrarian republic. The two resulting factions disagreed over economic and foreign policy. The French Revolution intensified the divisions: while Hamilton argued against American support for the French in their war with England, Jefferson pressed the administration to support their fellow revolutionaries. Washington managed to steer a neutral course in this European conflict. By the end of Washington's second term, the United States had expanded its borders, negotiated with Spain for access to the Mississippi River, and under Hamilton's guidance, it had established a national bank at the center of an economic system that promoted market-oriented growth. The departing Washington urged Americans to continue to cooperate and cautioned them not to allow competing visions of America's future to harm the new nation.

CHRONOLOGY
From Revolution to Nationhood

1770s	State constitutions developed
1776	Oversight in New Jersey constitution gives property-holding women the right to vote
1781	States ratify Articles of Confederation
	Cornwallis surrenders at Yorktown
1784–1787	Northwest Ordinances
1786	Annapolis Convention
	Shays's Rebellion
1787	Constitutional Convention
1787–1788	States ratify U.S. Constitution
1789	First congressional elections
	George Washington inaugurated as first president
	Judiciary Act of 1789
1791	First Bank of the United States chartered
	Bill of Rights added to Constitution
	Alexander Hamilton's *Report on Manufactures*
1792	Washington reelected
1793	Genêt affair
	Jefferson resigns as secretary of state
1794	Whiskey Rebellion in Pennsylvania
	Battle of Fallen Timbers
1795	Congress approves Jay's Treaty
	Treaty of San Lorenzo
1796	Washington's Farewell Address

Study Tools

FOCUS QUESTIONS

If you have mastered this chapter, you should be able to answer these questions and to explain the terms that follow the questions.

1. ☆ *What types of legislatures did the states create?*
2. ☆ *What were the major elements of the Articles of Confederation?*
3. ☆ *What problems arose in ratifying the Articles?*
4. ☆ *What problems faced the Confederation?*
5. ☆ *What gains did nationalists expect from a stronger central government?*
6. ☆ *How did the Confederation establish relations with other nations?*
7. ☆ *What major compromises did the framers make in writing the new constitution?*
8. ☆ *What safeguards did James Madison see in his "checks and balances" system?*
9. ☆ *What were the Antifederalists' arguments against the Constitution? What were the Federalists' arguments in its favor?*
10. ☆ *What was the outcome of the ratification process?*
11. ☆ *How did Alexander Hamilton's expectations for the new nation differ from those of Thomas Jefferson? What were the consequences of this conflict of vision?*
12. ☆ *How did the French Revolution affect Washington's diplomatic policy?*

KEY TERMS

John Dickinson   *(p. 161)*
Articles of Confederation   *(p. 161)*
proportional representation   *(p. 162)*
Robert Morris   *(p. 164)*
tariff   *(p. 164)*
Northwest Ordinances   *(p. 164)*
Treaty of Fort Stanwix   *(p. 165)*
Hopewell Treaties   *(p. 165)*
John Jay   *(p. 166)*
Barbary pirates   *(p. 166)*
Daniel Shays   *(p. 167)*
nationalists   *(p. 167)*
James Madison   *(p. 168)*
Great Compromise   *(p. 169)*
Three-Fifths Compromise   *(p. 169)*
Electoral College   *(p. 170)*
ratifying conventions   *(p. 170)*
Federalists/Antifederalists   *(p. 171)*

Federalist Papers   *(p. 172)*
cabinet   *(p. 174)*
Judiciary Act of 1789   *(p. 174)*
Bill of Rights   *(p. 174)*
Federalists   *(p. 175)*
Republicans   *(p. 175)*
sectionalism   *(p. 175)*
Report on Public Credit   *(p. 175)*
Bank of the United States   *(p. 177)*
French Revolution   *(p. 177)*
Reign of Terror   *(p. 177)*
Edmond Genêt   *(p. 177)*
Democratic-Republican societies   *(p. 178)*
Whiskey Rebellion   *(p. 178)*
Treaty of San Lorenzo   *(p. 179)*
Jay's Treaty   *(p. 180)*
Battle of Fallen Timbers   *(p. 180)*
Treaty of Greenville   *(p. 180)*

 CourseMate   Go to the History CourseMate website for primary source links, study tools, and review materials for this chapter. www.cengagebrain.com

8

The Early Republic, 1796–1804

Behind the Stories

I often have to remind myself that the Founders, whom I am used to seeing immortalized as marble statues, were just people. Like our political leaders today they had faults, uncertainties, biases, and lack of foresight. At the same time, they understood that they occupied a peculiar place in history and were conscious of their legacy. For example, historians have learned that in retirement Thomas Jefferson, to enhance his reputation, edited file copies of letters he had sent earlier in his life. This willful manipulation of the historical record aggravates the already difficult task of sorting out our past, yet it makes the people who set the nation on its initial course all the more fascinating and the history they made all the more worthy of reexamination.

Too often we treat this era in our history as something, like the likenesses of the Founders themselves, carved in stone. Realizing that the Founders themselves were uncertain about where the nation was to go makes clear that we can never accept uncritical assertions about their intentions. As a historian, I must wade through intentional deceptions, naïve misrepresentations, expressions of confusion and uncertainty, and try to piece together how it all happened, constantly reexamining what I thought I knew.

Much that you will read in the chapter to come has changed considerably from what was in earlier editions of this book. This reflects neither a previous lack of judgment on my part nor a desire to make changes for their own sake. It results instead from our inability to write the ultimate version of any historical era; our story must change as we learn new things about what happened in the past.

—C.L.M.

Individual Choices
George Logan

Even the suggestion of the United States fighting a war presented a serious problem for George Logan. Like many descendants of Pennsylvania's first families, Logan was a Quaker and was morally opposed to war. His father, a conscientious objector during the Revolutionary War, had sent him to study medicine in Scotland and Paris while the war continued. Returning to the United States in 1780, George learned that his family was dead and that much of the considerable Logan estate had been destroyed.

Logan turned to farming to support himself and then, in 1785, to politics, winning a seat in the Pennsylvania assembly. Ever a critic of Federalist economic and diplomatic strategies, he followed his friend Thomas Jefferson when the Republican faction became an opposition party.

By 1798, Logan seemed well on his way to recovering the fortune and prominence that the war had taken. But then a diplomatic crisis with France made war again seem inevitable. Recalling his father's frustration as the colonies were drawn into war in 1776, Logan made a fateful choice: he risked his property, his reputation, even his life, to prevent another war.

"George Logan" by Gilbert Stuart

"George Logan" by Gilbert Stuart. Courtesy of the Philadelphia History Museum at the Atwater Kent, The Historical Society of Pennsylvania Collection.

Quietly Logan began selling off property to raise cash to support a private peace effort. He then went to his friend Jefferson, who gave him letters of introduction to important people in France. Government agents learned of Logan's aims and put him under surveillance, but he slipped their noose and sailed for Germany during the summer of 1798. There he met with the marquis de Lafayette, who used his influence to get Logan into France and arranged an audience for him with the French foreign minister, Talleyrand.

Facing a formidable coalition of antirevolutionary European powers, the last thing Talleyrand wanted was to further alienate the only other democratic nation in the world. Meeting with Talleyrand and other French officials in early August, Logan capitalized on this fact. He told them that most Americans supported democracy in France but warned that French actions in what was being called the Quasi-War were undermining that support. He assured them that if this conflict were ended, American sentiments would again favor France. Talleyrand was convinced, assuring Logan that France would be happy to meet with a peace delegation if Adams would send one.

One of the fathers of the American Revolution, John Adams seemed the perfect choice to step into the presidency when George Washington chose to step down at the end of his second term. Though many were comforted by Adams's conservative statesmanship, the rigid New Englander was poorly qualified to deal with the partisan politics that came to haunt his administration. Library of Congress.

Playing a complicated diplomatic game, French foreign minister **Charles Maurice de Talleyrand-Périgord** declined to receive Pinckney and the peace delegation. As weeks passed, three businessmen residing in Paris, whose international trading profits stood at risk, offered themselves as go-betweens in solving the stalemate. According to Pinckney's report, these men suggested that if the Americans were willing to pay a bribe to key French officials and guarantee an American loan of several million dollars to France, the three businessmen would be able to get them a

■ **Charles Maurice de Talleyrand-Périgord** French foreign minister appointed by the revolutionary government in 1797; he later aided Napoleon Bonaparte's overthrow of that government and served as his foreign minister.

■ **XYZ affair** A diplomatic incident in which American envoys to France were told that the United States would have to loan France money and bribe government officials as a precondition for negotiation.

■ **Quasi-War** Diplomatic crisis triggered by the XYZ affair; fighting occurred between the United States and France between the early summer of 1798 and the official end of the conflict in September 1800, but neither side issued a formal declaration of war.

naturalized Granted full citizenship (after having been born in a foreign country).

hearing. Offended at such treatment, Pinckney broke off diplomatic relations. Reporting the affair to President Adams, Pinckney refused to name the would-be go-betweens, calling them only "X," "Y," and "Z."

Americans' response to the **XYZ affair** was overwhelming. France's diplomatic slight seemed a slap in the face to a new nation seeking international respect. In Philadelphia, people paraded in the streets to protest French arrogance. The crowds chanted Pinckney's reported response: "No, no, not a sixpence!" This wave of patriotism overcame the spirit of division that had plagued the Adams administration, giving the president a virtually unified Congress and country. In the heat of the moment, Adams pressed for increased military forces, and in short order Congress created the Department of the Navy and appropriated money to start building a fleet of warships. Then, on July 7, 1798, Congress rescinded all treaties with France and authorized privateering against French ships. Congress also created a standing army of twenty thousand troops and ordered that the militia be expanded to thirty thousand men. Washington added his prestige to the effort by coming out of retirement to lead the new army, with Hamilton as his second-in-command. Although running sea battles between French and American ships resulted in the sinking or capture of many vessels on both sides, Congress shied away from actually declaring war, which led to the conflict being labeled the **Quasi-War**.

The Home Front in the Quasi-War

Federalists immediately seized upon the war as a means to crush their political enemies. In Congress, they began referring to Jefferson and his supporters as the "French Party" and accused the vice president and his faction of treason whenever they advised a moderate course. Arguing that the presence of this "French Party" constituted a danger to national security, congressional Federalists proposed a series of new laws to destroy all opposition to their conception of true republicanism.

One source of opposition was **naturalized** American citizens. The revolutionary promises of "life, liberty, and the pursuit of happiness" had attracted many immigrants to the United States. They were drawn to Jefferson's political rhetoric—especially his stress on equal opportunity and his attacks on aristocracy. In 1798 Federalists in Congress passed three acts designed to counter political activities by immigrants. The Naturalization Act extended the residency requirement for citizenship from five to fourteen years. The Alien Act authorized the president to deport any foreigner he judged "dangerous to the peace and safety of the United States." The Alien Enemies Act permitted the president to imprison or banish any foreigner he considered dangerous during a national emergency. The Naturalization Act was designed to prevent recent immigrants from supporting the Republican cause by barring them from the political process. The other two acts served as a constant reminder that the president or his agents could arbitrarily imprison or deport any resident alien who stepped out of line.

The other source of support for Jefferson was a partisan Republican press, which attempted to balance the biased news and criticism spewing forth from Federalist news sources with biased accounts of its own. To counter this, congressional Federalists passed the Sedition Act. In addition to outlawing conspiracies to block the enforcement of federal laws, the Sedition Act prohibited the publication or utterance of any criticism of the government or its officials that would bring either "into contempt or disrepute." In the words of one Federalist newspaper, "It is patriotism to write in favour of our government, it is **sedition** to write against it." Federalists brandished the law against all kinds of criticism directed toward either the government or the president, including perfectly innocent political editorials. Not surprisingly, most of the defendants in the fifteen cases brought by federal authorities under the Sedition Act were prominent Republican newspaper editors.

Republicans complained that the **Alien and Sedition Acts** violated the Bill of Rights, but Congress and the federal judiciary, controlled as they were by Federalists, paid no attention. Dissidents had little choice but to take their political case to the state governments, which they did in the fall of 1798. One statement, drafted by Madison, came before the Virginia legislature, and another, by Jefferson, was considered in Kentucky.

Madison and Jefferson based their **Virginia and Kentucky Resolutions** on the Tenth Amendment, contending that powers not specifically granted to the federal government under the Constitution or reserved to the people in the Bill of Rights fell to the states. By passing laws such as the Alien and Sedition Acts that were not explicitly permitted in the text of the Constitution, Congress had violated the states' rights. The two authors differed, however, in how the states should respond. For his part, Madison asserted that when the majority of states agreed that a federal law had violated their Tenth Amendment rights, they could collectively overrule federal authority. But Jefferson argued for the principle of **interposition**, recognizing each state's "natural right" to interpose its authority between the federal government and its own citizens.

The Virginia and Kentucky Resolutions passed in their respective state legislatures, but no other states

The majority of Americans were scandalized by the XYZ affair and convinced that French radicalism and corruption threatened their security. In this cartoon from 1798, the French Directory is depicted as a five-headed monster threatening the American delegation with a dagger. In the background French dignitaries share a feast at the base of the guillotine. Such images ginned up American resentment as the Quasi-War unfolded.

followed suit. Even within Kentucky and Virginia, great disagreement arose over how far state authority should extend. Nevertheless, this response to the Federalists' use of federal power brought the disputed relationship between federal law and **states' rights** into national prominence.

Another bone of contention was the methods used to finance the Quasi-War with France and the impact these methods had on various groups of Americans. Consistent with Hamilton's views on finance, tariffs and excises were to be the primary source of revenue, and they had the greatest impact on people

sedition Conduct or language inciting rebellion against the authority of a state.

■ **Alien and Sedition Acts** Collectively, the four acts—Alien Act, Alien Enemies Act, Naturalization Act, and Sedition Act—passed by Congress in 1798 designed to prevent immigrants from participating in politics and to silence the anti-Federalist press.

■ **Virginia and Kentucky Resolutions** Statements that the Virginia and Kentucky legislatures issued in 1798 in response to the Alien and Sedition Acts; they asserted the right of states to overrule the federal government.

Interposition To Jefferson, the principle of interposition meant that states had the right to use their sovereign power as a barrier between the federal government and the states' citizens when the natural rights of those citizens were at risk.

■ **states' rights** The political position in favor of limiting federal power to allow the greatest possible self-government by the individual states.

who needed manufactured or imported items but had little hard cash. In addition, Federalists imposed a tax on land, hitting cash-poor farmers especially hard. In 1799 farmers in Northampton County, Pennsylvania, refused to pay the tax and began harassing tax collectors. Several tax resisters were arrested, but local Federalist John Fries raised an armed force to break them out of jail. Later, federal troops sent by Adams to suppress what was characterized as **Fries's Rebellion** arrested Fries and two of his associates. Charged with treason, the three were tried in federal court, found guilty, and condemned to death.

Settlement with France

The Federalists' seeming overreaction to French provocation and domestic protest alienated increasing numbers of Americans. Adams himself was eager to end the conflict, and when George Logan sent news from France that Foreign Minister Talleyrand was asking that a new American delegation be sent, Adams seized the opportunity to end the Quasi-War. Telling the Federalist-dominated Congress that he would give them the details later, Adams instructed the American minister to the Netherlands, William Vans Murray, to go immediately to Paris. As rumors of negotiations began to circulate, Hamilton and his supporters became furious, all but accusing Adams of treason. This gave the president the ammunition he needed: he fired Hamilton loyalists Pickering, Wolcott, and McHenry and then embarrassed the Federalist judiciary by granting a presidential pardon to John Fries and his fellow Pennsylvania rebels.

Adams's diplomatic appeal to France was well timed. When Murray and his delegation arrived in Paris in November 1799, they found that whatever ill feeling might have existed toward the United States had been swept away. On November 9, 1799, **Napoleon Bonaparte** had overthrown the government that was responsible for the XYZ affair. Napoleon was more interested in establishing an empire in Europe than in continuing an indecisive conflict with the United States. After some negotiation, Murray and Napoleon drew up and signed the Convention of Mortefontaine, ending the Quasi-War on September 30, 1800.

■ **Fries's Rebellion** A tax revolt by Pennsylvania citizens in 1799 that was suppressed by federal forces; leader John Fries was condemned to death for treason but received a presidential pardon from John Adams.

■ **Napoleon Bonaparte** General who took control of the French government in November 1799, at the end of France's revolutionary period; he eventually proclaimed himself emperor of France and conquered much of the continent of Europe.

THE "REVOLUTION OF 1800"

☆ How did Federalists respond to losing the election of 1800? What does this response reveal about their political attitudes?

☆ What did Thomas Jefferson mean by the statement "Every difference of opinion is not a difference of principles"?

☆ How did Jefferson's vision for America differ from that of Hamilton, Adams, and other Federalists?

According to the partisan press, the political situation in 1800 was as simple as the contrast between the personalities of the major presidential candidates. The Republican press characterized Adams as an aristocrat and claimed that his efforts to expand the powers of the federal government were really attempts to rob citizens of freedom and turn the United States back into a colony of England. In contrast, the Republican press characterized Jefferson as a man of the people, sensitive to the appeals of southern and western agricultural groups who felt perpetually ignored or abused by northeastern elites. According to Federalist newspapers, however, Vice President Jefferson was a dangerous radical and an atheist. In the eyes of the Federalists, Adams was a man whose policies and steady-handed administration would bring stability and prosperity, qualities that appealed to manufacturers and merchants in New England. The rhetoric became so hateful that even Adams and Jefferson got caught up in it—the old friends stopped speaking to each other; nearly twenty years passed before they renewed their friendship.

The Lesser of Republican Evils

As the election of 1800 approached, the split between Adams and Hamilton widened. Both agreed on the necessity of dumping Jefferson as vice president, putting forward Charles Cotesworth Pinckney, hero of the XYZ affair, to replace him. But Adams's behavior in the wake of George Logan's mission to France had angered Federalists; they now wanted Adams to be gone as well. Having gotten Pinckney into the Electoral College balloting, Hamilton again tried to steal the 1800 election. As before, he advised delegates to withhold votes, but this time he engaged in direct lobbying, even writing a pamphlet in which he questioned Adams's suitability for the presidency.

Hamilton's methods backfired again: Federalists cast one more vote for Adams than for Pinckney. But more important, Hamilton's scheming and his faction's consistent promanufacturing stance had so alienated southern Federalists that many chose to support Jefferson. With Jefferson pulling in the southern vote and his running mate—Burr again—pulling in

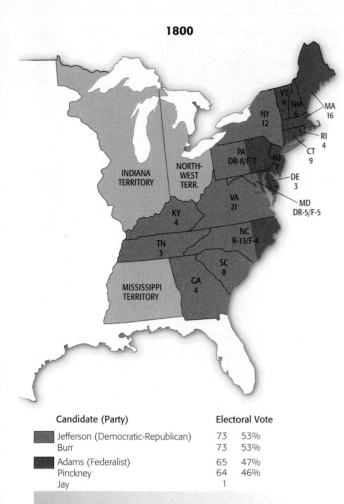

1800

Candidate (Party)	Electoral Vote	
Jefferson (Democratic-Republican)	73	53%
Burr	73	53%
Adams (Federalist)	65	47%
Pinckney	64	46%
Jay	1	

MAP 8.1 Election of 1800
The political partnership between Thomas Jefferson and Aaron Burr allowed the Republicans to unseat Federalist John Adams in the election of 1800. As this map shows, only New England voted as a bloc for the Federalist, while Burr's political home, New York, went entirely to Jefferson.
Copyright © Cengage Learning

the craftsmen and small-farm vote in New York and Pennsylvania, the Republicans outscored the Federalists by 16 votes in the Electoral College. But that still did not settle the election. Burr and Jefferson won the same number of electoral votes, throwing the contest into the still Federalist-dominated House of Representatives (see Map 8.1).

Federalists in the House now faced the task of choosing between two men whom most of them viewed as being dangerous radicals bent on destroying the Federalists' hard work. Indecision was plain: in ballot after ballot over six grueling days early in 1801, neither Jefferson nor Burr could win the necessary majority. Eventually, two things combined to break the deadlock. First, Hamilton convinced several Federalists that even though Jefferson's rhetoric was dangerous, the Virginian was a gentleman of property and

integrity—a suitable guardian under classical republican theory—whereas Burr was "the most dangerous man of the community." Second, intent on preventing a "legislative usurpation" of the popular will, Virginia and Pennsylvania mobilized their militias. As Delaware senator James Bayard described the situation, "we must risk the Constitution and a Civil War or take Mr. Jefferson." Finally, on the thirty-sixth ballot, on February 17, 1801, Jefferson emerged as the winner.

Federalists and Republicans agreed about very little, but the threat of civil war frightened both factions equally. Not long after Jefferson's election, both parties aligned briefly to pass the **Twelfth Amendment** to the Constitution, which requires separate balloting in the Electoral College for president and vice president, thereby preventing deadlocks like the one that nearly wrecked the nation in 1800.

Federalist Defenses and a Loyal Opposition

The Federalists had outmaneuvered themselves in the election of 1800, but they were not about to leave office without erecting some defenses for the political and economic machinery they had constructed. The Federalist-controlled judiciary, which had proved its clout during the controversy over the Alien and Sedition Acts, appeared to offer the strongest bulwark to prevent Republicans from tampering with the Constitution. Thus, during their last days in office, the Federalist **lame ducks** in Congress passed the **Judiciary Act of 1801**, which greatly expanded the federal court system. President Adams then rushed to fill all these positions with loyal Federalists, signing appointments right up to midnight on his last day in office. The appointments came in such large numbers and so late in the day that **John Marshall**, Adams's secretary of state, was unable to deliver all the appointment letters before his own term ran out. But Marshall did deliver one letter promptly: the one addressed to himself, making him chief justice of the Supreme Court.

Painted while he was at the height of his power and influence, this portrait of Chief Justice John Marshall captures the jurist's imposing presence—he dominated the Supreme Court and American constitutional law for over thirty years after his appointment in 1801, setting many precedents that remain in force today.

© Boston Athenaeum/The Bridgeman Art Library International.

Considering the ill will evident in the Alien and Sedition Acts and the presidential electioneering, Jefferson's inaugural address was oddly **conciliatory**. "We are all Republicans; we are all Federalists," Jefferson said, seeming to abandon partisan politics and align himself with those who had recently labeled him a "contemptible hypocrite." In his mind, all Americans shared the same fundamental principles—the principles of 1776. But even Jefferson considered the election of 1800 a revolution—"as real a revolution in the

conciliatory Striving to overcome distrust or to regain good will.

opposition party A political party opposed to the party or government in power.

urbanization The growth of cities in a nation or region and the shifting of the population from rural to urban areas.

principles of our government as that of 1776 was in its form."

Jefferson was right in many respects about the revolutionary nature of the election of 1800. Although his inaugural address preached kinship between Federalists and Republicans, the new president repeatedly criticized his opponents for their lack of faith in democracy and the American people. "If there be any among us who would wish to dissolve this Union or to change its republican form," he said, "let them stand undisturbed as monuments of the safety with which error of opinion may be tolerated, where reason is left free to combat it."

As a result of Jefferson's reassuring address, the nation began to share the president's view that "every difference of opinion is not a difference of principles." Even extreme Federalists such as Fisher Ames came to understand that a "party is an association of honest men for honest purposes." Ames went on to describe how a loyal **opposition party** should behave. "We are not to revile or abuse magistrates, or lie even for good cause," he said. "We must act as good citizens, using only truth, and argument, and zeal to impress them." With parties such as these, a system of loyal opposition could become a permanent part of a republican government without risk to security or freedom. And in keeping with the two-party spirit and Jefferson's philosophical commitment to free speech, Congress eliminated the Alien and Sedition Acts.

Jefferson's Vision for America

Jefferson had a strong, positive vision for the nation, and the party made every effort to put his policies into effect. The greatest dangers to a republic, he believed, were (1) high population density and the social evils it generated, and (2) the concentration of money and power in the hands of a few. Accordingly, Jefferson wanted to steer America away from the large-scale, publicly supported industry so dear to Hamilton and toward an economy founded on yeoman farmers—men who owned their own land, produced their own food, and were beholden to no one. Such men, Jefferson believed, could make political decisions based solely on pure reason and good sense.

But Jefferson was not naive. He knew Americans would continue to demand the comforts and luxuries found in industrial societies. His solution was simple. In America's vast lands, he said, a nation of farmers could produce so much food that "its surplus [could] go to nourish the now perishing births of Europe, who in return would manufacture and send us in exchange our clothes and other comforts." Overpopulation and **urbanization**—the twin causes of corruption in Europe—would not occur in America, for here, Jefferson said, "the immense extent of uncultivated and fertile lands enables every one who will labor, to marry young, and to raise a family of any size."

It Matters Today

The Peaceful Transit of Power

Beginning with debates over the ratification of the Constitution and continuing with ever-increasing stridency through the Quasi-War, questions about the legitimacy of opposition politics ran rampant. Many among the nation's founders wondered if *loyal* opposition was even a possibility. In 1798, one Federalist in Congress accused the Republican opposition of outright treason, charging that they "believe it to be their duty to do all in their power to overturn the whole system, to effect which, they may think a French army and a French invasion necessary." Republican John Nicholas countered that the Federalists were far more dangerous than the French, seeking to "subvert all the liberties of our country," and many suspected that they were not above using a British army to attain that end. Such charges and countercharges became increasingly strident as the presidential election approached in 1800, and many feared that a truly contested election would result in civil war. Despite these realistic fears, the election came and went, the Federalists were swept from power, and both parties settled into a comfortable, though seldom affable, pattern of permanent opposition. With a few minor exceptions, the two-party political system has dominated the political process ever since, and while claims of treason or of subverting liberties continue to muddle our political rhetoric, the precedent of a peaceful transit of power set in the election of 1800 remains fundamental to our success as a nation.

- Consider the impact of a two-party political system on national life. Has the impact been generally positive? Why or why not?
- Though the two-party system has dominated politics in the United States, there have been some significant exceptions. Examine a period during which there was either only one political party or more than two parties and analyze what caused this exception and how it played out.

Making such a system work, however, would require a radical change in economic policy. The government would have to let businesses make their own decisions and succeed or fail in a marketplace free of government interference. In an economy with absolutely free trade and an open marketplace, the iron law of **supply and demand** would determine the cost of goods and services. This view of the economy was a direct assault on mercantilist notions of governments controlling prices and restricting trade to benefit the nation-state.

REPUBLICANISM IN ACTION

★ *What legal maneuvers did Republicans initiate to deal with defenses Federalists put in place in 1801? What were the political and constitutional consequences?*

★ *What policies did Jefferson pursue to carry out his vision for the country? What obstacles did he encounter?*

When Jefferson assumed office, he ushered a new spirit into national politics and the presidency. A combination of circumstances moved him to lead a much simpler life than had his predecessors. For one thing, he was the first president to be inaugurated in the new national capital, the still largely uncompleted Washington City, which afforded quite different and much more limited **amenities**. Washington lacked the taverns and entertaining social circles that both previous capitals, New York and Philadelphia, had offered. Personal preferences also moved him in a simpler direction. He refused, for example, to ride in a carriage, choosing to go by horseback through Washington's muddy and rutted streets. He sometimes entertained with startling informality, wearing frayed slippers and work clothes, and seated his guests at a round table so that no one might be seen as more important than the others.

But this show of simplicity and his conciliatory inaugural address were somewhat misleading. Jefferson was a hardworking partisan politician and

---

■ **supply and demand** The two factors that determine price in an economy based on private property: (1) how much of a commodity is available (supply), and (2) how many people want it (demand).

amenities Conveniences, comforts, and services.

Suffering a lifelong sensitivity to cold as well as a dislike for formality, Thomas Jefferson usually chose to dress practically, in fairly plain clothes that kept him warm. This 1822 portrait by Thomas Sully captures the former president in his customary greatcoat, unadorned suit, and well-worn boots.

administrator whose main objective was to turn the nation around to his vision of republican virtue with all possible speed. He quickly launched a program to revamp the American economy and give the United States a place in the international community. Along the way, he captured many Americans' affection and their political loyalty but also alienated those who did not share his vision or who lacked his zeal.

constitutionality Accordance with the principles or provisions of the Constitution.

justice of the peace The lowest level of judge in some state court systems, usually responsible for hearing small claims and minor criminal cases; because the District of Columbia is a federal territory rather than a state, the justice of the peace for that district is a federal appointee.

■ *Marbury v. Madison* Supreme Court decision (1803) declaring part of the Judiciary Act of 1789 unconstitutional, thereby establishing an important precedent in favor of judicial review.

precedent An event or decision that may be used as an example in similar cases later on.

judicial review The power of the Supreme Court to review the constitutionality of laws passed by Congress and by the states.

manifesto A written statement publicly declaring the views of its author.

Assault on Federalist Defenses

Aware of the partisan purpose behind the Judiciary Act of 1801 and Adams's midnight appointments, Republicans chose to wage an equally aggressive partisan war to reverse Federalist control of the justice system. In January 1802, Republicans in Congress proposed the repeal of the 1801 Judiciary Act, arguing that the expanded court system was unnecessary. Federalists countered that repealing the act would violate the separation of powers. Congress proceeded anyway, replacing the Judiciary Act of 1801 with the Judiciary Act of 1802, and awaited the response of the Federalist courts.

The **constitutionality** of the new Judiciary Act was never tested, but the power of the judicial branch to interpret and enforce federal law did become a major issue the following year. On taking office, Jefferson's secretary of state, James Madison, held back the appointment letters that John Marshall had been unable to deliver before the expiration of his term. One jilted appointee was William Marbury, who was to have been **justice of the peace** for the newly created District of Columbia in which Washington was located. Marbury, with the support of his party, filed suit in the Supreme Court. According to Marbury, the Judiciary Act of 1789 gave the federal courts the power to order the executive branch to deliver his appointment.

Marbury v. Madison was Chief Justice Marshall's first major case, and in it he proved his political as well as his judicial ingenuity. Marshall was keenly aware that in a direct confrontation between the executive and judicial branches, the judiciary was sure to lose. Rather than risking a serious blow to the dignity of the Supreme Court, Marshall ruled in 1803 that the Constitution contained no provision for the Supreme Court to issue such orders as the Judiciary Act of 1789 required and that therefore the law was unconstitutional.

This decision put Jefferson and Madison in a difficult political position. On one hand, the authors of the Virginia and Kentucky Resolutions were on record for arguing that the states and not the courts should determine the constitutionality of federal laws. But political realities forced them to accept Marshall's decision in this case if they wanted to block Adams's handpicked men from assuming lifetime appointments in powerful judicial positions. Although this **precedent** for **judicial review** did not immediately invalidate the principles set forth in Jefferson's and Madison's earlier **manifestos**, it established the standard that federal courts, rather than states, could decide the constitutionality of acts of Congress.

Marshall's decision in *Marbury v. Madison* gave the Republicans the power to withhold undelivered letters of appointment from the Adams administration, but it gave them no power to control the behavior of judges whose appointments were already official. Thus, in the aftermath of the Marbury decision, Republican radicals in Congress decided to take aim at particularly partisan Federalist judges.

John Pickering of New Hampshire was an easy first target. Mentally ill, he was known to rave incoherently both on and off the bench, usually about the evils of Jefferson and liberal republicanism. No one, not even staunch Federalists, doubted that the man was incompetent, but it was far from certain that he had committed the "high crimes and misdemeanors" for which he was **impeached** in 1803. Whether he had or not, the Senate found him guilty and removed him from office.

Emboldened by that easy victory and armed with a powerful precedent, radical Republicans took on Supreme Court justice Samuel Chase. Chase was notorious for making partisan decisions—such as condemning John Fries to death—and for using the federal bench as an anti-Republican soapbox. Unlike Pickering, Chase defended himself very competently, making the political motivations behind the impeachment effort obvious to all observers. In the end, both Federalists and many Republicans voted to dismiss the charges, returning Chase to his position on the Supreme Court. The failure to impeach Chase demonstrated that the political structure was not going to tip decisively to either side and made Jefferson's inaugural statement of principle a guideline for political reality: both sides would have to compromise in charting the course for the nation.

Implementing a New Economy

Still, Republicans were determined on one partisan agenda item: tearing down Hamilton's economic structure and replacing it with a new one more consistent with Jefferson's vision. Responsibility for planning and implementing this economic policy fell to Treasury Secretary **Albert Gallatin**. Gallatin's first effort as Secretary of the Treasury was to try to settle the nation's debts. His ambitious goal was to make the United States entirely debt free by 1817. With Jefferson's approval, Gallatin implemented a radical course of budget cutting, going so far as to close several American embassies overseas to save money. At home, Gallatin and Jefferson pared administrative costs by reducing staff and putting an end to the fancy receptions and other social events that President Adams had so enjoyed. The administration cut the military by half, reducing the army from four thousand to twenty-five hundred men and the navy from twenty-five ships to a mere seven.

But Gallatin's cost cutting did much more than just reduce the national budget. First, Gallatin was able to mask the firing of loyal Federalists still employed in civil service in a seemingly nonpartisan appeal to fiscal responsibility. He accomplished another ideological

goal by reducing the overall federal presence, putting more responsibilities onto the states, where Jefferson's philosophy said they belonged. In addition, Gallatin's plan called for a significant change in how the government raised money. In 1802 the Republican Congress repealed all **internal taxes**, leaving customs duties and the sale of western lands as the sole sources of federal revenue. With this one sweeping gesture, Gallatin struck a major blow for Jefferson's economic vision by tying the nation's financial future to westward expansion and foreign trade. But this vision would soon face serious challenges.

Threats to Jefferson's Vision

One threat to Jefferson's commitment to foreign trade came from pirates who patrolled the northern coast of Africa from Tangier to Tripoli, controlling access to the Mediterranean Sea. Ever since gaining independence, the United States had in effect been bribing the Barbary pirates not to attack American ships. By 1800, fully a fifth of the federal budget was earmarked for this purpose, a cost Gallatin wished to see eliminated as he tried to balance the nation's books. To Jefferson, principle was as important as financial considerations. Deciding on war, Jefferson asserted presidential privilege as commander in chief to dispatch navy ships to the Mediterranean in 1801.

What followed was a fiasco from anyone's point of view. After some indecisive engagements between the American fleet and the pirates, Jefferson's navy suffered a major defeat with the capture of a prize warship, the *Philadelphia,* and its entire crew. A bold but unsuccessful attempt to invade Tripoli by land across the Libyan Desert led only to a threat to kill the crew of the *Philadelphia* and other hostages. The war dragged along until 1805, when the United States finally negotiated peace terms, agreeing to pay $60,000 for the release of the hostages and accepting the pirates' promise to stop raiding American shipping.

In the meantime, France and Spain posed a serious threat to Jefferson's dream of rapid westward expansion. As settlers continued to pour into the region between the Appalachian Mountains and the Mississippi River,

impeach To formally charge a public official with criminal conduct in office; once the House of Representatives has impeached a federal official, the official is then tried in the Senate on the stated charges.

■ **Albert Gallatin** Treasury secretary in Jefferson's administration; he favored limited government and reduced the federal debt by cutting spending.

internal taxes Taxes collected directly from citizens, like Alexander Hamilton's various excise taxes, as opposed to tariffs or other taxes collected in connection with foreign trade.

Although Jefferson largely failed in efforts to stop Barbary pirate looting against American shipping in the Mediterranean, the struggle provided a wonderful training ground for future military leaders. Young naval commander Stephen Decatur was one such figure. Decatur led his men in boarding a pirate ship and engaged in hand-to-hand fighting against the crew, eventually winning the fight despite having been shot through the arm.

Naval Historical and Heritage Command.

the commercial importance of that inland waterway increased. Whoever controlled the mouth of the Mississippi—the place where it flows past New Orleans and into the Gulf of Mexico and the open seas—would have the power to make or break the interior economy.

In accordance with the Treaty of San Lorenzo (1795), Spain had granted American farmers the right to ship cargoes down the Mississippi without paying tolls and had given American merchants permission to **transship** goods from New Orleans to Atlantic ports without paying export duties. In 1800, however, Napoleon had traded some of France's holdings in southern Europe to Spain in exchange for Spain's land in North America. The United States had no agreement with France concerning navigation on the Mississippi, so

transship To ship cargo to a port and then transfer it to other ships for transport to a final destination; cargoes shipped by barge down the Mississippi River to New Orleans were then loaded onto ocean-going vessels bound for American ports along the Atlantic coast.

■ **Saint-Domingue** Caribbean island originally named Hispaniola by Christopher Columbus and also known as Santo Domingo; today shared by the nations of Haiti and the Dominican Republic.

■ **François Dominique Toussaint Louverture** Black revolutionary who liberated the island of Saint-Domingue, only to see it reinvaded by the French in 1802.

■ **Louisiana Purchase** The U.S. purchase of Louisiana from France for $15 million in 1803; the Louisiana Territory extended from the Mississippi River to the Rocky Mountains.

the deal between Spain and France threatened to scuttle American commerce on the river. Anxiety over this issue turned to outright panic when, preparatory to the transfer of the land to France, Spanish officials suspended free trade in New Orleans.

Jefferson responded on two fronts. Backing away from his usual anti-British position, he announced, "The day France takes possession of New Orleans we must marry ourselves to the British fleet and nation," and he dispatched James Monroe to talk with the British about a military alliance. He also had Monroe instruct the American minister to France, Robert Livingston, that he could spend as much as $2 million to try to purchase New Orleans and as much adjacent real estate as possible.

Napoleon may have been considering the creation of a Caribbean empire when he acquired Louisiana from Spain, but a series of setbacks prevented his following through, including a slave revolt on the island of **Saint-Domingue** led by **François Dominique Toussaint Louverture**.

Stymied in the Caribbean, Napoleon turned his full attention back to extending his holdings in Europe and was seeking funds to finance a continental war. Thus, by the time Monroe and Livingston entered into negotiations with the French in 1803, Napoleon had instructed Foreign Minister Talleyrand to offer the whole of Louisiana to the Americans for $15 million.

Pushing Westward

Although Livingston and Monroe had been authorized to spend only $2 million for the purchase of Louisiana, they jumped at Talleyrand's offer. The president was overjoyed. The deal contained three important benefits for Jefferson and the nation. It removed one European power—France—from the continent and saved Jefferson from having to ally the United States with Britain. It secured the Mississippi River for shipments of American agricultural products to industrial Europe. And it doubled the size of the United States, opening uncharted new expanses for settlement by yeoman farmers.

The **Louisiana Purchase** was immensely popular among most Americans, but it raised significant ideological and constitutional questions. Some Federalists *and* Republicans questioned whether the United States could acquire this territory and its many residents without becoming an empire—something entirely at war with the rhetoric of our Revolution against the British. To this Jefferson responded by spinning the term "empire" into the phrase "empire of liberty," emphasizing that the new territory would

In the Wider World

aid Americans in securing and extending the benefits of our revolutionary tradition. Members of both parties also pointed out that the framers of the Constitution had made no provision for the acquisition of new territories by the United States, saying that the nation was prohibited from extending westward beyond its then-current boundaries without specific constitutional authorization. Again Jefferson parried with rhetoric, saying: "Strict observance to the written laws is doubtless one of the high duties of a good citizen, but it is not the highest. The laws of necessity, of self-preservation, of saving our country when in danger, are of a higher obligation." In the end, Jefferson got his way: Congress voted overwhelmingly for ratification of the treaty in November 1803.

Even before the Louisiana Purchase, "laws of necessity" had led Jefferson to exert presidential power in an unusual way. Although Spanish, French, and American fur traders, outlaws, and soldiers of fortune had crisscrossed Louisiana over the years, little systematic exploration had been done. When rumors of the land transfer between France and Spain began circulating, Jefferson started preparations for a covert spy mission. In a series of confidential letters, Jefferson instructed his private secretary, **Meriwether Lewis**, to form a party that would pretend to be on a scientific expedition into Louisiana. Their primary mission, however, would be to note the numbers of French, Spanish, and other agents in the area, along with the numbers and condition of the Indians, and to chart major waterways and other important strategic sites (see Map 8.2). They were also to open the way for direct dealings between the Indians and the United States, undermining the Indians' relations with the Spanish and French whenever possible. Early in 1803, months before ratifying the Louisiana Purchase, Congress secretly granted the funds necessary to finance the mission.

Lewis, his co-commander **William Clark**, and the rest of the Corps of Discovery set out by boat in the spring of 1804. Pushing its way up the Missouri River, the party arrived among the Mandan Indians (see page 11) in present-day North Dakota in the late fall. They chose to winter among the Mandans, a decision that may have ensured the expedition's success. The Mandans were a settled agricultural group who had been farming along the upper Missouri for over a thousand years. Their villages, which offered food and shelter for the wandering hunting tribes, became hubs in the evolving Plains trading and raiding system after the arrival of horses (see page 45 and Map 2.3). By wintering with the Mandans, the expedition came into contact with many of the Indian and European groups that participated in the complex economy of the West. Lewis and Clark acted on Jefferson's secret instructions by learning all they could from the Mandans and their visitors about the fur trade, the nature of military alliances, and the tribes that lived farther west.

One particularly important contact Lewis and Clark made during the Mandan winter was with a French trapper named Charbonneau and his Shoshone wife, **Sacajawea**. Between the two of them, Sacajawea and Charbonneau spoke several of the languages understood by the Indians in the Far West and possessed knowledge about the geography and

■ **Meriwether Lewis** Jefferson aide who was sent to explore the Louisiana Territory in 1803; he later served as its governor.

■ **William Clark** Soldier and explorer who joined Meriwether Lewis as co-leader on the expedition to explore the Louisiana Territory; he was responsible for mapmaking.

■ **Sacajawea** Shoshone woman who served as guide and interpreter on the Lewis and Clark expedition.

MAP 8.2 Louisiana Purchase and Lewis and Clark Expedition
As this map shows, President Jefferson added an enormous tract of land to the United States when he purchased Louisiana from France in 1803. The president was eager to learn about the new territory, sending the Lewis and Clark expedition to collect information. The expedition also sought to commit Indian groups along their path to alliances with the United States and to undermine French, Spanish, and British relations with the Indians, even in those areas that were not officially part of the United States. Copyright © Cengage Learning

the various peoples in the area. With their help, Lewis and Clark were able to make contact with the Shoshones, who aided them in crossing the Rocky Mountains. From there, the expedition passed from Indian group to Indian group along a chain of friendship. Following this chain of Indian hospitality, the expedition finally reached the Pacific Ocean in November 1805.

CHALLENGE AND UNCERTAINTY IN JEFFERSON'S AMERICA

★ *How did American life change during Jefferson's presidency?*

★ *How did Native Americans and African Americans figure into Jefferson's vision of America? How did each group respond to their circumstances?*

Jefferson's policies not only put the nation on a new road politically and economically but also brought a new spirit into the land. The Virginian's commitment

to opportunity and progress, to openness and frugality, offered a stark contrast in approach and style to the policies of his predecessors. The congressional elections of 1802 and the presidential election in 1804 proved Jefferson's popularity and the Republican Party's strong appeal. Nevertheless, some disturbing social and intellectual undercurrents began to surface during his second term. National expansion strained conventional social institutions as white farmers, entrepreneurs, and adventurers seized the opportunities that Republican economic and expansion policies offered. Adding to the strain was the fact that the Jeffersonian spirit was more of a promise than a commitment: Jefferson's vision for the republic excluded many.

The Heritage of Partisan Politics

The popularity of Jefferson's party was abundantly clear in 1804. Jefferson had won an extremely narrow victory in 1800, and his Republican Party had won significant but hardly overwhelming majorities in Congress. The congressional elections of 1802, however,

One of the key objectives for the Lewis and Clark Expedition was to map portions of the newly acquired Louisiana Territory. Here we see a copy of William Clark's map of their journey rendered by map publisher Samuel Lewis. In order to draw accurate maps—not to mention finding their way—the expedition carried sophisticated navigation hardware like the chronometer and box compass shown here. The original chronometer (now lost) was the single-most expensive item carried by the explorers on their way west. Map copied by Samuel Lewis in 1814, from an original by William Clark.The Tracy W. McGregor Library of American History, Special Collections, University of Virginia, Charlottesville, Virginia; compass: Division of Politics and Reform, National Museum of American History, Smithsonian Institution; chronometer: Department of Work and Industry, National Museum of American History, Smithsonian Institution.

had virtually eclipsed Federalist power, and Federalists faced the presidential election of 1804 with dread. Former president John Adams commented, "The power of the Administration rests upon the support of a much stronger majority of the people throughout the Union than the former administrations ever possessed since the first establishment of the Constitution."

Despite an abiding faith in the emerging two-party system, staunch Federalist congressman Fisher Ames withdrew from public life, followed by John Jay and other prominent leaders. Charles Cotesworth Pinckney, however, stepped forward to head the Federalists' 1804 presidential ticket. For the vice presidency, the Federalists chose Rufus King, a defender of the notion of loyal opposition and the two-party system. But Federalists had trouble identifying issues on which to build a viable platform. Pinckney accused Jefferson of violating his own political principles by exerting the federal authority to purchase Louisiana, which was not explicitly granted in the Constitution. Beyond that, there was little to complain about: the economy had continued to grow at the same rate during Jefferson's tenure in office as it had under the Federalists. Such economic growth permitted Jefferson to maintain a favorable **balance of payments** throughout his first administration, a feat the Federalists had never achieved. And with Gallatin's help, Jefferson

had proved his fiscal responsibility by building up a multimillion-dollar Treasury surplus. The enormous scope of Jefferson's successes and the limited scope of his opponent's platform helped swing the election of 1804 firmly over to the Republicans. Jefferson won 162 electoral votes to Pinckney's 14, carrying every state except Connecticut and Delaware.

Westward Expansion and Social Stress

A baby boom had followed the Revolution, and as new territories opened in the West, young people streamed into the region at a rate that alarmed many. This had an unsettling effect on communities in the East. During the eighteenth century, older people maintained authority by controlling the distribution of land to their children. With only so much worthwhile land to go around, sons and daughters lived with and worked for their parents until their elders saw fit to deed property over to them. As a result, children living in the East generally did not become independent—that is, they did not become church members, marry, or

balance of payments The difference between a nation's total payments to foreign countries and its total receipts from abroad.

Challenge and Uncertainty in Jefferson's America **199**

The Mississippi River drainage system was the only reliable transportation route for Americans moving into the West during the early 1800s. Farmers moved produce to market on keelboats like the one depicted here. Above decks, cargo and livestock endured weather and exposure to mosquitoes and other river menaces. Below decks, however, there was a cabin-like environment where people could eat, drink, and sleep in comfort during the trip downriver. One problem with this mode of transport was that the current on the giant river made upstream travel impossible during much of the year, so boats like this one were often sold for lumber after they reached New Orleans.

operate their own farms or businesses—until they were in their thirties. Economic opportunities available in the West, however, lessened young people's need to rely on their parents for support and lowered the age at which they began to break away. Breathing the new air of independence, intrepid young people not only migrated west but also challenged their parents' authority at home, upsetting social and political traditionalists. Business interests in the East were also upset as they witnessed westward expansion drawing off population, which in time would drive up the price of labor and reduce profits.

Conditions out west were even less stable as rapid growth put enormous stress on conventional institutions. The population of Ohio, for example, grew from 45,000 in 1800 to 231,000 in 1810, and similar rates of growth occurred in the new states of Tennessee and Kentucky and in territories from Louisiana north to Michigan and west to Missouri. Authorities in the West found these increases challenging as they tried to deal with the practical matters of maintaining governments, economies, and peaceful relations among

the new settlers and between the settlers and neighboring Indians.

Most of the people who moved west looked forward to achieving the agrarian self-sufficiency that Jefferson advocated, but life in the West was far more complicated. Inexpensive, reliable transportation was impossible in the vast, rugged interior, and Jefferson's notion of breadbasket America trading with industrial Europe was doomed without it. No navigable streams ran eastward from America's interior across the Appalachians to the Atlantic, and the ridges of those mountains made road building extremely difficult.

Only two reliable routes existed for transporting produce from the interior to shipping centers in the East. The Ohio-Mississippi-Missouri drainage system provided a reliable watercourse, and huge cargoes flowed along its stream. Shipping goods on the Mississippi, however, was dangerous and expensive. Because of the river's strong current, loads could be shipped only one way—downstream. Rafts were built for the purpose and then were broken up and sold for lumber in New Orleans. Shippers had to return home by foot.

On both legs of the journey, travelers risked attack by river pirates, Indians, and sickness. Moreover, it was virtually impossible for shippers to take manufactured goods back with them because of the condition of the roads and the distances involved. The other river route—the St. Lawrence River, flowing east from the Great Lakes to the northern Atlantic—presented similar problems. In addition, that river passed through British Canada and therefore was closed to American commercial traffic.

As a result of geographical isolation and the rapid pace of settlement, the economy in the West became highly localized. Settlers arriving with neither food nor seed bought surplus crops produced by established farmers. The little capital that was generated in this way supported the development of local industries in hundreds of farming villages. Enterprising craftsmen ranging from **coopers** to **wheelwrights** produced hand-manufactured items on demand. As long as people kept moving into an area, local economies boomed. But when new arrivals slowed and then stopped, the market for surplus crops and local manufactures collapsed, and the economy went bust. Swinging from boom to bust and back again became a way of life in newly settled areas.

Along with economic instability, social instability was also common. The odd mixture of ethnic, religious, and national groups found in western villages did little to bring cohesiveness to community life.

The Religious Response to Social Change

The changes taking place in the young republic stirred conflicting religious currents. One was liberalism in religious thought. The other was a new **evangelicalism**.

Born of the Enlightenment (see pages 90–91) in France, Scotland, and England, liberal religious thought emphasized the connection between **rationalism** and faith. To rationalists like both Jefferson and Adams, the possibility that a being as perfect as God might behave irrationally was unthinkable. In fact, for such men, the more plain, reasonable, and verifiable religious claims were, the more likely it was that they emanated from God. Less perfect than God, it was man who had cluttered the plain revealed truth with irrational claims and insolvable mysteries. For his part, Jefferson was so convinced of this logic that he edited his own version of the Bible, keeping only the moral principles and the solid historical facts and discarding anything supernatural.

This liberal creed led many, including Jefferson, to abandon organized religion altogether. Not all liberals were so quick to bolt organized worship, however. John Adams, for example, continued to adhere to New England Congregationalism, but he and others used their influence to promote a young and more liberal clergy who sought to insert a heavy dose of rationalism into the old Puritan structure. Rejecting

such traditional mysteries as the **Trinity** and the literal divinity of Christ, **Unitarianism** expanded inside Congregational churches during the years just before and following the American Revolution. Liberal influence within Congregationalism became so prominent in New England that Unitarians were able to engineer the election of their own **Henry Ware** as the senior professor of theology at Harvard College, formerly the educational heart of orthodox American Protestantism. Though outraged, more traditional Congregationalists did little immediately to oust liberals from their churches. In the decades to come, however, doctrinal disagreements between the parties led to virtual religious warfare.

While deism and Unitarianism were gaining strong footholds in eastern cities, disorder, insecurity, and missionizing activities were helping to foster a very different kind of religious response in the West. Although Methodists, Baptists, Presbyterians, and evangelical Congregationalists disagreed on many specific principles, they all emphasized the spirited preaching that could bring about the emotional moment of conversion—the moment of realization that without the saving grace of God, every soul is lost. Each of these denominations concentrated on training a new, young ministry and sending it to preach in every corner of the nation. In this way, another religious awakening swept across America, beginning in Cane Ridge, Kentucky, in 1801 and spreading throughout the South and West.

The new evangelicalism stressed the individual nature of salvation but at the same time emphasized the importance of Christian community. Looking back to the first generation of Puritans in America, evangelicals breathed new life into the old Puritan

cooper A person who makes or repairs wooden barrels.

wheelwright A person who makes or repairs wheels for carts, wagons, or other vehicles.

evangelicalism A Protestant religious persuasion that emphasizes the literal truth of the Gospels and salvation through faith alone; in the early nineteenth century, it became infused with increasing amounts of romantic emotionalism and an emphasis on converting others.

rationalism The theory that the exercise of reason, rather than the acceptance of authority or spiritual revelation, is the only valid basis for belief and the best source of spiritual truth.

Trinity The Christian belief that God consists of three divine persons: Father, Son, and Holy Spirit.

■ **Unitarianism** A religion that denies the Trinity, teaching that God exists only in one person; it also stresses individual freedom of belief and the free use of reason in religion.

■ **Henry Ware** Liberal Congregationalist who was elected senior theologian at Harvard College in 1805, making Unitarianism the dominant religious view at the previously orthodox stronghold.

Evangelical denominations gained ever wider followings during the early nineteenth century as the uncertainties accompanying rapid expansion and social change took their toll. Both black and white communities engaged in enthusiastic worship. This painting, attributed to Russian travel writer and artist Pavel Svinin, captures an African American Methodist service that Svinin attended in 1811. "Black Methodists Holding a Prayer Meeting" by Pavel Petrovich Svinin (1787/88–1839), 1811–ca.1813. Watercolor and pen and black ink on off-white wove paper, 6 9/16 x 9 15/16 in. (16.6 x 25.3 cm.). Rogers Fund, 1942 (42.95.19). The Metropolitan Museum of Art, New York, NY, U.S.A. Image copyright © The Metropolitan Museum of Art/Art Resource, New York.

notion of God's plan for the universe and the leading role that Americans were to play in its unfolding. As early nineteenth-century Presbyterian divine Lyman Beecher put it, "It was the opinion of [Jonathan] Edwards that the millennium would commence in America . . . all providential signs of the times lend corroboration to it."

In addition to numerous official evangelical councils and conventions, hundreds of informal associations came together to carry out what they characterized as God's plan for America. These organizations helped counterbalance the forces of extreme individualism and social disorder by providing ideological underpinnings for the expansive behavior of westerners and a sense of mission to ease the insecurities produced by venturing into the unknown. They also provided an institutional framework that brought some stability to communities in which traditional controls were lacking. These attractive features helped evangelicalism to sweep across the West. During the early nineteenth century, it became the dominant religious persuasion in that region.

Exceptions in Jefferson's Vision

Jefferson's policies enabled many Americans to benefit from the nation's development, but they certainly did not help everyone. Neither Native Americans nor African Americans had much of a role in Jefferson's republic, and each group was subject to different forms of unequal treatment. And women were to occupy a special, but far from equal place in the envisioned society.

A slaveholder himself, Jefferson expressed strong views about African Americans. In his *Notes on the State of Virginia* (1781), Jefferson asserted that blacks were "inferior to whites in the endowments both of body and mind." Even when presented with contrary evidence, like the case of well-respected African American mathematician, astronomer, and engineer Benjamin Banneker, Jefferson remained unmoved. "I have a long letter from Banneker," Jefferson told his friend Joel Barlow, "which shows him to have had a mind of very common stature indeed."

Jefferson was convinced, and stated publicly on many occasions, that the white and black races could not live together without inevitably polluting both. This was the key reason for what little opposition he voiced to slavery and for his continued involvement in various projects to remove African Americans by colonizing them in Africa. And yet despite this attitude, many of his contemporaries believed that he kept a slave mistress, Sally Hemings, by whom he fathered several children, a contention that modern DNA evidence has demonstrated as credible. Even so, almost no documentary evidence about the relationship exists despite the fact that hundreds of the nation's most prolific writers (and gossips) passed through Jefferson's home regularly. Circumstantial evidence, however, suggests that their relationship was an exclusive one and lasted for a long time. And traditions passed down through generations of Sally Hemings's descendants claim that theirs was a sentimental, even romantic bond.

Given his belief in racial inequality, it seems contradictory that Jefferson could have had a long-term affectionate relationship with an African American woman. If so, it reflects equally deep-seated contradictions that shot through American society at the time. Truly a man of his century and his social class, Jefferson was convinced that women, like slaves, existed to serve and entertain men. For example, when asked if a woman could hold public office, Jefferson replied, "The appointment of a woman to office is an innovation for which the public is not prepared, nor am I." Thus his entanglement with Hemings, who probably was the half-sister of Jefferson's deceased wife, seemed no more unequal or unnatural than his marriage. But while the relationship may have seemed perfectly natural behind closed doors, the race code to which Jefferson gave voice in his various publications and official utterances defined it as entirely unacceptable in public. This rigid separation between public and private behavior led Jefferson to keep the relationship secret, and his friends and family—even most of his political enemies—joined him in a conspiracy of silence. This, too, reflected broader social ambiguities, contradictions that defined the sex lives of masters and slaves in Jefferson's South.

Throughout the Jeffersonian era, the great majority of African Americans lived in that South, and most of them were slaves. But during the late eighteenth century, conditions for slaves underwent some serious modifications and the number of free blacks increased steadily. In northern states like New York and Pennsylvania slavery was in the process of gradual legislative abolition, and even the plantation states showed increasing flexibility in dealing with slavery, as some elite southerners began to recognize the unprofitability, though generally not the immorality, of the institution. After Virginia authorized owners to free their slaves in 1782, Delaware and Maryland soon did likewise. But an event that took place in 1800 revealed that slavery would continue to be a controversial issue and source of enormous anxiety.

In the more relaxed racial atmosphere that was coming into existence in late-eighteenth-century Virginia, skilled slave workers like a blacksmith named Gabriel, owned by a Henrico County planter named Thomas Prosser, exercised significant freedom, hiring himself out for wages and learning to read and write. Gabriel came into contact with a wide variety of people and learned about the promises of greater freedom mouthed by Jeffersonian reformers and of the successful slave revolution in Saint-Domingue. Frustrated by the impotence of Republican rhetoric and emboldened by Toussaint's Louverture's successes, Gabriel enlisted at least two white partners and a number of fellow slaves to wage an armed revolt. On August 30, they armed themselves in preparation to invade nearby Richmond, but torrential rainfall bogged down the effort. Eventually Gabriel, along with his two brothers and twenty-four other slaves, were captured and hanged. It appears that Virginia governor James Monroe was aware that there were white participants, but did not pursue the evidence in fear that the information would hurt Jefferson's election efforts.

Gabriel's Rebellion had a chilling effect on race relations throughout the country. In Virginia and throughout the slave South, new restrictions were placed on the freedoms accorded to both enslaved and free African Americans. Even in northern states blacks were not permitted to testify in court, vote, attend schools, or exercise other fundamental freedoms accorded to whites. Even churches were often closed to blacks who wished to worship.

Some African Americans began to respond to systematic exclusion and to express their cultural and social identity by forming their own institutions. In Philadelphia, tension between white and free black Methodists led former slave Richard Allen to form the Bethel Church for Negro Methodists in 1793. Two years later, Allen became the first black deacon ordained in America. Ongoing tension with the white Methodist hierarchy, however, eventually led Allen to secede from the church and form his own **African Methodist Episcopal Church** (Bethel) in 1816. Similar controversies in New York led black divine James Varick to found an African Methodist Episcopal Church (Zion) in that city in 1821.

African American leadership was not confined to religious and intellectual realms. **James Forten**, for example, a free-born African American, followed up on his experience as a sailor in the Revolutionary navy with a career as a sail maker in Philadelphia. Despite both overt and subtle racial discrimination, he acquired his own company in 1798, eventually becoming a major employer of both African American and white workers. Though himself a Quaker, Forten often cooperated with Richard Allen but did not subscribe to projects designed to separate the races, working consistently—even to the point of petitioning Congress and the Pennsylvania assembly—to pass laws ensuring desegregation and equal treatment. In cooperation with other African American entrepreneurs, such as Boston's Paul Cuffe, Forten invested expertise, capital, and personal influence in an effort to create jobs for black city-dwellers and opportunities for budding black businessmen. Despite these efforts, the overall racial atmosphere in Jefferson's America significantly limited the number of African American leaders who attained positions of wealth or influence.

Jefferson thought differently of Native Americans than he did of African Americans. He considered Indians to be "savages" but was not convinced that they were biologically inferior to Europeans: "They are formed in mind as well as in body," he said, "on the same module with the 'Homo Sapiens Europaeus.'" Jefferson attributed the differences between Indians and Europeans to what he termed the Indians' cultural retardation. He was confident that if whites lifted

■ **Gabriel's Rebellion** Attempted slave revolt led by a slave blacksmith in 1800; although a failure, the affair led to greater restrictions on African Americans both slave and free in the South.

■ **African Methodist Episcopal Church** African American branch of Methodism established in Philadelphia in 1816 and in New York in 1821.

■ **James Forten** African American entrepreneur with a successful sail-making business in Philadelphia who provided leadership for black business enterprises and advocated both racial integration and equal rights during the Jeffersonian era.

Library of Congress.

Unlike many of his contemporaries, Thomas Jefferson was convinced that the American Indians could eventually become full participants in the American republic. Members of the "Five Civilized Tribes" (Cherokee, Choctaw, Chickasaw, Creek, and Seminole) often owned large plantations and practiced lifestyles not unlike those of their white neighbors. Unfortunately, Jefferson's hopes fell before the racism and greed of white settlers. Even sophisticated leaders like Cherokee chief Tah Chee, pictured here, were driven from their land; he and his band eventually took up residence in Texas to escape persecution in their native Arkansas.

Indians out of their uncivilized state and put them on an equal footing with Europeans, Indian populations would grow, their physical condition would improve, and they would be able to participate in the yeoman republic on an equal footing with whites.

acculturation Changes in the culture of a group or an individual as a result of contact with a different culture.

Jefferson's Indian policy reflected this attitude. Jefferson created a series of government-owned trading posts at which Indians were offered goods at cheap prices. He believed that Indians who were exposed to white manufactures would come to agree that white culture was superior and would make the rational decision to adopt that culture wholesale. At the same time, both the government and right-minded philanthropists should engage in instructing Native Americans in European methods of farming, ensuring that these former "savages" would emerge as good, Republican-voting frontier farmers. Until this process of **acculturation** was complete, however, Jefferson believed the Indians, like children, should be protected from those who might take advantage of them or lead them astray. Also like children, the Indians were not to be trusted to exercise the rights and responsibilities of citizenship. Thus Indian rights were left to the whims of the Senate—which drafted and ratified Indian treaties—and of the army—which enforced those treaties.

The chief problem for Jeffersonian Indian policy was not the Indians' supposed cultural retardation but their rapid modernization. Among groups such as the Cherokees and Creeks, members of a rising new elite led their people toward greater prosperity and diplomatic independence. Alexander McGillivray of the Creeks, for example, deftly manipulated American, French, and Spanish interests to Creek advantage while building a strong economic base founded on both communally and privately owned plantations. In similar fashion, the rising Cherokee elite in 1794 established a centralized government that began pushing the Cherokees into a new era of wealth and power.

Although Jefferson might have greeted such acculturation with enthusiasm, the Indians' white neighbors generally did not. Envisioning all-out war between the states and the Indians—war that his reduced government and shrunken military was helpless to prevent—Jefferson advanced an alternative. Having acquired Louisiana, Jefferson suggested the creation of large reserves to which Indians currently residing within states could relocate, taking themselves out of state jurisdictions and removing themselves from the corrupting influence of the "baser elements" of white society. Although he did not advocate the use of force to move Indians west of the Mississippi, he made every effort to convince them to migrate. This idea of segregating Native Americans from other Americans formed the basis for Indian policy for the rest of the century.

Individual Voices

Congress Debates **George Logan's Mission to France**

Even before any official news had reached Washington, rumors were flying about George Logan's trip to France to negotiate an end to the diplomatic crisis that was plaguing the nation. Less than a month after Logan had set off for Europe, Federalists in Congress proposed a new law that would make any such efforts at unofficial peace-making a federal crime. Republican representative Albert Gallatin urged patience: wait for the president to present the facts to Congress as he had promised to do. But the Federalists persisted, leading Gallatin to ask why they were so eager to criminalize Logan's actions. Whether Gallatin was genuinely curious or was engaging in political rhetoric, in a moment of heated candor, Massachusetts Federalist Harrison G. Otis blurted out the answer. His outburst reveals what was really at work inside the radical circle, helping historians interpret Federalist motives.

❶ What is Otis saying here? What does he perceive as the motive behind the Republican criticism of a bill to outlaw acts like Logan's?

❷ This speech is quoted from *The Debates and Proceedings in the Congress of the United States*, the official record of Congress from 1789 through 1824. In this source, speeches were generally reported in the third person; hence Otis is referred to as "he."

❸ What is Otis saying was the actual motivation for proposing this bill? What conclusions can you draw from this statement about the nature of partisan politics in 1798? To what extent is such political practice in play today?

Again: it is insisted that the secret of the resolution on the table, was to perpetuate the division of party, and that, although but few real causes of dissension remain, yet we are determined to throw down the gauntlet and excite the greatest possible irritation. ❶ This accusation he denied. ❷ He did not believe that the resolution was introduced with any such design; but if such had been the object of the mover, the blame would not attach to him or to his friends. They might even then have justified themselves upon principles of self-defence. He appealed to the whole House that, within a few days after the commencement of this session, they were threatened with a notice that motions might be expected in favor of repealing the Alien and Sedition acts; which could owe their origin to no other intention but that of inflaming the public mind, and of persevering in the endeavor to expose the Administration and its friends to odious imputations. Therefore we should stand acquitted, if, instead of giving time to our adversaries to furnish their weapons, and carry war into our borders, we had seized this occasion to strike the first blow. ❸

Study Tools

SUMMARY

Americans faced a difficult choice in 1796: to continue in a Federalist direction with John Adams or to move into new and uncharted regions of republicanism with Thomas Jefferson. Factionalism and voter indecision led to Adams's election as president and Jefferson's as vice president. The split outcome frightened Federalists, and they used every excuse to make war on their political opponents. Diplomatically, they let relations with France sour to the point that the two nations were at war in all but name. At home, they used repressive measures such as the Alien and Sedition Acts to try to silence opponents, and they imposed tariffs and taxes that were hateful to many. Reminded of what they had rebelled against in the Revolution, in 1800 the American people decided to give Jefferson and the Republican faction a chance.

Although Jefferson called the election "the revolution of 1800," even hard-line Federalists such as Hamilton were sure that the general direction in government would not change. Just to be safe, however, Federalists stacked the court system so that Republicans would face insurmountable constraints if they tried to change government too much.

Jefferson's inaugural address in 1801 seemed to announce an end to partisan warfare, but both Madison and hard-line Republicans in Congress attempted to restrict Federalist power in the court system. The Republican program, however, was not entirely negative. Jefferson looked toward a future in which most Americans could own enough land to produce life's necessities for themselves and were beholden to no one and thus free to vote as their consciences and rationality dictated. To attain this end, Jefferson ordered massive reductions in the size of government, the elimination of internal federal taxes, and rapid westward expansion, including the purchase of the vast territory called Louisiana. For some the outcome was a spirit of excitement and optimism, but not everyone was so hopeful. Many were unsure and fearful of the new order's novelty and of the stresses that rapid expansion engendered; social change disrupted lives and communities.

Jefferson clearly wanted most Americans to share in the bounty of an expanded nation, but not all were free to share equally. For American Indians, the very success of Jefferson's expansion policy meant a contraction in their freedom of action. African Americans also found that the equality Jefferson promised to others was not intended for them, though many like Benjamin Banneker and Paul Cuffe grasped for it anyway. As to women, they were encouraged to play an active role in the new nation but were expected to do so only through their roles as wives and mothers.

CHRONOLOGY
Partisan Tension and Jeffersonian Optimism

1796	George Washington's Farewell Address
	First contested presidential election: John Adams elected president, Thomas Jefferson vice president
1797	XYZ affair
1798	Quasi-War with France begins
	Alien and Sedition Acts
	Kentucky and Virginia Resolutions
	George Logan's mission to France
1799	Napoleon seizes control in France
1800	Convention of Mortefontaine ends Quasi-War
1801	Jefferson elected president in House of Representatives; Burr vice president
	Judiciary Act of 1801
	John Marshall becomes chief justice
	War begins between American navy ships and Barbary pirates
	Outdoor revival meeting at Cane Ridge, Kentucky
1802	Congress repeals all internal taxes
	Congress repeals Judiciary Act of 1801
	French invade Saint-Domingue
1803	*Marbury v. Madison*
	Louisiana Purchase
1804	Twelfth Amendment ratified
	Jefferson reelected
1804–1806	Lewis and Clark expedition
1816	African Methodist Episcopal Church formed in Philadelphia

Study Tools

FOCUS QUESTIONS

If you have mastered this chapter, you should be able to answer these questions and to explain the terms that follow the questions.

1. ☆ *How did Federalists manipulate the crisis with France in 1798 for their own political advantage?*

2. ☆ *What steps did Republicans take to counter Federalist manipulations?*

3. ☆ *How did Federalists respond to losing the election of 1800? What does this response reveal about their political attitudes?*

4. ☆ *What did Thomas Jefferson mean by the statement "Every difference of opinion is not a difference of principles"?*

5. ☆ *How did Jefferson's vision for America differ from that of Hamilton, Adams, and other Federalists?*

6. ☆ *What legal maneuvers did Republicans initiate to deal with defenses Federalists put in place in 1801? What were the political and constitutional consequences?*

7. ☆ *What policies did Jefferson pursue to carry out his vision for the country? What obstacles did he encounter?*

8. ☆ *How did American life change during Jefferson's presidency?*

9. ☆ *How did Native Americans and African Americans figure into Jefferson's vision of America? How did each group respond to their circumstances?*

KEY TERMS

Aaron Burr *(p. 186)*

Charles Cotesworth Pinckney *(p. 187)*

Charles Maurice de Talleyrand-Périgord *(p. 188)*

XYZ affair *(p. 188)*

Quasi-War *(p. 188)*

Alien and Sedition Acts *(p. 189)*

Virginia and Kentucky Resolutions *(p. 189)*

states' rights *(p. 189)*

Fries's Rebellion *(p. 190)*

Napoleon Bonaparte *(p. 190)*

Twelfth Amendment *(p. 191)*

Judiciary Act of 1801 *(p. 191)*

John Marshall *(p. 191)*

supply and demand *(p. 193)*

Marbury v. Madison *(p. 194)*

Albert Gallatin *(p. 195)*

Saint-Domingue *(p. 196)*

François Dominique Toussaint Louverture *(p. 196)*

Louisiana Purchase *(p. 196)*

Meriwether Lewis *(p. 197)*

William Clark *(p. 197)*

Sacajawea *(p. 197)*

Unitarianism *(p. 201)*

Henry Ware *(p. 201)*

Gabriel's Rebellion *(p. 203)*

African Methodist Episcopal Church *(p. 203)*

James Forten *(p. 203)*

Go to the History CourseMate website for primary source links, study tools, and review materials for this chapter. www.cengagebrain.com

Tecumseh . . .

Hopes for a unified Indian resistance died with Tecumseh, and his mutilated body foreshadowed the future for the Indian land base. Stinging from military defeats and with no more strong voices urging common cause, the once-cosmopolitan world of the Indian interior became what whites imagined it to be: isolated tribes constantly warring among themselves. Expansionists like Harrison used this desperation to play one group off against another, carving piece after piece out of the Indian domain until, by 1850, virtually no Indians remained in the territory Tecumseh had tried to preserve.

Tecumseh's situation in Indiana reflected many of the more troubling problems that beset the nation during the opening decades of the nineteenth century. Sitting at the juncture of three worlds—the dynamic republican world of Jeffersonian America, the European imperial world in Canada, and his own Native American world—Tecumseh perceived that unless something happened soon, all three worlds were heading for crisis.

Jefferson had set an ambitious agenda for the country that was extremely popular with many Americans, but it created serious stresses within the nation and across the world. Along the Atlantic frontier, imperial powers such as Great Britain and France challenged Jefferson's commitment to open trade and freedom of the seas. A war of words, blustering threats, and some open confrontations pushed the United States increasingly toward crisis and triggered economic disaster. Along the western frontier, a variety of Indian groups opposed Jefferson's vision of rapid westward expansion. Here too, verbal and some armed conflicts engendered an air of crisis. And to many, including Harrison, these seemed not to be isolated phenomena. Convinced that a conspiracy was afoot between Indian dissidents like Tecumseh and imperial agents from Great Britain, an increasing number of Jeffersonians demanded aggressive action.

No one could stem the tide of crisis. Harrison finally took matters over the edge: his attack on Prophetstown precipitated a general call for a war that set the nation on a new course altogether.

secede To withdraw formally from membership in a political union; threats of secession were used frequently during the early nineteenth century to bring attention to political issues.

■ Essex Junto A group of political conspirators who sought power outside of the regular political process—composed of radical Federalists in Essex County, Massachusetts, who at first advocated constitutional changes that would favor New England politically and later called for New England and New York to secede from the United States.

TROUBLING CURRENTS IN JEFFERSON'S AMERICA

☆ How did varying regional interests complicate Jefferson's political situation during his second term as president?

☆ How did European politics affect the American economy between 1804 and 1808?

Jefferson's successes, culminating in his victory in the 1804 election, seemed to prove that Republicans had absolute control over the nation's political reins. But factions challenging Jefferson's control were forming. A small but vocal coalition of disgruntled Federalists threatened to **secede** from the Union. Even within his own party, Jefferson's supremacy eroded and dissidents emerged. Diplomatic problems joined domestic ones to trouble Jefferson's second administration.

Emerging Factions in American Politics

The Federalists' failure in the election of 1804 nearly spelled the troubled party's demise. With the West and the South firmly in Jefferson's camp, disgruntled New England Federalists found their once-dominant voice being drowned out by those who shared Jefferson's rather than Hamilton's view of America's future (see pages 174–175). Proclaiming that "the people of the East cannot reconcile their habits, views, and interests with those of the South and West," Federalist leader Timothy Pickering advocated radical changes in the Constitution that he thought might restore balance. Among other things, northeasterners demanded much stricter standards for admitting new states in the West and the elimination of the Three-Fifths Compromise. Pickering brought together a tight political coalition called the **Essex Junto** to press for these changes.

Regional fissures began to open inside Jefferson's party as well. Throughout Jefferson's first administration, some within his party, especially those from the South, criticized the president for turning his back on republican principles by expanding federal power and interfering with states' rights. One of Jefferson's most vocal critics was his cousin **John Randolph**.

On the eve of the 1804 election, the two Virginia Republicans clashed over the **Yazoo affair**, a complicated legal tangle arising from land fraud in Georgia. Traditional Republicans thought the matter should have been worked out at the state level. Jefferson, however, chose to involve the federal courts in the affair. He irritated Randolph again in 1806 by approaching Congress for a $2 million appropriation to be used to win French influence in convincing Spain to sell Florida to the United States. Citing these and other perceived violations of republican principles, Randolph announced, "I found I might co-operate or be an honest man." Randolph chose honesty, splitting with Jefferson to form a third party, the **Tertium Quid**, which fractured the Republicans' united political front.

A second fissure in the party opened over controversial vice president Aaron Burr's political scheming. Upset that Burr had not conceded the presidency immediately after the tied Electoral College vote in 1800, Jefferson snubbed him for four years and then dropped him as vice-presidential nominee in 1804. With Burr in political limbo, Pickering saw an opportunity: he offered to help Burr become governor of New York if Burr would commit the state to the Essex Junto. Mainstream New York Federalists were furious, especially Alexander Hamilton, who was quoted by the press as saying that Burr was "a dangerous man, and one who ought not to be trusted with the reins of government." Burr lost the election in a landslide. Never willing to accept defeat gracefully, he challenged Hamilton to a duel. Hamilton was personally opposed to dueling, but in the honor-driven culture that permeated early nineteenth-century politics, he could not refuse. An excellent shot, Burr put a bullet through Hamilton's liver and into his spine, killing him.

Though his political career was now in shambles, Burr was not finished meddling in the nation's future. Calling in outstanding political favors, he arranged for James Wilkinson to become governor of the Louisiana Territory. To this day, no one is entirely certain what Wilkinson and Burr had in mind, but it appears that they intended to carve out a personal domain in the borderland between American and Spanish territories in the Mississippi region. In 1805, Burr ventured west, sailing down the Mississippi to recruit associates. Amid rumors of intrigue, federal authorities received a letter from Wilkinson late in 1806 implicating Burr in a "deep, dark, wicked, and widespread conspiracy" against the United States. Learning that Wilkinson had turned him in, Burr tried to reach Spanish Florida but was captured early in 1807 and put on trial for treason.

Burr's trial provided an open arena for Jefferson and his critics to air their views on such touchy subjects as presidential power, westward expansion, and national loyalty. Jefferson used the powers of his office to pardon conspirators who would testify against Burr and he leaked information that made his former vice president look guilty. Chief Justice John Marshall presided over the case, and citing Marshall's earlier support for George Washington's assertion of presidential privilege during investigations into Jay's Treaty, Jefferson refused court orders to deliver evidence from presidential records that might have aided Burr's case. Marshall, making clear that he believed Burr was the victim, not the perpetrator, of a conspiracy, retaliated by applying Jefferson's position of strict constitutional constructionism. He advised the jury that treason consisted of, and *only* of, "levying war against the United States or adhering to their enemies." Burr had done neither, and so the jury was forced to acquit, to the glee of Jefferson's critics.

The Problem of American Neutrality

Internal tensions in American politics were matched by growing stress in the nation's diplomatic and economic relations. Jefferson's economic successes had been the product of continuing warfare in Europe. With their fleets engaged in naval battles, their people locked in combat, and their lands crisscrossed by opposing armies, Europeans needed American ships and the fruits of American labor, especially food. American neutrality ensured continued prosperity as long as the contending parties in Europe agreed to recognize that neutrality.

Americans immediately grasped at this opportunity. An upsurge in European campaigning in 1803 helped raise the total value of American exports by over 65 percent. A significant proportion of the increase came from the shipment of foreign goods to foreign markets by way of neutral American ports: sugar from the Caribbean, for example, frequently passed through the United States on its way to Europe. These so-called reexports rose in value from $14 million in 1803 to $60 million in 1807, prompting a rapid growth in earnings for American shipping. In 1790, net income from shipping amounted to a mere $5.9 million; by 1807 the volume had surged to $42.1 million.

■ **John Randolph** Virginia Republican politician who believed in limited government and objected to several of Jefferson's policies.

■ **Yazoo affair** Corrupt deal in which the Georgia legislature sold a huge tract of public land to speculators for a low price but later overturned the sale; the basis for the Supreme Court case of *Fletcher v. Peck*, discussed in detail in Chapter 10.

■ **Tertium Quid** Republican faction formed by John Randolph to protest Jefferson's plan for acquiring Florida from Spain; the name is Latin and means a "third thing," indicating Randolph's rejection of both the Federalist and Republican parties.

The impressment of sailors into the British navy from American ships was one of the more prominent causes of the War of 1812. This 1790 engraving shows an American sailor being seized at gunpoint while those who might try to assist him are elbowed aside.

Prospects seemed bright for America's economic and diplomatic future and for Jefferson's dream of agricultural America feeding overcrowded, war-torn Europe. But politicians in both England and France cared about their own military victories, not about American prosperity. Their decisions, especially those relating to neutral shipping, constantly threatened to disrupt American trade and created an atmosphere of hostility.

Another source of tension was **impressment**. For decades, British sailors had protested the exceedingly cruel conditions and low pay in His Majesty's navy by jumping ship in American ports and enlisting as merchant sailors on American vessels. Strapped for mariners by renewed warfare, England pursued a vigorous policy of reclaiming British sailors after 1803, even if they were on neutral American ships and, more provocatively, even if they had become citizens of the United States. It is estimated that the British abducted as many as eight thousand sailors from American ships between 1803 and 1812. The loss of so many seamen hurt American shippers economically, but it wounded American pride even more. Like the XYZ affair, impressment seemed to be a direct denial of the United States' status as a legitimate nation.

Economic Warfare

Pressure on American neutrality increased after 1805, when a military deadlock emerged in the European war: Britain was supreme at sea, while France was in control on the ground. The war then changed from one of military campaigning to one of diplomatic and economic maneuvering. Seeking to close off foreign supplies to England, in November 1806 Napoleon issued the **Berlin Decree**, barring ships that had anchored at British harbors from entering ports controlled by France. The British Parliament responded by issuing a series of directives that permitted neutral ships to sail to European ports only if they first called at a British port to pay a transit tax. It was thus impossible for a neutral ship to follow the laws of either nation without violating the laws of the other. All this European blustering, however, had little immediate effect on the American economy. From the issuance

■ **impressment** Procedure permitted under British maritime law that authorized commanders of warships to force English civilian sailors into military service.

■ **Berlin Decree** Napoleon's order declaring the British Isles under blockade and authorizing the confiscation of British goods from any ship found carrying them.

of the Berlin Decree to the end of 1807, American exports and shipping rose more than they had risen during any similar period.

But such good fortune was not to last. Seeking to break France's dependence on America as a source for food and other supplies, Napoleon sought an alliance with Russia, and in the spring of 1807 his diplomatic mission succeeded. Having acquired an alternative source for grain and other foodstuffs, Napoleon immediately began enforcing the Berlin Decree, hoping to starve England into submission. The British countered by stepping up enforcement of their European blockade and aggressively pursuing impressment to strengthen the Royal Navy.

The escalation in both France's and Britain's economic war efforts quickly led to confrontation with Americans and a diplomatic crisis. A pivotal event occurred in June 1807. The British **frigate** *Leopard*, patrolling the American shoreline, confronted the American warship *Chesapeake*. The *Leopard* ordered the American ship to halt and hand over any British sailors on board. When the *Chesapeake*'s captain refused, the *Leopard* fired several **broadsides**, crippling the American vessel, killing three sailors, and injuring eighteen. The British then boarded the *Chesapeake* and dragged off four men, three of whom were naturalized citizens of the United States. Americans were outraged.

Americans were not the only ones galvanized by British aggression. Shortly after the *Chesapeake* affair, word arrived in the United States that Napoleon had responded to Britain's belligerence by declaring a virtual economic war against neutrals. In the **Milan Decree**, he vowed to seize any neutral ship that so much as carried licenses to trade with England. What was worse, the Milan Decree stated that ships that had been boarded by British authorities—even against their crew's will—were subject to immediate French capture.

Many Americans viewed the escalating French and English sanctions as insulting treachery that cried out for an American response. The *Washington Federalist* newspaper observed, "We have never, on any occasion, witnessed . . . such a thirst for revenge." But Jefferson stayed calm. He had insisted on inexpensive government, lobbied for American neutrality, and hoped for renewed prosperity through continuing trade with Europe. War would destroy his entire agenda. But clearly Jefferson had to do something.

Believing that Europeans were far more dependent on American goods and ships than Americans were on European money and manufactures, Jefferson chose to violate one of his cardinal principles: the U.S. government would interfere in the economy to force Europeans to recognize American neutral rights. In December 1807, the president announced the **Embargo Act**, which would, in effect, close all American foreign trade as of January 1 unless the Europeans agreed to recognize America's neutral rights.

CRISES IN THE NATION

★ How did Jefferson's economic and Indian policies influence national developments after 1808?

★ How did problems in Europe, coupled with the actions of frontier politicians such as William Henry Harrison, lead the nation into war in 1812?

Jefferson's reaction to European aggression immediately began strangling American trade and with it America's domestic economy. In addition, European countries still had legitimate claims on much of North America, and the Indians who continued to occupy most of the continent could pose a serious threat to the United States if properly motivated. While impressment, blockade, and embargo paralyzed America's Atlantic frontier, a combination of European and Indian hostility along the western frontier added to the air of national emergency. The resulting series of domestic crises played havoc with Jefferson's vision of a peaceful, prosperous nation.

Economic Depression

Although Jefferson felt justified in suspending free trade to protect neutral rights, the result was the worst economic depression since the founding of the British colonies in North America. Critics such as John Randolph pronounced Jefferson's solution worse than the problem—like trying "to cure corns by cutting off the toes." And while Jefferson's "damn-bargo," as critics called it, was only halfheartedly enforced, the economy slumped disastrously. Taken together, all American exports fell from $109 million to $22 million, and net earnings from shipping fell by almost 50 percent. During 1808, earnings from legitimate business enterprise in America declined to less than a quarter of their value in 1807.

The depression shattered economic and social life in many eastern towns. It has been estimated that thirty thousand sailors were thrown out of work and that as many as a hundred thousand people employed in support industries were laid off. During 1808 in

frigate A very fast warship, rigged with square sails and carrying from thirty to fifty cannon on two gun decks.

broadside The simultaneous discharge of all the guns on one side of a warship.

■ **Milan Decree** Napoleon's order authorizing the capture of any neutral vessels sailing from British ports or submitting to British searches.

■ **Embargo Act** Embargo (a government-ordered trade ban) announced by Jefferson in 1807 to pressure Britain and France to accept neutral trading rights; it went into effect in 1808 and closed down all U.S. foreign trade.

New York City alone, 120 businesses went bankrupt, and the combination of unemployment and business failure led to the imprisonment of twelve hundred New Yorkers for debt. New England, where the economy was almost entirely dependent on foreign trade, was hit harder still. In light of Jefferson's policies and the collapsing economy, the extremism expressed by the Essex Junto three years earlier began to sound reasonable.

New Englanders screamed loudest about the impact of the embargo, but southerners and westerners were just as seriously affected by it. The economy of the South had depended on the export of staple crops like tobacco since colonial times and was rapidly turning to cotton. There, embargo meant near-death to all legitimate trade. In response to the loss of foreign markets, tobacco prices fell from $6.75 per hundredweight to $3.25, and cotton from 21 to 13 cents per pound. In the West, wholesale prices for agricultural products spiraled downward also. Overall, the prices of farm products were 16 percent lower between 1807 and 1811 than they had been between 1791 and 1801. At the same time, the price of virtually every consumer item went up. For example, the price of building materials—hardware, glass, and milled lumber—rose 11 percent during the same period, and the price of textiles climbed 20 percent. In fact, the only consumer item that did not go up in price was the one item farmers did not need to buy: food. Faced with dropping incomes and soaring costs, farmers probably felt the trade restrictions more profoundly than others.

Rather than blaming their problems on the Republican administration, however, disaffected farmers directed their anger at the British. Frontiersmen believed, rightly or wrongly, that eliminating British interference with American trade would restore the boom economy that had drawn so many of them to the edge of American settlement. Thus westerners banded together to raise their voices in favor of war against Britain.

Political Upheaval

Despite the escalating crisis in the country, Jefferson remained popular and powerful, but like Washington, he chose to step down from the presidency after serving two terms, making it clear to party officials that he favored James Madison to replace him. Although Madison and Jefferson had much in common and were longtime friends, they seemed very different from each other. Few could say they knew Madison well, but those who did found him captivating: a man of few words but of piercing intellect and unflinching conviction. Those less well acquainted with him thought the quiet Virginian indecisive: where Jefferson tended to act on impulse, Madison approached matters of state as he approached matters of political philosophy—with caution, patience, and reason.

Dissatisfied with Jefferson's policies, both southern and northeastern party members contested Madison's succession. The Tertium Quid challenged Jefferson's authority in the **party caucus** and tried to secure the nomination for the stately and conservative **James Monroe**. Jefferson managed to hold the party's southern wing in line, but northeasterners, stinging under the pressure of the embargo, bucked the decision of the party caucus and nominated their own presidential candidate: New Yorker George Clinton. Although Clinton polled only six electoral votes, his nomination was a sign of growing divisions over the problems that the United States faced in 1808. Despite all the political contention, Madison also easily defeated his Federalist opponent, Charles Cotesworth Pinckney. But Federalist criticism of Jefferson's policies, especially of the embargo, was finding a growing audience as the depression deepened, and in the congressional elections the Republicans lost twenty-four seats to Federalists.

During Madison's first two years in office, lack of any progress toward resolving the nation's woes seemed to confirm critics' perception of his indecisiveness. Nevertheless, Republicans actually made gains in the congressional elections in 1810: they regained fourteen of the seats they had lost in the House in 1808 and picked up two additional Senate seats. But this was no vote of confidence in Madison. Though the new congressmen were Republicans, sixty-three of them did not support Madison or his commitment to a conciliatory policy toward the British. These new members of Congress were mostly very young, extremely patriotic, and represented frontier constituents who were being ravaged by the agricultural depression. In the months to come, their increasingly strident demands for aggressive action against England earned them the nickname **War Hawks**.

The Rise of the Shawnee Prophet

A key reason for War Hawk militancy was the unsettled conditions along the western frontier. Relations with Indians in the West had been peaceful since the Battle of Fallen Timbers in 1794. The Shawnees and other groups had been thrown off their traditional

party caucus A meeting of members of a political party to decide on questions of policy, leadership, or candidates running for office.

■ **James Monroe** Republican politician from Virginia who served in diplomatic posts under George Washington, John Adams, and Thomas Jefferson; he later became the fifth president of the United States.

■ **War Hawks** Members of Congress elected in 1810 from the West and South who campaigned for war with Britain in the hopes of stimulating the economy and annexing new territory.

homelands in Ohio by the Treaty of Greenville and forced to move to new lands in Indiana. There, food shortages, disease, and continuing encroachment by settlers caused many young Indians to lose faith in their traditional beliefs and in themselves as human beings.

In the midst of the crisis, one disheartened, diseased alcoholic rose above his afflictions to lead the Indians into a brief new era of hope. Like others of his generation, Lalawethika felt increasingly hopeless, turned to alcohol, and finally in 1805 became critically ill. He claimed that he remembered dying and meeting the Master of Life and then awoke cured of his illness. Launching a full-fledged religious and cultural revival designed to teach the ways revealed to him by the Master of Life, he adopted the name Tenskwatawa ("the Way"). Whites called him **The Prophet**.

Blaming the decline of his people on their adoption of white ways, the Prophet taught them to go back to their traditional lifestyle—to discard whites' clothing, religion, and especially alcohol—and live as their ancestors had lived. He also urged his followers to unify against the temptations and threats of white exploiters and to hold on to what remained of their lands. If they followed his teachings, the Prophet insisted, the whites would vanish from their world. In 1807 the Prophet established a religious settlement, Prophetstown, on the banks of Tippecanoe Creek in Indiana Territory. This community was to serve as a center for the Prophet's activities and as a living model for revitalized Indian life.

Although the Prophet preached a message of ethnic pride, nonviolence, and passive resistance, as white settlers continued to pressure his people, he began to advocate more forceful solutions. In a speech to an intertribal council in April 1807, he suggested for the first time that warriors unite to resist white expansion. Although he did not urge his followers to attack the whites, he made it clear that the Master of Life would defend him and his followers if war were pressed on them.

Prophecy and Politics in the West

While Tenskwatawa continued to stress spiritual means for stopping white aggression, his brother Tecumseh pushed for a more political course of action. Seven years older than the Prophet, Tecumseh had always inclined more toward politics and warfare. Known as a brave fighter and a persuasive political orator, Tecumseh traveled throughout the western frontier, working out political and military alliances designed to put a stop to white expansion once and for all. Although he did not want to start a war against white settlers, Tecumseh exhorted Indians to defend every inch of land that remained to them.

Tecumseh's plan might have brought about his brother's goals. Faced by a unified defensive line of Indians stretching along the American frontier from Canada to the Gulf of Mexico, the United States probably would have found it virtually impossible to expand any farther, and the Indian confederacy would have become a significant force in America's future. Concerns soon led to rumors that the Shawnee leader was a British agent and that his activities were an extension of some hidden international plot. Though wrong, such theories helped to escalate the air of crisis in the West and in the nation at large.

Indiana governor William Henry Harrison had good reason to advance the impression of a conspiracy between Tecumseh and the British. Harrison and men like him believed the United States had the right to control all of North America and, accordingly, to brush aside anything standing in the way (see Map 9.1). Britain and the Indians were thus linked in their minds. Both were seen as obstacles to national destiny, and many War Hawks prayed for the outbreak of war between the United States and the British with the Indians in between. Such a war would provide an excuse to attack the Indians and dispossess them of their land. In addition, a war would justify invading and seizing Canada, fulfilling what many considered a logical but frustrated objective of the American Revolution. Taking Canada from the British would open rich timber, fur, and agricultural lands for American settlement. More important, it would secure American control of the Great Lakes and St. Lawrence River—potentially a very valuable shipping route for agricultural produce.

Choosing War

With the nation reeling from the economic squeeze of the embargo, Congress replaced it with the **Non-Intercourse Act** early in 1809. The new law forbade trade only with England and France and gave the president the power to reopen trade if either of the combatants lifted its restrictions against American shipping. Even though this act was much less restrictive than the embargo, American merchants were relieved when it expired in the spring of 1810. At that

■ **The Prophet (Tenskwatawa)** Shawnee religious visionary who called for a return to Indian traditions and founded the community of Prophetstown on Tippecanoe Creek in Indiana.

■ **Non-Intercourse Act** 1809 law reopening trade with all nations except France and Britain and authorizing the president to reopen trade with them if they lifted restrictions on American shipping.

MAP 9.1 **Tecumseh's Potential Alliance**
Between 1806 and the outbreak of the War of 1812, Tecumseh traveled up and down the Trans-Appalachian
West recruiting allies for a unified Indian confederacy to oppose any further American westward expansion.
Had Tecumseh succeeded, the history of the United States would undoubtedly have been very different.
Copyright © Cengage Learning

point, Congress passed an even more permissive boy-cott, **Macon's Bill No. 2**. According to this new law, merchants could trade with the combatants if they wanted to take the risk, but if either France or England lifted its blockade, the United States would stop trading with the other.

Hoping to cut England off from needed outside supplies, Napoleon responded to Macon's Bill in August by promising to suspend French restrictions on American shipping while secretly ordering the continued seizure of American ships. Despite Napoleon's devious intentions, Madison sought to use the French peace overture as a lever: he instructed the American mission in London to tell the British that he would close down trade with them unless they joined France in dropping trade restrictions. Sure that Napoleon was lying, the British refused, backing the president into a diplomatic corner. In February 1811, the provisions

■ **Macon's Bill No. 2** 1810 law that offered exclusive trading rights to France or Britain, whichever recognized American neutral rights first.

Although they had enormous respect for each other, Indiana territorial governor William Henry Harrison and Tecumseh were both ferocious when it came to defending their political and diplomatic positions. This painting of their confrontation at the 1810 peace conference held at Vincennes makes this point clearly. The two never actually came to blows at this meeting or at another held one year later, but they never were able to find common ground.

of Macon's Bill forced Madison to close trading with Britain for its failure to remove economic sanctions, stepping up tensions all around.

Later in the year, events in the West finally triggered a crisis. The origin of the problem was an agreement, the Fort Wayne Treaty, signed in the fall of 1809 between the United States and representatives of the Miami, Potawatomi, and Delaware Indians. In return for an outright bribe of $5,200 and individual **annuities** ranging from $250 to $500, accommodationists among these three tribes sold over 3 million acres of Indian land in Indiana and Illinois—land already occupied by many other Indian groups.

In August 1810, Tecumseh met with Governor Harrison in Vincennes, Indiana, to denounce the Fort Wayne Treaty. Harrison insisted that the agreement was legitimate. Speaking for those whose lands had been sold out from under them, Tecumseh said, "They want to save that piece of land, we do not wish you to take it. . . . I want the present boundary line to continue. Should you cross it, I assure you it will be productive of bad consequences." But Harrison refused to budge.

The Vincennes meeting convinced the Indians that they must prepare for a white attack. Tecumseh traveled up and down the American frontier, enlisting additional allies in his growing Indian confederacy. Meanwhile, Harrison grew more and more eager to attack the Indians before they could unite fully. He got his chance when a second peace conference in the summer of 1811 also failed. Citing the failed peace effort and sporadic skirmishes between frontier settlers and renegade bands of Indians, none of which were connected to Tecumseh, Harrison ordered an attack. On November 7, in the so-called **Battle of Tippecanoe**, an army of enraged frontiersmen burned Prophetstown. Then, having succeeded in setting the Indian frontier ablaze, Harrison called for a declaration of war against the Indians and the British.

annuity An allowance or income paid annually.

■ **Battle of Tippecanoe** Battle near Prophetstown in 1811, where American forces led by William Henry Harrison defeated the followers of the Shawnee Prophet and destroyed the town.

While the army experienced a string of embarrassing losses during the opening days of the War of 1812, the navy outperformed all expectations. This contemporary engraving celebrates the victory of the USS *United States* over the British HMS *Macedonian*. In a protracted battle, the Americans splintered the British ship with seventy broadsides, capturing her as a prize of war.

ca. 1813 engraving. The Granger Collection, New York.

the Republican congressmen—mostly those from New York and New England—rallied around New Yorker DeWitt Clinton. Like his uncle George Clinton, DeWitt Clinton was a Republican who favored Federalist economic policies and agreed with New England Federalists that the war was unnecessary. Most Federalists supported Clinton, and the party did not field a candidate of its own.

The campaign's outcome mirrored the congressional vote on the war bill earlier in the year. New York and New England rallied behind Clinton. The South and West continued to support Madison, the Republicans, and war. Madison won, but his share of electoral votes had fallen from 72 percent in 1808 to 58.9 percent. At the same time, Republican Party strength in the House dropped by over 13 percent, and in the Senate by about 8 percent.

"one of our stoutest frigates," the H.M.S. *Guerrière*. The *United States,* under the command of Stephen Decatur, both endured and delivered horrific broadsides while subduing the British *Macedonian.* The carnage Decatur described when he boarded the crippled vessel was typical of naval warfare at the time: "fragments of the dead scattered in every direction, the decks slippery with blood." American privateers also enjoyed success, capturing 450 British merchant ships valued in the millions during the first six months of the war.

American naval victories were all that kept the nation's morale alive in 1812. Former Treasury secretary Albert Gallatin summarized the nation's humiliating military efforts: "The series of misfortunes exceeds all anticipations made even by those who had least confidence in our inexperienced officers and undisciplined men." The land war had been, as another politician recalled, a "miscarriage, without even the heroism of disaster." Vowing to reverse the situation, Congress increased the size of the army to fifty-seven thousand men and offered a $16 bonus to encourage enlistments.

Thus in 1812 Madison stood for reelection at a time when the nation's military fate appeared uncertain and his own leadership equally so. Although the majority of his party's congressional caucus supported him for reelection, nearly a third of

The War Continues

When military campaigning resumed in the spring of 1813, it appeared that the U.S. Army would fare as badly as it had the previous fall. Fighting resumed when British colonel Henry Proctor and Tecumseh, with a joint force of nine hundred British soldiers and twelve hundred Indians, laid siege to Harrison's command camped at Fort Meigs on the Maumee Rapids in Ohio. An army of twelve hundred Kentucky militiamen finally arrived and drove the enemy off but were so disorganized that they lost nearly half their number in pursuing the British and Indian force. Harrison was shocked, proclaiming the Kentuckians' "excessive ardour scarcely less fatal than cowardice." Having escaped virtually unscathed, Proctor and Tecumseh continued to harass American forces through the summer. Then, with winter approaching, the British and Indians withdrew to Canada. Harrison, who had been busy raising additional troops, decided to pursue.

No doubt Harrison's new effort would have proved as fruitless as his earlier ones, but an unexpected event turned the odds in his favor. One key problem plaguing Harrison and other commanders in the field was that the British controlled the Great Lakes and so could depend on an uninterrupted supply line. In contrast, American forces and their supplies moved along undeveloped roads and were easy targets for

Indian and British attackers. **Oliver Hazard Perry**, a young naval tactician, had been given command of a small fleet assigned to clear the lakes of British ships. He got his chance at Put-in-Bay on Lake Erie in September 1813. Two hours of cannon fire left Perry's **flagship**, the *Lawrence*, nearly destroyed, and 80 percent of the crew lay dead or wounded. Perry refused to surrender. He slipped off his damaged vessel and took command of another ship standing nearby. What remained of his command then sailed back into the heart of the British force and after three hours of close combat subdued and captured six British ships. Perry immediately sent a note to Harrison stating, "We have met the enemy and they are ours."

Buoyed by this news, Harrison's army closed in on Proctor and Tecumseh at the Thames River, about 50 miles northeast of Detroit, on October 5. The British force faced a piercing cavalry charge and, lacking naval support, abandoned their Indian allies and fled. The Indians held out longer, but when word spread that Tecumseh had been killed, they melted into the woods, leaving the body of their fallen leader to be torn apart by the victorious Americans.

Another war front had also opened farther south during 1813. Although the Creek Confederacy as a whole wished to remain neutral, one faction calling themselves the Red Sticks had allied with Tecumseh in 1812. In the summer of 1813, Red Stick leader William Weatherford led a force against Fort Mims, killing all but about thirty of the more than three hundred occupants. The so-called Fort Mims massacre enraged whites in the Southeast. In Tennessee, twenty-five hundred militiamen rallied around **Andrew Jackson**, a young brawler and Indian fighter. Already called "Old Hickory" because of his toughness, Jackson made a bold promise: "The blood of our women & children shall not call for vengeance in vain." In the course of that summer and fall, Jackson's frontier ruffians fought multiple engagements against the Red Stick Creeks, driving them into hiding.

While these battles raged on land, the British shut down American forces at sea. Embarrassed by the success of Old Ironsides and the other American frigates, the British admiralty ordered that "the naval force of the enemy should be quickly and completely disposed of" and sent sufficient ships to do the job. The American naval fleet and **merchant marine** found themselves bottled up in port by the world's strongest navy.

The Politics of War

The war had wound down for the winter by the time Congress reconvened in December 1813, but the outlook was not good. President Madison tried to be optimistic. Recalling the victories during the year, he said, "The war, with its **vicissitudes**, is illustrating the capacity and destiny of the United States to be a great, a flourishing, and a powerful nation." Madison's optimism seemed justified later in December when the British offered to open direct peace negotiations with the Americans. The president quickly formed a peace commission, but until its work was done, Madison and Congress still had to worry about the practical issues of troops and money, both of which were in critically short supply.

Despite increases in army pay and bonuses for new recruits, enlistments were falling off in 1813. Congressional Republicans responded by adding further enticements, including grants of 160 acres of land in the western territories. Congress also authorized the president to extend the term of enlistment for men already in service. By 1814, the army had increased to more than sixty-two thousand men but Congress had not figured out how to pay them.

Traditional enemies of internal taxes, the Republicans faced a dilemma: in the federal budget for 1814 the government's income would be approximately $16 million, but its expenses would amount to over $45 million. Congress had already passed a set of new taxes and could not imagine explaining another increase to their constituents. So congressional Republicans decided to borrow instead, authorizing a $35 million deficit.

Adding to the money problem, the United States, to this point in the war, had permitted neutral nations to trade freely in American ports, carrying American exports to England and Canada and English goods into eastern U.S. ports. As a result American food was rolling directly into British military commissaries, strengthening the enemy's ability and will to fight.

In a secret message to Congress, the president proposed an absolute embargo on all American ships and goods—neither were to leave port. Federalists, especially those from New England, screamed in protest. They called the proposal "an engine of tyranny." But congressional Republicans passed the embargo a mere eight days after Madison submitted it. What emerged, the **Embargo of 1813**, was the most far-reaching trade

■ **Oliver Hazard Perry** American naval officer who led the fleet that defeated the British in the Battle of Put-in-Bay during the War of 1812.

flagship The ship that carries the fleet commander and bears the commander's flag.

■ **Andrew Jackson** General who defeated the Creeks at Horseshoe Bend in 1814 and the British at New Orleans in 1815; he later became the seventh president of the United States.

merchant marine A nation's commercial ships.

vicissitudes Sudden or unexpected changes in circumstances.

■ **Embargo of 1813** An absolute embargo on all American trade and British imports.

In frustration at failing to capture members of the U.S. government, the British pillaged Washington in August 1814 and then burned the public buildings. This painting captures the disordered scene as city-dwellers try to quench the flames while the capitol building blazes in the background.

restriction bill ever passed by Congress. It confined all trading ships to port, and even fishing vessels could put to sea only if their masters posted sizable **bonds**. Government officials charged with enforcing the new law had unprecedented **discretionary powers**. The impact was devastating: the embargo virtually shut down the New England and New York economies, and it severely crippled the economy of nearly every other state.

New British Offensives

While Congress debated matters of finance and trade restrictions, events in Europe were changing the entire character of the war. On March 31, 1814, the British and their allies took Paris, forcing Napoleon to

bond A sum of money paid as bail or security.
discretionary powers Powers to be used at one's own judgment; in government, powers given to an administrative official to be used without outside consultation or oversight.

abdicate his throne. Napoleon's defeat left the United States as Great Britain's sole military target. Republican Joseph Nicholson expressed a common lament when he observed, "We should have to fight hereafter not for 'free Trade and sailors rights,' not for the Conquest of the Canadas, but for our national Existence." As Nicholson feared, a flood of combat-hardened British veterans began arriving in North America, and the survival of the United States as an independent nation was indeed at issue. By the late summer of 1814, British troop strength in Canada had risen to thirty thousand men. From this position of power, the British prepared a chain of three offensives to bring the war to a quick end.

In the first of these, twenty British warships and several troop transports sailed up Chesapeake Bay toward Washington, D.C. The British arrived outside Washington at midday on August 24. The troops defending the city could not withstand the force of hardened British veterans, but they slowed the invasion long enough for the government to escape.

As part of a three-pronged British offensive designed to bring the war to an end, Governor-General George Prevost led an invasion from Canada into New York. As illustrated here, In the Battle of Plattsburgh, American defenders were able to defeat the British support fleet and turn back the invasion.

Angered at being foiled, the British sacked the city, torching most of the buildings. They then moved on toward the key port city of Baltimore.

At Baltimore, the British navy had to knock out Fort McHenry and take the harbor before the army could take the city. On September 13, British ships armed with heavy **mortars** and rockets attacked the fort. Despite the pounding, when the sun rose on September 14, the American flag continued to wave over Fort McHenry. The sight moved a young prisoner of war held on a British ship, **Francis Scott Key**, to record the event in a poem that was later set to music and became the national anthem of the United States. Having failed to reduce the fort, the British were forced to withdraw, leaving Baltimore undisturbed.

While this strike at the nation's midsection was raging, Sir George Prevost, governor-general of Canada, massed ten thousand troops for an invasion in the north. The British force arrived just north of Plattsburgh, New York, on September 6, where it was to join the British naval fleet that controlled Lake Champlain. However, a small American flotilla under the command of Lieutenant Thomas Macdonough outmaneuvered the imposing British armada and forced a surrender on September 11. Prevost had already begun his attack against the defenders at Plattsburgh, but when he learned that the British lake fleet was defeated, he lost his nerve and ordered his men to retreat.

On yet another front, the British pressed an offensive against the Gulf Coast designed to take pressure off Canada and close transportation on the Mississippi River. The defense of the Gulf Coast fell to Andrew Jackson and his Tennesseans. Having spent the winter raising troops and collecting supplies, in March 1814 Jackson and his army of four thousand militiamen and Cherokee volunteers resumed their mission to punish the Red Stick Creeks. Learning that the Red Sticks had established a camp on the peninsula formed by a bend in the Tallapoosa River, Jackson led his men on a forced march to attack. On March 27 in what was misleadingly called the **Battle of Horseshoe Bend**, Jackson's force trapped the Creeks and slaughtered nearly eight hundred people, destroying Red Stick opposition and severely crippling Indian resistance in the South.

After the massacre at Horseshoe Bend, Jackson moved his army toward the Gulf of Mexico, where a British offensive was in the making. Arriving in New Orleans on December 1, he found the city ill prepared to defend itself. The local militia, consisting mostly of French and Spanish residents, would not obey American officers. "Those who are not for us are against us, and will be dealt with accordingly,"

mortar A portable, muzzle-loading cannon that fires large projectiles; traditionally used against fixed fortifications.

■ **Francis Scott Key** Author of "The Star-Spangled Banner," which chronicles the British bombardment of Fort McHenry in 1814; Key's poem, set to music, became the official U.S. national anthem in 1931.

■ **Battle of Horseshoe Bend** Attack in 1814 in which Tennessee militia massacred Creek Indians in Alabama, ending Red Stick resistance to white westward expansion.

Jackson proclaimed. He turned increasingly to unconventional sources of support. Free blacks in the city formed a regular army corps, and Jackson created a special unit of black refugees from Saint-Domingue. He also accepted a company of river pirates under the command of **Jean Lafitte**, awarding them a blanket pardon for all past crimes. "Hellish Banditti," Jackson himself called them, but the pirate commander and the general hit it off so well that Lafitte became Jackson's constant companion during the campaign.

Having pulled his ragtag force together, Jackson settled in to wait for the British attack. On the morning of January 8, 1815, it came. The British force, commanded by General Edward Pakenham, emerged from the fog at dawn, directly in front of Jackson's defenses. Waiting patiently behind hastily constructed barricades, Jackson's men began firing cannon, rifles, and muskets as the British moved within range. According to one British veteran, it was "the most murderous fire I have ever beheld before or since."

When it was all over, more than two thousand British troops had been killed or wounded in the **Battle of New Orleans**. This was by far the most successful battle fought by American forces during the War of 1812. But ironically, it was fought after the war was over.

The War's Strange Conclusion

While the British were closing in on Washington in the summer of 1814, treaty negotiations designed to end the war were beginning in Ghent, Belgium. Confident that their three-pronged attack against the United States would soon knock the Americans out of the war, the British delegates were in no hurry to end it by diplomacy. They refused to discuss substantive issues, insisting that all of the matters raised by Madison's peace commission were nonnegotiable.

At that point, however, domestic politics in England began to play a deciding role. After nearly a generation of armed conflict, British taxpayers were war weary. As one official put it, "Economy & relief from taxation . . . are the real objects to which public attention

is turned." The failures at Plattsburgh and Baltimore made it appear that the war would drag on at least another year, adding another $44 million to the British tax burden. Moreover, continuation of the American war was interfering with Britain's European diplomacy: "We do not think the Continental Powers will continue in good humour with our Blockade of the whole Coast of America," one British diplomat observed. Speaking for the military, the **Duke of Wellington** reviewed British military successes and failures in the American war and advised his countrymen, "You have no right . . . to demand any **concession** . . . from America."

In the end, the **Treaty of Ghent**, completed on December 24, 1814, simply restored diplomatic relations between England and the United States to what they had been prior to the outbreak of war. The treaty said nothing about impressment, blockades, or neutral trading rights. Neither military action nor diplomatic finagling netted Canada for the War Hawks. And the treaty did nothing about the alleged conspiracies between Indians and British agents. Although Americans called the War of 1812 a victory, they actually won none of the prizes that Madison's war statement had declared the nation was fighting for.

PEACE AND THE RISE OF NEW EXPECTATIONS

☆ How did events during the War of 1812 help to move the American economy in new directions after peace was restored?

☆ How did changes in the economy affect the institution of slavery and the lives of slaves?

Despite repeated military disasters, loss of life, and diplomatic failure, the war had a number of positive effects on the United States. Just to have survived a war against the British was enough to build national confidence, but to have scored major victories such as those at Plattsburgh, Baltimore, and especially New Orleans was truly worth boasting about. Americans emerged from the conflict with a new sense of national pride and purpose. And many side effects from the fighting itself gave Americans new hopes and stimulated new plans.

New Expectations in the Northeastern Economy

Although trading interests in the Northeast suffered following Jefferson's embargo and were nearly ruined by the war and Madison's embargo, a new avenue of economic expansion opened in New England: cut off from European manufactured goods, Americans started to make more textiles and other items for themselves.

Luddites

As Americans began to embrace mechanized manufacturing, many in Great Britain were protesting its unsettling impact. During 1811 and 1812, men calling themselves Luddites—a name taken from a fictional leader, "King Ludd"—began attacking and destroying mechanized factories. Although we now use the term Luddite to describe people who oppose modernization, that was not the point among the original Luddites. It took no special training, no craft skill, to run a power loom, and so weavers and other traditional craftsmen found themselves losing status, wages, and control over their own labor. They protested these losses by destroying the machines they blamed for demeaning them. The Luddites were eventually put down by the British military, and in 1812 Parliament passed the Frame Breaking Act, which made destroying factory equipment an offense punishable by death.

Samuel Slater, an English immigrant who had been trained in manufacturing in Britain, introduced the use of machines for spinning cotton yarn to the United States in 1790. His mill was financially successful, but few others tried to copy his enterprise. Even with shipping expenses, tariffs, and other added costs, buying and selling machine-made British cloth was still more practical than investing large sums at high risk to build competing factories in the United States. And after 1800, Jefferson's economic policies discouraged such investment. But his embargo changed all that. After it went into effect in 1808, British fabrics became increasingly unavailable, and prices soared. Slater and his partners moved quickly to expand their spinning operations to fill the void. And now his inventiveness was widely copied.

Another entrepreneur, Francis Cabot Lowell, went even further than Slater. On a trip to England in 1810, he engaged in wholesale industrial espionage, making detailed notes and sketches of British textile-manufacturing practices and machinery. Returning to the United States just before war broke out in 1812, Lowell formed the Boston Manufacturing Company. In 1813 the company used the plans Lowell had smuggled back to the United States to build a factory in Waltham, Massachusetts. The new facility included spinning machines, power looms, and all the equipment necessary to **mechanize** every stage in the production of finished cloth, bringing the entire process under one roof. Like Slater's innovations, Lowell's too were soon duplicated by economically desperate New Englanders.

The spread of textile manufacturing was astonishing. Prior to 1808, only fifteen cotton mills had been built in the entire country. But between the passage of the embargo and the end of 1809, eighty-seven additional mills had sprung up, mostly in New England. And when war came, the pace increased, especially when Lowell's idea of a factory mechanizing production through finished cloth proved to be highly efficient and profitable. The number of people employed in manufacturing increased from four thousand in 1809 to perhaps as many as a hundred thousand in 1816. In the years to come, factories in New England and elsewhere supplied more and more of the country's consumer goods.

New Opportunities in the West

Different kinds of development took place in the West following the war. Settlers poured into western regions in astounding numbers. The population of Ohio had already soared from 45,000 in 1800 to 231,000 in 1810, but it more than doubled again by 1820, reaching 581,000. Indiana, Illinois, Missouri, and Michigan experienced similar growth. Most of those who flooded into the newly opened West were small farmers, but subsistence agriculture was not the only economic opportunity that drew expectant Americans into the region.

One of the designs behind the Lewis and Clark expedition had been to gain entry for the United States into the burgeoning economy in North America's interior. That economy was complex, with many commodities being traded, and few entirely understood all of its intricacies. There was one facet, though, that was well known and very desirable to entrepreneurs: the brown gold of beaver, otter, and other animal furs. Even before the War of 1812, John Jacob Astor, a German immigrant, announced that he intended to establish "a range of Posts or Trading houses" along the route that Lewis and Clark had followed from St. Louis to the Pacific (see Map 8.2, page 198).

mechanize To substitute machinery for human labor.

The outcome of Whitney's inventiveness was the rapid spread of short-staple cotton throughout inland South Carolina and Georgia. Then, just as it seemed that the southern economy was about to bloom, embargo and war closed down exports to England. Although some cotton growers were able to shift sales from England to the rising new factories in New England, a true explosion of growth in cotton cultivation had to await war's end.

With the arrival of peace and the departure of the British naval blockade, cotton growing began to spread at an astounding rate. Southerners rushed into frontier areas, spreading cotton agriculture into Alabama and Mississippi and then into Arkansas and northern Louisiana. Even the Mississippi River seemed to present no serious barrier to this runaway expansion. In 1821 Spanish authorities gave long-time western land speculator Moses Austin permission to settle three hundred American families within a 200,000-acre tract in Texas between the Brazos and Colorado Rivers. When the elder Austin died, his son, **Stephen F. Austin**, took over the enterprise and was able to offer families large plots of land for a filing fee of only 12½ cents an acre. "I am convinced," he exclaimed, "that I could take on fifteen hundred families as easily as three hundred if permitted to do so." Throughout the 1820s and 1830s, Austin and other *empresarios* helped thousands of hopeful cotton capitalists to expand into Mexican territory. As a result of this expansion, the South's annual cotton crop grew by leaps and bounds. By 1840, annual exports reached nearly a million and a half bales, and increasing volumes were consumed within the United States by the mushrooming textile factories in the Northeast.

COTTON-GIN—GINNING COTTON.

Photo by MPI/Getty Images.

The invention of the cotton gin and the spread of cotton agriculture throughout the American South created an enormous new demand for slave workers and changed the nature of their work. A handful of slaves (only two in this illustration of the process) could comb through large amounts of fiber, but it took armies of field workers to produce the raw cotton that kept the machinery (and the plantation system) working.

Reviving and Reinventing Slavery

Before the emergence of cotton, when the South's agricultural system was foundering, many southerners began to question the use of slaves. In 1784 Thomas Jefferson proposed (but saw defeated) a land ordinance that would have prohibited slavery in all of the nation's territories after 1800. Some southern leaders advocated abolishing slavery and transporting freed blacks to Africa. But the booming southern economy after the War of 1812 required more labor than ever. As a result, African American slavery expanded as never before.

Viewed side by side, a map showing cotton agriculture and one showing slave population appear nearly identical (see Map 9.3). In the 1820s, when cotton production was most heavily concentrated in South Carolina and Georgia, the greatest density of slaves occurred in the same area. During the 1840s, as cotton growing spread to the West, slavery followed. By 1860, both cotton growing and slavery appear on the map as a continuous belt stretching from the Carolinas through Georgia and Alabama and on to the Mississippi River.

■ **Stephen F. Austin** American colonizer in Texas and later a leading voice in the Texas Revolution.

empresario In the Spanish colonies, a person who organized and led a group of settlers in exchange for land grants and the right to assess fees.

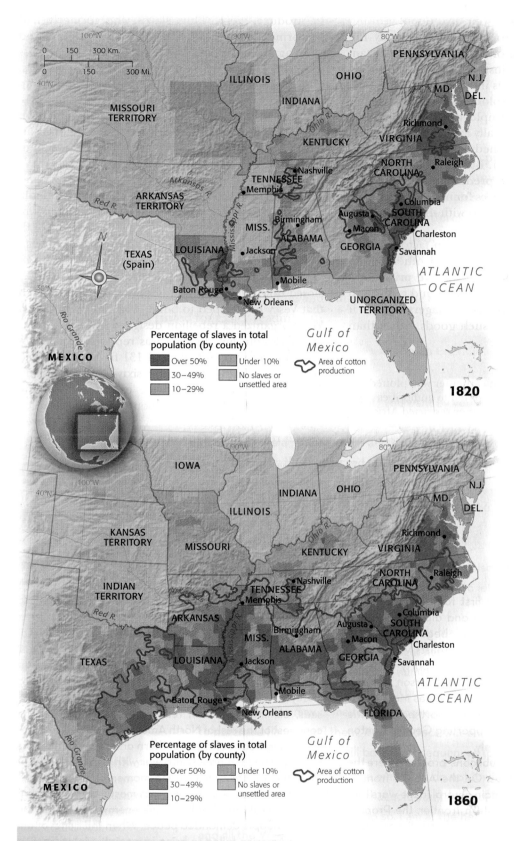

MAP 9.3 Cotton Agriculture and Slave Population

Between 1820 and 1860, the expansion of cotton agriculture and the extension of slavery went hand in hand. As these maps show, cotton production was an isolated activity in 1820, and slavery remained isolated as well. By 1860, both had extended westward. Copyright © Cengage Learning

Consistent with views expressed in the *Argus*, the Bucktails emphasized grassroots community organizing along with strong party principles and strict party discipline. Candidates were to be selected at party conventions and, once named, supported universally by all party members regardless of family or other connections. Failure to adhere to the party line would be punished by being stripped of office or denied political appointments; loyalty, on the other hand, would be rewarded by favors from the party. Using these tactics, by 1820 Van Buren was able to pull together a statewide political machine that unseated the Clintons.

The new kind of politics that Van Buren invented was enormously appealing to a restless generation who wanted to break into the political game. The grassroots style of organization began spreading, as did Van Buren's ideas about how to structure a political party (see the Individual Voices feature at the end of this chapter for one illustration of his thinking). In 1828 he became a leading light in launching an anti-establishment national organization that hitched its political star to the charismatic war hero Andrew Jackson. What emerged was the new, modern style of politics that we have taken for granted for two centuries.

Martin Van Buren was typical of a growing number of Americans in politics. Like his contemporaries Henry Clay and William Henry Harrison, Van Buren made politics a career from very early in life. Unlike them, Van Buren was a political outsider with no family or other coattails to ride into the political arena. But during the 1820s more and more Americans gained access to the levers of government. In this highly charged atmosphere, matters of state became for the first time in the nation's history a topic for debate among people from all regions and from a broad cross-section of occupations and communities. They found the sort of grassroots party organization Van Buren had created enormously appealing. Politics for these newly enfranchised voters was not some gentleman's game but a form of personal combat designed to make their own lives better and to test their wills and their loyalties. Clearly a new day was dawning for American politics and for the whole of American society as well.

AN "ERA OF GOOD FEELINGS"

★ What were the sources for Americans' optimism as they emerged from the War of 1812 and how did the American government capitalize on this optimism?

★ How did new developments in the nation influence foreign affairs?

James Madison had been the butt of jokes and the cause of dissension within his own party during the War of 1812, but he emerged from the war with considerable political clout. Although his fellow Republicans considered his wartime policies indecisive, after the war Madison immediately seized the political initiative to inaugurate vigorous new diplomatic and domestic programs. His successor, James Monroe, then picked up the beat, pressing on with a new nationalistic Republican agenda. The nationalism that arose after the war seemed to bring political dissension to a close; a Federalist newspaper in Boston proclaimed the dawn of an "**Era of Good Feelings**."

The "American System" and New Economic Direction

The nation was much more unified politically in 1815 than it had been for years. The war's outcome and the growth that began to take place immediately following the peace settlement had largely silenced Madison's critics within the Republican Party. And during the waning days of the war, extreme Federalists had so embarrassed their party that they were at a severe political disadvantage.

The Essex Junto was primarily responsible for the Federalists' embarrassment. The junto had capitalized on the many military blunders and growing national debt to cast Republicans in a bad light and was drawing increasing support in the Northeast. In mid-December 1814 they staged the **Hartford Convention**, voting to secede from the Union unless Congress repealed the Embargo of 1813 and passed the slate of constitutional reforms the junto had been pushing since its formation. However, many viewed the Federalists' efforts as either foolish or treasonous, and party popularity underwent a steep decline.

Facing no meaningful opposition, Madison chose in December 1815 to launch an aggressive new domestic policy. He challenged Congress to correct the economic ills that had caused the depression and helped to propel the nation into war. He also encouraged the states to invest in the nation's future by financing transportation systems and other internal improvements. Former critics such as DeWitt Clinton, **Henry Clay**, and **John C. Calhoun** quickly rallied behind the president and his nationalistic economic and political agenda.

Clay took the lead. He had come to Congress as one of the War Hawks in 1810 and had quickly become the dominant voice among the younger representatives. Born in Virginia in 1777, Clay had moved to the wilds of Kentucky to practice law and carve out a career in politics. He was fantastically successful, becoming Speaker of the Kentucky state assembly when he was only 30 years old and winning a seat in the House of Representatives four years later. He became Speaker of the House during the prewar crisis. Now aligning himself firmly with the new economic agenda, Clay became its champion, calling it the **American System**.

What congressional Republicans had in mind was to create a national market economy. In the colonial period and increasingly thereafter, local market economies grew up around the trading and manufacturing centers of the Northeast. Individuals in these areas produced single items for cash sale and used the cash they earned to purchase goods produced by others. Specialization was the natural outcome. Farmers, for example, chose to grow only one or two crops and to sell the whole harvest for cash, which they used to buy various items they had once raised or made for themselves. Clay and others wanted to see such interdependence on a much larger scale. They envisioned a time when whole regions would specialize in producing commodities for which the geography, climate, and the temperament of the people was most suitable. Agricultural regions in the West, for example, would produce food for the industrializing Northeast and the fiber-producing South. The North would depend on the South for efficiently produced cotton, and both South and West would depend on the Northeast for manufactured goods. Advocates of the American System were confident that the balance eventually established among regions would free the nation as a whole from economic dependence on Europe.

Nationalists recognized that one of the first steps in bringing all this about would have to be a national banking authority. Republicans had persistently opposed the Bank of the United States and had killed it in 1811, but the postwar call for a unified national economy prompted Republicans to press again for a national currency and for a national bank to regulate its circulation. In 1816 Calhoun introduced legislation chartering a Second Bank of the United States, which Congress approved overwhelmingly. The Second Bank had many of the same powers and responsibilities as the first. Congress provided $7 million of its $35 million in opening capital and appointed one-fifth of its board of directors. The Second Bank opened for business in Philadelphia on January 1, 1817.

Proponents also saw improvements in transportation and communications as essential. Announcing that they would "bind the republic together with a perfect system of roads and canals," Republicans in Congress put forward a series of proposals designed to achieve this result.

Finally, they advocated **protective tariffs** to help the fledgling industries that had hatched during the war. Helped by the embargoes, American cotton-spinning plants had increased rapidly between 1808 and 1815. But with the return of open trade at war's end, British merchants dumped accumulated inventories of cotton and woolen cloth onto the U.S. market. Although some New England voices protested tariffs as unfair government interference, most northeasterners supported protection. Most southerners and westerners, however, remained leery of its impact on consumer prices. Still, shouting with nationalistic fervor about American economic independence, westerners like Clay and southerners like Calhoun were able to raise enough support to pass Madison's proposed **Tariff of 1816**, opening the way for continued tariff legislation in the years to come.

■ **"Era of Good Feelings"** The period from 1816 to 1823, when the decline of the Federalist Party and the end of the War of 1812 gave rise to a time of political cooperation.

■ **Hartford Convention** A meeting held late in 1814 at which Federalist extremists threatened secession from the Union unless their political demands were met.

■ **Henry Clay** Former congressional War Hawk who became the leading advocate for nationalistic reforms following the War of 1812. He remained in politics well into the 1850s, holding many government offices.

■ **John C. Calhoun** Congressman and constitutional scholar from South Carolina who, with Henry Clay and others, pushed for a nationalist agenda after the War of 1812. He later rejected nationalism and became a leading advocate for states' rights.

■ **American System** An economic plan sponsored by nationalists in Congress; it was intended to capitalize on regional differences to spur U.S. economic growth and the domestic production of goods previously bought from foreign manufacturers.

protective tariff Tax on imported goods intended to make them more expensive than similar domestic goods, thus protecting the market for goods produced at home.

■ **Tariff of 1816** First protective tariff in U.S. history; its purpose was to protect America's fledgling textile industry.

Before the transportation revolution, traveling was highly risky and uncomfortable. This painting shows a rather stylish stagecoach, but its well-dressed passengers are clearly being jostled. Note how the man in the front seat is bracing himself, while the man behind him loses his hat under the wheels.

The popularity of these measures was apparent in the outcome of the 1816 elections. The Republican caucus nominated Virginian James Monroe who won by a decisive electoral majority: 184 votes to Federalist Rufus King's 34. Congressional Republicans enjoyed a similar sweep, winning more than three-fourths of the seats in the House of Representatives and the Senate. Presented with such a powerful mandate and the political clout necessary to carry it out, Republicans immediately set about expanding on the new nationalistic agenda.

The Transportation Problem

It was clear to many after the War of 1812 that only the large-scale resources available to state and federal governments could make a practical difference in the transportation picture. Immediately after the war, Calhoun introduced legislation in Congress to finance a national transportation program. Congress approved, but Madison vetoed the bill, stating that the Constitution did not authorize federal spending on projects designed to benefit individual states. But Calhoun finally won Madison's support by convincing the president that a government-funded national road between Cumberland, Maryland, and Wheeling, Virginia, was a military and postal necessity and therefore the initial federal expenditure of $30,000 for the **Cumberland Road** was constitutional. Construction began in 1815.

Although people and light cargoes might move efficiently along the proposed national road, water transportation remained the most economical way to ship bulky freight. Unfortunately, with few exceptions, navigable rivers and lakes did not link up conveniently to form usable transportation networks. Before the War of 1812, some Americans had considered canals as a likely solution, but enormous costs and engineering problems had limited canal construction to less than 100 miles. After the war, however, the entry of the state and federal governments into transportation development opened the way to an era of canal building.

◘ **Cumberland Road** The initial section of what would be called the "National Road," a highway built with federal funds; this section stretched from Cumberland, Maryland, to Wheeling, Virginia. Later the road would be extended to Vandalia, Illinois, and beyond.

New York State was most successful at canal development. Though Governor DeWitt Clinton hoped to cash in on federal money, Van Buren blocked that move, convincing the state legislature to issue bonds instead. In 1817 the state started work on a canal that would run more than 350 miles from Lake Erie at Buffalo to the Hudson River at Albany. Three thousand workers dug the huge ditch and built the **locks**, dams, and **aqueducts** that would eventually form the **Erie Canal**. The last leg was completed in 1825, and the first barge made its way from Buffalo to Albany and then on to New York City.

Canals were really little more than extensions of natural river courses, and fighting the currents of great rivers remained a problem. Pushed along by current and manpower, a barge could make the trip south from Pittsburgh to New Orleans in about a month. Returning north, against the current, took more than four months, if a boat could make the trip at all. In 1807, however, Robert Fulton's 160-ton steam-powered ship, the *Clermont*, ran upstream from New York City to Albany in an incredibly quick thirty-two hours. Unfortunately, the design of the *Clermont* made it impractical for most of America's rivers. After the war Henry M. Shreve borrowed the hull design of the shallow-draft, broad-beamed keelboats that had been sailing up and down inland streams for generations. Shreve added two lightweight steam engines, each one driving an independent side wheel. He also added an upper deck for passengers, creating the now-familiar multistoried steamboats of southern lore. Funded by merchants in Wheeling, Virginia—soon to be the western terminus for the Cumberland Road—Shreve successfully piloted one of his newly designed boats upriver, from Wheeling to Pittsburgh. Then, in 1816, he made the first successful run south, all the way to New Orleans.

Legal Anchors for New Business Enterprise

President Madison had raised serious constitutional concerns when Henry Clay and his congressional clique proposed spending federal money on road development. Though Calhoun was able to ease the president's mind on this specific matter, many constitutional issues needed clarification if the government was going to play the economic role that nationalists envisioned.

In 1819 the Supreme Court took an important step in clarifying the federal government's role in national economic life. The case arose over an effort by the state of Maryland to raise money by placing **revenue stamps** on federal currency. When a clerk at the Bank of the United States' Baltimore branch, James McCulloch, refused to apply the stamps, he was indicted by the state. In the resulting Supreme Court case, ***McCulloch v. Maryland*** (1819), the majority ruled that the states could not impose taxes on federal institutions and that McCulloch was right in refusing to comply with Maryland's revenue law. But more important, Chief Justice John Marshall wrote, "The Constitution and the laws made in pursuance thereof are supreme: that they control the constitution and laws of the respective states, and cannot be controlled by them." With this, Marshall declared his binding opinion that federal law was superior to state law in all matters.

Marshall reinforced this principle five years later in the landmark case of ***Gibbons v. Ogden*** (1824). In 1808 the state of New York had recognized Robert Fulton's accomplishments in steamboating by granting him an exclusive contract to run steamboats on rivers in that state. Fulton then used this monopoly power to sell licenses to various operators, including Aaron Ogden, who ran a ferry service between New York and New Jersey. Another individual, Thomas Gibbons, was also running a steamboat service in the same area, but he was operating under license from the federal government. When Ogden accused Gibbons of violating his contractual monopoly in a New York court, Gibbons took refuge in federal court. It finally fell to Marshall's Supreme Court to resolve the conflict. Consistent with its earlier decision, the Court ruled in favor of Gibbons, arguing that the New York monopoly conflicted with federal authority and was therefore invalid. In cases of interstate commerce, it ruled, Congress's authority "is complete in itself" and the states could not challenge it.

But it was going to take more than federal authority and investment to revolutionize the economy. Private money would be needed as well, and that too required some constitutional clarification. At issue were contracts, the basis for all business transactions, and their security from interference by either private or public challengers.

---

lock A section of canal with gates at each end, used to raise or lower boats from one level to another by admitting or releasing water; locks allow canals to compensate for changes in terrain.

aqueduct An elevated structure raising a canal to bridge rivers, canyons, or other obstructions.

■ **Erie Canal** A 350-mile canal stretching from Buffalo to Albany; it revolutionized shipping in New York State.

revenue stamps Stickers affixed to taxed items by government officials indicating that the tax has been paid.

■ ***McCulloch v. Maryland*** Supreme Court case (1819) in which the majority ruled that federal authority is superior to that of individual states and that states cannot control or tax federal operations within their borders.

■ ***Gibbons v. Ogden*** Supreme Court case (1824) in which the majority ruled that the authority of Congress is absolute in matters of interstate commerce.

It Matters Today

The Federal Role in Interstate Commerce

Gibbons v. Ogden (1824) established a strong precedent that had far-reaching consequences. At the time of the ruling, interstate commerce was fairly inconsequential; most people in the United States depended on themselves and their immediate neighbors for their needs. But with this ruling in place, as interstate commerce expanded, the power of the federal government expanded, too. It is now virtually impossible to engage in any sort of activity that does not involve interstate commerce. Even in the most private and intimate moments of our lives, objects we use often were manufactured, in whole or in part, in another state; if not, they likely were carried to our local community on interstate highways; and in all cases they were paid for using federal reserve notes. Marshall's decision granting absolute federal authority over interstate commerce thus justified central government jurisdiction over a wide variety of our everyday activities. For example, many civil rights cases during the 1960s and after landed in federal court because interstate commerce was involved.

- Reflecting upon the development of canal and road systems during the early nineteenth century, how did the Supreme Court's decisions concerning interstate commerce and federal supremacy influence the way the nation developed?

- Choose an activity in which you engage on a regular basis—an athletic event, cultural activity, religious act, or something entirely personal and private; virtually anything—and examine what role interstate commerce plays in it. In what ways might the involvement of interstate commerce give the federal government the right to influence or even control that activity? Do you think that degree of influence is justified?

One case from before the war was important in clarifying how federal authorities would deal with matters of contract. The issue was the Yazoo affair, in which the Georgia state legislature had contracted to sell vast tracts of land to private investors. The decision by the legislature to overturn that contract led to a great deal of political fuss, but it created a legal problem also: could a state legislature dissolve an executed contract? This came before Marshall's Court in 1810 with the case of ***Fletcher v. Peck*** (1810). In this case, the Court ruled that even if the original contract was fraudulently obtained, it still was binding and that the state legislature had no right to overturn it. Nor, it ruled in a later case, could a state modify a standing contract. That case, ***Dartmouth College v. Woodward*** (1819), involved Dartmouth College's founding charter, which specified that new members of the board of trustees were to be appointed by the current board. In 1816 the New Hampshire state legislature tried to take over the college by passing a bill that would allow the state's governor to appoint board members. The college brought suit, claiming that its charter was a legal contract and that the legislature had no right to abridge it. Announcing the Court's decision, Marshall noted that the Constitution protected the sanctity of contracts and that state legislatures could not interfere with them.

These and other cases helped ease the way for the development of new business ventures. With private contracts and federal financial bureaus safe from state and local meddling and the superiority of Congress in interstate commerce established, businesses had the security they needed to expand into new areas and attempt to turn Clay's dream of a national market economy into a reality. And private investors knew that their involvement in often risky ventures was protected, at least from the whims of politicians.

■ ***Fletcher v. Peck*** Supreme Court case (1810) growing out of the Yazoo affair in which the majority ruled that the original land sale contract rescinded by the Georgia legislature was binding, establishing the superiority of contracts over legislation.

■ ***Dartmouth College v. Woodward*** Supreme Court case (1819) in which the majority ruled that private contracts are sacred and cannot be modified by state legislatures.

James Monroe and the Nationalist Agenda

While Congress and the courts were firmly in the hands of forward-looking leaders, the presidency passed in 1816 to the seemingly old-fashioned James

The Granger Collection, New York.

With a long and distinguished career as a diplomat behind him, the handsome and elegant James Monroe brought a statesmanlike demeanor into the White House. He managed to soothe long-standing disputes between various political factions, ushering in what would be called "The Era of Good Feelings."

Monroe. Personally conservative, Monroe nonetheless was a strong nationalist as well as a graceful statesman. He had served primarily as a diplomat during the contentious period that preceded the War of 1812, and as president he turned his diplomatic skills to the task of calming political disputes. He was the first president since Washington to take a national goodwill tour, during which he persistently urged various political factions to merge their interests for the benefit of the nation at large.

Monroe's cabinet was well chosen to carry out the task of smoothing political rivalries while flexing nationalistic muscles. He selected John Quincy Adams, son and heir of Yankee Federalist John Adams, as secretary of state because of his diplomatic skill and to win political support in New England. Monroe tapped southern nationalist John C. Calhoun for secretary of war and balanced his appointment with that of southern states' rights advocate William C. Crawford

as secretary of the treasury. With his team assembled, Monroe launched the nation on a course designed to increase its control over the North American continent and improve its position in world affairs.

Madison had already taken steps toward initiating a more aggressive diplomatic policy, setting the tone for the years to come. Taking advantage of U.S. involvement in the War of 1812, Barbary pirates (see page 196) had resumed their raiding activity against American shipping. In June 1815, Madison ordered a military force back to the Mediterranean to put an end to those raids. Naval hero Stephen Decatur returned to the region with a fleet of ten warships. Training his guns on the port of Algiers itself, Decatur threatened to level the city if the pirates did not stop raiding American shipping. The Algerians and the rest of the Barbary pirates signed treaties ending the practice of exacting **tribute**. They also released all American hostages and agreed to pay compensation for past seizures of American ships. Celebrating the victory, Decatur gave voice to a militant new American nationalism, proclaiming, "Our Country! In her intercourse with foreign nations may she always be in the right; but our country, right or wrong."

Monroe maintained Madison's firm stand as he attempted to resolve important issues not settled by earlier administrations. Secretary of State Adams began negotiating for strict and straightforward treaties outlining America's economic and territorial rights.

The first matter Adams addressed were the loose ends left dangling by the Treaty of Ghent (1814). One problem had been the **demilitarization** of the Great Lakes boundary between the United States and British Canada. In the 1817 Rush-Bagot Agreement, both nations agreed to cut back their Great Lakes fleets to only a few vessels. A year later, the two nations drew up the Convention of 1818: the British agreed to honor American fishing rights in the Atlantic, to recognize the 49th parallel as the boundary between the Louisiana Territory and Canada, and to occupy the Oregon Territory jointly with the United States.

With these northern border issues settled, Adams set his sights on defining the nation's southern and southwestern frontiers. Pirates and other renegades used Florida as a base for launching raids against American settlements and shipping, and runaway slaves found it a safe haven in their flight from southern plantations. Reflecting on the situation in December 1817, General Andrew Jackson wrote to the president advocating the invasion of Spanish

tribute A payment of money or other valuables that one group makes to another as the price of security.

demilitarization The removal of military forces from a region and the restoration of civilian control.

Florida. A short time later, Secretary of War Calhoun ordered Jackson to lead a military expedition into southern Georgia, but Jackson crossed the border and forced the Spanish government to flee. Though some recommended that the general be severely disciplined, Adams saw an opportunity to settle the Florida border issue. He announced that Jackson's raid was an act of self-defense that would be repeated unless Spain could police the area adequately. Fully aware that Spain could not guarantee American security, Adams knew that the Spanish would either have to give up Florida or stand by and watch the United States take it by force. Understanding his country's precarious position, Spanish minister Don Luis de Onís chose to cede Florida in the **Adams-Onís Treaty** of 1819. The United States got all of Florida in exchange for releasing Spain from $5 million in damage claims resulting from border raids.

Spain's inability to police its New World territories also led to a more general diplomatic problem. As the result of Spain's weakness, many of its colonies in Latin America had rebelled and established themselves as independent republics. Fearful of the anticolonial example being set in the Western Hemisphere, several European powers were poised to help Spain reclaim its overseas empire. Neither England, which had developed a thriving trade with the new Latin American republics, nor the United States wanted recolonization to occur. In 1823 the British foreign minister proposed that the United States and England form an alliance to end European meddling in Latin America. Adams protested that America would be reduced to a "cock-boat in the wake of the British man-of-war," suggesting instead a **unilateral** statement saying that "the American continents by the free and independent condition which they have assumed, and maintain, are henceforth not to be considered as subject for future colonization by any European power."

Monroe remained undecided. He trusted Adams's judgment but did not share the secretary of state's confidence in the nation's ability to fight off European colonization without British help. Monroe nevertheless conceded the nationalistic necessity for the United States to "take a bolder attitude . . . in favor of liberty." In November 1823 European support to restore Spain's colonies was faltering, so with the immediate threat removed, Monroe announced that the United States would regard any effort by European countries "to extend their system to any portion of this hemisphere as dangerous to our peace and safety." He went on to define any attempt at European intervention in the affairs of the Western Hemisphere as a virtual act of war against the United States.

The **Monroe Doctrine** was exactly the proud assertion of principle "in favor of liberty" that Monroe had deemed necessary. It immediately won the support of the American people. Like Decatur's "Our country, right or wrong" speech, it seemed to announce the arrival of the United States on the international scene.

DYNAMIC GROWTH AND POLITICAL CONSEQUENCES

★ How did the global economic situation combine with postwar economic optimism to lead to economic panic in 1819?

★ How did economic growth and panic contribute to sectional conflict and political contention?

After the **Napoleonic wars** ended in 1815, Europeans continued to need American food and manufactures as they rebuilt a peacetime economy. Encouraged by a ready European market and expanding credit offered by both public and private banks, budding southern planters, northern manufacturers, and western and southwestern farmers embarked on a frenzy of speculation. They rushed to borrow against what they were sure was a golden future to buy equipment, land, and slaves.

Although all shared the same sense of optimism, entrepreneurs in the North, West, and South had different ideas about the best course for the American economy. As the American System drew the regions together into increasing mutual dependency, the tensions among them increased as well. As long as economic conditions remained good, there was little reason for conflict, but when the speculative boom collapsed, sectional tensions increased dramatically.

The Panic of 1819

Earlier changes in federal land policy had contributed to the rise of speculation. In 1800 and again in 1804, Congress had passed bills lowering the minimum number of acres of federal land an individual could purchase and the minimum price per acre. After 1804 the minimum purchase became 160 acres and the

■ **Adams-Onís Treaty** Treaty between the United States and Spain in 1819 that ceded Florida to the United States, ended any Spanish claims in Oregon, and recognized Spanish rights in the American Southwest.

unilateral Undertaken or issued by only one side and thus not involving an agreement made with others.

■ **Monroe Doctrine** President Monroe's 1823 statement declaring the Americas closed to further European colonization and discouraging European interference in the affairs of the Western Hemisphere.

■ **Napoleonic wars** Wars in Europe waged by or against Napoleon Bonaparte between 1803 and 1815.

minimum price, $1.64 per acre. The bill also permitted farmers to pay the government in **installments**. For most Americans, the minimum investment of $262.40 was still out of reach, but the installment option encouraged many to take the risk and buy farms they could barely afford.

Land speculators complicated matters considerably. Taking advantage of the new land prices, they too jumped into the game, buying land on credit. Unlike farmers, however, speculators never intended to put the land into production. They hoped to subdivide it and sell it to people who could not afford to buy 160-acre lots directly from the government. Speculators also offered installment loans, pyramiding the already huge tower of debt.

Banks—both relatively unsupervised state banks and the Second Bank of the United States—then added to the problem. Farmers who bought land on credit seldom had enough cash to purchase farm equipment, seed, materials for housing, and the other supplies necessary to put the land to productive use. So the banks extended liberal credit on top of the credit already extended by the government and by land developers. Farmers thus had acreage and tools, but they also had an enormous debt.

Several developments in the international economy combined to undermine the nation's tower of debt. The economic optimism that fed the speculative frenzy rested on profitable markets. But as the 1810s drew to a close and recovery began in Europe, the profit bandwagon began to slow, and optimism to slip. Not only was Europe able to supply more of its own needs, but Europeans were also importing from other regions of the globe. Led by Great Britain, European nations were establishing colonies in Asia, Africa, and the Pacific. In addition, the recent independence of many of Europe's Latin American colonies deprived the Europeans of the gold and silver that had driven international economics since the discovery of America. Europe became less and less dependent on American goods and, at the same time, less and less able to afford them. Thus the bottom began to fall out of the international market that had fueled speculation within the United States.

Congress noted the beginning of the collapse late in 1817 and tried to head off disaster by tightening credit. The government stopped installment payments on new land purchases and demanded that they be transacted in hard currency. The Second Bank of the United States followed suit in 1818, demanding immediate repayment of loans in either gold or silver. State banks then followed and were joined by land speculators. Instead of curing the problem, however, tightening credit and recalling loans drove the economy over the edge. The speculative balloon burst, leaving nothing but a mass of debt behind. This economic catastrophe became known as the **Panic of 1819**.

Before the adoption of modern bankruptcy laws, it was common for people to be put in prison when they could not pay their debts. One impact of the Panic of 1819 was a huge upturn in such imprisonments. Newspapers like *The Remembrancer, or Debtors Prison Recorder*, which began publication with this issue on April 8, 1820, called for reform in debtor laws and also reported gruesome stories about the sufferings of previously respectable people who found themselves in debtors' prison through no fault of their own.
Debtors Prison Recorder, Vol. 1., No. 1, New York, Saturday, April 8, 1820.

Six years of economic depression followed the panic. As prices declined, individual farmers and manufacturers, unable to repay loans for land and equipment, faced **repossession** and imprisonment for debt. In Cincinnati and other agricultural cities, bankruptcy sales were a daily occurrence. In New England

installments Partial payments of a debt made at regular intervals until the entire debt is repaid.

■ **Panic of 1819** A financial panic that began when the Second Bank of the United States tightened credit and recalled government loans.

repossession The reclaiming of land or goods by the seller or lender after the purchaser fails to pay installments due.

and the West, factories closed, throwing both employees and owners out of work. In New York and other manufacturing and trading cities, the ranks of the unemployed grew steadily. The number of **paupers** in New York City nearly doubled between 1819 and 1820, and in Boston thirty-five hundred people were imprisoned for debt. Shaken by the enormity of the problem, John C. Calhoun observed in 1820: "There has been within these two years an immense revolution of fortunes in every part of the Union; enormous numbers of persons utterly ruined; multitudes in deep distress."

Economic Woes and Political Sectionalism

Despite Monroe's efforts to merge southern, northern, and nationalist interests during the Era of Good Feelings, the Panic of 1819 drove a wedge between the nation's geographical sections. The depression touched each of the major regions differently, calling for conflicting solutions. For the next several years, the halls of Congress rang with debates rooted in each section's particular economic needs.

Tariffs were one proven method for handling economic emergencies, and as the Panic of 1819 spread economic devastation throughout the country, legislators from Pennsylvania and the Middle Atlantic states, southern New England, and then Ohio and Kentucky began clamoring for protection. Others disagreed, turning tariffs into the issue that would pit region against region more violently than any other during these years.

Farmers were split on the tariff issue. Irrespective of where they lived, so-called yeoman farmers favored a free market that would keep the price of the manufactures they had to buy as low as possible. In contrast, the increasing number of commercial farmers—those who had chosen to follow Henry Clay's ideas and were specializing to produce cash crops of raw wool, hemp, and wheat—joined mill owners, factory managers, and industrial workers in supporting protection against the foreign dumping of such products. So did those westerners who were producing raw minerals such as iron and tin that were in high demand in the industrializing economy.

Southern commercial farmers, however, did not join with their western counterparts in favoring protection. After supporting the protective Tariff of 1816, Calhoun and other southerners became firm opponents of tariffs. Their dislike of protection reflected a complex economic reality. Britain, not the United States, was the South's primary market for raw cotton and its main supplier of manufactured goods. Protective tariffs raised the price of such goods as well as the possibility that Britain might enact a **retaliatory tariff** on cotton imports from the South. If that happened, southerners would pay more for manufactures but receive less profit from cotton.

When, in 1820, northern congressmen proposed a major increase in tariff rates, small farmers in the West and cotton growers in the South combined to defeat the measure. Northerners then began engaging in **log rolling** with congressmen from the West. The northerners supported one bill that lowered the minimum price of public land to $1.25 per acre and another that allowed farmers who had bought land before 1820 to pay off their debts at the reduced price. The bill also extended the time over which those who were on the installment plan could make payments. Then, in 1822, northerners backed a bill authorizing increased federal spending on the Cumberland Road, an interest vital to westerners. The strategy succeeded: in 1824 western congressmen repaid northern manufacturing interests by voting for a greatly increased tariff.

This victory demonstrated an important new political reality. Of the six western states admitted to the Union after 1800, three—Ohio, Indiana, and Illinois—were predominantly farming states, split between commercial and nonspecialized farming. The other three—Louisiana, Mississippi, and Alabama—were increasingly dominated by cotton growing. As long as northern commercial interests could pull support from Ohio, Indiana, and Illinois, the balance of power in Congress remained relatively even. But new expansion in either the North or South had the potential to tip the political scale. As all three regions fought to implement specific solutions to the nation's economic woes, the regional balance of power in Congress became a matter of crucial importance.

The Missouri Compromise

The delicate balance in Congress began to wobble immediately in 1819 when the Missouri Territory applied for statehood. New York congressman James Tallmadge, Jr., realized that if Missouri was admitted

paupers A term popular in the eighteenth and nineteenth centuries to describe poor people; cities like New York and Boston often registered paupers so as to provide local relief.

retaliatory tariff A tariff on imported goods imposed neither to raise revenue nor control commerce but to retaliate against tariffs charged by another nation.

log rolling The trading of favors, such as vote trading, by legislators to obtain passage of bills that would otherwise lack sufficient votes to pass.

MAP 10.1 Missouri Compromise and Representative Strength
The Missouri Compromise fixed the boundary between free and slave territories at 36°30' north latitude.
This map shows the result both in geographical and political terms. While each section emerged from the
compromise with the same number of senators (24), the balance in the House of Representatives and Electoral
College tilted toward the North. Copyright © Cengage Learning

as a free state, its economy would resemble the economies of states in the Old Northwest, and its congressmen would be susceptible to northern log rolling. This realization led Tallmadge to propose Missouri be closed to slavery. Southerners likewise understood that if Missouri was admitted as a slave state, it would undoubtedly support the southern position on tariffs and other key issues. They unified to oppose the **Tallmadge Amendment**.

Both sides in the debate were deeply entrenched, but in 1820 Henry Clay suggested a compromise. Late in 1819, Maine applied for admission to the United States. The compromise proposed by Clay was to admit Missouri as a slave state and Maine as a free state. Clay also proposed that after the admission of Missouri, slavery be banned forever in the rest of the Louisiana Territory above 36°30' north latitude, the line that formed Missouri's southern border (see Map 10.1). With this provision, Congress approved the **Missouri Compromise**, and the issue of slavery in the territories faded—for a while.

New Politics and the End of Good Feelings

Conducted in the midst of the Missouri crisis, the presidential election of 1820 went as smoothly as could be: Monroe was reelected with the greatest majority ever enjoyed by any president except George Washington. Despite economic depression and sectional strife, the people's faith in Jefferson's party and his successors nominated by the party caucus remained

■ **Tallmadge Amendment** An amendment to a statehood bill for Missouri proposed by New York congressman James Tallmadge, Jr., that would have banned slavery in the new state; it created a deadlock in Congress that necessitated the Missouri Compromise.

■ **Missouri Compromise** Law proposed by Henry Clay in 1820 admitting Missouri to the Union as a slave state and Maine as a free state and banning slavery in the Louisiana Territory north of latitude 36°30'.

situation: northeastern Jacksonians would win increasing support from manufacturing interests in their region by appearing to support tariffs; southern and western Jackson supporters could take credit for sinking tariff increases, cementing support in their districts; and Adams, who had promised increases as part of his political agenda, would appear ineffectual. But Calhoun and his fellow conspirators had miscalculated: when the tariff package came to the floor in May 1828, key northeastern congressmen engineered its passage. The resulting **Tariff of Abominations** was not what Calhoun had expected, but it served his ends by establishing tariff rates that were unpopular with almost every segment of the population, and the unpopular president would bear the blame.

Democratic Styles and Political Structure

Adams's demeanor and outlook compounded his problems. He seemed more a man of his father's generation than of his own. The enormous economic and demographic changes that occurred during the first decades of the nineteenth century created a new political climate, one in which Adams's archrival Andrew Jackson felt much more at ease than did the stiff Yankee who occupied the White House.

One of the most profound changes in the American political scene was an explosion in the number of voters. Throughout the early years of the republic's history, voting rights were limited to white men who held real estate. In a nation primarily of farmers, most men owned land, so the fact of limited suffrage raised little controversy. But as economic conditions changed, a smaller proportion of the population owned farms, and while bankers, lawyers, manufacturers, and other such men often were highly educated, economically stable, and politically concerned, their lack of real estate barred them from political participation. Not surprisingly, such elite and middle-class men urged suffrage reform. In 1800 only three of the sixteen states had no property qualifications for voting, and another three permitted taxpayers to vote even if they did not own real property. By 1830, only five of the twenty-four states retained property qualifications, nine required tax payment only, and ten made no property demands at all. The raw number of voters grew enormously and rapidly. In 1824, 356,038 men cast ballots for the presidency. Four years later, more than three times that number voted. In addition, states increasingly dropped property qualifications for officeholding as well as voting, opening new opportunities for breaking the gentlemanly monopoly on political power. Of course, all of the states continued to bar women from voting, and most refused the ballot to African Americans, whether free or slave.

Political opportunists were not slow to take advantage of the new situation. Men such as New Yorker Martin Van Buren quickly came to the fore, organizing political factions into tightly disciplined local and statewide units. Opposing Governor DeWitt Clinton's faction in New York, Van Buren molded disaffected Republicans into the so-called Bucktail faction. In 1820 the Bucktails used a combination of political patronage—the ability of the party in power to distribute government jobs—**influence peddling**, and fiery speeches to draw newly qualified voters into the political process and swept Clinton out of office.

Many new voters were gratified at finally being allowed to participate in politics but sensed that their participation was not having the impact it should. They resented the "corrupt bargain" that had denied the presidency to the people's choice—Andrew Jackson—in the election of 1824. Voters in upstate New York and elsewhere pointed at organizations such as the **Masons**, claiming that they used secret signs and rituals to ensure the election of their own members, thwarting the popular will. In the fall of 1826, William Morgan, a New York bricklayer, decided to publish some of the organization's secrets. Morgan was promptly arrested—charged with owing a debt of $2.69—and jailed. What happened after that remains a mystery. Some unknown person paid Morgan's debt, and he was released. But as he emerged from jail, he was seized, bound and gagged, and dragged into a carriage that whisked him out of town. He was never seen again.

Morgan's disappearance caused a popular outcry, and political outsiders demanded a complete investigation. When no clues turned up, many assumed that a Masonic conspiracy was afoot. Within a year, opportunistic young politicians, including New Yorkers Thurlow Weed and William Seward and Pennsylvanian **Thaddeus Stevens**, had harnessed this political anxiety by forming the **Antimasonic Party**. Based exclusively on the alienation felt by small craftsmen, farmers, and other

---

■ **Tariff of Abominations** Tariff package designed to win support for anti-Adams forces in Congress; its passage in 1828 discredited Adams but set off sectional tension over tariff issues.

influence peddling Using one's influence with people in authority to obtain favors or preferential treatment for someone else, usually in return for payment.

Masons An international fraternal organization with many socially and politically prominent members, including a number of U.S. presidents.

■ **Thaddeus Stevens** Opportunistic politician who was one of the founders of the Antimasonic Party; he later became a leader of the "Conscience Whigs" and later still became one of the key organizers of the Republican Party. During and after the Civil War, he was the leader of the Radical Republican faction in Congress.

■ **Antimasonic Party** Political party formed in 1827 to capitalize on popular anxiety about the influence of the Masons; it opposed politics-as-usual without offering any particular substitute.

As suffrage requirements loosened, politics went from being a sedate parlor game among gentlemen to a rough-and-tumble contest that often spilled out into the streets of the nation's cities and villages. This painting by George Caleb Bingham captures the colorful spirit of the new politics in depicting a county election in early nineteenth-century Missouri.

marginalized groups, the Antimasons had no platform beyond their shared opposition to conspiracies they were sure were directed against political transparency. The Antimasonic Party was, in effect, a political party whose sole cause was to oppose political parties.

What was happening in New York was typical of party and antiparty developments throughout the country. As the party of Jefferson dissolved, a tangle of political factions broke out across the nation. This was precisely the sort of petty politics that Adams disdained, but the chaos suited a man like Jackson perfectly. So, while the Antimasons were busy pursuing often highly fanciful conspiracy theories, Van Buren was busy forging with the hero of New Orleans an alliance that would fundamentally alter American politics.

The Rise of "King Andrew"

Within two years of Adams's election, Van Buren had brought together northern outsiders like himself, dissident southern Republicans like John C. Calhoun, and western spokesmen like **Thomas Hart Benton** of Missouri and John H. Eaton of Tennessee into a new political party. Calling themselves Democratic-Republicans—the **Democratic Party** for short—this party railed against the neofederalism of Clay's and Adams's National Republican platform. The Democrats called for a return to Jeffersonian simplicity, states' rights, and republican principles. Behind the scenes, however, they employed the tight organizational discipline and manipulative techniques that Van Buren had used to such good effect against the Clintons in New York. Lining up behind the recently defeated popular hero Andrew Jackson, the new party appealed to both opportunistic political outsiders and democratically inclined new voters. In the congressional elections of 1826, Van Buren's coalition drew the unqualified support of both groups, unseating enough National Republicans to gain a twenty-five-seat majority in the House of Representatives and an eight-seat advantage in the Senate.

■ **Thomas Hart Benton** U.S. senator from Missouri and legislative leader of the Democrats; he was a champion of President Jackson and a supporter of westward expansion.

■ **Democratic Party** Political party that brought Andrew Jackson into office; it recalled Jeffersonian principles of limited government and drew its support from farmers, craftsmen, and small businessmen.

by Jackson's decision to abandon his predecessors' practice of regularly seeking his cabinet members' advice on major issues: the president called virtually no cabinet meetings and seldom asked for his cabinet's opinion. Instead, he surrounded himself with an informal network of friends and advisers. This so-called **Kitchen Cabinet**, under the deft leadership of Van Buren, worked closely with the president on matters of both national policy and party management.

Jackson's relationship with everyone in government was equally unconventional. He was known to rage, pout, and storm at suspected disloyalty. Earlier presidents had at least pretended to believe in the equal distribution of power among the three branches of government, but Jackson avowed that the president was the only member of the government elected by all the people, making it clear that he would stand in opposition to both private and congressional opponents. Reflecting his generally testy relationship with the legislative branch, he vetoed more bills than all his predecessors combined. Nor did he feel any qualms about standing up to the judiciary. Such arrogant assertions of executive power led Jackson's opponents to call the new president "King Andrew."

THE REIGN OF "KING ANDREW"

☆ How did regional conditions influence the national divisions reflected in the Bank War and the nullification crisis?

☆ What was President Jackson's role in shaping U.S. Indian policy?

Jackson had promised the voters "retrenchment and reform." He delivered retrenchment, but reform was more difficult to arrange. Jackson tried to implement reform in four broad areas: (1) the nation's banking and financial system, (2) internal improvements and public land policy, (3) Indian affairs, and (4) the collection of revenue and enforcement of federal law. The steps that Jackson took appealed to some of his supporters but strongly alienated others. Thus, as Jackson tried to follow through on his promise to reform the nation, he nearly tore the nation apart.

■ **Kitchen Cabinet** President Jackson's informal advisers, who helped him shape both national and Democratic Party policy.
■ **Nicholas Biddle** President of the Second Bank of the United States; he struggled to keep the bank functioning when President Jackson tried to destroy it.
specie Coins minted from precious metals.

Jackson and the Bank

The Second Bank of the United States was an essential part of the American System. In addition to serving as the depository for federal funds, the Second Bank issued national currency, which could be exchanged directly for gold, and it served as a national clearinghouse for notes issued by state and local banks. In that capacity, the Second Bank could regulate currency values and credit rates and help to control the activities of state banks by refusing to honor their notes if the banks lacked sufficient gold to back them. The Second Bank could also police state and local banks by calling in loans and refusing credit—actions that had helped bring on the Panic of 1819 and had made the Second Bank very unpopular.

In 1823 **Nicholas Biddle** became president of the bank. An able administrator and talented economist, Biddle enforced firm and consistent policies that restored some confidence in the bank and its functions. But many Americans still were not ready to accept the notion of an all-powerful central banking authority. The vast majority did not understand the function of the Second Bank, viewing it as just another instrument for helping the rich get richer. These critics tended instinctively to support the use of **specie**. Other critics, including many state bankers, opposed the Second Bank because they felt that Biddle's controls were too strict and that they were not receiving their fair share of federal revenues. Speculators and debtors also opposed the bank: when they gambled correctly, they could benefit from the sort of economic instability the bank was designed to prevent.

Hoping that Democratic Party discipline would break down before the upcoming presidential election, Jackson's opponents in Congress proposed to renew the bank's twenty-year charter four years early. Congress passed the renewal bill, and as expected, Jackson vetoed it, but an anticipated rift between Jackson and congressional Democrats did not open. The president stole the day by delivering a powerful veto message geared to appeal to the mass of Americans on whose support his party's congressmen depended. In line with his political supporters, Jackson denounced the Second Bank for serving the interests of "the few at the expense of the many" and injuring "humbler members of society—the farmers, the mechanics, and laborers—who have neither the time nor the means of securing like favors to themselves."

Although the charter was not renewed, the Second Bank could operate for four more years on the basis of its unexpired charter. Jackson, however, wanted to "deprive the conspirators of the aid which they expect from its money and power." Withdrawing federal deposits would do just that, although doing so was illegal. Jackson nonetheless ordered Treasury

Published in 1833, this political cartoon entitled "The Diplomatic Hercules [Andrew Jackson] Attacking the Political Hydra [The Second Bank of the United States]" illustrates why the Bank War enhanced rather than hurt Jackson at the polls. Many voters saw the bank as a monster that used its tentacles of complicated financial policy to choke common people while enriching the speculators and merchants who supported it.

Secretary Louis McLane to make the withdrawals. When he refused, the president fired him and replaced him with William J. Duane, who also refused. Jackson quickly fired him too and appointed Kitchen Cabinet member Roger B. Taney to head the Treasury Department. Taney chose to step around the law rather than breaking it by paying the government's bills from existing accounts in the Second Bank while placing all new deposits in so-called **pet banks**.

Powerless to stop Taney's diversion of federal funds, Biddle sought to replace dwindling assets by raising interest rates and calling in loans owed by state banks. In this way, the banker believed, he would not only head off the Second Bank's collapse but also trigger a business panic that might force the government to reverse its course. "Nothing but the evidence of suffering . . . will produce any effect," Biddle said as he pushed the nation toward economic instability. Biddle was correct that there would be "evidence of suffering," but the full effect of the **Bank War** would not be felt until after the reign of "King Andrew" had ended.

The Nullification Crisis

Southern concerns about banking and rising tariffs reflected the South's abiding political and economic posture during the Jackson administration. For years,

southerners had complained that tariffs discriminated against them. From their point of view, they were paying at least as much in tariffs as the North and West but were not getting nearly the same economic benefits. The banking system, too, seemed to benefit others more than it did them.

This matter had come to a head in 1829 when the impact of the ill-considered Tariff of Abominations (1828) began to be felt throughout the nation. The new tariffs roused loud protest from states such as South Carolina, where soil exhaustion and declining agricultural prices were putting strong economic pressure on men who were deeply invested in land and slaves. Calhoun, who took office as Jackson's vice president in 1829, spearheaded the protest.

Though it guarded the author's identity, the South Carolina legislature published Calhoun's *South*

■ **pet banks** State banks into which Andrew Jackson ordered federal deposits to be placed to help deplete the funds of the Second Bank of the United States.

■ **Bank War** The political conflict that occurred when Andrew Jackson tried to destroy the Second Bank of the United States, which he thought represented special interests at the expense of the common man.

Carolina Exposition and Protest in 1828, fanning the flames of sectionalism. Calhoun's **nullification** sentiments reflected notions being expressed throughout the nation. And as Calhoun's pamphlet circulated to wider and wider audiences, nationalists such as Clay and Jackson grew more and more anxious about the potential threat to federal power. The test came in 1830, when Senator Robert Y. Hayne of South Carolina and Senator **Daniel Webster** of Massachusetts entered into a debate over Calhoun's ideas. Hayne zealously supported Calhoun; Webster appealed to nationalism. Jackson soon made his opinion known at a political banquet, offering the toast, "Our Federal Union—It must be preserved," indicating that he would brook no nullification arguments. Calhoun, who was sitting near the president, then rose and countered Jackson's toast with one of his own: "The Union—next to our liberty most dear." For Jackson, who valued loyalty above all else, his vice president's insubordination was inexcusable. Still, two years passed before the crisis finally came.

In 1832 nullification advocates in South Carolina called for a special session of the state legislature, which voted overwhelmingly to nullify the despised tariff. The legislature also elected Hayne, nullification's most prominent spokesman, as governor and named Calhoun as his replacement in the Senate. The vice president, who realized that he would not be Jackson's running mate in the coming election, finally admitted writing the *Exposition and Protest* and resigned from the vice presidency to lead the pro-nullification forces from the Senate floor.

Jackson quickly proved true to his toast of two years before. Bristling that nullification violated the Constitution and was "destructive of the great object for which it was formed," Jackson immediately reinforced federal forts in South Carolina and sent warships to guarantee the tariff's collection. He also asked Congress to pass a "force bill" giving him the power to invade the rebellious state if doing so proved necessary to carry out federal law. In hopes of placating southerners and winning popular support in the upcoming election, Congress passed a lowered tariff, but it also voted to give Jackson the power he requested.

South Carolina nullifiers immediately called a new convention, which withdrew its nullification of the previous tariff but passed a resolution nullifying the force bill. Because Jackson no longer needed the force bill to apply federal law and collect the new tariff, he chose to ignore this action. Thus there was no real resolution to the problem, and the gash over federal versus states' rights remained unhealed. The wound continued to fester until it was finally cauterized thirty years later by civil war.

Jackson and the West

Although Jackson was a westerner, his views on federal spending for roads, canals, and other internal improvements seemed based more on politics than on ideology or regional interest. For example, when Congress passed a bill calling for federal money to build a road in Kentucky—from Maysville, on the Ohio border, to Lexington—Jackson vetoed it, claiming that it would benefit only one state and was therefore unconstitutional. But three practical political issues influenced his decision. First, party loyalists in places such as Pennsylvania and New York, where Jackson hoped to gain support, opposed federal aid to western states. Second, Lexington was the hub of Henry Clay's political district, and by denying aid that would benefit that city, Jackson was putting his western competitor in political hot water. Finally, Jackson's former congressional district centered on Nashville—already the terminus of a national road and therefore a legitimate recipient of federal funds. Thus Jackson could lavish money on his hometown while seeming to stand by strict constitutional limitations on federal power.

Disposing of the **public domain** was the other persistent problem Jackson faced. By the time he came to power, land policy had become a major factor in sectional politics. Currying support from western voters, Jackson abandoned his predecessors' notion that public land sales should profit the government, taking the position that small farmers should be able to buy federal land for no more than it cost the government to **survey** the plot and process the sale.

Jackson thus directed Congress that "public lands shall cease as soon as practicable to be a source of revenue," and western Jacksonians responded immediately. One of them, Senator Thomas Hart Benton of Missouri, proposed in 1830 that the price of government land be dropped gradually from $1.25 to just 25 cents an acre and that any lands not sold at that price simply be given away. He also suggested that squatters—people who were currently settled illegally on public land—be given the first chance to buy the tract where they were squatting when the government offered it for sale.

Such measures pleased Jackson's western supporters but frightened easterners and southerners. His supporters in the East and South feared that migration

nullification Refusal by a state to recognize or enforce a federal law within its boundaries.

■ **Daniel Webster** Massachusetts senator and lawyer who was known for his forceful speeches and considered nullification a threat to the Union.

public domain Land owned and controlled by the federal government.

survey To determine the area and boundaries of land through measurement and mathematical calculation.

"The Squatters" by George Caleb Bingham (1811–1879), 1850, oil on canvas, Museum of Fine Arts, Boston, Bequest of Henry Lee Shattuck in memory of the late Ralph W. Gray. 1871.154. Photograph © 2011. Museum of Fine Arts, Boston.

Throughout the West, people without money simply camped on publicly owned land. This painting by George Caleb Bingham captures one such family as they pause outside their log cabin. Western politicians like Thomas Hart Benton argued that such "squatters" had a legitimate right to claim the land they settled and fought for legislation protecting squatters' rights.

Kickapoos, Sauks, Foxes, and Winnebagos were living settled and stable lives along the northern frontier.

Throughout the 1820s, the federal government tried to convince tribes along the frontier to move farther west. Promised money, new land, and relief from white harassment, many Indian leaders agreed. Others, however, resisted, insisting that they stay where they were. The outcome was terrible factionalism within Indian societies as some lobbied to sell out and move west while others fought to keep their lands. Playing on this factionalism, federal Indian agents were able to extract land cessions that consolidated the eastern tribes onto smaller and smaller holdings. One such transaction, the 1825 Treaty of Indian Springs, involved fraud and manipulation so obnoxious that President Adams overturned the ratified treaty and insisted on a new one.

Adams at least paid lip service to honest dealings with the Indians and the sanctity of treaties. Jackson scoffed at both. In 1817 he had told President Monroe, "I have long viewed treaties with the Indians an absurdity not to be reconciled to the principles of our government." As president, Jackson advocated removing all the eastern Indians to the west side of the Mississippi, by force if necessary (see Map 10.4). Following Jackson's direction, Congress passed the **Indian Removal Act** in 1830, appropriating the funds necessary to purchase all of the lands held by Indian tribes east of the Mississippi River and to pay for their resettlement in the West.

It did not take Jackson long to begin implementing his new authority. When white farmers penetrated Sauk Indian territory during the summer of 1831, the Jackson administration authorized federal troops to forcibly move the entire band of more than a thousand Indian men, women, and children across the Mississippi.

At the same time, whites were exerting similar pressure on the southern tribes. The case of the Cherokees provides an excellent illustration of the new, more aggressive attitude toward Indian policy. Having allied with Jackson against the Creeks in 1813, the Cherokees

would give the West an even bigger say in the nation's economic and political future. In addition, southerners were concerned that Congress would replace revenues lost from the sale of public land by raising tariffs, threatening the South's economic relationship with Europe. Northerners were afraid that as people moved west, the drain on population would drive up the price of labor, increasing the cost of production and lowering profits. The result was nearly three years of debate in Congress. A frustrated Henry Clay, desperate to save any scrap of his economic plans for the nation, suggested that the distribution of public land be turned over to the states. Congress, relieved to have the matter taken out of its hands, passed Clay's bill in 1833, but Jackson vetoed it.

Jackson and the Indians

At the end of the War of 1812, the powerful Cherokees, Choctaws, Seminoles, Creeks, and Chickasaws—the so-called **Five Civilized Tribes**—numbered nearly seventy-five thousand people and occupied large holdings within the states of Georgia, North and South Carolina, Alabama, Mississippi, and Tennessee. These Indians had embraced Jefferson's vision of acculturation but were seen as an obstruction to westward migration, especially by grasping planters on the make who coveted Indian land for cotton fields. A similar situation prevailed in the Northwest. Though neither as numerous nor as Europeanized as the Civilized Tribes, groups such as the Peorias, Kaskaskias,

■ **Five Civilized Tribes** Term used by whites to describe the Cherokee, Choctaw, Seminole, Creek, and Chickasaw Indians, many of whom were planters and merchants.

■ **Indian Removal Act** Law passed by Congress in 1830 providing for the removal of all Indian tribes east of the Mississippi and the purchase of western lands for their resettlement.

emerged from the War of 1812 with their lands pretty well intact, and a rising generation of accommodationist leaders pushed strongly for the tribe to embrace white culture. In the early 1820s the Cherokees created a formal government with a bicameral legislature, a court system, and a professional, salaried civil service. In 1827 the tribe drafted and ratified a written constitution modeled on the Constitution of the United States. In the following year the tribe began publication of its own newspaper, the *Cherokee Phoenix,* printed in both English and Cherokee, using the alphabet devised earlier in the decade by tribal member **George Guess (Sequoyah)**.

Rather than winning the acceptance of their white neighbors, however, those innovations led to even greater friction. From the frontiersmen's point of view, Indians were supposed to be dying out, disappearing into history, not founding new governments and competing successfully for economic power. Thus

in 1828 the Georgia legislature nullified the Cherokee constitution. In the following year, gold was found on Cherokee land. As more than three thousand greedy prospectors violated tribal territory, the state of Georgia extended its authority over the Cherokees and ordered all communal tribal lands seized.

That was the first in a series of laws that the Georgia legislature passed to make life as difficult as possible for the Cherokees in hopes of driving them out of the state. When Christian missionaries living with the tribe protested the state's actions and encouraged the Cherokees to seek federal assistance, Georgia passed a law that required teachers among the Indians to obtain licenses from the state—a law expressly designed to eliminate the missionaries' influence. When two missionaries, Samuel Austin Worcester and Elizur Butler, refused to comply, a company of Georgia militia invaded the Cherokee reservation, arrested the teachers, and marched them off to jail.

MAP 10.4 Indian Removal
The outcome of Andrew Jackson's Indian policy appears clearly on this map. Between 1830 and 1835, all of the Civilized Tribes except Osceola's faction of Seminoles were forced to relocate west of the Mississippi River. Thousands died in the process. © *Martin Gilbert,* The Routledge Atlas of American History, *Fourth Edition, ISBN:* 0415281512 HB & 0415281520 PB. Copyright © Cengage Learning

It is easy to gloss over the brutality that was part of removing the Cherokees and other Indians from the Southeast during the 1830s, but this blockhouse at the former site of Fort Marr in Tennessee provides gruesome testimony to the actualities of the "Trail of Tears." It was one of four corner guard towers that were connected by high walls that contained Indians waiting to be transported to Indian Territory. Confinement often lasted for months, during which time food, fresh water, adequate shelter, and sanitary facilities were either minimal or not supplied at all. Armed sentinels in the blockhouses could shoot through specially drilled gun ports if the Indian detainees protested their inhumane treatment.

Two notable lawsuits came out of the combined efforts of the missionaries and Cherokees to get justice. In the first case, **Cherokee Nation v. Georgia** (1831), the Cherokees claimed that Georgia's action in extending authority over them and enforcing state law within Cherokee territory was illegal because they were a sovereign nation in a treaty relationship with the United States. The U.S. Supreme Court refused to hear this case. Speaking for the Court, Chief Justice John Marshall stated that the Cherokee Nation was neither a foreign nor a domestic state but was a "domestic dependent nation" and as such had no standing in federal court.

As American citizens, however, Worcester and Butler did have legitimate standing under federal law, and in 1832 Marshall was able to render a decision in the case of **Worcester v. Georgia**. In this case, the Court ruled that the Cherokee Nation was a distinct political community recognized by federal authority and that Georgia did not have legitimate power to pass laws regulating Indian behavior or to invade Indian land. He thus declared all the laws Georgia had passed to harass the Cherokees null and void and ordered the state to release Worcester and Butler from jail.

Although the Cherokees had grounds for celebration, their joy was short-lived. Jackson refused to use any federal authority to carry out the Court's order. When the Cherokees and their sympathizers pressed Jackson on the matter, he claimed that he was powerless to help and that the only way the Indians could

■ **George Guess (Sequoyah)** Cherokee silversmith and trader who created an alphabet that made it possible to transcribe the Cherokee language according to the sounds of its syllables.

■ **Cherokee Nation v. Georgia** Supreme Court case (1831) concerning Georgia's annulment of all Cherokee laws; the Supreme Court ruled that Indian tribes did not have the right to appeal to the federal court system.

■ **Worcester v. Georgia** Supreme Court case (1832) concerning the arrest of two missionaries to the Cherokees in Georgia; the Court found that Georgia had no right to rule in Cherokee territory.

Study Tools

SUMMARY

With the end of the War of 1812, President Madison and the Republicans promoted a strong agenda for the nation. Joining with former critics such as Henry Clay and John C. Calhoun, Madison pushed for a national market economy by sponsoring federal legislation for a national bank, controlled currency, and tariff protection for American industry. In addition, Madison gave free rein to nationalists such as Stephen Decatur, John Quincy Adams, and Andrew Jackson, who succeeded in enhancing the nation's military reputation and expanding its sphere of influence.

While the nation moved forward in accomplishing its diplomatic goals, the Republicans' economic agenda suffered from a lack of viable transportation and communication systems. Expecting quick and enormous profits, New York built the Erie Canal, the first successful link between the increasingly urban and manufacturing East and the rural, agricultural West. Convinced finally that transportation improvements were necessary for carrying out the work of the government, Madison and his successors joined with state officials to begin the process of building a truly national system of roads and canals.

But what had begun as an age of optimism closed in a tangle of conflict and ill will. A much-hoped-for prosperity dissolved in the face of shrinking markets, resulting in economic panic in 1819 and a collapse in the speculative economy. Economic hard times, in turn, triggered increased competition between the nation's geographical sections, as leaders wrestled for control over federal power in an effort to rid particular areas of economic despair. Supporters of the American System tried to craft a solution, but their compromise did not entirely satisfy anyone. And in the sea of contention that swelled around the Missouri Compromise, the Era of Good Feelings collapsed.

Meanwhile, an army of newly enfranchised voters, common men of moderate means, distressed by what seemed an elite conspiracy to run American affairs, swept the gentlemanly John Quincy Adams out of office

CHRONOLOGY
New Optimism and a New Democracy

1810	*Fletcher v. Peck*
1814	Treaty of Ghent ends War of 1812
1814–1815	Hartford Convention
1815	Government funds Cumberland Road
	Stephen Decatur defeats Barbary pirates
1816	Tariff of 1816
	First successful steamboat run, Pittsburgh to New Orleans
	James Monroe elected president
1817	Second Bank of the United States opens
1818	Andrew Jackson invades Spanish Florida
1819	*McCulloch v. Maryland*
	Adams-Onís Treaty
	Panic of 1819
1820	Monroe reelected
	Missouri Compromise
1823	Monroe Doctrine
1824–1828	Suffrage reform triples voter population
1825	House of Representatives elects John Quincy Adams president
	Completion of Erie Canal
1826	Disappearance of William Morgan and beginning of Antimasons
1827	Ratification of Cherokee constitution
1828	Tariff of Abominations
	Jackson elected president
	Publication of Calhoun's *The South Carolina Exposition and Protest*
	First issue of the *Cherokee Phoenix*
1830	Webster-Hayne debate
	Indian Removal Act
1831	Federal removal of Sauks and Choctaws
1832	*Worcester v. Georgia*
	Bank War
	Nullification crisis
	Sauk massacred while resisting removal
	Seminole War begins
1836–1838	Federal removal of Creeks, Chickasaws, and Cherokees

Study Tools

and replaced him with the more exciting and presumably more democratic Andrew Jackson. Backed by a political machine composed of northern, western, and southern interests, Jackson had to juggle each region's financial, tariff, and Indian policy demands while trying to hold his political alliance and the nation together. The outcome was a series of regional crises—the Bank War, nullification, and Indian removal—that alienated each region and together constituted a crisis of national proportions.

FOCUS QUESTIONS

If you have mastered this chapter, you should be able to answer these questions and to explain the terms that follow the questions.

1. ☆ *What were the sources for Americans' optimism as they emerged from the War of 1812 and how did the American government capitalize on this optimism?*

2. ☆ *How did new developments in the nation influence foreign affairs?*

3. ☆ *How did the global economic situation combine with postwar economic optimism to lead to economic panic in 1819?*

4. ☆ *How did economic growth and panic contribute to sectional conflict and political contention?*

5. ☆ *What factors helped change Americans' political options during the mid-1820s?*

6. ☆ *How did the election of Andrew Jackson in 1828 reflect those new options?*

7. ☆ *How did regional conditions influence the national divisions reflected in the Bank War and the nullification crisis?*

8. ☆ *What was President's Jackson role in shaping U.S. Indian policy?*

KEY TERMS

DeWitt Clinton *(p. 235)*
"Era of Good Feelings" *(p. 236)*
Hartford Convention *(p. 236)*
Henry Clay *(p. 237)*
John C. Calhoun *(p. 237)*
American System *(p. 237)*
Tariff of 1816 *(p. 237)*
Cumberland Road *(p. 238)*
Erie Canal *(p. 239)*
McCulloch v. Maryland *(p. 239)*
Gibbons v. Ogden *(p. 239)*
Fletcher v. Peck *(p. 240)*
Dartmouth College v. Woodward *(p. 240)*
Adams-Onís Treaty *(p. 242)*
Monroe Doctrine *(p. 242)*
Napoleonic wars *(p. 242)*
Panic of 1819 *(p. 243)*
Tallmadge Amendment *(p. 245)*
Missouri Compromise *(p. 245)*

Virginia Dynasty *(p. 246)*
Tariff of Abominations *(p. 248)*
Thaddeus Stevens *(p. 248)*
Antimasonic Party *(p. 248)*
Thomas Hart Benton *(p. 249)*
Democratic Party *(p. 249)*
Kitchen Cabinet *(p. 252)*
Nicholas Biddle *(p. 252)*
pet banks *(p. 253)*
Bank War *(p. 253)*
Daniel Webster *(p. 254)*
Five Civilized Tribes *(p. 255)*
Indian Removal Act *(p. 255)*
George Guess (Sequoyah) *(p. 256)*
Cherokee Nation v. Georgia *(p. 257)*
Worcester v. Georgia *(p. 257)*
Treaty of New Echota *(p. 258)*
Trail of Tears *(p. 258)*
Osceola *(p. 258)*

 CourseMate Go to the History CourseMate website for primary source links, study tools, and review materials for this chapter. www.cengagebrain.com

This early photograph, taken on a South Carolina plantation before the Civil War, freezes slave life in time, giving us a view of what slave cabins looked like, how they were arranged, how the largest majority of slaves dressed, and how they spent what little leisure time they had.

Furnishings in slave houses were usually fairly crude and often crafted by the residents themselves. Bedding normally consisted of straw pallets stacked on the floor or occasionally mounted on rough bedsteads. Other furnishings were equally simple—rough-hewn wooden chairs or benches and plank tables. Clothing was also very basic. One Georgia planter itemized the usual yearly clothing allowance for slaves: "two suits of cotton for spring and summer, and two suits of woolen for winter; four pair of shoes and three hats." Women commonly wore simple dresses or skirts and blouses, while children often went naked in the summer and were fitted with long, loose hanging shirts during the colder months.

lockjaw A popular name for tetanus, an often fatal disease resulting primarily from deep wounds.

cholera An infectious disease of the small intestines contracted mainly from bacteria in untreated water.

endemic Present in a particular group of people or geographical area.

It appears that the slave diet, like slave clothing and housing, was sufficient but not particularly pleasing. One slave noted that there was "plenty to eat sich as it was," but in summer flies swarmed all over the food. Her master, she said, would laugh about that, saying the added nutrition provided by the flies "made us fat." Despite justified complaints, slaves in the American South ate significantly more meat than workers in the urban North. In addition to meat, slaves consumed milk and corn, potatoes, peas and beans, molasses, and fish. The planter usually provided this variety of food, but owners also occasionally permitted slaves to hunt and fish and to collect wild roots, berries, and vegetables.

Although the diet provided to slaves kept them alive, the southern diet in general lacked important nutrients, and diet-related diseases plagued southern communities. Slaves were also subject to occupational ailments like hernia, pneumonia, and **lockjaw**. Because of inadequate sanitation, slaves also suffered from dysentery and **cholera**. Cardiovascular (heart and circulatory) diseases were also **endemic** among slaves. Recent research reveals that most slave children were undernourished because slaveowners would not allocate enough food for people who did not work. Once children were old enough to work, however, they had access to a very high-calorie diet. Such early malnutrition followed by an abrupt switch to a high-calorie and often high-fat diet may well have led to the high incidence of heart attacks, strokes, and similar ailments that the historical record indicates among slaves. And given the balance-sheet mentality among plantation owners, this phenomenon may not have been unwelcome. Old people who could not work hard were, like children, a liability; thus having slaves die from circulatory disease in middle age saved planters from unnecessary expenditures later on.

As to the work itself, cotton planting led to increasing concentration in the tasks performed by slaves. A survey of large and medium-size plantations during the height of the cotton boom shows that the majority of slaves (58 percent of the men and 69 percent of the women) were employed primarily as **field hands**. Of the rest, only 2 percent of slave men and 17 percent of slave women were employed as **house slaves**. The remaining 14 percent of slave women were employed in nonfield occupations such as sewing, weaving, and food processing. Seventeen percent of slave men were employed in nonfield activities such as driving wagons, piloting riverboats, and herding cattle. Another 23 percent were managers and craftsmen.

The percentage of slave craftsmen was much higher in cities, where slave **artisans** were often allowed to hire themselves out on the open job market in return for handing part of their earnings over to their owners. In Charleston, Norfolk, Richmond, and Savannah, slave artisans formed **guilds**. Feeling threatened by their solidarity, white craftsmen appealed to state legislatures and city councils for restrictions on slave employment in skilled crafts. Such appeals, and the need for more and more field hands, led to a decline in the number of slave artisans during the 1840s and 1850s.

Whether on large plantations or small farms, the burden of slavery was a source of constant stress for both slaves and masters in the newly evolving South. The precarious nature of family life, the ever-present threat of violence, and the overwhelming sense of powerlessness weighed heavily on slaves. Among masters, the awareness that they often were outnumbered and thus vulnerable to organized slave rebellion was a source of anxiety. Locked into this fear- and hate-laden atmosphere, everyone in the cotton South was drawn into what would become a long-lasting legacy of racial tension and distrust.

THE MANUFACTURING EMPIRE IN THE NORTHEAST

★ How did manufacturing and the nature of work change in the United States after 1820?

★ In what ways did the American system of manufacturing change the traditional pattern of U.S. foreign trade?

★ How did the developing factory system affect the lives of artisans, factory owners, and middle-class Americans?

Although the South changed radically during the opening years of the nineteenth century, one thing persisted: the economy remained rooted in households. Before the 1820s, households in the North also produced most of the things they used. For example, more than 60 percent of the clothing that Americans wore was spun from raw fibers and sewn by women in their own homes. Some householders even crafted sophisticated items—furniture, clocks, and tools—but skilled artisans usually made such products. These craftsmen, too, usually worked in their homes, assisted by family members and an extended family of artisan employees: apprentices and **journeymen**.

Beginning with the cotton-spinning plants that sprang up during the War of 1812, textile manufacturing led the way in pushing production out of the home (see page 225): from 1820 onward, manufacturing increasingly moved into factories, and cities began to grow up around the factories. Such changes severed the intimate ties between manufacturers and workers, and both found themselves surrounded by strangers in the new urban environments. "In most large cities there may be said to be two nations, understanding as little of one another, having as little intercourse, as if they lived in different lands," said one insightful observer. "This estrangement of men from men, of class from class, is one of the saddest features of a great city."

field hands People who did agricultural work such as planting, weeding, and harvesting.

house slaves People who did domestic work such as cleaning and cooking.

artisan A person who works at a craft, such as a blacksmith, cabinet maker, or stone mason.

guild An association of craftspeople with the same skills who join together to protect their common interests.

journeyman A person who has finished an apprenticeship to learn a trade or craft and is a qualified worker in the employ of another.

With two wives and several children to help share the burden of work, this Mormon settler was in a good position to do well, even in the harsh conditions that prevailed in the near-desert environment of Utah. Sensitive to disapproval from more traditional Christians, families like this tended to associate exclusively with other Mormons and pressured outsiders to leave as quickly as possible.

Intercultural cooperation also characterized the early history of Texas settlement. Spanish and then Mexican officials aided the empresarios, hoping that the aggressive Americans would form a frontier line between southern Plains Indians and prosperous silver-mining communities south of the **Rio Bravo**. Tensions rose, however, as population increased. Despite the best efforts of the Mexican government to encourage Hispanics to settle in Texas, fully four-fifths of the thirty-five hundred land titles perfected by the empresarios went to non-Hispanics. Cultural insensitivity and misunderstanding created disharmony between **Texians** and **Tejanos** and each tended to cling to their own ways.

The Mormon Community

Physical conditions in the Great Basin led to a completely different social and cultural order in that area. Utah is a high-desert plateau where water is scarce and survival depends on careful management. The tightly ordered community of Mormons was perfectly suited to succeed in such an inhospitable place.

Mormons followed a simple principle: "Land belongs to the Lord, and his Saints are to use so much as they can work profitably." The church measured off plots of various sizes, up to 40 acres, and assigned them to settlers on the basis of need. Thus a man with several wives, a large number of children, and enough wealth to hire help might receive a grant of 40 acres, but a man with one wife, few children, and little capital might receive only 10. The size of a land grant determined the extent to which the recipient was obligated to support community efforts. When the church ordered the construction of irrigation systems or other public works, a man who had been granted 40 acres had to provide four times the amount of labor as one who had been granted 10 acres. Like settlers elsewhere, the Mormons in Utah joined in community work parties, but cooperation among them was more rigidly controlled and formal.

Mormons had their own peculiar religious and social culture, and because of their bad experiences in Missouri and Illinois, they were unaccepting of strangers. The General Authorities of the church made every effort to keep Utah an exclusively Mormon society, welcoming all who would embrace the new religion and its practices but making it difficult for non-Mormons to stay in the region. The one exception was the American

Rio Bravo The Spanish and then Mexican name for the river that now forms the border between Texas and Mexico; the Rio Grande.

Texians Non-Hispanic settlers in Texas in the nineteenth century.

Tejanos Mexican settlers in Texas in the nineteenth century.

Denver Public Library, Western History Division.

Transoceanic Steamers

Experiments with large oceangoing steamships began early in the nineteenth century, but progress remained slow and no regular steam shipping service among the world's continents emerged. This situation ended in 1838 when two companies competing for a contract to carry mail across the Atlantic engaged in the first transoceanic steamboat race. The *Sirius* and the *Great Western* both departed from Great Britain in April. The *Sirius* took eighteen days to arrive in New York, more than twenty days faster than the average passage for sailing ships. But the *Great Western* arrived after only fifteen days. Despite these breathtaking performance records, neither company got the contract: flaws were found in both ships and both companies temporarily delayed negotiations. In the meantime, Canadian-born Samuel Cunard used a network of personal connections to seize the contract. Over the next century the Cunard Line would push steam shipping around the world.

Indian population. Because Indians—defined by the Book of Mormon as descendants of the Lamanites, a lost tribe of Israel—occupied a central place in Mormon sacred literature, the Mormons practiced an accepting and gentle Indian policy. Like other missionaries, Mormons insisted that Indians convert to their religion and lifestyle, but the Mormon hierarchy used its enormous power in Utah to prevent private violence against Indians whenever possible.

Tying the West to the Nation

Rapid expansion created an increased demand for reliable transportation and communications between the new regions in the West and the rest of the nation. An early first step in meeting this demand was building the so-called National Road, which between 1815 and 1820 snaked its way across the Cumberland Gap in the Appalachian Mountains and wound from the Atlantic shore to the Ohio River at Wheeling, Virginia. By 1838 this state-of-the-art highway—with its evenly graded surface, gravel pavement, and stone bridges—had been pushed all the way to Vandalia, Illinois. Within a few more years, it reached St. Louis, the great jumping-off point for the Far West.

At the same time, a series of other roads was beginning to merge into a transportation network. The so-called Military Road connecting Nashville to New Orleans also earned federal funding, as did the Nashville Road that, in turn, connected Nashville to Knoxville, where a traveler could pick up the Great Valley Road to Lynchburg, Virginia, and from there the Valley Turnpike, which connected with the Cumberland Road. Eventually towns from Portland, Maine, to Saint Augustine, Florida, and from Natchez, Mississippi, to New Haven, Connecticut, were linked by intersecting highways (see Map 11.2). Increasing numbers of people used these new roads to head west looking for new opportunities. Farmers, craftsmen, fur hunters, and others already settled in the West used them too, moving small loads of goods to the nearby towns and small cities that always sprang up along the unfolding transportation routes. But the new roads did little to advance large-scale commerce. Heavy and bulky products were too expensive to move: at a minimum, hauling a ton of freight along the nation's roads cost 15 cents a mile. At that rate, the cost of shipping a ton of oats from Buffalo to New York City amounted to twelve times the value of the cargo.

But the new roads also linked rural America to an ever-expanding network of waterways that made relatively inexpensive long-distance hauling possible. Completed in 1825, the Erie Canal revolutionized shipping: the cost of transporting a ton of oats from Buffalo to Albany fell from $100 to $15, and the transit time dropped from twenty days to just eight. All of New York State celebrated. The spectacular success of the Erie Canal prompted businessmen, farmers, and politicians throughout the country to promote canal building. State governments offered exclusive charters to canal-building companies, giving them direct financial grants, guaranteeing their credit, and easing their way in every possible manner. The result was an explosion in canal building that lasted through the 1830s (see Map 11.2).

This new mobility did not come cheaply. Canals cost as much as $20,000 to $30,000 a mile to build, and financing was always a problem. Hoping for large profits, entrepreneurs such as John Jacob Astor invested heavily in canal building. Before 1836, careful investors could make a 15 to 20 percent return on capital in canal building, but after that, most canal companies faced bankruptcy, as did the states that had helped finance them.

revolution, however, made quite a difference in how quickly news got around. After the Erie Canal opened, letters posted in Buffalo could reach New York City within six days and might get to New Orleans within two weeks.

As the nation expanded, and as economics and social life became more complicated, Americans felt growing pressure to keep up with news from across the nation and its new territories. Transportation improvements helped them do so by moving printed matter faster and more cheaply. At the same time, revolutions in printing technology and paper production significantly lowered the cost of printing and speeded up production. Organizations such as the American Bible Society and the American Tract Society joined newspaper and magazine publishers in producing a flood of printed material. In 1790 the 92 newspapers being published in America had a total **circulation** of around 4 million. By 1835 the number of periodicals had risen to 1,258, and circulation had surpassed 90 million.

The explosion in the volume and velocity of communications was enhanced by an even greater revolution in information technology that was in its starting phases. In the mid-1830s, Samuel F. B. Morse began experimenting with the world's first form of electronic communication: the **electric telegraph**. Morse developed a code consisting of dots (short pulses) and dashes (longer pulses) that represented letters of the alphabet. With this device, a skilled operator could quickly key out long messages and send them at nearly the speed of light. Over the next several years, Morse worked on improvements to extend the distance that the impulses would travel along the wires. Finally, in 1843, Congress agreed to finance an experimental telegraph line from Washington, D.C., to Baltimore. Morse sent his first message on the experimental line on May 24, 1844. His message, "What hath God wrought!" was a fitting opening line for the telecommunications revolution.

circulation The number of copies of a publication sold or distributed.

■ **electric telegraph** Device invented by Samuel F. B. Morse in 1836 that transmits coded messages along a wire over long distances; the first electronic communications device.

Individual Voices

Elizabeth Yale Hancock's Application to Be a Missionary

Entire segments of the American population have long been invisible to historians because they left behind few written records. Young, nonelite women are particularly absent from the historical record. Elizabeth Yale Hancock is a welcome exception. In her months-long correspondence with the American Board of Commissioners for Foreign Missions, she tells us much about herself, relating various experiences she had had during her life that qualified her to go to "the heathen," and revealing her attitudes toward the work. The following passage from one of those letters is especially revealing about her attitudes and her approach to her future as a missionary and provides a window through which we may glimpse the world of other mostly invisible young people of that time.

❶ What do we learn about the missionary Mrs. Sutphen's attitudes toward the people she had been sent to work with in Turkey? What do we learn about Hancock's attitudes? Both were hired as missionaries and maintained in the field. What does this tell us about the ABCFM's views on missionary behavior and approaches?

❷ What does Hancock's underlining of the phrase "without their consent" suggest about how committed she is to becoming a missionary? In the rest of this passage, how does she justify such defiance of her parents' authority?

When I was in Clinton an acquaintance of mine recd. a letter from Mrs. Sutphen (now Mrs. Morgan, Turkey) & she wrote that when she was in America she had often thought it would be a privilege to instruct the heathen, but when the native women came into her house—were so curious to examine every thing, would take down her hair &c. she would become impatient.

I think from the experience I have had with <u>nearly</u> that class (for here on the borders of Canada there are some as ignorant, perhaps, as there) that I should enjoy their native simplicity to the life, & be more useful in such a place than any where else. **❶** As to the sacrifice, <u>I think I have counted the cost</u>. To leave my aged parents <u>without their consent</u>—to leave this land of light & privileges would cost a struggle, yet I could do it <u>cheerfully if God requires it</u>. I have halted a great deal upon this question. I am willing to brave the dangers & endure the trials <u>if God will go with me</u>, but I <u>am not</u> willing to run without being sent. **❷** I know that my being so illy prepared both spiritually & mentally for such a work, are mighty reasons against any of the funds of the Board being employed in sending me, but shall I abandon the idea? This is a question I have not felt competent to decide, nor do I wish the responsibility of deciding it. After much thought & prayer I have concluded to refer the question to God in this way, by offering myself to the Board, & have prayed that the answer I receive from the Board may be <u>God's answer</u>. **❸**

❸ By what mechanism is Hancock determining what she should do? If this is typical, what does it tell us about women's decision making during this era?

Study Tools

SUMMARY

Although seemingly the most old-fashioned region of the country, the South that emerged during the years leading up to 1840 was a profoundly different place from what it had been before the War of 1812. As an industrial revolution overturned the economies in Great Britain and the American Northeast, economic options for southerners also changed radically. Although elite southerners clothed their new society in romanticized medieval garb, they were creating an altogether new kind of economy and society. The efficient production of cotton by the newly reorganized South was an essential aspect of the emerging national market economy and a powerful force in the Great Transformation.

Change in the North was more obvious, as factories replaced craft shops and cities replaced towns. The new economy and new technology created wonderful new opportunities but also imposed serious constraints. A revamped social structure replaced the traditional order as unskilled and semiskilled workers, a new class of clerks, and the genteel elite carved out new lives. As in the South, the outcome was a remarkable transformation in the lives of everyone in the region.

Meanwhile, the westward movement of Americans steadily gained momentum. Some successful entrepreneurs such as William Henry Ashley made enormous profits from their fur-trading empires. Land speculators and gold seekers, too, helped open areas to settlement. Such pioneers were usually followed by distinct waves of migrants who went west in search of land and opportunity. In Texas, Oregon, California, Utah, and elsewhere in the West, communities sprang up like weeds. Here they interacted—and often clashed—with one another, with those who had prior claims to the land, and with the land itself. As a result, a variety of cultures and economies developed in the expansive section of the country.

Tying the regions together, a new network of roads, waterways, and communications systems accelerated the process of change. After 1840, it was possible to ship goods from any one section of the country to any other, and people in all sections were learning more about conditions in far distant parts of the growing nation. Often this new information promised prosperity, but it also made more and more people aware of the enormity of the transformation taking place and the glaring differences between regions. The twin outcomes would be greater integration in the national economy and increasing tension between mutually dependent participants in the new marketplace.

CHRONOLOGY
The Dawn of Modernization

Year	Event
1821	William Becknell opens Santa Fe Trail to American traders
1822	John H. Hall perfects interchangeable parts for gun manufacturing
1828	Baltimore and Ohio Railroad commissioned
1830	Church of Latter-day Saints (Mormons) founded in New York
1830–1840	Ten-year immigration figure for United States exceeds 500,000
1835	Number of U.S. periodicals exceeds 1,250, with combined circulation of 90 million
1836	Samuel F. B. Morse invents electric telegraph / Bronson Alcott's *Conversations with Children on the Gospels*
1838	National Road completed to Vandalia, Illinois / First mass-produced brass clock
1839	John Sutter founds New Helvetia / Mormons build Nauvoo, Illinois
1841	Congress passes preemption bill
1844	Murder of Joseph Smith
1847	Mormons arrive in Utah
1848	Gold discovered in California

FOCUS QUESTIONS

If you have mastered this chapter, you should be able to answer these questions and to explain the terms that follow the questions.

1. ★ *Why did living conditions for southerners—black and white—change after 1820?*

2. ★ *How did elite white southerners respond to the change? How did their response affect slaves, free blacks, and poor whites?*

3. ★ *How did manufacturing and the nature of work change in the United States after 1820?*

4. ★ *In what ways did the American system of manufacturing change the traditional pattern of U.S. foreign trade?*

5. ★ *How did the developing factory system affect the lives of artisans, factory owners, and middle-class Americans?*

6. ★ *How did most Americans imagine "the West"? To what extent were their imaginings accurate?*

7. ★ *Who generally were the first pioneers to move into the West? How did they and those who followed actually move westward and establish communities there?*

KEY TERMS

Cotton Belt *(p. 265)*

slave codes *(p. 267)*

putting-out system *(p. 270)*

interchangeable parts *(p. 270)*

blue-collar workers *(p. 274)*

white-collar workers *(p. 275)*

voluntary association *(p. 276)*

cult of domesticity *(p. 277)*

extractive industry *(p. 278)*

forty-niners *(p. 279)*

Joseph Smith Jr. *(p. 279)*

Brigham Young *(p. 280)*

Great Salt Lake *(p. 280)*

Great Basin *(p. 280)*

Oregon Country *(p. 280)*

Oregon Trail *(p. 280)*

preemption bill *(p. 280)*

Junípero Serra *(p. 282)*

Californios *(p. 283)*

John Sutter *(p. 283)*

Baltimore and Ohio Railroad *(p. 287)*

electric telegraph *(p. 288)*

 CourseMate Go to the History CourseMate website for primary source links, study tools, and review materials for this chapter. www.cengagebrain.com

12 Responses to the Great Transformation, 1828–1848

Behind the Stories

A number of years ago, a counselor friend introduced me to a concept he used when working with people facing crises. It seems that in some versions of Chinese calligraphy the word "crisis" is represented by two characters, one meaning "danger" and the other meaning "opportunity." He told his patients that in any crisis one must create strategies for dealing with the dangers but never lose sight of the opportunities. I was so taken with this idea that I had it tattooed on my arm as a reminder of what a crisis really is. The rise of modern America in the era covered by this chapter might be called

a crisis, and historians have been torn as to whether this was primarily an era of great progress, characterized by improved economic productivity and political inclusion, or one of disastrous conflict, characterized by racial, class, and ethnic strife. Actually it was both, as my counselor friend explained: crisis always consists of both danger and opportunity. And in their various reactions to the great transformations taking place in this era, Americans had to deal with both. In the process, they created many of the fundamental structures on which our current society is based.

—C.L.M.

Individual Choices
Lydia Sigourney

Lydia Howard Huntley's father was a gardener and handyman on the estate of a Connecticut matron. But his employer recognized a budding talent in the young girl and encouraged her. Under the older woman's patronage, Lydia began writing poetry and essays at a young age, and when the time came, her sponsor's patrician family saw to it that the girl received the solid education thought fitting for young ladies in New England. Like many young women of modest means in her generation, Lydia followed up her education by becoming a teacher and then, with the help of her benefactors, started an academy for young women in Hartford. Her educational career culminated with the publication in 1815 of collected teaching materials under the title *Moral Pieces, in Prose and Verse.*

Shortly after reaching this pinnacle, she met and married a Hartford area widower, Charles Sigourney. Now a married woman, Lydia gave up her career in teaching and writing to devote herself to service as a wife. However, her desire to write continued. For years she published poems and short prose pieces anonymously, much to the chagrin of her conservative husband, and contrary to the standards of Christian reformers (see the Individual Voices feature at the end of this chapter). However, her husband's declining fortunes and her parents' failing health led Lydia to rebel against conventions and begin selling her work and trading on her name. Between 1833 and 1835, she sold nine books under her own name and a number of articles and other pieces to well-known periodicals. In the process, she became the first American woman to earn an entirely independent living as a commercial writer.

Though Edgar Allan Poe and other critics called her work shallow and **mawkish** and certainly would not classify her with Longfellow and other of her male contemporaries, her work may have had a greater influence in her own time than did theirs. Focusing on themes that were popular among women of the elite and emerging middling classes, her words and sentiments helped to form a literary basis for female

Lydia Sigourney

Watkinson Library, Trinity College, Hartford, Connecticut.

mawkish Mushy, exaggerated, and insincere sentimentality.

culture during the middle decades of the nineteenth century. Awareness of a literature designed especially for them also encouraged many young women to pursue and attain literacy. In part because of writers like Lydia Sigourney, women's literacy grew at a revolutionary pace: from about 50 percent of that of white males in 1780 to over 90 percent by 1850. As Lydia Sigourney chose to write and take credit for her writing, a generation of American women chose to read, and American society and culture was forever changed in the process.

Lydia Sigourney reflected many of the forces that were shaping America in the years before midcentury. These were years of both growing anxiety and growing hopefulness. Anxiety was rising over the industrialization and urbanization that was sweeping across the American North and by the expansion of cotton capitalism in the American South. She shared with born-again Christians, transcendentalists, socialists, and other communitarians a belief in human perfectibility that drove them all into a frenzy of work and experimentation. In northern cities, on southern plantations, and at western revival meetings, members of all social classes were crafting cultural expressions designed to give meaning to their lives and lend shape to a society that seemed to be losing all direction. At the same time, ambitious politicians were recreating the art of politics in line with new economic and cultural imperatives. A new, modern, and much more complicated America clearly was in the making.

And looming over it all was the promise and the challenge of the American West. For many, the West offered a destination for those who sought wealth or free expression. For others, the region provided an arena in which to contest economic and political issues facing the nation at large. Most agreed that the nation's destiny lay in the largely unexplored region, but exactly how this destiny was to unfold remained murky and divided loyalties at every level of society.

■ romanticism Artistic and intellectual movement characterized by interest in nature, emphasis on emotion and imagination over rationality, and rebellion against social conventions.

■ Ralph Waldo Emerson Philosopher, writer, and poet whose essays and poems made him a central figure in the transcendentalist movement and an important figure in the development of literary expression in the United States.

REACTIONS TO CHANGING CONDITIONS

☆ How did developments in American arts and letters reflect the spirit of change during the Jacksonian era?

☆ To what extent did international forces influence American cultural expressions?

As industrialization and urbanization mushroomed in the Northeast, cotton cultivation and its peculiar cultural and labor systems expanded across the South, and hundreds of communities grew up in the West. At the same time, however, increasing economic interdependence between regions and revolutionary transportation and communications systems pulled the geographically expansive nation closer together. These opposing forces helped define not only the social and political tendencies throughout the country but also the trends that would shape a distinctive American culture.

Romanticism and Genteel Culture

Underlying the new mood in American culture was an artistic and philosophical attitude that swept across the Atlantic and found a fertile new home in North America. **Romanticism**, the European rebellion against Enlightenment reason (see page 90), stressed the heart over the mind, the wild over the controlled, the mystical over the rational. The United States, with its millions of acres of wilderness, was the perfect setting for romanticism to flower. Many of the era's leading intellectuals emphasized the positive aspects of life in the United States, celebrating it in new forms of religious thought, literary presentation, and artistic expression that won broad recognition among the genteel and middle classes.

This new influence had its earliest impact in the religious realm. Reeling under the shock of social change that was affecting every aspect of life, many young people sought a religious anchor to engender some stability. Many, especially in the rising cities in the Northeast, found a voice in New Englander **Ralph Waldo Emerson**.

It Matters Today

The Spread of Mass Literacy

During the colonial and early national eras, literacy beyond basics like signing your name was reserved to a small number of elite people in American society. Books were expensive, and newspapers were few in number; there was little opportunity for most people to read and little incentive for them to do so.

During the early nineteenth century, however, the spread of public education, creation of literary and self-improvement societies, and mass publication of books and magazines caused an upsurge in both the availability and demand for literacy. Many saw in universal literacy a device that would ensure continuation of the American democratic republic, and writers like Lydia Sigourney saw in it a burgeoning marketplace for making personal fortunes. For their part, young men and women saw in literacy an opportunity to break away from traditional roles in a traditional political and economic system to forge new lives in a new society. From this era onward, Americans took widespread literacy among all classes for granted as part of our national life.

- What developments arose during the early nineteenth century that helped to produce mass literacy in the United States?
- How would American society today be different if only a wealthy elite minority could read? How would your life be different in such a society?

Pastor of the prestigious Second Unitarian Church in Boston, Emerson experienced a religious crisis in 1831 when his young wife, Ellen Louisa, died. Looking for new inspiration, he traveled to Europe where he met the famous Romantic writers William Wordsworth and Thomas Carlyle, who influenced him to seek truth in nature and spirit rather than in rationality and order. Emerson combined this Romantic influence with his already strong Unitarian leaning, creating a new philosophical creed called **transcendentalism**. Recovered from his grief, he returned to the United States to begin a new career as an essayist and lecturer, spreading the transcendentalist message.

"Historical Christianity has fallen into the error that corrupts all attempts to communicate religion," Emerson told the students at the Harvard Divinity School in 1838. "Men have come to speak of revelation as somewhat long ago given and done, as if God were dead." But for Emerson, God was "everywhere active, in each ray of the star, in each wavelet of the pool." Only through direct contact with the transcendent power in the universe could men and women know the truth.

Emerson's writings were in tune with the cultural and economic currents of his day. In celebrating the individual, Emerson validated the surging individualism of Jacksonian America. In addition, because each person had to find his or her own path to knowledge, Emerson could extol many of the disturbing aspects of modernizing America as potentially liberating forces. Rather than condemning the money grubbing that many said characterized Jacksonian America, Emerson stated that money represented the "prose of life" and was, "in its effects and laws, as beautiful as roses."

Emerson not only set the tone for American philosophical inquiry but also suggested a bold new direction for American literature. His 1837 address at Harvard University entitled "The American Scholar" was a declaration of literary independence from European models. Young American writers responded enthusiastically. During the twenty years following this speech, Henry David Thoreau, Walt Whitman, Henry Wadsworth Longfellow, and other writers and poets elaborated the nationalistic and transcendentalist gospels, emphasizing the uniqueness of the individual and the role of literature as a vehicle for self-discovery and national expression. "I celebrate myself, and sing myself," Whitman wrote. They also carried the Romantic message, celebrating the primitive and the common. Longfellow sang the praise of the village blacksmith, and in "I Hear America Singing," Whitman conveyed the poetry present in the everyday speech of America's common folk.

Perhaps the most radical of the transcendentalists was Emerson's good friend and frequent houseguest **Henry David Thoreau**. Emerson and his other followers made the case for self-reliance, but Thoreau embodied it, camping on the shore of Walden Pond near Concord, Massachusetts, where he did his best to

■ **transcendentalism** A philosophical and literary movement asserting that God exists within human beings and in nature, and that intuition is the highest source of knowledge, opening the way to the *transcendent*—that which lies beyond the range of normal experience.

■ **Henry David Thoreau** Writer and naturalist and friend of Ralph Waldo Emerson; his best-known work is *Walden* (1854).

This 1827 painting by Thomas Cole, capturing a scene from James Fenimore Cooper's *Last of the Mohicans*, illustrates the romantic mood during the early nineteenth century. In line with artistic romanticism, nature dwarfs all else. Even a large Indian camp seems insignificant in size, lost in an exaggerated image of the mountains in the Hudson River region of New York.

"Last of the Mohicans" by Thomas Cole. Fenimore Art Museum, Cooperstown, New York.

live independent of the rapidly modernizing market economy. "I went to the woods because I wished to live deliberately," Thoreau wrote, "and not, when I came to die, discover that I had not lived."

Among women who were seeking meaning through their writing, Margaret Fuller was the leading transcendentalist. After demonstrating her own equality by editing the transcendentalist magazine *The Dial* as well as serving as chief literary critic for the *New York Tribune*, Fuller advocated for women's rights in her *Woman in the Nineteenth Century* (1845).

But the most popular women writers of the day were those who were most successful at communicating the sentimentalized role for the new genteel woman. Lydia Sigourney was one of the first American women to carve out an independent living as a writer. Catharine Beecher was another writer who enjoyed enormous success for her practical advice guides aimed at making women more effective homemakers. The novels of women writers E. D. E. N. Southworth and Susan Warner were among the most popular books published in the first half of the nineteenth century.

Other authors joined Sigourney, Southworth, and Warner in pushing American literature in Romantic

directions. James Fenimore Cooper and Nathaniel Hawthorne each helped to popularize American themes and scenes in their writing. Even before Emerson's "American Scholar," Cooper had launched a new sort of American novel and American hero. Cooper's *The Pioneers* (1823) was the first of five novels featuring Natty Bumppo, a frontiersman whose rough-hewn virtues were beloved by Romantics and popularly associated with the American frontier. Nathaniel Hawthorne explored different American literary themes. In *Twice-Told Tales* (1837), Hawthorne presented readers with a collection of moral **allegories** stressing the evils of pride, selfishness, and secret guilt among puritanical New Englanders. He brought these themes to fruition in his novel *The Scarlet Letter* (1850), in which adulteress Hester Prynne overcomes shame to gain redemption, while her secret lover, Puritan minister Arthur Dimmesdale, is destroyed by his hidden sins.

George Bancroft did for American history what novelists like Cooper did for American literature. Bancroft set out in 1834 to capture the history of the United States from its first settlement, a story that eventually filled ten volumes when he completed it in 1874. Focusing on strong leaders who carried out God's design by bringing liberty into the world, Bancroft made clear that the middle-class qualities of individualism, self-sufficiency, and a passionate love of liberty were the essence of the American experience and the American character. Bancroft's history became the definitive work of its kind, influencing generations of American students and scholars in their interpretations of the nation's past.

The drive to celebrate American scenes and the young nation's uniqueness also influenced the visual arts during this period. Neoclassicism, a style influenced by Enlightenment rationalism that emphasized the simple, logical lines found in Greek and Roman art, dominated the art scene at first. Artists often used classical imagery in their portrayals of contemporary figures and events. Horatio Greenough's statue of George Washington, for example, presented the nation's first president wrapped in a toga, looking like a Roman statesman. After 1825, however, classical scenes were gradually being replaced by American ones. Englishman Thomas Cole came to the United States in 1818

allegory A story in which characters and events stand for abstract ideas and suggest a deep, symbolic meaning.

hoping to find a romantic paradise. Cole was disappointed by the neoclassical art scene in Philadelphia, but eventually found the paradise he was seeking in the Hudson River valley. There he began painting romantically exaggerated renderings of the landscape. The refreshing naturalness and Americanness of Cole's paintings attracted a large following, and other artists took up the style. This group of landscapists is known as the **Hudson River school**, after the area where most of them painted.

The paintings of George Caleb Bingham exemplify another movement in American art that reflected the temper of the time. Bingham was born in Virginia and educated for a time in Pennsylvania before he went west to Missouri. There he painted realistic pictures of common people engaged in everyday activities. The flatboat men, marketplace-dwellers, and electioneering politicians in Bingham's paintings were artistic testimony to the emerging democratic style of America in the Jacksonian period (see illustrations on pages 249 and 255).

Anti-Catholic and anti-immigrant feelings often caused rioting in American cities during the 1830s and 1840s. In 1834, street violence escalated into a full-fledged riot in Massachusetts, leading to the burning of a Catholic convent in Charlestown, a Boston suburb. This engraving, which adorned the covers of a number of pamphlets that purported to tell the true lurid story of the events surrounding the fire, shows the convent ablaze as fire companies try in vain to smother the flames. Though the most notorious event of this kind that occurred during this era, this riot was anything but exceptional. "The Nun of St. Ursula: Burning of the Convent" by Harry Hazel.

Culture Among Workers and Slaves

Most genteel people in the antebellum era would have denied that working people, whether wage-earning immigrants in northern cities or slaves in the South, had a "culture." But each of these groups crafted viable cultures that suited their living and working conditions and were distinct from the genteel culture of their owners or supervisors.

Wretched living conditions and dispiriting poverty encouraged working-class people in northern cities to choose social and cultural outlets that were very different from those of upper- and middle-class Americans. Offering temporary relief from unpleasant conditions, drinking was the social distraction of choice. Whiskey and gin were cheap and available during the 1820s and 1830s as western farmers used the new roads and canals to ship distilled spirits to urban markets. In the 1830s, consumers could purchase a gallon of whiskey for 25 cents.

Even activities that did not center on drinking tended to involve it. While genteel and middle-class people remained in their private homes reading Sigourney or Hawthorne, working people attended popular theaters cheering entertainments designed to appeal to their less polished tastes. **Minstrel shows** featured fast-paced music and raucous comedy. Plays, such as Benjamin Baker's *A Glance at New York in 1848*, presented caricatures of working-class "Bowery B'hoys" and "G'hals" and of the well-off Broadway "pumpkins" they poked fun at. To put the audience in the proper mood, theater owners sold cheap drinks in the lobby or in basement pubs. Alcohol was also sold at sporting events that drew large working-class audiences—bare-knuckle boxing contests, for instance, where the fighting was seldom confined to the boxing ring.

Stinging from their low status in the urbanizing and industrializing society, angry about living in hovels, and freed from inhibitions by hours of drinking, otherwise rational workingmen often pummeled one another to let off steam. And in working-class neighborhoods, where police forces were small, fist-fights often turned into brawls and then into riots pitting Protestants against Catholics, immigrants against the native-born, and whites against blacks.

■ **Hudson River school** The first native school of landscape painting in the United States (1825–1875); it attracted artists rebelling against the neoclassical tradition.

minstrel show A variety show in which white actors made up as blacks presented jokes, songs, dances, and comic skits.

be raised to purchase their freedom, the freed slaves should immediately be shipped to Africa.

Most preachers active in the Second Great Awakening supported the idea of colonization, but a few individuals pressed for more radical reforms. The most vocal leader among the antislavery forces during the early nineteenth century was **William Lloyd Garrison**. In 1831 he founded the nation's first prominent abolitionist newspaper, *The Liberator*. In it he advocated immediate emancipation for African Americans, with no compensation for slaveholders. In the following year, Garrison founded the New England Anti-Slavery Society and then, in 1833, the national American Anti-Slavery Society.

At first, Garrison stood alone. Some Christian reformers joined his cause, but the majority held back. In eastern cities, workers lived in dread of either enslaved or free blacks flooding in, lowering wages, and destroying job security. In western states, farmers feared that competition could arise from a slaveholding aristocracy. In both regions, white supremacists argued that the extension of slavery beyond the Mississippi River and north of the **Mason-Dixon Line** would eventually lead to blacks mixing with the white population, a possibility they found extremely distasteful. Thus most whites detested the notion of immediate emancipation, and radical abolitionists at this early date were almost universally ignored or, worse, attacked when they denounced slavery. Still, support for the movement gradually grew. In 1836 petitions flooded into Congress demanding an end to the slave trade in Washington, D.C. Not ready to engage in an action quite so controversial, Congress passed a **gag rule** that automatically **tabled** any petition to Congress that addressed the abolition of slavery. The rule remained in effect for nearly a decade. Many state assemblies followed suit, but not all governments remained closed to the discussion of slavery. In these state battles, a new group often led the fight against slavery: women.

Having assumed the burden of eliminating sin from the world back in the 1830s (see pages 276–277), many evangelical women became active in the antislavery cause. Moved by their activism, in 1840 Garrison proposed that a woman be elected to the executive committee of the American Anti-Slavery Society. And later that year women were members of Garrison's

■ **William Lloyd Garrison** Abolitionist leader who founded and published *The Liberator*, an antislavery newspaper.

■ **Mason-Dixon Line** The boundary between Pennsylvania and Maryland; it marked the northern division between free and slave states before the Civil War.

gag rule A rule that limits or prevents debate on an issue.

table Action by a legislative body (Congress, for example) to postpone debate on an issue until a positive vote removes the topic from the table.

Though they were often in the majority in the various reform movements that arose during the 1830s and 1840s, women were consistently denied leadership roles and forbidden to express their views in public. In 1848, a number of women led by reformers Lucretia Mott and Elizabeth Cady Stanton (pictured here) brought attention to their unequal status by holding a Women's Rights Convention in Seneca Falls, New York. This marked the beginning of a self-conscious movement designed to win full equality for women in the United States, an objective for which women continue to struggle today.

delegation to the first World Anti-Slavery Convention in London, but British antislavery advocates considered the presence of women inappropriate and refused to seat them.

One prominent female abolitionist, Angelina Grimké, gave voice to her contemporaries' frustration at such treatment: "Are we aliens, because we are women? . . . Have women no country—no interests staked in public weal [welfare]—no liabilities in the common peril—no partnership in a nation's guilt and shame?" In that same year, her sister Sarah went further, writing a powerful indictment against the treatment of women in America and a call for equality. In *Letters on the Equality of the Sexes and the Condition of Woman*, Sarah proclaimed, "The page of history teems with woman's wrongs . . . and it is wet with woman's tears." Women must, she said, "arise in all the majesty of moral power . . . and plant themselves, side by side, on the platform of human rights, with man, to whom they were designed to be companions, equals and helpers in every good word and work."

Like Sarah Grimké, many other women backed away from male-dominated causes and began advancing their own cause. In 1848 two women who had been excluded from the World Anti-Slavery Convention, **Lucretia Mott** and **Elizabeth Cady Stanton**, called concerned women to a convention at Seneca Falls, New York, to discuss their common problems. At Seneca Falls, they presented a Declaration of Sentiments that cited "the history of repeated injuries and usurpations on the part of man toward woman, having in direct object the establishment of an absolute tyranny over her." The convention adopted eleven resolutions relating to equality under the law, rights to control property, and other prominent gender issues. A twelfth resolution, calling for the right to vote, failed to receive unanimous endorsement.

Free and Slave Labor Protests

Like the predominantly white and middle-class women who were founding female protest movements in America, some northern workers and southern slaves began to perceive their miseries as the product of their exploitation by others. In view of their grim working and living conditions, it is not surprising that some manufacturing workers and slave laborers protested their situations and embraced increasingly active strategies for dealing with them.

The first organized labor strike in America took place in 1806, when a group of journeymen shoemakers stopped work to protest the hiring of unskilled workers to perform some tasks that higher-paid journeymen and apprentices had been doing. The strike failed when a New York court declared the shoemakers' actions illegal, but in the years to come many other journeymen's groups would try the same tactic. Industrialization robbed them of their status as independent contractors, forcing many to become wage laborers, and they bemoaned their loss of power in having to accept owner-dictated hours, conditions, and wages for the work they performed.

Unlike the British Luddites (see page 225), journeymen simply asked for decent wages and working conditions and some role in decision making. Throughout the industrializing cities of the Northeast and the smaller manufacturing centers of the West, journeymen banded together in **trade unions**: assemblies of skilled workers grouped by specific occupation. During the 1830s, trade unions from neighboring towns merged with one another to form the beginnings of a national trade union movement. In this way, house carpenters, shoemakers, and other craft workers established national unions through which they attempted to enforce uniform wage standards in their industries. In 1834 journeymen's organizations from a number of industries joined to form the **National Trades' Union**, the first labor organization in the nation's history to represent many different crafts.

Not surprisingly, factory owners, bankers, and others who had a vested interest in keeping labor cheap used every device available to prevent unions from succeeding. Employers formed manufacturing associations to resist union activity and used the courts to keep organized labor from disrupting business. Despite such efforts, a number of strikes affected American industries during the 1830s. In 1834 and again in 1836, women working in the textile mills in Lowell, Massachusetts, closed down production in the face of wage reductions and rising boarding house rates. Such demonstrations of power by workers frightened manufacturers, and gradually employers replaced native-born women in the factories with immigrants, who were less liable to organize successfully and, more important, less likely to win approval from sympathetic judges or consumers.

Still, workers won some small victories in the battle to organize. A significant breakthrough finally came in 1842 when the Massachusetts Supreme Court decided in the case of **Commonwealth v. Hunt** that Boston's journeymen boot makers were within their rights to organize "in such manner as best to subserve their own interests" and to call strikes. By that time, however, economic changes had so undermined labor's ability to withstand the rigors of strikes and court cases that legal protection became somewhat meaningless.

Though never as violent as those of the Luddites, not all labor protests were peaceful. In 1828, for example, immigrant weavers protested the pitiful wages paid by Alexander Knox, New York City's leading textile employer. Storming Knox's home to demand higher pay, the weavers invaded and vandalized his house and beat Knox's son and a cordon of police guards. The rioters then marched to the garret and basement homes of weavers who had refused to join the protest and destroyed their looms.

Unlike workers in the North, who at least had some legal protections and civil rights, slaves had nothing but their own wits to protect them against a society that classed them as disposable personal property. Slaves were skilled at the use of **passive resistance**. The importance of passive resistance was evident in the folk tales and songs that circulated

■ **Lucretia Mott** Quaker minister who founded the Philadelphia Female Anti-Slavery Society (1833) and co-organized the Seneca Falls Women's Rights Convention in 1848.

■ **Elizabeth Cady Stanton** Pioneering woman suffrage leader, co-organizer of the first Women's Rights Convention, held in Seneca Falls, New York, in 1848.

trade union A labor organization whose members work in a specific trade or craft.

■ **National Trades' Union** The first national association of trade unions in the United States; it was formed in 1834.

■ ***Commonwealth v. Hunt*** Landmark decision by the Massachusetts Supreme Court making unionization legal in that state.

passive resistance Resistance by nonviolent methods.

Thurlow Weed's skillful political manipulation had pulled in a wide range of people who were disgusted with what Jefferson had called "political party tricks," and the convention drew a broad constituency. Using all his charm and influence, Weed cajoled the convention into nominating William Wirt, a respected lawyer from Maryland, as its presidential candidate.

Antimasons fully expected that when the Republicans met in convention later in the year, they would rubber-stamp the Antimasonic nomination and present a united front against Jackson. But the Republicans, fearful of the Antimasons' odd combination of **machine politics** and antiparty paranoia, nominated Clay as their standard-bearer. The Republicans then issued the country's first formal **party platform**, a ringing document supporting Clay's economic ideas and attacking Jackson's use of the **spoils system**.

Even having two anti-Jackson parties in the running did not satisfy some. Distrustful of the Antimasons and put off by Clay's nationalist philosophy, southerners in both parties refused to support any of the candidates. They finally backed nullification advocate John Floyd of Virginia.

Lack of unity contributed to disaster for Jackson's opponents. Wirt and Floyd received votes that might have gone to Clay. But even if Clay had gotten those votes, Jackson's popularity and the political machinery that he and Van Buren controlled would have given him the victory. The president was reelected with a total of 219 electoral votes to Clay's 49, Wirt's 7, and Floyd's 11. Jackson's party lost five seats in the Senate but gained six in the House of Representatives. Despite unsettling changes in the land and continuing political chaos, the people still wanted the hero of New Orleans as their leader.

The New Political Coalition

If one lesson emerged clearly from the election of 1832, it was that Jackson's opponents needed to pull together if they expected to challenge the growing power of "King Andrew." Imitating names used by political organizations in Great Britain, Clay and his associates began calling Jackson supporters Tories—supporters of the king—and calling themselves Whigs.

machine politics The aggressive use of influence, favors, and tradeoffs by a political organization, or "machine," to mobilize support among its followers.

party platform A formal statement of the principles, policies, and promises on which a political party bases its appeal to the public.

■ **spoils system** System associated with American politics in which a political party, after winning an election, gives government jobs to its supporters as a reward for working toward victory.

■ **Whig Party** Political party started in 1834 as an anti-Jackson coalition, charging "King Andrew" with executive tyranny.

BORN TO COMMAND.

OF VETO MEMORY.

HAD I BEEN CONSULTED.

KING ANDREW THE FIRST.

© Collection of the New-York Historical Society

Calling themselves Whigs after the English political party that opposed royal authority, Henry Clay, John C. Calhoun, and Daniel Webster joined forces to oppose what they characterized as Andrew Jackson's kingly use of power. This lithograph from 1834 depicting Jackson in royal dress stepping on the Constitution expresses their view quite vividly.

The antimonarchical label stuck, and the new party formed in 1834 was called the **Whig Party**.

The Whigs eventually absorbed all the major factions that opposed Jackson. At the heart of the party were Clay supporters: advocates of strong government and the American System in economics. The nullifiers in the South, however, quickly came around when Clay and Calhoun found themselves on the same side in defeating Jackson's appointment of Van Buren as American minister to England. This successful campaign, combined with Calhoun's growing awareness that Jackson was perhaps more dangerous to his constituents' interests than was Clay, led the southerner and his associates into the Whig camp. The Antimasons joined because their disgust at Jackson's use of patronage and back-alley politics—not to mention the fact that he was a Mason—overcame their distrust of Clay's party philosophy. A final major group to rally to the Whigs were evangelicals who disapproved of Jackson's personal lifestyle, his views on slavery, his Indian policy, and his refusal to involve government in their moral causes. The orderly and sober society that Clay and the Whigs envisioned appealed to such people.

The congressional elections in 1834 provided the first test for the new coalition. In this first electoral contest, the Whigs won nearly 40 percent of the seats in the House of Representatives and more than 48 percent in the Senate. Clearly cooperation was paying off.

Van Buren in the White House

Jackson had seemed to be a tower of strength when he was first elected to the presidency in 1828, but by the end of his second term, he was nearly 70 years old and plagued by various ailments. Old Hickory decided to follow Washington's example and not run for a third term. Instead, Jackson used all the power and patronage at his command to ensure that Martin Van Buren, his most consistent loyalist, would win the presidential nomination at the Democratic Party convention.

Van Buren was a skilled organizer whose ability to create unlikely political alliances had earned him the nickname "the Little Magician." Throughout Jackson's first term, Van Buren had headed the Kitchen Cabinet and increasingly became Jackson's chief political henchman. In 1832 Jackson had repaid his loyalty by making him vice president, with the intention of launching him into the presidency.

Meanwhile, Clay and his Whig associates were hatching a plot to deny the election to the Democrats. Instead of holding a convention and thrashing out a platform, the Whigs let each region's party organization nominate its own candidates. Whig leaders hoped a large number of candidates would confuse voters and throw the election into the House of Representatives, where skillful political management and Van Buren's unpopularity might unseat the Democrats. As a result, four **favorite sons** ran on the Whig ticket. Daniel Webster of Massachusetts represented the Northeast. Hugh Lawson White, a Tennessean and former Jackson supporter, ran for the Southwest. South Carolina nullifier W. P. Mangum represented the South. William Henry Harrison, former governor of Indiana Territory and victor at the Battle of Tippecanoe in 1811, was tapped to represent the Northwest.

Weed underestimated the Democrats' hold on the minds of the voters. Van Buren captured 765,483 popular votes—more than Jackson had won in the previous election—but his performance in the Electoral College was significantly weaker than Jackson's had been. Van Buren squeaked by with a winning margin of less than 1 percent, but it was a victory, and the presidential election did not go to the House of Representatives.

It became clear from the beginning that Van Buren's presidency would be a troubled one. As soon as he assumed office, the nation was hit by another terrible financial crisis. The **Panic of 1837** was a direct outcome of the Bank War and Jackson's money policies,

but it was Van Buren who would take the blame. The crisis had begun with Nicholas Biddle's manipulation of credit and interest rates in an effort to discredit Jackson and have the Second Bank rechartered in spite of the president's veto. Jackson had added to the problem by removing paper money and credit from the economy in an effort to win support from hard-money advocates. Arguing that he wanted to end "the monopoly of the public lands in the hands of speculators and capitalists," Jackson had issued the **Specie Circular** on August 15, 1836. From that day forward payment for public land had to be made in specie.

The contraction in credit and currency had the same impact in 1836 as it had in 1819: the national economy collapsed. By May 1837, New York banks were no longer accepting any paper currency, and soon all banks had adopted the policy of accepting specie only. Unable to pay back or collect loans, buy raw materials, or conduct any other sort of commerce, hundreds of businesses, plantations, farms, factories, canals, and other enterprises spiraled into bankruptcy. More than a third of the population was thrown out of work, and people who were fortunate enough to keep their jobs found their pay reduced by as much as 50 percent. Fledgling industries and labor organizations were cast into disarray, and the nation sank into both an economic and an emotional depression.

As credit continued to collapse through 1838 and 1839, President Van Buren tried to address the problems. First, he extended Jackson's hard-money policy, which caused the economy to contract further. Next, in an effort to keep the government solvent, Van Buren cut federal spending to the bone, shrinking the money supply even more. Then, to replace the stabilizing influence lost when the Second Bank was destroyed, he created a national treasury system endowed with many of the powers formerly wielded by the bank. The new regional treasury offices accepted only specie in payment for federal lands and other obligations and used that specie to pay federal expenses and debts. As a result, specie was sucked out of local banks and local economies. While fiscally sound by the wisdom of the day, Van Buren's decisions only made matters worse for the average person and drove the last nail into his political coffin.

---

favorite son A candidate nominated for office by delegates from his or her own region or state.

■ **Panic of 1837** An economic collapse that came as the result of Andrew Jackson's fiscal policies and led to an extended national economic depression.

■ **Specie Circular** Order issued by President Jackson in 1836 stating that the federal government would accept only specie— gold and silver—as payment for public land; one of the causes of the Panic of 1837.

The Granger Collection, New York.

A BEAUTIFUL GOBLET OF WHITEHOUSE CHAMPAGNE

AN UGLY MUG OF LOG-CABIN HARD CIDER

Democrats tried to discredit Whig candidate William Henry Harrison by characterizing the one-time Ohio governor as an unsophisticated backwoods hick, funny considering that he was the son of one of the first families of Virginia. Whigs responded by characterizing Martin Van Buren as an urban sophisticate, out of touch with everyday people, also funny, considering that he was the son of a rural tavern keeper. This clever pull card illustrates the Whig view: with the pull lever in one position, Van Buren smiles as he sips "Whitehouse champagne" (*left*); pull the lever and he grimaces at the taste of simple "log cabin hard cider."

The Log Cabin and Hard Cider Campaign of 1840

The Whigs had learned their lesson in the election of 1836: only a unified party could possibly destroy the political machine built by Jackson and Van Buren. As the nation sank into depression, the Whigs determined to use whatever means were necessary to break the Democrats' grip on the voters and were prepared to line up behind a single candidate.

Once again, Henry Clay hoped to be the party's nominee, but Thurlow Weed convinced the party that William Henry Harrison would have a better chance in the election. For Harrison's running mate, the party chose **John Tyler**, a Virginia senator who had bolted from Jackson's Democratic Party during the Bank War. Weed clearly hoped that the Virginian would draw votes from the planter South while Harrison carried the West and North.

■ **John Tyler** Virginia senator who left the Democratic Party after conflicts with Andrew Jackson; he was elected vice president in 1840 and became president when William Henry Harrison died in office.

Although the economy was in bad shape, the Whig campaign avoided addressing any serious issues. Instead, the Whigs launched a smear campaign against Van Buren. Although he was the son of a lowly tavern keeper, the Whig press portrayed him as an aristocrat whose expensive tastes were signs of dangerous excess during an economic depression. Harrison really was an aristocrat, but the Whigs played on the Romantic themes so popular among their genteel and middle-class constituents by characterizing him as a simple frontiersman—a Natty Bumppo—who had risen to greatness through his own efforts. Whig claims were so extravagant that the Democratic press soon satirized Harrison in political cartoons showing a rustic hick swilling hard cider. The satire backfired. Whig newspapers and speechmakers seized on the image and sold Harrison, the longtime political insider, as a simple man of the people.

Van Buren had little with which to retaliate. Harrison had a distinguished political and military career behind him. Tyler, too, was well respected. And Van Buren had simply not done a good job of addressing the nation's pressing economic needs. Voters cried out for change and Van Buren could not offer them one. The combination of political dissatisfaction and

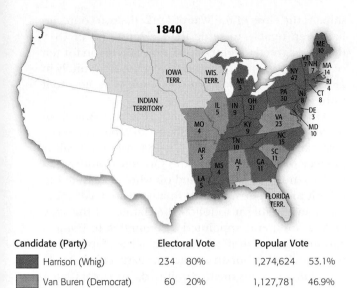

1840

Candidate (Party)	Electoral Vote		Popular Vote	
Harrison (Whig)	234	80%	1,274,624	53.1%
Van Buren (Democrat)	60	20%	1,127,781	46.9%
Territories				

MAP 12.2 Election of 1840

Although the difference in popular votes between William Henry Harrison and Martin Van Buren was small in the election of 1840, Harrison won a landslide victory in the Electoral College. This map shows why. After floundering through several elections, the Whig Party was finally able to organize a national coalition, giving it solid victories in all of the most populous regions of the country. Only the Far West, which was still sparsely settled, voted as a block for Van Buren. Copyright © Cengage Learning

campaign hype brought the biggest voter turnout to that time in American history: nearly twice as many voters came to the polls in 1840 as had voted in 1836. And while Harrison won only 53 percent of the popular vote, Weed's successful political manipulations earned the Whigs nearly 80 percent of the electoral votes, sweeping the Democrats out of the White House (see Map 12.2).

THE TRIUMPH OF MANIFEST DESTINY

★ What forces in American life contributed to the concept of manifest destiny?

★ To what extent did the actions taken by American settlers in Oregon and Texas reflect the ideal of manifest destiny?

The key to Harrison's success was the Whig Party's skillful manipulation of the former general's reputation as a frontiersman and popular advocate for westward expansion. With politics bogged down in debates over tariffs, states' rights, public finance, and dozens of other practical, if boring policy matters, the nationalistic appeal of seizing and occupying the West brought

an air of excitement to public discourse. It was this allure that helped to draw out the thousands of new voters in 1840 and would provide a new basis for political cooperation and contention in the years to come.

The Rise of Manifest Destiny

The new spirit that came to life in American politics and rhetoric in the years after 1840 found expression in a single phrase: manifest destiny. To some extent, manifest destiny can be traced back to the sense of mission that had motivated colonial Puritans (see page 63). Like John Winthrop and his Massachusetts Bay associates, many early nineteenth-century Americans believed they had a duty to go into new lands. During the antebellum period, romantic nationalism, land hunger, and the evangelicalism of the Second Great Awakening shaped this sense of divine mission into a new and powerful commitment to westward expansion. As the American Board of Commissioners for Foreign Missions noted in its annual report for 1827, "The tide of emigration is rolling westward so rapidly, that it must speedily surmount every barrier, till it reaches every habitable part of this continent." The power of this force led many to conclude that the westward movement was not just an economic process but was part of a divine plan for North America and the world.

Not surprisingly, the earliest and most aggressive proponents of expansion were Christian missionary organizations, whose many magazines, newsletters, and reports were the first to give it formal voice. Politicians, however, were not far behind. Democratic warhorse and expansion advocate Thomas Hart Benton of Missouri borrowed both the tone and content of missionary rhetoric in his speeches promoting generous land policies, territorial acquisition, and even overseas expansion. In 1825, for example, Benton argued in favor of American colonization of the Pacific coast and eventually of Asia, bringing "great and wonderful benefits" to the western Indians and allowing "science, liberal principles in government, and true religion [to] cast their lights across the intervening sea."

Expansion to the North and West

One major complication standing in the way of the nation's perceived manifest destiny was that other countries already owned large parts of the continent. The continued presence of the British, for example, proved to be a constant source of irritation. During the War of 1812, the War Hawks had advocated conquering Canada and pushing the British from the continent altogether. Although events thwarted this ambition, many continued to push for that objective by either legal or extralegal means.

MAP 12.3 Oregon Territory
This map shows the changing boundaries and shifting possession of the Oregon Country. As a result of Polk's aggressive stance and economic pressures, Britain ceded all land south of the 49th parallel to the United States in 1846. Copyright © Cengage Learning

Legend:
Focus of dispute by 1846
Area of original dispute over Oregon

One source of dispute between the United States and Great Britain was the **Oregon Question**. The vast Oregon tract had been claimed at one time or another by Spain, Russia, France, England, and the United States (see Map 12.3). By the 1820s, only England and the United States continued to contest for its owner-

ship. At the close of the War of 1812, the two countries had been unable to settle their claims, and in 1818 they had agreed to joint occupation of Oregon for ten years. They extended this arrangement indefinitely in 1827, with the **proviso** that either country could end it with one year's notice.

Oregon's status as neither British nor American presented its occupants with an unstable situation. One early incident occurred in 1841 when a wealthy pioneer died and because the Oregon Country had no laws, no guidelines existed on who was entitled to inherit his property. Settlers finally created a **probate court**, instructing it to follow the statutes of the state of New York, and appointed a committee to frame a constitution and draft a basic code of laws. Opposition from the British put an end to this early effort at self-rule, but the movement continued. Two years later, Americans began agitating again, this time because of wolves preying on their livestock. They held a series of "Wolf Meetings" in 1843 to discuss joint protection and resolved to create a civil government. Although the British tried to prevent it, the assembly passed the **First Organic Laws of Oregon** on July 5, 1843, making Oregon an independent republic in all but name. Independence, however, was not the settlers' long-term goal. The document's preamble announced that the code of laws would continue in force "until such time as the United States of America extend their jurisdiction over us."

Revolution in Texas

Similar problems faced American settlers who had taken up residence in Spain's, then Mexico's territories in the Southwest. Although the Spanish and then the Mexican government had invited Anglo-Americans to settle in the region, these pioneers generally ignored Mexican customs and disregarded Mexican law. This was particularly the case after 1829, when Mexico began attaching duties to trade items moving between the region and the neighboring United States. Mexico also abolished importing slaves. Bad feelings grew over the years, but the distant and politically unstable Mexican government could do little to enforce laws and customs. In addition, despite the friction between cultures in Texas, many Tejanos were disturbed by the corruption and political instability in Mexico City and were as eager as their Texian counterparts to participate in the United States' thriving cotton market.

Assuming responsibility for forging a peaceful settlement to the problems between settlers in Texas and the Mexican government, Stephen F. Austin went to Mexico City in 1833. While Austin was there, **Antonio López de Santa Anna** seized power. Although he had supported Mexico's republican constitution, adopted in 1824, Santa Anna had since come to the conclusion that Mexico was not ready for democracy. Upon

■ **Oregon Question** The question of the national ownership of the Pacific Northwest; the United States and England renegotiated the boundary in 1846, establishing it at 49° north latitude.

proviso A clause making a qualification, condition, or restriction in a document.

probate court A court that establishes the validity of wills and administers the estates of people who have died.

■ **First Organic Laws of Oregon** A constitution adopted by American settlers in the Oregon Country on July 5, 1843, establishing a government independent from Great Britain and requesting annexation by the United States.

■ **Antonio López de Santa Anna** Mexican general who was president of Mexico when he led an attack on the Alamo in 1836; he again led Mexico during its war with the United States in 1846–1848.

Following the Battle of San Jacinto, Texas forces captured Mexican president Antonio López de Santa Anna as he tried to escape disguised as a private. Brought to Sam Houston, who had been wounded in the battle, Santa Anna conveyed his formal surrender. A month later, the captured president signed the Treaty of Velasco, granting Texas its independence in exchange for his own release and return to Mexico.

assuming power, he suspended the constitution, dismissed Congress, and set himself up as the self-declared "Napoleon of the West."

Throughout Mexico, former revolutionaries and common citizens who had anticipated democracy were outraged by Santa Anna's actions. To the south, in Yucatán and elsewhere, provinces openly rebelled. The same potential existed along the northern frontier as well. Trying to avoid an open break, Austin met with Santa Anna in 1834 and presented several petitions advocating reforms and greater self-government in Texas, but Santa Anna made it clear that he intended to exert his authority over the region. On his arrival back in Texas in 1835, Austin declared, "War is our only recourse." He was immediately made chairman of a committee to call for a "Consultation" of delegates from all over Texas.

Mexican officials, viewing the unrest in Texas as rebellion against their authority, issued arrest warrants for all the Texas troublemakers they could identify and **deployed** troops to San Antonio. Austin's committee immediately sent out word for Texans to arm themselves. The **Texas Revolution** started quickly thereafter when the little town of Gonzales refused to surrender a cannon to Mexican officials on September 29, 1835.

Angered by the rebellion, Santa Anna personally led the Mexican army into Texas, arriving in San Antonio on February 23, 1836 (see Map 12.4). Knowing that Santa Anna was on his way, Texas militia commander William Travis moved his troops into the **Alamo**. On March 6 Santa Anna ordered an all-out assault and despite staggering casualties was able to capture the former mission. Most of the post's defenders were killed in the assault, and Santa Anna executed those who survived the battle, including former American congressman and frontier celebrity Davy Crockett. While Travis, Crockett, and others struggled at the Alamo, General **Sam Houston**

deploy To position military resources (troops, artillery, equipment) in preparation for action.

■ **Texas Revolution** A revolt by American colonists in Texas against Mexican rule; it began in 1835 and ended with the establishment of the Republic of Texas in 1836.

■ **Alamo** A fortified Franciscan mission at San Antonio, where Santa Anna's forces wiped out rebellious Texas defenders in 1836.

■ **Sam Houston** American general and politician who fought in the struggle for Texas's independence from Mexico and became president of the Republic of Texas.

MAP 12.4 Texas Revolution
This map shows troop movements and the major battles in the Texas Revolution, as well as the conflicting boundary claims made by Texans and the Mexican government. The Battle of San Jacinto and the Treaty of Velasco ended the war, but the conflicting land claims continued when Mexico repudiated the treaty. Copyright © Cengage Learning

was busy rounding up troops for a more general war against the invading Santa Anna.

Despite the loss at the Alamo, Texans continued to underestimate Santa Anna's strength and his resolve to put down the rebellion. After a series of

■ **Treaty of Velasco** Treaty that Santa Anna signed in May 1836 after his capture at the San Jacinto River; it recognized the Republic of Texas, but the Mexican congress later rejected it.

filibuster To use obstructionist tactics, especially prolonged speechmaking, to delay legislative action.

■ **Webster-Ashburton Treaty** 1842 treaty that established the present border between Canada and northeastern Maine.

defeats, however, the Texans scored a stunning victory on April 21 at the San Jacinto River and captured Santa Anna. In exchange for his release, in May 1836 Santa Anna signed the **Treaty of Velasco**, officially recognizing Texas's independence and acknowledging the Rio Grande as the border between Texas and Mexico.

As in Oregon, many leaders in Texas hoped their actions would lead to swift annexation by the United States. In 1838 Houston, by then president of the Republic of Texas, invited the United States to annex Texas. Because all of Texas lay below the Missouri Compromise line (see Map 10.1, page 245), John Quincy Adams, now a Whig member of the House of Representatives, **filibustered** for three weeks against the acquisition of such a massive block of potential slave territory. Seeking to avoid national controversy, Congress refused to ratify the annexation treaty.

The Politics of Manifest Destiny

Although Adams was typical of one wing of the Whig coalition, he certainly did not speak for the majority of Whigs on the topic of national expansion. The party of manufacturing, revivalism, and social reform inclined naturally toward the blending of political, economic, and religious evangelicalism that was manifest destiny. William Henry Harrison himself, the united party's first national candidate, was a colorful figure in American westward expansion (see Chapter 10), and his political campaign in 1840 celebrated the simple virtues of frontier life. When Harrison died soon after taking office in 1841, his vice president, John Tyler, picked up the torch of American expansionism.

Tyler was a less typical Whig than even Adams. A Virginian and a states' rights advocate, he had been a staunch Democrat until the nullification crisis, when he bolted the party to protest Jackson's strong assertion of federal power (see pages 253–254). As president, Tyler seemed still to be more Democrat than Whig. Although he had objected to Jackson's use of presidential power, like Old Hickory, Tyler as president was unyielding where ideology was concerned. He vetoed high protective tariffs, internal improvement bills, and attempts to revive the Second Bank of the United States. Tyler's refusal to promote Whig economic policies led to a general crisis in government in 1843, when his entire cabinet resigned over his veto of a bank bill.

Tyler did share his party's desire for expansion, however. He assigned his secretary of state, Daniel Webster, to negotiate a treaty with Britain to settle disputes over the Canadian border. The resulting **Webster-Ashburton Treaty** (1842) gave a large chunk of Lower Canada to the United States and finalized the nation's northeastern border. In that same year, Tyler also adopted an aggressive stance

In the Wider World

Russian Imperial Expansion

As the United States pushed westward toward the Pacific, Russia was expanding its borders southward toward the Mediterranean. And like the United States, the Russians faced serious resistance from indigenous tribes and neighboring nations. Beginning in the 1820s and lasting for over thirty years, tribal groups in the Caucasus Mountains fought a protracted guerrilla war, killing thousands of Russian soldiers yearly. Despite such drastic losses, vast superiority in numbers and technology finally brought victory to the Russians in the late 1850s, and places like Dagestan, Chechnya, and Ossetia were grafted onto the growing empire. Like contemporary Americans, Russians were sure that they were participating in an exceptional mission, a manifest destiny, and when it was over the Tsar's forces declared pride in having "civilized" and "domesticated" a savage frontier. Ironically, throughout the United States, newspapers and magazines condemned Russian aggression, ignoring the amazing parallels between that behavior and their own.

on the Oregon Question by appointing Elijah White, one of the organizers of the Wolf Meetings, as the federal Indian agent for the region, undercutting British authority.

Tyler also pushed a forceful policy toward Texas. In 1842 Sam Houston repeated his invitation for the United States to annex Texas, only to be rebuffed by Secretary of State Webster, a New Englander who shared Adams's views. When Webster resigned with the other cabinet officers in 1843, however, Tyler replaced him with fellow Virginian Abel P. Upshur, who immediately reopened the matter of Texas annexation.

Negotiations between Houston's representatives and Tyler's secretary of state—Upshur at first, then, after Upshur's death, John C. Calhoun—led to a treaty of annexation on April 11, 1844. In line with the Treaty of Velasco, the annexation document named the Rio Grande as the southern boundary of Texas. Annexation remained a major arguing point between proslavery and antislavery forces, however, and the treaty failed ratification in the Senate. The issue of Texas annexation then joined the Oregon Question as a major campaign issue in the presidential election of 1844.

Expansion and the Election of 1844

As the Whigs and the Democrats geared up for a national election, it became clear that expansion would be the key issue. This put the two leading political figures of the day, Democrat Martin Van Buren and Whig Henry Clay, in an uncomfortable position. Van Buren was on record as opposing the extension of slavery and was therefore against the annexation of Texas. Clay, the architect of the American System, was opposed to any form of uncontrolled expansion, especially if it meant fanning sectional tensions, and

he too opposed immediate annexation of Texas. Approaching the election, both issued statements to the effect that they would back annexation only with Mexico's consent.

Clay's somewhat ambiguous stance on expansion contrasted sharply with Tyler's efforts to advance the cause of manifest destiny. However, President Tyler's constant refusal to support the larger Whig political agenda led the party to nominate Clay anyway. Van Buren was not so lucky. The strong southern wing of the Democratic Party was so put off by Van Buren's position on slavery that it blocked him, securing the nomination of Tennessee congressman **James K. Polk**.

The Democrats based their platform on the issues surrounding Oregon and Texas. They implied that the regions rightfully belonged to the United States, stating "that the *re-occupation* of Oregon and the *reannexation* of Texas at the earliest practicable period are great American measures." Polk vowed to stand up to the British by claiming the entire Oregon Country up to 54°40′ north latitude and to defend the territorial claims of Texas. For his part, Clay continued to waffle on expansionism, emphasizing economic policies instead.

The election demonstrated the people's commitment to manifest destiny. Clay was a national figure, well respected and regarded as one of the nation's leading statesmen, whereas Polk was barely known outside Tennessee. Still, Polk polled 40,000 more

■ **James K. Polk** Tennessee congressman who was a leader of the Democratic Party and the dark-horse winner of the presidential campaign in 1844.

This campaign banner celebrating the Democratic candidacy of James K. Polk and George M. Dallas subtly conveys the party's platform. Surrounding Polk's picture are twenty-five stars, one for each state in the Union. Outside the corner box, a twenty-sixth star stands for Texas, which Polk promised to annex.

Collection of David J. and Janet L. Frent.

popular votes than Clay and garnered 65 more electoral votes. Seeing the election as a political barometer, outgoing president Tyler prepared a special message to Congress in December 1844 proposing a **joint resolution** annexing Texas. Many congressmen who had opposed annexation could not ignore the clear mandate given to manifest destiny in the presidential election, and the bill to annex Texas passed in February 1845.

Holding to the position he had taken prior to the election, in his annual message for 1845 Polk asked Congress to end the joint occupation of Oregon. Referring to the largely forgotten Monroe Doctrine,

joint resolution A formal statement adopted by both houses of Congress and subject to approval by the president; if approved, it has the force of law.

the president insisted that no nation other than the United States should be permitted to occupy any part of North America and urged Congress to assert exclusive control over the Oregon Country even if doing so meant war.

Neither the United States nor Britain intended to go to war over Oregon. The only issue—where the border would be—was a matter for the bargaining table, not the battlefield. Recalling the rhetoric that had gotten him elected, Polk insisted on 54°40′. The British lobbied for the Columbia River as the boundary, but their position softened quickly. The fur trade along the Columbia was in rapid decline and had become unprofitable by the early 1840s. As a result, in the spring of 1846, the British foreign secretary offered Polk a compromise boundary at the 49th parallel. The Senate recommended that Polk accept the offer, and a treaty settling the Oregon Question was ratified on June 15, 1846.

Individual Voices

The American Tract Society: The Moral Threat from Reading Fiction

As mass literacy spread throughout the nation, a culture war began to emerge. Producers of popular magazines and booksellers sought to tap into a burgeoning new market by pumping out both classic and new works of fiction. But Christian reformers, like those who founded and financed the American Tract Society, feared that such frivolous literature would undermine the nation's morals and compromise the republic itself. To counter this threat, dozens of benevolent organizations put out volumes of "uplifting" literature, often at very low prices or for free, in an effort to drive sinful fiction off the market. Ironically, by flooding the marketplace with easy-to-read inexpensive texts, the Tract Society actually helped to expand literacy and the demand for an ever greater variety of written work.

❶ What is it about fiction that the governors of the American Tract Society find objectionable?

❷ Why does the publication of fiction in cheap forms present a particular threat to American morals and stability?

❸ How does the American Tract Society feel about a free market in literature? What role should publishers have played in American society?

❹ How did the Tract Society characterize the relationship between fictional literature and alcohol? Why were these particularly dangerous, in their view?

Fiction also lamentably pervades our own country: deluding our youth with dreams of unreal bliss; pandering to the taste of the licentious; seducing the innocent; profaning all sacred things; prostituting the press, and sacrificing the welfare, temporal and eternal, of thousands, for the sake of pecuniary gain. **❶** Not only is the gilded volume furnished for the wealthy and tasteful, but leaves rudely and roughly printed and thrown together find acceptance with the novel reader. **❷** Corrupt European writers, with principles as base as their imaginations are vivid, and with pretended sympathy for the depraved masses to whose level their publications tend to debase their readers, have found eager publishers among those from whom we might have hoped better things, and too many readers and admirers in all parts of our country. **❸** This misnamed "literature" had demoralized thousands of the unsuspecting, and is known to have been the occasion of ruin to many of both sexes by its polluting pages. Its ravages are scarcely less wide spread than those of intemperance: like ardent spirits, producing inattention to present duties; deadening the conscience to the claims of the gospel; undermining or counteracting influences that might result, with the divine blessing, in the salvation of the soul. An immense proportion of the issues of the popular press are of this sort, too vast a proportion for the temporal or spiritual well-being of this reading nation, or for the safety of institutions based on sound intelligence and virtue of the people. **❹**

Study Tools

SUMMARY

Americans responded in many different ways to the many unsettling changes that had been taking place as part of the Great Transformation. Different economic classes responded by creating their own cultures and by adopting specific strategies for dealing with anxiety. Some chose violent protest, some passive resistance. Some looked to heaven for solutions and others to earthly utopias. And out of this complex swirl, something entirely new and unexpected emerged: a new America, on its way to being socially, politically, intellectually, and culturally modern.

A new generation emerged that grasped greedily at the new opportunities offered by new economic and cultural arrangements. Literacy grew as never before in the nation's history and with it a thirst for new knowledge. Book publishers, magazine editors, and charitable societies competed to meet this new demand for information and entertainment. And this group of young readers sought to express itself not only in literature, but in politics as well. As expanding media made more people aware of issues taking place nationwide, they were drawn into politics as never before. In the presidential election of 1840 almost two and a half million men cast ballots, more than a million more than had voted four years earlier.

In that election, William Henry Harrison, a man who had become a national figure by fighting against Indian sovereignty and for westward expansion, swept a new sentiment into national politics. Increasingly Americans came to believe that the West would provide the solutions to the problems ushered in during the Great Transformation. In the short term, this notion led to an exciting race by Americans toward the Pacific. But different visions about how the West would solve the nation's problems soon added to the ever-growing air of crisis.

CHRONOLOGY
Modernization and Rising Stress

1821	Charles G. Finney experiences a religious conversion
1823	James Fenimore Cooper's *The Pioneers*
1825	Thomas Cole begins Hudson River school of painting Robert Owen establishes community at New Harmony, Indiana
1826	Shakers have eighteen communities in the United States
1831	Nat Turner's Rebellion William Lloyd Garrison begins publishing *The Liberator*
1832	Jackson reelected
1833	Lydia Sigourney publishes bestsellers *Letters to Young Ladies* and *How to Be Happy* George Bancroft publishes volume 1 of his American history Formation of National Trades' Union Formation of Whig Party
1835	Texas Revolution begins
1836	Congress passes the gag rule Martin Van Buren elected president
1837	Horace Mann heads first public board of education Panic of 1837 Ralph Waldo Emerson's "American Scholar" speech Senate rejects annexation of Texas
1838	Emerson articulates transcendentalism Sarah Grimké publishes *Letters on the Equality of the Sexes and the Condition of Women*
1840	Log cabin campaign William Henry Harrison elected president
1841	Brook Farm established Death of President Harrison; John Tyler becomes president
1842	*Commonwealth v. Hunt*
1843	Dorothea Dix advocates state-funded insane asylums Oregon adopts First Organic Laws
1844	James K. Polk elected president
1845	United States annexes Texas Term "manifest destiny" coined
1846	Oregon boundary established

Study Tools

FOCUS QUESTIONS

If you have mastered this chapter, you should be able to answer these questions and to explain the terms that follow the questions.

1. ☆ *How did developments in American arts and letters reflect the spirit of change during the Jacksonian era?*

2. ☆ *To what extent did international forces influence American cultural expressions?*

3. ☆ *What did Jackson's opponents hope to accomplish when they built their coalition to oppose the Democrats? How successful were they?*

4. ☆ *What forces in American life contributed to the concept of manifest destiny?*

5. ☆ *To what extent did the actions taken by American settlers in Oregon and Texas reflect the ideal of manifest destiny?*

KEY TERMS

romanticism   *(p. 294)*

Ralph Waldo Emerson   *(p. 294)*

transcendentalism   *(p. 295)*

Henry David Thoreau   *(p. 295)*

Hudson River school   *(p. 297)*

"Negro spiritual"   *(p. 299)*

New Harmony   *(p. 299)*

Brook Farm   *(p. 299)*

Charles Fourier   *(p. 299)*

Oneida Community   *(p. 299)*

Shakers   *(p. 300)*

Joseph Tracy   *(p. 300)*

Charles Grandison Finney   *(p. 300)*

Second Great Awakening   *(p. 301)*

Christian benevolence movement   *(p. 302)*

Dorothea Dix   *(p. 302)*

temperance movement   *(p. 303)*

Horace Mann   *(p. 303)*

American Colonization Society   *(p. 303)*

William Lloyd Garrison   *(p. 304)*

Mason-Dixon Line   *(p. 304)*

Lucretia Mott   *(p. 305)*

Elizabeth Cady Stanton   *(p. 305)*

National Trades' Union   *(p. 305)*

Commonwealth v. Hunt   *(p. 305)*

spoils system   *(p. 308)*

Whig Party   *(p. 308)*

Panic of 1837   *(p. 309)*

Specie Circular   *(p. 309)*

John Tyler   *(p. 310)*

Oregon Question   *(p. 312)*

First Organic Laws of Oregon   *(p. 312)*

Antonio López de Santa Anna   *(p. 312)*

Texas Revolution   *(p. 313)*

Alamo   *(p. 313)*

Sam Houston   *(p. 313)*

Treaty of Velasco   *(p. 314)*

Webster-Ashburton Treaty   *(p. 314)*

James K. Polk   *(p. 315)*

 CourseMate   Go to the History CourseMate website for primary source links, study tools, and review materials for this chapter. www.cengagebrain.com

13 Sectional Conflict and Shattered Union, 1848–1860

Behind the Stories

A Civil War—states divided against other states, families divided among themselves, brothers killing brothers in grisly hand-to-hand combat. Over a four-year period, it would claim more American lives and break more American bodies than any other war in the nation's history. How could this have happened?

Because the antebellum period is my primary area of interest, this is a question I have asked myself many, many times. And it is one that has haunted all historians of the prewar era. Immediately after the war, writers in the North blamed southerners for their antiquated and immoral practice of slavery. Southerners countered by blaming selfish northern industrial and commercial interests for wanting to colonize the South to enhance their own profits. During the early decades of the twentieth century, some historians identified key structural problems in the Constitution that

were beyond compromise. Others emphasized that a "bumbling generation" of American politicians was incapable of effecting reasonable compromises. More recently, some pointed to fundamental contradictions between northern and southern versions of capitalism, a structural contest that only a war could resolve. And in the last few years, historians have dusted off a version of the "bumbling generation" argument by claiming that an excess of democracy led to emotional rather than rational approaches to national problems.

I go back and forth, and as you read this chapter you will encounter evidence that might be used to support any of these arguments. I encourage you not to leap to conclusions prematurely, but to analyze this evidence and come to informed conclusions about why this terrible event happened.

—C.L.M.

Individual Choices
Frederick Douglass

In 1838, Frederick Douglass, a slave living in Baltimore, decided that he would try to escape. This was no sudden impulse; Douglass had been thinking about freedom for most of his life. As a young boy he told his white friends, "You will be free as soon as you are twenty-one, *but I am a slave for life!*" And he had tried once before to make his way to freedom, but was captured and returned to his owner. Though his master threatened to sell him to a cotton plantation in Alabama, Douglass's intelligence and skills were worth more in Baltimore: he was made an apprentice at the local shipyard, eventually becoming a master ship caulker. His productivity earned him a lot of freedom: he made his own contracts, set his own work schedule, and collected his own earnings. "I was now of some importance to my master," Douglass recalled. "I was bringing him from six to seven dollars per week." But he also remembered his liberty. "I have observed this in my experience of slavery," Douglass commented, "that whenever my condition was improved, instead of its increasing my contentment, it only increased my desire to be free."

Using a wide network of personal connections, Douglass raised money and secured forged documents that entitled him to pass unmolested through slave territory. On September 3, Douglass disguised himself as a merchant sailor and made his way northward, arriving in New York City early on the morning of September 4. Although he had a couple of close calls, Douglass's escape had succeeded.

Douglass now was free, but the promised land of the nonslave North proved disappointing. Moving to the town of New Bedford, Massachusetts, where he hoped to earn a living in the boatyards, Douglass found that "such was the strength of prejudice against color, among the white caulkers, that they refused to work with me, and of course I could get no employment." For three years he was forced to do odd jobs to keep himself and his wife alive. "There was no work

Frederick Douglass

Samuel J. Miller, American, 1822-1888, Frederick Douglass, 1847-52, Cased half-plate daguerreotype, plate: 14 x 10.6 cm (5 ½ × 4 1/8 in.), mat opening: 12.1 c 8.8 cm (4 ¾ × 3 ½ in.), (6 x 4 ¾ x ½ in.), plate in closed case: 15.2 × 12 × 1.4 cm (6 × 4 ¾ × ½ in.), plate in open case: 15.2 × 24.2 cm (6 × 9 ½ × ¾ in.), Major Acquisitions Centennial Endowment, 1996.433, The Art Institute of Chicago. Photography © The Art Institute of Chicago.

An American private, Samuel E. Chamberlain, made this drawing of the Battle of Buena Vista. Present at the battle, Chamberlain watched as Mexican forces overran an artillery emplacement. The Americans eventually turned the tide, and the battle came out a draw. Even so, troops under Santa Anna were forced to retreat into the Mexican interior, spoiling the general's hope for a quick and easy victory against the invading Americans.

Serious political combat began in August 1846 when David Wilmot, a Democratic representative from Pennsylvania, proposed an amendment to the war appropriations bill that "neither slavery nor involuntary servitude shall ever exist" in any territory gained in the War with Mexico. The **Wilmot Proviso** twice passed in the House of Representatives but both times failed in the Senate, where equal state representation gave the South a stronger position. The House finally decided in April to appropriate money for the war without stipulating whether or not slavery would be permitted.

While all this political infighting was going on in Washington, D.C., a real war was going on in the Southwest. In California, American settlers rallied in open rebellion in the Sacramento Valley and declared independence in June 1846. They crafted a flag depicting a grizzly bear and announced the birth of the Bear Flag Republic. Frémont's force rushed to join the Bear Flag rebels, and when the little army arrived in Monterey on July 19, they found that the Pacific fleet had already acted on Polk's orders and seized the city. The Mexican forces were in full flight southward.

To round out the greater southwestern strategy, Polk ordered Colonel Stephen Kearny to invade New Mexico on May 15. After leading his men across 800 miles of desert to Santa Fe, Kearny found a less-than-hostile enemy. Members of the interracial upper class of Santa Fe had already expressed interest in joining the United States and given the opportunity, they surrendered without firing a shot.

Within a short time, all of the New Mexico region and California were securely in the hands of U.S. forces. In Texas, however, Zachary Taylor faced more serious opposition. Marching across the Rio Grande, Taylor headed for the regional capital of Monterrey, capturing the city in September 1846. Because of his military successes, Taylor became a political threat to Polk within the party. In an attempt to undermine Taylor's political appeal, Polk turned the war effort over to **Winfield Scott**, ordering him to gather an army, drawing men from Taylor's and other forces, and sail to Veracruz. From there the army was to move inland to take Mexico City (see Map 13.1).

■ **Wilmot Proviso** 1846 measure that would have closed any territory acquired from Mexico to slavery; it was defeated in the Senate.

■ **Winfield Scott** Virginia soldier and statesman who led troops in the War of 1812 and the War with Mexico; he was still serving as a general at the start of the Civil War.

Planning to crush Taylor's remaining force and then wheel around to attack Scott, General Santa Anna and his numerically superior army encountered Taylor at Buena Vista in February 1847. Tired and dispirited from a forced march across the desert, the Mexican army was in no shape to fight, but Santa Anna ordered an attack anyway. Tactically speaking, the **Battle of Buena Vista** was a draw, but it was a strategic victory for the Americans: Taylor's fresher troops stalled Santa Anna's forces, permitting Scott's army to capture Veracruz on March 9. Marching and fighting their way to Mexico City, Scott's force captured it on September 13, 1847.

With Mexico City, all of Texas, New Mexico, and California in American hands, the direction of treaty talks should have been fairly predictable. Scott's enormous success, however, caused the Mexican government's collapse, leaving no one to negotiate with American peace commissioner Nicholas Trist. The Mexican government eventually elected a new president, and finally, on February 2, 1848, Trist and the Mexican delegation signed the **Treaty of Guadalupe Hidalgo**, granting the United States all the territory between the Nueces River and the Rio Grande and between there and the Pacific. In exchange, Trist agreed that the United States would pay Mexico $15 million and would pay any **war reparations** owed to Americans.

Polk was very angry when he heard the terms of the treaty, believing that the sweeping American victory justified annexing all of Mexico. In Congress, however, many antislavery voices protested bringing so much potential slave territory into the Union. Others opposed the annexation because they feared that Mexico's largely Roman Catholic population might be a threat to Protestant institutions in the United States. Still others, many of whom had opposed the war to begin with, had moral objections to taking any territory by force. Perhaps more convincing than any of these arguments, however, was that the war had cost a lot of money, and congressmen were unwilling to allocate more if peace was within reach. With these considerations in mind, the Senate approved the treaty by a vote of 38 to 14.

Politicizing Slavery: The Election of 1848

The American victory in the War with Mexico was an enormous shot in the arm for American nationalism and manifest destiny, but it also brought the divisive issue of slavery back into mainstream politics to a degree unknown since the Missouri Compromise. Of course, being opposed to the expansion of slavery was not the same thing as opposing the institution itself, and antislavery sentiments were still not widespread among the American people during the 1840s. However, as the debates over the Mexican War indicate, abolitionist voices were getting more politically insistent. Despite strong and sometimes violent opposition, the abolition movement had continued to grow, especially among the privileged and educated classes in the Northeast. Throughout the 1830s, evangelicals increasingly stressed the sinful nature of slavery, urging the immediate, uncompensated liberation of slaves.

But the leading voice among the abolitionists, William Lloyd Garrison, consistently alienated his followers. Calling the Constitution "a covenant with death and an agreement with hell," Garrison burned a copy of it, telling his followers, "so perish all compromises with tyranny," and he urged them to have no dealings with a government that permitted so great an evil as slavery. Citing the reluctance of most organized churches to condemn slavery outright, Garrison urged his followers to break with them as well. He also offended many of his white evangelical supporters by associating with and supporting free black advocates of abolition.

During the 1830s, even moderates within the abolition movement had celebrated Frederick Douglass, **Sojourner Truth**, and other African American abolitionists, welcoming them as members of the American Anti-Slavery Society. But more insistent black voices frightened white abolitionists. African American abolitionist David Walker cried, "The whites want slaves, and want us for their slaves, but some of them will curse the day they ever saw us." Walker advocated that African Americans should "kill or be killed." Another black spokesman, Henry Highland Garnet, proclaimed, "Strike for your lives and liberties. Now is the day and hour. Let every slave in the land do this and the days of slavery are numbered. Rather die freemen than live to be slaves."

Garrison's sentiments mobilized some, but most of his followers were more conservative. In 1840 this and other controversial issues caused many of those moderates to bolt from Garrison's American Anti-Slavery

- **Battle of Buena Vista** Battle in February 1847 during which U.S. troops led by Zachary Taylor forced Santa Anna's forces to withdraw into the interior of Mexico.
- **Treaty of Guadalupe Hidalgo** Treaty (1848) in which Mexico gave up Texas above the Rio Grande and ceded New Mexico and California to the United States in return for $15 million.

war reparations Payments made to settle damage and injury claims resulting from a war; usually paid by the losing side.

- **Sojourner Truth** Abolitionist and feminist who was freed from slavery in 1827 and became a leading preacher against slavery and for the rights of women.

Sojourner Truth was a remarkable woman for her time, or for any time. One anecdote claims that a white policeman in New York state demanded that she identify herself. Using her cane to thrust herself upright to her full six feet of height, she boomed out the same words that God used to identify himself to Moses: "I am that I am." The policeman was unnerved and scurried away. Showing such bravery and pride in both her race and sex, it is little wonder that she commanded great respect in both antislavery and women's rights circles throughout her lifetime.

Society to form the more temperate American and Foreign Anti-Slavery Society. This new group forged strong ties with mainstream politicians and church leaders who, while opposed to any extension of slavery and sympathetic to moderate abolitionist proposals, had been relatively silent because of Garrison's reputation for radicalism.

Efforts by moderate antislavery supporters to bring limited abolitionism into the political mainstream meshed with the political aspirations of both those who opposed slavery's expansion primarily for political and economic reasons and those who were motivated by purely ethical concerns. Moderates in 1840

■ **Liberty Party** The first antislavery political party; it was formed in Albany, New York, in 1840.

■ **Free-Soil Party** Successor to the Liberty Party, launched in Buffalo, New York, in 1848; fielded presidential candidates in 1848 and 1852.

challenged both Whig and Democrat ambivalence by forming the **Liberty Party**.

Specifically disavowing Garrison's radical aims, Liberty Party leaders argued that slavery would eventually die on its own if it could be confined geographically. In addition, the Liberty Party called for the abolition of slavery in Washington, D.C., and in all the territories where it already existed. Though certainly more popular than Garrison's radical appeals, this moderate message drew little open political support: in 1840 Liberty Party presidential candidate James G. Birney garnered only about 7,000 votes. But in 1844, when he again ran on the Liberty Party ticket, he won 62,000 popular votes. Clearly a moderate antislavery position was becoming more acceptable.

Even in the face of such evidence, both major parties continued to practice the politics of avoidance. Suffering ill health, Polk chose not to run for a second term in 1848, leaving the Democrats scrambling for a candidate. They chose Lewis Cass of Michigan—a longtime moderate on slavery issues—as their presidential candidate and balanced the ticket with General William Butler of Kentucky. The Whigs hoped to ride a wave of nationalism following the War with Mexico by running military hero Zachary Taylor, a Louisianan and a slaveholder, for president and moderate New Yorker Millard Fillmore for vice president. Not satisfied with either party's candidates, a number of anti-slavery advocates banded together to launch yet another third party, the **Free-Soil Party**, and promoted Martin Van Buren as its candidate. Adopting the slogan "free soil, free speech, free labor, and free men," this new coalition avoided taking a radical stand on the issue of slavery itself but was firm about excluding slavery from the territories. When all the votes were counted, Taylor came out the winner with Cass a very close second, but the Free-Soilers netted nearly 10 percent of all votes cast.

Disaffected Voices and Political Dissent

It did not take long after the election of 1848 for cracks in the system to become more prominent. In an effort to compete with Democrats in northeastern cities, the Whigs had tried to win Catholic and immigrant voters away from the rival party. The strategy backfired. Not only did the Whigs not attract large numbers of immigrants, they also alienated two core groups among their existing supporters. One such group was artisans, who saw immigrants as the main source of their economic and social woes. The other was Protestant evangelicals, to whom Roman Catholic Irish and German immigrants symbolized all that was threatening to the American republic. Whig leaders could do little to address these voters' immediate concerns, and increasing numbers left the Whig Party to

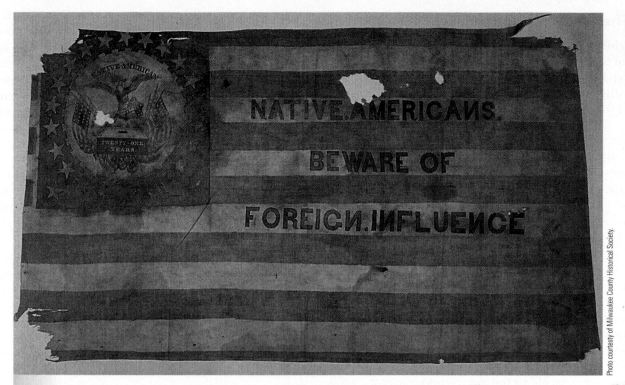

Photo courtesy of Milwaukee County Historical Society.

Convinced that slavery and other sectional issues were blinding Americans to the true dangers stemming from uncontrolled immigration and foreign influence, the Know-Nothing Party ran Millard Fillmore for president in 1856. Banners like this one warned Americans and solicited their votes. Fillmore succeeded in getting 21 percent of the popular vote.

form state and local coalitions more in tune with their hopes and fears.

One of the most prominent of these locally oriented groups was the anti-Catholic, anti-immigrant group that sprung up in New York but soon spread nationally. Bearing close ties, in terms of both leadership and attitudes, with the Antimasons, this loosely knit political network grafted **xenophobic** views onto strong antiparty sentiments, alleging wholesale voter fraud and government corruption by both major parties. They insisted that issues of slavery and sectionalism dominating national political debate were nothing but devices being used by political insiders and the established parties to divert ordinary Americans from real issues of concern and that immigration, loss of job security, urban crowding and violence, and political corruption were the true threats to American liberties. Behind it all was a perceived Catholic plot to overthrow democracy in the United States. Seeking to protect their members from this conspiracy, leaders told them to say "I know nothing" if they were questioned about the organization or its political intrigues, hence their name: the **Know-Nothings**. Increasingly after 1848, these secretive groups became more public and more vocal, promoting a twenty-one-year naturalization period, a ban against naturalized citizens

holding public office, and the use of the Protestant Bible in public schools. As future president Rutherford B. Hayes noted, these people were expressing a "general disgust with the powers that be."

Many Know-Nothings had deep ties with the evangelical Protestant movement and indeed represented one dimension of Christian dissent, but not all Protestant dissenters shared their single-mindedness. In addition to Catholicism and immigration, many evangelicals pointed to slavery, alcohol, and religious heresy as threats to the nation's moral fiber. In their efforts to create moral government and to direct national destiny, these reformers advocated social reform through both religious and political action. Overall, however, progress seemed slow, and like Know-Nothings and others, Christian reform advocates became increasingly impatient with the traditional political parties.

xenophobic Fearful of or hateful toward foreigners or those seen as being different.

■ **Know-Nothings** Members of anti-Catholic, anti-immigrant organizations who eventually formed themselves into a national political party.

The Politics of Compromise

While dissidents of various types attacked the political parties from outside, problems raised by national expansion were continuing to erode party unity from within. Immediately after Zachary Taylor's election in 1848, California's future became a new divisive issue.

California presented a peculiar political problem. Once word reached the rest of the nation that California was rich with gold, politicians immediately began grasping for control over the newly acquired territory. Although large parts of the area lay below the 36°30' line that the Missouri Compromise had set for slavery expansion, that legislation had applied only to territory acquired in the Louisiana Purchase, and the failure of Congress to pass Wilmot's Proviso left the question of slavery in the new territories wide open.

Having been primarily responsible for crafting the earlier compromise (see pages 244–245), Henry Clay took it upon himself to find a solution. Clay was convinced that any successful agreement would have to address all sides of the issue. He thus proposed a complex **omnibus bill** to the Senate on January 20, 1850.

California would enter the Union as a free state, but the slavery question would be left to **popular sovereignty** in all other territories acquired through the Treaty of Guadalupe Hidalgo. The bill also directed Texas to drop a continuing border dispute with New Mexico in exchange for federal assumption of Texas's public debt. Then, to appease abolitionists, Clay called for an end to the slave trade in Washington, D.C., and balanced that with a clause popular with southerners: a new, more effective **fugitive slave law**.

Though Clay was trying to please all sectional interests, the omnibus bill satisfied no one; Congress debated it without resolution for seven months. Finally, in July 1850, Clay's proposals were defeated. The 73-year-old political veteran left the capital tired and dispirited, but **Stephen A. Douglas** of Illinois set himself to the task of reviving the compromise. Using practical economic arguments and backroom political arm twisting, Douglas proposed each component of Clay's omnibus package as a separate bill, steering it forward toward a comprehensive compromise. Finally, in September, Congress passed the **Compromise of 1850** (see Map 13.2).

MAP 13.2 The Compromise of 1850
The acquisition of Texas and California brought a showdown between North and South over representation in the national government. As this map shows, the Compromise of 1850 permitted Texas and California to be admitted to the Union without seriously undermining the balance of power in the Senate. In the House of Representatives, however, the balance favored the North. Copyright © Cengage Learning

Who said I would not make a NO PARTY President? I defy you to show any party action here.

WILMOT PROVISO.

SOUTHERN RIGHTS.

How much do you weigh? Eight dollars a day... Whack fol de rol!

My patience is as inexhaustible as the public treasury.

I said that we'd be even with you.

We can wait as long as they can.

We hold our own.

That's like what we calls in old England, a glass of 'alf and 'alf.

CONGRESSIONAL SCALES,
A TRUE BALANCE.

The question of how territory acquired in the war with Mexico might unbalance the nation politically weighed heavily on people's minds as the nation entered the 1850s. In this cartoon, lithographer Nathaniel Currier—who later would found the famous graphic art company Currier and Ives—illustrates the problem. Trying himself to balance the Wilmot Proviso against southern rights, the president seeks to keep congressional representatives from the North and the South in balance as well.

to focus on other major changes in national life.

A Changing Political Economy

In the years following the Compromise of 1850, American economic and territorial growth continued to play a destabilizing role in both national and regional development. Most notably, during the 1850s industrial growth accelerated, further altering the nation's economic structure. By 1860 less than half of all northern workers made a living from agriculture as northern industry became more concentrated. Steam began to replace water as the primary power source, and factories were no longer limited to locations along rivers and streams. The use of interchangeable

The Compromise of 1850 did little to relieve underlying regional differences and only aggravated political dissent. That slaveowners could pursue runaway slaves into northern states and return them into bondage brought slavery too close to home for many northerners. Many joined both antislavery and evangelical Whigs in chafing at this provision and increasingly joined forces with African Americans to seek solutions outside the political realm. Throughout the 1850s, both white and African American activists helped slaves escape from the South through a covert network of hiding places called the **Underground Railroad** (see Map 12.1, page 306). Individuals like **Harriet Tubman** conducted slaves along routes through American territory made hostile by the fugitive slave law and on to safety in Canada. Nor did southerners find any reason to celebrate: admission of another nonslave state further drained their power in Congress and slavery had gained no positive protection, either in the territories or at home. Still, the compromise created a brief respite from the slavery-extension question at a time when the nation's attention increasingly needed

omnibus bill A piece of legislation with many parts.

■ **popular sovereignty** In the debate over slavery, the principle that the citizens of each state should determine, by popular vote, whether to permit slavery.

■ **fugitive slave law** Law providing for the return of escaped slaves to their owners.

■ **Stephen A. Douglas** Illinois senator who tried to reconcile northern and southern differences over slavery through the Compromise of 1850 and the Kansas-Nebraska Act.

■ **Compromise of 1850** Plan intended to reconcile North and South on the issue of slavery; it recognized the principle of popular sovereignty and included a strong fugitive slave law.

■ **Underground Railroad** The secret network of northerners who helped fugitive slaves escape to Canada or to safe areas in free states.

■ **Harriet Tubman** One of the most famous and most effective of the many African American "conductors" on the Underground Railroad; she is thought to have been personally responsible for leading at least three hundred slaves into freedom.

New technologies responded to but also drove an economic revolution in the United States during the decades just prior to the Civil War. Power looms in the Northeast, cotton gins in the South, and farming machinery in the West increased productivity and launched the emergence of a national capitalist economy. The complicated intersection between economies is illustrated by this engraving of farm implement inventor Cyrus McCormick showing both his inventions and the enormous factory needed to manufacture them.

The Granger Collection, New York.

hungry for southern fiber, lent vitality to the continued growth of the cotton kingdom and the slave labor system that gave it life. Northern political leaders visualized an industrial nation based on free labor, but that view ran counter to the southern elites' ideals of **agrarian capitalism** based on slavery. In the West, most continued to believe in the Jeffersonian ideal of an agricultural nation of small and medium-size farms and could not accept either industrial or cotton capitalism as positive developments.

agrarian capitalism A system of agriculture based on the efficient, specialized production of crops intended to generate profits rather than subsistence.

Political Instability and the Election of 1852

Dynamic economic progress improved material life throughout the nation, but it also raised serious questions about what course progress should take. As one clear-sighted northern minister pointed out in 1852, the debate was not about whether America should pursue progress but about "different kinds and methods of progress." Contradictory visions of national destiny were about to cause the breakdown of the existing party system.

Slavery seemed to loom behind every debate, but most Americans, even southerners, had no personal investment in the institution. Two-thirds of southerners owned no slaves, tolerating the institution but having only fleeting contact with the great plantations and their peculiar labor system. Northerners, too, were largely indifferent. Men like young Illinois state congressman **Abraham Lincoln** believed the institution was wrong but were not inclined to do anything about it. What mattered to these people was not slavery but autonomy—control over local affairs and over their own lives.

The slavery question challenged notions of autonomy in both the North and the South. In their widely disseminated rhetoric, abolitionists expanded the specter of the Slave Power conspiracy, especially in the aftermath of the Compromise of 1850. Growing numbers perceived this conspiracy as intent on imposing southern ways and installing southern elites or their sympathizers in seats of power in every section of the nation. Whether farmers in Illinois or artisans in Pennsylvania, common people stood ready to resist a southern takeover of local institutions. Likewise, common people in the South feared interference from outsiders in view of the ever more vigorous antisouthern crusade by northern radicals.

After the Compromise of 1850 momentarily eased regional fears, sectional tensions flamed anew in 1852 with the publication of *Uncle Tom's Cabin* by **Harriet Beecher Stowe**. Stowe portrayed the darkest inhumanities of southern slavery in the first American novel to include African Americans as central characters. *Uncle Tom's Cabin* sold 300,000 copies in its first year. Adapted for the stage, it became one of the most popular plays of the period. The book stirred public opinion and breathed new life into antislavery sentiments, leading Free-Soilers and so-called **conscience Whigs** to renew their efforts to limit or end slavery. When these activists saw that the Whig Party was incapable of addressing the slavery question in any effective way, they began to look for other political options.

Superficially, the Whigs seemed well organized and surprisingly unified as a new presidential election approached in 1852. Zachary Taylor had died in office in July 1850, and they nominated General Winfield Scott, Taylor's rival for fame in the War with Mexico. The Democrats remained divided through forty-nine ballots, unable to decide among Lewis Cass of Michigan, Stephen A. Douglas of Illinois, and **James Buchanan** of Pennsylvania. They finally settled on the virtually unknown **Franklin Pierce** of New Hampshire, who pledged to uphold the Compromise of 1850 and keep slavery out of politics. This promise was enough to bring Martin Van Buren back to the Democrats, and he brought many Free-Soilers back with him. Many others, though, abandoned Van Buren and joined forces with conscience Whigs.

Scott was a national figure and a distinguished military hero, but Pierce gathered 254 electoral votes to Scott's 42, exposing the disarray in the Whig Party. Splits between "cotton" and "conscience" groups splintered Whig unity, and regional tension escalated as Free-Soil rhetoric clashed with calls for extending slavery. Confrontations between Catholics and Protestants and between native-born and immigrant laborers caused bitter animosity. In the North, where immigration, industrialization, and antislavery sentiment were most prevalent and economic friction most pronounced, massive numbers of voters, believing the Whigs incapable of addressing current problems, deserted the party.

Increasing Tension under Pierce

The Democratic Party and Franklin Pierce also felt the pressures of a changing electorate. Pierce was part of the **Young America Movement**, which, as

Harriet Beecher Stowe's *Uncle Tom's Cabin* was the first American novel that featured African American characters in prominent roles. It was issued in various editions with many different covers, but most of them featured the lead character, Uncle Tom—another first in American publishing. This particular cover, from an early "Young Folks' Edition" of the book, depicts the stooped old man with his owner's young, sympathetic daughter. Collection of Picture Research Consultants and Archives.

■ **Abraham Lincoln** Illinois lawyer and politician who in a losing senatorial campaign in 1858 argued against popular sovereignty in debates with Stephen Douglas; he was elected president in 1860.

■ **Harriet Beecher Stowe** American novelist and abolitionist whose novel *Uncle Tom's Cabin* fanned antislavery sentiment in the North.

■ **conscience Whigs** Members of the Whig Party who supported moderate abolitionism, as opposed to cotton Whigs, members who opposed abolitionism.

■ **James Buchanan** Pennsylvania senator who was elected president in 1856 after gaining the Democratic nomination as a compromise candidate.

■ **Franklin Pierce** New Hampshire lawyer and Democratic politician nominated as a compromise candidate and elected president in 1852.

■ **Young America Movement** A political movement popular among young voters during the 1840s and early 1850s, advocating free-market capitalism, national expansionism, and American patriotism.

a whole, tried to ignore the slavery issue, advocating romantic and aggressive nationalism, manifest destiny, and republican revolutions throughout the Americas. In line with the Young America agenda, Pierce emphasized expansion; choosing a route for a transcontinental railroad became the keystone in his agenda for the nation.

Southerners knew that a railroad based in the South would channel the flow of gold from California through their region and would also allow new settlement and cotton agriculture to spread beyond the waterways that had proved necessary for expansion so far. Eventually the new territories would become states, increasing the South's national political power.

That model of development was totally unacceptable to several groups: to northern evangelicals, who viewed slavery as a moral blight on the nation; to Free-Soil advocates, who believed the spread of slavery would degrade white workers; and to northern manufacturers, who wanted to maintain dominance in Congress to ensure continued economic protection. In May 1853, only two months after assuming office, Pierce inflamed all of these groups by sending James Gadsden, a southern railroad developer, to Mexico to purchase a strip of land lying below the southern border of the New Mexico Territory. Any rail line built westward from a southern city to California would have to cross that land, and Pierce and his southern supporters wanted to make sure it was part of the United States. The **Gadsden Purchase**, signed on December 30, 1853, added 29,640 square miles of land to the United States for a cost of $10 million. It also finalized the southwestern border of the United States.

The Gadsden Purchase prompted proponents of a southern route for the transcontinental railroad, led by Secretary of War **Jefferson Davis**, to push for government sponsorship of the project. Having invested his own money in more northerly rail development, Illinois senator Stephen A. Douglas blocked Davis's efforts and pushed for a route westward from

his home town of Chicago. But this route would have to pass through Indian Territory that was not open to rail development. To rectify this problem, Douglas introduced a bill on January 4, 1854, incorporating the entire northern half of Indian Territory into a new federal entity called Nebraska.

Douglas knew that he would need both northern and southern support to get his bill through Congress, and he sought to silence possible opposition by proposing that the slavery question in the territory be left to popular sovereignty—let the voters of Nebraska decide. When southerners pointed out that the proposed territory was above the Missouri Compromise line and that Congress might prohibit popular sovereignty from functioning, Douglas responded that the Compromise of 1850 superseded the 1820 Missouri Compromise. But to calm southerners he finally supported an amendment to his original bill dividing the territory in half—Nebraska in the north and Kansas in the south (see Map 13.3). The amended legislation—called the **Kansas-Nebraska Act**—rested on the assumption that popular sovereignty would lead to slavery in Kansas and free labor in Nebraska.

TOWARD A HOUSE DIVIDED

☆ How did various political coalitions react to the Kansas-Nebraska Act?

☆ What was the effect on the national political climate?

Once again slavery threatened national political stability. In the North, opponents of the bill formed local coalitions to defeat it. On January 24, 1854, a group of Democrats including Salmon P. Chase, Gerrit Smith, Joshua Giddings, and **Charles Sumner** published "The Appeal of the Independent Democrats in Congress, to the People of the United States." They called the bill an "atrocious plot" to make Nebraska a "dreary region of despotism, inhabited by masters and slaves." On February 28, opponents of the Kansas-Nebraska bill met in Ripon, Wisconsin, and recommended the formation of a new political party. Similar meetings took place in several northern states as opposition to the bill grew. In the wake of these meetings, the existing party system collapsed and a new one arose to replace it.

A Shattered Compromise

Despite this strong opposition, Douglas and Pierce rallied support for the Kansas-Nebraska Act. On May 26, 1854, after gaining approval in the House

■ **Gadsden Purchase** A strip of land in present-day Arizona and New Mexico that the United States bought from Mexico in 1853 to secure a southern route for a transcontinental railroad.

■ **Jefferson Davis** Secretary of war under Franklin Pierce; he later became president of the Confederacy.

■ **Kansas-Nebraska Act** 1854 law creating the Kansas and Nebraska territories and allowing residents to decide whether to allow slavery within their borders.

■ **Charles Sumner** Co-founder of the Republican Party and a strong advocate for abolition and racial equality; he was brutally beaten by a southern congressman in 1856 after delivering a speech attacking the South.

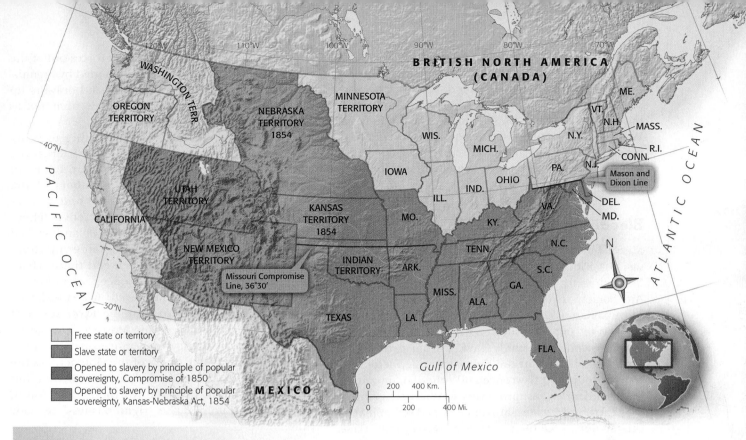

MAP 13.3 The Kansas-Nebraska Act
This map shows Stephen Douglas's proposed compromise organizing the vast territory separating the settled northern United States from California and Oregon. Designed in part to win profitable rail connections for Douglas's home district in Illinois, the Kansas-Nebraska Act stirred a political crisis by repealing the Missouri Compromise and replacing it with popular sovereignty. Copyright © Cengage Learning

Map legend:
- Free state or territory
- Slave state or territory
- Opened to slavery by principle of popular sovereignty, Compromise of 1850
- Opened to slavery by principle of popular sovereignty, Kansas-Nebraska Act, 1854

of Representatives, the bill passed the Senate, and Pierce soon signed it into law. Passage of the act crystallized northern antislavery sentiment. To protest, many northerners threatened **noncompliance** with the fugitive slave law of 1850. As Senator William Seward of New York vowed, "We will engage in competition for the virgin soil of Kansas, and God give the victory to the side which is stronger in numbers as it is in right."

Antislavery forces, however, remained divided into at least three major groups. The Free-Soil contingent opposed any extension of slavery but did not necessarily favor abolishing the institution. The other two groups—Garrisonians and evangelicals—wanted immediate abolition but disagreed on many particulars. William Lloyd Garrison and his followers believed that slavery was the primary evil facing the nation, while evangelicals agreed that slavery was evil, but believed it was one among many vices undermining the virtuous republic. All three groups constantly agitated against slavery and what they perceived as southern control of national politics. They weakened

the Democratic Party's strength in the North but could not bring themselves to align behind a single opposition party.

Actions perceived as further evidence of the Slave Power conspiracy also undermined Democratic unity. Private armies, led by adventurers like **William Walker**, invaded territories in Latin America and the Caribbean, which many in the North concluded were Slave Power efforts. In this atmosphere, President Pierce unintentionally undermined the party by pushing for the purchase of Cuba from Spain. When the Spanish refused, three of Pierce's European

noncompliance Failure or refusal to obey a law or request.
■ **William Walker** Nineteenth-century American military adventurer whose private army invaded several Latin American countries and seized Nicaragua in 1856; he was executed in Honduras in 1860.

ministers met in Ostend, Belgium, in October 1854, and secretly drafted a justification for taking Cuba by force. When the so-called **Ostend Manifesto** became public in 1855, many northerners were convinced that Pierce and the Democratic Party approved of Walker-like adventurism to expand slavery. These perceptions stirred antislavery anxieties and fueled the growth of the newly formed anti-Democratic coalitions.

Bleeding Kansas

Meanwhile, political friction was about to ignite Kansas. In April 1854, abolitionist Eli Thayer of Worcester, Massachusetts, organized the New England Emigrant Aid Society to encourage antislavery supporters to move to Kansas. They reasoned that flooding a region subject to popular sovereignty with right-minded residents could effectively "save" it from slavery. This group eventually sent two thousand armed settlers to Kansas, founding Lawrence and other communities. With similar designs, proslavery southerners, particularly those in Missouri, also encouraged settlement in the territory. Like their northern counterparts, these southerners came armed and ready to fight for their cause.

President Pierce appointed governors in both Kansas and Nebraska and instructed them to organize elections for territorial legislatures. As proslavery and antislavery settlers vied for control of Kansas, the region became a testing ground for popular sovereignty. When the vote came on March 30, 1855, a large contingent of armed slavery supporters from Missouri—so-called border ruffians—crossed into Kansas and cast ballots for proslavery candidates. According to later Senate investigations, 60 percent of the votes cast were illegal. These unlawful ballots gave proslavery supporters a large majority in the Kansas legislature. They promptly expelled all abolitionist legislators and enacted the Kansas Code—a group

of laws meant to drive all antislavery forces out of the territory. Antislavery advocates responded by organizing their own free-state government and drawing up an alternative constitution, which they submitted to the voters.

Bloodshed soon followed. Attempting to bring the conflict to conclusion, proslavery territorial judge Samuel LeCompte called a grand jury of slavery supporters that indicted members of the free-state government for treason and sent a **posse** of about eight hundred men to Lawrence. There they "arrested" the antislavery forces and sacked the town, burning buildings and plundering shops and homes. The violence did not end there. Hearing news of the "Sack of Lawrence," **John Brown**, an antislavery zealot, murdered five proslavery men living along the Pottawatomie River south of Lawrence. This "Pottawatomie Massacre" triggered a series of episodes in which more than two hundred men were killed. Much of the violence was the work of border ruffians and zealots like Brown, but to many people in both the North and the South, the events symbolized the "righteousness" of their cause.

The Kansas issue also led to violence in Congress. During the debates over the admission of the territory, Massachusetts senator Charles Sumner made insulting remarks about South Carolina and its 60-year-old senator Andrew Butler. Butler was out of town, but Butler's nephew, Representative Preston Brooks, accosted Sumner and beat him nearly to death with a cane. Though **censured** by the House of Representatives, Brooks was overwhelmingly reelected by his home district and openly praised for his actions—he received canes as gifts from admirers all over the South.

Meanwhile the presidential election of 1856 was approaching. The Pierce administration's actions, southern expansionism, and the Kansas-Nebraska controversy swelled the ranks of dissenters like those who had convened in Ripon. Now formally calling themselves the **Republican Party**, these northern and western groups began actively seeking support. Immigration also remained a major issue, but the Know-Nothings, despite their success at the local and state levels, split over slavery at their initial national convention in 1855; many then joined Republican coalitions, though some loyalists proceeded to nominate Millard Fillmore. John C. Frémont, a moderate abolitionist who had achieved fame as the "liberator of California," won the Republican nomination. For their part, the Democrats rejected both Pierce and Douglas and nominated James Buchanan from Pennsylvania, selecting John C. Breckinridge of Kentucky as Buchanan's running mate to balance the ticket between the North and the South.

■ **Ostend Manifesto** Declaration by American foreign ministers in 1854 that if Spain refused to sell Cuba, the United States might be justified in taking it by force.

posse A group of citizens deputized by a court or peace officer to assist in law enforcement.

■ **John Brown** Abolitionist who fought proslavery settlers in Kansas in 1855; he was hanged for treason after seizing the U.S. arsenal at Harpers Ferry in 1859 as part of an effort to liberate southern slaves.

censure To issue an official rebuke, as by a legislature to one of its members.

■ **Republican Party** Political party formed in 1854 that opposed the extension of slavery into the western territories.

The election became a contest for party survival rather than a national referendum on slavery. Buchanan received 45 percent of the popular vote and 163 electoral votes. Frémont finished second with 33 percent of the popular vote and 114 electoral votes. Fillmore received 21 percent of the popular vote but only 8 electoral votes. Frémont's surprisingly narrow margin of defeat demonstrated the appeal of the newly formed Republican coalition to northern voters. The Know-Nothings disappeared and never again attempted a national organization.

Bringing Slavery Home to the North

On March 4, 1857, James Buchanan became president of the United States. The 65-year-old Pennsylvanian had begun his political career in Congress in 1821 and owed much of his success to southern support. His election came at a time when the nation needed strong leadership, but Buchanan seemed unable to provide it. Despite his campaign promise to emphasize national unity, he proved incapable of achieving a unifying compromise. His attempt to preserve the politics of avoidance only strengthened radicalism in both the North and the South. **Regionalism** colored all political issues, and every debate became a contest between competing social, political, and economic ideologies.

Though Buchanan's shortcomings contributed to the rising crisis, an event occurred within days of his inauguration that sent shock waves through the already troubled nation. **Dred Scott**, a slave once owned by army surgeon John Emerson, sued for his freedom. Scott's attorney argued that between 1831 and 1833, Emerson had taken Scott with him during various military postings to areas where the Missouri Compromise banned slavery, making Scott a free man. When, after nearly six years in the Missouri courts, the state supreme court rejected this argument in 1852, Scott, with the help of abolitionist lawyers, appealed to the United States Supreme Court. In a 7-to-2 decision, the Court ruled against Scott. Chief Justice Roger B. Taney, formerly a member of Andrew Jackson's Kitchen Cabinet and a stalwart Democrat, argued that in the eyes of the law slaves were not people but property; as such, they could not be citizens of the United States and had no right to petition the Court. Taney then ignited a

Federal officials often found themselves in an awkward position as civil war threatened in Kansas during the 1850s. Here, Colonel Edwin Vose Sumner, commander of Fort Leavenworth and an opponent of slavery, acts upon orders from the proslavery territorial government to break up an antislavery convention in Topeka in 1856. Sumner prevented the meeting from convening, but refused to disarm the conventioneers, winning three cheers from the assembled crowd.

political powder keg by ruling that Congress had no constitutional authority to limit slavery in a federal territory, thereby declaring the Missouri Compromise unconstitutional.

While southerners generally celebrated the decision, antislavery forces and northern evangelical leaders called the *Dred Scott* decision a mockery of justice and a crime against a "higher law." Some radical abolitionists argued that the North should separate from the Union. Others suggested impeaching the Supreme Court. Already incensed by events in Kansas, antislavery leaders predicted that the next move by the Slave Power conspiracy would be to get the Supreme Court to strike down antislavery laws in northern states.

Meanwhile, the Kansas issue still burned. That very few slaveholders actually moved into the territory did nothing to deter proslavery leaders, who met in Lecompton, Kansas, in June 1857 to draft a state

regionalism Loyalty to the interests of a particular region of the country.
■ **Dred Scott** Slave who sued for his liberty in the Missouri courts, arguing that four years on free soil had made him free; the Supreme Court's 1857 ruling against him negated the Missouri Compromise.

It Matters Today

The *Dred Scott* Case

Frederick Douglass was disappointed to discover that freedom for African Americans did not also mean equality. This personal revelation was soon reinforced by one of the most important cases ever to reach the Supreme Court. Denying once and for all that freedom and equality for people of African heritage were identical, the Court's decision in *Dred Scott v. Sanford* declared that because no state at the time that the Constitution was ratified had included African Americans as citizens, then no one of African descent could become a citizen of the United States. Ever! It would take the Thirteenth, Fourteenth, and Fifteenth Amendments to the Constitution to remove the legal justification behind the Court's opinion, but even these did not reverse the racism underlying the decision. The *Dred Scott* case and the amendments designed to correct the constitutional defects that led to it still play a key role in dozens of cases in the nation's courts each year as men and women of many backgrounds seek to make real the tie between freedom and equality that Dred Scott and Frederick Douglass only dreamed of.

- To what extent do you think that the *Dred Scott* case made Civil War in the United States inevitable? Explain.
- Choose a post–Civil War court case dealing with racial equality issues (the American Civil Liberties Union and other organizations as well as the federal government maintain catalogues of important cases). In what ways does the case you have chosen reflect the *Dred Scott* case and the constitutional amendments passed in response? Assess the continuing legacy of this case in American life and justice.

---

constitution favoring slavery. When the **Lecompton constitution** was submitted for voters' approval, antislavery forces protested by refusing to vote, so it was easily ratified. But when it was revealed that more than two thousand nonresidents had voted illegally, both Republicans and northern Democrats in Congress roundly denounced it. The Buchanan administration joined southerners in support of admitting Kansas to the Union as a slave state and managed to push the statehood bill through the Senate, but the House of Representatives rejected it. Congress then returned the Lecompton constitution to Kansas for another vote. This time Free-Soilers participated in the election and defeated the proposed constitution. Kansas remained a territory.

Growing Friction and Expanding Violence

The *Dred Scott* decision dangerously accelerated the ever-expanding debate between North and South. Both the Kansas controversy and Dred Scott

■ **Lecompton constitution** State constitution written for Kansas in 1857 at a convention dominated by proslavery forces; it would have allowed slavery, but Kansas voters rejected it.

undermined the Democratic commitment to popular sovereignty. Entertaining presidential ambitions, party leader Stephen Douglas sought a solution that might win him both northern and southern support in a run for that office in 1860. His immediate goal, however, was reelection to the Senate.

Illinois Republicans selected Abraham Lincoln to run against Douglas for the Senate in 1858. Born on the Kentucky frontier in 1809, Lincoln had accompanied his family from one failed farm to another, picking up schooling in Indiana and Illinois as opportunities arose. As a young man he worked odd jobs—farm worker, ferryman, flatboatman, surveyor, and store clerk. He was eventually elected to the Illinois legislature and began a serious study of law. A strong Whig, Lincoln followed Henry Clay's economic philosophy and steered a middle course between the "cotton" and "conscience" wings of the Whig Party. Lincoln acknowledged that slavery was evil but contended that it was the unavoidable consequence of black racial inferiority. The only way to get rid of the evil, he believed, was to prevent the expansion of slavery into the territories, forcing it to die out naturally.

Lincoln was decidedly the underdog in the contest with Douglas and sought to improve his chances by challenging the senator to a series of debates. Douglas agreed. During the debate at Freeport, Lincoln asked

Hoping to trigger a full-scale revolt against slavery, Kansas radical John Brown seized the federal armory at Harpers Ferry, Virginia, on October 16, 1859. Federal troops stormed the hostage armory and dislodged Brown's insurgents. Here Marines lead the captured men out of the building. Brown and several other participants in the raid were eventually hanged, becoming martyrs to the antislavery cause.

engraving from Frank Leslie's Illustrated Newspaper/Private Collection/The Bridgeman Art Library International.

Douglas to explain how the people of a territory could exclude slavery in light of the *Dred Scott* ruling. Douglas's reply became known as the **Freeport Doctrine**. Slavery, he said, needed the protection of "local police regulations." In any territory, citizens opposed to slavery could elect representatives who would "by unfriendly legislation" prevent the introduction of slavery. Lincoln did not win Douglas's Senate seat, but the debate drew national attention to the Illinois race, and Lincoln won recognition as an up-and-coming Republican figure.

Southerners bristled at claims by Lincoln and others that slavery was immoral. Charles C. Jones and other southern evangelical leaders, for example, offered a religious defense of slavery, arguing that whites had a moral responsibility to care for blacks and instruct them in the Christian faith. However, many southerners, like some of their Republican opponents, were less interested in the slaves than in how slavery affected white society and white labor. Southern apologists contended that whites in the South enjoyed a greater degree of freedom than northern whites because slaves did all the demeaning work, freeing whites for more noble pursuits. Moreover, southern lawyer George Fitzhugh argued, both the North and the South relied equally on a subjugated work force. The only meaningful difference between northern **wage slaves** and southern slaves, Fitzhugh concluded, was that northerners accepted no responsibility for housing and feeding their work force, condemning laborers to suffer at below-subsistence conditions.

Northern radicals increasingly called for a violent response to the Slave Power movement, and in 1857 Kansas zealot John Brown came to the East to oblige them. He convinced several prominent antislavery leaders to finance a daring plan to raise an army of slaves in an all-out insurrection against their masters. Brown and a small party of followers attacked the federal arsenal at **Harpers Ferry**, Virginia, on October 16, 1859, attempting to seize weapons. The arsenal proved an easy target, but no slaves joined the uprising. Local citizens surrounded the arsenal, firing on Brown and his followers until federal troops commanded by Colonel **Robert E. Lee** arrived. On October 18, Lee's forces battered down the barricaded

■ **Freeport Doctrine** Stephen Douglas's belief, stated at Freeport, Illinois, that a territory could exclude slavery by writing local laws or regulations that made slavery impossible to enforce.

wage slaves Workers who, though legally free, are underpaid, trapped in debt, and living in extreme poverty.

■ **Harpers Ferry** Town in present-day West Virginia and site of the U.S. arsenal that John Brown briefly seized in 1859.

■ **Robert E. Lee** A Virginian with a distinguished career in the U.S. Army who later assumed command of the Confederate army in Virginia during most of the Civil War.

entrance and arrested Brown. He was tried, convicted of treason, and hanged on December 2, 1859.

Brown's raid on Harpers Ferry captured the imagination of radical abolitionists. Republican leaders denounced it, but other northerners proclaimed Brown a martyr. Church bells tolled in many northern cities on the day of his execution. In New England, Ralph Waldo Emerson proclaimed Brown "that new saint." Such reactions caused many appalled southerners—even very moderate ones—to seriously consider **secession**. In Alabama, Mississippi, and Florida, state legislatures resolved that a Republican victory in the upcoming presidential election would provide sufficient justification for such action.

THE DIVIDED NATION

☆ *In what ways was the presidential election in 1860 an outcome of the realignment of the party system during the 1850s?*

☆ *Why did the election results have the political effects that they did?*

The Republicans were a new phenomenon on the American political scene: a purely regional political party. Rather than making any attempt to forge a national coalition, the party drew its strength and ideas almost entirely from the North. The Republican platform—"Free Soil, Free Labor, and Free Men"—stressed the defilement of white labor by slavery and contended that the Slave Power conspiracy was eroding the rights of free whites everywhere. By taking up a cry against "Rum, Romanism, and Slavery," the Republicans drew former Know-Nothings and temperance advocates into their ranks. The Democrats hoped to maintain a national coalition, but as the nation approached a new presidential election, their hopes began to fade.

The Dominance of Regionalism

During the Buchanan administration, Democrats found it increasingly difficult to achieve national party unity. Facing Republican pressure in their own states, northern Democrats realized that any concession to southern Democratic demands for extending

or protecting slavery would cost them votes at home. In April 1860, as the party convened in Charleston, South Carolina, each side was ready to do battle for its political life.

The fight began when northern supporters of Stephen A. Douglas championed a popular sovereignty position. Southern radicals demanded a plank calling for the legal protection of slavery in the territories. After heated debates, neither side would compromise. When the delegates finally voted, the Douglas forces carried the day. Disgusted delegates from eight southern states walked out of the convention. Shocked, the remaining delegates adjourned; they would reconvene in Baltimore in June. Most southern delegates boycotted the Baltimore proceedings, and Douglas easily won the Democratic presidential nomination with moderate southerner Herschel V. Johnson of Georgia as his running mate. Hoping to attract moderate voters from both the North and the South, the party's final platform supported popular sovereignty and emphasized allegiance to the Union.

The southern Democratic contingent met one week later, also in Baltimore, and nominated Vice President John C. Breckinridge of Kentucky as its presidential candidate and Joseph Lane of Oregon as his running mate. The southern Democrats' platform vowed support for the Union but called for federal protection of the right to own slaves in the territories and for the preservation of slavery where it already existed.

In May 1860, a group of former Whigs and Know-Nothings along with some disaffected Democrats convened in Baltimore and formed the **Constitutional Union Party**. They nominated John Bell, a former southern Know-Nothing and wealthy slaveholder from Tennessee, and Edward Everett of Massachusetts, a former Whig leader, as his running mate. Hoping to resurrect the politics of compromise, the party resolved to take no stand on the sectional controversy and pledged to uphold the Constitution and the Union and to enforce the laws of the nation.

Having lost most of its moderates to the Constitutional Union coalition and having virtually no southerners in its ranks to start with, the Republican convention faced few ideological divisions, but personality conflicts were rife. The front-runner for the Republican nomination appeared to be William Seward of New York. A former Whig and longtime New York politician, Seward had actively opposed any extension of slavery during the early 1850s but had switched to the popular-sovereignty position during the Kansas controversy. Several other Republican favorites—Salmon P. Chase of Ohio, Simon Cameron of Pennsylvania, and Edward Bates of Missouri—agreed with Seward's position but sought the nomination for themselves.

secession Withdrawal from the nation.

■ **Constitutional Union Party** Political party that organized on the eve of the Civil War with no platform other than preservation of the Constitution, the Union, and the law.

THE POLITICAL QUADRILLE
Music by Dred Scott

As this cartoon makes clear, the *Dred Scott* case set the agenda for the presidential election of 1860. Here Scott provides the music as each of the four presidential candidates dances with a partner who symbolizes his perceived political orientation. John C. Breckinridge (upper left) dances with fellow southern Democrat James Buchanan, illustrating his alignment with southern proslavery hard-liners. John H. Bell (lower right) dances with a Native American, symbolizing his nativist Know-Nothing affiliations, suggesting avoidance of the slavery issue. Meanwhile, Stephen A. Douglas (lower left) escorts a disheveled Irishman, suggesting his alignment with northeastern urban interests including immigrants and other "undesirables." Finally, Abraham Lincoln (upper right) is seen with an African American woman, an obvious reference to his party's perceived abolitionist leanings.

Eventually, however, Abraham Lincoln emerged as Seward's major competition. Many delegates considered Seward too radical and his campaign manager, Thurlow Weed (see page 308), was perceived by many as a corrupt opportunist. Lincoln, in contrast, had a reputation for integrity and had not seriously alienated any of the Republican factions. He won the nomination on the third ballot.

The Election of 1860

The 1860 presidential campaign began as several separate contests. Lincoln and Douglas competed for northern votes; the Republicans were not even on the ballot in the **Deep South**. Douglas proclaimed himself the only national candidate but received most of his support from northerners who feared the consequences of a Republican victory. By the same token, Breckinridge and the southern Democrats expected no support in the North. Bell and the Constitutional

Unionists attempted to campaign in both regions but attracted mostly southern voters anxious to stave off disunion.

Slavery and sectionalism were the key issues. Even when a congressional investigation revealed evidence of graft, bribery, and shady dealings in the Buchanan administration, Republicans linked these charges to the supposed Slave Power conspiracy. The slaveholding elite, they contended, not only had attempted to subvert liberty but had used fraudulent means to keep the Democrats in power. "Honest Abe Lincoln," the man of the people, would lead the fight against the forces of slavery and corruption. This argument drew

> **Deep South** The region of the South farthest from the North, usually said to include the states of Alabama, Florida, Georgia, Louisiana, Mississippi, and South Carolina.

1860

Candidate (Party)	Electoral Vote		Popular Vote	
Lincoln (Republican)	180	59.4%	1,865,593	39.8%
Douglas (Northern Democrat)	12	3.9%	1,382,713	29.5%
Breckinridge (Southern Democrat)	72	23.8%	848,356	18.1%
Bell (Constitutional Union)	39	12.9%	592,906	12.6%
Territories, no returns				

MAP 13.4 Election of 1860

The election of 1860 confirmed the worst fears expressed by concerned Union supporters during the 1850s: changes in the nation's population made it possible for one section to dominate national politics. As this map shows, the Republican and southern Democratic parties virtually split the nation, and the Republicans were able to seize the presidency.

Copyright © Cengage Learning

in many northern voters, including a lot of former Know-Nothings. Sensing that Lincoln would win the North, Douglas launched a last-ditch effort to win the election and hold the Union together by pushing his campaign into the South. As the election drew near, the likelihood of a Republican victory deeply alarmed southerners. Even moderate southerners started to believe that the Republicans intended to crush their way of life and to enslave southern whites economically while freeing southern blacks. Northern qualms were aroused as well when the pro-Democrat *New York Herald* contended that the election of Lincoln would bring "hundreds of thousands" of slaves north to compete with whites for jobs, resulting in "African amalgamation with the fair daughters of the Anglo-Saxon, Celtic, and Teutonic races."

■ **John J. Crittenden** Kentucky senator who made an unsuccessful attempt to prevent the Civil War by proposing a series of constitutional amendments protecting slavery south of the Missouri Compromise line.

Seeking to counter such scare tactics, national Republican leaders forged a platform that advocated limits on slavery's expansion but contained no planks seeking an end to slavery in areas where it already existed. They also called for higher tariffs (to appeal to northern industrialists) and for internal improvements and public lands legislation (to appeal to westerners). Particularly in the Midwest, party leaders worked hard to portray themselves as "the white man's party." In line with the position Lincoln had taken in his 1858 debates with Douglas, Republicans argued that excluding slavery meant excluding blacks from competition with whites. These tactics alienated a few abolitionists but persuaded many northerners and westerners to support the party.

On November 6, 1860, Abraham Lincoln was elected president of the United States with 180 electoral votes—a clear majority—but only 40 percent of the popular vote. Lincoln carried all the northern states, California, and Oregon (see Map 13.4). Douglas finished second with 29 percent of the popular vote but just 12 electoral votes. He won only Missouri. Bell won the 39 electoral votes of Virginia, Kentucky, and Tennessee. Breckinridge, as expected, carried the Deep South but tallied only 72 electoral votes and 18 percent of the popular vote nationwide. For the first time in American history, a purely regional party held the presidency. The Republicans, who had made no effort to win votes in the South, also swept congressional races in the North and secured a large majority in the House of Representatives for the upcoming term.

The First Wave of Secession

After the Republican victory, southern sentiment for secession snowballed, especially in the Deep South. The Republicans were a "party founded on a single sentiment," stated the *Richmond Examiner:* "hatred of African slavery." The *New Orleans Delta* agreed, calling the Republicans "essentially a revolutionary party." But this party now controlled the national government. To a growing number of southerners, the Republican victory was proof that secession was the only alternative to political domination. Most Republicans did not believe that the South would actually leave the Union: Seward had ridiculed threats of secession and Lincoln believed that the "people of the South" had "too much sense" to launch an "attempt to ruin the government." During the campaign, he had promised "no interference by the government, with slaves or slavery within the states," and he continued to urge moderation.

In a last-ditch attempt at compromise, **John J. Crittenden** proposed a block of constitutional amendments that could never be repealed on December 18, 1860. These called for extending the Missouri

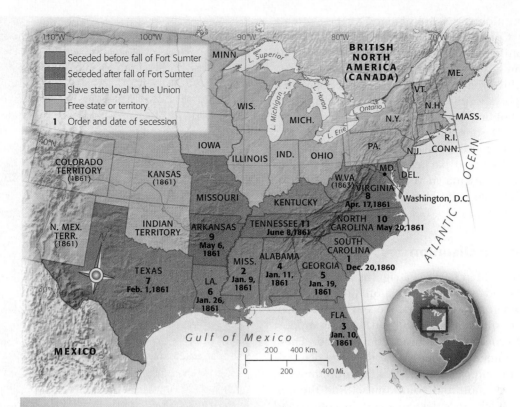

MAP 13.5 Secession
This map shows the breakup of the Union begun by South Carolina's secession in December 1860. The Cotton Belt followed South Carolina's lead in January, and the rest of the confederate states joined them later in the spring of 1861. Free states then aligned to oppose southern secession, while the border states and inland territories were caught in the middle. Copyright © Cengage Learning

Compromise line westward across the continent, forbidding slavery north of the line, and protecting slavery to the south; maintaining the interstate slave trade; and requiring federal compensation to slave-owners who were unable to recover fugitive slaves from northern states. Surprisingly, this plan appealed to some northerners, especially businessmen who feared that secession would cause a major depression. Lincoln warned, however, that such a plan would "lose us everything we gained by the election." The Senate defeated Crittenden's proposal by a vote of 25 to 23.

Meanwhile, on December 20, 1860, delegates in South Carolina met to consider seceding from the Union. South Carolina had long been a hotbed of resistance to federal authority, and state officials determined to take action to protect slavery before the newly elected Republican administration came to power. Amid general jubilation, South Carolina delegates voted unanimously to dissolve their ties with the United States. Just as the radicals hoped, other southern states followed. During January 1861, delegates convened in Mississippi, Florida, Alabama, Georgia, and Louisiana and voted to secede (see Map 13.5).

On February 4, 1861, delegates from the six seceding states and from several states still considering secession met in Montgomery, Alabama, and formed the **Confederate States of America**. During the several weeks that followed, the provisional congress drafted a constitution, and the six Confederate states ratified it on March 11, 1861.

The Confederate constitution emphasized the "sovereign and independent character" of the states and guaranteed the protection of slavery in any new territories acquired. It allowed tariffs solely for the purpose of raising government revenue and prohibited government funding of internal improvements. It also limited the president and vice president to a single six-year term. A cabinet composed of six executive department heads rounded out the executive branch. In all other respects, the Confederate government was identical to that in the United States. In fact, the

■ **Confederate States of America** Political entity formed by the seceding states of South Carolina, Georgia, Florida, Alabama, Mississippi, and Louisiana in February 1861; Texas, Virginia, Arkansas, Tennessee, and North Carolina joined later.

U.S. Constitution was acknowledged as the supreme law in the Confederacy except in those particulars where it conflicted with provisions in the Confederate Constitution.

While this process was under way, the Confederate cause got a significant boost when Texas, which had been holding back, declared itself part of the new nation. Despite unionist pleas from Governor Sam Houston, the heavily populated cotton-growing region in the eastern part of the state opted to join neighboring Louisiana in rebellion, and the rest of the state followed suit. The Confederacy now numbered seven states.

Responses to Disunion

Even as late as March 1861, a significant number of southerners did not favor secession. John Bell and Stephen Douglas together had received more than 50 percent of southern votes in 1860, winning support from southerners who desired compromise. These "plain folk" joined together with some large planters, who stood to suffer economic loss from disunion, in calls for moderation and compromise. And the border states, which were less invested in cotton and had numerous ties with the North, were not strongly inclined toward secession. In February, Virginia had called for a peace conference to meet in Washington in an effort to forestall hostilities, but this attempt, like Crittenden's effort, also failed to hold the Union together.

The division in southern sentiments was a major stumbling block to the election of a Confederate president. Many moderate delegates to the constitutional convention refused to support radical secessionists, believing them to be equally responsible with the Republicans for initiating the crisis. The convention remained deadlocked until two pro-secession Virginia attendees nominated Mississippi moderate Jefferson Davis as a compromise candidate.

Davis appeared to be the ideal choice. Austere and dignified, he had not sought the job but seemed extremely capable of handling it. A West Point graduate, he served during the War with Mexico, was elected to the Senate soon afterward, then left the Senate in 1851 to run unsuccessfully for governor in Mississippi. After serving as secretary of war under Franklin Pierce, he returned to the Senate in 1857. Although Davis had long championed southern interests and owned many slaves, he was no romantic, fire-eating secessionist. Before 1860 he had been a strong **Unionist**, arguing only that the South be allowed to maintain its own economy, culture, and institutions,

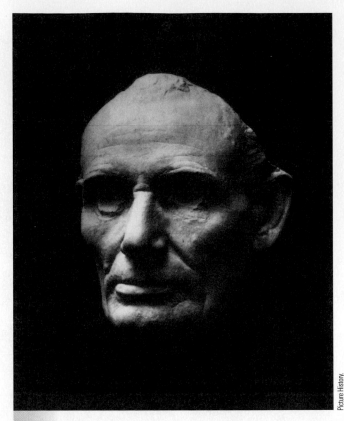

Picture History.

A few months before being nominated by the Republican Party as its presidential candidate, Abraham Lincoln permitted Illinois artist Leonard Volk to cast the future president's face in plaster. Preserved for all these years, this casting and the many reproductions that have been struck from it remain the most accurate picture we have of Lincoln before the secession crisis tore the nation apart. Captured in time, we can see the noble and serious man whose unflinching determination saw the nation through its worst historical crisis. As the many hundreds of photographs and other images of Lincoln during his presidency attest, he would never look this young and confident again.

including slavery. He had supported the Compromise of 1850. When he had fought for a southern route for a transcontinental railroad as secretary of war, he believed that it would benefit the South economically, but he also felt that it would tie the whole nation more firmly together. Like many of his contemporaries, however, Davis had become increasingly alarmed by the prospect of declining southern political power. Immediately after Mississippi's declaration of secession, Davis resigned his Senate seat and threw in with the Confederacy.

To moderates like Davis, the presidential election of 1860 was simply a forceful demonstration that unless the South took a strong stand against outside interference, the region would no longer be able to control its own internal affairs. The initial northward tilt in the Senate created by California's admission

Unionist Loyal to the United States of America.

in 1850 had been aggravated in 1858 by the admission of Minnesota and by Oregon's statehood in 1859. Southerners, Davis believed, needed to act in concert to convince northerners to either leave the South alone or face the region's withdrawal from the nation. "To rally the men of the North, who would preserve the government as our fathers found it," Davis proclaimed, "we . . . should offer no doubtful or divided front."

Elected provisional president of the Confederate States of America unanimously on February 9, 1861, Davis addressed the cheering crowds in Montgomery a week later and set forth the Confederate position: "The time for compromise has now passed," he said. "The South is determined to maintain her position, and make all who oppose her smell Southern powder and feel Southern steel." In his inaugural address several days later, he stressed a desire for peace but reiterated that the "courage and patriotism of the Confederate States" would be "found equal to any measure of defense which honor and security may require."

Northern Democrats and Republicans alike watched developments in the South with dismay. President Buchanan argued that secession had no constitutional validity and that any state leaving the Union did so unlawfully, but he also asserted that the federal government had no constitutional power to "coerce a State" to remain in the Union. He blamed the crisis on "incessant and violent agitation on the slavery question," chiding northerners for disregarding fugitive slave laws and calling for a constitutional amendment protecting slavery.

Waiting to assume the office he had just won, Lincoln wrestled with the twin problems of what he would do about secession and slavery. On one hand, he directly opposed Buchanan's position, stating that "My opinion is that no state can, in any way, lawfully get out of the Union, without the consent of the others." But he was more moderate where slavery was concerned, writing to reassure southerners that "a republican administration" would not "directly or indirectly, interfere with their slaves, or with them, about their slaves."

Before he could do anything else, Lincoln first had to unite his party. In an attempt to appease all the Republican factions, he chose his cabinet with great care. His vice president, Hannibal Hamlin of Maine, had supported Lincoln but was also a friend of William Seward and had been chosen to balance the ticket factionally. Lincoln continued this balancing act with cabinet appointments for his four main rivals for nomination. Seward received the job of secretary of state. Edward Bates of Missouri became attorney general and Simon Cameron of Pennsylvania secretary of war. Salmon P. Chase of Ohio became secretary of the Treasury. Despite Lincoln's evenhandedness, his political balancing act was not easy to maintain. Chase and Seward, for instance, had a long history of political infighting and hated each other. That Lincoln would appoint Chase to any position so angered Seward that he threatened to resign, and Lincoln had to persuade him to remain.

THE NATION DISSOLVED

★ What problems confronted Abraham Lincoln and Jefferson Davis in March 1861?

★ How did their actions contribute to the escalating national crisis?

Abraham Lincoln was inaugurated on March 4, 1861. In his inaugural address he repeated themes that he had been stressing since the election: no interference with slavery in states where it existed, no extension of slavery into the territories, and no tolerance of secession. Lincoln believed that the nation remained unbroken, and he pledged to see "that the laws of the Union be faithfully executed in all the States." This policy, he continued, necessitated "no bloodshed or violence, and there shall be none, unless it is forced upon the national authority." If war came, he argued, it would be over secession, not slavery, for the federal government had a duty to maintain the Union by any means, including force.

Lincoln, Sumter, and War

Lincoln's first presidential address drew mixed reactions. Most Republicans found it firm and reasonable, applauding its tone. Union advocates in both the North and the South thought the speech held promise for the future. Even former rival Stephen Douglas stated, "I am with him." Moderate southerners commended Lincoln's "temperance and conservatism" and believed the speech was all "any reasonable Southern man" could have expected. Confederates and their sympathizers, however, branded the speech a "Declaration of War."

But war was brewing even before Lincoln assumed office. In December 1860, South Carolina officials ordered the state militia to seize two federal forts—Fort Moultrie and Castle Pinckney—and the federal arsenal at Charleston. In response, Major Robert Anderson moved all federal troops from Charleston to **Fort Sumter**, an island stronghold in Charleston Harbor. The Confederate congress demanded that President

■ **Fort Sumter** Fort at the mouth of the harbor of Charleston, South Carolina, scene of the opening engagement of the Civil War in April 1861.

Study Tools

SUMMARY

The war with Mexico that began in 1846 raised, and then the Compromise of 1850 failed to alleviate, regional tension and debates. Slavery dominated the political agenda. The Whig Party, strained by fragmentation among its factions, disintegrated, and two completely new groups—the Know-Nothings and the Republicans—competed to replace it. A series of events—including the Kansas-Nebraska Act and the *Dred Scott* decision—intensified regional polarization, and radicals on both sides fanned the flames of sectional rivalry. Even the Democratic Party could not hold together, splitting into northern and southern wings. By 1859, the young Republican Party, committed to restricting slavery's expansion, seemed poised to gain control of the federal government. Fearing that the loss of political power would doom their way of life, southerners recoiled in terror. Neither side felt it could afford to back down.

With the election of Abraham Lincoln in 1860, six southern states withdrew from the Union. Last-minute efforts at compromise failed, and on April 12, 1861, five weeks after Lincoln's inauguration, Confederate forces fired on federal troops at Fort Sumter in Charleston Harbor. Lincoln believed that he had to call the nation to arms, and this move forced wavering states to choose sides. Internal divisions in Virginia, Tennessee, Maryland, Kentucky, and Missouri brought further violence and military action. Before summer, a second wave of secession finally solidified the lineup and established the boundary lines between the two competing societies. The stakes were set, the division was complete: the nation was poised for the bloodiest war in its history.

CHRONOLOGY
Toward a Shattered Union

1846	War with Mexico begins
1848	Treaty of Guadalupe Hidalgo
	Zachary Taylor elected president
	Immigration to United States exceeds 100,000
1850	Compromise of 1850
	Zacharay Taylor dies; Millard Fillmore becomes president
1852	First railroad line completed to Chicago
	Harriet Beecher Stowe's *Uncle Tom's Cabin*
	Franklin Pierce elected president
	Whig Party collapses
	Know-Nothing Party emerges
1853	Gadsden Purchase
1854	Republican Party formed
	Kansas-Nebraska Act
	Ostend Manifesto
1855	Proslavery posse sacks Lawrence, Kansas
1856	James Buchanan elected president
1857	*Dred Scott* decision
1858	Lincoln-Douglas debates
1859	John Brown's raid on Harpers Ferry
1860	Abraham Lincoln elected president
	Crittenden compromise fails
1861	Confederate States of America formed
	Fort Sumter shelled

Study Tools

FOCUS QUESTIONS

If you have mastered this chapter, you should be able to answer these questions and to explain the terms that follow the questions.

1. ☆ How did the war with Mexico and its outcomes influence politics over the following decade?

2. ☆ What new political options affected the political system during the 1850s? In what ways?

3. ☆ How did various political coalitions react to the Kansas-Nebraska Act?

4. ☆ What was the effect on the national political climate?

5. ☆ In what ways was the presidential election in 1860 an outcome of the realignment of the party system during the 1850s?

6. ☆ Why did the election results have the political effects that they did?

7. ☆ What problems confronted Abraham Lincoln and Jefferson Davis in March 1861?

8. ☆ How did their actions contribute to the escalating national crisis?

KEY TERMS

Zachary Taylor   (p. 323)

John C. Frémont   (p. 323)

Wilmot Proviso   (p. 324)

Winfield Scott   (p. 324)

Battle of Buena Vista   (p. 325)

Treaty of Guadalupe Hidalgo   (p. 325)

Sojourner Truth   (p. 325)

Liberty Party   (p. 326)

Free-Soil Party   (p. 326)

Know-Nothings   (p. 327)

popular sovereignty   (p. 328)

fugitive slave law   (p. 328)

Stephen A. Douglas   (p. 328)

Compromise of 1850   (p. 328)

Underground Railroad   (p. 329)

Harriet Tubman   (p. 329)

John Deere   (p. 331)

Cyrus McCormick   (p. 331)

Abraham Lincoln   (p. 333)

Harriet Beecher Stowe   (p. 333)

conscience Whigs   (p. 333)

James Buchanan   (p. 333)

Franklin Pierce   (p. 333)

Young America Movement   (p. 333)

Gadsden Purchase   (p. 334)

Jefferson Davis   (p. 334)

Kansas-Nebraska Act   (p. 334)

Charles Sumner   (p. 334)

William Walker   (p. 335)

Ostend Manifesto   (p. 336)

John Brown   (p. 336)

Republican Party   (p. 336)

Dred Scott   (p. 337)

Lecompton constitution   (p. 338)

Freeport Doctrine   (p. 339)

Harpers Ferry   (p. 339)

Robert E. Lee   (p. 339)

Constitutional Union Party   (p. 340)

John J. Crittenden   (p. 342)

Confederate States of America   (p. 343)

Fort Sumter   (p. 345)

Richmond   (p. 347)

CourseMate

Go to the History CourseMate website for primary source links, study tools, and review materials for this chapter. www.cengagebrain.com

14 A Violent Choice: Civil War, 1861–1865

Behind the Stories

It may strike you that this chapter does not focus exhaustively upon military details. To be honest, I am not a military historian and am not as fascinated as some by tactics and strategies. I tend to agree with Ulysses S. Grant and William Tecumseh Sherman that war is not a glamorous spectacle and should not be celebrated as such. Certainly there was gallantry, pageantry, and enormous bravery—all worth recording. But my objective in this chapter is to trace the more general history of all the American people: those who fought and those for whom the fighting was little more than a distant echo. My question is what difference all of these experiences have made to our lives in the United States today.

Obviously I cannot go into detail about every battle, every legislative vote, every family decision, or any number of thousands of events that were important to the everyday experiences of Americans during this terrible and revolutionary time. I hope, however, that the information presented will guide you to a fuller understanding of the era and inspire you to pursue the aspects you find most compelling, whether those follow horses and battles, the consumer price of sugar, or the aspirations of newly freed slaves.

—C.L.M.

Individual Choices
Susie King Taylor

Born a slave in 1848, young Susie Baker attended an illegal school for slave children in Savannah, Georgia, where, by the age of 14, she had learned everything her teachers could offer. Then war came. Early in 1862 Union forces attacked the Georgia coast. Powerless and fearful of what the future might hold, many slaves left the city. Eventually a Union gunboat picked up Susie and a number of "**contrabands**" and ferried them to a Yankee encampment on St. Simon's Island. Before long the community of displaced former slaves exceeded six hundred. Discovering that Susie could read and write, Union officials asked her to open the first legally sanctioned school for African Americans in Georgia.

At St. Simon's Susie married another contraband named Edward King. Like many in the camp, King wanted to fight for his freedom. Finally, Union Captain C. T. Trowbridge arrived on the island with a request for volunteers. Though they were offered no pay, no uniforms, and no official recognition, King and his friends eagerly joined up. Trowbridge drilled them during the day while Susie tutored them at night. Finally, in October, the brigade got uniforms and official recognition (though still no pay) and went off to war. Susie decided to go with them.

She spent the rest of the war traveling with the troops, tending to their wounds, their clothes, and their minds. Then the war ended, and her husband died. She taught school for a while, and though she eventually remarried and settled in the North, she never forgot her wartime experiences (see the Individual Voices feature at the end of this chapter).

"These things should be kept in history before the people," she declared, and she made it her business to tell the story. "There has never been a greater war in the United States than the one of 1861, where so many lives were lost—not men alone but noble women as well." Her efforts and those of people like her, people who made hard choices and wrenching sacrifices, had wrought a revolution. "What a wonderful revolution!" she concluded.

Susie King Taylor

Library of Congress.

contrabands Term coined by Gen. Benjamin F. Butler to describe fugitive slaves who sought refuge among Union troops in the South.

Writing of the Civil War, Susie King Taylor described it as a "revolution." To her mind, the mind of a former slave, that revolution was the liberation of the slaves. But when Jefferson Davis and southerner leaders spoke of a revolution, it was against a domineering North that they compared to the England of George III. Lincoln, meanwhile, spoke of a revolution being waged by a rebellious South that would destroy the Union and the Constitution with it.

Many shared the perception that this was a revolutionary moment, but disillusionment seemed to wait behind every event. The South would find it more and more difficult to withstand the superior manpower and resources controlled by the Union. And the North would suffer frustrations of its own as President Lincoln's generals let opportunity after opportunity slip by. In desperation, Lincoln would finally redefine the war by invoking Taylor's revolutionary cause, issuing the Emancipation Proclamation. From that point forward, hopes for a peaceful resolution evaporated: both sides would demand total victory or total destruction.

The war would affect many people in many different ways. For some, like Susie King Taylor, it would afford great opportunities for advancement. For others, it would be a long, torturous ordeal. But one thing was true for everyone and for the nation at large: nothing would be the same after the conflagration was over. Truly it would be a revolution.

THE POLITICS OF WAR

★ *What problems did Abraham Lincoln and Jefferson Davis face as they led their respective nations into war?*

★ *How did each chief executive deal with those problems?*

Running the war posed complex problems for both Abraham Lincoln and Jefferson Davis. At the outset, neither side had the experience, soldiers, or supplies to wage an effective war, and foreign diplomacy and international trade were vital to both. But perhaps the biggest challenge confronting both Davis and Lincoln

brigade A military unit consisting of two or more regiments and composed of between 1,500 and 3,500 men.

was internal politics. Lincoln had to contend not only with northern Democrats and southern sympathizers but also with divisions in his own party. Not all Republicans agreed with the president's war aims. Davis also faced internal political problems. The Confederate constitution guaranteed a great deal of autonomy to the Confederate states, and each state had a different opinion about war strategy and national objectives.

Union Policies and Objectives

Abraham Lincoln took the oath of office in March 1861, but Congress did not convene until July. In effect, Lincoln ruled by executive proclamation for three months, vastly expanding the wartime powers of the presidency. Lincoln called for seventy-five thousand militiamen from the states to put down the rebellion. And ignoring specific constitutional provisions, he suspended the civil rights of citizens in Maryland when it appeared likely that the border state would join the Confederacy. At various times during the war, Lincoln would resort to similar invasions of civil liberties when he felt that dissent threatened either domestic security or the Union cause.

Having assumed nearly absolute authority, Lincoln faced the need to rebuild an army in disarray. When hostilities broke out, the Union had only sixteen thousand men in uniform, and nearly one-third of the officers resigned to support the Confederacy. What military leadership remained was aged: seven of the eight heads of army bureaus had been in the service since the War of 1812, including General in Chief Winfield Scott, who was 74 years old. Only two Union officers had ever commanded a **brigade**, and both were in their seventies. Weapons were old, and supplies were low. On May 3, Lincoln again exceeded his constitutional authority by calling for regular army recruits to meet the crisis. "Whether strictly legal or not," he asserted, such actions were based on "a popular demand, and a public necessity," and he expected "that Congress would readily ratify them."

Lincoln had also ordered a naval blockade of the Confederate states, which became an integral part of the Union strategy devised by the aged Winfield Scott. Scott ordered that the blockade of southern ports be combined with a strong Union thrust down the Mississippi River, the primary artery in the South's transportation system. This strategy would break the southern economy and split the Confederacy into two isolated parts. Like many northerners, Scott believed that economic pressure would bring southern moderates forward to negotiate a settlement and perhaps return

Richard Carlile.

© Bettmann/Corbis.

"It is easy to understand how men catch the contagion of war," civilian relief worker Mary Ashton Rice Livermore asserted. Many on both sides certainly caught it during the opening days of the Civil War. These two Union cavalrymen (left) and Confederate infantrymen (right), volunteered for service and obviously were eager to fight. Such enthusiasm seldom lasted long as days and weeks of boredom, often accompanied by disease, punctuated by brief but heated battles, caused enormous anxiety that eroded their fighting spirit.

to the Union. A war-fevered northern press ridiculed what it called the **anaconda plan**.

When Congress finally convened on July 4, 1861, Lincoln explained his actions and reminded congressmen that he had neither the constitutional authority to abolish slavery nor any intention of doing so. Rebellion, not slavery, had caused the crisis, he said, and the seceding states must be brought back into the Union, regardless of the cost. "Our popular government has been called an experiment," he argued, and the point to be settled now was "its successful maintenance against a formidable internal attempt to overthrow it." On July 22 and 25, 1861, both houses of Congress passed resolutions validating Lincoln's actions.

This seemingly unified front lasted only a short time. Viewing vengeance as the correct objective, **Radical Republicans** pressured Congress to create a special committee to oversee the conduct of the war. Radical leader Thaddeus Stevens of Pennsylvania

(see page 248) growled, "If their whole country must be laid waste, and made a desert, in order to save this union, so let it be." Stevens and the Radicals pressed for and passed a series of confiscation acts that inflicted severe penalties against individuals in rebellion. Treason was punishable by death, and anyone aiding the Confederacy was to be punished with imprisonment, attachment of property, and confiscation of slaves. All persons living in the eleven seceding states, whether

■ **anaconda plan** Winfield Scott's plan (named after a snake that smothers prey in its coils) to blockade southern ports and take control of the Mississippi River, thus splitting the Confederacy, cutting off southern trade, and causing an economic collapse.

■ **Radical Republicans** Republican faction that tried to limit presidential power and enhance congressional authority during the Civil War; Radicals opposed moderation toward the South or any toleration of slavery.

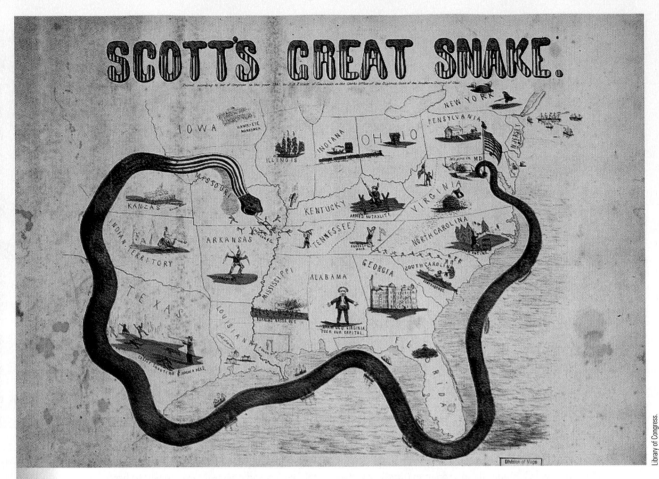

SCOTT'S GREAT SNAKE.

Though many northerners thought it was too passive, General Winfield Scott's "anaconda plan" was actually very well conceived. As this 1861 lithograph shows, Scott called for a naval blockade of the South and seizure of the Mississippi River, shutting down transportation routes to ruin the Confederate economy. Scott retired at the end of the war's first year, but his plan continued to shape the Union's overall strategy.

loyal to the Union or not, were declared enemies of the Union and subject to the provisions of the law.

The Radicals splintered any consensus Lincoln might have achieved in his own party, and northern Democrats railed against his accumulation of power. To keep an unruly Congress from undermining his efforts, Lincoln shaped early Union strategy to appease all factions and used military appointments to smooth political feathers. His attitudes frequently enraged radical abolitionists, but Lincoln maintained his calm in the face of their criticism and merely reinforced his intentions. "What I do about slavery and the colored race," he stated in 1862, "I do because it helps to save the Union; and what I forbear, I forbear because I do not believe it would help to save the Union."

Nevertheless, Lincoln had far greater physical and human resources at his command than did the Confederates (see Table 14.1). The Union was home to more than twice as many people as the Confederacy, had vastly superior manufacturing and transportation systems,

and enjoyed almost a monopoly in banking and foreign exchange. Lincoln also had a well-established government structure and formal diplomatic relations with other nations of the world. Still, these advantages could not help the war effort unless properly harnessed.

Confederate Policies and Objectives

At the start of the war, the Confederacy had no army, no navy, no war supplies, no government structure, no foreign alliances, and a political situation as ragged as the Union's. Each Confederate state had its own ideas about the best way to conduct the war. After the attack on Fort Sumter, amassing supplies, troops, ships, and war materials was the main task for Davis and his cabinet. Politics, however, influenced southern choices about where to field armies and who would direct them, how to run a war without offending state leaders, and how to pursue foreign diplomacy.

TABLE 14.1 Comparison of Union and Confederate Resources

	UNION (23 STATES)	CONFEDERACY (11 STATES)
Total population	20,700,000	9,105,000[a]
Manufacturing establishments	110,000	18,000
Manufacturing workers	1,300,000	110,000
Miles of railroad	21,973	9,283
Troop strength (est.)	2,100,000	850,000

Source: Data from *Battles and Leaders of the Civil War* (1884–1888; reprinted ed., 1956).

[a]Includes 3,654,000 blacks, most of them slaves and not available for military duty.

The Union naval blockade posed an immediate problem. The Confederacy had no navy and no capacity to build naval ships. But it did have the extremely resourceful Stephen Mallory as secretary of the navy. Under Mallory's direction, southern coastal defenders converted river steamboats, tugboats, and **revenue cutters** into harbor patrol gunboats, and they developed and placed explosive mines at the entrances to southern harbors.

Confederates pinned their main hope of winning the war on the army. Fighting for honor was praiseworthy behavior in the South, and southerners strongly believed they could "lick the Yankees" despite their disadvantage in manpower and resources. Thousands volunteered before the Confederate war department was even organized. By the time Lincoln issued his call for seventy-five thousand militiamen, the Confederates already had sixty thousand men in uniform.

Despite this rush of fighting men, the South faced major handicaps. Even with the addition of the four Upper South states (Virginia, North Carolina, Tennessee, and Arkansas), as of 1860, the South built only 4 percent of all locomotives and only 3 percent of all firearms manufactured in the United States. The North produced almost all of the country's cloth, **pig iron**, boots, and shoes. Early in the war, the South could produce enough food but lacked the means to transport it where it was needed.

The miracle worker in charge of supplying southern troops with weapons and ammunition was Josiah Gorgas, who became chief of **ordnance** in April 1861. Gorgas purchased arms from Europe while his ordnance officers bought or stole copper pots and tubing to make **percussion caps**, bronze church bells to make cannon, and lead weights to make bullets. He built factories and foundries to manufacture small arms. But despite his extraordinary skill, he could not supply all of the Confederate troops. When the Confederate congress authorized the enlistment of four hundred thousand additional volunteers in 1861, the war department had to turn away more than half of the enlistees because it lacked equipment for them.

Internal politics also plagued the Davis administration. First, he alienated his high-spirited populace by advocating a defensive war in the belief the Union would give up if the war was made too costly. As one southern editor put it, the "idea of waiting for blows, instead of inflicting them is altogether unsuited to the genius of our people." But even a defensive posture proved hard to maintain. Despite the shortage of arms, state governors hoarded weapons seized from federal arsenals for their own state militias and demanded that their states' borders be protected, spreading troops dangerously thin.

The Diplomatic Front

Perhaps the biggest challenge facing the Confederacy was gaining international recognition and foreign aid. The primary focus of Confederate foreign policy was Great Britain. For years, the South had been exporting huge amounts of cotton to Britain, and many southerners felt that formal recognition of Confederate independence would immediately follow secession. Political and economic realities as well as ethical issues doomed them to disappointment. After all, the Union was still an important player in international affairs, and the British were not going to risk offending the emerging industrial power without good cause. Also, many English voters were morally opposed to slavery and would have objected to an open alliance with the

revenue cutter A small, lightly armed boat used by government customs agents to apprehend merchant ships violating customs laws.

pig iron Crude iron, direct from a blast furnace, that is cast into rectangular molds called pigs in preparation for conversion into steel, cast iron, or wrought iron.

ordnance Weapons, ammunition, and other military equipment.

percussion cap A thin metal cap containing an explosive compound, needed to fire the guns used in the Civil War.

slaveholding Confederacy. On May 13, 1861, Queen Victoria proclaimed official neutrality but granted **belligerent status** to the South.

The British pronouncement set the tone for other European responses and was much less than southerners had hoped for. But Britain's rejection of Lincoln's position that the conflict was a rebellion against duly authorized government was also a blow to the North. Lincoln could do little but accept British neutrality. In November 1861, however, an incident at sea nearly scuttled British-American relations. James Murray Mason, the newly appointed Confederate emissary to London, and John Slidell, the Confederate minister to France, were traveling to their posts aboard the *Trent*, a British merchant ship bound for London. After the *Trent* left Havana, the U.S. warship *San Jacinto* stopped the British ship. Mason, Slidell, and their staffs were removed from the *Trent* and taken to Boston as prisoners of war.

Northerners celebrated the action, but the British viewed the *Trent* affair as aggression against a neutral government, a violation of international law, and an affront to their national honor. Lincoln ordered the release of the prisoners and apologized to the British, handling the incident so adroitly that the public outcry was largely forgotten when Mason and Slidell arrived in London.

The Union's First Attack

Like most southerners, northerners were confident that military action would bring the war to a quick end. General Irvin McDowell made the first move when his troops crossed into Virginia (see Map 14.1 and Table 14.2). McDowell's troops, though high-spirited, were poorly trained and undisciplined. They

belligerent status Recognition that a participant in a conflict is a nation engaged in warfare rather than a rebel against a legally constituted government; full diplomatic recognition is one possible outcome.

■ **Bull Run** A creek in Virginia not far from Washington, D.C., where Confederate soldiers forced federal troops to retreat in the first major battle of the Civil War, fought in July 1861.

■ **Thomas J. Jackson** Confederate general nicknamed "Stonewall"; he commanded troops at both battles of Bull Run and was mortally wounded by his own soldiers at Chancellorsville in 1863.

■ **George B. McClellan** U.S. general tapped by Lincoln to organize the Army of the Potomac; a skillful organizer but slow and indecisive as a field commander. He replaced Winfield Scott, who retired at the end of 1861, as general in chief of Union forces.

■ **Army of the Potomac** Army created to guard the U.S. capital after the Battle of Bull Run in 1861; it became the main Union army in the East.

TABLE 14.2 Battle of Bull Run, July 22, 1861

	UNION ARMY	CONFEDERATE ARMY
Commanders	Irvin McDowell	P. G. T. Beauregard
Troop strength	17,676	18,053
Killed	460	387
Wounded	1,124	1,582
Captured	1,312	13
Total losses	2,896	1,982

Source: Data from *Battles and Leaders of the Civil War* (1884–1888; reprinted ed., 1956).

ambled along as if they were on a country outing, allowing P. G. T. Beauregard enough time to position his troops in defense of a vital rail center near Manassas Junction along a creek called **Bull Run**.

McDowell attacked on Sunday, July 21, and maintained the offensive most of the day. He seemed poised to overrun the Confederates until southern reinforcements under **Thomas J. Jackson** stalled the Union advance. Jackson's unflinching stand at Bull Run earned him the nickname "Stonewall," and under intense cannon fire, Union troops panicked and began fleeing into a throng of northern spectators who had brought picnic lunches and settled in to watch the battle. Thoroughly humiliated before a hometown crowd, Union soldiers retreated toward Washington. Jefferson Davis immediately ordered the invasion of the Union capital, but the Confederates were also in disarray and made no attempt to pursue the fleeing Union forces.

This battle profoundly affected both sides. In the South, the victory stirred confidence that the war would be short and victory complete. Northerners, disillusioned and embarrassed, pledged that no similar retreats would occur. Under fire for the loss, Lincoln removed McDowell and appointed **George B. McClellan**. McClellan was to create the **Army of the Potomac** to defend the capital from Confederate attack and spearhead any offensives into Virginia. Lincoln also replaced Secretary of War Simon

MAP 14.1 Union Offensives into Virginia, 1861–1862
This map shows two failed Union attempts to invade Virginia: the Battle of Bull Run (July 1861) and
the Peninsular Campaign (August 1862). Confederate victories embarrassed the richer and more
populous Union. The map also shows the Battle of Antietam (September 1862), in which the Union
army under General George McClellan finally defeated Confederate troops under Robert E. Lee.

Copyright © Cengage Learning

Cameron with Edwin Stanton, a politician and lawyer
from Pennsylvania.

General McClellan's strengths were in organization and discipline. Both were sorely needed.
Before Bull Run, Union officers had lounged
around Washington while largely unsupervised raw
recruits in army camps received no military instruction. Under McClellan, months of training turned
the 185,000-man army into a well-drilled and efficient unit. Calls to attack Richmond began anew,
but McClellan, seemingly in no hurry for battle,
continued to drill the troops and remained in
the capital. Finally on January 27, 1862, Lincoln
called for a broad offensive, but his general in chief
ignored the order and continued to delay.

FROM BULL RUN TO ANTIETAM

★ *How did military action during the opening years of
the war affect the people's perceptions of the war in
the North and South?*

★ *Why did Lincoln issue the Emancipation
Proclamation when and in the way he did?
What sorts of responses did it elicit?*

Reorganizing the military and forming the Army of
the Potomac did not accomplish Lincoln's goal of
toppling the Confederacy quickly and bringing the
rebellious South back into the Union. In the second
year of the war, frustration followed frustration as
Confederate forces continued to outwit and outfight

Angered by years of systematic mistreatment at the hands of federal authorities, many Native Americans in Indian Territory were eager to enlist for service with the Confederacy. Confederate president Jefferson Davis chose his Indian agents carefully to take advantage of this much-needed source of aid. As this daguerreotype illustrates, Davis's diplomacy was highly successful; many young Indians flocked to Confederate recruitment rallies to join the army. Wisconsin Historical Society.

In the border state of Missouri, the conflict rapidly degenerated into guerrilla warfare. Confederate William Quantrill's Raiders matched atrocities committed by Unionist guerrilla units called Jayhawkers. Union officials seemed unable to stop the ambushes, arson, theft, and murder, and Missouri remained a lawless battleground throughout the war.

Both the United States and the Confederacy coveted the western territories nearly as much as they did the border states. In 1861 Confederate Henry Hopkins Sibley recruited thirty-seven hundred Texans and marched into New Mexico, defeating a Union force at Valverde, but his losses were high. Needing provisions to continue the operation, he sent units to raid abandoned Union storehouses at Albuquerque and Santa Fe, but withdrawing federal troops had burned whatever supplies they could not carry. The small Confederate force at Santa Fe encountered a much larger federal force and won a miraculous victory, but the effort left the Confederates destitute of supplies. Under constant attack, the starving Confederate detachment evaded Union troops and retreated back into Texas.

Confederate leaders sought alliances with several Indian tribes in the newly settled Indian Territory south of Kansas. Many of the residents there had endured the Trail of Tears (see pages 256–258) and had no particular love for the Union. If these Indian tribes aligned with the Confederacy, they not only could supply troops but might also form a buffer between Union forces in Kansas and the thinly spread Confederate defenses west of the Mississippi River. President Davis appointed General Albert Pike, an Arkansas lawyer who had represented the Creeks in their battle against removal in the 1830s, as special commissioner for the Indian Territory in March 1861. Pike negotiated with several tribes and on October 7 signed a treaty with members of the Cherokee, Choctaw, Creek, Chickasaw, and Seminole tribes that granted the Indians more nearly equal status—at least on paper—than any previous federal treaty, and it guaranteed that Indians would be asked to fight only to defend their own territory. One Cherokee leader, Stand Watie, became a Confederate general and distinguished himself in battle.

numerically superior and better-equipped federal troops. After Bull Run it was clear that the war would be neither short nor glorious. Military, political, and diplomatic strategies became increasingly entangled as both North and South struggled for the major victories that would end the war.

The War in the West

While the war in the East slid into inactivity, events in the West seemed almost as futile for the Union forces.

Struggle for the Mississippi

Union efforts in the west were dictated largely by Scott's anaconda plan as **Ulysses S. Grant** moved against southern strongholds in the Mississippi Valley in 1862. On February 6, he took Fort Henry along the Tennessee River and ten days later captured Fort Donelson on the Cumberland River near Nashville, Tennessee (see Map 14.2). In this one swift stroke, Grant successfully penetrated Confederate western defenses and brought Kentucky and most of Tennessee under federal control.

Confederate general Albert Sidney Johnston finally reorganized the retreating southern troops while Grant was waiting for reinforcements. Early on April 6, to Grant's surprise, Johnston attacked at Pittsburg Landing, Tennessee, near a small country meetinghouse called Shiloh Church (see Table 14.3). Some Union forces under General **William Tecumseh Sherman** were driven back, but the Confederate attack soon lost momentum as Union defenses stiffened. The **Battle of Shiloh** raged until midafternoon. When Johnston was mortally wounded, General Beauregard took command and by day's end believed the enemy defeated. But Union reinforcements arrived during the night, and the next morning Grant counterattacked, pushing the Confederates back.

The losses on both sides were staggering. The Battle of Shiloh made the reality of war apparent to everyone but made a particularly strong impression

MAP 14.2 The War in the West, 1862-1863
This map illustrates the anaconda plan at work. The Union navy closed southern harbors while Grant's troops worked to seal the northern end of the Mississippi River.

Copyright © Cengage Learning

TABLE 14.3 Battle of Shiloh, April 6–7, 1862

	UNION ARMY	CONFEDERATE ARMY
Commanders	William Tecumseh Sherman	Albert Sidney Johnston (killed)
	Ulysses S. Grant	P. G. T. Beauregard
Troop strength	75,000	44,000
Killed	1,754	1,723
Wounded	8,408	8,012
Captured, missing	2,885	959
Total losses	13,047	10,694

Source: Data from *Battles and Leaders of the Civil War* (1884–1888; reprinted ed., 1956).

■ **Ulysses S. Grant** U.S. general who, after a series of victories in the Mississippi Valley, became general in chief of the Union army in 1864; he later became president of the United States.

■ **William Tecumseh Sherman** U.S. general who supported Grant in the West; later captured Atlanta, Georgia, and led a destructive march to the Atlantic coast.

■ **Battle of Shiloh** Battle in Tennessee in April 1862 that ended with an unpursued Confederate withdrawal; both sides suffered heavy casualties for the first time, but neither side gained ground.

Desperate to break the grip of the Union anaconda, the Confederate navy converted the captured Union ship U.S.S. *Merrimac* into the ironclad C.S.S. *Virginia*. Virtually immune to any weapon carried by Union frigates, the *Virginia* dominated the sea-lanes out of Norfolk Harbor. The Union navy eventually completed construction of its own ironclad, the U.S.S. *Monitor*, which defeated the *Virginia* in a dramatic sea battle, eliminating that weapon from the Confederate arsenal.

on the common soldier. After Shiloh, one Confederate wrote: "Death in every awful form, if it really be death, is a pleasant sight in comparison to the fearfully and mortally wounded." Few people foresaw that the horrible carnage at Shiloh was but a taste of what was to come.

Farther south, Admiral David G. Farragut led a fleet of U.S. Navy gunboats against New Orleans, the commercial and banking center of the South, and on April 25 forced the city's surrender. Farragut then sailed up the Mississippi, hoping to take the well-fortified city of **Vicksburg**, Mississippi. He scored several victories, but at Port Hudson, Louisiana, the combination of Confederate defenses and shallow water forced him to halt. Meanwhile, on June 6, Union gunboats destroyed a Confederate fleet at Memphis, Tennessee, and brought the upper Mississippi under Union control. Vicksburg remained the only major obstacle to Union control over the entire river (see Map 14.2).

Lee's Aggressive Defense of Virginia

The anaconda plan was well on its way to cutting the Confederacy in two, but the general public in the North thought that the path to real victory led to Richmond, capital of the Confederacy. Confederates, too, realized that Richmond would be an important prize for the North and took dramatic steps to keep their capital city out of enemy hands.

In an effort to skirt Confederate defenses, when McClellan finally acted on Lincoln's insistence for action, he executed a surprise move by transporting the entire Army of the Potomac by ship to Fort Monroe, Virginia, to attack Richmond from the south. Initiating what would be called the **Peninsular Campaign**, the army marched up the peninsula between the York and James Rivers (see Map 14.1 on page 359). In typical fashion, McClellan proceeded cautiously. The outnumbered Confederate forces took advantage

■ **Vicksburg** City that was key to control of the Mississippi River, held by the Confederates until mid-1863.

■ **Peninsular Campaign** McClellan's attempt in the spring and summer of 1862 to capture Richmond by advancing up the peninsula between the James and York Rivers; Confederate forces under Robert E. Lee drove his troops back.

of his indecision and twice slipped away, retreating toward Richmond while McClellan followed. Hoping to overcome the odds by surprising his opponent, General Joseph E. Johnston, commander of the Confederate Army of Northern Virginia, wheeled about and attacked at Seven Pines on May 31. Though the battle was indecisive—both sides claimed victory—it halted McClellan's progress and disabled Johnston, who was seriously wounded.

With McClellan stalled, Confederate stalwart Stonewall Jackson staged a brilliant diversionary thrust down the Shenandoah Valley toward Washington. Jackson, who had grown up in the region, seemed to be everywhere at once. In thirty days, he and his "foot cavalry" marched 350 miles, defeated three Union armies in five battles, captured and sent back to Richmond a fortune in provisions and equipment, inflicted twice as many casualties as they received, and confused and immobilized Union forces in the region.

Meanwhile, McClellan was marking time near Richmond while waiting for reinforcements. With Johnston wounded, Davis had been forced to replace him, choosing Robert E. Lee. Daring, bold, and tactically aggressive, Lee enjoyed combat, pushed his troops to the maximum, and was well liked by those serving under him. He had an uncanny ability to read the character of his opponents, predict their maneuvers, and exploit their mistakes. It now fell to Lee to deal with the invading Yankees. In a move that became typical of his generalship, Lee split his forces and attacked from all sides over a seven-day period in August, forcing McClellan into a defensive position. The Peninsular Campaign was over. The self-promoting Union general had been beaten in part by his own indecisiveness.

Fed up with McClellan, Lincoln ordered the Army of the Potomac back to Washington and gave command to General John Pope, who soon encountered Lee's army again at the Manassas rail line on August 30. The Confederates pretended to retreat, and when Pope followed, Lee soundly defeated Lincoln's new general in the **Second Battle of Bull Run**. Thoroughly disappointed with Pope's performance, but lacking any other viable replacement, Lincoln once again named McClellan commander of the Army of the Potomac.

Lee's Invasion of Maryland

Feeling confident after the second victory at Bull Run, Lee devised a bold offensive against Maryland. On September 4, he crossed the Potomac, formulating an intricate offensive by dividing his army into three separate attack wings. But someone was careless—Union soldiers found a copy of Lee's detailed instructions wrapped around some cigars at an abandoned Confederate campsite. If McClellan had acted swiftly on this intelligence, he could have crushed Lee's army piece

by piece, but he waited sixteen hours before advancing. By then, Lee had learned of the missing orders and quickly withdrew. Lee reunited some of his forces at Sharpsburg, Maryland, around **Antietam Creek** (see Map 14.1). There, on September 17, the Army of the Potomac and the Army of Northern Virginia engaged in the bloodiest single-day battle of the Civil War.

The casualties in this one battle were more than double those suffered in the War of 1812 and the War with Mexico combined. "The air was full of the hiss of bullets and the hurtle of grapeshot," one Union soldier said, and "the whole landscape turned red." The bitter fighting exhausted both armies. After a day of rest, Lee retreated across the Potomac. Stonewall Jackson, covering Lee's retreat, soundly thrashed a force that McClellan sent in pursuit. But for the first time, General Lee experienced defeat.

Although Lee's offensive had been thwarted, Lincoln was not pleased with the performance of his army and its leadership. He felt that McClellan could have destroyed Lee's forces if he had attacked earlier or, failing that, had pursued the fleeing Confederate army. He fired McClellan again, this time for good, and placed Ambrose E. Burnside in command.

Burnside moved his forces to the east bank of the Rappahannock River overlooking **Fredericksburg**, Virginia (see Map 14.3), where he delayed for almost three weeks. Lee used the time to fortify the heights west of the city with men and artillery. On December 13, in one of the worst mistakes of the war, Burnside ordered a day-long frontal assault. The results were devastating. Federal troops, mowed down from the heights, suffered tremendous casualties, and once again the Army of the Potomac retreated to Washington.

Diplomacy and the Politics of Emancipation

The first full year of the war ended with mixed results for both sides. Union forces in the West had scored major victories, breaking down Confederate defenses and taking Memphis and New Orleans. But the failure of the Army of the Potomac under three different generals seemed to outweigh those successes. Lee's victories, however, carried heavy casualties, and the

■ **Second Battle of Bull Run** Union defeat near Bull Run in August 1862; Union troops led by John Pope were outmaneuvered by Lee.

■ **Antietam Creek** Site of a battle that occurred in September 1862 when Lee's forces invaded Maryland; both sides suffered heavy losses, and Lee retreated into Virginia.

■ **Fredericksburg** Site in Virginia of a Union defeat in December 1862 that demonstrated the incompetence of the new Union commander, Ambrose E. Burnside.

MAP 14.3 Fredericksburg, Chancellorsville, and Gettysburg
This map shows the campaigns that took place during the winter of 1862 and spring of 1863, culminating in the Battle of Gettysburg (July 1863). General Meade's victory at Gettysburg may have been the critical turning point of the war.
Copyright © Cengage Learning

South's ability to supply and deploy troops was rapidly diminishing. A long, drawn-out conflict favored the Union unless Jefferson Davis could secure help for the Confederacy from abroad.

The Confederacy still expected British aid, but nothing seemed to shake Britain's commitment to neutrality. To some extent, this resistance was due to the efforts of Charles Francis Adams, Lincoln's ambassador in London, who demonstrated his diplomatic

■ **Emancipation Proclamation** Lincoln's order abolishing slavery as of January 1, 1863, in states "in rebellion" but not in border territories still loyal to the Union.

skill repeatedly during the war. Also, Britain possessed a surplus of cotton and did not need southern supplies, neutralizing the South's only economic lever and frustrating Davis's diplomatic goals.

Radical Republicans were also frustrated. No aspect of the war was going as they had expected. They had hoped that the Union army would defeat the South in short order. Instead the war effort was dragging on. More important from the Radicals' point of view, nothing was being done about slavery. They pressed Lincoln to take a stand against slavery, and they pushed Congress for legislation to prohibit slavery in federal territories.

Politically astute as always, Lincoln acted to appease the Radical Republicans, foster popular support in the North for the war effort, and increase favorable sentiment for the Union cause abroad. During the summer of 1862, he drafted a proclamation freeing the slaves in the Confederacy and submitted it to his cabinet. Cabinet members advised that he postpone announcing the policy until after the Union had achieved a military victory. On September 22, five days after the Battle of Antietam, Lincoln unveiled the **Emancipation Proclamation**, which would abolish slavery in the states "in rebellion" on January 1, 1863.

Although the Emancipation Proclamation was a major step toward ending slavery, it actually freed no slaves. The proclamation applied only to slavery in areas controlled by the Confederacy, not in any area controlled by the Union. Some found this exception troubling, but the president's reasoning was sound. He could not afford to alienate the four slave states that had remained in the Union, nor could he commit any manpower to enforce emancipation in the areas that had been captured from the Confederacy. Lincoln made emancipation entirely conditional on a Union military victory, a gambit designed to force critics of the war, whether in the United States or Great Britain, to rally behind his cause.

Whether or not it was successful as a humanitarian action, issuing the Emancipation Proclamation at the time he did and in the form he did was a profoundly successful political step for Lincoln. Although a handful of northern Democrats and a few Union military leaders called it an "absurd proclamation of a political coward," more joined Frederick Douglass in proclaiming, "We shout for joy that we live to record this righteous decree." Meanwhile, some in Britain pointed to the paradox of the proclamation: it declared an end to slavery in areas where Lincoln could not enforce it, while having no effect on slavery in areas where he could. But even there, most applauded the document and rallied against recognition of the Confederacy.

Still, Lincoln's new general in chief, Henry Halleck, was chilled by the document. As he explained to Grant, the "character of the war has very much changed within the last year. There is now no possible hope of reconciliation." The war was now about slavery as well as secession, and the Emancipation Proclamation committed the Union to conquering the enemy. As Lincoln told one member of his cabinet, the war would now be "one of subjugation."

THE HUMAN DIMENSIONS OF THE WAR

★ How did the burdens of war affect society in the North and the South?

★ How did individuals and governments in both regions respond to those burdens?

The Civil War imposed tremendous stress on American society. As the men marched off to battle, women faced the task of caring for families and property alone. As casualties increased, the number of voluntary enlistments decreased, and both sides searched for ways to find replacements for dead and wounded soldiers. The armies constantly demanded not only weapons and ammunition but also food, clothing, and hardware. Government spending was enormous, and inflation soared as both governments printed paper money to pay their debts. Society in both North and South changed to meet an array of hardships as individuals facing unfamiliar conditions attempted to carry on their lives amid the war's devastation.

Instituting the Draft

By the end of 1862, heavy casualties, massive desertion, and declining enlistments had depleted both armies. Although the North had a much larger population to draw from, its enlistments sagged with its military fortunes during 1862. More than a hundred thousand Union soldiers were absent without official leave. Most volunteers had enlisted in 1861 for limited terms, which would soon expire. Calling on state militias netted few replacements because the Democrats, who made tremendous political gains at the state level in 1862, at times refused to cooperate. To bypass state officials and ensure enough manpower Congress passed the **Conscription Act** in March 1863. In effect, the law made all single men between the ages of 20 and 45 and married men between 20 and 35 eligible for service. Government agents collected names in a house-to-house survey, and draftees were selected by lottery.

The conscription law did offer "escape routes." Drafted men could avoid military service by providing—that is, hiring—an "acceptable substitute" or by paying a $300 fee to purchase exemption. The burden of service thus fell on farmers and urban work-ers who were already suffering from high taxation and inflation caused by the war. Added to that was workers' fear that multitudes of former slaves freed by the Emancipation Proclamation would pour into the already crowded job market, further lowering the value of their labor. Overall, the urban poor felt a sense of alienation, which exploded in the summer of 1863.

The trouble started on July 13 in New York City. Armed demonstrators protesting unfair draft laws engaged in a spree of violence, venting their frustration over the troubles plaguing working people. During three nights of rioting, white workingmen beat many African Americans and lynched six. The Colored Orphan Asylum and several homes owned by blacks were burned. Mobs ransacked businesses owned by African Americans and by people who employed them. Irish men and women and members of other groups that seemed to threaten job security also felt the fury as mobs attacked their churches, businesses, and homes. The rioters also expressed their frustration against Republican spokesmen and officials. Republican journalist **Horace Greeley** was **hanged in effigy**, and the homes of other prominent Republicans and abolitionists were vandalized. Protesting draft exemptions for the rich, rioters also set upon well-dressed strangers on the streets. After four days of chaos, federal troops put down the riot. Fearful of future violence, the city council of New York City voted to pay the $300 exemption fee for all poor draftees who chose not to serve in the army.

The Confederacy also instituted a draft after the first wave of enlistments dried up. Conscription in the South, as in the North, met with considerable resentment and resistance. Believing that plantations were necessary to the war effort and that slaves would not work unless directly overseen by masters, in 1862 Confederate officials passed the **Twenty Negro Law**, which exempted planters owning twenty or more slaves from military service. Like the exemptions in the

■ **Conscription Act** Law passed by Congress in 1863 that established a draft but allowed wealthy people to escape it by hiring a substitute or paying the government a $300 fee.

■ **Horace Greeley** Journalist and politician who helped found the Republican Party; his newspaper, the *New York Tribune*, was known for its antislavery stance.

hang in effigy To hang, as if on a gallows, a crude likeness or dummy—an effigy—representing a hated person.

■ **Twenty Negro Law** Confederate law that exempted planters owning twenty or more slaves from the draft on the grounds that overseeing farm labor done by slaves was necessary to the war effort.

Angered by the fact that rich men were virtually exempt from the draft, frightened by the prospect of job competition from freed southern slaves, and frustrated by the lack of resolution on the battlefield, workingmen took to the streets in New York City during the summer of 1863 to protest against the war. Well-dressed men, African Americans, and leading war advocates were the main targets of mob violence during three nights of uncontrolled rioting. As this illustration shows, federal troops finally put down the rioting in a series of battles around the city. An unknown number of people were killed and injured.

North, the southern policy fostered the feeling that the poor were going off to fight while the rich stayed safely at home. The law was modified in 1863, requiring exempted planters to pay $500, and in 1864, the number of slaves required to earn an exemption was lowered to fifteen. Nevertheless, resentment continued to smolder.

Wartime Economy in the North and South

In his 1864 message to Congress, Abraham Lincoln stated that the war had not depleted northern resources. Although the president exaggerated a bit, the statement contained some truth. Northern industry and population did grow during the Civil War. Operating in cooperation with government, manufacturing experienced a boom. Manufacturers of war supplies benefited from government contracts. Textiles and shoemaking boomed as new labor-saving devices improved efficiency and increased produc-

■ **Homestead Act** Law passed by Congress in 1862 that promised ownership of 160 acres of public land to any citizen or would-be citizen who lived on and cultivated the land for five years.

■ **greenbacks** Paper money issued by the Union; it was not backed by gold.

tion. Congress stimulated economic growth by means of subsidies and land grants to support a transcontinental railroad, higher tariffs to aid manufacturing, and land grants that states could use to finance higher education. In 1862 Congress passed the **Homestead Act** to make land available to more farmers. The law granted 160 acres of the public domain in the West to any citizen or would-be citizen who lived on, and improved, the land for five years.

Of course, the economic picture was not entirely positive. The Union found itself resorting to financial tricks to keep the economy afloat. Facing a cash-flow emergency in 1862, Congress passed the Legal Tender Act, authorizing Treasury Secretary Salmon Chase to issue $431 million in paper money, known as **greenbacks**, that was backed not by gold but only by the government's commitment to redeem the bills. Financial support also came through selling bonds. In the fall of 1862, Philadelphia banker Jay Cooke started a bond drive. More than $2 billion worth of government bonds were sold, and most of them were paid for in greenbacks. These emergency measures helped the Union survive the financial pressures created by the war, but the combination of bond issues and unbacked currency set up a highly unstable situation that came back to haunt Republicans after the war.

The South, an agrarian society, began the war without an industrial base. In addition to lacking transportation, raw materials, and machines, the South lacked managers and skilled industrial workers. The Confederate government intervened more directly in the economy than did its Union counterpart, offering generous loans to new or existing companies that would produce war materials. Josiah Gorgas started government-owned production plants in Alabama, Georgia, and South Carolina. These innovative programs, however, could not compensate for inadequate prewar industrialization.

The supply of money was also a severe problem in the South. Like the North, the South tried to ease cash-flow problems by printing paper money, eventually issuing more than $1 billion in unbacked currency. The outcome was runaway inflation. By the time the war ended, southerners were paying more than $400 for a barrel of flour and $10 a pound for bacon.

Southern industrial shortcomings severely handicapped the army. Many Confederate soldiers were barefoot because shoes were in such short supply. Ordnance was always in demand. Northern plants could produce more than five thousand muskets a day; Confederate production never exceeded three hundred. The most serious shortage, however, was food. Although the South was an agricultural region, most of its productive acreage was devoted to cotton, tobacco, and other crops that were essential to its overall economy but not edible. Corn and rice were the primary food products, but supplies were continually reduced by military campaigns and Union occupation of farmlands. Hog production suffered from the same disruptions, and while Southern cattle were abundant, most were range stock grown for hides and tallow rather than for food. Hunger became a miserable part of daily life for the Confederate armies.

Civilians in the South suffered from the same shortages as the army. Because of prewar shipping patterns, the few rail lines that crossed the Confederacy ran north and south. Distribution of goods became almost impossible as invading Union forces cut rail lines and disrupted production. The flow of cattle, horses, and food from the West diminished when Union forces gained control of the Mississippi. Imported goods had to evade the Union naval blockade. Southern society, cut off from the outside world, consumed its existing resources and found no way to obtain more.

Women in Two Nations at War

Because the South had fewer men than the North to send to war, a larger proportion of southern families were left in the care of women. Some women successfully supported their families. Others struggled in complete poverty amid the ravages of war. One

woman wrote to the Confederacy's secretary of war, pleading that he "discharge" her husband so that "he might do his children some good" rather than leaving them "to suffer." Some disregarded the authorities. "Desert again, Jake," one shouted to her husband, who was being drafted for the second time. Most southern women, however, supported the war effort. Women became responsible for much of the South's agricultural and industrial production, overseeing crops and laboring in the fields, working in factories, managing estates, and operating businesses while, in most cases, also running the household—and waiting for the dreaded message that a husband or child would not return from the front. As one southern soldier wrote, women bore "the greatest burden of this horrid war."

Women in the North served in much the same capacity as their southern counterparts. They maintained families and homes alone, working to provide income and raise children. Although they did not face the shortages and ravages of battle that made life so hard for southern women, they did work in factories, run family businesses, teach school, and supply soldiers. Many served in managerial capacities or as writers and civil servants. Even before the war ended, northern women were going south to educate former slaves and help them find a place in American society. Women thus assumed new roles that helped prepare them for greater involvement in social and political life after the war.

Women from both South and North actively participated in the war itself. Many women on both sides served as scouts, couriers, and spies; and more than four hundred disguised themselves as men and served as active soldiers until they were discovered. General William S. Rosecrans expressed dismay when one of his sergeants was delivered of "a bouncing baby boy," which was, the general complained, "in violation of all military regulations." Army camps frequently included officers' wives, female employees, camp followers, and women who came to help in whatever way they could. Susie King Taylor served the 33rd U.S. Colored Troops for four years and three months without pay, teaching the men to read and write and binding up their wounds.

Free Blacks, Slaves, and War

As Susie King Taylor observed, the Civil War marked a revolution for African Americans, but radical changes were not always for the better. At first, many free blacks attempted to enlist in the Union army but were turned away. In 1861 General Benjamin F. Butler began using runaway slaves, called contrabands, as laborers. Several other northern commanders quickly adopted the practice. As the number of contrabands increased,

Women served in many different capacities during the Civil War. An unknown number of them actually dressed as men to join the fighting. Frances Clayton was one of the few documented cases of such Civil War gender-bending.

however, the Union grappled with problems of housing and feeding them.

In the summer of 1862, Congress authorized the acceptance of "persons of African descent" into the armed forces, but enlistment remained low. After the Emancipation Proclamation, Union officials actively recruited former slaves, raising troops from among the freedmen and forming them into regiments known as the U.S. Colored Troops. Some northern state governments sought free blacks to fill state draft quotas; agents offered generous bonuses to those who signed up. By the end of the war, about 180,000 African Americans had enlisted in northern armies; by 1865, almost two-thirds of Union troops in the Mississippi Valley were black.

At first, African American regiments were used as laborers rather than being allowed to fight. But several black regiments, when finally allowed into battle, performed so well that they won grudging respect. These men fought in 449 battles in every theater of the war and had a casualty rate 35 percent higher than white soldiers. Still, discrimination was the rule, not the exception. Army officials discriminated

against African American soldiers in a variety of ways. Units were segregated, and until 1864, blacks were paid less than whites. All black regiments had white commanders; only one hundred African Americans were commissioned as officers, and none ever received a commission higher than major. And Confederates violently resented the Union's use of these troops: African American soldiers suffered atrocities because some Confederate leaders refused to take black prisoners. At Fort Pillow, Tennessee, for example, Confederate soldiers massacred more than a hundred African American soldiers who were trying to surrender. In all, about sixty-eight thousand black Union soldiers were killed or wounded in battle, and twenty-one were awarded the Congressional Medal of Honor.

The war effort in the South relied heavily on the slave population, mostly as producers of food and as military laborers. Slaves constituted more than half of the work force in armament plants and military hospitals. Though crucial to the southern war effort, slaves suffered more than other southerners in the face of food shortages and other privations. And after

Eager to fill constantly depleting army ranks, Union officials appealed to African Americans to volunteer for military service. This recruiting poster, which bore the legend "Come Join Us, Brothers," presents a glorified vision of what conditions were like for black units. One accurate detail is that the only officer in the scene is white; in fact, hardly any African Americans were permitted to command troops during the Civil War.

Lincoln issued the Emancipation Proclamation, fears of slave revolts prompted whites to institute harsh security procedures. Hungry and even less free than usual, slaves became the greatest unsung casualties of the war.

Life and Death at the Front

Many volunteers on both sides in the Civil War had romantic notions about military service. Most were disappointed. Life as a common soldier was anything but glorious. Letters and diaries written by soldiers tell of long periods of doing nothing in overcrowded camps, interrupted only by furious spells of dangerous action.

Though life in camp was tedious, it could be nearly as dangerous as time spent on the battlefield. Problems with supplying safe drinking water and disposing of waste constantly plagued military leaders. Diseases such as dysentery and **typhoid fever** frequently swept through unsanitary camps. And in the overcrowded conditions that often prevailed, smallpox and other contagious diseases passed rapidly from person to person. At times, as many as a quarter of the uninjured people in camps were disabled by one or another of these ailments.

Lacking in resources, organization, and expertise, the South did little to upgrade camp conditions. In the North, however, women drew on the organizational skills they had gained as antebellum reformers and created voluntary organizations to address the problem. At the local level, women like Mary Livermore and

typhoid fever An infectious disease transmitted through contact with contaminated water, milk, or food; causes severe intestinal distress and high fever.

In the Wider World

Jane Hoge created small relief societies designed to aid soldiers and their families. Gradually these merged into regional organizations that would take the lead in raising money and implementing large-scale public health efforts, both in the army camps and at home. Mental health advocate and reformer Dorothea Dix (see page 302) was also one of these crusaders. In June 1861, President Lincoln responded to their concerns by creating the **United States Sanitary Commission**, a government agency responsible for advising the military on public health issues and investigating sanitary problems. "The Sanitary," as it was called, put hundreds of nurses into the field, providing much-needed relief for overburdened military doctors.

Nurses on both sides showed bravery and devotion. Often working under fire at the front and with almost no medical supplies, these volunteers nursed sick and wounded soldiers, watched as they died not only from their wounds but also from infection and disease, and offered as much comfort and help as they could. **Clara Barton**, known as the "Angel of the Battlefield," recalled "speaking to and feeding with my own hands each soldier" as she attempted to nurse them back to health. Hospitals were unsanitary, overflowing, and underfunded.

■ **United States Sanitary Commission** Government commission established by Abraham Lincoln to improve public health conditions in military camps and hospitals.

■ **Clara Barton** Organizer of a volunteer service to aid sick and wounded Civil War soldiers; she later founded the American branch of the Red Cross.

rifled Having a series of spiral grooves inside the barrel of a gun that cause the projectile to spin, giving it greater range and accuracy.

The numbers of wounded who filled the hospital tents was unprecedented, largely because of technological innovations in weaponry that had taken place during the antebellum period. New **rifled** muskets had many times the range of the old smooth-bore weapons used during earlier wars—the effective range of the Springfield rifle used by many Union soldiers was 400 yards, and a stray bullet could still kill a man at 1,000 yards. Waterproof cartridges, perfected by gunsmith Samuel Colt, made these weapons much less prone to misfire and much easier to reload. And at closer range, the revolver, also perfected by Colt, could fire six shots without any reloading. Rifled artillery also added to the casualty count, as did exploding artillery shells, which sent deadly shrapnel ripping through lines of men.

Many surgeons at the front lines could do little more than amputate limbs to save lives. Hospitals, understaffed and lacking supplies and medicines, frequently became breeding grounds for disease. The war exacted a tremendous emotional toll on everyone, even on those who escaped physical injury. As one veteran put it, soldiers had seen "so many new forms of death" and "so many frightful and novel kinds of mutilation."

Conditions were even worse in prison camps. Throughout much of the war, an agreement provided for prisoner exchanges, but that did not prevent overcrowding and unsanitary conditions. And as the war dragged on, the exchange system stopped working effectively. In part the program collapsed because of the enormity of the task: moving and accounting for the large numbers of prisoners presented a serious organizational problem. Another contributing factor, though, was the refusal by Confederate officials to exchange African American prisoners of war—those

In 1862, photographer Mathew Brady put on a public display of battlefield scenes in his New York gallery that brought the war home to civilians as nothing had before. The *New York Times* proclaimed: "Mr. Brady has done something to bring home to us the terrible reality and earnestness of war. If he has not brought bodies and laid them on our dooryard and along the streets, he has done something very like it."

who were not slaughtered like the men at Fort Pillow were enslaved. Also, late in the war, Union commanders suspended all prisoner exchanges in hopes of depriving the South of much-needed replacement soldiers.

The most notorious of the Civil War prison camps was **Andersonville**, in northern Georgia, where thousands of Union captives languished in an open stockade with only a small creek for water and virtually no sanitary facilities. Without enough food to feed its own armies and civilian population, the Confederacy could allocate little food for its overcrowded prison camps. Designed to house 10,000 men, Andersonville held more than 33,000 prisoners during the summer of 1864. As many as 100 men died of disease and malnutrition within its walls each day; estimates put the death toll at that one prison at nearly 14,000 over the course of the war.

Even death itself came to be redefined, as 8 percent of the white male population in the United States between the ages of 13 and 43 died in such a short time and in such grisly ways. People at the front reported being numbed by the horror. One army surgeon reported, "I pass over the putrefying bodies of the dead . . . and feel as . . . unconcerned as though they were two hundred pigs." Nor was distance any insulation from the horrors of death. The new art of photography brought graphic images of the gruesome carnage directly into the nation's parlors. "Death does not seem half so terrible as it did long ago," one Texas woman reported. "We have grown used to it."

■ **Andersonville** Confederate prisoner of war camp in northern Georgia where some fourteen thousand Union prisoners died of disease and malnutrition.

Waging Total War

★ *What factors contributed to the Union's adoption of a total war strategy after 1863?*

★ *Was total war justifiable in light of the human and property damage it inflicted and the overall consequences it achieved? Why or why not?*

As northerners anticipated the presidential election of 1864, Lincoln faced severe challenges on several fronts. The losses to Lee and Jackson in Virginia and the failure to catch Lee at Antietam had eroded public support. Many northerners resented the war, conscription, and abolitionism. Others feared Lincoln's powerful central government.

Northern Democrats advocated a peace platform and turned to George B. McClellan, Lincoln's ousted general, as a potential presidential candidate. Lincoln also faced a challenge from within his own party. Radical Republicans, who felt he was too soft on the South and unfit to run the war, began planning a campaign to win power. They championed the candidacy of John C. Frémont, who had become an ardent advocate of the complete abolition of slavery.

Lincoln's Generals and Southern Successes

The surest way for Lincoln to stop his political opponents was through military success. After Burnside's disaster at Fredericksburg, Lincoln demoted him and elevated General Joseph Hooker. Despite Hooker's reputation for bravery in battle—his nickname was "Fighting Joe"—Lee soundly defeated his forces at **Chancellorsville** in May 1863 (see Map 14.3 and Table 14.4). After Hooker had maneuvered Lee into a corner, Stonewall Jackson unleashed a vicious attack, and Fighting Joe simply "lost his nerve," according to one of his subordinates. Hooker resigned, and Lincoln replaced him with General George E. Meade.

Chancellorsville was a devastating loss for the North, but it was perhaps more devastating for the Confederates. After he led the charge that unnerved Hooker, Jackson's own men mistakenly shot him as he rode back toward his camp in the darkness. Doctors amputated Jackson's arm in an attempt to save his life. "He has lost his left arm," moaned Lee, "but I have lost my right." Eight days later, Jackson died of pneumonia.

■ **Chancellorsville** Site in Virginia where in May 1863 Confederate troops led by Lee defeated a much larger Union force.

■ **Gettysburg** Site in Pennsylvania where in July 1863 Union forces under General George Meade defeated Lee's Confederate forces, turning back Lee's invasion of the North.

TABLE 14.4 Battle of Chancellorsville, May 1–4, 1863

	UNION ARMY	CONFEDERATE ARMY
Commanders	Joseph Hooker	Robert E. Lee
Troop strength	75,000	50,000
Killed	1,606	1,665
Wounded	9,762	9,081
Captured, missing	5,919	2,018
Total losses	17,287	12,764

Source: Data from *Battles and Leaders of the Civil War* (1884–1888; reprinted ed., 1956).

Despite that loss, at a meeting of Confederate leaders in Richmond, Lee proposed another major invasion of the North, arguing that such a maneuver would allow the Confederates to gather supplies and might encourage the northern peace movement, revitalize the prospects of foreign recognition, and perhaps capture the Union capital. Confederate leaders agreed and approved Lee's plan.

The Army of Northern Virginia met only weak opposition as it crossed the Potomac River and marched into Union territory (see Map 14.3). In Maryland and Pennsylvania the troops seized livestock, supplies, food, clothing, and shoes. Learning that a Union contingent was in the area of **Gettysburg**, Pennsylvania, and believing them to be weaker than they were, on June 29 Lee moved to engage the Federals. Meade, whose Army of the Potomac had been trailing Lee's army as it marched north from Chancellorsville, immediately dispatched a detachment to reinforce Gettysburg. On the following day, the two armies began a furious three-day battle.

Arriving in force on July 1, Meade took up an almost impregnable defensive position on the hills along Cemetery Ridge. The Confederates hammered both ends of the Union line but could gain no ground. On the third day, Lee ordered a major assault on the middle of the Union position. Eleven brigades, more than thirteen thousand men, led by fresh troops under Major General George E. Pickett, tried to cross open ground and take the hills held by Meade, while Major J. E. B. "Jeb" Stuart's cavalry attacked from the

TABLE 14.5 Battle of Gettysburg, July 1–3, 1863

	UNION ARMY	CONFEDERATE ARMY
Commanders	George E. Meade	Robert E. Lee
Troop strength	75,000	50,000
Killed	3,155	3,903
Wounded	14,529	18,735
Captured, missing	5,365	5,425
Total losses	23,049	28,063

Source: Data from *Battles and Leaders of the Civil War* (1884–1888; reprinted ed., 1956).

east. Lee made few strategic mistakes during the war, but Pickett's charge was foolhardy. Meade's forces drove off the attack. The whole field was "dotted with our soldiers," wrote one Confederate officer. Lee met his retreating troops with the words "It's all my fault, my fault." Losses on both sides were high (see Table 14.5), but Confederate casualties exceeded twenty-eight thousand men, more than half of Lee's army. Lee retreated, his invasion of the North a failure.

On the heels of this major victory for the North came news from Mississippi that Vicksburg had fallen to Grant's siege on July 4 (see Map 14.2). Sherman had been beating back Confederate forces in central Mississippi, and Union guns had been shelling the city continuously for nearly seven weeks, driving residents into caves and barricaded shelters. But it was starvation and disease that finally subdued the defenders. Then on July 9, after receiving news of Vicksburg's fate, Port Hudson, the last Confederate garrison on the Mississippi River, also surrendered. The "Father of Waters," said Lincoln, "again goes unvexed to the sea."

Despite jubilation over the recent victories, Lincoln and the North remained frustrated. After Gettysburg, Lincoln waited for word of Lee's capture, believing it would signal the end of the rebellion. But like McClellan, Meade failed to pursue the retreating Confederates. When the president learned of Lee's escape, he said in disbelief, "Our Army held the war in the hollow of their hand and they would not close it."

Disappointment in Tennessee also soon marred the celebration over Gettysburg and Vicksburg. Union general William S. Rosecrans had taken the rail center of Chattanooga, but on September 18, Braxton Bragg's forces attacked Rosecrans at Chickamauga Creek. Rosecrans scurried back to refuge in Chattanooga, leaving troops in place to cover his retreat. This force, under the command of George H. Thomas, delayed the Confederate offensive and, in the words of one veteran, "saved the army from defeat and rout." Bragg nonetheless was able to follow and laid siege to Chattanooga from the heights of Missionary Ridge and Lookout Mountain, overlooking the city.

With Lee and his army intact and Rosecrans pinned down in Tennessee, the war, which in July had appeared to be so nearly over, was, in Lincoln's words, "prolonged indefinitely." Lincoln needed a new kind of general.

Grant, Sherman, and the Invention of Total War

Among the available choices, Grant had shown the kind of persistence and boldness Lincoln thought necessary. Lincoln placed him in charge of all Union forces in the West on October 16. Grant immediately replaced Rosecrans with the more intrepid and decisive Thomas. Sherman's troops joined Thomas under Grant's command on November 14. This united force rid the mountains above Chattanooga of Confederate strongholds and drove Bragg's forces out of southern Tennessee. Confederate forces also withdrew from Knoxville in December, leaving the state under Union control.

While fighting raged in Tennessee, Lincoln took a break from his duties in the White House to participate in the dedication of a national cemetery at the site where, just months before, the Battle of Gettysburg had taken the lives of thousands. In the speech he delivered on November 19, 1863, Lincoln dedicated not only the cemetery but the war effort itself to the fallen soldiers, and also to a principle. "Fourscore and seven years ago," Lincoln said, "our fathers brought forth on this continent a new nation, conceived in liberty and dedicated to the proposition that all men are created equal." Though delivered in a low voice that most of the crowd could not hear, the **Gettysburg Address** was circulated in the media and

■ **Gettysburg Address** A speech given by Abraham Lincoln on November 19, 1863, dedicating a national cemetery in Gettysburg, Pennsylvania; it expressed Lincoln's maturing view of the war and its purpose.

At Gettysburg, a series of battles like the one shown here—this one on the first day of the fighting—cost Confederate General Robert E. Lee more than half of his entire army and forced his retreat into Virginia.

galvanized many Americans who had come to doubt the war's purpose.

Delighted with Grant's successes in Tennessee, Lincoln promoted him again on March 10, 1864, this time to general in chief. Grant immediately left his command in the West to prepare an all-out attack on Lee and Virginia, authorizing Sherman to pursue a campaign into Georgia.

In Grant and Sherman, Lincoln had found what he needed. On the surface, neither seemed a likely candidate for a major role in the Union army. Both were West Point graduates but left the army after the War with Mexico to seek their fortunes. Neither had succeeded in civilian life: Grant was a binge drinker who had accomplished little, and Sherman had failed as a banker and a lawyer. Both were "political generals," owing their Civil War commissions to the influence

of friends or relatives. Despite their checkered pasts, these two men invented a new type of warfare that eventually brought the South to its knees. Grant and Sherman were willing to wage **total war** to destroy the South's will.

One of Grant's first acts was to cut the supply of Confederate soldiers by suspending prisoner of war exchanges. He understood that one outcome of this policy would be slow death by starvation for Union prisoners, but he reasoned that victory was his primary goal and that suffering and death were unavoidable in war. Throughout the remainder of the war, this single-mindedness pushed Grant to make decisions that cost tens of thousands of lives on both sides.

On May 4, Grant and Meade moved toward Richmond and Robert E. Lee. The next day, Union and Confederate armies collided in a tangle of woods called The Wilderness, near Chancellorsville (see Map 14.4). Two days of bloody fighting followed. Grant decided to skirt Lee's troops and head for Richmond, but Lee anticipated the maneuver and blocked Grant's route at Spotsylvania. Twelve days of fighting ensued. Grant again attempted to move around Lee, and again Lee anticipated him. On June 1, the two armies met at **Cold Harbor**, Virginia. After each side had consolidated its position, Grant ordered a series of frontal attacks against the

■ **total war** War waged with little regard for the welfare of troops on either side or for enemy civilians; the objective is to destroy both the human and the economic resources of the enemy.

■ **Cold Harbor** Site at which Grant ordered a doomed assault on Lee's center that cost enormous Union casualties, one of a series of battles in the spring of 1864 in which Grant, accepting unspeakable carnage, tried to maneuver his army past Lee's.

MAP 14.4 The Final Virginia Campaign, 1864–1865
This map shows the series of battles during the late spring of 1864 in which Grant's army suffered staggering casualties but finally drove Lee into retreat. After holding out for months behind heavy fortifications in Petersburg, Lee made a daring attempt to escape in April 1865 but was headed off by General Philip Sheridan's troops. Grant quickly closed in on the greatly weakened Confederate army, forcing Lee's surrender. Copyright © Cengage Learning

entrenched Confederates on June 3. Lee's veteran troops waited patiently in perhaps the best position they had ever defended, while Union soldiers expecting to die marched toward them. The assault failed amid unspeakable slaughter.

One southerner described Grant's assaults as "inexplicable and incredible butchery." Many of the young federal attackers at Cold Harbor had pinned their names on their shirts in the hope that their shattered bodies might be identified after the battle. Casualties on both sides at Spotsylvania and Cold Harbor were staggering, but Union losses were unimaginably horrible. As one Confederate officer put it, "We have met a man, this time, who either does not know when he is whipped, or who cares not if he loses his whole army." During the three encounters, Grant lost a total of sixty thousand troops, more than Lee's entire army. Said Lee, "This is not war, this is murder." But Grant's seeming wantonness was calculated, for the Confederates lost more than twenty-five thousand troops. And Grant knew, as did Lee, that the Union could afford the losses but the Confederacy could not.

After Cold Harbor, Grant steered the Union army toward Petersburg, south of Richmond, to try to take the vital rail center and cut off the southern capital. But Lee rapidly shifted the **vanguard** of his troops, beat back Grant's advance, and occupied Petersburg. Grant bitterly regretted this failure, feeling that he could have ended the war. Instead, the campaign settled into a siege that neither side wanted.

The Election of 1864 and Sherman's March to the Sea

Lincoln was under fire from two directions. On May 31, 1864, the Republicans met in Cleveland and dumped him from the ticket, officially nominating John C. Frémont as their presidential candidate. Lincoln

vanguard The foremost unit in any army advancing into battle.

Disliked by most of his fellow officers because of his coarse behavior and binge drinking, Ulysses S. Grant had the right combination of daring, unconventionality, and ruthlessness to wear down Robert E. Lee's forces in Virginia and finally defeat the Confederate army.

National Archives.

supporters, who began calling themselves the Union Party, held their nominating convention in June and renominated Lincoln. To attract Democrats who still favored fighting for a clear victory, Union Party delegates dumped Republican Vice President Hannibal Hamlin and chose **Andrew Johnson**, a southern Democrat, as Lincoln's running mate. Then, in August, the Democratic National Convention met at Chicago. The Democrats pulled together many **Copperheads** and other northerners who were so upset by the heavy casualties that they were determined to stop the war, even at the cost of allowing slavery to continue. The Democrats selected McClellan as their presidential candidate and included a peace plank in their platform. Thus Lincoln sat squarely in the middle between one group that castigated him for pursuing the war and

■ **Andrew Johnson** Tennessee senator who became Lincoln's running mate in 1864 and who succeeded to the presidency after Lincoln's assassination.

■ **Copperheads** Derogatory term (the name of a poisonous snake) applied to northerners who supported the South during the Civil War.

■ **March to the Sea** Sherman's march through Georgia from Atlanta to Savannah in late 1864, during which Union soldiers carried out orders to destroy everything in their path.

another group that rebuked him for failing to punish the South vigorously enough.

Jefferson Davis's administration also faced serious criticism as deprivation and military losses mounted. In an effort to solve their mutual problems, Lincoln and Confederate vice president Alexander H. Stephens had conversations about negotiating a settlement. Lincoln stated his terms: reunion, abolition, and amnesty for Confederates. Stephens balked, pointing out that "amnesty" applied to criminals and that the South had "committed no crime." The only possible outcomes of the war for the South, he concluded, were independence or extermination, even if it meant enduring the sight of "every Southern plantation sacked and every Southern city in flames." The words proved prophetic.

Grant had instructed Sherman "to get into the interior of the enemy's country as far as you can, inflicting all the damage you can against their war resources." Sherman responded with a vengeance. Slowly and skillfully his army advanced southward from Tennessee toward Atlanta, one of the South's few remaining industrial centers (see Map 14.5). Confederate general Joseph E. Johnston repeatedly retreated to keep Sherman from annihilating his army. President Davis then replaced Johnston with John Bell Hood, who vowed to take the offensive. Hood attacked, but Sherman inflicted such serious casualties that Hood had to retreat to Atlanta.

For days Sherman shelled Atlanta and wrought havoc in the surrounding countryside. When a last-ditch southern attack failed, Hood evacuated the city on September 1. Sherman's victory caused tremendous despair among Confederates but gave great momentum to Lincoln's reelection campaign. Also boosting Lincoln's reelection efforts was General Philip Sheridan's campaign in the Shenandoah Valley, an important source of food for Lee's army. Adopting the same sort of devastating tactics that Sherman used so successfully, Sheridan's men lived off the land and destroyed both military and civilian supplies whenever possible. Accepting high casualties, Sheridan drove Confederate forces from the region in October, laying waste to much of Lee's food supply in the process.

These victories proved the decisive factor in the election of 1864. Sherman's and Sheridan's successes defused McClellan's argument that Lincoln was not competent to direct the Union's military fortunes and quelled much antiwar sentiment in the North. Equally discredited, the Radical Republican platform and the Frémont candidacy disappeared before election day. When the votes were counted, Lincoln learned that he had defeated McClellan—by half a million popular votes and by a landslide margin of 212 to 21 in the Electoral College.

The southern peace movement had viewed a Democratic victory as the last chance to reach a settlement. Without it, all hope of negotiation appeared lost. Amid the bleak prospects, animosity toward Jefferson Davis increased in the South. But with Lee's forces still in Petersburg and Hood's in Georgia, southern hopes were dimmed but not extinguished.

Sherman soon grew bored with the occupation of Atlanta and posed a bold plan to Grant. He wanted to ignore Hood and go on the offensive, cutting "a swath through to the sea." "I can make Georgia howl," he promised. Despite some misgivings, Grant agreed and convinced Lincoln.

A week after the election, Sherman began preparing for his 300-mile **March to the Sea** (see Map 14.5). His intentions were clear. "We are not only fighting hostile armies, but a hostile people," he stated. By devastating the countryside and destroying the South's ability to conduct war, he intended to break down southerners' will to resist. "We cannot change the hearts of those people of the South," he concluded, but we can "make them so sick of war that generations would pass away before they would again appeal to it." With that, he burned most of Atlanta and then set out on his march to the coastal town of Savannah. His troops plundered and looted farms and towns on the way, foraging for food and supplies and destroying everything in their path. Sherman entered Savannah unopposed on December 21.

The March to the Sea completed, Sherman turned north. In South Carolina, the first state to secede and fire shots, Sherman's troops took special delight in ravaging the countryside. When they reached Columbia, flames engulfed the city. With the state capital in flames, Confederate forces in South Carolina abandoned their posts, moving north to join with Joseph E. Johnston's army in an effort to stop Sherman from crossing North Carolina

MAP 14.5 Sherman's Campaign in the South
This map shows how William Tecumseh Sherman's troops slashed through the South, destroying both civilian and military targets and reducing the South's will to continue the war. Copyright © Cengage Learning

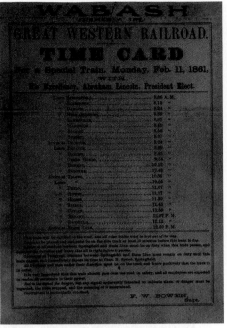

The nation's mood shifted from celebration to shock when it learned that President Lincoln had fallen to an assassin's bullet. His funeral provided an occasion for the entire country to mourn, not only his death but also the deaths of hundreds of thousands of Americans who had fallen in the Civil War. A rail car pulled by an armored military locomotive carried the president's body on a route that retraced his 1860 campaign throughout the North. In large cities, Lincoln's body was paraded through the streets in mourning processionals. Throughout the countryside, however, people lined the tracks at all hours of the day and night waiting for the train to pass so they could pay tribute to their fallen leader.

Jefferson Davis remained in hiding and called for guerrilla warfare and continued resistance. But one by one, the Confederate officers surrendered to their Union opponents. On May 10, Davis was captured near Irwinville, Georgia. Andrew Johnson, who had assumed the presidency upon Lincoln's death, issued a statement to the American people that armed rebellion against legitimate authority could be considered "virtually at an end." The last Confederate general to lay down his arms was Cherokee leader Stand Watie, who surrendered on June 23, 1865.

The price of victory was high for both the winner and the loser. More than 350,000 Union soldiers had been killed in action. No exact figures exist for the Confederacy, but southern casualties probably equaled or exceeded those of the Union. The war had wrecked the economy of the South. Union military campaigns had wiped out most southern rail lines, destroyed the South's manufacturing capacity, and severely reduced agricultural productivity. Both sides had faced rising inflation during the war, but the Confederacy's actions to supply troops and keep the war effort going had bled the South of most of its resources and money. Secession had been defeated, but reunion remained a distant and difficult objective.

Individual Voices

Susie King Taylor: Reflection on Racial Prejudice

Like all African Americans, Susie King Taylor had a deep personal investment in the outcome of the American Civil War. A slave herself, she ran away to the Union lines seeking asylum and, like many other "contrabands," joined the Union cause. Unlike most others, however, Taylor recorded her experiences during the war, giving her contemporaries and modern historians a unique insight into the accomplishments and disillusionments that came with fighting for the freedom and equality that the war seemed to promise. She continued to record her thoughts through later life. At the end of the Spanish-American War (1898), Taylor reflected on the impact of American racial prejudice on Cubans and the ongoing denial of justice to African Americans.

1 In Taylor's mind, what conditions did the end of the Spanish-American War leave unresolved? What does this say about her perceptions concerning her role in the Civil War?

2 In 1886, Taylor was one of the co-founders of the Women's Relief Corps, an organization devoted to aiding Civil War veterans and furthering recognition for American soldiers. She was the president of the Massachusetts auxiliary in 1898, leading the organization to send aid to soldiers in the Spanish-American War.

With the close of the Spanish war, and on the entrance of the Americans into Cuba, the same conditions confront us as the war of 1861 left. The Cubans are free, but it is a limited freedom, for prejudice, deep-rooted, has been brought to them and a separation made between the white and black Cubans, a thing that had never existed between them before; but to-day there is the same intense hatred toward the negro in Cuba that there is in some parts of this country **1**

I helped to furnish and pack boxes to be sent to the soldiers and hospitals during the first part of the Spanish war; **2** there were black soldiers there too. At the battle of San Juan Hill, they were in the front, just as brave, loyal, and true as those other black men who fought for freedom and the right; and yet their bravery and faithfulness were reluctantly acknowledged, and praise grudgingly given. **3** All we ask for is "equal justice," the same that is accorded to all other races who come to this country, of their free will (not forced to, as we were), and are allowed to enjoy every privilege, unrestricted, while we are denied what is rightfully our own in a country which the labor of our forefathers helped to make what it is.

3 What is Taylor suggesting here about the way in which the contributions of African American Civil War veterans were regarded? What does this suggest about her motivations for writing about her experiences in that war?

Study Tools

SUMMARY

Both the Union and the Confederacy entered the war in 1861 with glowing hopes. Jefferson Davis pursued a defensive strategy, certain that northerners would soon tire of war and let the South withdraw from the Union. Abraham Lincoln countered by using the superior human, economic, and natural resources of the North to strangle the South into submission. But both leaders became increasingly frustrated during the first year of the war.

For Lincoln, the greatest frustration was military leadership. Beginning with the first Battle of Bull Run, Union forces seemed unable to win any major battles. Although Union forces under Ulysses S. Grant's command scored victories in the Mississippi Valley, the Federals were stalemated. Robert E. Lee and Thomas "Stonewall" Jackson seemed able to defeat any Union general that Lincoln sent to oppose them.

The war's nature and direction changed after the fall of 1862, however. Lee invaded Maryland and was defeated at Antietam. Despite this crushing loss, Union generals still failed to capture Lee or to subdue Confederate forces in Virginia. Still angered by military blundering, political attacks, and popular unrest, Lincoln issued the Emancipation Proclamation in an effort to undermine southern efforts and unify northern ones. After the proclamation, the only option for either side was total victory or total defeat.

After further reversals in the spring of 1863, Union forces turned the tide in the war by defeating Lee's army at Gettysburg and taking Vicksburg to gain full control of the Mississippi. With an election drawing near, Lincoln spurred his generals to deal the death blow to the Confederacy, and two in particular rose to the occasion. During the last half of 1864, William Tecumseh Sherman wreaked havoc, making Georgia "howl." And Grant, in a wanton display of disregard for human life, drove Lee into a defensive corner. In November, buoyed by Sherman's victories in Georgia, Lincoln was reelected.

Suffering was not confined to those at the front. Governments in both the North and the South had to dig deep into depleting economic resources to keep the war effort going. Inflation plagued both nations, and common people faced hunger, disease, and lawlessness. Riots broke out in major cities, including New York. But throughout the country many people responded heroically to their own privations and to suffering at the front. Women such as Clara Barton and others faced up to epidemics, enemy gunfire, and gender bias to institute public health standards and bring solace to suffering civilians and soldiers alike.

As hope dwindled for the South in the spring of 1865, Lee made a final desperate effort to keep the flagging Confederacy alive, racing to unify the last surviving remnants of the once-proud southern army. But Grant closed a net of steel around Lee's troops, forcing surrender. Lincoln immediately promoted a gentle policy for reunion, but his assassination ended this effort. The saintly American hero was gone, leaving a southern Democrat—Andrew Johnson—as president and a nation reeling in shock. The war was over, but the issues were still unresolved.

Study Tools

CHRONOLOGY
War Between the States

1861	Lincoln takes office and runs Union by executive authority until July
	Fort Sumter falls
	Battle of Bull Run
	McClellan organizes the Union army
1862	Grant's victories in Mississippi Valley
	Battle of Shiloh
	U.S. Navy captures New Orleans
	Peninsular Campaign
	Battle of Antietam
	African Americans permitted in Union army
1863	Emancipation Proclamation takes effect
	Union enacts conscription

	Battle of Chancellorsville and death of Stonewall Jackson
	Union victories at Gettysburg and Vicksburg
	Draft riots in New York City
1864	Grant invades Virginia
	Sherman captures Atlanta
	Lincoln reelected
	Sherman's March to the Sea
1865	Lee abandons Petersburg and Richmond
	Lee surrenders at Appomattox Courthouse
	Lincoln proposes a gentle reconstruction policy
	Lincoln assassinated

FOCUS QUESTIONS

If you have mastered this chapter, you should be able to answer these questions and to explain the terms that follow the questions.

1. ☆ *What problems did Abraham Lincoln and Jefferson Davis face as they led their respective nations into war?*

2. ☆ *How did each chief executive deal with those problems?*

3. ☆ *How did military action during the opening years of the war affect the people's perceptions of the war in the North and South?*

4. ☆ *Why did Lincoln issue the Emancipation Proclamation when and in the way he did? What sorts of responses did it elicit?*

5. ☆ *How did the burdens of war affect society in the North and the South?*

6. ☆ *How did individuals and governments in both regions respond to those burdens?*

7. ☆ *What factors contributed to the Union's adoption of a total war strategy after 1863?*

8. ☆ *Was total war justifiable in light of the human and property damage it inflicted and the overall consequences it achieved? Why or why not?*

Study Tools

KEY TERMS

anaconda plan *(p. 355)*

Radical Republicans *(p. 355)*

Bull Run *(p. 358)*

Thomas J. Jackson *(p. 358)*

George B. McClellan *(p. 358)*

Army of the Potomac *(p. 358)*

Ulysses S. Grant *(p. 361)*

William Tecumseh Sherman *(p. 361)*

Battle of Shiloh *(p. 361)*

Vicksburg *(p. 362)*

Peninsular Campaign *(p. 362)*

Second Battle of Bull Run *(p. 363)*

Antietam Creek *(p. 363)*

Fredericksburg *(p. 363)*

Emancipation Proclamation *(p. 364)*

Conscription Act *(p. 365)*

Horace Greeley *(p. 365)*

Twenty Negro Law *(p. 365)*

Homestead Act *(p. 366)*

greenbacks *(p. 366)*

United States Sanitary Commission *(p. 370)*

Clara Barton *(p. 370)*

Andersonville *(p. 371)*

Chancellorsville *(p. 372)*

Gettysburg *(p. 372)*

Gettysburg Address *(p. 373)*

total war *(p. 374)*

Cold Harbor *(p. 374)*

Andrew Johnson *(p. 376)*

Copperheads *(p. 376)*

March to the Sea *(p. 377)*

John Wilkes Booth *(p. 379)*

 CourseMate

Go to the History CourseMate website for primary source links, study tools, and review materials for this chapter. www.cengagebrain.com

15

Reconstruction: High Hopes and Shattered Dreams, 1865–1877

Behind the Stories

For four long, bloody years of civil war, the armies of the North and South slogged through battle after battle. Toward the end of the war, Union armies smashed across the South, leaving wreckage in their wake: shelled buildings, ravaged farms, twisted railroad tracks. Slavery—the dominant economic and social institution in many parts of the South—collapsed.

The end of the war brought many questions. What would be the future status of African Americans? How would the South be reintegrated into the federal union? What would happen to those who had supported the Confederacy? Thousands of voices across the nation proposed very different answers.

Historians use the term *Reconstruction* to describe the years after the Civil War, from 1865 to 1877. In evaluating Reconstruction, historians focus on several central changes:

- The restoration of the federal union.
- Significant changes in the relationship between the federal government and the

states, and in the relative power of the president and Congress.

- The end of slavery and the experience of African Americans, most of them former slaves.
- The restructuring of race relations, especially in the South.
- Major changes in the politics, economy, and social structure of the South.

The Civil War and Reconstruction, like the American Revolution, form a dividing point in American history, a time when Americans made important and long-lasting choices about their future. Such dividing points attract historians, who seek to understand the momentous decisions that were being made. Historians of Reconstruction have largely agreed that the most ambitious efforts for restructuring race relations and southern politics ended in failure, but they have disagreed on the reasons for failure. As you read this chapter, think about these questions and about the long-term effects of Reconstruction on all Americans.

—R.W.C.

Individual Choices
Blanche K. Bruce

On a cold January day in 1875, Blanche Kelso Bruce, a former slave, raised his right hand to take the oath of office as U.S. senator from Mississippi, the second African American to become a U.S. senator. In the previous fifteen years, Bruce had seen the Civil War, the Emancipation Proclamation, and amendments to the Constitution that ended slavery and guaranteeed the citizenship and voting rights of the former slaves. For many Americans, black and white, the world had been turned upside down during those years, and the swearing-in of Bruce as a U.S. senator was but one more momentous change.

Library of Congress.

Blanche K. Bruce

Bruce was born into slavery in 1841. His mother, Polly Bruce, was a slave, daughter of a black slave woman and a white man. Bruce's father was also white—probably his master. In the language of the day, that made Bruce a "quadroon," three-quarters white. He later recalled that his master had treated him well, and that he was taught to read. He read widely, despite having no formal schooling. His master moved the household a good deal while Bruce was growing up, ending in Missouri.

With the beginning of civil war, Bruce reached a momentous decision: "I would emancipate myself." He went west to Kansas, then returned to Missouri several years later. He briefly attended Oberlin College in Ohio, hoping to become a minister, but quit when his funds ran out. Learning of opportunities in the postwar South, Bruce made another momentous decision: he would try his luck in the South. When he arrived in Bolivar County, Mississippi, where blacks accounted for about 90 percent of the population, Bruce had only seventy-five cents in his pocket but was ambitious, intelligent, and made friends easily. His next major decision was to go into politics. He was elected sheriff in 1871, reelected in 1873, and also served as county superintendent of schools. In 1874, the state legislature elected Bruce, just thirty-two years old, to the U.S. Senate. He became the first African American to serve a full term in the Senate, and the only one until the 1960s.

Blanche K. Bruce . . .

When white supremacists took power in Mississippi, Bruce protested (see the Individual Voices feature at the end of this chapter), but to no avail. When Bruce completed his Senate term in 1881, Democrats committed to white supremacy held sway across the South. Bruce, however, continued to be an important Republican Party leader in Washington, D.C., and in Mississippi, where he eventually owned thousands of acres of fertile farm land. A consummate politician, known for his tact and skills at persuasion, he always insisted that African Americans were "an integral part" of American society and would make "slow and painful" progress toward equality. He also sought to remain on good terms with Republican leaders who increasingly ignored the plight of southern African Americans, and he thereby drew criticism from some black leaders for being too accommodating.

Bruce was not the only African American who claimed freedom while the war was raging. That experience was repeated time and time again, with many variations, all across the South. Those many individual decisions were made legal by the Emancipation Proclamation, enforced by the presence of Union armies, and made permanent by the Thirteenth Amendment to the Constitution. The **freed people** now faced a wide range of new decisions—where to live, where to work, how to create their own communities.

The war left many parts of the South in a shambles. One-fifth of southern white men of military age did not survive the war, and some of those who survived lost arms or legs. As white southerners grieved for their dead and were dismayed by their ravaged countryside, many were also deeply troubled by the **emancipation** of 4 million slaves. In 1861, fears for the future of slavery caused the South to attempt to **secede**. With the end of the war, fears became reality. The end of slavery forced southerners of both races to develop new social, economic, and political patterns.

The years following the war were a time of physical rebuilding throughout the South, but the term **Reconstruction** refers primarily to the rebuilding of the federal union and to the political, economic, and social changes that came to the South as it was restored to the nation. Reconstruction involved some of the most momentous questions in American history: How was the defeated South to be treated? What was to be the future of the 4 million former slaves? Should key decisions be made by the federal government or in state capitols and county courthouses throughout the South? Which branch of the government was to establish policies?

As the dominant Republicans turned their attention from waging war to reconstructing the Union, they wrote into law and the Constitution new definitions of the Union itself. They also defined the rights of the former slaves and the terms on which the South might rejoin the Union. And they permanently changed the definition of American citizenship.

Most white southerners disliked the new rules emerging from the federal government, and some resisted. Disagreement over the future of the South and the status of the former slaves led to conflict between the president and Congress. A temporary result of this conflict was a more powerful Congress and a less powerful executive. A lasting outcome of these events was a significant increase in the power of the federal government and new limits on local and state governments.

Reconstruction significantly changed many aspects of southern life. In the end, however, Reconstruction failed to fulfill many African Americans' hopes for their lives as free people.

---

freed people Former slaves; *freed people* is the term used by historians to refer to former slaves, whether male or female.

emancipation The release from slavery.

secede To withdraw from an organization; the attempted withdrawal of eleven southern states from the United States in 1860–1861, giving rise to the Civil War.

■ **Reconstruction** Term applied by historians to the years 1865–1877, when the Union was restored after the Civil War; important changes were made to the federal Constitution, and relations between the races were transformed in the South.

PRESIDENTIAL RECONSTRUCTION

★ *What did Presidents Lincoln and Johnson seek to accomplish for the South? How did white southerners respond to those efforts?*

On New Year's Day, 1863, the Emancipation Proclamation took effect. More than four years earlier, **Abraham Lincoln** had insisted that "this government cannot endure permanently half slave and half free.... It will become all one thing, or all the other." With the Emancipation Proclamation, President Lincoln began to make the nation all free. At the time, however, the proclamation did not affect any slave because it abolished slavery only in territory under Confederate control, where it was unenforceable. But every advance of a Union army after January 1, 1863, brought emancipation to the slaves of the Confederacy.

Republican War Aims

For Lincoln and the Republican Party, freedom for the slaves became a central concern partly because **abolitionists** were influential within the party. The Republican Party had promised only to prohibit slavery in the territories during its 1860 electoral campaign, and Lincoln initially defined the war as one to maintain the Union. Some leading Republicans, however, favored abolition of slavery everywhere. As Union troops moved into the South, some slaves, like Blanche Bruce, simply walked away from their owners. Many sought safety with the Union army. Soon former slaves became Union soldiers as well. Abolitionists throughout the North—including **Frederick Douglass**, an escaped slave and an important leader of the abolition movement—began to argue that emancipation would be meaningless unless the government guaranteed the civil and political rights of the former slaves. Thus some Republicans expanded their definition of war objectives to include abolishing slavery, extending citizenship for the former slaves, and guaranteeing the equality of all citizens before the law. At the time, these were extreme views on abolition and equal rights, and the people who held them were called **Radical Republicans**, or simply Radicals.

Thaddeus Stevens, 73 years old in 1865, was the leading Radical in the House of Representatives. He had made a successful career as a Pennsylvania lawyer and iron manufacturer before winning election to Congress in 1858. Born with a clubfoot, he identified with those outside the social mainstream. He became a compelling spokesman for abolition and an uncompromising advocate of equal rights for African Americans. A masterful parliamentarian, he was known for his honesty and sarcastic wit. From the beginning of the war, Stevens urged that the slaves be not

Library of Congress.

Thaddeus Stevens, seen here at the height of his power, was the leader of the Radical Republicans in the House of Representatives. He died in 1868. At his request, he was buried in a cemetery that did not discriminate on the basis of race.

only freed but also armed to fight the Confederacy. By the end of the war, some 180,000 African Americans, the great majority of them freedmen, had served in the Union army and a few thousand in the Union navy. Many more worked for the army as laborers.

Charles Sumner of Massachusetts, a prominent Radical in the Senate, had argued for **racial integration** of Massachusetts schools in 1849 and won election to

■ **Abraham Lincoln** (1809–1865) Sixteenth president of the United States, who presided over the Union during the Civil War, initiated Reconstruction, and was assassinated shortly after beginning his second term as president.

abolitionist An individual who condemns slavery as morally wrong and seeks to abolish (eliminate) slavery.

■ **Frederick Douglass** (c. 1818–1895) Escaped slave who became a leader of the abolition movement and later an important African American leader and Republican politician.

■ **Radical Republicans** A group within the Republican Party during the Civil War and Reconstruction that advocated abolition of slavery, citizenship for the former slaves, and sweeping alteration of the South.

racial integration Equal opportunities to participate in a society or organization by people of different racial groups; the absence of race-based barriers to full and equal participation.

the U.S. Senate in 1851. The Senate's foremost champion of abolition, he suffered a severe beating in 1856 because of an antislavery speech. After emancipation, Sumner, like Stevens, fought for full political and civil rights for the freed people.

Stevens, Sumner, and other Radicals opposed slavery not only on moral grounds but also because they believed free labor was more productive. Slaves worked to escape punishment, they argued, but free workers worked to benefit themselves. Eliminating slavery and instituting a free-labor system in its place, they claimed, would benefit everyone by increasing the nation's productivity. Free labor not only contributed centrally to the dynamism of the North's economy, they argued, but was crucial to democracy itself. "The middling classes who own the soil, and work it with their own hands," Stevens once proclaimed, "are the main support of every free government." Not all Republicans agreed with the Radicals. All Republicans objected to slavery, but not all Republicans were abolitionists. Similarly, not all Republicans wanted to extend full citizenship rights to the former slaves. Some favored rapid restoration of the South to the Union so that the federal government could concentrate on stimulating the nation's economy and developing the West. Such Republicans are usually referred to as **moderates**.

Lincoln's Approach to Reconstruction: "With Malice Toward None"

After the Emancipation Proclamation, President Lincoln and the congressional Radicals agreed that abolition of slavery had to be a condition for the return of the South to the Union. Major differences soon appeared, however, over other terms for reunion and the roles of the president and Congress in establishing those terms. In his second inaugural address, a month before his death, Lincoln defined the task facing the nation:

> With malice toward none; with charity for all; with firmness in the right, as God gives us to see the right, let us strive on to finish the work we are in: to bind up the nation's wounds; to care for him who shall have borne the battle, and for his widow and orphan, to do all which may achieve and cherish a

just and lasting peace among ourselves, and with all nations.

Lincoln began to rebuild the Union on the basis of these principles. As soon as Union armies occupied portions of southern states, he appointed temporary military governors for those regions and tried to restore civil government as quickly as possible.

Drawing on the president's constitutional power to issue **pardons** (Article II, Section 2), Lincoln issued a Proclamation of **Amnesty** and Reconstruction in December 1863. Often called the "Ten Percent Plan," it promised a full pardon and restoration of rights to those who swore their loyalty to the Union and accepted the abolition of slavery. Only high-ranking Confederate leaders were not eligible. Once those who had taken the oath in a state amounted to 10 percent of the votes cast by that state in the 1860 election, the pardoned voters were to write a new state constitution that abolished slavery, elect state officials, and resume self-government. Some Radicals considered Lincoln's approach too lenient. When they tried to set more stringent standards, Lincoln blocked them, fearing their plan would slow restoration of civil government and perhaps lengthen the war.

Under Lincoln's Ten Percent Plan, new state governments were established in Arkansas, Louisiana, and Tennessee during 1864 and early 1865. In Louisiana, the new government denied voting rights to men who were one-quarter or more black. Radicals complained, but Lincoln urged patience, suggesting the reconstructed government in Louisiana was "as the egg to the fowl, and we shall sooner have the fowl by hatching the egg than by smashing it." Radicals, however, concluded that freed people were unlikely to receive equitable treatment from state governments formed under the Ten Percent Plan. Some moderates agreed and moved toward the Radicals' position that only **suffrage** could protect the freedmen's rights and that only federal action could guarantee black suffrage.

Abolishing Slavery Forever: The Thirteenth Amendment

Amid questions about the rights of freed people, congressional Republicans prepared the final destruction of slavery. The Emancipation Proclamation had been a wartime measure, justified partly by military necessity. It never applied in Union states. State legislatures or conventions abolished slavery in West Virginia, Maryland, Missouri, and the reconstructed state of Tennessee. In early 1865, however, slavery remained legal in Delaware and Kentucky, and prewar state laws—which might or might not be valid—permitted slavery in the states that had seceded. To destroy slavery forever, Congress in January 1865 approved the **Thirteenth Amendment**, which read simply, "Neither slavery nor

moderates People whose views are midway between two extreme positions; in this case, Republicans who favored some reforms but not all the Radicals' proposals.

pardon A governmental directive canceling punishment for a person or people who have committed a crime.

amnesty A general pardon granted by a government, especially for political offenses.

suffrage The right to vote.

■ **Thirteenth Amendment** Constitutional amendment, ratified in 1865, that abolished slavery in the United States and its territories.

These white southerners are shown taking the oath of allegiance to the United States in 1865, as part of the process of restoring civil government in the South. Union soldiers and officers are administering the oath.

Library of Congress.

involuntary servitude, except as a punishment for crime whereof the party shall have been duly convicted, shall exist within the United States, or any place subject to their jurisdiction."

The Constitution requires any amendment to be ratified by three-fourths of the states—then 27 of 36. By December 1865, only 19 of the 25 Union states had ratified the amendment. The measure passed, however, when 8 of the reconstructed southern states approved it. In the end, therefore, the abolition of slavery hinged on action by reconstructed state governments in the South.

Andrew Johnson and Reconstruction

In April 1865, shortly after the surrender of the main Confederate army, Lincoln was assassinated by a supporter of the Confederacy. Vice President **Andrew Johnson** became president. Johnson never had the opportunity to attend school and spent his early life in a continual struggle against poverty. As a young man in Tennessee, he worked as a tailor, then turned to politics. His wife, Eliza McCardle Johnson, tutored him in reading, writing, and arithmetic. A Democrat,

Johnson was elected to Congress and later was governor before winning election to the U.S. Senate in 1857. His political support came primarily from small-scale farmers and working people. The state's elite of plantation owners usually opposed him. Johnson, in turn, resented their wealth and power, and blamed them for secession and the Civil War.

Johnson was the only southern senator who rejected the Confederacy. Early in the war, Union forces captured Nashville, the capital of Tennessee, and Lincoln appointed Johnson as military governor. Johnson dealt harshly with Tennessee secessionists, especially wealthy planters. Radical Republicans approved. Johnson was elected vice president in 1864, receiving the nomination in part because Lincoln wanted to appeal to Democrats and Unionists in border states.

■ **Andrew Johnson** (1808–1875) Seventeenth president of the United States, who was elected vice president in 1864, became president after Lincoln's assassination, and was impeached, but not removed from the presidency, owing to conflicts with Congress.

In the Wider World

Abolition of Slavery Around the World

By abolishing slavery, the United States followed the lead of most of the nations of Europe and Latin America. Slavery had existed throughout human history, but in the eighteenth century, Enlightenment thinkers began to criticize slavery as violating human rights. At the same time, some religious groups, notably the Quakers, began to work for abolition. The table that follows summarizes information on the abolition of slavery in other parts of the world. Space does not permit listing all nations, but the table shows general patterns.

Though illegal, **chattel slavery** still exists in some parts of Africa and the Middle East, notably Mauritania and Sudan. In other places, people still work in conditions approaching slavery, through forced prostitution, debt bondage, and forced-labor camps.

Year	Event
1587	Slave trade abolished in Japan
1772	Slavery abolished in England and Wales
1794	Slavery abolished in France and French colonies; later restored in the colonies
1807	British navy begins operations to end the international slave trade
1808	United States prohibits importation of slaves
1820s	Slavery abolished in most Spanish-speaking Latin American nations
1833	Slavery abolished within the British Empire
1848	Slavery again abolished within the French Empire
1861	Abolition of serfdom in Russia
1863	Emancipation Proclamation (United States); slavery abolished within the Dutch Empire
1865	Thirteenth Amendment (United States)
1876	Slavery abolished within the Ottoman Empire
1888	Slavery abolished in Brazil
1910	Slavery abolished in China
1926	Thirty-five nations sign a Convention to Suppress the Slave Trade and Slavery
1948	United Nations adopts the Universal Declaration of Human Rights, including a call for abolition of slavery and the slave trade
1962	Abolition of slavery in Saudi Arabia

When Johnson became president, Radicals hoped he would join their efforts to transform the South. Johnson, however, was strongly committed to **states' rights** and opposed the Radicals' objective of a powerful federal government. "White men alone must manage the South," Johnson announced, although he recommended limited political roles for the freedmen. Self-righteous and uncompromising, Johnson saw the major task of Reconstruction as **empowering** the region's white middle class and excluding wealthy planters from power.

Johnson's approach to Reconstruction differed little from Lincoln's. Like Lincoln, he relied on the president's constitutional power to grant pardons. He wanted a quick restoration of the southern states to the Union, and he granted amnesty to most former Confederates who pledged loyalty to the Union and support for emancipation. In one of his last actions as president, he granted full pardon and amnesty to all southern rebels, although the Fourteenth Amendment prevented him from restoring their right to hold office.

Johnson appointed **provisional** civilian governors for the southern states not already reconstructed. He instructed them to reconstitute state government and to call constitutional conventions of delegates elected by pardoned voters. Some provisional governors, however, appointed former Confederates to state and local offices, outraging those who expected Reconstruction to bring to power loyal Unionists committed to a new southern society.

chattel slavery The condition in which one person is legally defined as the personal property of another person.

states' rights A political position favoring limitation of the federal government's power and the greatest possible self-government by the individual states.

empower To increase the power or authority of some person or group.

provisional Temporary.

The Southern Response: Minimal Compliance

Johnson expected the state constitutional conventions to abolish slavery within each state, ratify the Thirteenth Amendment, renounce secession, and **repudiate** their state's war debts. The states were then to hold elections and resume their places in the Union. State conventions during the summer of 1865 usually complied with these requirements, some grudgingly. Every state, however, rejected black suffrage.

By April 1866, a year after the close of the war, all the southern states had fulfilled Johnson's requirements for rejoining the Union and had elected legislators, governors, and members of Congress. Johnson had hoped for the emergence of new political leaders in the South, but was dismayed at the number of rich planters and former Confederate officials who won state contests.

Most white southerners, however, viewed Johnson as their protector, standing between them and the Radicals. His support for states' rights and his opposition to federal determination of voting rights led white southerners to expect that they would shape the transition from slavery to freedom—that they, and not Congress, would define the status of the former slaves.

Before emancipation, slaves typically made their own clothing or received the used outfits of their owners and overseers. With emancipation, freed people with an income could afford to dress more fashionably. The Harry Stevens family probably put on their best clothes for a visit to the photographer G. Gable in 1866. G. Gable, Summer Scene, 1866. Albumen silver print from glass negative. Image: 5.7 x 9.2 cm. (2 ¼ x 3 5/8 in.). Recto: "Harry Stevens". Gilman Collection, Purchase, The Horace W. Goldsmith Foundation Gift, through Joyce and Robert Menschel, 2005 (2005.100.277)/The Metropolitan Museum of Art, New York NY, U.S.A. Image copyright © The Metropolitan Museum of Art/Art Resource, New York.

FREEDOM AND THE LEGACY OF SLAVERY

★ *What seem to have been the leading objectives among freed people as they explored their new opportunities?*

★ *How do the differing responses of freed people and southern whites show different understandings of the significance of emancipation?*

As state conventions wrote new constitutions and politicians argued in Washington, African Americans throughout the South set about creating new, free lives for themselves. In the antebellum South, all slaves and most free African Americans had led lives tightly constrained by law and custom. They were permitted few social organizations of their own. Not surprisingly, the central theme of the black response to emancipation was a desire for freedom from white control, for **autonomy** as individuals and as a community. The prospect of autonomy touched every aspect of life—family, churches, schools, newspapers, and a host of other social institutions. From this ferment of freedom came new, independent black institutions that provided the basis for southern African American communities. At the same time, the economic life of the South had been shattered by the Civil War and was being transformed by emancipation. Thus white southerners also faced drastic economic and social change.

Defining the Meaning of Freedom

At the most basic level, freedom came every time an individual slave stopped working for a master and claimed the right to be free. Thus freedom did not come to all slaves at the same time or in the same way. For some, freedom came before the Emancipation Proclamation when, like Blanche Bruce, they walked away from their owners, crossed into Union-held territory, and asserted their liberty. Toward the end of the war, as civil authority broke down throughout much of the South, many slaves declared their freedom

repudiate The act of rejecting the validity or authority of something; to refuse to pay.

autonomy Control of one's own affairs.

and left the lands they had worked when they were in bondage. Some left for good, but many remained nearby, though with a new understanding of their relationship to their former masters. For some, freedom did not come until ratification of the Thirteenth Amendment.

Across the South, the approach of Yankee troops set off a joyous celebration—called a Jubilee—among those who knew that their enslavement was ending. As one Virginia woman remembered, "Such rejoicing and shouting you never heard in your life." Once the celebrating was over, however, the freed people had to decide how best to use their freedom.

The freed people expressed their new status in many ways. Some chose new names to symbolize their new beginning. Many freed people changed their style of dress, discarding the cheap clothing provided to slaves. Some acquired guns. A significant benefit of freedom was the ability to travel without a pass and without being checked by the **patrollers** who had enforced the **pass system**.

Many freed people took advantage of this new opportunity to travel. Indeed, some felt they had to leave the site of their enslavement to experience full freedom. One freed man later recalled that he refused to work for his last owner, not because he had anything against him but because he wanted "to take my freedom." A freed woman said, "If I stay here I'll never know I'm free." Most traveled only short distances, to find work or land to farm, to seek family members separated from them by slavery, or for other well-defined reasons.

The towns and cities of the South attracted some freed people. The presence of Union troops and federal officials promised protection from the random violence against freed people that occurred in rural areas. In March 1865, Congress created the **Freedmen's Bureau** to assist the freed people in their transition to freedom. In cities and towns, this agency offered assistance with finding work and necessities. Cities and towns also held black churches, newly established schools, and other social institutions, some begun by free blacks before the war. Some African Americans came to towns and cities looking for work. Little housing was available, however, so freed people often crowded into hastily built shanties. Sanitation was poor and disease a common scourge. Such conditions improved only very slowly.

Creating Communities

During Reconstruction, African Americans created their own communities with their own social institutions, beginning with family ties. Joyful families were sometimes reunited after years of separation caused by the sale of a spouse or children. Other people spent years searching for lost family members.

The new freedom to conduct religious services without white supervision was especially important. Churches quickly became the most prominent social organizations in African American communities. Churches were, in fact, among the very first social institutions that African Americans fully controlled. During Reconstruction, black denominations, including the African Methodist Episcopal, African Methodist Episcopal Zion, and several Baptist groups (all founded before the Civil War), grew rapidly in the South. Black ministers helped congregation members adjust to the changes that freedom brought, and ministers often became key leaders within developing African American communities.

Throughout the cities and towns of the South, African Americans—especially ministers and church members—created schools. Setting up a school, said one, was "the first proof" of independence. Many new schools were for both children and adults, whose literacy and learning had been restricted by laws prohibiting education for slaves. The desire to learn was widespread and intense. One freedman in Georgia wrote to a friend: "The Lord has sent books and teachers. We must not hesitate a moment, but go on and learn all we can."

Before the war, free public education had been limited in much of the South and was absent in many places. When African Americans set up schools, they faced severe shortages of teachers, books, and schoolrooms—everything but students. As abolitionists and northern reformers tried to assist the transition from slavery to freedom, many of them also focused first on education.

The Freedmen's Bureau played an important role in organizing and equipping schools. Freedmen's Aid Societies sprang up in most northern cities and, along with northern churches, collected funds and supplies for the freed people. Teachers—mostly white women, often from New England, and often acting on religious impulses—came from the North. Northern aid societies and church organizations, together with the Freedmen's Bureau, established schools to train black teachers. Some of those schools evolved into black colleges. By 1870, the Freedmen's Bureau supervised more than 4,000 schools, with more than

patrollers During the era of slavery, white guards who made the rounds of rural roads to make certain that slaves were not moving about the countryside without written permission from their masters.

pass system Laws that forbade slaves to travel without written authorization from their owners.

■ **Freedmen's Bureau** Agency established in 1865 to aid former slaves in their transition to freedom, especially by administering relief and sponsoring education.

Churches were the first institutions to be completely controlled by African Americans, and ministers were influential figures in the African American communities that emerged during Reconstruction. This photograph of the Colored Methodist Episcopal mission church in Hot Springs, Arkansas, was first published in 1898 in *The History of the Colored Methodist Episcopal Church in America*.

9,000 teachers and 247,000 students. Still, in 1870, only one-tenth of school-age black children were in school.

African Americans created other social institutions in addition to churches and schools, including **fraternal orders**, **benevolent societies**, and newspapers. By 1866, the South had ten black newspapers, led by the *New Orleans Tribune,* and black newspapers played important roles in shaping African American communities.

In politics, African Americans' first objective was recognition of their equal rights as citizens. Frederick Douglass insisted, "Slavery is not abolished until the black man has the ballot." In 1865, political conventions of African Americans attracted hundreds of leaders of the emerging black communities. They called for equality and voting rights, and pointed to black contributions in the American Revolution and the Civil War as evidence of patriotism and devotion. They also appealed to the nation's republican traditions, in particular the Declaration of Independence and its dictum that "all men are created equal."

Land and Labor

Former slaveowners reacted to emancipation in many ways. Some tried to keep their slaves from learning of their freedom. Very few white southerners welcomed the end of slavery, and few former slave owners provided financial assistance to their former slaves.

Many freed people looked to Union troops for assistance. When General William T. Sherman led his victorious army through Georgia in the closing months of the war, thousands of African American men, women, and children claimed their freedom and followed in the Yankees' wake. Their leaders told Sherman that they wanted to "reap the fruit of our own labor." In January 1865, Sherman issued Special Field Order No. 15, setting aside the Sea Islands and land along the South Carolina coast for freed families. Each family, he specified, was to receive 40 acres and the loan of an army mule. By June, the area had filled with forty thousand freed people settled on 400,000 acres of "Sherman land."

Sherman's action encouraged African Americans to expect that the federal government would redistribute land throughout the South. "Forty acres and a mule" became a rallying cry. Only land, Thaddeus Stevens proclaimed, would give freed people control of their own labor. "If we do not furnish them with homesteads," Stevens said, "we had better left them in bondage."

By the end of the war, the Freedmen's Bureau controlled some 850,000 acres of land abandoned by former owners or confiscated from Confederate leaders. In July 1865, General Oliver O. Howard, head of the bureau, directed that this land be divided into 40-acre plots to be given to freed people. However, President Johnson ordered Howard to halt **land redistribution** and to reclaim land already handed over and return it to its former owners. Johnson's order displaced thousands of African Americans who had already taken their 40 acres. Those who had expected land of their own felt betrayed. One later recalled that they had expected "a heap from freedom dey didn't git."

The congressional act that created the Freedmen's Bureau authorized it to assist white refugees. In a few places, white recipients of aid outnumbered the freed blacks. A large majority of southern whites had never

fraternal order A men's organization, often with a ceremonial initiation, that typically provided rudimentary life insurance; many fraternal orders had auxiliaries for female relatives of members.

benevolent society An organization dedicated to some charitable purpose.

land redistribution The division of land held by large landowners into smaller plots that are turned over to landless people.

During Reconstruction, the freed people gave a high priority to schools, often with the assistance of the Freedmen's Bureau and northern missionary societies. This teacher and her barefoot pupils were photographed in the 1870s, in Petersburg, Virginia. In such schools, one teacher typically taught grades 1–8. Daylight is coming through the shutter behind the teacher's right shoulder. Note, too, the gaps in the floorboards and the benches for the students, which seem to have been constructed from logs.

owned slaves, and some had opposed secession. The outcome of the war, however, meant that some lost their livelihood, and many feared they would have to compete with the freed people for farmland or wage labor. Like the freed people, many southern whites lacked the means to farm on their own. When the Confederate government collapsed, Confederate money became worthless. This sudden reduction in the amount of money in circulation, together with the failure of southern banks and the devastation of the southern economy, meant that the entire region was short of **capital**.

Sharecropping slowly emerged across much of the South, derived from the central realities of southern agriculture. Much of the land was in large holdings, but the landowners had no one to work it. Capital was scarce. Many landowners lacked cash to hire farm workers. Many families, both black and white, wanted to raise their own crops with their own labor but had no land, no supplies, and no money. Under sharecropping, an individual—usually a family head—signed a contract with a landowner to rent land as home and farm. The tenant—the sharecropper—was to pay, as rent, a share of the harvest. The share might amount to half or more of the crop if the landlord provided mules, tools, seed, and fertilizer as well as land. Many landowners thought that sharecropping encouraged tenants to be productive, to get as much value as possible from their shares of the crop.

Southern farmers—black or white, sharecroppers or owners of small plots—often found themselves in debt to a local merchant who advanced supplies on credit. In return for credit, the merchant required a lien (a legal claim) on the growing crop. Many landlords ran stores that they required their tenants to patronize. Often the share paid as rent and the debt owed the store exceeded the value of the entire harvest. Furthermore, many rental contracts and **crop liens** were automatically renewed if all debts were not paid at the end of a year. Thus, in spite of their efforts to achieve greater control over their lives and labor, many southern farm families, black and white alike,

capital Money, especially the money invested in a commercial enterprise.

sharecropping A system for renting farmland in which tenant farmers give landlords a share of their crops, rather than cash, as rent.

crop lien A legal claim to a farmer's crop, similar to a mortgage, based on the use of crops as collateral for extension of credit by a merchant.

Sharecropping gave African Americans some control over their labor, but also contributed to the South's dependence on one-crop agriculture and helped to perpetuate rural poverty. This family of sharecroppers near Savannah, Georgia, was photographed picking cotton in the late 1860s.

found themselves trapped by sharecropping and debt. Still, sharecropping gave freed people more control over their daily lives than had slavery.

Landlords could exercise political as well as economic power over their tenants. Until the 1890s, casting a ballot was an open process, and any observer could see how an individual voted (as illustrated on page 402). Thus, when a landlord or merchant advocated a particular candidate, the unspoken message was often an implicit threat to cut off credit at the store or to evict a sharecropper if he did not vote accordingly. Such forms of economic **coercion** could undercut voting rights.

The White South: Confronting Change

The Civil War and the end of slavery transformed the lives of white southerners as well as black southerners. For some, the changes were nearly as profound as for the freed people. Savings vanished. Some homes and other buildings were destroyed. Thousands left the South.

Before the war, few white southerners had owned slaves, and very few owned large numbers. Distrust or even hostility had always existed between the privileged planter families and the many whites who farmed small plots. Some regions populated by small-scale farmers had resisted secession, and some welcomed the Union victory and supported the Republicans during Reconstruction. Some southerners also welcomed the prospect

of the economic transformation that northern capital might bring.

Most white southerners, however, shared what one North Carolinian described in 1866 as "the bitterest hatred toward the North." Even people with no attachment to slavery detested the Yankees who so profoundly changed their lives. For many white southerners, the "lost cause" of the Confederacy came to symbolize their defense of their prewar lives, not an attempt to break up the nation or protect slavery. During the early phases of Reconstruction, most white southerners apparently expected that, except for slavery, things would soon be put back much as they had been before the war.

In late 1865 and 1866, the newly organized state legislatures passed **black codes** defining the new legal status of African Americans. These regulations varied from state to state, but every state placed significant restrictions on black people. Various black codes required African Americans to have an annual employment contract, limited them to agricultural work, forbade them from moving about the countryside without permission, restricted their ownership of land, and provided for forced labor by those guilty of **vagrancy**—which usually meant anyone without a job. Taken together, the black codes represented an effort by white southerners to define a legally subordinate place for African Americans and to put significant restrictions on their newly found freedom.

Some white southerners used violence to coerce freed people into accepting a subordinate status within the new southern society. Violence and terror became closely associated with the **Ku Klux Klan**, a secret organization formed in 1866 and led by a former Confederate general. The turn to terror suggests that Klan members felt themselves largely powerless through normal politics, and used terror to create a climate of fear among their opponents. Most Klan members were small-scale farmers and workers, but the leaders were often prominent within their own communities—one Freedmen's Bureau agent observed, "The most respectable citizens are engaged in it." Klan groups existed throughout the South, but operated with little central control. Their major goals

coercion Use of threats or force to compel action.

black codes Laws passed by the southern states after the Civil War restricting freed people; in general, the black codes limited the civil rights of freed people and defined their status as subordinate to whites.

vagrancy The legal condition of having no fixed place of residence or means of support.

■ **Ku Klux Klan** A secret society organized in the South after the Civil War to restore white supremacy by means of violence and intimidation.

In this picture, the artist has portrayed a Republican leader, white grocer John Campbell, pleading for mercy from a group of bizarrely dressed Klansmen in Moore County, North Carolina, on August 10, 1871. The Klansmen flogged Moore before releasing him. Curiously, the artist depicted Campbell as an African American.

The Granger Collection, New York.

were to restore **white supremacy** and to destroy the Republican Party. Other, similar organizations also formed and adopted similar tactics.

Klan members were called ghouls. Officers included cyclops, night-hawks, and grand dragons, and the national leader was called the grand wizard. Klan members covered their faces with hoods, wore white robes, and rode horses draped in white as they set out to intimidate black Republicans and their white allies. Klan members also attacked less politically prominent people, whipping African Americans accused of not showing sufficient deference to whites. Nightriders also burned black churches and schools. By such tactics, the Klan devastated Republican organizations in many communities.

white supremacy The racist belief that whites are inherently superior to other races and are therefore entitled to rule over them.

civil rights The rights, privileges, and protections that are a part of citizenship.

CONGRESSIONAL RECONSTRUCTION

☆ *Why did congressional Republicans take control over Reconstruction policy? How successful were they?*

☆ *How did the Fourteenth and Fifteenth Amendments change the nature of the federal union?*

The black codes, violence against freed people, and the failure of southern authorities to stem the violence turned northern opinion against President Johnson's lenient approach to Reconstruction. Increasing numbers of moderate Republicans accepted the Radicals' arguments that the freed people required greater federal protection, and congressional Republicans moved to take control of Reconstruction. When stubborn and uncompromising Andrew Johnson ran up against stubborn and uncompromising Thaddeus Stevens, the nation faced a constitutional crisis.

Challenging Presidential Reconstruction: The Civil Rights Act of 1866

In December 1865, the Thirty-ninth Congress (elected in 1864) met for the first time. Republicans outnumbered Democrats by more than three to one. President Johnson proclaimed Reconstruction complete and the Union restored, but few Republicans agreed. Events in the South had convinced most moderate Republicans of the need to protect free labor in the South and establish basic rights for freed people. Most also agreed that Congress could withhold representation from the South until reconstructed state governments met these conditions.

On the first day of the Thirty-ninth Congress, moderate Republicans joined Radicals to exclude newly elected congressmen from the South. Citing Article I, Section 5, of the Constitution (which makes each house of Congress the judge of the qualifications of its members), Republicans set up a Joint Committee on Reconstruction to evaluate the qualifications of the excluded southerners and to determine whether the southern states were entitled to representation. In the meantime, the former Confederate states had no representation in Congress.

Congressional Republicans also moved to provide more assistance to the freed people. Moderates and Radicals approved a bill extending the Freedmen's Bureau and giving it more authority against racial discrimination. When Johnson vetoed it, Congress drafted a slightly revised version. Republicans also produced a **civil rights** bill, a far-reaching measure that extended citizenship to African Americans and defined some of the rights guaranteed to all citizens. Johnson vetoed both the civil rights bill and the revised Freedmen's Bureau bill, but Congress passed both over his veto. With creation of the Joint Committee on Reconstruction and passage of the Civil Rights and Freedmen's Bureau acts, Congress took control of Reconstruction.

The Civil Rights Act of 1866 defined all persons born in the United States (except Indians not taxed) as citizens and listed certain rights of all citizens, including the right to testify in court, own property, make contracts, bring lawsuits, and enjoy "full and equal benefit of all laws and proceedings for the security of person and property." This was the first effort to define in law some of the rights of American citizenship. It placed significant restrictions on state actions on the grounds that the rights of national citizenship took precedence over the powers of state governments. The law expanded federal powers in unprecedented ways and challenged traditional concepts of states' rights. Though the law applied to all citizens, its most immediate consequence was to benefit African Americans.

Debate in Congress focused on the freed people. Some supporters saw the Civil Rights Act as a way to secure freed people's basic rights. For other Republicans, the bill carried broader implications because it empowered the federal government to force states to abide by the principle of equality before the law. They applauded its redefinition of federal-state relations. Senator Lot Morrill of Maine described it as "absolutely revolutionary" but added, "Are we not in the midst of a revolution?"

When President Johnson vetoed the bill, he argued that it violated states' rights. By defending states' rights and confronting the Radicals, Johnson may have hoped to generate enough political support to elect a conservative Congress in 1866 and to win the presidency in 1868. He probably expected his veto to turn voters against the Radicals. Instead, the veto led most moderate Republicans to abandon hope of cooperating with him. In April 1866, when Congress passed the Civil Rights Act over Johnson's veto, it was the first time ever that Congress had overridden a presidential veto of major legislation.

Defining Citizenship: The Fourteenth Amendment

Leading Republicans worried that the Civil Rights Act could be amended or repealed by a later Congress or declared unconstitutional by the Supreme Court. Only a constitutional amendment, they concluded, could permanently safeguard the freed people's rights as citizens.

The **Fourteenth Amendment** began as a Radical proposal for a constitutional guarantee of equality before the law. However, the final wording—the longest of any amendment—resulted from many compromises. Section 1 of the amendment defined American

citizenship in much the same way as the Civil Rights Act of 1866, then specified that

> No State shall make or enforce any law which shall abridge the privileges or immunities of citizens of the United States; nor shall any State deprive any person of life, liberty, or property, without due process of law; nor deny to any person within its jurisdiction the equal protection of the laws.

The Constitution and Bill of Rights prohibit federal interference with basic civil rights. The Fourteenth Amendment extends this protection against action by state governments.

The amendment was vague on some points. For example, it penalized states that did not **enfranchise** African Americans by reducing their congressional and electoral representation, but it did not specifically guarantee to African Americans the right to vote.

Not everyone approved of the final wording. Charles Sumner condemned the provision that permitted a state to deny suffrage to male citizens if it accepted a penalty in congressional representation. Woman suffrage advocates, led by **Elizabeth Cady Stanton** and **Susan B. Anthony**, complained that the amendment, for the first time, introduced the word *male* into the Constitution in connection with voting rights.

Despite such concerns, Congress approved the Fourteenth Amendment by a straight party vote and sent it to the states for ratification. Tennessee promptly ratified the amendment, became the first reconstructed state government to be recognized by Congress, and was exempted from most later Reconstruction legislation.

Although Congress adjourned in the summer of 1866, the nation's attention remained fixed on Reconstruction. In May and July, in Memphis and New Orleans, bloody riots aimed at African Americans turned more moderates against Johnson's Reconstruction policies. Some interpreted congressional elections that fall as a referendum on Reconstruction and the Fourteenth Amendment, pitting Johnson against the Radicals. Republicans swept the 1866 elections, outnumbering Democrats 143 to 49 in the new House of Representatives, and 42 to 11 in the Senate.

■ **Fourteenth Amendment** Constitutional amendment, ratified in 1868, defining American citizenship and placing restrictions on former Confederates.

enfranchise To grant the right to vote to an individual or group.

■ **Elizabeth Cady Stanton** A founder and leader of the American woman suffrage movement from 1848 (date of the Seneca Falls Conference) until her death in 1902.

■ **Susan B. Anthony** Tireless campaigner for woman suffrage and close associate of Elizabeth Cady Stanton.

It Matters Today

The Fourteenth Amendment

The Fourteenth Amendment is one of the most important sources of Americans' civil rights, next to the Bill of Rights (the first ten amendments). One key provision in the Fourteenth Amendment is the definition of American citizenship. Previously, the Constitution did not address that question. The Fourteenth Amendment cleared up any confusion about who was, and who was not, a citizen.

The amendment also specifies that no state could abridge the liberties of a citizen "without due process of law." Until this time, the Constitution and the Bill of Rights restricted action by the *federal* government to restrict individual liberties. The Supreme Court has interpreted the Fourteenth Amendment to mean that the restrictions placed on the federal government by the First Amendment also limit state governments—that no *state* government may abridge freedom of speech, press, assembly, and religion.

The Supreme Court continues to interpret the Fourteenth Amendment when it is presented with new cases involving state restrictions on the rights of citizens. For example, in *Roe v. Wade* (1973), the Supreme Court cited the due process clause among other provisions of the Constitution to conclude that state laws may not prevent women from having abortions. In *Lawrence v. Texas* (2003), the Court cited the Fourteenth Amendment to conclude that states may not punish adults for engaging in consensual sexual activities. Current arguments over same-sex marriage often focus on the equal-protection clause of the Fourteenth Amendment.

- Look up the Fourteenth Amendment in the back of this book. How does the Fourteenth Amendment define citizenship? Using an online newspaper, can you find recent proposals to change the definition of American citizenship?
- What current political issues may lead to court cases in which the Fourteenth Amendment is likely to be invoked?

Lyman Trumbull, senator from Illinois and a leading moderate, voiced the consensus of congressional Republicans: Congress should now "hurl from power the disloyal element" in the South.

Radicals in Control

As congressional Radicals struggled with President Johnson over control of Reconstruction, it became clear that the Fourteenth Amendment might fall short of ratification. Rejection by ten states could prevent its acceptance. By March 1867, the amendment had been rejected by twelve states—Delaware, Kentucky, and all the former Confederate states except Tennessee. Moderate Republicans who had expected the Fourteenth Amendment to be the final Reconstruction measure now became receptive to other proposals that the Radicals put forth.

On March 2, 1867, Congress overrode Johnson's veto of the Military Reconstruction Act, which divided the Confederate states (except Tennessee) into five military districts. Each district was to be governed by a military commander authorized by Congress to use military force to protect life and property. These ten states were to elect delegates and hold constitutional conventions, and all adult male citizens were to vote, except former Confederates who were barred from office under a provision of the proposed Fourteenth Amendment. The constitutional conventions were then to create new state governments that permitted black suffrage, and the new governments were to ratify the Fourteenth Amendment. Congress would then evaluate whether those state governments were ready to regain representation in Congress.

Congress had wrested a major degree of control over Reconstruction from the president, but it was not finished. The Command of the Army Act specified that the president could issue military orders only through the General of the Army—Ulysses S. Grant, considered an ally of Congress—and that the General of the Army could not be removed without Senate permission. Congress thereby blocked Johnson from direct communication with military commanders in the South. The Tenure of Office Act specified that officials appointed with the Senate's consent were to remain in office until the Senate approved a

Tickets such as these were in high demand, for they permitted the holder to watch the proceedings as the Radical leaders presented their evidence to justify removing Andrew Johnson from the presidency.

Collection of David J. and Janice L. Frent.

successor, thereby preventing Johnson from removing federal officials who opposed his policies. Johnson understood both measures as invasions of presidential authority.

Early in 1867, some Radicals began to consider impeaching President Johnson. The Constitution (Article I, Sections 2 and 3) gives the House of Representatives exclusive power to **impeach** the president—that is, to charge the chief executive with misconduct. The Constitution specifies that the Senate shall hold a trial on those charges, with the chief justice of the Supreme Court presiding. If found guilty by a two-thirds vote of the Senate, the president is removed from office.

When Johnson directly challenged Congress over the Tenure of Office Act by removing Edwin Stanton as secretary of war, Johnson's opponents now claimed he had violated the law. When the House Judiciary Committee failed to bring impeachment charges, the Joint Committee on Reconstruction, led by Thaddeus Stevens, took over. On February 24, 1868, the House adopted eleven articles, or charges, nearly all based on the Stanton affair. The actual reasons the Radicals wanted Johnson removed were clear to all: they disliked him and his actions.

To convict Johnson and remove him from the presidency required a two-thirds vote by the Senate. Johnson's defenders argued he had done nothing to warrant impeachment. The Radicals' legal case was weak, but they urged senators to vote on whether they wished Johnson to remain as president. Republican unity unraveled when some moderates, fearing the precedent of removing a president for such flimsy reasons, joined with Democrats to defeat the Radicals. The vote was 35 in favor of conviction and 19 against, one vote short of the required two-thirds. By this tiny margin, Congress endorsed the principle that it should not remove the president from office simply because members of Congress disagree with or dislike the president.

Political Terrorism and the Election of 1868

The Radicals' failure to unseat Johnson left him with less than a year remaining in office. As the election approached, the Republicans nominated Ulysses S. Grant for president. A war hero, popular throughout the North, Grant committed himself to the congressional view of Reconstruction. The Democrats nominated Horatio Seymour, a former governor of New York, and denounced Reconstruction.

In the South, the campaign stirred up fierce activity by the Ku Klux Klan and similar groups. **Terrorists** assassinated an Arkansas congressman, three members of the South Carolina legislature, and several other Republican leaders. Throughout the South, mobs attacked Republican offices and meetings, and sometimes attacked any black person they could find. Such coercion had its intended effect at the ballot box.

Despite such violence, many Americans may have anticipated a calmer political future. In June 1868 Congress had readmitted seven southern states that met the requirements of congressional Reconstruction. In July, the secretary of state declared the Fourteenth Amendment ratified. In November, Grant easily won the presidency, carrying twenty-six of the thirty-four states and 53 percent of the vote.

Voting Rights and Civil Rights

With Grant in the White House, Radical Republicans moved to secure voting rights for all African Americans. The states still defined voting rights. Congress had required southern states to enfranchise black males as the price of readmission to the Union, but only seven northern states had taken that step. Further, any state that had enfranchised African Americans could change its law at any time. In addition to the principled arguments of Douglass and other Radicals, many Republicans concluded that they needed to guarantee black suffrage in the South if they were to continue to win presidential elections and enjoy majorities in Congress.

To secure suffrage rights for all African Americans, Congress approved the **Fifteenth Amendment** in February 1869. The amendment prohibited both federal and state governments from restricting a person's

impeach To charge a public official with improper, usually criminal, conduct.

terrorists Those who use threats and violence to achieve ideological or political goals.

■ **Fifteenth Amendment** Constitutional amendment, ratified in 1870, that prohibited states from denying the right to vote because of a person's race or because a person had been a slave.

right to vote because of "race, color, or previous condition of servitude." Like the Fourteenth Amendment, the Fifteenth marked a compromise between moderates and Radicals. Some African American leaders argued for language guaranteeing voting rights to all male citizens, because prohibiting some grounds for **disfranchisement** might imply the legitimacy of other grounds. Some Radicals tried, unsuccessfully, to add "**nativity**, property, education, or religious beliefs" to the prohibited grounds. Democrats condemned the Fifteenth Amendment as a "revolutionary" attack on states' authority to define voting rights.

Elizabeth Cady Stanton, Susan B. Anthony, and other advocates of woman suffrage opposed the amendment because it ignored restrictions based on sex. For nearly twenty years, the cause of women's rights and the cause of black rights had marched together. Once black male suffrage came under discussion, however, this alliance began to fracture. The break between the women's movement and the black movement was eventually papered over, but the wounds never completely healed.

Despite such opposition, within thirteen months the proposed amendment received the approval of enough states to take effect. Success came in part because Republicans, who might otherwise have been reluctant to impose black suffrage in the North, concluded that the future success of their party required black suffrage in the South.

The Fifteenth Amendment did nothing to reduce the violence—especially at election time—that had become almost routine in the South after 1865. When Klan activity escalated in the elections of 1870, southern Republicans looked to Washington for support. In 1870 and 1871, Congress adopted several Enforcement Acts—often called the Ku Klux Klan Acts—to enforce the Fourteenth and Fifteenth Amendments.

Despite many obstacles, the prosecution of Klansmen began in 1871. Across the South hundreds were indicted, and many were convicted. In South

This engraving appeared on the cover of *Harper's Weekly* in November 1867. It shows black men lined up to cast their ballots. The artist has shown first an older workingman, with his tools in his pocket; and next a well-dressed, younger man, probably a city-dweller and perhaps a leader in the emerging black community; and next a Union soldier. Voting was open. Voters received a ballot (a "party ticket") from a party campaigner and deposited that ballot in a ballot box, in full sight of all. Voting was not secret until much later.

The Granger Collection, New York.

disfranchisement The taking away of an individual's or group's right to vote.

nativity Place of birth.

discrimination Denial of equal treatment based on prejudice or bias.

■ **Civil Rights Act of 1875** Law passed by Congress in 1875 prohibiting racial discrimination in selection of juries and in transportation and other businesses open to the general public.

public accommodations Hotels, bars and restaurants, theaters, and other places set up to do business with anyone who can pay the price of admission.

Carolina, President Grant declared martial law. By 1872, federal intervention had broken much of the strength of the Klan. (The Klan that appeared in the 1920s, covered in Chapter 21, was a new organization that borrowed the regalia and tactics of the earlier organization.)

Congress passed one final Reconstruction measure. Charles Sumner introduced a bill prohibiting **discrimination** in 1870 and in each subsequent session of Congress until his death in 1874. On his deathbed, Sumner urged his visitors to "take care of the civil-rights bill," begging them, "Don't let it fail." Approved after Sumner's death, the **Civil Rights Act of 1875** prohibited racial discrimination in the selection of juries and in public transportation and **public accommodations**.

This lithograph from 1883 depicts prominent African American men, most of whom had leading roles in Black Reconstruction. Frederick Douglass is in the center. Left of him is Louisiana Governor P. B. S. Pinchback. In the upper right is U.S. Senator Blanche K. Bruce.

BLACK RECONSTRUCTION

★ What major groups made up the Republican Party in the South during Reconstruction? Compare their reasons for being Republicans, their relative size, and their objectives.

★ What were the most lasting results of the Republican state administrations?

Congressional Reconstruction set the stage for new developments at state and local levels throughout the South. African Americans never completely controlled any state government but did form a significant element in the governments of several states. years when African Americans participated prominently in state and local politics are usually called **Black Reconstruction**. It began with efforts by African Americans to take part in politics as early as 1865 and lasted for more than a decade. A few African Americans continued to hold elective office in the South after 1877, but by then they could do little to bring about significant political change. Map 15.1 indicates the proportion of African Americans in each of the southern states, and also the years when each state was under a Reconstruction state government.

The Republican Party in the South

Nearly all African Americans who participated actively in politics did so as Republicans, and they formed the large majority of the Republican Party in the South. Nearly all black Republicans were new to politics, and they often braved considerable personal danger by participating in a party that many white southerners equated with the conquering Yankees.

Suffrage made politics a centrally important activity for African American communities. The state constitutional conventions that met in 1868 included 265 black delegates. Only in Louisiana and South Carolina were half or more of the delegates black. With suffrage established, southern Republicans began to elect African Americans to public office. Between 1869 and 1877, fourteen black men served in the national House of Representatives, and Mississippi sent two African Americans to the U.S. Senate.

Across the South, six African Americans served as lieutenant governors, and one of them, P. B. S. Pinchback, succeeded to the governorship of Louisiana. More than six hundred black men served in southern state legislatures during Reconstruction, but only in South Carolina did African Americans have a majority in the state legislature. Elsewhere they formed part of a Republican majority but rarely held key legislative positions. Only in South Carolina and Mississippi did legislatures elect black presiding officers.

Although politically inexperienced, most African Americans who held office during Reconstruction had some education. Of the eighteen who served in statewide offices, all but three are known to have been born free. P. B. S. Pinchback, for example, was educated in Ohio and served in the army as a captain before entering politics in Louisiana. Most black politicians first achieved prominence through service with the army, the Freedmen's Bureau, the new schools, or the religious and civic organizations of black communities.

Throughout the South, Republicans gained power only by securing support from some white voters. These white Republicans are usually remembered by the names fastened on them by their political opponents: "carpetbaggers" and "scalawags." Both groups included idealists who hoped to create a new southern society, but both also included opportunists expecting to exploit politics for personal gain.

Southern Democrats applied the term **carpetbagger** to northern Republicans who came to the South after

■ **Black Reconstruction** The period of Reconstruction when African Americans took an active role in state and local government.

carpetbagger Derogatory term for the northerners who came to the South after the Civil War to take part in Reconstruction.

Confederate states, 1861–1865

July 24, 1866   Date of readmission to the Union

Oct. 4, 1869   Date of reestablishment of conservative rule

New state and date of admission to Union

New territory and date of organization

Black population as percentage
of total population, 1880

50% or more

30–50%

10–30%

MAP 15.1 African American Population and the Duration of Reconstruction
This map shows the proportion of African Americans in the South, and also includes the dates when each of the former Confederate states was under a Reconstruction state government. Does the map suggest any relationship between the proportion of a state's population that was African American and the amount of time that the state spent under a Reconstruction state government? Copyright © Cengage Learning

the war, regarding them as second-rate schemers—outsiders with their belongings packed in a cheap carpet bag. In fact, most northerners who came south were well-educated men and women from middle-class backgrounds. Most men had served in the Union army and moved south before blacks could vote. Some were lawyers, businessmen, or newspaper editors. Whether as investors in agricultural land, teachers in the new schools, or agents of the Freedmen's Bureau, most hoped to transform the South by creating new institutions based on northern models, especially free labor and free public schools. Few in number, transplanted northerners nonetheless took leading roles in state constitutional conventions and state legislatures. Some were also prominent advocates of economic modernization.

Southern Democrats reserved their greatest contempt for those they called **scalawags**, slang for someone unscrupulous and worthless. Scalawags were

scalawag Derogatory term for white southerners who aligned themselves with the Republican Party during Reconstruction.

Bags made of carpeting, like this one, were inexpensive luggage for traveling. Southern opponents of Reconstruction fastened the label "carpetbaggers" on northerners who came south to participate in Reconstruction, suggesting that they were cheap opportunists. Collection of Picture Research Consultants and Archives.

The Hampton Normal and Agricultural Institute was founded in 1868 with financial assistance from the Freedmen's Bureau and the American Missionary Association. It educated African American males for jobs in agriculture or industry and women as homemakers. As a normal school, it also trained teachers. One of Hampton's most prominent graduates was Booker T. Washington (discussed in Chapter 17), who attended shortly after this picture was taken around 1870.

white southerners who became Republicans. They included many southern Unionists, who had opposed secession, and others who thought the Republicans offered the best hope for economic recovery. Scalawags included merchants, artisans, and professionals who favored a modernized South. Others were small-scale farmers who saw Reconstruction as a way to end political domination by the plantation owners.

The freedmen, carpetbaggers, and scalawags who made up the Republican Party in the South hoped to inject new ideas into that region. They tried to modernize state and local governments and make the postwar South more like the North. They repealed outdated laws and established or expanded schools, hospitals, orphanages, and penitentiaries.

Creating Public Education, Fighting Discrimination, and Building Railroads

Free public education was perhaps the most enduring legacy of Black Reconstruction. Reconstruction constitutions throughout the South required tax-supported public schools. Implementation, however, was expensive and proceeded slowly. By the mid-1870s, only half of southern children attended public schools.

In creating public schools, Reconstruction state governments faced a central question: would white and black children attend the same schools? Many African Americans favored racially integrated schools. Southern white leaders, including many southern white Republicans, argued that integration would destroy the fledgling public school system by driving whites away. In consequence, no state required school integration. Similarly, southern states set up separate black normal schools (to train schoolteachers) and colleges.

On balance, most blacks probably agreed with Frederick Douglass that separate schools were "infinitely superior" to no public education at all. Some found other reasons to accept segregated schools—separate black schools gave a larger role to black parents, and they hired black teachers.

Creating and operating two educational systems, one white and one black, was costly, and funds were always limited. Black schools almost always received fewer dollars per student than white schools. Despite their accomplishments, the segregated schools institutionalized discrimination.

Reconstruction state governments moved toward protection of equal rights in other areas. Southern Republicans often wrote into their new state

William Mahone, shown here at about the time he served in the U.S. Senate from Virginia, had been a railroad developer in Virginia before the Civil War. Educated at Virginia Military Institute, Mahone became a major general in the Confederate army during the Civil War. At the end of the war, he again became head of a railroad company. He also became involved in state politics, creating a coalition of African Americans, white Republicans, and conservative Democrats that took control of state government and elected Mahone to the U.S. Senate, where he usually caucused with the Republicans.

and West—often meant encouraging railroad construction. In the South, as elsewhere, some state governments granted land to railroads, or lent them money, or committed the state's credit to **underwrite** bonds for construction. Sometimes they promoted railroads without planning adequately or determining whether companies were financially sound. Some railroad projects failed as companies squandered funds without building rail lines. During the 1870s, only seven thousand miles of new track were laid in the South, compared with forty-five thousand miles elsewhere in the nation. Even that was a considerable accomplishment for the South, given its dismal economic situation.

Railroad companies sometimes sought favorable treatment by bribing public officials. All too many officeholders—South, North, and West—accepted their offers. Given the excessive favoritism that most public officials showed to railroads, revelations and allegations of corruption became common from New York City to Mississippi to California.

Southern politics proved especially ripe for corruption as government responsibilities expanded rapidly and created new opportunities for scoundrels. Too many Reconstruction officials—white and black—saw politics as a way to improve their own finances. One South Carolina legislator bluntly described his attitude toward electing a U.S. senator: "I was pretty hard up, and I did not care who the candidate was if I got two hundred dollars." Corruption was usually nonpartisan, but it seemed more prominent among Republicans because they held the most important offices.

constitutions prohibitions against discrimination and protections for civil rights. Some Reconstruction state governments enacted laws guaranteeing **equal access** to public transportation and public accommodations. Elsewhere, efforts to pass equal access laws foundered on the opposition of southern white Republicans, who often joined Democrats to favor **segregation**. Such conflicts pointed up the internal divisions within the southern Republican Party. Even when equal access laws were passed, they were often not enforced.

Republicans everywhere sought to use government to encourage economic growth and development. Promoting economic development—North, South,

THE END OF RECONSTRUCTION

★ What major factors brought about the end of Reconstruction? Evaluate their relative significance.

★ Many historians began to reevaluate their understanding of Reconstruction during the 1950s and 1960s. Why do you suppose that happened?

From the beginning, most white southerners resisted the new order that the conquering Yankees imposed on them. Initially, resistance took the form of black codes and the Klan. Later, some southern opponents of Reconstruction developed new strategies, but terror remained an important instrument of resistance.

The "New Departure" and the 1872 Presidential Election

By 1869, some leading southern Democrats had abandoned their resistance to change, deciding instead to accept some Reconstruction measures and African American suffrage. At the same time, they also tried to secure restoration of political rights for former Confederates. Behind this **New Departure** for southern Democrats lay

equal access The right of any person to make use of a public facility, such as streetcars, as freely as any other person.

segregation Separation on account of race or class from the rest of society, such as the separation of blacks from whites in most southern school systems.

underwrite To assume financial responsibility for; here, to guarantee the purchase of bonds so that a project can go forward.

■ **New Departure** Strategy adopted by some leading southern Democrats of cooperating with some Reconstruction measures in the hope of winning compromises favorable to their party.

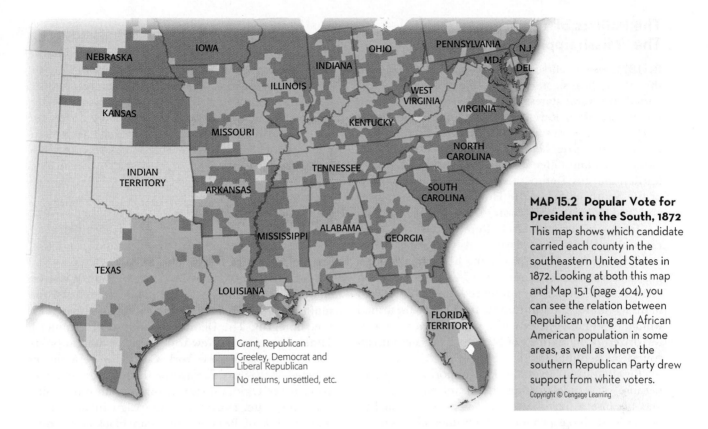

MAP 15.2 Popular Vote for President in the South, 1872 This map shows which candidate carried each county in the southeastern United States in 1872. Looking at both this map and Map 15.1 (page 404), you can see the relation between Republican voting and African American population in some areas, as well as where the southern Republican Party drew support from white voters.

Grant, Republican

Greeley, Democrat and Liberal Republican

No returns, unsettled, etc.

Copyright © Cengage Learning

the belief that continued resistance would only cause more regional turmoil and prolong federal intervention.

Sometimes southern Democrats supported conservative Republicans for state and local offices instead of members of their own party, hoping to defuse concern in Washington and dilute Radical influence in state government. This strategy appeared first in Virginia, where William Mahone, a former Confederate general, railroad promoter, and leading Democrat, forged a broad political **coalition** that accepted black suffrage. In 1869 Mahone's organization elected as governor a northern-born banker and moderate Republican. Mahone got state support for his railroad plans, and Virginia avoided Radical Republican rule.

Coalitions of Democrats and moderate Republicans won in Tennessee in 1869 and in Missouri in 1870. Elsewhere leading Democrats also accepted black suffrage but attacked Republicans for raising taxes, increasing state spending, and corruption. Such campaigns brought a positive response from many taxpayers because southern tax rates had risen significantly to support the new schools, railroad subsidies, and other modernizing programs. The victories of several so-called **Redeemers** and New Departure Democrats in the early 1870s also coincided with renewed terrorist activity aimed at Republicans. The worst single incident occurred in 1873. A group of armed freedmen fortified the town of Colfax, Louisiana, to hold off Democrats who were planning to seize the county government. After a three-week siege, well-armed whites overcame the black defenders and killed 280 African Americans.

Leading Democrats rarely endorsed such bloodshed, but they reaped political advantages from it.

The New Departure movement coincided with a nationwide division within the Republican Party. The Liberal Republican movement attracted moderates, concerned that the Radicals had gone too far. Others opposed Grant on issues unrelated to Reconstruction, especially growing evidence of corruption.

Horace Greeley, editor of the *New York Daily Tribune*, won the Liberal nomination for president in 1872. An opponent of slavery before the Civil War, Greeley had given strong support to the Fourteenth and Fifteenth Amendments. But he had sometimes taken puzzling positions, including a willingness to let the South secede. His unkempt appearance and whining voice conveyed little of a presidential image. One political observer described him as "honest, but . . . conceited, fussy, and foolish." Greeley had long ripped the Democrats in his newspaper columns, but the Democrats nonetheless nominated him in an effort to defeat Grant. Grant won convincingly, carrying 56 percent of the vote and winning every northern state and ten of the sixteen southern and border states (see Map 15.2).

coalition An alliance, especially a temporary one of different people or groups.

■ **Redeemers** Southern Democrats who hoped to bring the Democratic Party back into power and to suppress Black Reconstruction.

The Politics of Terror: The "Mississippi Plan"

By 1872, nearly all southern whites had abandoned the Republicans, and Black Reconstruction had ended in several states. African Americans, however, maintained their Republican loyalties. As Democrats worked to unite all southern whites behind their banner of white supremacy, the South polarized politically along racial lines. Elections in 1874 proved disastrous for Republicans: Democrats won more than two-thirds of the South's seats in the House of Representatives and "redeemed" several more states.

Terrorism against black Republicans and their remaining white allies played a role in some Democratic victories in 1874. Where the Klan had worn disguises and ridden at night, by 1874 Democrats often formed rifle companies, put on red-flannel shirts, and marched and drilled in public. In some areas, armed whites prevented African Americans from voting or terrorized prominent Republicans, especially African American Republicans.

Republicans in 1874 also lost support in the North because of scandals within the Grant administration and because a major economic **depression** that had begun in 1873 was producing high unemployment. In the 1874 elections, Democrats won control of the House of Representatives for the first time since the 1850s and could block any new Reconstruction proposals.

During 1875 in Mississippi, political violence reached such levels that the use of terror to overthrow Reconstruction became known as the **Mississippi Plan**. Democratic rifle clubs broke up Republican meetings and attacked Republican leaders. One black Mississippian described the election as "the most violent time we have ever seen." When Mississippi's carpetbagger governor, Adelbert Ames, requested federal help, President Grant declined. Grant feared that the southern Reconstruction governments had become so discredited that further federal military intervention might endanger the election prospects of Republican candidates in the North.

The Democrats swept the Mississippi elections, winning four-fifths of the state legislature. When the legislature convened, it impeached and removed from office Alexander Davis, the black Republican lieutenant governor, on grounds no more serious than those brought against Andrew Johnson. Facing similar action, Governor Ames resigned and left the state. Ames had foreseen the result during the campaign when he wrote, "A revolution has taken place—by force of arms."

The Troubled Presidential Election of 1876

In 1876, on the centennial of American independence, the nation stumbled through a deeply troubled—and potentially dangerous—presidential election. As revelations of corruption in the Grant administration multiplied, both parties sought candidates known for their integrity. The Democrats nominated Samuel J. Tilden, governor of New York, who had fought political corruption in New York City. The Republicans selected **Rutherford B. Hayes**, a Civil War general and governor of Ohio, who was virtually unknown outside his home state. During the campaign in the South, intimidation of Republicans, both black and white, continued in many places.

The first election reports indicated a victory for Tilden (see Map 15.3). In addition to the border states and South, he also carried New York, New Jersey, and Indiana. Tilden received 51 percent of the popular vote versus 48 percent for Hayes.

State Republican officials still controlled the counting and reporting of ballots in South Carolina, Florida, and Louisiana, and those three states could change the Electoral College majority from Tilden to Hayes. Charging voting fraud, Republican election boards in those states rejected enough ballots so that the official count gave Hayes narrow majorities and thus a one-vote margin of victory in the Electoral College. Crying fraud in return, Democratic officials in those states submitted their own versions of the vote count. Angry Democrats vowed to see Tilden inaugurated, by force if necessary. Some Democratic newspapers ran headlines that read "Tilden or War."

For the first time, Congress faced the problem of disputed electoral votes that could decide the outcome of an election. To resolve the challenges, Congress created a commission of five senators, five representatives, and five Supreme Court justices. The Republicans had a one-vote majority on the commission.

As commission hearings droned on through January and into February 1877, informal discussions took place among leading Republicans and Democrats. The result has often been called the **Compromise of 1877**.

Southern Democrats demanded an end to federal intervention in southern politics but insisted on

depression A period of economic contraction, characterized by decreasing business activity, falling prices, and high unemployment.

■ **Mississippi Plan** Use of threats, violence, and lynching by Mississippi Democrats in 1875 to intimidate Republicans and bring the Democratic Party to power.

■ **Rutherford B. Hayes** (1822–1893) Seventeenth president of the United States; Ohio governor and former Union general, president when Reconstruction ended.

■ **Compromise of 1877** Name applied by historians to resolution of the disputed presidential election of 1876; it gave the presidency to the Republicans and made concessions to southern Democrats.

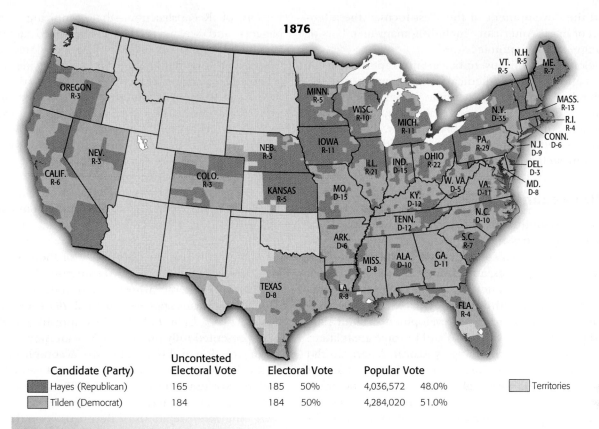

1876

Candidate (Party)	Uncontested Electoral Vote	Electoral Vote		Popular Vote	
Hayes (Republican)	165	185	50%	4,036,572	48.0%
Tilden (Democrat)	184	184	50%	4,284,020	51.0%

Territories

MAP 15.3 Election of 1876
The end of Black Reconstruction in the South combined with Democratic gains in the North to give a popular majority to Samuel Tilden, the Democratic candidate. The disputed electoral vote was ultimately resolved in favor of Rutherford B. Hayes, the Republican. Copyright © Cengage Learning

federal subsidies for railroad construction and waterways in the South. And they wanted one of their own as postmaster general because that office held the key to most federal patronage. In return, southern Democrats seemed willing to abandon Tilden's claim to the White House. The Compromise of 1877, however, was never set down in one place or agreed to by all parties.

By a straight party vote, the commission confirmed the election of Hayes. Soon after his inauguration, the new president ordered the last of the federal troops withdrawn from the South. The era of a powerful federal government pledged to protect "equality before the law" for all citizens was over. The last three Republican state governments fell in 1877, giving the Democrats, the self-described party of white supremacy, control in every southern state. One Radical journal bitterly concluded that African Americans had been forced "to relinquish the artificial right to vote for the natural right to live." In parts of the South thereafter, election fraud and violence became routine. A Mississippi judge acknowledged in 1890 that "since 1875 . . . we have been preserving the ascendancy of the white people by . . . stuffing ballot boxes, committing perjury and here and there in the state carrying the elections by fraud and violence."

Reconstruction was over. The Civil War was more than ten years in the past. Many moderate Republicans had hoped that the Fourteenth and Fifteenth Amendments and the Civil Rights Act would guarantee black rights without a continuing federal presence in the South. Southern Democrats persistently argued—on paltry evidence—that carpetbaggers and scalawags were all corrupt, that they manipulated black voters, that African American officeholders were ignorant and illiterate, and that southern Democrats wanted only honest self-government. The truth of the situation made little difference.

Northern Democrats had always opposed Reconstruction and readily adopted the southern Democrats' version of reality. Such portrayals found growing acceptance among other northerners too, for many had shown their own racial bias when they resisted black suffrage and kept their public schools segregated. In 1875, when Grant refused to use federal troops to protect black rights, he declared that "the whole public are tired out with these . . . outbreaks in the South." He was quoted widely and with approval throughout the North. In addition, a major depression in the mid-1870s, unemployment and labor disputes, the growth of industry, the emergence of big business, and the development of the West focused the attention of many Americans, including many members of Congress, on economic issues.

Some Republicans, to be certain, kept the faith of their abolitionist and Radical forebears and hoped the federal government might again protect black rights. After 1877, however, though Republicans routinely condemned violations of black rights, few Republicans showed much interest in using federal power to prevent such outrages.

After Reconstruction

After 1877, southern Democrats moved to establish new systems of politics and race relations. Most Redeemers worked to reduce taxes, dismantle Reconstruction legislation and agencies, and eliminate meaningful black participation in politics. They also began the process of turning the South into a one-party region, a situation that reached its fullest development around 1900 and persisted until the 1950s and in some areas later.

Voting and officeholding by African Americans did not cease in 1877, but without federal enforcement of black rights, the threat of violence and the potential for economic retaliation by landlords and merchants sharply reduced meaningful political involvement by African Americans. Efforts to mobilize black voters posed dangers to candidates and voters, and many black political leaders concluded that their political survival depended on favors from influential white Republicans or even from Democratic leaders. The public schools survived, segregated and underfunded, but presenting an important opportunity. Many Reconstruction-era laws remained on the books. Until about 1890, many theaters, bars, restaurants, hotels, streetcars, and railroads continued to serve African Americans without discrimination. White supremacy had been established by force of arms, however, and blacks exercised their rights at the sufferance of the dominant whites.

After 1877, Reconstruction was held up as a failure. Although far from accurate, the southern whites'

version of Reconstruction—that conniving carpetbaggers and scalawags had manipulated ignorant freedmen—appealed to many white Americans throughout the nation, and it gained widespread acceptance among many novelists, journalists, and historians. William A. Dunning endorsed that interpretation in his history of Reconstruction, published in 1907. Thomas Dixon's popular novel *The Clansman* (1905) inspired the highly influential film *The Birth of a Nation* (1915). Historically inaccurate and luridly racist, the book and the movie portrayed Ku Klux Klan members as heroes who rescued the white South, and especially white southern women, from domination and debauchery at the hands of depraved freedmen and carpetbaggers.

Against this pattern stood some of the first black historians, notably George Washington Williams, a Union army veteran whose two-volume history of African Americans appeared in 1882. *Black Reconstruction in America,* by W. E. B. Du Bois, appeared in 1935. Both presented fully the role of African Americans in Reconstruction and pointed to the accomplishments of the Reconstruction state governments and black leaders. Not until the 1950s and 1960s, however, did large numbers of American historians begin to reconsider their interpretations of Reconstruction. Historians today recognize that Reconstruction was not the failure that had earlier been claimed. The creation of public schools was the most important of the changes in southern life produced by the Reconstruction state governments. At a federal level, the Fourteenth and Fifteenth Amendments eventually provided the constitutional leverage to restore the principle of equality before the law that so concerned the Radicals. Historians also recognize that Reconstruction collapsed partly because of internal flaws, partly because of divisions within the Republican Party, and partly because of the political terrorism unleashed in the South and the refusal of the North to commit the force required to protect the constitutional rights of African Americans.

Individual Voices

Senator **Blanche K. Bruce**, Selection from a Speech Before the Senate, 1876

Bruce became a U.S. senator in early 1875. Later that year, the "Mississippi Plan" brought white-supremacist Democrats to power. When Congress reconvened, Bruce sought an investigation of the 1875 Mississippi election. This primary source gives historians one reaction of a leader of the African American community to the fraud and violence that brought an end to Black Reconstruction.

1 Does Bruce present the issue as a question of the rights of African Americans?

2 How does this paragraph indicate Bruce's reputation for tact and diplomacy rather than confrontation? What is the audience he identifies?

3 How does Bruce explain the preference of African Americans for the Republican Party? What does this paragraph tell you about Bruce's approach to race relations?

The conduct of the [1875] election in Mississippi . . . [has] put in question and jeopardy the sacred rights of the citizens; and the investigation contemplated in the pending resolution has for its object not the determination of the question whether the offices shall be held . . . by democrats or republicans, but the higher and more important end, the protection in all their purity and significance of the political rights of the people and the free institutions of the country.

The evidence in hand and accessible will show [that] threats and violence were practiced directly upon the masses of voters in such measures and strength as to produce grave apprehensions for their personal safety and as to deter them from the exercise of their political franchises. . . . **1**

I ask Senators to believe that no consideration of fear or personal danger has kept us quiet and forbearing under the provocations and wrongs that have so sorely tried our souls. But feeling kindly toward our white fellow-citizens, appreciating the good purposes and politics of the better classes, and, above all, abhorring a war of races, we determined to wait until such time as an appeal to the good sense and justice of the American people could be made. **2**

The sober American judgment must obtain in the South as elsewhere in the Republic, that the only distinction upon which parties can be safely organized and in harmony with our institutions are differences of opinion relative to principles and policy of government . . . [D]ifferences of religion, nationality, or race can neither with safety nor propriety be permitted for a moment to enter into the party contests of the day. The unanimity with which the colored voters act with a party is not referable to any race prejudice. . . . They deprecate the establishment of the color line by the opposition, not only because the act is unwise and wrong in principle, but because it isolates them from the white men of the South, and forces them, in sheer self-protection and against their inclination, to act seemingly upon the basis of a race prejudice that they neither respect nor entertain. **3** . . . [They] recognize the equality of citizenship and the right of every man to hold, without proscription any position of honor and trust to which the confidence of the people may elevate him. . . .

SUMMARY

At the end of the Civil War, the nation faced difficult choices regarding the restoration of the defeated South and the future of the freed people. Committed to ending slavery, President Lincoln nevertheless chose a lenient approach to restoring states to the Union, partly to persuade southerners to abandon the Confederacy and accept emancipation. When Johnson became president, he continued Lincoln's approach.

The end of slavery brought new opportunities for African Americans, whether or not they had been slaves. Taking advantage of the opportunities that freedom opened, they tried to create independent lives for themselves, and they developed social institutions that helped to define black communities. Because few managed to acquire land of their own, most became either sharecroppers or wage laborers. White southerners also experienced economic dislocation, and many also became sharecroppers. Most white southerners expected to keep African Americans in a subordinate role and initially used black codes and violence toward that end.

In reaction against the black codes and violence, Congress took control of Reconstruction and passed the Civil Rights Act of 1866, the Fourteenth Amendment, and the Reconstruction Acts of 1867. An attempt to remove Johnson from the presidency was unsuccessful.

Additional federal Reconstruction measures included the Fifteenth Amendment, laws against the Ku Klux Klan, and the Civil Rights Act of 1875. Several of these measures strengthened the federal government at the expense of the states.

Enfranchised freedmen, white and black northerners who moved to the South, and some southern whites created a southern Republican Party that governed most southern states for a time. The most lasting contribution of these state governments was the creation of public school systems. Like government officials elsewhere, however, some southern politicians fell prey to corruption.

In the late 1860s, many southern Democrats chose a "New Departure": they grudgingly accepted some features of Reconstruction and sought to recapture control of state governments. By the mid-1870s, however, southern politics turned almost solely on race. The 1876 presidential election was very close and hotly disputed. In the end, Hayes took office and ended Reconstruction. Without federal protection for their civil rights, African Americans faced terrorism, violence, and even death if they challenged their subordinate role. With the end of Reconstruction, the South entered an era of white supremacy in politics and government, the economy, and social relations.

CHRONOLOGY
Reconstruction

1863	Emancipation Proclamation
1864	Lincoln reelected
1865	Freedmen's Bureau created
	Civil War ends
	Andrew Johnson becomes president
	Thirteenth Amendment (abolishing slavery) ratified
1866	Ku Klux Klan formed
	Congress takes control over Reconstruction
1867	Military Reconstruction Act
1868	Impeachment and acquittal of President Johnson
	Fourteenth Amendment (defining citizenship) ratified
	Grant elected president
1869–1870	Victories of "New Departure" Democrats in some southern states
1870	Fifteenth Amendment (guaranteeing voting rights) ratified
1870–1871	Ku Klux Klan Acts
1872	Grant reelected
1875	Civil Rights Act of 1875
	Mississippi Plan ends Reconstruction in Mississippi
1876	Disputed presidential election
1877	Compromise of 1877; Hayes becomes president
	End of Reconstruction

Study Tools

FOCUS QUESTIONS

If you have mastered this chapter, you should be able to answer these questions and to explain the terms that follow the questions.

1. ☆ *What did Presidents Lincoln and Johnson seek to accomplish for the South? How did white southerners respond to those efforts?*

2. ☆ *What seem to have been the leading objectives among freed people as they explored their new opportunities?*

3. ☆ *How do the differing responses of freed people and southern whites show different understandings of the significance of emancipation?*

4. ☆ *Why did congressional Republicans take control over Reconstruction policy? How successful were they?*

5. ☆ *How did the Fourteenth and Fifteenth Amendments change the nature of the federal union?*

6. ☆ *What major groups made up the Republican Party in the South during Reconstruction? Compare their reasons for being Republicans, their relative size, and their objectives.*

7. ☆ *What were the most lasting results of the Republican state administrations?*

8. ☆ *What major factors brought about the end of Reconstruction? Evaluate their relative significance.*

9. ☆ *Many historians began to reevaluate their understanding of Reconstruction during the 1950s and 1960s. Why do you suppose that happened?*

KEY TERMS

Reconstruction *(p. 388)*

Abraham Lincoln *(p. 389)*

Frederick Douglass *(p. 389)*

Radical Republicans *(p. 389)*

Thirteenth Amendment *(p. 390)*

Andrew Johnson *(p. 391)*

Freedmen's Bureau *(p. 394)*

Ku Klux Klan *(p. 397)*

Fourteenth Amendment *(p. 399)*

Elizabeth Cady Stanton *(p. 399)*

Susan B. Anthony *(p. 399)*

Fifteenth Amendment *(p. 401)*

Civil Rights Act of 1875 *(p. 402)*

Black Reconstruction *(p. 403)*

New Departure *(p. 406)*

Redeemers *(p. 407)*

Mississippi Plan *(p. 408)*

Rutherford B. Hayes *(p. 408)*

Compromise of 1877 *(p. 408)*

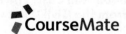 **CourseMate**

Go to the History CourseMate website for primary source links, study tools, and review materials for this chapter. www.cengagebrain.com

16

The Nation Industrializes, 1865–1900

Behind the Stories

After the Civil War, Americans experienced not only the hopes and frustrations of Reconstruction but also major economic and social transformations. At the end of the war, more than half of all Americans worked in agriculture, and three-fourths of Americans lived in rural areas or villages with fewer than 2,500 people. By 1920, more than half of all Americans lived in urban areas, and as many Americans worked in manufacturing as in agriculture. Americans also experienced a revolution in transportation and communication as steam engines, the **telegraph**, and later radio brought them closer to each other and the rest of the world.

When students study the years 1865–1900, they often see these great changes as inevitable. To see these changes as inevitable, however, prevents us from understanding both the amazement and the apprehension that Americans felt at the time. Henry Adams lived from 1838 to 1918; he spent much of his life writing history. In 1900, as he pondered the power of electricity and the mysteries of the atom, he concluded that recent advances in science and technology carried more far-reaching implications than anything in the previous sixteen centuries. The transformation of America during these years has engaged many historians. They have tried to understand those changes by seeking answers to such questions as: How can we explain the rapid pace of change? How do we understand such dynamic entrepreneurs as Andrew Carnegie, Thomas Edison, and John D. Rockefeller? How did the rise of large-scale manufacturing change Americans' lives? How did Americans respond to new urban, industrial, and technological realities?

The next three chapters explore historians' answers to those and other questions. We'll look at the transformation of the nation from agricultural to industrial, and from rural to urban. Most important, we'll examine how Americans created those changes, reacted to those changes, and sought more control over their new situation.

—R.W.C.

414

Individual Choices
John D. Rockefeller

For a generation of Americans, the name Rockefeller was synonymous with aggressive competition and monopoly. John D. Rockefeller was born in upper New York State in 1839 and educated in Cleveland, Ohio. After working as a bookkeeper, he became a partner in a grain and livestock business in 1859 and earned substantial profits during the Civil War. His attention was soon drawn to the oil-refining business, a major new enterprise in Cleveland.

The refining business was uncertain and highly competitive, and Rockefeller set out to stabilize his operations by reducing the competition. He joined with others to create a **cartel**, and then negotiated an astounding deal with the railroads that served Cleveland. Because the three major railroads that served Cleveland were highly competitive among themselves, Tom Scott, head of the Pennsylvania Railroad, proposed a plan that would have guaranteed each railroad a stable share of the shipping by the Rockefeller cartel, called the South Improvement Company in Scott's plan. Under Scott's plan, the three railroad companies would double their prices for carrying petroleum products to $2.56 per barrel, but would give the South Improvement Company a rebate of $1.06 per barrel and also pay the South Improvement Company $1.06 per barrel for petroleum products that any other petroleum refining company shipped on the railroads! The railroads were also to provide the South Improvement Company with complete information on all petroleum products shipped by its competitors. In return, the South Improvement Company would divide its business among the three railroads, with the Pennsylvania Railroad getting a double share.

John D. Rockefeller

Courtesy of the Rockefeller Archive Center.

telegraph Apparatus used to communicate at a distance over a wire, usually in Morse code.

■ **cartel** A group of separate companies within an industry that cooperate to control the production, pricing, and marketing of goods within that industry; also called a pool.

When news of this leaked out in 1872, other refining companies raised a great outcry, which led the railroad companies to promise to treat all shippers equally. Rockefeller pursued other means to reduce competition. In the end, though, Rockefeller's Standard Oil still managed to receive favorable treatment from the railroads and soon controlled 90 percent of the refining capacity in the entire country, making it one of a few genuine monopolies of the era (see the Individual Voices feature at the end of this chapter). Rockefeller emerged as the first American billionaire and the richest person in U.S. history. After his retirement in the mid-1890s, he devoted much of his attention to giving away his fortune, especially for research.

Rockfeller's rise to wealth came amidst an economy that was being dramatically and profoundly transformed. The changes in the nation's economy far exceeded the wildest expectations of Americans living in 1865. Many Americans probably anticipated economic growth, but few imagined that steel production could increase a thousand times by 1900, or that railroads could operate nearly six times as many miles of track, or that farmers could triple their harvests. These economic changes and many others were the result of decisions by many individuals—where to seek work, where to invest, whether to expand production, how to react to a business competitor, whom to trust.

Many Americans also made choices about competition and cooperation. As the industrial economy took off, many people found themselves in a love-hate relationship with competition. Andrew Carnegie, leader of the new steel industry, loved it, arguing that competition "insures the survival of the fittest" and "insures the future progress of the race" by producing the highest quality, largest quantity, and lowest prices. Other entrepreneurs saw competition as the most unpredictable factor they faced and a serious constraint on economic progress. Carnegie's zeal for competition was unusual. Although many entrepreneurs publicly applauded the idea of the "survival of the fittest," most loved competition only in the abstract and preferred to find alternatives to it in their own business affairs.

Other Americans also found themselves making choices regarding cooperation. Individualism was deeply entrenched in the American psyche, yet the increasing complexity of the economy presented repeated opportunities for cooperation. Railroad executives, as in the example of the South Improvement Company, sometimes cooperated by dividing a market rather than competing in it. Wage earners sometimes joined together to demand better wages or working conditions. The result of these many decisions was the industrialization of the nation and the transformation of the economy.

FOUNDATION FOR INDUSTRIALIZATION

★ *What factors encouraged economic growth and industrial development after the Civil War?*

By 1865, conditions in the United States were ripe for rapid industrialization. A wealth of natural resources, a capable work force, an agricultural base that produced enough food for a large urban population, and favorable governmental policies combined to lay the foundation.

Resources, Skills, Capital, and New Federal Policies

At the end of the Civil War, **entrepreneurs** could draw on vast and virtually untapped natural resources. Americans had long since plowed the fertile farmland of the Midwest (where corn and wheat dominated) and the South (where cotton was king). They had just begun to farm the rich soils of Minnesota, Nebraska, Kansas, Iowa, and the Dakotas, as well as the productive valleys of California and Oregon. Through the central part of the nation stretched vast grasslands that received too little rain for most farming but were well suited for grazing. The Pacific Northwest, the western Great Lakes region, and the South all held extensive forests untouched by the lumberman's saw.

The nation was also rich in mineral resources. Before the Civil War, the iron **industry** had developed in Pennsylvania as a result of easy access to iron ore and coal. Pennsylvania was also the site of early efforts to tap

entrepreneur A person who takes on the risks of creating, organizing, and managing a business enterprise.

industry A basic unit of business activity in which the various participants do similar activities; for example, the railroad industry consists of railroad companies and the firms and factories that supply their equipment.

Edwin L. Drake (foreground, right) stands in front of the first oil well in the United States, near Titusville, Pennsylvania. The well was drilled in 1858, but this photo was taken several years later. Drake pioneered the technology necessary for successful drilling, but was unable to translate this to financial success. Others copied his drilling techniques and by the early 1870s, the Titusville region was producing 5.8 million barrels of oil per year.

underground pools of crude oil. The California gold rush, beginning in 1848, had drawn many people west, and some of them found great riches. At the end of the war, other minerals lay unused or undiscovered across the country, including iron ore, coal, oil, gold and silver, and copper. Many of these natural resources were far from population centers, and their use awaited adequate transportation facilities. Exploitation of some of these resources also required new technologies.

A skilled and experienced work force was also essential for economic growth. In the 1790s and early nineteenth century, New Englanders had developed manufacturing systems based on **interchangeable parts** (first used for guns and clocks) and factories for cotton cloth. These accomplishments gave them a reputation for "Yankee ingenuity"—a talent for devising new tools and inventive methods. Such skills and problem-solving abilities were not limited to New England—they were key ingredients in nearly all large-scale manufacturing because early factories

usually relied on skilled **artisans** to supervise less-skilled workers in assembling products. Some of the early artisans and factory owners came from Great Britain, the world's first industrial nation.

Another crucial element for industrialization was capital. Before the Civil War, capital became centered in the seaport cities of the Northeast—Boston, New York, and Philadelphia, especially—where prosperous merchants invested their profits in banks and factories. Banks were important instruments for mobilizing capital. Before the war, some bankers had begun to specialize in arranging financing for large-scale enterprises, and some had opened offices in Britain to tap sources of capital there. **Stock exchanges** had also developed long before the Civil War as important institutions for raising capital for new ventures.

Still another important element for rapid economic development was favorable governmental policies. When Republicans took command of the federal government in 1861, they were immediately faced with the need to wage war against the Confederacy. At the same time, however, they forged new policies to stimulate economic growth, beginning with a new **protective tariff** in 1861. The tariff increased the price of imports to equal or exceed the price of American-made goods, thereby protecting domestic products from foreign competition and encouraging investment in manufacturing. Tariff rates changed periodically, but the protective tariff remained central to federal economic policy for more than a half-century.

New federal land policies also stimulated economic growth. At the beginning of the Civil War, the federal government claimed a billion acres of land as federal property—the **public domain**—half of the land area of the nation. Republicans used the public domain to encourage economic development in several ways. The **Homestead Act** (1862) provided that any person could receive free as much as 160 acres (a quarter of a square mile) of government land by building a house, living on the land for five years, and farming

interchangeable parts Identical mechanical parts that can be substituted for one another.

artisan A skilled worker, whether self-employed or working for wages.

stock exchange A place where people buy and sell stocks (shares in the ownership of companies); stockholders may participate in election of the company's directors and share in the company's profits.

■ **protective tariff** A tax placed on imported goods for the purpose of raising the price of imports as high as or higher than the prices of the same item produced within the nation.

public domain Land claimed by the federal government.

■ **Homestead Act** Act of Congress in 1862 offering 160 acres of designated public lands to any citizen who lived on and improved the land for five years.

MAP 16.1 Expansion of Agriculture, 1860–1900
The amount of improved farmland more than doubled during these years as western lands were brought under cultivation and other land was cultivated more intensely. Copyright © Cengage Learning

1860
Area of most intensive agriculture
Improved land

1900
Area of most intensive agriculture
Improved land

it. The **Land-Grant College Act** (1862)—often called the Morrill Act for its sponsor, Senator Justin Morrill of Vermont—gave land to each state to fund a public university, which was required to provide education in engineering and agriculture and to train military officers. Also in 1862, Congress approved land grants for the first transcontinental railroad, and more land grants to railroads followed.

■ **Land-Grant College Act** Act of Congress in 1862 that gave land to states to be used to fund public universities that were to offer courses in engineering and agriculture and to train military officers.

The Transformation of Agriculture

The expanding economy rested on a highly productive agricultural base. Improved transportation—canals early in the nineteenth century and railroads later—speeded the expansion of agriculture by making it possible to move agricultural produce over long distances. Up to the Civil War, farmers had developed 407 million acres into productive farmland. During the next forty years, this figure more than doubled, to 841 million acres. Map 16.1 indicates where this growth occurred.

The federal government contributed to the rapid settlement of Kansas, Nebraska, the Dakotas, and Minnesota through the Homestead Act. Between

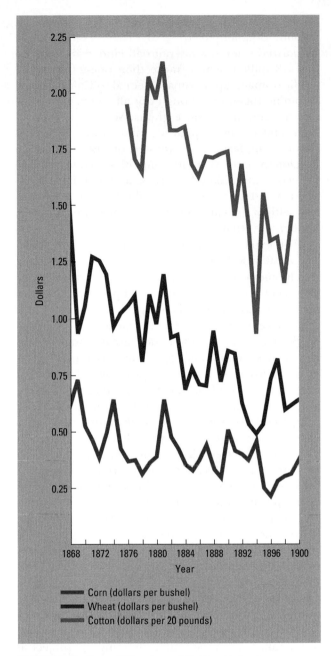

FIGURE 16.1 Corn, Wheat, and Cotton Prices, 1868–1900

From the late 1860s through the end of the century, prices for major crops fell. This graph shows the year-to-year fluctuations in prices and the general downward trend in prices for major crops.

Source: U.S. Department of Commerce, Bureau of the Census, Historical Statistics of the United States, Colonial Times to 1970, Bicentennial edition, 2 vols. (Washington: Government Printing Office, 1975), I: 510–512, 517–518.

1862 and 1890, 48 million acres passed from government ownership to private hands in this way. Other federally owned land could be purchased for as little as $1.25 per acre, and much more was obtained at this bargain price than was acquired free under the Homestead Act.

Production of leading commercial crops increased especially rapidly. When the total number of acres in farmland doubled, the number of acres planted in corn, wheat, and cotton more than tripled. New farming methods increased harvests even more—corn by 264 percent, wheat by 252 percent, and cotton by 383 percent. Through these years, farm output grew more than twice as much as the population.

As production of major crops rose, prices for them fell. Figure 16.1 shows the prices for wheat, corn, and cotton—the most significant commercial crops. Though several factors contributed to this decline in farm prices, the most obvious was that supply outpaced demand. Production increased more rapidly than the population (which determined the demand within the nation) and the demand from other countries. When American farmers received less for their crops, they often raised *more* in an effort to maintain the same level of income. To increase their harvests, they bought fertilizers and elaborate machinery. Between 1870 and 1890, the amount of fertilizer consumed in the nation more than quadrupled. And the more the farmers raised, the lower prices fell—and with them, the economic well-being of many farmers.

New machinery greatly increased the amount of land one person could farm. A single farmer with a hand-held scythe and cradle could harvest 2 acres of wheat in a day. Using the McCormick reaper (first produced in 1849), a single farmer and a team of horses could harvest 2 acres in an hour. For other crops too, a person with modern machinery could farm two or three times as much land as a farmer fifty years before.

Agricultural expansion also stimulated the farm equipment industry and, in turn, the iron and steel industry. Agricultural exports—cotton, tobacco, wheat, meat—spurred oceanic shipping and shipbuilding, and increased shipbuilding meant a greater demand for iron and steel. Railroads played a crucial role in the expansion and commercialization of agriculture by carrying farm products to distant markets and transporting fertilizer and machinery from factories to farming regions.

THE DAWN OF BIG BUSINESS

☆ What was the significance of the railroad and steel industries in the new industrial economy that emerged after the Civil War?

☆ How did investment bankers such as J. P. Morgan contribute to the new industrial economy?

To many Americans of the late nineteenth century, nothing symbolized economic growth so effectively as a locomotive—a huge, powerful, noisy, smoke-belching machine barreling forward. Railroads set much of the pace for economic expansion after the

Civil War. Growth of the rail network stimulated industries that supplied materials for railroad construction and operation—especially steel and coal—and industries that relied on railroads to connect them to the emerging national economy. Railroad companies also came to symbolize "big business"—companies of great size, employing thousands of workers, operating over large geographic areas—and some Americans began to fear their power.

Railroads: The First Big Business

Before the Civil War, much of the nation's commerce moved on water—on rivers, canals, and coastal waterways. At the end of the Civil War, the nation still lacked a comprehensive national transportation network. Railroads clearly had that potential, but railway companies operated on tracks of varying **gauges**, which made the transfer of railcars from one line to another impossible. Few railway bridges crossed major rivers. Until 1869, no railroad connected the eastern half of the country to the booming Pacific Coast region.

By the mid-1880s, all the elements were in place for a national rail network. The first transcontinental rail line was completed in 1869, connecting California to Omaha, Nebraska, and ultimately to eastern cities. Within the next twenty-five years, four more rail lines linked the Pacific Coast to the eastern half of the nation. Between 1865 and 1890, railroads grew from 35,000 miles of track to 167,000 miles (see Map 16.2). By the mid-1880s, major rivers had been bridged. Companies had replaced iron rails with steel ones, allowing them to haul heavier loads. New inventions increased the speed, carrying capacity, and efficiency of trains. In 1886 the last major lines converted to a standard gauge, making it possible to transfer railcars from one line to another simply by throwing a switch. Entrepreneurs could now think in terms of a national economic system in which raw materials and finished products moved easily from one region to another.

Railroads, especially in the West, expanded with generous governmental assistance. In the **Pacific Railway Act** of 1862, Congress provided the Union Pacific and Central Pacific companies not only with sizable loans but also with 10 square miles of the public domain for every mile of track laid—an amount doubled in 1864. By 1871, Congress had authorized some seventy railroad land grants, involving 128 million acres—more than one-tenth of the public domain, approximately equal to Colorado and Wyoming together—though not all companies qualified to claim their entire grants. Most railroads sold their land to raise capital for railroad operations. By encouraging farmers, businesses, or organizations to develop the land, railroad companies tried to build up the economies along their tracks and thereby to boost the demand for their freight trains to haul supplies to new settlers and carry settlers' products (wheat, cattle, lumber, ore) to market.

The expansion of railroads created the potential for a nationwide market, stimulated the economic development of the West, and created a demand for iron, steel, locomotives, and similar products. Railroad companies also provided an organizational model for newly developing industrial enterprises.

Because they spanned such great distances and managed so many employees and so much equipment, railroads encountered problems of scale that few companies had faced before but that other industrial entrepreneurs soon had to address. Railroad companies also required a much higher degree of coordination and long-range planning than most previous businesses. Earlier companies typically operated at a single location, but railroads functioned over long distances and at multiple sites. They had to keep up numerous maintenance and repair facilities and maintain many stations to receive and discharge freight and passengers. Financial transactions carried on over hundreds of miles by scores of employees required a centralized accounting office. One result was development of a company bureaucracy of clerks, accountants, managers, and agents. Railroads became training grounds for administrators, some of whom later entered other industries. Indeed, the experience of the railroads was central in defining the subject of business administration when it began to be taught in colleges at the turn of the century.

Railroads faced higher **fixed costs** than most previous companies. These costs included payments on debts and the expense of maintaining and protecting far-flung equipment and property. To pay their fixed costs and keep profits high, railroad companies tried to operate at full capacity whenever possible. Doing so, however, often proved difficult. Where two or more lines competed for the same traffic, one might choose to cut rates in an effort to lure business from the other. But if the other company responded with cuts in its rates, neither stood to gain significantly more business, and both took in less income. Competition between railroad companies sometimes became so intense that no line could show a profit.

---

gauge In this usage, the distance between the two rails making up railroad tracks.

■ **Pacific Railway Act** Act of Congress in 1862 that gave loans and land to the Central Pacific and Union Pacific Railroad companies to subsidize construction of a rail line between Omaha and the Pacific Coast.

fixed costs Costs that a company must pay even if it closes down all its operations—for example, interest on loans, debt payments, and property taxes.

MAP 16.2 Railroad Expansion and Railroad Land Grants
Railroad expansion produced the transportation base for an industrial economy. Note the high density of rail lines in the Northeast and Midwest. This map also shows federal land grants to railroads. The map at lower left shows a typical survey township within the area of a railroad land grant. The railroad company typically received every odd-numbered section (one square mile). Within the land grant, the price of the remaining federal land was doubled. Thus, the total income to the federal government was only slightly affected by the land grant.
Copyright © Cengage Learning

Legend:
— Railroads in 1870
— Railroads in 1920
■ Federal land grants "primary" limits
■ Federal land grants area forfeited within "primary" limits

Some railroad operators chose to defuse intense competition by forming a **pool**. In a pool, the railroads agreed to divide the existing business among themselves and not to compete on rates. The most famous was the Iowa Pool, made up of railroads running between Chicago and Omaha, across Iowa. Formed in 1870, the Iowa Pool operated until 1874, and some pooling continued until the mid-1880s. Few pools lasted very long. Often one or more pool members tired of a restricted market share and broke the pool arrangement in an effort to expand, thereby setting off a new price war. When a pooling arrangement became known, it brought loud complaints from customers, who concluded that they paid higher rates because of the pool.

pool An agreement among businesses in the same industry to divide up the market and charge equal prices instead of competing; another name for a cartel.

By the late nineteenth century, many Americans equated the locomotive—a huge, powerful, noisy, smoke-belching machine—with economic growth and progress. Some associated the locomotive with the power of the new industrial corporations that were transforming the economy. This photo, from 1900, shows the Northern Pacific railway company's first North Coast Limited passenger train.

To compete more effectively, railroads adjusted their rates to attract companies that did a great deal of shipping. Such favored customers sometimes received a rebate. Large shipments sent over long distances cost the railroad companies less per mile than small shipments sent over short distances, so companies developed different rate structures for long hauls and short hauls. Thus the largest shippers, with the power to secure rebates and low rates, could often ship more cheaply than small businesses and individual farmers. Railroad companies defended the differences on the basis of differences in costs, but small shippers who paid high prices saw themselves as victims of rate discrimination.

Railroads viewed state and federal governments as sources of valuable subsidies. At the same time, they constantly guarded against efforts by their customers to use government to restrict or regulate their enterprises—by outlawing rate discrimination, for example. Companies sometimes campaigned openly to secure the election of friendly representatives and senators and to defeat unfriendly candidates. They maintained well-organized operations to **lobby** public officials in Washington, D.C., and in state capitals. Most railroad companies issued free passes to public officials—a practice that reformers attacked as bribery. Some railroads won reputations as the most influential political power in entire states—the Southern Pacific in California, for example, or the Santa Fe in Kansas.

Stories of railroad officials bribing politicians became commonplace after the Civil War. The Crédit Mobilier scandal (discussed in Chapter 18) touched some of the most influential members of Congress in the 1870s. A decade later, Collis P. Huntington of the Southern Pacific Railroad candidly explained his expectations regarding public officials: "If you have to pay money to have the right thing done, it is only just and fair to do it." For Huntington, "the right thing" meant favorable treatment for his company.

Politically powerful or not, railroads produced significant change. Between 1850 and 1880, railroads transformed Chicago from a town of 30,000 residents to the nation's fourth-largest city, with a half-million people. By 1890, it was second only to New York in population, and in 1900 it claimed 1.7 million people.

lobby To try to influence the thinking of public officials for or against a specific cause.

Chicago was perhaps the most important single center for the nation's rail traffic in the late nineteenth century. This lithograph shows Chicago's Grand Passenger Station in 1880 and advertises some of the many rail connections possible through this station—to Kansas City, Denver, and San Francisco. Note also the many forms of street transportation in front of the station, including a coach, several varieties of carriages, and bicycles.

Thanks in part to local promoters and in part to geography, Chicago emerged as the rail center not just of the Midwest but of much of the nation. By 1880, more than twenty railroad lines and 15,000 miles of tracks connected Chicago with nearly all of the United States and much of Canada. The boom in railroad construction during the 1880s only reinforced the city's prominence. Entrepreneurs in manufacturing and commerce soon developed new enterprises based on Chicago's unrivaled location at the hub of a great transportation network.

Chicago's rail connections made it the logical center for the new business of **mail-order sales**. Central location and rail connections also made Chicago a major manufacturing center. By the 1880s, Chicago's factories produced more farm equipment than those of any other city, and its iron and steel production rivaled that of Pittsburgh. Other leading Chicago industries produced railway cars and equipment, metal products, a wide variety of machinery, and clothing. The city also claimed the title of the world's largest grain market.

Location and rail lines made Chicago the nation's largest center for **meatpacking**. Livestock from across the Midwest and from as far as southern Texas was unloaded in Chicago's Union Stockyards—over 400 acres of railroad sidings, chutes, and pens filled with cattle, hogs, and sheep. Huge slaughterhouses flanking the stockyards received a steady stream of live animals and disgorged an equally steady stream of fresh, canned, and processed meat. The development in the 1870s of refrigeration for railroad cars and ships permitted fresh meat to be sent throughout the nation and to Europe.

Railroads, Investment Bankers, and "Morganization"

Railroads expanded significantly in the 1880s, but some lines earned little profit. Some traversed sparsely populated areas of the West. Others spread into areas already saturated by rail service. In the 1880s,

■ **mail-order sales** The business of selling goods using the mails; mail-order houses send out catalogs, customers submit orders, and products are delivered, all by mail.

meatpacking The business of slaughtering animals and preparing their meat for sale as food.

a few ambitious, talented, and occasionally unscrupulous railway executives maneuvered to produce great regional railway systems. The Santa Fe and the Southern Pacific, for example, came to dominate the Southwest, and the Great Northern and the Northern Pacific held sway in the Northwest. The Pennsylvania and the New York Central controlled much of the shipping in the Northeast. By consolidating lines within a region, railway executives tried to create more efficient systems with less duplication, fewer price wars, and more dependable profits.

Railroads required far more capital than most manufacturing concerns. Even railroads that received government subsidies required large amounts of private capital. The railroads' huge appetite for capital made them the first American businesses to seek investors on a nationwide and international scale. Those who invested their money could choose to buy either stocks or **bonds**. Sales of railroad stocks provided the major activity for the New York Stock Exchange through the second half of the nineteenth century.

To raise the enormous amount of capital necessary for construction and consolidation, railroad executives turned increasingly to **investment banks**. By the late 1880s, **John Pierpont Morgan** had emerged as the nation's leading investment banker. Born in Connecticut in 1837, he was the son of a successful merchant who turned to banking. After schooling in Switzerland and Germany, young Morgan began working in his father's bank in London. In 1857 he moved to New York, where his father had arranged a banking position for him.

Morgan's experience and growing stature in banking gave him access to capital within the United States and abroad, in London and Paris. His investors wanted to put their money where it would be safe and give them a reliable **return**. Morgan therefore tried to stabilize the railroad business, especially the cutthroat rate competition that often resulted when several companies served one market. Railroad companies that turned to Morgan for help in raising capital found that Morgan wanted a say in their management. He insisted that companies seeking his help reorganize to simplify corporate structures and to combine small lines into larger, centrally controlled systems.

bonds A certificate of debt issued by a government or corporation guaranteeing payment of the original investment plus interest at a specified future date.

investment bank An institution that acts as an agent for corporations issuing stocks and bonds.

■ **John Pierpont Morgan** The most prominent and powerful American investment banker in the late nineteenth century.

return The yield on money that has been invested in an enterprise. Today, companies typically pay a dividend (a proportionate share of the profits) to their stockholders each quarter.

J. P. Morgan, Sr., was at the pinnacle of his power when this photograph was taken around 1900. Morgan seems to exude both power and anger. The anger may reflect his anxiety over being photographed. Morgan was very sensitive about his appearance, especially his nose. He suffered from *acne rosacea*, which made his nose large and misshapen.

He often demanded a seat on the board of directors as well, to guard against risky decisions in the future. Some began to refer to this process as "Morganization," and "Morganized" lines soon included some of the largest in the country. A few other investment bankers followed similar patterns.

Andrew Carnegie and the Age of Steel

The new, industrial economy rode on a network of steel rails, propelled by locomotives made of steel. Steel plows broke the tough sod of the western prairies. Skyscrapers, which first appeared in Chicago in 1885, relied on steel frames as they boldly shaped urban skylines. Steel, a relative latecomer to the industrial revolution, defined the age.

Made by combining carbon and molten iron and then burning out impurities, steel has greater strength, resilience, and durability than iron. This superior metal was difficult and expensive to make until the 1850s, when Henry Bessemer in England

This lithograph shows Andrew Carnegie's Homestead Works, one of the largest manufacturing plants in the nation, as of the early 1890s.

and William Kelly in Kentucky independently discovered ways to make steel in large quantities at a reasonable cost. Even so, the first Bessemer or Kelly process plants did not begin production in the United States until 1864. In that year, the entire nation produced only 10,000 tons of steel.

In 1875, just south of Pittsburgh, Pennsylvania, **Andrew Carnegie** drew upon a loan from J. P. Morgan's father's bank to construct the nation's largest steel plant, employing 1,500 workers. From then until 1901 (when the plant had grown to more than eight thousand workers), Carnegie held the central place in the steel industry. Born in Scotland in 1835, Carnegie and his penniless parents came to the United States in 1848. Young Andrew worked first in a textile mill, then as a messenger in a telegraph office. He soon became a telegraph operator, then the personal telegrapher for a high official of the Pennsylvania Railroad. Carnegie rose rapidly within that company and became a superintendent (a high management position) at the age of 25. At the end of the Civil War, he devoted his full attention to the iron and steel industry, in which he had previously invested money. He quickly applied to his own companies the management lessons he had learned with the railroad.

Carnegie's basic rule was "Cut the prices; scoop the market; run the mills full." An aggressive competitor, he repeatedly cut costs so that he might show a profit while charging less than his rivals. He usually chose to undersell competitors rather than cooperate with them. In 1864, steel rails sold for $126 per ton; by 1875, Carnegie was selling them for $69 per ton. Driven by improved technology and Carnegie's competitiveness, steel prices fell to $29 a ton in 1885 and less than $20 a ton in the late 1890s. Carnegie was the largest steel manufacturer in the United States,

though his company accounted for only a quarter of the nation's production. By 1900, the nation produced nearly 10 million tons of steel each year, more than any other nation.

Carnegie's company was larger and more complex than any manufacturing enterprise in pre–Civil War America. In its own day, however, other companies operated plants that were as complex, and several challenged it in size. By 1880, five steel companies had more than 1,500 employees, as did several textile mills and a locomotive factory. The size of such operations continued to grow. In 1900 the three largest steel plants each employed 8,000 to 10,000 workers, and seventy other factories employed more than 2,000, producing everything from watches to locomotives, from cotton cloth to processed meat.

Carnegie and other entrepreneurs transformed the organizational structure of manufacturing. They often joined a range of operations formerly conducted by separate businesses—acquisition of raw materials, processing, distribution of finished goods—into one company, achieving **vertical integration**. Companies usually developed vertical integration to ensure steady operations and to gain a competitive advantage. Control over the sources and transportation of

■ **Andrew Carnegie** Scottish-born industrialist who made a fortune in steel and believed the rich had a duty to act for the public benefit.

vertical integration The process of bringing together into a single company several of the activities involved in creating a manufactured product, such as acquiring raw materials, manufacturing products, and marketing, selling, and distributing finished goods.

raw materials, for example, guaranteed a reliable flow of crucial supplies at predictable prices. Such control may also have denied materials to a competitor.

Steel plants stood at one end of a long chain of operations that Carnegie owned or controlled: iron ore mines in Minnesota, a fleet of ships that transported iron ore across the Great Lakes, hundreds of miles of railway lines, tens of thousands of acres of coal lands, ovens to produce coke (coal treated to burn at high temperatures), and plants for turning iron ore into bars of crude iron. Carnegie Steel was vertically integrated from the point where the raw materials came out of the ground through the delivery of steel rails and beams.

Survival of the Fittest?

The concentration of power and wealth during the late nineteenth century generated extensive comment and concern. One prominent view on the subject was known as **Social Darwinism**, reflecting its roots in Charles Darwin's work on evolution. In his book *On the Origin of Species* (published in 1859), Darwin concluded that creatures compete with one another for survival in an often inhospitable environment, and those that survive are those that have, through mutation and inheritance, developed the traits best adapted to their surroundings. Such adaptation, he suggested, leads to the evolution of different species, each uniquely suited to a particular ecological niche.

Two philosophers, Herbert Spencer, writing in England in the 1870s and after, and William Graham Sumner, writing in the United States in the 1880s and after, put their own interpretations on Darwin's reasoning and applied it to the human situation, producing Social Darwinism (a philosophical perspective that bore little relation to Darwin's original work). Social Darwinists contended that competition among people, and by extension among powerful entrepreneurs, produced "progress" through "survival of the fittest" and that unrestrained competition provided the best route for improving humankind and advancing civilization. Further, they argued that efforts to ease the harsh impact of competition only protected the unfit and thereby worked to the long-term

disadvantage of all. When applied to government, this notion became a form of **laissez faire**.

The wealthiest entrepreneurs, though, could be inconsistent. Carnegie, for example, embraced Spencer's arguments but also preached what he called the **Gospel of Wealth**: the idea that the wealthy should return their riches to the community. Carnegie spent his final eighteen years giving away his fortune. He funded 3,000 public library buildings and 4,100 church organs all across the nation, gave gifts to universities, built Carnegie Hall in New York City, and created several foundations. Like Carnegie, other great entrepreneurs of that time gave away vast sums to promote learning and research—even as some of them also built ostentatious mansions, threw extravagant parties, and otherwise flaunted their wealth.

Although many Americans subscribed to the vision of Social Darwinism propounded by Spencer and Sumner, many others did not. Entrepreneurs themselves sometimes welcomed some forms of government intervention in the economy—from railroad land grants to the protective tariff to suppression of strikes—although most agreed with the Social Darwinists that government should not assist the poor and destitute.

Other Americans disagreed with the Social Darwinists' equating of laissez faire with progress. Henry George, a San Francisco journalist, pointed out in *Progress and Poverty* (1879) that "amid the greatest accumulations of wealth, men die of starvation," and concluded that "material progress does not merely fail to relieve poverty—it actually produces it." Lester Frank Ward, a sociologist, in 1886 posed a carefully reasoned refutation of Social Darwinism, suggesting that biological competition produced bare survival, not civilization. Civilization, he argued, derived not from "aimless competition" but from rationality and cooperation.

EXPANSION OF THE INDUSTRIAL ECONOMY

★ How and why did companies expand their operations and control within an industry?

★ In what ways was the economy of the South distinctive?

Innovative technologies and the integrated railway network began to change the ways that Americans shopped for goods from clothing to food to home lighting products. John D. Rockefeller took the lead in bringing vertical and horizontal integration to the production of kerosene and other petroleum products, and other entrepreneurs created similar corporate structures in other consumer-goods industries.

■ **Social Darwinism** The philosophical argument, inspired by Charles Darwin's theory of evolution, that competition in human society produced "the survival of the fittest" and therefore benefited society as a whole; Social Darwinists opposed efforts to regulate competitive practices.

laissez faire The principle that the government should not interfere in the workings of the economy.

■ **Gospel of Wealth** Andrew Carnegie's idea that all possessors of great wealth have an obligation to spend or otherwise disburse their money to help people help themselves.

5 Sale to consumer

4 Transportation
(finished products
go to retail stores)

3 Processing
(refineries transform crude
oil into kerosene, lubricating
oil, and paraffin)

2 Transportation of raw materials
(crude oil moves to refineries)

1 Production of raw materials
(oil is pumped out of the ground)

Vertical integration

Horizontal integration

● Steps in petroleum production/distribution

FIGURE 16.2 Vertical and Horizontal Integration of the Petroleum Industry
This diagram represents the petroleum industry before Standard Oil achieved its dominance. The symbols represent different specialized companies, each engaged in different steps in the production of kerosene. Rockefeller entered the industry by investing in a refinery, and first expanded *horizontally* by absorbing several other refineries (indicated by the blue band). His Standard Oil Company then practiced *vertical integration* (indicated by the green band) by acquiring oil leases, oil wells, pipelines, advantageous contracts with railroads, and eventually even retail stores. For a time, Standard Oil controlled nearly 90 percent of the industry.

Standard Oil: Model for Monopoly

Just as Carnegie provided a model for other steel companies and for heavy industry in general, John D. Rockefeller revolutionized the petroleum industry and provided a model for other consumer-goods industries. The major product of oil refining was kerosene, which transformed home lighting as kerosene lamps replaced candles and oil lamps. Rockefeller, in 1863, invested his wartime profits in a **refinery**. After the war, he bought control of more refineries and incorporated them as Standard Oil in 1870.

The refining business was relatively easy to enter and highly competitive. Aggressive competition became a distinctive Standard Oil characteristic. Recognizing that technology could bring a competitive advantage, Rockefeller recruited experts to make Standard the most efficient refiner. He secured favorable treatment from railroads by offering a heavy volume of traffic on a predictable basis. He usually sought to persuade his competitors to join the cartel he was creating. If they refused, he sometimes tried to drive them out of business.

By 1881, following a strategy of **horizontal integration**, Rockefeller and his associates controlled some forty refineries, with about 90 percent of the nation's refining capacity. Standard also moved toward vertical integration by gaining control of oil fields, building transportation facilities (including pipelines and oceangoing tanker ships), and creating retail marketing operations (see Figure 16.2). By the early 1890s,

refinery An industrial plant that transforms raw materials into finished products; a petroleum refinery processes crude oil to produce a variety of products for use by consumers.

horizontal integration Merging one or more companies doing the same or similar activities as a way of limiting competition or enhancing stability and planning.

It Matters Today

Standard Oil had achieved almost complete vertical and horizontal integration of the American petroleum industry—a virtual **monopoly** over an entire industry.

Between 1879 and 1881, Rockefeller and his associates centralized decision making among all their companies by creating the Standard Oil Trust. The **trust** was a new organizational form designed to get around state laws that prohibited one company from owning stock in another. To create the Standard Oil Trust, Rockefeller and others who held shares in the individual companies exchanged their stock for trust certificates issued by Standard Oil. Standard Oil thus controlled all the individual companies, though technically it did not own them. Eventually, new laws in New Jersey made it legal for corporations chartered in New Jersey to own stock in other companies. So Rockefeller set up Standard Oil of New Jersey as a **holding company** for the companies in the trust.

Once Standard Oil achieved its near-monopoly, it consolidated its operations by closing older refineries and building larger plants that incorporated the newest technology. Such innovations reduced the cost of producing petroleum products by more than two-thirds, leading to a decline by more than half in the price paid by consumers of fuel and home lighting products. Standard also took a leading role in the world market, producing nearly all American petroleum products sold in Asia, Africa, and Latin America during the 1880s. Rockefeller retired from active participation in business in the mid-1890s.

Standard's monopoly was short-lived, because of the discovery of new, rich oil fields in Texas and elsewhere at the turn of the century. New companies tapped those fields and quickly followed their own paths to vertical integration. Nonetheless, the "Rockefeller interests" (companies dominated by Rockefeller or his managers) steadily gained in power. They included the National City Bank of New York (an investment bank second only to the House of Morgan), railroads, mining, real estate, steel plants, steamship lines, and other industries.

Thomas Edison and the Power of Innovation

By the late nineteenth century, most American entrepreneurs had joined Rockefeller and Carnegie in viewing technology as a powerful competitive device. Railroads wanted more powerful locomotives, roomier freight cars, and stronger rails so they could carry more freight at a lower cost. Steel companies demanded larger and more efficient furnaces to make more steel more cheaply. Ordinary citizens as well as famous entrepreneurs seemed infatuated with technology. One invention followed another: an ice-making machine in 1865, the vacuum cleaner in 1869, the telephone in

monopoly Exclusive control by an individual or company of the production or sale of a product.

trust A legal arrangement in which an individual (the trustor) gives control of property to a person or institution (the trustee); in the late nineteenth century, a legal device to get around state laws prohibiting a company chartered in one state from operating in another state, and often synonymous in common use with *monopoly*; first used by John D. Rockefeller to consolidate Standard Oil.

holding company A company that exists to own other companies, usually through holding a controlling interest in their stocks.

In the Wider World

Cartels

Though American entrepreneurs sometimes cooperated through pools or cartels, such efforts rarely lasted very long, unless they took legal form as a trust or holding company. In contrast, cartels emerged as a more typical form of business cooperation in Germany, which was also undergoing rapid industrialization in the late nineteenth century.

By 1905, nearly 400 industrial cartels were operating in Germany and were especially prominent in the coal, iron, and steel industries and in chemicals. By then, there were also at least forty international cartels, typically including companies from neighboring European countries. The first attempt at a global cartel, initiated by a French company in 1887 in an effort to monopolize worldwide production of copper, included participation by companies in France, Germany, Spain, and the United States. It briefly controlled three-quarters of the world's supply of copper but lasted only until 1889.

1876, the phonograph in 1878, the electric light bulb in 1879, an electric welding machine in 1886, and the first American-made gasoline-engine automobile in 1895, to name only a few. By 1900, many Americans had come to expect a steady flow of ever more astounding creations, especially those that could be purchased by the middle and upper classes.

This photograph from 1893 shows Thomas A. Edison in his laboratory, the world's leading research facility when it opened in 1876. By creating research teams, the Edison laboratories could pursue several projects at once. They developed a dazzling stream of new products, most based on electrical power.

Many new inventions relied on electricity, and in the field of electricity one person stood out: **Thomas A. Edison**. Born in 1847, he secured the first of his thousand-plus **patents** at age 22. In 1876 Edison set up the first modern research laboratory, and he opened a new and improved facility in 1887. Edison promised "a minor invention every ten days and a big thing every six months," and he backed up his words with results. His laboratories invented or significantly improved electrical lighting, electrical motors, the storage battery, the electric locomotive, the phonograph, the microphone, and many other products. Research and development by Edison's laboratories and others soon translated into production and sales. Nationwide, sales of electrical equipment were insignificant in 1870 but reached nearly $2 million ten years later and nearly $22 million in 1890.

Such sales meant that generating and distribution systems had to be constructed, and wires to carry electrical current had to be installed along city streets and in homes. The pace of this work picked up appreciably after Nikola Tesla demonstrated the superiority of alternating current (AC) to direct current (DC) for transmitting power over long distances. Edison's distribution networks had relied on DC, which had limited their range.

Early developers of electrical devices and electrical distribution systems needed major financial assistance, and investment bankers came to play an important role in public utilities industries. General Electric, for

Thomas A. Edison American inventor, especially of electrical devices, among them the phonograph and the light bulb.

patent A government statement that gives the creator of an invention the sole right to produce, use, or sell that invention for a set period of time.

example, developed out of Edison's company through a series of **mergers** arranged by J. P. Morgan.

Selling to the Nation

The expansion of manufacturing in the 1880s accelerated earlier trends toward new and more affordable consumer goods. Large, vertically integrated manufacturers of consumer products often competed to sell items that differed little from one another and that cost virtually the same to produce. Such companies frequently competed not on the basis of price but through advertising.

By the late nineteenth century, advertisements in newspapers and magazines had become large and complex as manufacturers relied on large-scale advertising to promote a host of mass-produced consumer goods, including **patent medicines**, clothing, books, packaged foods, soap, and petroleum products. In some cases—notably cigarettes—advertising greatly expanded the market for the product. After the federal Patent Office registered the first **trademark** in 1870, companies rushed to develop brands and logos that they hoped would distinguish their products from nearly identical rivals.

Along with advertising came new ways of selling. Previously, most people expected to purchase goods directly from artisans who made items on order (shoes, clothes, furniture), or from door-to-door peddlers (pots and pans), or in small specialty stores (hardware, dry goods) or general stores. In urban areas following the Civil War, the first American **department stores** appeared and flourished, offering a wide range of choices in ready-made products—fashionable clothing, household furnishings, shoes, and much more. Department stores' products, unlike the wares in most previous retail outlets, not only had clearly marked prices but also could be returned or exchanged if the customer were dissatisfied. R. H. Macy's in New York City, Jordan Marsh in Boston, Marshall Field in Chicago, and similar stores relied heavily on newspaper advertising to attract large numbers of customers, especially women, from throughout the city and its suburbs. They targeted middle- and upper-class women, but the stores also appealed to young, single women who worked for wages and had an eye for the fashions that were now within their financial reach. Young, single women also often found white-collar jobs as clerks in the new department stores.

The variety presented by department stores paled when compared with the vast array of goods available through the new mail-order catalogs. Led by two Chicago companies, Montgomery Ward (which issued its first catalog in 1872) and Sears, Roebuck and Co. (whose first general catalogs appeared in 1893), mail-order houses aimed at rural America. They offered a wider range of choices than most rural-dwellers had ever before seen—everything from hams to hammers, handkerchiefs to harnesses.

Department stores and mail-order houses became feasible because manufacturers had begun to produce many types of consumer goods in huge volumes. Mail-order houses also depended on railroads and the U.S. mail to deliver their catalogs and products across great distances, and department stores relied on railroads to bring goods from distant factories. Together, advertising, mail-order catalogs (in rural areas), and the new department stores (in urban areas) began to change not only Americans' buying habits but

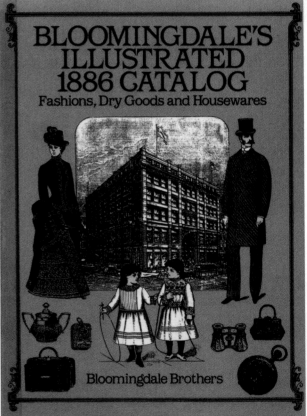

Sears and Roebuck and Montgomery Ward were not the only companies to reach out to consumers by using mail-order catalogs. This Bloomingdale's catalog from 1886 featured fashionable clothing and housewares.

merger The joining together of two or more organizations.

patent medicine A medical preparation that is advertised by brand name and available without a physician's prescription.

trademark A name or symbol that identifies a product and is officially registered and legally restricted for use by the owner or manufacturer.

■ **department store** Type of retail establishment that developed in cities in the late nineteenth century and featured a wide variety of merchandise organized in separate departments.

also their thinking about what they expected to buy ready-made.

Economic Concentration in Consumer-Goods Industries

Carnegie, Rockefeller, Edison, Morgan, and a few others redefined the expectations of American entrepreneurs and provided models for their activities. In a number of consumer-goods industries, massive, complex companies—vertically integrated, sometimes horizontally integrated, often employing extensive advertising—appeared relatively suddenly in the 1880s.

The American Sugar Refining Company, created in 1887, imitated Rockefeller's organization to control three-quarters of the nation's sugar-refining capacity by the early 1890s. In the 1880s, James B. Duke used efficient machinery, extensive advertising, and vertical integration to become the largest manufacturer of cigarettes. In 1890 he merged with his four largest competitors to create the American Tobacco Company, which dominated the cigarette industry. Gustavus Swift in the early 1880s began to ship fresh meat from his slaughterhouse in Chicago to markets in the East, using his own refrigerated railcars. He eventually added refrigerated storage plants in several cities, along with a sales and delivery staff. Other meatpacking companies followed Swift's lead. By 1890, half a dozen firms dominated meatpacking. Such a market, in which a small number of firms dominate an industry, is called an **oligopoly**. Oligopolies were (and are) more typical than monopolies.

Some of the new manufacturing companies did not sell stock or use investment bankers to raise capital. Standard Oil, like Carnegie Steel, never "went public"—that is, Rockefeller never used the stock exchange to raise capital. Instead, he expanded either through mergers or by making purchases capitalized by his profits. Rockefeller and his associates, like Carnegie and his partners, concentrated ownership and control in their own hands. So did many others among the new manufacturing companies. As late as 1896, the New York Stock Exchange sold stock in only twenty manufacturing concerns.

Gradually, however, with the passing of the first generation of industrial empire builders, ownership grew apart from management. Many new business executives were professional managers. Ownership rested among hundreds or thousands of stockholders, all of whom wanted a reliable return on their investment, even though the vast majority remained uninvolved with business operations. The huge size of the new companies also meant that most managers rarely saw or talked with most of their employees. Careful **cost analysis**, the desire for efficiency, and the need to pay shareholders regular **dividends** led many companies to treat most of their employees as expenses to be increased or cut as necessary, with little regard to the effect on individuals.

Laying the Economic Basis for a New South

The term **New South** usually refers to efforts by some southerners to modernize their region during the years after Reconstruction. Some advocates of the New South promoted a more diverse economic base, with more manufacturing and less reliance on a few staple agricultural crops, as a way to strengthen the southern economy and integrate it more thoroughly into the national economy.

Foremost among proponents of the New South was **Henry Grady**, who built the *Atlanta Constitution* into a powerful regional newspaper in the 1880s. Like Chicago, Atlanta grew as a railroad center. Though destroyed by Sherman's troops in 1864, Atlanta rebuilt quickly. It became the capital of Georgia in 1877. Thanks in part to Grady's skillful journalism, the city emerged as a symbol of the New South—a center for transportation, industry, and finance.

The importance of railroads in spurring Atlanta's growth was no coincidence. After the Civil War, inadequate transportation, especially railroads, posed a critical limit on the South's economic growth. During the 1880s, however, southern railroads more than doubled their miles of track. In the 1890s, J. P. Morgan led in reorganizing southern railroads into three large systems, dominated by the Southern Railway. With the emergence of better rail transportation, some entrepreneurs began to consider introducing new industries.

Some southerners had long advocated that their cotton be manufactured into cloth in the South, rather than in the New England textile mills that had been using southern cotton since early in the century. The southern cotton textile industry finally boomed during the 1880s and 1890s. The South counted 161 textile mills in 1880 and 400 in 1900. The new mills had more modern equipment and were larger and more productive than the mills of New England.

---

oligopoly A market or industry dominated by a few firms (from Greek words meaning "few sellers"); more common than a *monopoly* (from Greek words meaning "one seller").

cost analysis Study of the cost of producing manufactured goods to find ways to cut expenses.

dividend A share of a company's profits received by a stockholder.

■ **New South** Late-nineteenth-century term used by some southerners to promote the idea that the South should become industrialized, have a more diverse agriculture, and be thoroughly integrated into the economy of the nation.

■ **Henry Grady** Prominent Atlanta newspaper publisher and leading proponent of the concept of a New South.

They also had cheaper labor costs, partly because they relied on child labor. Similar patterns characterized the emergence of cigarette manufacturing as another new southern industry. In the end, these enterprises did little to improve the lives of many southerners. Most of the new companies paid low wages, and some located in the South specifically to take advantage of its cheap, unskilled, nonunion labor.

Other southerners tried to diversify the region's agriculture and to reduce its dependence on cotton and tobacco. Such efforts, however, ran up against the cotton textile and cigarette industries, both of which built factories in the South to be near their raw materials. Thus southern agriculture changed little: owners and sharecroppers farmed small plots, obligated by their rental contracts or crop liens to raise cotton or tobacco. In parts of the South, farmers became even more dependent on cotton than they had been before the Civil War. Parts of Georgia, for example, produced almost 200 percent more cotton in 1880 than in 1860.

Of greater potential to transform part of the South was the iron and steel industry that emerged in northern Alabama. Dominated by the Tennessee Coal, Iron, and Railroad Company, the industry drew on coal from Tennessee and Alabama mines and iron ore from northern Alabama. By the late 1890s, Birmingham, Alabama, had become one of the world's largest producers of pig iron. In 1897, the first southern steel mill opened in Ensley, Alabama, and soon established itself as a serious rival to those of the North. In 1907, J. P. Morgan arranged the merger of the Tennessee Company into his United States Steel Corporation.

The turn of the century also saw the beginning of a southern oil industry near Beaumont, Texas, with the tapping of the Spindletop Pool—so productive the press labeled it "the world's greatest oil well." The center of petroleum production now shifted from the Midwest to Texas, Oklahoma, and Louisiana, where important discoveries also came in 1901. In addition to attracting attention from Standard Oil, the new discoveries prompted the growth or creation of new companies, notably Gulf and Texaco.

Great Plains High grassland of western North America, stretching north to south across the center of the nation; it is generally level, treeless, and fairly dry.

tipis Conical tents made from buffalo hide and used as a portable dwelling by Indians on the Great Plains.

■ **horse culture** The nomadic way of life of those American Indians, mostly on the Great Plains, for whom the horse brought significant changes in their ability to hunt, travel, and make war.

■ **Lakota** A large confederation of Siouan-speaking Indian peoples, nomadic buffalo hunters, who lived on the northern Great Plains.

confederacy An organization of separate groups who have allied for mutual support or joint action.

INCORPORATING THE WEST INTO THE NATIONAL ECONOMY

☆ What were the causes and outcomes of the Indian wars of the late nineteenth century? Could they have been avoided?

☆ What were the major ways in which the West was incorporated into the national economy?

As Rockefeller was monopolizing the petroleum industry and Edison was perfecting the light bulb, the U.S. Army was subduing the last Indian resistance in the West. Before the Civil War, the issue of slavery had blocked efforts at the economic development of the West. The secession of the southern states permitted the Republicans who took over the federal government to open the West to economic development, through such measures as the Pacific Railway Act and the Homestead Act. The end result was the incorporation of the West into the emerging national industrial economy.

War for the West

When Congress decided to use the public domain—western land—to encourage economic development, most white Americans considered the West to be largely vacant. In fact, American Indians lived throughout most of the West. The most tragic outcome of the development of the West was the upheaval in the lives of the Native Americans who lived there.

At the end of the Civil War, as many white Americans began to move west, the acquisition of horses and guns had long since transformed the lives of western Native Americans. The transformation was most dramatic among tribes living on or near the **Great Plains** (see Map 16.3). This vast, relatively flat, and treeless region was the rangeland of huge herds of buffalo. Horses found their way onto the Great Plains slowly, trickling northward from Spanish settlements in what is now New Mexico and reaching the upper plains in the mid-eighteenth century. By that time, French and English traders working northeast of the plains had begun to provide guns to the Indians in return for furs. Together, horses and guns transformed the culture of some Plains tribes.

Although the possession of horses might confer status, among most of the Plains Indians a person achieved high social standing not by accumulating possessions but by sharing. Francis La Flesche, son of an Omaha leader, learned from his father that "the persecution of the poor, the sneer at their poverty is a wrong for which no punishment is too severe." His mother reinforced the lesson: "When you see a boy barefooted and lame, take off your moccasins and give them to him. When you see a boy hungry, bring him to your home and give him food."

The Native American peoples of the plains included both farmers and nomadic hunters. The farmers lived most of the year in large permanent villages. Among this group were the Arikaras, Pawnees, and Wichitas (parts of the Caddoan language family) and the Mandans, Hidatsas, Omahas, Otos, and Osages (who spoke Siouan languages). Women raised corn, squash, pumpkins, and beans, and gathered wild fruit and vegetables. Men hunted and fished near their villages and cultivated tobacco. Before the arrival of horses, twice a year entire villages went, on foot, on extended hunting trips for buffalo. During these hunts, the people lived in **tipis**, cone-shaped tents of buffalo hide that were easy to move. Acquisition of horses changed the culture of these Indians only slightly.

The horse revolutionized the lives of other Plains Indians. Because a hunter on horseback could kill twice as many buffalo as one on foot, the horse substantially increased the number of people the plains could support. The horse also increased mobility, permitting a band to follow the buffalo as they moved across the grasslands. Some groups abandoned farming and became nomadic, living in tipis year-round and following the buffalo herds. By the early nineteenth century, the **horse culture** existed throughout the Great Plains. The largest groups practicing this lifestyle included—from north to south—the Blackfeet, Crows, Lakotas, Cheyennes, Arapahos, Kiowas, and Comanches.

The **Lakotas**, largest of all the groups, were the westernmost members of a group of Native American peoples often called Sioux—a name applied to them by the French. Their name for themselves can be translated as *allies*, reflecting their organization as a **confederacy**. The Lakotas shared a common

MAP 16.3 The West in the Late Nineteenth Century

This map indicates major geographic features of the West in the late nineteenth century, including topography, major cities, subregions, cattle trails, and the major transcontinental railroads that had been completed by the 1890s. Mining areas are also shown for three important metals are also shown. Copyright © Cengage Learning

John Mix Stanley painted this buffalo hunt in 1845, dramatically illustrating how the horse increased the ability of Native American hunters to kill buffalo. A hunter on foot could not have approached closely enough to drive a lance into a buffalo's heart.

language, but the northern Cheyenne were generally considered members of the Lakota confederacy by the mid-nineteenth century.

Before 1851, federal policymakers had considered the region west of Arkansas, Missouri, Iowa, and Minnesota and east of the Rocky Mountains to be a permanent Indian country. But farmers bound for Oregon and gold seekers on their way to California carved trails across the central plains, and in 1851 Congress approved a new policy, designed in part to open the central plains as a railroad route to the Pacific. The new policy promised each tribe a definite territory "of limited extent and well-defined boundaries," within which the tribe was to live. The government was to supply whatever needs the tribes could not meet themselves. Federal officials first planned large reservations taking up much of the Great Plains.

tannery An establishment where animal skins and hides are made into leather.

guerrilla warfare A method of warfare in which small bands of fighters in occupied territory harass and attack their enemies.

As more easterners thronged westward, conflicts erupted along the trails. In April 1868, many members of the northern Plains tribes met at Fort Laramie and signed treaties creating a Great Sioux Reservation on the northern plains. They believed that they retained "unceded lands" for hunting in the Powder River country—present-day northeastern Wyoming and southeastern Montana. In return, the army abandoned its posts along the Bozeman Trail, a victory for the Lakotas and Cheyennes.

The creation of the new reservation was part of a larger plan. With the end of the Civil War in 1865, railroad construction crews prepared to build westward. Federal policymakers tried to head off hostilities by carving out a few great western reservations. The remainder of the West was to be opened for development—railroad building, mining, and farming. Native Americans on the reservations were to receive food and shelter, and agents were to teach them how to farm and raise cattle.

Other treaties were negotiated in 1867 and 1868 in fulfillment of the new policy. In 1867 a conference at Medicine Lodge Creek produced treaties by which the major southern Plains tribes accepted reservations in what is now western Oklahoma (see Map 16.4).

In May 1868 the Crows agreed to a reservation in Montana. In June 1868 the Navajos accepted a large reservation in the Southwest. Given the fluid structure of authority among most Indian peoples, however, those who signed the treaties did not necessarily obligate those who did not.

As some federal officials were negotiating these treaties, other federal officials were permitting and even encouraging white hunters to kill the buffalo—for sport, for meat, and for hides purchased by **tanneries** in the East. In the mid-1870s more than 10 million buffalo were killed and stripped of their hides, which sold for a dollar or so. The southern herd was wiped out by 1878, the northern herd by 1883. Only two thousand survived, the remnant of a species whose numbers once seemed as vast as the stars. Given the importance of the buffalo in the lives of the Plains Indians, their way of life was doomed once the slaughter began.

Some members of the southern Plains tribes refused to accept the terms of the Medicine Lodge Creek treaties and continued to live in their traditional territory. Resisting efforts to move them onto the reservations, they occasionally attacked stagecoach stations, ranches, travelers, and military units. After a group of southern Cheyennes inflicted heavy losses on an army unit, General William Tecumseh Sherman, the Civil War general and now head of the army, decreed that all Native Americans not on reservations "are hostile and will remain so till killed off."

Sherman's response was the usual reaction of a conventional military force to **guerrilla warfare**: concentrate the friendly population in defined areas (in this case, reservations) and then open fire on anyone outside those areas. In the winter of 1868–1869, the army launched a southern campaign under the command of General Philip Sheridan, another Union

MAP 16.4 Indian Reservations

This map indicates the location of most western Indian reservations in 1890, as well as the Great Sioux Reservation before it was broken up and severely reduced in size. Note how development of reservations on the northern plains and others on the southern plains opened the central plains for railroad construction and agricultural development. Copyright © Cengage Learning army veteran, who directed his men to "destroy their villages and ponies, to kill and hang all warriors, and bring back all women and children." The brutality that ensued convinced most southern Plains tribes to abandon further resistance.

In the early 1870s, however, sizable buffalo herds still roamed west and south of Indian Territory, in the Red River region of Texas. Though this was not reservation land, the Medicine Lodge Creek treaties permitted Indians to hunt there. When white buffalo hunters began work there in 1874, young men from the Kiowa, Comanche, and southern Cheyenne tribes attacked them. Sheridan responded with another **war of attrition**, destroying tipis, food, and animals. When winter came, the cold and hungry Indians surrendered to avoid starvation. War leaders were imprisoned in Florida, far from their families. Buffalo hunters then quickly exterminated the remaining buffalo on the southern plains.

On the northern plains, many Lakotas and some northern Cheyennes, led by **Crazy Horse** and **Sitting Bull**, lived on unceded hunting lands in the Powder River region. Complicating matters further, gold was discovered in the Black Hills, in the heart of the Great Sioux Reservation, in 1874, touching off an invasion of Indian land by miners. As the Northern Pacific Railroad prepared to lay track in southern Montana, federal authorities determined to force all Lakota and Cheyenne people onto the reservation, triggering a conflict sometimes called the **Great Sioux War**.

Military operations in the Powder River region began in the spring of 1876. Sheridan ordered troops to enter the area from three directions and converge on the Lakotas and Cheyennes. The offensive went dreadfully wrong when Lieutenant Colonel George A. Custer, without waiting for the other units, sent his Seventh Cavalry against a major village that his scouts had located. The encampment, on the **Little Big Horn River**, proved to be one of the largest ever on the northern plains. Custer unwisely divided his force, and more than two hundred men, including Custer, met their deaths.

That winter, U.S. soldiers unleashed another campaign of attrition on the northern plains. Troops defeated some Indian bands. Hunger and cold drove others to surrender. Crazy Horse and his band held out until spring and surrendered only when told that they could live in the Powder River region. A few months later, Crazy Horse was killed when he resisted being put into an army jail. Sitting Bull and his band escaped to Canada and remained there until 1881, when he finally surrendered. The government cut up the Great Sioux Reservation into several smaller units and took away the Powder River region, the Black Hills (which the Lakotas considered sacred), and other lands. After the Great Sioux War, no Native American group could muster the capacity for sustained resistance. Small groups occasionally left their reservations but were promptly tracked down by troops. In 1877 an effort to move the Nez Perces to a new reservation in western Idaho led to a battle in which a small group of Nez Perces defeated a larger group of U.S. troops and local civilian volunteers. Led by **Chief Joseph**, the Nez Perces then attempted to flee to Canada. Between July and early October, they evaded the army as they traveled east and north. More than two hundred members of the band died along the way. In the end, Joseph surrendered on the condition that the Nez Perces be permitted to return to their previous home. Federal officials sent the Nez Perces to faraway Indian Territory, where, in an unfamiliar climate, many died of disease.

The last sizable group to resist confinement was Geronimo's band of Chiricahua Apaches, who long managed to elude the army in the mountains of the Southwest. They finally gave up in 1886, and the men were sent to prison in Florida.

The last major confrontation between the army and Native Americans came in 1890, in South Dakota. Some Lakotas had taken up a new religion, the **Ghost Dance**, which promised to restore the buffalo and sweep away the whites. Fearing an uprising, federal authorities ordered the Lakotas to stop the ritual and, concerned that Sitting Bull might encourage defiance, ordered his arrest. He was killed when some of his followers resisted. A small band of Lakotas, led by Big Foot, fled but was surrounded by the Seventh Cavalry near **Wounded Knee Creek**. When one Lakota refused

war of attrition A form of warfare based on deprivation of food, shelter, and other necessities; if successful, it drives opponents to surrender out of hunger or exposure.

■ **Crazy Horse** Lakota war leader who resisted white encroachment in the Black Hills and fought at the Little Big Horn River in 1876.

■ **Sitting Bull** Lakota war leader and holy man; also fought at Little Big Horn.

■ **Great Sioux War** War between the U.S. Army and the tribes that took part in the Battle of Little Big Horn; it ended in 1881 with the surrender of Sitting Bull.

■ **Little Big Horn River** River in Montana where in 1876 Lieutenant Colonel George Custer attacked a large Indian encampment; Custer and most of his force died in the battle.

■ **Chief Joseph** Nez Perce chief who led his people in an attempt to escape to Canada in 1877; after a grueling journey they were forced to surrender and were exiled to Indian Territory.

■ **Ghost Dance** Indian religion centered on a ritual dance; it held out the promise of an Indian messiah who would banish the whites, bring back the buffalo, and restore the land to the Indians.

■ **Wounded Knee Creek** Site of a conflict in 1890 between a band of Lakotas and U.S. troops, sometimes characterized as a massacre because the Lakotas were so outnumbered and overpowered; the last major encounter between Indians and the army.

Library of Congress.

This photo shows the insensitive treatment of the Lakotas who died at Wounded Knee. They were buried in a mass grave, still frozen as they had fallen.

to surrender his gun, both Indians and soldiers fired their weapons. The soldiers, with their vastly greater firepower, quickly prevailed. As many as 250 Native Americans died, as did 25 soldiers.

The events at Wounded Knee marked the symbolic end of armed conflict on the Great Plains. Once the federal government began to encourage rapid economic development in the West, displacement of the Indians was probably inevitable. From the beginning, the Indians faced overwhelming odds—they had a superior knowledge of the terrain, superior horsemanship and mobility, and great courage, but the U.S. Army had superior numbers and superior technology. The army was also often able to find allies among Native American groups who were traditional enemies of the defiant tribes.

Transforming the West: Railroads, Cattle, and Mining

Long before the last battles between the army and the Indians, the incorporation of the West into the national economy was well under way. Railroad construction played a major role. In the eastern United States, railroad construction usually meant connecting established population centers. Eastern railroads moved through areas with developed economies, connected major cities, and hauled freight to and from the many towns along their lines. At the end of the Civil War, this situation existed almost nowhere in the West.

Most western railroads were built first to connect the Pacific Coast to the eastern half of the country. Only slowly did they begin to find business along their routes. Railroad promoters understood that a transcontinental line was unlikely at first to carry enough freight to justify the high cost of construction. Thus they turned to the federal government for assistance. The Pacific Railway Act of 1862 provided loans and 10 square miles (later increased to 20) of the public domain for every mile of track laid. In this way, federal lawmakers sought to tie California and Nevada, with their rich deposits of gold and silver, to the Union and to stimulate the rapid economic development of other parts of the West.

Two companies received this federal support: the Union Pacific, which began laying tracks westward from Omaha, Nebraska, and the Central Pacific, which began building eastward from Sacramento,

California. Construction began slowly, partly because crucial supplies—rails and locomotives—had to be brought to each starting point from the eastern United States, either by ship around South America to California or by riverboat to Omaha. Both lines experienced labor shortages. The Union Pacific solved its labor shortages only after the end of the Civil War, when former soldiers and construction workers flooded west. Many were Irish immigrants. The Central Pacific filled its work gangs earlier by recruiting Chinese immigrants. By 1868, Central Pacific construction crews totaled six thousand workers, Union Pacific crews five thousand.

The sheer cliffs and rocky ravines of the Sierra Nevadas slowed construction of the Central Pacific. Chinese laborers sometimes dangled from ropes to create a roadbed by chiseling away the solid rock face of a mountain. Because the companies earned their federal subsidies by laying track, construction became a race in which each company tried to build faster than the other. In 1869, with the Sierras far behind, the Central Pacific boasted of laying 10 miles of track in a single day. The tracks of the two companies finally met at Promontory Summit, north of Salt Lake City (see Map 16.3), on May 10, 1869. Other lines followed during the next twenty years, bringing most of the West into the national market system.

Westerners greeted the arrival of a railroad in their communities with joyful celebrations, but some soon wondered if they had traded isolation for dependence on a greedy monopoly. The Southern Pacific, successor to the Central Pacific, became known as the "Octopus" because of its efforts to establish a monopoly over transportation throughout California. It had a reputation for charging the most that a customer could afford. James J. Hill of the Great Northern, in contrast, was called the "Empire Builder" for his efforts to build up the economy and prosperity of the region alongside his rails, which ran west from Minneapolis to Puget Sound. Whether "Octopus" or "Empire Builder," railroads provided the crucial transportation network for the economic development of the West. In their wake, cattle raising, mining, farming, and lumbering all expanded rapidly.

Millions of cattle roamed the ranges of south Texas. Cattle had first been brought into south Texas—then part of New Spain (Mexico)—in the eighteenth century. The environment encouraged the herds to

When the Central Pacific and Union Pacific companies raced to build their part of the first transcontinental railroad, Chinese laborers were responsible for some of the most dangerous construction on the Central Pacific route through the Sierra Nevadas. This photograph was apparently taken by a photographer for the Union Pacific when the two lines joined near Promontory Summit, in Utah Territory.

Denver Public Library, Western History Collection.

multiply, and Mexican ranchers developed an **open-range** system. The cattle grazed on unfenced grasslands and *vaqueros* (cowboys) hearded the half-wild longhorns from horseback. Many practices that developed in south Texas were subsequently transferred to the range-cattle industry, including **roundups** and **branding**.

At the end of the Civil War, 5 million cattle ranged across Texas. And in the slaughterhouses of Chicago, cattle brought ten times their price in Texas or more. To get cattle from south Texas to markets in the Midwest, Texans herded cattle north from Texas through Indian Territory (now Oklahoma) to the railroads being built westward. Half a dozen cowboys, a cook, and a foreman (the trail boss) could drive one or two thousand cattle. Between 1866 and 1880, some 4 million cattle plodded north from Texas.

As railroad construction crews pushed westward, cattle towns sprang up—notably Abilene and Dodge City, Kansas. In cattle towns, the trail boss sold his herd and paid off his cowboys, most of whom quickly headed for the saloons, brothels, and gambling houses. Eastern journalists and writers of **dime novels** discovered and embroidered the exploits of town marshals like James B. "Wild Bill" Hickok and Wyatt Earp, giving them national reputations—deserved or not—as "town-tamers" of heroic dimensions. In fact, the most important changes in any cattle town came when middle-class residents—especially women—organized churches and schools, and were determined to create law-abiding communities like those from which they had come.

Most Texas cattle were loaded on eastbound trains, but some continued north to where cattlemen had virtually free access to vast lands still in the public domain. One result of these "long drives" was the extension of open-range cattle raising from Texas into the northern Great Plains. By the early 1870s, the profits in cattle raising on the northern plains attracted attention in the East, England, and elsewhere among investors eager to make a fortune. Some brought in new breeds of cattle, which they bred with Texas longhorns, producing hardy range cattle that yielded more meat.

By the early 1880s so many cattle ranches were operating that beef prices began to fall. Then, in the severe winter of 1886–1887, uncounted thousands of cattle froze or starved to death on the northern plains. Many investors went bankrupt. Cattle raising lost some of its romantic aura and afterward became more of a business than an adventure. Surviving ranchers fenced their ranges and made certain that they could feed their herds during the winter.

Another important change, both on the northern plains and in the Southwest, was the rise of sheep raising. By 1900, Montana had more sheep than any other state, and the western states accounted for more than half of the sheep raised in the nation.

At some time in the 1870s, these cowboys put on good clothes and sat for a photographer before a painted background. They probably worked together and were friends. Most cowboys were young African Americans, Mexican Americans, or poor southern whites.

Collection of William Gladstone.

As the cattle industry grew, the cowboy became a popular **icon**. Fiction after the 1870s, and motion pictures later, created the cowboy image: a brave, white, clean-cut hero who spent his time outwitting rustlers and rescuing fair-haired white women from snarling villains. In fact, most real cowboys were young and unschooled; many were African Americans or of Mexican descent, and others were former Confederate soldiers. On a cattle drive, they worked long hours (up to twenty a day), faced serious danger if a herd

open range Unfenced grazing lands on which cattle ran freely and cattle ownership was established through branding.

roundup A spring event in which cowboys gathered together the cattle herds, branded newborn calves, and castrated most of the new young males.

branding Burning a distinctive mark into an animal's hide using a hot iron as a way to establish ownership.

dime novel A cheaply produced novel of the mid-to-late nineteenth century, often featuring the dramatized exploits of western gunfighters.

icon A symbol, usually one with virtues considered worthy of imitating.

stampeded, slept on the ground, and ate biscuits and beans. They earned about a dollar a day and spent much of their working time in the saddle with no human companionship.

Just as railroads made possible the cattle drives, so too did railroad construction advance the expansion of mining. Discoveries of precious metals and valuable minerals in the mountainous regions of the West inevitably prompted the construction of rail lines to the sites of discovery, and the rail lines in turn permitted rapid exploitation of the mineral resources by bringing in supplies and heavy equipment. The mining industry changed rapidly. Solitary prospectors panning for gold in mountain streams gave way to corporations and wage workers. Mining operations quickly became vertically integrated, including mines, ore-crushing mills, railroads, and companies that supplied fuel and water for mining.

In most parts of the West, the exhaustion of surface deposits led to construction of underground shafts and tunnels. Such operations required elaborate machinery to move men and equipment thousands of feet into the earth and to keep the tunnels cool, dry, and safe. By the mid-1870s, some Nevada silver mines boasted the most advanced mining equipment in the world. There, temperatures soared to 120 degrees in shafts more than 2,200 feet deep. Mighty air pumps circulated air from the surface to the depths, and ice was used to reduce temperatures. Massive water pumps kept the shafts dry. Powerful drills speeded the removal of ore, and enormous ore-crushing machines operated day and night on the surface. In Butte, Montana, a gold discovery in 1864 led to discoveries of copper, silver, and zinc in what has been called the richest hill on earth. Mine shafts there reached depths of a mile and required 2,700 miles of tunnels.

Western miners organized too, forming strong unions. Beginning in Butte and spreading throughout the major mining regions of the West, miners' unions secured wages five to ten times higher than what miners in Britain or Germany earned.

aridity Dryness; lack of enough rainfall to support trees or woody plants.

meridian One of the imaginary lines representing degrees of longitude that pass through the North and South Poles and encircle the Earth.

ecosystem A community of animals, plants, and microorganisms, considered together with the environment in which they live.

Bohemia A region of central Europe now part of the Czech Republic.

Transforming the West: Farming and Lumbering

Railroad construction also facilitated the expansion of western farming. After the Civil War, the land most easily available for new farms stretched southward from Canada through the current state of Oklahoma. Mapmakers in the early nineteenth century had labeled this region the Great American Desert. It was not a desert—some parts were very fertile—but west of the line of **aridity**, roughly the 98th or 100th **meridian** (see Map 16.5), sparse rainfall limited farming. Farmers who followed traditional farming practices risked not only failing but also damaging a surprisingly fragile **ecosystem**.

After the Civil War, farmers pressed steadily westward, spurred by the offer of 160 acres of free land under the Homestead Act or lured by railroad advertising that promised fertile and productive land at little cost. Those who came to farm were as diverse as the nation itself. Thousands of African Americans left the South, seeking farms of their own. Immigrants from Europe—especially Scandinavia, Germany, **Bohemia**, and Russia—also flooded in. Most homesteaders, however, moved from areas a short distance to the east, where farmland had become too expensive for them to buy.

Single women could and did claim their own land. Sometimes the wife of a male homesteader did the same, claiming 160 acres in her own name next to the claim of her husband. By one estimate, one-third of all homestead claims in Dakota Territory were held by women in 1886. Some single women seem to have seen homesteading as a speculative venture, intending to sell the land and use the money for such purposes as starting a business, paying college tuition, or creating a nest egg for marriage.

The Homestead Act had clear limits, however. The 160 acres that it provided were sufficient for a farm only east of the line of aridity. West of that line, it was often possible to raise wheat, but most land required irrigation for other crops or was suitable only for cattle raising, which required much more than 160 acres.

Federal officials were sometimes lax in enforcing the Homestead Act's requirements. Some cattle ranchers manipulated the law by having their cowboys file claims and then transfer the land to the rancher after they received title to it. Or ranchers claimed the land along both sides of streams, knowing that surrounding land was worthless without access to water, and thus they could control the whole watershed without establishing ownership.

Those who complied with the requirement to build a house and farm the land often faced an unfamiliar environment. The plains were virtually barren of trees. The new plains settlers, therefore, scavenged

MAP 16.5 Rainfall and Agriculture, ca. 1890
The agricultural produce of any given area depended on the type of soil, the terrain, and the rainfall. Most of the western half of the nation received relatively little rainfall. The line of aridity, beyond which many crops require irrigation, lies between 28 inches and 20 inches of rain annually. Copyright © Cengage Learning

for substitutes for the construction material and fuel that eastern pioneers obtained without cost from the trees on their land. Initially, many families carved homes out of the land itself. Some tunneled into the side of a low hill to make a cavelike dugout. Others cut the tough prairie **sod** into blocks and laid them like bricks to make the walls of a house. Many combined dugout and sod construction. "Soddies" became common throughout the plains but seldom made satisfactory dwellings. For fuel to use in cooking or heating, women burned dried cow dung or sunflower stalks.

Plains families looked to technology to meet many of their needs. Barbed wire, first patented in 1874, provided a cheap and easy alternative to wooden fences. The barbs effectively kept ranchers' cattle off farmland. Ranchers eventually used it, too, to keep their herds from straying. Much of the plains had abundant groundwater, but the **water table** was

deeper than in the East, so settlers used windmills to pump the water. Because the sod was so tough, special plows were developed to make the first cut through it. These plows were so expensive that most farmers hired a specialist (a "sodbuster") to break their sod.

The most serious problem for pioneers on the Great Plains was a much-reduced level of rainfall compared with eastern farming areas. During the late 1870s and into the 1880s, when the central plains were farmed for the first time, the area received unusually

sod A piece of earth on which grass is growing; the dense sod of the plains was tough and fibrous with roots, dead grass from previous growing seasons, and hard-packed soil.

water table The level at which the ground is completely saturated with water.

Omer M. Kem (standing, slicing watermelon) posed for the photographer with his children and aged father outside his sod house in Custer County, Nebraska, in 1886. Four years later, Kem was elected to the U.S. House of Representatives as a Populist, representing the grievances of western farmers. The photographer, Solomon Butcher, compiled pictures illustrating the nature of life on what one historian termed "the sod-house frontier."

heavy rainfall. Then, in the late 1880s, rainfall fell below normal, and crop failures drove many homesteaders off the plains. By one estimate, half of the population of western Kansas left between 1888 and 1892. Only after farmers learned better techniques of dry farming, secured improved strains of wheat (some brought by **Russian-German** immigrants), and began to practice irrigation did agriculture become viable. Even so, farming practices in some western areas failed to protect soil that had formerly been covered by natural vegetation. This exposed soil became subject to severe wind erosion in years of low rainfall.

Throughout the Northeast and Middle West, the family farm was the typical agricultural unit. In the South after the Civil War, family-operated farms, whether run by owners or by sharecroppers, also became typical. Very large farming operations in those areas tended to be exceptions. In California and some other parts of the West, however, agriculture sometimes involved huge areas, the intensive use of heavy equipment, and wage labor. Today agriculture on such a large scale is known as **agribusiness**.

Wheat was the first major crop for which farming could be entirely mechanized. By 1880, in the Red River Valley of what is now North Dakota and in the San Joaquin Valley in central California, wheat farms were as large as 100 square miles. Such farming businesses required major capital investments in land, equipment, and livestock. One Dakota farm required 150 workers during spring planting and 250 or more

Russian-German Refers to people of German ancestry living in Russia; most had come to Russia in the eighteenth century at the invitation of the government to develop agricultural areas.

agribusiness A large-scale farming operation typically involving considerable land-holdings, hired labor, and extensive use of machinery; may also involve processing and distribution as well as growing.

Mechanization greatly increased the amount of land that an individual could farm. This 1878 lithograph depicts a California crew setting a world's record for the amount of wheat harvested in a single day.

at harvest time. By the late 1880s, some California wheat growers were using huge steam-powered tractors and **combines**.

Most of the great Dakota wheat farms had been broken into smaller units by the 1890s, but in some parts of California agriculture flourished on a scale unknown in most parts of the country. One California company, Miller and Lux, held more than a million acres, scattered throughout three states. Though California wheat raising declined in significance by 1900, large-scale agriculture employing many seasonal laborers became established for several other crops.

Growers of fruits and similar crops tended to operate small farms, but they still required a large work force at harvest time to pick the crops quickly so that they could be shipped to distant markets while still fresh. Fruit raising spread rapidly as California growers took advantage of refrigerated railroad cars and ships. By 1892, fresh fruit from California was for sale in London.

The coastal areas of the Pacific Northwest (see Map 16.5) are very different from other parts of the West. There, heavy winter rains and cool, damp, summer fogs nurture thick stands of evergreens, especially tall Douglas firs and coastal redwoods. The growth of California cities and towns required lumber, and it came first from the coastal redwoods of central and northern California. When the most accessible stands of timber had been cut, attention shifted north to Oregon and Washington. Seattle developed as a lumber town from the late 1850s onward, as companies in San Francisco helped to finance an industry geared to providing lumber for California cities. By the late nineteenth century, some companies had become vertically integrated, owning **lumber mills** along the northwest coast, a fleet of schooners that hauled rough lumber down the coast to California, and lumberyards in the San Francisco Bay area.

As railroads extended into the Pacific Northwest (see Map 16.3), they promoted the development of the lumber industry by offering cheap rates to ship logs. Lumber production in Oregon and Washington boomed, leaving behind treeless hillsides subject to severe erosion during heavy winter rains. Westerners

combine A large harvesting machine that both cuts and threshes grain.

lumber mill A factory or place where logs are sawed into rough boards.

committed to rapid economic development seldom thought about ecological damage, for the long-term cost of such practices was not immediately apparent.

Water and Western Development

It has been said that, in the West, "whiskey is for drinking, water is for fighting over." Throughout much of the West, water was scarce but crucial to economic development. Mining used large amounts of water for cooling the mines and separating valuable ore from worthless rock. On the Great Plains, a cattle rancher claimed grazing land by controlling a stream. In the West, competition for water sometimes produced conflict—usually in the form of courtroom battles.

In many parts of the West, irrigation was vital to the success of farming. As early as 1899, irrigated land in the eleven westernmost states produced $84 million in crops. Although individual entrepreneurs and companies undertook significant irrigation projects, the magnitude of the task led many westerners to look for federal assistance, just as they had sought federal assistance for railroad development. "When Uncle Sam," wrote one irrigation proponent, "waves his hand toward the desert and says, 'Let there be water!' we know that the stream will obey his commands." The National Irrigation Association, created in 1899, organized lobbying efforts, producing the **Reclamation Act** in 1902. Under that law, the Reclamation Service became a major power in the West as it moved the region's water to areas where it could be used for irrigation. Reclamation projects sometimes drew criticism, however, for disproportionately benefiting large landowners.

Lack of water potentially posed stringent limits on western urban growth. Beginning in 1901, San Francisco sought federal permission to create a reservoir by damming the Hetch Hetchy Valley, on federal land adjacent to Yosemite National Park in the Sierra Nevadas. Opposition came from the **Sierra Club**, formed in 1892 and dedicated to preserving Sierra Nevada wilderness. Congress finally approved the project in 1913, and the enormous construction task took more than twenty years to complete. Los Angeles resolved its water problems in a similar way, by diverting the water of the Owens River to its use— even though Owens Valley residents tried to dynamite the **aqueduct** in resistance.

Despite potential water worries, between the end of the Civil War and 1900, San Francisco emerged as the **metropolis** of the West and was long unchallenged as the commercial, financial, and manufacturing center for much of the region west of the Rockies. Building on the city's role as the major port on the Pacific Coast, San Francisco bankers played key roles

San Francisco rapidly emerged as the metropolis of the western United States. This 1905 photograph shows a San Francisco policeman talking to a young girl at one of the city's busiest intersections. Note the cable car on the right.

in development in the West, channeling profits from gold and silver mining into railroad and steamboat lines and manufacturing enterprises. By the 1880s, San Francisco was home to foundries that produced locomotives, technologically advanced mining equipment, agricultural implements for large-scale farming, and ships. Not until 1900 did a few other western cities—Denver, Salt Lake City, Seattle, Portland, and especially Los Angeles—seriously challenge the economic dominance of San Francisco.

BOOM AND BUST: THE ECONOMY FROM THE CIVIL WAR TO WORLD WAR I

★ What were the major changes in the U.S. economy from the Civil War to World War I?

The nation grew dramatically in the late nineteenth and early twentieth centuries. Between 1865 and 1920, the population increased by nearly 200 percent, from 36 million to 106 million. During the same years, railroad mileage increased by more than 1,000 percent. The output of manufacturing increased by a similar margin. Agricultural production grew far faster than the population. Perhaps most significantly, the total domestic product, per capita, in constant dollars, nearly tripled. (Figure 16.3 presents some of these patterns.)

Cycles of Growth and Depression in the 1870s and 1880s

Much of this growth was sporadic. Economic historians think of the economy as developing through a cycle in which periods of **expansion** (growth) alternate with times of **contraction** (**recession** or **depression**, characterized by high unemployment and low productivity). Though this alternation between expansion and contraction is predictable, there is no predictability or regularity to the duration of any given up or down period. During the late nineteenth century, contractions were sometimes severe, producing widespread unemployment and distress. After 1865, a postwar recession lasted until late 1867, reflecting sharp dislocations as the economy shifted from wartime production to other ventures. This was followed by several short expansions and contractions. A major depression began in October 1873 and lasted until March 1879. The period from 1879 to 1893 was generally one of expansion (105 months of growth), spurred in particular by railroad construction, but growth was interrupted three times by contractions (totaling 61 months), two of them quite short.

During boom periods, companies advertised for workers and ran their operations at full capacity.

When the demand for manufactured goods fell, companies reduced production, cutting hours of work or dismissing employees as they waited for business to pick up. Some businesses shut down temporarily; others closed permanently.

Thus Americans living in the late nineteenth and early twentieth centuries came to expect that hard times were likely in the future, regardless of how prosperous life seemed at the moment. Until the early twentieth century, federal intervention in the economy was limited largely to stimulating growth through the protective tariff and land distribution programs, but state and federal governments provided no unemployment benefits. Unemployed workers had little to fall back on besides their savings or the earnings of other family members, though some churches and private charity organizations gave out food. Families who failed to find work might go hungry or even become homeless. In a depression, jobs of any sort were scarce, and competition for every opening was intense. Most adult Americans therefore understood the wisdom of saving up for hard times, whether or not they were able to do so.

The depression that began in 1873 was both severe and long-lasting. Between 1873 and 1879, 355 banks closed down, a number equivalent to one bank in nine that existed in 1873. State and federal governments did nothing to save failing banks. Given the crucial role of banks as a source of credit for industry and agriculture, bank failures led to a credit contraction that, in turn, significantly delayed recovery. Nearly 54,000 businesses failed—equivalent to one in nine operating in 1873.

No reliable unemployment data exist, but evidence indicates that the contraction hit urban wage

■ **Reclamation Act** Law passed by Congress in 1902 that provided funding for irrigation of western lands and created the Reclamation Service to oversee the process.

Sierra Club Environmental organization formed in 1892; now dedicated to preserving and expanding parks, wildlife, and wilderness areas.

aqueduct A pipe or channel designed to transport water from a remote source, usually by gravity.

metropolis An urban center, especially one that is dominant within a region.

■ **expansion** In the economic cycle, a time when the economy is growing, characterized by increased production of goods and services and usually by low rates of unemployment.

■ **contraction** In the economic cycle, a time when the economy has ceased to grow, characterized by decreased production of goods and services and often by high rates of unemployment.

■ **recession/depression** A recession is an economic contraction of relatively short duration; a depression is an economic contraction of longer duration.

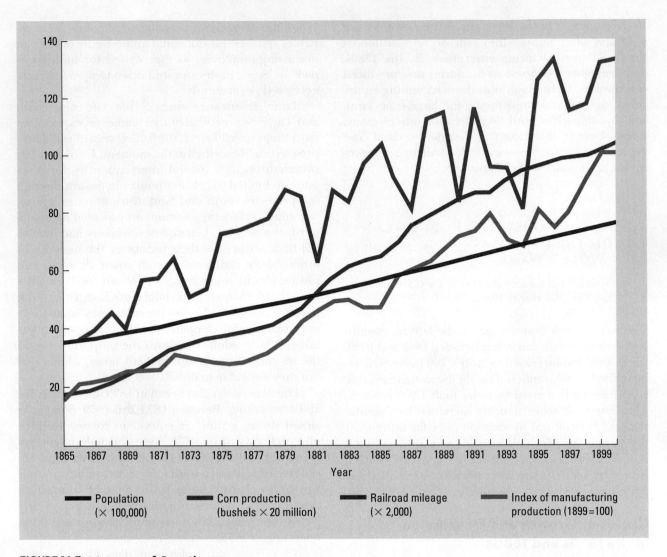

FIGURE 16.3 Measures of Growth, 1865–1900
Though many measures of economic productivity are related to population size, this graph shows how several measures of economic productivity grew more rapidly than did the population.

Source: U.S. Department of Commerce, Bureau of the Census, Historical Statistics of the United States, Colonial Times to 1970, Bicentennial edition, 2 vols. (Washington: Government Printing Office, 1975), I: 8, 510–512; 2: 667, 727–731.

earners especially hard. Many lost their jobs or suffered a reduced workweek. Workers who kept their jobs saw their daily wages fall 17–18 percent from 1873 to 1878 or 1879. One Massachusetts worker described the consequences for his family in 1875:

> I have six children. . . . Last year three of my children were promoted [to the next grade in school], *and I was notified to furnish different books.* [Schoolchildren then were responsible for providing their own textbooks.] *I wrote a note to the school committee, stating that I was not able to do so. . . . I then received a*

note stating that, unless I furnished the books called for, I must keep my children at home. I then had to reduce the bread for my children and family, in order to get the required books to keep them at school. Every cent of my earnings is consumed in my family; and yet I have not been able to have a piece of meat on my table twice a month for the last eight months.

Thus, though long-term economic trends reflect dramatic growth, the short-run boom-and-bust nature of the economy repeatedly claimed its victims.

Economic Collapse and Depression in the 1890s

Another major depression began in January 1893 and lasted (despite a brief upswing) until June 1897. It began when the Reading Railroad declared bankruptcy. A **financial panic** quickly set in. One business journal reported in August that "never before has there been such a sudden and striking cessation of industrial activity." Everywhere, industrial plants shut down in large numbers. More than fifteen thousand businesses failed in 1893, more proportionately than in any year since the depression of the 1870s.

At the time, no one understood why the economy collapsed so suddenly and completely. In retrospect, two important underlying weaknesses seem to have contributed: the slowing of both agricultural expansion and railroad construction. Railroad building drove the industrial economy in the 1880s, but slowed and then fell by half between 1893 and 1895. The decline in railroad construction initiated a domino effect, toppling industries that supplied the railroads, especially steel. Production of steel rails fell by more than a third, and thirty-two steel companies closed their doors. (Figure 16.3 shows the drop in manufacturing in the mid-1890s.) Some railway companies found they lacked sufficient traffic to pay their fixed costs, especially their obligations to bondholders, requiring them to declare bankruptcy. By 1894, almost one-fifth of the nation's railroad mileage had fallen into bankruptcy. Banks with investments in railroads and steel companies collapsed. One bank out of every ten failed between 1893 and 1897. Bank failures further contracted credit, limiting the possibilities for new investments that would spur expansion.

No agency kept careful national records on unemployment, but a third or more of the workers in manufacturing may have been out of work. During the winter of 1893–1894, Chicago counted one hundred thousand unemployed—roughly two workers out of five. Many who kept their jobs received smaller paychecks as employers cut wages and hours.

The depression produced widespread suffering. Many who lost their jobs had little to fall back on except charity. Newspapers told of people who chose suicide when faced with the dire options of starving to death or stealing food. Many men and some women left home desperate to find work, hoping to send money to their families as soon as they could. Some walked the roads, and others hopped on freight trains, riding in **boxcars**.

The "Merger Movement"

As the economy finally revived in the late 1890s, Americans witnessed an astonishing number of mergers in manufacturing and mining—a "merger movement" that lasted from 1898 until 1902. The high point came in 1899, with 1,208 mergers involving $2.3 billion in capital. The merger movement resulted partly from economic weaknesses revealed by the railroad companies. The threat of vicious competition among reviving manufacturing companies prompted reorganization there too.

The most prominent of the new corporations was United States Steel. As the economy edged out of the depression, J. P. Morgan began combining separate steel-related companies to create a vertically integrated operation. Andrew Carnegie had never carried vertical integration to the point of manufacturing final steel products such as wire, barrels, or tubes. By vertically integrating to include that last step, Morgan threatened to close off a significant part of Carnegie's market. Faced with the formidable prospect of having to build his own manufacturing plants for finished products, Carnegie sold all his holdings to Morgan for $480 million. In 1901 Morgan combined Carnegie's company with his own to create United States Steel, the first corporation capitalized at over a billion dollars (see Figure 16.4).

As with railroad reorganization in the 1880s, investment bankers usually sought two objectives in reorganizing an industry: first, to make the industry stable so that investments would yield predictable dividends, and second, to make the industry efficient and productive so that dividends would be high. Toward that end, investment bankers not only drove the mergers but also placed their representatives on the boards of directors of the newly created companies, to guarantee that those two objectives were top priority. By 1912, the three leading New York banking firms together occupied 341 directorships in 112 major companies. Investment bankers argued that benefits from their activities extended far beyond the dividends that shareholders received. One of Morgan's

financial panic Widespread anxiety about financial and commercial matters; in a panic, investors often sold large amounts of stock to cut their own losses, which drove prices much lower. Banks often called in their loans, forcing investors to sell assets at reduced prices, further driving down stock prices.

boxcars An enclosed railroad car with sliding side doors, used to transport freight.

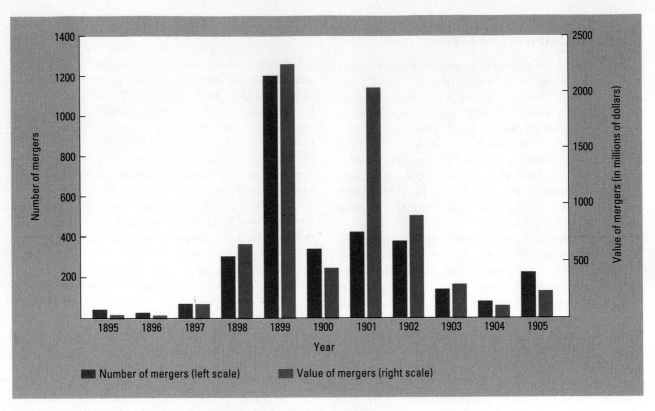

FIGURE 16.4 Recorded Mergers in Mining and Manufacturing, 1895–1905
The last few years of the 1890s and early 1900s witnessed the "merger movement," a restructuring of significant parts of corporate America. Note how the creation of United States Steel, the first "billion-dollar corporation," affects the bar for value for 1901.

associates predicted in 1901 that as a result of mergers and restructuring, "production would become more regular, labor would be more steadily employed at better wages, and panics caused by over-production would become a thing of the past."

In fact, the new industrial combinations failed to produce long-term economic stability. The economy continued to alternate between expansion and contraction. After the severe depression of 1893–1897, for example, a period of general expansion was interrupted by downturns in 1903, 1907–1908, 1910–1911, and 1913–1914. Morgan's hopes for stability through centralized control failed to be realized, but his activities and those of his contemporaries created many of the characteristics of modern business. Many industries were oligopolistic, dominated by a few vertically integrated companies, and the stock market had moved beyond the sale of railroad securities to play an important role in raising capital for industry.

Individual Voices

John D. Rockefeller Explains the Inevitability of Big Business

Rockefeller retired in the mid-1890s and devoted much of his time thereafter to philanthropy. He also took the time to write some reminiscences, which were published as *Random Reminiscences of Men and Events*. This excerpt provides Rockefeller's view on the origins of Standard Oil's monopoly over petroleum. The full text of Rockefeller's book is available online in several places.

The excerpt tells us much about Rockefeller's thinking and practices. Efficiency and economy were central to Rockefeller's vision for success in a highly competitive industry. For Rockefeller, these goals were often to be achieved through technology. In significant part, it was Standard Oil's extension of its operations to the retail level, and the aggressive competitiveness displayed at the retail level, that gave the company its reputation for ruthlessness, and here we get an idea of why Rockefeller took this approach. We also learn part of Rockefeller's argument for the inevitability of the development of big business and of monopolies and oligopolies.

❶ Here Rockefeller lays out a classic case of overproduction. What does the law of supply and demand, from basic economics, suggest for such a situation?

❷ This is Rockefeller's explanation for the origins of the cartel that became Standard Oil. How does he explain the willingness of other petroleum refiners to join him?

❸ Compare Rockefeller's use of technology as a competitive device with the practices of other entrepreneurs, especially Carnegie and Edison.

❹ Having brought former competitors together in a cartel, and having constructed technologically advanced refineries, Standard Oil now faced what problem? How did they solve the problem?

The cleansing of crude petroleum was a simple and easy process, and at first the profits were very large. Naturally, all sorts of people went into it: the butcher, the baker, and the candlestick-maker began to refine oil, and it was only a short time before more of the finished product was put on the market than could possibly be consumed. The price went down and down until the trade was threatened with ruin. . . . **❶**

This great depression led to consultations with our neighbors and friends in the business in the effort to bring some order out of what was rapidly becoming a state of chaos. To accomplish all these tasks of enlarging the market and improving the methods of manufacture in a large way was beyond the power or ability of any concern as then constituted. It could only be done, we reasoned, by increasing our capital and availing ourselves of the best talent and experience. **❷**

It was with this idea that we proceeded to buy the largest and best refining concerns and centralize the administration of them with a view to securing greater economy and efficiency. **❸** . . . To get the advantage of the facilities we had in manufacture, we sought the utmost market in all lands—we needed volume. **❹** To do this we had to create selling methods far in advance of what then existed; we had to dispose of two, or three, or four gallons of oil where one had been sold before. . . .

It is too late to argue about advantages of industrial combinations. They are a necessity. And if Americans are to have the privilege of extending their business in all the states of the Union, and into foreign countries as well, they are a necessity on a large scale, and require the agency of more than one corporation. **❺**

❺ Does it seem likely that the improved quality and quantity of consumer goods in the late nineteenth century could have been possible without the development of large corporations? Why or why not?

Study Tools

SUMMARY

After 1865, large-scale manufacturing developed quickly in the United States, built on a foundation of abundant natural resources, a pool of skilled workers, expanding harvests, and favorable government policies. The outcome was the transformation of the U.S. economy.

Entrepreneurs improved and extended railway lines, creating a national transportation network. Manufacturers and merchants now began to think in terms of a national market for raw materials and finished goods. Railroads were the first businesses to grapple with the many problems related to size, and they made choices that other businesses imitated. Investment bankers, notably J. P. Morgan, led in combining separate rail companies into larger and more profitable systems. Steel was the crucial building material for much of industrial America, and Andrew Carnegie revolutionized the steel industry. He became one of the best known of many entrepreneurs who developed manufacturing operations of unprecedented size and complexity.

What Carnegie did in steel, John D. Rockefeller did in oil. Others followed their lead, producing oligopoly and vertical integration in many industries. Technology and advertising emerged as important competitive devices. One important result was the introduction of both a wide range of new consumer goods and new ways for consumers to purchase. Some southerners promoted the creation of a New South through industrialization and a more diversified agricultural base. The outcome was mixed—the South did acquire significant industry, but the region's poverty was little reduced.

Federal policymakers hoped for the rapid development of the West and often used the public domain to accomplish that purpose. Native Americans, especially those of the Great Plains, seemed to pose an obstacle to industrial development, but most were defeated by the army and relegated to reservations. Throughout the West, railroad construction overcame the vast distances, making possible cattle raising on the western Great Plains, farming in the central part of the nation, extensive mining, and lumbering. In California especially, landowners transformed western agriculture into a large-scale commercial undertaking. Water posed a significant constraint on economic development in many parts of the West, prompting efforts to reroute natural water sources.

Throughout the late nineteenth century, the economy moved through cycles of expansion and contraction, with especially severe depressions in the 1870s and 1890s. At the end of the 1890s, a large number of mergers in mining and manufacturing were seen as having the potential to stabilize the economy, but ultimately failed to do so.

CHRONOLOGY

1850s	Development of Bessemer and Kelly steel-making processes
1861	Protective tariff
1862	Land-Grant College Act, Homestead Act, Pacific Railroad Act
1865	Civil War ends
1866–1880	Cattle drives north from Texas
1867–1868	Treaties establish major western reservations
1869	First transcontinental railroad completed
1870	Standard Oil incorporated
1870s–1880s	Extension of farming to Great Plains
1872	Montgomery Ward opens first U.S. mail-order business
1873–1879	Depression

1874	American Indian resistance ends on southern plains
1875	Andrew Carnegie opens nation's largest steel plant
1876	Alexander Graham Bell invents the telephone Indian victory in Battle of Little Big Horn
1879	Invention of the incandescent light bulb
1880s	Railroad expansion and consolidation Standard Oil Trust organized
1882–1885	Recession
1883	Northern Pacific Railroad completed to Portland
1887	American Sugar Refining Company formed
1890	Conflict at Wounded Knee Creek
1902	Reclamation Act

Study Tools

FOCUS QUESTIONS

If you have mastered this chapter, you should be able to answer these questions and to identify the terms that follow the questions.

1. ★ *What factors encouraged economic growth and industrial development after the Civil War?*

2. ★ *What was the significance of the railroad and steel industries in the new industrial economy that emerged after the Civil War?*

3. ★ *How did investment bankers such as J. P. Morgan contribute to the new industrial economy?*

4. ★ *How and why did companies expand their operations and control within an industry?*

5. ★ *In what ways was the economy of the South distinctive?*

6. ★ *What were the causes and outcomes of the Indian wars of the late nineteenth century? Could they have been avoided?*

7. ★ *What were the major ways in which the West was incorporated into the national economy?*

8. ★ *What were the major changes in the U.S. economy from the Civil War to World War I?*

KEY TERMS

cartel *(p. 415)*

protective tariff *(p. 417)*

Homestead Act *(p. 417)*

Land-Grant College Act *(p. 418)*

Pacific Railway Act *(p. 420)*

mail-order sales *(p. 423)*

John Pierpont Morgan *(p. 424)*

Andrew Carnegie *(p. 425)*

Social Darwinism *(p. 426)*

Gospel of Wealth *(p. 426)*

department store *(p. 430)*

New South *(p. 431)*

Henry Grady *(p. 431)*

horse culture *(p. 433)*

Lakota *(p. 433)*

Crazy Horse *(p. 436)*

Sitting Bull *(p. 436)*

Great Sioux War *(p. 436)*

Little Big Horn River *(p. 436)*

Chief Joseph *(p. 436)*

Ghost Dance *(p. 436)*

Wounded Knee Creek *(p. 436)*

Reclamation Act *(p. 444)*

expansion *(p. 445)*

contraction *(p. 445)*

recession/depression *(p. 445)*

 CourseMate Go to the History CourseMate website for primary source links, study tools, and review materials for this chapter. www.cengagebrain.com

17 Life in the Gilded Age, 1865–1900

Behind the Stories

Historians often call the late nineteenth century the Gilded Age, after *The Gilded Age: A Tale of Today*, a novel by Samuel L. Clemens and Charles Dudley Warner, published in 1873. In the novel—the first for either writer—Clemens and Warner satirized the business and politics of their day. You'll remember Clemens better by his pen name, Mark Twain, which he used as the author of *Tom Sawyer, Huckleberry Finn*, and other classics.

Using "the Gilded Age" to refer to the years from the late 1860s through the 1890s suggests the gleam of a surface gilded with a thin coating of gold that covers a cheap base metal underneath. Among the aspects of late-nineteenth-century life that might justify the label "gilded" were the dramatic expansion of the economy, the spectacular accomplishments of new technologies, the extravagant wealth and great power of the new industrial entrepreneurs, and the rapid economic development of the West. Just below that glittering surface lay the grim realities of life for most industrial workers and the plight of racial and ethnic minorities. You will encounter the varied layers of Gilded Age America in this chapter, which explores changes in people's lives during the thirty-five years after the Civil War.

Historians have identified four great transformations of American life between 1865 and 1900—industrialization, urbanization, immigration, and the development of the West. Each of these great changes carried profound implications for Americans living then—and since. This is the second chapter that addresses these changes in American life following the Civil War. Chapter 16, the previous chapter, looked at some of the changes brought by industrialization, especially the emergence of large-scale business and manufacturing. After you learn about new social patterns in this chapter, you'll next explore changes in politics and foreign relations in Chapter 18.

—R.W.C.

Individual Choices
Frank Roney

Frank Roney arrived in New York in 1868. Born in Ireland in 1841, he served a seven-year apprenticeship to become a skilled (journeyman) iron molder. (Iron molders make objects of cast iron by heating iron until it melts and pouring it into molds.) Some of the experienced iron molders from whom Roney learned his trade also taught him about the Friendly Society of Iron Molders, the trade union for molders. When Roney was arrested for joining the struggle for Irish independence from England, the judge gave him a choice: go to prison or leave Ireland. Roney was soon headed to America.

Frank Roney

Roney found that many American foundry workers lacked the self-respect he associated with his craft. In Ireland, molders "worked rationally, intelligently, and well," but "American molders seemed desirous of doing all the work required as if it were the last day of their lives." Roney learned that many American workers were paid by the piece rather than by the day, so the more work they did, the more they were paid. Roney was appalled. For him, being a skilled iron molder was a mark of status. He found the pace maintained by American workers to be both physically exhausting and personally degrading, and he refused to work under those conditions.

When Roney was fired from a job in Chicago for refusing to work overtime without extra pay, he moved to Omaha, worked in the shops of the Union Pacific Railroad, and became an officer in Iron Molders Union No. 190. William Sylvis, national president of this union, was also head of the National Labor Union, which sponsored the National Labor Reform Party. Roney eagerly joined, hoping the new party might end poverty. In this he was disappointed, and he continued west, arriving in San Francisco in 1875.

In San Francisco, working in the largest foundry in the West, Roney was again disgusted by the other workers, as made clear in the Individual Voices feature at the end of this chapter. "They labored hard of their volition," he wrote, "and displayed an eagerness most discouraging to one who wished to see each of them [behave like] a man." Manliness, for Roney, involved dignity: "Men who work as hacks and drudges are not those from whom to expect high thoughts or ideas of social improvement." He became active in the local molders' union and set out, in the shop and in union meetings, to persuade his fellow workers by word and deed to recognize the evils of "rushing" and competing with one another. Gradually, he sensed some success, and with it came the growth of the union. Roney helped to form the Trades and Labor Assembly, a central body for trade unions, and became a leader of organized labor in the city. Under his leadership, many San Francisco unions gained members and strength. Union activism, however, cost Roney his job. Eventually he chose to end his union work to devote his attention to his family.

Frank Roney's experiences as an immigrant, city-dweller, blue-collar worker, westerner, and union activist all involve major areas of change in American life following the Civil War. American cities grew rapidly, and technology made cities ever more exciting places, with skyscrapers, self-propelled streetcars, and electric lights. Technology joined with industry to produce such new marvels for urban consumers as telephones, phonographs, and cameras. In the midst of this growth, however, many new immigrants found themselves living in urban slums. Recent historians have looked at the ways in which urban, middle-class women began to take a greater interest in such social problems, prompting the emergence of women's groups devoted to reform. Like Roney, workers in the new industrial economy often found themselves working long hours under sometimes dangerous conditions. Like some entrepreneurs, some workers turned to combination to improve their lot, by forming unions.

THE NEW URBAN AMERICA

★ What were the key factors in the transformation of American cities in the late nineteenth century?

★ What important new social patterns emerged in urban areas in the late nineteenth century?

During the late nineteenth century, American cities boomed in size. Chicago doubled to take second rank, behind New York. In just ten years, Brooklyn grew by more than 40 percent, St. Louis by nearly 30 percent, and San Francisco by almost as much. Cities not only added more people but also expanded upward and outward, and became more complex, both socially and economically. The burgeoning cities presented new vistas of opportunity for some, especially the middle class. In the new urban environments, some women questioned traditionally defined gender roles, as did gays and lesbians. But as cities grew, so did the population of their most disadvantaged residents.

The New Face of the City

Many Americans were fascinated by their burgeoning cities. Cities boasted technological innovations that many equated with progress, but the lure of the city

walking city Term describing cities before changes in urban transportation permitted cities to expand beyond the distance that a person could easily cover on foot.

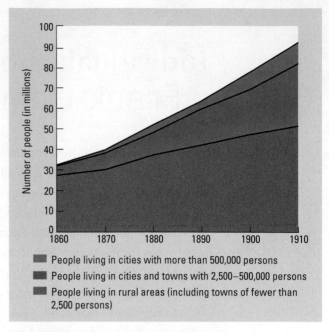

- People living in cities with more than 500,000 persons
- People living in cities and towns with 2,500–500,000 persons
- People living in rural areas (including towns of fewer than 2,500 persons)

FIGURE 17.1 Urban and Rural Population of the United States, 1860–1910
Although much of the population increase between 1860 and 1910 came in urban areas, the number of people living in rural areas increased as well. Notice, too, that the largest increase was in towns and cities that had between 2,500 and 500,000 people.

Source: U.S. Bureau of the Census, Department of Commerce, Historical Statistics of the United States, 2 vols. (Washington, D.C.: U.S. Government Printing Office, 1975), Series A-58, A-59, A-69, A-119.

stemmed from more than telephones, streetcars, and technological gadgetry. Samuel Lane Loomis in 1887 listed the many activities to be found in cities: "The churches and the schools, the theatres and concerts, the lectures, fairs, exhibitions, and galleries . . . and the mighty streams of human beings that forever flow up and down the thoroughfares." Not every urban vista was so appealing. Some visitors were shocked and repulsed by the poverty, crime, and filth that cluttered the urban landscape.

Filled with glamour and destitution, cities grew rapidly. Cities with more than 50,000 people grew almost twice as fast as rural areas (see Figure 17.1). The nation had twenty-five cities that large in 1870, with a total population of 5 million. By 1890, fifty-eight cities had reached that size and held nearly 12 million people. Nearly all these cities were in the Northeast and near the Great Lakes. The mechanization of American agriculture meant that farming required fewer workers, so America's farmlands contributed significantly to the growth of the cities, along with immigration from outside the United States, especially Europe.

The growth of manufacturing went hand in hand with urban expansion. By the late nineteenth century, the nation had developed a manufacturing belt. This region, which included nearly all the largest cities as well as the bulk of the nation's manufacturing and finance, may be thought of as constituting the nation's urban-industrial "core" (see Map 17.1). Some of the cities in this region—notably Boston, New York, Baltimore, Buffalo, and St. Louis—had long been among the busiest ports in the nation. Now manufacturing also flourished there. Other cities developed as industrial centers from their beginnings. Some cities became known for a particular product—iron and steel in Pittsburgh, clothing in New York City, meatpacking in Chicago, flour milling in Minneapolis. A few cities, especially New York, stood out as major centers for finance.

As the urban population swelled and the urban economy grew more complex, cities expanded upward and outward. In the early 1800s, most cities measured only a few miles across, and most residents got around on foot. Historians call such places "**walking cities**." Buildings were rarely higher than four stories. Small factories existed here and there among warehouses and commercial offices near the docks. In the late nineteenth century, new technologies for construction and transportation transformed the cities.

Until the 1880s, construction techniques restricted building height because the lower walls carried the structure's full weight. William LeBaron Jenney designed the first skyscraper—ten stories high, erected in Chicago in 1885. Chicago architects also took the lead in designing other tall buildings, adapting Jenney's approach by using a steel frame to carry the weight instead of the walls. Economical and efficient, skyscrapers created unique city skylines.

MAP 17.1 Cities, Industry, and Immigration

This map presents major U.S. cities, areas where immigrants lived, and the urban-industrial core region that included most cities and manufacturing. Western counties are much larger than eastern counties and were much more sparsely populated, so the western counties that show large *proportions* of immigrants did not necessarily have *numbers* of immigrants comparable to eastern cities. Copyright © Cengage Learning

Louis Sullivan, one of the Chicago architects who first created skyscrapers, designed the Wainwright Building (St. Louis, 1890) with the intention of creating what he called a "proud and soaring thing." He also tried to design exteriors that reflected the interior functions, in keeping to his rule that "form follows function." The building was widely acclaimed and often imitated.

Just as steel-frame buildings allowed cities to grow upward, so new transportation technologies permitted cities to expand outward. In the 1850s, horses pulled the first streetcars over iron rails laid in city streets. By the 1870s and 1880s, some cities boasted streetcar lines powered by underground moving cables. Electricity, however, revolutionized urban transit. Frank Sprague designed a streetcar driven by an electric motor that drew its power from an overhead wire and first installed his system in Richmond, Virginia, in 1888. Within a dozen years, electric streetcars replaced nearly all horse cars and cable cars. In the early 1900s, some large cities, choked with traffic, began to move their electrical streetcars above or below street level, thereby creating elevated trains and subways. Thus elaborate networks of rails came to connect **suburbs**

■ **suburb** A residential area lying outside the central city; many residents of suburbs work and shop in the central city though living outside it.

infrastructure Basic facilities that a society needs to function, such as transportation systems, water and power lines, and public institutions such as schools, post offices, and prisons.

to central business districts. Middle-class women wearing white gloves and stylish hats rode on streetcars to well-stocked downtown department stores. Skilled workers took other streetcar lines to and from their jobs. Streetcars also carried the typists, bookkeepers, and corporate executives who filled the banks and offices in the city's center.

New construction technologies also launched bridges spanning rivers and bays that had once limited urban growth. When the Brooklyn Bridge was completed in 1883, it was hailed as a new wonder of the world. Other great bridges soon followed.

As bridges and streetcar lines pushed outward from the city center, cities annexed suburban areas. In 1860 Chicago had occupied 17 square miles; forty years later, it took in 190 square miles. Boston grew from 5 square miles to 39, and St. Louis from 14 square miles to 61. As streetcars expanded the city, suburban railroad lines began to bring more distant villages within commuting distance of urban centers. Wealthier residents who could afford the passenger fare now left the city at the end of the workday. As early as 1873, nearly a hundred suburban communities sent between five and six thousand commuters into Chicago each day, and by 1890 seventy thousand suburbanites were pouring in daily. At about the same time, commuter lines brought more than a hundred thousand workers daily into New York City just from its northern suburbs.

New suburbs ranged outward from the city center in order of wealth. Those who could afford to travel the farthest could also afford the most expensive homes. Those too poor to ride the new transportation lines lived in densely populated and deteriorating neighborhoods in the center of the city or clustered around industrial plants. Much of the burgeoning urban middle class lived between the two extremes, far enough from the central business district that many residents rode streetcars downtown to work or shop.

Caught up in headlong growth, cities and their **infrastructure** developed with only minimal planning. Local governments did little to regulate expansion or create building standards, leaving individual landowners, developers, and builders to make most decisions about land use and construction practices. Everywhere, builders and owners hoped to produce the most space for the least cost. Such profit calculations rarely left room for amenities such as varied designs or open space. Most of the great urban parks that exist today, including Central Park in New York City, Prospect Park in Brooklyn, and Golden Gate Park in San Francisco, were established on the outskirts of their cities, before the surrounding areas were developed.

Given the rapid and largely unplanned nature of most urban growth, city governments usually had difficulty meeting all the demands for expanded municipal utilities and services—fire and police protection, schools, sewage disposal, street maintenance, water supply.

Chicago streetcars, 1906. Streetcars made it possible for cities to expand dramatically. By 1900, Chicago took in 190 square miles, up from 17 square miles in 1860. "Streetcar suburbs" took in even more territory.

The quality and quantity of the water supply varied greatly from city to city. Some cities spent enormous sums to transport water over long distances, but water quality remained a problem in most locales. As city officials began to understand that germs caused diseases, some cities introduced filtration and **chlorination** of their water. Even so, by the early twentieth century, only 6 percent of urban residents received filtered water.

City residents also faced major obstacles in disposing of sewage, cleaning streets (especially given the ever-present horses), and removing garbage. Even when cities built sewer lines, they usually dumped the untreated sewage into some nearby body of water. The disgusted mayor of Cleveland in 1881 called the Cuyahoga River "an open sewer through the center of the city"; similar situations existed in most large cities.

Few city streets were paved, and most became mud holes in the rain, threw up clouds of dust in dry weather, and froze into deep ruts in the winter. Chicago in 1890 included 2,048 miles of streets, but only 629 miles were paved, typically with wooden blocks—and Chicago was not unusual. Only in the late nineteenth century did cities begin using asphalt paving. Sometimes it was easier to pave streets than to maintain them: after clearing garbage from a street

in the 1890s, one Chicagoan discovered pavement buried under 18 inches of trash.

City utilities and services, including gas, public transit, sometimes water, and later electricity and telephone service, were typically provided by private companies operating under **franchises** from the city. Entrepreneurs eagerly competed for such franchises, sometimes bribing city officials to secure them. As a result, new residential areas sometimes had gas lines before sewers, and streetcars before paved streets.

At first, urban growth seemed to outstrip the abilities of city officials and residents to provide for its consequences. Nonetheless, most city utilities and services improved significantly between 1870 and 1900. New York City created the first uniformed police force in 1845, and other cities followed. By 1871, major cities had switched from volunteer fire companies to paid, professional firefighters. The new system proved inadequate, however, in the Great Chicago Fire of

chlorination The treatment of water with the chemical chlorine to kill germs.

franchise Government authorization allowing a company to provide a public service in a certain area.

1871, which devastated 3 square miles, including much of the downtown, killed more than 250 people, and left 18,000 homeless. Such disasters spurred efforts to improve fire protection by better training and equipping firefighters and by regulating construction so that buildings were more fire-resistant. By 1900, most American cities had impressive firefighting forces. Chicago had more firefighters and fire engines than London, a city three times its size.

The New Urban Middle Class

The Gilded Age brought significant changes to the lives of many middle-class Americans, especially those who made up the army of accountants, lawyers, secretaries, agents, and managers who staffed developing corporate headquarters and professional offices in the rising central business districts. Streetcar lines allowed this growing middle class to live in expanding suburbs distinct from both the neighborhoods of the industrial working class and the enclaves of the wealthy.

Single-family houses set amid carefully tended lawns were common in many new middle-class neighborhoods or suburbs in the late nineteenth century. Such developments accelerated the tendency of American urban and suburban areas to sprawl for miles and have population densities much lower than those of European cities of the same time. Owning property had long been central to the American dream. In the late nineteenth century, the single-family house became the realization of that dream for many middle-class families. Many members of the middle class found it especially attractive to acquire that house in a suburb connected to the city by streetcar or commuter rail. Such suburbs allowed the urban middle class to avoid the congestion of the slums, the violence of labor conflicts, and the higher property taxes that funded city governments.

In the new middle-class suburbs and urban neighborhoods, many middle-class families employed a domestic servant to assist with household chores, and middle-class women often participated in social organizations outside the home. Unlike many working-class families, middle-class parents rarely expected their children to contribute to the family's finances.

Middle-class families provided the major market for an expansion of daily newspapers, which began to include sections designed to appeal to women—household hints, fashion advice, and news of women's organizations—along with sports sections aimed at men, and comics for the children. Urban middle-class households were also likely to subscribe to family magazines such as the *Ladies' Home Journal* and the *Saturday Evening Post*. Much of the advertising in such publications was aimed at the middle class, fostering the

From Blanche Cirker, ed., "Victorian House Designs" (Courtesy of Dover Publications, 1996).

As streetcars and commuter railway lines permitted some Americans to move to the suburbs, developers and contractors depicted houses in the midst of green trees and wide lawns where children could play. This house featured a kitchen and living room on the ground floor and three bedrooms on the upper floor. Twelve hundred dollars, the cost to build this house in 1887, did not include the cost of the land. Such a house was far beyond the reach of an average blue-collar worker. This illustration appeared in *Scientific American, Architects and Builders Edition*, June 1887.

emergence of what historians have called a **consumer culture** among middle-class women, who became responsible for nearly all their family's shopping.

Middle-class parents' concern for their children's education combined with other factors to produce important changes in American education. Between 1870 and 1900, most northern and western states and territories established school attendance laws, requiring children between certain ages (usually 8 to 14) to attend school for a minimum number of weeks each year, typically twelve to sixteen. The largest increase in school attendance was at the secondary level. There were fewer than 800 high schools in the entire nation in 1878, but 5,500 by 1898. The proportion of high school graduates in the population tripled in the late nineteenth century. By 1890, four-year, public high schools were to be found in urban areas throughout most of the country, except for the South (as discussed later in this chapter). The high school curriculum also changed, adding courses in the sciences, civics, business, home economics, and skills needed by industry, such as drafting, woodworking, and the mechanical trades. From 1870 onward, women outnumbered men among high school graduates. The growth of high schools, however, was largely an urban, middle-class phenomenon. In rural areas, few students continued beyond the eighth grade, and urban working-class youth often started working full-time at about the same age.

College enrollments also grew, with the largest gains in the new state universities created under the Land-Grant College Act of 1862. Even so, college students came disproportionately from middle-class and upper-class families and rarely from farms. The college curriculum changed from courses required of all students (Latin, Greek, mathematics, rhetoric, and religion) to a system in which students focused on a major. Land-grant universities were required to provide instruction in engineering and agriculture. Other new college subjects included economics, political science, modern languages, laboratory sciences, business administration, and teacher preparation. In 1870 the curricula in most colleges still resembled those of a century before. By 1900, curricula looked much like those today.

Despite the growing female majority through the high school level, far fewer women than men marched in college graduation processions. Only one college graduate in seven was a woman in 1870, and this ratio improved to only one in four by 1900 (see Figure 17.2). In 1879 fewer than half of the nation's colleges admitted women, although most public universities did so. Twenty years later, four-fifths of all colleges, universities, and professional schools enrolled women.

Regardless of such impressive gains for coeducation, some colleges remained all-male enclaves, especially prestigious private institutions such as

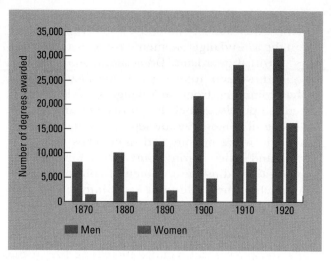

FIGURE 17.2 Number of First Degrees Awarded by Colleges and Universities, 1870–1920
This figure shows the change in the number of people receiving B.A., B.S., or other first college degrees, at ten-year intervals from 1870 to 1920. Notice that after 1890, the number of women increased more rapidly than the number of men.

Source: U.S. Department of Commerce, Bureau of the Census, Historical Statistics of the United States, Colonial Times to 1970, Bicentennial edition, 2 vols. (Washington, D.C.: Government Printing Office, 1975), 1: 385–386.

Harvard and Yale. Colleges exclusively for women began to appear after the Civil War, partly because so many colleges still refused to admit women and partly in keeping with the notion that men and women should occupy "separate spheres." Such institutions also provided opportunities for women as faculty members. The initial faculty of Vassar College, chartered in 1861, consisted of eight men and twenty-two women, including Maria Mitchell, a leading astronomer and the first female member of the American Academy of Arts and Sciences.

Redefining Gender Roles

Greater educational opportunities for women marked one part of a major reconstruction of gender roles. Throughout the nineteenth century, most Americans defined women's roles as those of wife and mother and guardian of the family, responsible for its moral, spiritual, and physical well-being. This emphasis on **domesticity** also permitted women to take important roles in the church

■ **consumer culture** A consumer buys products for personal use; a consumer culture emphasizes the values and attitudes that derive from the participants' roles as consumers.

■ **domesticity** The notion common throughout much of the nineteenth century that women should focus on the home, nurture of children, church, and school.

and the school. Business and politics, however, with their competition and potential for corruption, were thought to endanger women's roles as their families' spiritual guardians. Domesticity, some argued, required women to occupy a so-called **separate sphere**, immune from such dangers. Widely touted from the pulpits and in the journals of the day, the concepts of domesticity and separate spheres applied mostly to white middle- and upper-class women in towns and cities. Farm women and working-class women (including most women of color) witnessed too much of the world to fit easily into the patterns of dainty innocence prescribed by advocates of separate spheres.

The concepts of domesticity and, especially, separate spheres came under increasing fire in the late nineteenth century. One challenge came through education. As more and more women finished college, some entered the professions. In 1849 Elizabeth Blackwell became the first woman to complete medical school, and she helped to open a medical school for women in 1868. By the 1880s, some twenty-five hundred women held medical degrees. After 1900, however, medical schools imposed admission practices that sharply reduced the number of female medical students. In 1869, Arabella Mansfield became the first woman admitted to practice law, but the entire nation counted only sixty practicing women attorneys ten years later. Most law schools refused to admit women until the 1890s. Other professions also yielded very slowly to women seeking admission.

Professional careers attracted a few women, but many middle- and upper-class women in towns and cities became involved in other women's activities, especially women's clubs, which claimed 100,000 members nationwide by the 1890s. Ida Wells-Barnett, a crusader for black civil rights, actively promoted the development of black women's clubs. Such clubs often began within the separate women's sphere as forums for discussing literature or art, but they sometimes led women into reform activities in the public sphere. (Of course, women had publicly participated in reform before, especially in the movement to abolish slavery.)

■ **separate spheres** The notion that men should engage in the public sphere of business and politics but women should limit themselves to the private, domestic sphere. Women and some men increasingly challenged this idea in the late nineteenth century.

■ **Woman's Christian Temperance Union** (WCTU) Woman's organization founded in 1874 that opposed alcoholic beverages and supported reforms such as woman suffrage.

Masons The Ancient Free and Accepted Masons is one of the largest secret fraternal societies. The order uses allegorical rituals, open only to members, to teach moral values. It is limited to men but has auxiliaries open to women.

The **Woman's Christian Temperance Union** (WCTU) was organized in 1874 by women who regarded alcohol as the chief reason for men's neglect and abuse of their families. WCTU members committed themselves to total abstinence from all alcohol and sought to protect the home and family by converting others to abstinence and the legal prohibition of alcohol. The organization typically operated through old-stock Protestant churches—especially the Methodists, Presbyterians, Congregationalists, and Baptists. From 1879 until her death in 1898, Frances Willard was the driving force in the organization. Her personal motto was "Do everything," and she was untiring in her work for temperance. By the early 1890s, the WCTU claimed 150,000 members, making it the largest women's organization in the nation. Yet for Willard the organization remained very much devoted to the ideals of domesticity. She once offered a simple statement of purpose for the WCTU: "to make the whole world homelike."

Women's church organizations, clubs, and reform societies all provided experience in working together toward a common cause and sometimes in seeking changes in public policy. Through them, women cultivated leadership skills. These experiences and contacts contributed to the growing effectiveness of women's efforts to establish their right to vote. In 1882 the WCTU endorsed woman suffrage, the first support for that cause from a major women's organization other than those formed specifically to advocate woman suffrage.

Just as women's gender roles were undergoing reconstruction in the late nineteenth century, so too were those of men. In the early nineteenth century, manliness was defined largely in terms of "character," which included courage, honor, independence, duty, and loyalty (including loyalty to a political party), along with providing a good home for a family. With the growth of the urban industrial society, fewer men were self-employed (and thus no longer "independent"), and fewer men had the opportunity to demonstrate courage or boldness. The rise of big-city political organizations dominated by saloonkeepers and working-class immigrants caused some middle- and upper-class males to question older notions of party loyalty.

In response, some middle-class men turned to activities that emphasized male bonding or masculinity. Fraternal organizations modeled on the **Masons** multiplied in the late nineteenth century, usually providing both a ritualistic retreat to a preindustrial era and meager insurance benefits for widows and orphans. Professional athletics, including baseball and boxing, began to attract male spectators of all classes. The Young Men's Christian Association (YMCA) spread rapidly in American cities after the Civil War, emphasizing Christian values, physical fitness, and service. Wilderness camping and hunting—necessities for many Americans in earlier times—became a middle- and upper-class

The WCTU developed out of activities by women in various locations in the early 1870s. These early temperance advocates gathered outside saloons, sing hymns, and urge men to come out or not go in. This group of temperance workers was photographed in Mount Vernon, Ohio, around 1873 or 1874.

male sport, a demonstration of masculinity. Theodore Roosevelt claimed that hunting big game promoted the manly virtues of "nerve control" and "cool-headedness."

Emergence of a Gay and Lesbian Subculture

Urbanization and economic change contributed to the social redefinition of gender roles for middle-class women and men, but a quite different redefinition occurred at the same time, as burgeoning cities provided a setting for the development of gay and lesbian subcultures.

Homosexual behavior was illegal everywhere. At the same time, however, men and women engaged in a wide variety of socially acceptable same-sex relationships. The concept of separate spheres and the tendency for most schools and workplaces to be segregated by sex meant that many men and women spent much of their time with others of their own sex. Many occupations involved working closely with a partner, sometimes over long periods of time. Such partners—both male

or both female—could speak of each other with deep affection without violating prevailing social norms. Same-sex relationships may not have involved physical contact, although kisses and hugs—and sleeping in the same bed—were common expressions of affection among young women. Participants in such same-sex relationships did not consider themselves to be committing what the laws called "an unnatural act," and most married partners of the opposite sex.

Same-sex relationships that involved genital contact violated the law and the expectations of society. In rural communities, where most people knew one another, people physically attracted to those of their own sex apparently suppressed those desires or exercised them discreetly. The record of convictions for **sodomy** indicates that some failed to conceal their

sodomy Varieties of sexual intercourse prohibited by law in the nineteenth century, typically including intercourse between two males.

activities. A few men and somewhat more women changed their dress and behavior, passed for a member of the other sex, and married someone of their own sex.

In the late nineteenth century, in parts of the United States and Europe, burgeoning cities permitted an anonymity not possible in rural societies. Homosexuals and lesbians gravitated toward the largest cities and began to create distinctive **subcultures**. By the 1890s, one researcher reported that "perverts of both sexes maintained a sort of social set-up in New York City, had their places of meeting, and [the] advantage of police protection." Reports of regular homosexual meeting places—clubs, restaurants, steam baths, parks, streets—also issued from Boston, Chicago, New Orleans, St. Louis, and San Francisco. Although most participants in these subcultures were secretive, some flaunted their sexuality.

In the 1880s, physicians began to study members of these emerging subcultures and created medical names for them, including "homosexual," "lesbian," "invert," and "pervert." Earlier, law and religion had defined particular *actions* as illegal or immoral. The new, clinical definitions emphasized not the actions but instead the *persons* taking the actions. As medical and legal definitions shifted from actions to persons, the nature of same-sex relationships also changed. Once-acceptable behavior, including expressions of affection between heterosexuals of the same sex, became less common as individuals tried to avoid any suggestion that they were anything but heterosexual.

"How the Other Half Lives"

In 1890 Jacob Riis shocked many Americans with the revelations in *How the Other Half Lives*. Of New York City's million and a half inhabitants, Riis claimed, half a million (136,000 families) had begged for food at some time over the preceding eight years. Of these, more than half were unemployed, but only 6 percent were physically unable to work. Most of Riis's book described the appalling conditions of **tenements**—home, he claimed, to three-quarters of the city's population.

Strictly speaking, a tenement is a building occupied by three or more families, but the term came to imply overcrowded and badly maintained housing that was hazardous to the health and safety of its residents. Riis described the typical, cramped New York tenement of his day as

> a brick building from four to six stories high on the street, frequently with a store on the first floor. . . . Four families occupy each floor, and a set of rooms consists of one or two dark closets, used as bedrooms, with a living room twelve feet by ten. The staircase is too often a dark well in the center of the house . . . no direct through ventilation is possible.

Such buildings, Riis insisted, "are the hotbeds of the epidemics that carry death to rich and poor alike; the nurseries of pauperism and crime that fill our jails and police courts. . . . Above all, they touch the family life with deadly moral contagion." He especially deplored the harmful influence of poverty and miserable housing conditions on children and families.

Crowded conditions in working-class sections of large cities developed in part because so many of the poor needed to live within walking distance of sources of employment for various family members. By dividing buildings into small rental units, landlords packed in more tenants and collected more rent. To pay the rent, many tenants took in lodgers. Such practices produced shockingly high population densities in lower-income urban neighborhoods.

No other city was as densely populated as New York, but nearly all urban, working-class neighborhoods were crowded. Most Chicago stockyard workers, for example, lived in small row houses near the slaughterhouses. Many owned their own homes. A survey in 1911 revealed that three-quarters of the houses were subdivided into two or more living units, typically of four rooms each, and that a small shanty often sat in the backyard. More than half of all families took in lodgers, and lodgers who worked different shifts at the stockyards sometimes took turns sleeping in the same bed.

Few agreed on the causes of urban poverty, still fewer on its cure. Riis divided the blame among greedy landlords, corrupt officials, and the poor themselves. Henry George, a San Francisco journalist, in *Progress and Poverty*, pointed to the increase in the value of real estate due to urbanization and industrialization, which made it difficult or impossible for many to afford a home of their own. In contrast, the Charity Organization Society (COS), with chapters in a hundred cities by 1895, claimed that, in most cases, individual character defects produced poverty and that assistance for such people only rewarded immorality or laziness. Public or private help should be given only after careful investigation, the COS insisted, and only until the person secured work. Moreover, COS officials expected the recipients of aid to be moral, thrifty, and hardworking.

subculture A group whose members differ from the dominant culture in some values or interests but who share most values and interests with the dominant culture.

tenement A multifamily apartment building, often unsafe, unsanitary, and overcrowded.

This photograph from Jacob Riis's book *How the Other Half Lives* shows an interior court on the Lower East Side of New York City, open to the sky above. As the photograph suggests, such places were often the playground for children of the poor residents. On the far right is a water pump, probably the source of water for the residents. Adding such powerful visual images to Riis's book—possible because of new printing technologies—greatly increased their effectiveness in mobilizing reform.

NEW SOUTH, OLD PROBLEMS

★ *What new social patterns appeared in the South after the end of Reconstruction?*

★ *How did southern racial relations develop after the end of Reconstruction?*

Map 17.1 makes clear that the booming cities of the Gilded Age were located mostly in New England, the Middle Atlantic States, and the east North Central states. As discussed in Chapter 16, some southerners worked to promote a more diverse economic base, with more manufacturing and less reliance on a few staple agricultural crops; they and their neighbors—white and black alike—grappled, too, with the legacy of slavery, Civil War, Reconstruction, and poverty. In the end, white southerners created a racially segregated social structure that persisted with little change for more than a half-century.

Social Patterns in the New South

Of the nation's twenty-five largest cities in 1890, only New Orleans was located in the South, and no other southern city came close to its 242,000 people. Atlanta, which prided itself as the center of the New South and had nearly doubled in size between 1880 and 1890, counted nearly 81,000 people in 1890 but ranked only forty-first among the nation's cities. Birmingham, center of the developing southern iron and steel industry, grew by ten times between 1880 and 1900, but still ranked only one hundredth in the nation in size as late as 1900. Thus, while an urban middle class did develop and grow in the South, it was proportionately smaller than its counterpart to the north—and was sharply divided by the lines of race.

Education lagged throughout much of the South, especially in rural areas. Compared with much of the rest of the nation, fewer children attended school in

Library of Congress.

In 1908, Lewis Hine, an investigative photographer working for the National Child Labor Committee, documented the exploitation of American children. His photographs—some of which are among the most famous photographs ever taken—made clear that violations of child labor laws were widespread, and that child labor was robbing children of their youth, of education, and of opportunities for a better life. Hine recorded this information about the photo on the left: "Furman Owens, 12 years old. Can't read. Doesn't know his A, B, C's. Said, 'Yes I want to learn but can't when I work all the time.' Been in the mills 4 years, 3 years in the Olympia Mill. Columbia, S[outh].C[arolina]." For the photo on the right, Hine wrote, "The overseer said apologetically, 'She just happened in.' She was working steadily. The mills seem full of youngsters who 'just happened in' or 'are helping sister.' Newberry, S.C."

the South, where the school term was often limited to a few months, and school facilities were often inadequate. Few southern states had compulsory school attendance laws. Southerners were slow to create public high schools—as late as 1903, the entire state of Georgia had only four four-year, public high schools. Instead, most public schools stopped at the eighth grade, and private academies educated the children of the upper class. Some of the industries of the New South, especially textiles and cigarettes, were built on child labor, so many children worked instead of attending school. Seventy percent of southern cotton-mill workers were younger than 21, and most were under 14. Mostly girls, they worked 70-hour weeks and earned 10 to 20 cents a day. Not surprisingly, illiteracy remained much higher in the South than elsewhere in the nation. As late as 1900, 10 percent of the southern white population was illiterate, compared with fewer than 4 percent in the rest of the country. Illiteracy among African Americans was significantly higher—35 percent in the South, and 19 percent in the rest of the country.

Despite repeated backing for the idea of a New South by some southern leaders, and despite growth of some industry in the South, the late nineteenth century was also the time when the myths of the **Old South** and the **Lost Cause** reached into nearly every aspect of white southern life. Popular fiction and song, North and South, romanticized the pre–Civil War "Old South" as a place of gentility and gallantry, where "kindly" plantation owners cared for "loyal" slaves. The "Lost Cause" myth portrayed the Confederacy as a heroic, even noble, effort to retain the life and values of the Old South. Leading southerners—especially Democratic Party leaders—promoted the Lost Cause myth. Hundreds of statues of Confederate soldiers appeared on courthouse lawns, and gala commemorative events and organizations reflected devotion to the myth among many white southerners. One of the few dissenting voices was that of Samuel Clemens (Mark Twain).

The Second Mississippi Plan and the Atlanta Compromise

Although Reconstruction ended in 1877, the Civil Rights Act of 1875 should have protected African Americans against discrimination in public places. Some state laws required racial separation—for example, many states prohibited racial intermarriage. State or local law, or sometimes local practice, had produced racially separate school systems, churches, hospitals, cemeteries, and other voluntary organizations. Segregation

Old South Term for a romanticized view of the pre–Civil War South as a place of gentility and gallantry.

Lost Cause Term for a romanticized view of the Confederate struggle in the Civil War as a noble but doomed effort to preserve a way of life.

existed throughout the South, driven by local custom and the ever-present threat of violence against any African American who dared to challenge it. Restrictions on black political participation were also extralegal, enforced through coercion or intimidation.

Then, in the **Civil Rights Cases** of 1883, the U.S. Supreme Court ruled the Civil Rights Act of 1875 unconstitutional. The Court said that the "equal protection" promised by the Fourteenth Amendment applied only to state governments, not to individuals or companies. Though state governments were obligated to treat all citizens as equal before the law, private businesses need not do the same. Southern lawmakers soon began to require businesses to practice segregation. In 1887 the Florida legislature ordered separate accommodations on railroad trains. Mississippi passed a similar law the next year, and other southern states soon followed.

Mississippi whites took a more brazen step in 1890, holding a state constitutional convention to eliminate African Americans' participation in politics. The new provisions did not mention the word *race*. Instead, they imposed a **poll tax**, a literacy test, and other requirements for voting. Everyone understood, though, that these measures were designed to **disfranchise** black voters. Men who failed the literacy test could vote if they could understand a section of the state constitution or law when a local (white) official read it to them. The typical result was that the only illiterates who could vote were white. Most of the South watched this so-called Second Mississippi Plan unfold with great interest.

In 1895 a black educator signaled his apparent willingness to accept disfranchisement and segregation for the moment. Born into slavery in 1856, **Booker T. Washington** worked as a janitor while studying at Hampton Normal and Agricultural Institute in Virginia, a school that combined preparation for elementary school teaching with vocational education in agriculture and industrial work. Washington then taught at Hampton. In 1881 the Alabama legislature authorized a black **normal school** at Tuskegee. Washington became its principal, and he made Tuskegee Normal and Industrial Institute into a leading black educational institution.

In 1895 Atlanta hosted the Cotton States and International Exposition. The exposition directors invited Washington to speak at the opening ceremonies, hoping he could reach out to southern whites, southern blacks, and northern whites. Washington did not disappoint the directors. In his speech, he seemed to accept an inferior status for blacks for the present: "No race can prosper till it learns that there is as much dignity in tilling a field as in writing a poem. It is at the bottom of life we must begin, and not at the top." While implying that equal rights had to be earned, Washington also seemed to condone segregation: "In all things that are purely social, we can be as separate as the fingers, yet one as the hand in all things essential to mutual progress."

Booker T. Washington posed for this formal portrait around the time of his Atlanta address.

The speech—soon dubbed the **Atlanta Compromise**—won great acclaim. Southern whites were pleased to hear a black educator urge his race to accept segregation and disfranchisement. Northern whites too were receptive to the notion that the South would work out its race relations by itself. Until his death in 1915,

■ **Civil Rights Cases** Supreme Court decisions in 1883 that specified that private companies could legally discriminate against individuals based on race.

■ **poll tax** Annual tax imposed on each citizen; used in some southern states to disfranchise black voters, as the only penalty for not paying was loss of voting rights.

disfranchise To take away the right to vote.

■ **Booker T. Washington** Former slave who became an educator and founded Tuskegee Institute, a leading black educational institution; known as an advocate of accommodation with white southerners.

normal school Two-year school for training teachers for grades 1–8.

■ **Atlanta Compromise** Name applied by Booker T. Washington's critics to his 1895 speech urging African Americans to temporarily accept segregation and disfranchisement.

In the Wider World

Washington was the most prominent black leader in the nation, at least among white Americans.

Among African Americans, Washington's message found a mixed reception. Some accepted his approach as best for the moment. Others criticized him for sacrificing black rights. Henry M. Turner, a bishop of the African Methodist Episcopal Church in Atlanta, declared that Washington "will have to live a long time to undo the harm he has done our race." Privately, however, Washington never accepted disfranchisement and segregation as permanent fixtures in southern life.

Even as African Americans debated Washington's Atlanta speech, southern lawmakers were redefining the legal status of African Americans. State after state followed the lead of Mississippi and disfranchised black voters. Louisiana, in 1898, added the infamous **grandfather clause**, specifying that men who failed to meet new requirements could vote if their fathers or grandfathers had been eligible to vote in 1867 (before the Fourteenth Amendment extended the suffrage to African Americans). Thus, poor or illiterate whites could vote. Methods varied, but each southern state set up barriers to voting and then carved holes through which only whites could pass. Southern Democrats, who had long defined themselves as the "white man's party" or the party of white supremacy, also restricted their primaries and conventions to whites only. South

Carolina took this step first, in 1896, and other states followed.

Southern lawmakers also began to extend segregation by law, especially after the U.S. Supreme Court's decision in **Plessy v. Ferguson** (1896), involving a Louisiana law requiring segregated railroad cars. When the Court ruled that "separate but equal" facilities did not violate the equal protection clause of the Fourteenth Amendment, southern legislators applied that reasoning elsewhere, requiring segregation of almost everything—and especially public places such as parks and restaurants.

Violence against African Americans accompanied the new laws, providing an unmistakable lesson in the consequences of resistance. From 1885 to 1900, when the South was redefining relations between the races, the region witnessed more than twenty-five hundred deaths by lynching—about one every two days. The victims were almost all African Americans, and the largest numbers were in the states with the most black residents.

ETHNICITY AND RACE IN THE GILDED AGE

★ How did the expectations of European immigrants differ from their actual experiences?

★ Compare experiences of Chinese Americans, American Indians, Mexican Americans, and African Americans in the Gilded Age.

By 1890, immigrants made up more than 40 percent of the population of New York, San Francisco, and Chicago, and more than a third of the population in several other major cities. The United States has always attracted large numbers of immigrants, but never before experienced a flood of immigrants like that between the Civil War and World War I. Nearly all these immigrants came from Europe, and many

grandfather clause Louisiana rule that permitted a man to vote if his father or grandfather was eligible in 1867, allowing white men to circumvent rules disfranchising blacks; now refers to any law that exempts some people from current regulations based on past practice.

■ **Plessy v. Ferguson** Supreme Court decision in 1896 upholding a Louisiana law requiring segregation of railroad facilities; argued that "separate but equal" facilities were constitutional under the Fourteenth Amendment.

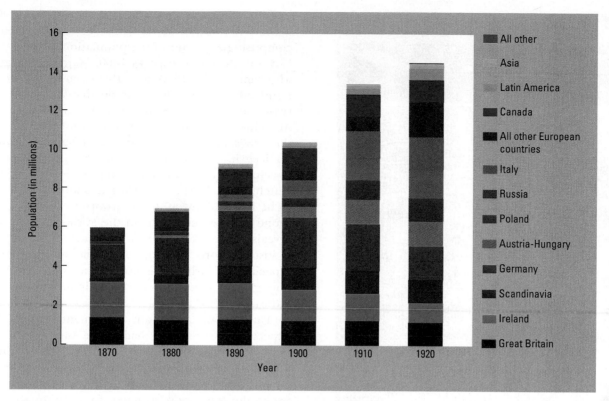

FIGURE 17.3 Foreign-Born Population of the United States, 1870–1920
This graph shows the largest foreign-born groups living in the United States at the time of the census every ten years. The number of foreign-born increased dramatically during these fifty years, and the foreign-born were increasingly diverse by country of origin.

Source: U.S. Department of Commerce, Bureau of the Census, Historical Statistics of the United States, Colonial Times to 1970, Bicentennial edition, 2 vols. (Washington, D.C.: Government Printing Office, 1975), 1: 116–117.

settled in cities. Significant numbers of immigrants also came from Asia, nearly all of whom settled in the West. At the same time, American Indians and Latinos in the Southwest, like African Americans in the South, faced new constraints on their choices and opportunities.

A Flood of Immigrants from Europe

The numbers of immigrants varied from year to year—higher in prosperous years, lower in depression years—but the trend was constantly upward. Nearly a quarter of a million arrived in 1865, two-thirds of a million in 1881, and a million in 1905. In the 1870s and 1880s, most immigrants came from Great Britain, Ireland, **Scandinavia**, Germany, and Canada, but after about 1890 increasing numbers arrived from southern and eastern Europe. By 1910, immigrants and their children made up more than 35 percent of the total population. Figure 17.3 shows the place of birth of the foreign-born population for the census years from 1870 through 1920. Note especially how the foreign-born population became increasingly diverse after 1890.

Immigrants left their former homes for a variety of reasons. In Ireland, for example, a fourfold population increase between 1750 and 1850 combined with changes in agriculture to push people off the land. Repeated failure of potato crops after 1845 produced widespread **famine** and starvation, greatly increasing migration. Similar population pressures in other parts of Europe, though without famine, produced significant population movements—from rural areas to cities, to other parts of Europe, to other parts of the world, including Canada, Argentina, and Australia.

The United States attracted the largest number and the greatest diversity of European immigrants. Some came because of the reputation of the United States for democracy and toleration of religious difference. But nearly all came because America was the "land of opportunity." They came, as one bluntly said,

Scandinavia The region of northern Europe consisting of Norway, Sweden, Denmark, and Iceland.

famine A serious and widespread shortage of food.

Ethnicity and Race in the Gilded Age   **467**

Railroad companies, seeking to sell their land grants, advertised in Europe for immigrants to buy farmland in the West. This poster, issued by the Burlington and Missouri Railroad, is in Czech, but the same poster was issued in German and Swedish. The sequence of drawings shows a six-year transition from bare prairie to prosperous farm. Such advertising helped to attract European immigrants to the north-central states (see Map 17.1).

for "jobs" and, as another declared, "for money." In fact, the reasons for immigrating to America varied from person to person, country to country, and year to year.

Irish immigrants, many desperately poor, arrived in greatest numbers before the Civil War, but Irish

manufacturing belt The region that included most factories and, in the late nineteenth century, also included most of the nation's large cities and railroad lines and much of its mining.

assimilation Among culturally distinct groups, the process of adopting the behaviors and values of the dominant society and its culture.

immigration continued at high levels until the 1890s. Many Irish settled in the cities of the Northeast, comprising a quarter of the population in New York City and Boston as early as 1860. Many immigrants who came in the 1870s and 1880s found that good farmland was available in the north-central states at reasonable prices or even free under the Homestead Act. One woman recalled that, in rural Nebraska in the 1880s, her family could attend Sunday church services in Norwegian, Danish, Swedish, French, Czech, or German, as well as English. Scandinavians, Dutch, Swiss, Czechs, and Germans were most likely to be farmers, but all those groups were also to be found in cities, especially in the Midwest. Map 17.1 reveals concentrations of immigrants in the urban-industrial core region, or **manufacturing belt**, especially in urban areas, but shows clearly that immigrant communities were not limited to cities or industrial areas.

Patterns of immigrant settlement reflect the expectations immigrants had about America, as well as opportunities they found when they arrived. After 1890, farmland was more difficult to obtain. The 1890s also marked a shift in the sources of immigration, with proportionately more coming from southern and eastern Europe and arriving with little or no capital. Newcomers after 1890 were more likely to find work in the rapidly expanding industries, especially mining, transportation, and manufacturing. Of course, there were many individual variations on these patterns. Some immigrants coming after 1890 intended to become farmers and succeeded. Many who came before 1890 became industrial workers or took other urban jobs.

In the nineteenth century, most old-stock Americans assumed that immigrants should quickly learn English, become citizens, and restructure their lives and values to resemble those of long-time residents. Most immigrants, however, resisted rapid **assimilation**. For the majority, assimilation took place over a lifetime or even over generations. Most retained elements of their own cultures even as they embraced their new lives in America. Their sense of identity drew on two elements—where they had come from and where they lived now—and they often came to think of themselves as hyphenated Americans: German-Americans, Irish-Americans, Norwegian-Americans.

On arriving in America, with its strange language and customs, many immigrants sought others who shared their cultural values, practiced their religion, and especially, spoke their language. Ethnic communities emerged wherever there were large numbers of immigrants. These communities played a significant role in newcomers' transition from the old country to America. They gave new immigrants a chance to learn about their new home with assistance from those who had come earlier. At the same time, newcomers could, without apology or embarrassment, retain cultural values and behaviors from their homelands. Foreign-language newspapers helped to connect the old country to the new, for they provided news from the old country as well as from other similar communities in the United States.

For members of nearly every **ethnic group**, religious institutions provided important building blocks of ethnic group identity. Protestant immigrant groups created new church organizations based on both theology and language. Catholic parishes in immigrant neighborhoods often took on the ethnic characteristics of the community, with services in the immigrants' language and special observances transplanted from the old country. Jewish congregations, too, often differed according to the ethnic background of their members.

Nativism

Though most immigrants changed their behavior, many old-stock Americans (including some only a generation removed from immigrant forebears themselves) expected immigrants to lay aside their previous identities and blend into prevailing cultural patterns. But many old-stock Americans fretted over the multiplication of German and Italian newspapers, feared to go into communities where they rarely heard an English sentence, and shuddered at the sprouting of Catholic schools. Such fears and misgivings fostered the growth of **nativism**: the view that old-stock values and social patterns were preferable to those of immigrants. Nativists argued that only their values and institutions were genuinely American, and they feared that immigrants threatened those traditions.

Nativism was often linked to anti-Catholicism. Irish and German immigrant groups, and later Italian and Polish groups, included large numbers of Catholics, and many old-stock Americans came to identify the Catholic Church as an immigrant church. The **American Protective Association** (APA), founded in 1887, loudly proclaimed itself the voice of anti-Catholicism. Its members pledged not to hire Catholics, not to vote for them, and not to strike with them. A half-million strong by 1894, APA members often tried to dominate the Republican Party—and succeeded in parts of the Midwest—before they died out by the late 1890s.

Jews, too, faced religious antagonism. In the 1870s, increasing numbers of organizations and businesses began to discriminate against Jews. Some employers refused to hire Jews. After 1900, such discrimination intensified. Many social organizations barred Jews from membership, and **restrictive covenants** kept them from buying homes in certain neighborhoods.

During the 1890s, a diverse political coalition emerged aimed at reducing immigration. Labor organizations began to look at immigrants as potential threats to jobs and wage levels. Some employers began to connect immigrants with unions and radicalism and to charge that unions represented foreign, un-American influences. Foreign-born radicals and **anarchists** were a special target, as newspapers claimed that "there is no such thing as an American anarchist." In 1901 Leon Czolgosz, an American-born anarchist with a foreign-sounding name, assassinated President William McKinley, and Congress promptly passed a bill barring anarchists from immigrating to the United States.

During the 1890s, nativism grew as the sources of European immigration began to shift from northwestern Europe to southern and eastern Europe, bringing larger numbers of Italians, Poles and other Slavs, and eastern European Jews. Anti-Catholicism and anti-Semitism combined to create a sense that these "**new immigrants**" were less desirable than "**old immigrants**" from northwestern Europe.

The arrival of many "new immigrants" after 1890 coincided with a growing tendency to glorify Anglo-Saxons (ancestors of the English) and accomplishments by the English and English Americans. Proponents of Anglo-Saxonism became alarmed by statistics showing old-stock Americans having fewer children than immigrants. Some voiced fears of "race suicide" in which Anglo-Saxons allowed themselves to be bred out of existence. With such anxieties feeding their prejudices, some nativists became blatant racists. By the 1890s, these economic, political, religious, and racist strains converged in demands that the federal government restrict immigration from Europe.

---

ethnic group A group that shares a racial, religious, linguistic, cultural, or national heritage.

■ **nativism** The view that old-stock values and social patterns were preferable to those of immigrants.

■ **American Protective Association** (APA) An anti-Catholic organization founded in Iowa in 1887 and active during the next decade.

restrictive covenant Provision in a property title restricting subsequent sale or use of the property, often specifying sale only to a white Christian.

anarchist A person who believes that all forms of government are oppressive and should be abolished.

"new immigrants" Newcomers from southern and eastern Europe who began to arrive in the United States in significant numbers during the 1890s and after.

"old immigrants" Newcomers from northern and western Europe who made up much of the immigration to the United States before the 1890s.

Immigrants to the Golden Mountain

The West has long had greater ethnic diversity than the rest of the nation (as illustrated in Figure 17.4). In 1900 the western half of the United States included more than 80 percent of all Native Americans, Mexican Americans, and Asian Americans. Between 1854 and 1882, some 300,000 Chinese immigrants entered the United States. Most came from southern China, which in the 1840s and 1850s suffered from political instability, economic distress, and famine. Among early Chinese immigrants who came as part of the California gold rush, California became known as *gam saan*, or "gold mountain." Many Chinese worked in mining or construction, especially western railroad building. Others worked as agricultural laborers and farmers, notably in California. Some made important contributions to crop development, especially fruit growing.

In San Francisco and elsewhere in the West, Chinese immigrants established **Chinatowns**—relatively autonomous and largely self-contained Chinese communities. In San Francisco's Chinatown, immigrants formed kinship organizations and district associations (whose members had come from the same part of China) to assist and protect each other. A confederation of such associations, the Chinese Consolidated Benevolent Association (often called the "Six Companies"), eventually dominated the social and economic life of Chinese communities in much of the West. Such communities were largely male, partly because immigration officials permitted only a few Chinese women to enter the country, apparently to prevent an American-born generation. As was true in many largely male communities, gambling and prostitution flourished, giving Chinatowns reputations as centers for vice.

Almost from the beginning, Chinese immigrants encountered discrimination and violence. During the Gold Rush, a California state tax on foreign-born miners posed a significant burden on Chinese (and also Latino) gold seekers. During the 1870s, many white workers blamed the Chinese for driving wages down and unemployment up. In fact, different economic factors depressed wage levels and brought unemployment, but white workers seeking a scapegoat instigated anti-Chinese riots in Los Angeles in 1871 and in San Francisco in 1877. In these riots, the message was usually the same: "The Chinese Must Go."

Chinatown A section of a city inhabited chiefly by people of Chinese birth or ancestry.

■ **Chinese Exclusion Act** Act of Congress (1882) prohibiting Chinese laborers from entering the United States; extended periodically until World War II.

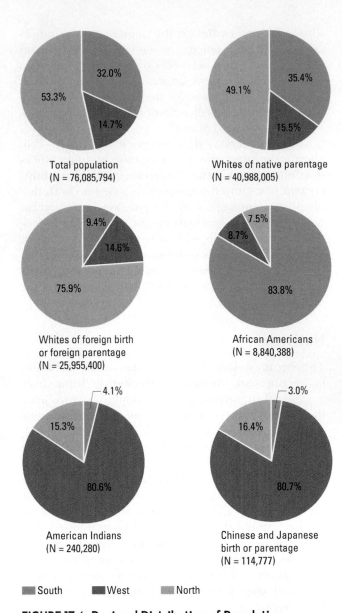

Total population
(N = 76,085,794)

Whites of native parentage
(N = 40,988,005)

Whites of foreign birth
or foreign parentage
(N = 25,955,400)

African Americans
(N = 8,840,388)

American Indians
(N = 240,280)

Chinese and Japanese
birth or parentage
(N = 114,777)

■ South ■ West ■ North

FIGURE 17.4 Regional Distribution of Population, by Race, 1900
These pie charts indicate the distinctiveness of the West with respect to race and ethnicity. Note that the West held about 15 percent of the nation's total population and about the same proportion of the nation's white population (including whites who were foreign-born or of foreign parentage) but included more than four-fifths of American Indians and those of Chinese and Japanese birth or parentage.

Source: Data from Twelfth Census of the United States: 1900 *(Washington, D.C., 1901), Population Reports, vol. 1, p. 483, Table 9.*

In 1882 Congress responded to repeated pressures from Pacific Coast unions by passing the **Chinese Exclusion Act**, prohibiting entry to all Chinese people except teachers, students, merchants, tourists, and officials. This was the first significant restriction on immigration. The law reaffirmed that Asian immigrants were not eligible to become naturalized citizens. Soon after, in 1885 anti-Chinese riots swept through much of the West. In Rock Springs, Wyoming

Territory, white coal miners burned the Chinatown and killed twenty-eight Chinese. In response, many Chinese retreated to the largest Chinatowns, and some returned to China.

In some parts of the West, the Chinese were subjected to segregation similar to that imposed on African Americans in the South, including residential and occupational segregation rooted in local custom rather than law. In 1871 the San Francisco school board barred Chinese students from that city's public schools. The ban lasted until 1885, when the parents of Mamie Tape convinced the courts to order the city to provide education for their daughter. The city then opened a segregated Chinese school. Segregated schools for Chinese American children were set up in a few other places in the West, but that school segregation began to break down in the 1910s and 1920s.

Organizations based on kinship, region, or occupation sometimes succeeded in fighting anti-Chinese legislation through the courts. When a San Francisco law restricted Chinese laundry owners, they brought a court challenge. In *Yick Wo v. Hopkins* (1886), the U.S. Supreme Court for the first time declared a licensing law unconstitutional because local authorities had used it to discriminate on the basis of race. The decision also extended the Fourteenth Amendment to cover immigrants who were not citizens.

When other immigrants began to arrive from Asia, they too concentrated in the West. Japanese immigrants started coming in significant numbers after 1890. From 1891 through 1907, nearly 150,000 arrived, most through Pacific Coast ports. Whites in the West, especially organized labor, viewed Japanese immigrants in much the same way as they had earlier immigrants from China—with hostility and scorn. Pushed by western labor organizations, President Theodore Roosevelt in 1907 negotiated an agreement with Japan to halt immigration of Japanese laborers.

Forced Assimilation

As headlines about the Great Sioux War, the Nez Perces, and Geronimo faded from the nation's newspapers, many Americans began to describe American Indians as a "vanishing race." But Indian people did not vanish. With the end of armed conflict, relations between Native Americans and the rest of the nation entered a new phase.

Well before the end of the Indian wars, federal policymakers began to implement plans to assimilate Native Americans into white society. Leading scholars, notably Lewis Henry Morgan of the Smithsonian Institution, viewed culture as an evolutionary process. They analyzed groups as being at one of three stages of development: savagery (hunters and gatherers), barbarism (those who farmed and made pottery), and civilization (those with a written language). All

peoples, they thought, were evolving toward "higher" cultural types. Most white Americans probably agreed that western Europeans and their descendants around the world had reached the highest level of development. Not until the 1890s did this perspective come under serious challenge, notably from Franz Boas, an anthropologist who held that every culture develops and should be understood on its own, rather than as part of an evolutionary chain.

Public support for changes in federal policy grew in response to speaking tours by American Indians and white reformers and to publication of several exposés, notably Helen Hunt Jackson's *A Century of Dishonor* (1881) and *Ramona* (a novel, 1884). Federal policymakers accepted reformers' arguments for speeding up the evolutionary process for Native Americans. Apparently no reformers or federal policymakers understood that American Indians had complex cultures that were very different from—but not inferior to—the culture of Americans of European descent.

Education was an important element in the reformers' plans for "civilizing" the Indians. Federal officials worked with churches and philanthropic organizations to establish schools distant from the reservations, where many Native American children were sent to live and study. Intending to assimilate their students into white society, teachers forbade Indian students to speak their languages, practice their religion, or otherwise follow their own cultural patterns. Other educational programs aimed to train adult Indian men to be farmers or mechanics. Federal officials also tried to prohibit some religious observances and traditional practices on reservations.

The **Dawes Severalty Act** (1887) was an important tool in the "civilizing" effort. Its objective was to make the Indians into self-sufficient, property-conscious, profit-oriented, individual farmers—model citizens of nineteenth-century white America. The law created a governmental policy of severalty—that is, individual ownership of land by Native Americans. Reservations were to be divided into individual family farms of 160 acres. Once each family received its allotment, surplus reservation land was to be sold by the government and the proceeds used for Indian education. This policy found enthusiastic support among both reformers urging rapid assimilation and westerners who coveted Indian lands.

Individual landownership, however, violated traditional Native American views that land was for the use of all and that sharing was a major obligation.

> ■ **Dawes Severalty Act** Law passed by Congress in 1887 intended to break up Indian reservations to create individual farms (holding land in severalty, that is, individually) rather than maintaining common ownership of the land.

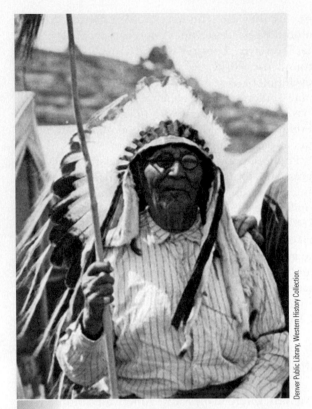

Denver Public Library, Western History Collection.

Luther Standing Bear was called Ota K'te when he was born in 1868, son of a chief who fought against Custer at the Battle of the Little Big Horn. Standing Bear attended the Carlisle Indian School in Pennsylvania, toured with a Wild West Show, became an actor, and belonged to the Actors' Guild (a union). He was also a hereditary chief of the Oglala Lakota. This photo, probably taken in Hollywood in the 1920s, shows him wearing a traditional Lakota headdress.

Susan La Flesche was the first Indian woman to graduate from medical college. Her sister, Susette, was a prominent advocate for Indian rights, and her brother, Francis, was a leading ethnologist. Well educated, they choose to live in and mediate between two societies—the Omaha and the whites. Nebraska State Historical Society.

Though some Indian leaders favored the Dawes Act, others urged Congress to defeat it. Delegates from the Cherokee, Creek, and Choctaw Nations bluntly told Congress, "Our people have not asked for or authorized this. . . . Our own laws regulate a system of land tenure suited to our condition."

Nonetheless, Congress approved the Dawes Act. The result bore out the warning of Senator Henry Teller of Colorado, who called it "a bill to despoil the Indians of their land." Once allotments to Indian families were made, about 70 percent remained of the reservation lands, much of which were sold. In the end, the Dawes Act did not end the reservation system, nor did it reduce the Indians' dependence on the federal government. It did separate the Indians from a good deal of their land.

Native Americans responded to their situation in various ways. Some tried to cooperate with the

peyote cult A religion that included ceremonial use of the hallucinogenic peyote cactus, native to Mexico and the Southwest.

assimilation programs. Susan La Flesche, for example, daughter of an Omaha leader, graduated from medical college in 1889 at the head of her class. But she disappointed her teachers, who wanted her to abandon Indian culture, when she set up her medical practice near the Omaha Reservation, treated both white and Omaha patients, took part in tribal affairs, and managed her land allotment and those of other family members. She also participated in the local white community through the temperance movement and sometimes by preaching in the local Presbyterian church.

Dr. La Flesche seems to have moved easily between two cultures. Some Native Americans preferred the old ways, keeping their children out of school and secretly practicing traditional religious ceremonies. Native American peoples' cultural patterns changed, but not always in the way federal officials anticipated. In Oklahoma, where groups with different traditional cultures lived in close proximity, people began to borrow cultural practices from others. In some places, Indians became part of the wage-earning work force near their reservations, sometimes against the wishes of reservation officials. In the late nineteenth century, the **peyote cult**, based on the hallucinogenic properties of the peyote cactus, emerged

Throughout the Southwest during the late nineteenth and early twentieth centuries, many Mexican American men found work as railway maintenance workers, called section hands. These Mexican American section hands were photographed in Arizona in 1904, traveling on a hand-truck to repair track.

as an alternative religion. It evolved into the Native American Church, combining elements of traditional Indian culture, Christianity, and peyote use.

Mexican Americans in the Southwest

The United States annexed Texas in 1845 and soon after acquired vast territories from Mexico at the end of the Mexican War. There large numbers of people lived who spoke Spanish, many of them **mestizos**—people of mixed Spanish and Native American ancestry. The treaties by which the United States acquired those territories specified that Mexican citizens living there automatically became American citizens.

Throughout the Southwest during the late nineteenth century, many Mexican Americans lost their land as the region attracted English-speaking whites (often called **Anglos** by those whose first language was Spanish). The Treaty of Guadalupe Hidalgo, which ended the war with Mexico, guaranteed Mexican Americans' landholdings, but the vagueness of Spanish and Mexican land grants encouraged legal challenges. Sometimes Mexican Americans were cheated out of their land through fraud.

The California gold rush, beginning in 1849, attracted fortune seekers from around the world, most from the eastern United States and Europe. In northern California, a hundred thousand gold seekers inundated the few thousand Mexican

Americans. People from Latin America who came to California as gold seekers were often driven from the mines by racist harassment and a tax on foreign miners. In southern California, however, there were fewer Anglos until late in the nineteenth century. There, **Californios** won election to local and state office, including Romualdo Pacheco, who served as state treasurer and lieutenant governor and succeeded to the governorship in 1875.

By the 1870s, many of the pueblos (towns created under Mexican or Spanish governments) had become **barrios**—some rural, some in inner cities. Such barrios somewhat resembled the ethnic neighborhoods created by European immigrants. Both had mutual benefit societies, political associations, and newspapers published in the language of the community, and the cornerstone of both was often a church. There was an important difference, however. European immigrants had come to a new land where they anticipated making changes in their own lives to

mestizo A person of mixed Spanish and Indian ancestry.

Anglos A term applied in the Southwest to English-speaking whites.

Californios The Spanish-speaking settlers of California and their descendants.

barrio A Spanish-speaking community, often a part of a larger city.

adjust. Barrio residents, in contrast, lived in regions that had been home to Mexicans for generations but now found themselves surrounded by English-speaking Americans who hired them for cheap wages, sometimes scorned their culture, and pressured them to assimilate.

In Texas, as in California, some **Tejanos** had welcomed the break with Mexico. Lorenzo de Zavala, for example, served briefly as the first vice president of the Texas Republic. By 1900, though, much of the land in south Texas had passed out of the hands of Tejano families—sometimes legally, sometimes fraudulently—but the new Anglo ranch owners usually maintained the social patterns characteristic of Tejano ranchers.

A large section of south Texas remained culturally Mexican, home to Tejanos and two-thirds of all Mexican immigrants who came to the United States before 1900. In the 1890s, one journalist described the area as "an overlapping of Mexico into the United States." During the 1860s and 1870s, conflict sometimes broke out as Mexican Americans challenged the political and economic power of Anglo newcomers. In social relations and in politics, all but a few wealthy Tejanos came to be subordinate to the Anglos, who dominated the regional economy and the professions.

In New Mexico Territory, **Hispanos** were clearly the majority throughout the nineteenth century. They consistently made up a majority in the territorial legislature and were frequently elected as territorial delegates to Congress (the only territorial position elected by voters). Anglos began to arrive in significant numbers with the first railroad in 1879. Although Hispanos were the majority, many lost their small landholdings in ways similar to patterns in California and Texas—except that some who enriched themselves in New Mexico were wealthy Hispanos.

Until 1910, the Latino population in the Southwest grew more slowly than the Anglo population. After 1910, however, that situation reversed itself as political and social upheavals in Mexico prompted massive migration to the United States. Probably a million people—equivalent to one-tenth of the entire population of Mexico in 1910—arrived over the next twenty years. More than half stayed in Texas, but significant numbers settled in southern California and elsewhere in the Southwest. Inevitably, this new stream of immigrants changed some of the patterns of ethnic relations that had characterized the region since the mid-nineteenth century.

Tejanos Spanish-speaking people born in Texas.

Hispanos The Spanish-speaking settlers of New Mexico and their descendants.

WORKERS ORGANIZE

★ How did industrialization affect those who worked in the new industries?

★ How did the various labor organizations define their membership and purpose? Does this help to explain their successes and shortcomings?

The rapid expansion of railroads, mining, and manufacturing created a demand for labor to lay the rails, dig the ore, tend the furnaces, and carry out a thousand other tasks. America's new workers—men, women, and children from many ethnic groups—came from across the nation and around the world. Despite hopes for a rags-to-riches triumph such as Andrew Carnegie's, very few rose from shop floor to manager's office.

Workers for Industry

The labor force grew rapidly after the Civil War, almost doubling by 1890. The largest increases occurred in industries undergoing the greatest changes (see Figure 17.5). Agriculture continued to employ the largest share of the labor force, ranging downward

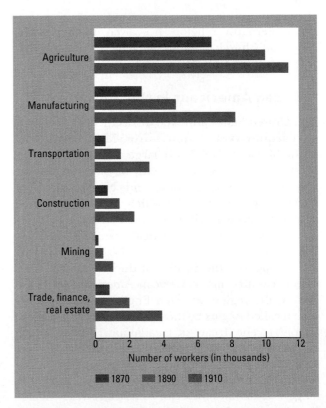

FIGURE 17.5 Industrial Distribution of the Work Force, 1870, 1890, 1910
The number of workers in every industry grew significantly after the Civil War. Though agriculture continued to employ more workers than any other industry, other industries were growing more rapidly than agriculture.

from more than half in 1870 to two-fifths in 1900, but the agricultural work force grew the least, proportionately, of all major categories of workers.

Some workers for the rapidly expanding economy came from within the nation, especially from rural areas. At the same time that mechanization was reducing the number of farm workers needed, farm birth rates remained high. Thus, throughout rural parts of New England and the Middle Atlantic states, many people found it difficult to make a living from agriculture and moved to urban or industrial areas.

The expanding economy, however, needed many more workers than the nation itself could supply. The large-scale immigration of the time contributed many adult males to the work force—especially in mining, manufacturing, and transportation. The expanding economy also pulled women and children into the industrial work force. A study in 1875 showed that the average male factory worker in Lawrence, Massachusetts, earned $500 per year. The study also showed that the average family in Lawrence required a minimum annual income of $600 to provide sufficient food, clothing, and shelter. Since Lawrence was fairly typical of much of the new industrial economy, this study and others in other cities indicate that workers' families often required two or more incomes.

By 1880, a million children (under the age of 16) worked for wages, the largest number in agriculture. Children worked in the fields and mills of the South, operated sewing machines in New York, and sorted vegetables in Delaware canneries. Others worked as newsboys, bootblacks, or domestic servants, and still others worked at home, alongside their parents who brought home **piecework**. Nationwide, most working children turned over their wages to their parents.

Most women who worked outside the home were unmarried. In 1890, 40 percent of all single women worked for wages, along with 30 percent of widowed or divorced women. Among married women, only 5 percent did so. Black women were employed at much higher rates in all categories. Some occupations came to be filled mainly by women. By 1900, females—adults and children—made up more than 70 percent of the work force in clothing factories, knitting mills, and other textile operations. Women also dominated certain types of office work, including more than 70 percent of the nation's secretaries and typists and 80 percent of telephone operators. However, as women moved into office work, displacing men, wage levels fell, along with the likelihood of promotion from clerical worker to managerial status. For women, office work usually paid less than factory work but was considered safer and of higher status.

Women and children workers almost always earned less than their male counterparts. In most industries, work was separated by age and gender, and adult males usually held the more skilled jobs

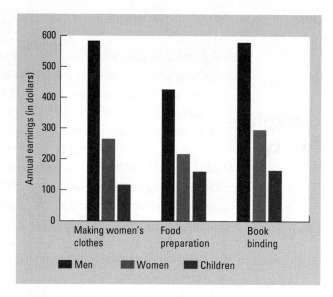

FIGURE 17.6 **Average Annual Earnings for Men, Women, and Children, in Selected Industries, 1890**

commanding the best pay. Even when men and women did the same work, they rarely received the same pay (see Figure 17.6). This wage differential was often explained by the argument that a man had to support a family, whereas a woman worked to supplement the income of her husband or father.

Not all women earned money through working for wages. Some women were self-employed, for example, in making and selling women's hats or dresses. In urban working-class neighborhoods, married or widowed women often rented a room to a boarder or charged to do other people's laundry or sewing. In rural areas, married women often kept chickens and sold eggs to supplement their family's income.

Because so many of the new industrial workers had been born into a rural society, either in the United States or in Europe, they found industrial work quite different from their previous work. Farm families might toil from sunrise to sunset, but they did so at their own speed, taking a break when they felt the need and adjusting the pace of their work to avoid exhaustion. Self-employed blacksmiths, carpenters, dressmakers, and other skilled workers also controlled the speed and intensity of their work, although, like the farmer, they might work long hours. Frank Roney considered this autonomy to be part of the dignity of labor. In many early factories, the skilled workers, such as Roney, often set the pace of work around them. They also earned more than other workers and were difficult to replace.

piecework Work for which someone is paid for the number of items turned out, rather than by the hour.

It Matters Today

Workplace Safety

The high rate of workplace fatalities in the early twentieth century has been reduced substantially by the combined efforts of employers, unions, individual workers, academic researchers, and government at all levels. In 1907, the worst year on record, 3,242 men and boys died in coal mining accidents, leading to establishment of the Federal Bureau of Mines to study and improve mine safety. Mining has remained among the most dangerous jobs throughout the twentieth century and since. The Federal Coal Mine Health and Safety Act of 1969 set federal mine safety standards and was followed by a 50 percent reduction in deaths over the next five years. Similarly, a 33 percent reduction in mining deaths followed further legislation, the Federal Mine Safety and Health Act of 1977. Still, an average of more than thirty miners have died each year in recent years.

- Laws regulating workplace safety remain politically controversial. Use online newspapers to research contention over the Occupational Safety and Health Act of 1970. What arguments are made by those who seek to modify such laws?

- Research the origins of workers' compensation laws. Why were they first developed? Why do they remain politically controversial today?

In the late nineteenth century, the workday in most industries averaged ten or twelve hours, six days a week. People expected to work long hours but found that industrial work controlled them, rather than the other way around. In many factories, the speed of the machines set the pace of the work, and machine speeds were often centrally controlled. If managers ordered a **speed-up**, workers worked faster. The job of the foreman was typically to demand faster and faster work. Ten- or twelve-hour days at a constant, rapid pace drained the workers. A woman textile worker in 1882 said, "I get so exhausted that I can scarcely drag myself home when night comes."

The pace of the work, together with inadequate safety precautions, contributed to a high rate of industrial accidents, injuries, and deaths. The first thorough study of workplace fatalities was not conducted until 1913, when the Bureau of Labor Statistics found 23,000 industrial deaths among a work force of 38 million, equivalent to 61 deaths per 100,000 workers. (Today there are about 4 deaths per 100,000 workers.) Injuries and disabilities were even more numerous. Those disabled by industrial accidents received no benefits from the federal government and rarely received anything from state or local government or from their employers. On the contrary, many businesses considered an on-the-job injury to be due to carelessness by the employee and grounds for firing.

Despite rags-to-riches success stories, extreme mobility was highly unusual. Nearly all successful business leaders, in fact, came from middle- or upper-class families. Few workers moved more than a step or so up the economic scale. An unskilled laborer might become a semiskilled worker, or a skilled worker might become a foreman, but few wage earners moved into the middle class. If they did, it was usually as the owner of a small and often struggling business.

The Origins of Unions and Labor Conflict in the 1870s

Just as the entrepreneurs of the late nineteenth century faced choices between competition and cooperation, so too did their employees. Like Frank Roney, some workers reacted to the far-reaching changes in the nature of work by joining with other workers in efforts to maintain or regain control over their working conditions.

Skilled workers remained indispensable in many fields. Only a skilled iron molder could set up the molds and know exactly when and how to pour molten iron into them. Only an experienced carpenter could build stairs or hang doors properly. Only a skilled typesetter could quickly transform handwritten copy into lines of lead type. Such workers took pride in the quality of their work and knew that their skill was crucial to their employer's success. One union leader was referring to such workers when he said, "The manager's brains are under the workman's cap."

Skilled workers formed the first unions, called **craft unions** or **trade unions** because membership was limited to skilled workers in a particular craft or trade. Before the Civil War, workers in most American cities created

speed-up An effort to make employees produce more goods in the same time or for the same pay.

■ **craft union, trade union** Labor union that organizes skilled workers engaged in a specific craft or trade.

local trade unions in attempts to regulate the quality of work, wages, hours, and working conditions within their craft. Local unions eventually formed national trade organizations—twenty-six of them by 1873, thirty-nine by 1880. They sometimes called themselves brotherhoods—for example, the United Brotherhood of Carpenters and Joiners, formed in 1881—and they drew on their craft traditions to forge bonds of unity.

The skills that defined craft unions' membership also provided the basis for their success. Skills that sometimes took years to develop made craft workers valuable to their employers and difficult to replace. Such unions often limited their membership not just to workers with particular skills but to white males with those skills. If most craft workers within a city belonged to the local union, a strike could badly disrupt or shut down the affected businesses. The strike, therefore, was a powerful weapon for skilled workers. Strikes most often succeeded in times of prosperity, when employers wanted to continue operating and were able financially to make concessions to workers. When the economy turned down and employers

reduced work hours or laid off workers, craft unions usually disintegrated because they could not use the strike effectively. Only after the 1880s did local and national unions develop strategies that permitted them to survive depressions.

Unskilled or semiskilled workers—the majority of employees in many emerging industries—lacked vthe skills that gave the craft unions their bargaining power. Without such skills, they could be replaced easily if they chose to strike. The most effective unions, therefore, were groups of skilled workers—sometimes called the "aristocracy of labor."

Shortly after the Civil War, in 1866, craft unionists representing a variety of local and national organizations joined with reformers to create the **National Labor Union** (NLU), headed by William Sylvis of the Iron Molders until his death in 1869. The NLU also included representatives of women's organizations and, after vigorous debate, decided to encourage the organization of black workers. The most important of the NLU objectives was to establish eight hours as the proper length for a day's work. In 1870 the NLU divided itself into a labor organization and a political party, the National Labor Reform Party, which Frank Roney joined so hopefully in Omaha. In 1872 the political party nominated candidates for president and vice president, but the campaign was so unsuccessful and divisive that neither the NLU nor the party met again.

In 1877, for the first time, the nation witnessed widespread labor strife. After the onset of depression in 1873, railroad companies reduced costs by repeatedly cutting wages. Railroad workers' pay fell by more than a third from 1873 to 1877. Union leaders talked of striking but failed to bring it off. Railway workers took matters into their own hands when companies announced additional pay cuts. On July 16, 1877,

■ **National Labor Union** (NLU) Federation of trade unions and reform societies organized in 1866; it lasted only six years but helped push through a law limiting government employees to an eight-hour workday.

This engraving depicts striking railroad workers in Martinsburg, West Virginia, as they stopped a freight train on July 17, 1877, in the opening days of the Great Railway Strike. Engravings such as this, showing strikers as heavily armed, may not have been accurate depictions of events. The technology of the day could not reproduce photographs in newspapers, so the public's understanding of events such as the 1877 strike was formed largely through artists' depictions.

some firemen and brakemen on the Baltimore & Ohio Railroad stopped work in Maryland. The next day, nearby in West Virginia, a group of railway workers refused to work until the company restored their wages. Members of the local community supported the strikers. The governor of West Virginia sent in the state **militia**, but the strikers prevented the trains from running. The governor then requested federal troops, and President Rutherford B. Hayes sent them.

Federal troops restored service on the Baltimore & Ohio, but the strike spread to other lines. Strikers shut down trains in Pittsburgh. When the local

militia refused to act against the strikers, the governor of Pennsylvania sent militia units from Philadelphia. When the militia killed twenty-six people, strikers and their sympathizers attacked the militia, forced the troops to retreat, and burned and looted railroad property throughout Pittsburgh.

Strikes erupted across Pennsylvania and New York and throughout the Midwest. Everywhere, the strikers drew support from their local communities. In various places, coal miners, factory workers, small business owners, farmers, black workers, and women demonstrated their solidarity with the workers. In St. Louis, local unions declared a **general strike** to secure the eight-hour workday and to end child labor. State militia, federal troops, and local police eventually broke up the strikes, but not before hundreds had lost their lives. By the strikes' end, railroad companies had suffered property damage worth $10 million, half of the losses in Pittsburgh.

The **Great Railway Strike of 1877** revealed widespread dislike for the railroad companies and

militia A volunteer military force, organized by state governments, consisting of civilians who agree to be mobilized in times of emergency; now superseded by the National Guard.

general strike A strike by members of all unions in a particular region.

■ **Great Railway Strike of 1877** Largely spontaneous strikes by railroad workers, triggered by wage cuts.

From "Puck", April 7, 1886.

Terence Powderly, in the center, advocates arbitration. The Knights of Labor urged that labor and management (identified here as "capital") should settle their differences this way, rather than by striking. Note how the cartoonist has depicted labor and management as of equal size, and given both of them a large weapon; management's club is labeled "monopoly" and labor's hammer is called "strikes." In fact, labor and management were rarely equally matched when it came to labor disputes in the late nineteenth century.

significant community support for striking workers. However, the strike alarmed many other Americans. Some considered the use of troops only a temporary expedient and, like President Hayes, hoped for "education of the strikers," "judicious control of the capitalists," and some way to "remove the distress which afflicts laborers." Others saw in the strike a forecast of future labor unrest, and they called for better means to enforce law and order.

Competing Labor Organizations in the 1880s

The Great Railway Strike of 1877 suggested that working people could unite across lines of occupation, race, and gender, but no organization drew on that potential until the early 1880s, when the **Knights of Labor** emerged as an alternative to craft unions.

The Knights grew out of an organization of Philadelphia garment workers formed in 1869. Abandoning their craft union origins, they proclaimed that labor was "the only creator of values or capital," and

they recruited members from what they considered "the producing class"—those who, by their labor, produced value. Anyone joining the Knights was required to have worked for wages at some time, but the organization specifically excluded only professional gamblers, stockbrokers, lawyers, bankers, and liquor dealers.

The Knights accepted African Americans as members, and some sixty thousand joined by 1886. After an organizer formed a local organization of women in 1881, the Knights officially opened their ranks to women and enrolled about fifty thousand by 1886. Some women and African Americans held local and regional leadership positions, and the Knights briefly appointed a woman as a national organizer. Through their activities, the Knights provided both

■ **Knights of Labor** Organization founded in 1869, open to all workers; membership peaked in 1886; members favored a cooperative alternative to capitalism.

women and African Americans with experience in organizing.

Terence V. Powderly, a machinist, directed the Knights from 1879 to 1893. Under his leadership, they focused on organization, education, and cooperation as their chief objectives. The Knights favored political action to accomplish such labor reforms as health and safety regulations, the eight-hour workday, prohibition of child labor, equal pay for equal work regardless of gender, and the graduated income tax. They also endorsed government ownership of the telephone, telegraph, and railroad systems. In 1878, 1880, and 1882, Powderly won election as mayor of Scranton, Pennsylvania, as the candidate of a labor party. Local labor parties often appeared in other cities where the Knights were strong.

A major objective of the Knights was "to secure to the workers the full enjoyment of the wealth they create." They committed themselves in 1878 to promote producers' and consumers' **cooperatives**, which they hoped would "supersede the wage-system." They established some 135 cooperatives by the mid-1880s, but few lasted very long. Most failed because of lack of capital, opposition from rival businesses, or poor organization.

Before the problems with their cooperatives became apparent, the Knights of Labor became the largest labor organization in the country, expanding from 9,000 members in 1879 to 703,000 in 1886. This meteoric growth suggested that many working people were seeking ways to respond to the emerging corporate behemoths or to regain some control over their own working lives. Though the rise of the Knights of Labor seemed to signal a growing sense of common purpose among many working people, labor organizations soon found themselves on the defensive and divided.

On May 1, 1886, some eighty thousand Chicagoans marched through the streets in support of an eight-hour workday, a cause that united many unions and radical groups. Three days later, Chicago police killed several strikers at the McCormick Harvester Works. Hoping to build on the May Day unity, a group of anarchists called a protest meeting for the next day at Haymarket Square. When police tried to break up the rally, someone threw a bomb at the officers. The police then opened fire on the crowd, and some protesters fired back. Eight policemen died, along with an unknown number of demonstrators, and a hundred people suffered injuries.

The Haymarket bombing sparked public anxiety and antiunion feelings. Employers who had previously opposed unions now tried to discredit them by playing on fears of terrorism. Some people who had supported union goals of better wages and working conditions now shrank back in horror. In Chicago, amid widespread furor over the violence, eight leading anarchists stood trial for inciting the bombing and, on flimsy evidence, were convicted. Four were hanged, one committed suicide, and three remained in jail until a sympathetic governor, John Peter Altgeld, released them in 1893.

Two weeks after the Haymarket bombing, trade union leaders met in Philadelphia to discuss the inroads that the Knights of Labor were making among their members. They proposed an agreement with the Knights: trade unions would recruit skilled workers, and the Knights would limit themselves to unskilled workers. The Knights refused, so the trade unions organized the **American Federation of Labor** (AFL). Membership in the AFL was limited to national trade unions. The combined membership of the thirteen founding unions amounted to about 140,000—only one-fifth of the number claimed by the Knights at the time.

Samuel Gompers became the AFL's first president. Born in London in 1850 to Dutch Jewish parents, he learned the cigarmaker's trade before coming to the United States in 1863. He joined the Cigarmakers' Union and became its president in 1877. Except for one year, Gompers continued as president of the AFL until his death in 1924. As AFL president, Gompers opposed labor involvement with radicalism or politics, and favored what he called "pure and simple" unionism: higher wages, shorter hours, and improved working conditions for union members, achieved not through politics but through the power of their organizations in relation to their employers. Though most AFL unions did not challenge capitalism, they repeatedly used strikes and sometimes engaged in long and bitter struggles with employers.

After the 1880s, the AFL suffered little competition from the Knights of Labor. The decline of the Knights came swiftly: 703,000 members in 1886; 260,000 in 1888; 100,000 in 1890. The failure of several strikes involving the Knights in the late 1880s cost them many supporters. Some who left were probably disappointed when a "cooperative commonwealth" was not quickly achieved. Some units of the Knights were organized like trade unions, and these groups

■ **Terence V. Powderly** Leader of the Knights of Labor from 1879 to 1893; three-term mayor of Scranton, Pennsylvania.

cooperative A business enterprise in which workers and consumers share in ownership and take part in management.

■ **American Federation of Labor** (AFL) National organization of trade unions founded in 1886; it used strikes and boycotts to improve the lot of craft workers.

■ **Samuel Gompers** First president of the AFL; sought to divorce labor organizing from politics and stressed practical demands involving wages and hours.

This drawing depicts U.S. troops firing on striking railroad workers in Chicago on July 7, 1894. The Pullman strike began with the employees of the Pullman plant near Chicago but affected rail traffic from New York to California. Because of Chicago's position as the center of so much of the nation's rail traffic, and because of the strength of the unions in that area, the Chicago area was the site of much of the violence of that strike. The intervention of U.S. troops, federal marshals, and the Illinois national guard effectively broke the strike by protecting strikebreakers.

often preferred the more practical AFL. The United Mine Workers of America switched from the Knights to the AFL in 1890 but retained some central principles of the Knights, including commitments to include both whites and African Americans and to organize all workers in coal mining, rather than only the most skilled.

Labor on the Defensive in the 1890s

In the 1890s, workers often found that even the largest unions could not withstand the power of the new industrial companies. A major demonstration of this power came in 1892 in Homestead, Pennsylvania, at the giant Carnegie Steel plant managed by Henry Clay Frick, Carnegie's partner. There a union had a contract with Carnegie Steel. When Frick proposed major wage cuts and the union balked, Frick locked out the union members and prepared to bring in replacements.

Frick had the Pinkerton National Detective Agency send three hundred guards to protect strikebreakers.

They arrived by riverboat, but ten thousand strikers and community supporters resisted when the private army tried to land. Shots rang out. In the ensuing battle, seven Pinkertons and nine strikers were killed, and sixty people were injured. The Pinkertons surrendered, leaving the strikers in control. Soon after, however, the governor of Pennsylvania sent in the state militia to patrol the city and protect the strikebreakers. The union never recovered. This crushing defeat suggested that no union could stand up to America's industrial giants, especially when they could call on the government for assistance.

A similar fate befell the most ambitious organizing drive of the 1890s. In 1893, under the leadership of **Eugene V. Debs**, railway workers launched the American Railway Union (ARU). Born in Indiana in 1855, Debs

■ **Eugene V. Debs** American Railway Union leader who was jailed for his role in the Pullman strike; later became a leading socialist and ran for president.

had served as an officer of the locomotive firemen's union. Railway workers had organized separate unions for engineers, firemen, switchmen, and conductors, but Debs hoped to bring all railway workers, skilled and unskilled, together into one union, thereby creating an **industrial union**. Success came quickly. Within a year, the ARU claimed 150,000 members and became the largest single union in the nation.

The twenty-four railway companies whose lines entered Chicago had formed the General Managers Association (GMA) to address common problems. Alarmed at the rise of the ARU, they found an opportunity to challenge the new union in 1894. Striking workers at the Pullman Palace Car Company, which manufactured luxury railway cars, asked the ARU to boycott Pullman cars—to disconnect them from trains and proceed without them. When the ARU agreed, the managers promised to fire any worker who observed the boycott. Their real purpose, as expressed by the GMA chairman, was to eliminate the ARU and "to wipe him [Debs] out."

Within a short time, all 150,000 ARU members were on strike in support of members who were fired for boycotting Pullman cars. Rail traffic in and out of Chicago ground to a halt, affecting railways from the Pacific Coast to New York. The companies found an ally in U.S. Attorney General Richard Olney, a former railroad lawyer. Olney obtained an **injunction** against the strikers on the grounds that the strike prevented delivery of the mail and also violated the Sherman Anti-Trust Act (discussed in the next chapter). President Cleveland then assigned thousands of **U.S. marshals** and federal troops to protect trains operated by strikebreakers. In response, mobs attacked railroad property, especially in Chicago, burning trains and buildings. ARU leaders condemned the violence, but a dozen people died before the strike finally ended. Union leaders, including Debs, were jailed, and the ARU was destroyed.

The depression that began in 1893 further weakened the unions. In 1894 Gompers acknowledged that nearly all AFL affiliates "had their resources greatly diminished and their efforts largely crippled" through lost strikes and unemployment. Nevertheless, the AFL hung on. By 1897, the organization claimed fifty-eight national unions with a combined membership of nearly 270,000.

■ **industrial union** A union that includes all of the workers, both skilled or unskilled, in a particular industry.

injunction A court order requiring an individual or a group to do something or to refrain from doing something.

U.S. marshal A federal law-enforcement official.

Individual Voices

Frank Roney Criticizes American Workers

Frank Roney left a long memoir of his experiences in Ireland and America, which was published in 1931. The following excerpt presents some of his views on work, manliness, and unions. From accounts such as these, historians find evidence about the nature of work, the way that people thought about gender roles, and the understandings that people had then about the role of unions.

❶ In Roney's descriptions of the workers in the New York stove-plate foundry and those in the Jersey City foundry, what evidence do you see for Roney's own understanding of what it meant to be a man? How would you characterize Roney's understanding, based on this evidence?

❷ Here, again, Roney gives an understanding of what he considered manly behaviour.

❸ Here Roney presents his notion of the purpose of a union, which he traces to William Sylvis. What is it? Is it primarily to secure improvements in wages?

On the morning of our arrival in New York harbour I was the very first on deck. . . . In my heart I hailed America as the Land of Liberty where all were equal and where poverty was unknown. . . .

[Roney began to seek employment in New York City.] *I peered into the semi-darkness and saw men, bare-headed and bare-footed. . . . I asked a bystander what was going on inside, and was told that it was a foundry. The information made me gasp. I had never seen or heard of a foundry like it, and became interested. To see men half nude, exerting themselves as these were doing in a place imperfectly lighted, black and dirty, and perspiring on this hot morning, was a revelation to me. If this was moulding in America, then I decided it were better for me to return to Ireland and go to prison and remain there rather than degrade myself as these free American citizens were doing. . . . I began to think that my exalted idea of man's equality in the American republic was rather mythical. . . .*

[Roney found a job in Jersey City.] *None of the wrecking and oppressive sordidness of the New York stove-plate moulders was visible in this foundry. It was a place for competent mechanics and not for slaves, voluntary or involuntary. There was nothing cringing or servile about the men who worked there nor was there anything domineering or exacting about the foreman. . . .* ❶

[Roney traveled west, eventually landing in San Francisco.] *I then went to the Union Iron Works and secured a job, although I had been advised of the tyrannous reputation of Mr. Dimmick, the foreman. I was a total stranger in the shop, which gave me a splendid opportunity to observe and study the men. The American style of working, which I had noticed in New York, St. Louis, and Chicago, consisted of competing to secure the favor of the foreman and through that means retain steady employment. It was carried to the limit in the Union Iron Works. No foreman was needed to urge these men to work to the point of exhaustion. They labored hard of their own volition and displayed an eagerness most discouraging to one who wished to see each of them occupy the niche of a man.* ❷ *. . . Men who work as hacks and drudges are not those from whom to expect high thoughts or ideas of social improvement. The conception of [William] Sylvis and those of his associates in forming the National Moulders' Union was that by association and an interchange of thought better notions of social improvement would be cultivated and something superior to a two-bit-a-day increase in wages would be firmly implanted in the minds of the members.* ❸ *. . .*

Study Tools

SUMMARY

In the Gilded Age, as industrialization transformed the economy, immigration and urbanization challenged many established social patterns. As rural Americans and European immigrants sought better lives in the cities, urban America changed dramatically. New technologies in construction, transportation, and communication produced a new urban geography with residential neighborhoods defined by economic status. Urban growth brought a new urban middle class. Education underwent far-reaching changes. Socially defined gender roles began to change as some women chose professional careers and took active roles in reform. Some men responded by redefining masculinity through organizations and athletics. Urbanization offered new choices to gay men and lesbians by making possible the development of distinctive urban subcultures. In response, medical specialists tried to define homosexuality and lesbianism.

The South shared in some of the changes of the Gilded Age, but lagged in others, notably education. The myths of the Old South and the Lost Cause obscured for some southerners the real source of their difficulties. Changes in state laws disfranchised black voters and other new laws legalized and extended racial segregation.

Many Europeans immigrated to the United States because of economic and political conditions in their homelands and their expectations of better opportunities in America. Immigrants often formed distinct communities, frequently centered on a church. The flood of immigrants spawned nativist reactions among some old-stock Americans. The West included immigrants from Asia, American Indians, and Latino peoples in substantial numbers. White westerners used politics and sometimes violence to exclude and segregate Asian immigrants. Federal policy toward American Indians proceeded from the expectation that they could and should be rapidly assimilated and must shed their separate cultural identities, but such policies largely failed. Latinos—descendants of those living in the Southwest before it became part of the United States and those who came later from Mexico or elsewhere in Latin America—often found their lives and culture under challenge.

Industrial workers had little control over the pace or hours of their work and often faced unpleasant or dangerous working conditions. Even so, people in both the United States and other parts of the world chose to migrate to expanding industrial centers from rural areas. The new work force included not only adult males but also women and children. Some workers formed labor organizations to seek higher wages, shorter hours, and better conditions. Trade unions, based on craft skills, were the earliest and most successful of such organizations. The Great Railway Strike of 1877 was the first indication of what widespread industrial strife could do to the nation's new transportation network based on railroads, and public officials resorted to federal troops to suppress the strike. Espousing cooperatives and reform, the Knights of Labor opened its

CHRONOLOGY

1862	Land-Grant College Act
1865	Civil War ends
1866	National Labor Union organized
1870	Populations in 25 cities exceed 50,000
1871–1885	Anti-Chinese riots across the West
1871	Great Chicago Fire
1872	Montgomery Ward opens first U.S. mail-order business
1873–1879	Depression
1874	Women's Christian Temperance Union founded
1877	Great Railway Strike
1881	669,431 immigrants enter United States / Publication of Helen Hunt Jackson's *A Century of Dishonor*
1886	Knights of Labor reaches peak membership / Haymarket Square bombing / American Federation of Labor founded
1887	American Protective Association founded / Dawes Severalty Act
1888	First electric streetcar system
1890	Populations in 58 cities exceed 50,000 / Second Mississippi Plan
1892	Homestead strike
1893–1897	Depression
1894	Pullman strike
1895	Booker T. Washington delivers Atlanta Compromise
1896	*Plessy v. Ferguson*

membership to the unskilled, to African Americans, and to women—groups usually not admitted to craft unions. The Knights died out after 1890. The American Federation of Labor was formed by craft unions, and its leaders rejected radicalism and sought instead to work within capitalism to improve wages, hours, and conditions for its members. Organized labor suffered two dramatic defeats in the 1890s, one at the Homestead steel plant in 1892 and the other over the Pullman car boycott in 1894.

FOCUS QUESTIONS

If you have mastered this chapter, you should be able to answer these questions and to explain the terms that follow the questions.

1. ☆ *What were the key factors in the transformation of American cities in the late nineteenth century?*

2. ☆ *What important new social patterns emerged in urban areas in the late nineteenth century?*

3. ☆ *What new social patterns appeared in the South after the end of Reconstruction?*

4. ☆ *How did southern racial relations develop after the end of Reconstruction?*

5. ☆ *How did the expectations of European immigrants differ from their actual experiences?*

6. ☆ *Compare experiences of Chinese Americans, American Indians, Mexican Americans, and African Americans in the Gilded Age.*

7. ☆ *How did industrialization affect those who worked in the new industries?*

8. ☆ *How did the various labor organizations define their membership and purpose? Does this help to explain their successes and shortcomings?*

KEY TERMS

suburb   *(p. 456)*

consumer culture   *(p. 459)*

domesticity   *(p. 459)*

separate spheres   *(p. 460)*

Woman's Christian Temperance Union   *(p. 460)*

Civil Rights Cases   *(p. 465)*

poll tax   *(p. 465)*

Booker T. Washington   *(p. 465)*

Atlanta Compromise   *(p. 465)*

Plessy v. Ferguson   *(p. 466)*

nativism   *(p. 469)*

American Protective Association   *(p. 469)*

Chinese Exclusion Act   *(p. 470)*

Dawes Severalty Act   *(p. 471)*

craft union, trade union   *(p. 476)*

National Labor Union   *(p. 477)*

Great Railway Strike of 1877   *(p. 478)*

Knights of Labor   *(p. 479)*

Terence V. Powderly   *(p. 480)*

American Federation of Labor   *(p. 480)*

Samuel Gompers   *(p. 480)*

Eugene V. Debs   *(p. 481)*

industrial union   *(p. 482)*

18 Politics and Foreign Relations in a Rapidly Changing Nation, 1865–1902

Behind the Stories

Chapters 16 and 17 presented the dramatic and far-reaching transformations that took place during the Gilded Age in economic and social patterns—industrialization, urbanization, immigration, and the development of the West. Many of those changes had the potential for conflict—for example, between railroad corporations and merchants who paid the railroads to deliver the goods they would sell, or between immigrants and nativists. Throughout American history, social and economic conflicts have often made their way into the political process—indeed, today most Americans have come to expect the federal government to address such issues. During much of the Gilded Age, however, federal politics seemed frozen, with little attention to the new corporate giants or to ethnic discord.

Historians have formulated differing explanations for the seeming irrelevance of politics in the 1870s and 1880s. Some historians in the 1930s and 1940s suggested that there was little difference between the two major parties and that both had been captured by big business. Some recent historians continue to make similar arguments. As you'll see in this chapter, my conclusion is different: there *were* important differences between the two major parties, and the long deadlock of politics was caused primarily because the two major parties were so closely balanced in strength that neither was able to put through its proposals for addressing the nation's problems. Other recent historians have drawn similar conclusions.

Historians agree that the 1890s were a decade of significant political change, though not all agree about how and why those changes came about. Some of those changes produced important features of our politics today. Furthermore, the political rhetoric of the 1890s still appears on occasion. About twenty years ago, at a time when the prices paid to farmers for corn were low, I was driving on a country road in Nebraska. In a field along the road I saw an old, rusting tractor. Propped on the tractor was a sign with hand-painted letters that read, "Raise Less Corn and More Hell"—political rhetoric from the 1890s being recycled to express political frustration and anger a century later.

—R.W.C.

486

Individual Choices
Carl Schurz

Born in what is now Germany, Carl Schurz became involved in politics as a student at the University of Bonn, in 1848, when he joined a failed revolution in support of greater democracy. Like other "48ers," he fled to the United States. Immediately drawn to the antislavery movement, he became a prominent campaigner for the new Republican Party, especially among German Americans. Schurz fought in the Union Army, reaching the rank of major general by the end of the Civil War. He served in the U.S. Senate from Missouri during 1869–1875, the first German American in that body, and President Rutherford B. Hayes appointed him Secretary of the Interior, a post he held during 1877–1881. Thereafter, as a nationally prominent journalist, he worked for civil service reform and, after 1898, against American acquisition of the Philippines and imperialism more generally.

In 1887, Hayes encouraged Schurz to write something to explain his political career because many politicians considered him an "enigma" and a "mystery." Hayes continued that "[T]he common explanation is, 'Well he is a German'— or 'He is a Free Trader.' 'He is a good man—an honest man—a man of extraordinary talents, but not a practical man in his political conduct.'"

Carl Schurz

In what way was Schurz not "practical"? Hayes specified that it was because Schurz was so lacking in "the strength of the tie which binds the average . . . American to his party. To break it is almost a crime."

Schurz entered American politics at a time when political parties were at their strongest, controlling nearly every aspect of political decision making. It was a time when all men were expected to have strong and continuing loyalty to a political party, and to "vote the party ticket straight"—that is, unquestioningly support their party's candidates. Those who broke with their party drew the contempt of mainstream politicians, who called them "political hermaphrodites," "eunuchs," and "man-milliners" (men who made women's hats), reflecting the extent to which being a loyal party member was closely tied to men's gender role.

For Schurz, however, loyalty to principles was more important than loyalty to party. During the presidency of U.S. Grant, Schurz broke with the Republican

487

Carl Schurz . . .

Party and led the Liberal Republican movement, which opposed Grant's reelection. He returned to Republican ranks, but refused to support the Republican presidential candidate in 1884. He then became the nation's best known independent, dividing his support for candidates on the basis of issues, especially civil service reform and, later, foreign policy, as made clear in the Individual Voices feature at the end of this chapter. His principled independence brought him many admirers, but he made even more enemies by his scathing criticism of those he considered unprincipled.

Schurz's political career came during a time when the nation's economy was changing at a breakneck pace, but when politics seemed to change very little. Americans expected that politics meant *party* politics and that all meaningful political choices came through the major parties. Any understanding of politics in this period must begin with political parties—what they were, what they did, what they stood for, and what choices they offered to voters. Yet from 1874 until the 1890s, there were few innovations in federal policies as the two major parties deadlocked. In foreign relations, too, things changed very little.

All that began to change in the 1890s, when political discontent in the West and South erupted into a new party, the People's Party, soon called the Populists. Politics crackled with new ideas and new alignments, shooting sparks in all directions. The 1896 presidential election was one of the most hard-fought in the nation's history. That election brought an end to the long political logjam, as Republicans emerged victorious and dominated politics for the next thirty-four years. And the 1890s ended with a war that ushered in a new role for the United States in world affairs, including the acquisition of new territorial possessions stretching nearly halfway around the world.

PARTIES, SPOILS, SCANDALS, AND STALEMATE, 1865–1880

★ What was the significance of political parties in the late nineteenth century?

★ Compare the presidencies from Grant through Cleveland. Which do you consider successful? Why?

Political parties were central to politics and government throughout most of the nineteenth century,

party convention Party meeting to nominate candidates for elective offices and adopt a platform.

caucus A meeting of people with a common political interest—for example, to choose delegates to a party convention.

platform A written statement of the principles, policies, and promises on which a political party appeals to voters.

but they were organized and behaved very differently from their counterparts today. Before looking at national politics, therefore, it is important to look first at political parties.

Parties, Conventions, and Patronage

After the 1830s, nominations for political offices came from **party conventions**. The process of selecting convention delegates began when neighborhood voters gathered in party **caucuses** to choose delegates to local conventions. Conventions took place at county, state, and national levels and for congressional districts and various state districts. At most conventions, the delegates listened to long-winded speakers glorifying their party and denouncing the opposition. They nominated candidates for elective offices or chose delegates to another convention further up the federal ladder. And they adopted a **platform**. Party leaders worked to negotiate compromises among major groups within their party, on both candidates and platform language, and such deal-making sometimes occurred in informal settings—perhaps hotel rooms thick with cigar smoke and cluttered with whiskey bottles. Such behind-the-scenes deal making reinforced the notion of political parties as all-male bastions into which no self-respecting women would venture.

After choosing their candidates, the parties launched their campaigns. Campaigns focused on party identity. Newspapers were the major source of news, and nearly every newspaper identified closely with a political party. The parties subsidized sympathetic newspapers, and the newspapers delivered both effusive support for their party and scathing attacks on the opposition. Before an election, local party organizations whipped up enthusiasm among party loyalists and tried to recruit new or undecided voters through parades, barbecues, and rallies capped by hours of speechmaking.

On election day, each party tried to mobilize all its supporters and make certain that they voted. This produced very high levels of voter participation—more than 80 percent of eligible voters cast their ballots in 1876. At polling places, party workers distributed lists, or "tickets," of their party's candidates, which voters

THIS IS NOT THE NEW YORK STOCK EXCHANGE, IT IS THE PATRONAGE EXCHANGE, CALLED U. S. SENATE.

This cartoon by James A. Wales appeared in the journal *Puck* in 1881, with the caption, "This is not the New York stock exchange, it is the patronage exchange, called U.S. Senate." It depicts senators spending all their time on patronage rather than national affairs. *Puck* was a favorite journal of the Mugwumps, who sharply criticized the patronage system. Library of Congress.

used as ballots. Voting was not secret until the 1890s. Before then, everyone could see which party's ticket a voter turned in (illustrations of voting appear on pages 402 and 500). The voting process discouraged voters from crossing party lines.

Once the votes were counted, newly elected presidents or governors or mayors began appointing their loyal supporters to government jobs, which were widely considered appropriate rewards for hard work during a winning campaign. Those appointed to such jobs were also expected to return part of their salaries to the party. This was called the **patronage system** or spoils system, after a statement by Senator William Marcy in 1831: "To the victor belong the spoils." Its defenders were labeled **spoilsmen**.

Party loyalists inevitably outnumbered the available jobs, so competition for appointments was fierce. When James A. Garfield became president in 1881, he was so overwhelmed with demands for jobs that he exclaimed in disgust, "My God! What is there in this place that a man should ever want to get into it?" Jobs in highest demand often involved purchasing or government contracts, which became another form of spoils, awarded to businessmen who supported the party. This system invited corruption. One Post Office official, for example, pressured **postmasters** across the country to buy clocks from one of his political associates. Such opportunities were limited only by the imagination of the spoilsmen.

Some critics, including Carl Schurz, argued that, by concentrating so much on patronage, politics ignored principles and issues and revolved instead around greed for office. The spoils system had many defenders, however. George W. Plunkitt, a longtime participant in New York City politics, explained, "You can't keep an organization together without patronage. Men ain't in politics for nothin'." Plunkitt described the reality: given the many party workers needed to identify supporters and mobilize voters, politics required some rewards.

In 1905, a newspaper reporter published a series of conversations with Plunkitt. His observations provide insights into the nature of urban politics and its relation to urban poverty. Born in a poor Irish neighborhood of New York City, Plunkitt left school early, entered politics, and eventually became a district leader of **Tammany Hall**, which dominated the city's

■ **patronage system** System that lets the winning party distribute appointed government jobs to loyal party members; also called the spoils system.

spoilsmen Derogatory term for defenders of the patronage or spoils system.

postmaster An official appointed to manage a local post office.

Tammany Hall New York City political organization that often dominated city and sometimes state politics by controlling the Democratic Party in New York City.

Democratic Party. Between 1868 and 1904, he served in several elected positions in state and city government. Plunkitt explained how he kept the loyalty of his neighborhood voters:

> Go right down among the poor families and help them in the different ways they need help. . . . It's philanthropy, but it's politics, too—mighty good politics. . . . The poor are the most grateful people in the world, and, let me tell you, they have more friends in their neighborhoods than the rich have in theirs. . . . The consequence is that the poor look up to George W. Plunkitt as a father, come to him in trouble—and don't forget him on election day.

Plunkitt typified many big-city politicians across the country. Throughout the late nineteenth century, urban politicians cultivated lower-income voters by addressing their needs directly and personally. They tried to build a personal rapport with the voters, and responded to the needs of the urban poor by providing an occasional basket of food or a job in some city department. In return, they wanted political loyalty. Such urban political organizations flourished during the years 1870–1910, and some survived long after that. Similar organizations—sometimes Republican but more often Democratic—emerged in nearly all large cities, based among lower-income voters, usually led by men of recent immigrant backgrounds. Where they amassed great power, their rivals denounced the leader as a boss and the organization as a **machine**.

In every city, opponents of the machine charged corruption. Some bosses accumulated sizable fortunes—sometimes through gifts or retainers from companies seeking franchises or city contracts (their critics called these bribes), sometimes through advance knowledge of city planning. Richard Croker, the boss of Tammany in the 1890s, accumulated an immense personal fortune, but he always insisted that he had never taken a dishonest dollar.

Above all, the bosses centralized political decision making. "There's got to be in every ward somebody that any bloke can come to," a Boston politician insisted, "to get help." If a pushcart vender needed a permit to sell tinware, or a railroad president needed permission to build a bridge, or a saloonkeeper wanted to stay open on Sunday in violation of the law, the machine could help them all—if they showed the proper gratitude in return.

machine When applied to urban political organizations, a derogatory term implying that the organization concentrated on patronage and graft to the exclusion of issues and principles.

prohibition A legal ban on the manufacture, sale, and use of alcoholic beverages.

Republicans and Democrats

Beneath the hoopla and interminable speeches, important differences characterized the major parties. Republicans pointed to their defense of the Union during the Civil War and claimed a monopoly on patriotism, arguing that Democrats—especially southern Democrats—had proven themselves disloyal. "Every man that shot a Union soldier," one Republican orator proclaimed, "was a Democrat." Such rhetoric was often called "waving the bloody shirt." Republicans in Congress voted generous pensions to disabled Union army veterans and the widows and orphans of those who died, and Republican leaders cultivated the Grand Army of the Republic (GAR), the organization of Union veterans, attending their meetings and urging them to "vote as you shot." Republican presidential candidates were usually Union veterans, as were many state and local officials throughout the North.

Republicans proudly claimed responsibility for prosperity, insisting that postwar economic growth resulted from their policies, especially the protective tariff. Republicans boasted that they were the party of decency and morality, and portrayed as typical Democrats "the old slave-owner and slave-driver, the saloon-keeper, the ballot-box-stuffer, the Kuklux [Klan], the criminal class of the great cities, the men who cannot read or write."

Where Republicans defined themselves in terms of what their party did and who they were, Democrats typically focused on what they opposed. Most leading Democrats stood firm against "governmental interference" in the economy, especially the protective tariff and land grants, equating government activism with privileges for a favored few. The protective tariff, they charged, protected manufacturers from international competition at the expense of consumers who paid higher prices. The public domain, they argued, should provide farms for citizens, not subsidies for railroad corporations. In general, Democrats favored a strictly limited role for the government in the economy.

Just as the Democrats opposed governmental interference in the economy, so too did they oppose governmental interference in social relations and behavior. In the North, especially in Irish and German communities, they condemned **prohibition**, which they called a violation of personal liberty. In the South, Democrats rejected federal enforcement of equal rights for African Americans, which they denounced as a violation of states' rights. There, Democrats stood for white supremacy.

Most voters developed strong loyalties to one party or the other, often on the basis of ethnicity, race, or religion. Nearly all Catholics and many Irish, German, and other immigrants supported the Democrats. Most southern whites supported the Democrats as the party of white supremacy. The Democrats' opposition to the

Thomas Nast, the most influential cartoonist of the 1870s and most talented cartoonist of his age, began using an elephant to symbolize the Republicans and a donkey for the Democrats. At the time, however, Republicans often preferred an eagle, and Democrats usually chose a rooster. (Left and right) Library of Congress.

protective tariff attracted entrepreneurs with interests in international commerce. The Democrats, all in all, comprised a diverse coalition, holding together primarily because their various components opposed government action on social or economic matters.

Outside the South, most old-stock Protestants voted Republican, as did most Scandinavian and British immigrants. Nearly all African Americans supported the Republicans as the party of emancipation, as did most veterans of the abolition movement. So many Union veterans supported the Republicans that someone suggested GAR stood for "generally all Republicans." Republicans usually carried New England, Pennsylvania, and much of the Midwest.

Republicans comprised the more coherent political organization, united around a set of policies that involved action by the federal government to foster economic growth and protect blacks' rights. The protective tariff and use of the public domain to encourage rapid economic development both involved positive governmental action. During Reconstruction, the dominant Republicans had changed the very nature of the federal government, redefining citizenship and relations between the federal government and the states. As one leading Republican put it, "The Republican party does things, the Democratic party criticizes." Neither party, however, proposed to regulate, restrict, or tax the new industrial corporations.

Grant's Troubled Presidency: Spoils and Scandals

Despite success as a general, Ulysses S. Grant seemed unprepared when he won the presidency in 1868. During his two terms in office (1869–1877), he usually deferred to Congress for domestic policymaking. Too often he appointed friends or acquaintances to posts for which they possessed few qualifications, and he proved too willing to believe their denials of wrongdoing. He failed to form a competent cabinet and faced constant turnover among his executive advisers. He did choose a highly capable secretary of state, Hamilton Fish, and eventually found in Benjamin Bristow a secretary of the treasury who vigorously combated corruption.

Congress supplied its full share of scandal. Visiting Washington in 1869, Henry Adams was surprised to hear a cabinet member bellow, "You can't use tact with a Congressman! A Congressman is a hog! You must take a stick and hit him on the snout!" Too many members of Congress behaved in ways that confirmed such cynical views. In 1868, before Grant became president, several congressional leaders became stockholders in the **Crédit Mobilier**, a company that

■ **Crédit Mobilier** Company created to build the Union Pacific Railroad; in a scandalous deal uncovered in 1872–1873, it sold shares cheaply to congressmen who approved federal subsidies for railroad construction.

the chief shareholders in the Union Pacific Railroad created and then gave a generous contract to build the railroad. Thus the company's leaders paid themselves handsomely to construct their own railroad. To prevent congressional scrutiny, the company sold shares at cut-rate prices to key congressmen. Revelation of these arrangements in 1872–1873 scandalized the nation. No sooner did that furor pass than Congress voted itself a 50 percent pay raise and made the increase two years retroactive. Only after widespread public protest did Congress repeal its "salary grab."

Public disgrace was not limited to the federal government or to Republicans. In New York City, the **Tweed Ring** scandal involved city and state officials accused of using bribery, **kickbacks**, and padded accounts to steal money from New York City and the state. At the center was **William Marcy Tweed**, whose name became synonymous with urban political corruption. Tweed entered New York City politics in the 1850s and became head of Tammany Hall in 1863. Labeled "Boss Tweed" by opponents, he and his associates built public support by spending tax funds on charities and giving to the poor from their own pockets—pockets filled with ill-gotten gains.

Under Tweed's direction, city government launched major construction projects: public buildings, streets, parks, and sewers. Much of the construction was riddled with corruption. Between 1868 and 1871, the Tweed Ring may have plundered $200 million from the city, mostly by giving bloated construction contracts to businesses that returned a kickback to the ring. In 1871 evidence of corruption led to Tweed's indictment and ultimately his conviction and imprisonment.

Grant easily won reelection in 1872, but the midterm elections of 1874 were a different story. The congressional scandals alienated some voters. Moreover, the depression that began in 1873 undercut

Republicans' claim to have produced prosperity. Throughout the South, political terrorism suppressed the Republican vote. As a result, Democrats took control of the House of Representatives. For twenty years, from 1874 until 1894, Democrats usually kept their majority in the House of Representatives. Though Republicans usually won the presidency, Democratic control of the House made it difficult or impossible for the Republicans to enact major legislation.

More scandals were to come. In 1875 Treasury Secretary Bristow revealed that a **Whiskey Ring** of federal officials and distillers, centered in St. Louis, had defrauded the government of millions of dollars in whiskey taxes. The 230 men indicted included several of Grant's appointees and even his private secretary. The next year, William Belknap, Grant's secretary of war, resigned shortly before he was impeached for accepting bribes.

The Politics of Stalemate, 1876–1889

From the mid-1870s through the 1880s, as the nation's economy and social patterns changed with astonishing speed, American politics seemed frozen in place. From the end of the Civil War to the mid-1870s, politics had revolved largely around issues of war and Reconstruction. By the late 1870s, other issues emerged as crucial, notably the economy and political corruption. After the mid-1870s, however, voters divided almost evenly between the two major political parties, beginning a long political **stalemate** during which neither party could enact its proposals.

Republican Rutherford B. Hayes became president after the closely contested election of 1876 (discussed in Chapter 15). His personal integrity and principled stand on issues helped restore his party's reputation after the embarrassments of the Grant administration. However, he faced a Democratic majority in the House of Representatives and significant opposition within his own party. Roscoe Conkling, a flamboyant senator and boss of New York's powerful and patronage-hungry Republican organization, became Hayes's harshest Republican critic after Hayes refused Conkling's demands regarding patronage. Hayes also estranged reformers by not seeking a full-scale revision of the spoils system. He did not seek reelection in 1880.

In 1880, the Republican nominating convention deadlocked between the supporters of James G. Blaine of Maine, a spellbinding orator who attracted loyal supporters and bitter enemies, and Conkling and his followers, who called themselves **Stalwarts** and wanted to nominate former president Grant. Eventually the deadlock produced a compromise, James A. Garfield, a congressman from Ohio. Born in a log cabin, Garfield had grown up in poverty. A minister, college president, and lawyer before the Civil War, he

■ **Tweed Ring** Name applied to the political organization of William Marcy Tweed. "Ring," in this context, means a group of people who act together to exercise control over something.

kickback An illegal payment by a contractor to the official who awarded the contract.

William Marcy Tweed New York City political boss who used the Tammany organization to control city and state government from the 1860s until his downfall in 1871.

Whiskey Ring Distillers and federal revenue officials in St. Louis who were revealed in 1875 to have defrauded the government of millions of dollars in whiskey taxes.

stalemate In chess, a situation where neither player can move, and therefore neither can win. Thus, any situation where neither side can gain an advantage.

Stalwarts Faction of the Republican Party led by Roscoe Conkling of New York; Stalwarts claimed to be the genuine Republicans.

Republicans circulated this cartoon in 1884, claiming that the Democrats' proposed tariff reform would threaten wages and endanger little children, but that Republicans' commitment to the protective tariff would protect wages and make families more secure.

became the Union's youngest major general. For vice president, the delegates tried to placate the Stalwarts by nominating Conkling's chief lieutenant, Chester A. Arthur.

Garfield won the popular vote by half a percentage point but won the electoral vote convincingly. He brought to the presidency a solid understanding of Congress and a studious approach to issues. Though he appointed Blaine as secretary of state, the most prestigious cabinet position, Garfield also hoped to work cooperatively with the Stalwarts. When Conkling arrogantly demanded his supporters be appointed to key federal positions, Garfield proved to be politically shrewder than any president since Lincoln. Humiliated, Conkling resigned from the Senate, and Garfield scored a victory for a stronger presidency.

On July 2, 1881, four months after taking office, Garfield was shot while walking through a Washington railroad station. His assassin, Charles Guiteau, a mentally unstable religious fanatic and disappointed office-seeker, claimed he had acted to save the Republican Party. Two months later, Garfield died of the wound—or of incompetent medical care.

Chester A. Arthur now became president. Probably best known as a member of the Conkling organization and a dapper dresser, Arthur soon showed, as one of his former associates said, that "He isn't 'Chet' Arthur any more; he's the President." In 1882 doctors diagnosed him as suffering from Bright's disease, a kidney condition that produced fatigue, depression,

and eventually death. Arthur kept the news secret from all but his family and closest friends. Despite political liabilities and his own physical limitations, Arthur proved more capable than anyone might have predicted.

In 1884, Blaine—charming and quick-witted— finally secured the Republican nomination. The Democrats chose Grover Cleveland, the governor of New York, who had earned a reputation for integrity and political courage by attacking Tammany Hall. Many Irish voters—a large component in Tammany— seemed attracted to Blaine. Seeking to tarnish Cleveland's image of integrity, Republicans trumpeted that Cleveland had fathered a child outside marriage by chanting, "Ma! Ma! Where's my pa?" The election hinged on New York State, where Blaine hoped to cut into the usually Democratic Irish vote. A few days before the election, however, Blaine was present when a preacher in New York City called the Democrats the party of "rum, Romanism [Catholicism], and rebellion." Blaine failed to respond quickly to this insult to his Irish Catholic supporters. Cleveland won New York by a tiny margin, and New York's electoral votes gave him victory.

Cleveland enjoyed support from many who opposed the spoils system, and he insisted on demonstrated ability in those he appointed to office. Staunchly committed to minimal government and cutting federal spending, Cleveland vetoed 414 bills—most granting pensions to individual Union veterans—twice as many

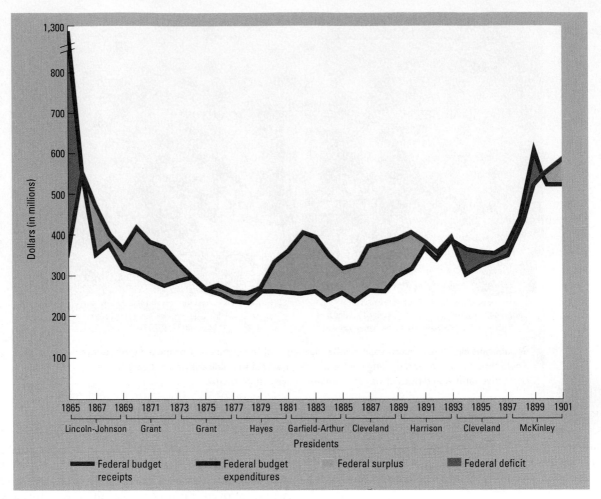

FIGURE 18.1 Federal Receipts and Expenditures, 1865–1901
The federal surplus usually shrank during economic downturns (mid-1870s and mid-1890s) and grew in more prosperous periods (1880s). During the Harrison administration, however, the surplus virtually disappeared, reflecting efforts to reduce income and increase expenditures.

Source: U.S. Department of Commerce, Bureau of the Census, Historical Statistics of the United States, Colonial Times to 1970, Bicentennial edition, 2 vols. (Washington, D.C.: U.S. Government Printing Office, 1975), 1: 1104.

vetoes as all previous presidents *combined*. Cleveland deferred to Congress regarding policymaking and approved several important measures produced by the Democratic House and Republican Senate, including the Dawes Severalty Act (discussed in Chapter 17) and the Interstate Commerce Act.

The Interstate Commerce Act grew out of political pressure from farmers and small businesses. In the early 1870s, several midwestern states passed laws regulating railroad freight rates (usually called Granger laws, discussed later in this chapter). In 1886,

however, the Supreme Court limited states' power to regulate railroad rates. In response, and amid protests over railroad rate discrimination, Congress passed the Interstate Commerce Act in 1887. The new law created the **Interstate Commerce Commission** (ICC), the first federal regulatory commission. Though the law prohibited pools and rebates and required that rates be "reasonable and just," the ICC had little real regulatory power until the Hepburn Act strengthened it in 1906.

Cleveland considered the nation's greatest problem to be the federal budget surplus. After the Civil War, the tariff usually generated more income than the country needed (see Figure 18.1). Worried that the surplus encouraged wasteful spending and that tariffs reduced competition among the developing industrial corporations, Cleveland demanded in

■ **Interstate Commerce Commission** (ICC) The first federal regulatory commission, created in 1887 to regulate railroads and require that rates be "reasonable and just."

1887 that Congress cut tariff rates. His action divided Democrats, but Cleveland provided little leadership. The House and Senate deadlocked, each writing a quite different version of tariff reform, and Congress then adjourned without taking any action. Cleveland's call for tariff reform came to nothing.

In the 1888 presidential election, Democrats renominated Cleveland, but he backed off from the tariff issue and did little campaigning. Republicans nominated Benjamin Harrison, senator from Indiana and a former Civil War general. Thoughtful and cautious, Harrison impressed many as cool and distant. Republicans campaigned vigorously in defense of the protective tariff, raising unprecedented amounts of campaign money from business leaders and issuing record amounts of campaign materials. Harrison received fewer votes than Cleveland (47.9 percent to Cleveland's 48.7 percent) but won in the Electoral College. As important for the Republicans as their narrow presidential victory, however, were the majorities they secured in the House and Senate.

Harrison and the Fifty-first Congress

With Harrison in the White House and Republican majorities in Congress, the Republicans set out to do a lot and to do it quickly. When the fifty-first session of Congress opened late in 1889, Harrison worked more closely with congressional leaders of his own party than any other president in recent memory. Democrats in the House of Representatives tried to delay, but Speaker Thomas B. Reed—an enormous man renowned for his wit—imposed new rules designed to speed up House business.

The Republicans first turned to tariff revision, to cut the troublesome federal surplus without reducing protection. Led by **William McKinley** of Ohio, the **House Ways and Means Committee** drafted a bill that moved some items to the free list (notably sugar, a major source of tariff revenue) but raised tariff rates on other items, sometimes so high as to be prohibitive. The House passed the **McKinley Tariff** in May 1890 and sent it on to the Senate.

The House also approved a federal elections bill, intended to protect the voting rights of African Americans in the South. Sponsored by Representative Henry Cabot Lodge of Massachusetts, the bill proposed federal supervision over congressional elections to prevent disfranchisement, fraud, or violence. Its Democratic opponents called it a "force bill," evoking memories of Reconstruction. After passing the House, the measure went to the Senate, where approval by the Republican majority seemed likely.

Harrison wanted the two bills passed as a party package, but Republicans feared that a Democratic **filibuster** against the elections bill would prevent passage of both measures. Despite protests by Lodge and others, a compromise emerged—Republicans would table the elections bill, and Democrats would not delay the tariff bill. Thus, Republicans sacrificed African Americans' voting rights to gain the revised tariff. Harrison signed the McKinley Tariff on October 1, 1890, and the revised tariff soon produced the intended result: it reduced the surplus by cutting tariff income.

The Senate, meanwhile, had been laboring over two measures named for Senator John Sherman of Ohio: the Sherman Silver Purchase Act (discussed shortly) and the **Sherman Anti-Trust Act**. The Anti-Trust Act, drafted by several Republican senators working with Harrison, was Republicans' response to concerns about monopolies. Approved overwhelmingly, the law declared that "every contract, combination in the form of trust or otherwise, or conspiracy, in restraint of trade or commerce among the several states, or with foreign nations, is hereby declared to be illegal." The law made the United States the first industrial nation to attempt to prevent monopolies, but it proved difficult to interpret and had little initial effect.

In ten months the Republicans passed what one Democrat called "a raging sea of ravenous legislation." In addition to the McKinley Tariff, the Sherman Anti-Trust Act, and the Silver Purchase Act, the record number of new laws included appropriations that laid the basis for a modern navy, a major increase in pension eligibility for disabled Union veterans and their dependents, statehood for North and South Dakota, Montana, Washington, Idaho, and Wyoming, and creation of territorial government in Oklahoma. Republicans hoped they had finally broken the political logjam that had clogged politics since 1875.

■ **William McKinley** (1843–1901) Twenty-fifth president. Served in the House of Representatives and as governor of Ohio before winning the presidency in 1896. Assassinated in 1901.

House Ways and Means Committee One of the most significant standing (permanent) committees of the House of Representatives, responsible for initiating all taxation measures.

■ **McKinley Tariff** Tariff passed by Congress in 1890 that sought not only to protect established industries but by prohibitory duties to stimulate the creation of new industries.

filibuster A speech by a bill's opponents to delay legislative action; usually applies to extended speeches in the U.S. Senate, which has no time limit on speeches and where a minority may therefore "talk a bill to death" by holding up all other business.

■ **Sherman Anti-Trust Act** Law passed by Congress in 1890 authorizing the federal government to prosecute any "combination" "in restraint of trade"; because of adverse court rulings, it had little initial effect.

It Matters Today

The Defeat of the Lodge Bill

CHALLENGES TO POLITICS AS USUAL

★ What were the major goals of the various reform groups?

★ Why were some reformers more successful than others?

Though political change seemed to move at a glacial pace in the Gilded Age, several groups challenged mainstream politics and sought new policies and new ways of making political decisions. Given the number of Americans still engaged in agriculture, it should not be surprising that farmers were prominent in several significant movements.

Grangers, Greenbackers, and Silverites

Crop prices fell steadily after the Civil War as production of wheat, corn, and cotton grew much faster than the population (see Figure 16.1, page 419). Some farmers, however, denied that prices were falling solely because of overproduction, pointing to the hungry and ragged residents of urban slums. Farmers condemned the monopolistic practices of **commodity markets** in Chicago and New York that determined crop prices. They knew that the bushel of corn they sold for 10 or 20 cents in October brought three or four times that amount in New York in December. When they brought their crops to market, however, farmers accepted the price that was offered because they needed cash to pay their debts and could not store their crops for later sale at a higher price.

Many farmers borrowed heavily to establish new farms after the Civil War. Falling prices magnified their indebtedness. Because crop prices sank lower and lower, farmers raised more and more just to pay their mortgages and buy necessities. Given the relation between supply and demand, the more they raised, the lower prices fell. They must have felt as if they were running faster and faster just to stay in the same place, and many found they could not keep up.

In addition, the railroads seemed to be greedy monopolies that charged as much as possible to deliver supplies to rural America and carry farm crops to market. It sometimes cost four times as much to ship freight in the West or South as in the East. Farmers also protested that the railroads dominated politics in many western and southern states and distributed free passes to politicians in return for favorable treatment.

Soon organizations began to address the scourges of falling prices and high railroad freight rates. The first was formed by Oliver H. Kelley in 1867. Officially

commodity market Financial market in which brokers buy and sell agricultural products in large quantities, thus determining the prices paid to farmers for their harvests.

called the Patrons of Husbandry, it was usually known as the **Grange** and extended full participation to women as well as men. Kelley saw the Grange as a social outlet for farm families and a way to educate them in new farming methods.

The Grange grew rapidly, especially in the Midwest and central South. In the 1870s, it became a leading proponent for cooperative buying and selling. Many local Granges set up cooperative stores (consumers' cooperatives), where members did their shopping and divided any profits among themselves. Some formed producers' cooperatives, in which farmers agreed to hold their crops back from market and jointly negotiate over prices. Two state Granges began manufacturing farm machinery, and Grangers planned for cooperative factories producing everything from wagons to sewing machines. Some Grangers formed mutual insurance companies, and a few experimented with cooperative banks.

The Grange defined itself as nonpartisan. However, as Grange membership boomed in the 1870s, its midwestern and western members moved toward political action. New political parties emerged in eleven states, usually called "Granger Parties." They demanded state legislation to prohibit railroad rate discrimination. Other groups, especially merchants, also sought such laws, but the Grangers were so prominent that the resulting state laws, most dating to 1872–1874, were usually called **Granger laws**. When the constitutionality of such regulation was challenged, the Supreme Court ruled, in *Munn v. Illinois* (1877), that businesses with "a public interest," including warehouses and railroads, "must submit to be controlled by the public for the common good."

The Grange reached its zenith in the mid-1870s. Hastily organized cooperatives soon encountered financial problems that were compounded by the national depression. As cooperatives collapsed, they often pulled down Grange organizations. Political activity brought some successes but also generated bitter internal disputes. The organization lost many members, and surviving Granges generally avoided both cooperatives and politics.

With the decline of the Grange, some farmers looked to **monetary policy** for relief. After the Civil War, most prices fell (a situation called **deflation**) because of increased production, more efficient techniques in agriculture and manufacturing, and the failure of the money supply to grow as rapidly as the economy. Deflation has always injured debtors

This poster appeared in 1869, shortly after the founding of the Grange. It depicts the farmer, in the center, as a member of the producing class with the caption, "I pay for all." Above him is a liberty cap, a symbol of freedom. Around the edge are a military officer ("I fight for all"), railroad magnate ("I carry for all"), physician ("I prescribe for all"), politician ("I legislate for all"), lawyer ("I plead for all"), merchant ("I trade for all"), and preacher ("I pray for all")—but the poster implies that all of them are living off the farmer's labor. Library of Congress.

■ **Grange** Organization for farmers that combined social activities with education about improved farming methods and cooperative economic efforts; formally called the Patrons of Husbandry.

■ **Granger laws** State laws regulating railroads, passed in several states in the 1870s in response to lobbying by the Grange and other groups.

monetary policy Now, the regulation of the money supply and interest rates by the Federal Reserve. Before 1913, federal monetary policy was largely limited to defining the medium of the currency (gold, silver, or paper) and the relations between the types of currency.

deflation Falling prices, a situation in which the purchasing power of the dollar increases; the opposite of deflation is inflation, when prices go up and the purchasing power of the dollar declines.

because it means that the money to pay off a loan has greater purchasing power (and so is harder to come by) than the money of the original loan. The Greenback Party argued that increasing the supply of money by printing more **greenbacks**, the paper money issued during the Civil War, would stabilize prices. They found a receptive audience among farmers in debt.

In the congressional elections of 1878, the Greenback Party received nearly a million votes and elected fourteen congressmen. In the 1880 presidential election, Greenbackers tried to attract urban workers by supporting the eight-hour workday, legislation to protect workers, and the abolition of child labor. They also called for regulation of transportation and communication, a **graduated income tax** (which they considered the fairest form of taxation), and woman suffrage. For president, they nominated James B. Weaver of Iowa, a Greenback congressman and former Union army general. He got only 3.3 percent of the vote. In 1884, the Greenbackers fared even worse.

The prevalent currency deflation also motivated those who wanted the government to resume issuing silver dollars. In 1873 Congress dropped the silver dollar from the list of approved coins, following the lead of Britain, Germany, and other European nations, which had specified that only gold was to serve as money. Some Americans believed that adhering to this **gold standard** was essential if American businesses were to compete effectively in international markets for capital and goods.

The Grange tries to awaken the public to the approaching locomotive (a symbol of monopoly power) that is bringing consolidation (mergers), extortion (high prices), bribery, and other evils. Railroad ties (the wooden pieces on which the rails rested) are sometimes called sleepers.

greenbacks Paper money, not backed by gold, that the federal government issued during the Civil War.

graduated income tax Tax based on income, such that the percentage of income paid as tax increases with income level, so that those with the lowest income pay the lowest percentage and those with higher incomes pay a larger percentage.

■ **gold standard** A monetary system based on gold, under which legal contracts typically called for the payment of all debts in gold, and paper money could be redeemed in gold at a bank.

Bland-Allison Act 1878 law providing for federal purchase of limited amounts of silver to be coined into silver dollars.

■ **Sherman Silver Purchase Act** 1890 law requiring the federal government to increase its purchases of silver to be coined into silver dollars.

■ **Mugwumps** Reformers, mostly Republicans, of the 1880s and 1890s who opposed political corruption and campaigned for reform, especially civil service reform, sometimes crossing party boundaries to achieve their goals.

Given major silver discoveries in the West, resuming silver coinage seemed a way to counteract deflation without resorting to greenbacks. Silver coinage quickly found support not just among farmers but also among silver mining interests. Members of this farming-mining coalition were soon called "silverites." In 1878, over Hayes's veto, Congress passed the **Bland-Allison Act** authorizing a limited amount of silver dollars. The act failed to counteract deflation, and satisfied neither silverites nor gold supporters. The **Sherman Silver Purchase Act** of 1890 increased the amount of silver to be coined, but both silverites and advocates of the gold standard still found it unsatisfactory.

Reforming the Spoils System

A very different set of reformers challenged the spoils system. Known as **Mugwumps** to their contemporaries and centered in Boston and New York, most were Republicans of high social status. Like Carl Schurz, they blamed many of the defects of politics on the spoils system, argued that eliminating patronage would drive out the machines and opportunists, and advocated a merit system based on a job seeker's ability to pass a comprehensive examination. As they did with others who broke with their party, party politicians sometimes questioned the Mugwumps' manhood.

The assassination of President Garfield by a disappointed office seeker spurred efforts to reform the patronage system. Sponsored by Senator George Pendleton (an Ohio Democrat), the **Pendleton Act** of 1883 created a merit system for filling federal positions. The new law designated certain federal positions, about 15 percent of the total, as "classified" and required these **classified civil service** positions to be filled only through competitive examinations. The law authorized the president to add positions to the classified list. Within twenty years, the law applied to 44 percent of federal employees. Most state and local governments eventually adopted merit systems as well.

Challenging the Male Bastion: Woman Suffrage

In the masculine political world of the Gilded Age, men were expected to display strong loyalty to a political party, but men considered women—who could not vote—to stand outside the party system. The concepts of domesticity and separate spheres dictated that women avoid politics, especially party politics. Some women nonetheless involved themselves in reform efforts, and a few even took part in party activities. In the late nineteenth century, some women also pushed for full political participation through the right to vote.

The struggle for woman suffrage was of long standing. In 1848 Elizabeth Cady Stanton and four other women organized the world's first Women's Rights Convention, held at Seneca Falls, New York. Their Declaration of Principles announced, in part, "It is the duty of the women of this country to secure to themselves their sacred right to the elective franchise." Stanton and Susan B. Anthony became the most prominent advocates for women's rights, especially voting rights, through the turn of the century. They convinced lawmakers to modify some laws that discriminated against women but failed to secure voting rights. During the nineteenth century, however, women increasingly participated in public affairs: in movements to abolish slavery, mobilize support for the Union, improve educational opportunities, end child labor, and more.

In 1866 Stanton and Anthony unsuccessfully opposed inclusion of the word *male* in the Fourteenth Amendment. In 1869 they formed the **National Woman Suffrage Association** (NWSA), with membership open only to women, and sought an amendment to the federal Constitution as the only sure route to woman suffrage. The NWSA built alliances with other reform and radical organizations and worked to improve women's status, promoting women's trade unions and lobbying for easier divorce laws and access to birth-control information. In contrast, the **American Woman Suffrage Association** (AWSA), organized by Lucy Stone and other suffrage advocates, also in 1869, concentrated strictly on winning the vote and avoided other issues. The two organizations merged in 1890 to become the National American Woman Suffrage Association.

The first victories for suffrage came in the West. In 1869, in Wyoming Territory, the territorial legislature extended the franchise to women. Wyoming women had forged a well-organized suffrage movement and persuaded some male legislators to support their cause. Some legislators also hoped that woman suffrage would attract more women to Wyoming, which at the time had about seven thousand men but only two thousand women. Thereafter, women in Wyoming Territory voted, served on juries, and held elective office. In 1889, when Wyoming asked for statehood, some congressmen balked at admitting a state with woman suffrage. Wyoming legislators, however, bluntly stated, "We will remain out of the Union a hundred years rather than come in without the women." Congress finally voted to approve Wyoming statehood—with woman suffrage—in 1890.

Utah Territory adopted woman suffrage in 1870. Mormon men formed the majority of Utah's voters, and Mormon women far outnumbered the relatively few non-Mormon women. By enfranchising women, Mormons strengthened their voting majority and may have hoped, at the same time, to silence those who claimed that **polygamy** degraded women. However, in an act aimed at the Mormons, Congress outlawed polygamy in 1887 and simultaneously disfranchised Utah women. Not until Utah became a state, in 1896, did its women regain the vote. In 1893, Colorado voters (all male) approved woman suffrage, making Colorado the first state to adopt woman suffrage through a popular vote. In addition to a well-organized campaign by Colorado women, their cause was assisted

---

■ **Pendleton Act** 1883 law that created the Civil Service Commission and instituted a merit system of competitive examinations for federal hiring and jobs.

classified civil service Federal jobs filled through the merit system instead of by patronage.

■ **National Woman Suffrage Association** (NWSA) Women's suffrage organization formed in 1869 and led by Elizabeth Cady Stanton and Susan B. Anthony; accepted only women as members and worked for suffrage and related issues such as unionizing female workers.

■ **American Woman Suffrage Association** (AWSA) Boston-based women's suffrage organization formed in 1869; it welcomed men and worked solely to win the vote for women.

polygamy The practice of a man having more than one wife; Mormons practiced polygamy, which they referred to as plural marriage, until 1890.

could vote in school elections in nine-teen states and on bond and tax issues in three.

Structural Change and Policy Change

Grangers, Greenbackers, local labor parties, the WCTU, Mugwumps, and advocates of woman suffrage all challenged basic features of the party-bound political system of the Gilded Age. They and other groups sought political changes that the major parties ignored: abolition of the spoils system, woman suffrage, prohibition, the secret ballot, regulation of business, an end to child labor, changes in monetary policy, and more.

Most of these groups called themselves reformers, meaning that they wanted to change the *form* of politics. Most reforms fall into one of two categories—structural change and policy change. Structural reform modifies the *structure* of political decision making, for example, the way in which public officials are selected or eligibility for voting. Advocates of woman suffrage and those seeking to eliminate the spoils system were seeking to change the *structure* of politics.

Policy issues, in contrast, have to do with the way that government uses its powers to accomplish particular objectives. The debate over federal economic policy in the Gilded Age provides an array of contrasting positions. Many Democrats favored a policy of laissez faire, believing that federal interference in the economy created a privileged class. Republicans used land grants and the protective tariff to encourage economic growth. Grangers wanted the government to regulate economic activity by prohibiting pools and rebates and setting railroad rates. Greenbackers wanted monetary policy to benefit debtors—or, as they would have put it, to stop benefiting lenders.

Groups seeking change may find they have little in common or may seek to cooperate with other groups. Frances Willard of the WCTU embraced a wide range of reforms. One key distinction between the National Woman Suffrage Association and the American Woman Suffrage Association was that the NWSA welcomed political alliances with groups who supported suffrage for all citizens. The AWSA feared such alliances might lose more support than they gained and focused narrowly on suffrage.

This sketch of women voting in Cheyenne, Wyoming Territory, appeared in 1888. In 1869, Wyoming became the first state or territory to extend suffrage to women. This drawing appeared shortly before Wyoming requested statehood, a request made controversial by the issue of woman suffrage.

Library of Congress.

by support from the new Populist Party (discussed in the next section). In Idaho, where both Mormon and Populist influences were strong, male voters approved woman suffrage in 1896. These western states were among the first places in the world to grant women equal voting rights with men.

Several states also began to extend limited voting rights to women, especially for school board elections and school bond issues. These concessions perhaps reflected the widespread assumption that women's gender roles included child rearing. By 1890, women

policy A course of action adopted by a government, usually pursued over a period of time and potentially involving several laws and agencies.

In the Wider World

Woman Suffrage

The following table presents the dates when women achieved the right to vote in all elections for various nations and parts of nations. Space does not a permit a complete list. Some places had restricted forms of woman suffrage before the dates indicated; for example, women could vote for school board members but not in any other elections in some American states. In New Jersey, women were accidentally granted the suffrage in 1776 through the use of the word "people" rather than "men," but this grant of suffrage was removed in 1807.

TABLE 18.1 Woman Suffrage Around the World

Year	Place	Year	Place
1838	Pitcairn Island	1934	Turkey, Cuba
1869	Wyoming Territory	1940	Quebec (completing full suffrage in all of Canada)
1870	Utah Territory (lost in 1887)	1945	France, Italy
1890	Wyoming (state)	1945	France, Italy
1893	Colorado, New Zealand	1946	Japan
1894	South Australia (limited voting since 1861)	1948	Belgium, Chile, Israel, Republic of Korea
1896	Idaho, Utah	1950	India
1899	Western Australia	1952	*United Nations Covenant on Political Rights calls for woman suffrage*
1902	New South Wales (Australia)	1952	Greece
1906	Finland	1953	Bolivia
1908	Australia (all states; federal voting in 1902)	1954	Colombia, Ghana
1910	Washington (state)	1956	Egypt, Pakistan
1911	California	1958	Mexico
1912	Arizona, Kansas, Oregon	1962	Algeria
1913	Alaska Territory, Illinois, Norway	1963	Iran, Morocco
1914	Montana, Nevada	1964	Afghanistan, Sudan
1915	Denmark, including Iceland	1971	Switzerland (all but one canton)
1916	Alberta, Manitoba, Saskatchewan (Canada)	1973	Syria (first gained in 1953 and lost soon after)
1917	New York, North Dakota, Nebraska, Rhode Island, British Columbia and Ontario (Canada), Russia	1974	Jordan, Portugal
1918	Michigan, Oklahoma, South Dakota, Austria, Germany, Poland	1976	Spain (gained in 1931 but lost following the Spanish civil war)
1919	Indiana, Maine, Missouri, Iowa, Minnesota, Ohio, Wisconsin, Tennessee, Netherlands	1977	Libya
1919	Indiana, Maine, Missouri, Iowa, Minnesota, Ohio, Wisconsin, Tennessee, Netherlands	1980	Iraq
1920	**United States of America,** Czechoslovakia	1990	Last Swiss canton approves full suffrage
1921	Sweden	2005	Kuwait
1922	Irish Free State (Ireland)	2010	United Arab Emirates (projected) Women barred from voting: Brunei (men also), Saudi Arabia
1928	United Kingdom	2010	United Arab Emirates (projected) Women barred from voting: Brunei (men also), Saudi Arabia
1932	Thailand, Brazil, Uruguay	2010	United Arab Emirates (projected) Women barred from voting: Brunei (men also), Saudi Arabia

Some groups combined structural and policy proposals. The tiny Prohibition Party wanted government to eliminate alcohol but also favored woman suffrage because they assumed that women voters would oppose alcohol. Thus, they promoted a structural reform, woman suffrage, in part to accomplish a policy reform, prohibition of alcohol. Advocates of woman suffrage also argued that enfranchising women would lead to a new approach to politics and to new policies.

One important structural change received widespread support from many political groups, and many states adopted it soon after its first appearance. The **Australian ballot**—printed and distributed by the government, not by political parties, listing all candidates of all parties, and marked in a private voting booth—was first adopted by Massachusetts in 1888. The idea quickly spread to all states and carried important implications for political parties. Now voters could easily cross party lines. No longer could party activists see which party's ballot a voter dropped into the ballot box. The switch to the Australian ballot and the Pendleton Act marked significant efforts to limit parties' power and influence.

POLITICAL UPHEAVAL IN THE 1890S

★ Which groups and issues led to the formation of the Populist Party?

★ What were the issues in the 1896 presidential election, and what were the short-term and long-term results?

In 1890–1891, farmers who felt hard-pressed by debts, low prices for their crops, and the monopoly power of the railroads formed the People's Party, or **Populists**, and won elections in several states. The Depression that began in 1893 set the stage for more political change, culminating in the 1896 presidential election, which made the Republicans the majority party for a generation.

■ **Australian ballot** A ballot printed by the government, rather than by political parties, and marked privately.

■ **Populists** Members of the People's Party; held their first presidential nominating convention in 1892; called for federal action to control big business and assist farmers and workers. The more general term **populist** refers to a politician who attacks, and seeks to mobilize people against, the existing power structure.

■ **Farmers' Alliances** Organizations of farm families in the 1880s and 1890s, similar to the Grange.

■ **antimonopolism** Opposition to great concentrations of economic power such as large corporations, as well as to actual monopolies.

The People's Party

Populism grew out of the economic problems of farmers, especially falling prices for crops, the economic power of the railroads, and currency issues. The Grange, the Greenback Party, and the silver movement in the late 1870s had expressed farmers' grievances, but those movements faded during the relatively prosperous 1880s. By 1890, however, falling crop prices and widespread indebtedness brought renewed concern among farmers.

In the 1880s, three new organizations emerged, all called **Farmers' Alliances**. One was centered in the north-central states. Another, the Southern Alliance, began in Texas in the late 1870s and spread eastward across the South. The Southern Alliance limited its membership to white farmers, but a third group, the Colored Farmers' Alliance, recruited southern black farmers. Like the Grange and Knights of Labor, the Alliances defined themselves as organizations of the "producing classes" and looked to cooperatives as a partial solution to their problems. Alliance stores were most common. The Texas Alliance also experimented with cooperative cotton selling, and some midwestern local Alliances tried cooperative grain storage and selling.

Local Alliance meetings featured social and educational activities. By the late 1880s, a host of weekly newspapers across the South and West presented Alliance views. One Kansas woman described the result: "People commenced to think who had never thought before, and people talked who had seldom spoken. . . . Thoughts and theories sprouted like weeds after a May shower."

The Alliances defined themselves as nonpartisan and expected their members to work within the major parties. This was especially important in the South, where any white person who challenged the Democratic Party risked being condemned as a traitor to both race and region. Many Midwestern Alliance leaders, however, came out of the Granger Party tradition, and some had been Greenbackers. During the winter of 1889–1890, corn prices had fallen so low that some farmers found it cheaper to burn their corn than to sell it and buy fuel. More and more Alliance members talked of political action.

Through the hot summer of 1890, Alliance members in Kansas, Nebraska, the Dakotas, Minnesota, and surrounding states formed new political parties to contest state and local elections. One explained that the political battle they waged was "between the insatiable greed of organized wealth and the rights of the great plain people." Women took a prominent part in Populist campaigning, especially in Kansas and Nebraska. Mary Elizabeth Lease was among the most effective.

Populists emphasized three elements in their campaigns: **antimonopolism**, government action on behalf of farmers and workers, and increased popular control of government. Their antimonopolism drew on their unhappy experiences with railroads, grain buyers, and manufacturing companies. It also derived from a long American tradition of opposition to concentrated economic power. Populists quoted Thomas Jefferson on the importance of equal rights for all, and they compared themselves to Andrew Jackson in his fight against the Bank of the United States.

"We believe the time has come," Populists proclaimed in 1892, "when the railroad companies will either own the people or the people must own the railroads." Their solution to the dangers of monopoly was government action on behalf of farmers and workers, including federal ownership of the railroads and the telegraph and telephone systems, and government alternatives to private banks. Currency inflation, through greenbacks, silver, or both, formed an important part of the Populists' platform, along with a graduated income tax. Through such measures, they hoped, in the words of their 1892 platform, that "oppression, injustice, and poverty shall eventually cease in the land." They hoped to gain support among urban and industrial workers by calling for the eight-hour workday and opposing companies' use of private armies in labor disputes.

Finally, the People's Party favored structural changes to make government more responsive to the people, including expansion of the merit system for government employees, election of U.S. senators by the voters instead of state legislatures, a one-term limit for the president, and the secret ballot. Many also favored woman suffrage. In the South, Populists posed a serious challenge to the prevailing patterns of politics by seeking to forge a political alliance of the disadvantaged of both races. Populists usually opposed disfranchisement of black voters.

Thus Populists wanted to use government to control, even to own, the corporate behemoths that had evolved in their lifetimes. They also deeply distrusted the old parties and wanted to increase the influence of the individual voter in political decision making.

The Elections of 1890 and 1892

Despite Republicans' hopes for breaking the political logjam during the Fifty-first Congress, they immediately found themselves on the defensive. The issues in the 1890 elections for members of the House of Representatives and for state and local offices varied by region. In the West, the Populists stood at the center of the campaign, lambasting both major parties for ignoring the needs of the people. In the South, Democrats held up Lodge's "force bill" as a warning of the potential dangers if southern whites should bolt the party of white supremacy. There, members

VOL. 20 NO. 50.   JUNE 6 1891   PRICE 10 CENTS.

A PARTY OF PATCHES.
Grand Balloon Ascension—Cincinnati, May 20th, 1891.

When the Populists launched their new party, one cartoonist depicted them as a hot-air balloon of political malcontents. This cartoon may have inspired Frank Baum, author of *The Wizard of Oz*, whose wizard arrived in Oz in a hot-air balloon launched from Omaha, site of the Populists' 1892 nominating convention.

of the Southern Alliance worked within the Democratic Party to secure candidates committed to the farmers' cause. In the Northeast, Democrats attacked the McKinley Tariff for producing higher prices for consumers. In the Rocky Mountain region, nearly all candidates pledged their support for unlimited silver coinage.

The new Populist Party scored several victories, marking it as the most successful new party since the Republicans in the 1850s. Kansas Republican Senator John J. Ingalls had dismissed Populists as "a sort of turnip crusade," but Populists won control of the Kansas legislature and elected a Populist to replace him in the Senate. Elsewhere Populists elected state legislators, members of Congress, and one other U.S. senator. All across the South, the Alliance claimed that successful candidates owed their victories to Alliance voters.

Everywhere Republicans suffered defeat, losing nearly half their seats in the House of Representatives. Many Republican candidates for state and local offices also lost. The losses bred dissension within the party, and President Harrison could not maintain party unity.

For the 1892 presidential election, the Republicans renominated Harrison though he aroused little

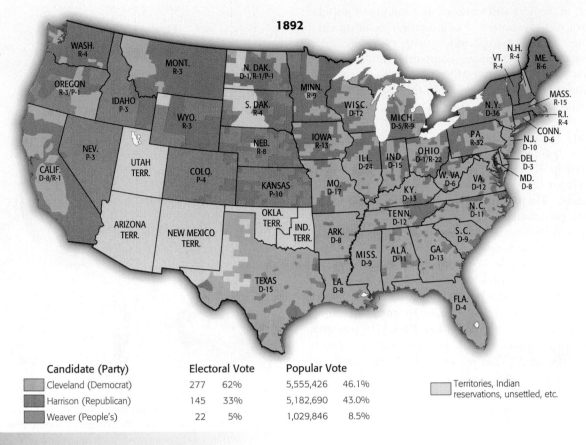

1892

Candidate (Party)	Electoral Vote		Popular Vote	
Cleveland (Democrat)	277	62%	5,555,426	46.1%
Harrison (Republican)	145	33%	5,182,690	43.0%
Weaver (People's)	22	5%	1,029,846	8.5%

Territories, Indian reservations, unsettled, etc.

MAP 18.1 Popular Vote for President, 1892
Support for the Populist Party's presidential candidate, James B. Weaver, was concentrated in the West and South. Nationwide, he received 8.5 percent of the vote. Copyright © Cengage Learning

enthusiasm among many party leaders. The Democrats again chose Grover Cleveland. Southern Alliance activists joined western Populists to form a national People's Party and nominated James Weaver, the Greenback presidential candidate in 1880. Democrats and Populists scored the most impressive victories. Cleveland became the only president in American history to win two nonconsecutive terms. Democrats kept control of the House of Representatives and won a majority in the Senate. Populists displayed particular strength in the West and South (see Map 18.1). The Democrats now found themselves where the Republicans had stood four years before: in control of the presidency and Congress.

Failure of the Divided Democrats

When Congress met in 1893, Democrats faced several controversial issues, especially silver coinage and the tariff. The depression that had begun earlier that year (discussed in Chapter 16) and rising unemployment also demanded attention. President Cleveland, holding to his party's traditional commitment to minimal

government and laissez faire, opposed any federal assistance to those in need. In the midst of financial crisis, Cleveland suffered a personal crisis—doctors detected cancer in his mouth. Fearing this news might lead to further financial panic, the president kept his surgery and recuperation secret.

Many business leaders argued that the Sherman Silver Purchase Act of 1890 had caused the gold drain that set off the depression, but many western and southern Democrats supported it as better than no silver coinage at all. Convinced that silver coinage had contributed to the economic collapse, Cleveland asked Congress to repeal the Silver Purchase Act. In the House of Representatives, most Republicans voted for repeal, but more than a third of the Democrats were opposed. In the Senate, Republicans supported Cleveland by 2 to 1, but Democrats divided almost evenly. Cleveland won but divided his own party, pitting the Northeast against the West and much of the South.

The Democrats also had to grapple with the tariff. After their harsh condemnation of the McKinley Tariff during the 1892 elections, they now had to do

In 1896, William Jennings Bryan (right), candidate for the Democratic, Populist, and Silver Republican parties, traveled eighteen thousand miles in three months. William McKinley (let), the Republican, stayed home in Canton, Ohio, greeting thousands of well-wishers.

better. The tariff bill produced by the House reduced duties, tried to balance sectional interests, and created an income tax to replace lost federal revenue. Senate Democrats, however, loaded on many amendments. Cleveland characterized the result as "party dishonor" and refused to sign it. It became law without his signature in 1894. (The Supreme Court soon declared the income tax unconstitutional.)

By 1894, many Americans were becoming concerned by growing signs of social disorder. Early that year, Jacob S. Coxey, an Ohio Populist, announced a march on Washington to promote public works programs to provide jobs to the unemployed. The response electrified the nation—by April, six thousand people were camped outside Washington. Soon after, the Pullman Strike shut down many of the nation's railroads until Cleveland deployed U.S troops and marshals against the strikers.

Voters recorded their disgust with the disorganized Democrats in the 1894 elections. Democrats lost everywhere but in the Deep South, giving up 113 seats in the House of Representatives. Populists made few gains and suffered some losses. Republicans scored their biggest gains ever, adding 117 House seats, and looked forward eagerly to the 1896 presidential election.

The 1896 Election and the New Republican Majority

Republicans confidently anticipated victory in the presidential election of 1896. They nominated William McKinley, a Union veteran who had risen to the rank of major. McKinley had served fourteen years in Congress (where he had specialized in the tariff) and two terms as governor of Ohio. Known as calm and competent, McKinley billed himself as the "Advance Agent of Prosperity." The Republican platform supported the gold standard and opposed silver, but McKinley preferred to focus on the tariff. When the convention voted against silver, several western Republicans walked out of the convention and out of the party.

When the Democratic convention met, silverites held the majority but were split among several candidates. Then the platform committee chose **William Jennings Bryan** of Nebraska to speak in a debate on silver. Blessed with a commanding voice, Bryan had

■ **William Jennings Bryan** Nebraska Democrat who advocated silver coinage, opposed imperialism, and ran for president unsuccessfully three times.

Political buttons with pins attached to the back were patented shortly before the 1896 presidential campaign, and they were in great abundance that year. The Bryan-Sewall button pictured shows a clock at 16 minutes to 1:00, a reference to the Democratic commitment to increase the coinage of silver dollars, with a ratio of 16:1—meaning that the amount of silver in a silver dollar would weigh 16 times the amount of gold in a gold dollar. The McKinley button depicts a bicycle wheel to proclaim support for McKinley by a wheelmen's club (bicyclists). Collection of Janice L. and David J. Frent.

won election to the House of Representatives in 1890 and 1892 and gained national attention for his eloquent defense of silver. His speech was masterful. Defining the issue as a conflict between "the producing masses" and "the idle holders of idle capital," he argued that the first priority of federal policy should be "to make the masses prosperous," rather than to benefit the rich in the hope that "their prosperity will leak through on those below." His closing rang defiant: "We will answer their demand for a gold standard by saying to them: You shall not press down upon the brow of labor this crown of thorns. You shall not crucify mankind upon a cross of gold." The speech provoked an enthusiastic half-hour demonstration in support of silver—and Bryan. Only 36 years old, Bryan soon won the presidential nomination

The Populists and defecting Republicans, who were quickly dubbed Silver Republicans, held nominating conventions next, amid frustration that the Democrats had stolen their thunder. Bryan favored silver, the income tax, and other reforms that Populists favored, and had worked closely with Populists. Populists gave him their nomination too, and Silver Republicans did the same. Subsequently, a group of Cleveland supporters nominated a Gold Democratic candidate.

Bryan and McKinley fought all-out campaigns but used sharply contrasting tactics. Bryan, vigorous and young, used his speaking voice as his greatest campaign tool. He spoke directly to the voters in four grueling train journeys through twenty-six states and more than 250 cities. Speaking to perhaps 5 million people in all, he stressed over and over that silver was the most important issue and that other reforms would follow once it was settled. Large crowds of excited and enthusiastic supporters greeted him nearly everywhere.

While McKinley himself campaigned from his home in Canton, Ohio, the Republicans flooded the country with speakers, pamphlets, and campaign paraphernalia, and also chartered trains and brought thousands of supporters to hear McKinley speak. Many business leaders feared that Bryan and silver coinage would bring financial collapse and opposed Bryan's other proposals, especially the income tax and lower tariff rates. McKinley's campaign played on such fears to secure a fund more than double any previous effort and many times what Bryan could raise.

McKinley won by the largest margin since 1872. As Map 18.2 shows, Bryan carried the South and most of the West. McKinley prevailed in the urban, industrial Northeast, and he carried nearly every major city. The crucial battleground was the Midwest, where McKinley carried not only the urban industrial regions but also many farming areas.

Bryan's defeat spelled the end of the Populist Party. Some Populists moved into Bryan's Democratic Party, but others tried to hold together the tattered remnants of Populism. A few joined the Socialist Party, some returned to the Republican Party, and a few simply ignored politics. The issues they had raised—control of huge corporations, the extension of democratic processes, a fair monetary system—lived on in politics. Their influence remained especially prominent in Bryan's wing of the Democratic Party.

Bryan had appealed most to debt-ridden farmers, western miners, and traditional Democrats in the South and big cities. McKinley forged a broader appeal by emphasizing the gold standard and protective tariff as keys to economic recovery. For many urban residents—workers and the middle class alike—silver seemed to promise only higher prices, but the protective tariff meant manufacturing jobs. McKinley also won, in part, by restraining his party's nativist tendencies and denouncing the anti-Catholic American Protective Association, thereby gaining support among some immigrants who approved of his stand on gold and the tariff.

McKinley's victory ushered in a new generation of Republican dominance of national politics. Republicans had majorities in the House of Representatives for twenty-eight of the thirty-six years after 1894, and in the Senate for thirty of those thirty-six years. Republicans won seven of the nine presidential elections between 1896 and 1932, and similar patterns of Republican dominance appeared in state and local government.

Bryan led the Democrats over much of the next sixteen years, and he and his allies moved the party away from its traditional commitment to minimal government. While retaining Democrats' opposition to monopoly and to government favoritism toward business, Bryan and other new Democratic leaders agreed that the solution to the problems of economic

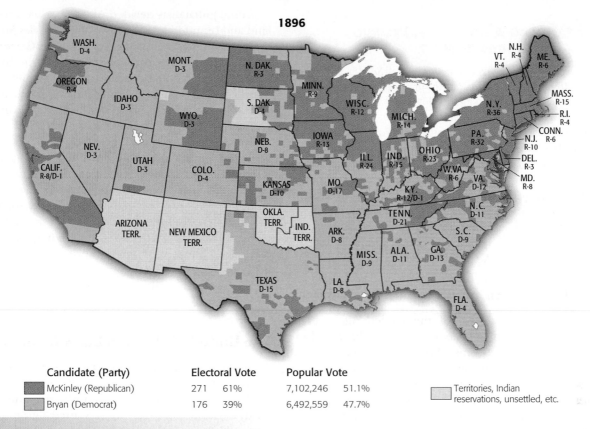

1896

Candidate (Party)	Electoral Vote		Popular Vote	
McKinley (Republican)	271	61%	7,102,246	51.1%
Bryan (Democrat)	176	39%	6,492,559	47.7%

Territories, Indian reservations, unsettled, etc.

MAP 18.2 Election of 1896
Bryan could not win with just the votes of the South and West, for they had few electoral votes. McKinley won in the urban, industrial core region and the more prosperous farming areas of the Midwest (compare Map 18.2 with Map 17.1 on page 455). Copyright © Cengage Learning

concentration lay in a more active government. "A private monopoly," Bryan never tired of repeating, "is indefensible and intolerable." Democrats nonetheless clung to their version of states' rights, which permitted southern Democrats to perpetuate white-supremacist regimes. And most northern Democrats continued to oppose nativism and such moral reforms as prohibition.

McKinley provided strong executive leadership and worked closely with congressional leaders of his party to develop new policies. In 1897 a revised protective tariff fulfilled one Republican campaign promise, driving tariff rates sharply higher and reducing tariff-free imports. The surplus disappeared as an issue partly because of large naval expenditures. In 1900 the **Gold Standard Act** wrote another Republican pledge into law.

Whether Republican or Democrat, many voters now held their party commitments less intensely than before. For most voters before 1890, ethnicity and party went hand in hand. Now voters sometimes felt pulled toward one party by their economic situation and toward the other party by their ethnicity. Such voters sometimes supported Republicans for some

offices and Democrats for others, choices now much easier because of the Australian ballot.

The political role of newspapers also changed. In the 1890s, William Randolph Hearst and Joseph Pulitzer took the lead in transforming urban newspapers into mass circulation dailies, competing for readership through eye-catching headlines and sensational stories. As they focused on increasing their circulation and advertising, they also played down their ties to political parties. Some journalists began to develop the idea of providing balanced political coverage.

American politics in 1888 looked much like American politics in 1876 or even 1844. But in the 1890s, American politics changed. In the early 1900s, the continued decline of political parties and partisan loyalties among voters combined with the emergence of organized interest groups to create even more change, producing the major structural features of American politics in the twentieth century.

Gold Standard Act Law passed by Congress in 1900 that made gold the monetary standard for all currency issued.

STANDING ASIDE FROM WORLD AFFAIRS, 1865–1889

★ How did American policymakers define the role of the United States in North America and other parts of the world during 1865-1889?

The years when domestic politics seemed deadlocked saw little change in the nation's relations with the rest of the world. The nation's role in world affairs was slight, and most Americans expected their nation to follow George Washington's advice to "steer clear of permanent alliances with any portion of the foreign world." The effect of America's economic transformation on its foreign relations, as on its domestic politics, was slow in appearing.

Alaska, Canada, and the *Alabama* Claims

William H. Seward, one of the Gilded Age's most capable secretaries of state, often voiced his belief in America's destiny to expand across the North American continent. When he learned in 1866 that Tsar Alexander II might sell Russian holdings in North America if the price were right, Seward made an offer, and in 1867, for slightly over $7 million, Alaska was in U.S. hands.

The Alaska treaty differed from earlier agreements acquiring territory in one significant way. Like previous treaties, it extended immediate citizenship to all inhabitants of the territory (except Indians), but unlike previous treaties, it carried no promise that the acquired territory would eventually become a state. This half-step away from earlier patterns of territorial expansion foreshadowed later patterns of colonial acquisition.

■ **William H. Seward** U.S. secretary of state under Lincoln and Johnson (1861–1869), a former abolitionist who had expansionist views and arranged the purchase of Alaska from Russia.

Senate Foreign Relations Committee A standing committees of the Senate; its chairman often wields considerable influence over foreign policy.

arbitration Process by which parties to a dispute submit their case to the judgment of an impartial person or group (the arbiter) and agree to accept the arbiter's decision.

■ **Monroe Doctrine** Pronouncement by President James Monroe in 1823 that the Western Hemisphere was off limits for future European colonial expansion.

■ **Benito Juarez** President of Mexico who led resistance to French troops occupying his country in 1864–1867; the first Mexican president of Indian ancestry.

Maximilian Austrian archduke appointed emperor of Mexico by Napoleon III, emperor of France; later executed by Mexican republicans.

Some journalists derided Alaska as a frozen wasteland and branded it "Seward's Folly." Charles Sumner, chairman of the **Senate Foreign Relations Committee**, voiced more enthusiasm, looking on the purchase of Alaska as a first step toward acquiring Canada. Sumner thought a second step might lie in claims against Great Britain arising out of the Civil War. Confederate warships, notably the *Alabama* and *Florida*, built in British shipyards and given refuge and repairs in British ports, had badly disrupted northern shipping. The United States claimed that Britain owed compensation for the damage done by the Confederate cruisers, and Sumner unrealistically suggested that Britain could meet this obligation by ceding all its North American possessions, including Canada, to the United States. Ultimately, however, the two countries agreed to **arbitration**, and the 1872 arbitration decision set $15.5 million as damages to be paid to the United States.

The United States and Latin America

After the Civil War, American diplomats took new interest in Latin America, partly because European powers were starting to exert influence there and partly because some Americans wanted a more prominent role there. In 1823 President James Monroe had announced that the United States would consider any attempt by a European power to colonize in North and South America to be a threat to the United States, but that the United States would neither interfere with existing colonies nor involve itself in European politics. Though later a linchpin of American policy, the **Monroe Doctrine** was rarely mentioned by presidents until the 1890s.

In 1861, as the United States lurched into civil war, France, Spain, and Britain sent a joint force to Mexico to collect debts that Mexico could not pay. Spain and Britain withdrew, but French troops remained despite resistance led by **Benito Juarez**, president of Mexico. Some of Juarez's political opponents cooperated with the French emperor, Napoleon III, to name Archduke **Maximilian** of Austria as emperor of Mexico. Maximilian, a young idealist, apparently believed that the Mexican people genuinely wanted him as their leader. He antagonized some conservative supporters with talk of reform but failed to win other support. In reality, Maximilian held power only because of the French troops.

Involved in its own civil war, the U.S. government recognized Juarez as president but could do little else. When the Civil War ended, however, Seward demanded that Napoleon III withdraw his troops, and underscored his demand by sending fifty thousand battle-hardened troops to the Mexican border. Napoleon III soon brought the French soldiers home.

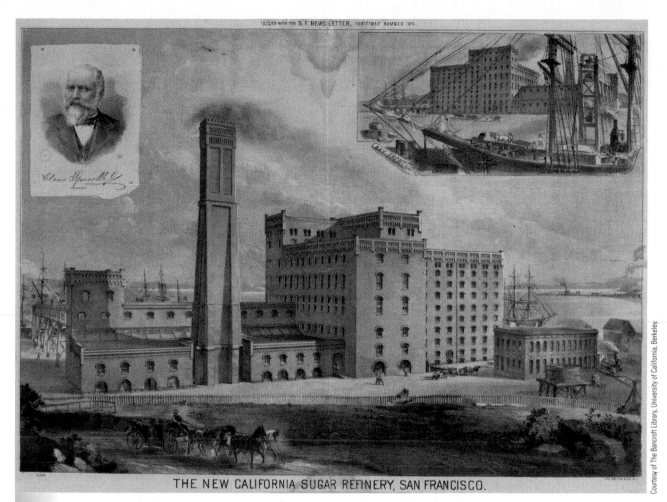

THE NEW CALIFORNIA SUGAR REFINERY, SAN FRANCISCO.

Claus Spreckels accomplished the vertical integration of the sugar industry. His operations began with sugar cane fields on the island of Maui and ended here in San Francisco, at a sugar refinery on the waterfront, where his coworkers could unload the raw sugar from Spreckels's ships and process it into refined sugar for sale in the American market. A similar chain of vertical integration still exists today.

Maximilian unwisely remained behind, where he was defeated in battle by Juarez and then executed. Seward did not cite the Monroe Doctrine, but the withdrawal of French troops in the face of American military force renewed respect in Europe for the role of the United States in Latin America.

Eastern Asia and the Pacific

Americans had long-standing commercial interests in eastern Asia. The China trade dated to 1784, and the first treaty between China and the United States, in 1844, included a provision granting **most-favored-nation status** to the United States. Goods from Asia and the Pacific accounted for 8 percent of U.S. imports after the Civil War. Exports were disappointing, however, and some Americans dreamed of selling to the millions of Chinese. American missionaries began to preach in China in 1830. Although they gained few converts, their lectures in the United States stimulated public interest in eastern Asia.

Japan and Korea had also refused to engage in trade, their way of deflecting Western influences and avoiding European power rivalries. In 1854 an American naval force convinced the Japanese government to open its ports to foreign trade. A similar navy action opened Korea in 1882.

Growing trade between eastern Asia and the United States fueled American interest in the Pacific. American commercial ships needed ports in the Pacific for supplies and repairs, and interest focused especially on Hawai'i. Hawai'i had attracted Christian missionaries from New England as early

most-favored-nation status In a treaty between nation A and nation B, the provision that commercial privileges extended by A to other nations automatically become available to B.

as 1819, shortly after King Kamehameha united the islands into one nation. The missionaries were first concerned with preaching the Gospel and convincing the unabashed Hawaiians to wear clothes, but later some missionaries and their descendants came to exercise great influence over several Hawaiian monarchs.

Ideally located for resupply of ships traveling the Pacific, after 1848 Hawai'i became a routine stop for ships sailing from New York around South America to San Francisco. As early as 1842, President John Tyler announced that the United States would not allow the islands to pass under the control of another power, but Britain and France continued to take a keen interest in them.

David Kalakaua became king of Hawai'i in 1874. During his reign, relations with the United States became much closer. Kalakaua became the first reigning monarch ever to visit the United States, in 1874. In 1875 he approved a treaty that gave Hawaiian sugar free access to the United States. The Hawaiian sugar industry then expanded rapidly as descendants of missionaries joined American companies in developing huge plantations. Soon Hawaiian sugar spawned a vertically integrated industry that included American-owned plantations, ships to carry raw sugar to the mainland, and sugar refineries in California—and the economies of the two nations became closely linked.

Despite these economic ties, relations between Kalakaua and the **haole** community of Hawai'i were never comfortable. Kalakaua wanted to preserve political power for **indigenous** Hawaiians, but *haoles* charged that he was ignoring the needs of business and the sugar plantations. In 1887 the news broke that Kalakaua had profited from bribery related to opium. Leaders of the *haole* community used that excuse to force a constitution on him, reducing his power. *Haoles* soon dominated much of the government. That same year, Kalakaua approved an extension of the treaty of 1875, with an additional provision giving the U.S. Navy exclusive rights to use Pearl Harbor. Among some members of the royal family, resentment festered over the new constitution, the Pearl Harbor provision, and especially the extent of *haole* control. Those resentments boiled over after Kalakaua's death in 1891.

haole Hawaiian word for persons not of native Hawaiian ancestry, especially whites.

indigenous Original to an area.

■ **Alfred Thayer Mahan** Naval officer and historian who stressed the importance of sea power in international politics and diplomacy.

☆ *How and why did some Americans' attitudes about the U.S. role in world affairs begin to change between 1889 and 1897?*

During the 1890s, America's involvement in world affairs changed in important ways. One element revolved around a new role for the U.S. Navy and the commissioning of modern ships able to carry it out. Another related to the emergence and acceptance of new concepts of America's global status and foreign policy.

Building a Modern Navy

Most presidents of the Gilded Age paid little attention to the army and navy. After the last Indian wars, the army was limited to a few garrisons, most near Indian reservations. Most federal decision-makers understood the role of the navy as limited to protecting American coasts. The navy's wooden sailing vessels deteriorated so badly that some ridiculed them as fit only for firewood. Not until 1882 did Congress authorize construction of two steam-powered cruisers—the first new ships in almost twenty years—and four more ships in 1883. Still, Secretary of the Navy William C. Whitney announced in 1885 that "we have nothing which deserves to be called a navy," and persuaded Congress to fund several more cruisers and the first two modern battleships.

Alfred Thayer Mahan played a key role in developing a modern navy. President of the Naval War College, Mahan exerted a powerful influence through lectures to navy officers, a book, *The Influence of Sea Power upon History* (1890), and articles in the press. Mahan argued that sea power had been the determining factor in European power struggles for the previous 150 years and explored the significance of geography, population, and government for establishing sea power. He advocated a large, modern navy centered on huge battleships capable of carrying American power to distant seas. He also stressed the need to establish and control a canal through Central America, command the Caribbean, dominate strategic locations in the Pacific, and create naval bases at key points.

In 1889, with Harrison in the White House and Republican majorities in both houses of Congress, Secretary of the Navy Benjamin F. Tracy urged Congress to modernize and significantly expand the navy. Tracy's ambitious proposal might have eliminated the federal budget surplus all by itself! Congress did

This engraving shows the launching of the battleship *Maine* at the New York Navy Yard in 1889. The *Maine* was the nation's first modern battleship and the prototype for those that followed.

not give him all he wanted but did vote funds for a modern navy centered on battleships. With construction under way on three battleships, Tracy happily announced that "we shall rule [the sea] as certainly as the sun doth rise!"

A New American Mission?

Mahan's strategic arguments and Tracy's battleship launchings came as some Americans began, in Mahan's phrase, to "look outward." Advocacy came from many sources: Protestant ministers, scholars, business figures, historians, politicians. Together they redefined the way many Americans, and American policymakers, viewed the nation's role in world affairs. Josiah Strong offered the perspective of a Protestant missionary, arguing that expansion of American Protestant ideals to the world constituted a Christian duty. "The world is to be Christianized and civilized," he predicted, adding that "commerce follows the missionary."

Social Darwinism and the notion of "progress" merged with a belief in the superiority of the Anglo-Saxons—the people of England and their descendants. In the 1880s, popular books claimed that Anglo-Saxons had demonstrated a unique capacity for civilization and had a duty to enlighten and uplift other peoples. Albert Beveridge, Republican senator from Indiana, blended some of these ideas with American nationalism when he proclaimed, "[God] has made us the master organizers of the world to establish system where chaos reigns." Rudyard Kipling, an English poet, in 1899 urged the United States to "take up the white man's burden," a phrase that came to describe a self-imposed obligation to go into distant lands, bring the supposed blessings of Anglo-Saxon civilization to their peoples, Christianize them, and sell them manufactured goods.

Today historians understand Anglo-Saxonism and the "white man's burden" as imbued with racism. Such views assumed that some people, by virtue of race, possessed a superior capability for self-government and cultural accomplishment. This thinking elevated only one cultural pattern as "civilization," dismissing all others as inferior and ignoring their cultural accomplishments.

Revolution in Hawai'i

New views on the strategic significance of the Pacific focused the attention of many Americans on Hawai'i when a revolution broke out there early in 1893. The revolution stemmed in part from changes in American tariff rates on sugar. In 1890, the McKinley Tariff provided that all sugar could enter the United States without paying a tariff. Previously only Hawaiian sugar had this privilege. Now it faced new competition, notably from Cuban sugar. Facing economic disaster, many Hawaiian planters began to discuss annexation to the United States.

In 1891 King Kalakaua died and was succeeded by his sister, **Lili'uokalani**, who hoped to restore Hawai'i to the indigenous Hawaiians and return political power to the monarchy. Some *haole* entrepreneurs feared that they might lose their political clout and economic holdings. On January 17, 1893, a group of plotters proclaimed a republic and announced they would seek annexation by the United States. John L. Stevens, the U.S. minister to Hawai'i, promptly ordered the landing of 150 U.S. Marines. Lili'uokalani surrendered, as she put it, "to the superior force of the United States." Stevens immediately recognized the new republic, declared it a **protectorate** of the United States, and raised the American flag.

The Harrison administration **repudiated** Stevens's overzealous deeds but opened negotiations with representatives of the new republic. The Senate received a treaty of annexation shortly before Cleveland became president. Cleveland was willing to consider annexing Hawai'i if the Hawaiian people requested it. However, he withdrew the annexation treaty temporarily, then learned the revolution would have failed had the marines not intervened. He asked the new officials to restore the queen. They refused, and Hawai'i continued as an independent republic, dominated by its *haole* business and planter community.

The Granger Collection, New York.

This painting of Queen Lili'uokalani dates to 1892. Lili'uokalani was a gifted musician and wrote the song "Aloha 'Oe," which is still performed today.

Crises in Latin America

Harrison and Cleveland disagreed regarding Hawai'i, but both presidents extended American involvement in Latin America.

In 1891 a mob in Chile set upon several American sailors on shore leave and beat them, injuring several and killing two. When the Chilean government gave no sign of apologizing, Harrison threatened "such action as may be necessary." When the Chilean government would not back down, Harrison responded with plans for a naval war. Chile then gave in, apologized, and promised to pay damages.

In 1895 and 1896, Cleveland also took the nation to the edge of war. At issue was an old boundary dispute between Venezuela and British Guiana. Venezuela proposed arbitration, which Cleveland also favored, but Britain refused. In July 1895, Secretary of State Richard Olney cited the Monroe Doctrine, demanded Britain submit to arbitration, and bombastically declared the United States preeminent

■ **Lili'uokalani** Last queen of Hawai'i, whose desire to restore land to the Hawaiian people and strengthen the monarchy prompted *haole* planters to remove her from power in 1893.

protectorate A country partially controlled by a stronger power and dependent on that power for protection from foreign threats.

repudiate To reject as invalid or unauthorized.

throughout the Western Hemisphere. Britain still refused. Cleveland then asked Congress for authority to determine the boundary and enforce it. Britain now faced the possibility of conflict with the United States—at a time when the British were increasingly concerned about the rising power of Germany and facing possible war in South Africa. Britain agreed to arbitration.

Both presidents behaved more forcefully than their predecessors since Seward stood up to Napoleon III in Mexico. However, where Seward's action had restored Mexican control over its own affairs, Harrison's heavy-handed threats toward Chile discouraged closer relations with Latin America. Cleveland, however, may have had some effect in persuading European imperial powers that the Western Hemisphere was off-limits in the ongoing scramble for colonies.

Cuba presented a very different situation. Cuba and Puerto Rico were all that remained of the once-mighty Spanish empire in the Americas, and Cubans had repeatedly rebelled against Spain. In the early 1890s, when the McKinley Tariff permitted Cuban sugar to enter the United States without charge, the Cuban sugar industry boomed. In 1894, though, the new tariff law restored a duty on Cuban sugar and depressed the island's economy. Fueled by economic distress, a new insurrection erupted against Spanish rule. Advocates of *Cuba libre* ("free Cuba") received support from sympathizers in the United States. In 1896, in response to the **insurgents'** guerrilla warfare, the Spanish commander, General Valeriano Weyler, established a **reconcentration** policy. The civilian population was ordered into fortified towns or camps. Everyone outside these fortified areas was considered an insurgent, subject to military action. Disease and starvation swept through the camps, killing many Cubans.

American newspapers—especially **Joseph Pulitzer's** *New York World* and **William Randolph Hearst's** *New York Journal*—presented Spanish atrocities in screaming headlines, sometimes exaggerating and sensationalizing their reporters' stories (a practice called **yellow journalism**). In response, many Americans began clamoring to rescue the Cubans.

Intent on avoiding American involvement, Cleveland proclaimed U.S. neutrality and warned Americans not to support the insurrection. When members of Congress pushed Cleveland to seek Cuban independence, he only urged Spain to grant concessions to the insurgents. Just as he had earlier opposed annexation of Hawai'i, Cleveland now resisted intervention in Cuba, fearing it might lead to annexation regardless of the will of the Cuban people. Nonetheless, by the time he left the presidency in early 1897, he suggested possible American intervention.

STRIDING BOLDLY IN WORLD AFFAIRS: MCKINLEY, WAR, AND IMPERIALISM, 1898–1902

☆ What led the United States into war with Spain?

☆ What new attitudes about America's role in world affairs appeared in the debate over acquiring new possessions?

In 1898 the United States went to war with Spain over Cuba. John Hay, the American ambassador to Great Britain, celebrated the conflict as "a splendid little war," and the description stuck. Some envisioned a quick war to save the suffering Cubans and establish a Cuban republic. Others saw war with Spain as an opportunity to seize territory and acquire an American colonial empire.

McKinley and War

William McKinley became president amid increasing demands for action regarding Cuba. He moved cautiously, gradually stepping up diplomatic efforts to resolve the crisis. In response, Spain softened the reconcentration policy and offered limited self-government but not independence. In February 1898, however, events scuttled progress toward a negotiated solution.

First, Cuban insurgents stole a letter from **Enrique Dupuy de Lôme**, the Spanish minister to the United States, and released it to the *New York Journal*. In it, de Lôme criticized President McKinley as "weak and a bidder for the admiration of the crowd." The letter also implied that the Spanish government's commitment to reform in Cuba was not serious. Although de Lôme immediately resigned, the letter aroused intense anti-Spanish feeling among many Americans.

insurgent Rebel or revolutionary; one involved in an insurrection or rebellion against constituted authority.

■ **reconcentration** Spanish policy in Cuba in 1896 that ordered the civilian population into fortified areas so as to isolate and annihilate the revolutionaries who remained outside.

Joseph Pulitzer Hungarian-born newspaper publisher whose *New York World* printed sensational stories about Cuba that helped precipitate the Spanish-American War.

William Randolph Hearst Publisher and rival to Pulitzer whose newspaper, the *New York Journal*, sensationalized and distorted stories and actively promoted war with Spain.

■ **yellow journalism** The use of sensational exposés, embellished reporting, and attention-grabbing headlines to sell newspapers.

Enrique Dupuy de Lôme Spanish minister to the United States whose letter criticizing President McKinley was stolen and printed in the *New York Journal*, increasing anti-Spanish sentiment.

On February 15, 1898, an explosion destroyed the USS *Maine* at Havana, Cuba. Many Americans blamed the Spanish government, although there was no evidence to suggest who was responsible.

A few days later, on February 15, an explosion ripped open the **USS Maine**, anchored in Havana Harbor. The battleship sank, killing more than 260 Americans. The yellow press accused Spain of sabotage but without evidence. An official inquiry blamed a submarine mine but could not determine its source. Years later, an investigation indicated that the blast was probably of internal origin, resulting from a fire. Regardless of how the explosion occurred, those advocating intervention now had a rallying cry: "Remember the *Maine!*"

McKinley extended his demands: an immediate end to the fighting, an end to reconcentration, measures to relieve the suffering, and **mediation** by

■ **USS Maine** American warship that exploded in Havana Harbor in 1898, inspiring the motto "Remember the *Maine!*" which spurred the Spanish-American War.

mediation An attempt to bring about the peaceful settlement of a dispute through the intervention of a neutral party.

armistice An agreement to halt fighting.

■ **Teller Amendment** Senate resolution in 1898 promising that the U.S. would not annex Cuba; introduced by Senator Henry Teller.

McKinley himself. He specified that one possible outcome of mediation might be Cuban independence. In reply, the Spanish government promised reforms, agreed to end reconcentration, and consented to cease fighting if the insurgents asked for an **armistice**—but said nothing about mediation by McKinley or independence for Cuba.

On April 11, McKinley sent a message to Congress stating that "the war in Cuba must stop" and asking for authority to act. Congress answered on April 19 with four resolutions: (1) declaring that Cuba was and should be independent, (2) demanding that Spain withdraw "at once," (3) authorizing the president to use force to accomplish Spanish withdrawal, and (4) disavowing any intention to annex the island. The first three resolutions amounted to a declaration of war. The fourth is usually called the **Teller Amendment** for its sponsor, Senator Henry M. Teller, a Silver Republican from Colorado. In response, Spain declared war.

Most Americans wholeheartedly approved what they understood to be a war undertaken to bring independence and aid to the long-suffering Cubans. Some, however, distrusted the McKinley administration's motives. The Teller Amendment reflected this concern that the McKinley administration might try to make Cuba an American possession rather than granting it independence.

The "Splendid Little War"

Americans' attention had been riveted on Cuba. Many were surprised that the first engagement in the war occurred in the **Philippine Islands**—nearly halfway around the world from Cuba. The Philippines had been a Spanish colony for three hundred years, but had rebelled repeatedly, most recently in 1896.

Some Americans understood the islands' strategic location with regard to eastern Asia—including Assistant Secretary of the Navy **Theodore Roosevelt**. In February 1898, six weeks before McKinley's war message to Congress, Roosevelt drew upon planning exercises by the Naval War College when he cabled George Dewey, the American naval commander in the Pacific, to crush the Spanish fleet at Manila Bay if war broke out.

At sunrise on Sunday, May 1, Dewey's squadron of four cruisers, two gunboats, and three support vessels steamed into the harbor and quickly destroyed or captured seven Spanish cruisers and four gunboats. The Spanish lost 161 men and 210 were wounded. The Americans lost one, a victim of heat prostration, and nine were wounded. Dewey instantly became a national hero.

Dewey's victory at Manila focused public attention on the western Pacific, raising the prospect of a permanent American presence there. This possibility, in turn, revived interest in the Hawaiian Islands as a base halfway to the Philippines. Anti-imperialist sentiment in the Senate made approval of an annexation treaty unlikely, so McKinley revived the joint-resolution precedent by which Texas had been annexed in 1844. Only a majority vote in both houses of Congress was required to adopt a joint resolution, rather than the two-thirds vote of the Senate needed to approve a treaty. Annexation of Hawai'i was accomplished on July 7.

Dewey's victory clearly demonstrated American naval superiority. In contrast, the Spanish army in Cuba outnumbered the entire American army by five to one and had years of experience fighting on the island. When McKinley called for volunteers, nearly a million men responded—five times as many as the army needed. Next the army began to train and supply the new recruits.

Sent to training camps in the South, the new soldiers found chaos and confusion. Food, uniforms, and equipment arrived at one location while the intended recipients stood hungry and idle at another. Uniforms were often of heavy wool, unsuited for the Cuban climate. Disease raged through some camps, killing many men. Others died from tainted food,

called "embalmed beef" by the troops. Some African American soldiers refused to comply with racial segregation, and many white southerners objected to the presence in their communities of uniformed and armed black men. Congress declared war in late April, but not until June did the first troop transports head for Cuba.

When they finally arrived in Cuba, American forces tried to capture the port city of Santiago, where the Spanish fleet had taken refuge. Inexperienced, poorly equipped, and unfamiliar with the terrain, the Americans landed some distance from Santiago and assaulted the fortified hills surrounding the city.

Theodore Roosevelt had resigned as assistant secretary of the navy to organize a cavalry unit known as the Rough Riders. At Kettle Hill, he led a successful charge of Rough Riders and regular army units, including parts of the Ninth and Tenth Cavalry, made up of African Americans. All but Roosevelt were on foot because their horses had not yet arrived. Driving the Spanish from the crest of Kettle Hill cleared a serious impediment to the assault on nearby San Juan Heights and San Juan Hill. Journalists loved Roosevelt—and newspapers all over the country declared him the hero of the Battle of San Juan Hill.

Nearly 10 percent of U.S. troops were killed or wounded during the first few days of the attack on Santiago. Worsening the situation, the surgeon in charge of medical facilities refused assistance from Red Cross nurses because he thought field hospitals were not appropriate places for women. He was later overruled. Red Cross nurses also helped care for injured Cuban insurgents and civilians.

Once American troops gained control of the high ground around Santiago harbor, the Spanish fleet tried to escape. A larger American fleet met them and duplicated Dewey's rout at Manila—every Spanish ship was sunk or run aground. The Spanish suffered 323 deaths, the Americans one.

Their fleet destroyed, surrounded by American troops, the Spanish in Santiago surrendered on July 17. A week later American forces occupied Puerto Rico. Spanish land forces in the Philippines surrendered when the first American troops arrived in mid-August. The "splendid little war" lasted only sixteen weeks. More than 306,000 men served in the American forces. Only 385 of them died in battle, but more than 5,000 died of disease and other causes.

Philippine Islands A group of islands in the Pacific Ocean southeast of China that came under U.S. control in 1898; an independent nation since 1946.

■ **Theodore Roosevelt** (1858–1919) Twenty-sixth president of the United States Politician and writer who advocated war against Spain in 1898; elected vice president in 1900; became president in 1901 upon McKinley's assassination.

Theodore Roosevelt's Rough Riders, on foot because there was not room aboard ship for their horses, are in the background of this depiction of the battle for Kettle Hill. The artist has put into the foreground members of the Ninth and Tenth Cavalry, African American units, who played a key role in that engagement, but one often overlooked because of the attention given Roosevelt.

The Treaty of Paris

On August 12, the United States and Spain agreed to stop fighting and hold a peace conference in Paris. The major question for the conference centered on the Philippines. Finley Peter Dunne, a popular humorist, parodied the national debate in a discussion between his fictional characters, Mr. Dooley (a Chicago saloonkeeper) and a customer named Hennessy. Hennessy insists that McKinley should take the islands. Dooley retorts that "it's not more than two months since you learned whether they were islands or canned goods," then confesses his own indecision: "I can't annex them because I don't know where they are. I can't let go of them because someone else will take them. . . . It would break my heart to think of giving people I've never seen or heard tell of back to other people I don't know. . . . I don't know what to do about the Philippines. And I'm all alone in the world. Everybody else has made up his mind."

McKinley voiced almost as many doubts as Mr. Dooley. At first, he seemed to favor only a naval base, leaving Spain in control elsewhere. However, Spanish authority collapsed by mid-August as Filipino insurgents took charge throughout the islands. Britain, Japan, and Germany watched carefully, and one or another seemed likely to step in if the United States withdrew. McKinley and his advisers decided that a naval base on Manila Bay would require control of the entire island group. No one seriously considered the Filipinos' desire for independence.

McKinley was well aware of the political and strategic importance of the Philippines for eastern Asia. He invoked other reasons, however, when he explained his decision to a group of visiting Methodists. He repeatedly prayed for guidance on the Philippine question, he told them. Late one night, he said, it came to him that "there was nothing left for us to do but to take them all, and to educate the Filipinos, and uplift and civilize and Christianize them and by God's

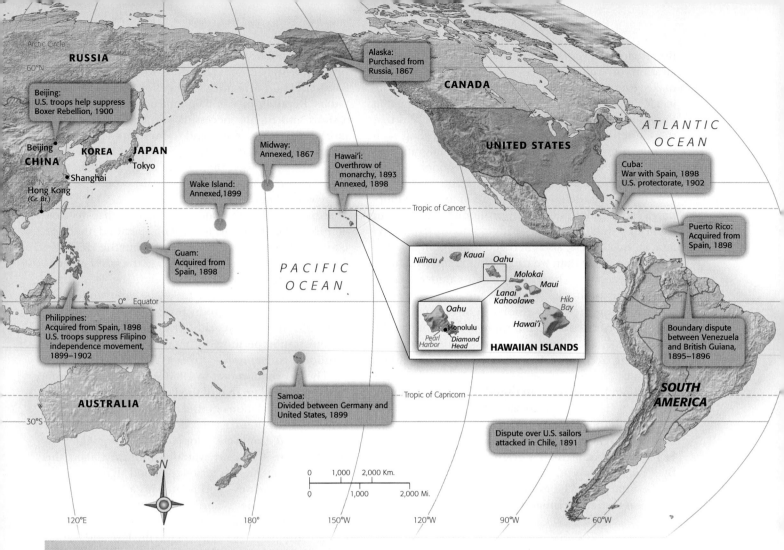

MAP 18.3 American Involvement in the Caribbean and Pacific

As a result of the war with Spain, the United States acquired possessions stretching nearly halfway around the world, from Puerto Rico to the Philippines. Note how the acquisition of various Pacific islands and island groups provided crucial "stepping stones" from the American mainland to eastern Asia. Copyright © Cengage Learning

Labels on map:

- Beijing: U.S. troops help suppress Boxer Rebellion, 1900
- Alaska: Purchased from Russia, 1867
- Midway: Annexed, 1867
- Wake Island: Annexed, 1899
- Hawai'i: Overthrow of monarchy, 1893 Annexed, 1898
- Cuba: War with Spain, 1898 U.S. protectorate, 1902
- Puerto Rico: Acquired from Spain, 1898
- Guam: Acquired from Spain, 1898
- Philippines: Acquired from Spain, 1898 U.S. troops suppress Filipino independence movement, 1899–1902
- Boundary dispute between Venezuela and British Guiana, 1895–1896
- Samoa: Divided between Germany and United States, 1899
- Dispute over U.S. sailors attacked in Chile, 1891

HAWAIIAN ISLANDS: Niihau, Kauai, Oahu, Molokai, Maui, Lanai, Kahoolawe, Hilo Bay, Hawai'i; Oahu, Honolulu, Pearl Harbor, Diamond Head

---

grace do the very best we could by them." In fact, most Filipinos had been Catholics for centuries, but no one ever expressed more clearly the concept of the "white man's burden."

Spain resisted giving up the Philippines, but McKinley was adamant. The Treaty of Paris, signed in December 1898, required Spain to surrender Cuba, cede Puerto Rico and Guam to the United States, and sell the Philippines for $20 million (see Map 18.3). For the first time in American history, a treaty acquiring new territory failed to confer U.S. citizenship on the residents. Nor did the treaty mention future statehood. Thus these acquisitions represented a new kind of expansion—America had become a colonial power.

The **Treaty of Paris** dismayed Democrats, Populists, and some conservative Republicans, sparking a public debate over acquisition of the Philippines in particular and **imperialism** in general. An anti-imperialist movement quickly formed, with William Jennings Bryan, Andrew Carnegie, Grover Cleveland, Carl Schurz, and Mark Twain among its outspoken proponents. The treaty, they argued, denied self-government for the newly acquired territories. For the United States to hold colonies, they claimed,

■ **Treaty of Paris** 1898 treaty ending the Spanish-American War, under which Spain granted independence to Cuba, ceded Puerto Rico and Guam to the United States, and sold the Philippines to the United States for $20 million.

imperialism The practice by which a nation acquires and holds colonies and other possessions, denies them self-government, and usually exploits them economically.

threatened the very concept of democracy. "The Declaration of Independence," warned Carnegie, "will make every Filipino a thoroughly dissatisfied subject." Others voiced racist arguments, claiming that Filipinos were incapable of self-government and that the United States would be corrupted by ruling such people. Union leaders, fearing Filipino migration to the United States, repeated arguments once used to secure Chinese exclusion.

Those who defended acquisition of the Philippines echoed McKinley's lofty pronouncements about America's duty. Albert Beveridge, senator from Indiana, among others, also cited economic benefits: "We are raising more than we can consume, making more than we can use. Therefore we must find new markets for our produce." Such "new markets" were not limited to the new possessions. A strong naval and military presence in the Philippines would make the United States a leading power in eastern Asia, thereby supporting access for American business to markets in China.

William Jennings Bryan urged senators to approve the treaty. That way, he reasoned, the United States alone could determine the future of the Philippines. Once the treaty was approved, he argued, the United States should immediately grant them independence. By a narrow margin, the Senate approved the treaty on February 6, 1899. Soon after, senators rejected a proposal for Philippine independence.

The New American Empire

Bryan hoped to make independence for the Philippines the central issue in the 1900 presidential election. He easily won the Democratic nomination for a second time, and the Democrats' platform condemned the McKinley administration for its "imperialism." Bryan found, however, that many conservative anti-imperialists would not support his candidacy because he still insisted on silver coinage and attacked big business.

■ **Platt Amendment** An amendment to the Army Appropriations Act of 1901, sponsored by Senator Orville Platt; set terms for the withdrawal of the U.S. Army from Cuba, effectively making the island an American proctectorate.

■ **Foraker Act** 1900 law establishing civilian government in Puerto Rico; provided for an elected legislature and a governor appointed by the U.S. president.

Insular Cases Supreme Court decision (1901) concerning Puerto Rico; held that people in new island territories did not automatically receive the constitutional rights of U.S. citizens.

■ **Emilio Aguinaldo** Leader of unsuccessful struggles for Philippine independence, first against Spain, then against the United States.

The Republicans renominated McKinley. For vice president, they chose Theodore Roosevelt, "hero of San Juan Hill." McKinley's reelection seemed unstoppable. Republican campaigners pointed proudly to a short and highly successful war, legislation on the tariff and gold standard, and the return of prosperity. Bryan repeatedly attacked imperialism. McKinley and Roosevelt never used the term at all and instead took pride in expansion. McKinley easily won a second term with 52 percent of the vote.

Now the United States had to organize its new empire. The Teller Amendment specified that the United States would not annex Cuba, but the McKinley administration refused to recognize the insurgents as the legitimate government. Instead, the U.S. Army took control. Among other tasks, the army undertook sanitation projects to reduce disease, especially yellow fever. After two years of army rule, the McKinley administration permitted Cuban voters to hold a constitutional convention.

The convention met in 1900 and drafted a constitution modeled on that of the United States. Nowhere did it define relations between Cuba and the United States. In response, the McKinley administration drafted, and Congress adopted, terms for Cuba to adopt before the army would withdraw. Called the **Platt Amendment**, the terms specified that (1) Cuba was not to make any agreement with a foreign power that impaired the island's independence, (2) the United States could intervene in Cuba to preserve Cuban independence and maintain law and order, and (3) Cuba was to lease facilities to the United States for naval bases and coaling stations. Cubans reluctantly agreed, changed their constitution, and signed a treaty with the United States stating the Platt conditions. In 1902 Cuba thereby became a protectorate of the United States.

The Teller Amendment did not apply to Puerto Rico. There, the army provided a military government until 1900, when Congress approved the **Foraker Act**. That act made Puerto Ricans citizens of Puerto Rico but not citizens of the United States. Puerto Rican voters could elect a legislature, but final authority rested with a governor and council appointed by the president of the United States. In 1901, in the **Insular Cases**, the U.S. Supreme Court confirmed the colonial status of Puerto Rico and, by implication, the other new possessions. The Court ruled that they were not equivalent to earlier territorial acquisitions and that their people did not possess the constitutional rights of citizens.

Establishment of civil government in the Philippines took longer. Between Dewey's victory and arrival of the first American soldiers three months later, a Philippine independence movement led by **Emilio Aguinaldo** established a provisional government and took control everywhere but Manila, which remained

Brown Brothers.

The Spanish banished Emilio Aguinaldo from the Philippines because of his opposition to Spanish rule. American naval officials returned him to the islands, where he helped to establish an independent Filipino government. This photograph was taken in 1900, when Aguinaldo was leading what many Filipinos considered a war for independence.

Congress set up a government for the Philippines similar to that of Puerto Rico. Filipinos became citizens of the Philippine Islands, but not of the United States. The president of the United States appointed the governor. Filipino voters elected one house in the two-house legislature, and the governor appointed the other. Both the governor and the U.S. Congress could veto laws passed by the legislature. **William Howard Taft**, governor from 1901 to 1904, tried to build local support for American control, secured limited land reforms, and started to build public schools, hospitals, and sanitary facilities. However, when the first Philippine legislature met, in 1907, more than half of its members favored independence.

The Open Door and the Boxer Rebellion in China

Late in 1899, Britain, Germany, and the United States signed the Treaty of Berlin, which divided **Samoa** between Germany and the United States. The new Pacific acquisitions of the United States—Hawai'i, the Philippines, Guam, and Samoa—all contained excellent sites for naval bases. Combined with the modernized navy, these acquisitions greatly strengthened American ability to assert power in the region and protect Americans' commercial access to eastern Asia. The United States now began to seek full participation in the East Asian **balance of power**.

Weakened by war with Japan in 1894–1895, the Chinese government could not resist European nations' demands for territory. Britain, Germany, Russia, and France had carved out **spheres of influence**—areas where they claimed special rights, usually a monopoly over trade, and sought to exclude other powers. The United States argued instead for

in Spanish hands until American troops arrived. Aguinaldo and his government wanted independence. When the United States determined to keep the islands, the Filipinos resisted.

Quelling what American authorities called the "Philippine insurrection" required three years (1899–1902), took the lives of 4,196 American soldiers, and perhaps 700,000 or more Filipinos (most through disease and other noncombat causes), and cost $400 million (twenty times the price of the islands). When some Filipinos resorted to guerrilla warfare, U.S. troops adopted practices similar to those Spain had used in Cuba. Both sides committed atrocities, and anti-imperialists pointed to brutal behavior by American troops as proof that a colonial policy was corrupting American values. American troops captured Aguinaldo in 1901, but resistance continued into mid-1902.

■ **William Howard Taft** Governor of the Philippines, 1901–1904; president of the United States, 1909–1913; chief justice of the Supreme Court, 1921–1930.

Samoa A group of volcanic and mountainous islands in the South Pacific.

balance of power In international politics, the notion that nations may restrict one another's actions because of the relative equality of their naval or military forces, either individually or through alliance systems.

sphere of influence A region where a foreign nation exerts significant authority.

A FAIR FIELD AND NO FAVOR!
UNCLE SAM: "I'M OUT FOR COMMERCE, NOT CONQUEST!"

In this 1899 cartoon celebrating the Open Door policy, Uncle Sam insists that other nations must compete fairly for China's commerce and not seize Chinese territory. In the background, John Bull (Britain) lifts his hat in approval. Library of Congress.

the "Open Door"—the principle that citizens of all nations should have equal status in seeking trade. American diplomats, however, began to fear the breakup of China into separate European colonies and the exclusion of American commerce.

In 1899 Secretary of State John Hay circulated a letter to Germany, Russia, Britain, France, Italy, and Japan, asking them to preserve Chinese sovereignty within their spheres of influence and not to discriminate against citizens of other nations engaged in commerce within their spheres. Hay wanted both to prevent the dismemberment of China and to maintain commercial access for American business throughout China. Some replies proved less than fully supportive, but Hay announced in a second letter that all had agreed to his "Open Door" principles. Hay's letters have usually been called the **Open Door notes**.

In 1900, a Chinese secret society tried to expel all foreigners from China. Because the rebels used a clenched fist as their symbol, westerners called them Boxers. The Boxers laid siege to the section of Beijing, the Chinese capital, that housed foreign **legations**. Hay feared that other powers might use the rebellion as a pretext to take control and divide China permanently. To block such a move, the United States took full part in an international military expedition to rescue the besieged foreign diplomats and to crush the **Boxer Rebellion**.

Although China did not lose territory, the intervening nations required it to pay an **indemnity**. After compensating U.S. citizens for their losses, the U.S. government returned the remainder of its indemnity to China. To show its appreciation, the Chinese government used the money to send Chinese students to study in the United States.

■ **Open Door notes** Diplomatic messages in 1899–1900 by which Secretary of State John Hay announced American support for Chinese autonomy and opposed efforts by other powers to carve China into exclusive spheres of influence.

legation Diplomatic officials representing their nation to another nation, and their offices and residences.

Boxer Rebellion Uprising in China in 1900 directed against foreign powers attempting to dominate China; suppressed by an international army including Americans.

indemnity Payment for damage, loss, or injury.

Individual Voices

Carl Schurz Comments on America's Changing Role in World Affairs, 1896–1899

Schurz maintained a strong interest in world affairs throughout his political career, serving on the Senate Foreign Relations Committee and later helping organize the Anti-Imperialist League. The following three selections, addressing major changes in America's role in world affairs during the 1890s, brought Schurz acclaim from other Mugwump types and from many Democrats. Such primary sources assist historians in understanding opposition to McKinley administration policies.

From a speech, January 2, 1896:

❶ *Jingo*, a term in general use in the 1890s, was applied to mindless, outspoken patriots, especially those advocating war.

❷ Do you think that Schurz had any particular events or individuals in mind in making this statement? Given the date, what are the possibilities?

❸ What action was pending in Congress at the time? How did Schurz hope to influence Congress?

❹ To whom is Schurz most likely referring here?

❺ Stephen Decatur, a naval officer, following the War of 1812, offered an after-dinner toast: "Our Country! In her intercourse with foreign nations may she always be in the right; but right or wrong, our country!" This has often been quoted as, "My country, right or wrong!"

What is the rule of honor to be observed by a power so strongly and so advantageously situated as this Republic is? . . . it should not, as our boyish jingoes ❶ wish it to do, swagger about among the nations of the world, with a chip on its shoulder, shaking its fist in everybody's face. . . . it should not, whenever its own notions of right or interest collide with the notions of others, fall into hysterics and act as if it really feared for its own security and its very Independence. ❷ . . . With all its latent resources for war, it should be the great peace power of the world. . . . Is not this peace with honor? There has, of late, been much loose speech about "Americanism." Is not this good Americanism? It is surely today the Americanism of those who love their country most.

From *Harper's Weekly*, April 16, 1898:

The man who in times of popular excitement boldly and unflinchingly resists hot-tempered clamor for an unnecessary war, ❸ and thus exposes himself to the opprobrious imputation of a lack of patriotism or of courage, to the end of saving his country from a great calamity, is, as to "loving and faithfully serving his country," at least as good a patriot as the hero of the most daring feat of arms, and a far better one than those who, with an ostentatious pretense of superior patriotism, cry for war before it is needed, especially if then they let others do the fighting. ❹

From a speech, October 17, 1899:

I confidently trust that the American people will prove themselves . . . too wise not to detect the false pride or the dangerous ambitions or the selfish schemes which so often hide themselves under that deceptive cry of mock patriotism: "Our country, right or wrong!" ❺ They will not fail to recognize that our dignity, our free institutions and the peace and welfare of this and coming generations of Americans will be secure only as we cling to the watchword of true patriotism: "Our country—when right to be kept right; when wrong to be put right." ❻

❻ Do these selections help you to understand Schurz's reputation for putting principle before party? What principles does he enunciate in these selections?

Study Tools

SUMMARY

In the late nineteenth century, political parties dominated politics. All elected public officials were nominated by party conventions and elected through party campaigns. Nearly all government jobs came through the spoils system. Republicans used government to promote rapid economic development, but Democrats argued for minimal government. Voters divided between the major parties largely along the lines of region, ethnicity, and race.

The presidency of Ulysses S. Grant was plagued by scandals. Thereafter, the closely balanced strengths of the two parties contributed to a long-term political stalemate. In 1889–1890, however, Republicans wrote most of their campaign promises into law.

Grangers, Greenbackers, and silverites challenged the major parties, appealing most to debt-ridden farmers. Mugwumps argued for the merit system in the civil service, accomplished through the Pendleton Act of 1883. By the late nineteenth century, a well-organized woman suffrage movement had emerged. A wide range of reform groups sought both structural changes and policy changes.

The 1890s saw major, long-lasting changes in American politics. A political upheaval began when western and southern farmers joined the Farmers' Alliances, then launched a new political party, the Populist Party. Elected in 1892, President Grover Cleveland failed to meet the political challenges of the depression that began in 1893; his party, the Democrats, lost badly in the 1894 congressional elections. In 1896 the Democrats nominated for president William Jennings Bryan, a supporter of silver coinage. The Republicans chose William McKinley, who favored the protective tariff. McKinley won, beginning a period of Republican dominance in national politics that lasted until 1930. Under Bryan's leadership, the Democratic Party promoted government action against monopolies and other powerful economic interests.

From 1865 to 1889, few Americans expected their nation to be significantly involved in world affairs outside North America. The United States did acquire Alaska, pressured the French to withdraw from Mexico, and took actions to encourage trade with eastern Asia. The kingdom of Hawai'i became closely integrated

CHRONOLOGY

1867	French troops leave Mexico
	United States purchases Alaska
1868	Ulysses S. Grant elected president
1869	National Woman Suffrage Association and American Woman Suffrage Association formed
	Wyoming Territory adopts woman suffrage
1872	Crédit Mobilier scandal
	Grant reelected
1872–1874	Granger laws
1873–1879	Depression
1877	Rutherford B. Hayes becomes president
1878	Greenback Party peaks
1880	James A. Garfield elected president
1881	Garfield assassinated
	Chester A. Arthur becomes president
1883	Pendleton Act
1884	Grover Cleveland elected president
1887	Interstate Commerce Act
1888	Benjamin Harrison elected president

1890	Sherman Anti-Trust Act
	Sherman Silver Purchase Act
	McKinley Tariff
	Significant increase in naval appropriation
	Lodge federal elections bill defeated
	Populist movement begins
1892	Cleveland elected president again
1893	*Haole* planters and businessmen proclaim Hawaiian republic
1893–1897	Depression
1895–1896	Venezuelan boundary crisis
1896	William Jennings Bryan's "Cross of Gold" speech
	William McKinley elected president
1898	War with Spain
	United States annexes Hawai'i
1899	Treaty of Paris ratified
	Open Door notes
1899–1902	Philippine insurrection
1900	McKinley reelected
1902	Civil government in the Philippines
	Cuba becomes a protectorate

Study Tools

with the American economy. During the early 1890s, the United States moved toward a new role in world affairs. Presidents Harrison and Cleveland asserted American power in Latin America.

A revolution in Cuba led the United States into a one-sided war with Spain in 1898, resulting in acquisition of the Philippines, Guam, and Puerto Rico. Congress annexed Hawai'i in the midst of the war, and the United States acquired part of Samoa in 1899. Filipinos resisted American authority, leading to a three-year war. With the Philippines and an improved navy, the United States gained new prominence in eastern Asia, especially in China, where the United States promoted the Open Door and American troops helped suppress the Boxer Rebellion.

FOCUS QUESTIONS

If you have mastered this chapter, you should be able to answer these questions and explain the terms that follow the questions.

1. ☆ What was the significance of political parties in the late nineteenth century?

2. ☆ Compare the presidencies from Grant through Cleveland. Which do you consider successful? Why?

3. ☆ What were the major goals of the various reform groups?

4. ☆ Why were some reformers more successful than others?

5. ☆ Which groups and issues led to the formation of the Populist Party?

6. ☆ What were the issues in the 1896 presidential election, and what were the short-term and long-term results?

7. ☆ How did American policymakers define the role of the United States in North America and other parts of the world during the period 1865–1889?

8. ☆ How and why did some Americans' attitudes about the U.S. role in world affairs begin to change between 1889 and 1897?

9. ☆ What led the United States into war with Spain?

10. ☆ What new attitudes about America's role in world affairs appeared in the debate over acquiring new possessions?

KEY TERMS

patronage system   (p. 489)

Crédit Mobilier   (p. 491)

Tweed Ring   (p. 492)

Interstate Commerce Commission   (p. 494)

William McKinley   (p. 495)

McKinley Tariff   (p. 495)

Sherman Anti-Trust Act   (p. 495)

Grange   (p. 497)

Granger laws   (p. 497)

gold standard   (p. 498)

Sherman Silver Purchase Act   (p. 498)

Mugwumps   (p. 498)

Pendleton Act   (p. 499)

National Woman Suffrage Association   (p. 499)

American Woman Suffrage Association   (p. 499)

Australian ballot   (p. 502)

Populists   (p. 502)

Farmers' Alliances   (p. 502)

antimonopolism   (p. 502)

William Jennings Bryan   (p. 505)

William H. Seward   (p. 508)

Monroe Doctrine   (p. 508)

Benito Juarez   (p. 508)

Alfred Thayer Mahan   (p. 510)

Lili'uokalani   (p. 512)

reconcentration   (p. 513)

yellow journalism   (p. 513)

USS Maine   (p. 514)

Teller Amendment   (p. 514)

Theodore Roosevelt   (p. 515)

Treaty of Paris   (p. 517)

Platt Amendment   (p. 518)

Foraker Act   (p. 518)

Emilio Aguinaldo   (p. 518)

William Howard Taft   (p. 519)

Open Door notes   (p. 520)

 CourseMate   Go to the History CourseMate website for primary source links, study tools, and review materials for this chapter. www.cengagebrain.com

Roosevelt acted as what he called "the steward of the people," mediating a conflict between organized interest groups in an effort to advance the public interest. In this and other ways he significantly changed both the office of the presidency and the authority of the federal government—and he did so consciously, as you will see in a passage from his memoirs at the end of the chapter.

Roosevelt became president at a time historians call the Progressive Era—a time when "reform was in the air," as one newspaper editor recalled. Reform was "in the air" almost everywhere, and many individuals and groups joined in, often with quite different expectations. Progressivism took shape through many decisions by voters and political leaders, but one question loomed behind many of those decisions: Should government play a larger role in the lives of Americans? This question lay behind debates over regulation of railroads in 1906 and regulation of banking in 1913, as well as behind proposals to prohibit alcoholic beverages and limit working hours of women factory workers.

Time after time, Americans chose a greater role for government. Often the consensus favoring government intervention was so broad that the only debate was over the form of intervention. As Americans gave government more power, they also tried to make government more responsive to ordinary citizens. They put limits on political parties and introduced ways for people to participate more directly in politics. The political changes of the Progressive Era, following on the heels of the political realignment of the 1890s, fundamentally altered American politics and government in the twentieth century and marked the birth of many aspects of modern American politics.

ORGANIZING FOR CHANGE

★ *What important changes transformed American politics in the early twentieth century?*

★ *What did women and African Americans seek to accomplish by creating new organizations devoted to political change?*

During the early twentieth century, politics expanded to embrace wide-ranging concerns raised by a complex assortment of groups and individuals. In the swirl of proponents and proposals, politics more than ever

before came to reflect the interaction of organized interest groups.

The Changing Face of Politics

As Americans entered the twentieth century, their lives were changing in important ways. The railroad, telegraph, and telephone transformed concepts of time and space and fostered formation of new organizations. Executives of new industrial corporations now thought in terms of regional or national markets. Union members allied with others of their trade in distant cities. Farmers in Kansas and Montana studied grain prices in Chicago and Liverpool. Physicians organized nationwide to establish higher standards for medical schools.

Manufacturers, farmers, merchants, carpenters, teachers, lawyers, physicians, and many others established or reorganized national associations to advance their economic or professional interests. Sometimes that meant seeking governmental assistance. As early as the 1870s, for example, associations of merchants, farmers, and oil producers had pushed for laws to regulate railroad freight rates.

Some graduates emerged from the recently transformed universities with the conviction that their knowledge and skills could improve society, and they formed professional associations to advance those objectives. Long-established church organizations sometimes fostered the emergence of new associations devoted to moral reform, especially prohibition. Some people formed groups with humanitarian goals such as ending child labor. Members of ethnic and racial groups set up societies to further their groups' interests. Reformers organized to limit the power of corporations or to defeat party bosses. Overlapping with many of these new associations were the organizational activities of women, including middle-class women, new college graduates, and factory and clerical workers.

Sooner or later, many of the new associations sought changes in laws to help them reach their objectives. Increasing numbers of citizens related to politics through such organized **interest groups**, even as the traditional political parties found they could no longer count on the voter loyalty typical of the Gilded Age.

■ **interest group** A coalition of people identified with a particular cause, such as an industry or occupational group, a social group, or a policy objective.

Many of these new groups optimistically believed that responsible citizens, acting together, assisted by technical know-how, and sometimes drawing on the power of government, could achieve social progress—improvement of the human situation. As early as the 1890s, some had begun to call themselves "progressive citizens." By 1910, many were simply calling themselves "progressives."

Historians use the term *progressivism* to signify three related developments during the early twentieth century: (1) the emergence of new concepts of the purposes and functions of government, (2) changes in government policies and institutions, and (3) the political agitation that produced those changes. A progressive, then, was a person involved in one or more of these activities. Many individuals and groups promoted their own visions of change, making progressivism a complex phenomenon. There was no single progressive movement. To be sure, an organized **Progressive Party** emerged in 1912, sputtered for a brief time after, but failed to capture the allegiance of all who called themselves progressives. Nonetheless, many aspects of progressivism reflected concerns of the urban middle class, especially urban middle-class women.

Progressivism appeared at every level of government—local, state, and federal. And progressives promoted a wide range of new government activities: regulation of business, moral revival, consumer protection, conservation of natural resources, educational improvement, tax reform, and more. Through all these avenues, they brought government more directly into the economy and more directly into the lives of most Americans.

"Spearheads for Reform": The Settlement Houses

During the 1890s, in several large cities, young college-educated men and women began to provide assistance for the poor. The **settlement house** idea originated in England in 1884, at Toynbee Hall, in London's slums, where idealistic university graduates lived among the poor and tried to help them. In 1886, young male college graduates opened a similar settlement house in New York City. In 1889 several women, graduates of Smith College (a women's college), opened another settlement house in New York.

Also in 1889, Jane Addams and Ellen Gates Starr opened **Hull House**, the first settlement house in Chicago. For many Americans, Jane Addams became synonymous with the settlement house movement and with reform more generally. Born in 1860 in a small town in Illinois, youngest daughter of a bank president, Addams attended college, then traveled in Europe. There she and Ellen Gates Starr, a friend from college, visited Toynbee Hall and learned about

Jane Addams, co-founder of Hull House, had become the most prominent settlement house worker in the country by the time she posed for this portrait around 1900.

its work with the poor. Inspired by that example, the two set up Hull House in a working-class, immigrant neighborhood in Chicago. They lived at Hull House for most of their lives, attracting impressive associates and making Hull House the best known example of settlement work. Hull House eventually offered a variety of services to the families of its neighborhood: a nursery, childcare, classes for mothers, a playground, a gymnasium, and adult education classes. Hull House activists also challenged the power of city bosses and lobbied state legislators, seeking cleaner streets, the abolition of child labor, health and safety regulations for factories, compulsory school attendance, and more. Their efforts brought national recognition and helped to establish the reputation of the settlement houses as what one historian called "spearheads for reform."

■ **Progressive Party** Political party formed in 1912 with Theodore Roosevelt as its candidate for president; it collapsed when Roosevelt returned to the Republicans in 1916.

settlement house Community center operated by resident social reformers in a poor urban neighborhood.

■ **Hull House** Settlement house founded by Jane Addams and Ellen Gates Starr in 1889 in Chicago.

Other settlement house workers across the country provided similar assistance to poor urban families: cooking and sewing classes, public baths, English lessons, and housing for unmarried working women. Some settlement houses were church sponsored. Nearly all tried to minimize class conflict because they agreed with Addams that "the dependence of classes on each other is reciprocal." Some historians have suggested that settlement house workers tried to bridge the gap between urban economic classes by imparting middle-class values to the poor and persuading the wealthy to help mitigate poverty. Such a view suggests that their efforts reflected urban middle-class anxieties over growing extremes of wealth and poverty. Other historians have noted that some settlement house workers drew on the bonds of gender solidarity to appeal to upper- and middle-class women for funds to assist working-class and poor women and children. Like Addams, many settlement house workers became forces for urban reform, promoting better schools, improved public health and sanitation, and honest government.

Settlement houses spread rapidly, with some four hundred operating by 1910. Three-quarters of settlement house workers were women, and settlement houses became the first institutions created and staffed primarily by college-educated women. They led to a new profession—social work. When universities began to offer study in social work (first at Columbia, in 1902), women tended to dominate that field, too. Women college graduates thus created a new and uniquely urban profession at a time when many careers remained closed to them.

Church-affiliated settlement houses often reflected the influence of the **Social Gospel**, a movement popularized by Protestant ministers concerned about urban social and economic problems. Washington Gladden, of Columbus, Ohio, called for "Applied Christianity," by which he meant the application to business of Christ's injunctions to love one another and to treat others as you would have them treat you. A similar strain of social activism appeared among Catholics, especially those inspired by Pope Leo XIII's 1891 *Rerum Novarium* ("Of New Things"), an **encyclical** urging greater attention to the problems of the industrial working class.

Women and Reform

The settlement houses are among many women's organizations that burst onto politics during the Progressive Era. By 1900 or so, a new ideal for women had emerged from the women's clubs, women's colleges, and settlement houses, and from discussions on national lecture circuits and in the press. The "New Woman" stood for self-determination rather than unthinking acceptance of roles prescribed by the concepts of domesticity and separate spheres. By 1910, this attitude, sometimes called **feminism**, was accelerating the transition from the nineteenth-century movement for suffrage to the twentieth-century struggle for equality and individualism.

Women's increasing control over one aspect of their lives is evident in the birth rate, which fell steadily throughout the nineteenth and early twentieth centuries as couples (or perhaps women alone) chose to have fewer children. Abortion was illegal, and state and federal laws banned distribution of information about contraception. In 1915 a group of women formed the National Birth Control League to seek repeal of laws prohibiting contraceptive information. In 1916 **Margaret Sanger**, a nurse practicing among the poor, attracted wide attention when she went to jail for informing women about birth control.

Other women formed organizations to advance specific causes. The National Consumers' League (founded in 1890) and the Women's Trade Union League (1903) tried to improve the lives of working women. Such efforts received a tragic boost in 1911 when fire roared through the Triangle Shirtwaist Company's clothing factory in New York City, killing 146 workers—nearly all young women—who were trapped in a building with no outside fire escapes and locked exit doors. The public outcry produced a state investigation and, in 1914, a new state factory safety law.

Some states passed laws to protect working women. In **Muller v. Oregon** (1908), the Supreme Court approved the constitutionality of one such law, limiting women's hours of work. Louis Brandeis, a lawyer working with the Consumers' League, defended the law by arguing that women needed special protection because of their social roles as mothers. Such arguments ran contrary to the New Woman's rejection of separate spheres and ultimately raised questions for women's drive for equality. At the time, however, the decision was widely hailed as a vital and necessary protection for women wage earners. By 1917, laws in thirty-nine states restricted women's working hours.

Though prominent in reform politics, most women could neither vote nor hold office. Support

■ **Social Gospel** A reform movement of the late nineteenth and early twentieth centuries, led by Protestant clergy who drew attention to urban problems and advocated for the poor.

encyclical A letter from the pope to Roman Catholic bishops, intended to guide them in their relations with the churches under their jurisdiction.

feminism The conviction that women are and should be the social, political, and economic equals of men.

■ **Margaret Sanger** Birth-control advocate who believed so strongly that information about birth control was essential to help women escape poverty that she violated laws against its dissemination.

■ *Muller v. Oregon* Supreme Court case in 1908, upholding an Oregon law that limited the hours of employment for women.

These union members carry banners mourning the deaths of the young women who died in the Triangle fire. Such demonstrations were both a form of grieving and also of demanding action to prevent any such disaster in the future. Among the witnesses to the fire was Frances Perkins, a settlement house worker who later became secretary of labor—and the first woman to serve in the president's cabinet—during the administration of Franklin D. Roosevelt. Perkins considered the fire an important turning-point in her life.

for suffrage grew, however, as more women recognized the need for political action to bring social change. By 1896, four western states had extended the vote to women (see pages 499–500). No other state did so until 1910, when Washington approved female suffrage. Seven more western states soon followed. In 1916 **Jeannette Rankin** of Montana—born on a ranch, educated as a social worker, experienced as a suffrage campaigner—became the first woman elected to the U.S. House of Representatives. Suffrage scored few victories outside the West, however.

Convinced that only a federal constitutional amendment would gain the vote for all women, the **National American Woman Suffrage Association** (NAWSA), led by Carrie Chapman Catt and Anna Howard Shaw, developed a national organization geared to lobbying in Washington, D.C. Alice Paul advocated public demonstrations and civil disobedience, tactics she learned from suffragists in England, where she had been a settlement house worker. In 1913 Paul formed the Congressional Union to pursue militant strategies. Some white suffragists tried to build an interracial movement for suffrage—NAWSA, for example, condemned

lynching in 1917—but most feared that attention to other issues would weaken their position.

Although its leaders were predominantly white and middle-class, the suffrage cause became a mass movement during the 1910s, mobilizing women of all ages and socioeconomic classes. Their opponents argued that voting would bring women into the male sphere, expose them to corrupting influences, and render them unsuitable as guardians of the moral order. Suffrage advocates turned that argument on its head, however, claiming that women would make politics more moral and family oriented. Others, especially feminists, argued that women should vote because they deserved full equality with men.

■ **Jeannette Rankin** Montana reformer and, in 1916, first woman elected to Congress; she worked for woman suffrage and to protect women in the workplace.

■ **National American Woman Suffrage Association** (NAWSA) Organization formed in 1890 that united the two major women's suffrage groups of that time.

This cartoon, entitled "The Awakening," shows a western woman, draped in a golden robe, bringing the torch of woman suffrage from the western states that had adopted suffrage to the eastern states that had not done so. In the dark eastern states, women eagerly reach toward the light from the West. Yellow had become a symbol of the suffrage movement.

Moral Reform

Other causes also stirred women to action. Moral reformers focused especially on banning alcohol—Demon Rum. The temperance movement dated to 1820s, but early temperance advocates worked to persuade individuals to give up strong drink. By the late nineteenth century, they looked to government to prohibit production, sale, or consumption of alcoholic beverages. Many saw prohibition as a progressive reform and expected government to safeguard what they saw as the public interest.

The drive against alcohol developed a broad base during the Progressive Era. Some old-stock Protestant churches—notably the Methodists—termed alcohol one of the most significant obstacles to a better society. Most adherents of the Social Gospel urged that prohibition could save the victims of industrialization and urbanization. Others emphasized protecting the family and home from the destructive influence of alcohol. Sociologists demonstrated links between liquor and prostitution, sexually transmitted diseases, poverty, crime, and broken families. Other evidence pointed to alcohol as contributing to industrial accidents, absenteeism, and inefficiency on the job.

By the late 1890s, the **Anti-Saloon League** became the model for successful interest-group politics. Proudly describing itself as "the Church in action against the saloon," the Anti-Saloon League usually operated through old-stock Protestant churches and focused on the saloon as corrupting not only individuals—men who neglected their families—but politics as well. Saloons, where political cronies struck deals and mingled with voters, had long been identified with big-city political machines.

The League endorsed only politicians who opposed Demon Rum, regardless of party or their stands on other issues. As the prohibition cause demonstrated growing political clout, more politicians lined up against the saloon. Between 1900 and 1917, voters adopted prohibition in nearly half of the states, including nearly all of the West and the South. Elsewhere, many towns and rural areas voted themselves "dry" under **local option laws**.

Opposition to prohibition came especially from immigrants, and their American-born descendants,

■ **Anti-Saloon League** Political interest group advocating prohibition, founded in 1895; it organized through churches.

local option laws A state law that permitted the residents of a town or city to decide, by an election, whether to ban liquor sales in their community.

from Ireland, Germany, and southern and eastern Europe who did not regard alcohol as inherently sinful. For them, beer or wine was an accepted part of social life. Companies that produced alcohol, especially beer-brewers, also organized to fight the prohibitionists. "Personal liberty" became the slogan for these "wets."

The drive against alcohol, ultimately successful at the national level, was not the only target for moral reformers. Reformers—including many women—tried to eliminate prostitution through state and federal legislation. Other moral reform efforts—to ban gambling or make divorces more difficult, for example—also represented attempts to use government power to regulate individual behavior.

Organizing Against Racism

During the Progressive Era, racial issues generally drew less attention than other causes. Only a few white progressives actively opposed disfranchisement and segregation in the South. Indeed, southern white progressives often took the lead in enacting discriminatory laws. Ray Stannard Baker was one of the few white progressives to examine the situation of African Americans. In his book *Following the Color Line* (1908), Baker asked, "Does democracy really include Negroes as well as white men?" For most white Americans, the answer appeared to be no.

Lynchings and violence continued as facts of life for African Americans. Between 1900 and World War I, lynchings claimed more than eleven hundred victims, most in the South. During the same years, race riots wracked several cities. In 1906 Atlanta erupted into a riot as whites randomly attacked African Americans, killing four, injuring many more, and vandalizing property. In 1908, in Springfield, Illinois (where Abraham Lincoln had made his home), a mob of whites lynched two black men, injured others, and destroyed black-owned businesses.

During the Progressive Era, some African Americans challenged the accommodationist leadership of Booker T. Washington. **W. E. B. Du Bois**, the first African American to receive a Ph.D. degree from Harvard, wrote some of the first scholarly studies of African Americans. He emphasized the contributions of black men and women, disproved racial stereotypes, and used his book *Souls of Black Folk* (1903) to criticize Washington and exhort African Americans to struggle for their rights "unceasingly." "The hands of none of us are clean," he argued, speaking to both whites and blacks, "if we bend not our energies to a righting of these great wrongs."

African American leaders organized in support of black rights. In 1905 Du Bois and others met in Canada, near Niagara Falls, and drafted demands for racial equality. In 1910 black and white delegates

A brilliant young intellectual, W. E. B. Du Bois had to choose between leading the life of a quiet college professor or challenging Booker T. Washington's claim to speak on behalf of African Americans.

Schomburg Center/Art Resource, New York.

formed the **National Association for the Advancement of Colored People** (NAACP), which provided important leadership in the fight for racial equality. Du Bois became the NAACP's director of publicity and research.

Ida B. Wells provided important leadership for the struggle against lynching. Born in Mississippi in 1862, she attended a school set up by the Freedmen's Bureau and worked as a rural teacher. Then, in Memphis, Tennessee, she began to write for a black newspaper and attacked lynching, arguing that several local victims had been targeted to eliminate successful black businessmen. When a mob

■ **W. E. B. Du Bois** African American intellectual and civil rights leader, author of important works on black history and sociology, who helped form and lead the NAACP.

■ **National Association for the Advancement of Colored People** (NAACP) Racially integrated civil rights organization founded in 1910; it continues to work to end discrimination.

■ **Ida B. Wells** African American reformer and journalist, prominent opponent of lynching and advocate for racial justice and woman suffrage; upon marrying in 1895, she became Ida Wells-Barnett.

An unknown photographer captured this lynching on film and preserved its brutality and depravity. Although there are many photographic records of lynch mobs, local authorities nearly always claimed that they were unable to determine the identity of those responsible for the murder.

Challenging Capitalism: Socialists and Wobblies

Many progressive organizations reflected middle- and upper-class concerns, such as businesslike government and greater reliance on experts. Not so the **Socialist Party of America** (SPA), formed in 1901. Proclaiming themselves the political arm of workers and farmers, the Socialists argued that industrial capitalism had produced "an economic slavery which renders intellectual and political tyranny inevitable." They rejected most progressive proposals as inadequate and called instead for workers to control the means of production. Most looked to the political process to accomplish this transformation.

The Socialists' best-known national leader was Eugene V. Debs, leader of the Pullman strike and virtually the only person able to unite the many socialist factions. Strong among immigrants, some of whom had become socialists in their native lands, the SPA attracted some trade unionists, municipal reformers, and intellectuals, including W. E. B. Du Bois, Margaret Sanger, and Upton Sinclair. The party also had some support among farmers, especially in Oklahoma and Kansas, where they attracted some former Populists.

Hundreds of cities and towns—ranging from Reading, Pennsylvania, to Milwaukee, Wisconsin, to Berkeley, California—elected Socialist mayors or council members. Socialists won election to state legislatures in several states. Districts in New York City and Milwaukee sent Socialists to the U.S. House of Representatives. Most Americans, however, had no interest in eliminating private property. Most progressive reformers looked askance at the Socialists and sometimes tried to undercut their appeal with reforms that addressed some of their concerns but stopped short of challenging capitalism.

In 1905 a group of unionists and radicals organized the **Industrial Workers of the World** (IWW, or "Wobblies"). IWW organizers boldly proclaimed, "We have been naught, we shall be all," as they set out to organize the most exploited unskilled and semiskilled workers. They aimed their message at **sweatshop** workers in eastern cities, **migrant** farm workers who harvested western crops, southern sharecroppers, women workers, African Americans, and immigrants from southern and eastern Europe. Such workers were usually ignored by the American Federation of Labor, which emphasized skilled workers, most of them white males. The Wobblies' objective was simple: when most workers had joined the IWW, they would call a general strike, labor would refuse to work, and capitalism would collapse.

The IWW did organize a few dramatic strikes and demonstrations and scored a handful of significant victories but made few lasting gains. More often, the IWW met brutal suppression by local authorities.

destroyed the newspaper office, she moved north. During the 1890s and early 1900s, Wells attacked lynching on speaking tours and in print. Eventually she persuaded some white northerners to recognize and condemn the horror of lynching. She lived in Chicago during the Progressive Era, where she promoted black women's clubs and a black settlement house. Initially a supporter of the NAACP, she came to regard it as too cautious.

■ Socialist Party of America (SPA) Political party formed in 1901 and committed to socialism—that is, government ownership of most industries.

Industrial Workers of the World (IWW) Radical workers' organization formed in 1905 to unite all wage-earners regardless of race, ethnicity, or gender, and committed to the destruction of capitalism.

sweatshop A shop or factory in which employees work long hours at low wages under poor conditions.

migrant Traveling from one area to another.

This design appeared originally on a "stickerette," a small poster (2″ × 3″) with glue on the back. When the glue was moistened, the poster could be stuck on a fence post or inside a boxcar (where migratory workers often traveled). Wobblies called the stickerettes "silent agitators." Courtesy of Labor Archives and Research Center, San Francisco State University.

THE REFORM OF POLITICS, THE POLITICS OF REFORM

★ *What did the muckrakers contribute to reform?*

★ *What characterized reforms of city and state government and what role did organized interest groups play?*

Progressivism emerged at all levels of government as cities elected reform-minded mayors and states swore in progressive governors. In their quest for change, reformers sometimes came up against the entrenched leaders of political parties and therefore sought to limit the power of those parties.

Exposing Corruption: The Muckrakers

Journalists prepared the ground for reform. By the early 1900s, magazine publishers discovered that their sales boomed when they presented dramatic exposés of political corruption, corporate wrongdoing, and other scandalous offenses. Such journalists acquired the name **muckrakers** in 1906 when President Theodore Roosevelt compared them to "the Man with the Muck-rake," a character in John Bunyan's classic allegory *Pilgrim's Progress*. Roosevelt intended the comparison as a criticism, but journalists proudly claimed the label.

McClure's Magazine led the surge in muckraking, especially after October 1902, when the magazine began a series by Lincoln Steffens on corruption in city governments. By early 1903, *McClure's* added a series by Ida Tarbell on Standard Oil and a piece revealing corruption and violence in labor unions. Sales of *McClure's* soared, and other journals—including *Collier's* and *Cosmopolitan*—copied its style, publishing exposés on patent medicines, fraud by insurance companies, child labor, and more.

Muckraking soon extended from periodicals to books. Many muckraking books were investigations into social problems. The most famous muckraking book, however, was a novel: *The Jungle,* by **Upton Sinclair** (1906). In following the experiences of fictional immigrant laborers in Chicago, Sinclair exposed the disgusting failings of the meatpacking industry. He described in chilling detail the afflictions of packinghouse workers—severed fingers, tuberculosis, blood poisoning. The nation was shocked to read of men who "fell into the vats" and "would be overlooked for days, till all but the bones of them had gone out to the world as Durham's Pure Leaf Lard!" Sinclair, a Socialist, hoped readers would recognize that the offenses he portrayed were the results of industrial capitalism.

The Jungle horrified many Americans. President Roosevelt appointed a commission to investigate its allegations, and the report confirmed Sinclair's charges. Congress responded with the **Pure Food and Drug Act**, banning impure and mislabeled food and drugs, and the **Meat Inspection Act**, requiring federal inspection of meatpacking—something the industry itself welcomed to reassure nauseated consumers. Sinclair, however, was disappointed because his revelations produced only regulation rather than converting readers to socialism. "I aimed at the public's heart," Sinclair later complained, "and by accident I hit it in the stomach."

■ **muckrakers** Progressive Era journalists who wrote articles exposing corruption in city government, business, and industry. In John Bunyan's *Pilgrim's Progress*, "the Man with the Muck-rake" is so preoccupied with raking through the filth at his feet that he didn't notice he was being offered a celestial crown in exchange for his rake.

■ **Upton Sinclair** Socialist writer and reformer whose novel *The Jungle* exposed unsanitary conditions in the meatpacking industry and advocated socialism.

■ **Pure Food and Drug Act** 1906 law forbidding sale of impure and improperly labeled food and drugs.

■ **Meat Inspection Act** 1906 law requiring federal inspection of meatpacking.

A NAUSEATING JOB, BUT IT MUST BE DONE

(President Roosevelt takes hold of the investigating muck-rake himself in the packing-house scandal.)

U.S. INSP'D AND CONDEMNED

Upton Sinclair's novel *The Jungle* (1906) prompted President Theodore Roosevelt to order an investigation of Sinclair's allegations about unsanitary practices in the meatpacking industry. Roosevelt then pressured Congress to approve new federal legislation to inspect meatpacking, including a stamp such as the one shown here.

Reforming City Government

By the time of Lincoln Steffens's first article (1902) on corruption in city government, advocates of **municipal reform** had already won office and brought changes to some cities, and municipal reformers soon appeared elsewhere.

Municipal reformers argued that eliminating corruption and inefficiency required changes in the structure of city government. City councils usually consisted of members elected from **wards** corresponding roughly to neighborhoods. Middle- and working-class wards usually dominated city councils. Reformers condemned the ward system as producing city council members unable to see beyond their own neighborhoods. Reformers also recognized that poor immigrant neighborhoods supported political bosses and machines despite their corruption. They argued that citywide elections, in which all city voters chose from one list of candidates, would produce city council members who could better address the problems of the city as a whole—men with citywide business interests, for example—and would undercut the influence of ward bosses and machines.

James Phelan of San Francisco was an early structural reformer. Son of a pioneer banker, he attacked corruption in city government and won election as mayor in 1896. He then spearheaded adoption of a new charter that strengthened the office of mayor and required citywide election of supervisors (equivalent to city council members).

Some municipal reformers proposed more fundamental changes in the structure of city government, notably the **commission system** and the **city manager plan**, which reflected many progressives' distrust of political parties and desire for expertise and efficiency. The commission system was first tried in Galveston, Texas, after a devastating hurricane and tidal wave in 1900. Typically, in commission systems, the city's voters elected a few commissioners, each

■ **municipal reform** Political activity intended to bring about changes in the structure or function of city government.

ward A division of a city or town, especially an electoral district, for administrative or representative purposes.

commission system System of city government in which executive and legislative powers are vested in a small elective board, each member of which supervises some aspect of city government.

city manager plan System of city government in which the city council hires a city manager who exercises broad executive authority.

of whom managed a specific city function. The city manager plan—an adaptation of the structure of the corporation—featured a professional city manager (similar to a corporate executive) appointed by an elected city council (similar to a corporate board of directors) to handle most municipal administration. In 1913 a serious flood prompted the citizens of Dayton, Ohio, to adopt a city manager plan, and other cities then followed.

A few reformers went beyond structural reform to advocate social reforms. Hazen Pingree, a successful businessman, attracted national attention as mayor of Detroit. Elected in 1889, he soon took on the city's gas, electric, and streetcar companies for overcharging customers and providing poor service. He responded to the depression of 1893 with community vegetable gardens and work projects for the unemployed. Samuel "Golden Rule" Jones, a prosperous manufacturer, won election as mayor of Toledo, Ohio, in 1897. He promoted free concerts, free public baths, childcare for working mothers, and the eight-hour workday for city employees. Phelan, Pingree, Jones, and a few others also advocated city ownership of utilities—the gas, water, electricity, and streetcar systems.

The Progressive Era also saw early efforts at city planning, as city officials began to designate separate zones for residential, commercial, and industrial use (first in Los Angeles, in 1904–1908). By 1910, a few cities had created city planning commissions. The emergence of **city planning** represents an important transition in thinking about government and the economy, for it emphasized expertise and presumed greater government control over use of private property.

The emergence of public health, mental health, social work, and other new professions led to efforts to use local government to solve the problems of an urban industrial society. Their objective was to use scientific and social scientific knowledge to control social forces and thereby to shape the future. New medical knowledge presented an opportunity to reduce disease on a significant scale. Public health emerged as a new medical field, combining the knowledge of the medical doctor with the insight of the social scientist and the skills of the corporate manager. New public health programs sought to wipe out **hookworm** in the South, **tuberculosis** in the slums, and sexually transmitted diseases. Social workers often found themselves allied with public health professionals in efforts to use local government to improve urban health and safety.

The public schools also attracted reformers. As university programs began graduating teachers and school administrators, these new professionals sought greater control over education. Professional educators often pushed for greater centralization and professionalization in school administration by reducing the role of local, usually elected, **school boards** and

by replacing elected school superintendents with appointed professionals. Professional educators also began to use recently developed intelligence tests to identify children unable to perform at average levels, and then to isolate them in special classes.

Reforming State Government

As reformers launched changes in many cities and as new professionals considered ways to improve society, **Robert M. La Follette** pushed Wisconsin to the forefront of reform. A Republican, he entered politics soon after graduating from the University of Wisconsin. He served three terms in Congress in the 1880s but found his political career blocked by the leader of the state Republican organization. He was firmly convinced of the need for reform when he finally won election as governor in 1900.

Conservative legislators, mostly Republicans, defeated La Follette's proposals to regulate railroad rates and to reduce the power of party bosses by replacing nominating conventions with the **direct primary**. La Follette threw himself into an energetic campaign to elect reformers to the state legislature. He earned the nickname "Fighting Bob" as he traveled the state and propounded his views. Most of his candidates won, and La Follette built a strong following among Wisconsin's farmers and urban wage earners, who reelected him in 1902 and 1904.

La Follette secured legislation to regulate corporations and political parties. Acclaimed as a "laboratory of democracy," Wisconsin adopted the direct primary, set up a commission to regulate railroads, increased taxes on corporations, enacted a merit system for state employees, and restricted lobbyists. In many of his efforts, La Follette drew on the expertise of faculty members at the University of Wisconsin. These reforms, along with reliance on experts, came to be

city planning The policy of planning urban development by regulating land use.

hookworm A parasite, formerly common in the South, that causes loss of strength.

tuberculosis An infectious disease that attacks the lungs; spread by unsanitary conditions and practices, such as spitting in public, it was common and often fatal in the nineteenth and early twentieth centuries and is reappearing today.

school board Policymakers who oversee the public schools of a local political unit.

■ **Robert M. La Follette** Progressive governor of Wisconsin; instituted direct primaries, tax reform, and anticorruption measures; later U.S. senator.

direct primary Election in which voters who identify with a specific party choose that party's candidates to run later in the general election.

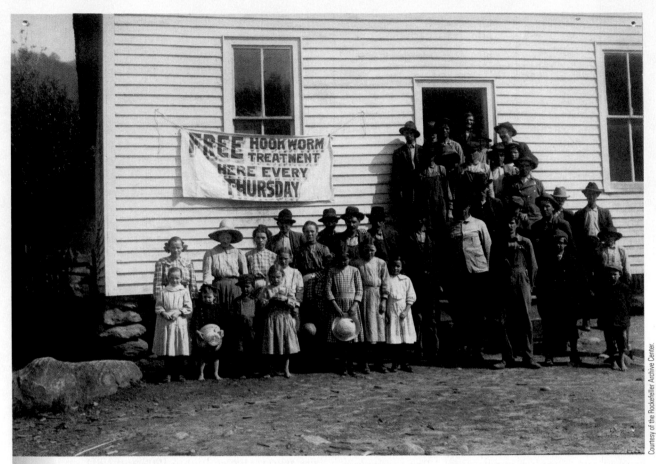

In 1909, John D. Rockefeller, Sr., contributed $1 million to create the Rockefeller Sanitary Commission for the Eradication of Hookworm Disease. The commission launched a public-health campaign in eleven southern states, including education and medical dispensaries to provide treatment. This photograph shows the dispensary and some of the patients in Greenbrier, Tennessee, in May 1914.

called the **Wisconsin Idea**. La Follette won election to the U.S. Senate in 1905 and remained a leading progressive voice there until his death in 1925.

La Follette's success prompted imitation elsewhere. In 1901 Iowans elected Albert B. Cummins governor, and Cummins launched a campaign against railroad corporations similar to La Follette's. He too went on to the Senate. Reformers won office in other states as well, but only a few matched La Follette's legislative and political success.

Progressivism came to California relatively late. Reformers accused the Southern Pacific Railroad of running a political machine that controlled the state by dominating the Republican Party. In 1910, **Hiram Johnson** ran for governor as a reformer and

won. California progressives produced a volume of reform that rivaled that of Wisconsin—regulation of railroads and public utilities, restrictions on political parties, protection for labor, conservation, and woman suffrage. Johnson appointed union leaders to state positions and promoted measures to benefit working people. California progressives in both parties, however, condemned Asian immigrants and Asian Americans, and progressive Republicans in 1913 pushed through a law that prohibited Asian immigrants from owning land in California.

Like La Follette, Johnson moved on to national politics. In 1912 he was the vice-presidential candidate of the new Progressive Party. Reelected governor in 1914, he won election to the U.S. Senate in 1916 and served there until his death in 1945.

Southern progressivism took up concerns similar to those that motivated reformers elsewhere and blended them with that region's racial politics. Often inspired by northern models of reform and by northern reform organizations or philanthropists, southern progressives promoted school and public

■ **Wisconsin Idea** Program of reform sponsored by La Follette in Wisconsin.

■ **Hiram Johnson** Governor of California; promoted many reforms, including regulation of railroads and measures to benefit labor.

Hiram Johnson campaigning at Lincoln, California, in 1914. Elected governor of California in 1910 as a progressive Republican, Johnson provided strong leadership for the state's progressives. In 1912, he was the vice-presidential candidate of the new Progressive Party, running with Theodore Roosevelt.

health reforms, limits on child labor, prohibition, and woman suffrage. Southern progressives could point to success in some states, especially on railroad regulation, prohibition, improved schools, and child labor laws. However, some southern reformers ran up against a long-standing insistence on local control. Given the South's one-party politics, the Democratic Party sometimes became the battleground between progressives and conservatives. Some southern reformers were also among the most demagogic advocates of white supremacy, pushing both corporate regulation and racist policies.

The Weakening of Parties and Rise of Organized Interest Groups

Like Wisconsin and California, other states moved to restrict political parties. Reformers charged that bosses and machines manipulated nominating conventions and public officials, and that bosses, in return for payoffs, used their influence on behalf of corporate interests. Articles by muckrakers and some highly publicized bribery trials convinced many voters

that the reformers were correct. The mighty party organizations that had dominated politics during the nineteenth century came under attack along a broad front.

Progressives nearly everywhere proposed measures to enhance the power of individual voters and reduce the power of party organizations. State after state adopted the direct primary, and many reformers sought to replace state patronage systems with the merit system. In many states, judgeships, school board seats, and educational offices were made nonpartisan.

A number of cities and states also adopted the **initiative** and **referendum**. The initiative permitted voters to adopt a new law directly: if enough voters signed a petition, the proposed law would be voted on at the next election; if approved by the voters, it became law. The referendum permitted voters, through a petition, to reject a law adopted by the legislature. Oregon voters approved these reforms in 1902, and Oregon reformers used the initiative to create new laws, giving the initiative and referendum so much national attention that they were sometimes called the Oregon System. Some states also adopted the **recall**, permitting voters, through petitions, to initiate a special election to remove an elected official from office. The direct primary, initiative and referendum, and recall are known collectively as **direct democracy** because they remove intermediate steps between the voter and final political decisions.

With the switch to direct primaries and the weakening of party organizations, campaigns focused more on individual candidates and less on parties. Candidates now appealed directly to voters rather than to party leaders and convention delegates. Individual candidates' personal organizations and advertising supplanted the armies of party retainers who had mobilized voters in the nineteenth century. At the same time, new voter registration laws and procedures disqualified some voters, especially transient workers. Voter turnout fell. Ironically, the emergence of new channels for political participation created the illusion of a vast outpouring of public involvement in politics—but proportionally fewer voters actually cast ballots.

initiative Procedure allowing voters to petition to have a new law placed on the ballot to be voted up or down, bypassing the legislature.

referendum Procedure whereby voters petition to have a legislative act submitted to the voters, who can overturn it.

recall Provision that permits voters, through petition, to hold a special election to remove an elected official from office.

■ **direct democracy** Provisions that permit voters to make political decisions directly, including the direct primary, initiative, referendum, and recall.

New avenues of political participation opened not only through direct democracy but also through organized interest groups who used politics to advance their agendas. Groups could cooperate when their political objectives coincided, as when merchants and farmers both favored regulation of railroad rates. Other times, they found themselves in conflict, perhaps over tariff policy. Within the many groups that advocated change, participants sometimes fought among themselves over which reform goals were most important and how to achieve them. Many groups adopted the tactics of the Anti-Saloon League—they ignored parties, pressured candidates to accept their group's position, and urged their members to vote only for approved candidates. In 1904, for example, the National Association of Manufacturers (NAM) targeted and defeated two pro-labor members of Congress, one in the House and one in the Senate. The American Federation of Labor (AFL) responded in 1906 with a similar strategy and elected six union members to the House of Representatives.

Organized interest groups often focused on the legislative process. They retained full-time representatives, or **lobbyists**, who urged legislators to support their group's position on pending legislation, reminded lawmakers of their group's electoral clout, and arranged campaign backing for those who supported their cause. Thus, as political parties became weaker, organized interest groups gained strength. Pushed one way by the AFL and the other by the NAM, under opposing pressure from the Anti-Saloon League and liquor interests, some elected officials came to see themselves less as loyal members of a political party and more as mediators among competing interest groups.

ROOSEVELT, TAFT, AND REPUBLICAN PROGRESSIVISM

★ *What did Theodore Roosevelt mean by a "Square Deal"? Do his accomplishments fit this description?*

★ *How did Roosevelt's presidency change the federal role in the economy and alter the presidency itself?*

When Theodore Roosevelt became president upon the death of William McKinley, he fascinated Americans—one visitor reported that the most exciting things he saw in the United States were "Niagara Falls and the President . . . both great wonders of nature!"

lobbyist A person who tries to influence the opinions of legislators or other public officials for or against a specific cause.

"TR" quickly became recognizable everywhere, as cartoonists delighted in sketching his bristling mustache, thick glasses, and toothy grin.

Roosevelt later wrote, "I cannot say that I entered the Presidency with any deliberately planned and far-reaching scheme of social betterment." Nonetheless, Americans soon saw Roosevelt as the embodiment of progressivism. In seven years, he changed the nation's domestic policies more than any president since Lincoln—and made himself a legend.

Roosevelt: Asserting the Power of the Presidency

Roosevelt was unlike most politicians of his day. He had inherited wealth and added to it from the many books he wrote. He saw politics as a duty to the nation rather than an opportunity for personal advancement, and he defined his politics in terms of character, morality, hard work, and patriotism. Uncertain whether to call himself a "radical conservative" or a "conservative radical," he considered politics the tool for forging an ethical and stable society. Confident in his own personal principles, Roosevelt did not hesitate to wield all the powers of the presidency. He especially liked to use the office as what he called a "bully pulpit" to publicize his concerns.

In his first message to Congress, in December 1901, Roosevelt sounded a theme that he repeated again and again: the growth of powerful corporations was "natural," but some exhibited "grave evils" that required correction. As Roosevelt later explained, "When I became President, the question as to the method by which the United States Government was to control the corporations was not yet important. The absolutely vital question was whether the Government had power to control them at all." He determined to establish that power.

The chief obstacle to regulating corporations was a Supreme Court decision, *United States v. E. C. Knight* (1895), preventing the Sherman Anti-Trust Act from being used against manufacturers. Roosevelt looked for an opportunity to challenge the *Knight* decision. In 1901, some of the nation's most prominent business leaders had joined forces to create the Northern Securities Company, creating a railroad monopoly in the Northwest. The *Knight* case involved manufacturing; the Northern Securities Company provided interstate transportation. If any industry could satisfy the Supreme Court that it fit the constitutional language authorizing Congress to regulate interstate commerce, Roosevelt believed, the railroads could.

Roosevelt's attorney general, Philander C. Knox, filed suit against the Northern Securities Company for violating the Sherman Act. Wall Street leaders condemned Roosevelt's action, but most Americans applauded to see the federal government finally challenge a powerful corporation. In 1904 the Supreme Court agreed that the Sherman Act could be applied to the Northern Securities Company and ordered it dissolved.

Bolstered by this confirmation of federal power, Roosevelt launched additional antitrust suits, but he used **trustbusting** selectively. Large corporations, he thought, were potentially beneficial. He thought regulation was preferable to breaking them up. Companies that met Roosevelt's standards of character and public service—and that acknowledged the power of the presidency—had no reason to fear antitrust action.

Roosevelt's willingness to act boldly was not limited to trustbusting. In time of crisis, he felt, the president should "do whatever the needs of the people demand, unless the Constitution or the laws explicitly forbid him to do it." As he illustrated in asserting new presidential powers to deal with the coal miners' strike in 1902, he intended to produce what he called a **Square Deal**, fair treatment for all parties.

The Square Deal in Action: Creating the Regulatory State

Roosevelt's trustbusting and handling of the coal strike brought him great popularity. In 1903 Congress approved several measures he requested or endorsed: an act to speed up prosecution of antitrust suits; creation of a cabinet-level Department of Commerce and Labor, including a bureau to investigate corporate activities; and the Elkins Act, which penalized railroads that paid rebates.

When Roosevelt sought election in 1904, he won by one of the largest margins up to that time—more than 56 percent of the popular vote. Elected in his own right, with a powerful demonstration of public approval, Roosevelt set out to secure meaningful regulation of the railroads, largest of the nation's big businesses.

Roosevelt and reformers in Congress wanted to regulate railroads' prices for both freight and passengers. In Roosevelt's year-end message to Congress in 1905, he asked for legislation to regulate railroad rates, open the financial records of railroads to government inspection, and increase federal authority in strikes involving interstate commerce. At the same time, the attorney general filed suits against some of the nation's largest corporations. Muckrakers (some of them Roosevelt's friends) fired off scathing exposés of railroads and attacks on Senate conservatives.

Although Roosevelt compromised on some issues, he got most of what he wanted. On June 29, 1906, Congress passed the **Hepburn Act**, allowing the Interstate Commerce Commission (ICC) to establish maximum railroad rates and to regulate other forms of transportation. The act also limited railroads' ability to issue free passes, a practice that reformers had

long considered bribery. The next day, on June 30, Congress approved the Pure Food and Drug Act and the Meat Inspection Act, the aftermath to Sinclair's stomach-turning revelations. Taken together, these three measures can be considered the beginning of the federal regulatory state.

Regulating Natural Resources

An advocate for strenuous outdoor activities, Roosevelt took great pride in establishing five national parks and more than fifty wildlife preserves to save what he called "beautiful and wonderful wild creatures whose existence was threatened by greed and wantonness." **Preservationists**, such as John Muir of the Sierra Club, applauded these actions and urged that such wilderness areas be kept forever safe from developers. Parks and wildlife refuges, however, were only part of Roosevelt's **conservation** agenda.

Roosevelt and **Gifford Pinchot**, the president's chief adviser on natural resources, believed conservation required not only preservation of wild and beautiful lands but also carefully planned use of resources. Trained in scientific forestry in Europe, Pinchot combined scientific expertise with a managerial outlook. He and Roosevelt withdrew large tracts of federal timber and grazing land from public sale or use. By careful management of these lands, they hoped to provide for the needs of both the present and the future. Roosevelt removed nearly 230 million acres from public sale, more than quadrupling the land under federal protection.

Roosevelt strongly supported the Reclamation Act of 1902, which set aside proceeds from federal land sales in sixteen western states to finance irrigation projects. The act established a commitment later greatly expanded: the federal government would construct western dams, canals, and other facilities

---

trustbusting Use of antitrust laws to prosecute and dissolve big businesses ("trusts").

■ **Square Deal** Theodore Roosevelt's term for his efforts to deal fairly with all.

■ **Hepburn Act** 1906 law authorizing the Interstate Commerce Commission to set maximum railroad rates and regulate other forms of transportation.

preservationist One who advocates reserving natural areas so as to protect them against human disturbance.

conservation The careful management of natural resources so that they yield the greatest benefit to present generations while maintaining their potential to meet the needs of future generations.

■ **Gifford Pinchot** Head of the Forestry Service from 1898 to 1910; promoted conservation and urged careful planning in the use of resources.

Gifford Pinchot believed in careful management of natural resources, including the preservation of some wilderness areas and carefully planned use of other resources. Head of the Forestry Service under Roosevelt, Pinchot influenced Roosevelt's conservation and preservation policies.

to support agriculture in areas of scant rainfall. Thus water, perhaps the most important natural resource in the West, came to be managed. Far from preserving the western landscape, federal water projects profoundly transformed it, vividly illustrating the vast difference between the preservation of wilderness that Muir advocated and the careful management of resources that Pinchot sought.

Taft's Troubles

Soon after Roosevelt won the election of 1904, he announced that he would not seek reelection in 1908. He remained immensely popular, however, and virtually named his successor. Republicans nominated William Howard Taft. A graduate of Yale and former federal judge, Taft had served as governor of the Philippines before joining Roosevelt's cabinet as secretary of war in 1904.

William Jennings Bryan, leader of the progressive wing of the Democratic Party, won his party's nomination for the third time. Roosevelt's popularity and strong endorsement of Taft carried the day. Taft won just under 52 percent of the vote, and Republicans kept control of the Senate and the House. Roosevelt turned over the presidency to Taft, then set off to hunt big game in Africa.

Taft's legalistic approach often appeared timid when compared with Roosevelt's boldness. But Taft's attorney general initiated some ninety antitrust suits in four years, twice as many as during Roosevelt's seven years. And Taft approved legislation to strengthen regulatory agencies.

During the Taft administration, progressives amended the Constitution twice. Reformers had long considered an income tax to be the fairest means of raising federal revenues. With support from Taft, enough states ratified the **Sixteenth Amendment** (permitting a federal income tax) for it to take effect in 1913. In contrast, Taft took no position on the **Seventeenth Amendment**, proposed in 1912 and ratified shortly after he left office in 1913. It changed the method of electing U.S. senators from election by

■ **Sixteenth Amendment** (1913) Constitutional amendment authorizing the federal government to establish an income tax.

■ **Seventeenth Amendment** (1913) Constitutional amendment requiring election of U.S. senators directly by the voters of each state, rather than by state legislatures.

WHITE HOUSE

G.O.P.

HE'S A GOOD THING PUSH HIM ALONG

This postcard depicts Roosevelt, in command of the Republican Party, persuading his friend William Howard Taft to run for president in 1908. Taft was not eager for that office, but Roosevelt convinced him to seek it. Taft was elected but proved a disappointment to Roosevelt.

state legislatures to election by voters, another long-time goal of reformers, who claimed that corporate influence and outright bribery had swayed state legislatures and shaped the Senate.

Roosevelt had left Taft a Republican Party divided between progressives and conservatives. Those divisions grew, and Taft increasingly sided with the conservatives. In 1909, he called on Congress to reform the tariff. The resulting Payne-Aldrich Tariff retained high rates on most imports, but Taft signed it. When Republican progressives protested, Taft became defensive, alienating them further by calling it "the best bill that the Republican party ever passed."

Republican progressives also attacked the high-handed exercise of power by Joseph Cannon, the conservative Speaker of the House of Representatives. Taft first favored the progressives, then backed off and made his peace with Cannon. Republican progressives then joined Democrats in a "revolt against Cannonism" that reduced the Speaker's powers.

A dispute over conservation further damaged Republican unity. Taft had kept Gifford Pinchot as head of the Forest Service, but Pinchot charged that Taft's secretary of the interior, Richard A. Ballinger, had weakened the conservation program. Taft concluded that Ballinger had done nothing improper. When Pinchot persisted, Taft fired him. By 1912, when Taft faced reelection, the Republican Party was in serious disarray, and he faced opposition from most progressive Republicans.

"Carry a Big Stick": Roosevelt, Taft, and World Affairs

★ What were Roosevelt's objectives for the United States in world affairs?

★ How did Roosevelt reshape American foreign policy?

Theodore Roosevelt not only remolded the presidency and established new federal regulatory authority, he also significantly expanded America's role in world affairs. Few presidents have had so great an influence. He once expressed his fondness for what he called a West African proverb: "Speak softly and carry a big stick; you will go far." As president, however, Roosevelt seldom spoke softly. Well read in history and current events, Roosevelt entered the presidency with definite ideas on the place of the United States in the world. As he advised Congress in 1902, "The increasing interdependence and complexity of international political and economic relations render it incumbent on all civilized and orderly powers to insist on the proper policing of the world." The United States, Roosevelt made clear, stood ready to do its share of "proper policing."

Taking Panama

While McKinley was still president, American diplomats began efforts to create a canal through Central America. Many people had long shared the dream of such a passage between the Atlantic and Pacific Oceans. A French company actually began construction in the late 1870s, but abandoned the project when the task proved too great.

During the Spanish-American War, the battleship *Oregon* took well over two months to steam from the West Coast around South America to join the rest of the fleet off Cuba. A canal would have cut the time to three weeks or less. McKinley pronounced an American-controlled canal "indispensable."

Experts identified two possible locations for a canal, Nicaragua and Panama (then part of Colombia). The Panama route was shorter, and the French company had completed some work there. **Philippe Bunau-Varilla**—formerly chief project engineer for the French effort, now a major stockholder—did his utmost to sell the French company's interests to the United States. Building through Panama, however, meant overcoming formidable mountains and fever-ridden swamps. Previous studies had preferred Nicaragua. Its geography posed fewer natural obstacles, and much of the route lay through Lake Nicaragua.

In 1902, shortly before Congress was to vote on the two routes, Bunau-Varilla distributed to senators a Nicaraguan postage stamp showing a smoldering volcano looming over a lake. Bunau-Varilla's lobbying—and his stamps—reinforced efforts by prominent Republican senators. The Senate approved the route through the Colombian state of Panama.

Negotiations with Colombia bogged down, then the Colombian government offered to accept limitations on its sovereignty in return for more money. Outraged, Roosevelt called the offer "pure bandit morality." Bunau-Varilla and his associates then encouraged and financed a revolution in Panama. Roosevelt ordered U.S. warships to the area to prevent Colombian troops from crushing the uprising. The revolution quickly succeeded. Panama declared its independence on November 3, 1903, and the United States immediately extended diplomatic recognition. Bunau-Varilla became Panama's minister to the United States and promptly signed a treaty that gave the United States much the same arrangement earlier rejected by Colombia.

MAP 19.1 The United States and the Caribbean, 1898–1917

Between 1898 and 1917, the United States expanded into the Caribbean by acquiring possessions and establishing protectorates. As a result, the United States became the dominant power in the region.

The **Hay–Bunau-Varilla Treaty** (1903) granted the United States perpetual control over the Canal Zone, a strip of Panamanian territory 10 miles wide, for a price of $10 million and annual rent of $250,000; it also made Panama the second American protectorate (Cuba was the first; see Map 19.1). The United States purchased the assets of the French company and began construction. Roosevelt considered the canal his crowning deed in foreign affairs. "When nobody else could or would exercise efficient authority, I exercised it," he wrote in his *Autobiography* (1913). He always denied any part in instigating the revolution, but he once bluntly claimed, "I took the canal zone."

Construction proved difficult. Just over 40 miles long, the canal took ten years to build and cost nearly $400 million. Completed in 1914, just as World War I began, it was considered one of the world's great engineering feats.

Making the Caribbean an American Lake

With canal construction under way, American policymakers considered how to protect it. Roosevelt determined to establish American dominance in the Caribbean and Central America, where the many harbors might permit a foreign power to prepare for a strike against the canal or even the Gulf Coast of the United States. Acquisition of Puerto Rico, protectorates over Cuba and Panama, and naval facilities in all three locations as well as on the Gulf Coast made the United States a powerful presence.

The Caribbean and the area around it contained twelve independent nations. Britain, France, Denmark, and the Netherlands held nearly all the smaller islands, and Britain had a coastal colony (British Honduras, now Belize). Several Caribbean nations had borrowed large amounts of money from European bankers, raising the prospect of intervention to secure loan payments. In 1902, Britain and Germany declared a blockade of Venezuela over such debts. In 1904, when several European nations hinted that they might intervene in the Dominican Republic, Roosevelt presented what became known as the **Roosevelt Corollary** to the Monroe Doctrine. He warned European nations against any intervention in the Western Hemisphere. If intervention by what he termed "some civilized nation" became necessary in the Caribbean or Central America to correct "chronic wrongdoing," Roosevelt insisted that the United States would handle it, acting as "an international police power."

Roosevelt acted forcefully to establish his new policy. In 1905 the Dominican Republic agreed to permit the United States to collect customs (taxes on imports, the major source of governmental revenue) and supervise government expenditures, including debt repayment, thereby becoming the third U.S. protectorate.

Roosevelt's successors, William Howard Taft and Woodrow Wilson, continued and expanded American domination in the Caribbean. The Taft administration encouraged American investments there, hoping that American investments would block investment by other nations and also stabilize and develop the Caribbean economies. Taft supported such "**dollar diplomacy**" (as his critics called it) throughout the region, especially in Nicaragua.

In 1912 Taft sent U.S. Marines to Nicaragua to suppress a rebellion against President Adolfo Díaz. They remained after the turmoil settled, ostensibly to guard the American legation but actually to prop up the Díaz government—making Nicaragua the fourth U.S. protectorate. A treaty was drafted giving the United States responsibility for collecting customs, but the Senate rejected it. At that point, the State Department, several American banks, and Nicaragua set up a **customs receivership** through the banks.

Roosevelt and Eastern Asia

In eastern Asia, Roosevelt built on the Open Door notes and American participation in the international force that suppressed the Boxer Rebellion. He was both concerned and optimistic about the rise of Japan as a major industrial and imperial power. Aware of Alfred Thayer Mahan's warnings that Japan posed a potential danger to the United States in the Pacific, Roosevelt hoped that Japan might exercise an international police power in its vicinity similar to that which the United States claimed under the Roosevelt Corollary.

In 1904 Russia and Japan went to war over **Manchuria**, part of northeastern China. Russia had pressured China to grant so many concessions in Manchuria that it seemed to be turning into a Russian colony. Russia

■ **Philippe Bunau-Varilla** Chief planner of the Panamanian revolt against Colombia and minister to the United States from the new Republic of Panama.

■ **Hay–Bunau-Varilla Treaty** 1903 treaty with Panama that granted the United States sovereignty over the Canal Zone in return for $10 million plus annual rent.

■ **Roosevelt Corollary** 1904 extension of the Monroe Doctrine announced by Theodore Roosevelt, in which he proclaimed the right of the United States to police the Caribbean area.

■ **dollar diplomacy** Name applied by critics to the Taft administration's policy of supporting U.S. investments abroad.

customs receivership An agreement whereby one nation takes over the collection of another nation's customs and exercises some control over that nation's expenditures of customs receipts, thus limiting the autonomy of the nation in receivership.

Manchuria A region of northeastern China.

Theodore Roosevelt, in his 1904 Corollary to the Monroe Doctrine, asserted that the United States was dominant in the Caribbean. Here a cartoonist capitalized on Roosevelt's boyish nature, depicting the Caribbean as Roosevelt's pond. Culver Pictures, Inc.

seemed also to have designs on Korea, nominally an independent kingdom. Japan saw Russian expansion as a threat to its own interests and responded with force. The Japanese scored smashing naval and military victories over the Russians but had too few resources to sustain a long-term war.

Roosevelt concluded that American interests were best served by reducing Russian influence in the region so as to maintain a balance of power. Such a balance, he thought, would be most likely to preserve nominal Chinese sovereignty in Manchuria. Early in the war, he indicated some support for Japan. As its resources ran low, Japan asked Roosevelt to act as mediator. The president agreed, concerned that a Japanese victory

■ **Treaty of Portsmouth** 1905 treaty, mediated by Roosevelt at a conference in Portsmouth, New Hampshire, ending the Russo-Japanese War.

gentlemen's agreement An agreement rather than a formal treaty; in this case, Japan agreed in 1907 to limit Japanese emigration to the United States.

might be as dangerous as Russian expansion. The peace conference took place in Portsmouth, New Hampshire. The **Treaty of Portsmouth** (1905) recognized Japan's dominance in Korea and gave Japan the southern half of Sakhalin Island and Russian concessions in southern Manchuria. Russia kept its railroad in northern Manchuria. China remained responsible for civil authority in Manchuria. For his mediation, Roosevelt received the 1906 Nobel Peace Prize.

In 1906–1907, Roosevelt mediated another dispute. The San Francisco school board ordered students of Japanese parentage to attend the city's segregated Chinese school. The Japanese government protested what it considered an insult, and Japanese newspapers even hinted at war. Roosevelt convinced the school officials to withdraw the order, in return for restrictions on Japanese immigration, and he negotiated a so-called **gentlemen's agreement** by which Japan agreed to limit the departure of laborers to the United States.

In 1908 the American and Japanese governments further agreed to respect each other's territorial possessions (the Philippines and Hawai'i for the United

"The Nations Pride"

This picture was issued as a penny postcard, expressing the nation's pride in the "Great White Fleet." The Post Office approved penny postcards in 1902, and the years 1905–1915 are sometimes considered the "golden age" for penny postcards. The one-penny price for postage made them highly affordable, and the wide variety of subjects available made them popular.

Collection of Picture Research Consultants and Archives.

States; Korea, Formosa, and southern Manchuria for Japan) and to honor as well "the independence and integrity of China" and the Open Door.

The United States and World Affairs, 1901–1913

Before the 1890s, the United States had few clear or consistent foreign-policy commitments or objectives. By 1905, the Philippines, Guam, Hawai'i, Puerto Rico, eastern Samoa, and the Canal Zone were highly visible evidence of a dramatic change in America's role in world affairs.

Central to that concept was a large, modern navy, without which every other commitment was merely a moral pronouncement. Roosevelt was so proud of the navy that in 1907 he dispatched sixteen battleships—painted white to signal their peaceful intent—on an around-the-world tour. Though Roosevelt claimed that he sent the Great White Fleet "to impress the American people," he was clearly interested in impressing other nations, especially Japan, and in demonstrating that the American navy was fully capable of moving quickly to distant parts of the globe.

The need to protect the canal led the United States to dominate the Caribbean and Central America, but the new American role also focused on the Pacific. As Mahan and others pointed out, the Pacific Ocean was a likely theater of twentieth-century conflict. Thus considerations of commercial enterprise, such as the China trade, coincided with naval strategy and led the United States to acquire possessions at key locations in the Pacific.

American policymakers' new vision of the world seemed to divide nations into broad categories. In one class were the "civilized" nations. In the other were those nations that Theodore Roosevelt described, at various times, as "barbarous," "impotent," or simply unable to meet their obligations. When dealing with "civilized" countries—the European powers, Japan, the large, stable nations of Latin America, Canada, Australia, New Zealand—American diplomats focused on finding ways to realize mutual objectives, especially arbitration of disputes. In eastern Asia, McKinley, Roosevelt, and Taft looked to a balance of power among the contending "civilized" powers as most likely to realize the American objective of maintaining the "open door" in China.

The conviction that arbitration was the appropriate means to settle disputes among "civilized" countries was widespread. An international conference in 1899 created a **Permanent Court of Arbitration** in the Netherlands, which provided neutral arbitrators for international disputes. Roosevelt and Taft tried to negotiate arbitration treaties with major powers, but the Senate refused for fear that arbitration might diminish the Senate's role in foreign relations.

The United States and Great Britain repeatedly used arbitration to settle their disputes. Throughout the late nineteenth and early twentieth centuries, American relations with Britain improved steadily, mostly due to British initiatives. The more Germany expanded its army and navy, the more British policymakers worked to improve relations with the United States, the only nation besides Britain with a navy comparable to Germany's. During America's war with Spain, Britain alone among the major European powers sided with the United States. By reducing its naval forces in the Caribbean, Britain delivered a clear signal—it not only accepted American dominance there but now depended on the United States to protect its holdings in the region.

■ **Permanent Court of Arbitration** Organization of about fifty member nations, created in the Netherlands in 1899 for the purpose of peacefully resolving international conflicts; also known as the Hague Court from its location.

In the Wider World

The Scramble for the Last Colonies

As the United States was consolidating its control over the Philippines and establishing its dominance in the Caribbean, other nations were scrambling for the last areas that could be claimed as colonies. Britain and France had constructed worldwide empires during the eighteenth and nineteenth centuries, and the Spanish and Portuguese empires were even older, though both lost their Latin American colonies in the nineteenth century. The Russian empire gained control over Central Asia during the nineteenth century and took concessions in northeastern China in the 1890s. Germany was unified as a nation only in 1871, and did not embark on colonialism until the 1880s. By then, little was left—a few areas in Africa and the Pacific and some concessions in China. Japan, too, came late to the scramble for colonies, taking Taiwan from China in the Sino-Japanese War (1894) along with parts of the Chinese mainland and Korea (previously independent), and engaging in the Russo-Japanese War (1905) over control of Manchuria.

WILSON AND DEMOCRATIC PROGRESSIVISM

☆ What choices confronted American voters in the presidential election of 1912?

☆ How did Wilson's views on reform evolve from 1912 through 1916 and how did his administration change the federal government's role in the economy?

The presidential election of 1912 marks a moment when Americans actively and seriously debated their future. All three nominees were well educated and highly literate. Roosevelt and Wilson had written respected books on American history and politics. They approached politics with a sense of destiny and purpose, and they talked frankly to the American people about their ideas for the future.

Debating the Future: The Election of 1912

As Taft watched the Republican Party unravel, Theodore Roosevelt was hunting in Africa and then hobnobbing with European leaders. When he returned in 1910, he undertook a speaking tour and proposed a broad program of reform he labeled the **New Nationalism**. In the 1910 congressional elections,

■ **New Nationalism** Reform program that Theodore Roosevelt advocated before and during his unsuccessful bid to regain the presidency in 1912.

credentials committee Party convention committee that settles disputes arising when rival delegations from the same state demand to be seated.

■ **Bull Moose Party** Popular name given to the Progressive Party in 1912.

Republicans fared badly, plagued by divisions within their party and an economic downturn. For the first time since 1892, Democrats won a majority in the House of Representatives. Democrats, including Woodrow Wilson in New Jersey, also won a number of governorships. Many Republican progressives now looked to Robert La Follette to wrest the Republican nomination from Taft in 1912. Roosevelt had lost confidence in Taft, but he considered La Follette too radical and irresponsible. Finally, in February 1912, Roosevelt announced he would oppose Taft for the Republican presidential nomination.

In the thirteen states with direct primaries, Roosevelt won 278 delegates to the national nominating convention to 48 for Taft and 36 for La Follette. However, Taft had all the advantages of an incumbent president in control of the party machinery. At the Republican convention, many states sent rival delegations, one pledged to Taft and one to Roosevelt. Taft's supporters controlled the **credentials committee** and gave most contested seats to Taft delegates. Roosevelt's supporters stormed out, complaining that Taft was stealing the nomination. The remaining delegates nominated Taft on the first ballot.

Roosevelt refused to accept defeat. "We stand at Armageddon," he thundered, invoking the biblical prophecy of a final battle between good and evil. "And," he continued, "we battle for the Lord." His supporters quickly formed the Progressive Party, nicknamed the **Bull Moose Party** after Roosevelt's boast that he was "as fit as a bull moose." At their convention, they sang "Onward, Christian Soldiers" and issued a platform based on the New Nationalism, including tariff reduction, regulation of corporations, a minimum wage, an end to child labor, woman suffrage, and the initiative, referendum, and recall. Women were prominent at the Progressive convention and helped draft the platform—especially the

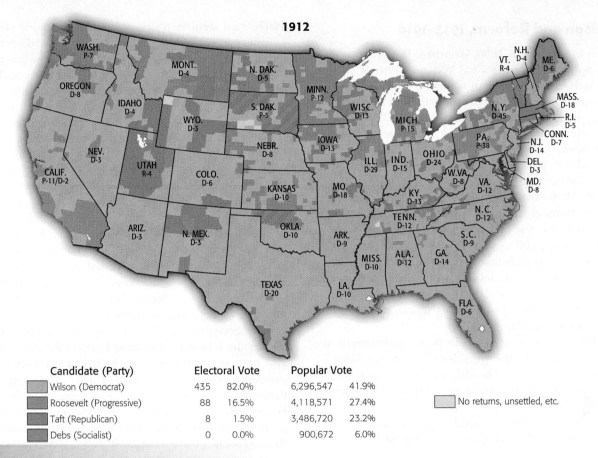

1912

Candidate (Party)	Electoral Vote		Popular Vote	
Wilson (Democrat)	435	82.0%	6,296,547	41.9%
Roosevelt (Progressive)	88	16.5%	4,118,571	27.4%
Taft (Republican)	8	1.5%	3,486,720	23.2%
Debs (Socialist)	0	0.0%	900,672	6.0%

No returns, unsettled, etc.

MAP 19.2 Election of 1912, by Counties
The presidential election of 1912 was complicated by the campaign of former president Theodore Roosevelt, running as a Progressive. Roosevelt's campaign split the usual Republican vote without taking away much of the usual Democratic vote. Copyright © Cengage Learning

sections dealing with labor. Jane Addams addressed the convention to second the nomination of Roosevelt.

Democrats were overjoyed, certain that the Republican split gave them their best chance at the presidency in twenty years. Their nomination was hotly contested, requiring forty-six ballots to nominate Woodrow Wilson. Their platform attacked monopolies, favored limits on campaign contributions by corporations, and called for tariff reductions. Wilson labeled his program the **New Freedom**. Afterward, Wilson met with **Louis Brandeis**, a Boston attorney and leading critic of corporate consolidation, who convinced him to center his campaign on the issue of big business.

Much of the campaign focused on Roosevelt and Wilson. Roosevelt argued that the behavior of corporations was the problem, not their size, and that regulation was the solution. Wilson followed Brandeis's lead and depicted monopoly itself as the problem. Breaking up monopolies and restoring competition, he argued, would benefit consumers because competition would yield better products and lower prices. Wilson also pointed to what he considered the most serious flaw in regulation: as long as monopolies faced regulation, they

would seek to control the regulator—the federal government. Only antitrust actions, Wilson argued, could protect democracy from this threat. Taft was the most conservative of the candidates. Eugene V. Debs, the Socialist candidate, rejected both regulation and antitrust actions and argued for government ownership of monopolies.

The real contest was between Roosevelt and Wilson. In the end, Wilson received nearly all the usual Democratic vote and won with 42 percent of the total. Democrats also won sizable majorities in both houses of Congress. Roosevelt and Taft split the traditional Republican vote, 27 percent for Roosevelt and 23 percent for Taft. Debs, with only 6 percent, placed first in a few counties and city precincts (see Map 19.2).

■ **New Freedom** Reform program that Woodrow Wilson advocated during his 1912 presidential campaign, including reducing tariffs and prosecuting trusts.

■ **Louis Brandeis** Lawyer and reformer who opposed monopolies and defended individual rights; in 1916 he became the first Jewish justice on the Supreme Court.

Wilson and Reform, 1913-1916

Born in Virginia in 1856, Woodrow Wilson grew up in the South during the Civil War and Reconstruction. His father, a Presbyterian minister, impressed on him lessons in morality and responsibility that remained with him his entire life. Wilson earned a Ph.D. in political science from Johns Hopkins University, and his first book, *Congressional Government,* analyzed federal lawmaking. A professor at Princeton University after 1890, he became president of Princeton in 1902.

In 1910, conservatives who controlled the New Jersey Democratic Party picked Wilson to run for governor because of his reputation as a conservative and a good public speaker. He won the election but shocked his party's leaders by embracing reform. As governor, he led the legislature to adopt several progressive measures, and his record won support from many Democratic progressives when he sought the 1912 presidential nomination.

Wilson firmly believed in party government and an active role for the president in policymaking. He wanted to work closely with Democrats in Congress and succeeded to such an extent that, like Roosevelt, he changed the nature of the presidency itself. Confident in his oratorical skills, he became the first president since John Adams to address Congress in person.

Wilson first tackled tariff reform, arguing that high tariff rates helped breed monopolies by reducing competition. Despite opposition from manufacturers, Congress passed the **Underwood Tariff** in October 1913, establishing the most significant reductions since the Civil War. To offset federal revenue losses, the Underwood Act implemented the income tax recently authorized by the Sixteenth Amendment.

Wilson and the Democrats next took up banking. The national banking system dated to 1863, and periodic economic problems—most recently, a panic in 1907—had demonstrated the system's major shortcomings: it had no real center to provide direction and no way to adjust the money supply (the amount of money available in the economy as cash and in bank accounts). A congressional investigation also revealed the concentration of great power in the hands of a few investment bankers. Conservatives, led by Carter Glass of Virginia, joined with bankers in proposing a more centralized system with minimal federal regulation. Progressive Democrats, especially William Jennings Bryan (now Wilson's secretary of state) and Louis Brandeis, favored strong federal regulation.

The debate ended in compromise. In December 1913, Wilson approved the **Federal Reserve Act**, establishing twelve regional Federal Reserve Banks. These were "bankers' banks," institutions where commercial banks kept their reserves. All national banks were required to belong to the Federal Reserve System. The participating banks owned all the stock in their regional Federal Reserve Bank and named two-thirds of its board of directors; the president named the other third. The regional banks were to be regulated and supervised by the Federal Reserve Board, a new federal agency with members chosen by the president. Economists agree that creation of the Federal Reserve system was the most important single measure to come out of the Wilson administration.

In 1913, Congress also fulfilled a Democratic campaign promise by creating a separate cabinet-level Department of Labor, and in 1914 Congress passed the **Clayton Antitrust Act**, which prohibited specified business practices, including **interlocking directorates** among large companies that could be proven to inhibit competition. It exempted farmers' organizations and unions from antitrust prosecution under the Sherman Act. The antitrust sections in the final version of the Clayton Act, however, did little to break up big corporations. Instead of breaking up big business, Wilson now moved closer to Roosevelt's position favoring regulation. Wilson also supported passage of the **Federal Trade Commission Act** (1914), a regulatory measure intended to prevent unfair methods of competition.

During his first year in office, Wilson drew sharp criticism from some northern social reformers when his appointees (especially southern Democrats) initiated racial segregation in several federal agencies. As a southerner himself, Wilson undoubtedly believed in segregation even though he resisted his party's most extreme racists. Wilson was surprised at the swell of protest, not just from African Americans but also from some white progressives in the North and Midwest. He never designated a change in policy, but the process of segregating federal facilities slowed significantly.

Underwood Tariff 1913 law that substantially reduced tariffs and made up for the lost revenue by imposing a graduated income tax.

■ **Federal Reserve Act** 1913 law establishing twelve regional Federal Reserve Banks to hold the cash reserves of commercial banks and a Federal Reserve Board to regulate aspects of banking.

■ **Clayton Antitrust Act** 1914 law banning monopolistic business practices such as price fixing and interlocking directorates; also exempted farmers' organizations and unions from antitrust prosecutions.

interlocking directorates Situation in which the same individuals sit on the boards of directors of various companies in one industry.

■ **Federal Trade Commission Act** 1914 law outlawing unfair methods of competition in interstate commerce and creating a commission appointed by the president to investigate illegal business practices.

The Federal Reserve Act

The Federal Reserve Act stands as the most important domestic act of the Wilson administration, for it still provides the basic framework for the nation's banking and monetary system. Though the original act of 1913 has been amended many times, the Federal Reserve System remains an independent entity within the federal government, having both public purposes and private aspects.

Congress has charged the Federal Reserve to carry out the nation's monetary policy, including regulating the money supply and interest rates to accomplish the goals of maximum employment, stable prices, and moderate long-term interest rates. The Federal Reserve also supervises and regulates banks and financial institutions to ensure their safety and soundness. (Chapter 22's It Matters Today feature, page 626, discusses the Fed's role in recent economic events.)

- Look at a basic macroeconomics textbook for its description of the role of the Federal Reserve. How does that text present its functions? How does "the Fed" seek to control inflation?
- Look at an online newspaper and find the most recent story about the Federal Reserve Board or the chairman of "the Fed." What does the story imply about the significance of the Federal Reserve for American business?

Though many progressives applauded Wilson for tariff reform, the Federal Reserve Act, and the Clayton Act, some progressives criticized his appointees to the Federal Trade Commission and the Federal Reserve Board as being too sympathetic to business and banking. Moreover, Wilson considered federal action to outlaw child labor to be unconstitutional, and he questioned the need to amend the Constitution for woman suffrage. The approach of the 1916 presidential election seems to have spurred Wilson to reconsider. In 1912 he had received less than half of the popular vote and had won the White House only because the Republicans split. As the 1916 election approached, Wilson joined progressives in pushing measures intended to secure his claim as the true voice of progressivism and to capture progressive voters.

In January 1916, Wilson nominated Louis Brandeis for the Supreme Court. Brandeis's reputation as a staunch progressive and critic of business aroused intense opposition from conservatives, but he was confirmed in June 1916. Wilson followed up with support for several reform measures—credit facilities for farmers, workers' compensation for federal employees, and the elimination of child labor. Under threat of a railroad strike, Congress passed and Wilson signed the Adamson Act, securing an eight-hour workday for railroad employees.

The presidential election of 1916 was conducted against the background of war in Europe (covered in the next chapter). Wilson's shift toward social reform helped solidify his support among progressives. His support for organized labor earned him strong backing among unionists, and labor's votes probably ensured his victory in a few states, especially California. In states where women could vote, many of them seem to have preferred Wilson, probably because he backed issues of interest to women, such as outlawing child labor and keeping the nation out of war. In a very close election, Wilson won with 49 percent of the popular vote to 46 percent for Charles Evans Hughes, a progressive Republican.

NEW PATTERNS IN CULTURAL EXPRESSION

★ Did developments in cultural expression draw more from American sources or European sources?

★ How did social and technological changes contribute to new patterns in mass entertainment?

The changes sweeping American society also affected cultural expression. Shortly after 1900, the director of the nation's most prominent art museum, the Metropolitan Museum of New York, observed "a state of unrest" in art, literature, music, painting, and sculpture. Unrest meant change, and Americans at that time witnessed dramatic changes in art, literature, and music—many of them directly influenced by the new urban industrial society, and some of them reflecting the concerns of the Progressive Era.

Realism, Impressionism, and Ragtime

At the turn of the century, American novelists increasingly turned to a realistic—and sometimes critical—portrayal of life. The towering figure of the era remained **Mark Twain** (pen name of Samuel L. Clemens), whose novel *The Adventures of Huckleberry Finn* (1885) may be read at many levels, from a nostalgic account of boyhood to profound social satire. In this masterpiece, Twain reproduced the everyday speech of unschooled whites and blacks, poked fun at social pretensions, scorned the Old South myth, and challenged racially biased attitudes toward African Americans. Twain continued as an important social commentator until his death in 1910. The novels of William Dean Howells and Henry James, in contrast, presented restrained, realistic portrayals of upper-class men and women, and Kate Chopin sounded feminist themes in *The Awakening* (1899), dealing with repression of a woman's desires. Stephen Crane, Theodore Dreiser, and Frank Norris showed the influence of Émile Zola, a prominent French novelist, as they sharpened the critical edge of fiction. In Crane's *Maggie: A Girl of the Streets* (1893), urban squalor, alcohol, and callous men drive a young woman to prostitution. Norris's *The Octopus* (1901) portrayed the abusive power of a railroad over farmers.

As American literature moved toward realism and social criticism during these years, many American painters looked for inspiration to French **impressionism**, which emphasized less an exact reproduction of the world and more the artist's impression of it. Mary Cassatt was the only American—and one of only two women—to rank among the leaders of impressionism, but she lived and painted mostly in France. Among prominent impressionists working in the United States was Childe Hassam, who often depicted urban scenes. Attention to the city was also characteristic of work by Robert Henri, John Sloan, and others labeled the **Ash Can School** because of their preoccupation with everyday urban life and people. Their work has been considered the artistic counterpart to critical realism in literature.

Mary Cassatt created this portrait of a mother and child in 1897. Cassatt was the only American woman to have a major role in French impressionism; some of her paintings were included in the Armory Show of 1913. Unlike other leading impressionists, her work often focused on women and children.

© Réunion des Musées Nationaux/Art Resource, New York.

In 1913 the most widely publicized art exhibit of the era permitted Americans to view works by the most innovative European painters. Known as the Armory Show for its opening in New York's National Guard Armory (it was later displayed in Chicago and Boston), the exhibit presented works by Pablo Picasso, Henri Matisse, Marcel Duchamp, Wassily Kandinsky, and others. Sophisticated critics and popular newspapers alike dismissed them as either insane or anarchists. One reviewer scornfully suggested that Duchamp's cubist painting *Nude Descending a Staircase* be retitled "explosion in a shingle factory." The abstract, modernist style, however, became firmly established by the 1920s.

As with painting, many aspects of American music derived from European models. John Philip Sousa, who produced well over a hundred works between the 1870s and his death in 1932, was the most popular American composer of the day, best known for his stirring patriotic marches. Perhaps more significant in the long run was the African American composer Scott Joplin. Born in Texas, Joplin had formal instruction in the piano, then traveled through black com-

This photo shows a small part of the crowd at the New York Polo Grounds, watching the final game for the 1908 National League pennant, between the Chicago Cubs and the New York Giants. The Cubs won, and went on to beat the Detroit Tigers in the World Series. How is this crowd different from the crowd at a baseball game today?

munities from New Orleans to Chicago where he encountered **ragtime** music. He soon began to write his own. In 1899 he published "Maple Leaf Rag" and quickly soared to fame as the leading ragtime composer in the country. Though condemned by some as vulgar, ragtime contributed significantly to the later development of jazz (discussed in Chapter 21).

Mass Entertainment in the Early Twentieth Century

By 1900, changes in transportation (the railroads) and communication (telegraph and telephone) combined with increased leisure time among the middle class and some skilled workers to foster new forms of entertainment.

Traveling dramatic and musical troupes had long entertained some Americans, but now booking agencies could schedule such groups into nearly every corner of the country. Traveling actors, singers, and other performers offered everything from Shakespeare to **slapstick**, from opera to **melodrama**.

Other traveling spectacles also took advantage of improved transportation and communication to establish regular circuits, including circuses and Wild West shows. A less sensational traveling show but one of the most popular was the **Chautauqua**, a blend of inspirational oratory, educational lectures, and entertainment.

During the late nineteenth century, a quite different form of mass entertainment appeared— professional baseball. Teams traveled by train from city to city, and urban rivalries built loyalty among fans. In 1876 team owners formed the National League as

ragtime Style of popular music characterized by a syncopated rhythm and a regularly accented beat; considered the immediate precursor of jazz.

slapstick A rowdy form of comedy marked by crude practical jokes and physical humor, such as falls.

melodrama A sensational or romantic stage play with exaggerated conflicts and stereotyped characters.

Chautauqua A traveling show offering educational, religious, and recreational activities, part of a nationwide movement of adult education that began in the town of Chautauqua, New York.

At the center of the Columbian Exposition of 1893 was a great water-filled basin, with an elaborate sculpture representing Columbus at one end and this dramatic, 65-foot-tall depiction of the republic at the opposite end. The sculptor, Daniel Chester French, represented the American republic with one hand on a pole with a liberty cap at its end and with the other hand holding a globe surmounted by an American eagle. Though this view shows the entire statue as golden, in fact the head and arms were an ivory color and the rest of the statue was gilded. The statue may still be seen in Chicago's Jackson Park.

a cartel to dominate the industry by excluding rival clubs from their territories and controlling the movement of players from team to team. Because African Americans were barred from the National League, separate black clubs and Negro leagues emerged. In the 1880s and 1890s, the National League warded off challenges from rival leagues and defeated a players' union. Not until 1901 did another league—the American League—successfully organize. In 1903 the two leagues merged into a new, stronger cartel and staged the first World Series—in which the Boston Red Sox beat the Pittsburgh Pirates. As other professional spectator sports developed, they often imitated the organization, labor relations, and racial discrimination first established in baseball.

Celebrating the New Age

In 1893, when the World's Columbian Exposition opened in Chicago, Hamlin Garland, a writer living there, wrote to his parents in South Dakota, "Sell the cook stove if necessary and come. . . . You must see

this fair." Between 1876 and World War I, Americans repeatedly held great expositions, beginning with one in Philadelphia in 1876 that commemorated the centennial of independence and concluding with one in San Francisco in 1915 that celebrated the opening of the Panama Canal. Others took place in Atlanta, Buffalo, Omaha, Portland (Oregon), San Diego, and St. Louis. The most impressive and influential was the Columbian Exposition in Chicago, marking the four hundredth anniversary of Columbus's voyage to the New World.

These expositions typically featured vast exhibition halls where companies demonstrated their latest technological marvels, artists displayed their creations, and farmers presented their most impressive produce. In other halls, states and foreign nations showcased their accomplishments. The exhibits nearly always expressed the conviction that technology and industry would inevitably improve the lives of all. After 1898, most also included demeaning exhibits of "savage" or "barbarian" people from the nation's new overseas possessions.

Behind the gleaming machines in the imitation marble palaces, however, lurked troubling questions that never appeared in the exhibits glorifying "Progress." What should be the working conditions of those whose labor created such technological marvels? Were democratic institutions compatible with the concentration of power and control in industry and finance or with the acquisition of colonies?

PROGRESSIVISM IN PERSPECTIVE

★ *Was progressivism successful? How do you define success?*

★ *How did progressivism affect modern American politics?*

The Progressive Era began with efforts at municipal reform in the 1890s and sputtered to a close during World War I. Some politicians who called themselves progressives remained in prominent positions afterward, and progressive concepts of efficiency and expertise continued to guide government decision making. But American entry into the war in 1917 diverted attention from reform, and by the end of the war political concerns had changed. By the mid-1920s, many of the major leaders of progressivism had passed from the political stage.

The changes of the Progressive Era transformed American politics and government. Before the Hepburn Act and the Federal Reserve Act, the federal government's role in the economy consisted largely of distributing land grants and setting protective tariffs. After the Progressive Era, the federal government became a significant and permanent player in the economy, regulating a wide range of economic activity and enforcing laws to protect consumers and some workers. The income tax quickly became the most significant source of federal funds. Without the income tax, it is impossible to imagine the many activities that the federal government has assumed since then—from vast military expenditures to social welfare to support for the arts. Since the 1930s, the income tax has sometimes been an instrument of social policy,

by which the federal government has redistributed income.

During the Progressive Era, political parties declined in significance, and political campaigns focused increasingly on personality and advertising. These patterns accelerated in the second half of the twentieth century under the influence of television and public opinion polling. Organized pressure groups have proliferated and become ever more important. Women's participation in politics has continued to increase, especially in the last third of the twentieth century and the first decade of the twenty-first.

The assertion of presidential authority by Theodore Roosevelt and Woodrow Wilson reappeared in the presidency of Franklin D. Roosevelt (1933–1945). The two Roosevelts and Wilson transformed Americans' expectations regarding the office of the presidency itself. Throughout the nineteenth century, Congress had dominated the making of domestic policy. During the twentieth century, Americans came to expect domestic policy to flow from forceful executive leadership in the White House.

Finley Peter Dunne, the political humorist, realized that change is an integral part of American politics. He quoted this conversation between a woman who ran a boarding house and one of her lodgers:

> "I don't know what to do," says she. "I'm worn out, and it seems impossible to keep this house clean. What is the trouble with it?"
>
> "Madam," says my friend Gallagher, . . . "the trouble with this house is that it is occupied entirely by human beings. If it was a vacant house, it could easily be kept clean."

Thus, Dunne concluded about progressive reform, "The noise you hear is not the first gun of a revolution. It's only the people of the United States beating a carpet." In fact, however, the most important changes of the Progressive Era were more than just housekeeping—they may not have been revolutionary, but they laid the basis for many aspects of our modern politics and government.

Individual Voices

Theodore Roosevelt Asserts Presidential Powers

Theodore Roosevelt was one of the nation's most informed presidents. He read widely, especially in history and natural history, and he wrote extensively on those topics. In Roosevelt's *Autobiography* (1913), he discussed some of his ideas about the nature of the presidency. Such writings—autobiographies, memoirs, letters, and the like—are valuable sources for historians seeking to understand the motivation of people in past times.

❶ Which of Roosevelt's actions were "things not previously done by a President"?

❷ What can you find about the presidencies of Jackson, Lincoln, and Buchanan that would support Roosevelt's views?

❸ Can you find examples of such behavior in U.S. foreign affairs? In domestic policy? Can you find contrary examples? How successful was Roosevelt in meeting his own standard?

❹ Who might have felt threatened by these views? What dangers might result from Roosevelt's views of sweeping presidential powers?

The most important factor in getting the right spirit in my Administration, next to the insistence upon courage, honesty, and a genuine democracy of desire to serve the *plain* people, was my insistence upon the theory that the executive power was limited only by specific restrictions and prohibitions appearing in the Constitution or imposed by the Congress under its Constitutional powers. . . . I declined to adopt the view that what was imperatively necessary for the Nation could not be done by the President unless he could find some specific authorization to do it. . . . I did and caused to be done many things not previously done by the President and the heads of the departments. **❶** I did not usurp power, but I did greatly broaden the use of executive power. . . . I did not care a rap for the mere form and show of power; I cared immensely for the use that could be made of the substance. . . .

There have long been two schools of political thought. . . . The course I followed, of regarding the executive as subject only to the people, and, under the Constitution, bound to serve the people affirmatively in cases where the Constitution does not explicitly forbid him to render the service, was substantially the course followed by both Andrew Jackson and Abraham Lincoln. Other honorable and well-meaning Presidents, such as James Buchanan, took the opposite and, as it seems to me, narrowly legal view that the President is the servant of Congress rather than of the people, and can do nothing, no matter how necessary it be to act, unless the Constitution explicitly commands the action. **❷** Most able lawyers who are past middle age take this view. . . .

In foreign affairs the principle from which we never deviated was to have the Nation behave toward other nations precisely as a strong, honorable, and upright man behaves in dealing with his fellow-men. . . . **❸**

In internal affairs I cannot say that I entered the Presidency with any deliberately planned and far-reaching scheme of social betterment. I had, however, certain strong convictions. . . . I was bent upon making the Government the most efficient possible instrument in helping the people of the United States to better themselves in every way, politically, socially, and industrially. I believed with all my heart in real and thoroughgoing democracy, and I wished to make this democracy industrial as well as political. . . . I believed that the Constitution should be treated as the greatest document ever devised by the wit of man to aid a people in exercising every power for its own betterment, and not as a straitjacket cunningly fashioned to strangle growth. . . . **❹**

Study Tools

SUMMARY

Progressivism, a phenomenon of the late nineteenth and early twentieth centuries, refers to new concepts of government, to changes in government based on those concepts, and to the political process by which change occurred. Those years marked a time of political transformation brought about by many groups and individuals who approached politics with often contradictory objectives. Organized interest groups became an important part of this process. Women broke through long-standing constraints to take a more prominent role in politics. The Anti-Saloon League was the most successful of several organizations that appealed to government to enforce morality. Some African Americans fought segregation and disfranchisement, notably W. E. B. Du Bois and the NAACP. Socialists and the Industrial Workers of the World saw capitalism as the source of many problems, but few Americans embraced their radical solutions.

Political reform took place at every level, from cities to states to the federal government. Muckraking journalists exposed wrongdoing and suffering. Municipal reformers introduced modern methods of city government in a quest for efficiency and effectiveness. Some tried to use government to remedy social problems by employing the expertise of new professions such as public health and social work. Reformers attacked the power of party bosses and machines by reducing the role of political parties.

At the federal level, Theodore Roosevelt set the pace for progressive reform. Relishing his reputation as a trustbuster, he challenged judicial constraints on federal authority over big business and promoted other forms of economic regulation, thereby increasing government's role in the economy. He also regulated the use of natural resources. His successor, William Howard Taft, failed to maintain Republican Party unity and eventually sided with conservatives against progressives.

Roosevelt played an important role in defining America's status as a world power, as he secured rights to build a U.S.-controlled canal through Panama and established Panama as an American protectorate. The Roosevelt Corollary declared that the United States was the dominant power in the Caribbean and Central America. In eastern Asia, Roosevelt tried to bolster the Open Door policy by maintaining a balance of power. Roosevelt and others sought arbitration treaties with leading nations but failed because of Senate opposition. Faced with the rise of German military and naval power, Great Britain improved relations with the United States.

In 1912 Roosevelt led a new political party, the Progressives, making that year's presidential election a three-way contest. Roosevelt called for regulation of big business, but Wilson, the Democrat, favored breaking up monopolies through antitrust action. Wilson won the election but soon preferred regulation over antitrust actions. He helped to create the Federal Reserve System to regulate banking nationwide. As the 1916 election approached, Wilson also pushed for social reforms in an effort to unify all progressives behind his leadership.

The new urban, industrial, multiethnic society contributed to critical realism in literature, new patterns in painting, and ragtime music, although many creative artists continued to look to Europe for inspiration. Urbanization and changes in transportation and communication also fostered the emergence of a mass entertainment industry.

Progressive reforms made a profound impression on later American politics. In many ways, progressivism marked the origin of modern American politics and government.

Study Tools

CHRONOLOGY
The Progressive Era

1885	Mark Twain's *The Adventures of Huckleberry Finn*
1890	National American Woman Suffrage Association formed
1893	World's Columbian Exposition, Chicago
1895	Anti-Saloon League formed
	United States v. E. C. Knight
1898	War with Spain
1899	Permanent Court of Arbitration (the Hague Court) created
	Scott Joplin's "Maple Leaf Rag"
1900	Robert M. La Follette elected governor of Wisconsin
	President William McKinley reelected
1901	Socialist Party of America formed
	McKinley assassinated; Theodore Roosevelt becomes president
1902	Muckraking journalism begins
	Antitrust action against Northern Securities Company
	Roosevelt intervenes in coal strike
	Reclamation Act
1903	W. E. B. Du Bois's *Souls of Black Folk*
	Panama becomes a protectorate
	Hay–Bunau-Varilla Treaty; work begins on Panama Canal
1904	Roosevelt Corollary
	Roosevelt elected president
1905	Industrial Workers of the World organized
	Roosevelt mediates Russo-Japanese War
	Dominican Republic becomes third U.S. protectorate
1906	Upton Sinclair's *The Jungle*
	Hepburn Act
	Meat Inspection Act
	Pure Food and Drug Act

1908	*Muller v. Oregon*
	Race riot in Springfield, Illinois
	William Howard Taft elected president
1910	National Association for the Advancement of Colored People formed
	Hiram W. Johnson elected governor of California
1911	Fire at Triangle Shirtwaist factory
1912	Progressive ("Bull Moose") Party formed
	Wilson elected president
	Nicaragua becomes a protectorate
1913	Sixteenth Amendment (federal income tax) ratified
	Seventeenth Amendment (direct election of U.S. senators) ratified
	Federal Reserve Act
	Armory Show
1914	Clayton Antitrust Act
	Federal Trade Commission Act
	Panama Canal completed
1915	National Birth Control League formed
1916	Louis Brandeis appointed to the Supreme Court
	Jeannette Rankin of Montana becomes first woman elected to U.S. House of Representatives
	Wilson reelected
1917	United States enters World War I

FOCUS QUESTIONS

If you have mastered this chapter, you should be able to answer these questions and to identify the terms that follow the questions.

1. ☆ *What important changes transformed American politics in the early twentieth century?*

2. ☆ *What did women and African Americans seek to accomplish by creating new organizations devoted to political change?*

3. ☆ *What did the muckrakers contribute to reform?*

4. ☆ *What characterized reforms of city and state government and what role did organized interest groups play?*

5. ☆ *What did Theodore Roosevelt mean by a "Square Deal"? Do his accomplishments fit this description?*

Study Tools

6. ★ *How did Roosevelt's presidency change the federal role in the economy and alter the presidency itself?*

7. ★ *What were Roosevelt's objectives for the United States in world affairs?*

8. ★ *How did Roosevelt reshape American foreign policy?*

9. ★ *What choices confronted American voters in the presidential election of 1912?*

10. ★ *How did Wilson's views on reform evolve from 1912 through 1916 and how did his administration change the federal government's role in the economy?*

11. ★ *Did developments in cultural expression draw more from American sources or European sources?*

12. ★ *How did social and technological changes contribute to new patterns in mass entertainment?*

13. ★ *Was progressivism successful? How do you define success?*

14. ★ *How did progressivism affect modern American politics?*

KEY TERMS

interest group *(p. 526)*

Progressive Party *(p. 527)*

Hull House *(p. 527)*

Social Gospel *(p. 528)*

Margaret Sanger *(p. 528)*

Muller v. Oregon *(p. 528)*

Jeannette Rankin *(p. 529)*

National American Woman Suffrage Association *(p. 529)*

Anti-Saloon League *(p. 530)*

W. E. B. Du Bois *(p. 531)*

National Association for the Advancement of Colored People *(p. 531)*

Ida B. Wells *(p. 531)*

Socialist Party of America *(p. 532)*

muckrakers *(p. 533)*

Upton Sinclair *(p. 533)*

Pure Food and Drug Act *(p. 533)*

Meat Inspection Act *(p. 533)*

municipal reform *(p. 534)*

Robert M. La Follette *(p. 535)*

Wisconsin Idea *(p. 536)*

Hiram Johnson *(p. 536)*

direct democracy *(p. 537)*

Square Deal *(p. 539)*

Hepburn Act *(p. 539)*

Gifford Pinchot *(p. 539)*

Sixteenth Amendment *(p. 540)*

Seventeenth Amendment *(p. 540)*

Philippe Bunau-Varilla *(p. 542)*

Hay–Bunau-Varilla Treaty *(p. 543)*

Roosevelt Corollary *(p. 543)*

dollar diplomacy *(p. 543)*

Treaty of Portsmouth *(p. 544)*

Permanent Court of Arbitration *(p. 545)*

New Nationalism *(p. 546)*

Bull Moose Party *(p. 546)*

New Freedom *(p. 547)*

Louis Brandeis *(p. 547)*

Federal Reserve Act *(p. 548)*

Clayton Antitrust Act *(p. 548)*

Federal Trade Commission Act *(p. 548)*

Mark Twain *(p. 550)*

Ash Can School *(p. 550)*

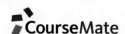 **CourseMate**

Go to the History CourseMate website for primary source links, study tools, and review materials for this chapter. www.cengagebrain.com

20 The United States in a World at War, 1913–1920

Behind the Stories

Some historians have looked at World War I—which, before World War II, was usually called the Great War—as the beginning of a struggle over the center of Europe, a struggle that began in 1914 with World War I, resumed in 1939 with World War II (Chapter 23), and then transitioned into the Cold War that lasted until the Berlin Wall came down in 1989 (Chapters 24–28). In these struggles, the military power of the United States proved decisive in blocking first Germany and then the Soviet Union from taking over western Europe.

Journalists and others have also declared the twentieth century "the American Century," a time in which American dominance was established culturally and militarily.

In both of these perspectives, World War I forms the crucial turning point. Until then, the United States had usually, often unthinkingly, followed George Washington's advice to avoid "permanent alliances with any portion of the foreign world." After World War I, the United States found it impossible to stay out of the affairs of Europe, even when it tried. And after World War II, the United States formed a series of permanent alliances, stretching around much of the world.

World War I did not just change the role of the United States in the world. It changed much of the world. In this chapter, you'll read about world events that pulled the United States into war in Europe, and about the destruction of old empires and the rise of new states as a consequence of that war. This chapter builds on the accounts of America in world affairs in the previous two chapters. You may want to review the final sections of Chapter 18, dealing with the war with Spain and America's acquisition of a colonial empire, and the part of Chapter 19 dealing with foreign affairs under Presidents Roosevelt and Taft.

—R.W.C.

Individual Choices
Charles Young

In 1917, Lieutenant Colonel Charles Young was the highest-ranking African American in the U.S. Army. Like other aspects of American life, the army was segregated. When the United States went to war against Germany, many African Americans expected Young to command a division, made up of the four black regular army regiments, and to take a prominent role in the war in Europe. Young also wanted to do this. He was a patriotic army officer, eager to carry out the duties for which he had prepared. But he also wanted to show that a black commanding officer and black soldiers were fully as capable as white troops of confronting an enemy under fire.

Growing up in Ohio, the son of former slaves, Young considered his father's Union Army service as a "heritage of honor" and secured an appointment to West Point through his academic accomplishments. After graduating, he was assigned to the 10th Cavalry, one of the army's two black cavalry units. He later taught military science at Wilberforce University in Xenia, Ohio, a leading black university.

During the war with Spain, Young commanded a battalion of black volunteers, but his unit was not sent into action. He was then assigned to the 9th Cavalry and sent to the Philippines to help suppress the resistance to American rule (see pages 518–519). Afterward, he received diplomatic assignments in Haiti and Liberia. In 1913, he was back with the 10th Cavalry and participated in Pershing's expedition into Mexico (discussed in this chapter). As a major, Young was superior to several white officers, some of whom complained about taking orders from an African American.

Charles Young

When the war with Germany came, Young, now a lieutenant colonel, hoped to command. However, all four black units in the regular army were assigned to duties far from Europe, and Young was given a medical retirement. Unwilling to accept that status, Young rode his horse nearly 500 miles to prove his physical fitness. He was returned to active duty and promoted to colonel, but too late to take part in the war. In 1919, he was again assigned to diplomatic duty, again in Liberia. He died there of a kidney infection in 1923.

Charles Young's experience was part of larger patterns of discrimination against African Americans. Though a capable and experienced officer, he was often given teaching or diplomatic duties rather than command of troops, most likely to prevent him from giving orders to white officers. It must have seemed deeply ironic for Young and other African Americans to read that President Wilson defined the war as a struggle for "the principle of justice to all peoples and nationalities, and their right to live on equal terms of liberty and safety with one another" (see the Individual Voices feature at the end of this chapter). In 1919, when asked about plans for a monument to African Americans who had died in the military, Young may have been reflecting on Wilson's statement when he suggested that the most fitting commemoration would not be a monument but instead "liberty, justice, equal opportunities and educational facilities, the suppression of lynching by making it a federal crime and the abolition of [segregated railroad] cars."

On June 28, 1914, a Serbian terrorist killed Archduke Franz Ferdinand, heir to the throne of Austria-Hungary, and his wife, Sophie. The royal couple was visiting Sarajevo, in Bosnia-Herzegovina, which Austria had recently annexed against the wishes of the neighboring kingdom of Serbia. In response to the assassinations, Austria first consulted with its ally Germany and then made stringent demands on Serbia. Serbia sought help from Russia, which was allied with France. Tense diplomats invoked elaborate, interlocking alliances. Huge armies began to move. By August 4, most of Europe was at war.

Before those events, many Americans had concluded that war among what Theodore Roosevelt called the world's "civilized" nations had become unthinkable. Given the widely held expectation that war had become obsolete, many Americans were shocked, saddened, and repelled when the leading "civilized" nations of the world—all of which had been busily accumulating arsenals—lurched into war.

When the nations of Europe went to war, the United States was no minor player on the international scene. Between 1898 and 1908, America acquired the Philippines and the Panama Canal, came to dominate the Caribbean and Central America, and actively participated in the balance of power in eastern Asia. The three presidents of the Progressive Era—Roosevelt, William Howard Taft, and Woodrow Wilson—agreed wholeheartedly that the United States should exercise a major role in world affairs.

INHERITED COMMITMENTS AND NEW DIRECTIONS

★ In what new directions did Wilson steer U.S. foreign policy before the coming of war in Europe?

When Woodrow Wilson entered the White House in 1913, he expected to spend most of his time dealing with domestic issues. Although well read on international affairs, he had neither significant international experience nor set foreign policies. For secretary of state he chose William Jennings Bryan, who also had devoted his political career to domestic matters and had little experience in foreign relations. Both men were devout Presbyterians, sharing a confidence that God had a plan for humankind and specifically for the United States. Both hoped—perhaps naively—that they might make the United States a model among nations for peaceful settlement of international disputes. Initially, Wilson fixed his attention on the three regions of greatest American involvement: Latin America, the Pacific, and eastern Asia. There, he tried to balance the anti-imperialist principles of his Democratic Party against the expansionist practices of his Republican predecessors. He marked out some new directions but in the end extended many previous commitments.

Anti-Imperialism, Intervention, and Arbitration

Wilson's Democratic Party had opposed many of the foreign policies of McKinley, Roosevelt, and Taft, especially imperialism. Secretary of State Bryan was a leading anti-imperialist who had criticized Roosevelt's "Big Stick" in foreign affairs. During the Wilson administration, the Democrats wrote into law a limited version of their opposition to imperialism. In 1916 Congress established a bill of rights for residents of the Philippines, provided more autonomy, and promised eventual independence. The next year, Congress made Puerto Rico an American territory and extended American citizenship to its residents.

Democrats had criticized Roosevelt's actions in the Caribbean, but Wilson eventually intervened more in Central America and the Caribbean than any previous administration. In Nicaragua, where Taft had used marines to prop up the rule of President Adolfo Diaz, Wilson sought more authority for the United States. Senate Democrats rejected his efforts, reminding him of their party's opposition to further protectorates. Even so, Bryan negotiated a treaty in 1914 that gave the United States significant concessions, including the right to build a canal through Nicaragua.

Haiti owed a staggering debt to foreign bankers, and its government was extremely unstable. When a mob killed the president in 1915, Wilson sent in the marines. A treaty followed, making Haiti a protectorate in which American forces controlled most aspects of government until 1933. Wilson sent marines into the Dominican Republic in 1916, and U.S. naval officers exercised control there until 1924. In 1917, the United States bought the Virgin Islands from Denmark for $25 million. Thus, Wilson made few changes in previous policies regarding American dominance of the Caribbean.

Wilson and Bryan did, however, bring a new approach to the arbitration of international disputes. Roosevelt's and Taft's secretaries of state had sought arbitration treaties, but the Senate had refused to accept them. Bryan drafted a model treaty and first obtained approval from the Senate Foreign Relations Committee. The Senate ultimately ratified treaties with twenty-two nations. All featured a "cooling-off" period for disputes, typically a year, during which the nations agreed to seek arbitration instead of going to war. These treaties marked the beginning of efforts by Wilson to redefine international relations, substituting rational negotiations for raw power.

Wilson and the Mexican Revolution

In Mexico, Wilson attempted to influence internal politics but eventually found himself on the verge of war. **Porfirio Díaz** had ruled Mexico for a third of a century, supported by great landholders, the church, and the military. During his rule, many American companies invested in Mexico. However, discontent was growing among peasants, workers, and intellectuals. Rebellion broke out, and Díaz resigned in 1911. Francisco Madero, a leading advocate of reform, assumed the presidency but failed to unite the country. Conservatives feared Madero as a reformer, but radicals dismissed him as too timid. In some places, peasant armies demanding *tierra y libertad* ("land and liberty") attacked the mansions of great landowners. In February 1913, conservatives joined with the commander of the army, General **Victoriano Huerta**, to overthrow Madero. Huerta took control of the government and had Madero executed.

Most European governments extended diplomatic recognition to Huerta because his government clearly held power in Mexico City. Wilson faced that decision soon after his inauguration. American companies with investments in Mexico urged recognition because they considered Huerta likely to protect their holdings. Wilson, however, considered Huerta a murderer and privately vowed "not to recognize a government of butchers." In public, Wilson announced he withheld recognition because Huerta's regime did not rest on the consent of the governed.

Wilson's addition of an ethical dimension to diplomatic recognition constituted something new in

MAP 20.1 The United States and the Mexican Revolution
This map shows the locations of key events during the U.S. troubles with Mexico from 1913 to 1917.
Copyright © Cengage Learning

foreign policy. Previous American presidents had automatically extended diplomatic recognition to governments in power. Wilson's approach, sometimes labeled "missionary diplomacy," implied that the United States would discriminate between virtuous and corrupt governments. Telling one visitor, "I am going to teach the South American republics to elect good men," Wilson waited for an opportunity to act against Huerta. In the meantime, anti-Huerta forces led by **Venustiano Carranza** made significant gains.

In April 1914, Mexican officials in Tampico arrested some American sailors. The city's army commander immediately released them and apologized, but Wilson used the incident to justify ordering the U.S. Navy to occupy **Veracruz**, the leading Mexican port (see Map 20.1). Veracruz was the major

Porfirio Díaz Mexican soldier and politician who became president after a coup in 1876 and ruled Mexico until overthrown in 1911.

■ **Victoriano Huerta** Mexican general who overthrew President Francisco Madero in 1913 and established a military dictatorship until 1914.

■ **Venustiano Carranza** Mexican revolutionary leader who helped to lead armed opposition to Victoriano Huerta, became president in 1914, and was overthrown in 1920.

Veracruz Major port city, located in east-central Mexico on the Gulf of Mexico; in 1914, the U.S. Navy occupied the port.

Francisco "Pancho" Villa and his troops in 1914; Villa and his army helped overthrow the regimes of Porfirio Díaz and Victoriano Huerta. In an effort to topple the administration of Venustiano Carranza, Villa tried to incite a war between the United States and Mexico.

faced armed opposition, however, from **Francisco "Pancho" Villa** in northern Mexico and Emiliano Zapata in the south. When Villa suffered setbacks, he apparently set out to involve Carranza in a war with the United States. Villa's men murdered several Americans in Mexico and then, in March 1916, raided across the border and killed several Americans in New Mexico. With Carranza's reluctant approval, Wilson sent an expedition of nearly seven thousand men, commanded by General John J. Pershing, into Mexico to punish Villa. Villa evaded the American troops, but drew them ever deeper into Mexico, alarming Carranza.

When a clash between Mexican government forces and American soldiers produced deaths on both sides, Carranza asked Wilson to withdraw the American troops. Wilson refused. Only in early 1917, when Wilson recognized that America might soon go to war with Germany, did he pull back the troops, leaving behind deep resentment and suspicion toward the United States.

THE UNITED STATES AND THE GREAT WAR, 1914–1917

★ Why did Wilson proclaim American neutrality? How did Americans respond?

★ What made neutrality difficult?

★ How did Wilson justify going to war?

At first, Americans paid little attention to the assassinations at Sarajevo. When Europe plunged into war, however, Wilson and all Americans faced difficult choices.

The Great War in Europe

Throughout much of the nineteenth and early twentieth centuries, most European governments had encouraged their citizens to identify strongly with their nation, thereby cultivating the intense patriotism known as nationalism. Within the ethnically diverse empires of Austria-Hungary, Russia, and Turkey, a different sort of nationalism fueled hopes for independence based on language and culture. Ethnic antagonisms and aspirations were especially powerful in the **Balkan Peninsula**, where the Ottoman (Turkish) Empire had lost territory as several groups had established their independence. Some of the new Balkan states were weak, however, attracting the neighboring Austrian and Russian empires. As Austria-Hungary sought to annex new territories, Russia claimed the role of protector of other **Slavic** peoples.

source of the Huerta government's revenue (from customs) and the landing point for most government military supplies. The occupation cut these off. However, it cost more than a hundred Mexican lives and turned many Mexicans against Wilson for violating their sovereignty. Without munitions and revenue, Huerta fled the country in mid-July. Wilson withdrew the last American forces from Veracruz in November.

Carranza succeeded Huerta as president, and Wilson officially recognized his government. Carranza

■ **Francisco "Pancho" Villa** Mexican bandit and revolutionary who raided into New Mexico in 1916, prompting the U.S. government to send troops into Mexico.

Balkan Peninsula Region of southeastern Europe; included several relatively new and sometimes unstable states in the early twentieth century.

Slavic Ethnic and linguistic groups, mainly in eastern and central Europe; includes Bulgarians, Croats, Czechs, Poles, Russians, Serbs, Slovaks, Ukrainians, and others.

During the same years, competition for world markets and territory spawned an unprecedented arms buildup. By the 1870s, Germany had the most powerful army in Europe and had set out to make its navy as powerful as Britain's. By 1900, most European powers had a professional officer corps and **universal military service**. Technology produced new and powerful weapons, including the machine gun, and designers quickly adapted automobiles and airplanes for combat. The major powers of Europe had avoided war with one another since 1871, when Germany had humiliated France. But they continued to prepare for war. Eventually European diplomats constructed two major alliance systems: the Triple Entente (Britain, France, and Russia) and the Triple Alliance (Germany, Austria-Hungary, and Italy). Britain was also allied with Japan.

Called the "powder keg of Europe," the Balkans lived up to their explosive nickname in 1914. The assassinations at Sarajevo grew out of a territorial conflict between Austria-Hungary and Serbia. Russia, alarmed over Austrian expansion into the Balkans, presented itself as the protector of Serbia. Austria first assured itself of Germany's backing, then declared war on Serbia. Russia confirmed France's support, then **mobilized** its army in support of Serbia. Germany declared war on Russia on August 1 and on France soon after. German strategists planned to bypass French defenses along their border by invading **neutral** Belgium (see Map 20.2). Britain entered the war in defense of Belgium. By August 4, much of Europe was at war. Eventually Germany and Austria-Hungary combined with Bulgaria and the Ottoman Empire to form the **Central Powers**. Italy abandoned its Triple Alliance partners and joined Britain, France, Russia, Romania, and Japan as the **Allies**.

At first, Secretary of State Bryan tried to take a hopeful view of events in Europe. "It may be," he suggested, "that the world needed one more awful object lesson to prove conclusively the fallacy of the doctrine that preparedness for war can give assurance for peace." Sir Edward Grey, Britain's foreign minister, was less optimistic as he mourned to a friend, "The lamps are going out all over Europe. We shall not see them lit again in our lifetime." Grey proved a more accurate prophet than Bryan.

The Germans expected to roll through Belgium, small and militarily weak, and quickly defeat France. The Belgians resisted long enough for French and British troops to block the Germans. The opposing armies then settled into defensive lines across 475 miles of Belgian and French countryside, extending from the English Channel to the Alps (see Map 20.2). By the end of 1914, the **western front** consisted of elaborate networks of trenches on both sides, separated by a desolate no man's land filled with coils of barbed wire, where any movement brought a burst of machine-gun fire. As the war progressed, terrible new weapons—poison gas, aerial bombings, tanks—took thousands of lives but failed to break the deadlock.

American Neutrality

Wilson's initial reaction to the European conflagration revealed his own deep religious beliefs—he wrote privately of his confidence that "Providence has deeper plans than we could possibly have laid for ourselves." On August 4, he announced that the United States was neutral. Later, on August 19, he urged Americans to be "neutral in fact as well as in name . . . impartial in thought as well as in action."

Wilson hoped not only that America would remain neutral but also that he might serve as peacemaker. Such hopes proved unrealistic. The warring nations wanted to gain territory, and only a decisive victory could accomplish that. The longer they fought, the more territory they wanted. So long as they saw a chance of winning, they had no interest in the appeals of any would-be peacemakers.

Wilson's hope that Americans could remain impartial was also unrealistic. Though few Americans wanted to go to war, most probably sided with the Allies. England had cultivated American friendship for decades, and trade and finance united many of their business leaders. French assistance during the American Revolution helped to fuel support for France. And the martyrdom of Belgium aroused American sympathy. Allied **propagandists** worked hard to generate anti-German sentiment in America, publicizing—and exaggerating—German atrocities and portraying the war as a conflict between civilized peoples and barbarian **Huns**.

universal military service Governmental policy requiring all adult males (or, rarely, all adults) to serve in the military for some period of time.

mobilize To make ready for combat or other forms of action.

neutral A nation not aligned with either side in a war; traditionally, neutral nations could engage in certain types of trade with nations at war.

■ **Central Powers** In World War I, Germany, Austria-Hungary, Bulgaria, and the Ottoman Empire.

■ **Allies** In World War I, Britain and its Commonwealth, France, Russia, Italy, Romania, Japan, Serbia, and Belgium.

■ **western front** In World War I, the zone of fighting in France and Belgium.

propagandist One who provides information in support of a cause, especially one-sided or exaggerated information.

Hun Disparaging term applied to Germans during World War I, derived from warlike people who invaded Europe in the fourth and fifth centuries.

MAP 20.2 The War in Europe, 1914–1918
This map identifies the two great military coalitions, the Central Powers and the Allies, and charts the development of the war. Note Russia's losses by the Treaty of Brest-Litovsk as compared with the armistice line (the line between the two armies when Russia sought peace). Copyright © Cengage Learning

Triple Entente and its Allies
Central Powers
Neutral nations
Greatest extent of territory gained by Germany-Austria
Battle line

Germany, 1914
German offensive, 1915
Greatest extent of territory gained by Germany, Sept. 1914
Front at beginning of 1915

German offensive, Summer 1918
Armistice line, November 1918
Major battle

Treaty of Brest-Litovsk, March 1918

Armistice line, December 1917

Farthest Russian advance, 1914

British blockade line

Western front

Italian front

Balkan front

Not all Americans sympathized with the Allies. Nearly 8 million of the 97 million people in the United States had one or both parents from Germany or Austria. Not surprisingly, many of them objected to depictions of their cousins as bloodthirsty barbarians. Many of the 5 million Irish Americans disliked England for ruling their ancestral homeland.

Neutral Rights and German U-Boats

Wilson and Bryan agreed that the United States should remain neutral but took different approaches to that goal. Bryan proved willing to sacrifice traditional neutral rights if insistence on those rights seemed likely to pull the United States into the conflict. Wilson, in contrast, stood firm on maintaining traditional neutral rights, a posture that actually favored the Allies.

Bryan initially opposed loans to **belligerent** nations as incompatible with neutrality. Wilson agreed at first, then realized that the ban hurt the Allies more. He then agreed to permit buying goods on credit. Eventually, he dropped the ban on loans, partly because neutrals had always been permitted to lend to belligerents and partly, perhaps, because the freeze endangered the stability of the American economy.

Traditional neutral rights included freedom of the seas: neutrals could trade with all belligerents. When both sides turned to naval warfare to break the deadlock on the western front, Wilson found himself defending the rights of neutral shipping to both Britain and Germany.

Britain commanded the seas and tried to redefine neutral rights by blockading German ports and neutral ports from which goods could reach Germany (see Map 20.3), and by expanding definitions of **contraband** to include anything that might indirectly aid Germany—even cotton and food. Britain extended the right of belligerent nations to stop and search neutral ships for contraband by insisting that large, modern ships could not be searched at sea and must be escorted to port, thus imposing costly delays.

Germany also challenged neutral rights, declaring a blockade of the British Isles, to be enforced by its submarines, called **U-boats**. Because U-boats were relatively fragile, a lightly armed merchant ship might sink one that surfaced and ordered the merchant ship to stop in the traditional manner. Consequently, submarines struck from below without warning. Britain began disguising its ships by flying the flags of neutral countries, so Germany declared that neutral flags no longer guaranteed protection.

Wilson had issued token protests over Britain's practices but strongly denounced those of Germany. Because Germany's violations of neutrality produced loss of life, he considered them to be significantly

MAP 20.3 The War at Sea
This map shows the contending definitions of war zones at sea by Great Britain and Germany. Both initially sought to prevent war materials from reaching enemy ports, but both soon sought to prevent virtually all shipping to enemy ports. Copyright © Cengage Learning

different from Britain's, which caused only financial hardship. On February 10, 1915, Wilson warned that the United States would hold Germany to "strict accountability" for its actions and would do everything necessary to "safeguard American lives and property" and maintain American rights on the high seas. On May 7, 1915, a German U-boat torpedoed the British passenger ship ***Lusitania***. More than a thousand people died, including 128 Americans. Americans reacted with shock and horror. Upon learning that *Lusitania* carried ammunition and other contraband, Bryan urged restraint in protesting to Germany. Wilson, however, sent a strong message that stopped just short of demanding an end to submarine attacks on merchant ships. The German response was noncommittal. When Wilson composed an even stronger protest,

belligerent A nation formally at war.

contraband Goods prohibited from being imported or exported; in time of war, contraband included materials of war.

■ **U-boat** A German submarine (in German, *Unterseeboot*)

■ ***Lusitania*** British passenger liner sunk by a German submarine in 1915, creating a diplomatic crisis between the United States and Germany.

New York newspapers carried warnings from the German embassy about the dangers of trans-Atlantic travel, but the passengers who boarded the *Lusitania* on May 1, 1915, probably paid little attention. The ship was sunk on May 7. Of the 1,959 passengers and crewmembers, 1,198 died, including 128 Americans.

Bryan feared it would lead to war. He resigned as secretary of state rather than sign it.

Robert Lansing, Bryan's successor, strongly favored the Allies. Where Bryan had counseled restraint, Lansing urged a show of strength. U-boat attacks continued. Wilson sent more protests but knew most Americans opposed going to war over that issue. Then a U-boat sank the unarmed French ship *Sussex* in March 1916, injuring several Americans. Wilson warned Germany that if unrestricted submarine warfare did not stop, the United States would sever diplomatic relations—the last step before declaring war. Germany responded with the **Sussex pledge**: U-boats would no longer strike noncombatant vessels without warning, provided the United States convinced the Allies to obey "international law." Wilson accepted the pledge but did little to persuade the British to change tactics.

The war strengthened America's economic ties to the Allies. Exports to Britain and France soared from $756 million in 1914 to $2.7 billion in 1916. American companies exported $6 million worth of explosives in 1914 and $467 million in 1916. Even more significant was the transformation of the United States from a debtor to a **creditor nation**. By April 1917, American bankers had loaned more than $2 billion to the Allied governments. However, the British blockade stifled Americans' trade with the Central Powers, which fell from around $170 million in 1914 to almost nothing two years later.

Wilson concluded that the best way to maintain American neutrality was to end the war. He sent his closest confidant, Edward M. House, to London and Berlin early in 1916 to present proposals for peace and for a league of nations to maintain peace in the future. House received no encouragement from either side and concluded that they were not interested in negotiations.

Some Americans had begun to demand "preparedness"—a military buildup. In response, in the summer of 1916, Congress appropriated the largest naval expenditures in peacetime history and approved the National Defense Act, which doubled the size of the army. Wilson accepted both measures.

The Election of 1916

By embracing preparedness, Wilson defused an issue that might otherwise have helped the Republicans in the 1916 presidential campaign. The Democrats

■ Sussex pledge German promise in 1916 to stop sinking merchant ships without warning if the United States would compel the Allies to obey "international law."

creditor nation A nation whose citizens or government have loaned more money to the citizens or governments of other nations than the total amount that they have borrowed from the citizens or governments of other nations.

nominated Wilson for a second term, and they campaigned on their domestic reforms and preparedness programs, frequently repeating the slogan "He kept us out of war."

Republicans nominated Charles Evans Hughes, a Supreme Court justice and former governor of New York with a reputation as a progressive. Hughes avoided taking a clear position on preparedness and neutrality, hoping for support both from German Americans upset with Wilson's harshness toward Germany and from those who wanted maximum assistance for the Allies. As a result, he failed to present a compelling alternative to Wilson.

The vote was very close. Most voters identified themselves as Republicans, and Wilson needed support from some of them. He won by uniting the always-Democratic South with the West, much of which was progressive. Wilson also received significant backing from unions, socialists, and women in states where women could vote. In the end, Wilson received 49 percent of the vote to 46 percent for Hughes.

The Decision for War

After the election, events moved very quickly. In January 1917, Wilson spoke to the Senate on the need to achieve and preserve peace. The galleries were packed as he eloquently called for an international organization to keep peace in the future. He urged that the only lasting peace would be a "peace without victory" in which neither side exacted gains from the other. He called for government by consent of the governed, freedom of the seas, and reductions in armaments. Wilson acknowledged privately that he had aimed his speech toward "the people of the countries now at war," hoping to build public pressure on those governments to seek peace. He won praise from **left-wing** opposition parties in several countries, but the British, French, and German governments had no interest in "peace without victory."

At the same time, the German government decided to resume unrestricted submarine warfare. They expected this would bring the United States into the war but gambled on being able to defeat the British and French before American troops could make a difference. When Germany announced it was resuming unrestricted submarine warfare, Wilson broke off diplomatic relations. German U-boats began immediately to devastate Atlantic shipping.

A few weeks later, on March 1, Wilson released a decoded message from the German state secretary for foreign affairs, **Arthur Zimmermann**, to the German minister in Mexico. Zimmermann proposed that, if the United States went to war with Germany, Mexico should join with Germany and attack the United States. Zimmermann promised that if Germany and Mexico won, Mexico would recover its "lost provinces" of Texas, Arizona, and New Mexico. Zimmermann also proposed that Mexico should encourage Japan to enter the war against the United States. The British intercepted the message and gave it to Wilson.

Zimmermann's suggestions outraged Americans, increasing public support for a proposal to arm American merchant ships for protection against U-boats. A few senators, mostly progressives, blocked the measure, arguing that it was safer to bar merchant ships from the war zone. Wilson then acted on his own and authorized merchant ships to be armed.

By March 21, German U-boats had sunk six American ships. Wilson could avoid war only by backing down from his insistence on "strict accountability." He did not retreat. Wilson's major objective in going to war was not to protect American commerce with the Allies, but to defeat German autocracy and militarism and to put the United States, and himself, in a position to determine the terms of peace. On April 2, 1917, Wilson asked Congress to declare war on Germany and tried to unite Americans in a righteous, progressive crusade. Condemning German U-boat attacks as "warfare against mankind," he proclaimed, "The world must be made safe for democracy." He promised that the United States would fight for self-government, "the rights and liberties of small nations," and a league of nations to "bring peace and safety to all nations and make the world itself at last free."

Not all members of Congress agreed that war was necessary; nor were all ready to join Wilson's campaign to transform the world. During the debate, Senator George W. Norris, a progressive Republican from Nebraska, best voiced the opposing arguments. The nation, he argued, was going to war "upon the command of gold" to "preserve the commercial right of American citizens to deliver munitions of war to belligerent nations." In the Senate, Norris, Robert La Follette, and four others voted no, but eighty-two senators voted for war. Jeannette Rankin of Montana, the first woman in the House of Representatives, was among those who said no when the House voted 373 to 50 for war. In December, Congress also declared war against Austria-Hungary.

---

left-wing Not conservative; usually implies socialist or other radical leanings.

■ **Arthur Zimmermann** German foreign-affairs official who proposed in 1917 that if the United States declared war on Germany, Mexico should become a German ally, win back Texas, Arizona, and New Mexico, and persuade Japan to go to war with the United States.

THE HOME FRONT

★ *How successful was the federal government in mobilizing the economy and society to support the war?*

★ *How did the war affect Americans, especially women, African Americans, and opponents of war?*

Historians call World War I the first "total war" because it was the first war to demand mobilization of an entire society and economy. The war altered nearly every aspect of the economy as the progressive emphasis on expertise and efficiency produced unprecedented centralization of economic decision making. Mobilization extended beyond war production to the people themselves and especially to shaping their attitudes toward involvement in the war.

Mobilizing the Economy

The ability to wage war effectively depended on a fully engaged industrial economy. Thus warring nations sought to direct economic activities toward supplying their war machines. In the United States, railway transportation delays, shortages of supplies, and the sluggish pace of some manufacturing led to increased federal direction over transportation, food and fuel production, and manufacturing. This was not unusual among the nations at war and in fact was probably less extreme than in other nations. Even so, the extent of direct federal control over so much of the economy has never been matched since World War I.

Though unprecedented, much of the government intervention was also voluntary. Business enlisted as a partner with government and supplied its cooperation and expertise. Some prominent entrepreneurs volunteered their services for a dollar a year. Much of the wartime centralization of economic decision making came through new agencies composed of government officials, business leaders, and prominent citizens.

■ **War Industries Board** Federal agency headed by Bernard Baruch that coordinated American production during World War I.

daylight saving time Setting of clocks ahead by one hour to provide more daylight at the end of the day during late spring, summer, and early fall.

■ **National War Labor Board** (NWLB) Federal agency created in 1918 to resolve wartime labor disputes.

collective bargaining Negotiation between the representatives of organized workers and their employer to determine wages, hours, and working conditions.

■ **Herbert Hoover** U.S. food administrator during World War I; later secretary of commerce (1921–1928) and president (1929–1933).

The **War Industries Board** supervised production of war materials. At first, it had only limited success in increasing productivity. Then, in early 1918, Wilson appointed Bernard Baruch, a Wall Street financier, to head the board. By pleading, bargaining, and sometimes threatening, Baruch usually persuaded companies to meet production quotas, allocate raw materials, develop new industries, and streamline operations. Though Baruch once threatened steel company executives with a government takeover, he accomplished most goals without coercion. And industrial production increased by 20 percent.

Efforts to conserve fuel included the first use of **daylight saving time**. To improve rail transportation, the federal government consolidated the country's railroads and ran them for the duration of the war. The government also took over the telegraph and telephone system and launched a huge shipbuilding program to expand the merchant marine.

The **National War Labor Board** (NWLB), created in 1918, endorsed **collective bargaining** to facilitate production by resolving labor disputes. The board also helped to settle labor disputes. Never before had a federal agency interceded this way. The board gave some support for an eight-hour workday in return for a no-strike pledge from unions.

Most unions promised not to strike for the duration of the war, and many of them secured contracts with significant wage increases. Union membership boomed from 2.7 million in 1916 to more than 4 million by 1919. Most union leaders fully supported the war. Samuel Gompers, president of the AFL, called it "the most wonderful crusade ever entered upon in the whole history of the world." Nevertheless, many workers felt that their purchasing power was not keeping pace with increases in prices.

Demands for increased production at a time when millions of men were marching off to war opened many opportunities for women. Employment of women in factory, office, and retail jobs had increased before the war, and the war accelerated those trends. Some of the new, wartime union members were women. At the war's end, many women's wartime jobs returned to male hands, but in office work and some retail positions women continued to predominate after the war.

One crucial American contribution to the Allies was food, for the war severely disrupted European agriculture. Wilson appointed as food administrator **Herbert Hoover**, who had already won wide praise for directing the relief program in Belgium when America was still neutral. Now he both promoted increased food production and also urged families to conserve food through Meatless Mondays and Wheatless Wednesdays and by planting "war gardens" to raise vegetables. Farmers brought large areas under

Labor shortages attracted new people into the labor market and opened up some jobs to women and members of racial minorities. In May 1918, these women worked in the Union Pacific Railroad freight yard in Cheyenne, Wyoming.

cultivation for the first time. Food shipments to the Allies tripled.

Some progressives urged that the Wilson administration pay for the war by taxing the wartime profits and earnings of corporations. That did not happen, but taxes—especially the new income tax—did account for almost half of the $33 billion the United States spent on the war between April 1917 and June 1920. The government borrowed the rest, much of it through **Liberty Loan** drives. Rallies, parades, and posters pushed all Americans to buy "Liberty Bonds." Groups such as the Red Cross and the YMCA urged people to donate time and energy in support of American soldiers.

Mobilizing Public Opinion

Not all Americans supported the war. Some German Americans were reluctant to send their sons to war against their cousins. Some Irish Americans became even more hostile to Britain after English troops brutally suppressed an attempt at Irish independence in 1916. The Socialist Party openly opposed the war, and Socialist candidates dramatically increased

their share of the vote in several places in 1917—to 22 percent in New York City and 34 percent in Chicago—suggesting that their antiwar stance attracted many voters.

To mobilize public opinion in support of the war, Wilson created the Committee on Public Information, headed by George Creel. Creel set out to sell the war to all Americans. The **Creel Committee** eventually counted 150,000 lecturers, writers, artists, actors, and scholars championing the war and whipping up hatred of the "Huns." Social clubs, movie theaters, and churches all joined what Creel called "the world's greatest adventure in advertising." "Four-Minute Men"—volunteers ready to make a short patriotic

■ **Liberty Loan** One of four bond issues floated by the U.S. Treasury Department from 1917 to 1919 to help finance World War I.

■ **Creel Committee** The U.S. Committee on Public Information (1917–1919), headed by journalist and editor George Creel; it used films, posters, pamphlets, and news releases to mobilize American public opinion in favor of World War I.

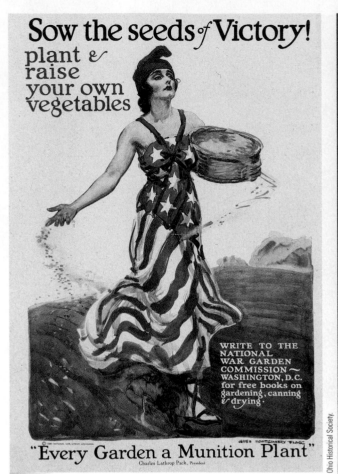

Sow the seeds *of* Victory!
plant *&* raise your own vegetables

WRITE TO THE NATIONAL WAR GARDEN COMMISSION ~ WASHINGTON, D.C. for free books on gardening, canning *&* drying.

"Every Garden a Munition Plant"
Charles Lathrop Pack, President

James Montgomery Flagg created this poster in 1918, showing Columbia, a traditional symbol for America, sowing grain as a way of appealing to American women to contribute to victory by raising and preserving food for their families. Columbia was usually garbed in an American flag, wearing a red liberty cap, a traditional symbol of freedom.

REMEMBER BELGIUM

Buy Bonds
Fourth
Liberty
Loan

This poster by Ellsworth Young, also from 1918, encouraged Americans to buy Liberty Bonds (that is, loan money to the government) by emphasizing the image of the vicious and brutal Hun, part of a larger process of demonizing the people of the Central Powers.

speech any time and place a crowd gathered—made 755,190 speeches.

Wilson's war message had stressed that "We have no quarrel with the German people," but wartime propaganda quickly moved toward demonizing all things German, and wartime patriotism sparked extreme measures against those considered "slackers" or pro-German. "Woe to the man or group of men that seeks to stand in our way," warned Wilson. "He who is not with us, absolutely and without reserve of any kind," echoed former president Theodore Roosevelt, "is against us, and should be treated as an alien enemy."

"Americanization" drives promoted rapid assimilation among immigrants. Some states prohibited the use of foreign languages in public. Officials removed German books from libraries and sometimes publicly burned them. Some communities banned music by Bach and Beethoven and dropped German classes from their schools. Even words became objectionable: sauerkraut became "liberty cabbage." Sometimes mobs hounded people with German names and occasionally attacked or even lynched people suspected of antiwar sentiments.

Civil Liberties in Time of War

Not only German Americans but also pacifists, socialists, and other radicals became targets for government repression and **vigilante** action. Congress passed the

vigilante A person who takes law enforcement into his or her own hands, usually on the grounds that normal law enforcement has broken down.

In the Wider World

Demonizing the Enemy

The United States was not the only belligerent to demonize the enemy. Propaganda that dehumanized the enemy made it easier to hate them and make sacrifices to destroy them. Labeling Germans as Huns apparently began in Britain, to identify them with brutal barbarians who invaded Europe in the Dark Ages. As Huns, they were threats to western civilization, rather than the source of great music, art, and literature. An Australian poster showed an ape-like brute wearing a German spiked helmet, his hands and forearms drenched in blood, grasping at the entire globe. British posters luridly described atrocities committed by "Huns," including an account of a German nurse pouring water on the ground rather than give it to a wounded British soldier. A Canadian poster showed a dying woman at sea, victim of a German U-boat attack, with the caption "Kultur [the German word for culture] vs. Humanity."

Espionage Act in 1917 and the **Sedition Act** in 1918, prohibiting interference with the draft and outlawing criticism of the government, the armed forces, or the war effort. Violators faced large fines and long prison terms. Officials arrested fifteen hundred people for violating these acts, including Eugene V. Debs, leader of the Socialist Party. The Espionage Act authorized the postmaster general to bar objectionable publications from the mail. By the war's end, he had denied mailing privileges to some four hundred periodicals, including, at least temporarily, the *New York Times* and other mainstream publications.

When opponents of the war challenged the Espionage Act as unconstitutional, the Supreme Court ruled that freedom of speech was never absolute. Just as no one has the right to falsely shout "Fire!" in a theater and create panic, said Justice Oliver Wendell Holmes, Jr., so in time of war no one has a constitutional right to say anything that might endanger the security of the nation. The Court also upheld the Sedition Act.

The Industrial Workers of the World (IWW) made no public pronouncement against the war, but most Wobblies probably opposed it. IWW members and leaders quickly came under attack from employers, government officials, and vigilantes, most of whom had disliked the IWW before the war. In September 1917, Justice Department agents raided IWW offices nationwide and arrested IWW leaders, who were sentenced to jail for up to twenty-five years and fined millions of dollars. Deprived of most leaders and virtually bankrupted, the IWW never recovered.

A few Americans protested the abridgment of civil liberties. One group formed the Civil Liberties Bureau—forerunner of the American Civil Liberties

Union. Most Americans, however, did not object to the repression, and many who did kept silent.

The Great Migration and White Reactions

In 1910, about 90 percent of all African Americans lived in the South, 75 percent in rural areas. By 1920, as many as a half-million had moved north in what has been called the **Great Migration**. Many went to the industrial cities of the Midwest. Gary, Indiana, showed one of the greatest gains—1,284 percent between 1910 and 1920. New York City, Philadelphia, and Los Angeles also attracted many blacks. Several factors produced this migration, but the most important were the brutality and hardships of southern life and the economic opportunities in the cities of the North. "Every time a lynching takes place in a community down South," said T. Arnold Hill of Chicago's Urban League, "colored people will arrive in Chicago within two weeks."

Perhaps the most significant factor in the Great Migration was American industry's desperate need for workers. The labor needs of northern cities attracted hundreds of thousands of African Americans seeking

■ **Espionage Act** 1917 law mandating severe penalties for anyone found guilty of interfering with the draft or encouraging disloyalty to the United States.

■ **Sedition Act** 1918 law supplementing the Espionage Act by extending the penalty to anyone deemed to have abused the government.

■ **Great Migration** Movement of about a half-million black people from the rural South to the urban North during World War I.

Labor shortages and high wages drew African Americans from the South to the North. This family, including members of three generations, posed for a photographer upon their arrival in Chicago from the South as part of the Great Migration during World War I.

better jobs and higher pay. In the North, one could earn almost as much in a day as in a week in the South. While they found better wages, they also found racial discrimination in housing and in access to many jobs. New black neighborhoods developed in some cities where African Americans were able to find housing.

Racial conflicts erupted in several cities at the northern end of the Great Migration trail, as whites attacked individual African Americans or tried to burn their neighborhoods. One of America's worst race riots swept through the industrial city of East St. Louis, Illinois, on July 2, 1917. Thousands of black laborers, most from the South, had settled there during the previous two years. Thirty-nine

African Americans perished in the riot, and six thousand lost their homes. Incensed that such brutality could occur just weeks after the nation's moralistic entrance into the war, W. E. B. Du Bois charged, "No land that loves to lynch [black people] can lead the hosts of Almighty God," and the NAACP led a silent protest parade of ten thousand people through **Harlem**.

PLANNING FOR PEACE IN THE MIDST OF WAR

★ *What role did American ships and troops play in the war?*

★ *How and why did Wilson keep America's participation in the war separate from the Allies?*

Some who supported the war expected that the United States would send only supplies and not soldiers, but it quickly became clear that the United

Harlem A section of New York City in the northern part of Manhattan; it became one of the largest black communities in the United States.

States needed to mobilize troops. The army, however, was tiny compared with the armies contesting in Europe. Millions of men and thousands of women had to be inducted, trained, and transported to Europe.

Mobilizing for Battle

The navy was large and powerful after nearly three decades of shipbuilding, and preparedness measures in 1916 further strengthened it. The American and British navies' convoy technique, in which several cargo or passenger ships traveled together under the protection of destroyers, helped to cut shipping losses in half by late 1917. By spring 1918, U-boats ceased to pose a significant danger.

In April 1917, the combined strength of the U.S. Army and National Guard stood at only 372,000 men. Many men volunteered but not enough. In May, Congress passed the **Selective Service Act**, requiring men aged 21 to 30 (later extended to 18 to 45) to register with local boards to determine who would be drafted (that is, called to duty). The law exempted those who opposed war on religious grounds, but such **conscientious objectors** were sometimes badly treated.

Few people demonstrated against the draft, and most seemed to accept it as efficient and fair. Twenty-four million men registered, and 2.8 million were drafted—about 72 percent of the entire army. By the end of the war, the combined army, navy, and Marine Corps counted 4.8 million members.

No women were drafted, but almost 13,000 served in the navy and marines, most in clerical capacities. For the first time, women held naval and marine rank and status. The army, however, refused to enlist women, considering it too "radical." Nearly 18,000 women served as army nurses, but without army rank, pay, or benefits. At least 5,000 civilian women also served in France, the largest number through the Red Cross, which helped to staff hospitals and rest facilities.

Nearly 400,000 African Americans served during World War I. Almost 200,000 served overseas, but most were assigned to menial tasks. Nonetheless, nearly 30,000 fought on the front lines. Emmett J. Scott, an African American and former secretary to Booker T. Washington, became special assistant to the secretary of war, responsible for African Americans. Nevertheless, black soldiers were often treated as second-class citizens. They served in segregated units in the army, were limited to food service in the navy, and were excluded altogether from the marines. More than six hundred African Americans earned commissions as officers, but the army refused to put a black officer in authority over white officers. White officers commanded most black troops.

About 10,000 American Indians served in the army during World War I, including John Miller (*left*) and Charlie Wolf, members of the Omaha tribe. Some Indians who went to war first underwent tribal ceremonies, long unpracticed, that prepared warriors for battle, thus helping preserve traditional customs. Indians' participation in the war led to increased demands for full citizenship and enfranchisement for all American Indians.

Nebraska State Historical Society.

Americans "Over There"

Shortly after the United States entered the war, a new song by George M. Cohan rocketed to national popularity:

> *Over there, over there,*
> *Send the word, send the word over there,*
> *The Yanks are coming, the Yanks are coming,*
> *And we won't come back 'til it's over over there.*

■ **Selective Service Act** Law passed by Congress in 1917 establishing compulsory military service for men aged 21 to 30.

conscientious objector Person who refuses to bear arms or participate in military service because of religious beliefs or moral principles.

Keystone View Company Publisher COPYRIGHTED MADE IN U.S.A. Manufacturers

Meadville, Pa., New York, N.Y., Portland Oregon, London, Eng., Sydney, Aus.

Collection of George Kimball/Picture Research Consultants and Archives.

19100—Our Answer to the Kaiser—3,000 of America's Millions Eager to Fight for Democracy.

This is a stereoscope photograph. Such photographs were taken by a special camera with two lenses a short distance apart. When viewed through a stereoscope (a device found in most middle-class homes in the early twentieth century), the two photographs produced a three-dimensional image. The caption of this photo is "Our Answer to the Kaiser—3,000 of America's Millions Eager to Fight for Democracy."

A few Yanks—troops in the **American Expeditionary Force** (AEF)—arrived in France in June 1917, commanded by General John J. Pershing, recently returned from Mexico. Most American troops, however, were still to be inducted, supplied, trained, and transported across the Atlantic.

Throughout the war, Wilson held the United States apart from the Allies, referring to the United States as an Associated Power, rather than one of the Allies. He also insisted that American troops have their own sector of the western front. This distinction stemmed from his distrust of Allied war aims and his wish to make the American contribution to victory as prominent as possible so as to maximize American influence at the peace conference.

As American troops trickled into France in mid-1917, the Allies were stretched thin. French and British offensives in spring and summer 1917 had failed,

and the Italians suffered a major defeat late in the year. After disastrous losses, Russia withdrew from the war late in 1917, permitting German commanders to shift troops to the western front (see Map 20.2). Hoping to win the war before Americans could make a difference, the Germans planned a massive offensive for spring 1918.

The German thrust came in Picardy with sixty-four divisions smashing into the French and British lines and attempting to advance along the Marne River. By late May, the Germans were within 50 miles of Paris. As French officials considered evacuating the capital, all available troops, including AEF units, were rushed to the front. At Château-Thierry and at Belleau Wood, AEF troops took 8,000 casualties during a month-long battle over a single square mile of wheat fields and woods. Of 310,000 AEF troops who fought in the Marne region, 67,000 were killed or wounded. The German advance failed.

The Allies then launched a counteroffensive in July as American troops poured into France, topping a million. In September Pershing launched a successful offensive against the St. Mihiel **salient** (see Map 20.2). AEF forces then joined a larger Allied offensive in the Meuse River–Argonne Forest region, the last major assault of the war and one of the fiercest battles in American military history.

■ **American Expeditionary Force** (AEF) American army commanded by General John J. Pershing that served in Europe during World War I.

salient In military usage, a portion of one's front line that projects into enemy territory. In this instance, it was a German salient that projected into the Allied front line.

© Bettmann/Corbis.

HOW 'YA GONNA KEEP 'EM
DOWN ON THE FARM
(AFTER THEY'VE SEEN PAREE ?)

WORDS BY
JOE YOUNG &
SAM M. LEWIS
MUSIC BY
WALTER DONALDSON

Brown University Library.

A black bandleader, James Reese Europe (*left*), went to France as a lieutenant, commanding a machine-gun company, and saw frontline action. He and other black musicians were reassigned to present musical entertainment behind the lines, becoming among the first to play jazz in France. Upon returning to the United States in 1919, he and his band recorded "How 'Ya Gonna Keep 'Em Down on the Farm After They've Seen Paree?" Many groups recorded the popular song, but black musicians may have given it a different emphasis: how can black soldiers be "kept down" after experiencing less oppressive racial patterns in France?

On October 8, Corporal Alvin York, a skilled sharpshooter from the Tennessee mountains, was in the Argonne Forest. His unit came under fire and most were wounded or killed. York, however, coolly practiced his mountaineer sharpshooting, single-handedly killing twenty-five enemy soldiers and silencing thirty-five machine guns. He and the six surviving members of his unit took 132 prisoners. York received the Congressional Medal of Honor, the Croix de Guerre (France's highest decoration), and similar awards from other nations. York's courage and coolness were not unique among the Americans in the Meuse–Argonne campaign—Harry J. Adams, with only an empty pistol, captured 300 prisoners; Hercules Korgia, captured by the Germans, persuaded his captors to become his prisoners; and Samuel Woodfill single-handedly took out five machine guns.

By late October, German military leaders were urging an armistice. Fighting ended at 11:00 A.M., November 11, 1918. By then, nearly 9 million combatants had died: Germany lost 1.8 million, Russia 1.7 million, France 1.4 million, Austria-Hungary 1.1 million, the British Empire 1.1 million. Of the 4.5 million who served in the French army, 31 percent were killed and 44 percent were wounded. American losses were small in comparison—365,000 **casualties**, including 126,000 deaths. Some 800,000 civilians from the Central Powers died of famine resulting from the British blockade. Millions of other civilians, worldwide, died from war-related causes, including starvation and disease. A global **influenza** epidemic in 1918 and 1919 killed 20–40 million people or perhaps more, more than died in the war, including 500,000 Americans.

Some white Americans, including some military officers, worried that experiences in France might

casualty A member of the military lost through death, wounds, injury, sickness, or capture.

influenza Contagious viral infection characterized by fever, chills, congestion, and muscular pain, nicknamed "the flu"; an unusually deadly strain of the H1N1 subtype, usually called "Spanish flu," swept across the world in 1918 and 1919.

This painting by Isaac I. Brodsky depicts Vladimir Lenin addressing workers at the Putilov Works in Petrograd (now St. Petersburg) in 1917. Workers from this factory gave crucial support to the Russian revolutions of 1917. The Communists saw art as a major tool for building public support, and Brodsky became a leader in the rise of Socialist Realism after Joseph Stalin came to power in the late 1920s.

© Bettmann/Corbis.

cause African American soldiers to resist segregation at home. In August 1918, AEF headquarters secretly requested that the French not prominently commend black units. The French, however, awarded the **Croix de Guerre** to several all-black units that had

distinguished themselves in combat and presented awards to individual soldiers for acts of bravery and heroism. When the Allies staged a grand victory parade down Paris's Champs Élysées, the British and French contingents included all races and ethnicities, but American commanders directed that no African American troops take part.

Bolshevism, the Secret Treaties, and the Fourteen Points

In March 1917, before the United States entered the war, war-weary and hungry Russians deposed their **tsar** and created a provisional government. In November, a group of radical socialists, the **Bolsheviks**, seized power. Soon renamed Communists, the Bolsheviks condemned capitalism and imperialism and sought to destroy them. **Vladimir Lenin**, the Bolshevik leader, initiated peace negotiations with the Germans. The **Treaty of Brest-Litovsk**, in March 1918, was harsh and humiliating, requiring Russia to surrender vast

Croix de Guerre French military decoration for bravery in combat; in English, "the Cross of War."

tsar The monarch of the Russian Empire; also spelled *czar.*

■ **Bolsheviks** Radical socialists, later called Communists, who seized power in Russia in November 1917. (The Bolshevik revolution has been called the October Revolution based on the calendar used in Russia at the time.)

■ **Vladimir Lenin** Leader of the Bolsheviks and head until 1924 of the Soviet Union, the state that grew out of the revolution.

■ **Treaty of Brest-Litovsk** March 1918 treaty between Germany and Russia allowing Russia to withdraw from World War I; Russia gave up vast territories.

territories—Finland, its Baltic provinces, parts of Poland and Ukraine—a third of its population, half of its industries, its most fertile agricultural land, and a quarter of its territory in Europe.

The Bolsheviks condemned the war as a scramble for imperial spoils, and in December 1917, before their treaty with Germany, they published the secret treaties by which the European Allies had agreed to divide colonies and territories of the defeated Central Powers among themselves. These exposés strengthened Wilson's intent to keep American war aims separate and to impose his war objectives on the Allies.

On January 8, 1918, Wilson spoke to Congress. He denounced both the secret treaties and the harsh terms the Germans were demanding from Russia. American war goals, he proclaimed, derived from "the principle of justice to all peoples and nationalities, and their right to live on equal terms of liberty and safety with one another, whether they be strong or weak." Seeking to seize the initiative, he presented fourteen objectives, soon called the **Fourteen Points**. Points one through five provided a general context for lasting peace: no secret treaties, freedom of the seas, reduction of barriers to trade, reduction of armaments, and adjustment of colonial claims based partly on the interests of colonial peoples. Point six called for other nations to withdraw from Russian territory and to welcome Russia "into the society of free nations." Points seven through thirteen addressed particular situations: return of territories France had lost to Germany in 1871 and self-determination in Central Europe and the Middle East. The fourteenth point called for "a general association of nations" that could afford "mutual guarantees of political independence and territorial integrity to great and small states alike."

Showing little enthusiasm, the Allies accepted Wilson's Fourteen Points as starting points for discussion. When the Germans asked for an end to the fighting, however, they made clear that their request was based on the Fourteen Points.

THE PEACE CONFERENCE AND THE TREATY

☆ How successful was Wilson at the peace conference?

☆ What caused the defeat of the treaty?

With the war over, Wilson hoped that the peace process would not sow the seeds of future wars. He hoped, too, to create an international organization to keep the peace. Most of the Allies, however, were more interested in grabbing territory and punishing Germany.

The World in 1919

In December 1918, Wilson sailed for France—the first American president to go to Europe while in office and the first president to negotiate directly with other world leaders. Wilson brought along reports from some 150 experts on European history, culture, **ethnology**, and geography who had been working since the fall of 1917 on plans for the postwar era. In France, Italy, and Britain, huge welcoming crowds cheered the great "peacemaker from America."

Delegates to the peace conference assembled amid the collapse of ancient empires and the birth of new republics. The Austro-Hungarian Empire had crumbled, producing the new nations of Poland and Czechoslovakia and the republics of Austria and Hungary. The German monarch, Kaiser Wilhelm, had **abdicated**, and a republic was forming. In January 1919, communists tried unsuccessfully to seize power in Berlin. Throughout the ruins of the Russian Empire, ethnic groups were proclaiming independent republics (most eventually incorporated into the Soviet Union, often by the Bolsheviks' **Red Army**). The Ottoman Empire was collapsing, too, as Arabs, with aid from Britain and France, overthrew Turkish rule in many areas.

Throughout Europe and the Middle East, national **self-determination** and sometimes government by the consent of the governed—part of Wilson's design for the postwar world—seemed to be lurching into reality. Nor were the British and French colonial empires immune, for both faced growing independence movements among their many possessions.

In Russia, civil war raged between the Bolsheviks and their opponents. When the Bolsheviks left the

■ **Fourteen Points** President Wilson's statement of war goals, including arms reduction, national self-determination, and a league of nations.

ethnology The study of ethno-cultural groups.

abdicate To relinquish a high office; usually said only of monarchs.

Red Army The Bolsheviks' army, created to defend the Communist government during their civil war and to reestablish control over parts of the Russian Empire that tried to create separate republics in 1917 and 1918; it was the army of the Soviet Union throughout its existence.

self-determination The freedom of a given people to determine their own political status.

world war, the Allies pushed Wilson to join them in intervening in Russia, ostensibly to protect war supplies from falling into German hands. In mid-1918, Wilson sent American troops as part of Allied expeditions to northern Russia and eastern Siberia. In Siberia, his intent was primarily to head off a Japanese grab of Russian territory. Lenin had initially accepted the intervention in northern Russia as necessary, but the purpose of the Allied intervention soon changed to support for the foes of the Bolsheviks. By late 1918, Wilson was expressing concern over what he called "mass terrorism" directed by the Bolsheviks toward "peaceable Russian citizens." Before the last American troops withdrew from northern Russia in May 1919 and from eastern Siberia in early 1920, they had engaged in conflict with units of the Red Army.

Wilson at Versailles

The peace conference opened on January 18, 1919, just outside Paris, at the glittering Palace of Versailles, once home to French kings. Representatives attended from all nations that had declared war against the Central Powers, but major decisions were made by the Big Four: Wilson, David Lloyd George of Britain, Georges Clemenceau of France, and Vittorio Orlando of Italy. Germany was excluded. Terms of peace were to be imposed, not negotiated. Russia, too, was absent, on the grounds that it had withdrawn from the war and made a separate peace with Germany. Although Russia was barred from Versailles, anxiety about Bolshevism hung over the proceedings, especially affecting decisions about central and eastern Europe.

Wilson quickly realized that European leaders were more interested in their own national interests than in his Fourteen Points. Clemenceau, nicknamed "the Tiger," remembered Germany's humiliating defeat of France in 1871 and hoped to disable Germany

so thoroughly that it could never again threaten his nation. Lloyd George agreed with many of Wilson's goals but felt he carried orders from British voters to exact heavy **reparations** from Germany. Orlando insisted on the territorial gains promised when Italy joined the Allies in 1915. Various Allies were also expecting to gain territories promised in the secret treaties. In addition, the European Allies feared the spread of Bolshevism and intended to create buffers to keep it at bay.

Facing the insistent and acquisitive Allies, Wilson had to compromise. He did secure a **League of Nations**. Instead of "peace without victory," however, the **Treaty of Versailles** imposed harsh victors' terms, requiring Germany to accept the blame for starting the war, pay reparations to the Allies (the exact amount to be determined later), and surrender all its colonies along with Alsace-Lorraine (which Germany had taken from France in 1871) and other European territories (see Map 20.4). The treaty deprived Germany of its navy and merchant marine and limited its army to 100,000 men. German representatives signed on June 28, 1919.

Wilson reluctantly agreed to the massive reparations but insisted that colonies taken from Germany and territories taken from the Ottoman Empire should not go permanently to the Allies. Called **mandates**, they were to be administered by one of the Allies on behalf of the League of Nations and were to move toward independence. In nearly every case, however, the mandate went to the nation slated to receive the territory under the secret treaties. Wilson blocked Italy's most extreme territorial demands but gave in on others. The peace conference recognized new republics in Central Europe, thereby creating a so-called quarantine zone between Russian Bolshevism and Western Europe. The treaty ignored those people—from Ireland to Vietnam—seeking the right of self-determination in colonies held by one of the victorious Allies. Japan failed to secure a statement supporting racial equality.

Though Wilson compromised on most of his Fourteen Points, every compromise intensified his commitment to the League of Nations. The League, he hoped, would not only resolve future controversies without war but also solve problems created by the compromises. Even so, Wilson had to threaten a separate peace with Germany before the Allies agreed to incorporate the **League Covenant** into the treaty. Wilson was especially committed to Article 10 of the League Covenant—he called it the League's "heart." It specified that League members agreed to protect one another's independence and territory against external attacks and take joint action against aggressors.

reparations Payments as compensation for damages.

■ **League of Nations** A world organization created by the Versailles peace conference to promote peace and international cooperation.

■ **Treaty of Versailles** Treaty in 1919 ending World War I; it imposed harsh terms on Germany, created territorial mandates, and created the League of Nations.

mandate A territory that the League of Nations authorized a member nation to administer and move toward independence.

League Covenant The constitution of the League of Nations, part of the 1919 Treaty of Versailles.

MAP 20.4 Postwar Boundary Changes in Central Europe and the Middle East

This map shows the boundary changes in Europe and the Middle East that resulted from the defeat of Austria-Hungary, Germany, Russia, and the Ottoman Empire. Copyright © Cengage Learning

Boundaries of German, Russian, Austro-Hungarian, and Ottoman Empires in 1914
Areas lost by Austro-Hungarian Empire
Areas lost by Russian Empire
Areas lost by German Empire
Areas lost by Bulgaria
Areas lost by Ottoman Empire
Demilitarized Zones
Areas controlled under mandates from the League of Nations, 1920
Boundaries of 1926

GREAT BRITAIN

NORWAY

SWEDEN

FINLAND

North Sea

DENMARK

Baltic Sea

Leningrad (St. Petersburg)

ESTONIA

LATVIA

LITHUANIA

NETHERLANDS

London

Free city of Danzig

EAST PRUSSIA

GERMANY

BELGIUM

RUHR

Berlin

POLAND

RUSSIAN EMPIRE
(later Union of Soviet Socialist Republics)

Paris

FRANCE

LUXEMBOURG

LORRAINE

ALSACE

SWITZ.

CZECHOSLOVAKIA

Vienna

AUSTRIA

HUNGARY

ROMANIA

Aral Sea

ITALY

Corsica

YUGOSLAVIA

Danube R.

Volga R.

60°N

60°E

50°N

40°N

Rome

MONTENEGRO
(To Yugoslavia 1921)

SERBIA

BULGARIA

Black Sea

Caspian Sea

Sardinia

ALBANIA

Istanbul (Constantinople)

GREECE

Sicily

OTTOMAN EMPIRE
(later Republic of Turkey)

TUNISIA
(France)

Mediterranean Sea

Crete

Dodecanese
(Italy)

Cyprus
(Gr. Br.)

Annexed by Turkey 1939

SYRIA
(French Mandate)

Euphrates R.

Tigris R.

PERSIA
(IRAN)

LEBANON
(French Mandate)

IRAQ
(MESOPOTAMIA)
(British Mandate)

PALESTINE
(British Mandate)

TRANSJORDAN
(British Mandate)

KUWAIT
(Gr. Br.)

NEUTRAL ZONES

Persian Gulf

BAHRAIN

QATAR

LIBYA
(Italy)

N

EGYPT
(Independent 1922)

Nile R.

Red Sea

HEJAZ
(Independent 1916; to Nejd 1925)

NEJD
(SAUDI ARABIA)

TRUCIAL OMAN

0   200   400 Km.

0   200   400 Mi.

It Matters Today

Redrawing the Map of the Middle East

Several current nations in the Middle East arose from mandates created through the League of Nations. During the war, Britain assisted Arabs to revolt against the Ottoman Empire and encouraged their desires for self-determination. However, Britain and France secretly agreed to divide much of the Ottoman Empire between them. At stake, the British knew, was oil.

Britain and France largely drew the boundaries of Iraq, Syria, Lebanon, Palestine, and Trans-Jordan (now Jordan), but not based on Wilson's goal of self-determination. Britain received the League mandate for Iraq, which Britain created by combining parts of the Ottoman Empire that included known oilfields.

In 1932, Iraq achieved independence under a king chosen by the British, who continued to wield influence. The new nation experienced conflict between Sunni and Shia, and Kurds in the north resisted their inclusion in Iraq. The government was unstable from 1920 until Saddam Hussein consolidated his power in the 1970s.

- How do decisions made at Versailles influence world affairs today?
- Do more research on Iraq from 1920 onward. In 2003, would you have assumed that removing Saddam Hussein would produce a stable, democratic government? Why or why not?

The Senate and the Treaty

While Wilson was in Paris, opposition to his plans was brewing at home. The Senate, controlled by Republicans since the 1918 elections, had to approve any treaty.

Presented with the treaty, the Senate split into three groups. **Henry Cabot Lodge**, chairman of the Senate Foreign Relations Committee, led the largest faction, called reservationists after the reservations, or amendments, to the treaty that Lodge developed. Article 10 of the League Covenant especially bothered Lodge, for he feared it might commit American troops to war without congressional approval. A small group called irreconcilables, mostly Republicans, opposed any American involvement in European affairs. A third Senate group, nearly all Democrats, supported the president and his treaty.

Wilson decided to appeal directly to the American people. In September 1919, he undertook an arduous speaking tour—9,500 miles with speeches in twenty-nine cities. The effort proved too demanding for his fragile health. Soon after, he suffered a serious stroke. Half-paralyzed and weak, Wilson could fulfill few duties. His wife, Edith Bolling

■ **Henry Cabot Lodge** Republican senator from Massachusetts; as chair of the Senate Foreign Relations Committee, led efforts to modify American participation in the League of Nations.

Wilson, exercised what she later called a "stewardship," strictly limiting her ailing husband's contact with the outside world.

Lodge proposed that the Senate accept the treaty with reservations. Some of his amendments were minor, but others would have permitted Congress to block action under Article 10. Wilson refused any compromise. On November 19, 1919, the Senate defeated the treaty with the Lodge reservations by votes of 39 to 55 and 41 to 50, with the irreconcilables joining the president's supporters in opposition. Then the Senate defeated the original version of the treaty by 38 to 53, with the irreconcilables joining the reservationists in voting no.

The treaty came to a vote again in March 1920. By then, some treaty supporters had concluded that the League could never be approved without Lodge's reservations, so they joined the reservationists to produce a vote of 49 in favor to 35 opposed—still short of the two-thirds majority required. Enough Wilson loyalists—following their stubborn leader's order not to compromise—joined the irreconcilables to defeat the treaty once again. The United States did not join the League of Nations.

Legacies of the Great War

Wilson had appealed to progressives' optimism and confidence in claiming that the United States was going to make the world "safe for democracy." One of his supporters even spoke of the "war to end war." Just as progressives defined their domestic policies in terms of progress, democracy, and social justice, so Wilson tried to invest his foreign policy with enlightened values. In doing so, however, he fostered unrealistic expectations that world politics might be transformed overnight.

Many Americans became disillusioned by the Allies' cynical opportunism. The war to make the world "safe for democracy" turned out to be a chance for Italy to annex Austrian territory and for Japan to seize German concessions in China. And the "war to end war" spun off several wars in its wake: Romania invaded Hungary in 1919, Poland invaded Russia in 1920, the Russian civil war continued until late 1920, and Greece and Turkey battled until 1923.

The peace conference left unresolved many problems. Wilson's promotion of self-government and self-determination encouraged aspirations for independence throughout the Allies' colonies and among the new League mandates. Some of the new nations of Central Europe, supposedly based on ethnic self-determination, actually included different and sometimes antagonistic ethnic groups. Above all, the war and the treaty contributed to economic and political instability in much of Europe, making it a breeding ground for totalitarian and nationalistic movements that eventually generated another world war.

AMERICA IN THE AFTERMATH OF WAR, NOVEMBER 1918–NOVEMBER 1920

★ How did Americans react to the outcome of the war and the events of 1919?

★ How did the events of 1917–1920 affect the 1920 presidential election?

Almost as soon as French church bells pealed for the armistice, the United States began to demobilize. By November 1919, nearly 4 million men and women were out of uniform. Industrial demobilization occurred even more quickly, as officials canceled war contracts. The year 1919 saw both the return of American troops from Europe and also raging inflation, massive strikes, bloody race riots, widespread fear of radical **subversion**, violations of civil liberties—and two new constitutional amendments that embodied important elements of progressivism, prohibition, and woman suffrage.

"HCL" and Strikes

Inflation—described in newspapers as "HCL" for "High Cost of Living"—was the most pressing single problem Americans faced after the war. Between 1913

JOBS for FIGHTERS

BUREAU for RETURNING SOLDIERS and SAILORS -- **WALK IN**

U.S. Employment Service and Co-operating Agencies

HONORABLE DISCHARGE

WELCOME

Gordon Grant Capt. USA

If You Need a Job
If You Need a Man
Inform the Official Central Agency
The Service is Free
The United States Employment Service
Bureau for Returning Soldiers and Sailors

United States Department of Labor—United States Employment Service   THOMSEN-ELLIS CO. Baltimore, Md.

The federal Employment Service assisted returning soldiers and sailors to find jobs. Unemployment for 1918 and 1919 was less than 2 percent, but rose above 5 percent in 1920 and to nearly 12 percent in 1921.

and 1919, prices almost doubled. When the armistice ended unions' no-strike pledge, unions made wage demands to match the soaring cost of living. In 1919, however, employers were ready for a fight.

Many companies wanted to return labor relations to prewar patterns. They blamed wage increases for

subversion Efforts to undermine or overthrow an established government.

inflation, and some linked unions to "dangerous foreign ideas" from Bolshevik Russia. In February 1919, Seattle's Central Labor Council called out the city's unions in a five-day general strike to support shipyard workers. Seattle's mayor branded the strike a Bolshevik plot. Boston's police struck in September 1919 after the police commissioner fired nineteen policemen for joining a union. The governor of Massachusetts, Calvin Coolidge, called out the national guard to maintain order and break the union. "There is no right to strike against the public safety by anybody, anywhere, anytime," he proclaimed. By mid-1919, many unionists concluded that conservative politicians were joining business leaders to block union organizing and roll back wartime gains.

The largest and most dramatic strike came against United States Steel. Few steelworkers were represented by unions after the 1892 Homestead strike. Steel companies often hired recent immigrants, keeping steelworkers divided by language. Most steelworkers put in twelve-hour workdays. Wages had not increased as fast as inflation—or as fast as company profits. In 1919 the AFL launched an ambitious unionization drive in the steel industry, and many steelworkers responded eagerly.

Steel industry leaders refused to deal with the new organization. The workers went on strike in late September, demanding union recognition, collective bargaining, the eight-hour workday, and higher wages. The company blamed the strike on radicals and mobilized public opinion against the strikers. Company guards protected strikebreakers, and U.S. military forces moved into Gary, Indiana, to help round up "the Red element." By January 1920, after eighteen workers had been killed and hundreds beaten, the strike was over and the unions were ousted.

Red Scare

The steel industry's charges of Bolshevism to discredit strikers came as many government and corporate leaders were declaiming against the dangers of Bolshevism at home and abroad. A few anarchist

bombers contributed to stirring up a widespread frenzy aimed at rooting out subversive radicals. In late April 1919, thirty-four bombs addressed to prominent Americans—including J. P. Morgan, John D. Rockefeller, and Supreme Court Justice Oliver Wendell Holmes—were discovered in various post offices after the explosion of two others addressed to a senator and Seattle's mayor. In June, bombs in several cities damaged buildings and killed two people. Probably the work of a few anarchists, the bombs fueled fears of a nationwide conspiracy against the government.

Attorney General A. Mitchell Palmer organized an anti-Red campaign, hoping that success might bring him the 1920 presidential nomination. "Like a prairie fire," Palmer claimed, "the blaze of revolution was sweeping over every American institution." He appointed **J. Edgar Hoover**, a young lawyer, to head an antiradical unit in the Justice Department's Bureau of Investigation, the predecessor of the Federal Bureau of Investigation. In November 1919, Palmer launched the first of what were soon called the **Palmer raids** to arrest suspected radicals. Authorities rounded up some five thousand people by January 1920. Although officials found few firearms and no explosives, the raids led to the **deportation** of several hundred aliens with some tie to radicalism. The rest were released.

State legislatures produced their own antiradical measures, including criminal syndicalism laws—measures criminalizing the advocacy of Bolshevik, IWW, or anarchist ideologies. In January 1920, the assembly of the New York state legislature expelled five members elected as Socialists, solely because they were Socialists.

After a wide range of respected public figures denounced the legislature's action as undemocratic, public opinion regarding the **Red Scare** began to shift. With the approach of May 1, a day of celebration for radicals, Palmer issued dramatic warnings about a general strike and bombings. When nothing happened, many concluded that the radical threat might have been overstated.

As the Red Scare sputtered to an end, in May 1920, police in Massachusetts arrested **Nicola Sacco** and **Bartolomeo Vanzetti**, Italian-born anarchists, and charged them with robbery and murder. Despite inconclusive evidence and the men's protestations of innocence, a jury found them guilty, and they were sentenced to death. Many argued that they had been convicted because of their political beliefs and Italian origins, and that they had not received a fair trial because nativism and antiradicalism had infected the judge and jury. Over loud protests at home and abroad, both men were executed in 1927. Historians continue to debate the evidence, many arguing that Sacco was probably guilty and Vanzetti innocent, and others insisting both were innocent and that the state police concealed evidence.

■ **J. Edgar Hoover** Head of an antiradical unit in the Justice Department in 1919; head of the FBI from 1924 until his death in 1972.

■ **Palmer raids** Government raids on individuals and organizations in 1919 and 1920 to search for radicals.

deportation Expulsion of an undesirable alien from a country.

■ **Red Scare** Wave of antiradicalism in the United States in 1919 and 1920.

■ **Nicola Sacco** and **Bartolomeo Vanzetti** Italian anarchists convicted in 1921 of murder and theft; despite public protests, they were electrocuted in 1927.

Alleged subversives, arrested in one of the Palmer raids in New York City in November 1919, are shown here leaving police wagons on their way to Ellis Island, where they were held pending deportation proceedings.

Race Riots and Lynchings

The racial tensions of the war years continued into the postwar period. Black soldiers encountered more acceptance and less discrimination in Europe than they had ever known at home. In May 1919, the NAACP journal *Crisis* expressed what the more militant returning soldiers felt:

> We return. We return from fighting. We return fighting. Make way for Democracy! We saved it in France, and by the Great Jehovah, we will save it in the U.S.A., or know the reason why.

Some whites, however, greeted returning black troops with furious violence intended to restore prewar race relations. Southern mobs lynched ten black soldiers, some still in uniform. In all, rioters lynched more than seventy blacks in the first year after the war and burned eleven victims alive.

Rioting also struck outside the South. In July 1919, violence reached the nation's capital, where white mobs, including many soldiers and sailors, attacked blacks throughout the city for three days, killing several. The city's African Americans organized their own defense, sometimes arming themselves. In Chicago in late July, war raged between white and black mobs for nearly two weeks, despite efforts by the national guard. The rioting caused thirty-eight deaths (fifteen white, twenty-three black). A thousand families—nearly all black—were burned out of their homes. In Omaha in September, a mob tried to hang the mayor when he bravely stood between them and a black prisoner accused of rape. Police saved the mayor but not the prisoner.

By the end of 1919, race riots had flared in more than two dozen places. The year saw not only rampant lynchings but also the appearance of a new Ku Klux Klan (discussed in the next chapter). Despite violence and coercion directed at African Americans, some things had changed. As W. E. B. Du Bois observed, black veterans "would never be the same again. You cannot ask them to go back to what they were before. They cannot, for they are not the same men."

Amending the Constitution: Prohibition and Woman Suffrage

At the end of the war, two of the great campaigns of the Progressive Era finally realized their goals. Both had roots in the nineteenth century, both attracted numerous supporters during the Progressive Era, and both received a boost by the war. Prohibition was adopted as the **Eighteenth Amendment** to the Constitution, and woman suffrage as the Nineteenth Amendment.

Pushed by the Anti-Saloon League, Congress passed a temporary prohibition measure in 1917. A more important victory came when Congress adopted and sent to the states the Eighteenth Amendment, prohibiting the manufacture, sale, or transportation of alcoholic beverages. Intense and single-minded lobbying persuaded three-fourths of the state legislatures to ratify the amendment in 1919. It took effect in January 1920.

The cause of woman suffrage also received a boost from the war, as suffrage advocates added women's contributions to the war effort to their previous arguments (discussed in Chapters 17–19). In June 1919, by a narrow margin, Congress proposed the **Nineteenth Amendment**, to enfranchise women, and sent it to the states for ratification. After a grueling, state-by-state battle, ratification came in August 1920. Though many women by then already exercised the franchise, especially in western states, ratification meant that the electorate for the 1920 elections was significantly expanded.

The Election of 1920

Republicans confidently expected to regain the White House in 1920. The Democrats had lost their congressional majorities in the 1918 elections, and postwar misgivings and disillusionment often focused on Wilson. One reporter described the stricken president as the "sacrificial whipping boy for the present bitterness."

Any competent Republican nominee was practically guaranteed election. Several candidates attracted significant support, notably former army chief of staff General Leonard Wood, Illinois governor Frank Lowden, and California senator Hiram Johnson. However, no candidate counted a majority

■ **Eighteenth Amendment** (1919) constitutional amendment forbidding the manufacture, sale, or transportation of alcoholic beverages.

■ **Nineteenth Amendment** (1919) constitutional amendment prohibiting restrictions on voting on account of sex.

in the convention. Months earlier, Harry Daugherty, campaign manager for Ohio senator Warren G. Harding, had foreseen a deadlock and had predicted that it would be broken by a compromise candidate, chosen at about "eleven minutes after two o'clock" in the morning, when "fifteen or twenty men, bleary-eyed and perspiring profusely from the heat" chose a compromise candidate. And so it was. A small group of party leaders met late at night in a smoke-filled hotel room and picked Harding. Even some of his supporters were unenthusiastic—one called him "the best of the second-raters." For vice president, the Republicans nominated Calvin Coolidge, the governor who had broken the Boston police strike.

The Democrats also suffered severe divisions. After forty-four ballots, they chose James Cox, governor of Ohio, as their presidential candidate. For vice president, they nominated Franklin D. Roosevelt, Wilson's assistant secretary of the navy and a remote cousin of Theodore Roosevelt.

Usually described as good-natured and likable—and sometimes as bumbling—Harding had published a small-town newspaper in Ohio until his wife, Florence, and some of his friends pushed him into politics. Eventually winning election to the Senate, unhappy with his marriage, Harding apparently took pleasure from a series of mistresses. The press knew of Harding's liaisons but never reported them.

During the campaign, an uproar arose over a claim that Harding's ancestry included African Americans. The story spread rapidly, and a reporter asked Harding, "Do you have any Negro blood?" Harding replied mildly, "How do I know, Jim? One of my ancestors may have jumped the fence." The allegation, and Harding's response to it, apparently did not hurt his cause. Most of Harding's campaign reflected his promise to "return to normalcy."

After the stress of the war and the postwar years, voters enthusiastically endorsed returning to "normalcy." Harding took thirty-seven of the forty-eight states and 60 percent of the popular vote—the largest popular majority up to that time. Wilson had hoped for a "solemn referendum" on the League of Nations, but the election proved more a reaction against the war launched with lofty ideals that turned sour at Versailles, the high cost of living, and the strikes and riots of 1919. Americans, it seemed, had had enough of idealism and sacrifice for a while.

Individual Voices

Woodrow Wilson Proposes His Fourteen Points

President Woodrow Wilson spoke to a joint session of Congress on January 8, 1918, and presented his objectives for peace, including his Fourteen Points. This is a condensed version of that speech. Historians understand that Wilson was writing to persuade many audiences: Congress, the American people, the Allies, the Central Powers—and later historians.

❶ To what events does this passage refer? To whom is it directed?

It will be our wish and purpose that the processes of peace, when they are begun, shall be absolutely open. . . . The day of conquest and aggrandizement is gone by; so is also the day of secret [treaties]. . . . ❶

What we demand in this war . . . is that the world be made fit and safe to live in; and particularly that it be made safe for every peace-loving nation which, like our own, wishes to live its own life, determine its own institutions, be assured of justice and fair dealing by the other peoples of the world as against force and selfish aggression. All the peoples of the world are in effect partners in this interest. . . . ❷ The program of the world's peace, therefore, is our program; and that program, the only possible program, as we see it, is this:

❷ How do these statements compare with the Treaty of Versailles?

I. Open covenants of peace, openly arrived at, after which there shall be no private international understandings of any kind but diplomacy shall proceed always frankly and in the public view.

II. Absolute freedom of navigation upon the seas, outside territorial waters. . . .

III. The removal, so far as possible, of all economic barriers and the establishment of an equality of trade conditions among all the nations.

IV. Adequate guarantees given and taken that national armaments will be reduced to the lowest point consistent with domestic safety.

V. A free, open-minded, and absolutely impartial adjustment of all colonial claims, based upon a strict observance of the principle that . . . the interests of the populations concerned must have equal weight with the equitable claims of the government whose title is to be determined. . . . ❸

❸ What are the connections among Points I through V, the causes of the war in 1914, and the reasons for American's entrance into the war?

[Points VI–XIII laid out specific territorial restorations or adjustments.]

XIV. A general association of nations must be formed under specific covenants for the purpose of affording mutual guarantees of political independence and territorial integrity to great and small states alike. . . .

For such arrangements and covenants we are willing to fight and to continue to fight until they are achieved; but only because we wish the right to prevail and desire a just and stable peace such as can be secured only by removing the chief provocations to war. . . .

❹ Was Wilson creating unrealistic expectations with such statements?

An evident principle runs through the whole program I have outlined. It is the principle of justice to all peoples and nationalities, and their right to live on equal terms of liberty and safety with one another, whether they be strong or weak. . . . ❹

❺ Compare Wilson's reasons for committing America to war with Charles Young's reasons for wanting to go war.

The people of the United States could act upon no other principle. . . .

The moral climax of this the culminating and final war for human liberty has come. . . . ❺

Study Tools

SUMMARY

Woodrow Wilson took office expecting to focus on domestic policy, not world affairs. He fulfilled some Democratic Party commitments to anti-imperialism but intervened extensively in the Caribbean. He also intervened in Mexico but failed to accomplish all his objectives there.

When war broke out in Europe in 1914, Wilson declared the United States to be neutral, and most Americans agreed. German submarine warfare and British restrictions on commerce, however, threatened traditional definitions of neutrality. Wilson secured a German pledge to refrain from unrestricted submarine warfare. He was reelected in 1916 on the argument that "he kept us out of war." Shortly after he won reelection, the Germans violated their pledge, and in April 1917 Wilson asked for war against Germany.

The war changed most aspects of America's economic and social life. The federal government developed a high degree of centralized economic planning, and tried to mold public opinion and restrict dissent. When the federal government backed collective bargaining, unions registered important gains. In response to labor shortages, more women and African Americans entered the industrial work force, and many African Americans moved to northern and midwestern industrial cities.

Germany launched an offensive in 1918, hoping to achieve victory before Americans could make a difference. However, the AEF helped to break the German advance, and the Germans surrendered. In his Fourteen Points, Wilson expressed his goals for peace.

Facing opposition from the Allies, Wilson compromised at the Versailles peace conference but hoped that the League of Nations would maintain the peace. Fearing obligations that League membership might place on the United States, enough senators opposed the treaty to defeat it. Thus the United States did not become a member of the League.

The end of the war brought disillusionment and high prices, many strikes, a Red Scare, and race riots and lynchings. In 1920 the nation returned to its previous Republican majority when it elected Warren G. Harding, a mediocre conservative, to the White House.

CHRONOLOGY
The United States and World Affairs, 1913–1920

1912	Woodrow Wilson elected president
1913	Victoriano Huerta takes power in Mexico; Wilson denies recognition
1914	U.S. Navy occupies Veracruz
	War in Europe, United States declares neutrality
	Stalemate on the western front
1915	German U-boat sinks the *Lusitania*
	United States occupies Haiti
1915–1920	Great Migration
1916	U.S. troops pursue Pancho Villa into Mexico
	Wilson reelected
1917	Wilson calls for "peace without victory"
	Germany resumes submarine warfare
	Overthrow of tsar of Russia
	United States declares war on Germany
	Race riot in East St. Louis
	Bolsheviks seize power in Russia, publish secret treaties, withdraw Russia from the war
	Railroads placed under federal control
1918	Wilson presents Fourteen Points to Congress
	Germans launch offensive but fail; Allies launch successful counteroffensive
	U.S. troops sent to northern Russia and Siberia
	Armistice in Europe
1918–1919	Worldwide influenza epidemic
1919	Signing of Treaty of Versailles
	Eighteenth Amendment (prohibition) approved
	Race riots
	Major strikes
1919–1920	Red Scare, Palmer raids
1920	Senate defeats Versailles for second and final time
	Nineteenth Amendment (woman suffrage) approved
	Warren G. Harding elected president

Study Tools

FOCUS QUESTIONS

If you have mastered this chapter, you should be able to answer these questions and to identify the terms that follow the questions.

1. ☆ *In what new directions did Wilson steer U.S. foreign policy before the coming of war in Europe?*

2. ☆ *Why did Wilson proclaim American neutrality? How did Americans respond?*

3. ☆ *What made neutrality difficult?*

4. ☆ *How did Wilson justify going to war?*

5. ☆ *How successful was the federal government in mobilizing the economy and society to support the war?*

6. ☆ *How did the war affect Americans, especially women, African Americans, and opponents of war?*

7. ☆ *What role did American ships and troops play in the war?*

8. ☆ *How and why did Wilson keep America's participation in the war separate from the Allies?*

9. ☆ *How successful was Wilson at the peace conference?*

10. ☆ *What caused the defeat of the treaty?*

11. ☆ *How did Americans react to the outcome of the war and the events of 1919?*

12. ☆ *How did the events of 1917–1920 affect the 1920 presidential election?*

KEY TERMS

Victoriano Huerta *(p. 561)*

Venustiano Carranza *(p. 561)*

Francisco "Pancho" Villa *(p. 562)*

Central Powers *(p. 563)*

Allies *(p. 563)*

western front *(p. 563)*

U-boat *(p. 565)*

Lusitania *(p. 565)*

Sussex pledge *(p. 566)*

Arthur Zimmermann *(p. 567)*

War Industries Board *(p. 568)*

National War Labor Board *(p. 568)*

Herbert Hoover *(p. 568)*

Liberty Loan *(p. 569)*

Creel Committee *(p. 569)*

Espionage Act *(p. 571)*

Sedition Act *(p. 571)*

Great Migration *(p. 571)*

Selective Service Act *(p. 573)*

American Expeditionary Force *(p. 574)*

Bolsheviks *(p. 576)*

Vladimir Lenin *(p. 576)*

Treaty of Brest-Litovsk *(p. 576)*

Fourteen Points *(p. 577)*

League of Nations *(p. 578)*

Treaty of Versailles *(p. 578)*

Henry Cabot Lodge *(p. 580)*

J. Edgar Hoover *(p. 582)*

Palmer raids *(p. 582)*

Red Scare *(p. 582)*

Nicola Sacco and Bartolomeo Vanzetti *(p. 582)*

Eighteenth Amendment *(p. 584)*

Nineteenth Amendment *(p. 584)*

Go to the History CourseMate website for primary source links, study tools, and review materials for this chapter. www.cengagebrain.com

21 Prosperity Decade, 1920-1928

Behind the Stories

As you'll recall from the past three chapters, Americans had been grappling with important issues of public policy from the early 1890s through World War I. Reform had been "in the air," and various causes had attracted many Americans as advocates or supporters. The Great War had ratcheted expectations and emotions even higher. At the war's end, it seemed almost as if someone had poked a hole in a balloon—much of the optimism and enthusiasm seemed to rush out of public life all at once.

Historians have sometimes argued over what happened to progressivism in the 1920s. Some have suggested that the excesses of the war, the disappointments of Versailles, and the many small wars that followed the Great War had bred skepticism of any progressive rhetoric. Some have argued that progressivism was still alive but that conservatism had momentarily taken the upper hand. Others have proposed that progressivism splintered—that the progressive emphasis on efficiency and expertise continued as an important value in American life, especially in American business, and that leaders of business appropriated that aspect of progressive rhetoric and made it their own. Moral reformers could take great pride in their accomplishments, especially prohibition. But the women who had united behind the banner of suffrage now splintered into competing groups. Perhaps most importantly, instead of listening to stirring political speeches in their leisure time, many Americans now had other choices—taking the family car for a drive, going to the movies, or listening to the new radio at home.

In this chapter, we focus on the big economic and social changes during the 1920s. The 1920s ended with a great economic depression, caused in major part by weaknesses in the economy during the "prosperity decade." In the next chapter, you'll be thinking back to this one as you read about how those weaknesses contributed to the crash, and how the politics of the 1930s focused on fixing them.

—R.W.C.

Chapter Outline

Individual Choices
Clara Bow

At the age of 21, Clara Bow became the "It" Girl—star of the movie *It*, loosely based on Elinor Glyn's novel. "It" was sex appeal, or in Glyn's words, "an inner magic, an animal magnetism." And Clara Bow, the "It" Girl, was the most popular movie star of the late 1920s.

Clara Bow

Clara was born in Brooklyn in 1905. Her father frequently abandoned Clara and her schizophrenic mother, who showed no affection for her daughter. Clara grew up streetwise, able to defend herself with her fists. She left school at 13, began to work, and decided to become a movie actress. Clara's mother threatened to kill her if she persisted with acting, but was confined to a mental institution in 1922 and died soon after. Left alone, Clara was raped by her father.

Bow landed a contract with a Hollywood studio by the time she was 17 and appeared in thirty-five movies before reaching the age of 21. In the early 1920s, some films were emphasizing sexuality to attract audiences, as can be seen in the advertising in the Individual Voices feature at the end of this chapter. Thus, though Bow's first substantial role was as a tomboy, by 1925 her studio labeled her "the hottest jazz baby in films." The *New York Times* agreed: "She radiates an elfin sensuousness." *It*, released in 1927, clinched her fame as the essential **flapper**. F. Scott Fitzgerald claimed that "Clara Bow is the quintessence of what the term 'flapper' signifies . . . pretty, impudent, superbly assured, as worldly-wise, briefly-clad and 'hard-berled' [tough] as possible." He added that thousands of young women were now "patterning themselves after her."

On the screen, Bow was flirtatious and sensuous, conscious of her sexuality and willing to use it, and aggressive in accomplishing her goal. In the process, she usually revealed as much skin as the censors permitted. She lived in much the same way, attracting Hollywood's handsomest men, making them her lovers, and discarding them for someone new. Perhaps reflecting on her parents' marriage, she told a reporter, "Marriage ain't woman's only job no more. . . . I wouldn't give up *my* work for marriage."

Despite her huge popularity and succession of famous lovers, Bow remained deeply lonely. Her working-class behavior and speech and the gossip about her sex life made her a social outcast in Hollywood. When silent films gave way to the talkies, the looming overhead microphone became her

flapper In the 1920s, a young woman with short hair and short skirts who flaunted her avant-garde dress and behavior.

enemy, reminding her of her childhood stutter and threatening her self-confidence. She made successful talking movies, but several public scandals led to cancellation of her studio contract. At the age of 25, Clara Bow seemed a has-been.

She married actor Rex Bell and moved to a remote ranch in Nevada. She starred in two films in 1933, both successful at the box office and with the critics. But Bow was done with Hollywood. Eventually she was diagnosed with schizophrenia and depression. She later returned to live in solitude in Los Angeles and died there in 1965. In 1957, a poll of surviving silent-film directors, actors, and cameramen placed Clara Bow a close second to Greta Garbo as the greatest actress of the silent films.

Called the "Jazz Age" and the "Roaring Twenties," the 1920s sometimes seem a swirl of conflicting images. Flappers—symbolized by Clara Bow—were flaunting new freedoms for women while prohibition, although poorly enforced, seemed an effort to preserve nineteenth-century values. The booming stock market promised prosperity to all with money to invest even as thousands of farmers abandoned the land because they could not survive financially. Business leaders celebrated the booming economy while many wage earners in manufacturing endured the destruction of their unions and saw their legal protections evaporate. White-sheeted Klansmen marched as self-proclaimed defenders of Protestant American values and white supremacy, but African American art, literature, and music were flowering.

Amid these seeming paradoxes, the economy roared along like a shiny new roadster, fueled by easy credit and consumer spending, virtually unregulated.

THE BULLISH DECADE

★ What was the basis for the economic expansion of the 1920s?

★ What weaknesses existed within the economy?

By 1920, the American economy had been thoroughly industrialized, with most industry controlled by large corporations run by professional managers. During the 1920s, the rise and growth of the automobile industry dramatized the new prominence of industries producing **consumer goods**. This significant change in direction carried implications for advertising, banking, and even the stock market.

consumer goods Products such as clothing, food, automobiles, and radios, intended for purchase and use by individuals or households, as opposed to products such as steel beams, locomotives, and electrical generators.

The Economics of Prosperity

With the end of the war in 1918, the government cancelled most orders for war supplies, from ships to uniforms. Large numbers of recently discharged military and naval personnel swelled the ranks of job seekers. However, no immediate economic collapse ensued. Given wartime shortages and overtime pay, many Americans had been earning more than they could spend. At the end of the war, their spending helped to delay the postwar slump until 1920 and 1921. The gross national product (GNP) dropped by only 4.3 percent between 1919 and 1920, then fell by 8.6 percent between 1920 and 1921. During the war, unemployment affected only about 1 percent of the work force. The jobless rate increased to 5 percent in 1920 and 12 percent in 1921. Some employers also cut hours and wages. Figure 21.1 presents earnings for three groups of Americans and indicates the impact of recession in the early 1920s. In the end, reduced earnings, unemployment, and declining demand halted the rampaging inflation of 1918 and 1919.

The economy quickly rebounded. Gross domestic product increased by 15 percent between 1921 and 1922, a bigger jump than during the booming war years. Unemployment remained at 2–5 percent from 1923 through 1929, and prices for most manufactured goods remained relatively stable. Thus many Americans seemed slightly better off by 1929 than in 1920.

Targeting Consumers

By the 1920s, many business leaders understood that persuading Americans to buy their products was crucial to keeping the economy healthy. In 1921 General Foods Company invented Betty Crocker to give its baking products a womanly, domestic image. In 1924 General Mills first advertised Wheaties as the "Breakfast of Champions," tying breakfast cereal to star athletes. Americans responded by buying those products and many others, all with their own creative

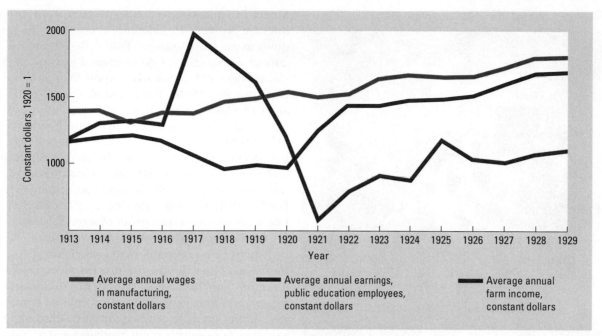

FIGURE 21.1 Patterns of Annual Income for Three Groups of Americans, 1913–1929
This graph depicts the patterns of annual income for three different groups of Americans. Income has been converted to constant dollars; that is, the dollar amounts are adjusted for changes in the purchasing power of the dollar. The year 1920 is used as the base year for calculating the value of the dollar. Wages for manufacturing workers rose during the war years, leveled during the recession of the early 1920s, then rose again. For public education employees—mostly teachers—real earnings fell dramatically with the inflation of the war years and the postwar recession, then rose to parallel those of manufacturing workers. Farmers had a boom in income during the war, then saw their real earnings plunge at the end of the war with only a modest recovery after the recession of the early 1920s.

Source: U.S. Department of Commerce, Bureau of Census, Historical Statistics of the United States, Colonial Times to 1970, Bicentennial Edition, 2 vols. (Washington, D.C.: Government Printing Office, 1975), I: 167, 170, 483.

pitches. "We grew up founding our dreams on the infinite promises of American advertising," Zelda Sayre Fitzgerald later wrote.

The marketing of Listerine provided a model for others. Listerine had been devised as a general antiseptic, but in 1921 Gerard Lambert developed a more persuasive—and profitable—approach when he plucked the obscure term *halitosis* (bad breath) from a medical journal. Through aggressive advertising, he fostered anxieties about the effect of halitosis on popularity and made millions by selling Listerine to combat the condition. Until then, few Americans had been concerned about freshening their breath. Now other entrepreneurs rushed to sell products by defining needs that consumers had not previously identified.

Changes in fashion encouraged increased consumption. Short hairstyles for women led to development of hair salons and stimulated sales of the recently invented **bobby pin**. Cigarette advertisers began to target women, as when the American Tobacco Company urged women to "Reach for a Lucky instead of a sweet" to attain a fashionably slim figure. Disposable products promoted regular, recurring consumer buying. Technological advances in the processing of

wood cellulose fiber led in 1921 to the marketing of Kotex, the first manufactured disposable sanitary napkin, and in 1924 to the first disposable handkerchiefs, later known as Kleenex tissues.

Technological advances also contributed to the growth of consumer-oriented manufacturing. In 1920 about one-third of all residences had electricity. By the end of the decade, electrical power had reached nearly all urban homes but fewer than 10 percent of farm homes. As the number of residences with electricity increased, advertisers stressed that housewives could save time and labor by using electric washing machines, irons, vacuum cleaners, and toasters. Between 1919 and 1929, consumer expenditures for household appliances grew by more than 120 percent.

Increased consumption encouraged changes in spending habits. Before the war, most families saved their money until they could pay cash for what they needed. In the 1920s many retailers encouraged buyers to "Buy now, pay later." Many consumers did so, taking home a new radio and worrying about paying

bobby pin Small metal hair clip with ends pressed tightly together, designed for holding short or "bobbed" hair in place.

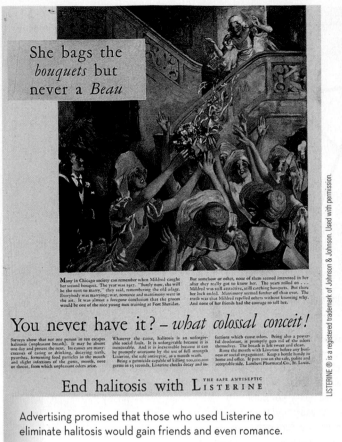

She bags the *bouquets* but never a *Beau*

You never have it? – *what colossal conceit!*

End halitosis with LISTERINE THE SAFE ANTISEPTIC

Advertising promised that those who used Listerine to eliminate halitosis would gain friends and even romance.

for it tomorrow. By the late 1920s, about 15 percent of all retail purchases were made through the **installment plan**, especially furniture, phonographs, washing machines, and refrigerators. Charge accounts in department stores also became popular, and **finance companies** (which made loans) grew rapidly.

The Automobile: Driving the Economy

The automobile epitomized the consumer-oriented economy of the 1920s. Early automobiles were luxuries, but **Henry Ford** developed a mass-production system that drove down production costs.

Ford, a former mechanic, built his success on the **Model T**, introduced in 1908. As early as 1918, the

installment plan A way of paying for a purchase over time, so that the price of the product is spread over several payments, typically due monthly.

finance company Business that makes loans to clients based on some form of collateral, such as a new car, thus allowing a form of installment buying when sellers do not extend credit.

■ **Henry Ford** Inventor and manufacturer, founded the Ford Motor Company in 1903 and pioneered mass production of autos.

Model T Lightweight automobile that Ford produced from 1908 to 1927 and sold at the lowest possible price on the theory that an affordable car would be more profitable than an expensive one.

Model T dominated the market. By 1927, Ford had produced more than 15 million of them. "Get the prices down to the buying power," Ford ordered, and his dictatorial management style combined with technological advances and high worker productivity to bring the price of a new Model T as low as $290 by 1927 (equivalent to $3,400 today). It was a dream come true for many Americans. Families came to love their ungraceful but reliable "Tin Lizzies," so named because of their lightweight metal bodies. The Model T sacrificed style and comfort for durability, ease of maintenance, and the ability to handle almost any road. It made Henry Ford a folk hero—a wealthy one. By 1925, Ford Motor Company showed a daily profit of some $25,000.

Ford's company provides an example of efforts by American entrepreneurs to reduce labor costs by improving efficiency. In the process, work on Ford's assembly line became a thoroughly dehumanizing experience. Ford workers were prohibited from talking, sitting, smoking, singing, or even whistling while working. As one critic put it, workers were to "put nut 14 on bolt 132, repeating, repeating, repeating until their hands shook and their legs quivered."

Still, Ford paid his workers well, and they could increase their pay by completing Americanization classes. Ford workers earned enough to buy their own Model T. Ford's high wages pushed other automakers to increase pay for their workers, to keep them from defecting to Ford. Auto workers thus came to enjoy some of the consumer buying previously restricted to middle- and upper-income groups.

Competition helped to keep auto prices low. Other automobile companies challenged Ford's predominance, notably General Motors (GM), founded by William Durant in 1908, and Chrysler, created by Walter Chrysler in 1925. GM and Chrysler adopted many of Ford's production techniques, but their cars also offered more comfort and style than the Model T. Ford ended production of the Model T in 1927, when Chevrolet passed Ford in sales. The next year, Ford introduced the Model A, which incorporated some features promoted by his competitors.

Advertising made the automobile the symbol not only of the ability of Americans to acquire material goods but also of technology, progress, and the freedom of the open road. American consumers were receptive. By the late 1920s, about 80 percent of the world's registered vehicles were in the United States. By then, America's roadways sported nearly one automobile for every five people.

The automobile industry often led the way in devising new sales techniques. By 1927 two-thirds of all American automobiles were sold on credit. GM began introducing new models every year, encouraging owners to keep up with changes in design, color, and optional features. Small automakers soon found they could not compete with Chrysler, Ford, and GM—the

From the Collections of the Henry Ford Museum and Greenfield Village.

Model A Fords are under production at Ford's main assembly plant in 1928. Assembly-line workers repeated the same task on car after car, as the line moved 6 feet per minute. Ford pioneered the assembly line to reduce cost and reliance on skilled workers.

accelerated, continuing earlier patterns toward greater economic concentration. By 1930, 5 percent of American corporations were receiving 85 percent of all net corporate income, up from 78 percent in 1921.

Ford and Giannini were not the only entrepreneurs to emerge as popular and respected public figures. Perhaps the ultimate glorification of the entrepreneur came in 1925, in a book entitled *The Man Nobody Knows*. The author, Bruce Barton, founder of a leading advertising agency, suggested that Jesus Christ could best be understood as a business executive who "had picked up twelve men from the bottom ranks of business and forged them into an organization that conquered the world." Portraying Jesus' parables as "the most powerful advertisements of all time," Barton's book led the nonfiction bestseller lists for two years.

Big Three. By 1929, the Big Three were making 83 percent of all cars manufactured in the country. The industry had become an oligopoly.

Changes in Banking and Business

Just as Henry Ford brought automobiles within reach of most Americans, so **A. P. Giannini** did something similar for banking. The son of Italian immigrants, Giannini founded the Bank of Italy in 1904 as a bank for shopkeepers and workers in San Francisco's Italian neighborhood. Until then, most banks had only one location, in the center of a city, and limited their services to businesses and substantial citizens. Giannini brought his bank to ordinary people by opening branches near people's homes and workplaces. Called the greatest innovator in twentieth-century American banking, Giannini broadened the base of banking by encouraging working people to open small checking and savings accounts and to borrow for such purposes as car purchases. In the process, his bank—renamed the Bank of America—became the third largest in the nation by 1927.

Giannini's bank and Ford's auto factory survived as relics of family management in a new world of modern corporations with large bureaucracies. Ownership and control continued to grow apart, as salaried managers came to run most big businesses.

Even though the number of corporations increased steadily throughout the 1920s, corporate mergers also

"Get Rich Quick"—Speculative Mania

During the 1920s, the stock market captured people's imagination as the fast track to riches. Stock market speculation—buying a stock with the expectation of selling it at a higher price—ran rampant. Articles in popular magazines proclaimed that everyone could participate and get rich quickly. By 1929, 4 million Americans owned stock, equivalent to about 10 percent of American households.

Just as Americans purchased cars and radios on the installment plan, some also bought stock on credit. One could purchase stock listed at $100 a share with as little as $10 down and the other $90 "on margin"—owed to the stockbroker. If the stock price advanced to $150, the investor could sell, pay off the broker, and gain a profit of $50 (500 percent!) on the $10 investment. Unfortunately, if the stock price fell to $50, the investor would still owe $90 to the broker. In fact, fewer than 1 percent of stock buyers purchased on margin, and the margin rarely exceeded 50 percent. More people borrowed money to buy stocks, but buying stocks with borrowed money carried the same potential for disaster as buying on margin.

■ **A. P. Giannini** Italian American who changed banking by opening multiple branches and encouraging small accounts and personal loans.

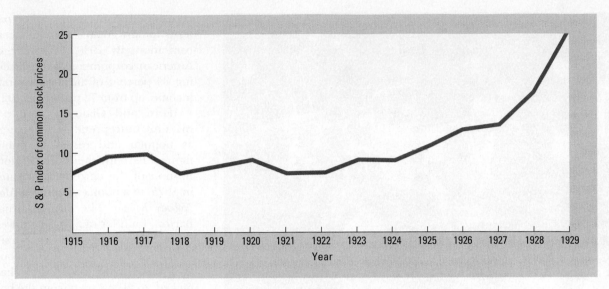

FIGURE 21.2 Stock Prices, 1915–1929
This graph shows the Standard & Poor index of common stock prices, with 1941–1942 as the base years (the index = 10 for those years). Figures for other years show stock prices in comparison to the base year. The Great Bull Market began in late 1924/early 1925 and roared upward until late 1929.

Source: U.S. Department of Commerce, Bureau of Census, Historical Statistics of the United States, Colonial Times to 1970, Bicentennial Edition, 2 vols. (Washington, D.C.: Government Printing Office, 1975), II: 10-4.

Driven partly by real economic growth and partly by speculation, stock prices rose higher and higher (see Figure 21.2). Common stock prices tripled between 1920 and 1929. As long as the market stayed **bullish** and stock prices kept climbing, prosperity seemed endless.

The ever-rising stock prices and corporate dividends of the 1920s encouraged creation of holding companies. Samuel Insull created a vast empire of electrical utilities companies. Much of his enterprise—and others like it—consisted of holding companies, which existed solely to own the stock of another company, some of which existed primarily to own the stock of yet another company. The entire structure rested on the dividends produced by the underlying **operating companies**. Those dividends enabled the holding companies to pay dividends on their bonds. Any interruption in the dividends from the operating companies could bring the collapse of the entire pyramid, swallowing up the investments of speculators.

Although the stock market held the nation's attention as the most popular path to instant riches, other speculative opportunities abounded. A land boom developed when people poured into Florida, especially Miami, attracted by the climate, the beaches,

bullish Optimistic or confident; regarding stocks, stock prices go up in a bull market and down in a bear market.

operating company A company that directly sells goods or services, as opposed to a holding company that exists to own other companies.

and the ease of travel from the cities of the chilly Northeast. Speculators bought land—almost any land—expecting its value would soar. Stories circulated of land that increased 1,500 percent in value over ten years. Like stocks, land was bought with borrowed money. Early in 1926, the population influx slowed. The boom began to falter, then collapsed when a hurricane slammed into Miami. By 1927, many Florida land speculators were facing bankruptcy.

Agriculture: Depression in the Midst of Prosperity

Prosperity never extended to most farmers, and farmers made up nearly 30 percent of the work force in 1920. During the war, many farmers expanded operations in response to government demands for more food, and exports of farm products nearly quadrupled. After the war, European farmers resumed production, exports of farm products fell, and agricultural prices dropped. Throughout the 1920s, American farmers consistently produced more than the domestic market could absorb, causing prices to fall.

The average farm's net income for the years 1917 to 1920 ranged between $1,196 and $1,395 (in current dollars) per year. Farm income fell to a dreadful $517 in 1921, then slowly rose, but never reached 1917–1920 levels until World War II. Although farmers' net income fell in the immediate postwar years and never recovered to prewar levels, their mortgage payments more than doubled over prewar levels, partly because of debts incurred to expand wartime production. Tax increases, purchases of tractors and trucks—now necessities on most farms—and the cost of fertilizer and other supplies bit further into farmers' meager earnings.

As the farm economy continued to hemorrhage, the average value of an acre of farmland fell by more than half between 1920 and 1928. The average farm was actually less valuable in 1928 than in 1912. Thousands of people left farming each year, and the proportion of farmers in the work force fell from nearly 30 percent to less than 20 percent. The 1920s were not the prosperity decade for rural America.

THE "ROARING TWENTIES"

★ *What groups most challenged traditional social patterns during the 1920s?*

★ *What role did technology play in social change during the 1920s?*

"The world broke in two in 1922 or thereabouts," wrote novelist Willa Cather, and she didn't like what came after. F. Scott Fitzgerald, another novelist, agreed with the date but embraced the change. He believed 1922 marked "the peak of the younger generation," who brought about an "age of miracles"—that, he admitted,

became an "age of excess." Evidence of sudden and dramatic social change was easy to see, from automobiles, radios, and movies to a new youth culture and an impressive cultural outpouring by African Americans.

Putting a People on Wheels: The Automobile and American Life

The automobile profoundly changed Americans' lives. Highways significantly shortened the travel time from rural areas to cities, reducing the isolation of farm life. One farm woman, when asked why her family had an automobile but no indoor plumbing, responded, "Why, you can't go to town in a bathtub." Trucks allowed farmers to take more products to market more quickly and conveniently than before. Tractors expanded the amount of land that one family could cultivate. By reducing the need for human labor, gasoline-powered farm vehicles stimulated migration to urban areas.

The automobile changed city life even more profoundly. The 1920 census, for the first time, recorded more Americans living in urban areas (places having 2,500 people or more) than in rural ones. As the automobile freed suburbanites from their dependence on commuter rail lines, new suburbs mushroomed, with most of the growth in single-family houses. From

This postcard shows Grauman's Chinese Theater around the time of its opening in 1927. Probably the most lavish theater constructed during the 1920s, when ornate theaters appeared in most cities, "the Chinese" cost $2 million (equivalent to more than $24 million today). Only the biggest stars could set their footprints in the floor of the theater's courtyard.

1922 through 1928, construction began on an average of 883,000 new homes each year. New home construction rivaled the auto industry as a major driving force behind economic growth.

The automobile soon demonstrated its ability to strangle urban traffic. One response was the development of traffic lights. Various versions were tried, but the four-directional, three-color traffic light first appeared in Detroit in 1920. Traffic lights spread rapidly to other large cities, but traffic congestion nonetheless worsened. By 1926, cars in the evening rush hour in Manhattan crawled along at less than 3 miles per hour—slower than a person could walk—and many commuters had returned to trains and subways.

Los Angeles: Automobile Metropolis

Manhattan was not designed to handle automobile traffic, but the fastest-growing major city of the early twentieth century—Los Angeles—was. The popula-

tion of Los Angeles increased tenfold between 1900 and 1920, then more than doubled by 1930, reaching 2.2 million. Expansion of citrus-fruit raising, major oil discoveries, and the development of the motion-picture industry laid an economic foundation for rapid population growth in southern California. Manufacturing also expanded—during the 1920s, the city moved from twenty-eighth to ninth place among American cities based on manufacturing.

Lack of sufficient water threatened to limit growth until city officials diverted the Owens River to Los Angeles through a 233-mile-long aqueduct, opened in 1913. Throughout the 1920s, southern California promoters attracted hundreds of thousands of people by presenting an image of perpetual summer, tall palm trees lining wide boulevards filled with automobiles, fountains gushing water into the sunshine, and broad sandy beaches.

Los Angeles boomed as the automobile industry was promoting the notion of a car for every family and real-estate developers were pushing the ideal of

Several of the biggest stars owed their fame to their sex appeal. Clara Bow was the "It" girl, and "It" meant sex appeal. Rudolph Valentino was the leading male sex star of the 1920s. This poster advertises *The Sheik* (1921), a movie so popular and influential that handsome young men came to be referred to for a time as sheiks.

the single-family home. By 1930, 94 percent of all residences in Los Angeles were single-family homes, an unprecedented level for a major city, and Los Angeles had the lowest urban population density of any major city in the nation.

Life in Los Angeles came to be organized around the automobile. The first modern supermarket, offering "one-stop shopping," appeared there, and the "Miracle Mile" along Wilshire Boulevard was the first large shopping district designed for the automobile. Such innovations set the pace for new urban development everywhere. The *Los Angeles Times* put it this way in 1926: "Our forefathers in their immortal independence creed set forth 'the pursuit of happiness' as an inalienable right of mankind. And how can one pursue happiness by any swifter and surer means . . . than by the use of the automobile?" By then, Los Angeles had one automobile for every three residents, twice the national average.

A Homogenized Culture Searches for Heroes

Los Angeles was the capital of the movie industry. By the mid-1920s, most towns of any size boasted at least one movie theater, and movie attendance increased rapidly from a weekly average of 40 million people in 1922 to 80 million in 1929—the equivalent of two-thirds of the total population. As Americans all across the country laughed or wept at the same movie, this new medium helped to **homogenize** the culture, that is, to make it more uniform by breaking down differences based on region or ethnicity.

Radio also contributed to greater homogeneity. The first commercial radio station began broadcasting in 1920. Within six years, 681 were operating. By 1930, 40 percent of all families had radios, including half of urban families. Other important factors in promoting more homogeneity included the automobile, which cut travel time, and new laws that sharply reduced immigration.

Radio and film joined newspapers and magazines in creating and publicizing national trends and fashions as Americans pursued one fad after another. In 1924, crossword puzzles captured the attention of many Americans, and contract bridge, a card game, became the rage in 1926. Such fads created markets for new consumer goods, from crossword dictionaries to folding card tables.

The media also helped to make spectator sports an obsession. Baseball had long been the preeminent national sport, and radio began to broadcast baseball games nationwide. Other sports now vied with baseball for fans' attention—and dollars. Most Americans in the 1920s were familiar with the exploits of Lou Gehrig and Babe Ruth on the baseball diamond, Jack Dempsey

Charles Lindbergh chose photo settings in which he appeared to be alone with his plane, thereby emphasizing the individual nature of his flight. This photo was taken before his historic solo flight across the Atlantic.

and Gene Tunney in boxing, and Bobby Jones, a golfer. Gertrude Ederle won national acclaim in 1926 when she became the first woman to swim the English Channel and did so two hours faster than any previous man. The rapid spread of movie theaters created a new category of fame—the movie star. Charlie Chaplin, Buster Keaton, Harold Lloyd, and others brought laughter to the screen. Tom Mix was the best known movie cowboy. In addition to Clara Bow, sex made a star of Theda Bara, the **vamp**, and Rudolph Valentino soared to fame as a male sex symbol, with his most famous film, *The Sheik*, set in a fanciful Arabian desert.

The greatest popular hero of the 1920s, however, was neither athlete nor actor but a small-town airmail pilot—**Charles Lindbergh**. At the time, aviation was barely out of its infancy. A few transatlantic flights had been logged by 1926, but the longest nonstop flight before 1927 was from San Diego to New York—2,500 miles.

homogenize To make something uniform throughout.

vamp A woman who uses her sexuality to entrap and exploit men.

■ **Charles Lindbergh** American aviator who made the first solo transatlantic flight in 1927 and became an international hero.

Lindbergh, in 1927, set his sights on the $25,000 offered by a New York hotel owner to the pilot of the first successful nonstop flight between New York and Paris—3,500 miles. His plane, *The Spirit of St. Louis*, was a stripped-down, one-engine craft. In a sleepless, 33½-hour flight, Lindbergh earned both the $25,000 and the adoration of crowds on both sides of the Atlantic. In an age devoted to materialism and dominated by a corporate mentality, Lindbergh's accomplishment suggested that old-fashioned individualism, courage, and self-reliance could still triumph over odds and adversity.

Alienated Intellectuals

Other Americans, too, went to Paris and other European cities in the 1920s, but for different reasons than Lindbergh. These **expatriates** left the United States to escape what they considered America's intellectual shallowness, dull materialism, and spreading uniformity. As Malcolm Cowley put it in *Exile's Return* (1934), his memoir of life in France, "by expatriating himself, . . . the artist can break the puritan shackles, drink, live freely, and be wholly creative." Paris in the 1920s, he added, "was a great machine for stimulating the nerves and sharpening the senses."

Sinclair Lewis and H. L. Mencken did not move to Paris but became leading critics of middle-class materialism and uniformity. Lewis, in *Main Street* (1920), presented small-town, middle-class existence as not just boring but stifling. In *Babbitt* (1922), Lewis presented a suburban businessman (George Babbitt) as narrow-minded and complacent, speaking in clichés and buying every gadget on the market. H. L. Mencken, editor of *The American Mercury*, relentlessly pilloried the "booboisie," jeered at all politicians, and celebrated only writers who shared his disdain for most of American life.

Others added to the critique of modern life. In *The Waste Land* (1922), T. S. Eliot, an American poet who fled to England, presented modernity as sterile and futile. F. Scott Fitzgerald, in *The Great Gatsby* (1925), portrayed the pointless lives of wealthy pleasure seekers and their careless disregard for life and values. Ernest Hemingway, in *The Sun Also Rises* (1926), depicted disillusioned and jaded expatriates.

expatriate A person who takes up long-term residence in a foreign country.

■ **Sinclair Lewis** Novelist who satirized middle-class America in works such as *Babbitt* (1922); the first American to win the Nobel Prize for literature.

■ **Harlem Renaissance** Literary and artistic movement in the 1920s, centered in Harlem, in which black writers and artists celebrated African American life.

Renaissance Among African Americans

For the most part, despair and disillusionment troubled white writers and intellectuals. Such sentiments were rarely apparent in the striking outpouring of literature, music, and art by African Americans in the 1920s.

African Americans continued to move from the South to northern cities in the 1920s. Harlem, the largest black neighborhood in New York City, came to symbolize the new urban life of African Americans. The term **Harlem Renaissance**, or Negro Renaissance, refers to a literary and artistic movement in which black artists and writers insisted on the value of black culture and drew upon African and African American traditions in their writing, painting, and sculpture. Black actors, notably Paul Robeson, now appeared in serious theaters and earned acclaim for their abilities. Earlier black writers, especially Alain Locke, James Weldon Johnson, and Claude McKay, encouraged and guided the novelists and poets of the Harlem Renaissance.

Among the movement's poets, Langston Hughes became the best known. Born in Joplin, Missouri, in 1902, Hughes began to write poetry in high school, briefly attended college, then worked and traveled in Africa and Europe. By 1925, he was a significant figure in the Harlem Renaissance, sometimes reading his poetry to the musical accompaniment of jazz. Some of his works present images from black history, vividly depict racism, or look to the future with an expectation for change, as in "I, Too" (1925):

> *I, too, sing America.*
> *I am the darker brother.*
> *They send me*
> *To eat in the kitchen*
> *When company comes,*
> *But I laugh,*
> *And eat well,*
> *And grow strong.*
> *Tomorrow*
> *I'll sit at the table*
> *When company comes. . . .**

Other important writers included Zora Neale Hurston, who came from a poor southern family, won a scholarship to Barnard College, and began her long writing career with several short stories in the 1920s. Jean Toomer's novel *Cane* (1923), dealing with African Americans in rural Georgia and Washington, D.C.,

---

*"I, Too" from *The Collected Poems of Langston Hughes* by Langston Hughes, edited by Arnold Rampersad with David Roessel, Associate Editor, copyright © 1994 by the Estate of Langston Hughes. Used by permission of Alfred A. Knopf, a division of Random House, Inc. and Harold Ober Associates.

The original cover for *The Weary Blues* (1926), Langston Hughes's first book of poetry, which included some of the first blues that Hughes ever heard, dating to his childhood in Lawrence, Kansas. Hughes's references to the blues and the cover design evoke the connection between music and poetry that was part of the Harlem Renaissance.

This was the cover of the March 1925 issue of *Survey Graphic*, a popular magazine of the period. *Survey Graphic* devoted the entire issue to Harlem and the emergence of new consciousness among its African American residents.

has been praised as "the most impressive product of the Negro Renaissance."

The 1920s have been called the Jazz Age. African American musicians in southern cities, especially New Orleans, developed **jazz** in the early twentieth century, drawing from several strains in African American music, particularly the blues and ragtime. Jazz moved north, began to attract white audiences in the 1910s, and influenced white composers, notably George Gershwin, whose *Rhapsody in Blue* (1924) brought jazz into the symphony halls. Some attacked the new sound, claiming it encouraged people to abandon self-restraint, especially with regard to sex. Despite— or perhaps because of—such condemnation, the wail of the saxophone became as much a part of the 1920s as the roar of the roadster and the flicker of the movie projector.

The great black jazz musicians of the 1920s— Louis "Satchmo" Armstrong, Bessie Smith, Fletcher Henderson, Ferdinand "Jelly Roll" Morton, and

others—drew white audiences into black neighborhoods to hear them. Harlem came to be associated with exotic nightlife and glittering jazz clubs. Edward "Duke" Ellington came to lead the Cotton Club band in 1927 and began to develop the works that made him one of America's most respected composers.

Few African Americans experienced the glitter of the Cotton Club, but one Harlem black leader affected black people throughout the country and beyond. **Marcus Garvey**, born in Jamaica, advocated a form of **black separatism**. His organization, the Universal Negro Improvement Association

■ **jazz** Style of music developed in America in the early twentieth century, characterized by strong, flexible rhythms and improvisation on basic melodies.

■ **Marcus Garvey** Jamaican black nationalist active in America in the 1920s.

■ **black separatism** A strategy of creating separate black institutions, based on the assumption that African Americans can never achieve equality within white society.

"Jelly Roll" Morton, born Ferdinand Joseph Lemott, was a leading figure in jazz. Shown here with the Hot Peppers, Morton called himself "the Originator of Jazz," and his "Jelly Roll Blues" may be the first jazz composition ever published.

(UNIA), founded in 1914, stressed racial pride, the importance of Africa, and racial solidarity across national boundaries. Garvey supporters urged blacks around the world to help Africans overthrow colonial rule and build a strong Africa. Garvey's message of racial pride and solidarity attracted wide support among African Americans, especially in the cities. However, black integrationist leaders, especially W. E. B. Du Bois of the NAACP, opposed Garvey's separatism and argued that the first task facing blacks was integration and equality in the United States. Garvey and Du Bois each labeled the other a traitor to his race. Garvey was convicted of mail fraud in 1923 due to irregularities in his fundraising. After two years in jail, he was deported to his native Jamaica.

"Flaming Youth"

African Americans created jazz, but those who danced to it, in the popular imagination of the 1920s, were white—a male college student, clad in a stylish raccoon-skin coat with a hip flask of illegal liquor in his pocket, and his female counterpart, the uninhibited flapper, with bobbed hair and a daringly short skirt. This stereotype of "flaming youth"—the title of a popular novel—reflected far-reaching changes among many white, college-age youths of middle- or upper-class background.

In the 1920s adolescence emerged as a separate subculture. The booming economy allowed more middle-class families to send their children to college. Before World War I, just over 3 percent of people aged 18 to 24 were in college. By 1930, that proportion had more than doubled, with larger increases among women, and women were receiving 40 percent of all bachelor's degrees. Students reshaped colleges into youth centers, where football games and dances assumed as much significance as examinations and term papers.

Young women who captured public attention with their clothes and behavior were called flappers because of the flapping sound made by their fashionably unfastened galoshes. They scandalized their elders with skirts that stopped at the knee, stockings rolled below the knee, short hair often dyed black, and generous amounts of rouge and lipstick. Many observers assumed that their outrageous look reflected outrageous behavior—that young women were abandoning their parents' moral values. In fact, women's sexual activity outside marriage began to increase before the war, especially among working-class women and radicals. "Dating," too, owed its origins to prewar working-class young people. In the 1920s, these behaviors appeared among college and high school students from middle-class families. About half of the women who came of age during the 1920s had intercourse before marriage, a marked increase from prewar patterns.

Such changes in behavior were often linked to the automobile. It brought greater freedom to young people, for there they had no chaperone and could go where they wanted. Sometimes they went to a **speakeasy** (where illegal alcohol was sold). Before Prohibition, few women entered saloons, but men and women alike went to speakeasies to drink, smoke, and dance to jazz. While some adults criticized the frivolities of the young, others emulated them, launching the first American youth culture. F. Scott Fitzgerald later called the years after 1922 "a children's party taken over by elders."

speakeasy A place that illegally sells liquor and sometimes offers entertainment.

TRADITIONAL AMERICA ROARS BACK

★ *Why and how did some Americans try to restore traditional social values during the 1920s?*

Most Americans embraced cars, movies, and radios, but many felt threatened by the pace of change and the upheaval in social values that seemed centered in the cities. In nearly every case, though, efforts to stop the tide of change appeared in both cities and rural areas, and many of those efforts dated to the prewar era. In the 1920s, several movements seeking to restore elements of an older America came to fruition at the same time as Fitzgerald's "age of excess."

Prohibition

The **Eighteenth Amendment** (Prohibition) came to symbolize many of the efforts to preserve white, old-stock, Protestant values. Prohibition did reduce drinking somewhat, but many Americans simply ignored it, and it grew less popular the longer it lasted. By 1926, a poll indicated that only 19 percent

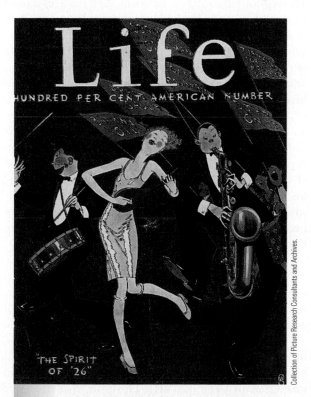

On the 150th anniversary of the Declaration of Independence, *Life* presented this cover parodying the famous painting *The Spirit of '76* by depicting "The Spirit of '26"—an uninhibited flapper with a jazz saxophonist and drummer, and banners with the snappy sayings of the day. The caption reads: "1776-1926: One Hundred and Forty three Years of LIBERTY and Seven Years of PROHIBITION."

Collection of Picture Research Consultants and Archives.

of Americans supported Prohibition, 50 percent wanted the amendment modified, and 31 percent favored outright **repeal**. Prohibition, however, remained the law, if not the reality, from 1920 until 1933, when the Twenty-first Amendment finally did repeal it.

Prohibition was never well enforced anywhere, partly because of the immensity of the task and partly because Congress never provided enough money for serious federal enforcement. In 1923 a federal agent visited major cities to see how long it took to find an illegal drink: 35 seconds in New Orleans, 3 minutes in Detroit, and 3 minutes and 10 seconds in New York City.

Previously, neighborhood saloons had often attracted working-class and lower-middle-class men, but the new speakeasies were often more glamorous, drawing an upper- and middle-class clientele, women as well as men. **Bootlegging**—production and sale of illegal beverages—flourished. Some bootleggers brewed only small amounts of beer and sold it to their neighbors. In the cities, bootlegging provided criminals with a fresh and lucrative source of income, part of which they used to buy influence in city politics and protection from police.

In Chicago, **Al Capone**'s gang counted nearly a thousand members and, in 1927, took in more than $100 million (equivalent to $1.2 billion today)— $60 million of it from bootlegged liquor. Capone faced competition from other gangs, and gang warfare raged across Chicago throughout the 1920s, producing some five hundred slayings. In 1931 federal officials finally managed to convict Capone—of income-tax evasion—and sent him to prison.

Elsewhere, other gangsters—many of recent immigrant background, including Italians, Irish, Germans, and Jews—also found riches in bootlegging, gambling, prostitution, and **racketeering**. Through racketeering they gained power in some labor unions. The gangs, killings, and corruption confirmed other Americans' long-standing distrust of cities and immigrants, and they clung to the vision of a dry America as the best hope for renewing traditional values.

■ **Eighteenth Amendment** (1919) constitutional amendment forbidding the manufacture, sale, or transportation of alcoholic beverages.

repeal The act of canceling a law or regulation; repeal of a constitutional amendment requires a new amendment.

bootlegging Illegal production, distribution, or sale of liquor.

■ **Al Capone** Italian-born American gangster who ruthlessly ruled the Chicago underworld until imprisoned in 1931.

racketeering Crimes such as extortion, loansharking, and bribery, sometimes behind the front of a seemingly legitimate business or union.

Fundamentalism and the Campaign Against Evolution

Fundamentalism, a movement within Protestant Christianity, represented another effort to maintain traditional values. Where Christian modernists tried to reconcile their religious beliefs with modern science, fundamentalists rejected anything—including science—they considered incompatible with the Scriptures. Every word of the Bible, they argued, is the revealed word of God. The fundamentalist movement grew throughout the first quarter of the twentieth century, led by figures such as Billy Sunday, a baseball player turned evangelist.

In the early 1920s, some fundamentalists focused on **evolution** as contrary to the Bible. Biologists cite evolution to explain how living things developed over millions of years. The Bible, however, states that God created the world and all living things in six days. Fundamentalists saw in evolution not just a challenge to the Bible's account of creation but also a challenge to religion itself.

William Jennings Bryan, former Democratic presidential candidate and secretary of state, fixed on the evolution controversy after 1920. His energy, eloquence, and enormous following guaranteed that the issue received wide attention. "It is better," Bryan wrote, "to trust in the Rock of Ages than to know the age of rocks." Bryan played a central role in the most famous dispute over evolution—the Scopes trial.

In March 1925, the Tennessee legislature made it illegal for public school teachers to teach evolution. When the American Civil Liberties Union (ACLU) offered to defend a teacher willing to challenge the law, John T. Scopes, who taught biology in Dayton, accepted. Bryan volunteered to assist the local prosecutors, who faced an ACLU defense team

that included the famous attorney **Clarence Darrow**. Bryan claimed that the only issue was the right of the people to regulate public education as they saw fit, but Darrow insisted he was there to prevent "ignoramuses from controlling the education of the United States."

The court proceedings were carried nationwide via radio. Toward the end of the trial, in a surprising move, Darrow called Bryan to the witness stand as an authority on the Bible. Under Darrow's withering questioning, Bryan revealed that he knew little about findings in archaeology, geology, and linguistics that cast doubt on Biblical accounts, and he also admitted, to the dismay of many fundamentalists, that he did not always interpret the words of the Bible literally. "Darrow never spared him," one reporter wrote. "It was masterful, but it was pitiful." Bryan died a few days later. Scopes was found guilty, but the Tennessee Supreme Court threw out his sentence on a technicality, preventing appeal.

Nativism, Immigration Restriction, and Eugenics

Throughout the 1920s, nativism and discrimination were widespread. **Restrictive covenants** attached to real-estate titles prohibited future sale to particular groups, typically African Americans and Jews. Exclusive colleges placed quotas on the number of Jews admitted each year, and some companies refused to hire Jews. In 1920 Henry Ford accused Jewish bankers of controlling the American economy, then suggested an international Jewish conspiracy to control virtually everything from baseball to bolshevism. After Aaron Sapiro, an attorney, sued Ford for defamation and challenged him to prove his claims, Ford retracted his charges and apologized in 1927. Ethnic hostility sometimes turned violent, as when rioting townspeople beat and stoned Italians in West Frankfort, Illinois, in 1920.

Laws to restrict immigration resulted in significant part from nativist anxieties that immigrants, especially those from southern and eastern Europe, were transforming the United States. Advocates of restriction redoubled their efforts in response to an upsurge in immigration after the war—430,000 in 1920 and 805,000 in 1921, with more than half from southern and eastern Europe. Efforts to cut off immigration were not new. However, the presence of many German Americans during the war with Germany, the Red Scare and fear of foreign radicalism, and the continued influx of poor immigrants at a time of growing unemployment came together with nativism after the war. Congress reacted, limiting immigration with a temporary measure in 1921, then in 1924 passing a permanent law, the **National Origins Act**, which restricted total immigration to

---

■ **fundamentalism** Originally an early twentieth-century Protestant Christian religious movement that emphasized the literal truth of the Bible and opposed efforts to reconcile the Bible with scientific knowledge; applied today to any religious movement based on uncompromising adherence to a set of principles.

■ **evolution** The central organizing principle of the biological sciences, which holds that genetic change in organisms over generations can produce new species; it includes the concept that humans evolved from nonhuman ancestors.

■ **Clarence Darrow** A leading trial lawyer of the early twentieth century, who often defended those challenging the status quo.

restrictive covenant Provision in a property title that prohibits subsequent sale to specified groups, especially people of color and Jews.

■ **National Origins Act** 1924 congressional act establishing quotas for immigration to the United States; it limited immigration from southern and eastern Europe and prohibited immigration from Asia.

It Matters Today

150,000 per year. Quotas for each country were set at 2 percent of the number of Americans whose ancestors came from that country, but all Asians were excluded. In attempting to freeze the ethnic composition of the nation, the law reflected the arguments of those nativists who contended that immigrants from southern and eastern Europe and Asia made less desirable citizens than people from northern and western Europe. However, the law permitted unrestricted immigration from Canada and Latin America.

In its transparent effort to restrict immigration from southern and eastern Europe while admitting larger numbers from northern and western Europe, the National Origins Act also reflects the concerns of one group of **eugenics** advocates. The eugenics movement developed in the late nineteenth and early twentieth century; its proponents hoped to use genetics to improve the human race by selective breeding. Some eugenicists argued that most southern and eastern Europeans showed undesirable genetic traits, and therefore favored barring them from immigration. Other eugenicists focused on mental ability or mental illness to argue that those with "undesirable" traits should not be permitted to marry or should be sterilized. In 1927, the U.S. Supreme Court approved a Virginia law permitting the state to sterilize those considered mentally retarded; such state laws were widespread by the 1920s, and most continued in force until the 1960s.

The Ku Klux Klan

Nativism, anti-Catholicism, anti-Semitism, and fear of radicalism all contributed to the spectacular growth of the Ku Klux Klan in the early 1920s. The original Klan, created during Reconstruction to intimidate former slaves, had long since died out. But D. W. Griffith's hugely popular film *The Birth of a Nation*, released in 1915, glorified the old Klan.

The new Klan claimed to be devoted to traditional American values, old-fashioned Protestant Christianity, and white supremacy; it opposed Catholics, Jews, immigrants, and blacks, along with bootleggers, corrupt politicians, and gamblers. Growth came slowly at first but surged to 5 million members nationwide by 1925.

The Klan was strong in the South, Midwest, West, and Southwest, and in towns and cities as well as rural areas. Klan members participated actively

---

eugenics The notion that information about genetics should be used to improve the human race.

This image is from a Ku Klux Klan pamphlet published in the mid-1920s.

NEW SOCIAL PATTERNS IN THE 1920S

★ What continuities and changes characterized racial and ethnic relations during the 1920s?

★ Is it appropriate to describe the 1920s as "the lean years" for working people?

★ How did gender roles and definitions change in the 1920s?

The Harlem Renaissance and Klan nightriders represent polar extremes of racial relations in the 1920s. For most people of color, the realities of daily life fell somewhere in between. For working people, the 1920s represented what one historian has termed "the lean years" when earlier gains were lost and unions remained on the defensive. For women, the 1920s opened with the political victory of suffrage, but the unity mustered in support of that measure soon broke down.

Ethnicity and Race: North, South, and West

Discrimination against Jews, violence against Italians, and the Klan's appeal to white Protestants all point to the continuing significance of ethnicity in American life during the 1920s. Throughout the decade, racial relations remained deeply troubled at best, violent at worst.

The Harlem Renaissance helped produce greater appreciation for black music and other accomplishments, but racial discrimination still confronted most African Americans, no matter where they lived. A few gained better jobs by moving north, but many found work only in low-paying service occupations. In nearly every city, social pressures and restrictive covenants limited access to desirable housing. Those who did succeed sometimes became targets for racial hostility, like the black physician whose home was attacked by a white mob when he moved into a white Detroit neighborhood in 1925. A race riot devastated Tulsa, Oklahoma, in 1921, leaving nearly 40 confirmed dead (with blacks outnumbering whites by more than two to one), hundreds injured, and 1,400 black businesses and homes burned. Rumors circulated of hundreds more buried in mass graves.

The NAACP continued to lobby for a federal anti-lynching law, but southern legislators defeated each attempt, arguing against any federal interference in the police power of the states. In its efforts to combat lynching, the NAACP worked to educate the public by publicizing violence against blacks.

In the eastern United States, North, and South, race relations usually meant black-white relations. In the West, race relations were always more complex, and became more so in the years around World War I, when Filipinos began to arrive in Hawai`i and on the West Coast. Most of them worked in agriculture and

in local politics, and Klan leaders exerted powerful political influence in some communities and state governments, notably Texas, Oklahoma, Kansas, Oregon, and Indiana. In Oklahoma, the Klan led a successful impeachment campaign against a governor who tried to restrict it. In Oregon, the Klan claimed responsibility for a 1922 law aimed at eliminating Catholic schools. (The Supreme Court ruled the law unconstitutional.) Many local and state elections in 1924 divided along pro- and anti-Klan lines.

Extensive corruption underlay the Klan's self-righteous rhetoric. Some Klan leaders joined primarily for personal gain, both legal (from recruiting) and illegal (mostly from political payoffs). Some shamelessly violated the morality they preached. In 1925, D. C. Stephenson, Grand Dragon of Indiana and a nationally prominent Klan leader, was convicted of second-degree murder after the death of a woman who had accused him of raping her. When the governor refused to pardon him, Stephenson produced records proving the corruption of the governor, a member of Congress, the mayor of Indianapolis, and other officials. Klan membership fell sharply amid factional disputes and further evidence of fraud and corruption.

African Americans intensified their efforts to end lynching. This protest was held in Washington, D.C., in 1922. The NAACP's efforts to secure a federal anti-lynching law were repeatedly defeated by southerners in Congress.

aboard ships. Sikhs from India also entered the West Coast work force, mainly as agricultural laborers.

California had long led the way among western states with laws discriminating against Asian Americans. By the 1920s, other western states had copied California laws forbidding Asian immigrants to own or lease land. Westerners, especially Californians, also had a lengthy record of violence against Asians. In 1930, for example, a white mob killed a Filipino farm worker in Watsonville, California.

Some Asian immigrants and Asian Americans fought discrimination through the courts, but with little success. In the early 1920s, the U.S. Supreme Court affirmed that only white persons and persons of African descent could become naturalized citizens, denying citizenship to persons born in Asia. The U.S. Supreme Court also ruled that Mississippi could require a Chinese American schoolchild to attend a segregated school established for African Americans.

Beginnings of Change in Federal Indian Policy

During the 1920s, several events began to converge in support of changes in federal policy toward American Indians. In the early 1920s, Interior Secretary Albert Fall tried to lease parts of reservations to white developers and to extinguish Pueblo Indians' title to lands along the Rio Grande. Fall's proposals, especially the Pueblo land issue, led directly to organization by John Collier of the **American Indian Defense Association** (AIDA), in 1923.

Collier, a social worker, and the AIDA soon emerged as leading voices for changes in federal Indian policy. They sought better health and educational services on reservations, creation of tribal governments, tolerance of Indian religious ceremonies and other customs, and an end to land allotments—all in all, changes away from the policy of forced assimilation toward a policy of recognizing Indian cultures and values. Political pressure by AIDA and similar groups, along with political efforts by Indians themselves, secured several new laws favorable to Indians, including full citizenship for all Native Americans. These efforts laid the basis for a significant shift in federal policy in the 1930s.

Mexican Americans

California and the Southwest have been home to many Mexican and Mexican American families since the region was part of Mexico. Those states attracted growing numbers of Mexican immigrants after 1910. Many Mexicans went north, most to Texas and California, to escape the revolution and civil war that devastated their nation from 1910 into the 1920s. Nearly 700,000 Mexicans legally entered the United States between 1910 and 1930, and probably the same number came illegally.

■ **American Indian Defense Association** (AIDA) Organization founded in 1923 to defend the rights of American Indians; it pushed for an end to land allotment and a return to tribal government.

These sugar-beet fieldworkers near Fort Collins, in northern Colorado, about 1928, include men, women, and boys. Unlike most previous ethnic groups who worked in western agriculture, Mexicans often came as families and often worked in the fields as family units.

The agricultural economies of the Southwest were changing. By 1925, the Southwest was relying on irrigation to produce 40 percent of the nation's fruits and vegetables, crops that were highly labor-intensive. By the late 1920s, Mexicans made up 80 to 85 percent of farm laborers in that region. At the same time, the southwestern states also experienced large increases in their Anglo populations. These changes in population and economy reshaped relations between Anglos and Mexicans.

In south Texas, many Anglo newcomers looked on Mexicans as what one Anglo called a "partly colored race," and white newcomers tried to import elements of southern black-white relations, including disfranchisement and segregation. Disfranchisement was unsuccessful, but some schools were segregated despite Mexican opposition. The League of United Latin American Citizens (LULAC) could sometimes halt discrimination by businesses—but only occasionally.

In California, Mexican workers' efforts to organize and strike for better pay and working conditions were often broken quickly and brutally by local authorities or growers' private guards. Leaders were likely to be deported. Nevertheless, Mexican labor had become vital to agriculture, and growers opposed any restrictions on immigration from Mexico—the National

Origins Act of 1924 permitted unlimited immigration from the Western Hemisphere.

Not all immigrants from Mexico stayed in the Southwest. As the doors to European immigration closed with the new immigration law, midwestern manufacturers began to recruit Mexican workers to work in steel mills, meatpacking plants, and auto factories. By 1930, significant numbers of Mexican Americans were to be found in such industrial cities as Chicago, Detroit, and Gary.

Labor on the Defensive

Difficulties in establishing unions among Mexican workers mirrored a larger failure of unions in the 1920s. When unions tried to recover lost purchasing power by calling strikes in 1919 and 1920, nearly all failed. After 1921, employers increasingly challenged Progressive Era legislation benefiting workers. The Supreme Court responded by limiting workers' rights, voiding laws that eliminated child labor, and striking down minimum-wage laws for women and children.

Many companies undertook anti-union drives. Arguing that unions were unnecessary and either corrupt or radical, some employers used the term **American Plan** to describe their refusal to deal with unions. At the same time, some companies began to provide workers with programs such as insurance, retirement pensions, cafeterias, paid vacations, and stock purchase plans, an approach sometimes called **welfare capitalism**. Such innovations stemmed from both genuine concern about workers' well-being and the expectation that such improvements would increase productivity and discourage unionization.

■ **American Plan** Term used by some employers in the 1920s to describe their policy of refusing to negotiate with unions.

■ **welfare capitalism** Program adopted by some employers to provide employee benefits such as lunchrooms, paid vacations, bonuses, and profit-sharing plans.

The 1920s marked the first period of prosperity since the 1830s when union membership declined, falling from 5 million in 1920 to 3.6 million in 1929, a 28 percent decline at a time when the total work force increased by 15 percent. AFL leaders, insisting on separate unions for each skill group, made no serious effort to organize the great mass-production industries. Some unions suffered from internal battles—the International Ladies' Garment Workers' Union lost two-thirds of its members during power struggles between Socialists and Communists.

The Communists sought power within other unions, but the membership of the **Communist Party of the United States** (CP) never approached the numbers claimed by the Socialist Party before World War I. In 1929 the CP counted only 9,300 members. Always closely tied to the leadership of the Soviet Union, the CP labored strenuously to organize workers throughout the 1920s but had little success.

Changes in Women's Lives

The attention given to the flapper should not detract from important changes in women's gender roles during these years. Significant changes occurred in two arenas: family and politics.

Marriage among white middle-class women and men came increasingly to be valued as companionship between two partners. Although the ideal of marriage was often expressed in terms of man and woman taking equal responsibility for a relationship, the actual responsibility for the smooth functioning of the family typically fell on the woman.

Many women in the 1920s seem to have increased their control over decisions about childbearing. Usually in American history, prosperity brings increases in the birth rate. In the 1920s, however, changing social values together with more options for birth control resulted in fewer births. Women who came of childbearing age in the 1910s and 1920s are distinctive in three ways when compared with women of both earlier and later periods: (1) they had fewer children on average, (2) more of them had no children at all, and (3) far fewer had very large families (see Figure 21.3).

■ **Communist Party of the United States** (CP) Party organized in 1919, devoted to replacing capitalism and private property with their version of socialism.

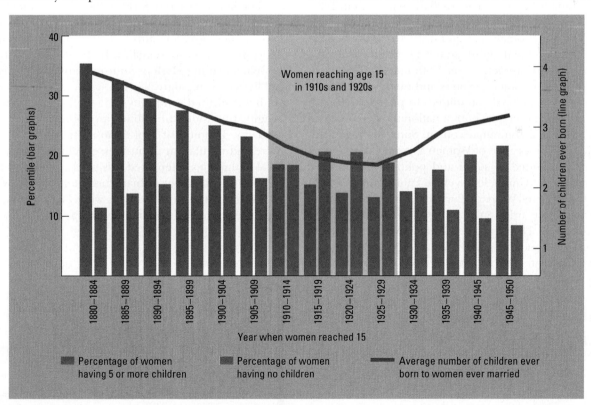

FIGURE 21.3 Changing Patterns of Childbearing Among Women
This figure depicts three different choices regarding family size: (1) the number of children born to women ever married, (2) the percentage of women ever married having large families, and (3) the percentage of women ever married having no children at all. Childbearing ages are considered to be between 15 and 45.

Sources: Series B42–48, U.S. Bureau of the Census, Historical Statistics of the United States, Colonial Times to 1970, Bicentennial Edition, 2 vols. (Washington, D.C.: U.S. Government Printing Office, 1975), I: 53;. Table 270, U.S. Bureau of the Census, 1980 Census of Population (Washington, D.C.: U.S. Government Printing Office, 1984), 1–103.

This declining birth rate reflected, in part, some success for earlier efforts to secure wider availability of birth-control information and devices, for example, diaphragms, but it is also typical that the birth rate falls as a society becomes more urban. The birth-control movement also gained the backing of some male physicians and became a more respectable, middle-class reform movement. By 1925, the American Medical Association had declared its support for birth control, and the Rockefeller Foundation began to fund medical research into contraception methods. Nevertheless, until 1936, federal law restricted public distribution of information about contraception, and many women continued to rely on illegal abortions to terminate unwanted pregnancies. In Clara Bow's Hollywood, abortions became almost routine as a way for actresses to meet their contractual obligations to perform in films and to avoid public scandal.

Throughout the 1920s, working-class women still struggled to stretch their finances to cover their families' needs. As before, some women and children worked outside the home because the family needed additional income. The proportion of women working for wages remained quite stable during the 1920s, at about one in four. The proportion of married women working for wages increased, though, from 23 percent of the female labor force in 1920 to 29 percent in 1930.

After the implementation of the Nineteenth Amendment (woman suffrage) in 1920, the unity of the suffrage movement disintegrated in disputes over the proper role for women voters. Both major political parties welcomed women as voters and modified the structure of their national committees to provide that each state be represented by both a national committeeman and a national committeewoman. Some suffrage activists joined the League of Women Voters, a nonpartisan group committed to social and political reform. The Congressional Union, led by Alice Paul, converted itself into the National Woman's Party and, after 1923, focused its efforts on securing an **Equal Rights Amendment** to the Constitution. The League of Women Voters disagreed, arguing that such an amendment would endanger laws providing protection for women.

Development of Gay and Lesbian Subcultures

In the 1920s, gay and lesbian subcultures became more established and relatively open in several cities. *The Captive,* a play about lesbians, opened in New York in 1926, and some movies included unmistakable homosexual references. Novels with gay and lesbian characters were published in the late 1920s and early 1930s. In Chicago, the Society for Human Rights was organized to advocate equal treatment. A relatively open gay and lesbian community emerged in Harlem, where some prominent figures of the Renaissance were gay or bisexual. The annual Hamilton Lodge drag ball in Harlem attracted as many as seven thousand revelers and spectators of all races.

At the same time, however, more and more psychiatrists and psychologists were labeling homosexuality a **perversion**. By the 1920s, the work of **Sigmund Freud** had become well known, and most psychiatrists and psychologists labeled homosexuality a sexual disorder that required a cure, though no "cure" ever proved viable. Thus Freud's theories may have been liberating for heterosexual relations, but they proved harmful for same-sex relations.

The new medical definitions were slow to work their way into the larger society. The armed forces, for example, continued previous practices, making little effort to prevent homosexuals from enlisting and taking disciplinary action only against behavior that clearly violated the law.

The late 1920s and early 1930s brought increased suppression of gays and lesbians. New state laws gave police greater authority to prosecute open expressions of homosexuality. In 1929 Adam Clayton Powell, a leading Harlem minister, launched a highly publicized campaign against gays. Motion-picture studios instituted a morality code that, among its wide-ranging provisions, prohibited any depiction of homosexuality. The end of Prohibition after 1933 brought increased regulation of businesses selling liquor, and local authorities often used this power to close establishments with gay or lesbian customers. Thus, by the 1930s, many gays and lesbians were becoming more secretive about their sexual identities.

■ **Equal Rights Amendment** Proposed constitutional amendment, first advocated by the National Woman's Party in 1923, to give women in the United States equal rights under the law.

perversion Sexual practice considered abnormal or deviant.

■ **Sigmund Freud** Prominent Austrian psychoanalyst, known for his theory that the sex drive underlies much individual behavior.

THE POLITICS OF PROSPERITY

☆ Compare the attitude of the Harding and Coolidge administrations toward the economy with the attitude of the Roosevelt and Wilson administrations.

☆ How did the third-party candidacy of La Follette in 1924 resemble that of Roosevelt in 1912 and the Populists in 1892?

Sooner or later, nearly all the social and economic developments of the 1920s found their way into politics, from highway construction to prohibition, from immigration restriction to the teaching of evolution, from farm prices to lynching. After 1918, the Republicans resumed the majority role they had exercised from the mid-1890s to 1912, and they continued as the unquestioned majority throughout the 1920s. Progressivism largely disappeared, although some veteran progressives, led by Robert La Follette and George Norris, persisted in seeking to limit corporate power. The Republican administrations of the 1920s shared a faith in the ability of business to establish prosperity and benefit the American people and considered government the partner of business, not its regulator.

Harding's Failed Presidency

Elected in 1920, Warren G. Harding looked presidential—handsome, gray-haired, dignified, warm, outgoing—but had little intellectual depth. For some of his appointments, he chose the most respected leaders of his party, including Charles Evans Hughes for secretary of state, Andrew Mellon for secretary of the Treasury, and Herbert Hoover for secretary of commerce. Harding, however, was most comfortable playing poker with his friends, and he gave hundreds of government jobs to his cronies and political supporters. They turned his administration into one of the most corrupt in American history. As their misdeeds began to come to light, Harding put off taking action until after a trip to Alaska. During his return, on August 2, 1923, he died when a blood vessel burst in his brain.

The full extent of corruption became clear after Harding's death. Albert Fall, secretary of the interior, had accepted huge bribes from oil companies for leases on federal oil reserves at Elk Hills, California, and Teapot Dome, Wyoming. Attorney General Harry Daugherty and others pocketed payoffs to approve the sale of government-held property for less than its value. Daugherty may also have protected bootleggers. The head of the Veterans Bureau swindled the government out of more than $200 million. In all, three cabinet members resigned, four officials went to jail, and five men committed suicide. As if the financial dishonesty were not enough, in 1927 Nan Britton published a book claiming that she had been Harding's mistress, had borne his child, and had carried on trysts with him in the White House.

In the midst of these scandals, hard-pressed and debt-ridden farmers turned to the federal government for help. In 1921 farm organizations worked with senators and representatives to form a bipartisan **Farm Bloc**, which promoted legislation to assist farmers. The bloc enjoyed a substantial boost in the 1922 elections, when distraught farmers across the Midwest turned out conservatives and elected candidates attuned to farmers' problems. Congress passed a few assistance measures in the early 1920s, but none

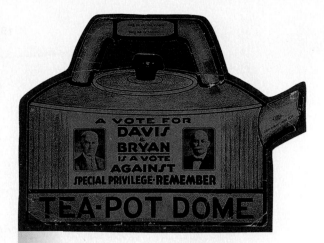

In 1924, the Democrats tried to capitalize on the Republicans' embarrassment over the Teapot Dome scandal. They received little response because the death of Harding brought Calvin Coolidge to the presidency, and Coolidge's personal honesty and morality were unquestioned. Collection of David J. and Janice L. Frent.

addressed the central problems of overproduction and low prices. By 1922, some farm organizations joined with unions, especially unions of railroad workers, to form the Conference for Progressive Political Action and agitate for a new Progressive Party.

The Three-Candidate Presidential Election of 1924

When Harding died, Vice President Calvin Coolidge became president. Fortunately for the Republican Party, the new president exemplified honesty, virtue, and sobriety. In 1924 Republicans quickly chose Coolidge as their candidate for president.

The Democratic convention, however, sank into a long and bitter deadlock. Since the Civil War, the party had divided between southerners (mostly Protestant and committed to white supremacy) and northerners (often city-dwellers and of recent immigrant descent, including many Catholics). In 1924 the Klan was approaching its peak membership and exercised significant influence among many Democratic delegates from the South and parts of the Midwest.

Many northern Democrats wanted to nominate **Al Smith** for president. Highly popular as governor

■ **Farm Bloc** Bipartisan group of senators and representatives formed in 1921 to promote legislation to assist farmers.

■ **Al Smith** New York governor who unsuccessfully sought the Democratic nomination for president in 1924 and was the unsuccessful Democratic candidate for president in 1928; his Catholicism and desire to repeal Prohibition were political liabilities.

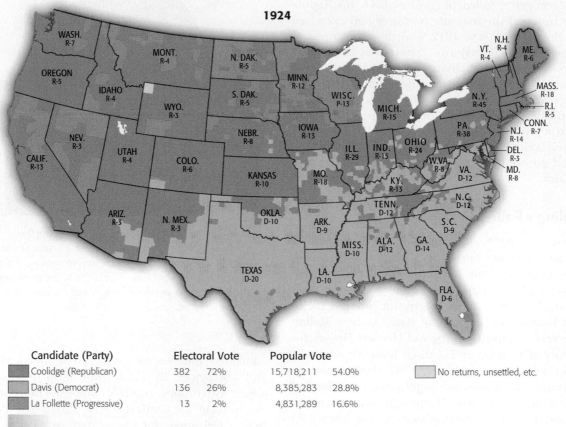

1924

Candidate (Party)	Electoral Vote		Popular Vote	
Coolidge (Republican)	382	72%	15,718,211	54.0%
Davis (Democrat)	136	26%	8,385,283	28.8%
La Follette (Progressive)	13	2%	4,831,289	16.6%

No returns, unsettled, etc.

MAP 21.1 Election of 1924, by County

The presidential election of 1924 was complicated by the campaign of Senator Robert La Follette of Wisconsin, who ran as a Progressive. Much of his support came from the north-central and northwestern regions where the agricultural economy was most hard-hit. Compare this map to Maps 18.1 and 19.2. Copyright © Cengage Learning

of New York, Smith epitomized urban, immigrant America. Catholic and the son of immigrants, he was everything the Klan—and most of the southern convention delegates—opposed. After nine hot days of stalemate and 103 ballots, the exhausted Democrats turned to a virtually unknown compromise candidate, John W. Davis, who had served in the Wilson administration, then became a corporate lawyer. All in all, the convention seemed to confirm the observation by the contemporary humorist Will Rogers: "I belong to no organized political party. I am a Democrat."

Surviving progressives welcomed the independent candidacy of Senator Robert M. La Follette, nominated by a new Progressive Party formed by farmers, unions, and reformers. The La Follette Progressives attacked big business and promoted collective bargaining, reform of politics, public ownership of railroads and water power, and a public referendum on questions of war and peace. La Follette was the first presidential candidate to be endorsed by the American Federation of Labor.

Republican campaigners largely ignored Davis and focused on portraying La Follette as a dangerous radical. Coolidge claimed the key issue was "whether America will allow itself to be degraded into a communistic or socialistic state" or "remain American." Coolidge won with nearly 16 million votes and 54 percent of the total. Davis held on to most traditional Democratic voters, especially in the South, receiving 8 million votes and 29 percent. La Follette carried only his home state of Wisconsin but garnered almost 5 million votes, 17 percent, and did well both in urban working-class neighborhoods and in parts of the rural Midwest and Northwest (see Map 21.1).

The Politics of Business

Committed to limited government and content to let problems work themselves out, Coolidge tried to reduce the significance of the presidency—and succeeded. He announced that "the business of America is business" and believed that the free market would best sustain economic prosperity for all. As president, he set out to prevent government from interfering with business.

Coolidge had little sympathy for efforts to secure federal help for the faltering farm economy. Congress

This cartoon depicts Coolidge playing praise of big business. Big business, dressed like a flapper, wildly dances the Charleston and sings, "Yes Sir, He's My Baby."

tried to address low prices for farm products and persistent agricultural surpluses with the **McNary-Haugen bill**, which would have created federal price supports and authorized the government to buy farm surpluses and sell them abroad. The Farm Bloc pushed the bill through Congress in 1927, but Coolidge vetoed it. The same thing happened in 1928. In contrast, the **Railway Labor Act of 1926** drew on wartime experiences to establish collective bargaining for railroad employees. Passed by overwhelming margins in Congress, the new law met most of the railway unions' demands and effectively removed them from politics.

Andrew Mellon, one of the wealthiest men in the nation, served as secretary of the Treasury throughout the 1920s. Acclaimed by Republicans and business leaders as the greatest secretary of the Treasury since Alexander Hamilton, Mellon argued that high taxes on the wealthy stifled the economy. He secured tax breaks for the affluent, arguing that they would benefit everyone through "productive investments" of the tax savings. Herbert Hoover, secretary of commerce under Harding and Coolidge, urged Coolidge to regulate the increasingly wild use of credit, which contributed to rampant stock market speculation, but Coolidge refused.

Coolidge cut federal spending and staffed federal agencies with people who shared his distaste for too much government. Unlike Harding, Coolidge found honest and competent appointees. Like Harding, he

named probusiness figures to regulatory commissions and put conservative, probusiness judges in the courts. The *Wall Street Journal* described the outcome: "Never before, here or anywhere else, has a government been so completely fused with business."

The 1928 Campaign and the Election of Hoover

In August 1927, President Coolidge told reporters, "I do not choose to run in 1928," stunning the country and his party. Secretary of Commerce Herbert Hoover immediately declared his candidacy, and Republicans found him an ideal candidate, representing what most Americans believed was best about the United States: individual effort and honestly earned success.

Son of a Quaker blacksmith from Iowa, Hoover was orphaned at 10 and grew up believing that hard work was the only way to success. Graduating from Stanford University, he traveled the world as a mining engineer and became a millionaire. When World War I broke out, he turned to public service, organizing relief for Belgium. "This man is not to be stopped anywhere under any circumstance," the Germans noted on his passport. When the United States entered the war, President Wilson named Hoover to head the U.S. Food Administration. By the end of the war, Hoover emerged as an international hero. As secretary of commerce under Harding and Coolidge, he attracted wide support in the business community for his efforts to encourage economic growth through associationalism—voluntary cooperation among otherwise competing groups.

In launching his campaign before thousands of supporters gathered in the Stanford football stadium, Hoover sounded the theme of his candidacy: "We in America today are nearer to the final triumph over poverty than ever before."

The Democrats nominated Al Smith—like Hoover, a self-made man. Unlike Hoover, who had gone to Stanford, Smith's education came on the streets of New York City and as part of Tammany Hall, the Democratic machine that ran the city. As a reform-minded, progressive governor of New York, Smith streamlined state government, improved its efficiency, and supported legislation to set a minimum wage and maximum hours of work and to establish state ownership of hydroelectric plants.

In many places, Smith became the main issue in the campaign. Opponents attacked his Catholic religion, his big-city background, his opposition to Prohibition,

> ■ **McNary-Haugen bill** Farm relief bill providing for government purchase of crop surpluses; Coolidge vetoed it in 1927 and in 1928.
> ■ **Railway Labor Act of 1926** Federal law guaranteeing collective bargaining for railroad employees.

his Tammany connections, and even his New York accent. Anti-Catholic sentiment burned hotly in parts of the country, often fanned by remnants of the Klan. Evangelist Billy Sunday called Smith supporters "damnable whiskey politicians, bootleggers, crooks, pimps and businessmen who deal with them." Thus, for many voters, the choice seemed to be between a candidate who represented hard work and the pious values of small town, old-stock, Protestant America and a candidate who represented Catholics, foreigners, machine politics, and the ugly problems of the cities.

Hoover won easily, with 58 percent of the popular vote. Prosperity and the nation's long-term Republican majority probably would have spelled victory for any competent Republican. Smith's religion and anti-Prohibition stance cost him in the South, where Hoover carried areas that had not voted Republican since Reconstruction. Smith brought Democratic gains in northern cities, partly by drawing to the polls Catholic voters, especially women who had not previously voted.

The first president born west of the Mississippi River, Hoover came to the presidency with definite ideas about both domestic and foreign policy. He set out to be an active president. The role of government, he believed, was to promote cooperation. He warned that once government, especially the federal government, stepped in to solve problems directly, the people gave up some of their freedom, and government became part of the problem. Hoover recognized that the federal government had a responsibility to help find solutions to social and economic problems, but the key word was *help*: Hoover looked to the government to help but not to solve problems by itself.

THE DIPLOMACY OF PROSPERITY

★ What role did the United States play in world affairs during the 1920s?

★ How successful was Hughes at the Washington Naval Conference?

Two realities shaped American foreign policy in the 1920s: rejection of Woodrow Wilson's internationalism and a continuing quest for economic expansion by American business. As president, Harding dismissed any American role in the League of Nations and refused to accept the Treaty of Versailles. Undamaged

unilateral An action taken by a country by itself, as opposed to actions taken jointly with other nations.

multilateral Involving more than two nations (when two nations are involved, the term is *bilateral*).

■ **isolationism** The notion that the United States should avoid political, diplomatic, and military entanglements with other nations.

by the war, American firms outproduced and outtraded the rest of the world. U.S. trade amounted to 30 percent of the world's total, and American firms produced more than 70 percent of the world's oil and almost 50 percent of the world's coal and steel. American bankers loaned billions of dollars to other nations, expanding the global economy.

Harding and Coolidge had neither expertise nor interest in foreign affairs, so they left most foreign policy decisions to their secretaries of state, Charles Evans Hughes and Frank Kellogg. Both were capable men interested in developing American business and influence abroad through what historians have called "independent internationalism." Independent (or **unilateral**) internationalism had two central thrusts: avoidance of **multilateral** commitments—sometimes called **isolationism**—and expansion of economic opportunities overseas. The Commerce and State Departments promoted American business activities worldwide and encouraged private investments in Japan and China. American officials worked to allow U.S. oil companies to drill in Iran, Iraq, the Persian Gulf region, and Saudi Arabia. Their efforts to expand Americans' economic position in Latin America and Europe were quite successful. As president, Hoover and his secretary of state, Henry L. Stimson, followed a similar approach.

The United States and Latin America

When Harding took office in 1921, the United States had troops stationed in Cuba, Panama, Haiti, the Dominican Republic, and Nicaragua (see Map 21.2). During the presidential campaign, Harding had criticized Wilson's "bayonet rule" in Haiti and the Dominican Republic and expressed his intention to end those occupations. To maintain American dominance in the Caribbean, however, U.S. officials wanted stable and friendly local governments. Therefore, American administrators kept some control over national finances and trained each nation's national guard to act as its police force. American troops left Cuba in 1922, the Dominican Republic in 1924, Nicaragua in 1932, and Haiti in 1934. In the Dominican Republic and in Haiti, however, the United States kept control of the customhouse—and tariff revenues—until the 1940s.

When American troops withdrew from the Dominican Republic and Haiti, they left better roads, improved sanitation systems, governments favorable to the United States, and well-equipped national guards. But the years of occupation had not advanced the educational systems, the national economies, or most residents' standard of living. Nor did the United States do much to promote democracy, favoring stability instead—even if it meant accepting dictators such as Rafael Trujillo, who seized power in the Dominican Republic in 1930 and ruled brutally until his death in 1961.

UNITED STATES

ATLANTIC OCEAN

40°N

Cuba
Platt Amendment, 1902–1934
U.S. troops, 1906–1909, 1912, 1917–1922
U.S. companies invest in sugar

Havana, Cuba
U.S. upholds right of intervention at
Pan American Conference, 1928

MEXICO

Gulf of Mexico

Haiti
U.S. troops, 1915–1934
U.S. financial supervision, 1916–1941

BAHAMA IS.
(Gr. Br.)

Mexico
U.S. companies' investments, including railroads
and oil
Constitution of 1917 challenges U.S. interests
Nationalization of foreign oil companies, 1938

Havana **CUBA**

DOMINICAN REP.

Dominican Republic
U.S. troops, 1916–1924
U.S. financial supervision, 1905–1941
Trujillo era, 1930–1961

20°N

HAITI

VIRGIN IS. (U.S./Gr. Br.)

Guatemala
United Fruit Company, coffee
investments

BRITISH
HONDURAS (Gr. Br.)

JAMAICA
(Gr. Br.)

PUERTO RICO
(U.S.)

Virgin Islands
U.S. possession since 1917

HONDURAS

Caribbean Sea

GUATEMALA

NICARAGUA

El Salvador
U.S. companies invest in coffee

EL SALVADOR

COSTA RICA

TRINIDAD
(Gr. Br.)

Puerto Rico
U.S. possession since 1898
Jones Act grants U.S. citizenship, 1917

PANAMA

VENEZUELA

BR. GUIANA (Gr. Br.)
DUTCH GUIANA (Neth.)

Honduras
United Fruit Company investments

FRENCH GUIANA (Fr.)

COLOMBIA

Nicaragua
U.S. financial supervision, 1911–1925
U.S. troops, 1912–1925, 1927–1933
War against Sandino, 1925–1933
Somoza era, 1936–1979

ECUADOR

Venezuela
U.S. companies
invest in oil

Equator–0°

Amazon R.

Panama
U.S. acquired Canal Zone,1903

BRAZIL

PERU

PACIFIC OCEAN

BOLIVIA

Chile
U.S. companies invest
in copper mining

Paraná R.

20°S

PARAGUAY

N

CHILE

URUGUAY

ARGENTINA

0   500   1000 Km.

0   500   1000 Mi.

40°S

40°W

FALKLAND ISLANDS
(Gr. Br.)

80°W   60°W

MAP 21.2   The United States and Latin America Between the Wars

During the 1920s, the United States played an active role throughout Central America and the Caribbean and,
to a lesser extent, in South America. This sometimes included military intervention, but during the 1920s, political
and economic pressures largely replaced military force as the means for protecting U.S. interests.

Dwight Morrow, U.S. ambassador to Mexico, and Mexican president Plutarco Calles (*right*), shaking hands. Morrow proved a highly successful ambassador, defusing tensions between the two countries. At Morrow's invitation, Charles Lindbergh visited Mexico. While he was there, he met Morrow's daughter Anne; they were married in 1929.

© Bettmann/Corbis.

In Nicaragua, American forces left in 1925 but returned in mid-1926 to protect the pro-American government when civil war broke out. Coolidge sent Henry L. Stimson to negotiate a peace agreement that ended most fighting in 1927. However, **Augusto Sandino**, who wanted to rid Nicaragua of American influence, rejected the peace agreement and continued guerrilla warfare.

Elsewhere in Latin America, American involvement was not military, but commercial. Throughout Central America, American firms such as the United Fruit Company purchased thousands of acres for plantations to produce, especially bananas and coffee,

for the American and European market. United Fruit came to exercise a powerful influence in several Central American countries. In Venezuela and Colombia, American oil companies, with State Department help, negotiated contracts for drilling rights, outmaneuvering European oil companies. U.S. investments in Latin America rose from nearly $2 billion in 1919 to over $3.5 billion in 1929.

Oil played a key role in relations with Mexico. The Mexican constitution of 1917 limited foreign ownership, and Mexico moved to **nationalize** its subsurface resources, including oil. American businessmen strongly objected. By 1925, American oilmen and some members of the Coolidge administration called for military action to protect American oil interests in Mexico, But Coolidge sent Dwight W. Morrow—a college friend—as ambassador to Mexico with instructions "to keep us out of war with Mexico." Morrow understood Mexican nationalism and pride, knew some Spanish, and cultivated a personal relationship with Mexican president Plutarco Calles. He succeeded in reducing tensions and delayed nationalization of oil until 1938. Following the election of 1928, president-elect Hoover undertook a goodwill tour of eleven Latin American countries, seeking better relations.

America and the European Economy

World War I shattered much of Europe physically and economically. The American economy soared to unprecedented heights, however, and the United States became the world's leading creditor nation. After the war, Republican leaders joined with business figures to expand exports and restrict imports. In 1922 the **Fordney-McCumber Tariff** set the highest rates ever for most imported industrial goods. The tariff not only limited European imports but also made it difficult for Europeans to acquire the dollars needed to repay their war debts to the United States.

While Harding and Coolidge sought debt repayment, Secretary of State Hughes and Secretary of Commerce Hoover worked to expand American economic interests in Europe, especially Germany. They believed that if Germany recovered economically and paid its $33 billion war reparations, other European nations would also recover and repay their debts. With government encouragement, over $4 billion in American investments flowed into Europe, doubling American investments there. General Motors purchased Opel, a German automobile firm. Ford built the largest automobile factory outside the United States, in England, and constructed a tractor factory in the Soviet Union.

Even so, Germany could not make its reparation payments, defaulting in 1923 to France and Belgium. France responded by sending troops to occupy Germany's **Ruhr Valley**, a key economic region, igniting an international crisis. Hughes sent Charles G. Dawes, a Chicago banker and prominent Republican, to resolve

■ **Augusto Sandino** Nicaraguan guerrilla leader who resisted Nicaraguan and American troops from 1925 to 1933 and was murdered in 1934 by order of Anastasio Somoza, whose family remained in power until 1979, when they were ousted by rebels calling themselves Sandinistas.

nationalize To convert an industry or enterprise from private to government ownership and control.

■ **Fordney-McCumber Tariff** Protective tariff passed by Congress in 1922 that raised tariff rates to record levels and provoked foreign reprisals.

Ruhr Valley Region surrounding the Ruhr River in northwestern Germany, containing major industrial cities and valuable coal mines.

In the Wider World

the situation. Under the **Dawes Plan**, American bankers loaned $2.5 billion to Germany for economic development, and the Germans promised to pay $2 billion in reparations to the European Allies, who, in turn, were to pay $2.5 billion in war debts to the United States. This circular flow of capital was the subject of jokes at the time but worked fairly well until 1929, when the Depression ended nearly all loans and payments.

Encouraging International Cooperation

Committed to independent internationalism, Republican policymakers of the 1920s also understood that some international cooperation was necessary to achieve policy goals and solve international problems. On such issues, they were willing to cooperate with other nations and enter into international agreements, but only with the understanding that the United States was not entering an alliance or otherwise agreeing to commit resources or troops in defense of another nation.

Disarmament was such an issue. The destruction caused by World War I had spurred pacifism and calls for disarmament. In the United States, support for arms cuts was widespread and vocal. In early 1921, Senator William E. Borah of Idaho suggested an international conference to reduce the size of the world's navies. Fearing that naval expenditures would prevent tax cuts, Treasury Secretary Mellon and many members of Congress joined the disarmament chorus.

American policymakers had other reasons for promoting disarmament, notably concerns about Japan. The United States and Britain had the largest navies, roughly equal in strength, and had no interest in further naval construction. Japan, the next largest naval power, wanted to expand its navy. Americans worried that Japanese pressures on China could endanger Chinese territory and the Open Door policy. Harding and Hughes therefore agreed to host international discussions on limiting the size of navies and ensuring the status quo in China. In November 1921, Harding invited the major naval powers to Washington to discuss reducing "the crushing burdens of military and naval establishments."

When the delegates assembled for the **Washington Naval Conference**, Hughes shocked them with a radical proposal: scrap nearly 2 million tons of warships, mostly battleships. He also called for a ten-year ban on naval construction and limits on the size of navies that would keep the Japanese well behind the British and Americans. Hughes suggested a ratio of 5 to 5 to 3 for the United States, Britain, and Japan, with Italy and France allocated 1.7 each. Hughes's plan gained immediate support among the American public and most of the nations attending—but not Japan. The Japanese called it an insult and demanded equality. Discussions dragged on for two months, but the Japanese finally agreed. U.S. intelligence had broken the Japanese diplomatic code, so Hughes knew that the Japanese delegates had orders to concede if he held firm.

In February 1922, the United States, Britain, Japan, France, and Italy agreed to build no more **capital ships** for ten years and to abide by the 5:5:3:1.7:1.7 ratio for future shipbuilding. A British observer commented that Hughes had sunk more British ships in one speech "than all the admirals of the world." The powers also agreed to prohibit the use of poison gas and not to

■ **Dawes Plan** Arrangement for collecting World War I reparations from Germany; it scheduled annual payments and stabilized German currency.

■ **Washington Naval Conference** International conference in 1921–1922; produced agreements to limit naval armaments and prevent conflict in East Asia and the Pacific.

capital ships A navy's largest, most heavily armed ships; at the Washington Naval Conference, capital ships were those over 10,000 tons and carrying guns with at least an 8-inch bore.

Several members of the advisory committee to the U.S. delegation to the Washington Naval Conference, appointed by President Harding to advise the official delegates from various perspectives and help publicize the conference. The committee included a few business leaders, two labor leaders, four leaders of women's organizations, General John J. Pershing (*second from the left*), Secretary of Commerce Herbert Hoover (*far right*), and several former members of Congress, mostly Republicans but including a few Democrats and progressives. Katherine Philips Edson (*fourth from the left*) was an important leader of California progressivism.

attack one another's Asian possessions. The **Nine-Power Pact** affirmed the sovereignty and territorial boundaries of China and guaranteed equal commercial access to China, thereby maintaining the Open Door.

Hughes considered the meetings successful, though critics complained that there were no enforcement provisions and no mention of smaller ships, including submarines. Other attempts to reduce armaments had mixed outcomes. In 1930, Britain, the United States, and Japan established ratios for cruisers and destroyers similar to those of the Washington Conference. By the mid-1930s, however, Japan's demands for naval equality ended British and American cooperation and spurred new naval construction by all three.

Many Americans and Europeans applauded the achievements of the Washington Naval Conference but wanted to go further. In 1923 Senator Borah introduced a resolution in the Senate to outlaw war. In 1924 La Follette campaigned for a national referendum as

a requirement for declaring war. In 1927 the French foreign minister, Aristide Briand, suggested a pact formally outlawing war between the France and the United States, privately hoping such an agreement would commit the United States to aid France if attacked. Secretary of State Kellogg instead suggested a multinational statement opposing war, thereby removing any hint of an American commitment to any nation. On August 27, 1928, the United States and fourteen other nations, including Britain, France, Germany, Italy, and Japan, signed the Pact of Paris, or **Kellogg-Briand Pact**, renouncing war "as an instrument of national policy" and agreeing to settle disputes peacefully. Eventually sixty-four nations signed, but the pact included no enforcement provisions, and nearly every **signatory** reserved its right to self-defense.

Thus, late in 1928, American independent internationalism seemed a success. Investments and loans by American businesses were fueling an expansive world economy and contributing to American prosperity. Avoiding entangling alliances, the United States had protected its Asian and Pacific interests against Japan, while protecting China and promoting disarmament and world peace. In Latin America, the United States had withdrawn some troops from the Caribbean, avoided intervention in Mexico, and tried to broker a peace in Nicaragua. Foreign policies based on economic expansion and noncoercive diplomacy appeared to be establishing a promising era of cooperation and peace in world affairs.

■ **Nine-Power Pact** 1922 agreement by Britain, France, Italy, Japan, the United States, China, the Netherlands, Portugal, and Belgium to recognize China and affirm the Open Door.

■ **Kellogg-Briand Pact** 1928 treaty by fifteen nations, including Britain, France, Germany, the United States, and Japan, renouncing war as a means of solving international disputes.

signatory One who has signed a treaty or other document.

Individual Voices

Sexuality and Innuendo in Movie Advertising

The great popularity of movies in the 1920s means that social historians are interested in the messages conveyed by the films and ways that the films may have influenced people's behavior. The relatively rapid growth of motion pictures was also accompanied by the appearance of movie ads in newspapers, like the ones shown here, and the advertising posters shown earlier in the chapter. These ads survive as useful sources even if the films, in some cases, no longer exist. The ads also tell us what the filmmakers thought would make people want to buy tickets.

Flaming Youth, at Loew's State theater, ad in *Los Angeles Times;* December 31, 1923.

❶ What do these ads suggest regarding the depiction of sexuality in these films?

❷ The 1925 film *Quo Vadis* was one of several based on the novel by that name by Henryk Sienkiewicz. Set in ancient Rome, the novel depicts the love between a young Christian woman and an upper-class Roman. Can you tell from this ad that the original novel was about the spiritual power of Christianity?

Quo Vadis, at the Apollo theater, ad in *New York Times,* March 1, 1925.

❸ How would you determine whether the movies were as titillating as their advertising suggests? Keep in mind that not all films have survived from the 1920s.

❹ Could these films have contributed to changing attitudes toward sexuality? How could you research such a hypothesis?

617

Study Tools

SUMMARY

The 1920s were a decade of prosperity. Unemployment was low, productivity grew steadily, and many Americans fared well. Sophisticated advertising campaigns created bright expectations, and installment buying freed consumers from paying cash. Many consumers bought more and bought on credit—stimulating manufacturing and expanding personal debt. Expectations of continuing prosperity also encouraged speculation. The stock market boomed, but agriculture did not share in this prosperity.

During the Roaring Twenties, Americans experienced significant social change. The automobile, radio, and movies, abetted by immigration restriction, produced a more homogeneous culture. Many American intellectuals, however, rejected the consumer-oriented culture. During the 1920s, African Americans produced an outpouring of significant art, literature, and music. Some young people rejected traditional constraints, and one result was the emergence of a youth culture.

Not all Americans embraced change. Some tried instead to maintain or restore earlier cultural values. The outcomes were mixed. Prohibition was largely unsuccessful. Fundamentalism grew and prompted a campaign against the teaching of evolution. Nativism helped produce significant new restrictions on immigration. The Ku Klux Klan, committed to nativism, traditional values, and white supremacy, experienced nationwide growth until 1925, but membership declined sharply thereafter.

Discrimination and occasional violence continued to affect the lives of people of color. Federal Indian policy had long stressed assimilation and allotment, but some groups successfully promoted different policies based on respect for Indian cultural values. Immigrants from Mexico came especially to California, Texas, and the Southwest. Some Mexicans working in agriculture tried, in vain, to organize unions. Nearly all unions faced strong opposition from employers. Some older gender roles for women broke down as women gained the right to vote and exercised more control over having children. A gay and lesbian subculture became more visible, especially in cities.

The politics of the era were marked by greater conservatism than before World War I. Warren G. Harding was a poor judge of character, and some of his appointees accepted bribes and disgraced their chief. Harding and his successor, Calvin Coolidge, expected government to act as a partner with business, and their economic policies minimized regulation and encouraged speculation. With some exceptions, progressive reform disappeared from politics, and efforts to secure federal assistance for farmers failed. The federal government was strongly conservative, staunchly probusiness, and

CHRONOLOGY
America in the 1920s

1908	Henry Ford introduces Model T
	General Motors formed
1914	Universal Negro Improvement Association founded
1914–1918	War in Europe
1920	Eighteenth Amendment (Prohibition) takes effect
	Nineteenth Amendment (women suffrage) takes effect
	Warren G. Harding elected president
1920–1921	Nationwide recession
1921	Farm Bloc formed
1921–1922	Washington Naval Conference
1922	Fordney-McCumber Tariff
	Sinclair Lewis's *Babbitt*
1923	Harding dies; Calvin Coolidge becomes president
	Jean Toomer's *Cane*
	American Indian Defense Association formed
	France occupies Ruhr Valley
1923–1927	Harding administration scandals revealed

1924	National Origins Act
	Coolidge elected
	Full citizenship for American Indians
	Dawes Plan
	U.S. forces withdraw from Dominican Republic
1924–1929	Great Bull Market
1925	Scopes trial
	F. Scott Fitzgerald's *The Great Gatsby*
	Ku Klux Klan claims 5 million members
1926	Florida real-estate boom collapses
	Railway Labor Act of 1926
1927	Charles Lindbergh's transatlantic flight
	Duke Ellington conducts jazz at Cotton Club
1928	Ford introduces Model A
	Kellogg-Briand Pact
	Herbert Hoover elected
1929	Great Depression begins

unwilling to regulate economic activity. Herbert Hoover defeated Al Smith in the 1928 presidential election, in which the values of an older, rural America seemed to be pitted against those of the new, urban, immigrant society.

During the 1920s, the United States followed a policy of independent internationalism that stressed voluntary cooperation among nations, while at the same time enhancing opportunities for American business around the world. Relations with Latin America improved somewhat, and the Washington Naval Conference held out the hope for preventing a naval arms race.

FOCUS QUESTIONS

If you have mastered this chapter, you should be able to answer these questions and to explain the terms that follow the questions.

1. ☆ *What was the basis for the economic expansion of the 1920s?*

2. ☆ *What weaknesses existed within the economy?*

3. ☆ *What groups most challenged traditional social patterns during the 1920s?*

4. ☆ *What role did technology play in social change during the 1920s?*

5. ☆ *Why and how did some Americans try to restore traditional social values during the 1920s?*

6. ☆ *What continuities and changes characterized racial and ethnic relations during the 1920s?*

7. ☆ *Is it appropriate to describe the 1920s as "the lean years" for working people?*

8. ☆ *How did gender roles and definitions change in the 1920s?*

9. ☆ *Compare the attitude of the Harding and Coolidge administrations toward the economy with the attitude of the Roosevelt and Wilson administrations.*

10. ☆ *How did the third-party candidacy of La Follette in 1924 resemble that of Roosevelt in 1912 and the Populists in 1892?*

11. ☆ *What role did the United States play in world affairs during the 1920s?*

12. ☆ *How successful was Hughes at the Washington Naval Conference?*

KEY TERMS

Henry Ford (p. 592)

A. P. Giannini (p. 593)

Charles Lindbergh (p. 597)

Sinclair Lewis (p. 598)

Harlem Renaissance (p. 598)

jazz (p. 599)

Marcus Garvey (p. 599)

black separatism (p. 599)

Eighteenth Amendment (p. 601)

Al Capone (p. 601)

fundamentalism (p. 602)

evolution (p. 602)

Clarence Darrow (p. 602)

National Origins Act (p. 602)

American Indian Defense Association (p. 605)

American Plan (p. 606)

welfare capitalism (p. 606)

Communist Party of the United States (p. 607)

Equal Rights Amendment (p. 608)

Sigmund Freud (p. 608)

Farm Bloc (p. 609)

Al Smith (p. 609)

McNary-Haugen bill (p. 611)

Railway Labor Act of 1926 (p. 611)

isolationism (p. 612)

Augusto Sandino (p. 614)

Fordney-McCumber Tariff (p. 614)

Dawes Plan (p. 615)

Washington Naval Conference (p. 615)

Nine-Power Pact (p. 616)

Kellogg-Briand Pact (p. 616)

 CourseMate Go to the History CourseMate website for primary source links, study tools, and review materials for this chapter. www.cengagebrain.com

22

The Great Depression and the New Deal, 1929–1939

Behind the Stories

On October 24, 1929, the stock market crashed. Then it fell repeatedly over the next days and months. At first, the crash seemed like a sudden rainstorm after which sunshine would return. But the storm intensified, reaching hurricane force. The Great Depression devastated the economy and people's lives, affecting all Americans—rich, poor, and in between. Out of the economic chaos came a new president, Franklin D. Roosevelt, and his program for relief, recovery, and reform called the New Deal.

The Great Depression and the New Deal loomed large in my family's stories. In 1931, when my mother was 12 years old, her parents lost their farm because they could not make their mortgage payments. They moved to town, and my grandfather worked at whatever he could find. One summer, when he was in his early 50s, he worked for the WPA, building stone steps up a steep hill. Later, he

found a job taking care of motor vehicles at a CCC camp. (The WPA and CCC were government-funded work programs.) Later, whenever anyone suggested that WPA workers had loafed on the job, my mother was always quick to explain that her father came home from his WPA job so exhausted he could hardly move. The New Deal had kept food on her family's table and a roof over their heads at a time when they had no other source of income.

My mother's family was not unusual. Many Americans struggled to survive during the 1930s. The New Deal restored some economic security for many of those most disadvantaged, but it was not without critics, then and later.

Though both political parties eventually accepted much of the New Deal, the role of the federal government in the economy and in people's lives continues to divide the country politically, culturally, and socially.

—R.W.C.

Individual Choices
Frances Perkins

On February 22, 1933, President-elect Franklin D. Roosevelt asked Frances Perkins to be secretary of labor in his administration. Initially trained as a social worker, Perkins had been deeply affected by the Triangle Shirtwaist fire tragedy in 1911 (discussed in Chapter 19). Perkins had served Roosevelt in a similar capacity when he was governor of New York, and she said yes on the condition that she be allowed to push for specific legislation, especially old-age pensions, a minimum wage, and the abolition of child labor. Roosevelt agreed but warned her that she should not "expect too much help" from him. She accepted, becoming the first woman to serve in a president's cabinet.

Frances Perkins

As secretary of labor, Perkins played key roles in programs to assist the unemployed. But her central goal was to create a system that provided social insurance. In 1934, she helped draft a bill that provided unemployment compensation, retirement pensions for elderly workers, and aid for poor children. In securing passage of the Social Security Act of 1935, Perkins made difficult choices. For fiscal and political reasons, the final bill required that workers pay into the system instead of having benefits paid out of taxes. Perkins wanted medical coverage, too, but it was excluded, owing largely to opposition by the medical profession. After hundreds of speeches, like the one excerpted in the Individual Voices feature at the end of this chapter, and countless congressional committee hearings, the bill passed, and the relationship between the federal government and the people fundamentally changed.

Perkins also wanted federal standards for workers' wages and hours of work. No "self-supporting and self-respecting democracy," she argued, could justify any "economic reason for chiseling workers' wages or stretching workers' hours." The Fair Labor Standards Act of 1938 answered these concerns and also barred industrial child labor. Opponents called it too much government intrusion, but the act protected more than 12 million workers. Perkins left office in 1945 but remained an advocate for workers and their families until her death in 1965.

621

When the stock market crashed and depression set in, President Herbert Hoover fought the economic collapse with concepts and policies he expected would produce recovery—but he failed. As the number of the unemployed and underemployed soared, many Americans faced economic insecurity. Some feared that basic social and political structures might collapse, but Americans proved resilient.

In 1932, amid the unemployment and spreading bank failures, Franklin D. Roosevelt was elected president. He proved willing to use all the powers of government to combat the Depression and institute changes. With the New Deal, his administration unleashed a flood of legislation intended to provide immediate relief, bring long-term recovery, and institute permanent reform. The New Deal proved highly popular with American voters. Critics, however, abounded on both the **right** and **left**. On the left, some argued that Roosevelt's program was too timid in redistributing resources, too hesitant in promoting equality, too limited in its regulation and planning. On the right, many saw the New Deal as too intrusive, creating a federal monster that threatened individual, property, and entrepreneurial rights. Should government promote human rights over property rights? Should it assist the disadvantaged at the expense of others? How should the Constitution be applied to circumstances unforeseen when it was written? These are not new questions, but the New Deal set the stage for many of the nation's political, economic, and social debates from then to now.

By the late 1930s, the New Deal was sputtering to an end. It had not restored prosperity, but unemployment was down, and many people now felt they had a new social "safety net." The New Deal changed the definition of "liberalism," remade the political landscape, and permanently expanded the responsibilities and power of the federal government. Roosevelt was revered and reviled, but no one denied his impact.

right, left When applied to politics, *right* refers to conservative or reactionary positions, and *left* refers to liberal or radical positions; *right-wing* and *left-wing* are common variants.

■ **Great Depression** The years 1929 to 1941 when the economy of the United States suffered a major contraction, millions were unemployed, and thousands of businesses went bankrupt; President Hoover used the term *depression* rather than the more traditional *panic* in hopes that it would reduce the public's fears.

credit crunch (or credit crisis) A significant reduction in the availability of credit, caused by changes in banks' lending policies.

THE ECONOMIC CRISIS AND HOOVER'S RESPONSE

★ What was the effect of the stock market crash on the American economy, and what major economic weaknesses contributed to the crash and the Great Depression?

★ How did Hoover try to deal with the Depression? How successful were his efforts?

Campaigning for the presidency in 1928, Herbert Hoover had promised a "New Day" for America, but his sweeping victory was more a vote for the status quo. The United States had experienced almost a decade of economic growth, and people voted for Hoover expecting that trend to continue. The outcome was much different, as the nation was soon tested by economic and social trauma.

The Crash and the Great Depression

Hoover took office as president in the midst of rising stock prices, shiny new cars, and rapidly expanding suburbs that seemed to verify his observation about "the final triumph over poverty." But behind the rush for homes, radios, and vacuum cleaners were serious economic weaknesses, some of which were already becoming visible. Less than eight months later, on "Black Thursday," October 24, 1929, the stock market crashed. The value of stocks plummeted, and across the country frenzied brokers rushed to place sell orders. Few places were untouched. In the mid-Atlantic, on board the passenger liner *Berengaria*, Helena Rubenstein watched stock prices fall and finally sold 50,000 shares of Westinghouse Company. She had lost more than a million dollars in a few hours. The market rebounded a bit on Friday but crashed again on Monday. The next day—"Black Tuesday"—prices plunged and continued to fall throughout the year. Within the first week of the crash, stocks fell by a total of $30 billion. Thousands who had speculated on an ever rising market were ruined. Stories circulated of New York hotel clerks asking guests whether they wanted rooms for sleeping or jumping. In fact, nationwide, the suicide rate increased by almost 50 percent in 1929, as compared to the previous eight years. The Dow Jones Industrial Averages measure the stock market performance of selected major stocks. From a high point of 381.17 on September 3, 1929, the Dow fell to a low of 41.22 on July 8, 1932. Similar losses occurred in stock markets around the world. The Dow did not recover to pre-1929 levels until the 1950s.

The crash was a starting point for the **Great Depression**, but it was a catalyst, not the cause. The Depression resulted from uneven economic growth, overproduction, a poor distribution of income, excessive credit buying, and a **credit crunch** resulting from serious weaknesses in the banking system. The prosperity of the 1920s had in part rested on expanding industries—especially construction, automobiles, movies, and electronics—that pushed the rest of the economy forward. By 1927, most of those industries were slowing down. Construction starts, for example, fell from 11 billion to 9 billion units between 1926 and 1929, causing producers of household merchandise to reduce production. The expansion of the 1920s had been uneven. Older industries, including railroads, textiles, and iron and steel had barely made a profit, while mining suffered steady losses. Workers in those industries saw little increase in wages or standards of living. The postwar economic expansion completely bypassed agriculture, and farmers watched their incomes and property values slip to about half of their wartime highs. Compounding these problems, credit had virtually dried up in rural America, as five thousand banks, many in rural areas, closed between 1921 and 1928. By the end of 1928, thousands of people had left their farms, and agriculture was approaching an economic crisis.

Another weakness of the economy lay in the distribution of wealth. Economists estimate that, in 1929, the richest 5 percent of Americans received about one-third of all income, much of which was in the form of interest, dividends, and rent. Given the amount of wealth in the hands of those few, reductions in spending or investment by the wealthiest could have a disproportionate effect on the entire economy. Much of the $30 billion loss in stock values represented losses for the wealthiest. The distribution of wealth affected consumer spending in other ways as well. In the late 1920s, the Brookings Institution judged that an annual salary of $2,500 provided an American family a comfortable standard of living. It also found that 70 percent of American families earned less than that amount. When Hoover took office, many people were buying on credit, especially through installment buying (discussed in the preceding chapter). Americans had spent about $100 million buying on credit in 1919, but ten years later that amount had soared over $7 billion. Still, few worried as long as the economy seemed stable, unemployment remained low, and Americans had confidence in the economy. All that changed with the stock market crash.

The stock market crash undermined economic confidence and highlighted the weaknesses of the economy. A soaring stock market was a symbol of a vigorous economy, but the market's continued fall made investors and business leaders wary. Reduced demand led manufacturers to cut production and lay off workers or reduce hours. As more and more people found themselves out of work or with smaller paychecks, they cut back consumer purchases and stopped buying on credit, thereby further reducing demand. They often found that they could not make their installment payments, so they lost their car or radio.

As the economy spiraled downward, the banking system appeared to be collapsing. Too many banks had made risky loans and now found that they could not collect on them. As rumors circulated of a bank's instability, customers lined up at teller windows to empty their accounts. As such "runs" on banks intensified, more and more banks were unable to meet their obligations, declared bankruptcy, and closed their doors. Many thousands of depositors lost their savings, jarring the well-being of many upper- and middle-class families.

As some banks closed their doors and others struggled to remain open, the nation entered a credit crunch. Unable to collect on many of their current loans, bankers became highly cautious about making new loans—and credit dried up. In the midst of this, the Federal Reserve *raised* interest rates, which further discouraged borrowing. Many Americans dumped their stocks for whatever they could get and refused to invest in the stock market so long as it kept falling. Because economic growth and expansion require access to both credit from banks and funds from the sale of stocks, the entire economy lurched toward paralysis.

By 1933, American exports were at their lowest level since 1905, nearly ninety thousand businesses had failed, and corporate profits were down 60 percent. Unemployment rose from 3 percent in 1929 to 9 percent in 1930 and to 25 percent by 1933, with much higher rates in manufacturing areas. American industry, according to *Fortune*, suffered 46 percent unemployment, but in many areas it was much worse. In Gary, Indiana, nearly the entire working class was out of a job by 1932. (Map 22.1 presents state-level data on unemployment.) Nine thousand banks had closed, with depositors losing $2.5 billion. The drastic decline in the value of stocks, the closing of banks, and actions by the Federal Reserve all contributed to a serious shrinkage in the money supply, causing deflation. Average annual income dropped 35 percent—from $2,300 to $1,500—by 1933. Prices for most products began to fall, reducing income to both merchants and producers, but the decline in income and uncertainties about the overall economy meant that people were unable or unwilling to buy even at reduced prices. Automobile purchases dropped by 75 percent.

Other industrial nations also experienced economic contraction and significant unemployment. During the last half of the 1920s, the European economy was recovering from the devastation of the Great War, greatly aided by over $5.1 billion dollars borrowed from American sources. However, by the end of 1928, American investors were already reducing

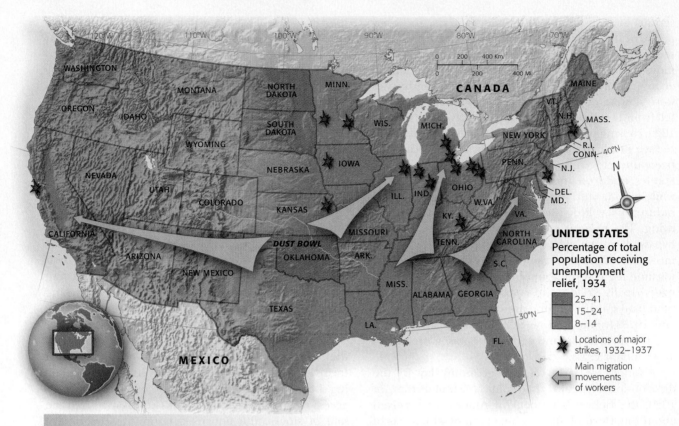

MAP 22.1 The Great Depression and Unemployment
As Herbert Hoover confronted Franklin D. Roosevelt in the race for the presidency in 1932, the nation was experiencing the highest unemployment since statistics began to be collected. This map shows the percentage of the work force unemployed by state during this period. Source: Data: *Statistical Abstract of the United States 1935*; Map: Copyright © Cengage Learning

their loans to Europe. The onset of the Depression in the United States made the international credit contraction much worse. As the Depression spread, many nations, including the United States, raised tariffs to protect their industries from foreign goods. The 1930 Smoot-Hawley Tariff set the highest tariff rates in U.S. history. While these actions may have protected domestic markets, they also undermined world trade—including American exports. World trade slowed to a crawl by 1931.

Hoover's Response to Economic Crisis

At first, the most common response to the plunge in stock prices was that voiced by Secretary of the Treasury Andrew Mellon, who stated that the economy remained strong, that the market plunge was temporary, and that it would actually strengthen the economy. Though many experts argued that the free-market sysem would eventually heal itself, Hoover disagreed. He summoned the nation's economic leaders, asking them to help absorb the economic shock by reducing profits rather than cutting jobs and wages. At the same time, he urged Congress, states, and cities to increase spending on **public works projects**, including government buildings and highways, to stimulate the economy. He called on local groups to raise money to help the unemployed. The Agricultural Marketing Act (1929) tried to address farmers' problems with the creation of a Farm Board to help support agricultural prices. Despite some initial successes, these efforts did little to counteract the credit crunch and produced no sustained recovery. As profits declined, businesses cut production, reduced wages, and laid off workers. Agricultural prices continued to collapse, and state, local, and private efforts to aid the growing number of unemployed were overwhelmed (see Figure 22.1).

■ **public works projects** Construction projects financed by public funds and carried out by federal, state, or local governments.

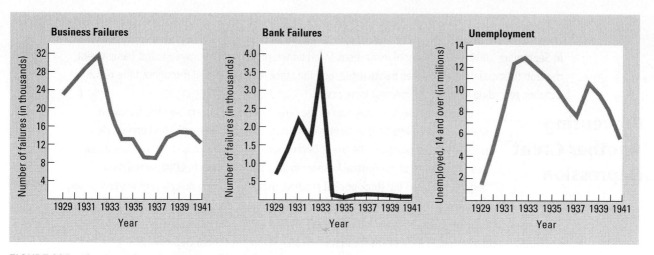

FIGURE 22.1 Charting the Economics of the Depression
Between 1929 and 1933, the number of people unemployed and of bank and business failures steadily increased.
As the New Deal began, not only did the statistics improve, but for many a sense of hope also emerged.

With the country slipping further into the Depression, Hoover took new steps in 1931, some of which finally addressed the credit crunch. He asked Congress for banking reforms, financial support for home mortgages, the creation of the **Reconstruction Finance Corporation** (RFC), and higher taxes to pay for it all. Congress responded in 1932 with the **Glass-Steagall Act**, which encouraged lending, and the **Federal Home Loan Bank Act**, which allowed homeowners to remortgage their homes at lower rates and payments. Hoover intended the RFC to be the major tool to fight the Depression by pumping money into the economy. Created in 1932—several years after the beginning of the credit crunch that was producing economic paralysis—the RFC used federal funds to provide loans to banks, railroads, and large corporations to prevent their collapse and expand their operations. Hoover and his advisers hoped the benefits of this expansion would "trickle down" to workers and the unemployed through higher wages and new jobs. But the RFC came years too late and, even then, was slow to begin operations. It did loan over $805 million within its first five months, but with little apparent effect on the economy. Critics branded the program "welfare for the rich" and insisted Hoover do more for the poor and unemployed. Hoover opposed federal relief to the poor, however, believing that it was too expensive and eroded the work ethic. But as unemployment reached nearly 25 percent and pressure mounted from Congress and the public, he accepted an Emergency Relief Division within the RFC to provide $300 million in loans to states to pay for relief. Yet few states wanted to put themselves more deeply in debt by borrowing, and 90 percent of the relief fund was still intact by the end of 1932. Whether for recovery or relief, the RFC proved to be too little and too late to resolve the economic crisis.

The onslaught of the Depression changed Hoover's and the nation's fortunes. Many Americans blamed the president and the Republicans for the worsening economy and for callousness toward the hardships besetting the country. As people who lost their homes began to live in shantytowns on the outskirts of many cities, the head of publicity for the Democratic National Committee sarcastically dubbed them "**Hoovervilles**," and the name stuck.

■ **Reconstruction Finance Corporation** (RFC) Organization established in 1932 at Hoover's request to promote economic recovery; it provided emergency financing for banks, life insurance companies, railroads, and farm mortgage associations; continued and expanded as part of the New Deal.

Glass-Steagall Act 1932 law that expanded credit through the Federal Reserve System.

Federal Home Loan Bank Act 1932 law that established twelve banks across the nation to assist institutions making home loans in an effort to reduce foreclosures and to stimulate the construction industry.

Hooverville Crudely built camp set up by the homeless on the fringes of a town or city during the Depression.

In September 2008, major financial institutions faced bankruptcy owing to unwise loans. Panic swept through financial markets. Fifteen banks failed, and the stock market crashed throughout the month of October, recording some of the greatest losses ever.

Preventing Another Great Depression

Ben Bernanke was chairman of the Federal Reserve System (see the feature It Matters Today, page 549). A former economics professor, Bernanke had previously researched the causes of the Great Depression. The key factor, he had concluded, had been the failure of the Federal Reserve to stop bank failures. In 2008, when banks began to fail and the stock market crashed, Bernanke moved quickly and worked closely with Henry Paulson, secretary of the treasury, to prevent some bank failures and to secure approval of hundreds of billions of dollars of federal loans to and investments in key financial institutions to keep them stable and discourage a credit crunch that could lead to another Great Depression.

- Do newspaper accounts from September and October 2008 draw comparisons to the events of 1929?
- Can you find other examples when historical analysis, such as that of Bernanke, has affected recent governmental policies?

Some farmers began to take matters into their own hands. In October 1931, when an Iowa bank **foreclosed** on a mortgage and held an auction sale of the farmer's land and equipment, other farmers used their numbers and threats of violence to force a "penny auction" that returned the foreclosed farm to its owners for a fraction of its value. Penny auctions quickly spread across the Midwest. In Ohio, for example, one farmer, backed by a crowd of angry neighbors, regained his farm for a high bid of $1.90 to settle a mortgage of $800. In the summer of 1932, some midwestern farmers joined the **Farmers' Holiday Association**, led by Milo Reno. Reno called on farmers to "stay home, buy nothing, sell nothing," to push up prices by destroying their crops rather than selling them. Many farmers responded not just by withholding their own produce from market but also by setting up roadblocks to prevent other

foreclose To confiscate property when mortgage payments are delinquent; in the 1930s, it was typical to auction off all foreclosed assets.

■ **Farmers' Holiday Association** Organization of farmers that called on members to take direct action—such as destroying crops and resisting foreclosures—to protest the plight of agriculture and the lack of government support.

Chicago History Museum/Chicago Daily News Collection negative number DN-0093996.

The Great Depression produced large-scale unemployment that reached 25 percent in 1933; across the nation people scrambled to find other sources of income. In this picture a World War I vet sells apples on the street in Chicago.

Unable to get adequate prices for their products, these dairymen chose to dump their milk rather than sell it.

farmers from selling theirs. By 1932, Communist Party organizers were signing up members among desperate farmers. Farmers were not alone. Across the nation, strikes, protest rallies, "bread marches," and rent riots took place as citizens demanded more jobs, higher wages, and relief payments. Overall, the Communist Party signed up nearly 20,000 new members between 1931 and 1932, though most dropped out after a short time.

A major protest took place in the spring and summer of 1932 when thousands of World War I veterans, usually called the **Bonus Army**, converged on Washington, D.C., to demonstrate support for the "bonus bill," which promised early payment of veteran's bonuses originally scheduled for 1945. The marchers, some with their families, set up a Hooverville across from Congress at Anacosta Flats. When the bill failed, most left, but nearly ten thousand stayed behind. In late July, Hoover ordered the army to remove them. Led by Army Chief of Staff General Douglas MacArthur, troops armed with cavalry sabers, rifles, tear gas, and fixed bayonets evicted the veterans and their families and burned their shelters. Over one hundred veterans were injured and two were killed, but rumors quickly swelled those numbers and intensified the public's angry reaction. Upon hearing of the army's action, the governor of New York, Franklin D. Roosevelt, exclaimed, "This will elect me."

THE ELECTION OF 1932 AND THE EARLY NEW DEAL

★ How did the New Deal's "First Hundred Days" represent a change in the role of the federal government?

★ What were the initial responses to New Deal measures?

Like the elections of 1860 and 1896, the election of 1932 was one of the great turning points in American political history. Since 1860, Republicans had usually been able to win the White House and set the agenda for national politics. After 1932, however, the Democrats, under the leadership of Franklin D. Roosevelt, created bold new policies and established themselves as the majority party for a generation.

The Roosevelt Landslide

Nearly any Democratic candidate could have defeated Hoover in 1932, but the Democrats nominated an exceptional politician in Franklin D. Roosevelt, born

■ **Bonus Army** Unemployed World War I veterans who marched to Washington in 1932 to demand early payment of a promised bonus; Congress refused, and the army evicted protesters who remained.

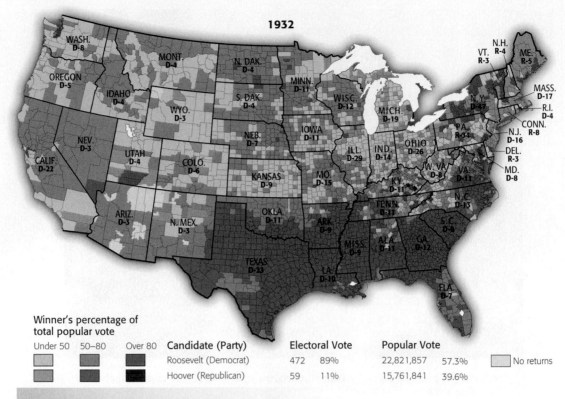

1932

Winner's percentage of total popular vote

Under 50	50–80	Over 80	Candidate (Party)	Electoral Vote		Popular Vote			No returns
			Roosevelt (Democrat)	472	89%	22,821,857	57.3%		
			Hoover (Republican)	59	11%	15,761,841	39.6%		

MAP 22.2 Presidential Election, 1932, Popular Vote by County
In the election of 1932, Franklin D. Roosevelt, promising a New Deal for Americans beleaguered by the continuing economic catastrophe, won 42 of 48 states. Minor party candidates drew about 3 percent of the vote.

into wealth and educated at the exclusive Groton School and Harvard College. After graduation, with a recognizable name, Roosevelt entered New York politics. Tall, handsome, charming, and a good speaker, he became assistant secretary of the navy (a position his distant cousin Theodore had once held) in the Wilson administration, then won the Democratic nomination for vice president in 1920. Though he and presidential candidate James Cox lost, his political future looked bright. Then, in 1921, he was stricken with polio and paralyzed from the waist down. Greatly aided by his wife, Eleanor, he kept his political career alive and in 1928 won the governorship of New York. Roosevelt was one of the few governors to mobilize his state's limited resources to help the unemployed and poor. Although the results were modest, his efforts suggested a caring and energetic leader—a champion of the "forgotten man." The opposite image stuck to Hoover, who seemed to have little concern for the 11 million unemployed Americans.

■ **New Deal** Implying a fresh start, this term became the best known name for Roosevelt's policies to combat the Depression.

When nominated for president in 1932, Roosevelt broke with all precedents and flew to Chicago to give his acceptance speech to the convention. Establishing a theme for the coming campaign, Roosevelt emphatically announced that he and the Democratic Party had no fear of breaking with "all foolish traditions" and closed by promising a "new deal for the American people." The media quickly picked up the term, and Roosevelt's campaign acquired a memorable slogan: the **New Deal**. Although his speech offered no concrete solutions to the nation's problems, it promised hope and instilled the belief that Roosevelt would move the nation along new paths.

During the campaign, Roosevelt tried to avoid any commitments and policy proposals that might offend voters. He supported direct federal relief while promising to balance the budget, but mostly he stressed hope and the prospect of change. Hoover claimed that the campaign was "more than a contest between two men," that it was "a contest between two philosophies of government." The electorate chose the philosophy of Roosevelt and the Democratic Party. Across the nation, people voted for Democrats at every level, from local to national. Roosevelt won in a landslide, with 57 percent of the vote to 40 percent for Hoover, who carried only six states (see Map 22.2).

After his bout with polio in 1921, Roosevelt could walk using braces and supports but usually used a wheelchair—yet few pictures exist of him in a wheelchair because news photographers generally respected his wish not to be photographed that way. Here he relaxes at his family estate at Hyde Park in New York State.

1933—The First Hundred Days

In the four months between the election and Inauguration Day, Americans eagerly waited for the New Deal to start even as the economy worsened. Many expected that Roosevelt and his advisers, labeled by the press as the Brain Trust because the group included several college professors, were developing a plan to restore prosperity. In fact, Roosevelt's advisers were frequently at odds about which path to follow. Some, like Rexford Tugwell and Raymond Moley, supported a collective approach, working with business through joint economic planning. Others, like Harry Hopkins, Eleanor Roosevelt, and Frances Perkins, advocated social programs. All agreed, however, that the worst path was doing nothing.

Roosevelt took office on March 4, as many of the country's banks seemed in danger of closing. Millions listened to the radio and heard the president reassure Americans that they had "nothing to fear but fear itself" and promise that the economy would revive. "We must act quickly," he specified, adding that he would call Congress into emergency session to deal with the banking crisis. On March 6, Roosevelt—soon widely referred to as FDR—declared a national **Bank Holiday**, closing all the country's banks. Three days later, as freshmen congressmen were still finding their seats, the president presented Congress with the **Emergency Banking Bill**. Without even seeing a written version of the bill, Democrats and Republicans gave Roosevelt what he wanted in less than four hours. The new law required a federal inspection before banks could reopen, thus reassuring depositors that those that reopened were safe, and it allowed the Federal Reserve and the Reconstruction Finance Corporation (held over from the Hoover administration) to prop up the nation's banking system by providing funds and buying stocks of some banks. On Sunday evening, March 12, Roosevelt took to the radio in the first of his **fireside chats**. He told the nation that the federal government was solving the banking crisis and banks would be safe again, adding that "It is safer to keep your money in a reopened bank than under the mattress." Over 60 million Americans listened to the speech, and most believed him. On the following day in Atlanta, for example, deposits outnumbered withdrawals by over 3 to 1. Within a month, nearly 75 percent of the nation's banks were operating again.

The New Deal had begun. Riding a wave of popular support and great expectations, Roosevelt faced a unique political climate of almost total **bipartisanship**. Some Republicans even enthusiastically embraced aspects of the New Deal. Within its **First Hundred Days**, the Roosevelt administration and Congress created a long list of new federal agencies and programs. A few carried out traditional Democratic Party goals, such as the repeal of Prohibition, but most were aimed at relief, recovery, and reform.

Bank Holiday Temporary closure of banks throughout the country by executive order of President Roosevelt in March 1933.

Emergency Banking Bill (Act) 1933 law that permitted sound banks to reopen and allowed the government to supply funds to prop up some banks.

■ **fireside chats** Radio talks in which President Roosevelt promoted New Deal policies and reassured the nation; Roosevelt delivered twenty-eight fireside chats.

bipartisanship In American politics, when the two major parties work together cooperatively to resolve issues.

■ **First Hundred Days** The opening period of Roosevelt's administration, during which the president and Congress developed an unprecedented number of measures aimed at relief for the unemployed and economic recovery.

Among the first bills Roosevelt offered Congress was the **Agricultural Adjustment Act** (AAA), intended to bring the recovery of agriculture. Passed by Congress on May 12, the act created the Agricultural Adjustment Administration (AAA), which paid farmers to reduce production as a way of cutting the surpluses that drove down prices for farm produce. Focusing on wheat, cotton, corn, rice, tobacco, hogs, and dairy products, a planning board determined the amount to be removed from production. The program was to be funded by a special tax on industrial food processors. Some critics argued that the AAA gave too much power to the government. Others complained that it did nothing to help small farmers, sharecroppers, and tenant farmers, or to make surplus food available for the needy.

The AAA addressed the problems of agriculture, and the Roosevelt administration next turned to industrial recovery. The **National Industrial Recovery Act** (NIRA) was approved in June, with Roosevelt calling it the "most important and far reaching legislation passed by the American Congress." The act, a compromise among Roosevelt's advisers who had advocated two quite different approaches, incorporated both approaches by creating two new agencies, the **National Recovery Administration** (NRA) and the **Public Works Administration** (PWA).

The NRA, led by Hugh Johnson, a former army general, sought to stimulate the economy through national economic planning by establishing, industry by industry, codes that set prices, production levels, and wages. Business supported the NRA because it allowed **price fixing** that raised both prices and profits.

- **Agricultural Adjustment Act** (AAA) Law passed by Congress in 1933 to bring the recovery of agriculture through planning and subsidies to reduce production.

National Industrial Recovery Act (NIRA) Law passed by Congress in 1933 establishing the National Recovery Administration to promote planning in industry and the Public Works Administration to create jobs.

- **National Recovery Administration** (NRA) Agency created by the NIRA to supervise the drafting and implementation of national industrial codes.

- **Public Works Administration** (PWA) Headed by Harold Ickes, secretary of the interior, the PWA sought to increase employment and to stimulate economic recovery by constructing major public works.

price fixing The artificial setting of commodity prices.

- **Tennessee Valley Authority** (TVA) Independent public corporation created by Congress in 1933 to plan the development of the Tennessee River valley region, especially through flood control and dams that generated electricity.

Labor was attracted by Section 7a, which gave workers the right to organize unions and bargain collectively, outlawed child labor, and established minimum wages and maximum hours of work. By early 1935, some 700 industries with 2.5 million workers were displaying a poster with a blue eagle that meant they were covered by NRA codes.

The PWA took a different approach, stimulating recovery by putting federal funds into major construction projects, thereby providing jobs directly for construction workers and more jobs in the industries that supplied construction materials. These jobs would then stimulate demand for consumer products and create still more jobs. The PWA was, by far, the largest federal public works program up to that time and still ranks as one of the largest ever. Administered by the Department of the Interior, the PWA was slow to begin operations, partly because the projects required significant planning and partly because the secretary of the interior, "Honest Harold" Ickes, was scrupulous about preventing any waste or graft. Nonetheless, over six years PWA spent some $6 billion (equivalent to almost $100 billion today), usually in cooperation with state and local governments, funding some 34,000 projects, including roads, bridges, giant electricity-generating dams, 70 percent of all new school buildings, one-third of all new hospital buildings, two aircraft carriers, and much more.

One of the most innovative programs of the First Hundred Days was the **Tennessee Valley Authority** (TVA). The goal was to develop a regional approach to planning and development for a rural and impoverished region of 40,000 square miles including parts of seven states. The most immediate benefit was to provide jobs repairing and building dams and improving flood controls. But the TVA did much more. The TVA improved the navigability of hundreds of miles of rivers and lakes and reduced soil erosion. TVA dams provided electricity through federally owned and operated hydroelectric systems (see Map 22.3), making possible the introduction of electricity to many rural areas. The TVA also provided a model for other federal dam-building projects, especially in the West, that provided water and electricity for economic development. Critics of the New Deal opposed such government-owned agencies as socialist.

Recovery was one thrust of Roosevelt's offensive against the Depression. He had campaigned on the slogan of helping the "forgotten man," and in March 1933 unemployment was at a historic high—25 percent of the work force. In industrial states such as New York, Ohio, Pennsylvania, and Illinois, unemployment pushed toward 33 percent and was even higher in some manufacturing centers. Recognizing that

MAP 22.3 The Tennessee Valley Authority
One of the most ambitious New Deal Projects was developing the Tennessee Valley. This map shows the various components of the TVA. Copyright © Cengage Learning

state and private relief sources could not cope with people's needs, Roosevelt proposed and Congress enacted federal relief programs. Though all were temporary measures, they established a new role for the federal government. By the end of the decade, about 46 million people had received some form of relief support.

The first relief program was the **Civilian Conservation Corps** (CCC), passed on March 31, 1933. It established several thousand army-style camps to house, employ, and provide a healthy, moral environment for unemployed urban males aged 18 to 25. Within months it had enrolled over 300,000 men, paying them $30 a month, $25 of which had to be sent to their parents. By 1941, more than 3 million men had received employment through the CCC camps. The "Conservation Army" built and improved national park facilities, constructed roads and firebreaks, worked to control erosion, dug irrigation ditches, fought forest fires, and planted trees. In the camps, 35,000 men were taught to read.

The CCC reached only a small percentage of those needing relief. To widen the range of assistance, the Roosevelt administration created the **Federal Emergency Relief Administration** (FERA). FERA pro-

vided states with money for their relief needs. In some cases it bypassed state and local governments and instituted federally administered programs. One such FERA program opened special centers to provide housing, meals, and medical care for many of the homeless roaming the nation. In the program's first year of operation, it cared for as many as 5 million people. One man who had been riding the rails was pulled off a train in Omaha and taken to a transient camp where he was deloused and given a bath, a bed, and food. "We ate a great meal," he recalled years later. "We thought we'd gone to heaven." In other programs, half a million people attended literacy classes and 1 million received vaccinations and immunizations.

■ **Civilian Conservation Corps** (CCC) Organization created by Congress in 1933 to hire young unemployed men for conservation work, such as planting trees, digging irrigation ditches, and maintaining national parks.

■ **Federal Emergency Relief Administration** (FERA) Agency created in May 1933 to provide direct grants to states and municipalities to spend on relief.

Here, Civilian Conservation Corps workers plant seedlings to reforest an area destroyed by fire.

The **Civil Works Administration** (CWA) was a temporary measure to help the unemployed through the winter of 1933–34 by hiring 4 million jobless people for federal, state, and local work projects. Though critics argued that the CWA sometimes created meaningless jobs, the goal of the program was to provide work to as many unemployed people as possible, and CWA projects did result in many permanent public works.

Civil Works Administration (CWA) Emergency unemployment relief program in the winter of 1933–34.

Home Owners' Loan Corporation (HOLC) Government agency created in 1933 that refinanced nonfarm home mortgages and loaned money to pay property taxes and make repairs.

Federal Deposit Insurance Corporation (FDIC) Agency created by the Banking Act of 1933 to insure deposits up to a fixed sum in banks of the Federal Reserve System and state banks that chose to participate.

Securities and Exchange Commission (SEC) Agency created by the Securities Exchange Act (1934) to license stock exchanges and supervise their activities.

Federal Housing Administration (FHA) Agency created by the National Housing Act (1934) to insure loans made by banks and other institutions for new home construction, repairs, and improvements.

■ **American Liberty League** Conservative organization established in 1934 to oppose New Deal policies; conducted an extensive media campaign funded by powerful corporations.

The list of new programs approved during the "hundred days" did not end there. The **Home Owners' Loan Corporation** (HOLC), established in May 1933, permitted homeowners to refinance their mortgages at lower interest rates through the federal government. Before it stopped making loans in 1936, the HOLC had refinanced 1 million homes, including 20 percent of all mortgaged urban homes. To correct problems within the banking industries, the Banking Act of 1933 gave more power to the Federal Reserve System and created the **Federal Deposit Insurance Corporation** (FDIC), which provided federal insurance for those who deposited money in member banks. In less than six months, 97 percent of all commercial banks had joined the system.

The special session and first session of the Seventy-third Congress met for 102 days, but this period quickly became known as the Hundred Days. Never before had such a long list of major legislation been passed in so short a time. Since 1933, journalists have popularized the notion that a new president should be judged on the basis of his accomplishments during his first hundred days in office, and an activist president is always compared to FDR. However, such comparisons rarely take into account the seriousness of the crisis facing the president and Congress in 1933 or the unusual degree of bipartisanship that characterized much of the hundred days.

1934—Year of Turmoil

The New Deal started with almost total support in Congress and among the people. However, as the economy began to improve, opposition emerged. By mid-1933, most Republicans and some conservative Democrats opposed relief programs, federal spending, and increased governmental controls over business. A few new policies were approved in 1934, notably creation of the **Securities and Exchange Commission** (SEC), to regulate stock markets, and the National Housing Act, which set up the **Federal Housing Administration** (FHA) to make home loans more available. But in that year conservative Democrats, including Al Smith, the 1928 presidential candidate, joined with representatives of several major corporations to establish the **American Liberty League**, which opposed New Deal policies through an extensive media campaign funded mostly by the Du Pont family and leaders of other powerful corporations.

In the Wider World

Many vocal conservatives fumed that Roosevelt threatened free enterprise, if not capitalism. The Hearst newspaper chain instructed its editors to tell the public that the New Deal was a "raw deal" and that Roosevelt was leading the nation into socialism. The Communist Party, meanwhile, stridently attacked the New Deal as a tool of big business that was pushing the nation toward fascism. By late 1934, Communists claimed 25,000 members and 6,000 youth members; half of the members were unemployed, but the Communists also claimed an additional 50,000 followers in Communist-controlled unions and organizations of the unemployed.

A major target of anti-New Dealers was the NRA, which ran into trouble almost from the beginning. As implementation proceeded, support for NRA programs waned, and critics soon dubbed it the "National Run Around." Workers complained that NRA codes set wages too low and hours too long, and that employers resisted unionization. One woman textile worker wrote to the president that her husband was "laid off, for no other reason than they got a union hear [*sic*] and My Husband became president of it." Consumers grumbled that the NRA caused prices to rise without creating any noticeable growth in wages or jobs. Farmers griped that NRA-generated price increases ate up any AAA benefits they received. Some businesses resisted the restrictions and regulations in NRA codes and questioned the government's right to impose such controls.

The NRA's Section 7a had raised workers' expectations by ensuring their right to organize, but they were disappointed in the actual support for their unions. As union membership grew, many thousands of workers in 1934 walked picket lines in nearly two thousand strikes in almost every city. Thirty thousand cab drivers shut down New York City's taxis in late January and most of February. Between January and early May, more than 80,000 coal miners walked out in a half-dozen separate strikes in nine states. Nearly 40,000 auto workers struck, sometimes only for a day, at nine plants in four states. Several hundred thousand textile workers walked out in six states, the largest of all the strikes in 1934, but were unsuccessful in gaining union recognition. Nearly 22,000 longshore and maritime workers were more successful after tying up shipping on the entire Pacific Coast for three months. A strike by Minneapolis Teamsters eventually gained union recognition and led to the first organization of over-the-road drivers (truckers driving between cities). Communists or other Marxists were prominent in some of those strikes.

The organizing drives and strikes often met stubborn resistance from employers and local officials. Between July 1 and the end of 1933 alone, before the biggest wave of strikes even began, the American Civil Liberties Union counted fifteen strikers killed, two hundred injured, and hundreds arrested and a half-dozen deployments of National Guard troops. Further, the ACLU claimed, the NRA lacked "the will or the power to overcome the defiance of employers." "Labor's rights to meet, organize and strike have been widely violated," the ACLU concluded. Further violence came in 1934, and in some places, notably San Francisco and Minneapolis, there were brief general strikes when all those cities' unions stopped work to protest the killing of strikers.

By 1934, too, several figures began to attract significant attention by arguing that the New Deal had not gone far enough. At three o'clock every Sunday afternoon, **Father Charles Coughlin**, a Roman Catholic priest, used the radio to preach to nearly 30 million

Father Charles Coughlin Roman Catholic priest whose influential radio addresses in the 1930s at first emphasized social justice but eventually became anti-Semitic.

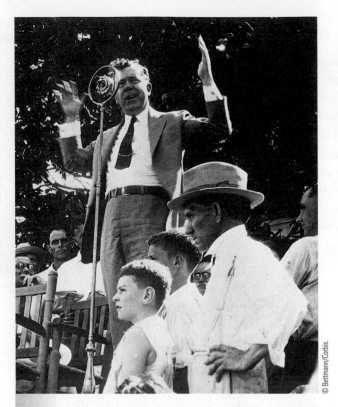

In 1934, Huey Long, a fiery politician from Louisiana, claimed that Roosevelt was not helping ordinary Americans. Long proclaimed his support for the "little man" with the slogan, "Every man a king." Before Long could become a real political threat to Roosevelt, he died of gunshot wounds, the victim of an assassin, in September 1935.

up over 4 million members throughout the country. Dr. Francis Townsend advocated an old-age pension plan to provide every American aged 60 and older with a monthly pension check for $200. To qualify, individuals could not work and had to spend the money within a month. Thousands of Townsend clubs sprang up with an estimated membership of several million, including sixty members of Congress.

Upton Sinclair, the socialist who had exposed the unsanitary conditions in meatpacking with his novel, *The Jungle* (1905), won the Democratic nomination for governor of California in 1934, arguing for a program he called "End Poverty in California," or EPIC, which proposed to take over idle factories and farmland for use by the unemployed. When Sinclair lost the election, he broadened his EPIC program to "End Poverty in Civilization" and sought to build a national movement.

Amid the attacks on the New Deal and the problems with the NRA, the first real measure of voter sentiment came in the 1934 state and congressional elections. Democrats had a one-vote majority in the House of Representatives after the 1930 elections, and Roosevelt's landslide victory in 1932 boosted them to a 313–117 majority. Most politicians and journalists expected the 1934 congressional elections to follow the usual off-year pattern in which the president's party lost seats. In 1934, however, Democrats made further gains, now outnumbering Republicans by 320 to 103 in the house and 60–35 in the Senate. Roosevelt, it seemed, had become immensely popular despite all the criticism from the right and left.

Americans. Formerly a strong supporter of Roosevelt, the "radio priest" now turned against the New Deal and advocated a guaranteed annual income, the redistribution of wealth, tougher antimonopoly laws, and the nationalization of banking. His attacks on Roosevelt also began to carry anti-Semitic overtones. His organization, the National Union for Social Justice, soon claimed 5 million members. **Huey Long**, a flamboyant senator from Louisiana, proposed a dramatic "**Share Our Wealth**" plan: every family would receive an annual check for $2,000, a home, a car, a radio, and a college education for each child, all to be funded by taxing the rich, including confiscating all income over $1 million. Share Our Wealth societies quickly signed

THE LATER NEW DEAL, 1935–1939

★ *What new reforms came during the Second Hundred Days, and how did they differ from those of the First Hundred Days?*

★ *What happened to restrict expansion of the New Deal after 1936?*

Roosevelt was encouraged by the strong endorsement of the New Deal apparent in the 1934 election results, looked forward to expanding the New Deal, and became less willing to cooperate with the conservatives and business leaders who had moved into the opposition. At the same time, he was also concerned that recovery was not progressing as rapidly as desired and that the New Deal had not provided sufficient help to the unemployed.

1935—The Second Hundred Days

Despite the huge Democratic majorities in Congress, the early months of 1935 registered little new legislation, and FDR himself provided scant leadership. He did launch one new initiative when he asked Congress

■ **Huey Long** Louisiana governor, then U.S. senator, who ran a powerful political machine and whose advocacy of redistribution of income was gaining him a national political following at the time of his assassination in 1935.

Share Our Wealth Movement launched by Huey Long that sprang up around the nation in the 1930s urging the redistribution of wealth through government taxes or programs.

to provide more **work relief**. Months later, Congress responded by allocating nearly $5 billion for relief and creating a new agency, the **Works Progress Administration** (WPA). **Harry Hopkins**, the former social worker whom FDR put in charge of the WPA, set out to put the unemployed to work. (WPA programs are discussed later in this chapter.)

Beyond the WPA, Roosevelt seemed uncertain where to turn next. He anxiously watched both Huey Long and the Supreme Court. He considered Long dangerous because of his contempt for democracy in Louisiana, where he completely controlled state politics, and his demagogic appeals for national support. If Long were to run as a third-party candidate in 1936 and unite the supporters of Coughlin, Townsend, and Sinclair, he might be able to win the presidency or, at the least, throw the election to a Republican. The Supreme Court was also a source of anxiety because many New Deal programs were coming under challenge for their constitutionality. Then, on May 27, 1935, in *Schechter Poultry Corporation v. the United States*, the Supreme Court ruled that the NRA was unconstitutional because it improperly delegated legislative authority to the executive branch and exceeded congressional authority to regulate only interstate commerce. Roosevelt furiously exclaimed that the Court still had a "horse and buggy" mentality.

Roosevelt now seized the initiative, calling on Congress a few days later to pass several pieces of legislation. Members of Congress had been planning to go home and avoid the steamy Washington summer but now stayed in session and, over the next three months, passed some of the most significant legislation of the twentieth century.

The establishment of a federal old-age and survivor insurance program set the tone of the **Second Hundred Days** and significantly modified the government's role in society. Frances Perkins (see the Individual Choices feature) was the driving force behind the **Social Security Act** (1935). She had been working on the bill since early 1933, and now that Roosevelt gave it his full support it moved toward passage. The act's most controversial element was a pension plan for retirees 65 or older. The program was to begin in 1937, and initial benefits would vary depending on how much an individual paid into the system.

Compared to Perkins's original plan or to many existing European systems, the Social Security system was limited and conservative. It failed to cover domestic and agricultural laborers and provided no health insurance. Roosevelt insisted that workers should pay for their old-age pensions, saying, "We put those payroll contributions there so as to give the contributors a legal, moral, and political right to collect their pensions and unemployment benefits. With those taxes in there, no damn politician can ever scrap my social

Michigan artist Alfred Castagne sketching Works Progress Administration (WPA) construction workers, 1939. The WPA provided a wide variety of jobs, from those requiring little or no previous training to jobs for artists and classical musicians.

security program." For Americans, the new Social Security program provided not only old-age pensions but also federal aid to families with dependent children and to the disabled, and it helped fund state-run systems of unemployment compensation. Within two years, every state was part of the unemployment compensation system, paying between $15 and $18 a week in unemployment compensation and supplying support to over 28 million people. Passage of the Social Security Act established a major new function for the federal government and is one of the most durable legacies of the New Deal. Since its inception, amendments have changed the method of payments, instituted cost-of-living increases, and added medical

work relief Government programs to provide paid work for the unemployed.

■ **Works Progress Administration** (WPA) Agency established in 1935 and headed by Harry Hopkins that hired the unemployed for a wide variety of programs, including construction, conservation, and art.

Harry Hopkins Close adviser to Roosevelt during his four administrations. He headed several New Deal agencies, including the Works Progress Administration.

■ *Schechter Poultry Corporation v. the United States* Supreme Court decision (1935) declaring the NRA unconstitutional because it improperly delegated legislative authority to the executive and regulated commerce within a state.

■ **Second Hundred Days** Period in 1935 during which Roosevelt proposed and Congress passed landmark legislation including the Social Security Act and National Labor Relations Act.

■ **Social Security Act** 1935 law creating unemployment, old-age, and disability insurance and providing for child welfare.

coverage. Millions of Americans have benefited from the system. Though controversial for years after its passage, no one has seriously argued for dismantling the program for many decades.

The next bill that Roosevelt called on Congress to approve was the National Labor Relations Act (NLRA). Largely the work of Senator Robert Wagner of New York and called the **Wagner Act**, it strengthened unions by putting the power of government behind workers' right to organize and to bargain collectively with their employers over the terms and conditions of their employment. It created the National Labor Relations Board as a new regulatory agency to oversee labor relations and ensure workers' rights, including their right to conduct elections to determine union representation and to prevent unfair labor practices, such as firing or **blacklisting** workers for union activities. The act excluded workers in agriculture and service industries. Nonetheless, the Wagner Act altered the relationships among business, labor, and the government and, in a very real way, redistributed economic power from employers to unions.

The final bill that Roosevelt pushed was a revision of income tax rates for those making over $50,000 a year. Often called the "Wealth Tax Act," it was intended to increase federal revenues to pay for such new programs as the WPA. Taken together with WPA, the Wealth Tax Act provides the first significant example of a federal redistributive policy—taxing the wealthy to provide work relief for the unemployed. Social Security also had some modestly redistributive features. Since 1935, a modest level of redistribution has been a continuing feature of federal economic policy.

The New Deal in Action

By 1935 and 1936, the New Deal had touched the lives of a large majority of Americans and changed the United States in important ways (see Table 22.1). The activities of New Deal agencies were so widespread and various that it is possible to describe only some of the most prominent.

■ **Wagner Act** The National Labor Relations Act, a law passed by Congress in 1935 that defined unfair labor practices and protected unions against coercive measures such as blacklisting.

blacklisting Practice in which businesses share information to deny employment to workers known to belong to unions.

■ **National Youth Administration** (NYA) Program established in 1935 to provide employment for young people and help needy high school and college students.

■ **Mary McLeod Bethune** African American educator who, as director of the Division of Negro Affairs within the NYA, was a strong and vocal advocate for equality of opportunity for African Americans during the New Deal.

In the West, several huge dam construction projects significantly changed the course of rivers. Boulder Dam, on the Colorado River, later renamed Hoover Dam, was begun during the Hoover administration to generate electricity and to provide water to southern California. In Washington and Oregon, the PWA funded the massive Grand Coulee Dam on the Columbia River, the largest electrical power facility in the United States, providing the foundation for economic development in that region. The Fort Peck Dam in Montana, a PWA project on the Missouri River, was the largest earthen dam in the world when it was completed in 1939. The Central Valley Project in central California began with WPA funding and built dams, reservoirs, and irrigation canals.

The WPA employed over 2.1 million people a year between 1935 and 1938. Many did manual labor, building roads, schools, and other public facilities in partnership with local governments. The WPA sought to pay wages higher than relief payments but lower than local wages. Wages for nonwhites and women were the exception, generally exceeding the local rate. The WPA did not duplicate the PWA. Its projects usually spent less on materials than the PWA, and often created less durable structures.

The WPA was more than construction—it also created jobs for professionals, writers, artists, actors and actresses, and musicians. Unemployed historians, writers, and teachers conducted oral interviews, including sessions with nearly every living ex-slave, and wrote state and local histories and guidebooks. Theater groups and orchestras toured towns and cities, performing Shakespeare and Beethoven. By 1939 an estimated 30 million people had watched a WPA production. Unemployed artists created works for public buildings. Some Americans objected to actors, artists, and writers receiving aid, arguing that their labor was not real work. But Hopkins bluntly responded, "Hell, they got to eat just like other people."

The WPA also made special efforts to help women, members of racial and ethnic minority groups, students, and young adults. Prodded by Eleanor Roosevelt, the WPA employed between 300,000 and 400,000 women a year. Some were hired as teachers and nurses, but the majority, especially in rural areas, worked on sewing and canning projects. Efforts to ensure African American employment met with success in the northeastern states but were less successful in the South. The **National Youth Administration** (NYA), created in 1935 and directed by Aubrey Williams, developed a successful program to aid college and high school students and young people not in school. **Mary McLeod Bethune**, an African American educator, directed the NYA's Division of Negro Affairs. Through determination and constant, skillfully applied pressure, she obtained support for

TABLE 22.1 Selected Major Legislation of the New Deal

YEAR	NEW DEAL PROGRAMS	PURPOSE
1933	March 9–June 16: The "First Hundred Days"	
	Emergency Banking Relief Act	Stabilize banking
	Civilian Conservation Corps	Put young men to work on conservation projects
	Federal Emergency Relief Act	Supplement state and local relief efforts
	Agricultural Adjustment Act	Bring agricultural recovery through limiting production
	Tennessee Valley Authority	Plan economic development of Tennessee River Valley
	Home Owners Refinancing Act	Assist homeowners to prevent foreclosures
	Banking Act of 1933	Establish FDIC to insure bank deposits and stabilize banking
	National Industrial Recovery Act, Title I: National Recovery Administration	Create industry-wide codes of fair competition to plan recovery of industries
	National Industrial Recovery Act, Title II: Public Works Administration	Stimulate economy through public works projects
1934	Securities and Exchange Act	Regulate issuance of corporate stocks and bonds
	Indian Reorganization Act	Restore tribal government, halt some forced assimilation programs
1935	Emergency Relief Appropriations Act (ERAA)	Establish Works Progress Administration to work with state and local governments to provide jobs to the unemployed
	June–August: the "Second Hundred Days"	
	National Labor Relations Act (Wagner Act)	Regulate labor relations and collective bargaining
	Social Security Act	Provide old-age pensions, unemployment compensation, support for the disabled
	Revenue Act of 1935 ("Wealth Tax Act")	Increase taxes on upper incomes to pay for relief and recovery programs

black schools and colleges and increased the number of African Americans enrolled in vocational and recreational programs.

While the WPA was intended primarily for relief, the Wagner Act was a major reform. It came at a time when organized labor was at a crossroads. The unions that made up the American Federation of Labor (discussed in Chapter 17) had organized many skilled workers but not those of the major mass-production industries—steel, automobiles, rubber, textiles—and had generally avoided unskilled or less skilled workers. Some AFL unions limited their membership to whites or males. John L. Lewis of the United Mine Workers (coal miners), an industrial union that originated in the Knights of Labor, had insisted on the inclusion of Section 7a in the NRA and had used it to launch a successful organizing drive among coal miners. He argued that the AFL should organize the large mass-production industries on an industrial model, with one union for all workers in the industry, regardless of skill. That approach violated the long-standing AFL policy of separate unions for each skill group. When the AFL leaders turned Lewis down, in 1935, he formed the Committee on Industrial Organization (CIO) within the AFL. Composed of several AFL affiliates committed to the industrial model, the CIO launched organizing drives in the automobile, steel, rubber, electrical equipment, and textile industries. The Wagner Act gave their efforts important federal support. Most AFL craft unions opposed Lewis's efforts, and after marking important victories in the automobile and steel industries in 1937, Lewis led the CIO unions out of the AFL in 1938. They formed the **Congress of Industrial Organizations** and began to charter new industrial unions. Some of the AFL unions, notably the Carpenters, Machinists, and Teamsters, launched their own organizing drives, sometimes on an industrial model. Under the Wagner Act, unions nearly doubled their membership in five years, and the percentage of the **private-sector** work force in unions eventually reached an all-time high of 39 percent in 1958.

Like industrial workers, many farmers put their trust in Roosevelt and the New Deal. By 1935, the AAA appeared to be working as farm prices climbed and the purchasing power of farmers increased (see Figure 22.2). But there was a cost. Tenant farmers and sharecroppers usually received no share of the AAA payments paid to their landlords and sometimes found themselves evicted from their farms—a million by the end of 1935—so that landlords could obtain payment for taking the land out of production. In 1936, the New Deal plan for agriculture collapsed when the Supreme Court ruled that the AAA's production quotas and special tax on processing companies were unconstitutional in *United States v. Butler*. Quickly, the administration turned to other programs, including the **Soil Conservation and Domestic Allocation Act**, to reduce production.

In 1938, Congress approved a second Agricultural Adjustment Act that reestablished the principle of federal quotas on production, acreage reduction, and subsidies. By 1939, farm income had more than doubled since 1932, with the government providing over $4.5 billion in aid to farmers. Initially intended as a short-term measure, federal farm subsidies have

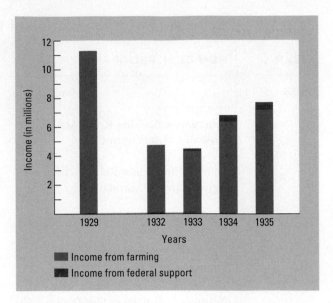

FIGURE 22.2 Farm Income, 1929–1935
Prices for farm products fell rapidly as the Depression set in, but by 1933, with support from New Deal programs, some farm incomes were rising. Some of the increase was a direct result of government payments.

Source: *U.S. Department of Commerce, Historical Statistics of the United States, Colonial Times to 1970, Bicentennial Edition, 2 vols. (Washington, D.C.: U.S. Government Printing Office, 1975), 1: 483–484.*

continued and significantly changed the relationship between agricultural producers and the federal government.

Nature also helped take land out of production as drought devastated a five-state region in the southern Great Plains (see Map 22.4). Above-average rainfall previously had encouraged the extension of wheat farming, but in the early 1930s reduced rainfall led to crop failure. The drought continued for several years, becoming the worst in U.S. history. Then high winds swept across the drought-plagued land, generating gigantic dust storms that could stretch more than 200 miles across and over 7,000 feet high. A reporter labeled the region the **Dust Bowl**. Millions of tons of topsoil blew away, much of it all the way to the Atlantic Ocean. Beginning in 1937, New Deal programs planted trees in shelterbelts across the drought-ravaged region and taught farmers new farming techniques, reducing erosion by two-thirds within a short time.

By the mid-1930s, thousands of farm families displaced by drought, technology, Depression, or the AAA headed for California, hoping to start over. Many of them found work as seasonal agricultural workers, following the crops, picking peaches and peas, grapes and plums. Few Californians greeted them warmly. The Los Angeles police chief sent police units to the state border to encourage them to turn back. Usually denigrated as Okies regardless of the state from which they came, they encountered miserable living conditions.

■ **Congress of Industrial Organizations** Labor organization established in 1938 by a group of unions that left the AFL to unionize workers by industry rather than by trade.

private sector Businesses owned by shareholders or individuals.

■ *United States v. Butler* Supreme Court decision (1936) declaring the Agricultural Adjustment Act invalid on the grounds that it unconstitutionally extended the powers of the federal government.

Soil Conservation and Domestic Allocation Act Legislation passed by Congress in 1935 and 1936 that sought to prevent soil erosion by paying farmers to replace soil-depleting crops with grasses and other crops that would help to hold the soil.

■ **Dust Bowl** Region devastated by drought and dust storms that began in the early 1930s; the worst years (1936–1938) saw over sixty major storms per year, seventy-two in 1937.

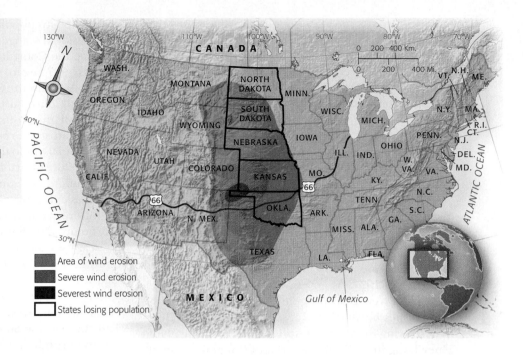

MAP 22.4 The Dust Bowl
Throughout the 1930s, sun and wind eroded millions of acres of cropland, sending millions of tons of topsoil into the air in gigantic dust clouds. This map shows the regions most affected by the Dust Bowl and decreases in population, and Route 66, which many traveled west to California. Copyright © Cengage Learning

Area of wind erosion
Severe wind erosion
Severest wind erosion
States losing population

Most migratory labor camps lacked even rudimentary sanitation, and most migratory labor families could not afford proper diets or health care. A survey of a thousand migratory children in the San Joaquin valley during 1936–37 found 831 with medical problems, most caused by malnutrition or poor hygiene.

California's migratory farm workers were among those who benefited from the work of the Resettlement

Administration (RA), created by executive order in 1935. The RA sought to address rural poverty everywhere in the country—western migrant farm workers, southern sharecroppers, and other impoverished farm families—by helping them to establish new working lives in planned communities or, in a few cases, communal farms. The Resettlement Administration only touched a small percentage of those in need before it was absorbed by a new agency, the Farm Security Administration (FSA), in 1937, which continued its work. In California, the RA began to construct migrant labor camps with adequate sanitation and housing, and the FSA continued that work.

Rural Americans everywhere benefited from the **Rural Electrification Administration** (REA), created in 1935. Utility companies had refused to extend electrical service to much of rural America, arguing that rural areas could not be profitable. In 1935, only 10.5 percent of farms had electricity. The REA bypassed private utility companies by aiding in the formation of rural electrical cooperatives. Within just five years, the REA had extended electrical service to a million more farms, 25 percent of the total. By 1950, 90 percent of farms were electrified. The electrification of rural America helped integrate those areas into modern culture. Electricity improved education, health, and sanitation, and encouraged the diversification of agriculture

The Dust Bowl was a major ecological disaster that swept across the Great Plains, devastating farms and families. One storm in 1935 displaced more dirt than was removed in building the Panama Canal. In this picture a young boy in Cameron County, Oklahoma, stands in the dust.

■ **Rural Electrification Administration** (REA) Government agency established in 1935 to loan money to rural cooperatives to produce and distribute electricity.

and the introduction of new industries. It lessened the drudgery of farm life, giving families running water and access to a variety of electrical appliances. Within eight months of receiving electricity, new consumers bought an average of $180 in appliances—with the two most common an electric iron and a radio.

The Election of 1936 and the Waning of the New Deal

By the end of 1935, Roosevelt had effectively reasserted his leadership and popularity. The chances of a successful Republican or third-party challenge to the president were remote. In a less than enthusiastic convention, Republicans nominated **Alfred Landon** of Kansas, one of the few Republican governors reelected in 1934. As governor, he had accepted and used most New Deal programs, but in keeping with party wishes he attacked Roosevelt and the New Deal as destroying the values of America. After the death of Huey Long in 1935, Townsend and Coughlin formed a third party, the Union Party, but posed no threat to Roosevelt's reelection. Roosevelt followed a wise path, reminding voters of the New Deal's achievements and denouncing big business as greedy. Roosevelt won with the largest percentage of the vote up to that time. Landon carried Maine and Vermont.

The Democratic victory demonstrated not only the personal appeal of Roosevelt but also an acceptance of an activist government that could provide social and economic benefits. Roosevelt's second inaugural address, sometimes referred to as the "one-third speech," raised expectations of a Third Hundred Days. "I see millions of families trying to live on incomes so meager that the pall of family disaster hangs over them day by day," he announced. "I see one-third of a nation ill-housed, ill-clad, ill-nourished." The words seemed to promise new legislation aimed at helping the poor and the working class.

A Third Hundred Days failed to materialize. Instead of promoting new social legislation, Roosevelt

first pitched his popularity against the Supreme Court. The president's anger at the Court had been growing since the Court had invalidated the NRA and the AAA. As 1937 began, legal challenges to the TVA, the Wagner Act, and the Social Security Act were on their way to the Court. Further, there had been not a single vacancy on the Court during Roosevelt's first term, a highly unusual occurrence. Fearing the Court was determined to undo the New Deal, Roosevelt proposed to enlarge the Court. His rationale was that the Court's elderly judges were unable to keep up with their work, and he asked Congress for authority to add a new justice for every one over age 70 who had served on the Court more than ten years. His real objective was obvious to all—he wanted to be able to add enough justices to protect the New Deal from the Court's conservative majority.

The **court-packing plan** proved a major political miscalculation. Several conservative Democrats, especially those in the South, saw an opportunity to break with the president and led opposition in the Senate. Roosevelt's effort was further weakened when enough justices changed sides that the Court upheld a state's minimum-wage law, the Wagner Act, and the Social Security system, something since called the **Judicial Revolution of 1937**. After Justice Willis Van Devanter, a conservative, announced his retirement, Roosevelt dropped his proposal and happily appointed Hugo Black, a New Deal senator from Alabama, to the Court. Before he left office, Roosevelt had appointed every member of the Court but one.

Another setback that snagged the Roosevelt agenda was a recession, dubbed **Roosevelt's recession** by critics. As the economy stabilized by 1937, industrial outputs reached their 1929 levels, and unemployment fell to 14 percent. Secretary of the Treasury Henry Morgenthau urged Roosevelt to reduce government spending and move toward a more balanced budget. Roosevelt agreed and cut back relief programs, releasing nearly 1.5 million workers from the WPA. But the economy was not strong enough to cope with reduced government spending and thousands of people seeking jobs. At the same time, the new Social Security payments somewhat reduced the paychecks of most employed people, causing some people to cut back purchases. Unemployment soared to 19 percent. The recovery collapsed, and in April 1938 Roosevelt restored spending. The WPA and other agencies rehired those released, but Roosevelt's image of being able to manage recovery was tarnished.

It was not just the court-packing plan and the recession that weakened the New Deal. Some Americans also opposed the higher taxes on the wealthy approved in 1935. Labor strife was increasing concern about unions and their relation to the New Deal. The United Automobile Workers, one of the new CIO unions, had occupied factories as part of a strike, and

Alfred Landon Kansas governor who ran unsuccessfully for president on the Republican ticket in 1936.

■ **court-packing plan** Roosevelt's effort in 1937 to expand the Supreme Court so that he could appoint more of its members; the proposal energized conservative opposition, hampering further New Deal legislation.

Judicial Revolution of 1937 Name sometimes applied to the change in direction by the Supreme Court in 1937, whereby it accepted the constitutionality of New Deal–type federal intervention in the economy.

■ **Roosevelt's recession** Economic downturn that occurred when Roosevelt, responding to improving economic figures, cut $4 billion from the federal budget, mostly by reducing relief spending.

such "sit-down" strikes alienated many who considered them violations of property rights. The public's mood had changed. The American people, Hopkins observed, were now "bored with the poor, the unemployed, and the insecure."

Despite waning support, the administration managed to pass two more significant pieces of legislation. In 1938, a second Agricultural Adjustment Act reestablished the principle of federally set quotas on specific commodities, acreage reduction, and subsidy payments. The **Fair Labor Standards Act**, also passed in 1938, addressed issues that Frances Perkins had long championed. It established forty-four hours as the standard workweek, set a minimum wage (25 cents an hour), and outlawed child labor (under age 16). With its minimum-wage provision, the act was especially beneficial to unskilled and nonunion workers and to workers from racial and ethnic minority groups. It was also the last piece of New Deal legislation.

In the November 1938 congressional elections, Roosevelt failed to get New Deal supporters elected, and Republicans increased their numbers and influence in Congress. Now conservative Democrats, mostly from the South, increasingly joined Republicans in a **conservative coalition** that could derail new liberal programs. Roosevelt recognized political reality and asked for no new domestic programs. The legislative New Deal was over, but the changes it generated remained part of the American social, economic, and political culture. By 1939, the economy was recovering, with some economic indicators reaching the point where they had been in 1929 and 1937, before the Roosevelt recession. But unemployment and underemployment persisted. Eight million were still unemployed, and there was no effort to provide more relief jobs or programs. Jobs and full "recovery" did not appear until 1942, when the United States mobilized for a second world war. Wartime spending finally propelled the American economy out of the Depression and to new levels of prosperity.

AMERICANS FACE THE DEPRESSION

★ How did Americans cope with the many challenges presented by the Great Depression?

★ What opportunities opened for women, African Americans, Latinos, Asian Americans, and Native Americans, and what challenges faced these groups during the 1930s?

★ How did the Depression and New Deal affect cultural expression?

One reason the New Deal was able to establish new patterns of government responsibility was that the Depression touched every segment of American life.

Poverty and hardship were no longer reserved for those viewed as unworthy or relegated to remote areas and inner cities. Now poverty included blue- and white-collar workers, and even some of the once-rich. Most Americans worried about their futures and economic insecurity—that the next day might bring a reduction in wages, the loss of a job, or the closing of a business.

"Making Do"

To help those facing economic insecurity, magazines and newspapers provided useful hints and "Depression recipes" that stretched budgets and included information about nutrition. According to home economists, a careful shopper could feed a family of five on as little as $8 (equivalent to $132 today) a week. This was comforting news for those with that much to spend, but for many families and for relief agencies $8 a week for food was beyond possibility. Before the New Deal, New York City provided only $2.39 a week for each family on relief. Things were bad, comedian Groucho Marx joked, when "pigeons started feeding people in Central Park."

Like New York, most towns and cities by 1933 had little ability to provide more than the smallest amount of relief and struggled unsuccessfully to maintain basic city services. Experiencing a shrinking tax base, local, county, and state governments not only cut back or eliminated relief but were sometimes forced to lay off teachers, policemen, and other workers. A city spokesman in Birmingham, Alabama, presented the choices: "I am as much in favor of relief . . . as anyone, but I am unwilling to continue this relief at the expense of bankrupting . . . Birmingham." Because state and local governments depended on property taxes, the New Deal indirectly provided assistance for local and state governments as the HOLC and the FHA saved homes, stimulated some new construction, and restored property tax bases. Federal agencies, especially the PWA and the WPA, not only provided many local civic improvements—schools, post offices, hospitals, other government buildings, roads, and bridges—but also reduced local relief responsibilities. Other federal programs also helped to lessen the burdens of local and state governments. In North Dakota, for example, it was estimated that two-thirds of the people drew some form of federal

■ **Fair Labor Standards Act** 1938 law that established a minimum wage and a maximum workweek and forbade labor by children under 16.

conservative coalition An informal cooperative relationship between conservative Democrats, mostly from the South, and Republicans, which often controlled Congress during the three or four decades following 1937.

Throughout the Depression, the most popular form of entertainment was probably the movies, providing escape from daily hardships into a fantasy world. At 20 cents a ticket, movies attracted as many as 75 million people a week, and theaters often offered the additional lure of drawings for prizes. In this photo, taken in 1938, a movie theater is showing *Room Service*, one of the Marx Brothers' madcap comedies, and *Flight to Fame*, a science-fiction thriller. Judging by the tangle of bicycles in front of the theater, the photo was likely taken during a Saturday matinee, a popular weekend pastime for young people. At the time, many movie theaters featured a bicycle rack in front, to accommodate their young patrons.

assistance. Thus, the New Deal drastically altered the relationship between local and national government. Increasingly people saw the national government as having an obligation to support families and communities against economic adversity.

"Use it up, wear it out, make it do, or do without" became the motto of most American families. In many working-class and middle-class neighborhoods, "making do" meant that many homes sprouted signs announcing a variety of services—household beauty parlors, kitchen bakeries, rooms for boarders. A Milwaukee woman recalled, "I did baking at home to supplement our income. I got 9 cents for a loaf of bread and 25 cents for an apple cake. . . . I cleared about $65 a month." A sewing machine salesman commented that he was selling more and more machines to people who would not previously have done their own sewing. For farm families, feed sacks had long provided fabric for sewing, and companies now competed by printing attractive designs on their sacks. One woman remembered her mother making a pretty new school dress out of a sack that had "a sky-blue background with gorgeous mallard ducks on it."

Still, even with "making do," many families—especially in the working class—failed, first losing jobs, and then homes. Some families moved in with relatives. One man remembered that during the Depression most households were like his, "where father, mother, children, aunts, uncles and grandma lived together." Approximately one-sixth of America's urban families "doubled up." Millions of others took to the road. Over 3 million loaded their meager possessions on their jalopies and traveled across the country looking for a better life. Many found their families and lives torn apart. Some rode the rails, hitching rides in boxcars, living in Hoovervilles, begging and scrounging for food and supplies along the road. Records show increased numbers of suicides, admissions to state mental hospitals, and children placed in orphanages. Some worried about the psychological problems created as women and children replaced husbands and fathers as breadwinners. A social worker remembered, "I used to see men cry because they didn't have a job."

Despite the hardships and migrations, American society did not collapse, as some had predicted. The vast majority of Americans clung tightly to traditional social norms and even expanded family togetherness. Economic necessity kept families at home. They played cards and board games, read books and magazines, and tended vegetable and flower gardens. The game of Monopoly, which allowed players to fantasize about becoming millionaires and bankrupting the other players, zoomed to popularity in the mid-1930s. Church attendance rose, and the number of divorces declined. Fewer people got married, and the birth rate fell.

Discrimination and Depression

The Depression and the New Deal provided mixed experiences for women, African Americans, Asian Americans, Latinos, and American Indians. For the large majority of American males, their self-image included the responsibility of providing for their families. As unemployment rose, public opinion polls found that most people, including women, believed that men should have jobs. Some companies dismissed or refused to hire married women. The number of women in the professions declined from 14.2 to 12.3 percent. Teachers were particularly vulnerable. One survey found that, of 1,500 school districts, 77 percent did not hire married women, and 63 percent had fired women when they married. By 1932, 2 million women were out of work, and an estimated 145,000 women were homeless, wandering across America. But employment patterns were uneven. Women in low-paying and low-status jobs were less likely to be laid off and more likely to find employment. White women also took jobs traditionally held by African Americans, especially in domestic service.

Few working women, however, found that bringing home a paycheck changed their status or role within the family. Most husbands still expected to be the head of the household—to maintain authority and dominance within the home, even if unemployed. Few husbands helped with work around the house, as such work challenged their notions of masculinity. One husband agreed to help with the laundry but refused to hang the wash outside for fear that neighbors might see him. At home women renewed and reaffirmed traditional roles: they sewed, baked bread, and canned fruits and vegetables. At the same time, a woman's traditional role as mother continued to change somewhat—the birth rate continued to fall, as did family size, thus extending the patterns first seen in the 1920s of married couples having fewer children or even no children (as indicated in Figure 21.3, page 607). While some of the change was probably due to couples agreeing that they could not afford children at the time, in other cases it was undoubtedly due to decisions made by women. The declining size of families also resulted from the postponement

Giving Her a Lift to Town - - - - - - - - —By Knott

President Franklin D. Roosevelt campaigned on helping the "forgotten man." As shown in this political cartoon, as First Lady, Eleanor Roosevelt did not forget women. She worked diligently to ensure that they benefited from the New Deal and had access to government and the Democratic Party.

of marriage because of finances—the older a couple is when they marry, the fewer children they are likely to have. Through it all, women were often praised as pillars of stability in a changing and perilous society. One woman remembered, "I did what I had to do. I seemed to always find a way to make things work."

The Depression's economic impact intensified economic and social difficulties for African Americans, Latinos, and Asians, who faced increased racial hostility and demands that they give up their jobs to whites. In Tucson, Arizona, "Mexicans" were accused of "taking the bread out of our white children's mouths." Low-paying, frequently temporary jobs and high unemployment made life in Latino communities difficult. On farms in California, Mexican American workers were being replaced by Anglos, including those fleeing the Dust Bowl. Those managing to find work in the fields earned only $289 a year—about a third of what the government estimated it took to maintain a subsistence budget.

In the early 1930s, especially, the Immigration and Naturalization Service (INS) worked with local authorities to facilitate **repatriation** of Mexican nationals to Mexico. Some local and state agencies gave free transportation to the border for those willing to leave. In one Indiana town, Mexicans and Mexican Americans were denied relief and encouraged to board a special train to Mexico. "They weren't forcing you to leave," recalled one *repatriado*, "they gave you a choice, starve or go back to Mexico." In several cities, the INS conducted sweeps of Mexican American communities to scare Mexicans into leaving and to round up illegal immigrants for deportation. In Los Angeles such sweeps resulted in nearly ten thousand Mexicans and Mexican Americans boarding special trains bound for Mexico. Nationally, more than half a million had left by 1937.

There was no comparable effort to repatriate Asians living on the West Coast, but Asian immigrants and Asian Americans remained isolated and often received inadequate relief. In San Francisco, where nearly one-sixth of the Asian population picked up benefits, they received from 10 to 20 percent less than whites, probably because relief agencies subscribed to the stereotype that Asians could subsist on a less expensive diet. Hoping to remove economic and social barriers, some Asians intensified ongoing efforts to assimilate, becoming "200 percent Americans." The Japanese American Citizens League was organized in 1929 to overcome discrimination and oppose anti-Asian legislation, but by 1940 the group had made little headway.

Before 1929, African Americans working as sharecroppers, farm hands, and tenant farmers in the South were already experiencing depression conditions, earning only about $200 a year. Their lives worsened as farm prices continued to fall and as hard times and the AAA increased evictions during the Depression. Many migrated to urban areas, seeking more economic security. Cities, however, provided few opportunities because whites were taking jobs that, like domestic service jobs, were previously held by African Americans. In most cases, joblessness among African Americans in urban areas averaged 20 to 50 percent higher than for whites. Compounding the high unemployment, across the nation blacks faced increased

racial hostility, violence, and intimidation. In 1931 the attention of the nation was drawn to Scottsboro, Alabama, where nine black men had been arrested and charged with raping two white prostitutes. Although no physical evidence linked the men to the crime, a jury of white males did not question the testimony of the women and quickly found the so-called **Scottsboro Nine** guilty. Eight were sentenced to death; the ninth, a minor, escaped the death penalty. Through appeals, intervention by the Supreme Court, retrials, parole, and escape, all those convicted were free by 1950.

A New Deal for All?

Like the Depression, the New Deal affected women and members of racial and ethnic minority groups in different ways, but generally it inspired a belief that the Roosevelt government cared and was trying to improve their lives. Eleanor Roosevelt was at the center of this image of compassion. She frequently acted as the social conscience of the administration and prodded her husband and other New Dealers not to forget women and people of color. "I'm the agitator,"

Time Life Pictures/Getty Images.

When the Daughters of the American Revolution denied opera singer Marian Anderson the use of Constitution Hall because of her race, Eleanor Roosevelt arranged a public concert at the Lincoln Memorial that drew more than seventy-five thousand people.

repatriation The return of people to their nation of birth or citizenship; repatriation of Mexicans from the United States during the Depression was at its height from 1929 to 1931.

Scottsboro Nine Nine African Americans convicted of raping two white women in a freight train in Alabama in 1931; their case became famous as an example of racism in the legal system.

she once said. "He's the politician." She crossed the country meeting and listening to people. She received thousands of letters that described people's hardships and asked for help. Although she was rarely able to provide direct assistance, her replies emphasized hope and pointed to the changes being made by the New Deal.

Within the White House, she helped convene a special White House conference on the needs of women in 1933 and, with the help of Frances Perkins and other women in the administration, worked to ensure that women received more than just token consideration from New Deal agencies. Ellen Woodward, who served as assistant director of the FERA and the WPA, was successful in promoting a few women's programs—headed by women. Still, New Deal agencies frequently paid women less than men, and fewer women were enrolled in relief programs. Women made up only about 10 percent of the WPA's work force, and the largest number were in programs focused on traditional women's skills, such as sewing. Large numbers of female wage-earners were left outside the Social Security Act and the Fair Labor Standards Act because both excluded domestic workers and similar service occupations with large proportions of women. Yet, despite these shortcomings, the New Deal provided women with more programs and positions in government than at any previous time in American history.

For African Americans and Latinos, the Roosevelts and the New Deal provided a large amount of hope and a lesser amount of change. More African Americans than ever before were appointed to government positions. Mary Bethune in 1936 organized African Americans in the administration into a "**Black Cabinet**" that met in her home and acted as a semiofficial advisory commission on racial relations. "We must think in terms of a 'whole' for the greatest service of our people," she said. Among the most pressing needs, the Black Cabinet concluded, was access to relief and jobs. The New Deal provided both, but never to the extent needed. Some New Deal administrators, notably Interior Secretary Harold Ickes and Hopkins, took steps to ensure that the PWA, WPA, and other New Deal agencies included members of racial and ethnic minority groups, especially African Americans. In northern cities, the WPA and the PWA nearly eliminated discrimination from their programs, but they had less success in other parts of the nation, where skilled African American workers were often given menial minimum-wage jobs. Other agencies were less supportive. The Civilian Conservation Corps and the Tennessee Valley Authority practiced racial segregation and wage discrimination. Still, by 1938, nearly 30 percent of African Americans were receiving some federal relief, with the WPA alone supporting almost a million African American families.

Library of Congress.

Some WPA projects sought to teach new skills to the unemployed. This WPA project at Costilla, New Mexico, taught local women, many of them of Mexican ancestry, how to make rag rugs using a loom. This woman is running a shuttle through a warp.

But even in the best of cases, it was not enough. In Cleveland, 40 percent of PWA jobs were reserved for African Americans, but there, as across the nation, black unemployment and poverty remained higher than for whites.

FDR also refused to support civil rights legislation. When confronted by black leaders for his refusal to promote an antilynching law, Roosevelt explained, "If I come out for the anti-lynching bill now, they [powerful southern Democrats] will block every bill I ask Congress to pass. . . . I just can't take that risk." Eleanor Roosevelt was willing to take more risks and visibly supported equality for racial and ethnic minority groups. In 1939, when the Daughters of the American Revolution refused to allow renowned black opera singer Marian Anderson to sing at their concert hall in Washington, the First Lady resigned her membership and, with assistance from Ickes, arranged a public concert on the steps of the Lincoln Memorial. Anderson's performance before Lincoln's statue attracted more than seventy-five thousand people.

Latinos benefited from the New Deal in much the same way as African Americans. In New Mexico and other western states, the Depression curtailed much of the migratory farm work for Mexican American workers, devastating local economies. New Deal

■ **Black Cabinet** Semiofficial advisory committee on racial affairs organized by Mary McLeod Bethune in 1936 and made up of African American members of the Roosevelt administration.

agencies such as the CCC, PWA, and WPA provided welcome jobs and income. A worker in a CCC camp in northern New Mexico remembered, "I had plenty to eat, . . . I had brand new clothes when I went to the CCC camps." Throughout the Southwest, federal agencies not only included Mexican Americans but also sometimes paid wages that exceeded what they received in the private sector. The WPA paid $8.54 a week for unskilled labor, whereas a comparable job in the private sector would have yielded an average of $6.02 or less. Discrimination, however, was still practiced, often enhanced by language differences.

New Deal legislation helped union organizers trying to assist Latino workers throughout the West. San Antonio's Mexican American pecan shellers, mostly women, were among the lowest-paid workers in the country, earning less than 4 cents per pound of shelled pecans, which amounted to an annual wage of less than $180. In 1934, 1935, and again in 1938, union organizers, including local activist "Red" Emma Tenayuca, led the pecan shellers in strikes, finally gaining higher wages and union recognition in 1938, under the auspices of the recently chartered United Cannery, Agricultural, Packing, and Allied Workers of America (UCAPAWA), the CIO's industrial union for farm workers and food processing workers. The UCAPAWA, which included a number of Communists among its organizers, also organized Mexican women working in California canneries. Efforts to organize field workers, however, came up against strong opposition from local growers, organized in California as the Associated Farmers and backed by some of the most powerful corporations in the West.

Despite its limitations, the New Deal provided hope and support for many women and members of racial and ethnic minority groups, who in turn praised Roosevelt. "The WPA came along, and Roosevelt came to be a god," said one African American. "You worked, you got a paycheck, and you had some dignity." Politically, such sentiments were more than praise because, where they could vote, many women and members of racial and ethnic minority groups began to vote for Roosevelt and the Democratic Party. Blacks bolted the Republican Party and enlisted in extraordinary numbers in the Democratic Party. In the 1936 presidential election, Roosevelt carried every black ward in Cleveland and, nationally, received nearly 90 percent of the black vote. By 1939, the Democratic Party was providing a political vehicle for the aspirations of industrial workers, people of color, and farmers.

John Collier worked to ensure the passage of the Indian Reorganization Act. This photo shows a group of Navajos meeting with Collier to discuss government-imposed limitations on the number of sheep each Navajo could own.

Native Americans directly benefited from the New Deal. They had two strong supporters in Secretary of the Interior Ickes and Commissioner of Indian Affairs John Collier. Both opposed existing Indian policies that since 1887 had sought to destroy the reservation system and eradicate Indian cultures. At Collier's urging, Congress passed the **Indian Reorganization Act** in 1934. Designed to restore tribal sovereignty under federal authority, the act returned land and community control to tribal organizations, permitted Indian self-rule on a reservation if reservation residents so decided, and ended the process of allocating reservation lands in severalty (discussed in Chapter 17). Each tribe had to ratify the act to participate, and not all tribes did so. Seventy-seven rejected the changes, including the Navajos, the nation's largest tribe, although some of those who initially rejected the act later changed their decision.

To improve the squalid conditions on most reservations and to provide jobs, Collier organized a CCC-type agency for Indians and ensured that other New Deal agencies played a part in improving Indian lands and providing jobs. He also promoted Native American culture. Working with tribal leaders, Collier took measures to protect, preserve, and encourage Indian customs, languages, religions, and folkways. Reservation school curricula incorporated Indian languages and customs, and Native Americans could once more openly and freely exercise their religions. While a positive effort, the so-called Indian New Deal did

■ **Indian Reorganization Act** 1934 law that ended Indian allotment, returned surplus land to tribal ownership, and encouraged tribal self-government.

Part of a mural depicting California agriculture, painted by Maxine Albro in 1934 as part of one of the earliest New Deal art projects, funded by the CWA, in Coit Tower, San Francisco. Note the blue eagles of the NRA on the packing crates for the oranges. The white flowers are calla lilies and are likely an homage to Diego Rivera, who often included calla lilies in his paintings and whose Rockefeller Center mural was destroyed while the Coit Tower murals were in progress. Most of the dozen-plus artists working in Coit Tower consciously adopted Rivera's style. One small mural there was removed because it included a hammer and sickle, a symbol of communism.

little to improve the standard of living for most American Indians. Funds were too few, and the problems created by years of poverty and government neglect were too great. Some tribal leaders complained that Collier's programs had been drafted with little or no participation by Indians themselves. At best, the programs slowed a long-standing economic decline and allowed Native Americans to regain some control over their cultures and societies.

Cultural Expression in the Midst of Depression

The homogenization of culture that began in the 1920s due to the movies and radio continued in the 1930s. At the same time, however, there were significant changes in cultural expression. During the 1920s, many American writers and artists had rejected their consumer-oriented society, producing novels depicting hedonism or escapism (discussed in the previous chapter). Many leading writers of the 1930s changed that focus, portraying instead working people and their problems or looking for inspiration to figures in American history. Many artists turned to a more realistic style.

A generation of painters, some of whom produced works of social criticism during the 1930s, were influenced by Diego Rivera, a great Mexican muralist whose work in Rockefeller Center in New York City was destroyed in 1934 because of its Marxist politics. Other Depression-era artists, particularly those in the Federal Arts Project (FAP) of the WPA, depicted the lives of ordinary people or themes from American history, especially scenes of hardy white pioneers. By one count, FAP artists produced some 200,000 individual works of art—murals, paintings, and sculptures—nearly all intended for public display.

Novels during the 1930s were frequently critical of American society and politics. Some leading authors depicted inequities caused by capitalism, racism, and class differences. John Steinbeck defined the social protest novel of the 1930s. Among his early works, *Tortilla Flat* (1933) portrayed the lives of Mexican Californians and *In Dubious Battle* (1936) presented an apple-pickers' strike through the eyes of an idealistic young Communist. *The Grapes of Wrath* (1939), which won the Pulitzer Prize for the best novel of the year, presented the Joad family, who lost their farm in Oklahoma and migrated to California where their family disintegrated under the strain of life as migratory farm workers. Similar social criticism appeared in Erskine Caldwell's *Tobacco Road* (1932), about Georgia sharecroppers, and Richard Wright's *Native Son* (1940), a critique of racism that became the first Book of the Month Club selection by an African American author. Ernest Hemingway's *For Whom the Bell Tolls* (1940) depicted an American fighting fascism in the Spanish Civil War (discussed in the next chapter), a sharp contrast to the hedonism of his *The Sun Also Rises* (1926, discussed in the previous chapter).

Dorothea Lange began photographing the victims of the Depression in the early 1930s and continued that work with the Resettlement Administration and FSA. Lange was among the leading figures in creating the new genre of documentary photography. Her 1936 photograph of a migratory farm worker and her children, later entitled "Migrant Mother," emerged as the most famous and perhaps the most moving photograph of the era. Margaret Bourke-White joined Lange as a pioneer in documentary photography with dramatic photographs of the Fort Peck Dam and moving shots of the victims of the Depression.

As in the 1920s, movies remained popular, providing a welcome break from the woes of the Depression for many people. On a national average, 60 percent of the people saw a movie a week. In the 1920s, some films had glorified gangsters or reveled in the sexuality of such stars as Clara Bow. To head off pressure for federal regulation to prevent such films, the major studios in 1930 created the Motion Picture Production Code, which specified, among other things, that "the sympathy of the audience should never be thrown to the side of crime, wrongdoing, evil or sin." In the context of the Depression, many studio heads insisted that the public needed escapist entertainment to distract them from the Depression. Musical extravaganzas like *Forty-Second Street* (1933)

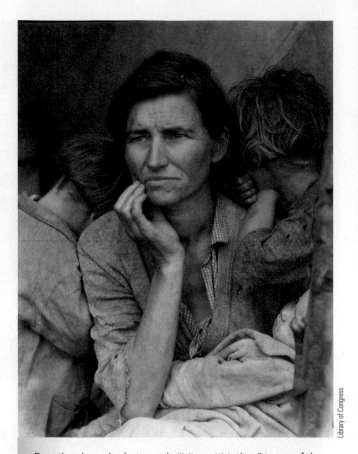

Library of Congress.

Dorothea Lange's photograph, "Migrant Mother," is one of the most famous in the history of photography. Her first caption was "Destitute peapickers in California; a 32 year old mother of seven children. February 1936." Lange later recalled taking her famous picture: "I saw and approached the hungry and desperate mother, as if drawn by a magnet. . . . She said that they had been living on frozen vegetables from the surrounding fields, and birds that the children killed. She had just sold the tires from her car to buy food." Lange's subject was Florence Owens Thompson, born in Oklahoma of Cherokee Indian descent. She and her husband came to California in the late 1920s and worked as farm laborers, traveling the state picking fruit and vegetables. Her daughter—the four-year-old child on the left—later remembered her as "a hard-working disciplinarian who loved red dresses and country music, drank Lucky Lager beer and chewed Garrett snuff [tobacco]."

and *Gold Diggers of 1933* (1933) fit the bill, as did the slapstick comedy of the Marx Brothers, whose *Duck Soup* (1933) is ranked among the best films of all time. Some disdain for the wealthy could be found in popular comedies that contrasted members of a snobby and selfish upper class with the honesty and common sense of ordinary people. Some westerns and gangster films were equally escapist, but others

WORLD'S HIGHEST STANDARD OF LIVING

There's no way like the American Way

Margaret Bourke-White was making a strong social statement in this 1937 photograph of flood victims in Louisville, Kentucky, waiting in line for food.

probed more deeply into the human condition. *Stagecoach* (1939), directed by John Ford, so defined the western genre that it inspired imitators for years after. Frank Capra directed several films that sympathized with the problems of ordinary people; *Mr. Smith Goes to Washington* (1939) showed a naïve but honest ordinary citizen battling political corruption. Hollywood occasionally produced films of social criticism, notably an adaptation of *The Grapes of Wrath* (1940), starring Henry Fonda. Charlie Chaplin's leftist politics were apparent in two important works, *Modern Times* (1936), portraying the dehumanizing tendencies of technology, and *The Great Dictator* (1940), which mocked and criticized Adolph Hitler.

Like movies, radio provided an escape from the concerns of the Depression. Nearly 90 percent of American households included a radio, suggesting that listening to the radio was nearly universal. "Gloom chasers"—that is, comedians, including Jack Benny and the comedy teams of George Burns and Gracie Allen and of Fibber McGee and Molly—filled the radio airways. Crime fighters were popular on the radio, and also in newspaper comic strips and comic books, where Dick Tracy (1931), Superman (1938), and Batman (1939) protected innocent victims from harm and oppression.

THE GREAT DEPRESSION AND NEW DEAL IN PERSPECTIVE

☆ *How did the Great Depression and New Deal affect Americans over the long run?*

A depression—a contraction of the economy causing significant unemployment and lasting several years—was nothing new. Americans had experienced serious photo by John Spence.

Some of the most visible legacies of the New Deal consist of the many public buildings and other public structures, from huge dams to city sidewalks, that were constructed by New Deal agencies. PWA structures were intended to be permanent, attractive additions to communities, and the large majority of them incorporated art, often in the form of murals. Many of the buildings were in an architectural style now often called PWA Moderne, which drew upon the Art Deco and Streamline Moderne styles of the period. This limestone bas-relief sculpture in the Art Deco style, presenting agricultural symbols, especially a woman sowing grain, forms the central decorative element for the Municipal Auditorium in Beatrice, a city of 11,000 people (1940 census) in southeastern Nebraska. The architect was Fred Organ but the identity of the sculptor has not been established. The building was constructed between 1938 and 1940 using local and PWA funds and is now on the National Register of Historic Places. The bas-relief remains the most significant public sculpture in a several-county area.

depressions every thirty to forty years since the 1830s. For generations, mothers had advised daughters always to save up for "hard times." The Great Depression confirmed that wisdom, and left its mark on a generation. For those who lived through the 1930s, "making do" became not just a way of surviving the depression, but a way of life that many continued long after the economy revived.

The New Deal also left its mark on a generation. Some spent the rest of their lives criticizing Roosevelt for destroying free enterprise. Others proudly voted Democratic because their families had survived financially only because of the New Deal. Democrats had been the minority from the election of Lincoln in 1860 until the election of Roosevelt in 1932. Thereafter, Democrats usually won the presidency until 1968, and usually controlled Congress until 1994. But the New Deal Democratic coalition was inherently unstable, including union members and small-scale farmers, southern white supremacists and African Americans in the cities of the north and west, and former socialists and states-rights conservatives.

The New Deal also left the permanent legacy of a more activist federal government—increased regulation of business, Social Security, the Wagner Act, the Fair Labor Standards Act, and more. Virtually no one at the beginning of the twenty-first century questions the appropriateness of a federal program benefiting the elderly or of a federally defined minimum wage. Similarly, Americans now expect that the federal government should take prompt action to prevent any future depression, reduce unemployment, and assist those most in need. Since Roosevelt, Americans have expected presidents, rather than Congress, to be the chief policymakers. In all these ways and more, the Great Depression and New Deal changed how Americans think about themselves and what they expect from their government.

Individual Voices

Frances Perkins Explains the Social Security Act

On September 2, 1935, Secretary of Labor Frances Perkins spoke over the radio to explain the importance of the recently passed Social Security Act. As the Social Security bill was being drafted and considered by Congress, it had come under attack from the right and the left. Conservatives argued that the bill imposed "big government" into an area best served by private and individual efforts. Liberals objected that it was not inclusive enough, leaving out large segments of the work force and providing no health benefits. Because Perkins's speech gave many Americans their first explanation of how the new act would change their lives, historians find in it important information both about the thinking of New Deal policymakers and about the ways that the Roosevelt administration wanted people to understand this new program.

1 What type of worker is most likely to receive a pension? What type of worker would be less likely?

2 In fact, many workers were not covered because of the political compromises necessary to pass the bill.

3 The Roosevelt administration believed that the Social Security program was an important reform in preventing another depression. Why would they believe that?

4 In what ways does Perkins's speech respond to the criticisms from conservatives? From liberals?

People who work for a living in the United States . . . can join with all other good citizens . . . in satisfaction that the Congress has passed the Social Security Act. . . . It provides for old-age pensions which mark great progress over the measures upon which we have hitherto depended in caring for those who have been unable to provide for the years when they no longer can work. It also provides security for dependent and crippled children, mothers, the indigent disabled and the blind.

Old-age benefits in the form of monthly payments are to be paid to individuals who have worked and contributed to the insurance fund in direct proportion to the total wages earned by such individuals in the course of their employment subsequent to 1936. The minimum monthly payment is to be $10, the maximum $85. These payments will begin in the year 1942 and will be to those who have worked and contributed. **1**

Because of difficulty of administration not all employments are covered in this plan at this time . . . but it is sufficiently broad to cover all normally employed industrial workers. . . . It is a sound and reasonable plan. . . . It does not represent a complete solution to the problems of economic security, but it does represent a substantial, necessary beginning. **2**

This is truly legislation in the interest of the national welfare . . . its enactment into law would not only carry us a long way toward the goal of economic security for the individual, but also a long way toward the promotion and stabilization of mass purchasing power without which the present economic system cannot endure. . . . **3**

The passage of this act . . . with so much intelligent public support is deeply significant of the progress which the American people have made in . . . using cooperation through government to overcome social hazards against which the individual alone is inadequate. **4**

Study Tools

SUMMARY

The Great Depression brought about significant changes in American life, altering expectations of government, society, and the economy. When Hoover assumed the presidency, most believed that the economy and quality of life would continue to improve. The Depression changed that. Flaws in the economy were suddenly exposed as the stock market crashed, legions of banks and businesses closed, unemployment soared, and people lost their homes and their hopes for the future.

More than previous presidents, Hoover expanded the role of the federal government to meet the economic and social crises. However, Hoover's measures, including the Reconstruction Finance Corporation, failed to stimulate a worsening economy.

Losing faith in Hoover, most Americans put their trust in Roosevelt and his promise of a New Deal. Roosevelt easily won the 1932 presidential election and took office amid widespread expectations for a major shift in the role of government. The First Hundred Days witnessed a barrage of legislation, most dealing with the immediate problems of unemployment and economic collapse. The Agricultural Adjustment Administration (AAA) and the National Recovery Administration (NRA) were designed to bring economic recovery, while programs such as the Civilian Conservation Corps (CCC) and Public Works Administration (PWA) were intended both to relieve unemployment and to stimulate the economy.

In 1935, assailed by both liberals and conservatives, Roosevelt responded with a second burst of legislation that focused more on putting people to work, economic redistribution, and social legislation, especially Social Security. New Deal programs touched the lives of many Americans, from unemployed laborers to unemployed artists, from struggling farmers to industrial workers. The overwhelming Democratic victory in 1936 confirmed Roosevelt's popularity. But FDR's ill-conceived court-packing plan, an economic downturn, labor unrest, and growing conservatism generated opposition to new legislation, and the New Deal wound down after 1938.

The Depression affected all Americans, as they had to adjust their values and lifestyles to meet the economic

CHRONOLOGY
Depression and New Deal

Year	Event
1928	Herbert Hoover elected president
1929	Stock market crash
	Mexican repatriation begins
	Depression deepens
1929–1933	Thousands of banks and businesses fail
	Unemployment rises from 9 to 25 percent
1931	Scottsboro Nine convicted
1932	Reconstruction Finance Corporation
	Bonus Army marches to Washington
	Franklin D. Roosevelt elected president
1933	Drought and wind create the Dust Bowl
	Franklin D. Roosevelt inaugurated
	New Deal begins
	National Bank Holiday
	First fireside chat
	First Hundred Days (March 9–June 16): CCC, AAA, TVA, HOLC, NRA, and PWA, repeal of Prohibition, Bank Act
1934	Huey Long's Share Our Wealth plan
	Indian Reorganization Act
	Securities and Exchange Commission (SEC) created
	American Liberty League established
	Dr. Francis Townsend's movement begins
	Federal Housing Administration
1935	Works Progress Administration created
	NRA ruled unconstitutional in *Schechter* case
	Second Hundred Days: Social Security, Wagner Act, Wealth Tax Act
	Rural Electrification Administration (REA) formed
	Long assassinated
	Committee on Industrial Organization (CIO) established
1936	AAA ruled unconstitutional in *Butler* case
	Roosevelt reelected
	"Black Cabinet" organized
1937	Court-packing plan
	"Roosevelt's recession"
1938	Fair Labor Standards Act
	Second AAA
	Congress of Industrial Organizations formed
1939	Marian Anderson's concert at Lincoln Memorial
	John Steinbeck's *The Grapes of Wrath*
1940	Richard Wright's *Native Son*

Study Tools

and psychological crisis. Lives were disrupted, homes and businesses lost, but most people learned to cope with the Great Depression and hoped for better times. Gender roles were affected by the depression as men lost their jobs. Members of racial and ethnic minority groups carried the extra burdens of discrimination, sometimes by New Deal agencies. During the 1930s, for the first time the federal government provided significant support to artists, writers, and musicians. While movies and radio often provided escape from daily worries, other forms of cultural expression focused on the problems faced by ordinary people.

The New Deal never fully restored the economy, but it engineered a profound shift in the nature of government and in society's expectations about the federal government's role in people's lives.

FOCUS QUESTIONS

If you have mastered this chapter, you should be able to answer these questions and to explain the terms that follow the questions.

1. ☆ *What was the effect of the stock market crash on the American economy, and what major economic weaknesses contributed to the crash and the Great Depression?*

2. ☆ *How did Hoover try to deal with the Depression? How successful were his efforts?*

3. ☆ *How did the New Deal's "First Hundred Days" represent a change in the role of the federal government?*

4. ☆ *What were the initial responses to New Deal measures?*

5. ☆ *What new reforms came during the Second Hundred Days, and how did they differ from those of the First Hundred Days?*

6. ☆ *What happened to restrict expansion of the New Deal after 1936?*

7. ☆ *How did Americans cope with the many challenges presented by the Great Depression?*

8. ☆ *What opportunities opened for women, African Americans, Latinos, Asian Americans, and Native Americans, and what challenges faced these groups during the 1930s?*

9. ☆ *How did the Depression and New Deal affect cultural expression?*

10. ☆ *How did the Great Depression and New Deal affect Americans over the long run?*

KEY TERMS

Great Depression *(p. 622)*

public works projects *(p. 624)*

Reconstruction Finance Corporation *(p. 625)*

Farmers' Holiday Association *(p. 626)*

Bonus Army *(p. 627)*

New Deal *(p. 628)*

fireside chats *(p. 629)*

First Hundred Days *(p. 629)*

Agricultural Adjustment Act *(p. 630)*

National Recovery Administration *(p. 630)*

Public Works Administration *(p. 630)*

Tennessee Valley Authority *(p. 630)*

Civilian Conservation Corps *(p. 631)*

Federal Emergency Relief Administration *(p. 631)*

American Liberty League *(p. 632)*

Huey Long *(p. 634)*

Works Progress Administration *(p. 635)*

Schechter Poultry Corporation v. the United States *(p. 635)*

Second Hundred Days *(p. 635)*

Social Security Act *(p. 635)*

Wagner Act *(p. 636)*

National Youth Administration *(p. 636)*

Mary McLeod Bethune *(p. 636)*

Congress of Industrial Organizations *(p. 638)*

United States v. Butler *(p. 638)*

Dust Bowl *(p. 638)*

Rural Electrification Administration *(p. 639)*

court-packing plan *(p. 640)*

Roosevelt's recession *(p. 640)*

Fair Labor Standards Act *(p. 641)*

Black Cabinet *(p. 645)*

Indian Reorganization Act *(p. 646)*

CourseMate

Go to the History CourseMate website for primary source links, study tools, and review materials for this chapter. www.cengagebrain.com

courts rejected the arguments of those Japanese Americans who challenged the wartime measures.

Released from Tule in 1946, Minoru went to college and graduated in 1949. Using his Japanese language skills, he took a civilian position with the Air Force Intelligence Service but lied on his application form, saying he was a U.S. citizen. He served in Korea and Japan, where, in 1954, his past caught up. He was dismissed from service and stripped of his U.S. passport. A man without a country, he enrolled at Tokyo University, majoring in Indian philosophy.

In 1955, he regained his citizenship when the Renunciation Law was thrown out by the Supreme Court. He returned to the United States and in 1963 took a position as a professor of Buddhist studies at the University of Wisconsin. He retired in 1999.

The Great Depression shook the world. Governments collapsed, and three nations emerged willing to use military force to achieve their goals. Japan led the way in 1931 when it annexed Manchuria. In 1935, Benito Mussolini shattered world peace by invading Ethiopia, which encouraged Adolf Hitler to begin taking action to restore Germany as a major power. The result would be a European-wide war in 1939.

Between 1933 and 1939, Roosevelt's primary concern was surviving the Great Depression and implementing his New Deal, but as international tensions increased he was forced to wrestle with how best to protect and improve U.S. economic and political positions abroad. While he would have liked to have more flexibility and to take a more active role in world affairs, he understood his actions were constrained by a public and Congress that remained strongly isolationist. The onslaught of the war in Europe in 1939, however, provided Roosevelt with new opportunities. Deciding that the United States must help Britain defeat Hitler, Roosevelt provided economic and military assistance to Britain. To check Japanese expansion, he used trade restrictions. Britain held on, but Japan's attack on Pearl Harbor indicated the failure of economic diplomacy in Asia.

The war restored American prosperity and increased presidential power. The mobilization of the U.S. resources resulted in full employment and unparalleled cooperation among business, labor, and government. Over 15 million Americans marched off to war. Those at home faced new challenges and opportunities. Roosevelt chose to allocate most of the nation's resources to defeat Hitler. Allied with Britain and the Soviet Union, the United States began its efforts to liberate Europe by invading North Africa and Italy before invading France. In the Pacific, the victory at Midway gave the United States a naval and air advantage that eventually allowed American forces to close the circle on Japan. By the end of May 1945, Hitler's Third Reich was in ruins, and American forces were on the verge of victory over Japan. Roosevelt's death left President Harry S Truman to chart the final paths to victory. To end the war as soon as possible, Truman approved the use of atomic bombs against Japan. The destruction of Hiroshima and Nagasaki led to Japan's surrender, the beginning of a new age of atomic energy, and the United States' emergence as a superpower.

THE ROAD TO WAR

★ How were Roosevelt's policies toward Latin America a continuation of Hoover's?

★ What obstacles did Roosevelt face in trying to implement a more assertive foreign policy from 1935 to 1939?

★ Following the outbreak of World War II in 1939, how did Roosevelt reshape American neutrality?

When Herbert Hoover became president in 1929, the world appeared stable and increasingly prosperous. He saw no reason to change foreign policy. The United States remained aloof from the world's political and diplomatic bickering. The onslaught of the Depression only strengthened most Americans' resolve to stay out of world affairs and attend to business at home. However, as the global depression deepened and governments changed, some nations sought solutions to their internal problems abroad. Japan was the first as it seized Manchuria in 1931.

Japan's economy rested in part on international commerce, and with the collapse of world trade many Japanese nationalists pursued other means to ensure economic vitality and power. They turned to Manchuria, a province of China situated north and west of Japanese-controlled Korea. It was rich in iron and coal, accounted for 95 percent of Japanese overseas investment, and supplied large amounts of foodstuffs. Equally important, Japan maintained an army in Manchuria to protect its interests. In September 1931, Japanese officers used the army to seize the province. The world, including the League of Nations, condemned Japan's aggression, but did little else as Japan created a new puppet nation, Manchukuo, under its control. Hoover instituted a policy of **non-recognition** of the new state. Humorist Will Rogers sarcastically noted that the world's diplomats would run out of stationery writing protests before Japan ran out of soldiers. Rogers was right. Japan's success strengthened its leaders' idea of a Japanese-dominated **Greater East Asian Co-Prosperity Sphere** and further increased tensions with China. Roosevelt maintained Hoover's policy of non-recognition, but dealing with an expansionist Japan would test Roosevelt's abilities to protect American interests.

Diplomacy in a Dangerous World

Roosevelt also continued Hoover's Latin American policy. Announcing a "Good Neighbor" policy, he affirmed that the United States had no right to militarily intervene in regional affairs. But events in Cuba and Mexico put nonintervention to the test. In 1933, political unrest weakened Cuba's oppressive president, Gerardo "the Butcher" Machado. Roosevelt sent special envoy Sumner Wells to convince Machado to resign. He grudgingly resigned, but Wells considered his successor, Ramón Grau San Martín, too radical and asked Roosevelt for armed intervention to remove him. Roosevelt refused but applied the non-recognition policy to the new regime. In Cuba, Wells turned to **Colonel Fulgencio Batista** and convinced him to oust Grau and establish a new government. Batista's regime was immediately recognized by the United States and received a favorable trade agreement.

Mexico in 1938 nationalized its foreign-owned oil properties. American oil interests argued that Mexico had no right to seize their properties, demanded their return, and asked that Roosevelt intervene, with military force if necessary. Roosevelt rejected the request. Instead, he accepted the principle of nationalization and sought a fair monetary settlement for the American companies. Not until 1941 did Mexico and the United States agree on the amount of compensation, but throughout, American relations with Mexico remained cordial. The **Good Neighbor policy** was also enhanced when Roosevelt visited the Caribbean and South America, Congress repealed the Platt Amendment in 1934,

and the United States affirmed at the 1938 Pan-American Conference that there were no acceptable reasons for armed intervention.

Roosevelt and Isolationism

While Roosevelt upheld nonintervention and American interests in Latin America, maintaining American interests around the world was becoming difficult. As tensions rose regarding Japan, in Europe **fascist** Germany and Italy were seeking to expand their influence and power. Adolf Hitler took office in 1933, promising to improve the economy and Germany's role in the world. Benito Mussolini, ruling Italy since 1921, argued that Italy needed to expand its influence abroad. As global tensions increased, U.S. isolationists were in full cry. In 1934, a congressional investigation chaired by Senator Gerald P. Nye of North Dakota alleged that America's entry into World War I had been engineered by arms manufacturers, bankers, and war profiteers—"the merchants of death." At the same time, public opinion polls revealed that a large majority of Americans believed that the nation's intervention in the war was a mistake and that the country should avoid any actions that might draw it into another conflict. Congress responded in August 1935 by enacting the **Neutrality Act of 1935**. It prohibited the sale of arms and munitions to any nation at war, whether aggressor or victim. It also permitted the president to warn Americans traveling on ships of belligerent nations that they sailed at their own

non-recognition A policy of not acknowledging changes in government or territory to show displeasure with the changes. In this way, the United States refused to accept the creation of Manchukuo.

■ **Greater East Asian Co-Prosperity Sphere** Japan's plan to create and dominate an economic and defensive union in East Asia, using force if necessary. In defending the concept, the Japanese compared it to the U.S. power in Latin America and advocated the idea of Asia for Asians.

■ **Colonel Fulgencio Batista** Dictator who ruled Cuba from 1934 through 1958; his corrupt, authoritarian regime was overthrown by Fidel Castro's revolutionary movement.

■ **Good Neighbor policy** An American policy toward Latin America that stressed economic ties and nonintervention; begun under Hoover but associated with Roosevelt.

■ **fascist** Refers to a political system led by a dictator having total control over society and the economy; facism places the needs of the nation above those of the individual and is often characterized by racism and organized violence against opposition.

■ **Neutrality Act of 1935** Act forbidding the sale and shipment of war goods to all nations at war and authorizing the president to warn U.S. citizens against traveling on belligerents' vessels, intended to keep America from being drawn into war.

WIR DANKEN UNSERM FÜHRER

To celebrate Hitler's peaceful acquisition of the Sudetenland from Czechoslovakia through negotiations at Munich, a grateful Germany printed postcards showing a map of the new territory with the caption of "We thank our Fuhrer."

risk. Roosevelt would have preferred **discriminatory neutrality** but, anxious to see the Second Hundred Days through Congress, he accepted political reality. When Italian troops invaded the poorly armed African nation of Ethiopia in October, Roosevelt immediately announced American neutrality, denying the sale of war supplies to either side. Moving beyond strict neutrality, he also asked, to no avail, that Americans implement a "moral embargo" against Italy to reduce the sale of nonwar goods, like coal and oil. Italy formally annexed Ethiopia in May 1936.

International tensions continued to heighten in 1936 when Japan stepped up construction of new warships, German troops violated the Treaty of Versailles by occupying the **Rhineland**, and civil war broke out between Nationalists led by Francisco Franco and the Republican government of Spain. With isolationism still strong, Congress modified the neutrality legislation (the Second Neutrality Act) to forbid U.S. involvement in civil wars and making loans to countries at war—whether victim or aggressor.

discriminatory neutrality Withholding aid and trade from one nation at war while providing them to another.

Rhineland Region of western Germany along the Rhine River, which under the terms of the Versailles Treaty was to remain free of troops and military fortifications.

With the peace seemingly slipping away, both political parties championed neutrality in the 1936 presidential elections. Roosevelt told an audience at Chautauqua, New York, that he hated war and that if it came to "the choice of profits over peace, the nation will answer—must answer—'We choose peace.'" The Republican candidate, Alfred Landon, was equally adamant that the Republicans were the best party to keep the nation out of war. Roosevelt easily defeated Landon. In 1937, the new Congress, with strong public support, passed another neutrality act. It required warring nations to pay cash for all "nonwar" goods and to carry them away on their own ships, and it barred Americans from sailing on belligerents' ships. Roosevelt would have liked more flexibility but appreciated that the law allowed the president to determine which nations were at war and which goods were nonwar goods.

Roosevelt used that provision in July 1937, following a Japanese invasion of northern China. Ignoring reality and disregarding protests, he refused to recognize that China and Japan were at war and allowed unrestricted American trade to continue with both nations. Hoping that isolationist views had softened, on October 5 Roosevelt suggested that the United States and other peace-loving nations should quarantine "bandit nations" that were contributing to "the epidemic of world lawlessness." The "quarantine speech" was applauded in many foreign capitals, but not in Berlin, Rome, or Tokyo, and not at home.

In the wider World

Fascism

Fascism is a term frequently tossed about by those discussing modern politics. But ask what it means and answers usually get vague and reference the governments of Hitler and Mussolini. Historically, it emerged as a political system in 1922 when Mussolini overthrew the existing Italian government. As a political philosophy that rejected liberal democratic-capitalism and communism, it spread widely throughout Europe between 1922 and 1945, an "era of fascism." With the war and defeat of Italy and Germany, facism lost its widespread appeal and ceased to be a mass movement.

As a political system facism's characteristics varied, but a core set of values helps provide a central definition. An authoritarian system led by one political party and a charismatic leader, it stressed the unity of the state and government leadership of the society and economy. It legitimized violence to achieve its ends, especially in Nazi Germany. Mussolini stated: "Everything within the state, nothing outside the state, nothing against the state."

The *Wall Street Journal* argued that Roosevelt should "stop . . . meddling: America Wants Peace." As Japan continued to gobble up Chinese territory, on December 12, 1937, Japanese aircraft strafed, bombed, and sank the American gunboat *Panay*. Two Americans died, and over thirty were wounded. Outraged, Roosevelt favored retaliatory action. The *Christian Science Monitor*, expressing public and congressional opinion, pointed out that the *Panay* was not the *Maine*. Realizing he had no support for initiating any action against Japan, Roosevelt accepted Japan's apology and payment of over $2 million in damages for the *Panay* attack.

As fighting raged on in China and Spain in 1938, Hitler pronounced his intentions to unify all German-speaking lands and create a new German empire, or *Reich*. He first annexed Austria and then incorporated the Sudeten region of western Czechoslovakia into the German Reich (see Map 23.1). With a respectable military force and defense treaties with France and the Soviet Union, the Czechoslovakian government was prepared to resist. However, France, the Soviet Union, and Britain wanted no confrontation with Hitler. Choosing a policy of **appeasement**, in late September Britain's prime minister, Neville Chamberlain, met with Hitler in Munich and accepted Germany's annexation of the Sudetenland. France concurred. Chamberlain returned to England promising the **Munich Agreement** had secured "peace for our time." Within Germany, Hitler stepped up the persecution of the country's nearly half-million Jews. In government-sponsored violence, synagogues and Jewish businesses and homes were looted and destroyed. Detention centers—concentration camps—at Dachau and Buchenwald soon confined over fifty thousand Jews. Thousands of German and Austrian Jews fled to other countries. Many applied to enter the United States, but most were turned away. Public opinion

polls found American anti-Semitism strong. One survey found that 85 percent of Protestants, 84 percent of Catholics, and even 25.8 percent of Jews in the United States opposed more Jewish refugees entering the country. The State Department, citing immigration requirements against admitting anyone who would become "a public charge," routinely denied entry to Jews whose property and assets had been seized by the German government. Roosevelt expressed concern, but Congress rejected efforts to change immigration restrictions. In all, only about sixty thousand Jewish refugees entered the United States between 1933 and 1938—many of them scientists, academics, and musicians.

Discussing world affairs in his 1939 State of the Union address, Roosevelt bolstered his own words by echoing Abraham Lincoln: "Events abroad have made it increasingly clear to the American people that the dangers within are less to be feared than dangers without. . . . This generation will nobly save or meanly lose the last best hope of earth." He then asked Congress to increase military spending for the construction of aircraft and to repeal the arms **embargo** section of the 1937 Neutrality Act. Congress rejected changing the neutrality law but approved money for aircraft

---

■ **appeasement** Granting concessions to potential enemies to maintain peace. Since the Munich agreement did not stop Hitler's aggression, appeasement has become a policy that most nations avoid.

■ **Munich Agreement** Agreement signed by Germany, Italy, France, and Britain in September 1938 allowing Germany to annex the part of Czechoslovakia called the Sudetenland.

embargo A ban on trade with a country or countries, covering all goods or certain items, usually ordered and enforced by a government.

MAP 23.1 German and Italian Expansion, 1933–1942

By the end of 1942, the Axis nations of Italy and Germany, through conquest and annexation, had occupied nearly all of Europe. This map shows the political and military alignment of Europe as Germany and Italy reached the limit of their power. Copyright © Cengage Learning

Legend:
- Greater Germany
- Italy, including occupied and annexed territories
- Satellite states of Germany, including annexed territory
- Areas under direct German control in the east
- Countries under German military occupation in the west
- Vichy France, nominally sovereign
- Area of German military operations in the east
- Neutral and non-belligerent states
- Opponents of Germany
- Boundary of Greater Germany
- Boundary of areas annexed diplomatically in 1938

EXTERMINATION AND CONCENTRATION CAMPS
- Poland before Sept. 1, 1939
- Extermination camp
- Concentration camp

In September 1939, Germany introduced the world to a new word and type of warfare, *Blitzkrieg*—lightning war. Combining the use of tanks, aircraft, and infantry, German forces quickly overran first Poland, then most of Western Europe. This picture shows a German victory parade in Warsaw, Poland.

Hugo Jaeger/Getty Images.

construction, some of which Roosevelt loaned to aircraft companies through the Reconstruction Finance Corporation. Boeing and Beechcraft, for example, received over $11 million to build long-range bombers in Wichita, Kansas.

In quick succession, events seemed to verify Roosevelt's prediction. Hitler ominously concluded a military alliance with Italy and a **German-Soviet Nonaggression Pact** with Stalin. He seized what remained of Czechoslovakia and demanded that Poland turn over to Germany the Polish Corridor, which connected Poland to the Baltic Sea. When Warsaw refused, Hitler invaded Poland on September 1, 1939. Two days later, Britain and France declared war on Germany. Within a matter of days, German troops overran nearly all of Poland. On September 17, Soviet forces entered the eastern parts of Poland as they had secretly agreed to do in the Nonaggression Pact.

War and American Neutrality

As war began in Europe, isolationism remained strong in the United States, with polls showing that sizeable majorities of Americans in every part of the country wanted the United States to stay out of the conflict. Roosevelt proclaimed neutrality, but was determined to do everything possible, short of war, to help the nations opposing Hitler. He called Congress into special session and asked that the cash-and-carry policy of the Neutrality Act of 1937 be modified to allow the sale of any goods, including arms, to any nation, provided the goods were paid for in cash and carried away on ships belonging to the purchasing country. A "peace bloc" argued that the request was a ruse to aid France and Britain and would drag America into the war, but Congress yielded to the president and passed the **Neutrality Act of 1939** in November. With this act, any nation could now buy weapons from the United States. Roosevelt also worked with Latin American

countries to establish a 300-mile neutrality zone around the Western Hemisphere, excluding Canada and other British and French possessions. Within the zone, patrolled by the U.S. Navy, warships of warring nations were forbidden.

Although neutral in appearance, both acts were designed to help France and England. While any nation could now buy weapons from the United States, German ships would be denied access to American ports by the British navy. The neutrality zone had to allow French and British warships to reach their possessions in the Western Hemisphere; therefore, it was only German warships that would be stopped by the U.S. Navy. If the navy happened to sink any German submarines, Roosevelt joked to his cabinet, he would apologize like "the Japs do, 'So sorry. Never do it again.' Tomorrow we sink two."

As 1940 began most people did not expect Roosevelt to run for a third term, nor did Roosevelt seem anxious to run. Yet he was worried about the direction of American foreign policy under someone else. He told the secretary of treasury: "I do not want to run unless . . . thing get very worse in Europe." Things got worse quickly. In April Hitler unleashed his forces on Denmark and Norway, which quickly fell. On May 10 the German offensive against France began with an invasion of Belgium and the Netherlands (see Map 23.1). On May 26 Belgian forces

■ **German-Soviet Nonaggression Pact** 1939 agreement in which Germany and the Soviet Union pledged not to fight each other and secretly arranged to divide Poland after Germany conquered it.

■ **Neutrality Act of 1939** Law repealing the arms embargo and authorizing cash-and-carry exports of arms and munitions even to belligerent nations.

surrendered, while French and British troops began their remarkable evacuation to England from the French port of Dunkirk. On June 10, Mussolini entered the war and invaded France from the southeast. Twelve days later, France surrendered, leaving Germany and Italy, called the **Axis powers**, controlling most of western and central Europe. Britain now faced the seemingly invincible German army and air force alone. England's new prime minister, Winston Churchill, pledged never to surrender until the Nazi threat was destroyed and pleaded with Roosevelt for immediate help. He needed ships, aircraft, weapons, and steel and other raw materials. Roosevelt made two decisions: to aid England and to run for a third term. In June, Republicans nominated Wendell Willkie, an ex-Democrat from Indiana. Roosevelt became the official Democratic candidate in July.

Between the convention and election day, events in Europe shaped much of the political debate. To prepare for the invasion of England, Hitler ordered the navy to block supplies coming to Britain and the air force to bomb targets throughout England. As Britain's Royal Air Force rose to fight the *Luftwaffe*, Churchill repeated his requests to Roosevelt for warships and aircraft. Across the United States, opinion polls showed public confusion about what course the country should take. A large majority favored the United States staying out of the war, but a slightly smaller majority approved giving Britain aid, and support for preparedness was increasingly bipartisan. Roosevelt, determined to aid Britain, promised help and asked Congress to increase the military budget. He supported a bipartisan bill to create the first peacetime military draft in American history. Isolationists opposed both actions, especially the draft. Senator Nye expressed the view of many, saying, "If we get into this war it will not be because the President tried to keep us out." But Nye and other isolationists were unable to prevent Congress from approving the draft and over $37 billion for military spending, more than the total cost of World War I.

In September, Roosevelt signed the **Burke-Wadsworth Act**, and the government began drafting men into the military in October. He also, by executive order, exchanged fifty old destroyers for ninety-nine-year leases on British military bases in Newfoundland, the Caribbean, and British Guiana. The public responded favorably, contributing to a 10 percent Roosevelt lead in the political race. With Willkie trailing in the polls, Republican leaders convinced him to attack Roosevelt for pushing the nation toward war. If Roosevelt was elected, he told a Baltimore audience, "you may expect war by April." Willkie's popularity surged. Roosevelt countered with a promise to American mothers: "Your boys are not going to be sent into any foreign wars." Roosevelt won easily, but his victory did not sweep other Democrats into office; Republicans gained seats in both the Senate and House of Representatives.

The Battle for the Atlantic

While Roosevelt relaxed in the Caribbean after the election, he received an urgent message from Churchill. Britain was out of money to pay for American goods, as required by the 1939 Neutrality Act, and needed credit to pay for supplies. He also asked Roosevelt to allow American ships to carry goods to England and for American help to protect merchant ships from German submarines. Roosevelt agreed, but knowing that the requests faced tough congressional and public opposition, he turned to his powers of persuasion. In his December fireside chat, he told his audience that if England fell, Hitler would surely attack the United States next. He urged the people to make the nation the "arsenal of democracy" and to supply Britain with all the material help it needed to defeat Hitler. He then presented Congress with a bill allowing the president to lend, lease, or in any way provide goods to any country considered vital to American security. The request drew the expected fire from isolationists. Senator Burton K. Wheeler from Montana called it a military Agricultural Adjustment Act that would "plow under every fourth American boy." Supporters countered with "Send guns, not sons." On March 11, 1941, the 60-year-old president breathed a sigh of relief when the **Lend-Lease Act** passed easily.

By the summer of 1941, the U.S. Navy's patrols of the neutrality zone overlapped Hitler's Atlantic war zone. It was only a matter of time until American and German ships confronted each other. Having called off the invasion of Britain, Hitler directed German forces into Yugoslavia, Greece, and North Africa. He also planned to crush the Soviets with the largest military force ever assembled on a single front. On June 22, 1941, German forces, supported by allied Finnish, Hungarian, Italian, and Romanian armies, opened the eastern front. Claiming he would join even the devil to defeat Hitler, Churchill made an ally of Stalin, while Roosevelt extended credits and lend-lease goods to the Soviet Union. Despite initial

■ **Axis powers** Coalition of nations that opposed the Allies in World War II, first consisting of Germany and Italy and later joined by Japan.

■ **Burke-Wadsworth Act** Law passed by Congress in 1940 creating the first peacetime draft in American history.

■ **Lend-Lease Act** 1941 law providing that any country whose security was vital to U.S. interests could receive arms and equipment by sale, transfer, or lease from the United States.

From 1940 to 1943, the *Unterseeboot* (U-boat) was Germany's primary weapon during the battle for the Atlantic, but by mid-1943, Allied countermeasures forced their withdrawal from most of the Atlantic. Nearly 800 of the 1,160 U-boats built during the war were sunk.

crushing victories in which German soldiers advanced within miles of Moscow, by November it was becoming clear that the Soviets were not going to collapse.

With the battle for the Atlantic reaching a tipping point and Germany rolling through Russia, Roosevelt and Churchill met secretly off the coast of Newfoundland (the Argentia Conference, August 9–12, 1941). Churchill pleaded for an American declaration of war, but Roosevelt's main concern was more political than strategic. He urged Churchill to subscribe to an **Atlantic Charter** that would highlight the distinctions between the open, cooperative world of the democracies and the closed, self-serving world of fascist expansion. Championing self-determination, freedom of trade and the seas, and the establishment of a "permanent system of general security" in the form of a new world organization, Roosevelt explained, would help Americans support entry into the war. Churchill agreed but reminded Roosevelt that Britain could not fully accept the goals of self-determination and free trade within its Commonwealth and the British Empire. Returning to London, Churchill told his ministers that Roosevelt meant to "wage war, but not declare it, and that he would become more and more provocative . . . to force an incident . . . which would justify him in opening hostilities."

On September 4, 1941, the United States moved a step closer to ending its neutrality. In the North Atlantic, near Iceland, the American destroyer *Greer* skirmished with a German U-boat. Neither ship was damaged, but Roosevelt used the skirmish to get Congress to amend the neutrality laws to permit armed U.S. merchant ships to sail into combat zones. In October, following an attack on the U.S.S. *Kearney* and the sinking of the U.S.S. *Reuben James*, Congress rescinded all neutrality laws and public opinion seemed to accept the prospect of war. Throughout the country, FBI agents instructed local officials in how to best deal with problems of a nation at war, including espionage and sabotage, air raids and blackouts, and even gas contamination. Roosevelt accepted the War Department's "Victory Program," which concluded that the United States would have to fight a two-front war against Germany and against Japan. It also stated that Hitler needed to be defeated before the Japanese, and that July 1943 was about the earliest date that American troops could be ready for any large-scale operation.

Pearl Harbor

Since 1937, Japanese troops had seized more and more of China, while the United States did little but protest. By 1940, popular sentiment favored not only beefing up American defenses in the Pacific but also using economic pressure to slow Japanese aggression. In July 1940, Roosevelt began placing restrictions on

■ **Atlantic Charter** Joint statement issued by Roosevelt and Churchill in 1941 to formulate American and British postwar aims of international economic and political cooperation.

MAP 23.2 Japanese Advances, December 1941–1942
Beginning on December 7, 1941, Japanese forces began carving out a vast empire, the Greater East Asian Co-Prosperity Sphere, by attacking American, British, Dutch, and Australian forces from Pearl Harbor to the Dutch East Indies. This map shows the course of Japanese expansion until the critical naval battles of the Coral Sea and Midway in the spring of 1942 halted Japanese advances in the Pacific. Copyright © Cengage Learning

Japanese-American trade, forbidding the sale and shipment of aviation fuel, steel, and scrap iron. Many Americans believed the action was too limited and pointed out that Japan was still allowed to buy millions of gallons of American oil, which it was using to "extinguish the lamps of China."

The situation in East Asia soon worsened when Japanese troops entered French Indochina (see Map 23.2), and Japan signed a defense treaty with Germany and Italy. America promptly strengthened its forces in the Philippines and tightened trade restrictions on Japan. Within the Japanese government some still hoped for an agreement with the United States and sought to negotiate. The subsequent discussions between Secretary of State Cordell Hull and Admiral Kichisaburo Nomura, Japan's ambassador to the United States, were confused and nonproductive. The lack of progress in the negotiations convinced many in the Japanese government

that war was unavoidable to break the "circle of force" that denied Japan its interests. High on the list of interests was control over Malaysia and the Dutch East Indies (Indonesia), sources of vital raw materials, including oil. Seizing those regions, they concluded, would probably involve fighting the United States.

For Minister of War Hideki Tojo, the choice was simple: either submit to American demands, giving up the achievements of the past ten years and accepting a world order defined by the United States, or safeguard the nation's honor and achievements by initiating a war. In his mind, war could be averted only if the United States released frozen Japanese assets, suspended aid to China, capped its military presence in the Pacific, and resumed full trade with Japan. Without these concessions, Japan would begin military operations in the first week of December. Negotiations remained stalled until November 26, when Hull made it clear that the United States would

Roosevelt called it a day of "infamy"—December 7, 1941, when Japanese planes attacked Pearl Harbor, Hawai`i, without warning and before a declaration of war. In this photo, the U.S.S. *West Virginia* sinks in flames, one of seven battleships sunk or badly damaged in the attack.

make no concessions and insisted that Japan withdraw from China.

On November 26, Admiral Isoroku Yamamoto dispatched part of the Japanese fleet, including six aircraft carriers, toward Hawai`i. American observers, however, focused on the activity of a larger part of the Japanese fleet, which joined troop ships in sailing on December 5 toward the South China Sea and the Gulf of Siam. At 7:49 A.M. December 7 (Hawaiian time), before Japan's declaration of war had been received in Washington, Japanese planes struck the American fleet anchored at Pearl Harbor. By 8:12, seven battleships of the American Pacific fleet lined up along Battleship Row were aflame, sinking, or badly damaged. Eleven other ships had been hit, nearly two hundred American aircraft had been destroyed, and twenty-five hundred Americans had lost their lives.

The attack on Pearl Harbor, however, was only a small part of Japan's strategy. Elsewhere that day Japanese planes struck Singapore, Guam, the Philippines, and Hong Kong. Everywhere, British and American positions in the Pacific and East Asia were being overwhelmed. Roosevelt declared that the unprovoked, sneak attack on Pearl Harbor made December 7 "a day which will live in infamy" and asked Congress for a declaration of war against Japan. Only Representative Jeannette Rankin of Montana, a pacifist, kept the December 8 declaration of war from being unanimous. Three days later, Germany and Italy declared war on the United States. In England Churchill "slept the sleep of the saved and thankful." He knew that with the economic and human resources of the United States finally committed to war, the Axis would be "ground to powder."

AMERICA RESPONDS TO WAR

★ *What actions did Roosevelt take to mobilize the nation for war and how did they affect the relationship between business and government?*

★ *What new social and economic choices did Americans confront during the war? How were different groups affected?*

Americans were angry and full of fight, and the attack on Pearl Harbor unified the nation as no other event had done. It was almost impossible to find an American isolationist as thousands of young men rushed to enlist. On December 8, 1,200 applicants besieged the navy recruiting station in New York City, some having waited outside the doors all night. Eventually

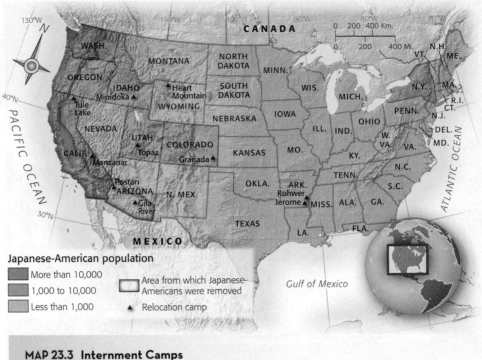

MAP 23.3 Internment Camps
This map shows the locations of the ten relocation centers, mostly in the West, used to house
Japanese Americans during World War II. Copyright © Cengage Learning

over 16.4 million Americans would serve in the armed forces during World War II.

The shock of Japan's attack on Pearl Harbor raised fears of further attacks, especially along the Pacific Coast. On the night of December 7 and throughout the next week, West Coast cities reported enemy planes overhead and practiced blackouts. Phantom Japanese planes were spotted above San Francisco and Los Angeles. The Rose Bowl game between Oregon State and Duke was moved from the bowl's home in Pasadena to Duke's stadium in Durham, North Carolina. Stores everywhere removed "made in Japan" goods from shelves. Alarm and anger were focused especially on Japanese Americans. Rumors circulated wildly that they intended to sabotage factories and military installations, paving the way for the invasion of the West Coast. Within a week, the FBI had arrested 2,541 citizens of Axis countries: 1,370 Japanese, 1,002 Germans, and 169 Italians.

■ *Issei* A Japanese immigrant to the United States.

■ **Executive Order #9066** President Roosevelt's order in 1942 authorizing the removal of "enemy aliens" from military areas; it was used to isolate Japanese Americans in internment camps.

■ **internment camps** Camps to which more than 110,000 Japanese Americans living in the West were moved soon after the attack on Pearl Harbor; Japanese Americans in Hawai'i were not confined in internment camps.

Japanese American Internment

There were nearly 125,000 Japanese Americans in the country, about three-fourths of whom were Nisei—Japanese Americans who had been born in the United States. The remaining fourth were Japanese immigrants, or **Issei**—officially citizens of Japan, although nearly all had lived in the United States prior to 1924 when Asians were barred from the country. Reflecting a popular view, General John L. De Witt, commanding general of the Western Defense District, stated, "We must worry about the Japanese all the time until he is wiped off the map." Echoing long-standing anti-Japanese sentiment, the West Coast moved to "protect" itself. Japanese Americans were fired from state jobs, and their law and medical licenses were revoked. Banks froze Japanese American assets, stores refused service, and loyal citizens vandalized Nisei and Issei homes and businesses. The few voices that came forward to speak on behalf of Japanese Americans were shouted down by those demanding their removal from the West Coast. On February 19, 1942, Roosevelt signed **Executive Order #9066**, which allowed the military to remove anyone deemed a threat from official military areas. When the entire West Coast was declared a military area, the eviction of those of Japanese ancestry from the region began. By the summer of 1942, over 110,000 Nisei and Issei had been transported to ten **internment camps** (see Map 23.3). When tested in court, the executive order was upheld by

It Matters Today

Internment

Does war or national crisis allow for the reduction and elimination of a person's rights, of a citizen's rights? During the war the government interned 110,000 people of Japanese ancestry because they were regarded as potential threats to American security. With the memory of Pearl Harbor still fresh, fears of spying and sabotage played a role; race, too was a factor. Many argued that the culture and values of Japan made the conflict a "race war" and that all Japanese, even those who were citizens, could not be trusted: "Once a Jap always a Jap!" The dissenting Justices in the *Korematsu* case believed internment was clearly a result of racism that violated the American concept of democracy and that the decision was the "legalization of racism." How a society acts in time of war often provides insights into not only the strengths of the nation but its weaknesses as well.

- Since the Al Qaeda attacks on September 11, 2001, the United States has fought a war on international terrorism and defined radical Islamic fundamentalism as a source of that terrorism. These actions have raised the issues of race, religion, and culture, and have led to comparisons to the treatment of the Nisei and the Issei during World War II. Are these comparisons valid? Why or why not?

the Supreme Court in *Korematsu v. the United States* in 1944 (see the Individual Voices feature, page 685).

The orders to relocate allowed almost no time to prepare. Families could pack only a few personal possessions and had to store or sell the rest of their property, including homes and businesses. Finding storage facilities was nearly impossible, and most families had to liquidate their possessions at ridiculously low prices. "It is difficult to describe the feeling of despair and humiliation experienced," one man recalled, "as we watched the Caucasians coming to look over all our possessions and offering such nominal amounts knowing we had no recourse but to accept." In the relocation it is estimated that Japanese American families lost from $810 million to $2 billion in property and goods.

Having disposed of a lifetime of possessions, Japanese Americans began the process of internment. Tags with numbers were issued to every family to tie to luggage and coats—no names, only numbers. "From then on," wrote one woman, "we were known as family #10710." In the camps, the Nisei and Issei were surrounded by barbed wire and watched over by guards. The internees were assigned to 20-by-25-foot apartments in long barracks of plywood covered with tarpaper, and each camp was expected to create a community complete with farms, shops, and small factories. Within a remarkably short time, they did. Making the desert bloom, by 1944 the internees at Manzanar, east of the Sierra in California's Owens Valley, were producing more than $2 million worth of agricultural products.

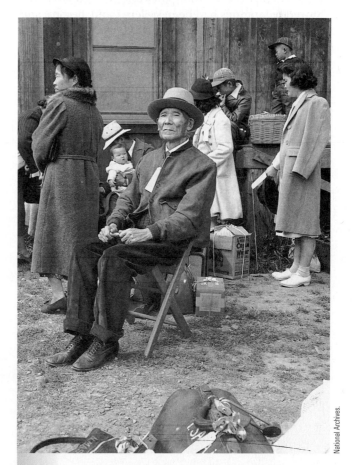

National Archives.

In February 1942, President Roosevelt signed an order sending all Japanese Americans living on the West Coast to internment camps. This photo, taken at a staging area for transportation to the internment camps, shows the quiet dignity of those waiting to be interned.

Some internees were able to leave the camps by working outside, supplying much-needed labor, especially farm work. By the fall of 1942, one-fifth of all males had left the camps to work. Others left for college or volunteered for military service. Japanese American units served in both the Pacific and European theaters, the most famous being the four-thousand-man 442nd Regimental Combat Team, which saw action in Italy, France, and Germany. The men of the 442nd would be among the most decorated in the army. Years later, in 2000, the federal government, citing racial bias during the war for the delay, awarded the Medal of Honor to twenty-one Asian Americans—most belonging to the 442nd Regiment. Included in the group was Daniel Ken Inouye, who was elected to the U.S. Senate from Hawai`i in 1960.

Aware of rabidly anti-Japanese public opinion, Roosevelt waited until after the off-year 1943 elections to allow internees who passed a loyalty review to go home. A year later, most of the camps were empty, each internee having been given train fare home and $25. Returning home, the Japanese Americans discovered that nearly everything they once owned was gone. Stored belongings had been stolen. Land, homes, and businesses had been confiscated by the government for unpaid taxes. Denied even an apology from the government, Japanese Americans nevertheless began to reestablish their homes and businesses. Decades later, in 1988, and after several lawsuits on behalf of victims, a semi-apologetic federal government paid $20,000 in compensation to each of the surviving sixty thousand internees.

Mobilizing the Nation for War

When President Roosevelt gave his first fireside chat following Pearl Harbor, "Dr. New Deal" became "Dr. Win the War." To produce the goods necessary for victory factories were to run twenty-four hours a day, seven days a week. Gone was the antibusiness attitude that had characterized much New Deal rhetoric, and in its place was the realization that only big business could produce the vast amount of armaments and supplies needed. Secretary of War Henry L. Stimson noted: "You have to let business make money out of the process or business won't work." Overall, the United States paid over $240 billion in defense contracts, with 82 percent of them going to the nation's top one hundred corporations. At the same time

more than half a million small businesses collapsed. Every part of the nation benefited from defense-based prosperity, but the South and the coastal West saw huge economic gains. The South experienced a remarkable 40 percent increase in its industrial capacity, and the West did even better.

Since 1929, the Depression and New Deal governmental programs had provided the West with important resources such as electricity, experience in large-scale production projects, and a growing population. Now, billions of dollars of government contracts flowed into the region, with California receiving nearly 40 percent of the total. Wrote one observer, "It was [as] if someone had tilted the country: people, money, and soldiers all spilled west."

Among the contractors, few outdid Henry J. Kaiser, "Sir Launchalot." He transformed the shipbuilding industry by constructing massive shipyards in California. By using **prefabricated** sections, he cut the time it took to build a merchant ship from about three hundred days to an average of eighty days in 1942. Nationally, by the end of 1942, one-third of all production was geared to the war, and the government had allocated millions of dollars to improve productivity by upgrading factories and generating new industries. When the war cut off some supplies of raw rubber, government and business cooperated to develop and produce synthetic rubber. By the end of the war, the United States had pumped more than $320 billion into the American economy, and the final production amounts exceeded almost everyone's expectations: U.S. manufacturers had built more than 300,000 aircraft, 88,140 tanks, and 86,000 warships. Neither Germany nor Japan could come close to matching the output of American products.

Millions of dollars were also spent on research and development (R&D) to create and improve a variety of goods from weapons to medicines. In "science cities" constructed by the government across the country, researchers and technicians of the **Manhattan Project** harnessed atomic energy and built an atomic bomb. Hundreds of colleges and universities and private laboratories, such as Bell Labs, received research and development grants. Improved radar and sonar allowed American forces to detect and destroy enemy planes and ships. New medical techniques and new, more effective medicines, including penicillin, saved millions of lives. Potent pesticides fought insects that carried typhus, malaria, and other diseases at home and overseas.

As the economy retooled to provide the machines of war, Roosevelt acted to provide government direction and planning. An array of governmental agencies and boards arose to regulate prices and production. The size of the federal bureaucracy grew 400 percent. The War Production Board (WPB) and the War Labor Board (WLB), both created in January 1942, sought to coordinate and plan production, establish the allotment of materials, and ensure harmonious labor

prefabricated Parts of an item that are manufactured in advance, usually in standardized sections for easy shipment and quick assembly.

■ **Manhattan Project** A secret scientific research effort begun in 1942 to develop an atomic bomb.

THE SUPREME TEST

"NOW, I'M GOING TO FIND OUT HOW GOOD YOU REALLY ARE!"

WAR OF MACHINES

AMERICA'S MECHANICAL GENIUS

MASS PRODUCTION

The ability to wage war rests on a nation's resources, not only of soldiers but of raw materials and production. In this political cartoon, the challenge is given, and over the next four years the United States easily produced more of the machines of war than either Germany or Japan.

Chicago History Museum, negative number ICHi-34717.

relations. An Office of Price Administration (OPA), established in 1941, tried to limit inflation and equalize consumption by setting prices and issuing ration books with coupons needed to buy a wide range of commodities, such as shoes, coffee, meat, and sugar. When the agencies failed to resolve problems and create a smoothly working economy, Roosevelt and Congress expanded the agencies' scope and created new ones. Seeking to improve coordination, in 1942 and 1943 Roosevelt added two new umbrella agencies, the Office of Economic Stabilization (OES) and the **Office of War Mobilization**. To direct both agencies, he appointed former Supreme Court justice James F. Byrnes. Armed with extensive powers and the president's trust, Byrnes became known as the "Assistant President." By the fall of 1943, production was booming, jobs were plentiful, wages and family incomes were rising, and inflation was under control. Even farmers were climbing out of debt as farm income had tripled since 1939.

The war provided full employment and new opportunities for labor organizations. Union leaders, in exchange for their agreements not to strike, expected industry to agree to union recognition, collective bargaining, **closed shops**, and increased wages. Others, however, argued that unions should be

forbidden to strike or otherwise hinder war production and should accept the open shop. In 1941, even before the United States entered the war, four thousand strikes had stopped work on defense production and had forced the government on one occasion—a strike at North American Aviation—to seize the plant and threaten the strikers with induction into the military if they did not return to work. Roosevelt hoped his war production agencies could find a middle ground between union advocates and opponents. In 1942 OPA, the WLB, and other agencies hammered out a compromise promoting union membership and accepting the closed shop and collective bargaining, while getting pledges from unions to control wages and oppose strikes.

While most workers and employers accepted the guidelines, others did not. Every year nearly 3 million workers went on strike or conducted work slowdowns. Most lasted only a brief time and did not jeopardize production, but several strikes were more serious, generating the wrath of the president, Congress, and the public and prompting government intervention. The most serious strike occurred in 1943 when CIO president and head of the United Mine Workers John L. Lewis demanded higher wages and safer working conditions. An angry president threatened to take over the mines. Congress wanted Lewis jailed as a traitor and pushed through, over the president's veto, the **Smith-Connally War Labor Disputes Act**. It gave the president the power to seize and operate any strikebound industries considered vital for war production. Eventually, the parties in the mine strike compromised, giving higher wages to the miners. By the end of the war, American workers had produced a massive amount of material and were receiving higher wages than ever before. Unions represented 35 percent of the labor force and had gained unprecedented influence.

Taxes were also up, reflecting Roosevelt's desire to fund the war through taxation. The 1942 and 1943 Revenue Acts increased the number of people paying taxes and raised rates. In 1939, 4 million Americans paid income taxes; by the end of the war, more than 40 million did so. Individuals making $500,000 or more a year paid 88 percent in taxes. Corporate

■ **Office of War Mobilization** Umbrella agency created in 1943 to coordinate the production, procurement, and distribution of civilian and military supplies.

closed shop A business or factory whose workers are required to be union members.

■ **Smith-Connally War Labor Disputes Act** 1943 law authorizing the government to seize plants in which labor disputes threatened war production.

FIGURE 23.1 The National Debt, 1940–1945
As the United States fought to defeat the Axis nations, its national debt soared. Rather than further raise taxes, the government chose to borrow about 60 percent of the cost. By the end of the war the debt had reached near $260 billion.

taxes averaged 40 percent, with a 90 percent tax on excess profits.

These tax changes moderately altered the basic distribution of income by reducing the proportion held by the upper two-fifths of the population—but tax revenues paid for only about half of the cost of the war. The government borrowed the rest. The national debt jumped from $40 billion in 1940 to near $260 billion by 1945 (see Figure 23.1). The most publicized borrowing effort encouraged the purchase of war bonds. Movie stars and other celebrities asked Americans to "do their part" and buy bonds. The public responded by purchasing more than $40 billion in individual bonds, but the majority of bonds—$95 billion—were bought by corporations and financial institutions.

Wartime Politics

As Roosevelt mobilized the nation for war, Republicans and conservative Democrats moved to bury what was left of the New Deal. People secure in their jobs were

■ **G.I. Bill** 1944 law to provide financial and educational benefits for American veterans after World War II; *G.I.* stands for "government issue."

■ **Harry S Truman** Democratic senator from Missouri whom Roosevelt selected in 1944 to be his running mate for vice president; in 1945, on Roosevelt's death, Truman became president.

no longer as concerned about social welfare programs. They griped about higher taxes, rents, and prices, the scarcity of some goods, and government inefficiency. Congressional elections in November 1942 continued the trend started in 1937 and returned more Republicans to Congress. A more conservative Congress axed the Civilian Conservation Corps (CCC), the Works Progress Administration (WPA), and the National Youth Administration (NYA) and slashed the budgets of other government agencies.

Roosevelt, seeking an unprecedented fourth term in 1944, hoped to recapture some social activism and called for the passage of an economic bill of rights that included government support for higher-wage jobs, home construction, and medical care, but his plea fell on deaf ears. Instead, Congress passed a smaller version that would reward veterans of the war. In June the **G.I. Bill** became law. It guaranteed a year's unemployment compensation for veterans while they looked for "good" jobs, provided economic support if they chose to go to school, and offered low-interest home loans.

Roosevelt brushed aside concerns about his age and health, but responding to conservatives in the party, he agreed to drop his liberal vice president, Henry Wallace, and replace him with a more conservative running mate. The choice was Senator **Harry S Truman** from Missouri. Roosevelt campaigned on a strong wartime economy, his record of leadership, and by November 1944, a successful war effort.

As their candidate, Republicans nominated Governor Thomas Dewey of New York, who attacked government inefficiency and waste, and argued that his youth, 42, made him a better candidate than Roosevelt. A Republican-inspired "whispering campaign" hinted that at 62 Roosevelt was ill and close to death. Voters ignored the rumors and reelected Roosevelt, whose winning totals, although not as large as in 1940, were still greater than pollsters had predicted and proved that Roosevelt still generated widespread support.

A People at Work and War

America's entry into the war changed nearly everything about everyday life. Government agencies set prices and froze wages and rents. Cotton, silk, gasoline, and items made of metal, including hair clips and safety pins, became increasingly scarce. By the end of 1942, most Americans had a ration book containing an array of different-colored coupons of various values that limited their purchases of such staples as meat, sugar, and gasoline. Explaining why most Americans received only 3 gallons of gasoline a week, Roosevelt noted that a bomber required nearly

1,100 gallons of fuel to bomb Naples, Italy, the equivalent of about 375 gasoline ration tickets. Speeding was unpatriotic as it wasted gas and rubber. Also, the War Production Board changed fashion to conserve fabrics. In men's suits, lapels were narrowed, and vests and pant cuffs were eliminated. The amount of fabric in women's skirts was also reduced, and the two-piece bathing suit was introduced as "patriotic chic." Families collected scrap metal, paper, and rubber to be recycled for the war effort and growing a **victory garden** became a symbol of patriotism. When some people complained about shortages and inconveniences, more would challenge, "Don't you know there's a war on?"

Even with rationing, most Americans were experiencing a higher-than-ever standard of living. Consumer spending rose by 12 percent, and Americans were spending more than ever on entertainment, from books to movies to horse racing. Included in those discovering prosperity were women, African Americans, Latinos, and Indians who by 1943 were being hired because of severe labor shortages. As noted, even the Nisei were allowed to leave their relocation camps when their labor was needed. To gain access to new jobs, 15 million Americans relocated between 1941 and 1945. Two hundred thousand people, many from the rural South, headed for Detroit, but more went west, where defense industries beckoned. Shipbuilding and the aircraft industry sparked boomtowns that could not keep pace with the growing need for local services and facilities. San Diego, California, once a small retirement community with a quiet naval base, mushroomed into a major military and defense industrial city almost overnight. Nearly fifty-five thousand people flocked there each year of the war, with thousands living in small travel trailers leased by the federal government for $7 a month. Mobile, Alabama; Norfolk, Virginia; Seattle, Washington; Denver, Colorado—all experienced similar rapid growth.

With the expanding populations, industrial war cities experienced massive problems providing homes, water, electricity, and sanitation. Crime flourished. Marriage, divorce, family violence, and juvenile delinquency rates soared. Contributing to the social problems of the booming cities were those posed by many unsupervised teenage children. Juvenile crime increased dramatically during the war, much of it blamed on lockout and latchkey children whose working mothers left them alone during their job shifts. In Mobile, authorities speculated that two thousand children a day skipped school, some going to movies but most just hanging out looking for something to do.

Particularly worrisome to authorities were those nicknamed "V-girls." Victory girls were young teens, sometimes called "khaki-wacky teens," who hung around gathering spots like bus depots and drugstores to flirt with GIs and ask for dates. Wearing hair ribbons, bobby sox, and saddle shoes, their young faces thick with makeup and bright red lipstick, V-girls traded sex for movies, dances, and drinks. Seventeen-year-old Elvira Taylor of Norfolk took a different approach—she became an "Allotment Annie." She simply married the soldiers and collected their monthly **allotment checks**. Eventually, two American soldiers at an English pub showing off pictures of their wives discovered they had both married Elvira! It turned out she had wed six servicemen.

New Opportunities and Old Constraints

Mobilization forced the restructuring and redirecting of economic and human resources. Families had to adjust to new challenges. Men and women confronted new roles and accepted new responsibilities, both on the home front and in the military. Like men, many women were anxious to serve in the military. But at first the armed forces did not employ women except as nurses. To expand women's roles, Congresswoman Edith Norse Rogers prodded Congress and the Army to create the Women's Auxiliary Army Corps (WAAC) in March 1942, which became the Women's Army Corps (WAC) a year later. Other services followed suit by creating the navy's Women Appointed for Volunteer Emergency Service (WAVES) and the Marines' Women's Reserve. Relegated to noncombat roles, most women served as nurses and clerical workers. But those in the Women's Airforce Service Pilots (WASPS) tested planes, ferried planes across the United States and Canada, and trained male pilots. At the marine flight-training center at Cherry Point, North Carolina, all the flight instructors were women. By war's end, over 350,000 women had donned uniforms, earned equal pay with men who held the same rank, and provided a new female image.

Women serving in the military were not the only break with tradition. With over 10 million men marching off to war, employers increasingly turned to women. The federal government supported the move with training and a campaign stressing that women could shorten the war if they joined the work force.

■ **victory garden** Small plot cultivated by a patriotic citizen during World War II to supply household food and allow farm production to be used for the war effort.

allotment checks Checks that a soldier's wife received from the government, amounting to a percentage of her husband's pay.

As during World War I, the Second World War opened up new job opportunities for women. In this picture, a real-life "Rosie the Riveter" works on the fuselage of a bomber.

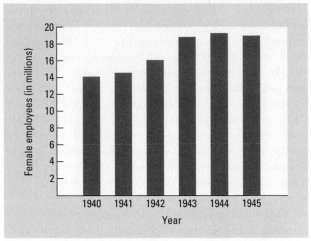

FIGURE 23.2 Women in the Work Force, 1940–1945
As men went to war, the nation turned increasingly to women to fill vital jobs. With government's encouragement, the number of women in the work force swelled from 14 million to nearly 20 million. With the war's end, however, many women left the workplace and returned to the home.

The image of **Rosie the Riveter** became the symbol of the patriotic woman doing her part. As more jobs opened, women filled them. A Billings, Montana newspaper noted, "petticoat troops are making forced landings in businesses and industry, and the situation is in hand." Increasingly women filled those jobs once held by men. In Detroit, women made up 56 percent of the labor force, while in Boeing's Seattle plant women filled 47 percent of the payroll. Women went to work for many reasons—some because of patriotism, but most because they wanted both the job and the wages. Leaving home, Peggy Terry worked in a munitions plant and considered it "an absolute miracle. . . . We made the fabulous sum of $32 a week. . . . Before, we made nothing." Other women left menial jobs for better-paying positions with industries and the federal government. By 1944, 37 percent of all adult women were working, almost 19.4 million (see Figure 23.2). Of these, the majority (72.2 percent) were married, and over half were 35 or older.

New opportunities did not diminish familiar constraints. Professional and supervisory positions remained dominated by men, and not all was rosy at work. Despite the labor shortage, male workers frequently resented and harassed women. "The hardest thing about the job," remembered one woman cab driver, "was the hostility of men toward women driving." Similar complaints echoed across the country

even as management and the media praised women's work ethics and abilities. Edsel Ford commented that women did the hardest welding and the most delicate jobs "superbly," while a Yellow Cab manager pointed out that women drivers had more "tact" and a "very, very low" accident rate. Keeping with tradition, women were generally paid less than men, even though the WLB promoted the idea of the same pay for the same job. Women with children faced the problem of daycare. Although the 1942 Lanham Act provided communities with federal funds for child care, there were never enough money, centers, or programs to meet the needs of working families. Many women who found it too difficult to balance family needs and work left their jobs. Finally, women worked under the reminder that despite their wishes, employers and most men expected them to return to their traditional roles at home when the war ended.

Those expectations proved correct. By the summer of 1945, many of the women found themselves among the unemployed. Shipyards and the aircraft plants dismissed nearly three-fourths of their women employees. In Detroit, the automobile industry executed a similar cut in women workers, from 25 to 7.5 percent. Those who managed to remain at work were frequently transferred to less attractive, poorly paying jobs. Thus, for most women, the war experience was mixed, with new choices cut short by changing circumstances.

The war also provided new opportunities for African Americans, but they were accompanied by racial and ethnic tensions and the knowledge that when the war ended, the opportunities were likely to vanish. Initially, many companies resisted hiring nonwhite workers. North American Aviation Company spoke for the

■ **Rosie the Riveter** A popular image symbolizing the patriotic woman working in industry to advance war production; the many women who entered the labor force were usually among the first let go at war's end.

aircraft industry when, in early 1942, it announced that it would not hire blacks "regardless of their training."

The antiblack bias began to change by mid-1942 for a variety of reasons. One was that African Americans were unwilling to be denied job opportunities. Even before the war, in early 1941, **A. Philip Randolph**, leader of the powerful Brotherhood of Sleeping Car Porters union, proposed that African Americans march on Washington to demand equality in jobs and the armed forces. To avoid such an embarrassing demonstration, Roosevelt issued Executive Order #8802 in June 1941, creating the **Fair Employment Practices Commission** (FEPC), and forbidding racial job discrimination by the government and companies holding government contracts. Bending under federal pressure and recognizing worsening labor shortages, businesses began to integrate their work forces.

In California, these pressures dissolved the color line by the end of 1942. West Coast shipyards were the first to integrate. When Lockheed Aircraft broke the color barrier in August, even North American Aviation grudgingly complied. Word soon spread to the South that blacks could find work in California, and between the spring of 1942 and 1945, more than 340,000 African Americans moved to Los Angeles. Overall, nearly 400,000 African Americans abandoned the South for the West. Thousands of others went north to cities such as Chicago and Detroit.

The FEPC and increased access to jobs did not mean that segregation and discrimination ended. Black wages rose from an average of $457 to $1,976 a year but remained only about 65 percent of white wages. To continue their quest for equality, blacks advocated the "Double V" campaign: victory over racist Germany and victory over racism at home. Membership of the NAACP and Urban League increased as both turned to public opinion, the courts, and Congress to attack segregation, lynching, the poll tax, and discrimination. In 1942 the newly formed **Congress of Racial Equality** (CORE) adopted the **sit-in** tactic to attempt to integrate public facilities. Led by black civil rights activist **James Farmer**, CORE integrated some public facilities in Chicago and Washington, although it failed in the South, where many CORE workers were badly beaten.

In many places across the nation, racial tensions increased as the population of African Americans grew. In Detroit, white workers went on strike when three black workers were promoted. A Justice Department examination reported, "White Detroit seems to be a particularly hospitable climate for native fascist-type movements." On a hot summer Sunday, June 20, 1943, the tensions in Detroit erupted into a major race riot. Before federal troops arrived on June 21 and restored order, twenty-five blacks and nine whites were dead.

The opportunities and difficulties of African Americans in uniform paralleled those of black civilians. Prior to 1940, blacks served at the lowest ranks and

in the most menial jobs in a segregated army and navy. The Army Air Corps and the Marines Corps refused to accept blacks at all. Compounding the problem, most in the military openly agreed with Secretary of War Henry L. Stimson when he asserted, "Leadership is not embedded in the Negro race." The manpower needs of war changed the role of the black soldier, opening up new ranks and occupations. In April 1942, Secretary of the Navy James Forrestal permitted black **noncommissioned officers** in the U.S. Navy, although blacks would wait until 1944 before becoming upper-rank officers. With only a small number of African American officers, in 1940 the army began to encourage the recruitment of black officers and promoted Benjamin O. Davis, Sr. from colonel to brigadier general. His son, **Benjamin O. Davis, Jr.**, was quickly promoted to lieutenant colonel and given command of the 99th Pursuit Squadron–the Tuskegee Airmen. Eventually six hundred African Americans were commissioned as pilots. The army also organized other African American units that fought in both the European and Pacific theaters of operations, such as the 371st Tank Battalion, which battled its way across France and into Germany and liberated the concentration camps of Dachau and Buchenwald.

Higher ranks and better jobs for a few still did not disguise that for most blacks, even officers, military life was often demeaning and brutal, and almost always segregated. In Indiana, more than a hundred black officers were arrested for trying to integrate an officers' club. Across the country, blacks objected to the Red Cross practice of segregating its blood supply. German prisoners of war held in Salina, Kansas, could eat at any local lunch counter and go to any movie theater, but their black guards could not. One dismayed soldier

■ **A. Philip Randolph** African American labor leader who organized a proposed 1941 march on Washington, which pressured Roosevelt to issue an executive order banning racial discrimination in government and defense industries, leading to cancellation of the march.

■ **Fair Employment Practices Commission** (FEPC) Commission established in 1941 to halt discrimination in war production and government.

■ **Congress of Racial Equality** (CORE) Civil rights organization founded in 1942 and committed to using nonviolent techniques, such as sit-ins, to end segregation.

sit-in The act of occupying seats or an area; a tactic used, for example, to protest segregation or strengthen the effect of a labor strike.

■ **James Farmer** Helped to organize the Congress of Racial Equality in 1942; led the organization from 1961 to 1966. In 1969 he became assistant secretary of health, education, and welfare.

noncommissioned officers Enlisted member of the armed forces who has been promoted to a rank such as corporal or sergeant, conferring leadership over others.

■ **Benjamin O. Davis, Jr.** Army Air Corps officer who commanded the Tuskegee Airmen and in 1954 became the first African American general in the U.S. Air Force.

National Archives.

About 700,000 African Americans served in segregated units in all branches of the military, facing discrimination at all levels. Among those units were the four squadrons of the Tuskegee Airmen commanded by General Benjamin O. Davis. "We fought two wars," commented Airman Louis Parnell, "one with the enemy and the other back home."

wrote, "The people of Salina would serve these enemy soldiers and turn away black American GIs. . . . If we were . . . in Germany, they would break our bones. As 'colored' men in Salina, they only break our hearts." In truth, many black soldiers had their bones broken, and their lives taken, on the home front. As in the civilian world, blacks in the military resisted discrimination and called on Roosevelt and the government for help. But their requests accomplished little.

Latinos, too, found new opportunities during the war while encountering continued segregation and hostility.

pachucos A Spanish term originally meaning "bandits," it became associated with juvenile delinquents of Mexican American heritage.

zoot suit A long jacket with wide lapels and padded shoulders, worn over pleated trousers pegged and cuffed at the ankle.

■ **braceros** (Spanish for "helping arms.") Mexican nationals who worked on U.S. farms beginning in 1942 because of the labor shortage during World War II; despite guarantees, their housing was usually substandard and their wages kept low.

■ **code talkers** Navajos serving in the U.S. Marine Corps who communicated by radio in their native language, undecipherable by the enemy.

Like other Americans, Latinos, almost invariably called "Mexicans" by their fellow soldiers, rushed to enlist as the war started. More than 300,000 Latinos served—the highest percentage of any ethnic community—and seventeen won the nation's highest award for valor, the Medal of Honor. Although they faced some institutional and individual prejudices in the military, Latinos, unlike African Americans and most Nisei, served in integrated units and generally faced less discrimination in the military than in society.

For those remaining at home, more jobs were available, but still Latinos almost always worked as common laborers and agricultural workers. In the Southwest, it was not until 1943 that the FEPC attempted to open semiskilled and skilled positions to Mexican Americans. Jobs drew Mexican Americans, like others, to cities, creating serious social tensions as well as significant shortages of farm workers across the Southwest. As Los Angeles' already large Latino population expanded, social tensions became especially acute between Anglos and young Mexican Americans, known as **pachucos**, who expressed their rejection of Anglo culture by wearing **zoot suits**. Newspapers fanned racial tensions with articles highlighting a Mexican crime wave and depicting the "zooters" as dope addicts and draft dodgers. In June 1943, Anglo mobs, including several hundred servicemen, descended on East Los Angeles for three successive nights. They dragged zoot suiters out of movies, stores, even houses, beating them and tearing apart their clothes. When the police acted, it was to arrest the victims—over six hundred Mexican American youths were taken into "preventive custody." The riot lasted a week. Afterward, the Los Angeles city council outlawed the wearing of zoot suits.

To relieve the need for agricultural workers, Washington turned to Mexico. Together they negotiated the *bracero* program. The agreement stipulated that the **braceros** receive fair wages and adequate housing, transportation, food, and medical care. But guarantees mattered little. Most ranchers and farmers paid low wages and provided substandard facilities. The average Mexican American family earned about $800 a year, well below the U.S. government's established $1,130 annual minimum standard for a family of five.

Jobs and higher wages were available to many American Indians during the war and lured more than forty thousand of them away from their reservations, many of whom never returned following the war. In addition, over twenty-five thousand Indians served in the military. Among the most famous were about four hundred Navajos who served as **code talkers** for the Marine Corps, using their native language as a secure means of communication. Although often called "chief," American Indians met little discrimination in the military. Whether in the armed forces or in the domestic work force, those who left the reservations saw their families' average incomes rise from $400 a year in 1941 to $1,200 in 1945, and many chose to assimilate into American culture, abandoning their old patterns of life.

Nearly invisible in society, homosexuals also served in the military. The official policy was not to enlist them, but the screening process was ineffective, merely asking if a person was a homosexual and looking only for effeminate behavior. Once enlisted, many gays and lesbians discovered that the military generally tolerated them unless they were caught in a sexual act. In a circular letter sent to military commanders, the surgeon general's office asked that homosexual relationships be overlooked as long as they did not disrupt the unit. During the war, gays' war records were much like those of other soldiers. "I was super patriotic," said one gay combat veteran.

Waging World War

☆ *What factors did Roosevelt consider in shaping America's strategy for global conflict?*

☆ *Why did Truman and his advisers choose to use the atomic bomb?*

In the days following Pearl Harbor, many Americans wanted the defeat of Japan to be the country's first priority. To Churchill's and Stalin's relief, however, Roosevelt remained committed to victory first in Europe. But what was the best strategy to defeat Hitler? The Soviets, fighting against 3.3 million Germans, called for a second front in northern Europe as soon as possible. The British considered an invasion across the English Channel into France too risky and promoted an easier and safer landing in western North Africa, Operation Torch, in 1942. Believing the people needed a victory anywhere, Roosevelt ignored opposition from his chiefs of staff and approved the operation.

As planning began for the invasion, the course of the war darkened for the Allies. German forces were advancing toward Egypt and penetrating deeper into the Soviet Union. In the Atlantic, German U-boats were sinking ships at an appalling rate. April and May 1942 saw the surrender of most American forces in the Philippines, and Japanese successes continued elsewhere in the Pacific. General Patrick Hurley admitted, "We were out-shipped, out-planed, out-manned, and out-gunned by the Japanese."

Halting the Japanese Advance

Despite the commitment to defeating Germany, the nation's first victory came in the Pacific on May 8, 1942, at the **Battle of the Coral Sea** (see Map 23.4). Having deciphered secret Japanese codes, American military planners successfully deployed carrier forces to intercept and halt a Japanese invasion fleet aimed at New Guinea. Soon after the Coral Sea success, again

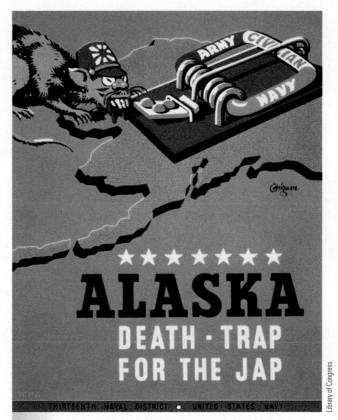

Library of Congress.

War posters often used exaggerated racial and ethnic stereotypes to show the enemy in the worst possible light. In this American poster the Japanese are depicted as rats—Japanese as monkeys was also a common form. The Japanese posters frequently showed Franklin D. Roosevelt as a horned demon, accompanied by an equally demonic Churchill.

reading top-secret Japanese messages, the United States learned of a Japanese thrust spearheaded by an aircraft carrier group aimed at **Midway Island**.

The Battle of Midway, June 4–6, 1942, helped change the course of the war in the Pacific. The air-to-sea battle was several hours old when a flight of American dive-bombers attacked the Japanese carriers in the middle of rearming and refueling their planes. Their decks cluttered with planes, fuel, and bombs, the Japanese carriers suffered staggering casualties and damage. Three immediately sank, and a fourth went down later in the battle. Although the

■ **Battle of the Coral Sea** U.S. victory in the Pacific in May 1942; it prevented the Japanese from invading New Guinea and thus isolating Australia.

■ **Midway Island** Strategically located Pacific island that the Japanese navy tried to capture in June 1942; warned about Japanese plans by U.S. naval intelligence, American forces repulsed the attack and inflicted heavy losses on Japanese planes and carriers.

MAP 23.4 Closing the Circle on Japan, 1942–1945
Following the Battle of Midway, American forces began the costly process of island-hopping with the invasion of Guadalcanal (August 1942). This map shows the paths of the American campaign in the Pacific, closing the circle on Japan. After atomic bombs destroyed Hiroshima and Nagasaki and the Soviet Union entered the war, Japan surrendered on August 14, 1945. Copyright © Cengage Learning

Americans lost the U.S.S. *Yorktown*, they had destroyed the carrier-based air superiority of the Japanese. In the war of machines, the United States quickly replaced the *Yorktown* and by the end of the war had constructed fourteen additional large carriers—Japan was able to build only six.

The next step in the Pacific was to begin an island-hopping campaign intended, eventually, to close in on Japan. **General Douglas MacArthur** and the army would advance toward the Philippines from the south. The navy, under the direction of Admiral Chester Nimitz, would seize selected islands and atolls in the Solomon, Marshall, Gilbert, and Mariana island groups, approaching the Philippines from the east (see Map 23.4). Both forces would join for the final attack on Japan. On August 7, 1942, soldiers of the 1st Marine Division waded ashore on **Guadalcanal Island** in the Solomons. Japan, considering the invasion to

■ **General Douglas MacArthur** Commander of American and Filipino troops in the Philippines when Japan took the islands in 1942, he led the forces that retook the islands in 1944; in 1945, as Supreme Commander for the Allied Powers (SCAP), he accepted Japan's formal surrender and subsequently oversaw the rebuilding of Japan.

■ **Guadalcanal Island** Pacific island secured by U.S. troops in February 1943, starting the process of taking strategic islands to close the circle on Japan.

Regarded by many as the turning point of the war in Europe, the Battle of Stalingrad lasted from July 1942 to February 1943, with much of the most brutal fighting occurring in the streets of the city during October and November 1942. Here Soviet soldiers battle in the ruins of the city in October. When German forces finally surrendered in January and February, Hitler said: "The God of War" has gone over to the other side.

be "the fork in the road that leads to victory for them or for us," furiously defended the island. Both sides suffered significant losses in the horrendous face-to-face combat that characterized the war in the Pacific. After heavy losses, the Japanese withdrew in early February.

Roads to Berlin

While American marines sweated in the jungles of Guadalcanal, British and American armies closed in on German forces in North Africa. With the British driving the Germans from Egypt westward, American troops landed in Morocco in November 1943 and pushed eastward. In early May 1943, the Americans linked up with the British, forcing 300,000 German troops to surrender (see Map 23.5).

German losses in North Africa were light compared with those in Russia, where Soviet and German forces were locked in a titanic struggle. Through the summer and fall of 1942, German armies advanced steadily, but during the winter the Soviet army drove them from the Caucasus oil fields and trapped them at Stalingrad. On February 2, 1943, after a three-month Soviet counteroffensive in the dead of winter, 300,000 German soldiers surrendered, their 6th Army having lost more than 140,000 men.

Although it was hard to predict in February, the tide of the war had turned in Europe. Soviet forces would continue to grind down the German army all the way to Berlin (see Map 23.5). But in February, Stalin knew only that the **Battle of Stalingrad** had cost the Russians dearly and that German strength was still formidable. He again demanded a second front in Western Europe. Again, he would be disappointed. Meeting with Churchill at Casablanca (January 1943), Roosevelt agreed with the British leader to invade Sicily and Italy, targets that Churchill called the "soft underbelly of the Axis." General Albert Wedemeyer expressed the U.S. military reaction to the Casablanca deal: "We lost our shirts . . . we came, we listened, and we were conquered."

The invasion of Sicily—Operation Husky—took place in early July 1943, and within a month the Allies controlled the island. In response, the Italians overthrew Mussolini and opened negotiations with Britain and the United States to change sides. Italy

■ **Battle of Stalingrad** Battle for the Russian city that was besieged by the German army in 1942 and recaptured by Soviet troops in 1943; regarded by many as the key battle of the European war.

MAP 23.5 The Fall of the Third Reich
In 1943 and 1944, the war turned in favor of the Allies. On the eastern front, Soviet forces drove the Germans back toward Germany. On June 6, 1944, D-Day, British, Canadian, and American forces landed on the coast of Normandy to begin the liberation of France. This map shows the course of the Allied armies as they fought their way toward Berlin. On May 7, 1945, Germany surrendered. Copyright © Cengage Learning

surrendered unconditionally on September 8. Immediately, German forces assumed the defense of Italy and halted the Allied advance just north of Salerno. Not until late May 1944 did Allied forces finally break through the German defenses in southern Italy. On June 4, U.S. forces under General Mark Clark entered

Rome. Two days later, the world's attention turned toward Normandy along the west coast of France. The second front demanded by Stalin had, at long last, begun (see Map 23.5).

In November 1943 the leaders of the **Grand Alliance**, Roosevelt, Churchill, and Stalin, had met in the Iranian capital of Tehran to discuss strategy and to consider the process of establishing a postwar settlement. The **Tehran Conference** was a productive meeting. The Allies made plans to coordinate a Soviet offensive with the Allied landings at Normandy and to work together to create a positive peace. Roosevelt was especially pleased because Stalin had agreed to support a new world organization and to enter the Japanese war once the battle with Hitler was over.

■ **Grand Alliance** A term used to refer to those allied nations working to defeat Hitler; often used to refer to the Big Three: Britain, the United States, and the Soviet Union.

■ **Tehran Conference** Meeting in Iran in 1943 at which Roosevelt, Churchill, and Stalin discussed the invasion of Western Europe and considered plans for a new international organization; Stalin also renewed his promise to enter the war against Japan.

The invasion of Normandy, France—**Operation Overlord**—was the grandest **amphibious** assault ever assembled: 6,483 ships, 1,500 tanks, and 200,000 men. Opposing the Allies were thousands of German troops behind the Atlantic Wall they had constructed along the coast to stop such an invasion. On D-Day, June 6, 1944, American forces landed on Utah and Omaha Beaches, while British and Canadian forces hit Sword, Gold, and Juno Beaches. At the landing sites, German resistance varied: the fiercest fighting was at Omaha Beach. One soldier from Arizona wrote:

> Let the thunder roll,
> Smoke and flame, will show th' way.
> I am the Beach at Omaha.
> The gates of hell are open wide,
> For all who come to play.
> The stakes are high,
> The game is death,
> No winners here today.

After a week of attacks and counterattacks, the five beaches were linked, and the Allied forces coiled to break through the German positions blocking the roads to the rest of France. On July 25, American soldiers pierced the stubbornly held German defensive lines at Saint-Lô. Paris was liberated on August 25, and in October, the Allies reached the west side of the Rhine River. From November 1944 to March 1945, American forces readied themselves to attack across the Rhine. At the same time, Allied bombers and fighter-bombers continued to bomb German-held Europe night and day. They destroyed vital industries and transportation systems as well as German cities. In one of the worst raids, during the night of February 13, 1945, three flights of British and American bombers set Dresden aflame, creating a firestorm that killed more than 135,000 civilians. Nearly 600,000 German civilians would die in Allied air raids, with another 800,000 injured.

With his cities being destroyed from the air and his forces crumbling in the east, Hitler approved a last-ditch attempt to halt the Allied advance in the west. Taking advantage of bad weather that grounded Allied aircraft, on December 16 German forces launched an attack through the Ardennes Forest designed to split American forces. It created a 50-mile "bulge" in the Allied lines. At Bastogne, a critical crossroads, American soldiers hung on until a relief column reached the city. When asked to surrender, General A. C. McAuliffe simply told the Germans, "Nuts." After ten days, the weather improved, and the German offensive slowed and was driven back. The Battle of the Bulge (see Map 23.5 inset) was the last major Axis counteroffensive on the western front. In March 1945, British and American forces crossed the Rhine and battled eastward. At the same time,

Soviet forces began the bloody, house-to-house conquest of Berlin. On April 25, American and Soviet infantrymen shook hands at the Elbe River 60 miles south of Berlin. Inside the city, Hitler committed suicide on April 30 and had aides burn his body. On May 8, 1945, German officials surrendered. The war in Europe was over.

Stresses in the Grand Alliance

As the Soviets pushed toward Berlin, they liberated parts of Poland, Romania, Bulgaria, Hungary, and Czechoslovakia. Following the Red Army were Soviet officials and Eastern European Communists who had lived in exile in the Soviet Union before and during the war. The Soviet goal was to establish new Eastern European governments that would be "friendly" to the Soviet Union. A Communist Lublin government (named after the town where the government was installed) was established in Poland, while in Romania and Bulgaria **"popular front"** governments, heavily influenced by local and returning Communist Party members, took command. Only Czechoslovakia and Hungary managed to establish non-Communist-dominated governments as the German occupation collapsed.

On February 4, 1945, the Big Three met at the Black Sea resort of **Yalta** amid growing Western apprehension about Soviet goals in Eastern Europe. Confident that he could work with Stalin, Roosevelt wanted to ensure that the Soviet Union would enter the war against Japan and maintain its support for a new United Nations. He also wanted the Soviets to show some willingness to modify their controls over Eastern Europe. Stalin's goals were Western acceptance of a Soviet sphere of influence in Eastern Europe, the weakening of Germany, and the economic restoration of the Soviet Union. Central to

■ **Operation Overlord** The Allied invasion of Europe on June 6, 1944—D-Day—across the English Channel to Normandy; D-Day is short for "designated day."

amphibious In historical context, a military operation that coordinates air, land, and sea military forces to land on a hostile shore.

popular front An organization or government composed of a wide spectrum of political groups; popular fronts were used by the Soviet Union in forming allegedly non-Communist governments in Eastern Europe.

■ **Yalta** Site in the Crimea of the last meeting, in 1945, between Roosevelt, Churchill, and Stalin; they discussed the final defeat of the Axis powers and the problems of postwar occupation. Among the most important issues were the Polish government, German reparations, and the formation of the United Nations.

As Allied armies fought their way closer to Berlin, Roosevelt, Churchill, and Stalin met at the Black Sea resort of Yalta in February 1945 to discuss military strategy and postwar concerns. Two months later, Roosevelt died and Harry S Truman assumed the presidency.

National Archives.

Allied differences over Eastern Europe was the nature of the Polish government. Roosevelt and Churchill considered the Lublin regime to be undemocratic and a puppet of the Soviet Union and instead supported a London-based government in exile. Stalin labeled the London-based government hostile to the Soviet Union and demanded a friendly government in Poland. After considerable acidic haggling, the powers compromised in language so vague that Admiral William Leahy, one of Roosevelt's primary advisers, ruefully noted it could be "stretched from Yalta to Washington" without breaking. Roosevelt reluctantly allowed the Lublin government to remain the center of a larger coalition government, with free elections to be held after the war. Poland's borders were shifted to the West, leaving the Soviets in control of those lands seized during their invasion of Poland in 1939. The agreement hardly applied the ideals of the Atlantic Charter, but Roosevelt concluded that it was the best he could do for Poland at the moment. Still Roosevelt had achieved two of his major goals: Stalin agreed to maintain Soviet support in defeating Japan and engage in a new world organization. Although disappointed over the continued Soviet domination of Eastern Europe, Roosevelt realized that little could be done to prevent the Soviet Union from keeping what it already had, or could easily take. He hoped that his goodwill would encourage Stalin to respond in kind, maintaining at least a semblance of representative government in Eastern Europe and continuing to cooperate with the United States.

Roosevelt returned from Yalta exhausted with rapidly failing health. Relaxing at Warm Springs, Georgia, the 63-year-old president suffered a cerebral hemorrhage on April 12, 1944, and died. Long-time political opponent Senator Robert Taft spoke for the nation: "He dies a hero of the war, for he literally worked himself to death in the service of the American people." Truman, a man few knew much about, was now president and determined to continue Roosevelt's road to victory.

The Holocaust

As Allied forces advanced into Germany, they and the world came to realize the full horror of the **Holocaust**. In 1941 the Nazi political leadership had ordered what it called the **Final Solution** to rid German-occupied

■ **Holocaust** Mass murder of European Jews and other groups systematically carried out by the Nazis during World War II.

■ **Final Solution** German plan to eliminate Jews through the use of special mobile execution forces or by mass executions within concentration camps; by the end of the war, the Nazis had killed 6 million Jews.

Hitler ordered the "Final Solution"—the extermination of Europe's Jews—soon after the United States entered the war. In this picture, German troops arrest residents of the Warsaw ghetto for deportation to concentration camps. Few would survive the camps, where over 6 million Jews died.

Europe of Jews. In concentration camps, Jews, along with homosexuals, gypsies, and the mentally ill, were brutalized, starved, worked as slave labor, and systematically exterminated. At Auschwitz, Nazis used gas chambers—disguised as showers—to execute 12,000 victims a day.

Reports of German brutalization of Jews in the concentration camps had circulated even before the war, but the Western governments and the press did little to expose or prevent the atrocities. Roosevelt, like other leaders, did not see a personal, political, diplomatic, or military need to make Holocaust information widely known; and he did not give the plight of the Jews or other refugees a high priority. Only in January 1944 did Roosevelt establish a **War Refugee Board**.

As British, American, and Soviet troops liberated the camps, reporters and photographers recorded the reality of the sweeping horrors found there. Among the American units freeing Jewish survivors at Buchenwald and Dachau were the African American 761st Tank Battalion and the Japanese American 522nd Field Artillery Battalion. One survivor at first thought that the Japanese had won the war, until realizing the soldiers were Americans. "I had never seen black men or Japanese," another recalled. "They were riding in

these tanks and jeeps; they were like angels who came down from heaven to save our lives." While thousands were saved, over 6 million Jews, nearly two-thirds of prewar Europe's Jewish population, were slaughtered in the death camps.

Closing the Circle on Japan

On May 8, 1945, V-E Day—celebrating victory in Europe—touched off parades and rejoicing in the United States. But Japan still had to be defeated. Japan's defensive strategy was simple: force the United States to invade a seemingly endless number of Pacific islands before it could launch an invasion against Japan, with each speck of land costing the Americans dearly in lives and materials. The American military, however, realized that it had to seize only the most strategic islands. With carriers providing mobile air superiority, the Americans could bypass and isolate others.

■ **War Refugee Board** Group created to rescue as many persecuted minorities of Europe as possible from Nazi oppression.

"Tarawa", painting by Tom Lovell, USMCR. Art Collection, National Museum of the Marine Corps, Triangle, Virginia.

On November 21, 1943, marines stormed ashore on the atoll of Tarawa, soon to be called, "Bloody Tarawa." The marines secured the island, but the cost was high. Of the five thousand marines who fought in the battle, more than one thousand were killed and another two thousand were wounded. Nearly all of the five thousand Japanese defenders died, many in a final "death charge."

Throughout 1943, U.S forces continued to advance toward the Philippines from the south. At the same time, far to the northeast, the U.S. Navy and the Marines Corps were establishing footholds in the Gilbert and Marshall Islands. Exemplifying the bitter fighting was "bloody Tarawa," where marines fought their way ashore on November 21, 1943. Overcoming five thousand well-entrenched Japanese troops, nearly all of whom fought to the death, American marines suffered nearly three thousand casualties. The Mariana Islands were next (see Map 23.4 on page 676). In the battle for Saipan, the Japanese lost 243 planes and three more aircraft carriers, while nearly thirty-two thousand Japanese defenders fought to the death. Shocking American troops, nearly two-thirds of the island's Japanese civilians, mostly women and children, committed suicide. Marines next seized the nearby islands of Tinian and Guam. By late summer of 1944, the southern and eastern approaches to the Philippines were in American hands.

Island bases added support facilities for bombing military and domestic targets in Japan, which began in February 1944. Long-range bombers, the B-29s, made devastating raids against Japanese cities, with the intention of weakening the Japanese will to resist. Although the estimated number of Japanese civilians killed in the bombing far exceeded the number of Japanese soldiers killed in combat, the raids did little to reduce Japanese citizens' support for the war or the government.

In October 1944, American forces landed on Leyte in the center of the Philippine archipelago. General MacArthur, who had evacuated the Philippines in March 1942, had fulfilled his promise to return. The Japanese navy moved to halt the invasion, and in the largest naval battle in history, the **Battle of Leyte Gulf** (October 23–25, 1944), American forces shattered what remained of Japanese air and sea power.

After the Battle of Leyte Gulf, the full brunt of the American Pacific offensive bore down on Iwo Jima and Okinawa, only 750 miles from Tokyo. To defend the islands, Japan made large-scale use of the *kamikaze* attack—in which pilots made suicide crashes on targets in explosive-laden airplanes. The American assault on Iwo Jima began on February 19, 1945, and before it ended on March 17, virtually all of the 21,000 Japanese defenders had fought to the death, and American losses approached one-third of the landing force: 6,821 dead and 20,000 wounded.

On Okinawa, from April through June, the carnage was even worse. While American forces took heavy losses along Japanese defensive lines, Japanese planes and *kamikazes* rained terror and destruction

■ **Battle of Leyte Gulf** Naval battle in October 1944 in which American forces near the Philippines crushed remaining Japanese air and sea power.

on the American fleet. But the Japanese air onslaughts became weaker each month as Japan ran out of planes and pilots. By the end of June, Okinawa was in American hands, but at a fearful price: 12,000 Americans, 110,000 Japanese soldiers, and 160,000 Okinawan and Japanese civilians dead.

Entering the Nuclear Age

The experience of Okinawa suggested to most American planners that any invasion of Japan would result in large numbers of American casualties. But by the summer of 1945, the United States had a possible alternative to invasion: a new and untried weapon—the atomic bomb. The A-bomb was the product of years of British-American research and development in the Manhattan Project. From the beginning of the conflict, science had developed and improved the tools of combat, providing, in addition to radar and sonar, flamethrowers, rockets, and a variety of other useful and frequently deadly products. But the most fearsome and secret of the projects was the drive started in 1941 to construct a nuclear weapon. Between then and 1945, the Manhattan Project scientists, led by physicists J. Robert Oppenheimer and Edward Teller, controlled a chain reaction involving uranium and plutonium to create the atomic bomb. By the time Germany surrendered, the project had consumed more than $2 billion, but the bomb was born. When it was tested at Alamogordo, New Mexico, on July 16, 1945, the results were spectacular. In the words of Brigadier General Leslie R. Groves, the U.S. Army engineer who headed the project: "The effect could well be called unprecedented, magnificent, beautiful, stupendous and terrifying. . . . The whole country was lighted by a searing light. . . . Thirty seconds after the explosion came . . . the air blast . . . followed almost immediately by the strong, sustained, awesome roar which warned of doomsday and made us feel that we puny things were blasphemous to dare tamper with the forces heretofore reserved to The Almighty." Word of the successful test was quickly relayed to Truman, who at the time was meeting with Churchill and Stalin at Potsdam, outside Berlin.

Before leaving for Potsdam, Truman had decided not to tell Stalin any details about the atomic bomb and to use it as soon as possible against Japan. Using the atomic bomb, he hoped, would serve two purposes. It would force Japan to surrender without an invasion, and it would impress the Soviets and, just maybe, make them more amenable to American views on the postwar world order.

On August 6, 1945, the world entered the atomic age when the city of Hiroshima was destroyed by an atomic bomb. "We had seen the city when we went in," said the pilot of the *Enola Gay*, "and there was nothing to see when we came back." The city and most of its people had died.

Soon after his arrival for the Potsdam Conference (July–August, 1945), Truman obtained confirmation from Stalin that the Soviet Union would enter the Japanese war in mid-August, and he informed Stalin about a new and powerful weapon to use against Japan. Stalin, who knew from spies that it was an atomic bomb, appeared unimpressed and told Truman to go ahead and use it. Working with Prime Minister Clement Attlee of Britain (who was told of the atomic bomb), Truman released the **Potsdam Declaration**, which called on Japan to surrender by August or face total destruction. The declaration reflected two developments—one Japan knew about, and the other it was soon to learn. Japanese officials had asked the "neutral" Soviets to try to persuade the Americans to consider negotiating a Japanese surrender. Stalin, Attlee, and Truman agreed instead to insist on unconditional surrender. In the Potsdam Declaration, the Japanese could read the rejection of their overture, but they had no way of knowing that the utter destruction referred to in the declaration meant the A-bomb. On July 25, Truman ordered the use of the atomic bomb as soon after August 3 as possible, provided the Japanese did not surrender.

■ **Potsdam Declaration** The demand for Japan's unconditional surrender, made near the end of the Potsdam Conference.

COUNTRY	DEAD
Soviet Union	8.6 million
China	1.3 million
Poland	130 thousand
Germany	3.6 million
Japan	1.75 million
Britain and Commonwealth	384 thousand
United States	292 thousand

World War II Deaths

Allied Military 25%

Axis Military 13%

Axis Civilians 4%

Allied Civilians 58%

FIGURE 23.3 Military War Dead

On the island of Tinian, B-29s were readied to carry the two available bombs to targets in Japan; a third was waiting to be assembled. A B-29 bomber named the *Enola Gay* dropped the first bomb over **Hiroshima** at 9:15 A.M. on August 6, 1945. Japan's eighth-largest city, Hiroshima had a population of over 250,000 and to that point had not suffered heavy bombing. In the atomic blast and fireball, almost 100,000 Japanese were killed or terribly maimed. Another 100,000 would eventually die from the effects of radiation. The United States announced that unless the Japanese surrendered immediately, they could "expect a rain of ruin from the air, the like of which has never been seen on this earth."

As Tokyo contemplated surrender, on August 8 the Soviets declared war and advanced into Japanese-held Manchuria. The next day a second atomic bomb destroyed **Nagasaki**. Nearly 60,000 people were killed.

■ **Hiroshima** Japanese city that was the target, on August 6, 1945, of the first atomic bomb, called "Little Boy."

■ **Nagasaki** City in western Japan devastated on August 9, 1945, by the second atomic bomb, called "Fat Man."

Although some within the Japanese army argued for continuing the fight, Emperor Hirohito, watching the Red Army slice through Japanese forces and afraid of losing more cities to atomic attacks, made the final decision. Japan must "bear the unbearable," he said, and surrender. On August 14, 1945, Japan officially surrendered, and the United States agreed to leave the position of emperor intact.

World War II was over, but much of the world lay in ruins. Some 50 million people, military and civilian, had been killed (see Figure 23.3). The United States was spared most of the destruction. It had suffered almost no civilian casualties, and its cities and industrial centers stood unharmed. In many ways, in fact, the war had been good to the United States. It had decisively ended the Depression, and although some economists predicted an immediate postwar recession, the overall economic picture was bright. Government regulation and planning for the economy that had their beginnings in the New Deal took root and flourished during the war. As the war ended, only a few wanted a return to the laissez-faire-style government that had characterized the 1920s. Big government was here to stay, and at the center of big government was a powerful presidency ready to direct and guide the nation.

Individual Voices

Justice Hugo Black Explains the Majority View
in *Korematsu v. United States*

Japanese American Fred Korematsu did not report for internment and was arrested in May 1942 and sentenced to five years' probation. While at the Topaz relocation camp, with the aid of the American Civil Liberties Union, he unsuccessfully appealed his conviction to the Supreme Court. In December 1944, in a split decision, the Court upheld his conviction. Justice Hugo Black, writing for the majority, found that the needs of war can abridge the rights of citizenship. Black's written majority opinion provides historians with insights into what the Court was thinking, but his arguments also reveal, and attempt to counter, ways in which some Americans might have disagreed.

① How does Minoru Kiyota match Justice Black's definition of disloyal? In what way was Fred Korematsu disloyal?

② Under what criteria did Justice Black dismiss race as a basis of the decision being contested by Korematsu?

③ What reasons does Justice Black use to prevent the use of hindsight? What does this view suggest about the Court's ability to reverse past decisions made by the government?

④ Why is the *Korematsu* decision important in defining limitations on civil rights and rights found in the Bill of Rights?

It should be noted . . . all legal restrictions which curtail the civil rights of a single racial group are immediately suspect. That is not to say that all such restrictions are unconstitutional. . . . Pressing public necessity may sometimes justify the existence of such restrictions. . . .

Exclusion of those of Japanese origin was deemed necessary because of the presence of . . . disloyal members of the group, most of whom we have no doubt were loyal to this country. . . . we could not reject the finding . . . that it was impossible to . . . [segregate] the disloyal from the loyal that we sustained the validity of the curfew order. . . . That there were members of the group who retained loyalties in Japan has been confirmed. . . . Approximately five thousand American citizens of Japanese ancestry refused to swear unqualified allegiance to the United States and to renounce allegiance to the Japanese Emperor. . . . **①**

We . . . are not unmindful of the hardships imposed. . . . But hardships are part of war. . . . Compulsory exclusion of large groups of citizens from their homes . . . is inconsistent with our basic governmental institutions. But when under conditions of modern warfare our shores are threatened by hostile forces, the power to protect must be commensurate with the threatened danger. . . .

It is said [this is a] . . . case of imprisonment of a citizen . . . solely because of his ancestry, without evidence or inquiry concerning his loyalty and good disposition towards the United States. . . . To cast this case into outlines of racial prejudice, without reference to the real military dangers which were presented, merely confuses the issue. Korematsu was not excluded from the Military Area because of . . . his race. He was excluded because we are at war with the Japanese Empire, because the properly constituted military authorities feared an invasion of our West Coast and felt constrained to take proper security measures, because they decided that the military urgency of the situation demanded that all citizens of Japanese ancestry be segregated from the West Coast. . . . **②** There was evidence of disloyalty . . . the military authorities considered that the need for action was great, and time was short. We cannot—by availing ourselves of the calm perspective of hindsight **③**—now say that at that time these actions were unjustified. **④**

685

Study Tools

SUMMARY

In 1929 Hoover believed that he would preside over a world at peace. But he and Roosevelt faced the collapse of the international system as Japan, Italy, and Germany increased their territories, influence, and power. Japan seized Manchuria and later invaded China, while Mussolini conquered Ethiopia, and Hitler created a new German empire. In the lengthening shadow of world conflict, the majority of Americans maintained isolationism, and Congress passed neutrality laws designed to keep the nation from involvement in the faraway conflicts. Even as Germany invaded Poland in 1939, most Americans were still anxious to remain outside the conflict. Roosevelt, however, chose to help those fighting Germany, linking the United States' economic might first to England and then to the Soviet Union.

Roosevelt also used economic and diplomatic pressures to halt Japan's expansion. But the pressure only heightened the crisis, convincing many in the Japanese government that the best choice was to attack the United States before it grew in strength. Japan's attack on Pearl Harbor on December 7, 1941, brought a fully committed American public and government into World War II.

Mobilizing the nation for war ended the Depression and increased government intervention in the economy. Another outcome of the war was a range of new choices for Americans in the military and the workplace. Japanese Americans, however, suffered a loss of freedom

CHRONOLOGY
A World at War

1929	Herbert Hoover becomes president
1931	Japan seizes Manchuria
1933	Franklin D. Roosevelt becomes president
	Hitler and Nazi Party take power in Germany
1934	Fulgencio Batista assumes power in Cuba
1935	First Neutrality Act
	Italy invades Ethiopia
1936	Germany reoccupies the Rhineland
	Italy annexes Ethiopia
	Spanish Civil War begins
	Second Neutrality Act
1937	Third Neutrality Act
	Roosevelt's quarantine speech
	Sino-Japanese War begins
1938	Germany annexes Austria and Sudetenland
	Munich Conference
1939	German-Soviet Nonaggression Pact
	Germany invades Poland; Britain and France declare war on Germany
	Neutrality Act of 1939
1940	Germany occupies most of Western Europe
	U.S. economic sanctions against Japan
	Burke-Wadsworth Act
	Destroyers-for-bases agreement
	Roosevelt reelected
1941	Lend-Lease Act
	Fair Employment Practices Commission created
	Germany invades Soviet Union

	Atlantic Charter
	U-boats attack U.S. warships
	Japan attacks Pearl Harbor; United States enters World War II
1942	War Production Board created
	Japanese conquer Philippines
	Japanese Americans interned
	Battles of Coral Sea and Midway
	Congress of Racial Equality founded
	U.S. troops invade North Africa
1943	U.S. forces capture Guadalcanal
	Soviets defeat Germans at Stalingrad
	Smith-Connally War Labor Disputes Act
	Detroit race riot
	U.S. and British forces invade Sicily and Italy; Italy surrenders
	Tehran Conference
1944	Operation Overlord—June 6 invasion of Normandy
	G.I. Bill becomes law
	U.S. forces invade the Philippines
	Roosevelt reelected
	Soviet forces liberate Eastern Europe
	Battle of the Bulge
1945	Yalta Conference
	Roosevelt dies; Harry S Truman becomes president
	United Nations created
	Germany surrenders; Potsdam Conference
	United States drops atomic bombs on Hiroshima and Nagasaki
	Japan surrenders

and property as the government placed them in internment camps.

Fighting a two-front war, American planners gave first priority to defeating Hitler. The effort began in North Africa in 1942, expanded to Italy in 1943, and to France in 1944. By the beginning of 1945, Allied armies were threatening Nazi Germany from the west and the east, and on May 8, 1945, Germany surrendered. In the Pacific theater, the victory at Midway in mid-1942 checked Japan's offensive and allowed the use of aircraft carriers to begin tightening the noose around the enemy. To bring the war to a close without a U.S. invasion, Truman elected to use the atomic bomb. Following the destruction of Hiroshima and Nagasaki, Japan surrendered on August 14, 1945, ending the war and for many Americans ushering in the beginning of "America's century."

FOCUS QUESTIONS

If you have mastered this chapter, you should be able to answer these questions and to identify the terms that follow the questions.

1. ☆ *How were Roosevelt's policies toward Latin America a continuation of Hoover's?*

2. ☆ *What obstacles did Roosevelt face in trying to implement a more assertive foreign policy from 1935 to 1939?*

3. ☆ *Following the outbreak of World War II in 1939, how did Roosevelt reshape American neutrality?*

4. ☆ *What actions did Roosevelt take to mobilize the nation for war and how did they affect the relationship between business and government?*

5. ☆ *What new social and economic choices did Americans confront during the war? How were different groups affected?*

6. ☆ *What factors did Roosevelt consider in shaping America's strategy for global conflict?*

7. ☆ *Why did Truman and his advisers choose to use the atomic bomb?*

KEY TERMS

Nisei   (p. 655)

Greater East Asian Co-Prosperity Sphere   (p. 657)

Colonel Fulgencio Batista   (p. 657)

Good Neighbor policy   (p. 657)

fascist   (p. 657)

Neutrality Act of 1935   (p. 657)

appeasement   (p. 659)

Munich Agreement   (p. 659)

German-Soviet Nonaggression Pact   (p. 661)

Neutrality Act of 1939   (p. 661)

Axis powers   (p. 662)

Burke-Wadsworth Act   (p. 662)

Lend-Lease Act   (p. 662)

Atlantic Charter   (p. 663)

Issei   (p. 666)

Executive Order #9066   (p. 666)

internment camps   (p. 666)

Manhattan Project   (p. 668)

Office of War Mobilization   (p. 669)

Smith-Connally War Labor Disputes Act   (p. 669)

G.I. Bill   (p. 670)

Harry S Truman   (p. 670)

victory garden   (p. 671)

Rosie the Riveter   (p. 672)

A. Philip Randolph   (p. 673)

Fair Employment Practices Commission   (p. 673)

Congress of Racial Equality   (p. 673)

James Farmer   (p. 673)

Benjamin O. Davis, Jr.   (p. 673)

braceros   (p. 674)

code talkers   (p. 674)

Battle of the Coral Sea   (p. 675)

Midway Island   (p. 675)

General Douglas MacArthur   (p. 676)

Guadalcanal Island   (p. 676)

Battle of Stalingrad   (p. 677)

Grand Alliance   (p. 678)

Tehran Conference   (p. 678)

Operation Overlord   (p. 679)

Yalta   (p. 679)

Holocaust   (p. 680)

Final Solution   (p. 680)

War Refugee Board   (p. 681)

Battle of Leyte Gulf   (p. 682)

Potsdam Declaration   (p. 683)

Hiroshima   (p. 684)

Nagasaki   (p. 684)

 CourseMate

Go to the History CourseMate website for primary source links, study tools, and review materials for this chapter. www.cengagebrain.com

24 Truman and Cold War America, 1945–1952

Behind the Stories

"IT'S WAR!" screamed the headlines of the *New York Times* in March 1946. Soviet tanks and troops were rolling toward the capital of Iran. As it turned out, the headline and story were wrong. There was no war—not in the traditional sense—but Americans knew that their hopes for a peaceful world were over. The Cold War was beginning, and although the United States and the Soviet Union never faced each other across the battlefield, their rivalry and hostility shaped the nation and the world.

What caused the Cold War? Most Americans replied: Soviet expansionism and aggression and U.S. unwillingness to appease a totalitarian state. Most historians agreed with that view until the 1960s when a group of revisionist historians examined newly released American primary sources. The revisionists' assessment varied, but emphasized a central theme that blamed the United States as much, if not more, for the origins of the Cold War. They described the United States as aggressively seeking an American-dominated world economic order and creating a national security state. Their critiques of American policies led to a bitter debate among historians that has outlasted the Cold War.

Still, as American soldiers returned home, international relations was not on many minds. There was too much to do—lives and families to begin or renew. Expectations and questions abounded. Would the changes generated by the New Deal and war remain? Would the government continue to play an active role in regulating business and the economy? Would women and minorities keep the benefits of the economic, social, and cultural changes generated by the war? How would new technology, especially the atom, change lives? Would Harry Truman lead the nation along the paths established by Roosevelt, would he oversee another return to "normalcy," or—as it turned out— would he follow a new course? What would be the effect of new attitudes and expectations generated by the developing Cold War? Chapter 24 begins to answer these questions as Americans moved into "America's century" and the "atomic age."

—J.G.

Individual Choices
Jackie Robinson

In high school and college Jackie Robinson proved he was a gifted athlete, but few would have thought those gifts would contribute to one of the most important choices in American sports. As this chapter's Individual Voices feature illustrates, great controversy surrounded the idea of African Americans playing in baseball's white major leagues and if Robinson was the best choice to cross the color line. In 1945, Branch Rickey, the president and general manager of the Brooklyn Dodgers, asked Robinson if he was "the right man" to play baseball in the Dodgers' system— to integrate major league baseball. What Rickey wanted to know was whether Robinson could take abuse, be someone "with guts enough not to fight back." Robinson said he could "turn the other cheek," and the deal was set. Robinson would get $600 a month to play with the Montreal Royals, a Dodgers farm team.

Jackie Robinson

At Muir Technical High School, Pasadena Junior College, and the University of California at Los Angeles, Robinson had excelled in athletics—lettering in four sports: track, baseball, football, and basketball. In 1941, he left UCLA before graduating to take a job but was soon drafted into the army. He applied to Officer Training Corps, which was accepting applications from African Americans for the first time, and received a commission as second lieutenant in 1943. He was assigned to a segregated tank regiment, but Robinson would not deploy to Europe and see combat. Involvement in an alleged racial incident and charges of insubordination resulted in a court martial that kept him stateside. Acquitted, Robinson was honorably discharged from the army in November 1944. He played professional baseball with the Kansas City Monarchs of the Negro League until he went to Montreal in 1945.

Spring training for the Royals was in Florida, and Robinson quickly experienced the racial hostility Rickey had predicted. He could not room at the team hotel, and some local officials cancelled games rather than let him play on their field. Robinson survived, and during the regular season Robinson led the Royals'

689

minor league in batting and was 1946's most valuable player. The following year, he was playing in the majors for the Dodgers.

On April 15, 1947, Robinson became the first African American player in major league baseball since the 1890s. He immediately faced racial tensions within the clubhouse and on the field. Team manager Leo Durocher made his views clear: "I do not care if the guy is yellow or black, or if he has stripes like a . . . zebra . . . I say he plays. What's more, I say he can make us all rich. And if any of you cannot use the money, I will see that you are all traded." When players threatened to strike rather than play against Robinson, the commissioner of baseball vowed to suspend them. These actions kept Robinson in the games but did not stop the verbal and physical abuse he received on and off the field. Robinson responded with his bat, fielding, and base-running, earning the Rookie of the Year title. The integration of major league baseball was history. Robinson played ten seasons with the Dodgers before retiring. He entered the Baseball Hall of Fame in 1962.

When World War II ended, Americans expected to return to a normal life, living in peace while they enjoyed the benefits of a consumer society. Many found jobs that allowed them to move to the suburbs and live the "American Dream." But world peace proved more elusive. By 1947, the United States and the Soviet Union were locked in a Cold War. Washington's policy was to contain Soviet power, first in Western Europe and then in Asia. When North Korea invaded South Korea, the Cold War suddenly became "hot" as President Truman committed American troops to halt Communist aggression.

The Cold War affected every aspect of American life. The growing fear of communism provided many with ammunition to attack ideas, institutions, and people they believed were too liberal. Conservatives and businesspeople asserted that unions had become too powerful—they needed to be restrained and purged of their Communist members. Southern whites charged that civil rights advocates were tainted with socialistic values. Across the nation, change and diversity were increasingly suspect. Spearheading America's defense against the dangers of communism were the House Un-American Activities Committee (HUAC) and Republican senator Joseph McCarthy. Both claimed that American institutions were rife with disloyal Americans whose values threatened the existence and soul of the nation.

The expanding Cold War also made it more difficult for Truman to introduce or expand on New Deal–style programs. Calls for civil rights, a national health system, and expansions of existing programs proved too expensive and too liberal for many. Truman had to accept the "politics of the possible," a moderate agenda that pleased neither ardent liberals nor staunch conservatives.

Despite concerns about communism, the majority of Americans looked forward to transitioning to a normal life. The G.I. Bill provided veterans with opportunities to improve their education, find a job, own a home. Those who had found new job opportunities during the war, however, faced a less optimistic future. They were expected to relinquish their wartime gains and return to their customary roles in American society. Still, many maintained a sense of optimism. Jackie Robinson was breaking the color line in professional baseball, and in the southwest federal courts were rejecting the separation of Mexican Americans and Anglos in public schools. Further, the skills, experiences, and self-confidence gained during the war could not be taken away. Even those returning to traditional roles did so with a stronger sense of self.

THE COLD WAR BEGINS

★ *What views and actions chosen by the Soviet Union and United States contributed to the Cold War?*

★ *How did the Truman administration seek to promote American global interests between 1947 and 1951 and why was the outcome in Asia less than satisfactory?*

★ *What events contributed to NSC 68 and how did it represent a change in strategy?*

Around the globe people hoped an enduring peace would follow the defeat of the Axis powers. But could the cooperative relationship of the Allies continue into the postwar era without a common enemy to unite them? Suspicion and distrust already had surfaced when Britain and the United States objected to the establishment of pro-Soviet governments in Eastern Europe, and President Harry S Truman appeared less willing than Roosevelt to place much trust in the Soviets. "The Soviet Union needs us more than we need them," Truman told a colleague. Although he was new to conducting foreign and domestic policies, Truman believed in the idea that at critical times individuals were called to rise to positions of leadership and to shape history. He was now in that situation. "The buck stops here," read a plaque in his office.

Truman and Paths to Peace

Truman and other American leaders identified two overlapping paths to peace: international cooperation and **deterrence** based on military strength. In 1944, as a means to achieve global cooperation and economic development, the International Monetary Fund and the World Bank were created, and at the Dumbarton Oaks conference delegates from the United States, China, Britain, and the Soviet Union mapped the basic structure of the **United Nations** (UN). Building on a series of high-level discussions in April 1945, a conference in San Francisco finished the task. It wrote the charter of the United Nations, an organization of six distinct bodies, the most important of which are the **General Assembly** and the **Security Council**. Composed of all member nations, the General Assembly was the weaker body with authority only to discuss issues, whereas resolving issues was the responsibility of the Security Council, composed of eleven nations. Six nations were elected by the General Assembly, but the real power was held by five permanent members: the United States, the Soviet Union, the United Kingdom, China, and France. To give the United Nations authority, the Security Council could apply economic and military pressures against other nations, but to protect their interests, each of the five permanent nations could veto Security Council decisions. When it was decided to house the headquarters of the UN in New York City, Truman noted that the center of Western civilization had shifted from Europe to the United States.

Still, Truman and most Americans chose not to rely solely on international cooperation for national security or maintaining peace. They concluded that the United States must continue to field a strong military force with bases around the globe, maintain its atomic monopoly, and take the lead in creating the conditions for an enduring peace. Drawing on lessons learned from World War II, most Americans believed aggressors should be halted, democratic governments supported, and a prosperous world economy created. These were the ideals of the Atlantic Charter, and most Americans saw them as fundamental values on which to construct peace.

In looking at international affairs, many Americans, including most in the Truman administration, saw the Soviet Union as a potential threat to world peace. It seemed that Moscow was ignoring the principles of the Atlantic Charter and following an "ominous course" in Eastern Europe that violated the Yalta agreements by creating undemocratic **puppet governments** and closing the region to free trade. By the end of 1945, Truman concluded that he was "tired of babying the Soviets." In February 1946, the State Department asked its Russia expert, George Kennan, to evaluate Soviet policy to determine its motivations and goals.

Kennan's "Long Telegram" described Soviet totalitarianism as internally weak. Soviet leaders, he said, held Communist ideology secondary to remaining in power, needing Western capitalism to serve as an enemy. But, he argued, Soviet leaders were not fanatics and would retreat when met with opposition. He recommended a policy of **containment**, meeting head-on any attempted expansion of Soviet power. His report immediately drew high praise from Washington's official circles. Soon thereafter, Truman adopted a policy designed to "set will against will, force against force, idea against idea . . . until Soviet expansion is finally worn down."

The Soviets had prewar and wartime experiences different from those of the United States and as a result had different postwar concerns and objectives. They wanted to be treated as a major power, to have Germany reduced in power, and to establish a "zone of security" with "friendly" governments in neighboring states. While accepting the United Nations, the Soviets preferred to work bilaterally and to rely on their own

---

deterrence Measures that a state takes to discourage attacks by other states, often including a military buildup.

■ **United Nations** (UN) International organization established in 1945 to maintain peace among nations and foster cooperation in human rights, education, health, welfare, and trade.

■ **General Assembly** Assembly of all members of the United Nations; it debates issues but neither creates nor executes policy.

■ **Security Council** The executive agency of the United Nations; today it includes five permanent members with veto power (China, France, the United Kingdom, Russia, and the United States) and ten members elected by the General Assembly for two-year terms.

puppet governments Governments imposed, supported, and directed by an outside force, usually a foreign power.

■ **containment** The U.S. policy of checking the expansion or influence of Communist nations by making strategic alliances, aiding friendly nations, and supporting weaker states in areas of conflict.

Joseph Stalin controlled the Soviet Union from 1926 until his death in 1953. His popular image was "Uncle Joe" during World War II, but by the time of the Truman Doctrine in March 1947, Stalin's image resembled Hitler's. Truman's first impression of the Soviet dictator, at Potsdam in July 1945, was that he was "dishonest but smart as hell" and they could work together. One of Truman's closest advisers bluntly stated that Stalin was "a liar and a crook."

resources. As 1946 began, Soviet officials warned of "capitalist encirclement" and accused the Truman administration of being less friendly than Roosevelt's. Moscow interpreted several American actions and policies as threatening and ideologically motivated. In September 1946, the Soviet ambassador in Washington, Nikolai Novikov, depicted the United States as globally aggressive, seeking to establish military bases around the world and to maintain a monopoly over atomic technology. He believed the United States was using its economic power to further its capitalistic goals while forcing other countries to adopt American interests, and he praised the Soviet Union for resisting the power and demands of the United States (see the Novikov Telegram above).

By the spring of 1946, fear of Soviet intentions was becoming a rising concern as Democrats and Republicans tried to educate the public about the Soviet threat to world stability. One of the most dramatic warnings, however, came from Winston Churchill on March 5, 1946, at Westminster College in Fulton, Missouri. With President Truman sitting beside him, the former prime minister of Britain decried Soviet expansionism and stated that an "**iron curtain**" had

■ **iron curtain** Name given to the military, political, and ideological barrier established between the Soviet bloc and Western Europe after World War II.

fallen across Europe (see Map 24.1). Churchill called for a "fraternal association of the English-speaking peoples" to halt the Russians. Truman thought it was a wonderfully eloquent speech and would do "nothing but good." Churchill, *Time* magazine pronounced, had spoken with the voice of a "lion."

As Churchill spoke, it appeared that an "American lion" was needed in Iran. During World War II, the Big Three had stationed troops in Iran to ensure the safety of lend-lease materials going to the Soviet Union. The troops were to be withdrawn by March 1946, but as that date neared, Soviet troops remained in northern Iran. Suddenly, on March 2, reports flashed from northern Iran that Soviet tanks were moving toward Tehran, the Iranian capital, as well as toward Iraq and Turkey. Some believed that war was imminent. Britain and the United States sent harshly worded telegrams to Moscow and petitioned the United Nations to consider an Iranian complaint against the Soviet Union. War did not break out, and Soviet forces soon evacuated Iran. The crisis was over, but it convinced many

MAP 24.1 Cold War Europe

Following World War II, Europe was divided by what Winston Churchill called the "iron curtain," which divided most of the continent politically, economically, and militarily into an eastern bloc (the Warsaw Pact) led by the Soviet Union and a western bloc (NATO) supported by the United States. This postwar division of Europe lasted until the collapse of the Soviet Union in the early 1990s. Copyright © Cengage Learning

Legend:
- $ Participants in the Marshall Plan
- Member of NATO,* formed in 1949
- Member of COMECON,** formed in 1949, and the Warsaw Pact, organized in 1955
- Member of the European Common Market, formed in 1958
- Iron Curtain

* North Atlantic Treaty Organization
** Council for Mutual Economic Assistance

ICELAND — Joined Common Market, 1973

UNITED KINGDOM — U.S. loan of $3.5 billion, 1946; Exploded first atomic bomb, 1952; Joined Common Market, 1973

NETHERLANDS — Joined Common Market, 1973

FRANCE — Exploded first atomic bomb, 1960; Withdrew from NATO, 1966

EAST GERMANY / West Berlin — Berlin blockade, 1948–1949

POLAND — Communist coup, 1948; U.S.S.R. invasion, 1968 (CZECHOSLOVAKIA)

UNION OF SOVIET SOCIALIST REPUBLICS — Exploded first atomic bomb, 1949

AUSTRIA — Joined NATO, 1955; Zones of occupation ended, 1955

HUNGARY — Revolution, 1956

YUGOSLAVIA — Tito-Stalin schism, 1948

ALBANIA — Left COMECON, 1961; Withdrew from WP, 1968

TURKEY — Truman Doctrine, 1947; Joined NATO, 1952

CYPRUS — Joined Common Market, 1981

GREECE — Truman Doctrine, 1947; Joined NATO, 1952; Joined Common Market, 1981

PORTUGAL — Joined Common Market, 1986

SPAIN — Joined NATO, 1982; Joined Common Market, 1986

693

Americans that war with the Soviets was possible. "Red Fascism" had replaced Nazi fascism, and for the sake of civilization there could be no more appeasement.

The Division of Europe

As the crisis in Iran receded, events in Europe assumed priority. A deepening economic crisis across Europe appeared to favor leftist parties and their assertion that state controls and state planning led to quicker economic recovery. But the most immediate trouble spots were in Greece and Turkey. The Soviets were pressuring Turkey to permit them some control over the Dardanelles, the straits linking the Black Sea to the Mediterranean. In Greece, a civil war raged between Communist-backed rebels and the British-supported conservative government. In February 1947, Britain informed Washington that it was no longer able to provide economic or military aid to the two nations and asked the United States to assume its role in the region to prevent Communist expansion. Truman eagerly assumed the responsibility of "world leadership with all of its burdens and all of its glory."

To convince Congress and gain public support for $400 million to support Greece and Turkey, Truman overstated the "crisis," presenting an image of the world under attack from the forces of evil. On March 12, 1947, he set forth the **Truman Doctrine**, offering an ideological, black-and-white view of world politics. He said it was the duty of the United States "to support free people" who resisted subjugation "by armed minorities or by outside pressure." Congress agreed and provided aid for Greece and Turkey. Bolstered by American support, Turkey resisted Soviet pressure and retained control over the straits, and the Greek government was able to defeat the Communist rebels in 1949.

Although the Truman administration asked Congress only to support Greece and Turkey, officials admitted among themselves that the request was just the beginning. "It happens that we are having a little trouble with Greece and Turkey at the present time," stated a War Department official, "but they are just one of the keys on the keyboard of this world piano."

On June 5, 1947, in a commencement address at Harvard, Secretary of State George Marshall uncovered more of the keyboard. He offered Europe a program of economic aid to restore stability and

Americans pictured the Soviets as aggressors seeking world domination. In a mirror image the Soviet magazine *Krokodil* pictures Truman armed with the atomic bomb and money leading his loyal followers, including Winston Churchill. *Krokodil, U.S.S.R.*

prosperity—the **Marshall Plan**. For the Truman administration, the difficult question was whether to include the Soviets and Eastern Europeans in the invitation. To allow the Soviets and their satellites to participate seemed contrary to the intent of the Truman Doctrine. Would a Congress that had just spent $400 million to keep Greece and Turkey out of Soviet hands be willing to provide millions of American dollars to the Soviet Union? But if the Soviets were excluded, the United States might seem to be encouraging the division of Europe, an image the State Department wanted to avoid. Chaired by Kennan, the State Department planning staff recommended that the United States take "a hell of a big gamble" and offer economic aid to all Europeans. Kennan believed the Soviets would reject the offer because it involved economic and political cooperation with capitalists. Thus, when Marshall spoke at Harvard, he invited all Europeans to work together and write a program "designed to place Europe on its feet economically."

The gamble worked. At a June 26, 1947, meeting in Paris of potential Marshall Plan participants, Soviet

■ **Truman Doctrine** Anti-Communist foreign policy announced by Truman that called for military and economic aid to countries whose political stability was threatened by communism.

■ **Marshall Plan** Program launched in 1948 to foster economic recovery in Western Europe in the postwar period through massive amounts of U.S. financial aid.

MAP 24.2 Cold War Germany
This map shows how Germany and Berlin were divided into temporary occupation zones, which were transformed by the Cold War into East and West Germany. In 1948, with the Berlin airlift, and again in 1961, with the erection of the Berlin Wall, Berlin became the flash point of the Cold War. With the end of the Cold War, the Berlin Wall was torn down in 1989, and in 1990 the two Germanys were reunified. Copyright © Cengage Learning

foreign minister Molotov rejected a British and French written proposal for an economically integrated Europe, joint economic planning, and a requirement to purchase mostly American goods. At first the Marshall Plan looked like a "tasty mushroom," commented one Soviet official, but on closer examination it turned out to be a "poisonous toadstool." The Soviets and the Eastern Europeans left the conference, and over the next ten months the Soviet Union took steps to solidify its control over its satellite states. In July 1947, Moscow announced the Molotov Plan, which further incorporated Eastern European economies into the Soviet system. Throughout the region non-Communist elements were expelled from governments, an effort that culminated in the February 1948 Soviet-engineered **coup** that toppled the Czechoslovakian government. "We are faced with exactly the same situation with which Britain and France were faced in 1938 and 1939 with Hitler," Truman announced. The Czech coup helped convince Congress to approve $12.5 billion in Marshall Plan aid to Western Europe.

In March 1948, the United States announced that the western zones of Germany were eligible for Marshall Plan aid, would hold elections to select delegates to a constitutional convention, and would adopt a standard currency. The meaning of these actions seemed clear: a West German state was being formed. Faced with the prospect of a pro-Western, industrialized, and potentially remilitarized Germany, Stalin reacted. On June 24, the Russians blockaded all land traffic to and from Berlin, which had been divided into British-, French-, Soviet-, and U.S.-controlled zones after the war. With West Berlin isolated 120 miles inside the Soviet zone of Germany (see Map 24.2), the Soviet goal was to force the West either to abandon the creation of West Germany or to face the loss of Berlin. Americans viewed the blockade as proof of Soviet hostility and were determined not to back down. Churchill affirmed the West's stand. We want peace, he stated, "but we should by now have learned that there is no safety in yielding to dictators,

coup Sudden overthrow of a government by a group of people, usually with military support.

It Matters Today

whether Nazi or Communist." "We are very close to war," Truman wrote in his diary.

American strategists confronted the dilemma of how to stay in Berlin and supply 2.4 million people without starting a shooting war. Although some recommended fighting across the Soviet zone to the city, Truman chose another option, one that would not violate Soviet-occupied territory or any international agreements. Marshaling a massive effort of men, provisions, and aircraft, British and Americans flew supply planes to three Berlin airports on an average of one flight every three minutes, month after month. To drive home to the Soviets the depth of American resolve, Truman ordered a wing of B-29 bombers, the "atomic bombers," to Britain. These planes carried no atomic weapons, but the general impression was that their presence lessened the likelihood of Soviet aggression.

The **Berlin airlift** was a victory for the United States in the Cold War. The increasing flow of supplies into West Berlin testified to America's resolve to stand firm against the Soviets and protect Western Europe. In May 1949, Stalin, finding no gains from the blockade, without explanation ended it and allowed land traffic to cross the Soviet zone to Berlin. The crisis swept away most congressional opposition to the Marshall Plan and the creation of West Germany and silenced those who had protested a permanent American military

■ **Berlin airlift** Response to the Soviet blockade of West Berlin in 1948 involving tens of thousands of continuous flights by American and British planes to deliver supplies.

When the Soviets blockaded the western zones of Berlin, in one of the first confrontations of the Cold War, the United States replied by staging one of the most successful logistical feats of the twentieth century, Operation Vittles, in which vital supplies were flown into the city. During the airlift's 321 days, American planes flew more than 272,000 missions and delivered 2.1 million tons of supplies.

Walter Sanders/Getty Images.

commitment to Western Europe. In June 1949, Congress approved American entry into the **North Atlantic Treaty Organization** (NATO), ensuring that American forces would remain in the newly created West Germany. The Mutual Defense Assistance Act passed in 1949 provided $1.5 billion in arms and equipment for NATO member nations. By 1952, 80 percent of American assistance to Europe was military aid.

A Global Presence

To facilitate fighting a global Cold War, Congress passed the National Security Act in 1947. It created the Air Force as a separate service and unified command of the military with a new cabinet position, the Department of Defense. To improve coordination between the State Department and the Department of Defense, the **National Security Council** (NSC) was formed to provide policy recommendations to the president. The act also established the Central Intelligence Agency to collect and analyze foreign intelligence information and to carry out covert actions believed necessary for American national security. By mid-1948, covert operations were increasing in scope and number, including efforts to influence Italian elections (a success) and to topple the communist Albanian government (a failure).

While the Truman administration's primary foreign-policy concern was Europe, it could not ignore the rest of the world. In Latin America, the administration encouraged private firms to develop the region and in 1947 helped organize the **Rio Pact**. It established the concept of collective security for Latin America and created a regional organization—the **Organization of American States** (OAS)—to coordinate common defense, economic, and social concerns.

In the Middle East, fear of future oil shortages led the United States to promote the expansion of American petroleum interests in Saudi Arabia, Kuwait, and Iran. At the same time, the United States became a powerful supporter of a new Jewish state to be created in Palestine. The area of Palestine had been administered by the British since the end of World War I and had experienced increasing tensions between the indigenous Arab population, the Palestinians, and a growing number of Jews, largely immigrants from Europe. As World War II ended, Britain faced growing pressure to create a new Jewish state in Palestine. Truman asked in August 1945 that at least 100,000 displaced European Jews be allowed to migrate to Palestine. Considering the Nazi terror against Jews, he believed that the Jews should have their own nation—a view strongly supported by a well-organized, pro-Jewish lobbying effort across the United States.

In May 1947, Britain turned the problem over to the United Nations, which voted to **partition** Palestine into Arab and Jewish states on May 14, 1948. Truman recognized the nation of Israel within fifteen minutes. War quickly broke out between Israel and the surrounding Arab nations—who refused to recognize the partition. Although outnumbered, the better-equipped Israeli army drove back the invading armies, and in January 1949 UN mediator **Ralph Bunche** arranged a cease-fire. When the fighting stopped, Israel had added 50 percent more territory to its emerging nation. No Palestinian state was created, and more than 700,000 Arabs left Israeli-controlled territory, many living as refugees in the Gaza Strip, Lebanon, Jordan, and Egypt. Bitter at the loss of what they regarded as their homeland, the majority of Palestinians and other Arabs were determined to destroy the Jewish state.

If Americans were pleased with events in Latin America and the Middle East, Asia provided several disappointments. Under American occupation, Japan's government was reshaped into a democratic system and placed safely within the American orbit, but diplomatic setbacks occurred in China and Korea. During World War II, the **Nationalist Chinese government** of Jiang Jieshi (Chiang Kai-shek) and the Chinese Communists under Mao Zedong (Mao Tse-tung) had collaborated to fight the Japanese. But when the war ended, old animosities quickly resurfaced, and civil war followed in February 1946. American supporters of Jiang, led by the "China Lobby," recommended that the United States increase its economic and military support for the Nationalist government, arguing that Soviet power threatened

■ **North Atlantic Treaty Organization** (NATO) Mutual defense alliance formed in 1949 among most of the nations of Western Europe and North America in an effort to contain communism.

■ **National Security Council** (NSC) Executive agency established in 1947 to coordinate the strategic and defense policies of the United States; it includes the president, vice president, and four cabinet members.

■ **Rio Pact** Considered the first Cold War alliance, it joined Latin American nations, Canada, and the United States in an agreement to prevent Communist inroads in Latin America and to improve political, social, and economic conditions among Latin American nations; it created the Organization of American States.

■ **Organization of American States** (OAS) An international organization composed of most of the nations of the Americas, including the Caribbean, that deals with the mutual concerns of its members; Cuba is not currently a member.

partition To divide a country into separate, autonomous nations.

■ **Ralph Bunche** An African American scholar, teacher, and diplomat. After negotiating a settlement ending the Arab-Israeli War, he received the Nobel Peace Prize in 1950.

■ **Nationalist Chinese government** The government of Jiang Jieshi, who fought the Communists for control of China in the 1940s; Jiang and his supporters were defeated and retreated to Taiwan in 1949, where they set up a separate government.

China and the rest of Asia as much as it did Europe. Truman and Marshall (who was now secretary of state) dreaded Communist success in China but questioned whether the corrupt and inefficient Nationalist government could ever effectively rule the vast country. While willing to continue some political, economic, and military support, neither wanted to commit American resources to an Asian war. Increasing U.S. aid would be like "throwing money down a rat hole," Truman told his cabinet.

Overmatched by an efficient and popular opponent and denied additional American support, Jiang's forces soon disintegrated, and in 1949 the Nationalist government fled to the island of Taiwan. Conservative Democrats and Republicans labeled the rout of Jiang a humiliating American defeat and complained that the Truman administration was too soft on communism. To quiet critics and to protect Jiang, Truman refused to recognize the People's Republic of China on the mainland and ordered the U.S. 7th Fleet to the waters near Taiwan.

Pressure to expand the containment policy beyond Europe intensified in late August 1949, when the Soviets detonated their own atomic bomb, shattering the American nuclear monopoly. A joint Pentagon–State Department committee, headed by Paul Nitze, concluded that the Soviets were driven by "a new fanatic faith, antithetical to our own," whose objective was to dominate the world, and might be able to launch a nuclear attack on the United States as early as 1954. The committee's report, **NSC Memorandum #68**, called for global containment and a massive buildup of American military force, amounting to an almost 400 percent increase in military spending for the next fiscal year, which would have raised military expenditures to nearly $50 billion. A separate report concluded that the projected mobilization of industry for the Cold War would reduce automobile construction by nearly 60 percent and cut production of radios and television sets to zero. Truman, worried about such an impact on the manufacture of domestic goods, eventually agreed to a "moderate" $12.3 billion military budget for 1950 that included building the

hydrogen bomb. Proponents of NSC 68 won the final argument on June 25, 1950, when North Korean troops stormed across the 38th parallel.

THE KOREAN WAR

☆ As the North Koreans invaded South Korea, why did Truman decide to refer the issue to the United Nations?

☆ What were Truman's and MacArthur's goals in Korea? What was the consequence of China's entry into the war?

When World War II ended, Soviet forces occupied Korea north of the 38th parallel (see Map 24.3) and American forces remained south of it, and by mid-1946, two Koreas existed. In the south was an American-supported Republic of Korea (ROK), led by Syngman Rhee, while in the north a Communist-backed Democratic People's Republic of Korea, headed by Kim Il Sung. In 1949 the Soviet and American forces withdrew, leaving behind two hostile regimes. Both claimed to be Korea's rightful government and launched raids across the border. The raids accomplished little except to kill more than 100,000 Koreans and to expand each side's military capabilities.

Having received approval from the Soviets, on June 25, 1950, Kim Il Sung launched a full-scale invasion of the south. Overwhelmed, South Korean forces rapidly retreated. Truman concluded that South Korea's survival required American intervention, but he feared that a congressional declaration of war against North Korea might trigger a Chinese and Soviet response. Instead, he asked the UN Security Council to intervene. The Security Council complied and called for a cease-fire, asking member nations to provide assistance to South Korea.

Halting Communist Aggression

American forces led by General Douglas MacArthur, officially under United Nations control, arrived in Korea in July but were unable to halt the North Korean advance. By the end of July, North Korean forces occupied most of South Korea. United Nations forces, including nearly 122,000 Americans and the whole South Korean army, held only the southeastern corner of the peninsula—the Pusan perimeter. In September the tide turned as seventy thousand American troops landed at Inchon, near Seoul, while UN forces advanced north from Pusan. The North Koreans fled back across the 38th parallel. Seoul was liberated on September 27. The **police action** had achieved its purpose: the South Korean government was saved, and the 38th parallel was again a real border.

■ **NSC Memorandum #68** Report concluding that the Soviets were seeking world domination and recommending large-scale increases in military spending, increased covert operations, reduced domestic programs, and increased taxes.

hydrogen bomb Nuclear weapon of much greater destructive power than the atomic bomb.

■ **police action** Official term used by the United States for its role in the Korean conflict because there was no formal declaration of war; the North Koreans called it "the Fatherland Liberation War."

Legend:
← United States and United Nations forces
← North Korean forces
← Intervention by Chinese forces, Oct. 1950

CHINA

U.S.S.R.

MANCHURIA

Chongjin

Hyesanjin

Kanggye

Chosan

Chosin Res.

Angtung
Sinuiju

Unsan

Farthest U.S. advance, Oct.–Nov. 1950

Hungnam

NORTH KOREA

Sea of Japan (East Sea)

Pyongyang ☆

Nan R.

Armistice line, July 7, 1953

38°N

Kaesong

38th Parallel

Panmunjom

U.S. landing Sept. 15, 1950

Inchon

☆ Seoul

Farthest Chinese/ North Korean advance, Jan. 1951

Han R.

U.N. advance, Sept.–Nov. 1950

Yongdok

Taejon

Pohang

36°N

Yellow Sea

Naktong R.

SOUTH KOREA

Taegu

Farthest North Korean advance, Sept. 1950

Pusan

Korea Strait

34°N

N

0   50   100 Km.
0   50   100 Mi.

126°E   128°E

MAP 24.3 The Korean War, 1950–1953

Seeking to unify Korea, North Korean forces invaded South Korea in 1950. To protect South Korea, the United States and the United Nations intervened, driving North Korean forces northward, and Truman sought to unify Korea under South Korea's government. But as UN and South Korean forces pushed toward the Chinese border, Communist China intervened, forcing UN troops to retreat. This map shows the military thrusts and counterthrusts of the Korean War until it stalemated roughly along the 38th parallel.

Copyright © Cengage Learning

Seeking to Liberate North Korea

Now, however, the South Korean leadership, MacArthur, Truman, and most Americans wanted to unify the peninsula under South Korean rule. Bending under American pressure, the United Nations on October 7 approved a new goal, to "liberate" North Korea from Communist rule. In mid-October UN forces pushed northward toward the Korean-Chinese border at the Yalu River. The Chinese threatened intervention if the invaders approached the border. Nevertheless, General MacArthur was supremely confident. Intelligence estimates said that any intervening Chinese forces would number less than 50,000 and easily be defeated. When American, British, and Korean forces advanced within a few miles of the Yalu River, nearly 300,000 Chinese soldiers entered the Korean Conflict.

Blowing their bugles, the Chinese attacked in waves, hurling grenades, taking massive casualties, and nearly trapping several American and South Korean units in the most brutal fighting of the war. UN forces fell back in bitter combat. The U.S. 1st Marine Division was nearly surrounded at the Chosin Reservoir. When asked about the marines retreating, General O. P. "Slam" Smith responded, "Gentlemen, we are not retreating. We are merely advancing in another direction." Within three weeks, the North Koreans and Chinese had shoved the UN forces back to the 38th parallel. American casualties exceeded twelve thousand, but the Chinese had lost three times as many.

Truman now abandoned the goal of a unified pro-Western Korea and sought a negotiated settlement, even if it left two Koreas. The decision was not popular. Americans wanted victory. Encouraged by public opinion polls and Truman's Republican critics, General MacArthur publicly objected to the limitations his commander-in-chief had placed on him. He put it simply: there was "no substitute for victory." Already displeased by MacArthur's arrogance, Truman replaced him with General Matthew Ridgeway.

The decision unleashed a storm of protest. Some called for Truman's impeachment, and Congress opened hearings to investigate the conduct of the war. MacArthur testified that expanding the war could achieve victory, while the administration argued that it might lead to a global nuclear war. The face-off between MacArthur and Truman produced no winner. Polls showed Truman's approval rating falling to a dismal 24 percent by late 1951. At the same time, MacArthur's hopes for a presidential candidacy collapsed because most Americans feared his aggressive policies might indeed result in World War III. By the beginning of 1952, the vast majority of Americans were simply tired of the "useless" conflict and wanted it to end.

The Korean front, meanwhile, stabilized along the 38th parallel as four-power peace talks among the

National Archives.

The Korean War was one of ebb and flow, advances and retreats up and down the rugged Korean peninsula. The war also sped the integration of the American armed forces as African American troops served and fought alongside other Americans.

United States, South Korea, China, and North Korea began on July 10, 1951. The negotiations did not go smoothly. While the powers postured and argued about prisoners, cease-fire lines, and a multitude of lesser issues, soldiers fought and died over scraps of territory. When the Eisenhower administration finally concluded the cease-fire on July 26, 1953, the Korean conflict had cost more than $20 billion and thirty-three thousand American lives, but it had left South Korea intact.

The "hot war" in Korea had far-reaching military and diplomatic results for the United States. The expansion of military spending envisioned by NSC 68 had occurred. In Europe, Truman moved forward to rearm West Germany and Italy. Throughout Asia and the Pacific, a large American presence was made permanent. In 1951 the United States concluded a settlement with Japan that kept American forces in Japan and Okinawa. The Australia–New Zealand–United States (ANZUS) treaty of 1951 promised American military protection to those countries. At the same time, the United States was increasing its military aid and commitments to Nationalist China and French **Indochina**. The containment policy had been expanded—formally and financially—to cover East Asia and the Pacific.

POSTWAR POLITICS

★ In what ways did Truman attempt to maintain and expand the New Deal? How did the fear of communism strengthen conservative opposition to his programs?

★ Why did Truman win the 1948 election?

When Roosevelt died, many wondered if Truman would continue the Roosevelt–New Deal approach to domestic policies. Would he work to protect the social and economic gains that labor, women, and minorities had earned during the war? Conservatives and some of Truman's friends predicted that the new president was "going to be quite a shock to those who followed Roosevelt–that the New Deal is as good as dead . . . and that the 'Roosevelt nonsense' was over." But Truman had no intention of extinguishing the New Deal.

Truman and Liberalism

In September 1945, Truman presented to Congress what one Republican critic called an effort to "out–New Deal the New Deal." Truman set forth an ambitious program designed to ease the transition to a peacetime economy and reenergize the New Deal. To prevent inflation and a recession, he wanted

Congress to continue wartime economic agencies to help control wages and prices. He also asked that the Fair Employment Practices Commission be renewed. Furthering the New Deal, he recommended an expansion of Social Security coverage and benefits, an increase in the minimum wage, the development of additional housing programs, and a national health system.

Opposing Truman's proposals was a conservative coalition of southern Democrats and Republicans who had successfully blocked extensions of the New Deal since 1937. They embarked on a campaign to persuade the American public of the dangers of Truman's "socialistic" program, which involved too much government, threatened private enterprise, and endangered existing class and social relations. "Public sentiment is everything," wrote an officer of Standard Oil. "He who molds public sentiment goes deeper than he who enacts statutes or pronounces decisions." A Truman official sadly agreed: "The consuming fear of communism fostered a widespread belief that change was subversive and that those who supported change were Communists or **fellow-travelers**."

Congress rejected or severely scaled back nearly all of Truman's proposals. Wartime economic controls and the Fair Employment Practices Commission quickly faded away. Congress spurned any idea of a national health program and substituted a program to build hospitals. While Congress and Truman disagreed over the domestic agenda, the country experienced economic and social dislocations caused by the conversion to a peacetime economy. Inflation quickly emerged as a principal issue, with prices rising 25 percent within 18 months after the defeat of Germany. Inflation, cuts in hours, and layoffs cut into many workers' purchasing power, reducing it for some by as much as 30 percent. The economic changes led to nearly 4.5 million workers staging more than five thousand strikes. United Automobile Workers (UAW) strikers wanted a 30 percent increase in wages and a guarantee that car prices would not rise—they got neither.

Unions hoped their strikes would save wages and expand their power, but the opposite occurred. Congress and state and local governments responded with antilabor measures designed to weaken unions

Indochina French colony in Southeast Asia, including present-day Vietnam, Laos, and Cambodia; it began fighting for its independence in the mid-twentieth century.

fellow-traveler Individual who sympathizes with or supports the beliefs of the Communist Party without being a member.

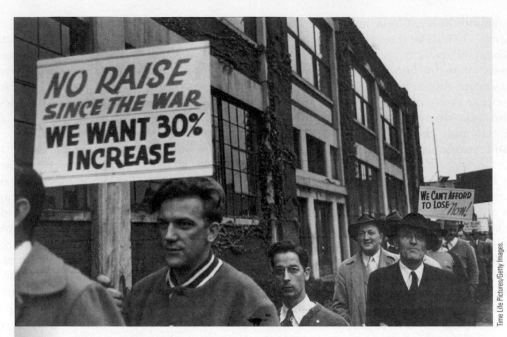

As the nation moved from a wartime to peacetime economy, workers initiated more than five thousand strikes. Pictured here are strikers in Detroit in 1945.

and end work stoppages. **Right-to-work laws** banned compulsory union membership (the closed shop) and in some cases provided legal and police protection for workers crossing picket lines. In the spring of 1946, Truman joined the attack. In April, he squared off against John L. Lewis and 400,000 striking United Mine Workers. Taking drastic action, the president seized the mines and ordered miners back to work. As miners returned to work, Truman pressured mine owners to meet most of the union's demands. When locomotive engineers walked off the job in May, Truman asked Congress for power to draft the strikers. The railroad strike was settled before Congress responded, but momentum mounted in Congress to take legislative action to control strikes and weaken unions.

Amid strikes, soaring inflation, divisions within Democratic ranks, and widespread dissatisfaction

with Truman's leadership—"to err is Truman" was a common quip—Republicans asked the public, "Had enough?" Voters responded affirmatively in 1946, filling both houses of the Eightieth Congress with more Republicans and anti–New Deal Democrats. Refusing to retreat, Truman opened 1947 by presenting Congress with a restatement of many of the programs he had offered in 1945. The political battle between the president and Congress fired up again. Congress rejected Truman's proposals, Truman vetoed 250 bills, and Congress overrode 12 of Truman's vetoes. Among the most critical vetoes cast by Truman and overridden by Congress was the **Taft-Hartley Act**. The Taft-Hartley Act, passed in June 1947, was a clear victory for management over labor. It banned the closed shop, prevented industry-wide collective bargaining, and legalized state-sponsored right-to-work laws that hindered union organizing. It also required that union officials sign **affidavits** that they were not Communists. Echoing Truman's actions in the coal strike, the law also empowered the president to use a court injunction to force striking workers back to work for an eighty-day cooling-off period. Privately, Truman supported much of the bill and cast his veto knowing it would be overridden. He also knew his veto would help "hold labor support" for his 1948 run for the presidency.

Truman's veto of Taft-Hartley was an easy political decision. In contrast, the issue of civil rights was extremely complex and politically dangerous. Democrats were clearly divided. Southern Democrats

■ **right-to-work laws** State laws that make it illegal for labor unions and employers to require that all workers be members of a union. Many state laws require that all employees, even those who are not union members, must benefit from contract agreements made between the union and the employer.

■ **Taft-Hartley Act** Law passed by Congress in 1947 banning closed shops, permitting employers to sue unions for broken contracts, and requiring unions to observe a cooling-off period before striking.

affidavit A formal, written legal document made under oath; those signing the document state that the facts in the document are true.

opposed any mention of civil rights, while African Americans and liberals, including Eleanor Roosevelt, demanded that Truman "speak" to the issue. Truman was cautious but supportive of civil rights and aware of Soviet criticism of American segregation. Confessing that he did not know how bad conditions were for African Americans and that "the top dog in a world . . . ought to clean his own house," Truman agreed in December 1946 to create a committee on civil rights to examine race relations in the country. The December 1947 report *To Secure These Rights* described the racial inequalities in American society and called on the government to take steps to correct the imbalance. Among its recommendations were the establishment of a permanent commission on civil rights, the enactment of anti-lynching laws, and the abolition of the poll tax. The committee also called for integration of the U.S. armed forces and support for integrating housing programs and education. Truman asked Congress in February 1948 to act on the recommendations, but provided no direction or legislation. After black labor leader A. Philip Randolph again threatened a march on Washington, in July 1948, Truman issued executive orders desegregating the armed forces and the federal work force. The navy and air force complied, but the army resisted until high casualties in Korea during the summer of 1950 forced the integration of black replacements into white combat units. Despite his caution, Truman had done more in the area of civil rights than any president since Lincoln, a record that ensured African American and liberal support for his 1948 bid to be elected president in his own right.

The 1948 Election

Republicans' hopes were high in 1948. They had done well in congressional elections in 1946 and 1947. To take on Truman they chose New York governor Thomas E. Dewey. He had lost to Roosevelt in 1944, but had earned a respectable 46 percent of the popular vote, and Truman was not Roosevelt. The Democrats were also mired in bitter infighting over the direction of domestic policy. Many Democratic liberals and minorities wished that Truman had pushed harder to sell his New Deal–type programs to the public and Congress. Truman worried that some liberals might switch their votes to Henry A. Wallace, the former vice president, who was running as a Progressive Party candidate. Southern Democrats, meanwhile, opposed any efforts to support organized labor or civil rights and walked out of the convention when a civil rights plank was inserted into the party's platform. Unwilling to support a Republican, they met in Birmingham

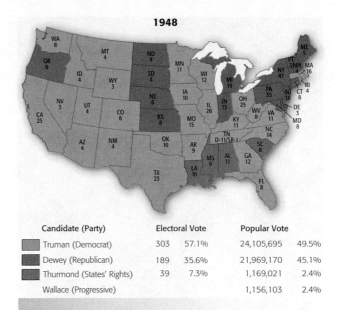

1948

Candidate (Party)	Electoral Vote		Popular Vote	
Truman (Democrat)	303	57.1%	24,105,695	49.5%
Dewey (Republican)	189	35.6%	21,969,170	45.1%
Thurmond (States' Rights)	39	7.3%	1,169,021	2.4%
Wallace (Progressive)			1,156,103	2.4%

MAP 24.4 Election of 1948
In the 1948 presidential election, Harry S Truman confounded the polls and analysts by upsetting his Republican opponent, Thomas Dewey, earning 50 percent of the popular vote and 57 percent of the electoral vote. Copyright © Cengage Learning

and organized the States' Rights Democratic Party, better known as the **Dixiecrat Party**, nominating South Carolina governor J. Strom Thurmond for president.

Confounding the pollsters, Truman defeated Dewey. His victory was a triumph for Roosevelt's New Deal coalition. Despite the Dixiecrats, most southerners did not abandon the Democratic Party. Thurmond carried only four southern states; Wallace carried none (see Map 24.4). Democrats also won majorities in Congress, and Truman hoped that in 1949 he would succeed with his domestic program, which he called the **Fair Deal**.

■ *To Secure These Rights* Created in December 1946 to investigate race relations, the President's Commission on Civil Rights issued this report a year later, making several recommendations to improve civil rights; Truman asked Congress to implement the recommendations, but Congress failed to act.

■ **Dixiecrat Party** Party organized in 1948 by southern delegates who refused to accept the civil rights plank of the Democratic platform; they nominated Strom Thurmond of South Carolina for president.

■ **Fair Deal** President Truman said that "every segment of the population" deserved a "fair deal" from the government. He hoped the Democratic majority would provide an expansion of New Deal programs, including civil rights legislation, a fair employment practices act, a system for national health insurance, and appropriations for education.

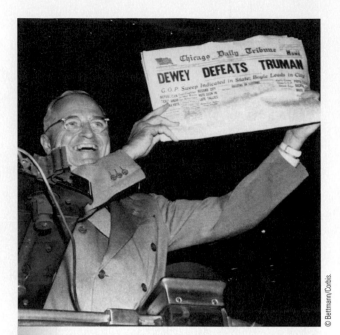

Many considered Harry S Truman's 1948 victory over Thomas E. Dewey a major political upset—nearly all of the major polls had named the Republican an easy winner. Here Truman holds up the *Chicago Tribune's* incorrect headline announcing Dewey's triumph.

In his inaugural address, Truman asked for increases in Social Security, public housing, and the minimum wage, the repeal of the Taft-Hartley Act, and the creation of a national health program. He also gave civil rights and federal aid to education a place on the national agenda. Rewarding farmers for their role in his victory, Truman submitted the Brannan Plan, which included federal benefits for small farmers. Congress responded favorably to Truman's programs in areas already well established by the New Deal: a 65-cent minimum hourly wage, funds for low- and moderate-income housing, and increases in Social Security coverage and payments. Proposals going beyond the scope of the New Deal encountered effective opposition from a coalition of southern Democrats and Republicans. A national health system and government intervention in education was communistic, said opponents, while civil rights efforts were part of a Communist conspiracy to undermine American unity. Adding their voices to the chorus, agribusiness leaders attacked the Brannan Plan as socialistic and class oriented.

■ **House Un-American Activities Committee** (HUAC)
Congressional committee, created in 1938, that investigated suspected Communists during the McCarthy era.

COLD WAR POLITICS

☆ *What fears and events heightened society's worries about internal subversion, and how did politicians respond to the public's concerns?*

☆ *Why and how did Joseph McCarthy become so powerful by 1952?*

Attacks on liberal programs as being socialistic or communistic were not new. But the developing Cold War intensified fears that Communists and their supporters were undermining American values and stability, leading to a second Red Scare. Some of the growing concerns were valid. The Soviets had a well-developed espionage system operating in the country, including within the atomic bomb program. Other concerns, though, arose from political opportunism and antiliberalism. Tobacco giant R. J. Reynolds characterized unionism as a step toward socialism in its multimillion-dollar public ad campaign to defeat the CIO's "Operation Dixie" effort to organize southern workers. In Pittsburgh, Pennsylvania, a local paper labeled those trying to integrate a public swimming pool "Commies." Across the country, neighborhoods and communities organized "watch groups," which screened books, movies, and public speakers and questioned teachers and public officials, seeking to ban or dismiss those considered suspect.

The Red Scare

Responding to increasing accusations, including those of the **House Un-American Activities Committee** (HUAC), that his administration tolerated Communist subversion, Truman moved to beef up the existing loyalty program by issuing Executive Order #9835, establishing the Federal Employee Loyalty Program. Attorney General Tom Clark provided a list of subversive organizations, and government administrators screened their employees for membership. But the program went beyond membership in one of the listed groups. If "reasonable grounds" existed for believing a federal employee was disloyal in belief or action, the employee could, after a hearing, be fired. Soon supervisors and workers began to accuse one another of "un-American" thoughts and activities. Between 1947 and 1951, the government discharged more than three thousand federal employees because of their supposed disloyalty. In almost every case, the accused had no right to confront the accusers or to refute the evidence. While the Soviets used American citizens to conduct espionage, few of those forced to leave government service were Communists.

Truman's loyalty program intensified rather than calmed fears, especially when Federal Bureau of Investigation (FBI) director J. Edgar Hoover proclaimed that there was one American Communist for every 1,814 loyal citizens, and Attorney General Clark warned that Communists were everywhere, "in factories, offices, butcher shops, on street corners, in private businesses," carrying "the germs of death for society." Grabbing headlines in 1947, HUAC targeted Hollywood, intent on removing people with liberal, leftist viewpoints from the entertainment industry and ensuring that the mass media promoted American capitalism and traditional American values. Just as World War II had mobilized the film industry, committee supporters believed, the Cold War necessitated that movies promote the "right" images. With much fanfare, HUAC called Hollywood notables to testify about Communist influence in the industry. Many of those called used the opportunity to prove their patriotism and to denounce communism. Actor Ronald Reagan, president of the Screen Actors Guild, denounced Communist methods that "sucked" people into carrying out "Red policy without knowing what they are doing" and testified that the Conference of Studio Unions was full of Reds.

Not all witnesses were cooperative. Some, including the "**Hollywood Ten**," took the Fifth Amendment and lashed out at the activities of the committee. Labeled "Fifth Amendment Communists," the ten were jailed for contempt of Congress and blacklisted by the industry. Eric Johnson, president of the Motion Picture Association, announced that Hollywood would produce no more films like *The Grapes of Wrath*, featuring the hardships of poor Americans or "the seamy side of American life." Moviemakers soon issued a new code—*A Screen Guide for Americans*—that demanded, "Don't Smear the Free Enterprise System"; "Don't Show That Poverty Is a Virtue."

Just before the election of 1948, HUAC zeroed in on spies within the government, bringing forth a number of informants who had been Soviet agents and were now willing to name others who allegedly had sold out the United States. The most sensational revelation came from a repentant ex-Communist named Whittaker Chambers. He accused **Alger Hiss**, a New Deal liberal and one-time State Department official, of being a Communist. At first Hiss denied knowing Chambers, but under interrogation by HUAC members, especially Congressman **Richard M. Nixon** of California, Hiss admitted an acquaintance with Chambers in the 1930s but denied he was or had been a Communist. When Hiss sued Chambers for libel, Chambers escalated the charges. He stated that Hiss had passed State Department secrets to

him in the 1930s, and he produced rolls of microfilm that he said Hiss had delivered to him. In a controversial and sensationalized trial, in 1949 Hiss was found guilty of **perjury** (the statute of limitations on espionage had expired) and sentenced to five years in prison.

As the nation followed the Hiss case, news of the Communist victory in China and the Soviet explosion of an atomic bomb heightened American fears. Many people believed that such Communist successes could have occurred only with help from American traitors. Congressman Harold Velde of Illinois proclaimed, "Our government from the White House down has been sympathetic toward the views of Communists and fellow-travelers, with the result that it has been infiltrated by a network of spies." Congress responded in 1950 by passing, over Truman's veto, the **McCarran Internal Security Act**. The law required all Communists to register with the attorney general and made it a crime to conspire to establish a totalitarian government in the United States. The following year the Supreme Court upheld the **Smith Act** (passed in June 1940), ruling that membership in the Communist Party was equivalent to conspiring to overthrow the American government and that no specific act of treason was necessary for conviction.

Congressman Velde's observation about spies seemed vindicated in February 1950, when **Julius and Ethel Rosenberg** were accused of being part of a Soviet

■ **Hollywood Ten** Ten screenwriters and producers who stated that the Fifth Amendment of the Constitution gave them the right to refuse to testify before HUAC in 1947. The House of Representatives disagreed and issued citations for contempt. Found guilty in 1948, the ten served from six months to a year in prison.

■ **Alger Hiss** State Department official accused in 1948 of being a Communist spy; he was convicted of perjury and sent to prison.

■ **Richard M. Nixon** Republican elected in 1945 to the House of Representatives; he earned national recognition as a member of HUAC through his investigation of alleged Soviet spy Alger Hiss; elected vice president in 1952 and president in 1968.

perjury The deliberate giving of false testimony under oath.

■ **McCarran Internal Security Act** Law passed by Congress in 1950 requiring Communists to register with the U.S. attorney general and making it a crime to conspire to establish a totalitarian government in the United States.

■ **Smith Act** The Alien Registration Act, passed by Congress in 1940, which made it a crime to advocate or to belong to an organization that advocates the overthrow of the government by force or violence.

■ **Julius and Ethel Rosenberg** Wife and husband who were arrested in 1950 and tried for conspiracy to commit espionage in 1951 after being accused of passing atomic bomb information to the Soviets; they were executed in 1953.

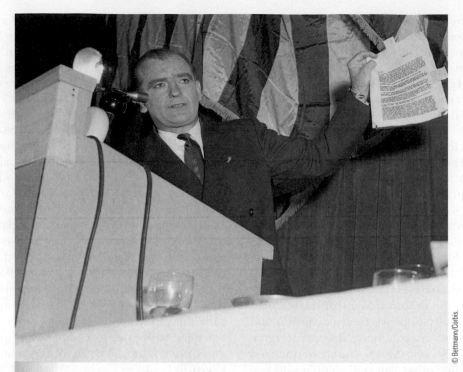

At the heart of the Red Scare was Senator Joseph McCarthy. Using inquisition-style tactics to attack his opponents, he became one of the most powerful politicians in the nation by 1952. In this picture from the 1952 presidential campaign, McCarthy waves a report on Democratic candidate Adlai Stevenson showing that he endorsed policies favoring the Soviets.

atomic spy ring. At trial in 1951, the prosecution alleged that the information the Rosenbergs passed to the Soviets was largely responsible for the successful Soviet atomic bomb. The Rosenbergs professed innocence but were convicted of espionage. (Soviet documents indicate that Julius Rosenberg was engaged in espionage but that Ethel was probably guilty only of being loyal to him. Documents concerning Hiss are inconclusive, continuing a spirited debate about his innocence.)

Joseph McCarthy and the Politics of Loyalty

Feeding on the furor over the enemy within, Republican senator **Joseph McCarthy** of Wisconsin emerged at the forefront of the anti-Communist movement. Running for the Senate in 1946, he invented a

■ **Joseph McCarthy** Republican senator from Wisconsin who in 1950 began a Communist witch-hunt that lasted until his censure by the Senate in 1954; *McCarthyism* is a term associated with attacks on liberals and others, often based on unsupported assertions and carried out without regard for basic liberties.

glorious war record for himself that included the nickname "Tail-gunner Joe" and several wounds—he even walked with a fake limp—to help himself win the election. In February 1950, he announced to a Republican women's group in Wheeling, West Virginia, that the United States was losing the Cold War because of traitors within the government. He claimed to know of 205 Communists working in the State Department.

His charges were examined by a Senate committee and shown to be at best inaccurate. When the chair of the committee, Democrat Millard Tydings of Maryland, pronounced McCarthy a hoax and a fraud, the Wisconsin senator countered by accusing Tydings of questionable loyalty. During Tydings's 1950 reelection campaign, McCarthy worked for his defeat, spreading false stories and even a faked photograph of the Democrat talking to Earl Browder, head of the American Communist Party. When Tydings lost by forty thousand votes, McCarthy's stature soared. The outbreak of the Korean War and the reversals at the hands of the Chinese only increased the senator's popularity. Few dared to oppose him and many supported his allegations. The Senate's most powerful Republican, Robert Taft of Ohio, slapped McCarthy on the back saying, "Keep it up, Joe."

By 1952, with the Korean Conflict stalemated, Truman's popularity was almost nonexistent, and Republicans were having a field day attacking "cowardly containment" and calling for victory in Korea. When Truman lost the opening presidential primary in New Hampshire, he withdrew from the race, leaving no clear choice for a Democratic candidate. Again, Republicans were sure voters would elect a Republican president—someone who, in Thomas Dewey's opinion, would "save the country from going to Hades in the hand basket of paternalism-socialism-dictatorship."

HOMECOMING AND SOCIAL ADJUSTMENTS

★ How did suburban America reflect the social and economic expectations of many Americans?

★ What adjustments did women and minorities have to make in postwar America?

With World War II over, Americans were eager to return home and resume normal lives. Organized "Bring Daddy Back" clubs flooded Washington with letters demanding a speedy return of husbands and fathers. By November 1945, 1.25 million GIs were returning home each month. For Americans entering the postwar world, the homecoming was buoyed with expectations and fraught with anxieties. The nation had experienced dramatic economic growth, but remembering the Depression, Americans wondered if the postwar economy would remain strong. Still, most were optimistic that any recession would be short-lived and they would be able to spend savings, find jobs, and enjoy the American dream. "Consumption is the frontier of the future," chirped one economic forecast.

Rising Expectations

Owning a home was for many the symbol of the American dream. Before 1945 the housing industry had focused on building custom homes or multi-family dwellings. But the postwar demand changed the housing industry. To meet the demand, William Levitt and other developers supplied mass-produced, prefabricated houses—the suburban **tract homes**. Using building techniques developed during the war, timber from his forests, and nonunion workers, Levitt boasted that he could construct an affordable house on an existing concrete slab in sixteen minutes. Standardized, with few frills, the house had two stories with four and a half rooms. Built on

tract homes Numerous houses of similar design built on small plots of land.

As World War II ended, Americans flocked to the suburbs, creating a demand for new housing—a demand matched by developers of planned communities like Levittown, Pennsylvania. Developers kept the cost of the homes down using uniformity of style and prefabricated materials.

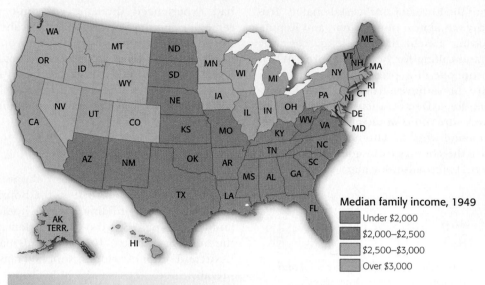

MAP 24.5 Postwar Affluence
Postwar America was characterized by a growing affluence as many Americans enjoyed the fruits of a booming economy, increasing family income, and a large variety of consumer goods.
Copyright © Cengage Learning

generous 60-by-100-foot lots, complete with a tree or two, Levitt homes cost slightly less than $8,000 and still provided Levitt with a $1,000 profit per house. The first Levittown sprang up in Hempstead, Long Island, and was a planned community with more than seventeen thousand homes, seven village greens, fourteen playgrounds, and nine swimming pools. Hundreds of look-alike suburban neighborhoods were soon built across the nation, contributing to a growing migration from rural and urban America to the suburbs (see Map 24.5).

Nowhere were tract homes more prominent than in southern California. During and after the war, networks of roads extended out from southern California cities, developing "satellite" economic centers, pulling businesses, homes, and industries away from the central cities. In Los Angeles this resulted in a 50 percent loss in sales and tax revenues, the reduction of public transportation, a loss of jobs, and a growing urban poverty rate. This pattern of development became

increasingly common across the country as suburbs multiplied.

Although part of the American dream, suburbs were not for everyone. Widespread discrimination kept some out by design. Whether it was the official policy of developers like Levitt, neighborhood covenants written to exclude minorities, or lack of home loans, almost every suburb in the nation was predominately white and Christian. Even though the Supreme Court ruled in *Shelly v. Kraemer* (1948) that restrictive housing covenants could not be enforced by lower courts, the decision failed to have much effect. Neither did the Court's decision to prevent banks and the FHA from rejecting home loan applications from minorities trying to buy houses in white neighborhoods. Real-estate agents continued to abide by the Realtors' Code of Ethics, which called it unethical to permit the "infiltration of inharmonious elements" into a neighborhood. Across the nation, fewer than 5 percent of suburban neighborhoods provided nonwhites access to the American dream house.

For many veterans a cozy home was only part of the postwar dream—so too was going to college. Armed with economic support through the G.I. Bill in September 1946, nearly 1 million veterans enrolled in college. New Jersey's Rutgers University saw its enrollment climb from seven thousand to sixteen

■ *Shelly v. Kraemer* Supreme Court ruling (1948) that barred lower courts from enforcing restrictive agreements that prevented minorities from living in certain neighborhoods; it had little impact on actual practices.

thousand. At Lehigh University in Pennsylvania, 940 veteran students outnumbered the 396 "civilians" and refused to don the traditional freshman beanie. Faculty and administrators soon discovered that veterans made exceptional students and rarely needed disciplinary action. Schools, responding to the influx of students, not only hired more faculty and built more facilities but also began providing special housing, daycare centers, and expanded health clinics for married students. By the time the G.I. Bill expired in 1952, over 2 million veterans, including sixty-four thousand women, had earned their degrees under its umbrella.

Veterans expected jobs, too, and most figured that "wartime" workers would relinquish their jobs and return to traditional roles. At first jobs were scarce. The cancellation of wartime contracts and the nationwide switch to domestic production resulted in 2.7 million workers being dismissed from their jobs within a month of Japan's surrender. Fortunately for veterans, the G.I. Bill provided unemployment compensation for a year until a job was found. And within a year, jobs were becoming more and more available. By 1947, 60 million people were working, 7 million more than at the peak of wartime production. But the work force had changed, with noticeably fewer women and minorities as industries and businesses resumed their prewar hiring habits.

"She's a gem—she used to work for Lockheed!"

Following World War II, a majority of women left the industrial work force and returned to the home and more "traditional" occupations. In this cartoon, a more affluent homemaker benefits from the wartime skills her new domestic servant acquired.

Ellen Kaiper Collection.

From Industrial Worker to Homemaker

"Last hired, first fired" fit the workplace as the war ended. Across the nation women, African Americans, and Latinos were told that they were no longer needed in the industrial workplace. In the aircraft and shipbuilding industries, companies drastically trimmed their work forces as wartime orders ended, dismissing most of the women and African Americans who had provided much-needed labor during the war. Mirroring the rest of the nation, in Seattle and Baltimore two-thirds of aircraft workers and one-third of the shipbuilding workers lost their jobs within one month after Japan's surrender. In the aircraft industry women had made up 40 percent of the work force, but by 1948 they numbered a mere 12 percent. For most women the loss of jobs was expected. "We will work as long as they need us," stated a woman

employee at Boeing, "and when we're through we will go back to our meals and dishes and children."

Indeed, most of society assumed that women would want to go back to domesticity. A *Fortune* poll in the fall of 1945 revealed that 57 percent of women and 63 percent of men believed that married women should not work outside the home. Other polls, however, found that a sizable majority of women, especially single women, wanted and needed to keep their jobs. One single woman asked simply: "What are we to do? I need a job badly." While the vast majority of women wanting to continue work hoped to stay in the same field, it was clear that employers had different expectations, and as rapidly as it had changed after 1942, the postwar workplace became highly gender

In the Wider World

oriented again. Those women finding or keeping work took lower-paying "female" jobs. Rosie the Riveter had become Fran the File Clerk, as wages declined from about $50 to $35 a week.

While some women struggled to find or keep jobs, society stressed a renewed social emphasis on femininity, family, and a woman's proper role. Psychiatrists and marriage counselors argued that men wanted their wives to be feminine and submissive, not fellow workers. Fashion designers, such as Christian Dior in his "New Look," lengthened skirts and accented waists and breasts to emphasize femininity. Marriage was more popular than ever: by 1950, two-thirds of the population was married and having children. Factors contributing to the rush to the altar were fears of "male scarcity" caused by war losses and a new attitude that viewed marriage as the ideal state for young people. Many women's magazines and marriage experts championed the idea that men should marry at around age 20 and women at age 18 or 19. With veterans returning home, with society celebrating family, and with prosperity increasing came the "**baby boom**" that would last for nearly twenty years. From a Depression level of under 19 births per 1,000 women per year, the birth rate rose to more than 25 births per 1,000 women by 1948 (see Figure 24.1).

Not all women accepted the role of contented, submissive wives and homemakers—the war experi-

ence had changed relationships. When one veteran informed his wife that she could no longer handle the finances because it was not "woman's work," she indignantly reminded him that she had successfully balanced the checkbook for four years and that his return had not made her suddenly stupid. Reflecting such tensions and too many hasty wartime marriages, the divorce rate rose dramatically. Twenty-five percent of all wartime marriages were ending in divorce in 1946, and by 1950 over a million GI marriages had dissolved. As the number of female heads of household rose, so also did the poverty and social stigma attached to single parenthood. Following her divorce, one suburban resident recalled that her neighbors "avoided" her and made remarks like "Why don't you get a job instead of taking tax monies?" She also noted that her children were singled out at school because they did not have a father at home.

Restrained Expectations

For Latinos the war years had brought many positive changes. Many experienced a higher degree of equality than before and, especially among Mexican Americans, there was more of a sense of being part of the United States, "American-ness." A wounded veteran and resident of El Paso, Texas, Moises Flores recalled: "I am proud to be an American. Sometimes I even call myself gringo, which I'm not. I'm still Mexican, but I'm an American first." The war also saw in many an increasing unwillingness to return to traditional roles. Antonio Campo, for one, had experienced a segregated life in Houston before the war. After the war he used the G.I. Bill to go to

■ **baby boom** Sudden increase in the birth rate that occurred in the United States after World War II and lasted until roughly 1964.

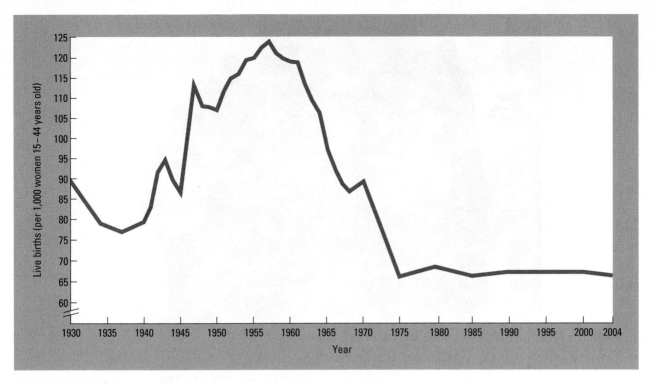

FIGURE 24.1 Birth Rate, 1930–2004
Between 1946 and 1964, rebounding from the low birth rate of the Depression, families chose to have more children. This increase is often called the "baby boom." In the 1960s, the birth rate slowed, and since the mid-1970s, it has remained fairly constant.

college and later ran for political office. When told in response to his activism, "If you don't like it, why don't you go back to Mexico?" he shot back: "I was born here in Texas. I went overseas and put my life on the line so you people can make decisions." He lost the election but, like many other Latinos, drew from the same desire for change that energized the League of United Latin American Citizens (LULAC) and the **American GI Forum** to attack discrimination throughout the West and Southwest. The American GI Forum, organized in Texas in early 1948 by Mexican American veterans, worked to secure for Latino veterans the benefits provided by the G.I. Bill and to develop leadership within the Mexican American population. In California and Texas, LULAC and the American GI Forum successfully used federal courts to correct school systems that segregated Latino from white children. In *Mendez v. Westminster* (1946) and in *Delgado v. Bastrop School District* (1948), federal courts ruled that school systems could not educate Mexican Americans separately from Anglos. Despite these rulings, throughout the Southwest and West, Latino students remained in predominantly "Mexican" schools and classrooms,

which perpetuated inferior educational opportunities and contributed to high dropout rates.

African Americans had experiences similar to those of Latinos and also exhibited a heightened degree of resistance to returning to old norms. Even as African Americans lost industrial and other higher-paying jobs as the war ended, some positive changes occurred. In the South, African American voter registration increased, primarily in the Upper South and in urban areas. In several northern cities, African Americans displayed their growing political voice by electing black representatives to local and state office and, in 1945, sent Adam Clayton Powell, Jr., to Congress from

■ **American GI Forum** Organization formed in Texas by Mexican American veterans to overcome discrimination and provide support; it led the court fight to end the segregation of Latino children in school systems in the West and Southwest.

■ *Mendez v. Westminster* **and** *Delgado v. Bastrop School District* Court cases that overturned the establishment of separate schools for Mexican American children in California and Texas.

In California and throughout the Southwest, Mexican American children were often segregated into "Mexican" schools. In this picture Mexican American students stand in front of their elementary school in Westminster, California. In 1946, a group of Mexican American families filed suit against the Westminster School District in Orange County, California, to allow their children to attend the "white" school. The California District Court, in *Mendez v. Westminster*, declared the practice of separating Mexican children illegal, ending *de jure* segregation in California. After an Appeals court upheld the decision in 1947, Governor Earl Warren ordered the integration of California schools. Arthur Palomino at Fremont School May 2, 1946, #35160004319183, Palomino Photo Collection; Mendez vs. Westminster Archive 2009.03r, Frank Mt. Pleasant Library of Special Collections and Archives, Chapman University, California.

New York. That same year, Jackie Robinson gained more national recognition when he began playing in the minor leagues.

While the postwar period generally saw significant loss of income and status for women, African Americans, and Latinos, their experiences had energized many to pursue their own vision of the American dream, one that included not only improved prosperity but an unfettered role in society and an unmuzzled voice in politics.

Individual Voices

The Sporting News Editorializes on **African Americans in Baseball**

The Sporting News (TSN), established in 1886 and called the "Bible of Baseball," was for decades the most important source for those seriously interested in the sport. Its editorials and articles shaped and expressed the public's views on sports. These editorials, separated by three years, discuss the integration of baseball. Each reflects the views of both the baseball insider and the general public and helps today's readers and historians better understand the attitudes and rationalizations regarding race in American society at the time.

❶ Why would the author believe that African American athletes in boxing (Lewis) and track (Owens) faced different issues than in baseball? In the first editorial, what do the editors of *TSN* believe is a primary reason why integration of baseball is a bad idea?

❷ What evidence does the second editorial give as to why it believes that Jackie Robinson is not a legitimate choice for the first African American to be integrated into the major leagues?

❸ Does the second editorial support the integration of baseball? How is the issue of race presented in the editorials?

❹ In what ways are the two editorials different in their view of the issue of the integration of baseball?

August 8, 1942: "No Good from Raising Race Issue"

There is no law against Negroes playing with white teams, nor whites with colored clubs, but neither has invited the other.... Other sports had their Joe Louis, Jesse Owens ... respected and honored by all races, but they competed under different circumstances from those dominating in baseball. **❶**

The baseball fan is a peculiar creature.... it's his inalienable right ... to criticize and jeer, in words that not always are ... the most gentlemanly. Not even a Ted Williams ... or a Babe Ruth is immune. It is not difficult to imagine what would happen if a player on a mixed team ... should throw a bean ball, strike out with the bases full or spike a rival. Clear-minded men of tolerance of both races realize the tragic possibilities and have steered clear of such complications.

November 1, 1945: "Montreal Puts Negro Player on Spot"

In signing Jack Roosevelt Robinson ... Branch Rickey ... touched off a powder keg in the South, unstinted praise in Negro circles and a northern conviction that the racial problem in baseball is as far from a satisfactory solution as ever.... Robinson ... is reported to possess baseball abilities which, were he white, would make him eligible for a trial with, let us say, the Brooklyn Dodgers' Class B farm at Newport News, if he were six years younger.

Here then is the picture which confronts the first Negro signed in Organized Ball ... (1) He is thrown into ... competition with a vast number of younger, more skilled and more experienced players. (2) He is ... too old.... (3) He is confronted with the sweat and tears of toil, with the social rebuff and the competitive heartaches which are inevitable for a Negro trailblazer in Organized Baseball. (4) He ... will be expected to demonstrate skills far beyond those he is reported to possess or to be able to develop.... **❷**

Granted that Robinson can "take it," insofar as points 2, 3 and 4 are concerned, the first factor alone appears likely to beat him down.... **❸**

The Sporting News believes that the attention which the signing of Robinson elicited in the press around the country was out of proportion to the actual vitality of the story ... [and] is convinced that those players ... who gave out interviews blasting the hiring of a Negro would have done a lot better ... if they had refused to comment.... "It's all right with me, just so long as Robinson isn't on our club"—the standard reply—is unsportsmanlike and, above all else, un-American. **❹**

Sources: Excerpt from "No Good from Raising Race Issue" from *The Sporting News*, August 8, 1942 and "Montreal Puts Negro Player on Spot" from *The Sporting News*, November 1, 1945.

Study Tools

SUMMARY

People hoped that the end of World War II would usher in a period of international cooperation and peace. This expectation vanished with the start of the Cold War. To protect the country and the world from Soviet expansion, the United States implemented a containment policy that was first applied to Western Europe but eventually included Asia as well. By the end of Truman's presidency, the United States viewed its national security in global terms and vowed to use its resources to combat the spread of Communist power.

At home Truman sought to expand on the New Deal but found success difficult. While existing New Deal programs such as Social Security, farm supports, and a minimum wage were extended, a conservative Congress blocked new programs. Linking liberal ideas and programs with communism, moderates and conservatives, with the House Un-American Activities Committee and Joseph McCarthy leading the way, promoted their own political, social, and economic interests.

Most Americans expected to enjoy an expanding postwar economy that would bring increased prosperity and more consumer goods. For many the vision of the suburbs with its stable family structure and new-model car in every garage seemed obtainable. Women were encouraged to return to "domestic" life and raise a family. Postwar America saw a rise in marriages and the start of a baby boom. But alongside these trends were an increasing number of divorces and women dissatisfied with their traditional roles.

While white families seemed poised to achieve the American dream, African Americans and Latinos found that discrimination undid many of the economic and social gains they had made during the war. Though forced into lesser jobs and still living in a socially segregated society, many saw changes that they hoped would bring economic and educational improvement as well as full political and civil rights.

CHRONOLOGY
From World War to Cold War

1945	United Nations formed
	Potsdam Conference
1946	Kennan's "Long Telegram"
	Churchill's "iron curtain" speech
	Iran crisis
	Construction begins on first Levittown
	Vietnamese war for independence begins
1947	Truman Doctrine
	Truman's Federal Employee Loyalty Program
	Taft-Hartley Act
	HUAC begins to investigate Hollywood
	Jackie Robinson joins Brooklyn Dodgers
	To Secure These Rights issued
	Rio Pact organized
1948	Communist coup in Czechoslovakia
	State of Israel founded
	Congress approves Marshall Plan
	Shelly v. Kraemer
	Truman defeats Dewey

1949	North Atlantic Treaty Organization created
	Berlin blockade broken by Allied airlift
	Soviet Union explodes atomic bomb
	Communist forces win civil war in China
	Alger Hiss convicted of perjury
1950	U.S. hydrogen bomb project announced
	McCarthy claims Communists riddle the State Department
	NSC 68
	Korean War begins
	McCarran Internal Security Act
1951	General MacArthur relieved of command
	Rosenbergs convicted of espionage
1953	Korean War armistice signed

Study Tools

FOCUS QUESTIONS

If you have mastered this chapter, you should be able to answer these questions and to explain the terms that follow the questions.

1. ☆ *What views and actions chosen by the Soviet Union and United States contributed to the Cold War?*

2. ☆ *How did the Truman administration seek to promote American global interests between 1947 and 1951 and why was the outcome in Asia less than satisfactory?*

3. ☆ *What events contributed to NSC 68 and how did it represent a change in strategy?*

4. ☆ *As the North Koreans invaded South Korea, why did Truman decide to refer the issue to the United Nations?*

5. ☆ *What were Truman's and MacArthur's goals in Korea? What was the consequence of China's entry into the war?*

6. ☆ *In what ways did Truman attempt to maintain and expand the New Deal? How did the fear of communism strengthen conservative opposition to his programs?*

7. ☆ *Why did Truman win the 1948 election?*

8. ☆ *What fears and events heightened society's worries about internal subversion, and how did politicians respond to the public's concerns?*

9. ☆ *Why and how did Joseph McCarthy become so powerful by 1952?*

10. ☆ *How did suburban America reflect the social and economic expectations of many Americans?*

11. ☆ *What adjustments did women and minorities have to make in postwar America?*

KEY TERMS

United Nations   *(p. 691)*

General Assembly   *(p. 691)*

Security Council   *(p. 691)*

containment   *(p. 691)*

iron curtain   *(p. 692)*

Truman Doctrine   *(p. 694)*

Marshall Plan   *(p. 694)*

Berlin airlift   *(p. 696)*

North Atlantic Treaty Organization   *(p. 697)*

National Security Council   *(p. 697)*

Rio Pact   *(p. 697)*

Organization of American States   *(p. 697)*

Ralph Bunche   *(p. 697)*

Nationalist Chinese government   *(p. 697)*

NSC Memorandum #68   *(p. 698)*

police action   *(p. 698)*

right-to-work laws   *(p. 702)*

Taft-Hartley Act   *(p. 702)*

To Secure These Rights   *(p. 703)*

Dixiecrat Party   *(p. 703)*

Fair Deal   *(p. 703)*

House Un-American Activities Committee   *(p. 704)*

Hollywood Ten   *(p. 705)*

Alger Hiss   *(p. 705)*

Richard M. Nixon   *(p. 705)*

McCarran Internal Security Act   *(p. 705)*

Smith Act   *(p. 705)*

Julius and Ethel Rosenberg   *(p. 705)*

Joseph McCarthy   *(p. 706)*

Shelly v. Kraemer   *(p. 708)*

baby boom   *(p. 710)*

American GI Forum   *(p. 711)*

Mendez v. Westminster and *Delgado v. Bastrop School District*   *(p. 711)*

Go to the History CourseMate website for primary source links, study tools, and review materials for this chapter. www.cengagebrain.com

25 Quest for Consensus, 1952–1960

Behind the Stories

What images do you conjure up when asked about the 1950s? You might think of things like sock hops, Elvis Presley, hula hoops, barbecues, cars with tail fins, and streets of tract homes with happy families headed to the shopping centers to buy the latest fashions or hit records. You might also think of President "I like Ike" Eisenhower, a smiling, grandfatherly president who liked to play golf and let the country run itself. If that is your vision, you wouldn't be wrong, but you wouldn't be totally correct, either.

Wedged between the turmoil of the 1940s and the 1960s, the fifties may appear a period of social and political calm and a triumph of American industrialization that created an affluent society. But the fifties were far from calm. People worried and faced social, cultural, and economic choices that were difficult and challenged existing perceptions. The optimism of progress was balanced with concerns about World War III and nuclear destruction. Affluent America was mocked by persistent pockets of poverty and the need to "keep up with the Joneses," which resulted in a growing number of wives and mothers taking jobs. Social and cultural norms were challenged by a civil rights movement, an emerging automobile and youth culture, and voices rejecting a mass-produced, cookie-cutter America.

Nowhere was the cry against conventionality louder than in the South, where two Americas stood in obvious sharp contrast. There, African Americans through personal acts of courage tested the status quo and the forces of segregation, and generated one of the most significant social and political changes of the twentieth century.

—J.G.

Individual Choices
Ray Kroc

It was astounding; a restaurant in southern California was ordering more milkshake machines. It had eight. Ray Kroc, who marketed Multimixers, wondered why. He went to see and found a small restaurant named McDonald's with customers flocking to windows to buy hamburgers, shakes, and fries.

The McDonald brothers had taken a typical drive-in restaurant and done something radical. They fired the carhops and opened take-out windows. They drastically reduced the menu and adopted an assembly-line technique that employed twelve men. The burgers were wrapped in paper, drinks were served in paper cups, and the order was put in paper bags. To attract families they removed cigarette machines and jukeboxes and emphasized quick service and cleanliness.

Kroc, who had no restaurant experience, made his choice. The McDonalds gave him the right to **franchise** the restaurant, provided he charge a low franchise fee and accept a service fee of less than 2 percent of the profits. He opened his first McDonald's in 1955 in Des Plaines, Illinois. Others followed, but profits lagged. Selling franchises was not making money.

Ray Kroc

Kroc decided to focus on profits rather than franchise sales. Watching the growth of suburbs and the rise of two-income, working families, he chose McDonald's locations near schools and churches. To improve profitability, he used regional suppliers and bought in bulk. As illustrated in the Individual Voices feature at the end of this chapter, Kroc developed a pattern for success. To ensure quality, consistency, and recognition, all the restaurants and menus would be the same. The food would be prepared and served the same way. Asked about his success, Kroc answered, "We take the hamburger business more seriously than anyone else." It was a successful formula not only for Kroc, who within four years franchised 738 McDonald's, but also for others who hoped to create an American icon like the Golden Arches. Yet the arches represented hometown America in a special way. Having seen a picture of a Big Mac, a platoon of soldiers in Vietnam wrote, "when we get back to the world . . . our first act [will be] going to McDonald's for a burger and a shake."

franchise Right granted by a company to an individual or group to sell the company's goods and services. The franchisee operates his or her business and keeps most of the profits, although the franchiser receives part of the profit and may establish rules and guidelines for running the business.

Republicans represented change. Most people expected less intervention in domestic affairs and more Cold War successes. They got less than expected. Recognizing that most New Deal–style programs were ingrained in society, Eisenhower knew he could modify but not dismantle them. Able to cut spending and reduce regulations, he also expanded government's role into new areas. In foreign policy, Eisenhower's New Look maintained the strategy of containment by stressing the use of nuclear weapons, alliances, and covert activities while saving money.

Americans also expected to enjoy the benefits of a growing economy with low unemployment and increasing wages. The focus of life centered on the suburban nuclear family: Dad at work, Mom at home nurturing "baby boom" children. Between child and adult, teenagers generated their own culture, merging consumerism, conformity, and rebelliousness as reflected in the growing popularity of rock 'n' roll. Optimists projected that most Americans had the chance to share in the American dream, even those not living in the suburbs. They promoted the popular image of consensus, or agreement, about the meaning and values of America.

The reality was different. Stresses existed within suburbia while race, gender, poverty, and prejudice kept many from fulfilling their hopes. But change seemed possible as groups formed grassroots organizations to advocate equality and access to a better life. Throughout the South, African Americans, supported by Supreme Court decisions, began to batter down the walls of legal segregation. Increasingly, politics and society found it hard to ignore long-standing contradictions in the country's democratic image.

POLITICS OF CONSENSUS

★ *What were the popular images of Eisenhower, and how did they compare with reality?*

★ *What constraints did Eisenhower face in trying to roll back New Deal programs?*

★ *How did Eisenhower alter the federal government?*

"Time for a change," cried Republicans in 1952. Politically wounded by the lingering war in Korea and the soft-on-communism label, the Democrats' twenty-year hold on the White House seemed in jeopardy. Bypassing would-be presidential candidate Senator Robert Taft, moderate Republicans turned to General Dwight David Eisenhower. Although politically inexperienced, "Ike" was well known, revered as a war hero, and carried the image of an honest man thrust into

public service. Skillfully gaining the nomination at the Republican convention, Eisenhower chose Richard M. Nixon of California as his vice-presidential running mate. Nixon was young and had risen rapidly in the party because of his outspoken anticommunism, made visible in the Hiss investigation. The Democrats nominated Adlai E. Stevenson, a liberal New Dealer and governor of Illinois.

Eisenhower Takes Command

The Republican campaign took two paths. One concentrated on the popular image of Eisenhower. Republicans introduced "spot commercials" on television that stressed his honesty, integrity, and "Americanness." Eisenhower crusaded for high standards and good government and posed as another George Washington. A war-weary nation applauded his promise to go to Korea "in the cause of peace." McCarthy, Nixon, and others took the second path, brutally attacking the Democrats' Cold War and New Deal records, blasting the Democrats as representing "plunder at home and blunder abroad." They boasted of "no Communists in the Republican Party," promised to roll back communism, and vowed to dismantle the New Deal. Stevenson's effort to "talk sense" to the voters stood little chance.

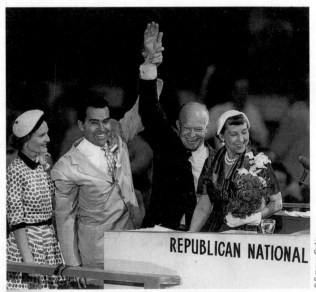

REPUBLICAN NATIONAL

© Bettmann/Corbis.

In this picture, the triumphant Republican nominees for the White House pose with smiles and wives—Pat Nixon and Mamie Eisenhower. Seen as a statesman and not a politician during the campaign, Eisenhower worked hard to ensure his nomination, then chose Richard Nixon to balance the ticket because he was a younger man, a westerner, and a conservative.

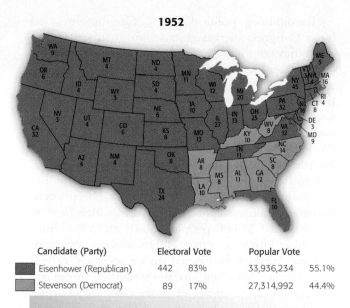

1952

Candidate (Party)	Electoral Vote		Popular Vote	
Eisenhower (Republican)	442	83%	33,936,234	55.1%
Stevenson (Democrat)	89	17%	27,314,992	44.4%

MAP 25.1 Election of 1952
Dwight David Eisenhower and the Republicans swept into office in 1952. Leading the ticket, Eisenhower swamped his Democratic opponent, Adlai Stevenson, and carried four southern states. In the 1956 presidential election, Eisenhower beat Stevenson by even larger margins—57.2 percent of the popular vote and 457 electoral votes, but Democrats retained a majority in Congress. Copyright © Cengage Learning

The campaign's only tense moment came with an allegation that Nixon had accepted gifts and money from business friends. To counter the accusations and stay on the ticket, Nixon used television. In the "Checkers speech," the teary-eyed candidate denied the fund existed and claimed that the only gift his family had ever received was a puppy, Checkers. His daughter loved the puppy, Nixon stated, and he would not make her give it back, no matter what it did to his career. It was an overly sentimental speech, but the public and Eisenhower rallied behind Nixon. Eisenhower buried Stevenson in popular and electoral votes (see Map 25.1), and his broad political coattails also swept Republican majorities into Congress. Four years later, the 1956 presidential election was a repeat of 1952, with Eisenhower receiving 457 electoral votes and again swamping Stevenson, who carried only seven southern states. But in 1956, the Republican victory was Eisenhower's alone, as Democrats maintained the majorities in both houses of Congress they had won in the 1954 midterm races.

During both of his administrations, Eisenhower was "Ike" to the public, a warm, friendly, grandfather figure who projected middle-class values and habits. Critics complained that he seemed almost an absentee president, often leaving the government in the hands of Congress and his cabinet while he played golf or bridge. But to those who knew and worked with him, he was far from bumbling or neglectful. In military fashion, Eisenhower relied on his staff to provide a full discussion of any issue. We had a "good growl," he would say after especially heated cabinet talks, but he made the final decisions, and he expected them to be carried out.

Dynamic Conservatism

Eisenhower wanted to follow a "middle course" that was "conservative when it comes to money and liberal when it comes to human beings." He believed that government should be run efficiently, like a successful business, and he staffed his cabinet with a majority of businessmen, most of whom were millionaires. Among the president's key priorities was to reduce spending and the presence of the federal government. Yet, like Truman, Eisenhower recognized the politics of the practical and understood that many New Deal agencies and functions could and should not be attacked. He told his brother that any political party that tried "to abolish Social Security, unemployment insurance, and eliminate labor laws and farm programs" would not be heard of again. He meant to pick and choose his domestic battles, staying to the right but still in the "vital center."

To balance the budget, Eisenhower used a "meat ax" on Truman's projected budgets. He dismissed 200,000 government workers, cut domestic spending by 10 percent, and slashed the military budget. His budget cutting gave Eisenhower a vehicle for reducing New Deal programs and returning control of some to local and state governance. Eisenhower thought he could eliminate or curtail the federal government's role in the areas of energy, the environment, and trusteeship over Indian reservations. Advocating private ownership and state responsibility, he signed legislation allowing private ownership of nuclear power plants and reducing federal control over the industry. Congress also approved legislation placing much of the nation's offshore oil sources under state authority and opening federal lands to lumber and mining companies.

Citing costs and expanding opportunities for Native Americans, Congress in 1954 passed a resolution establishing a termination program, which began to withdraw federal services and economic support to tribes, encouraged Indians to leave the reservations, and liquidated tribal lands and resources. The Klamath tribe in Oregon, for example, sold much of their ponderosa pine lands to lumber companies. Before the policy was reversed in the 1960s, sixty-one tribes were

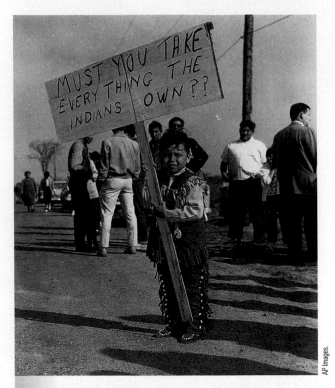

In line with his policy to reduce federal spending and controls, Eisenhower tried to turn Indian affairs over to the states and liquidate federal services and reservations. Between 1954 and 1960, sixty-one tribes were affected. This picture shows a 4-year-old Tuscarora boy protesting state and federal policies that attacked Indian rights.

involved. Some experienced short-term economic gains with the sale of valuable lands and resources, but long-term benefits failed to materialize. Reservations were poorer, and the nearly half of reservation Indians who had abandoned their reservations and moved to urban areas found that few jobs or opportunities were available.

■ **Federal Highway Act** Law passed by Congress in 1956, appropriating $32 billion for the construction of interstate highways.

■ ***Sputnik I*** The first artificial satellite launched into space, it weighed 184 pounds; this feat by the Soviet Union in October 1957 marked the beginning of the space race. A month later, ***Sputnik II,*** even larger, was launched, weighing 1,120 pounds and carrying a dog named Laika.

National Defense Education Act A ten-part act that sought to improve instruction in science, mathematics, and foreign languages and included federally backed low-interest loans to college students. Today those loans are known as the Federal Perkins Loans.

■ **National Defense Student Loans** Loans established by the U.S. government in 1958, designed to encourage the teaching and study of science and modern languages.

Recognizing political reality, Eisenhower stood by as Congress increased agricultural subsidies, the minimum wage (to $1.00 an hour), funds for urban development, and Social Security benefits. But he also expanded the role of government in new directions. In 1953, he created the Department of Health, Education and Welfare, directed by Oveta Culp Hobby, who had commanded the Women's Army Corps during World War II. Still, even public health was something Eisenhower felt was best left to states and communities. In 1955, Jonas Salk developed a vaccine for polio, and many called for a nationwide federal program to inoculate children against the disease, which in 1952 had infected 52,000 people, mostly children. However, Eisenhower, Secretary Hobby, and the American Medical Association rejected such a program, calling it socialistic. State and local vaccination programs did reduce the number of polio cases to less than one thousand annually by the 1960s.

There were also two new major government spending programs: the St. Lawrence Seaway Act (1954) and the **Federal Highway Act** (1956). The first funded joint U.S.-Canadian construction of an inland waterway connecting the Great Lakes with the Atlantic. The second provided funds to construct an interstate highway system; the military, Eisenhower maintained, needed such a nationwide transportation network, which would also meet the needs of an automobile-driven nation.

In 1957, Eisenhower again extended federal spending after the Soviet Union launched ***Sputnik I*** and ***Sputnik II*** into space. Not only did the nation seem vulnerable to Soviet missiles, but it appeared that the American education system was not putting enough effort into teaching mathematics and science. Eisenhower promptly asked Congress to provide money for public education and to create a new agency to coordinate the country's space program.

The **National Defense Education Act** of 1958 provided funds for public education to improve the teaching of math, languages, and science and set aside $295 million in **National Defense Student Loans** for college students. To improve the space program, Congress created the National Aeronautics and Space Administration (NASA), which unveiled Project Mercury with the goal of sending astronauts into space.

The Problem with McCarthy

With the Democrats defeated, Eisenhower and most Republicans thought McCarthy would end his crusade against Communists. But he continued to criticize the administration's foreign policy as soft on communism and to search for subversives. To weaken McCarthy's rhetoric, the administration, claiming loyalty issues, dismissed more than two thousand federal employees in 1953. None were proven to be Communists, but nearly all were Roosevelt and Truman appointees. When, in 1954, McCarthy claimed favoritism toward known Communists in the army, anti-McCarthy forces in Congress, quietly supported by Eisenhower, moved to defang the senator and established a committee to examine the senator's claims.

The American Broadcasting Company's telecast of the 1954 **Army-McCarthy hearings** allowed more than 20 million viewers to see McCarthy's ruthless bullying firsthand. When the army's lawyer, Joseph Welch, asked the brooding McCarthy, "Have you no sense of decency?" the nation burst into applause. McCarthy's power ebbed and several months later the Senate voted 67 to 22 to censure McCarthy's "unbecoming conduct." Drinking heavily, shunned by his colleagues, and ignored by the media, McCarthy died in 1957.

EISENHOWER AND WORLD AFFAIRS

★ *What were the weaknesses of the New Look and how did Eisenhower address them?*

★ *What tactics did the Eisenhower administration pursue in the "third world," especially in the Middle East and Latin America, to protect American interests?*

During the 1952 campaign, part of Eisenhower's popularity reflected the view that Republicans would conduct a more forceful foreign policy. Republican spokesmen promised the rollback of communism and the liberation of peoples under communist control. After his election Eisenhower kept his campaign promise to go to Korea. He went—for three days. Many expected him to find a means to win the conflict, but after visiting the front lines, he was convinced that a negotiated peace was the only solution. The problem was how to persuade the North Koreans and Chinese that a settlement would be in their best interests. Eisenhower, wary of being too assertive and too simplistic in approaching international problems, approached foreign policy as a realist. Despite the campaign rhetoric of liberation and rollback, he embraced the principle of containment and sought to modify it to match what he believed to be the nation's capabilities and needs. His new policy was called the **New Look**.

The New Look

The core of the New Look was nuclear deterrence—an enhanced arsenal of nuclear weapons and delivery systems—and the threat of **massive retaliation**.

In explaining the shift to more atomic weapons, Vice President Nixon stated, "Rather than let the Communists nibble us to death all over the world in little wars, we will rely . . . on massive mobile retaliation." Secretary of Defense Charles E. Wilson, noting that the nuclear strategy was cheaper than conventional forces, quipped that the policy ensured "more bang for the buck." Demonstrating the country's nuclear might, the United States exploded its first hydrogen bomb in November 1952 (the Soviets tested theirs in August 1953), expanded its arsenal of strategic nuclear weapons to six thousand, and developed tactical nuclear weapons of a lower destructive power that could be used on the battlefield.

The New Look was sold to the public as more positive than Truman's defensive containment policy, but insiders recognized that it had flaws. The central problem was where the United States should draw the massive-retaliation line: "What if the enemy calls our bluff? How do you convince the American people and the U.S. Congress to declare war?" asked one planner. The answer was to convince potential aggressors that the United States would strike back, raining nuclear destruction not only on the attackers but also on the Soviets and Chinese so that the bluff would never be called. This policy was called **brinkmanship**, because it required the administration to take the nation to the brink of war, trusting that the opposition would back down. Thus Secretary of State John Foster Dulles and Eisenhower indulged in dramatic speeches explaining that nuclear weapons were as usable as conventional ones. It was necessary "to remove the taboo" from using nuclear weapons, Dulles informed the press.

To prod the North Koreans and Chinese to sign a Korean truce agreement, Eisenhower used public and private channels to suggest that the United States might use atomic weapons. By July 1953, the strategy apparently had worked. A truce signed at Panmunjom ended the fighting and brought home

■ **Army-McCarthy hearings** Congressional investigations by Senator Joseph McCarthy televised in 1954; the hearings revealed McCarthy's villainous nature and ended his popularity.

■ **New Look** National security policy under Eisenhower that called for a reduction in the size of the army, development of tactical nuclear weapons, and the buildup of strategic air power to deploy nuclear weapons.

■ **massive retaliation** Term that Secretary of State John Foster Dulles used in a 1954 speech, implying that the United States was willing to use nuclear force in response to Communist aggression anywhere.

brinkmanship Practice of seeking to win disputes in international politics by creating the impression of being willing to push a highly dangerous situation to the limit.

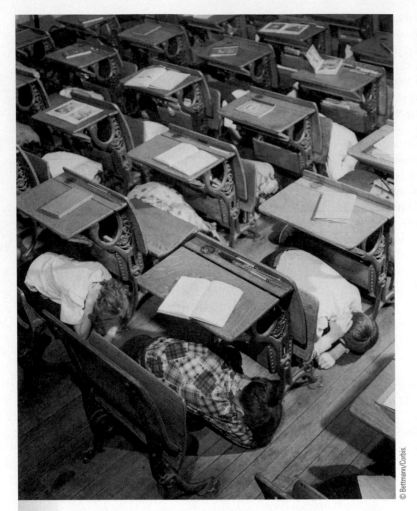

To protect themselves from the effect of a nuclear explosion, the government recommended that once the flash was seen or the warning signal was given, students should "duck and cover," assuming the fetal position and covering the head with their hands. Burt the Turtle became a popular mascot for the exercises that were practiced from 1951 to the mid-1980s. In this picture elementary school children in Ohio successfully practice "duck and cover."

© Bettmann/Corbis.

demilitarized zone An area in which military forces, operations, and installations are prohibited.

fallout shelters Underground shelters stocked with food and supplies that were intended to provide safety in case of atomic attack; *fallout* refers to the irradiated particles falling through the atmosphere after a nuclear attack.

B movies Poorer quality, more cheaply made films that were shown in addition to the main movies.

covert operation A program or event carried out in secret.

bilateral Involving two parties.

multilateral Involving more than two parties.

almost all the troops but left Korea divided by a **demilitarized zone**. Had the nuclear threat, "atomic diplomacy," worked? Some thought it had, but others pointed to Stalin's death in March 1953 and the resolution of central issues as more important. Still, Americans praised Eisenhower's new approach.

To strengthen the idea of "going nuclear" and make the possibility of World War III less frightening, the administration stressed that nuclear war was survivable. Public and private underground **fallout shelters**—well stocked with food, water, and medical supplies—could, it was claimed, provide safety against an attack. A 32-inch-thick slab of concrete, *U.S. News & World Report* related, could protect people from an atomic blast "as close as 1,000 feet away." Across the nation, civil defense drills were established for factories, offices, and businesses. "Duck-and-cover" drills were held in schools: when their teachers shouted "Drop!" students immediately got into a kneeling or prone position and placed their hands behind their necks.

While people were being convinced that they could survive a nuclear war, movies and novels showed the horror of nuclear death and destruction. Nevil Shute portrayed the extinction of humankind in his novel *On the Beach* (1957). In *Them!* (1954) and dozens of other **B movies**, giant ants and other hideous creatures mutated by atomic fallout threatened the world.

As with Korea, Eisenhower recognized the limits of American power—areas under Communist control could not be liberated, and a thermonuclear war would yield no winners. Consequently, the administration sought other ways to promote American power and influence, including alliances and **covert operations**. Alliances would identify areas protected by the American nuclear umbrella and would protect the United States from being drawn into limited "brushfire" wars. When small conflicts erupted, the ground forces of regional allies, perhaps supported with American naval and air strength, would snuff them out.

In Asia, Eisenhower concluded **bilateral** defense pacts with South Korea (1953) and Taiwan (1955) and a **multilateral** agreement, the Southeast Asia Treaty Organization (SEATO, 1954), that linked the United States, Australia, Thailand, the Philippines, Pakistan,

New Zealand, France, and Britain. In the Middle East, the United States officially joined Britain, Iran, Pakistan, Turkey, and Iraq in the **Baghdad Pact** in 1957, later called the Central Treaty Organization (CENTO) after Iraq withdrew in 1959. In Europe, the United States approved the rearming of West Germany in 1954 and welcomed it into NATO in 1958. In all, the Eisenhower administration signed forty-three pacts to help defend regions or individual countries from Communist aggression (see Map 25.2). In 1955, the Soviet Union created its own military alliance, the **Warsaw Pact**.

The Third World

In 1946, fifty-one nations, most located in Europe and the Western Hemisphere, signed the United Nations' charter. Over the next ten years, twenty-five more nations entered, about a third of them having achieved independence from European nations through revolution and political and social protests. By 1960, thirty-seven new nations existed in Africa, Asia, and the Middle East. For many of the emerging nations, independence did not bring prosperity or stability, and the so-called **third world** became part of the Cold War. Both the West and the Communist bloc competed for the "hearts and minds" of the emerging nations. Commenting on nationalistic movements in Latin America, Secretary of State Dulles said: "In the old days we used to be able to let South America go through the wringer of bad times . . . but the trouble is, now, when you put it through the wringer, it comes out red."

One solution to the problem was to use economic and military aid, political pressure, and the **Central Intelligence Agency** (CIA) to support those governments that were anti-Communist and provided stability, even if that stability was achieved through ruthless and undemocratic means. It seemed a never-ending and largely thankless task. "While we are busy rescuing Guatemala or assisting Korea and Indochina," Eisenhower observed, the Communists "make great inroads in Burma, Afghanistan, and Egypt." To meet the growing need, the CIA expanded by 500 percent and shifted its resources to covert activities—80 percent by 1957. In its conduct of activities, the CIA, headed by Allen Dulles, operated with almost no congressional oversight or restrictions.

Turmoil in the Middle East

In the Middle East, Arab nationalism, fired by anti-Israeli and anti-Western attitudes, posed a serious threat to American interests. Iran and Egypt offered the greatest challenges. In Iran, Prime Minister Mohammed Mossadegh had nationalized British-

owned oil properties and seemed likely to sell oil to the Soviets. Eisenhower considered him to be "neurotic and periodically unstable" and gave the CIA the green light to overthrow the Iranian leader and replace him with a pro-Western government. On August 18, 1953, Mossadegh was forced from office and was replaced by **Shah Mohammad Reza Pahlavi**, who awarded the United States 40 percent of Iranian oil production.

Egyptian leader Gamal Abdel Nasser, who assumed power in 1954, posed a similar problem. At first the United States hoped that Nasser would act as a stabilizing influence in the region and offered money and help to build the Aswan Dam on the Nile. But the U.S. attitude changed when Nasser's relations with Israel deteriorated and he denounced the Baghdad Pact and purchased arms from the Soviet bloc. Calling him an "evil influence," Eisenhower canceled the Aswan Dam project (July 1956). Days later, claiming the need to finance the dam, Nasser nationalized the Anglo-French–owned Suez Canal.

Israel, France, and Britain responded with military action to regain control of the canal. Eisenhower was furious. He disliked Nasser but could not approve armed aggression. Fearful that the Soviets were ready "to take any wild adventure" and intervene, Eisenhower moved rapidly to sponsor a UN General Assembly resolution (November 2, 1956) calling for an end to the fighting, the removal of foreign troops from Egyptian soil, and the assignment of a UN peacekeeping force there. Faced with worldwide opposition and intense pressure from the United States—including a threat to withhold oil shipments—France, Britain, and Israel withdrew their forces. Nasser regained control of the canal and, as Eisenhower had feared,

■ **Baghdad Pact** A regional defensive alliance signed between Turkey and Iraq in 1955; Great Britain, Pakistan, and Iran soon joined; the United States supported the pact but did not officially join until mid-1957.

■ **Warsaw Pact** A defense alliance among the Soviet Union and its Eastern European satellite nations, officially the Treaty of Friendship, Co-operation and Mutual Assistance; it was dissolved in 1991.

■ **third world** Developing nations that claimed to be independent of either the Western capitalist or Communist blocs; both sides tested this neutrality in the Cold War, as each used a variety of means to include third world nations in their camps.

■ **Central Intelligence Agency** (CIA) An agency created in 1947 to gather and evaluate military, political, social, and economic information on foreign nations.

■ **Shah Mohammad Reza Pahlavi** Iranian ruler who received the hereditary title *shah* from his father in 1941 and with CIA support helped oust the militant nationalist Mohammed Mossadegh in 1953.

MAP 25.2 Confrontation Cold War

During the Cold War, the United States attempted to construct a ring of containment around the Soviet Union and its allies, while the Soviets worked to expand their influence and power. This map shows the nature of this military confrontation—the bases, alliances, and flash points of the Cold War. Copyright © Cengage Learning

Legend

- NATO nations
- SEATO nations
- CENTO nations
- Warsaw Pact nations

- ■ Soviet military base
- ■ U.S. military base
- ● U.S. Strategic Air Command base
- ▲ U.S. Intercontinental Balistic Missile base
- U.S. naval fleet
- ★ Cold War point of conflict

Australia
New Zealand

Conflicts / Dates

CZECHOSLOVAKIA 1948, 1968
EAST GERMANY 1948–1949, 1953, 1958–1962
POLAND 1956
YUGOSLAVIA 1948–1953
HUNGARY 1956

GUATEMALA 1954
EL SALVADOR 1979–1992
NICARAGUA 1981–1990
PANAMA
CUBA 1961–1962
DOMINICAN REPUBLIC 1965–1966
GRENADA 1983
Puerto Rico (U.S.)

AFGHANISTAN 1979
IRAN 1945–1946, 1951–1953
IRAQ 1958
TURKEY 1945–1947
LEBANON 1958
GREECE 1946–1949
EGYPT 1956 1967 1973
SOMALIA 1970s–1980s
ETHIOPIA 1975–1991
DEMOCRATIC REPUBLIC OF THE CONGO 1961–1965
ANGOLA 1976–1992

SOUTH KOREA 1950–1953
FORMOSA (TAIWAN) 1958
Okinawa (U.S.)
LAOS 1960–1975
PHILIPPINES
SOUTH VIETNAM 1945–1954, 1957–1975
CAMBODIA 1969–1975
THAILAND
INDONESIA 1965

Map labels

PACIFIC OCEAN
ARCTIC OCEAN
ATLANTIC OCEAN
INDIAN OCEAN

HAWAI'I (U.S.)
ALASKA (U.S.)
CANADA
UNITED STATES
GREENLAND (DEN.)
ICELAND
Azores (Port.)

NORWAY
GREAT BRITAIN
DEN.
NETH.
BELG.
W. GER.
E. GER.
FRANCE
PORT.
SPAIN
ITALY
ALB.
POLAND
CZECH.
HUNG.
YUGO.
ROMANIA
BULG.
GREECE
MOROCCO
LIBYA
SAUDI ARABIA

SOVIET UNION
MONGOLIA
CHINA
JAPAN
PAKISTAN

1st fleet
2nd fleet
6th fleet
7th fleet

Distant Early Warning (DEW) Radar Line
Mid-Canada Radar Line
Pinetree Radar Line

Equator

150°W 120°W 90°W 30°W 0° 30°E 60°E 90°E 120°E 150°E
30°N 60°N

1000 Mi.
1000 Km.
500
0

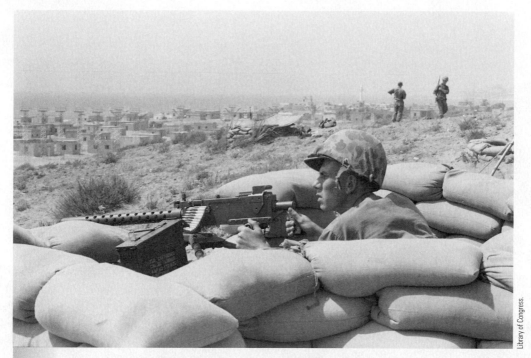

Implementing the Eisenhower Doctrine, American forces landed in Lebanon in July 1958, taking up positions around the city of Beirut. They landed and withdrew without incident.

emerged a major leader in the Arab world willing to accept Soviet support.

The outcome of the Suez War and the growth of Soviet influence in the Middle East forced Eisenhower to expand American interests in the region. To protect Arab friends from Communist-nationalist revolutions, he asked Congress for permission to commit American forces, if requested, to resist "armed attack from any country controlled by internationalism" (by *internationalism* Eisenhower meant the forces of communism). Congress agreed in March 1957, establishing the so-called **Eisenhower Doctrine** and providing $200 million in military and economic aid to improve military defenses in the nations of the Middle East.

It did not take long for the Eisenhower Doctrine to be applied. When an internal revolt threatened Jordan's King Hussein in 1957, the White House announced Jordan was "vital" to American interests, moved the U.S. 6th Fleet into the eastern Mediterranean, and supplied more than $10 million in aid. King Hussein put down the revolt, dismissed parliament and all political parties, and instituted authoritarian rule. A year later, when Lebanon's Christian president Camile Chamoun faced an uprising of Muslim nationalistic and anti-West elements, Eisenhower committed nearly fifteen thousand troops to protect the pro-American government. Within three months Washington, without firing a

shot, oversaw the formation of a new government and withdrew American forces.

A Protective Neighbor

During the 1952 presidential campaign, Eisenhower charged Truman with following a "Poor Neighbor policy" toward Latin America, allowing the development of economic problems and popular uprisings that had been "skillfully exploited by the Communists." He was most concerned about Guatemala, disapproving of the reformist president, Jacobo Arbenz, who had instituted agrarian reforms by nationalizing thousands of acres of land, much of it owned by the American-based United Fruit Company. These actions led to a CIA effort to remove Arbenz. A CIA-organized and -supplied rebel army led by Colonel Carlos Castillo Armas invaded Guatemala on June 18, 1954. Within weeks a new, pro-American government was installed in Guatemala City. But the effort failed to reduce social and economic inequalities or foster goodwill

■ **Eisenhower Doctrine** Policy formulated by Eisenhower of providing military and economic aid to Arab nations in the Middle East to help defeat Communist-nationalistic rebellions.

Considering Guatemalan president Jacobo Arbenz a threat to American interests, Eisenhower approved a CIA plan to fund and direct a force commanded by Colonel Castillo Armas to invade Guatemala and topple the elected government. In this picture, a group of Armas's soldiers prepare to leave for Guatemala City in June 1954. Speaking after Arbenz had fled, Secretary of State Dulles announced the people of Guatemala had "cured" the problem by themselves.

toward the United States. The next crisis was closer to home when a rebellion led by Fidel Castro toppled the Cuban government of Fulgencio Batista, who had controlled the island since the 1940s.

The corrupt and dictatorial Batista had become an embarrassment to the United States, and many Americans believed that Castro could be a pro-American reformist leader. By 1959, rebel forces had control of the island, but by midyear many of Castro's economic and social reforms were endangering American investments and interests, which dominated Cuba's economy. Concerned about Castro's political leanings, Washington tried to push Cuba in the right direction by applying economic pressure. In February 1960, Castro reacted to the American arm twisting by signing an economic pact with the Soviet Union.

Eisenhower seethed: Castro was a "madman . . . going wild and harming the whole American structure." In March, Eisenhower approved a CIA plan to prepare an attack against Castro. Actual implementation of the plot to overthrow the Cuban leader, however, was left to Eisenhower's successor.

The New Look in Asia

Korea was not the only problem in Asia that Eisenhower faced when he took office. Chinese threats continued toward Taiwan and its offshore islands, and a "war of national liberation" raged in French Indochina. In both cases, he continued Truman's policies—supporting the Nationalist Chinese and the French. By 1954, the struggle between France and the **Viet Minh** was not going well for Paris. Watching the French military position worsen, Eisenhower announced the **domino theory**, warning that if Indochina fell to communism, the loss "of Burma, of Thailand, of the [Malay] Peninsula, and Indonesia" would certainly follow, endangering Australia and New Zealand. To many it meant that the United States needed to take a more direct role in the conflict.

As Viet Minh forces launched murderous attacks on the beleaguered French fortifications at Dienbienphu, the French—and some members of the Eisenhower administration—wanted American intervention to save the garrison. Eisenhower rejected the idea, saying that "no military victory" was "possible in that kind of theater." The surrender of Dienbienphu on May 7, 1954, left the French and Eisenhower no option but to try to salvage a partial victory at an international conference in Geneva.

But the West could piece together no victory at Geneva either. The **Geneva Agreement** "temporarily" partitioned Vietnam along the 17th parallel and created the neutral states of Cambodia and Laos. Within two years, the two Vietnams were to hold elections to unify the nation, and neither was to enter into military alliances or allow foreign bases on its territory. American strategists called the settlement a "disaster"—half of Vietnam was lost to communism. Showing its displeasure, the United States refused to sign the agreement. Eisenhower immediately moved to support South Vietnam's new government and prime minister, Ngo Dinh Diem. With American blessings, Diem ignored the Geneva-mandated unification elections, quashed his political opposition, and in October 1955 staged a **plebiscite** that created the Republic of Vietnam and elected him president.

The Soviets and Cold War Politics

To strengthen the New Look deterrent capability, the Eisenhower administration developed a three-way system to deliver a nuclear attack on the Soviet Union and China. Efforts were intensified to develop an intercontinental and intermediate-range ballistic missile system that could be fired from land bases and from submarines. At the same time, the nation's bomber fleet was improved, introducing the jet-powered B-47. While deterrence was critical, Stalin's death in 1953 offered an opportunity to improve American-Soviet relations. When the Russian premier, Georgii Malenkov, called for "peaceful coexistence," Dulles dismissed the suggestion, but Eisenhower said they should assume that "Malenkov was a reasonable

man . . . and talk accordingly." He called on the Soviets to demonstrate their willingness to cooperate with the West. Malenkov responded positively and some headway followed when the Soviets removed their controls and troops from Austria, but overall, deep-seeded suspicions remained.

In 1955, as both nations continued to test their hydrogen bombs, Eisenhower agreed to a summit meeting in Geneva with the new Soviet leadership team of Nikolai Bulganin and **Nikita Khrushchev**, who had replaced Malenkov. Eisenhower expected no resolution of the two major issues—disarmament and Berlin—but saw the meeting as good public relations. He would make a bold disarmament initiative—the Open Skies proposal—that would earn broad international support. In a dramatic presentation, highlighted by a sudden thunderstorm that momentarily blacked out the conference room, Eisenhower asked the Soviets to share information about military installations and permit aerial reconnaissance to verify the information while work began on general disarmament. Bulganin voiced official interest, but Khrushchev considered the proposal a "very transparent espionage device." In the end, the Geneva Summit ended as most expected, with each side agreeing to disagree, although publicly both Eisenhower and the Soviets said the "spirit of Geneva" reduced East-West tensions.

The spirit of Geneva vanished when Soviet forces invaded Hungary in November 1956 to quell an anti-Soviet revolt. Many Americans favored supporting the Hungarian freedom fighters, but facing the Suez crisis and seeing no way to send aid to the Hungarians without risking all-out war, the administration only watched as the Soviets crushed the

- **Viet Minh** Vietnamese army made up of Communist and other nationalist groups led by Ho Chi Minh that fought from 1946 to 1954 for independence from French rule.
- **domino theory** The idea that if one nation came under Communist control, then neighboring nations would also fall to the Communists.
- **Geneva Agreement** Truce signed at Geneva in 1954 by French and Viet Minh representatives, dividing Vietnam along the 17th parallel into the Communist North and the anti-Communist South.
- **plebiscite** Special election that allows people to either approve or reject a particular proposal.
- **Nikita Khrushchev** Soviet leader who denounced Stalin in 1956 and improved the Soviet Union's image abroad; he was deposed in 1964, after six years as premier, for his failure to improve the country's economy.

In this cartoon, an American suburban family sits contentedly next to their cozy home with little concern about the delicate Cold War balance between peace and destruction. By 1953, both the United States and the Soviet Union had tested hydrogen bombs and seemed willing to use the A-bomb to protect national interests.

States in September 1959, and the two leaders met at a summit in Paris in May of 1960. But a "thaw" in the Cold War failed to materialize. Just as the summit began, the Soviets shot down an American U-2 spy plane over the Soviet Union and captured its pilot. At first, the United States claimed the U-2 was a stray weather plane, but the Soviets' display of the captured pilot and pictures of the plane's wreckage clearly proved otherwise. In Paris, Eisenhower took full responsibility but refused to apologize for such flights, which he contended were necessary to prevent a "nuclear Pearl Harbor." Khrushchev withdrew from the summit, and Eisenhower canceled his forthcoming trip to the Soviet Union.

Eisenhower remained popular, but the loss of the U-2, Soviet advances in missile technology and nuclear weaponry, and a Communist Cuba only 90 miles from Florida provided the Democrats with strong claims that the Republican administration had been deficient in meeting Soviet threats. In 1960, turning the Republicans' tactics of 1952 against them, Democrats cheerfully accused their opponents of endangering the United States by being too soft on communism.

revolt. Soviet-American relations cooled, and Eisenhower and Khrushchev jousted with each other over nuclear testing, disarmament, and Germany and Berlin. First one leader and then the other, with little belief in success, offered to end testing and reduce nuclear weapons if certain provisions were met. When in 1958 NATO agreed to include West Germany, the simmering issue of Berlin erupted. When the Soviets stated that Berlin was to be unified under East German control, Eisenhower, joined by the British and French, declared that their forces would remain in West Berlin.

Faced with unflinching Western determination, Khrushchev backed down and suggested that he and Eisenhower exchange visits and hold a summit meeting. East-West relations seemed to improve as Khrushchev took a twelve-day tour of the United

THE BEST OF TIMES

★ *What new economic factors contributed to prosperity in the 1950s?*

★ *What stresses and contradictions were at work beneath the placid surface of suburbia? Who voiced criticism and how did they express it?*

★ *Why were rock 'n' roll and rebellious teens seen as threats to social norms?*

According to the popular magazine *Reader's Digest,* in 1954 the average American male stood 5 feet 9 inches tall and weighed 158 pounds. He liked brunettes, baseball, bowling, and steak and French fries. In seeking a wife, he could not decide if brains or beauty was more important, but he definitely wanted a wife who could run a home efficiently. The average female was 5 feet 4 inches tall and weighed 132 pounds. She preferred marriage to career, but she wanted to remove the word *obey* from her marriage vows. Both man and

In the expanding suburbs of the 1950s, many women merged business with socializing by hosting Tupperware parties, introducing friends and neighbors to the newest ways to store leftovers.

to be regulated staffed regulatory agencies and cabinet positions. Secretary of Defense Wilson, the ex-president of General Motors, later voiced the common view: "What was good for our country was good for General Motors and vice versa." It was an era of "new economics" where, according to a 1952 ad in the *New York Times,* industry's "efforts are not in the selfish interest" but "for the good of many." The Advertising Council called the economic system "people's capitalism" and said it was creating "the highest standard of living ever known by any people . . . at any time." Not all agreed that the connections between government and business were without risk. In his farewell address, President Eisenhower warned of the power of the "military-industrial complex" and its potential threat to the "democratic process."

However, few Americans worried about military-industrial connections when corporate profits doubled between 1948 and 1958 and industrial wages steadily rose from about $55 to $80 a week over the decade. Nor was there much concern that corporations were getting bigger. Many companies were either closing their doors or merging into larger industries to create **conglomerates**. Expanding giant International Telephone and Telegraph, for example, was acquiring construction and insurance firms, food companies, hotels, and other companies not associated with communications.

The outcome of all this explosive business activity was that the GNP reached $500 billion in 1960, double its level in 1940. Exports also doubled, giving the nation a $5 billion trade surplus by 1960. For many Americans, the Depression and scarcities of the war were a thing of the past.

Central to the new economy was the automobile and those industries and jobs that made the car part

woman were enjoying life to the fullest, according to the *Digest,* and buying more of just about everything. The economy appeared to be bursting at the seams, providing jobs, good wages, a multitude of products, and profits.

The Web of Prosperity

The expanding economy was a result of big government, big business, and an expanding population. World War II and the Cold War had created military-industrial-governmental linkages that primed the economy through government spending, what some have labeled "military **Keynesianism**." National security needs by 1955 accounted for half of the U.S. budget—equaling about 17 percent of the gross national product—and exceeded the total net incomes of all American corporations.

The connection between government and business went beyond direct spending: millions of research and development dollars flowed into colleges and industries. The electronics industry drew 70 percent of its research money from the government, producing not only new scientific and military technology but marketable consumer goods like the transistor radio and televisions.

In addition, a revolving door seemed to connect government and business positions. Few saw any real conflict of interest even when those from businesses

■ **Keynesianism** The economic theories of Lord John Maynard Keynes (1883–1946), who promoted government intervention in the economy, arguing that expanding and contracting the money supply and regulating interest rates could stimulate economic growth during periods of recession and, when needed, reduce inflation.

conglomerates The combination of two or more firms engaging in entirely different businesses.

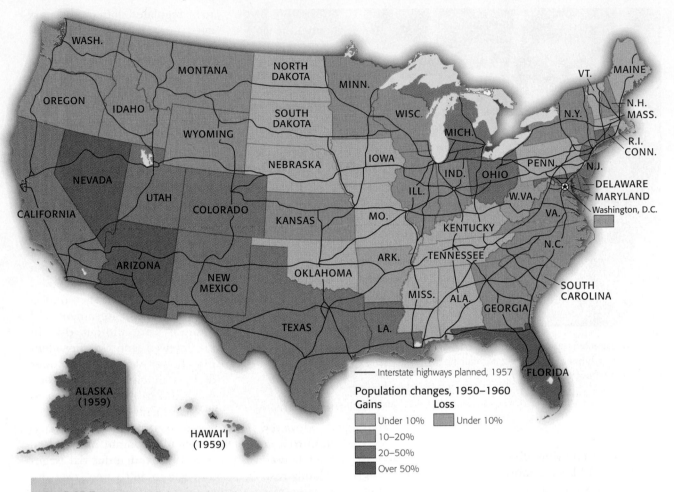

Population changes, 1950–1960
Gains   Loss
☐ Under 10%   ☐ Under 10%
☐ 10–20%
☐ 20–50%
☐ Over 50%

— Interstate highways planned, 1957

MAP 25.3 Movement Across America, 1950–1960
Americans were on the move during the 1950s. White Americans moved to the suburbs, especially in the South and West. Many African Americans left rural areas of the South; others moved against existing patterns of segregation. This map shows the web of interstate highways and population shifts during this period.
Copyright © Cengage Learning

of the American landscape. The more than $32 billion Eisenhower allocated to build an interstate highway system represented only a fraction of funds spent on road construction by all levels of government (see Map 25.3). New and better highways led to more cars, and more cars needed still more roads. By 1960, 75 percent of all Americans had at least one car and were driving millions of miles, stopping at newly constructed motels, amusement parks, shopping malls, drive-in theaters, and fast-food restaurants. Disneyland opened in 1955, with acres of parking lots to accommodate the family cars of people who entered the "Happiest Place on Earth." Within six months a

million people had visited the "Magic Kingdom." Meanwhile, McDonald's "drive-to" restaurants were changing the nation's eating habits, serving a million hamburgers a day by 1963.

The new economics of the 1950s also changed the nature of the work force and organized labor. In the wake of lost strikes and anti-union legislation in the late 1940s and facing workplace changes wrought by **automation**, unions altered their tactics. Beginning with a new contract with General Motors in 1950, union leaders dropped efforts to gain control over managerial decisions and focused on getting better wages and benefits. GM and other corporations responded by accepting collective bargaining and creating an economic/social safety net that included pensions and health care. Yet despite higher wages, the number of union workers in the work force fell to 31 percent by 1960. Much of the decline was a consequence of there

automation A process or system designed so that equipment functions automatically, often replacing workers with machines.

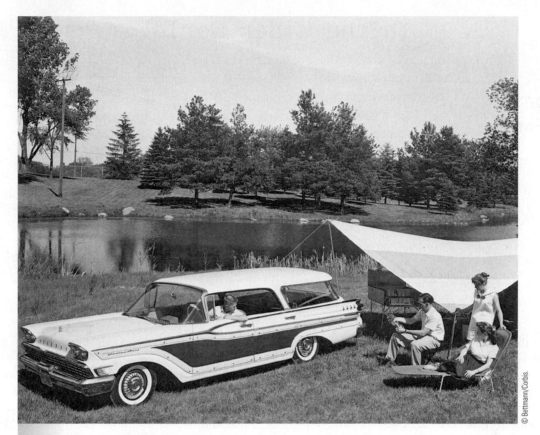

Throughout the 1950s, a popular image of the American dream was the family enjoying "togetherness" during a family picnic.

being fewer industrial workers as the economy shifted to public- and service-sector jobs. By 1956, white-collar workers outnumbered blue-collar workers. Neither the AFL nor the CIO, which merged in 1956, responded well to the shift, showing little interest in recruiting workers from the service sector.

Suburban and Family Culture

The suburban housing boom continued to spark the economy and, like the automobile, to shape the American landscape. "We were thrilled to death," recalled one newly arrived suburbanite. "Everyone was arriving with a sense of forward momentum. Everyone was taking courage from the sight of another orange moving van pulling in next door, a family just like us, unloading pole lamps and cribs and Formica dining tables like our own. . . ." Many of the families were moving into a new "ranch" or California-style home, designed to match the most modern family's needs. It was a single-story rectangular or L-shaped house with a simple floor plan, an attached garage, and a family room—sometimes complete with a television, now the focus of the house. Near the family room was the "modern" kitchen with its new appliances that made life easier for the stay-at-home housewife.

At the heart of the home was the American nuclear family. Families were the strength of the nation, and the number of families continued to grow, with the baby boom peaking at 4.3 million births in 1957. Within the family there were clearly defined roles. Husbands were the breadwinners and directed weekend events. Wives managed the home, cared for the children, and deferred to their husbands' decisions. "There was this pressure to be the perfect housekeeper," remembered one suburban wife. For guidance on how to raise babies and children, millions of Americans turned to Dr. Benjamin Spock's popular book *Baby and Child Care* (1946). A mother's love and positive parental guidance were keys to healthy and well-adjusted children. Strict rules and corporal punishment were to be avoided. To ensure proper gender identity, boys should participate in sports and outdoor activities, whereas girls should concentrate on their appearance and domestic skills. Toy guns and doctor bags were for boys; dolls, tea sets, and nurse kits were for girls. Conforming—being part of the group—was as important for parents as for children. Those not fulfilling those roles were suspected of being homosexual, immature, or simply irresponsible.

Television helped define suburban life. Developed in the 1930s, televisions were not widely available

In the Wider World

The Great Leap Forward

Concerned about the slow pace of Chinese economic growth, Mao Zedong began the Great Leap Forward in 1958 to mobilize the masses. Within a year, 700 million people were placed in more than 25,500 communes that served as centers of labor and production. Focused on grain and steel, goals were lofty, such as surpassing Britain as an industrial power in fifteen years. To expand steel production, "backyard steel furnaces" were constructed in villages, communes, and schools. Most of China's forests were destroyed to supply wood for the furnaces. From the communes, workers marched to work on farms and in factories and to build massive public works projects, like flood controls on the Yellow River. Despite claims of staggering production successes, the Great Leap Forward was an economic disaster that, combined with bad weather, resulted in "Three Hard Years" (1959–1962) of widespread starvation that claimed over 30 million victims. For Americans it was further proof that the Communist system was seriously flawed.

until after the war, and then they were very expensive. But as prices fell the number of homes with a television rocketed from about 9 percent in 1950 to nearly 90 percent by the end of the decade. At the same time, programming developed audience-oriented time slots with cartoons and westerns for children on weekend mornings and sports for dad on Saturday and Sunday afternoons. The most watched time-slot, however, was after dinner and designed for family viewing. By 1960 most people watched television five hours a day.

Among the most popular shows during the family time slot were situation comedies ("sitcoms") like *Father Knows Best* (1953) and *Leave It to Beaver* (1957). They depicted "normal" middle-class families that were white with hardworking fathers and attractive, stay-at-home mothers. The children, usually numbering between two and four, did well in school, rarely worried about the future, and provided humorous dilemmas for Mom to untangle with common sense and sensitivity. After the dislocations of the Depression and the war, stable households seemed to represent the strength and future of the country.

Part of the family's strength and stability, many argued, came from religious faith. "The family that prays together stays together," announced the Advertising Council. Church attendance reached a historic high of 59.5 percent in 1953, and that did not include those who attended religious revivals or listened to

religious radio and television programs. Religious leaders like the **Reverend Norman Vincent Peale** and Billy Graham were commonly rated as the most important members of society. Peale's message of Christian positive thinking as a means to improve both the individual and society found a wide audience. More conservative evangelists like Graham questioned society's materialism and stressed a higher level of personal morality, and they drew huge audiences in packed stadiums. While their views on religion and the problems facing America differed, religious leaders were unanimous on the need to promote faith to prevent the spread of Communism. In keeping with the spirit of the times, Congress added "under God" to the Pledge of Allegiance in 1954 and "In God We Trust" to the American currency in 1955.

Consumerism

Another dimension of suburbia was consumerism. Radio and television bombarded their audiences with images of products Americans supposedly needed. The average television watcher saw over five hours a week of ads enticing viewers to indulge themselves by buying goods that would improve their lives. New goods were a sign of success and a matter of status, and Americans were in a shopping mood. "Our old car just didn't cut it," remarked one new home owner. "A car was a real status symbol and who didn't want to impress the neighbors?"

To sell cars and other products, advertisers used images of youth, glamour, sex appeal, and sophistication. When market research showed that it was mostly the middle and upper classes who bought new cars, automobile makers closed the gap in size, equipment, and style between luxury and nonluxury cars. Their ads emphasized "modern" styles with fins and linked

■ **Reverend Norman Vincent Peale** Minister who told his congregations that positive thinking could help them overcome all their troubles in life; his book *The Power of Positive Thinking* was an immediate bestseller.

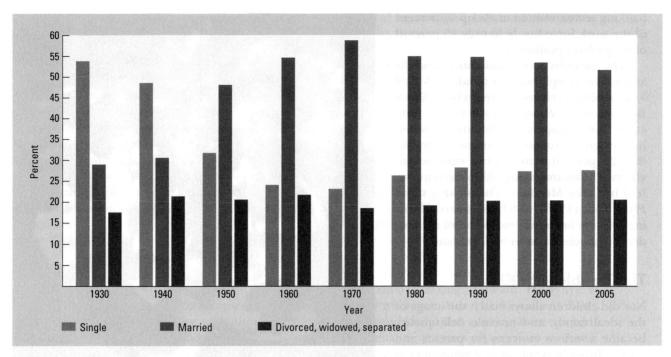

FIGURE 25.1 Marital Status of Women in the Work Force, 1930–2005
This figure shows the percentage of women in the work force from the Great Depression through 2005. While the number of women who fell into the category of divorced, widowed, and separated remained fairly constant, a significant shift occurred in the number of single and married women in the work force, with the number of single women declining as the number of married women increased.

Source: U.S. Department of Commerce, *Historical Statistics of the United States, Colonial Times to 1970,* Vol. I (Washington, D.C.: U.S. Government Printing Office, 1970), pp. 20–21, 131–132; and U.S. Department of Commerce, *Statistics of the United States, 1993* (Washington, D.C.: U.S. Government Printing Office, 1993), pp. 74, 399; U.S. Department of Commerce, *Statistical Abstract of the United States: 2003* (Washington, D.C.: U.S. Government Printing Office, 2003), pp. 390–391; Richard Smith and Susan Carlan, eds., *Historical Statistics of the United States: Earliest Times to the Present,* Vol. 2 (New York, Cambridge University Press, 2006), pp. 131–133.

the car to the idealized family that saw the "USA in their Chevrolet." The public responded, and a record 8 million new cars were sold by Detroit in 1955.

Increasingly, to pay for cars, televisions, washing machines, toys, and "Mom's night out," Americans were turning to credit, and a new form of credit was available—the all-purpose credit card. The Diner's Club credit card made its debut in 1950, followed by American Express and a host of other plastic cards. By 1958, credit purchases reached $44 billion, more than five times the amount bought on credit in 1946.

Another View of Suburbia

Unlike that of the families shown on television, life in the suburbs was not always idyllic or equal to expectations. "Togetherness" was more often seen on televisions than in real life. Studies found that of eighteen common household chores, men were willing to do three—lock up at night, do yard work, and make repairs—and that more than one-fifth of suburban

wives were unhappy with their marriages and lives. Many women complained of the drudgery and boredom of housework and the lack of understanding and affection from their husbands.

Responding to personal motives or economic needs, more married middle-class women were working outside the home, even those with young children (see Figure 25.1). While some sought self-fulfillment in careers, others worked to safeguard their family's existing **standard of living**. Most found part-time jobs or sales-clerk or clerical positions that paid low wages and provided few benefits. *Look* magazine, in a 1956 article, pointed out that about a third of the work force were women, most of whom were seeking to fill their "hope chest" or to buy "a new home freezer," and happily conceded "the top job rungs to men." Whether they conceded gracefully or not, in the

standard of living Level of material comfort as measured by the goods, services, and luxuries currently available and affordable.

households. Even with Social Security payments, as 1959 ended nearly 31 percent of those over 65 lived below the poverty line, with 8 million receiving less than $1,000 a year. Women heads of household contributed another 23 percent of those living in poverty, while throughout rural America, especially among small farmers and farm workers, poverty was common, with most earning $1,000 below the national average of about $3,500. In rural Mississippi, the annual per capita income was less than $900.

Poverty also increased in major cities as blacks and Latinos continued to migrate there. By 1960 half of all African Americans and nearly 80 percent of Latinos lived in urban centers. New York's Puerto Rican community, for example, increased more than 1,000 percent. In some cities, including Atlanta and Washington, D.C., African Americans became the majority, but they rarely exercised any political power proportionate to their numbers. No matter what the city, there was little economic opportunity; nonwhite unemployment commonly reached 40 percent.

At the same time, cities were less able or willing to provide services. Cities lost tax revenues and deteriorated at an accelerating rate as white middle- and working-class families moved into the suburbs and were followed by shopping centers and businesses. When funds were available for urban renewal and development, many city governments, like Miami and Los Angeles, used those funds to relocate and isolate minorities in specific neighborhoods away from developing entertainment, administrative, and shopping areas and upscale apartments. Cities also chose to build wider roads connecting the city to the suburbs rather than invest in mass transit within the city. In South and East Central Los Angeles, freeway interchanges gobbled up 10 percent of the housing space and divided neighborhoods and families. For nearly all minorities, discrimination and **de facto** segregation put upward mobility and escaping poverty even further out of reach.

de facto Existing in practice, though not officially established by law.

de jure According to, or brought about by, law, such as "Jim Crow" laws that separated the races throughout the South until passage of the 1964 Civil Rights Act.

■ *Brown v. Board of Education* 1954 case in which the Supreme Court ruled that separate educational facilities for different races were inherently unequal.

■ **Thurgood Marshall** Civil rights lawyer who argued thirty-two cases before the Supreme Court and won twenty-nine; he became the first African American justice of the Supreme Court in 1967.

■ **Earl Warren** Chief Justice of the Supreme Court from 1953 to 1969, under whom the Court issued decisions protecting civil rights, the rights of criminals, and First Amendment rights.

Integrating Schools

For many African Americans, poverty was just one facet of life. They also faced a legally sanctioned segregated society. Legal, or **de jure**, segregation existed not only in the South but also in the District of Columbia and several western and midwestern states. Changes had occurred, but most African Americans regarded them as minor victories, indicating no real shift in white America's racial views. By 1952 the NAACP had won cases permitting African American law and graduate students to attend white colleges and universities, even though the separate-but-equal ruling established in 1896 by the Supreme Court in *Plessy v. Ferguson* remained intact (see page 466).

A step toward more significant change came in 1954 when the Supreme Court considered the case of **Brown v. Board of Education**, *Topeka, Kansas*. The *Brown* case had started four years earlier, when Oliver Brown sued to allow his daughter to attend a nearby white school. The Kansas courts had rejected his suit, pointing out that the availability of a school for African Americans fulfilled the Supreme Court's separate-but-equal ruling. The NAACP appealed. In addressing the Supreme Court, NAACP lawyer **Thurgood Marshall** argued that the concept of "separate but equal" was inherently self-contradictory. He used statistics to show that black schools were *un*equal in financial resources and the quality and number of teachers. He also used a psychological study indicating that black children educated in a segregated environment suffered from low self-esteem. Marshall stressed that segregated educational facilities, even if physically similar, could never yield equal results.

In 1952 a divided Court was unable to make a decision, but two years later the Court heard the case again. Now sitting as chief justice was **Earl Warren**, the Republican former governor of California who had been appointed to the Court by Eisenhower in 1953. To the dismay of many who had considered Warren a legal conservative, the chief justice moved the Court down new judicial paths. Rejecting social and political consensus, the activist Supreme Court promoted new visions of society as it deliberated racial issues and individual rights. Reflecting the opinion of a unanimous Court, the *Brown* decision stated that "separate educational facilities are inherently unequal." While governor of California in 1947, Warren, following a federal court decision in *Mendez v. Westminister* (see page 711), had signed legislation ending segregation in education in the state's public schools. In 1955, in addressing how to implement *Brown*, the Court gave primary responsibility to local school boards. Not expecting integration overnight, the Court ordered school districts to proceed with "all deliberate speed." The justices instructed lower federal courts to monitor progress according to this vague guideline.

Reactions to the case were predictable. African Americans and liberals hailed the decision and hoped that segregated schools would soon be an institution of the past. Southern whites vowed to resist integration by all possible means. Virginia passed a law closing any integrated school. Southern congressional representatives issued the **Southern Manifesto**, in which they proudly pledged to oppose the *Brown* ruling. Eisenhower, who believed the Court had erred, refused to support the decision publicly.

While both political parties carefully danced around school integration and other civil rights issues, the school district in Little Rock, Arkansas, moved forward with "all deliberate speed." Central High School was scheduled to integrate in 1957. Opposing integration were the parents of the school's students and Governor Orval Faubus, who ordered National Guard troops to surround the school and prevent desegregation. When Elizabeth Eckford, one of the nine integrating students, walked toward Central High, National Guardsmen blocked her path as a hostile mob roared, "Lynch her! Lynch her!" Spat on by the jeering crowd, she retreated to her bus stop. Central High remained segregated.

For three weeks the National Guard prevented the black students from enrolling. Then on September 20 a federal judge ordered the integration of Central High School. Faubus complied and withdrew the National Guard. But segregationists remained determined to block integration and were waiting for the black students on Monday, September 23, 1957. When they discovered that the nine had slipped into the school unnoticed, the mob rushed the police lines and battered the school doors open. Inside the school, integrating student Melba Patella Beaus thought, "We were trapped. I'm going to die here, in school." Hurriedly, the students were loaded into cars and warned to duck their heads. School officials ordered the drivers to "start driving, do not stop. . . . If you hit somebody, you keep rolling, 'cause [if you stop] the kids are dead."

Integration had lasted almost three hours and was followed by rioting throughout the city, forcing the mayor to ask for federal troops to restore order. Faced with insurrection, Eisenhower, on September 24, nationalized the Arkansas National Guard and dispatched a thousand troops of the 101st Airborne Division to Little Rock. Speaking to the nation, the president emphasized that he had sent the federal troops not to integrate the schools but to uphold the law and to restore order. The distinction was lost on most white southerners, who fumed as soldiers protected the nine black students for the rest of the school year.

The following school year (1957–1958), the city closed its high schools rather than integrate them. To prevent such actions, the Supreme Court ruled

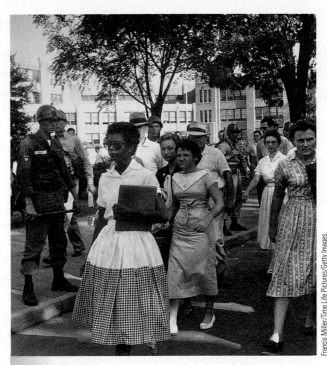

As Elizabeth Eckford approached Little Rock's Central High School, the crowd began to hurl curses, and a National Guardsman blocked her entrance into the school with his rifle. Terrified, she retreated down the street away from the threatening mob. Weeks later, this photograph was taken when Eckford, with army troops protecting her, finally attended—and integrated—Central High School.

Francis Miller/Time Life Pictures/Getty Images.

in **Cooper v. Aaron** (1959) that an African American's right to attend school could not "be nullified openly" or "by evasive schemes for segregation." Little Rock's high schools reopened, and integration slowly spread to the lower grades. But in Little Rock, as in other communities, many white families fled the integrated public schools and enrolled their children in private schools that were beyond the reach of the federal courts. With no endorsement from the White House and entrenched southern opposition, "all deliberate speed" amounted to a snail's pace. By 1965, less than 2 percent of all southern schools were integrated.

■ **Southern Manifesto** Statement issued by one hundred southern congressmen in 1954, after the *Brown v. Board of Education* decision, pledging to oppose desegregation.

■ **Cooper v. Aaron** Supreme Court decision (1958) that barred state authorities from interfering with desegregation either directly or through strategies of evasion.

It Matters Today

The Brown Decision

The *Brown v. Board of Education* decision by the Supreme Court remains a milestone in American history. "It is doubtful that any child may reasonably be expected to succeed in life if he is denied the opportunity of an education. Such an opportunity," the Court wrote, "is a right which must be made available to all in equal terms." It raised expectations, it desegregated public schools, but it also fell short of its expectations and has not provided effective integration or equality of education. Other cases have since tested the definitions of equality and the methods used to achieve racial diversity. Until the late 1970s, the Court's decisions upheld the view that race could be used as a determining factor to achieve racial diversity. However, since then, several of the Court's decisions have indicated that the use of race has discriminated against Caucasians—a reverse discrimination. Is there a way, one Justice recently asked, to decide when the "use of race to achieve diversity" is benign or discriminatory?

- Some argue that the Supreme Court should apply "color-blind" criteria when deciding if institutions and business can use race to create racial diversity. How does this view reflect the view of the original *Brown* decision?
- Research the issues behind the December 2006 Supreme Court cases involving the Seattle, Washington, and Louisville, Missouri, school districts. Compare the issues to the decisions made by the Court on the issue in June 2007.

The Montgomery Bus Boycott

While the nation responded to the *Brown* decision, other events involving civil rights grabbed national headlines, including the death of Emmett Till and the Montgomery bus boycott. In 1955, Till, an African American teenager from Chicago, visited relatives in Mississippi and was brutally tortured and murdered for speaking to a white woman—saying "Bye, baby"— without her permission. In the trial that followed, the two confessed murderers were acquitted. It was not an unexpected verdict in Mississippi, but it and the brutality of the murder shocked much of the nation.

Later in 1955, on December 1 in Montgomery, Alabama, **Rosa Parks** refused to give up her seat on a city bus so that a white man could sit. At 42, Mrs. Parks earned $23 a week as a seamstress, and she had not boarded the bus with the intention of disobeying the seating law, although she strongly opposed it. But that afternoon, her fatigue and humiliation were suddenly too much. She refused to move and was arrested.

Hearing of her arrest, local African American community leaders saw an opportunity to contest segregation. When the city and the bus company refused to consider a petition for more equitable bus seating, black leaders called for a boycott of the bus line.

On December 5, 1955, the night before the boycott began, nearly four thousand people filled and surrounded Holt Street Baptist Church to hear **Martin Luther King, Jr.**, the newly selected leader of the boycott movement—now called the Montgomery Improvement Association. The 26-year-old King firmly believed that the church had a social justice mission and that violence and hatred, even when considered justified, brought only ruin. In shaping that evening's speech, he wrestled with the problem of how to balance disobedience with peace, confrontation with civility, and rebellion with tradition—and his words overcame the contradictions, electrifying the crowd: "We are here this evening to say to those who have mistreated us so long that we are tired of being segregated and humiliated, tired of being kicked about by the brutal feet of oppression." King asked the crowd to boycott the buses, to protest

■ **Rosa Parks** Black seamstress who refused to give up her seat to a white man on a bus in Montgomery, Alabama, in 1955, triggering a bus boycott that energized the civil rights movement.

■ **Martin Luther King, Jr.** Ordained Baptist minister and civil rights leader committed to nonviolence; a brilliant orator, he led many of the important protests of the 1950s and 1960s.

(Left and right) AP Images.

On December 1, 1955, Rosa Parks made a fateful choice—she refused to give up her seat to a white man on a Montgomery, Alabama, bus. Her act of defiance ignited a grassroots effort by African Americans to eliminate discrimination, and with it Martin Luther King, Jr., emerged as a national leader for civil rights. These pictures show the Montgomery Police Department's mug shots of Parks and King, following their arrests. "I had no idea history was being made," Parks stated later. "I was just tired of giving in."

"courageously, and yet with dignity and Christian love," and when confronted with violence, to "bless them that curse you."

On December 6, Rosa Parks was tried, found guilty, and fined $10, plus $4 for court costs. She appealed, and the boycott, 90 percent effective, stretched into days, weeks, and finally months. Police issued basketfuls of traffic tickets to drivers taking part in the car pools that provided transportation for boycotters. Insurance companies canceled their automobile coverage, and acid was poured on their cars. On January 30, 1956, someone threw a stick of dynamite that destroyed King's front porch, almost injuring King's wife and a friend. King remained calm, reminding supporters to avoid violence and persevere. Finally, as the boycott approached its first anniversary, the Supreme Court ruled in *Gayle et al. v. Browser* (1956) that the city's and bus company's policy of segregation

was unconstitutional. "Praise the Lord. God has spoken from Washington, D.C.," cried one boycotter.

The Montgomery bus boycott shattered the traditional white view that African Americans accepted segregation, and it marked the beginning of a pattern of nonviolent resistance. Across the South thousands of African Americans were eager to take to the streets and to use the federal courts to achieve equality. Building on the energy generated by the boycott, in 1956, King and other black leaders formed a new civil rights organization, the **Southern Christian Leadership Conference** (SCLC).

■ **Southern Christian Leadership Conference** (SCLC)
Group formed by Martin Luther King, Jr., and others after the Montgomery bus boycott; it became the backbone of the civil rights movement in the 1950s and 1960s.

Ike and Civil Rights

As the Montgomery boycott steamrolled into the headlines month after month, from the White House came either silence or carefully selected platitudes. When asked, Eisenhower gave elusive replies: "I believe we should not stagnate. . . . I plead for understanding, for really sympathetic consideration of a problem. . . . I am for moderation, but I am for progress; that is exactly what I am for in this thing." Personally, Eisenhower believed that government, especially the executive branch, had little role in integration. Max Rabb, the president's adviser on minority affairs, thought the

■ **Civil Rights Act of 1957** Created the U.S. Commission on Civil Rights, which primarily investigated restrictions on voting, and the Civil Rights Division of the Department of Justice.

"Negroes were being too aggressive." On a political level, cabinet members and Eisenhower were disappointed in the low number of blacks who had voted Republican in 1952 and 1956.

But not all within the administration were unsympathetic toward civil rights. Attorney General Herbert Brownell drafted the first civil rights legislation since Reconstruction. The **Civil Rights Act of 1957** passed Congress after a year of political maneuvering, having gained the support of Democratic majority leader Lyndon B. Johnson of Texas. A moderate law, it provided for the formation of a Commission on Civil Rights and opened the possibility of using federal lawsuits to ensure voter rights. A second act passed Congress in 1960 that strengthened efforts to use the courts to gain voting rights, but like its predecessor, it was too weak to counter white opposition and violence in the South. Still, Congress had acted and many African Americans hoped that a new president might provide the needed leadership to achieve equal rights.

Individual Voices

Ray Kroc Explains the McDonald's Approach to Business

Around the world few symbols are better known than the Golden Arches of McDonald's. Since its humble origins in San Bernardino, California, more than thirty thousand restaurants now exist in 191 countries. Unlike the original reproduced here, today's McDonald's menus provide a wide variety of choices, from Big Macs to salads to vegetarian burgers in India and Shogun Burgers in Japan.

　　Ray Kroc's autobiography, *Grinding It Out*, provides insight not only into his personal climb to prominence but also into the many innovations he implemented that changed the economics of business. Kroc's innovations helped shape both the fast-food industry and the development of a consumer society based on large-scale retailing and marketing. The following excerpts demonstrate some of the techniques Kroc and McDonald's used that changed the world's eating habits and also provided a model for other mass-consumer retailers.

❶ Compare this original McDonald's menu to a menu at today's McDonald's. What do the differences suggest about McDonald's and American eating habits?

McDonald's Menu—1956 ❶

Hamburgers	15 cents	Root Beer	10 cents
Cheeseburgers	19 cents	Coke	10 cents
Malt Shakes	20 cents	Milk	10 cents
French Fries	10 cents	Coffee	10 cents
Orange	10 cents		

Source: "McDonald's menu from the 1950's" found in Pauline Maier, et al. *Inventing America: A History of the United States,* Vol 2, W. W. Norton, 2003, p. 1000.

It requires a certain kind of mind to see beauty in a hamburger bun. Yet, is it any more unusual to find grace in the texture and softly curved silhouette of a bun than [in] . . . the arrangement of textures and colors of a butterfly wing? Not if you are a McDonald's man. Not if you view the bun as an essential material in the art of serving a great many meals fast. Then this plump, yeasty mass becomes an object worthy of somber study. . . .

❷ In what other ways might McDonald's have lowered its costs to make its product more competitive?

　　We set the standards of quality and recommended methods for packaging. . . . Our stores are selling only nine items, and they were buying only thirty-five or forty items with which to make the nine. So a McDonald's restaurant's purchasing power . . . was concentrated. A McDonald's bought more buns, more catsup, more mustard, and so forth, and this gave it a terrific position in the marketplace for those items. We enhanced that position by figuring out ways a supplier could lower his costs, which meant . . . that he could afford to sell to a McDonald's for less. Bulk packaging was one way. . . . **❷**

❸ How does Ray Kroc's statement on American small business reflect the hopes and values of the 1950s in America?

　　. . . [A] McDonald's hamburger patty is a piece of meat with character. The first thing that distinguishes it from the patties that many other places pass off as hamburgers is that it is all beef. There are no hearts or other alien goodies ground into our patties. The fat content . . . is a prescribed nineteen percent. . . . We decided that our patties would be ten to a pound. . . . There was also a science in stacking patties. If you made the stack too high, the ones at the bottom would be misshapen and dried out. So we arrived at the optimum stack, and that determined the height of our meat suppliers' packages. . . .

❹ In this paragraph, Kroc provides a formula for McDonald's success, but would these aspects have been as important if he had not made the purchasing, packing, and marketing innovations that he did?

　　Since a McDonald's restaurant is a prime example of American small business in action, the husband-wife team is basic to us. Typically, the husband will look after operations and maintenance while his wife keeps the books and handles personnel. . . . **❸**

　　My way of fighting the competition is the positive approach. Stress your own strengths, emphasize quality, service, cleanliness and value, and the competition will wear itself out trying to keep up. **❹**

Source: Excerpt from Ray Kroc, *Grinding It Out: The Making of McDonald's* (Chicago: Henry Regnery Company, 1977)

Study Tools

SUMMARY

"Had enough?" Republicans asked voters in 1952. Voters responded by electing Eisenhower. Though promising change, Eisenhower in practice chose foreign and domestic policies that continued the basic patterns established by Truman. Republicans were able to cut domestic programs, but public acceptance of existing federal responsibilities prevented any large-scale dismantling of the New Deal. In foreign policy, the New Look relied on new tactics, but Eisenhower continued containment, expanding American influence in southern Asia and the Middle East. Although the Soviets spoke of peaceful coexistence, relations with the Soviet Union deteriorated over the decade, and Moscow seemed to score victories with *Sputnik* and in Cuba.

Reflecting the image of Ike in the White House, the 1950s spawned comforting, if not entirely accurate, images of America centered on affluent suburbs and a growing consumer culture. The postwar trend continued with white working-class and middle-class Americans fulfilling their expectations in a society shaped by cars, expanded purchasing power, and middle-class values. Critics argued that America's middle-class culture bred a social grayness and stifled individualism. Yet life in suburbia did not necessarily fit either the popular or the critics' image. Many people behaved contrary to the supposed norms of family and suburban culture. Teens and young adults, especially, turned to forms of expression that seemed to reject established norms and values.

Outside the suburbs another America existed, where economic realities, social prejudices, and entrenched politics blocked equality and upward mobility. Although declining, poverty persisted, especially in rural America and among minorities living in urban areas. While poverty remained largely ignored, it became increasingly difficult to ignore the actions taken by African Americans to overturn decades of segregation. By the end of the decade, civil rights had emerged as an issue that neither political party nor white, suburban America could avoid.

CHRONOLOGY
The Fifties

1950	Korean War begins
1951	Mattachine Society formed
	Alan Freed's "Moondog's Rock 'n' Roll Party"
1952	Dwight David Eisenhower elected president
	United States tests hydrogen bomb
1953	Korean armistice at Panmunjom
	CIA helps overthrow Mohammed Mossadegh in Iran
	Termination programs for American Indians implemented
	Earl Warren appointed chief justice of Supreme Court
	Father Knows Best debuts on television
	Department of Health, Education, and Welfare created
1954	*Brown v. Board of Education*
	Army-McCarthy hearings
	CIA helps overthrow Jacobo Arbenz in Guatemala
	Geneva Agreement (Vietnam)
	SEATO founded
1955	Montgomery bus boycott
	AFL-CIO merger
	Geneva Summit
	Montgomery, Alabama, bus boycott begins
1956	Federal Highway Act
	Southern Christian Leadership Conference formed
	Eisenhower reelected
	Suez crisis
	Soviets invade Hungary
	Elvis Presley records "Heartbreak Hotel"
1957	Little Rock crisis
	Civil Rights Act
	Eisenhower Doctrine
	United States joins Baghdad Pact
	Soviets launch *Sputnik*
	Baby boom peaks at 4.3 million births
1958	Berlin crisis
	United States sends troops to Lebanon
	National Defense Education Act
	NASA established
1959	Fidel Castro takes control in Cuba
	Nikita Khrushchev visits the United States
	Cooper v. Aaron
1960	Soviets shoot down U-2 and capture pilot
	Paris Summit

Study Tools

FOCUS QUESTIONS

If you have mastered this chapter, you should be able to answer these questions and to explain the terms that follow the questions.

1. ☆ *What were the popular images of Eisenhower, and how did they compare with reality?*

2. ☆ *What constraints did Eisenhower face in trying to roll back New Deal programs?*

3. ☆ *How did Eisenhower alter the federal government?*

4. ☆ *What were the weaknesses of the New Look and how did Eisenhower address them?*

5. ☆ *What tactics did the Eisenhower administration pursue in the "third world," especially in the Middle East and Latin America, to protect American interests?*

6. ☆ *What new economic factors contributed to prosperity in the 1950s?*

7. ☆ *What stresses and contradictions were at work beneath the placid surface of suburbia? Who voiced criticism and how did they express it?*

8. ☆ *Why were rock 'n' roll and rebellious teens seen as threats to social norms?*

9. ☆ *How did African Americans attack de jure segregation in American society during the 1950s?*

10. ☆ *What role did the federal government play in promoting civil rights?*

KEY TERMS

Federal Highway Act   *(p. 720)*

Sputnik I   *(p. 720)*

Sputnik II   *(p. 720)*

National Defense Student Loans   *(p. 720)*

Army-McCarthy hearings   *(p. 721)*

New Look   *(p. 721)*

massive retaliation   *(p. 721)*

Baghdad Pact   *(p. 723)*

Warsaw Pact   *(p. 723)*

third world   *(p. 723)*

Central Intelligence Agency   *(p. 723)*

Shah Mohammad Reza Pahlavi   *(p. 723)*

Eisenhower Doctrine   *(p. 725)*

Viet Minh   *(p. 727)*

domino theory   *(p. 727)*

Geneva Agreement   *(p. 727)*

Nikita Khrushchev   *(p. 727)*

Keynesianism   *(p. 729)*

Reverend Norman Vincent Peale   *(p. 732)*

Elvis Presley   *(p. 734)*

Beats   *(p. 735)*

Brown v. Board of Education   *(p. 736)*

Thurgood Marshall   *(p. 736)*

Earl Warren   *(p. 736)*

Southern Manifesto   *(p. 737)*

Cooper v. Aaron   *(p. 737)*

Rosa Parks   *(p. 738)*

Martin Luther King, Jr.   *(p. 738)*

Southern Christian Leadership Conference   *(p. 739)*

Civil Rights Act of 1957   *(p. 740)*

Go to the History CourseMate website for primary source links, study tools, and review materials for this chapter. www.cengagebrain.com

26 Great Promises, Bitter Disappointments, 1960–1968

Behind the Stories

John F. Kennedy's assassination, on November 22, 1963, remains a moment burned into the national memory—even today those who heard the news can tell you where they were. I was in geometry class, and I would soon wonder, as many others did and still do, whether the assassin, Lee Harvey Oswald, was acting alone or as part of a larger conspiracy. Why did he, or they, choose to kill the president?

In many ways our understanding of the 1960s is as uncertain as that of the assassination. Historians have no clear-cut definition of the 1960s. Disagreements abound. When did the "sixties" start and end? Were they the culmination of liberalism or its demise? Did a movement for civil rights turn into a revolutionary attack on the values and mores of society? Chapters 26 and 27 make the complexities of the sixties evident as events and issues interconnect. One useful way to understand the period is through the political and social lens of liberalism. Be aware, however, that unlike in previous decades, the momentum for change was pushed by strong grassroots movements. Grassroots expectations did not always jibe with the agenda of lawgivers. But for a while each supported the other, spurring the belief that political and social inequalities could be rectified.

The first half of the 1960s seemed full of successes: a war on poverty, tax cuts, civil rights legislation, medical care for the elderly and poor—New Deal liberalism was triumphant. But even as liberalism achieved new heights, disillusionment appeared. Were expectations too high? Some within the grassroots movements argued that racism, poverty, sexism, and gender bias continued. New voices emerged, pronouncing that society remained flawed, that liberalism had achieved no real expansion of equality or individual freedom. By 1966, successes receded and critiques of liberalism grew, merging with opposition to the war in Vietnam, contributing to a conservative backlash and resurgence.

—J.G.

744

Individual Choices
Eunice Kennedy Shriver

In 1963, Eunice Kennedy Shriver wrote that those with severe intellectual disabilities needed a champion to change the way that people viewed them. Following her death in 2009, a commentator wrote that the mentally challenged "don't catch many breaks" but that "one island of inclusion: the Special Olympics" existed "because Eunice Shriver . . . insisted on looking differently at disability. She offered love without pity, a chance to race and win, and to win just by racing."

Eunice Kennedy Shriver

Over the years, others commented that if she had been born a man, Eunice Kennedy would have been president. But for a girl born in 1921, even into the Kennedy household, a role in politics was not in the cards. Instead, she was encouraged to take an active role in what she called "social work." Her involvement with intellectual disability arose from two sources: her experiences with her intellectually disabled sister Rosemary and a prod from her father. In the 1950s, Joseph Kennedy, Sr., was considering using his Kennedy Foundation to support research on mental retardation and asked her and Sargent Shriver to investigate the possibilities. The results were her marriage to Shriver and a commitment to bettering the lives of the mentally challenged.

Their investigation found that what was referred to as mental retardation (MR) was largely ignored by the scientific community, institutions, and governmental agencies. They discovered that families with mentally retarded children were isolated and frequently "closeted" their children away from public view. They believed that MR needed to have a national priority, and Eunice Shriver was determined to see it through. In 1960, she prodded her brother, John Kennedy, who was running for president, to make children's health and MR part of his program. He agreed and over the next three years, she would needle, cajole, and lobby him to maintain his commitment to the mentally challenged. Robert Kennedy joked that the president said, ". . . give Eunice whatever she wants so I can get her off the phone and get on with the business of government."

She also lobbied Congress, medical researchers and institutions, and the public (as illustrated in the Individual Voices feature at the end of this chapter). It was her "sense of mission" that added the weight of the federal government to

Eunice Kennedy Shriver

improving the lives of those with mental disabilities. But government programs were only part of the solution. There was the issue of dignity. Popular perceptions of the mentally challenged needed to be changed. Families needed to stop hiding those afflicted. The cycle of social isolationism had to be broken. Eunice Shriver's solution would become the Special Olympics.

In 1962, Eunice Shriver created a day camp for children with mental disabilitiies at her Maryland home. "Camp Shriver" was a success and the idea spread. But she looked beyond localized day and summer recreational camps. She wanted a national venue that would be year-round and reach a wider public audience. In 1968, the Chicago Parks and Recreation Department sponsored a national track and field competition for children with mental retardation. Over nine hundred children from twenty-seven states and Canada competed, but only about twenty parents watched. "Parents had not yet learned they could be proud of their mentally retarded kids," observed one organizer. As the first competitions began, Eunice Shriver unexpectedly announced that the Kennedy Foundation would support "a national Special Olympics training program for all mentally retarded children everywhere," and that there would be an "international Special Olympics in 1970 and every two years thereafter." The result has significantly shifted the nation's attention and perception. Today, nearly 3 million athletes of all ages participate in Special Olympics sports training and competition in more than 180 countries.

The 1960s evoke visions of change, of protest marches, demonstrations, and governmental activism. It appeared that new opportunities existed to generate change through individual, group, and governmental action. Kennedy's election provided a symbol of youth and vigor and raised expectations that the activism in the streets would be joined by that of government.

The New Frontier promised prosperity and change, but strong political opposition in Congress made achieving new domestic goals difficult. Kennedy preferred foreign policy, finding fewer political constraints there. A staunch Cold Warrior, he promised to confront global communism and regain lost ground. His new strategy, called "flexible response," emphasized the developing regions of the world. Yet despite his efforts, the erection of the Berlin Wall, the Cuban missile crisis, and events in Vietnam heightened Cold War tensions while stretching American commitments.

Lyndon Johnson inherited Kennedy's agendas and added his own imprint. Prior to the 1964 presidential election, Johnson passed a civil rights bill and presented the nation with proposals for a Great Society. An onslaught of legislation that waged war on poverty and discrimination followed. Great Society measures increased education and welfare programs, expanded voting rights, and created a national system of healthcare for the aged and poor. By mid-decade liberalism was at high tide, and new voices were pushing for further reform and equality. Some of the voices were militant ones that divided and challenged the leadership and assumptions of liberalism.

THE POLITICS OF ACTION

★ How successful was the Kennedy administration in achieving its domestic agenda?

★ What form of African American activism pushed the civil rights movement forward, and how did Kennedy respond to those efforts?

■ **New Frontier** Program for social and educational reform put forward by President John F. Kennedy and largely resisted by Congress.

Republicans had every reason to worry as the 1960 presidential campaign neared. The last years of the 1950s were not kind to the Republican Party. Neither the president nor Republicans nor Congress appeared able to deal with the problems of the country—civil rights agitation, a slowing economy, and a soaring national debt that had reached $488 billion. Cold War victories seemed equally illusive as the Soviets launched *Sputnik* and gained a foothold in Cuba. Vice President Richard Nixon calculated the Republican candidate would have to get practically all Republican votes, more than half of the independents—and, in addition, the votes of 5 to 6 million Democrats to become president.

The 1960 Campaign

On the Democratic side stood John Fitzgerald Kennedy, a youthful, vigorous senator from Massachusetts. A Harvard graduate, Kennedy came from a wealthy Catholic family. Some worried about his young age (43) and lack of experience. Others worried about his religion—no Catholic had ever been elected president. To offset these possible liabilities, Kennedy astutely added the politically savvy Senate majority leader Lyndon Johnson of Texas to the ticket, called for a new generation of leadership, and suggested that those who were making religion an issue were bigots.

He challenged the nation to enter a **New Frontier** to improve the overall quality of life of all Americans, and to stand fast against the Communist threat. He offered action, and empowerment to the government, people, and institutions.

Facing Kennedy was Nixon. To distance himself from the image of Eisenhower's leadership, he promised a forceful, energetic presidency, vowing to improve the quality of life and support civil rights. To distinguish himself from Kennedy, he emphasized his executive experience and history of anticommunism. Several political commentators called the candidates "two peas in a pod" and speculated that the election would probably hinge on appearances more than on issues.

Trailing in the opinion polls and hoping to give his campaign a boost, Nixon agreed to televised debates. Kennedy seized the opportunity, recognizing that the candidate who appeared more calm and knowledgeable—more "presidential"—would "win" each debate. Before the camera's eye, in the war of images, Kennedy appeared fresh and confident and spoke directly to the camera. Nixon appeared tired and haggard and looked at Kennedy rather than the camera. The contrasts were critical. Unable to

The 1960 presidential race was at the time the closest in recent history, with many people believing that the outcome hinged on the public's perception of the candidates during their nationally televised debates. The majority of viewers believed that Kennedy (left) won the debates and looked more in control and presidential than Nixon.

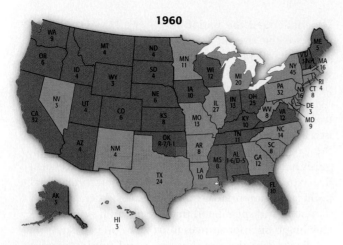

1960

Candidate (Party)	Electoral Vote		Popular Vote	
Kennedy (Democrat)	303	56.50%	34,226,731	49.7%
Nixon (Republican)	219	40.75%	34,108,157	49.5%
Byrd (Independent)	15	2.75%	501,643	0.7%

MAP 26.1 Election of 1960
Although Richard Nixon won in more states than John F. Kennedy, in the closest presidential election in the twentieth century, Kennedy defeated his Republican opponent by a slim 84 electoral votes and fewer than 119,000 popular votes. Copyright © Cengage Learning

see Nixon, the radio audience believed he won the debates, but to the 70 million television viewers, the winner was the self-assured Kennedy. The televised debates helped Kennedy, but victory depended on his holding the Democratic coalition together, maintaining southern Democratic support while wooing African American and liberal voters. The Texan Johnson used his political clout to keep the South largely loyal while Kennedy blasted the lack of Republican leadership on civil rights. Every vote was critical but when the ballots were counted, Kennedy had secured popular and electoral victories, although Nixon carried more states, 25 to 21 (see Map 26.1).

urban renewal Effort to revitalize run-down areas of cities by providing federal funding for the construction of apartment houses, office buildings, and public facilities.

■ **new economics** Planning and shaping the national economy through the use of tax policies and federal spending as recommended by Keynesian economics.

fiscal policy The use of government spending to stimulate or slow down the economy.

■ **sit-in** The act of sitting peacefully in an establishment to protest its policies—a tactic, used to protest segregation, that energized civil rights activism at the start of the 1960s.

The New Frontier

The weather in Washington was frigid when Kennedy gave his inaugural address, but his speech fired the imagination of the nation. He pledged to march against "the common enemies of man: tyranny, poverty, disease, and war itself." He then invited all Americans to participate, exhorting them to "ask not what your country can do for you; ask what you can do for your country." Believing that most of the nation's problems were "technical" and could be solved by experts, Kennedy selected advisers with know-how who were willing to take action. He chose from the ranks of Rhodes scholars, Harvard professors, and successful businessmen, including Ford Motor Company president Robert McNamara, who was tapped for secretary of defense. In a more controversial move, Kennedy named his brother Robert as attorney general. Many hailed Kennedy's choices as representing "the best and the brightest." But not everyone thought so. Referring to their lack of political background, Speaker of the House Sam Rayburn, a Democrat, remarked that he would "feel a whole lot better . . . if just one of them had run for sheriff once."

Kennedy asked Congress for a wide range of domestic programs, including a national health system and increased federal aid to education, but, like Truman, he received only modest results. By 1963, Congress had approved small increases in Social Security, the minimum wage (to $1.25 an hour), and a housing and **urban renewal** bill. He had better luck with the economy, which grew by 13 percent.

To spur the economy out of a recession that began in 1960, Kennedy turned to the "**new economics**" advocated by Walter Heller, his chairman of the Council of Economic Advisers. Heller recommended an aggressive Keynesian use of monetary and **fiscal policies** including tax cuts to stimulate the economy. While the new economics helped, it was the nearly 10 percent increase in defense spending that energized the economy. The Soviets were still leading the missile race, and Soviet cosmonaut Yuri Gagarin had recently orbited the earth. Congress also approved more money for NASA and the Apollo program to send a man to the moon and back. In 1969, after the expenditure of nearly $33 billion, Neil Armstrong would become the first human to step on the surface of the moon.

Kennedy and Civil Rights

When Kennedy was elected African Americans showed a guarded confidence that the new administration would take a more active role in aiding the civil rights movement. At the same time, most realized that the movement should not wait quietly for Kennedy to act. Civil rights activists continued to build on momentum created by the **sit-in** movement, which had begun in February

1960 when four black freshmen at North Carolina Agricultural and Technical College in Greensboro, North Carolina, decided to integrate the public lunch counter at the local F. W. Woolworth store (see Map 26.2). They entered the store, sat down at the lunch counter, and ordered a meal. Refused service, but not arrested, they sat until the store closed. The next day twenty black A&T students sat at the lunch counter demanding service.

The movement quickly spread to more than 140 cities, including some outside the South, in Nevada, Illinois, and Ohio. In some cities, including Greensboro, integration was achieved with a minimum of resistance. But elsewhere, particularly in the Deep South, thousands of participants in sit-ins were beaten and jailed. Most of those taking part were young and initially unorganized, but as the movement grew, civil rights groups moved to incorporate the new tactic and its practitioners. In April 1960, SCLC official Ella Baker helped form the **Student Nonviolent Coordinating Committee** (SNCC, pronounced "snick"), a new civil rights organization built around the sit-in movement. Although its statement of purpose emphasized nonviolence, SNCC members were more militant than other civil rights activists. As one stated, "We do not intend to wait placidly for those rights which are already legally and morally ours."

When Kennedy took office, the sit-in movement was spreading across the South as students from colleges and universities sought to integrate places of public accommodation. In this picture, whites harass students from Tougaloo College who are sitting-in at a Woolworth lunch counter in Jackson, Mississippi.

Despite the sit-ins, with southern Democrats entrenched in Congress, Kennedy saw little reason to "raise hell" and waste legislative efforts on civil rights. Instead, he relied on limited executive action, appointing African Americans to federal positions (more than any previous president), including NAACP lawyer Thurgood Marshall to the U.S. Court of Appeals. Civil rights activists applauded, but pointed out that Kennedy also appointed segregationists and was not rushing to fulfill his campaign pledge to ban segregation in federal housing. (Kennedy signed the order in November 1962.)

To prod executive action, James Farmer of the Congress of Racial Equality (CORE) announced a series of "**freedom rides**" to force integration in southern bus stations. In December 1960, the Supreme Court had ruled in *Boynton v. Virginia* that all interstate buses, trains, and terminals were to be desegregated, and Farmer intended to make that decision a reality. The buses of riders left Washington, D.C., in May 1961, headed toward Alabama and Mississippi (see Map 26.2). Trouble was anticipated, and in Anniston, Alabama, angry whites attacked the buses, setting them on fire and severely beating several freedom riders. "[I]t was going to be the end of me," one freedom rider recalled thinking when his

■ **Student Nonviolent Coordinating Committee** (SNCC) Organization formed in 1960 to give young blacks a greater voice in the civil rights movement; it initiated black voter registration drives, sit-ins, and freedom rides.

■ **freedom rides** An effort in which civil rights protesters rode buses throughout the South in 1961, despite attacks and arrests, seeking to achieve the integration of bus terminals.

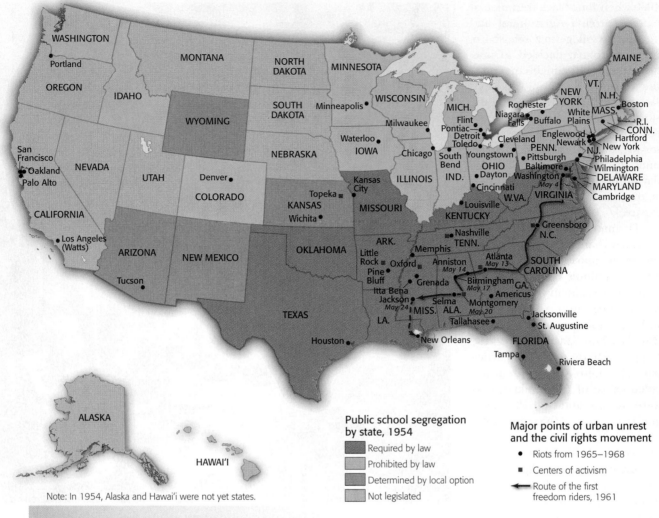

MAP 26.2 The Struggle for Civil Rights, 1960–1968
In the mid-1950s, African Americans confronted the system of prejudice and segregation that existed across the country. This map shows hot spots of civil rights activism and flash points of urban unrest from 1960 to 1968. Copyright © Cengage Learning

Public school segregation by state, 1954
- Required by law
- Prohibited by law
- Determined by local option
- Not legislated

Major points of urban unrest and the civil rights movement
- Riots from 1965–1968
- Centers of activism
- Route of the first freedom riders, 1961

Note: In 1954, Alaska and Hawai'i were not yet states.

bus caught fire. Some buses continued on to Birmingham where the savagery continued. As Farmer hoped, the violence forced the attorney general to place federal agents on the buses. Robert Kennedy also negotiated state and local protection for the riders through Alabama. When the buses arrived in Montgomery, Alabama, however, the police and National Guard escorts vanished, and a large mob attacked the riders and federal agents. Furious, the attorney general deputized local federal officials as marshals and

ordered them to escort the freedom riders to the state line, where Mississippi forces would take over. Battered and bloodied, the riders continued to the state capital, Jackson. There they were peacefully arrested for violating Mississippi's recently passed **public order laws**. The jails quickly filled as more freedom riders arrived and were arrested—328 by the end of the summer. The freedom rides ended in September 1961 when the administration declared that the Interstate Commerce Commission would uphold the Supreme Court decision prohibiting segregation. Faced with direct federal involvement, most state and local authorities desegregated bus and train terminals.

Robert Kennedy hoped similar direct involvement would ease the integration of the University of Mississippi by **James Meredith** in September 1962. A hundred federal marshals arrived to guard Meredith, but thousands of white students and nonstu-

public order laws Laws passed by many southern communities to discourage civil rights protests; the laws allowed the police to arrest anyone suspected of intending to disrupt public order.

■ **James Meredith** Black student admitted to the University of Mississippi under federal court order in 1962; in spite of rioting by racist mobs, he finished the year and graduated in 1963.

dents attacked Meredith and the marshals. Two people were killed, and nearly all the marshals were injured before five thousand army troops arrived and restored order. Protected by federal forces, Meredith finished the year. In May 1963, the University of Mississippi had its first African American graduate.

As Meredith prepared to graduate, Martin Luther King, Jr., organized a series of protest marches to overturn segregation in Birmingham. King expected a violent white reaction, which would force federal intervention and raise national awareness and support. On Good Friday, 1963, King led the first march. He was quickly arrested and, from his cell, wrote a nineteen-page "letter" defending his confrontational tactics. The "Letter from a Birmingham Jail" called for immediate and continuous peaceful civil disobedience. Freedom was "never given voluntarily by the oppressor," King asserted, but "must be demanded by the oppressed." Smuggled out of jail, read aloud in churches, and printed in newspapers across the nation, the letter rallied support for King's efforts.

In Birmingham the marches continued, and on May 3 young and old alike filled the city's streets. Sheriff "Bull" Connor's police attacked the marchers with nightsticks, attack dogs, and high-pressure fire hoses. Television caught it all, including the arrest of more than thirteen hundred battered and bruised children. Connor's brutality not only horrified much of the American public but also caused many Birmingham blacks to reject the tactic of nonviolence. The following day, some clashed with the police, and fearing more violence, King and Birmingham's business element met on May 10. To ease tensions, business owners agreed to hire black salespeople. But neither the agreement nor King's pleading halted the violence, and two days later President Kennedy ordered three thousand troops to Birmingham to maintain order and to uphold the integration agreement. "The sound of the explosion in Birmingham," King observed, "reached all the way to Washington."

Birmingham encouraged Kennedy to make civil rights a priority. In June 1963, he announced that America could not be truly free "until all its citizens were free" and sent Congress civil rights legislation

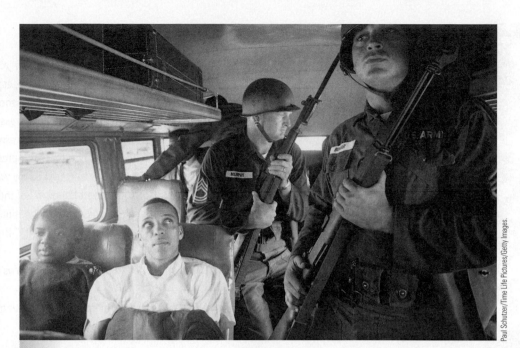

In May 1961, freedom riders left Washington, D.C., for New Orleans on a mission to integrate bus terminals along the way. At stops in Alabama and Mississippi, the buses and riders were attacked. After negotiations between the Kennedy administration and Mississippi officials, it was agreed that Mississippi National Guard members, as pictured here, would guarantee the safety of the riders by escorting them on the buses. As part of the agreement, the administration allowed Mississippi officials to arrest the riders once they reached Jackson, Mississippi, on charges of traveling "for the avowed purpose of inflaming public opinion."

that would mandate integration in public places. To pressure Congress to act on the bill, King and other civil rights leaders organized a **March on Washington**. During the August 28 march, King gave an address that electrified the throng. He warned about a "whirlwind of revolt" if black rights were denied. "I have a dream," he offered, "that my four little children will one day live . . . where they will not be judged by the color of their skin but by the content of their character. . . . that even Mississippi could become an oasis of freedom and justice" and that "all of God's children, black men and white men, Jews and Gentiles, Protestants and Catholics, will be able to join hands and sing . . . 'Free at last! Free at last! Thank God almighty, we are free at last!'" It was a stirring speech, but it did not move Congress to act. The civil rights bill stalled in committee, while in the South whites vowed to maintain segregation, and racial violence continued. In Birmingham, within weeks of King's speech, a church bombing killed four young black girls attending Sunday school.

■ **March on Washington** Meeting of a quarter of a million civil rights supporters in Washington in 1963, at which Martin Luther King, Jr., delivered his "I Have a Dream" speech.

It Matters Today

"Letter from a Birmingham Jail"

In 1963, Martin Luther King, Jr., wrote and smuggled out of a Birmingham jail a lengthy letter calling for support for his civil rights struggle. The letter was in response to those, especially within the clergy, who argued that his confrontational approach of disobedience generated too much backlash and that negotiation was a better course. He sought not only to address that issue of disobedience to "unjust laws," but to point out that he was a centrist in responding to segregation and discrimination. Working from an assumption that "[o]ppressed people cannot remain oppressed forever," King asserted that his path was the only way out of a "frightening racial nightmare." He rejected both "the do-nothingism" of those worn out and "drained of self-respect" by racism, and the angry voices of black nationalists, who had "lost faith in America [and] . . . concluded that the white man is an incurable 'devil.'" He offered choices—choices that are relevant today.

- How does one determine what laws are just and unjust? Can unjust laws be constitutionally correct?
- What issues in today's society and world present similar choices that King mentions in the letter? What alternatives really exist?

FLEXIBLE RESPONSE

★ How did Kennedy modify the strategy and tactics of Eisenhower's foreign policy?

★ What actions did Kennedy take in Latin America and Vietnam to promote American interests?

From day one, President Kennedy favored foreign over domestic policy. In his inaugural address, he dropped most of the material on domestic policy and concentrated on foreign policy, generating the powerful lines: "We shall pay any price, bear any burden, meet any hardship, . . . to assure the survival and success of liberty." Advised by his close circle of "action intellectuals," Kennedy was anxious to meet whatever challenges the United States faced.

To back up his foreign policies, Kennedy instituted a new defense strategy called **flexible response** and significantly expanded military spending to pay for it. Flexible response involved continuing support for NATO and other multilateral alliances, plus further development of nuclear capabilities and **intercontinental ballistic missiles** (ICBMs). Flexible response also centered on conventional, nonnuclear warfare. With increased budgets, each branch of the service sought new weapons and equipment.

The world's developing and third world nations were a special concern. Khrushchev had just announced Moscow's support for "wars of national liberation" as a means to expand communism, and Kennedy meant to thwart that threat. To strengthen pro-Western governments with advisers and to combat revolutionaries, special counterinsurgency forces, such as the Green Berets, were developed. The military commitment, though, was second to wider economic strategies that provided direct government aid and private investment to "friendly" nations. This effort also included the personal involvement of American volunteers participating in the **Peace Corps**. Beginning in March 1961, more than ten thousand idealistic young Americans enrolled for two years to help win the "hearts and minds" of what Kennedy called "the rising peoples" around the world, staffing schools, constructing homes, building roads, and making other improvements.

Confronting Castro and the Soviets

Castro's success in Cuba reinforced the idea that developing nations of Latin America and the Caribbean were important battlegrounds in the struggle against communism. Seeking a new approach to Latin

■ **flexible response** Kennedy's strategy of considering a variety of military and nonmilitary options when facing foreign-policy decisions.

intercontinental ballistic missiles (ICBMs) Missiles whose path cannot be changed once launched; their range can be from a few miles to intercontinental. In 2003 an estimated thirty-five nations had ballistic missiles.

■ **Peace Corps** Program established by President Kennedy in 1961 to send young American volunteers to other nations as educators, health workers, and technicians.

America, in 1961 Kennedy introduced the **Alliance for Progress**, a foreign-aid package promising more than $20 billion. In return, Latin American governments were to introduce land and tax reforms and commit themselves to improving education and their people's standard of living. Kennedy believed this plan could "successfully counter the Communists in the Americas." Results fell short of expectations. The United States granted far less aid than proposed, and Latin American governments implemented few reforms and frequently squandered the aid. Throughout the 1960s in Latin America, the gap between rich and poor widened, and the number of military dictatorships increased.

The Alliance for Progress, however, did not address the problem of Castro. Determined to remove the Cuban dictator, Kennedy implemented the Eisenhower administration's covert plan to topple him. In 1960, the Central Intelligence Agency (CIA) had begun training Cuban exiles and mercenaries for an invasion of Cuba, and Kennedy gave the green light to launch the mission in April 1961. On April 17, more than fourteen hundred "liberators" landed at the *Bahía de Cochinos*, the **Bay of Pigs**. Within three days Castro's forces had captured or killed most of the invaders. Kennedy took responsibility for the fiasco but indicated no regrets and vowed to continue the "relentless struggle" against Castro and communism. Responding to Kennedy's orders, U.S. planners devised **Operation Mongoose** and other operations that sponsored about thirty attempts to assassinate Castro and CIA-backed raids that destroyed roads, bridges, factories, and crops.

After the Bay of Pigs disaster, in early June 1961, Kennedy met with Soviet leader Nikita Khrushchev in Vienna. With both men eager to show their toughness, the issue of Berlin was especially worrisome, because Khrushchev was threatening to sign a peace treaty with East Germany that would give the East Germans full control of all four zones of the city.

Returning home, Kennedy asked for massive increases in military spending, tripled the draft, and called fifty-one thousand reservists to active duty. Back in Moscow, Khrushchev renewed atmospheric nuclear weapons testing and reaffirmed his determination to oust the Allies from Berlin. Kennedy responded by beginning American nuclear testing and voicing his strong support for West Berlin. Some within the administration advocated the use of force if the East Germans or the Soviets interfered with West Berlin. With both sides posturing, many feared armed confrontation.

In August 1961, the tension finally broke. The Soviets and East Germans suddenly erected a wall between East and West Berlin to block refugees fleeing East Germany and Eastern Europe. Although the **Berlin Wall** challenged Western ideals of freedom, it did not directly threaten the West's presence in West Berlin.

The Berlin crisis paled beside the possibility of nuclear confrontation over Cuba in October 1962. On October 14, an American U-2 spy plane discovered that medium-range nuclear missile sites were being built on the island. Launched from Cuba, such missiles would drastically reduce the time for mobilizing a U.S. counterattack on the Soviet Union. Kennedy promptly decided on a showdown with the Soviets and mustered a small crisis staff.

The military offered a series of recommendations ranging from a military invasion to a "surgical" air strike to destroy the missiles. These were rejected as too dangerous, possibly inviting a Soviet attack on West Berlin or on American nuclear missile sites in Turkey. President Kennedy, supported by his brother, the attorney general, decided to impose a naval blockade around Cuba until Khrushchev met the U.S. demand to remove the missiles. On Monday, October 22, Kennedy went on television and radio to inform the public of the missile sightings and his decision to quarantine Cuba. As 180 American warships got into position to stop Soviet ships carrying supplies for the missiles, army units converged on Florida. The **Strategic Air Command** (SAC) kept a fleet of nuclear-armed B-52 bombers in the air at all times. On Wednesday, October 24, confrontation and perhaps war seemed imminent as two Soviet freighters and a Russian submarine approached the quarantine line. Robert Kennedy recalled, "We were on the edge of a precipice with no way off." Voices around the world echoed his anxiety.

The Soviet vessels, however, stopped short of the blockade. Khrushchev had decided not to test Kennedy's will. After a series of diplomatic maneuvers, the two sides reached an agreement based on an October 26 message from Khrushchev: if the United States agreed not to invade Cuba, the Soviets would

■ **Alliance for Progress** Program proposed by Kennedy in 1961 through which the United States provided aid for social and economic programs in Latin American countries.

■ **Bay of Pigs** Site of a 1961 CIA-sponsored invasion of Cuba by Cuban exiles and mercenaries; the invasion was crushed within three days and embarrassed the United States.

■ **Operation Mongoose** Mission authorized by President Kennedy in November 1961, and funded with a $50 million budget, to create conditions for the overthrow of Castro.

■ **Berlin Wall** Wall between East and West Berlin that the Soviets erected during the 1961 Berlin crisis to stem the flow of refugees out of Eastern Europe.

Strategic Air Command (SAC) U.S. military unit formed in March 1946 to conduct long-range bombing operations anywhere in the world; its first strategic plan, completed in 1949, projected nuclear attacks on seventy Soviet cities. SAC was abolished in 1992 as part of the reorganization of the Department of Defense.

On October 22, 1963, at 7:00 P.M., a week after he was informed of Soviet missiles being placed in Cuba, President Kennedy addressed the nation, saying that there was "unmistakable evidence" that Moscow had placed missiles in Cuba and that he had ordered a "strict quarantine on all offensive military equipment" headed for Cuba. Here, customers of a furniture store cluster around the display television sets to listen to the president.

Ralph Crane/Time Life Pictures/Getty Images.

remove their missiles. Khrushchev sent another letter the following day that called for the United States to remove existing American missiles in Turkey. Kennedy ignored the second message, and the Soviets agreed to remove their missiles without a public link to missiles in Turkey. Keeping its unpublicized promise to the Soviets, the United States withdrew all of its missiles in Turkey and Italy by April 1963. The world breathed a collective sigh of relief. Kennedy basked in what many viewed as a victory in the **Cuban missile crisis**, but he recognized how near the world had come to nuclear war and concluded that it was time to improve Soviet-American relations. A "hot line" telephone link was established between Moscow and Washington to allow direct talks in case of another East-West crisis.

In a major foreign-policy speech in June 1963, Kennedy suggested an end to the Cold War and offered that the United States, as a first step toward improving relations, would halt its nuclear testing. By July, American-Soviet negotiations had produced the **Limited Test Ban Treaty**, which forbade those who signed to conduct nuclear tests in the atmosphere, in space, and under the seas. Underground testing was still allowed. By October 1963, one hundred nations had signed the treaty, although the two newest atomic powers, France and China, refused to participate and continued to test in the atmosphere.

Vietnam

South Vietnam represented one of the most challenging issues Kennedy faced. Like Eisenhower, Kennedy saw it as a place where the United States' flexible response could stem communism and develop a stable, democratic nation. But by 1961, President **Ngo Dinh Diem** was losing control of his nation. South Vietnamese Communist rebels, the **Viet Cong**, controlled a large portion of the countryside, having battled Diem's troops, the Army of the Republic of Vietnam (ARVN), to a standstill. Military advisers argued that American troops were necessary to turn the tide. Kennedy was more cautious. "The troops will march in, the bands will play," he said privately, "the crowds will cheer; and in four days

■ **Cuban missile crisis** Confrontation, seemingly threatening war, over Soviet missiles deployed in Cuba; the Soviets ultimately withdrew the missiles.

■ **Limited Test Ban Treaty** Treaty signed by the United States, the USSR, and nearly one hundred other nations in 1963; it banned nuclear weapons tests in the atmosphere, in outer space, and underwater.

■ **Ngo Dinh Diem** President of South Vietnam (1954–1963) who jailed and tortured opponents of his rule; he was assassinated in a coup in 1963.

Viet Cong Vietnamese Communist rebels in South Vietnam.

everyone will have forgotten. Then we will be told we have to send in more troops. It's like taking a drink. The effect wears off and you have to take another." The South Vietnamese forces would have to continue to do the fighting, but the president agreed to send more "advisers." By November 1963, the United States had sent $185 million in military aid and had committed sixteen thousand advisers to Vietnam—compared with only a few hundred in 1961.

The Viet Cong were only part of the problem. Diem's administration was unpopular, out of touch with the people, and unwilling to heed Washington's pleas for political and social reforms. Some were even concerned that Diem might seek an accord with North Vietnam, and by autumn of 1963, Diem and his inner circle seemed more a liability than an asset. American officials in Saigon secretly informed several Vietnamese generals that Washington would support a change of government. The army acted on November 1, killing Diem and installing a new military government. The change of government, however, brought neither political stability nor improvement in the ARVN's capacity to fight the Viet Cong.

Death in Dallas

With his civil rights and tax-cut legislation in limbo in Congress, Kennedy in late 1963 watched his popularity rating drop below 60 percent. He decided to visit Texas in November to try to heal divisions within the Texas Democratic Party. He was assassinated there on November 22, 1963. The police quickly captured the reputed assassin, Lee Harvey Oswald. Two days later a local nightclub owner and gambler, Jack Ruby, shot Oswald to death in the basement of the police station.

Many wondered whether Kennedy's assassination was the work of Oswald alone or part of a larger conspiracy. To dispel rumors, the government hastily formed a commission headed by Chief Justice Earl Warren to investigate the assassination and determine if others were involved. The commission hurriedly examined most, but not all available evidence and announced that Oswald was a psychologically disturbed individual who had acted alone. No other gunmen were involved, nor was there any conspiracy. While many Americans accepted the conclusions of the Warren Commission, others continued to find errors in the report and to suggest additional theories about the assassination.

Kennedy's assassination traumatized the nation. Many people idealized the fallen president as a brilliant, innovative chief executive who combined vitality, youth, and good looks with forceful leadership and good judgment. Lyndon B. Johnson, sworn in as president as he flew back to Washington on the plane carrying Kennedy's body, did not appear to be cut from the same cloth. Kennedy had attended the best eastern schools, enjoyed the cultural and social life associated with wealth, and surrounded himself with intellectuals. Johnson, a product of public schools and a state teachers college, distrusted intellectuals. Raised in the hill country of Texas, his passion was politics. By 1960, his congressional experiences were unrivaled: he had served in the House of Representatives and in the Senate, where he had become Senate majority leader. Johnson knew how to wield political power and get things done in Washington.

DEFINING A NEW PRESIDENCY

★ In what ways did the legislation associated with Johnson's Great Society differ from New Deal programs?

★ How did Johnson's War on Poverty and Great Society further the civil rights movement?

As president, Johnson described himself as a New Dealer and told one adviser that Kennedy was "a little too conservative to suit my taste." Johnson wanted to build a better society, "where progress is the servant of the neediest." Recognizing the political opening generated by the assassination, Johnson immediately committed himself to Kennedy's agenda, and in January 1964 he expanded on it by announcing an "unconditional war on poverty."

Old and New Agendas

Throughout 1964, Johnson transformed Kennedy's quest for action into his own quest for social reform. Wielding his considerable political skill, he moved Kennedy's tax cut and civil rights bill out of committee and toward passage. The Keynesian tax cut (the Tax Reduction Act) became law in February but the civil rights bill moved more slowly, especially in the Senate, where it faced a stubborn southern **filibuster**. Johnson traded political favors for Republican backing to silence the fifty-seven-day filibuster, and the **Civil Rights Act of 1964** became law on July 2. The act made it illegal to discriminate for reasons of race, religion, or gender in places and businesses that served the public. Putting force behind the law, Congress established a federal Fair Employment Practices Committee (FEPC) and empowered the executive branch to withhold federal funds from institutions that violated the act's provisions.

filibuster Using obstructionist tactics, especially prolonged speechmaking, to delay legislative action.

■ **Civil Rights Act of 1964** Law that barred segregation in public facilities and forbade employers to discriminate on the basis of race, religion, sex, or national origin.

By August 1964, the War on Poverty had begun, aimed at benefiting the 20 percent of the population who were classified as poor. In 1962, social critic Michael Harrington had alerted the public to widespread poverty in America with his book *The Other America.* Subsequently, the U.S. government, which defined the poverty line as $3,130 for an urban household of four and $1,925 for a rural family, found that almost 40 percent of the poor (15.6 million) were under the age of 18.

The **War on Poverty** was to be fought on two fronts: expanding economic opportunities and improving the social environment. The August 1964 Economic Opportunity Act established an Office of Economic Opportunity to coordinate a variety of programs that Johnson stated would "help more Americans, especially young Americans, to escape from squalor and misery." The cornerstones were education and job training. The Job Corps program enrolled unemployed teens and young adults (16 to 21) lacking skills, while Head Start reached out to disadvantaged pre-kindergarten children to provide important thinking and social skills. Another program, called Volunteers in Service to America (VISTA), sent service-minded Americans to help improve life in regions of poverty. Among the most ambitious programs was the Community Action Program (CAP), which allowed disadvantaged community organizations to target local needs by giving them direct access to federal funds. The program never met expectations, but it helped generate local activism and led to services like legal aid and community health clinics.

As the 1964 presidential election neared, Johnson was confident. He could claim credit for tax cuts, a civil rights bill, and starting a war on poverty. Public opinion polls showed significant support for the president in all parts of the nation, except the South.

Opposing Johnson's liberal programs were conservatives and Republicans energized by the emerging **New Right**. Intellectually led by William F. Buckley and the *National Review,* conservatives cried that liberalism was destroying vital traditional American values of localism, self-help, and individualism. They opposed

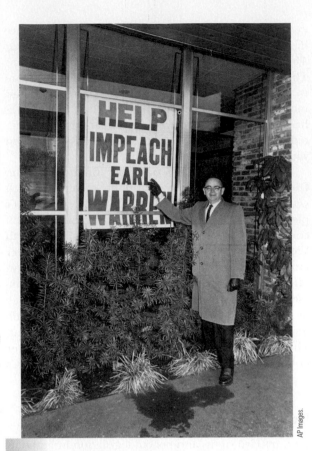

For many conservatives, Chief Justice Earl Warren was one of the most despised people in the country. In this picture Georgia Governor Lester Maddox calls for the impeachment of Warren. In 1968, Governor Maddox refused to fly the Georgia flag at half mast in honor of the death of Martin Luther King, Jr. Never impeached, Warren remained chief justice until he retired in 1969.

government activism, the growth of the welfare state, and the decisions of the Warren Court. From the mid-1950s through the 1960s, the Warren Court was at the forefront of liberalism, altering the obligations of the government and expanding the rights of citizens over the states's authority. Its decisions in the 1950s contributed to the legal base for the 1964 Civil Rights Act and began to reverse earlier decisions about the rights of those accused of crimes. Between 1961 and 1969, the Court issued over two hundred criminal justice decisions that, according to critics, hampered law enforcement. Among the most important were **Gideon** *v. Wainwright* (1963), **Escobedo** *v. Illinois* (1964), and **Miranda** *v. Arizona* (1966). In those rulings the Court declared that all defendants have a right to an attorney, even if the state must provide one, and that those arrested must be informed of their right to remain silent and to have an attorney present during questioning (the *Miranda* warning).

Further angering conservatives was a series of decisions that expanded freedom of expression, separated

■ **War on Poverty** Lyndon Johnson's program to help Americans escape poverty through education, job training, and community development.

■ **New Right** Conservative movement within the Republican Party that opposed liberal reforms of the 1960s, demanding less federal government interference with state and local power and a return to traditional values.

■ *Gideon, Escobedo, and Miranda* 1960s Supreme Court rulings declaring that the state must provide an attorney to any defendant who cannot afford one, and must inform those arrested of their right to remain silent and to have an attorney present during questioning.

President Johnson's Great Society greatly expanded the role of society in the lives of Americans through passage of civil rights, welfare, and education legislation. In this picture, President Johnson signs legislation establishing Medicare. His wife, Lady Bird, and Vice President Hubert Humphrey watch in the background.

church and state, and redrew voting districts. Especially onerous were two decisions in which the Warren Court applied the First Amendment—separation of church and state—to state and local actions that allowed prayer and Bible reading in public schools. Both decisions produced outcries of protest across the nation and from Democrats and Republicans in Congress. As Governor George Wallace of Alabama put it, "We find the court ruling against God." Congress introduced over 150 resolutions demanding that reading the Bible and praying aloud be permitted in schools. Still, the Court's decisions remained law, and communities and classrooms complied.

The New Right also complained that the Court's actions not only undermined the tradition of religion but condoned and promoted immorality. The Court weakened "community standards" in favor of broader ones regarding "obscene" and sexually explicit materials in *Jacobvellis v. Ohio* (1963). In the 1964 *Griswold v. Connecticut* decision, the Court attacked the state's responsibility to establish moral standards; it overturned Connecticut's laws that forbade the sale of contraceptives, arguing that individuals have a right to privacy that the state cannot abridge.

Leading the Republican assault against the values of liberalism was Senator **Barry Goldwater** of Arizona. Plainspoken and direct, Goldwater opposed the 1964 Civil Rights Act, "Big Government," and New Deal–style programs. Riding a wave of conservative and New

Right support, Goldwater seized the nomination for the presidency, launching an attack on liberalism and vowing to implement an anti-Communist crusade. When he appeared willing not only to commit American troops in Vietnam but also to use nuclear weapons against Communist nations, including Cuba and North Vietnam, Democrats quickly painted him as a dangerous radical. Johnson, meanwhile, promoted his Great Society and promised that "American boys" would not "do the fighting for Asian boys." Johnson won easily in a lopsided election.

Implementing the Great Society

Not only did Goldwater lose, but so too did many Republicans—moderates and conservatives—as more than forty new Democrats entered Congress. Armed with a seeming mandate for action, Johnson pushed forward legislation to enact his **Great Society**. He told aides that they must hurry before the natural opposition of politics returned. Between 1964 and 1968,

■ **Barry Goldwater** Conservative Republican senator from Arizona who ran unsuccessfully for president in 1964.

■ **Great Society** Social program that Johnson announced in 1964; it included the War on Poverty, protection of civil rights, and funding for education.

TABLE 26.1   War on Poverty and Great Society Programs, 1964–1966

1964	1965	1966
Tax Reduction Act	Elementary and Secondary Education Act	Demonstration Cities and Metropolitan Development Act
Civil Rights Act	Voting Rights Act	Motor Vehicle Safety Act
Economic Opportunity Act	Medical Care Act (Medicare and Medicaid)	Truth in Packaging Act
Equal Employment Opportunity Commission	Head Start (Office of Economic Opportunity)	Model Cities Act
Twenty-fourth Amendment	Upward Bound (Office of Economic Opportunity)	Clean Water Restoration Act
Job Corps (Office of Economic Opportunity)	Water Quality Act and Air Quality Act	Department of Transportation
Legal services for the poor	Department of Housing and Urban Development	
VISTA	National Endowment for the Arts and Humanities	
Wilderness Act	Immigration and Nationality Act	

more than sixty Great Society programs were put in place (see Table 26.1). Most sought to provide better economic and social opportunities by removing barriers thrown up by health, education, region, and race.

One of Johnson's goals was to further equality for African Americans. Within months of his election, he signed an executive order that, like the old Fair Employment Practices Commission, required government contractors to practice nondiscrimination in hiring and on the job. He also appointed the first African American to the cabinet, Secretary of Housing and Urban Development Robert Weaver; the first African American woman to the federal courts, Judge Constance Baker Motley; and the first African American to the Supreme Court, Justice Thurgood Marshall.

Blacks applauded the president's actions but realized that appointments and the civil rights act did not end discrimination or poverty and that large pockets of active opposition to civil rights remained—especially in

■ **Freedom Summer** Effort by civil rights groups in Mississippi to register black voters and cultivate black pride during the summer of 1964.

Alabama and Mississippi. A major goal was to expand black voting in the South. For nearly one hundred years, most southern whites had viewed voting as an activity for whites only and, through the poll tax and their control of the ballot, had maintained their political power and a segregated society. The ratification of the Twenty-fourth Amendment (banning the poll tax) in January 1964 was a major step toward dismantling that system, and by mid-1964 plans were under way to increase black voter registration. Bob Moses of SNCC organized a **Freedom Summer** in Mississippi. Whites and blacks opened "Freedom Schools" to teach literacy and black history, stress black pride and achievements, and help residents register to vote. In Mississippi, as in several other southern states, a voter literacy test required that all questions be answered to the satisfaction of a white registrar. Thus a question calling for "a reasonable interpretation" of an obscure section of the state constitution could be used to block blacks from registering.

In the face of white hostility, voter registration was dangerous work. "You talk about fear," an organizer told recruits. "It's like the heat down there, it's continually oppressive. You think they're rational. But, you know, you suddenly realize, they want to kill you." Indeed, from June through August of 1964,

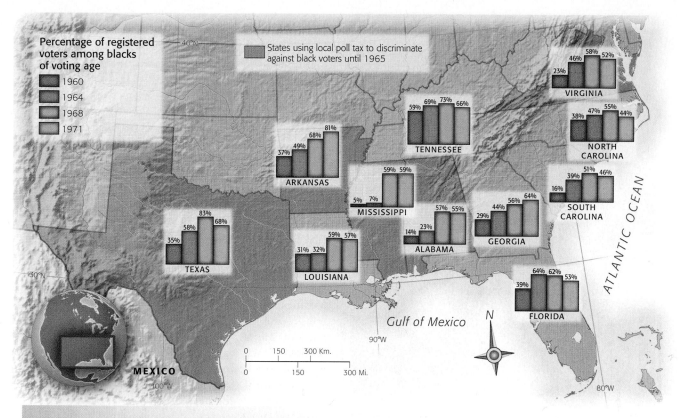

MAP 26.3 African Americans and the Southern Vote, 1960–1971

An important part of the civil rights movement was to reestablish the African American vote that had been stripped away in the South following Reconstruction. Between 1960 and 1971, with the outlawing of the poll tax and other voter restrictions, African American voter participation rose significantly across the South.

Copyright © Cengage Learning

more than thirty-five shooting incidents rocked Mississippi, and thirty buildings, many of them churches, were bombed. Hundreds were beaten and arrested, and three Freedom Summer workers were murdered. But the crusade drew national support and registered nearly sixty thousand new African American voters.

Keeping up the pressure, King announced a voter registration drive in Selma, Alabama, where only 2.1 percent of eligible black voters were registered. As expected, the police, led by Sheriff Jim Clark, confronted protesters, arresting nearly two thousand. King then called for a **freedom march** from Selma to Montgomery. On March 7, 1965, as scores of reporters watched, hundreds of freedom marchers faced fifty Alabama state troopers and Clark's mounted forces at Pettus Bridge. Firing tear gas and brandishing clubs, Clark's men chased the marchers down. Television coverage of the assault stirred nationwide condemnation of Clark's tactics and support for King and the marchers. When Alabama's staunch segregationist governor, George Wallace, told President Johnson that he could not provide protection for the marchers, Johnson ordered the National Guard, two army battalions, and 250 federal marshals to escort the protesters. The

march resumed on March 21 with about 3,200 marchers. When it arrived in Montgomery on March 27, more than 25,000 had joined.

Johnson used the violence in Selma to pressure Congress to pass the **Voting Rights Act** in August 1965. It banned a variety of methods that states had been using to deny the right to vote, including Mississippi's literacy test, and had immediate effect. Across the South, the percentage of African Americans registered to vote rose an average of 30 percent between 1965 and 1968 (see Map 26.3). In Mississippi, it went from 7 to 59 percent, and in Selma, more than 60 percent of qualified African Americans voted in 1968, stopping Sheriff Clark's bid for reelection.

■ **freedom march** Civil rights march from Selma to Montgomery, Alabama, in March 1965; the violent treatment of protesters by local authorities helped galvanize national opinion against segregationists.

■ **Voting Rights Act** 1965 law that outlawed literacy and other voting tests and authorized federal supervision of elections in areas where black voting had been restricted.

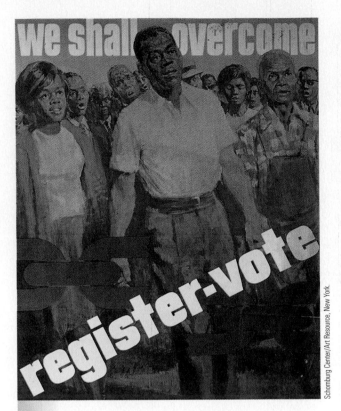

The summer of 1964 was called "Freedom Summer," as hundreds of civil rights volunteers—many of them college students—converged on Alabama and Mississippi to conduct voter registration drives. Many were beaten, some were jailed, and some lost their lives, but as Anne Moody wrote in her autobiography, *Coming of Age in Mississippi,* "threats did not stop them."

But civil rights legislation was only one of many facets of the Great Society. Several acts, like the Appalachian Regional Development Act (1965) and the Model Cities Act (1966), focused on developing economic growth in long-depressed regional and urban areas and on providing funds for housing and mass transit systems. In a related move, a cabinet-level Department of Housing and Urban Development was created in 1965.

Responding to rising environmental concerns, Johnson signed the Water Quality and Air Quality Acts in October 1965. Over the next three years, he would guide through Congress acts to expand wilderness

■ **Medicaid** Program of health insurance for the poor established in 1965; it provides states with money to buy healthcare for people on welfare.

■ **Medicare** Program of health insurance for the elderly and disabled established in 1965; it provides government payment for healthcare supplied by private doctors and hospitals.

areas, regulate waste removal, and remove billboards from federal highways.

Johnson also signed a major overhaul of the nation's immigration laws. The Immigration and Nationality Act of 1965 dropped the racial and ethnic discrimination in immigration policies that had been in effect since the 1920s. The act set a uniform yearly limit on immigration from any one nation, allowing for increased immigration from non-European parts of the world.

At the top of Johnson's priorities, however, were health and education. Above all, he wanted those two "coonskins on the wall." The Elementary and Secondary Education Act (1965) was the first general educational funding act by the federal government. It granted more than a billion dollars to public and parochial schools for textbooks, library materials, and special education programs. Poor and rural school districts were supposed to receive the highest percentage of federal support. But, as with many Great Society programs, implementation fell short of intention, and much of the money went to affluent suburban school districts. Johnson's biggest "coonskin" was the Medical Care Act (1965), which established **Medicaid** and **Medicare** to help pay healthcare costs for the elderly and individuals on welfare.

In 1966 Democrats were calling the Eighty-ninth Congress "the Congress of accomplished hopes." They were overly optimistic. Despite the flood of legislation, most of the Great Society's programs were underfunded and diminishing in popularity. Republicans and conservative Democrats had enough votes in Congress to effectively oppose further "welfare state" proposals. Supporting the opposition were the growing cost and dissatisfaction with the war in Vietnam, a backlash against urban riots and feminist militancy, and an expanding view that the federal government's efforts to wage war on poverty and build a "Great Society" were futile. Still, Johnson's programs had contributed to a near 10 percent decrease in the number of people living in poverty and a one-third drop in infant mortality. For African Americans statistics were also good: unemployment dropped over four years to 42 percent while average family income rose 53 percent.

NEW VOICES

★ *How did "new voices" conflict with traditional social norms, and what new organizations and agendas arose to provide a platform for those voices?*

★ *How did the urban riots and the emergence of the Black Power movement reflect a new agenda for the civil rights movement?*

By the end of 1965, legislation had ended de jure segregation and voting restrictions. Equality, however, depended on more than laws. Neither the Civil Rights Act nor the Voting Rights Act guaranteed justice, removed oppressive poverty, provided jobs, or ensured a higher standard of living. De facto discrimination and prejudice remained, and African American frustrations—born of raised expectations—soon changed the nature of civil rights protest and ignited northern cities. During the 1960s, more than a million mostly poor and unskilled African Americans left the South each year. Most sought a better life in northern and western cities, but they found soaring unemployment and cities unable or unwilling to provide adequate social services. Economics, not segregation, was the key issue: "I'd eat at your lunch counter—if only I had a job," spelled out the problem for many urban blacks. By the mid-1960s, the nation's cities were primed for racial trouble. Minor race riots occurred in Harlem and Rochester, New York, during the summer of 1964, but it was the Watts riot and militant new voices that shook the nation.

Urban Riots and Black Power

Within Los Angeles, the area of **Watts** had a largely African American population. Although Watts was a community having many well-maintained single-family homes and duplexes, its 250,000-plus residents gave it a population density more than four times higher than the rest of the city. Schools were overcrowded, and male unemployment hovered at 34 percent. Patrolling Watts was the nearly all-white L.A. police force, which had a reputation for racism and brutality.

In this climate, on August 11, 1965, an arrest of an African American for drunk driving led to an altercation that mushroomed into a riot. For thirty-six hours, rioters looted and set fire to stores, overturned and set ablaze cars, and attacked firefighters and police, who were unable to put out the flames or restore order. The costs of the riot were high: thirty-four dead, including twenty-eight African Americans, more than nine hundred injured, and $45 million in property destroyed. It also shattered the complacency of many whites who thought civil rights was just a southern problem.

For African Americans, Watts demonstrated a rejection of hopeful nonviolence and a demand for concrete changes. In 1964 Martin Luther King, Jr., had received the Nobel Peace Prize, but in 1965, when he spoke in Watts after the rioting, he was shouted down and jeered. "Hell, we don't need no damn dreams," one skeptic remarked. "We want jobs."

Competing with King were new voices like that of **Stokely Carmichael** who called on blacks to seek power through solidarity, independence, and, if necessary, violence. "I'm not going to beg the white man for anything I deserve," Carmichael announced in 1966. "I'm going to take it." SNCC and CORE quickly changed from biracial, nonviolent organizations to **Black Power** resistance movements that stressed Black Nationalism. The insistence on independence from white allies and the violent rhetoric widened the gap between moderates and radicals.

Joining the emergence of Black Power was the growing popularity and visibility of the Nation of Islam, or **Black Muslims**. Founded by Elijah Muhammad in the 1930s, the movement attracted mostly young males and demanded adherence to a strict moral code that prohibited the use of drugs and alcohol. Black Muslims preached black superiority and separatism from an evil white world. By the early 1960s, there were nearly a hundred thousand Black Muslims, including **Malcolm X**, who by 1952 had become one of the Black Muslims' most powerful and respected leaders. A mesmerizing speaker, he rejected integration with a white society that, he said, emasculated blacks by denying them power and personal identity. "Our enemy is the white man!" he roared. But in 1964 he reevaluated his policy. Though still a Black Nationalist, he admitted that to achieve their goals Black Muslims needed to cooperate with other civil rights groups and with some whites. He broke with Elijah Muhammad, and the defection cost him his life. On February 21, 1965, three Black Muslims assassinated him in Harlem.

Carmichael and Malcolm X represented only two of the strident African American voices advocating direct—and, if necessary, violent—action. The new leader of SNCC, H. Rap Brown, told followers to grab their guns and, if necessary, "shoot the honky." Brown's rhetoric was repeated in 1966 when Huey P. Newton, Eldridge Cleaver, and Bobby Seale organized the **Black Panthers** in Oakland, California. Although they pursued community action, such as developing school lunch programs, they were more noticeable

■ Watts Predominantly black neighborhood of Los Angeles where a race riot in August 1965 did $45 million in damage and took the lives of twenty-eight blacks.

■ Stokely Carmichael Civil rights activist who led SNCC and coined term "black power" to describe the need for blacks to use militant tactics to force whites to accept political and social change.

■ Black Power Movement begun in 1966 that rejected the nonviolent, coalition-building approach of traditional civil rights groups and advocated black control of black organizations; the self-determination approach was adopted by Latinos (Brown Power) and Native Americans (Red Power).

■ Black Muslims Popular name for the Nation of Islam, an African American religious group founded by Elijah Muhammad, which professed Islamic religious beliefs and emphasized black separatism.

■ Malcolm X Black activist who advocated black separatism as a member of the Nation of Islam; in 1963 he converted to orthodox Islam, and two years later was assassinated.

■ Black Panthers Black revolutionary party founded in 1966 that endorsed violence as a means of social change.

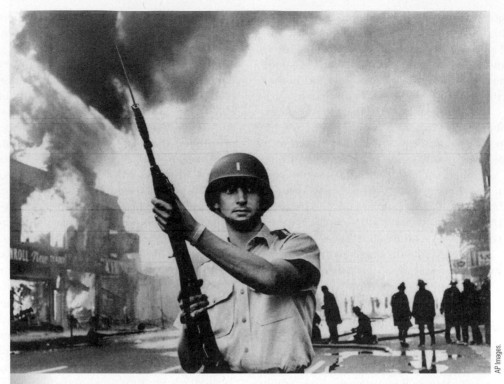

The July 1967 riot in Detroit was one of the most costly of the 1960s—five days of rioting left forty-three people dead (thirty-three of them African Americans), approximately one thousand injured and seven thousand arrested, and caused $40 to $80 million dollars in damage.

for being well armed and willing to use their weapons. FBI director J. Edgar Hoover called them "the most dangerous . . . of all extremist groups."

The spread of militant Black Nationalism paralleled a growing number of race riots that shook more than three hundred cities between 1965 and 1968. The summer of 1967 saw over seventy-five riots. The deadliest, in Detroit, killed forty-three people and destroyed millions of dollars in property. The next year, following the assassination of Martin Luther King, Jr., 350 American cities went up in flames of racial unrest. Stressing the need for social and economic justice, King had gone to Memphis to support striking sanitation workers. There, on April 4, 1968, he was killed by James Earl Ray.

The 1968 riots came as the Kerner Commission was releasing its report on the causes of urban unrest and making its recommendations for a solution. In 1967, Johnson had asked Governor Otto Kerner of Illinois to chair this commission, and the commission's report put the primary blame for unrest on the racist attitudes of white America. The study described two Americas, one white and one black, and concluded, "Pervasive discrimination and segregation in employment, education, and housing have resulted in the continuing exclusion of great numbers of Negroes from the benefits of economic progress." The study

recommended more government programs and spending to improve the lives of African Americans. But it fell on deaf ears. The urban violence and militant rhetoric had created a white backlash against civil rights and Great Society efforts. Governors Ronald Reagan (California) and Spiro Agnew (Maryland) blamed "mad dogs," "lawbreakers," and activists for the riots, and applauded FBI and police efforts to crack down on militants, especially members of the Black Panther Party, many of whom were arrested or killed in battles with authorities.

The civil rights movement had begun in the 1950s, but by the 1960s, African Americans were not alone in confronting the existing political and social norms. An increasing number of women were seeking to alter the status quo. And young adults, many of whom had been energized by the civil rights movement, now voiced demands for a more liberated society.

Rejecting the Feminine Mystique

By the end of the 1950s, the image of women as stay-at-home wives and mothers no longer matched the reality. Increasingly, women were entering the work force, graduating from college, getting divorces, and becoming heads of households. They also recognized that like African Americans they were frequently

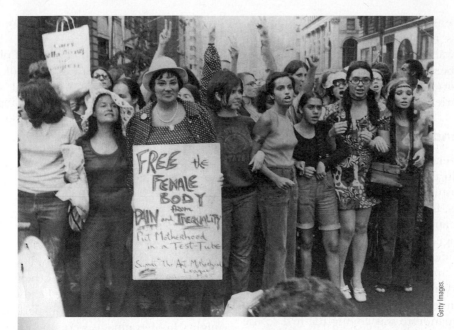

An avid supporter of women's rights, Bella Abzug (1920–1998) was elected to the House of Representatives in 1970 and a year later co-founded the National Women's Political Caucus.

treated as second-class citizens and faced discrimination based on gender. The 1963 report of the Presidential Commission on the Status of Women confirmed that women worked for less pay than white males (on average 40 percent less), were more likely to be fired or laid off, and rarely reached top career positions. It also indicated that throughout the country divorce, credit, and property laws generally favored men, and in several states women were not even allowed to serve on juries. The president's commission provided statistics, but it was **Betty Friedan's** 1963 bestseller *The Feminine Mystique* that many regard as the beginning of the women's movement. After reviewing the responsibilities of the housewife (making beds, grocery shopping, driving children everywhere, preparing meals and snacks, and pleasing her husband), Friedan asked: "Is this all?" She concluded that women needed to overcome the "feminine mystique" that promised them fulfillment in the domestic arts. She called on women to set their own goals and seek careers outside the home. Her book, combined with the presidential report, contributed to a renewed women's movement.

In 1963, Congress began to address women's issues when it passed the **Equal Pay Act**. Also engendering more activism was the passage of the 1964 Civil Rights Act with the inclusion of **Title VII**. The original version of the bill made no mention of discrimination on account of sex, but Representative Martha Griffins (D.–Michigan) joined with conservative Democrat Howard Smith of Virginia to add the word *sex* to the Civil Rights Act. As finally approved, Title VII prohibited discrimination on the basis of race, religion, creed, national origin, or sex.

Despite Title VII, the Equal Employment Opportunity Commission and the Johnson administration showed little interest in dealing with gender discrimination, leading women to form organizations to promote their interests and to persuade the government to enforce Title VII. The most prominent was the **National Organization for Women** (NOW), formed in 1966. With Betty Friedan as president, NOW launched an aggressive campaign to draw attention to sex discrimination and redress wrongs. It demanded an Equal Rights Amendment to the

■ **Betty Friedan** Feminist who wrote *The Feminine Mystique* in 1963 and helped found the National Organization for Women in 1966.

■ **Equal Pay Act** Forbids most employers to pay different wages, based on gender, for equal work. Some employers continued to pay lower wages to women, arguing that the jobs were not exactly equal.

■ **Title VII** Provision of the Civil Rights Act of 1964 that guarantees women legal protection against discrimination.

■ **National Organization for Women** (NOW) Women's rights organization founded in 1966 to fight discrimination against women and improve educational, employment, and political opportunities for women.

Constitution to ensure gender equality and pushed for easier access to birth-control devices and the right to have an abortion. NOW grew rapidly from about 300 members in 1966 to 175,000 in 1968. But the women's movement was larger than NOW and represented a variety of voices.

Rejecting Gender Roles

Some of those seeking change went beyond economics and politics in their critique of American society, taking aim at existing norms of sex and gender roles. Radical feminists, for example, called for a redefinition of sexuality and repudiated the moral rightness of family, marriage, and male domination in American society. "We identify the agents of our oppression as men. . . . We are exploited as sex objects, breeders, domestic servants and cheap labor," declared the Redstocking Manifesto in 1969. The New York group that issued the manifesto was among the first to use "**consciousness-raising**" groups to educate women about the oppression they faced because of the sex-gender system. Author Rita Mae Brown went further, advocating lesbian rights. Her acclaimed first novel, *Rubyfruit Jungle* (1973), presented lesbianism in a positive light and provided a literary basis for discussion of lesbian life and attitudes.

Brown joined a growing chorus of voices asking society to reconsider its views toward sexuality. Since the 1950s, gay and lesbian organizations had worked quietly to promote new attitudes toward same-sex orientation and to overturn laws that punished homosexual activities. But most gays remained in the closet, fearful of reprisals by the straight community and its institutions. The Stonewall Riot in 1969, however, brought increased visibility and renewed activism to the gay community.

The police raided the Stonewall Inn in New York City because it catered to a gay clientele. The raid resulted in an unexpected riot as gay patrons fought the police and were joined by other members of the community. After the riot, a Gay Manifesto called for homosexuals and lesbians to raise their consciousness and rid their minds of "garbage" poured into them by old values. "Liberation . . . is defining for ourselves

how and with whom we live. . . . We are only at the beginning."

Success came slowly, though. Polls in the early 1970s indicated that the majority of Americans still considered homosexuality immoral and even a disease. But by the mid-1970s, new polling showed a shift as a slight majority of Americans opposed job discrimination based on sexual orientation and appeared to show more tolerance of gay lifestyles. Responding to gay rights pressure in 1973, the American Psychiatric Association ended its classification of homosexuality as a mental disorder.

The Youth Movement

Within the 1960s movements for change, young adults in college were among the most active participants. By 1965, the baby boomers were heading off to college in record numbers. More than 40 percent of the nation's high school graduates were attending college, a leap of 13 percent from 1955. Graduate and professional schools were churning out unprecedented numbers of advanced degrees. Although the majority of young adults remained quite traditional, an expanding number began to question the goals of education. Students complained that higher education seemed sterile, an assembly line producing standardized products, not a crucible of ideas creating independent, thinking individuals. Many demanded more concern for the individual, more freedom of expression, and a more flexible curriculum.

Marches and sit-ins proliferated on campus to protest restrictions on student behavior and living arrangements, to seek a reduction in required courses, and to promote campuses as havens for free thought and a marshaling ground for efforts to change society. By the end of the decade, many colleges had given up the role of guardian for student behavior and decision making. They relaxed or eliminated dress codes, lifted dorm curfews and visitation restrictions, reduced the number of required courses, and introduced programs in nontraditional fields such as African American, Native American, and women's studies.

Across the country, campuses also served as venues for social and political debate and staging grounds for activism. At the University of Michigan in 1960, Tom Hayden and Al Haber organized **Students for a Democratic Society** (SDS). SDS members insisted Americans recognize that their affluent nation was also a land of poverty and want and that business and government chose to ignore social inequalities. In 1962 SDS issued its **Port Huron Statement**, which maintained that the country should reallocate its resources according to social need and strive to build "an environment for people to live in with dignity and creativeness." Accusing society of being "plastic" in its

consciousness-raising Achieving greater awareness of the nature of political or social issues through group interaction.

■ **Students for a Democratic Society** (SDS) Left-wing student organization founded in 1960 to criticize American materialism and work for social justice.

■ *Port Huron Statement* A 1962 critique of the Cold War and American materialism and complacency by Students for a Democratic Society; it called for "participatory democracy" and for universities to be centers of free speech and activism.

764 CHAPTER 26 Great Promises, Bitter Disappointments, 1960–1968

In the Wider World

Prague Spring, 1968

1968 was "the year of the barricades" as protests and rebellions erupted around the world challenging the status quo. One of the first occurred in January when Czech dissidents forced the resignation of the repressive government of Antonin Novotny, and Alexander Dubcek assumed the leadership of a reform movement. To put a "human face" on socialism, in April Dubcek issued the "Action Program," which began the process of allowing more freedom of expression, emphasizing increased private ownership, releasing political prisoners, and reducing the power of the central government.

Dubcek's problem was convincing the Soviet Union that the reforms did not challenge communism or Moscow's influence. In August, announcing the Brezhnev Doctrine, 200,000 Soviet and Warsaw Pact forces invaded Czechoslovakia. Despite pleas from Dubcek not to resist, seventy-two were killed and over five hundred wounded. The Prague Spring was over. Later, Dubcek was expelled from the Communist Party and assigned a job in forestry.

---

materialism, SDS and other youth activists represented an emerging **New Left** movement that maintained the threat to democracy came from liberals who had sold out to corporate America. "Corporate liberals" dominated the government, making just enough reforms to promote stability and profits while rejecting efforts to achieve social and economic equality. The liberal establishment could send thousands to kill in Vietnam, one New Left leader said, but would not "send 100 voter registrars . . . into Mississippi."

In 1964, at the University of California at Berkeley, administration efforts to limit political activity on and near campus sparked a **Free Speech Movement** with confrontation and protest. When student protesters seized the administration building, the police were called to remove the students. Barbara Zahn recalled: "I'm tired, dirty, scared, but most of all proud . . . we sit and we sing." She was also arrested, but the students succeeded. In January 1965 Berkeley allowed political activities on campus for the first time since the 1930s.

The Counterculture

Another, very visible, aspect of the youth movement was the emergence of a "counterculture." Rejecting the values of traditional society, by the mid-1960s "**hippies**" were replacing the "beats," adopting a lifestyle that emphasized personal freedom and a culture of opposition to "plastic" America. Some used drugs, especially marijuana, which they claimed reinforced ideals of peace, serenity, and self-awareness, and LSD or "acid," a dangerous and unpredictable hallucinogenic drug that alters perception. Many turned to religion to achieve a higher level of understanding, peace, and love. Non-Western mystic and religious practices like Zen Buddhism were widely adopted, while some found the "real" Jesus, whose original message, they argued, was altered by established religious institutions. Northern California became a center of the counterculture, especially in the Haight-Ashbury neighborhood of San Francisco. There, "beats" like Alan Ginsberg helped shape alternative lifestyles and culture. Elsewhere, groups abandoned the "old-fashioned" nuclear family and lived together as extended families on communes. In their communes and across the nation, those in the counterculture expressed nonconformity in their appearance, favoring long, unkempt hair and blue jeans or long flowered dresses, in their advocacy of sexual freedom, and in their music.

After the Supreme Court's 1964 decision in *Griswold v. Connecticut,* the availability of birth control, especially in the form of "the pill," contributed to a sexual revolution that spread far beyond the counterculture's advocacy of "free love." With fewer concerns of pregnancy, many women and men were willing to adopt less traditional relationships.

■ **New Left** An international movement in the 1960s primarily composed of intellectuals and college students that opposed "the Establishment" and its dominate political, economic, and social structures; in the United States it opposed the war in Vietnam and supported civil and individual rights.

■ **Free Speech Movement** Protest movement led by Mario Savio that began in 1964 at the University of California, Berkeley, when the administration prevented on-campus political activities; in January 1965 the administration lifted the ban and acknowledged students' freedom of speech.

■ **hippies** Members of the counterculture in the 1960s who rejected the competitiveness and materialism of American society and searched for peace, love, and autonomy.

To many, the counterculture was defined by "hippie" communes, where groups of young people left conventional society to establish alternative lifestyles, often close to nature, like the setting shown. In this picture, members of a commune use a bus named "The Road Hog" to participate in a Fourth of July parade in New Mexico.

Lisa Law/The Image Works.

Marriage was still popular, but living together emerged as an alternative, and for many women there was the image of the "single girl" popularized by Helen Gurley Brown's *Sex and the Single Girl* (1962) and articles aimed at the single market in the pages of *Cosmopolitan*. As Bob Dylan sang:

> Your sons and daughters
> Are beyond your command . . .
> For the times they are a changin'!*

Whether Dylan's lyrics or those of the Jefferson Airplane's "White Rabbit," whose pills could "make you larger" or "small," music provided a unifying medium not only for the counterculture but for the 1960s movements in general. Across the spectrum, musicians aimed their songs at large social and cultural issues like race, alienation, war, and love. Some musicians, including Bob Dylan and Joan Baez, challenged society with protest and antiwar songs rooted in folk music, but for the majority the evolving "rock" remained dominant. In 1964, the Beatles, an English

---

*From *The Times They Are A-Changin'* Copyright © 1963 by Warner Bros. Inc. Copyright renewed 1991 by Special Rider Music. All rights reserved. International copyright secured. Reprinted by permission.

■ **Woodstock** Free rock concert in Woodstock, New York, in August 1969; it attracted 400,000 people and was remembered as the classic expression of the counterculture.

group, exploded on the American music scene. They and their music mirrored the irreverence and values of the youth movement. They soon shared the stage with other British imports such as the Rolling Stones, whose behavior and songs depicted alienation and lack of social restraints. "Music," said one writer, was a liberating and revolutionary force that could "change the world." LSD advocate Timothy Leary merely proclaimed the Beatles "evolutionary agents sent by God."

In many ways the counterculture peaked in the summer of 1969, when musicians and an army of young adults converged on **Woodstock**, New York, for the largest free rock concert in history. For three days, through summer rains and deepening mud, more than 400,000 came together in a temporary open-air community, where many of the most popular rock 'n' roll bands performed day and night. Touted as three days of peace and love, sex, drugs, and rock 'n' roll, Woodstock symbolized the power of counterculture values to promote cooperation and happiness.

The spirit of Woodstock was fleeting. For most people, at home and on campus, the communal ideal was impractical, if not unworkable. Nor did the vast majority of young people who took up some counterculture notions completely reject their parents' society. Most stayed in school and continued to participate in the society they were criticizing. But parts of the youth movement and counterculture infiltrated into mainstream society and had a lasting impact.

Individual Voices

Eunice Kennedy Shriver Champions
New Perspectives

Because she was directly involved in promoting programs for those with intellectual disabilities, Eunice Kennedy Shriver provides the public as well as historians a window on how she sought to convince the public that those once referred to as "mentally retarded" should have the same rights as everyone else and that given the opportunities their successes benefited all of society.

"Challenges of the Mentally Retarded" appeared in the *New Catholic World* in 1976:

❶ Is it important that here and elsewhere in this document, Shriver uses familiar phrases from famous documents in American history? What is she attempting to accomplish by using such historical references?

❷ In what ways is Shriver making the point in this article that the quality of American society is determined by how it deals with all of its people?

❸ How do the accomplishments of individuals like Billy Bosquet reflect the differences between the Special and regular Olympics?

❹ Why do you think the "smiley games" are important to the issues presented in the previous excerpt?

How can we make sure that the mentally retarded people in our midst can be guaranteed their human rights? How can we make sure that their rights to life, liberty and the pursuit of happiness are protected? **❶**

... we are learning that, with the proper help and by any standards of worth, the mentally retarded have great value to our society. In their naïve innocence, they believe us when we talk about love, trust and sharing. In their striving to be what they think we are, they are devoted, hard-working and trusting. In the courage with which they face their handicaps and disabilities, they inspire us all to a new standard of achievement.

Yet, we are far from being truly civilized in our response to those who deviate from our social and intellectual norms. We deal with these people as clients or cases... even as we attempt to deal with their problems, a dehumanization process takes place....

So let us reaffirm our dedication to the rights of the handicapped, the weak and the mentally retarded in our midst.... Let us preserve our philosophic heritage which stated that "all men are endowed by their creator... with certain inalienable rights." And let us be sure... as for all other Americans, these inalienable rights include the right to life, education, health... the right to love, the right to work, the right... to be fully human in a humane and compassionate society. **❷**

"The Games Where Olympic Spirit Is All That Counts" was printed in the sports section of the *New York Times* in August 1983:

At a time when the ancient ideals of the Olympic Games have been obscured by politics and commercialism, many people have asked about the philosophy propelling the amazing progress of the Special Olympics.

What is the Special Olympics? It is the world's largest program of sports training and athletic competition for mentally retarded children and adults. Since its founding 15 years ago, as a single track and field event... it has grown to include more than a million athletes receiving year-round training and competition in 16 sports....

In today's world of sports, in which winning and the rewards of winning seem to be everything, Special Olympians strive for higher value.... It [is]... in the sportsmanship of Billy Bosquet of Massachusetts, who after having been moved from first to sixth... for running out of his lane, said: "Don't worry, I'll do it next time." **❸**

What lessons does the Special Olympics teach about the world?... It is that all human beings are created equal in the sense that each has the capacity and a hunger for moral excellence, for courage, for friendship and for love.... "This is the smiley games." **❹**

Sources: First selection: From Eunice Kennedy Shriver, "The Games Where Olympic Spirit Is All That Counts," *New York Times*, August 14, 1963. Copyright © 1963 by Special Olympics, Inc. Reprinted with permission. Second selection: From Eunice Kennedy Shriver, "Challenges of the Mentally Retarded," *New Catholic World*, 219 (September 1976), 200-203. Copyright © 1976 by Special Olympics, Inc. Reprinted with permission.

Study Tools

SUMMARY

John F. Kennedy's election generated a wave of optimism that individual, institutional, and governmental activism could combine to solve the nation's and the world's problems. This spirit fueled the New Frontier, the War on Poverty, and the Great Society. Many African Americans, in particular, looked to Kennedy and Johnson for legislation to end segregation and discrimination. Kennedy's domestic goals included a comprehensive civil rights bill and education and tax legislation, but the measures became mired in congressional politics and were never passed. Kennedy had to settle for modest legislative successes that merely expanded existing programs and entitlements (government programs and benefits provided to particular groups, such as the elderly, farmers, the disabled, and the poor).

Less constrained in his foreign policy, Kennedy implemented a more comprehensive, flexible strategy to confront communism. Confrontations over Berlin and Cuba, escalating arms and space races, and expanding commitments to Vietnam were accepted as part of the United States' global role and passed intact to Johnson.

President Johnson expanded Kennedy's domestic agenda. Announcing a War on Poverty and the formation of a Great Society, Johnson expanded New Deal liberalism into new areas of public policy. Between 1964 and 1966, Johnson pushed through Congress legislation that tackled poverty and discrimination, expanded educational opportunities, and created a national system of health insurance for the poor and elderly.

The decade's emphasis on activism encouraged more Americans to push their own agendas. As the civil rights movement focused more on economic and social issues, some African Americans rejected assimilation and more militantly demanded basic institutional changes. Drawing from the civil rights movement, a women's movement arose, demanding social, legal, and economic equality and questioning gender roles in a male-dominated society. Across the nation, young adults, especially those of college age, challenged traditional societal values and championed a more tolerant society.

CHRONOLOGY
New Frontiers

1960	Sit-ins begin
	SNCC formed
	Students for a Democratic Society formed
	John F. Kennedy elected president
1961	Peace Corps formed
	Alliance for Progress
	Bay of Pigs invasion
	Freedom rides begin
	Vienna summit
	Berlin Wall erected
1962	SDS's *Port Huron Statement*
	James Meredith enrolls at the University of Mississippi
	Cuban missile crisis
1963	Report on the status of women
	Betty Friedan's *The Feminine Mystique*
	Equal Pay Act
	Martin Luther King's "Letter from a Birmingham Jail"
	March on Washington
	Diem assassinated
	Kennedy assassinated; Lyndon Baines Johnson becomes president
1964	War on Poverty begins
	Freedom Summer
	Civil Rights Act
	Johnson elected president
1965	Malcolm X assassinated
	Selma freedom march
	Medicaid and Medicare
	Voting Rights Act
	Watts riot
	Water Quality and Air Quality Acts
1966	Black Panther Party formed
	National Organization for Women founded
1967	Urban riots in over 75 cities
1968	Martin Luther King, Jr., assassinated
1969	Woodstock
	Stonewall Riot
	Neil Armstrong sets foot on moon

Study Tools

FOCUS QUESTIONS

If you have mastered this chapter, you should be able to answer these questions and to identify the terms that follow the questions.

1. ☆ *How successful was the Kennedy administration in achieving its domestic agenda?*

2. ☆ *What form of African American activism pushed the civil rights movement forward, and how did Kennedy respond to those efforts?*

3. ☆ *How did Kennedy modify the strategy and tactics of Eisenhower's foreign policy?*

4. ☆ *What actions did Kennedy take in Latin America and Vietnam to promote American interests?*

5. ☆ *In what ways did the legislation associated with Johnson's Great Society differ from New Deal programs?*

6. ☆ *How did Johnson's War on Poverty and Great Society further the civil rights movement?*

7. ☆ *How did "new voices" conflict with traditional social norms, and what new organizations and agendas arose to provide a platform for those voices?*

8. ☆ *How did the urban riots and the emergence of the Black Power movement reflect a new agenda for the civil rights movement?*

KEY TERMS

New Frontier *(p. 747)*

new economics *(p. 748)*

sit-in *(p. 748)*

Student Nonviolent Coordinating Committee *(p. 749)*

freedom rides *(p. 749)*

James Meredith *(p. 750)*

March on Washington *(p. 751)*

flexible response *(p. 752)*

Peace Corps *(p. 752)*

Alliance for Progress *(p. 753)*

Bay of Pigs *(p. 753)*

Operation Mongoose *(p. 753)*

Berlin Wall *(p. 753)*

Cuban missile crisis *(p. 754)*

Limited Test Ban Treaty *(p. 754)*

Ngo Dinh Diem *(p. 754)*

Civil Rights Act of 1964 *(p. 755)*

War on Poverty *(p. 756)*

New Right *(p. 756)*

Gideon, Escobedo, and Miranda *(p. 756)*

Barry Goldwater *(p. 757)*

Great Society *(p. 757)*

Freedom Summer *(p. 758)*

freedom march *(p. 759)*

Voting Rights Act *(p. 759)*

Medicaid *(p. 760)*

Medicare *(p. 760)*

Watts *(p. 761)*

Stokely Carmichael *(p. 761)*

Black Power *(p. 761)*

Black Muslims *(p. 761)*

Malcolm X *(p. 761)*

Black Panthers *(p. 761)*

Betty Friedan *(p. 763)*

Equal Pay Act *(p. 763)*

Title VII *(p. 763)*

National Organization for Women *(p. 763)*

Students for a Democratic Society *(p. 764)*

Port Huron Statement *(p. 764)*

New Left *(p. 765)*

Free Speech Movement *(p. 765)*

hippies *(p. 765)*

Woodstock *(p. 766)*

CourseMate Go to the History CourseMate website for primary source links, study tools, and review materials for this chapter. www.cengagebrain.com

27

America Under Stress, 1967–1976

Behind the Stories

In France, Japan, Korea, Germany, and Czechoslovakia, 1968—"the year of the barricades"—was, declared *Time* magazine, "one tragic, surprising and perplexing thing after another." Not liking the word "perplexing," historians have offered various analyses of the year and examined and questioned its importance. Many accept 1968 as a turning point, but disagree on how much of a turn. Some see it as a moment of significant change—the end of an unsuccessful struggle between the "liberal movements" and the establishment. Others argue that it was more than a failure of liberal movements, pointing to the rise of a more dynamic conservatism offering its own agenda for the nation. While many suggest that the accepted social and cultural visions of the nation were being torn apart, others believe that the changes were minor and quickly merged within existing norms.

Still, there is another dimension to why 1968 appears to be so tumultuous—the media. Today with our 24/7 news channels, it is easy to forget how media communications shaped the visions of those experiencing the events. The use of communication satellites, portable television cameras, and videotape altered the immediacy of events, compressing them and generating opinions that shaped understanding. Vietnam became the first "living room" war, creating visions of war never before experienced by such a wide audience. Americans watched as civil rights activists were jailed and as African Americans rioted in the streets of the nation's cities. Robert Kennedy's assassination was caught on camera. The media made these and other events seem personal to those watching in a way never before experienced. Was the media recording events or defining them, and ultimately shaping their place in history?

In examining the materials found in Chapters 26 and 27 and looking back at 1968 over a forty year span, does that year represent a major change in direction, or is it a bridge connecting past and future? Having received an army commission in that "revolutionary year," I know that my perspectives have changed significantly over the years, and I wonder how the continued passage of time will further change my historical perspective and alter my understanding of 1968 and its importance.

—J.G.

Individual Choices
Dolores Huerta

Seeing the poverty of farm worker children, Dolores Huerta, a schoolteacher in Stockton, California, decided it was not enough to be a good teacher and chose in 1955 to work for the Community Service Organization (CSO), an activist organization working to help the poor. There, she met César Chávez and in 1962, they formed the National Farm Workers Association. As a union organizer, Huerta and her family experienced what "farm worker families go through every day of their lives"—poverty.

Dolores Huerta

Over the next forty-five years, she organized workers, led strikes, and stood in picket lines, oversaw a grape boycott, and negotiated contracts with growers. In the process, she and others sought to awaken the public and legislators to the many problems facing the farm workers (as illustrated in the Individual Voices feature at the end of this chapter). In the process Huerta was arrested twenty-two times, placed under FBI surveillance because of suspected Communist ties, and suffered a severe beating by a San Francisco police officer that ruptured her spleen.

But there were victories. Through negotiations with growers, she improved wages and working conditions—including portable toilets, health coverage, and the restriction of pesticides, especially DDT, which was completely banned in 1974. Huerta was instrumental in getting the California Agricultural Labor Relations Act (1975) passed, giving farm workers the right to organize and collectively bargain with employers. She remains involved in *La Causa* (discussed in this chapter), working for the rights of Latinos, workers, and women. Still supporting farm workers, in July 2006 she organized a march in Lamont, California, to gain "just wages."

ollowing the patterns set by other civil rights movements, Latinos and American Indians formed organizations to promote their interests—"Brown Power" and "Red Power" joined "Black Power" in contesting the status quo and adding to the political and social turmoil that characterized the 1960s. At the same time, while implementing his Great Society, Johnson committed to gradual **escalation** of American forces in South Vietnam. The goal was to convince North Vietnam that the cost of the war was too high. The strategy failed. Not only did North Vietnam meet escalation with escalation, but it was the United States that grew war weary.

For many, the election of 1968 was a referendum on the war. But to many others, it was a larger critique of liberal policies. Nixon promised to strengthen the nation by restoring national unity and global prestige and by reasserting traditional values. His call found support from a society fragmented by war, domestic unrest, and a declining economy.

As president, Nixon sought to alter American foreign policy and reshape politics. By 1972, he could point to several successes. American troops were being removed from Vietnam and he had implemented a policy of détente, improving relations with the Soviet Union and the People's Republic of China. Domestically, his choices showed flexibility, expanding some Great Society programs and following Keynesian guidelines to improve the economy while also implementing a "southern strategy" to draw white southerners to the Republican Party.

Nixon's popularity won him easy reelection. But behind the scenes he worked to ruin his political enemies, leading to the Watergate break-in and a bitter harvest: not only the unprecedented resignation of a president but a nationwide wave of disillusionment with politics and government. The unelected president, Gerald Ford, tried to heal the nation, but faced an uphill battle against a floundering economy and a politically cynical public. Although he gained few political victories, he gained his party's nomination for the 1976 presidential election.

■ **escalation** An increase in something; the term became associated with the steady increase in U.S. forces and the intensity of U.S. military activity in Vietnam.

■ **Mann Doctrine** U.S. policy outlined by Thomas Mann during the Johnson administration that called for stability in Latin America rather than economic and political reform.

JOHNSON AND THE WAR

★ How did Johnson modify Kennedy's policies toward Latin America and Southeast Asia?

★ What considerations led Johnson to expand America's role in Vietnam and how did the North Vietnamese respond to the changes?

As president, Lyndon Johnson inherited two foreign policy problems from Kennedy: Latin America and Vietnam. While not experienced in foreign affairs, Johnson was sure of one thing—he was not going to allow further erosion of American power.

In the Western Hemisphere, Castro's determination to export revolution appeared the biggest problem. Johnson continued Kennedy's economic boycott of Cuba and the CIA's efforts to destabilize the Castro regime. But he refocused Kennedy's Alliance for Progress. Stability became more important than reform. This new approach, labeled the **Mann Doctrine**, increased American military equipment and advisers in Latin America to help various regimes suppress disruptive elements they labeled "Communist." In 1965 the new policy led to direct military intervention in the Dominican Republic. There, supporters of deposed, democratically elected president Juan Bosch rebelled against a repressive, pro-American regime. Deciding that the pro-Bosch coalition was dominated by Communists and asserting the right to protect the Dominican people from an "international conspiracy," Johnson sent in twenty-two thousand American troops. They restored order; monitored elections that put a pro-American president, Joaquín Balaguer, in power; and left the island in mid-1966. Johnson claimed to have saved the Dominicans from communism, but many Latin Americans saw the American intervention only as an example of Yankee arrogance and intrusiveness.

Americanization of the Vietnam War

As Johnson took office, his advisers told him that the South Vietnamese government remained unstable, its army ineffective, and that the Viet Cong, supported by North Vietnam, appeared to be winning the conflict. There would be no improvement, they said, without a large and direct American involvement. Johnson felt trapped: "I don't think it is worth fighting for," he told an adviser, "and I don't think we can get out." "I am not going to be the president who saw Southeast Asia go the way China went," he asserted. In formulating policy, Johnson concluded that a gradual escalation of American force against North Vietnam and the Viet Cong would be the most effective course. It would pressure the North Vietnamese to halt their support of the Viet Cong while limiting domestic opposition.

He also wanted to wait until a Communist action justified U.S. retaliation before asking Congress for permission to use whatever force was necessary to defend South Vietnam.

The chance came off the coast of North Vietnam. On August 2, 1964, North Vietnamese torpedo boats skirmished with the American destroyer *Maddox* in the Gulf of Tonkin (see Map 27.1). On August 4, experiencing rough seas and poor visibility, radar operators on the *Maddox* and another destroyer, the *C. Turner Joy*, concluded that the patrol boats were making another attack. Confusion followed. Both ships fired at targets visible only on radar screens. Johnson immediately ordered retaliatory air strikes on North Vietnam and prepared a resolution for Congress. Although within hours he learned that the second incident probably had not occurred, Johnson told the public and Congress that Communist attacks against "peaceful villages" in South Vietnam had been "joined by open aggression on the high seas against the United States of America." On August 7, Congress approved the **Gulf of Tonkin Resolution**, allowing the United States "to take all necessary measures to repel" attacks against American forces in Vietnam and "to prevent further aggression." It was, in Johnson's terms, "like Grandma's nightgown, it covered everything." Public opinion polls showed strong support for the president, and only two senators opposed the resolution: Wayne Morse of Oregon and Ernest Gruening of Alaska.

Although the resolution gave Johnson freedom of action, he chose to wait until a Communist incident occurred before escalating and to begin with air attacks on targets in North Vietnam. The air offensive, Operation Rolling Thunder, began on March 2, 1965, with the 3rd Marine Division arriving a week later. By July, American planes were flying more than nine hundred missions a week, and a hundred thousand American ground forces had reached Vietnam. Near their bases, American forces patrolled aggressively, searching out the enemy. Johnson's strategy soon showed its flaws. Instead of reducing its support for the Viet Cong, North Vietnam committed units of the North Vietnamese army (NVA) to the fight. The U.S. commanding general in Vietnam, **William Westmoreland**, asked for more American soldiers to carry out larger land offensives. Reluctantly, Johnson gave the green light. Vietnam had become an American war.

Westmoreland intended to use overwhelming numbers and firepower to destroy the enemy and planned a large-scale sweep of the Ia Drang Valley in November 1965. Ten miles from the Cambodian border, the Ia Drang Valley contained no villages and was a longtime sanctuary for Communist forces. Airlifted into the valley to search out and destroy the enemy, air cavalry units soon came under fierce attack from North Vietnamese troops. The North Vietnamese commander Nguyen Huu remembered: "There was very vicious fighting . . . soldiers fought valiantly. They had no choice, you were dead if not." Both sides claimed victory and drew different lessons from the engagement. Examining the losses, 305 Americans versus 3,561 Vietnamese, American officials embraced the strategy of **search and destroy**—the enemy would be ground down. *Time* magazine named Westmoreland "Man of the Year" for 1965. Hanoi concluded its "peasant army" had withstood America's best firepower and had fought U.S. troops to a draw. The North Vietnamese were confident: the costs would be great, but they would wear down the Americans. Both sides, believing victory was possible, committed more troops and prepared for a lengthy war.

The war's intensity spiraled upward in 1966 and 1967. The United States and the North Vietnamese committed more troops, while American aircraft rained more bombs on North Vietnam and on supply routes, especially the **Ho Chi Minh Trail** (see Map 27.1). The bombing of North Vietnam produced great results—on paper. Nearly every target in North Vietnam had been demolished by 1968, but the North Vietnamese continued the struggle. China and the Soviet Union increased their support, while much of North Vietnamese industrial production moved underground. By mid-1966, it appeared to some in Washington that the war had reached a stalemate, with neither side able to win nor willing to lose. Some speculated that any victory would be a matter of will and feared that growing opposition to the war in the United States might be a deciding factor.

The Antiwar Movement

Throughout 1964, support at home for an American role in Vietnam was widespread. As the war escalated in 1965 a largely college-based opposition arose—with Students for a Democratic Society (SDS) the prime instigators. The University of Michigan held the first Vietnam "teach-in" to mobilize opposition to American policy on March 24, 1965. In April, SDS organized

■ **Gulf of Tonkin Resolution** 1964 congressional action authorizing the president to take any measures necessary to repel attacks against U.S. forces in Vietnam.

William Westmoreland Commander of all American troops in Vietnam from 1964 to 1968.

search and destroy Military strategy for ground operations in Vietnam during the Johnson administration; using mobility and superior fire power U.S. forces would attack the enemy in their territory with the goal of destroying as many as possible; the term "body count" became a means to explain the outcome of the operation.

■ **Ho Chi Minh Trail** Main route by which North Vietnamese soldiers and supplies reached South Vietnam; it ran through Laos and Cambodia.

Legend:
- Main area of confrontation
- Viet Cong base areas
- Communist supply route
- U.S. forces
- ★ Major battle

0   50   100 Km
0   50   100 Mi.

CHINA

Dien Bien Phu

MYANMAR
(BURMA)

Hanoi
Haiphong

U.S. air raids on Hanoi 1966, 1968, 1972

NORTH
VIETNAM

20°N

Gulf of Tonkin

Hainan

PLAIN OF JARS

Gulf of Tonkin, 1964

Vinh

Keo Nua Pass

LAOS

Vientiane

Mu Gia Pass

Demilitarized Zone

17°N

Demarcation Line, 1954

Hue Tet Offensive 1968

South China
Sea

Da Nang

THAILAND

My Lai Massacre 1968

15°N

Pleiku

Bangkok

CAMBODIA

CENTRAL
HIGHLANDS

Qui Nhon

Mekong

Ia Drang
Valley
1965

Ho Chi Minh Trail

SOUTH
VIETNAM

110°E

Phnom Penh

Saigon

Gulf of Thailand

Tet Offensive 1968

10°N

N

CA MAU
PENINSULA

Mekong
Delta

100°E

105°E

MAP 27.1 Southeast Asia and the Vietnam War

Following the French defeat at Dienbienphu in 1954, the United States committed itself to defending South Vietnam. This map shows some of the major battle sites of the Vietnam War from 1954 to the fall of Saigon and the defeat of the South Vietnamese government in 1975. Copyright © Cengage Learning a protest march of nearly twenty thousand past the White House, and by October its membership had increased 400 percent. But by mid-1966, SDS was only one of many groups and individuals demonstrating against the expanding war.

Those opposing the war fell into two major types who rarely agreed on anything other than that the war should be ended. Pacifists and radical liberals on the political left opposed the war for moral and ideological reasons. Others, as the American military commitment grew and the military draft claimed more young men, opposed the war for more pragmatic reasons: the draft, the loss of lives and money, and the inability of the United States either to defeat the enemy or to create a stable, democratic South Vietnam. A University of Michigan student complained that if he were drafted and spent two years in the army, he would lose more than $16,000 in income. "I know I sound selfish," he explained, "but . . . I paid $10,000 to get this education."

Yet college students and graduates were not the most likely to be drafted or go to Vietnam. Far more often, minorities and the poor served in Vietnam, especially in combat roles. African Americans constituted about 12 percent of the population but in Vietnam they made up nearly 50 percent of frontline units and accounted for about 25 percent of combat deaths. Stokely Carmichael and SNCC had opposed the war as early as 1965, but it was Martin Luther King, Jr.'s denunciation of the war in 1967 that made international headlines and shook the administration. King called the war immoral and said it was wrong to send young blacks to defend democracy in Vietnam when they were denied it in Georgia.

Johnson publicly dismissed critics, labeling King a "crackpot." But as the antiwar movement grew and public opinion polls registered increasing disapproval of the war effort, the administration responded with more direct action. **COINTELPRO** and **Operation Chaos** were implemented to infiltrate, spy on, discredit, and disrupt antiwar groups. Nevertheless, opposition to the war swelled. During "Stop-the-Draft Week" in October 1967 more than 10,000 demonstrators blocked the entrance of an induction center in Oakland, California, and over 200,000 people staged a massive protest march in Washington against "Lyndon's War."

Like the country, the administration was experiencing increasing disagreement about the course of the war. Hawks supported General Westmoreland's assertions that the war was being won but that more troops were needed to complete the job. Others, including Secretary of Defense Robert McNamara, were taking a different view. In November 1967, McNamara recommended a sharp reduction in the war effort, including a permanent end to the bombing of North Vietnam. Johnson rejected the idea, and McNamara left the administration. Still, Johnson decided to consider a "withdrawal strategy" that would reduce American support while the

THE AMERICANS ARE COMING

T. UNGERER

Library of Congress.

As the American involvement in Vietnam increased, so too did the opposition to the war. Some protesters argued that the Viet Cong were fighting for national independence, like the American revolutionaries. Here, a Vietnamese Paul Revere raises the alarm that the enemy is coming.

South Vietnamese assumed a larger role. But first it was necessary to commit more troops, intensify the bombing, and put more pressure on the South Vietnamese to make domestic reforms. "The clock is ticking," Johnson said.

TET AND THE 1968 PRESIDENTIAL CAMPAIGN

★ What were the political, social, and military outcomes of the Tet offensive?

★ What key issues shaped the 1968 campaign? What strategy did Richard Nixon use to win?

Johnson was correct: the clock was ticking—not only for the United States but also for North Vietnam. As Westmoreland reported success, North Vietnamese

■ **COINTELPRO** Acronym (COunterINTELligence PROgram) for an FBI program begun in 1956 and continued until 1971 that sought to expose, disrupt, and discredit groups considered to be radical political organizations; it targeted various antiwar groups during the Vietnam War.

■ **Operation Chaos** CIA operation within the country from 1965 to 1973 that collected information on and disrupted anti–Vietnam War elements; although it is illegal for the CIA to operate within the United States, it collected files on over seven thousand Americans.

leaders planned an immense campaign to capture South Vietnamese cities during **Tet**, the Vietnamese lunar New Year holiday.

The Tet Offensive

Catching American intelligence agencies and forces totally off guard, in January 1968, the Viet Cong struck forty-one cities throughout South Vietnam, including the capital, Saigon. In some of the bloodiest fighting of the war, American and South Vietnamese forces recaptured the lost cities and villages. It took twenty-four days to oust the Viet Cong from the old imperial city of Hue, leaving the city in ruins and costing more than 10,000 civilian, 5,000 Communist, 384 South Vietnamese, and 216 American lives. The Tet offensive was a military defeat for North Vietnam and the Viet Cong. It provoked no popular uprising against the South Vietnamese government, the Communists held no cities or provincial capitals, and they suffered staggering losses. Tet was, nevertheless, a "victory" for the North Vietnamese, for it seriously weakened American support for the war. Amid official pronouncements of "victory just around the corner," Tet destroyed the Johnson administration's credibility and inflamed a growing antiwar movement. The highly respected CBS news anchor Walter Cronkite had supported the war, but Tet changed his mind. He announced on the air that there would be no victory in Vietnam and that the United States should make peace. "If I have lost Walter Cronkite, then it's over. I have lost Mr. Average Citizen," Johnson lamented.

By March 1968, Johnson and most of his advisers had concluded that the war was not going to be won. In the words of the new secretary of defense, Clark Clifford, four years of "enormous casualties" and "massive destruction from our bombing" had not weakened "the will of the enemy" and a new strategy was needed. Johnson decided to send fewer troops than Westmoreland had asked for, seek a diplomatic end to the war, and place more responsibility on the South Vietnamese.

■ **Tet** The lunar New Year celebrated as a huge holiday in Vietnam; the Viet Cong–North Vietnamese attack on South Vietnamese cities during Tet in January 1968 was a military defeat for North Vietnam, but it seriously undermined U.S. support for the war.

■ **Eugene McCarthy** Senator who opposed the Vietnam War and made an unsuccessful bid for the 1968 Democratic nomination for president.

write-in campaign An attempt to elect a candidate in which voters are urged to write the name of an unregistered candidate directly on the ballot.

■ **Robert Kennedy** Attorney general during the presidency of his brother John F. Kennedy, elected to the Senate in 1964; his campaign for the presidency was gathering momentum when he was assassinated in 1968.

Unlike previous wars, Vietnam was a war without fixed frontlines. In this picture, marines work their way through the jungle south of the demilitarized zone (DMZ), trying to cut off North Vietnamese supplies and reinforcements moving into South Vietnam.

Larry Burrows/Time Magazine/Time Life Pictures/Getty Images.

Changing of the Guard

Two months after Tet came the first presidential primary in New Hampshire. There, Minnesota senator **Eugene McCarthy** was campaigning primarily on Johnson's record and conduct of the war. At the heart of his New Hampshire effort were hundreds of student volunteers who, deciding to "go clean for Gene," cut their long hair and shaved their beards. They knocked on doors and distributed bales of flyers and pamphlets touting their candidate and condemning the war. As McCarthy's antiwar candidacy strengthened, Johnson's advisers organized a **write-in campaign** for the president, who had not entered the primary. Johnson won by 6 percent of the votes, but political commentators named McCarthy the real winner. The results in New Hampshire prompted New York senator **Robert Kennedy** to announce his candidacy in mid-March. Watching his popularity decline and that of his opponents surge, Johnson decided not to run for the presidency.

On March 31, 1968, a haggard-looking president delivered a major televised speech announcing changes in his Vietnam policy. The United States would seek a political settlement through negotiations in Paris with the Viet Cong and North Vietnamese. The escalation of the ground war was over, and the South Vietnamese would take a larger role in the war. The bombing of northern North Vietnam would end, and a complete halt of the air war would follow the start of negotiations. At the end of his speech, Johnson calmly announced: "I shall not seek, and I will not accept, the nomination of my party for another term as president." Listeners were shocked. Although he later claimed that his fear of having a heart attack while in office was the primary reason for his decision not to run, nearly everyone agreed that the Vietnam War had ended Johnson's political career and undermined his Great Society.

The Election of 1968

There were now three Democratic candidates. McCarthy campaigned against the war and the "imperial presidency." Kennedy opposed the war, but not executive and federal power, and he called on the government to better meet the needs of the poor and minorities. Vice President Hubert H. Humphrey, running in the shadow of Johnson, stood behind the president's foreign and domestic programs.

By June, Kennedy was winning the primary race, drawing heavily from minorities and urban Democratic voters. But his candidacy abruptly ended when, after celebrating his victory in the California primary, Kennedy was shot by Sirhan Sirhan, a Jordanian immigrant. He died the next day. His death stunned the nation and ensured Humphrey's nomination. McCarthy continued his campaign but generated little support among party regulars. By the time of the national convention in Chicago in August, Humphrey had enough pledged votes to guarantee his nomination. Nevertheless, the convention was dramatic. Inside and outside the convention center, antiwar and anti-establishment groups demonstrated for McCarthy, peace in Vietnam, and social justice. By August 24, the second day of the convention, clashes between the police and protesters started and grew more belligerent every day. Protesters threw eggs, bottles, rocks, and balloons filled with water, ink, and urine at the police, who responded with tear gas and nightsticks. On August 28, the police indiscriminately attacked protesters and bystanders alike as television cameras recorded the scene. The violence in Chicago's streets overshadowed Humphrey's nomination.

The 1968 presidential campaign soon became a three-party race. Drawing on growing dissatisfaction with liberal social policies within Democratic

As governor of Alabama, George Wallace announced "segregation now, segregation tomorrow, segregation forever" and physically tried to stop the integration of the University of Alabama in 1963. In 1968, he bolted the Democratic Party to run for the presidency, hoping to force the election into the House of Representatives. He attacked liberalism and the youth culture, African Americans and integration, and hippies and the antiwar movement. He carried five southern states.

Howard Sochurek/Time Life Pictures/Getty Images.

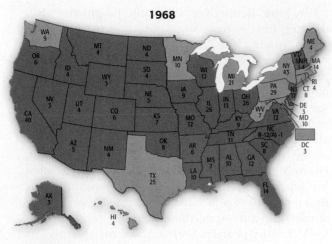

1968

Candidate (Party)	Electoral Vote		Popular Vote	
Nixon (Republican)	301	56.1%	31,710,470	43.4%
Humphrey (Democrat)	191	35.5%	30,898,055	42.3%
Wallace (American Independent)	46	8.4%	9,446,167	12.9%

MAP 27.2 Election of 1968

In winning the 1968 election against Hubert Humphrey, Richard Nixon received fewer popular votes than he did in 1960, when he won more than 34 million votes. But in the all-important electoral vote, Nixon easily defeated his Democratic rival. As they did in the 1960 election, some southerners, unwilling to vote for a Republican or a liberal Democrat, opted for a third choice, George Wallace.

Copyright © Cengage Learning

ranks, Governor **George Wallace** of Alabama left the Democratic Party and ran for president as the American Independent Party's candidate. He aimed his campaign at southern whites, blue-collar workers, and low-income white Americans, all of whom deplored the social unrest and "loss" of traditional American values. On the campaign trail, Wallace called for victory in Vietnam and gleefully attacked the counterculture and the "rich-kid" war protesters who avoided serving in Vietnam while the sons of working-class Americans died there. He also opposed federal civil rights and welfare legislation. Two months before the election, Wallace commanded 21 percent of the vote, according to national opinion polls. "On November 5," he confidently predicted,

■ **George Wallace** Conservative Alabama governor who opposed desegregation in the 1960s and ran unsuccessfully for the presidency in 1968 and 1972.

Sunbelt A region stretching from Florida in a westward arc across the South and Southwest.

"they're going to find out there are a lot of rednecks in this country."

Richard Nixon was the Republican candidate, having easily won his party's nomination. He focused his campaign on the need for effective international leadership, law and order, and the restoration of values. He denounced the four "Ps": pot, pornography, protesters, and permissiveness. On the critical issue of Vietnam, he offered no specifics but promised to "end the war and win the peace." Nixon won with a comfortable margin in the Electoral College, although he received only 43 percent of the popular vote (see Map 27.2). Together, Nixon and Wallace attracted almost 56 percent of the popular vote, which conservatives interpreted as wide public support for an end to liberal programs, a return to traditional values, and a major political realignment that emphasized the suburbs and the **Sunbelt**.

DEFINING THE AMERICAN DREAM

★ How did Latinos and Native Americans seek to address the problems they faced in American society?

★ How did the federal government respond to their efforts?

By 1968, there seemed little agreement on the nature of the American dream and the role of government in helping to achieve that end. From King to Carmichael, African Americans had confronted the old order with increasing militancy. But they were not alone. Like blacks, Latinos and American Indians remained near society's lowest levels of income and education. As the 1960s progressed, they too organized grassroots movements and confronted the status quo, demanding change.

The Emergence of *La Causa*

Initially enthusiastic about Kennedy, many Latino leaders were disappointed in his presidential actions. Few Hispanics were appointed to government positions, nor did there seem much interest in listening to Latino voices or promoting their civil rights. Federal agencies appeared to defer those issues to local and state governments, which frequently resisted Latino activism, especially by Mexican Americans, who despite being the largest minority in the western states, were still, according to one Mexican American leader, the "invisible minority."

Among the most invisible and poorest were those working in the fields. Trapped at the bottom of the occupational ladder, not covered by Social Security or minimum-wage and labor laws, unskilled and uneducated farm laborers—nearly one-third of all Mexican Americans—toiled long hours for low wages under often deplorable conditions. In 1962, drawing from a traditional base of farm worker organizations, **César Chávez** and Dolores Huerta organized farm workers in central California, creating the National Farm Workers Association (NFWA). The union gained national recognition three years later when it struck against the grape growers. The union demanded a wage of $1.40 an hour and asked the public to buy only union-picked grapes. After five years, the strike and the nationwide boycott forced most of the major growers to accept unionization and to improve wages and working conditions. Eventually, California and other states passed legislation to recognize farm workers' unions and to improve the wages and conditions of work for field workers, but agricultural workers, especially migrants, remain among the lowest-paid workers in the nation.

Chávez was central in promoting *La Causa* (Spanish for "the cause"), but he was not alone. Similar grassroot movements focusing on jobs, wages, and education were forming throughout the West and Southwest. Latino leaders like Rodolfo "Corky" Gonzales argued that discrimination and segregation barred their children from a decent education and that school districts needed to offer programs to meet the special needs of Hispanic students, including bilingual education.

In Los Angeles, Raul Ruiz told Mexican American students: "If you are a student you should be angry! You should demand! You should protest! You should organize for a better education!" He called for students to walk out of their classes if schools did not meet their demands. In 1967, "walkouts" spread in California and Texas. In the small South Texas school district of Edcouch-Elsa, Mexican American students walked out of the high school in November 1968. They demanded dignity, respect, and an end to "blatant discrimination," including corporal punishment—paddling—for speaking Spanish. The school board blamed "outside agitators" and suspended more than 150 students. But as in other school districts, the protests brought results. The Edcouch-Elsa school district implemented Mexican American studies and bilingual programs, hired Mexican American teachers, and created programs for migrant farm worker children, who moved from one school to another during picking season. Prominent in the growing grassroots militancy among Mexican Americans were young adults, who called themselves **Chicanos**. They stressed pride in their heritage and Latino culture and called for resistance to the dictates of Anglo society—"We're not in the melting pot. . . . Chicanos don't melt."

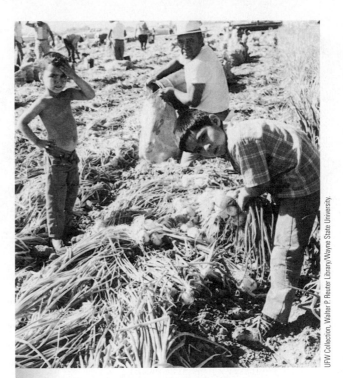

UFW Collection, Walter P. Reuter Library/Wayne State University.

For most Mexican American farm laborers, working in the fields was a family affair. Children as well as adults played a necessary economic role, traveling along with their families from location to location as the need for farm labor dictated. In this picture, children work in the onion fields of California.

It was not only in the West that Latinos were becoming more visible (see Map 27.3). In the urban Northeast, the Puerto Rican population had increased to about a million while economic opportunities declined as manufacturing jobs, especially in the garment industry, relocated to the Sunbelt or overseas. The Puerto Rican Forum attempted to coordinate federal grants and to find jobs, while the more militant Young Lords organized younger Puerto Ricans in Chicago and New York with an emphasis on their island culture and Hispanic heritage. "Brown Power" had joined Black Power, soon to be joined by "Red Power."

■ **César Chávez** Labor organizer who in 1962 founded the National Farm Workers Association; Chávez believed in nonviolence and used marches, boycotts, and fasts to bring moral and economic pressure to bear on growers.

■ **Chicano** A variation of *Mexicano*, a man or boy of Mexican decent. The feminine form is Chicana. Many Mexican Americans used the term during the late 1960s to signifiy their ethnic identity.

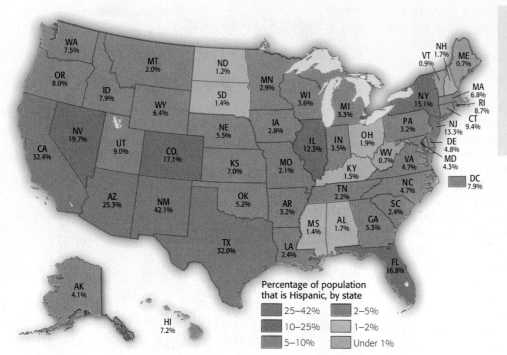

MAP 27.3 Changing Latino Population
Growing rapidly, the Latino population became the largest minority population in the United States by 2000, reaching 12.5 percent of the total population.
Copyright © Cengage Learning

Percentage of population that is Hispanic, by state
- 25–42%
- 10–25%
- 5–10%
- 2–5%
- 1–2%
- Under 1%

American Indian Activism

American Indians, responding to poverty, federal and state termination policies, and efforts by state government to seize land for development, organized and asserted their rights with new vigor in the 1960s. In 1961, reservation and nonreservation Indians met in Chicago to discuss problems and consider plans of action (see Map 27.4). They produced the "Declaration of Indian Purpose" that called for the end of the termination policies and for improved education, economic, and health opportunities. "What we ask of America is not charity, not paternalism" but that "our situation be recognized and be made a basis . . . of action." Presidents Kennedy and Johnson responded positively, ensuring that Indians benefited from New Frontier and Great Society programs. Johnson, in 1968, declared that Native Americans should have the same "standard of living" as the rest of the nation and signed the Indian Civil Rights Act. It officially ended the termination program and gave more power to tribal organizations.

■ **Russell Means** Indian activist who helped organize the seizures of Alcatraz and Wounded Knee.

Alcatraz Island Rocky island, formerly a federal prison, in San Francisco Bay occupied by Native American activists who demanded that it be made available to them as a cultural center.

■ **American Indian Movement** (AIM) Militant Indian movement founded in 1968 that was willing to use confrontation to obtain social justice and Indian treaty rights; organized the seizure of Wounded Knee.

Kennedy's and Johnson's support was a good beginning, but many activists wanted to redress old wrongs. The National Indian Youth Council called for "Red Power"—for Indians to use all means possible to resist further loss of their lands, rights, and traditions. They began "fish-ins" in 1964 when the Washington state government, in violation of treaty rights, barred Indians from fishing in certain areas. Protests, arrests, and violence continued until 1975, when the state complied with a federal court decision (*United States v. Washington*) upholding treaty rights. Indian leaders also demanded the protection and restoration of their water and timber rights and ancient burial grounds. Museums were asked to return for proper burial the remains and grave goods of Indians on display. But for most, the crucial issue was self-determination, which would allow Indians control over their lands and over federal programs that served the reservations.

In 1969 a group of San Francisco Indian activists, led by **Russell Means**, gained national attention by seizing **Alcatraz Island** and holding it until 1971 when, without bloodshed, federal authorities regained control. Two years later, in a more violent confrontation, **American Indian Movement** (AIM) leaders Means and Dennis Banks led an armed occupation of Wounded Knee, South Dakota, the site of the 1890 massacre of the Lakotas by the army (see page 436). AIM controlled the town for seventy-one days before surrendering to federal authorities. Two Indians were killed, and over 230 activists arrested, in the "Second Battle of Wounded Knee."

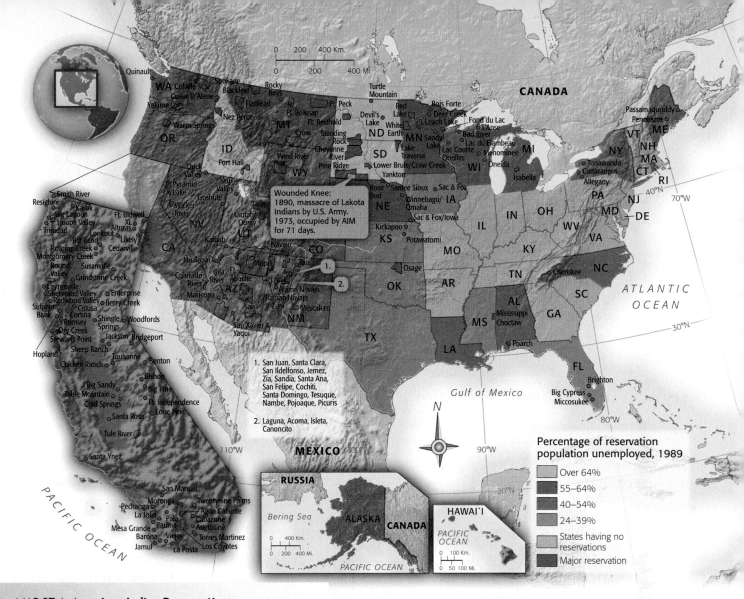

MAP 27.4 American Indian Reservations
In the seventeenth century, American Indians roamed over an estimated 1.9 billion acres, but by 1990 that area had shrunk to about 46 million acres spread across the United States. This area constitutes the federal reservation system. This map shows the location of most of the federal Indian reservations and highlights the high unemployment found on nearly every reservation. (*Note*: California is enlarged to show the many small reservations located there.) Copyright © Cengage Learning

President Nixon opposed AIM's actions at Wounded Knee but agreed that tribal and individual lives needed to be improved. He doubled funding for the Bureau of Indian Affairs, promoted tribal economies, and signed bills that returned 40 million acres of Alaskan land to Eskimos and other native peoples. In 1974 Congress passed the **Indian Self-Determination and Education Assistance Act**, giving tribes control and operation of many federal programs on their reservations. Tribal and pan-Indian movements sparked cultural pride and awareness. "We're a giant that's been asleep because we've been fed through our veins by the federal government," stated a Navajo leader. "But now that's ending, and we're waking up and flexing

muscles we never knew we had. And no one knows what we're capable of."

As federal courts asserted Indian treaty rights and tribes gained more control over their resources, some experienced economic growth and cultural revivals. Indian languages were revived and on many reservations disease and mortality rates declined, leading to population growth. Economically, some Indian tribes

Indian Self-Determination and Education Assistance Act 1974 law giving Indian tribes control over federal programs carried out on their reservations and increasing their authority in reservation schools.

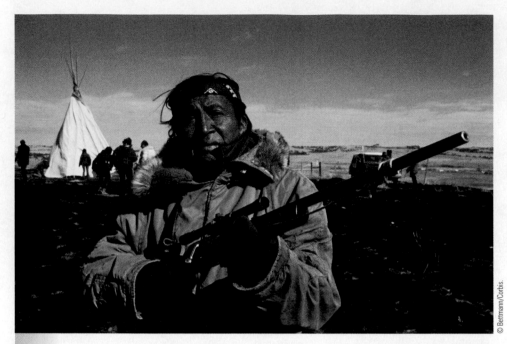

Oscar Bear Runner was one of two hundred Sioux organized by the American Indian Movement (AIM) who took over Wounded Knee, South Dakota, the site of the 1890 massacre, holding out for seventy-one days against state and federal authorities. The confrontation ended when one protester was killed and the federal government agreed to examine the treaty rights of the Oglala Sioux.

© Bettmann/Corbis.

greatly benefitted from the Indian Gaming Regulatory Act in 1988 that allowed reservations to open gaming casinos. By 2006 over 228 tribes had casinos earning over $23 billion. But profits are not equally distributed. Casinos near urban areas, like Mohegan Sun casino in Connecticut, do well while those in rural areas often struggle to break even. Consequently, few tribes see substantial economic gains and overall Indians remain the nation's most impoverished peoples.

NIXON AND THE WORLD

★ How did Richard Nixon plan to achieve an "honorable" peace in Vietnam?

★ How did Nixon's Cold War policies differ from those favored by earlier administrations?

In 1969 Nixon achieved the dream denied him in 1960—he was the president. Determined to be the center of decision making, he relied primarily on his own judgment and on a few close and loyal advisers.

■ **Henry Kissinger** German-born American diplomat who was President Nixon's national security adviser and secretary of state; he helped negotiate the cease-fire in Vietnam.

■ **Vietnamization** U.S. policy of scaling back American involvement in Vietnam and helping Vietnamese forces fight their own war.

For domestic affairs, he looked to John Mitchell, his attorney general, and longtime associates H. R. "Bob" Haldeman and John Ehrlichman. In foreign affairs, he tapped Harvard professor **Henry Kissinger** as his national security adviser and later made him secretary of state. In both domestic and foreign affairs, Nixon wanted to institute policies that would consolidate his presidency and strengthen the Republican Party.

Vietnamization

Vietnam was the foremost issue; it influenced nearly all others—the budget, public and congressional opinion, foreign policy, and domestic stability. Nixon needed a solution before he could move ahead on other fronts. The central question was not whether American troops should be withdrawn, but how best to do it while ensuring that the government of Nguyen Van Thieu remained intact and maintaining America's international and his own credibility. If the United States left Vietnam too abruptly, it would harm American relations. "A nation cannot remain great," Nixon said, "if it betrays its allies and lets down its friends."

The outcome was **Vietnamization**. Better-trained and better equipped South Vietnamese units would assume the bulk of the fighting as American troops left (see Figure 27.1). Changing the "color of bodies" and bringing American soldiers home, Nixon believed, would rebuild public support and diminish the crowds of protesters. Expanding the theme of

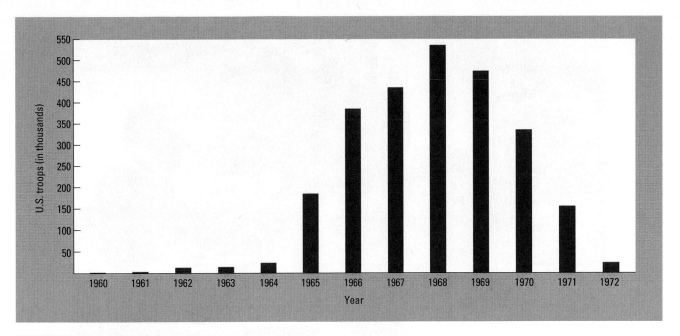

FIGURE 27.1 Troop Levels by Year, 1960–1972
For America, the Vietnam War went through two major phases: Americanization from 1960 to 1968 and Vietnamization from 1969 to 1972.

limiting American involvement, in July, the president announced the **Nixon Doctrine**: countries warding off communism would have to shoulder most of the military burden, with the United States providing political and economic aid and limited naval and air support.

Nixon publicly announced Vietnamization in the spring of 1969, telling the public that 25,000 American soldiers were coming home. Against a backdrop of some of the largest antiwar rallies in fall of 1969, Nixon worked to discredit protestors and called upon the Silent Majority to rally behind Vietnamization. "North Vietnam cannot defeat or humiliate" us, Nixon stated, "[o]nly Americans can do that." Nixon's approval rating soared after the speech and he was able to convince much of the media to alter their coverage of the war, downplaying the fighting and emphasizing "themes and stories under the general heading: We are on our way out of Vietnam." By the end of the year, American forces in Vietnam had declined by over 110,000, public opinion polls indicated support for Nixon's policy, and it appeared that the antiwar movement was losing momentum.

While Nixon's public Vietnam policy appeared to find approval at home, he and Kissinger quietly worked to improve relations with the Soviets and Chinese and to encourage them to reduce their support for North Vietnam. At the same time, Nixon ordered an expansion of the air war to support Vietnamization. Bombing of North Vietnam resumed and secret air attacks (Operation Menu) expanded the war by targeting enemy bases inside Cambodia and Laos. The air assault was part of a "madman strategy" that Nixon

designed to convince the North Vietnamese to negotiate. Nixon said he wanted Hanoi "to believe that I've reached the point where I might do anything to stop the war." "We'll just slip the word," Nixon told his advisers, "that 'for God's sake, you know Nixon. . . .We can't restrain him when he's angry—and he has his hand on the nuclear button.'"

The strategy did not work. The North Vietnamese believed that victory was only a matter of waiting until America was fed up with the war. Nixon remained committed to his strategy and in April 1970 ordered American troops to cross the border into Cambodia and destroy Communist bases and supply areas. The mission successfully demolished enemy bases and large amounts of supplies, but it also created a firestorm of protest in the United States.

A new wave of antiwar protests occurred around the country. Demonstrations against the war at the universities of Kent State (Ohio) and Jackson State (Mississippi) resulted in six dead students; eighty thousand protesters marched on the Capitol. The Senate overwhelmingly repealed the Gulf of Tonkin Resolution, which had provided the legislative foundation for the war, and forbade the further use of American troops in Laos or Cambodia.

■ **Nixon Doctrine** Nixon's policy of requiring countries threatened by communism to shoulder most of the military burden, with the United States offering mainly political and economic support.

Together, Richard Nixon and Secretary of State Henry Kissinger (shown here) sought to refocus American foreign policy by ending the war in Vietnam and improving relations with the Soviet Union and the People's Republic of China.

Adding to broadening opposition to the war, the release of the **Pentagon Papers** showed that American administrations from Truman to Nixon had not told the truth about Vietnam. Stories about drug use, **fragging**, and seemingly mindless slaughter strengthened the belief that the war was unraveling the morality of American soldiers. The court martial of Lieutenant William Calley, charged with murder, was a case in point. Calley's platoon had killed over five hundred men, women, and children in and around the village of **My Lai** in 1968. "This is not what the American soldier does," explained a helicopter pilot who had rescued some of the My Lai

Pentagon Papers Classified government documents on policy decisions leaked to the press by Daniel Ellsberg and printed by the *New York Times* in 1971.

fragging An effort to kill fellow soldiers, frequently officers, by using a grenade. It may have accounted for over a thousand American deaths in Vietnam.

■ **My Lai** Site of a massacre of South Vietnamese villagers by U.S. infantrymen in 1968. Of those brought to trial for the atrocity, only Lieutenant William Calley was found guilty of murder.

villagers. By early 1972, public opinion polls indicated that two-thirds of the American people wanted to get out of Vietnam.

Aware of declining support for the war in the United States and the weakness of South Vietnamese forces, North Vietnam in March 1972 launched its "Easter Offensive." Pushing aside Army of South Vietnam (ARVN) troops, Communist forces advanced toward Saigon. Nixon ordered massive bombing raids against North Vietnam and Communist forces in South Vietnam that enabled ARVN forces to regroup and drive back the North Vietnamese and encouraged the North Vietnamese to renew peace talks in Paris. In October, Kissinger announced "Peace is at hand," just in time for the 1972 presidential election.

South Vietnamese president Nguyen Van Thieu, however, rejected the plan. Reluctantly, Nixon supported Thieu, and he ordered the Christmas bombing of Hanoi and North Vietnam to convince Thieu that the United States would use its power to protect South Vietnam. After eleven days the bombing stopped. When talks resumed, Washington advised Thieu to accept the next peace settlement or fend for

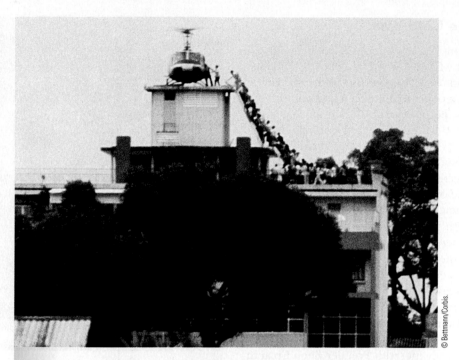

As North Vietnamese forces entered Saigon in April 1975, the last American evacuees left by helicopter. Here, they scramble to the roof of the Pittman apartments in Saigon; others left from the roof of the American embassy. Henry Kissinger asked the nation "to put Vietnam behind us."

himself. On January 27, 1973, Thieu accepted a peace settlement that did not differ significantly from the one offered in October. Nixon proclaimed peace with honor. The peace settlement imposed a cease-fire, removed the twenty-four thousand remaining American troops, and promised the return of American prisoners of war. The peace terms permitted the United States to end its role in the war. Because the settlement left North Vietnamese troops in South Vietnam, it did little to ensure the existence of Thieu's government or nation. When Haldeman asked Kissinger how long the South Vietnamese government could last, Kissinger answered bluntly, "If they're lucky, they can hold out for a year and a half."

To reassert congressional power to limit the president's war-making abilities, in November 1973, Congress passed over Nixon's veto the **War Powers Act**. The law requires the president to inform Congress within forty-eight hours of the deployment of troops overseas and to withdraw those troops within sixty days if Congress fails to authorize the action. As expected, North Vietnam continued to funnel men and supplies to the south, and in March 1975, they renewed the war. Congress refused to supply military aid and a month later, North Vietnamese troops entered Saigon. The Vietnam War ended as it had started, with Vietnamese fighting Vietnamese (see Table 27.1)

TABLE 27.1 The Vietnam Generation, 1964–1975

	MEN	WOMEN
Total in military service	8,700,000	250,000
Served in Vietnam	2,700,000	6,431
Killed in Vietnam	58,219	8
Wounded	303,000*	
Missing in action	2,330	1
Draft resisters (estimate)	570,000	—
Accused	210,000	—
Convicted	8,750	—

*Combined men and women
Source: Department of Defense and Veterans Administration.

■ **War Powers Act** 1973 law to prevent the president from involving the United States in war without authorization by Congress.

Modifying the Cold War

Ending the Vietnam War was a necessity in Nixon's grand plan to reshape the Cold War. An "era of confrontation" must give way to an "era of negotiation," Nixon said as he pursued **détente**, a policy that reduced tensions with the two Communist superpowers. China was the key to the strategy. The United States did not recognize the Beijing government and there had been no diplomatic contact since the end of the Chinese civil war in 1949. Establishing diplomatic connections with Communist China would provide new trade opportunities and would, in Nixon's and Kissinger's view, encourage the Soviets to improve their relations with the United States. The Soviets and Chinese had engaged in several bloody clashes along their border, and the Chinese hoped that better relations with the United States would help deter Soviet aggression. They also wanted access to American technology. Sending a signal to China, Nixon lowered restrictions on trade. The Chinese responded by inviting an American ping-pong team to tour China in April 1971. Three months later, Kissinger secretly met with Premier Zhou Enlai in Beijing. On Kissinger's return, Nixon stunned the world when he announced he would meet with Communist Party chairman Mao Zedong and Zhou in Beijing in February 1972. The first step in moving toward détente was in place. The second occurred in May when Nixon met Soviet President **Leonid Brezhnev**, saying their two nations should "live together and work together." The meeting was a success. Brezhnev obtained increased trade with the United States, especially much needed grain. The two superpower leaders also announced the **Strategic Arms Limitation agreement** (SALT I), which restricted antimissile sites and established a maximum number of intercontinental ballistic missiles (ICBMs) and submarine-launched ballistic missiles (SLBMs) for each side.

Nixon pursued détente with China and the Soviet Union, but in other areas of the world it was business as usual. In Latin America, he continued efforts to isolate Cuba and sought to remove the democratically elected socialist-Marxist government of **Salvador Allende** in

In efforts to redirect the Cold War, Nixon became the first president to visit China, meeting with Mao Zedong and Zhou Enlai in 1972. With regard to Chinese-Soviet relations, Nixon confided to Zhou that if Moscow marched either east or west, he was ready to "turn like a cobra on the Russians." Nixon's visit to China began the process of normalizing relations with the People's Republic of China that was finalized under Carter.

John Dominis/Time Life Pictures/Getty Images.

Chile. Kissinger thought they should not "let a country go Marxist just because its people are irresponsible." From 1970 to 1973, the United States openly and covertly worked to destabilize the Allende government and support his opponents until, in September 1973, the Chilean military stormed the presidential palace, killing Allende. The Nixon administration denied any direct American role in the coup but quickly recognized the repressive military government of General Augusto Pinochet, who promptly reinstated a free-market economy. Other Latin American dictators and the repressive governments of Iran and South Africa also received economic and military aid.

détente Relaxing of tensions between the superpowers in the early 1970s, which led to increased diplomatic, commercial, and cultural contact.

■ **Leonid Brezhnev** Leader of the Soviet Union (first as Communist Party secretary, and then also as president) from 1964 to his death in 1982; he worked to foster détente with the United States during the Nixon era.

■ **Strategic Arms Limitation agreement** (SALT I) Treaty between the United States and the Soviet Union in 1972 to limit offensive nuclear weapons and defensive antiballistic missile systems.

■ **Salvador Allende** Chilean president who was considered the first democratically elected Marxist to head a government; he was killed in a coup in 1973.

NIXON AND THE DOMESTIC AGENDA

☆ How did Nixon's policies dealing with the economy, welfare, and the environment reflect his pragmatic approach? What did he do to increase the base of the Republican Party?

☆ What actions led to the Watergate investigation and Nixon's resignation?

Like Kennedy, Nixon favored foreign over domestic affairs. He had a grand scheme for changing foreign policy, but no similar plan for domestic affairs. And he

It Matters Today

Banning DDT

In 1972, the United States banned the use of the pesticide DDT. Widely used in agriculture to protect crops from insects, it entered the food chain, creating medical problems in animals and humans. Momentum for the ban began with Rachel Carson's publication of *Silent Spring* (1962), which examined the effects of the chemical on nature and questioned societies' blind faith in technological progress. Since 1972, many other nations have stopped the use of DDT, and in 2008 the United Nations announced its goal to halt its worldwide use by 2020. Carson's views and the banning of DDT were, and continue to be, strongly criticized. Some have claimed that following her logic would mean returning to the "Dark Ages" when "insects and diseases . . . would . . . again inherit the earth" and that she is responsible for more deaths than Hitler.

- Should developed nations be able to dictate the ban of chemicals like DDT to countries that might benefit economically from using such toxic chemicals?
- The reference to Carson's killing of millions of people refers to deaths from malaria—a disease linked to mosquitoes—because DDT has been banned. Research the spread of malaria and the use of DDT since 1972 to determine if this accusation is valid.

was the first president since 1858 to take office without his own party controlling either house of Congress, which clearly complicated implementing traditional Republican agendas. Consequently, Nixon adopted a complex and pragmatic approach that balanced his desire to expand the Republican Party with an unexpectedly progressive social agenda.

Nixon as Pragmatist

Shocking many conservative Republicans, between 1969 and 1971, Nixon's administration adopted a surprisingly liberal agenda. It increased welfare support and approved legislation that enhanced the regulatory powers of the federal government. Food stamps became more accessible, and Social Security, Medicare, and Medicaid payments were increased. By 1972, for the first time since 1942, the government was spending more on social programs than on defense. Nixon's approaches to affirmative action and welfare were innovative and many considered them to be more liberal than conservative. Pat Buchanan, Nixon's speechwriter, considered Nixon "a fellow traveler of the right" but not a true conservative.

The "Philadelphia Plan," Nixon's affirmative action plan, paralleled earlier Democratic efforts. It required companies receiving federal contracts to file plans for hiring minority and women workers within 120 days of receiving the contract. It also required unions to open membership to more minorities. His effort to keep his campaign promise to fix the "welfare mess" was a pragmatic effort to replace "millions on welfare rolls"

with "millions on payrolls," keep the nuclear family intact, and eliminate many existing welfare agencies. The Family Assistance Plan that emerged in 1969 provided low-income families a direct monetary payment from the government, along with food stamps, as long as recipients worked or enrolled in job training programs. It was defeated by a coalition of conservatives and liberals in Congress in 1969 and again in 1971. Nixon blamed Congress, conservatives, and "damn social workers."

Like his predecessors, Nixon, too, expanded the federal government, creating the Occupational Safety and Health Administration (OSHA) and the **Environmental Protection Agency** (EPA). The modern environmental movement was gaining momentum when Nixon took office. Rachel Carson alerted the nation to the dangers of DDT in her book *Silent Spring* (1962) and touched off a wave of environmental concerns. By 1969, it was hard to ignore reports on urban air pollution, the ecological death of Lake Erie, and growing mountains of garbage everywhere. A national response came in April 1970, when communities and thousands of schools and colleges hosted Earth Day activities. It was the largest single-day demonstration in American history and showed a public deeply concerned about a worsening environment.

■ **Environmental Protection Agency** (EPA) Agency created to consolidate all major governmental programs controlling pollution and other programs to protect the environment.

On January 29, 1969, six miles off the coast of Santa Barbara, California, a Union Oil Co. platform oil spill occurred that in more than eleven days released over 200,000 gallons. The oil spill spread over 800 square miles and washed ashore along the California coast. In this picture, workers and volunteers work to clean up the oil-soaked beaches, and others sought to save oil-coated wildlife. President Nixon said the spill at Santa Barbara "touched the conscience of the American people."

Nixon was not an environmentalist and thought the movement was "overrated." But he recognized an emerging political issue. In July, he proposed the creation of the EPA to monitor and implement pollution standards. Congress approved it in December. Between 1970 and 1974, Congress and Nixon also approved a wide variety of environment legislation, including a Clean Air Act, Safe Drinking Water Act, and an Endangered Species Act. Watching the actions of OSHA, the EPA, and other regulatory agencies, many conservatives, including Nixon's economic adviser, complained that he was imposing the most "regulation on the economy . . . since the New Deal."

Nixon also proved flexible in economic matters. When he took office, he faced a budget deficit of nearly $25 billion and a climbing rate of inflation. Nixon cut spending, increased interest rates, and balanced the

budget in 1969. But economic recovery failed to follow, and inflation rose as economic growth slowed—giving rise to a new phenomenon, **stagflation**. By 1971, the economy was in its first serious recession since 1958. Unemployment and bankruptcies increased, but inflation still climbed, approaching 5.3 percent. Fearing that economic woes would erode his support, Nixon shifted his approach and asked for increased federal spending to boost recovery and for a wage and price freeze to stall inflation. Shocked conservatives complained bitterly at the betrayal of their values. But the economy responded positively as inflation and unemployment declined. Nonetheless, Nixon's battle with inflation was a losing one. Wages and prices climbed when Nixon lifted the wage and price freeze, and they soared in 1973 when Arab nations raised oil prices and limited oil sales to the United States (discussed later in this chapter).

Building the Silent Majority

While pursuing his pragmatic approach, Nixon was determined to expand and strengthen the Republican Party. To do this he looked at two regions, the Sunbelt and the South. He adopted a **"southern strategy"** to shatter the once solid Democratic South.

stagflation Persistent inflation combined with stagnant consumer demand and relatively high unemployment.

■ **southern strategy** A plan to entice southerners into the Republican Party by appointing white southerners to the Supreme Court and resisting the policy of busing to achieve integration.

In the rest of the Sunbelt, he hoped that Republican policies opposing liberal activism and supporting state authority would attract voters to the Republican Party. By opposing forced school integration and supporting neighborhood schools Nixon believed he could attract white southerners and many urban northern blue-collar workers to the Republican Party. He told Haldeman to "go for the Poles, Italians, Irish" but not "Jews or Blacks." In response to a 1969 request from Mississippi to postpone court-ordered integration of several school systems, Attorney General John Mitchell petitioned the Supreme Court for a delay. At the same time, the administration lobbied Congress for a revision of the 1965 Voting Rights Act that would have weakened southern compliance. Neither effort was successful. In October 1969, the Supreme Court unanimously decreed in *Alexander v. Holmes* that it was "the obligation of every school district to terminate dual school systems at once." The White House's support for de facto segregated neighborhood schools suffered another loss in 1971 when the Burger Court reaffirmed the use of busing to achieve integration in a North Carolina case, *Swann v. Charlotte-Mecklenburg*. The Nixon administration criticized the decisions but agreed to "carry out the law." By 1973, most African American children in the South were attending integrated public schools. Nixon was unable to slow the process of integration, but he won increasing political support among white southerners.

Another part of Nixon's political strategy was to stress his administration's support for law and order with the passage of anticrime legislation that would strengthen the criminal justice system and alter the liberal composition of the federal court system. He intended to appoint judges and justices who would be tougher on criminals and more narrowly interpret the Constitution. In 1969, Chief Justice Earl Warren retired, and Nixon nominated Warren Burger, a respected, conservative federal judge, who was easily confirmed by the Senate. Within months, another resignation gave Nixon a second chance to alter the Court. Merging his desire for a conservative judge with his southern strategy, Nixon first chose South Carolinian Clement Haynesworth and then G. Harrold Carswell of Florida for the position. The Senate rejected both nominees because of their lack of support for integration. On his third try, Nixon abandoned his southern strategy and chose Harry Blackmun, a conservative from Minnesota. Blackmun was confirmed easily. In 1971 Nixon appointed two more justices, Lewis Powell of Virginia and William Rehnquist of Arizona, creating a more conservative Burger Supreme Court.

An Embattled President

By the end of Nixon's first term, nearly 60 percent of respondents in national opinion polls approved of the president's record. The South was no longer solidly Democratic, and Sunbelt and blue-collar worker voters seemed to be supporting Republican issues and candidates. The economy, while still a worry, seemed under control. Diplomatically, Nixon had scored major successes with China and the Soviets, and a peace agreement in Paris seemed possible. Nixon projected that he would easily win reelection in 1972.

Meanwhile, Democrats were in disarray. Their most enthusiastic members appeared to be migrating to either the liberal Senator **George McGovern** or the conservative George Wallace. The newest category of voter, ages 18–21, voting for the first time as a result of the Twenty-sixth Amendment (ratified in 1971), seemed to be in McGovern's camp. When Senator McGovern won the nomination, George Wallace—confined to a wheelchair following an assassination attempt that left him paralyzed—again bolted the party to run as a third-party candidate on the American Independent ticket.

Despite almost certain victory, Nixon obsessed about enemies surrounding him. This preoccupation was not new but one that lay beneath the surface throughout his political career. Repeatedly, as president, he spoke about "screwing" his domestic enemies before they got him and how the press hated him. He warned his cabinet and staff that the press would "run lies about you . . . and the cartoonists will depict you as ogres." To combat his foes, Nixon kept an "enemies list," used illegal wiretaps and infiltration to spy on anti-administration organizations and people, and instructed the FBI, the Internal Revenue Service, and other governmental organizations to intimidate and punish his opponents. As the 1972 campaign began, Nixon and his campaign coordinators longed to humiliate their enemies and smash the Democrats. To achieve this, Nixon's staff and the **Committee to Re-elect the President** (CREEP), directed by John Mitchell, stepped outside the normal bounds of election behavior. A Special

■ **George McGovern** South Dakota senator who opposed the Vietnam War and was the unsuccessful Democratic candidate for president in 1972.

■ **Committee to Re-elect the President** (CREEP) Nixon's campaign committee in 1972, headed by John Mitchell, which enlisted G. Gordon Liddy and others to spy on the Democrats and break into the offices of the Democratic National Committee.

Despite his efforts to keep his role in the Watergate break-in hidden, the Watergate tapes and other testimony clearly indicated Nixon's direct role in the affair. When it became evident that he would be removed from office through the process of impeachment, he chose to resign from the presidency. In this picture taken on August 9, 1974, in the East Room of the White House, surrounded by his family, President Nixon informs his staff and others of his resignation.

Investigations Unit, known informally as the "Plumbers," conducted "dirty tricks" to disrupt the Democrats' activities. Seeking inside information on the opposition, CREEP approved a burglary of the Democratic National Committee headquarters in the **Watergate** building in Washington, D.C., to copy documents and tap phones.

On June 17, 1972, a Watergate security guard detected the burglars and notified the police. Five men were arrested carrying "bugging" equipment and two others were apprehended across the street. The burglars were soon linked to CREEP. Although the committee denied any connection to the burglary, both CREEP and the White House tried to disrupt any investigations and paid the suspects to help in the cover-up. "I want you all to stonewall it," Nixon told Mitchell. "Cover it up." The furor passed, and in November, Nixon buried McGovern in an ava-

lanche of electoral votes, winning every state except Massachusetts.

Despite Democrats still holding majorities in Congress, Nixon was overjoyed. "Seventy-three can be and should be the best year yet," he informed his cabinet. But his optimism faded as the cover-up unraveled. The burglars were convicted in January 1973. By then, *Washington Post* reporters Bob Woodward and Carl Bernstein, helped by "Deep Throat," a secret source inside the FBI, had uncovered a trail of "hush money" leading to CREEP and the White House. By May three separate investigations of the Watergate affair were under way. The most public was by a Special Committee of the Senate chaired by a Democrat, Senator Sam Ervin, Jr., of North Carolina, but the federal grand jury investigation led by Judge John Sirica and a Justice Department investigation conducted by Archibald Cox could result in criminal prosecutions.

Throughout the spring and summer, testimony linked the break-in and cover-up to CREEP and the executive branch. Trying to limit the damage, Nixon accepted the resignations of Haldeman, Ehrlichman, and others on his staff. "Until March, I remained convinced," he announced, that "the charges of involvement by . . . the White House staff were false." Nixon continued to deny he was involved, but his statements were less and less credible as the testimony unfolded,

■ **Watergate** Apartment and office complex in Washington, D.C., where CREEP "Plumbers" broke into the headquarters of the Democratic National Committee; its name became synonymous with the Nixon administration's involvement and the president's part in the cover-up that followed.

In the Wider World

Oil Shock

In 1973, the relationship between the Middle East and the rest of the world changed when OPEC raised the price of oil and implemented an embargo against nations supporting Israel during the Yom Kipper War. In addition to weakening American and European support for Israel, oil-producing countries wanted more control over the production and pricing structures of oil, which would mean more profits. As the shah of Iran explained, it was "only fair, from now on, you should pay more for oil. Let's say ten times more."

Suddenly the price of oil quadrupled to over $12 a barrel, and at the gas pump consumers faced a nearly 60 percent increase. New wealth flowed into coffers of the oil producers, their profits going from $22.5 billion in 1973 to $272 billion in 1980. At the same time, industrialized nations that depended on cheap oil experienced a global recession. The "lean times" had arrived, said one economist. OPEC's actions changed the world's economy as nations adjusted their priorities and energy policies, but it had no effect on the Yom Kipper War as Israeli forces defeated Egypt's and Syria's forces and annexed new territories.

---

especially after **John Dean** said he had discussed the break-in with Nixon as early as mid-1972.

In July 1973, the nature of the investigations changed when it was revealed that Nixon had secretly recorded meetings in the Oval Office, including those with Dean. Claiming executive privilege, Nixon refused demands for the tapes from Cox, Sirica, and Ervin. When Cox refused to drop his subpoena, Nixon ordered him fired. A firestorm of protest erupted, and the House Judiciary Committee started to gather evidence for impeachment proceedings. Adding to Nixon's woes in October, Vice President **Spiro Agnew** was forced to resign for accepting bribes while governor of Maryland. In keeping with the Twenty-fifth Amendment, Nixon appointed Agnew's successor, choosing Representative Gerald R. Ford of Michigan. Ford would be confirmed by Congress in December.

In March 1974, the Sirica grand jury investigating the Watergate break-in **indicted** Mitchell, Haldeman, and Ehrlichman and named Nixon as an "unindicted coconspirator." Nixon, under tremendous pressure, released transcripts of selected tapes. The outcome was devastating. The transcripts contradicted some official testimony, and Nixon's apparent callousness, lack of decency, and profane language shocked the nation. In July, the Supreme Court rejected Nixon's executive privilege position and ordered him to hand over all the tapes. Having ample evidence, the House Judiciary Committee charged Nixon with three impeachable crimes: obstructing justice, abuse of power, and defying subpoenas. Nixon's choices were to either resign or be impeached and removed from office. He resigned on August 9, 1974. Eventually, twenty-nine people connected to the White House were convicted of crimes related to Watergate and the 1972 campaign.

An Interim President

The nation's first unelected president, Gerald Ford, got off to a positive start. He was liked by members of both parties and considered an honest administrator by the public. But that quickly changed when he pardoned Nixon for any crimes he might have committed as president and seemed unable to deal with the problems facing the nation. The economy continued to slump, its decline quickened by the sharp rise in oil prices following the **Organization of Petroleum Exporting Countries'** (OPEC) embargo on the sale of oil to the United States in response to continuing American support

---

■ **John Dean** White House Counsel to President Nixon, Dean was involved in the Watergate break-in and cover-up; he became a prominent witness for the prosecution investigating the break-in and cover-up.

■ **Spiro Agnew** Vice president under Richard Nixon; he resigned in 1973 amid charges of illegal financial dealings during his governorship of Maryland.

indict To make a formal charge of wrongdoing against a person or party.

■ **Organization of Petroleum Exporting Countries** (OPEC) Economic alliance of oil-producing countries, mostly Arab, formed in 1960 to influence the world price of oil by controlling oil supplies; in 1973 OPEC members embargoed the sale of oil to countries allied with Israel.

for Israel in the ongoing conflict that had erupted into the **Yom Kippur War** in 1973. When Democrats, who won a record number of congressional seats in the 1974 elections, sponsored a bill to create jobs and increase spending, Ford resorted to the veto—which he would use to block thirty-seven bills. The result was political stalemate.

Despite relying heavily on Henry Kissinger, who was now national security adviser and secretary of state, Ford scored few foreign policy successes. Kissinger's efforts to negotiate a peace settlement in the Yom Kippur War and to reduce tensions in the Middle East earned him high praise. But little rubbed off on Ford, who could provide no help to Saigon as the North Vietnamese finished their conquest of South Vietnam, and whose handling of the Soviets alienated many within his own party. Trying to maintain the Nixon-Kissinger effort at détente with Moscow, he met with Soviet leader Brezhnev at Vladivostok in Siberia and in Helsinki, Finland. At the summits he made progress toward strategic arms limitation and improved East-West relations, but he received little credit at home, where his actions drew fire from those who wanted a tougher, more traditional Cold War policy toward the Soviet Union.

Among the most forceful Republican critics was presidential hopeful Ronald Reagan, who sought the Republican nomination in 1976. Representing the conservative wing of the party, he attacked détente as well as Ford's political ineffectiveness. Ford managed to eke out a victory at the convention, embracing a conservative agenda that called for smaller government and tougher policies toward communism.

■ **Yom Kippur War** On October 6, 1973, Egypt and Syria suddenly invaded Israel; after initial losses, the Israeli military defeated the Arab armies; with U.S. support, negotiations finally led to a cease-fire on October 22.

Individual Voices

Dolores Huerta on Winning Rights for Farm Workers

Union organizer Dolores Huerta spoke in 1978 to an audience at the University of California–Los Angeles, explaining the problems faced by farm workers and how the farm workers union she and César Chávez created managed to gain benefits for the workers. In this document, she presents an insider's view of the nature of the effort and why it was successful, but readers and historians need to be aware of how the university audience might have shaped the content and tone of the speech and her request.

❶ What types of benefits did unionization obtain for the workers and how did they compare to Chávez's and Huerta's goals for *La Causa*?

❷ According to the document, what contributed to the decision to turn to the national boycott of grapes?

❸ Why do you think that Huerta connects the efforts of the farm workers to those of the bus boycott?

❹ How does the phrase *"Sí se puede"* reflect the goal of the speaker and the nature of the farm workers' struggle?

There was a time when farm workers couldn't get any kind of welfare . . . if they were out of work. . . . Back in 1963, we did a big campaign and we got farm workers covered under welfare so if farm workers were out of work they could at least get welfare. . . . we have come a long way in the changes that have been made. The minimum wage for farm workers . . . in the places that we don't have the union are two dollars and fifty cents an hour and . . . where we have union contracts . . . farm workers' wages are three dollars and fifty-five cents an hour. **❶**

How were these change made? . . . The changes . . . were made by people that were like the poorest of all, people that didn't know how to read or write, people who had no resources, and when we think of the changes that we were able to make . . . it's really kind of a mindblower. About this time ten years ago, César Chávez started his first fast. . . . we had been on strike . . . for about . . . three years, and we still didn't have any contract. He . . . didn't eat for twenty-five days. And of course a lot of people thought he was crazy. . . . We sort of picked up on . . . César's fast, and then we thought, why couldn't the whole country do a little fast? Let's ask everyone not to eat grapes. That's kind of a simple thing, right? It doesn't take a lot, just don't eat grapes. **❷** And so we asked the whole country and the whole world not to eat grapes and they didn't. And as a result of . . . people not eating grapes, we had our first big national grape boycott and we got our first contract. That was a really simple thing, but it had tremendous impact. Because we were going to the heart of the growers, and that is their pocketbook. . . . they respond to only one thing and that is economic power. So, somehow, you have to hit them in that pocketbook where they have their heart and their nerves and then they feel the pain. . . . This is why . . . the Montgomery Bus Boycott was effective. . . . Because it hit them . . . [in] the pocketbook. **❸**

This country needs a lot of changes and we have to make them. . . . In Spanish, in our union, we have a saying. . . . We always say, *"Sí se puede."* It can be done, right? *Sí se puede* means it can be done. **❹**

Source: Speech by Dolores Huerta at the University of California, Los Angeles, February 22, 1978. From Mario T. Garcia, ed. *A Dolores Huerta Reader.* University of New Mexico Press, 2008. UCLA Chicano Studies Research Center Library and Archive.

Study Tools

SUMMARY

Following Kennedy's policies, President Johnson expanded American efforts to oppose communism around the world. In South Vietnam he implemented a series of planned escalations that Americanized the war. North Vietnam kept pace and showed no slackening of resolve or resources. Within the United States, however, as the American commitment grew, a significant antiwar movement developed. The combination of the Tet offensive and presidential politics divided the Democratic Party and compounded the divisions in American society.

By 1968, the country seemed aflame with urban riots and protests. Hispanics and Native Americans joined their voices with other groups demanding more recognition of their needs and calling upon the federal government for support. Those advocating social change, however, faced a resurgence of conservatism that helped elect Nixon. Seeking a strategy for withdrawing from Vietnam, Nixon implemented a policy of Vietnamization. To restructure the Cold War, he worked to improve relations with the Soviet Union and China. At home, Nixon charted a pragmatic course, switching between government activism and more traditional Republican policies, hoping to cement the Sunbelt and the South to the Republican Party.

Despite Nixon's domestic and foreign-policy successes, his desire to crush his enemies led to the Watergate scandal and his resignation. President Ford tried to restore confidence in government but faced too many obstacles. As the 1976 bicentennial election approached, the nation seemed mired in a slowing economy and public cynicism toward government and politics. Many wondered if the optimism that began the 1960s would ever return.

CHRONOLOGY
From Camelot to Watergate

1962	César Chávez and Dolores Huerta form National Farm Workers Association
1963	Lyndon B. Johnson becomes president
1964	Gulf of Tonkin Resolution
	Johnson elected president
1965	U.S. air strikes against North Vietnam begin
	American combat troops arrive in South Vietnam
	Anti-Vietnam "teach-ins" begin
	Dominican Republic intervention
1967	Antiwar march on Washington
1968	Tet offensive
	My Lai massacre
	Johnson withdraws from presidential race
	Robert Kennedy assassinated
	Mexican American student walkouts
	American Indian Movement founded
	Richard Nixon elected president
1969	Secret bombing of Cambodia
	First American troop withdrawals from Vietnam
	American Indians occupy Alcatraz
1970	U.S. troops invade Cambodia
	Kent State and Jackson State killings
	First Earth Day observed
	Environmental Protection Agency created
1972	Nixon visits China and Soviet Union
	Attempted assassination of George Wallace
	Watergate break-in
	Nixon reelected
	SALT I treaty
1973	Vietnam peace settlement
	"Second Battle of Wounded Knee"
	Watergate hearings
	Salvador Allende overthrown in Chile
	War Powers Act
	Arab oil boycott
1974	Nixon resigns
	Gerald Ford becomes president
1975	South Vietnam government falls to North Vietnamese

Study Tools

FOCUS QUESTIONS

If you have mastered this chapter, you should be able to answer these questions and to explain the terms that follow the questions.

1. ☆ *How did Johnson modify Kennedy's policies toward Latin America and Southeast Asia?*

2. ☆ *What considerations led Johnson to expand America's role in Vietnam and how did the North Vietnamese respond to the changes?*

3. ☆ *What were the political, social, and military outcomes of the Tet offensive?*

4. ☆ *What key issues shaped the 1968 campaign? What strategy did Richard Nixon use to win?*

5. ☆ *How did Latinos and Native Americans seek to address the problems they faced in American society?*

6. ☆ *How did the federal government respond to their efforts?*

7. ☆ *How did Richard Nixon plan to achieve an "honorable" peace in Vietnam?*

8. ☆ *How did Nixon's Cold War policies differ from those favored by earlier administrations?*

9. ☆ *How did Nixon's policies dealing with the economy, welfare, and the environment reflect his pragmatic approach? What did he do to increase the base of the Republican Party?*

10. ☆ *What actions led to the Watergate investigation and Nixon's resignation?*

KEY TERMS

escalation   *(p. 772)*

Mann Doctrine   *(p. 772)*

Gulf of Tonkin Resolution   *(p. 773)*

Ho Chi Minh Trail   *(p. 773)*

COINTELPRO   *(p. 775)*

Operation Chaos   *(p. 775)*

Tet   *(p. 776)*

Eugene McCarthy   *(p. 776)*

Robert Kennedy   *(p. 776)*

George Wallace   *(p. 778)*

César Chávez   *(p. 779)*

Chicano   *(p. 779)*

Russell Means   *(p. 780)*

American Indian Movement   *(p. 780)*

Henry Kissinger   *(p. 782)*

Vietnamization   *(p. 782)*

Nixon Doctrine   *(p. 783)*

My Lai   *(p. 784)*

War Powers Act   *(p. 785)*

Leonid Brezhnev   *(p. 786)*

Strategic Arms Limitation agreement   *(p. 786)*

Salvador Allende   *(p. 786)*

Environmental Protection Agency   *(p. 787)*

southern strategy   *(p. 788)*

George McGovern   *(p. 789)*

Committee to Re-elect the President   *(p. 789)*

Watergate   *(p. 790)*

John Dean   *(p. 791)*

Spiro Agnew   *(p. 791)*

Organization of Petroleum Exporting Countries   *(p. 791)*

Yom Kippur War   *(p. 792)*

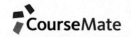 **CourseMate** Go to the History CourseMate website for primary source links, study tools, and review materials for this chapter. www.cengagebrain.com

28 New Economic and Political Alignments, 1976–1992

Behind the Stories

Since Chapter 22, the political story has focused on the liberalism generated by Democrats and the New Deal. In this chapter conservatism comes roaring back. Historians have termed this period the Reagan revolution, resurgent Republicanism, the conservative ascendancy or revival, and triumph of conservatism.

The 1980s were hard times for liberals. The cultural, economic, social, and political landscape of the country changed. Economically and socially, the intervention and regulations of New Deal and Great Society programs no longer made fiscal sense or guaranteed the preservation of the American dream, especially for the middle class. Culturally, the "American family" was rediscovered as

elements within conservatism called for government intervention to protect the morals and values of mainstream life.

But change is hard to control or predict and, as Democrats had, Republicans and conservatives found it difficult to maintain a single voice and project a national path that unified the nation. As you grapple with the next two chapters, consider the tones of conservative voices, how success—the rise to national power—opened divisions within the ranks, and how new issues altered national expectations. In examining the next twenty-plus years, are historians justified in using terms like "revolution," "triumph," or even "ascendency" when discussing either political party or political ideology?

—J.G.

Individual Choices
Franklin Chang-Dìaz

Twenty-one years separated the young child looking into space and the young man who looked down toward Latin America from space. Franklin Chang-Dìaz's wish had come true—he was an astronaut. It was January 1986, and he was on board the space shuttle *Columbia*, chasing Halley's Comet. As immigrants, Franklin Chang-Dìaz and Diameng Pa (see the Individual Voices feature at the end of this chapter) found opportunities in the United States that they otherwise could not have attained. Like countless other immigrants pursuing their own personal goals, neither Chang-Dìaz nor Diameng Pa expected an easy path, and both knew that they would have to work hard to make the most of, in Pa's words, "this generous privilege."

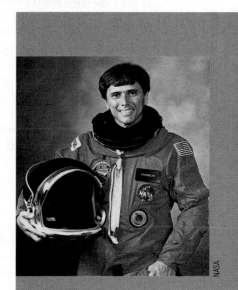

Franklin Chang-Dìaz

As a boy in Costa Rica, Chang-Dìaz had dreamed of exploring space. He left home for the United States in 1968, moved in with relatives, and enrolled in high school. With support from teachers, Chang-Dìaz received a scholarship to attend the University of Connecticut in the fall of 1969. He majored in engineering and graduated in 1973. To improve his chances of joining the National Aeronautics and Space Administration (NASA), he entered the Massachusetts Institute of Technology. In 1977 he received a doctorate in physics and immediately applied to the astronaut program. "All of a sudden the space program was so close, I felt I could touch it." But, his application was rejected.

Two years later, now a naturalized U.S. citizen, he applied again. One of four thousand applicants for nineteen open slots, he was selected. He was officially an astronaut by 1981, but disappointment followed. NASA found duties for him other than going into space. Finally, his dream came true, and he boarded the space shuttle *Columbia* for a six-day flight.

Chang-Dìaz made six additional flights, logging more than 1,600 hours in space, including 19 hours and 31 minutes in three spacewalks. Once asked about his journey from Costa Rica to Houston, he replied: "I cannot think of a better job. . . . I'm just having the time of my life. This is what I planned for all my life and I'm really enjoying it, and to me, I guess I feel I have the best of both worlds because I also continue my research, and so I am able to be a scientist at the same time that I am also an astronaut, and that is to me the perfect combination." Retired from NASA in 2005, Franklin Chang-Dìaz formed a company to develop a plasma-propelled rocket engine for space travel.

In 1976, Franklin Chang-Dìaz was full of optimism, but many Americans were not. A sluggish economy and rising unemployment seemed to make reaching the American dream more difficult. To many in the country liberalism was no longer the answer. Even the Democratic presidential candidate, Jimmy Carter, admitted that government could not solve every problem.

In office, Carter looked confused if not inept, unable to reverse the slowing economy or to fulfill liberal expectations on social issues. His foreign policy appeared unable to project American power or protect the nation's interests.

A hopeful nation chose Ronald Reagan president in 1980. Reagan promised changes that would restore American power and prosperity. His policies implemented a conservative agenda that replaced liberal economic and social policies and aggressively restored a Cold War foreign and military policy. Not all agreed with his choices. Critics charged his policies benefited the wealthy and abandoned support for minorities and the poor, and they warned of a growing national debt and trade deficits. But for most Americans, Reagan's policies worked. The economy rebounded and the country restored its preeminent role in the world with its victory in the Cold War.

In 1988, Americans sought to continue Reagan's approach by electing George Bush. He promised experienced and fiscally sound leadership, more concern for minorities and the poor, and continued American strength abroad. Taking office as the Soviet Union collapsed, he charted a foreign policy in a new international setting. He cautiously focused on supporting democratic change in Eastern Europe and Central America. When Iraq invaded Kuwait, he organized an international coalition, committed American forces, and liberated Kuwait. At home, however, he was unable to halt a deteriorating economy or meet the expectations of either liberals or conservatives. Still, as Bush campaigned for reelection, he hoped his foreign-policy successes would overcome the voters' concerns about the economy and carry him to victory. He had miscalculated. The Democratic candidate, William (Bill) Clinton, focused on the economy and swept into the presidency.

however, lurked a deepening sense of cynicism and uncertainty. President Ford's efforts to restore faith in government had not succeeded and the public's lack of trust and confidence only increased when the economy slowed. For the first time since the Depression, many parents worried that their children would not enjoy a higher standard of living. The optimism that had characterized the 1960s had faded into frustration and apathy.

The political forecast did not look especially promising as the two presidential contenders began their race for the White House. Polls showed that people liked Gerald Ford but considered him ineffective, while his Democratic opponent, James Earl Carter, who preferred to be called "Jimmy," boasted about his lack of political experience—aside from being a one-time governor of Georgia. Carter's nonpolitical, folksy background was refreshing, but some wondered whether he had the experience to lead Congress and the nation. Both men seemed full of good intentions but vague on the issues. Neither ignited the nation politically; even the televised debates were dull. In a very close election where only 54.4 percent of eligible voters cast ballots, Ford won more states but lost the electoral count to Carter by 56 votes. Giving one reason for the low voter turn-out, a Californian explained he did not want "to force a second-class decision on my neighbors."

Jimmy Carter arrived in the nation's capital in January 1977 brimming with enthusiasm. He stressed he was free of Washington politics and the lures of special interests. He pledged honesty and hard work and said he was determined to take different and more moral approaches in tackling foreign and domestic problems. With majorities in Congress, Democratic congressional leaders also were eager to assert their leadership. The problem was that Carter had little intention of playing politics as usual, which meant he would frequently ignore Congress. Democratic congressional leaders, in turn, announced that Congress had no intention of "rolling over and playing dead." The results were repeated conflicts between Congress and the president that left few satisfied.

THE CARTER PRESIDENCY

☆ *What problems did Carter face in implementing his domestic policies and why were many Democrats unhappy with his approach?*

☆ *What new directions in foreign policy did Carter take, especially in Central America and the Middle East?*

In 1976 the United States celebrated the two-hundredth anniversary of its independence. Amid the festivities and praise for its institutions and accomplishments,

Domestic Priorities

Carter faced an economic recession in 1977, and nearly everyone agreed that fixing the economy was a priority, but the question was how and at what expense to other issues. Fiscally conservative, Carter chose to attack the recession by raising interest rates, cutting taxes, and trimming federal spending, including budgets for social programs. He announced that liberalism had its limits and government could not "eliminate poverty or provide a bountiful economy." When he argued that improving regulatory agencies and better enforcing existing regulations and laws would produce better social results than costly expanded or new programs, many liberals and congressional Democrats disagreed and thought he was sacrificing social needs for the cause of **fiscal stringency**. Already unhappy with his approach and attitude, Democrats in Congress rebelled when Carter proposed a twenty-cent raise in the minimum wage, passing an increase of ninety-five cents instead.

The disagreement over the minimum wage was just one example. Ted Kennedy and liberal Democrats sought to push Carter forward on a variety of social fronts, including **affirmative action**. Since the mid-1960s, in an effort to provide more opportunities, many businesses and colleges had established affirmative action slots for minorities. But by the 1970s, a growing number of Americans believed these programs constituted preferential treatment for minorities that limited their own opportunities. In 1974 **Alan Bakke** sued the University of California at Davis Medical School for reverse discrimination. He claimed that he had been denied admission because he was white, and that in his place the medical school had accepted less-qualified African American students. When the case was heard by the Supreme Court in 1978, supporters of affirmative action pleaded with Carter to have the Justice Department back the university. The Justice Department did petition the Court to uphold the university's admissions program, but Carter's public statements that he hated "to endorse the proposition of quotas" seemed to undermine the administration's support for affirmative action. Bakke won his case in a 5-to-4 decision with the Court ruling that the university's admissions program created a quota system, which violated the Constitution. Bakke was admitted to the medical school and graduated in 1982.

Like those wanting Carter to fight harder for affirmative action, many women found his support for women's issues, including the ERA and freedom of choice regarding abortion, uneven and not strong enough. In 1972, Congress had proposed an **Equal Rights Amendment** (ERA) and sent it to the states for ratification. In two years, thirty-three of the needed thirty-eight states had approved the amendment and supporters were confident of its passage. But opposition stiffened under the leadership of conservative **Phyllis Schlafly**, who claimed the amendment diminished the rights and status of women and altered the "role of the American woman as wife and mother." Schlafly organized a "Stop-ERA" movement, drawing from white middle-class women who identified themselves as regular churchgoers. They pressured state legislatures to vote no on the ERA, and by 1974, ratification had been defeated in seventeen state legislatures. With passage stalled and the deadline for ratification (1979) approaching, pro-ERA groups asked Carter to endorse the amendment and an extension

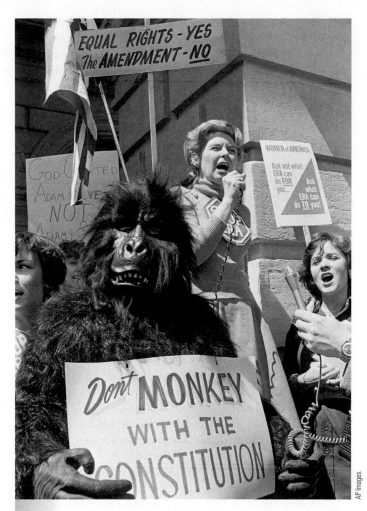

Phyllis Schlafly, pictured here outside of the Illinois capital, leads a group of anti-ERA protesters to encourage the state legislature not to ratify the Equal Rights Amendment. Illinois was one of fifteen states that never ratified the proposed amendment.

fiscal stringency The need because of real or perceived economic conditions to restrict, cut, or eliminate funding for programs.

affirmative action Policy that seeks to redress past discrimination through active measures to ensure equal opportunity, especially in education and employment.

■ **Alan Bakke** Student who filed a lawsuit against the University of California at Davis for reverse discrimination; he claimed he was denied admittance to medical school because of school policy that set aside admission slots for less qualified minorities; the Supreme Court agreed in 1978.

■ **Equal Rights Amendment** (ERA) Proposed constitutional amendment giving women equal rights under the law; Congress approved it in 1972, but it failed to achieve ratification by the required thirty-eight states.

■ **Phyllis Schlafly** Leader of the movement to defeat the Equal Rights Amendment; she believed that the amendment threatened the domestic role of women.

for ratification. Carter endorsed both and Congress extended the ratification process by thirty-nine months, but in the end, the amendment fell three states short of ratification. Many of its supporters complained that Carter might have taken a more active part in ensuring the amendment was ratified.

Conservative women had found a voice, and they quickly linked the ERA to abortion and other issues, creating a wider "pro-family" movement. In 1973, the Supreme Court in a 5-to-2 decision, *Roe v. Wade*, invalidated a Texas law that prohibited abortion. Justice Harry Blackmun, writing for the majority, held that "the right to privacy" gave women the freedom to choose to have an abortion during the first three months of pregnancy. The controversial ruling struck down laws in forty-six states that had made abortions nearly impossible to obtain legally except in cases of rape or to save the life of the mother.

Although most public opinion polls indicated that a majority of Americans favored giving women the right to choose an abortion, at least under some circumstances, many religious organizations worked with conservative groups to organize a **Right to Life movement** "opposing abortion rights on moral and legal grounds." It found common cause with the pro-family and anti-ERA movements in voicing a multifaceted critique of American society, feminism, and liberalism. Pointing out that the Great Society's Medicaid program paid out more than $45 million for abortion services in 1973, anti-abortion forces demanded that Congress pass the Hyde Amendment (1976), which prohibited the use of federal Medicaid

funds to pay for abortions. When Carter refused to oppose the Hyde Amendment, some within the NOW camp argued that their organization should support anyone but Carter in the forthcoming 1980 election.

For Carter the critical issue was not affirmative action or social legislation, but finding ways to stimulate economic growth. His approaches, as in the case of domestic issues, generated opposition from both Democrats and Republicans. Still, there was nearly unanimous agreement that it was important to reduce dependence on foreign oil, which supplied about 60 percent of the country's oil needs. Consequently, Carter's announcement that solving the **energy crisis** was the "moral equivalent of war" drew widespread applause. When Carter began to lay out his solutions, however, much of the applause quieted. Rather than stress more production of American-based gas and oil, he called for developing **alternative fuels** and for conservation, asking the nation to use less energy. Proponents of oil and gas production argued that alternative fuels were too expensive and could not meet the nation's demands. Nuclear energy, however, appeared a viable alternative—until March 1979, when a serious accident at **Three Mile Island** in central Pennsylvania released a cloud of radioactive gas and nearly caused a **meltdown**. No one was injured in the accident, but nuclear power now appeared a less attractive energy source, and more than thirty energy companies canceled their nuclear energy projects.

Overall, Carter offered Congress more than a hundred energy proposals, but Congress approved only fragments of them, including the formation of a cabinet-level Department of Energy. His pleas to the public to reduce their energy consumption by wearing sweaters, lowering their thermostats in winter, and using public transportation also found few takers. When Iran sparked another oil crisis in 1978, it was clear that the United States was still dependent on foreign oil and that the country had no real energy program. Nor had the economy improved, with inflation in 1980 at 14 percent—the highest rate since 1947—and unemployment reaching nearly 7.6 percent.

New Directions in Foreign Policy

Carter arrived at the White House wanting to reshape American foreign policy. Believing the nation's policies focused too much on Europe, the Cold War, and an "inordinate fear of communism," he wanted to provide a new path for the United States to lead by example and not through dominance. The "soul of our foreign policy," he said, should be **human rights**. But, it was easier to announce a new approach than to implement one. Carter never succeeded in developing a "thought-out and planned" approach to foreign policy and frequently received conflicting advice from

■ *Roe v. Wade* Supreme Court ruling that women have an unrestricted right to choose an abortion during the first three months of pregnancy.

■ **Right to Life movement** Anti-abortion movement that favors a constitutional amendment to prohibit abortion; some adherents grew increasingly militant during the 1980s and 1990s; also called the pro-life movement.

energy crisis Vulnerability to dwindling oil supplies, wasteful energy consumption, and potential embargoes by oil-producing countries.

alternative fuels Sources of energy other than coal, oil, and natural gas, such as solar, wind, geothermal, hydroelectric, and nuclear energy.

■ **Three Mile Island** Site of a nuclear power plant near Harrisburg, Pennsylvania; an accident at the plant in 1979 led to a release of radioactive gases and almost caused a meltdown.

meltdown Severe overheating of a nuclear reactor core, resulting in the melting of the core and the escape of life-threatening radiation.

human rights Basic rights and freedoms to which all human beings are entitled, such as the right to life and liberty, to freedom of thought and expression, and to equality before the law.

One of President Carter's greatest triumphs was the signing of the 1978 peace accords between Egyptian President Anwar Sadat and Israeli Prime Minister Menachem Begin. Sadat and Begin received the Nobel Peace Prize for their efforts.

his main foreign policy advisers, Secretary of State Cyrus Vance and National Security Adviser Zbigniew Brzezinski, who had decidedly different views on the conduct of foreign policy.

Despite highlighting human rights, Carter chose to denounce, apply sanctions, and reduce aid only to some governments that abused their citizenry but not all. Governments of El Salvador, Guatemala, Chile, Nicaragua, Uganda, the Soviet Union, and the minority white governments in southern Africa were among those targeted. But for repressive governments like those of the Philippines, Iran, and the People's Republic of China, it was business as usual, with Carter restoring full diplomatic relations with China in January 1979.

Seeking to reduce the tensions of the Cold War, Carter continued efforts to conclude a second arms limitation treaty and in June 1979, he and Brezhnev signed the second Strategic Arms Limitation Treaty (SALT II). It placed limits on the numbers of long-range bombers, missiles, and nuclear warheads each nation could deploy. But the treaty faced strong bipartisan opposition in the Senate, and when the Soviets invaded Afghanistan in December, Carter withdrew the treaty from consideration. Reverting to more traditional Cold War rhetoric, he labeled the invasion the "gravest threat to peace since 1945," imposed **economic sanctions** on the Soviets, and announced the United States would boycott the 1980 Moscow Olympic Games. Fearful that the Soviets would use Afghanistan as a "stepping stone" to Middle Eastern oil, Carter proclaimed the "**Carter Doctrine**," vowing "to repel by any means necessary, including the use of force" any attempt to take control of the Persian Gulf region. He also approved aid to the **mujahedeen**, Afghan rebels who were fighting the Soviets.

SALT II failed, but Carter notched two successes with the Panama Canal treaty and a peace agreement between Israel and Egypt. Both agreements charted new paths and matched Carter's goal of leading by

economic sanctions Trade restrictions imposed on a country that has violated international law.

■ **Carter Doctrine** Carter's announced policy that the United States would use force to repel any nation that attempted to take control of the Persian Gulf.

■ **mujahedeen** Afghan resistance group supplied with arms by the United States to assist in its fight against the Soviets following their 1979 invasion of Afghanistan.

In November 1979, Iranians seized the American embassy in Tehran and took sixty-six hostages. Thirteen were soon released through the efforts of Palestinian leader Yasir Arafat, but negotiations to release more failed. Held for more than a year, the hostages were set free as Ronald Reagan was being sworn in as president. When one hostage was asked if he would ever return to Iran, he said yes, but only in an American bomber.

Alain Mingam/Gamma.

example. For decades, Panamanians had argued and protested to gain control over the canal that split their nation. During the 1976 campaign, Carter had supported a treaty, even though the majority of Americans thought the Panama Canal should remain in American hands. Carter overcame bipartisan opposition, and in 1978 the Senate approved treaties giving Panama complete sovereignty over the canal in 2000.

Carter's persistence also was instrumental in working toward a peace agreement between Israel and its Arab neighbors (see Map 28.1). He invited Egyptian president Anwar Sadat and Israeli prime minister Menachem Begin to join him for peace talks at the presidential retreat at Camp David in Maryland. Surprisingly, both accepted, and at a series of meetings in September 1978, Carter shuttled between the two

leaders, smoothing relations and stressing his personal commitment to both nations. The outcome was a set of carefully crafted agreements by which Egypt recognized Israel's right to exist and Israel returned the Israeli-occupied Sinai Peninsula to Egypt. It took several months to finalize the **Camp David Accords**, but on March 26, 1979, Carter looked on as Begin and Sadat signed the first peace treaty between an Arab state and Israel.

The Soviet intervention in Afghanistan and the Carter Doctrine were responses to more than just events in Afghanistan. Both the Americans and the Soviets were reacting to the revolution in Iran, which had toppled the pro-American ruler, Mohammad Reza Shah Pahlavi, in early 1979. The shah, restored to power by the United States in 1953, was America's staunchest ally in the Persian Gulf region. But his authoritarian rule had generated widespread opposition led by Iran's religious leaders, especially the **Ayatollah Ruhollah Khomeini**, who assumed power during the revolution and established an Islamic fundamentalist state.

Tensions between Iran and the United States increased as the anti-Western revolutionary government called the United States the main source of evil in the world. On November 4, after the exiled shah entered a New York hospital for cancer treatment, an angry mob stormed the American embassy in Tehran taking sixty-six American hostages.

As the world watched televised pictures of the hostages, Carter received conflicting options from Vance and Brzezinski. Brzezinski recommended using military force to free the hostages, but Carter agreed with Vance and opted for negotiations. For a while it seemed the right choice; thirteen hostages, mostly women and African Americans, were released. But when further discussions failed, with his popularity falling to nearly 30 percent, Carter ordered a military rescue mission. It failed, losing three helicopters in a violent dust storm in Iran. In late 1980, Canadian and Algerian diplomatic efforts obtained the release of the remaining hostages, who were set free on January 20, 1981, the day Carter left the presidency, ending 444 days of captivity.

■ **Camp David Accords** Treaty, signed at Camp David in 1978, under which Israel returned territory captured from Egypt and Egypt recognized Israel as a nation; most of the Arab world denounced the agreement and Egyptian leader Sadat.

■ **Ayatollah Ruhollah Khomeini** Religious leader of Iran's Shiite Muslims; after toppling the shah in 1979, the ayatollah (a title of respect given to a high-ranking Shiite religious authority and leader) established a new constitution that gave him supreme power.

BULGARIA

Black Sea

RUSSIA

KAZAKHSTAN

UZBEKISTAN

GEORGIA

• Ankara

TURKEY

ARMENIA **AZERBAIJAN**

Caspian Sea

TURKMENISTAN

CHINA

Soviet occupation, 1979–1989
U.S. aid to rebels, 1980s

CYPRUS

Crete

20°E

Mediterranean Sea

30°N

U.S. troops, 1958, 1983–1984

SYRIA

• Damascus

Euphrates R.

Tigris R.

Tikrit •

Kirkuk •

Fallujah •

Baghdad •

IRAQ

IRAN

• Tehran

Mazar-e
Sharif •

AFGHANISTAN

Herat •

• Kabul

• Islamabad

PAKISTAN

Kandahar •

• Quetta

30°N

LEBANON

ISRAEL

Tel Aviv •

• Amman

JORDAN

Basra •

U.S. arms sales, 1955–1978:
$20.8 billion
Shah overthrown, 1979
American hostages taken,
1979–1981

LIBYA

Cairo •

EGYPT

KUWAIT

• Kuwait

Persian Gulf

U.S. and allies launch
First U.S.-Iraq War, 1991

• Karachi

INDIA

Nile R.

Tropic of Cancer

Aswan
Dam •

Red Sea

30°E

20°N

U.S. arms sales, 1980s,
during Iran-Iraq War
Iraq invades Kuwait, 1990

Manama •

BAHRAIN

Doha •

QATAR

Dubayy •

• Abu Dhabi

**UNITED ARAB
EMIRATES**

Strait of Hormuz

• Muscat

• Riyadh

SAUDI ARABIA

OMAN

Arabian Sea

70°E

• Mecca

Oil embargo, 1973
Source of 17% of U.S. oil imports
in 1975
Largest buyer of U.S. arms, 1978

SUDAN

ERITREA

40°E

YEMEN

Sana •

60°E

50°E

• Mukalla

Key / Legend:

■ Jewish state after UN partition
of Palestine, 1947

■ Israel after War of 1948–1949

■ Area controlled by Israel after
Six-Day War, 1967

■ Israeli-occupied area after
Yom Kippur War, 1973

By Egyptian-Israeli agreements of 1975 and
1979, Israel withdrew from the Sinai in 1982.
In 1981 Israel annexed the Golan Heights.
Through negotiations between Israel and
the PLO, Jericho and the Gaza Strip were
placed under Palestinian self-rule, and Israeli
troops were withdrawn in 1994. In 1994
Israel and Jordan signed an agreement
opening their borders and normalizing their
relations.

LEBANON

Beirut •

Damascus •

SYRIA

Haifa •

GOLAN
HEIGHTS

*Sea
of Galilee*

Tel Aviv •

WEST
BANK

Jordan R.

32°E

ISRAEL

Jerusalem •

Gaza •

*Dead
Sea*

• Aden

DJIBOUTI

• Djibouti

Gulf of Aden

*Socotra
(Yemen)*

10°N

ETHIOPIA

SOMALIA

U.S. troops assist in relief
of famine, 1992–1993; U.S.
troops withdrawn, 1994

*INDIAN
OCEAN*

*Mediterranean
Sea*

Port Said •

JORDAN

E G Y P T

*Suez
Canal*

Cairo •

Suez •

Key:

■ Members of the Organization of
Petroleum Exporting Countries
(OPEC)

⚑ Oil field

0   250   500 Km.
0   250   500 Mi.

Nile R.

• Elath

**SINAI
PENINSULA**

**SAUDI
ARABIA**

**ARAB-ISRAELI
CONFLICT**

Mogadishu •

0° Equator

Gulf of Suez

Sharm
el-Sheikh •

28°E

N

32°E

Red Sea

MAP 28.1   The Middle East

Since 1946, the United States has tried to balance its support for Israel with its need for oil from the Arab states.
To support its interests in this volatile region, the United States has provided large amounts of financial and
military aid to some nations while also seeking to create peace talks between Israel and its Arab neighbors and
the Palestinians.   Copyright © Cengage Learning

★ *What issues contributed to the emergence of the New Right, and how did the New Right help shape the 1980 election?*

★ *What is "Reaganomics," and what were the consequences of Reagan's economic policies?*

While liberals disagreed with Carter's view that liberalism had its limits, growing numbers of people were going even farther and agreeing with the ex-governor of California, Ronald Reagan, that the central "problem" facing the nation was liberalism. Reagan said the federal government was too big, too inefficient, and too expensive, and that liberal programs actually harmed those who worked hard, saved their money, and paid their taxes. But there was also a new, sharper edge to the criticisms voiced by an emerging New Right that placed its emphasis on social and moral issues.

The New Right

The New Right emerged as a coalition of conservative grassroots movements that believed the social and governmental liberal activism of the 1960s had weakened the national identity, contributed to a moral breakdown, and threatened "to destroy everything that is good and moral here in America." To save America, advocates of the New Right proclaimed the 1980 election needed to be a triumph of conservatism. Seeking to tap into the discontent voiced by many blue-collar and suburban voters, the New Right challenged the liberal use of government to induce social equality. It passionately claimed that liberalism sought to alter the foundation of the American family by promoting abortion rights, feminism, the ERA, and homosexuality.

Highly visible among New Right groups were evangelical Christian sects, many of whose ministers were **televangelists**—preachers who used radio and television to spread the gospel. Receiving donations that exceeded a billion dollars a year, they did not hesitate to mix religion and politics. Jerry Falwell's **Moral Majority** promoted New Right views on more than five hundred television and radio stations. Reaching millions of Americans, Falwell called on listeners to wage political war against liberal government officials whose views on the Bible, homosexuality, prayer in school, abortion, and communism were too liberal. Falwell told his listeners to get people "saved, baptized, and registered."

In the 1970s, the "electronic church" began to draw audiences of over 100 million viewers and listeners. Televangelists like Jerry Falwell, pictured here, shaped the "moral majority" by damning liberalism, feminism, homosexuality, and the teaching of evolution. The media pulpit, he stated, not only allowed explaining "the issues" but permitted endorsing "candidates, right there in church on Sunday morning."

© Wally McNamee/Corbis.

The New Right generated new levels of political activism, and its message found a growing audience among many working-class and young Americans who believed that their taxes were too high and were not being efficiently or correctly used. Throughout the 1970s, state and local taxes had risen while at the federal level Social Security taxes, now including Medicare, grew by 30 percent and income taxes, pushed by an inflation-fueled "**bracket creep**," increased by as much as 20 percent. Taxes and government spending, especially for social programs, were rapidly becoming broad-based issues. In California, Republicans and Democrats joined forces and used a referendum in 1978 to pass **Proposition 13**, which placed limits on property taxes and state spending. It "isn't just a tax revolt," observed a Carter official, "it is a revolution against government."

Promising to restore America by reducing government involvement and embracing the social positions of the New Right, Ronald Reagan benefited from the conservative resurgence. He attacked Carter's domestic and foreign policy record and offered to restore the nation's economy, power, and pride. Embracing the image of the "citizen politician, speaking out for the . . . common sense of everyday Americans," Reagan quipped, "A recession is when your neighbor loses his job. A depression is when you lose yours. A recovery is when Jimmy Carter loses his."

Reagan's message not only energized traditional Republicans and the New Right, but also resonated with many Democrats and independents, especially those living in the Sunbelt. By 1980, the Sunbelt's population not only exceeded that of the industrial North and East but it had taken the lead in opposing the cost and intrusive power of the federal government. As the November election approached, the central question was not if Reagan would win, but what the size of his majority would be and how many Republicans his **political coattails** would carry into office. When the votes were counted, Reagan had received an impressive 51 percent of the popular vote and an even more impressive 91 percent of the electoral count. The coattails had worked as well, with Republicans keeping their majority in the Senate and substantially narrowing the Democratic majority in the House of Representatives.

Reaganism

Called the "Great Communicator" by the press, Reagan brought to the White House an unusual ability to convey his views and agenda to the American public. The New Right and conservatives were expectant as he took office. He had campaigned not just on restoring prosperity and cutting intrusive government, but also on promoting traditional American values and strengthening the family. In office, however, Reagan

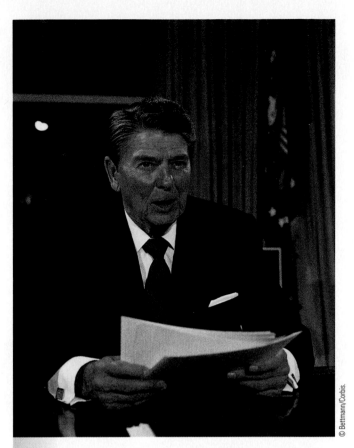

A former radio sports announcer, movie star, and host of television shows, Ronald Reagan used television and radio very effectively to outline his visions of American domestic and foreign policies. Because of his communication style, he was called "the Great Communicator."

© Bettmann/Corbis.

disappointed the New Right by choosing to concentrate on the economy and foreign policy. The administration's economic plan was simple: cut the number and cost of social programs, increase military spending, and reduce taxes and government restrictions. "If we can do that, the rest will take care of itself," Reagan's chief of staff, James A. Baker, III, argued.

televangelist Protestant evangelist minister who conducts televised worship services; many such ministers used their broadcasts as a forum for promoting conservative values.

■ **Moral Majority** Conservative religious organization led by televangelist Jerry Falwell; it had an active political lobby opposing abortion, homosexuality, and the Equal Rights Amendment.

bracket creep Inflation of salaries pushing individuals into higher tax brackets.

■ **Proposition 13** 1978 measure adopted by referendum in California that cut local property taxes by more than 50 percent.

political coattails Term referring to the ability of a presidential candidate to attract voters to other office seekers from the same political party.

Calling the formula for restoring economic vitality **supply-side economics**, the Reagan administration fought inflation by keeping interest rates high—they spiked at 18 percent, the highest in the twentieth century—and promoted economic growth by reducing federal regulations, taxes, and social programs. In implementing **Reaganomics**, over $25 billion was slashed from federal spending on social programs, including programs like food stamps and **Aid to Families with Dependent Children**. Federal controls over business were reduced in a flurry of deregulation that affected industries like oil and gas, banking, and communications. To further stimulate growth, Secretary of the Interior James Watt opened federally controlled land, coastal waters, and wetlands to mining, lumber, oil, and gas companies—a policy strongly advocated by many in the West. At the same time, to help business growth, the Environmental Protection Agency relaxed enforcement of federal guidelines for reducing air and water pollution. Finally, the 1981 **Economic Recovery Tax Act** lowered income taxes and most business taxes by an average of 25 percent.

Reagan's economic policies were not immediately effective; indeed, the economy worsened, as unemployment climbed to over 12 percent, the **trade deficit** soared, and bankruptcies for small businesses and farmers increased. Also growing at an alarming rate was the **federal deficit**, pushed by declining tax revenues and increases in military spending and entitlement programs like social security. Reagan called for patience, assuring the public that his economic programs eventually would work.

As Reagan predicted, in 1983, the economy recovered. Inflation dropped to 4 percent and unemployment fell to 7.5 percent. Many, especially corporate leaders, loudly cheered Reaganomics, applauding deregulation. Deregulating of financial institutions was seen as especially positive because it spurred investment, which drove the stock market upward—the Great Bull Market. "I think we hit the jackpot," Reagan announced when in 1982 he signed the Garn–St. Germain Act, which expanded the types of loans that the **savings and loan industry** (S&Ls) could make beyond those for single-family homes.

The recession ended just in time for the 1984 election. Using the theme "Morning in America," Reagan's campaign projected continued economic growth and affirmed his commitment to a strong America abroad. Democrats nominated Carter's vice president and traditional liberal Walter Mondale, whom Republicans immediately defined as a "tax and spend" liberal. Hoping to energize voters, Mondale selected New York Representative Geraldine Ferraro as the nation's first female vice presidential nominee. His choice made political history but had no effect on the election. President Reagan scored an overwhelming victory, taking 59 percent of the popular vote and carrying every state except Mondale's Minnesota.

Reagan continued to push Reaganomics during his second term, but the results were mixed, and by 1987 the economy was showing important weaknesses. Concerns grew about the size of the federal deficit and a **national debt** that had reached new records, requiring 14 percent of the annual budget to pay the interest. Others feared that the recently deregulated savings and loan industry, because of its aggressive and risky investment and loan policies, was tottering on the verge of collapse. The warnings proved true when in 1989 many S&Ls, especially in the southwest, faced bankruptcy and asked the federal government to provide more than $500 billion to cover the losses. Adding to the economic problems, in 1989 the stock market, which had been climbing since 1983, suddenly fell, losing 23 percent of its value on October 19. Not since Black Thursday, in the 1929 crash preceding the Great Depression, had such panic struck the market.

■ **supply-side economics** Theory that reducing taxes on the wealthy and increasing the money available for investment will stimulate the economy and eventually benefit everyone.

■ **Reaganomics** Economic beliefs and policies of the Reagan administration, including the belief that tax cuts for the wealthy and deregulation of industry benefit the economy.

■ **Aid to Families with Dependent Children** A program created by the Social Security Act of 1935; it provided states with matching federal funds and became one of the states' main welfare programs.

■ **Economic Recovery Tax Act** 1981 law passed by Congress that cut income taxes over three years by 25 percent across the board and lowered the rate for the highest bracket from 78 percent to 28 percent.

trade deficit Amount by which the value of a nation's imports exceeds the value of its exports.

federal deficit The total amount of debt owed by the national government during a fiscal year.

savings and loan industry (S&Ls) Network of financial institutions originally founded to provide home mortgage loans; deregulation allowed S&Ls to provide loans for office buildings, shopping malls, and other commercial properties.

national debt The total amount of money owed by the United States to domestic and foreign creditors.

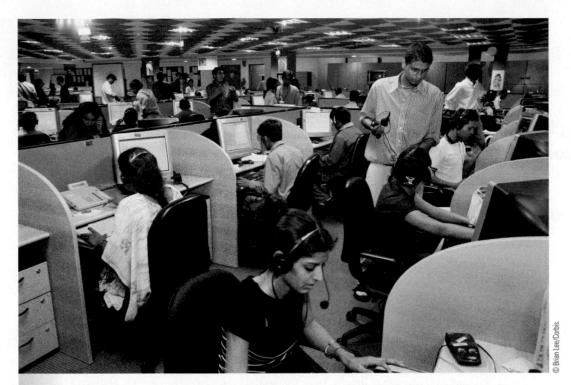

Part of globalization made possible by advanced telecommunications is the establishment of customer service centers in India that provide 24/7 answering and information services for American and British companies. In this picture dozens of Indians answer toll-free calls from English-speaking customers for a variety of American companies.

A Society and Economy in Transition

☆ *How was the changing U.S. economy affecting Americans?*

☆ *Who were the "new immigrants," and how were they received?*

More than Reagonomics shaped the economy. Since the Johnson administration, the American public and politicians had struggled with an economy that seemed to resist conventional solutions. In the first decades after 1946, the nation had experienced its longest era of consistent economic growth in its history, with the gross national product rising at an average annual rate slightly higher than 2.5 percent. This growth translated into higher-paying jobs, more home ownership, accessible college educations, and overall an expanding consumer society with rising expectations.

But by the early 1970s, economic growth had slowed, dipping to slightly over 1 percent, while the cost of living increased over 200 percent. In personal terms, this slowdown meant higher prices, fewer jobs, and for many, shattered expectations.

Many of the problems had roots in the shift from a manufacturing base to a service-based economy and in increasing **globalization**. Since the late 1960s, the expanding economies of West Germany, Japan, Korea, and Taiwan had begun to successfully compete for American domestic and foreign markets. Japanese goods were beginning to dominate the electronics industry and cut deeply into the American

globalization Interaction among countries worldwide in the free flow of trade, capital, ideas and information, and people.

In the Wider World

Deng Xiaoping's Economic Plan

Deng Xiaoping assumed leadership in China in 1978 and tackled China's economic problems, including massive poverty, announcing that "poverty is not socialism." He gave rural families land, offered incentives to improve and expand agricultural production, and allowed individual enterprise and small businesses under the "responsible system." Deng also invited foreign investment in jointly owned industries to produce goods primarily for the internal Chinese market but with an eye for foreign trade. He told the people not to be concerned whether policies were socialist or capitalist but only whether they made China prosperous. By the end of the 1980s, the Chinese economy was expanding rapidly, and economically the lives of most Chinese were improving. Agricultural production had increased by a third and China remained able to feed its own population. Privately owned automobiles did not exist in 1978, but twenty years later they numbered over a million, with ownership increasing by 12 percent a year. Deng died in 1997, but he had overseen China's emergence as an economic superpower.

automobile market. American companies that in 1946 had produced two-thirds of the world's steel by 1980 made only 15 percent. Aggravating the problem were higher oil prices and a growing national dependence on foreign oil.

To maintain profitability and survive in the global and what some called **postindustrial economy**, corporations devised new strategies. Many rid themselves of less profitable manufacturing operations and invested more heavily in service industries. General Electric, for example, once one of the largest American manufacturing firms, sold off most of its manufacturing divisions and moved its resources into the service sector by buying the entertainment giant RCA as well as a number of investment and insurance firms. Other companies closed less-productive plants and shifted their production to locales with lower operating costs. Many moved to southern and western states, but an increasing number of companies relocated overseas.

Across the country, but especially in the northeast, as American companies lost money, shed workers, and closed plants, an expanding "**Rust Belt**" formed. Philadelphia, from 1969 to 1981, lost 14 percent of its population and 42 percent of its factory jobs.

■ **postindustrial economy** An economy whose base is no longer driven by manufacturing but by service and information industries.

■ **Rust Belt** Industrialized Middle Atlantic and Great Lakes region whose old factories are barely profitable or have closed.

Pittsburgh, Cleveland, Detroit, and other Rust Belt cities also faced staggering economic losses as plants closed. But changes were felt everywhere. Suburban Lakewood, California, which had seen economic success for three decades after World War II, experienced economic decline when nearby defense-related and other industries relocated and downsized and stores like Walmart replaced higher-end department stores like Macy's.

With higher-paying manufacturing jobs on the decline, many Americans found new jobs in the service industry—which paid about one-third less and used more part-time help. Suddenly, McDonald's was one of the largest employers in the nation. Between 1980 and 1992, the average hourly wage of the American worker declined from $10.59 to $9.87. But the shift away from industry brought new opportunities for some, especially those able to participate in the expanding sector linked to advances in technology.

Technological developments by the mid-1970s were opening new fields and business opportunities, especially in communications and electronics. In part a by-product of military research and development, advances in miniaturization led to development in satellite transmissions, handheld calculators, videocassette recorders (VCRs), computers, and computer networks. With Apple and IBM leading the way, office and personal computers restructured the process of handling information and communications, spawning a new wave of "tech" companies and a new crop of millionaires such as Bill Gates. A Harvard dropout, Gates developed computer software, founded Microsoft in 1975, and became America's youngest billionaire.

Gates was not alone. It seemed that thousands of people were riding the now expanding economy to wealth and power, from inventors to financial "wizards" who brokered mergers. Stories of economic success filled the news media and the plots of television shows and movies, creating a money culture. "Buy high, sell higher," *Fortune* magazine proclaimed. The pursuit of wealth and the goods that it could buy became a lifestyle sought after by many young Americans, particularly the baby boomers, who were reaching their peak earning and spending years. Income-conscious college graduates hoping to become highly paid, aggressive professionals eagerly applied to law, business, and other postgraduate schools. Consequently, the number of doctors, lawyers, and MBAs (those with degrees as master's of business administration) swelled, while in the business world, many executive salaries broke $40 million. The 1980s were called by some the "Me Decade," and *Newsweek* declared 1984 the "Year of the **Yuppie**"—the young, upwardly mobile urban professional who was on the leading edge of the new economic vitality.

But for every Gates or successful yuppie, there seemed to be many more Americans whose economic realities were going in the other direction. Society seemed to be settling into a two-tiered structure with a widening gap separating rich and poor. Between 1980 and 1990, the percentage of the nation's wealth held by the richest 1 percent of American families climbed, but the other 99 percent of families saw their share of the nation's wealth decline. Put simply, the rich got richer and everyone else, on average, got poorer. The ranks of those in economic and social distress grew. Across the country, the number of homeless increased, placing more pressure on social programs even as their budgets were being reduced. The employed were not immune. With 15 percent blue-collar unemployment in Los Angeles, Juan Sanchez was happy to have a good job at a furniture factory, although he and his wife and three children were unable to afford a home and had to live in his brother-in-law's garage. Contributing to stresses on the two-tiered society was a new wave of immigrants who entered the United States following the passage of the 1965 Immigration and Nationality Act.

New Immigrants

The 1965 Immigration Act ended the national quota system established in the 1920s for immigration. A steady increase in the rate of immigration followed (see Figure 28.1). The 1965 act also set new criteria for immigration that favored those with family members in the United States and those having desired job skills and education. It set general annual immigration totals by nation (20,000 per nation) and hemispheric

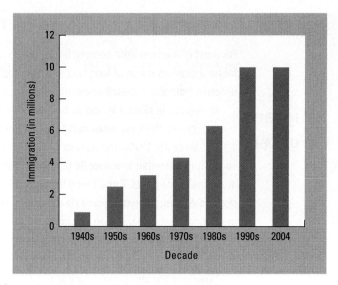

FIGURE 28.1 Immigration to the United States Since 1940

Since the 1940s, the number of immigrants coming to the United States has grown steadily. Changes in immigration laws in 1965 and 1990 not only allowed more immigrants to enter the country but also changed the point of departure for most of those immigrants from Europe to Latin America and Asia.

limits that for the first time set a ceiling on immigrants from the Western Hemisphere. The most immediate result was a change in the place of origin of those coming to the United States. Before the 1965 act, three of every four immigrants came from Europe, but within two decades, more than half of all immigrants arrived from the Caribbean and Latin America, with Asians immigrants becoming the second largest group, surpassing those arriving from Europe. Most came for the traditional reasons: jobs and security. Because the new immigration law favored those with education and skills, many filled the ranks of professionals and technicians, found well-paying jobs, and merged into American society. This appeared to be especially true of those from Japan, China, Korea, and India. But other Asians, especially those coming as refugees from Vietnam, Laos, and Cambodia, along with many from Latin America, arrived with little education or skills. They added to the tier of society that worked at low-paying, part-time jobs in the service and agriculture sectors. Mired in poverty, many had difficulty assimilating into American society and faced growing intolerance and hostility.

■ **yuppie** Young, upwardly mobile urban professional with a high-paying job and a materialistic lifestyle.

It Matters Today

Migrant Workers

For most of the twentieth century, farmers have relied on migrant workers to harvest crops. The life of migrant workers is one of long hours, low wages, and little respect. Working conditions are not much different from those described by John Steinbeck in *The Grapes of Wrath* (see page 648). A majority of migrant families live near or below the poverty line and face more health risks and shorter life expectancy than any other occupational group in the country.

Since the 1970s, the number of illegal immigrants working as migrants has increased steadily. Today, it is estimated that over 90 percent of migrants are foreign born and more than 65 percent are illegal immigrants. Those hiring these workers argue that not enough Americans are willing to do hard agricultural work. Some claim that the growers prefer foreign-born workers, including illegal immigrants, because they can pay lower wages and provide few benefits to workers who are not likely to complain about abusive treatment for fear of arrest and deportation.

- California has the highest percentage of foreign-born residents, causing a state senator to say: "We have the best benefit package . . . for illegal immigrants, so they come here." Do you think illegal immigrants should receive federal and state benefits like access to education, health care, and welfare?

By the mid-1980s, some critics of immigration, especially conservatives, voiced fears about the expanding cultural diversity that threatened their vision of an America centered on European culture. They pushed for Protestant Christian prayer in school and adoption of English as the official language of the United States. Other critics called for increased efforts to stop illegal immigration, especially from Latin America. The 1965 act's limit on immigrants from the Western Hemisphere led to an increased number entering the United States illegally. Most crossed over the border with Mexico and spread out across the country seeking jobs. They found employment as migrant farm workers, laborers, and workers in the service industry. By the mid-1980s, citing competition for jobs and increased social and welfare costs, many Americans called upon Congress to reduce the flow of illegals. Congress responded with the **Immigration Reform and Control Act**, which strengthened the U.S. Border Patrol and established stiffer punishments for employing illegal immigrants. But rather than deportation, the act offered amnesty

Latinos, Asians, and people from the Caribbean make up the majority of immigrants arriving in the United States today. Critics of immigration worry that these groups will not assimilate easily and want to limit further immigration. Supporters argue that assimilation is taking place and point to increased rates of nationalization and citizenship. Here, a Vietnamese family participates in the all-American sport of baseball (T-ball).

■ **Immigration Reform and Control Act** Law passed in 1986 that prohibits the hiring of illegal aliens; it offered amnesty and legal residence to any who could prove that they had entered the country before January 1982.

and possible citizenship to illegal immigrants who had arrived in the United States before 1982. Except for those who thereby became American citizens, few found much merit in the act, and as illegal immigration continued, so too did the calls for more assertive actions to prevent it.

Asserting World Power

★ What did the Reagan administration view as the main issue in world affairs, and how did it try to implement a more assertive foreign policy?

★ How and why did Reagan shift U.S.-Soviet policy during his second term?

Reagan's victories in 1980 and 1984 resulted not only from the popularity of his domestic agenda but also from public support for his views on the role of the United States in world affairs. Throughout the 1980 presidential campaign, the Republicans had hammered at Carter's ineffective foreign policy and at slipping American prestige in the world. Reagan promised to restore American power and influence. Although he had little expertise in foreign policy, Reagan held firm beliefs about America's role in the world and the importance of working from positions of military strength. The Soviets were the "focus of evil" in the world, an "evil empire," but he understood that the Soviet Union was weaker than the United States and that, when faced with strength, some in the Kremlin would be smart enough to negotiate. The United States "could outspend them forever," he explained, and when "we turn our full industrial might into an arms race, they cannot keep pace." The problem was how best to get to that point.

Cold War Renewed

The first step was to reverse Carter's policies that Reagan and his supporters thought made America look vulnerable. One way was to increase the offensive military's capabilities. A second was to develop and deploy a system of defense against Soviet missiles: the **Strategic Defense Initiative** (SDI). A compliant Congress quickly funded Reagan's military budget, adding more than $100 billion a year in appropriations. Congress also funded SDI research—more than $17 billion between 1983 and 1990—even as many scientists argued that the project was conceptually and technologically flawed and could not provide full protection against Soviet missiles.

To add more pressure on Soviet capabilities while projecting American strength, Reagan was determined to confront the Soviets and their minions around the globe. His program was labeled the "Reagan Doctrine," and he explained that as part of its "self-defense" and "mission," the United States would support "freedom fighters" and governments confronting communism, especially in the third world. In these "battles," Reagan supplied increasing amounts of economic and military aid, including covert operations in Afghanistan, Angola, Ethiopia, El Salvador, and Nicaragua. In the Caribbean, Reagan went further and approved a military strike against the island nation of **Grenada**. There, Reagan and his advisers believed, Soviet-Cuban influence was behind the building of an extended airport runway that could be used as a staging area for enemy aircraft. When the government, "a brutal gang of leftist thugs," seemed to threaten the freedom of nearly five hundred American students attending medical school on the island, Reagan ordered an invasion. On October 25, 1983, more than two thousand American soldiers quickly overcame minimal opposition, brought home the American students, and installed a pro-American government on the island. The administration basked in public approval.

Concern was growing, however, over Washington's efforts to fight Communist elements in Central America (see Map 28.2). Many in the administration believed that the Marxist Sandinista Nicaraguan government was part of a Soviet-Cuban effort to take over Central America and was exporting revolution to El Salvador, which was a key to the rest of the region. It was, they stated, a "textbook case of indirect armed aggression by Communists." Consequently, the Reagan administration increased its economic and military aid to the non-Communist government of El Salvador and discounted reports of human rights violations by "death squads" linked to the Salvadoran military. Concerns about abuses in El Salvador were linked to increasing opposition to Reagan's covert activities in Nicaragua.

Hoping to duplicate Eisenhower's success in toppling the Guatemalan government in 1954, Reagan supported organizing an army, the **Contras**, in neighboring Honduras that would overthrow the Sandinista government in Nicaragua. But public and congressional opposition arose in 1984 when the press uncovered large-scale American covert aid to the Contras, including the CIA's mining of Nicaraguan harbors. Many worried that Reagan's efforts in Central America would escalate, creating another Vietnam-like scenario. In response, Congress passed the **Boland Amendment**, which prohibited the CIA

■ **Strategic Defense Initiative** (SDI) Research program to create an effective laser-based defense against nuclear missile attack.

■ **Grenada** Country in the West Indies that achieved independence from Britain in 1974 and was invaded briefly by U.S. forces.

■ **Contras** Nicaraguan rebels, many of them former followers of Anastasio Somoza, fighting to overthrow the leftist Sandinista government.

■ **Boland Amendment** Motion, approved by Congress in 1984, that barred the CIA from using funds to give direct or indirect aid to the Nicaraguan Contras.

and other U.S. intelligence agencies from "directly or indirectly" supporting any military operations in Nicaragua. Reagan and CIA director William Casey ignored the intent of the amendment and found alternative ways to continue arming the Contras. One plan involved improving relations with Iran, which they hoped might have the added benefit of helping to reduce a spreading wave of terrorism throughout the Middle East.

Terrorism

Since the Iranians had seized American hostages, the problem of terrorism had gotten worse. Initially, it was primarily connected to the struggle between Israel and the **Palestine Liberation Organization** (PLO) and its Arab supporters. By the late 1970s, pro-Palestinian organizations were being supported by the ayatollah in Iran and **Muammar Qaddafi**, the ruler of Libya.

Throughout the Mediterranean region, terrorists kidnapped and killed Americans and Europeans, hijacked planes and ships, and attacked airports and other public places. Americans in Lebanon became direct targets on two occasions in 1983. In April Muslim terrorists attacked the American embassy in Beirut, killing 63 people, and six months later, a suicide bombing at the Marine barracks at the Beirut airport killed 241 Marines who were part of a United Nations (UN) peacekeeping force. Reagan vehemently denounced the terrorist attacks but found no solution to the problem except to remove American troops from Lebanon in January 1984.

The administration found a more satisfying response two years later when it bombed targets in Libya. Muammar Qaddafi was regarded as a major supporter of international terrorism, and when intelligence sources linked him to a bombing in West Berlin that killed two American soldiers, Reagan ordered

MAP 28.2 The United States and Central America and the Caribbean
Geographical nearness, important economic ties, security needs, and the drug trade continue to make Central America and the Caribbean a critical region for American interests. This map shows some of the American economic, military, and political actions taken in the region since the end of World War II. Copyright © Cengage Learning

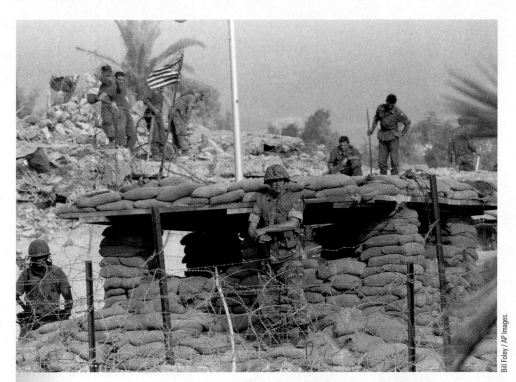

Like Eisenhower twenty-five years before, President Reagan in 1983 committed American troops to Beirut, Lebanon, as part of a peacekeeping operation. This intervention, however, was not successful. In October, terrorists blew up the marine barracks, killing 241. "Too few to fight and too many to die," said one congressional critic, as four months later Reagan withdrew the remaining American forces from the war-torn nation.

the raid on Libya. "You can run but you can't hide," he told terrorists. Neither the bombing nor Reagan's declaration deterred the terrorists, who continued their activities, especially in Lebanon. There, it was thought, one of the most active terrorist groups, Hezbollah, received direct support from Iran.

Trying to merge two problems, in 1985, American agents sought to gain the release of American hostages held in Lebanon by wooing Iran with the sale, through Israel, of weapons. In return for the weapons, Iran would use its influence to gain the release of the hostages, while the money paid for the arms would be sent to a Swiss bank account that could be used by the Contras. As news of this **Iran-Contra Affair** increased, it was clear that the administration had violated the Boland Amendment. Responding to growing public concern, Reagan appointed a special investigating commission, while Congress began its own investigation. By mid-1987, both investigations agreed that members of the CIA and the National Security Council (NSC) had acted independently, without the knowledge or approval of Congress, and had lied to Congress to hide their operation. Eventually, fourteen people were charged with committing crimes, and eleven—including several top-level advisers to Reagan—were convicted of

violating a variety of federal laws and were sentenced to prison terms. Investigators found no direct proof of Reagan's involvement in the affair but concluded that he had encouraged such illegal activities by ordering continued support for the Contras. Reagan's protest, "I just didn't know," made it appear that he was out of touch with and not in control of what his aides were doing.

■ **Palestine Liberation Organization** (PLO) Political and military organization of Palestinians, originally dedicated to opposing the state of Israel through terrorism and other means.

■ **Muammar Qaddafi** Political leader who seized power in a 1969 military coup and imposed a socialist regime and Islamic orthodoxy on Libya.

■ **Iran-Contra Affair** A secret effort by the Reagan administration to use arms sales to Iran to help free American hostages held in Lebanon and to fund the Contras in violation of the Boland Amendment; the program became public in 1986 and was terminated.

Reagan and Gorbachev

Until 1985, Reagan's foreign policy had focused on combating the power of the Soviet Union around the globe. Then, unexpectedly, the president executed a reversal of policy. Reagan and his advisers saw in the new Soviet leader **Mikhail Gorbachev** a true reformer committed to making fundamental changes in the Soviet Union and improving relations with the United States. Gorbachev released political prisoners, and with his policy of **perestroika** ("restructuring"), he began to restructure an economy that was stagnating under the weight of military spending and state planning. His policy of **glasnost** ("openness") initiated reforms that provided increased political and civil rights to the Soviet people. To demonstrate to the West that he was a new type of Soviet leader, Gorbachev unilaterally stopped nuclear testing and deployment of missiles in Eastern Europe and informed Reagan that he wanted to work "vigorously" to improve relations with the United States.

Reagan, too, wanted to improve relations, and he met with Gorbachev seven times between 1985 and 1989, with arms control the central issue. When the two leaders met in Reykjavik, Iceland, in October 1986, differences over SDI prevented an agreement to reduce strategic weapons. Both left the summit disappointed, but they agreed to keep working on arms limitations and in December 1987, they signed the **Intermediate Nuclear Force Treaty**, which removed their intermediate-range missiles from Europe. Soviet-American relations continued to improve as Gorbachev withdrew Soviet forces from Afghanistan and Reagan visited Moscow. Assessing the changes, Secretary of State George Shultz noted that the Cold War "was all over but the shouting."

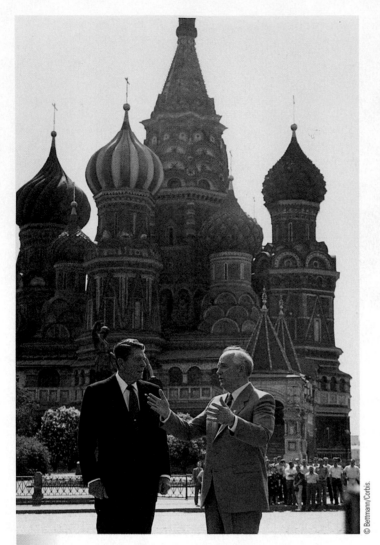

After declaring the Soviet Union an "evil empire" responsible for nearly all the world's problems, President Reagan reversed course in 1988 and opened productive discussions with Soviet reformer Mikhail Gorbachev. The outcome was an intermediate-range nuclear force treaty that helped to end the Cold War as well as to reduce the overall number of nuclear missiles. Here, the two superpower leaders pose in front of St. Basil's Cathedral in Moscow.

© Bettmann/Corbis.

■ **Mikhail Gorbachev** As Soviet General Secretary of the Communist Party he introduced political and economic reforms and then presided over the breakup of the Soviet Union; in 1991 he was forced from office.

perestroika Organizational restructuring of the Soviet economy and bureaucracy that began in the mid-1980s.

glasnost Official policy of the Soviet government under Gorbachev emphasizing freedom of thought and candid discussion of social problems.

■ **Intermediate Nuclear Force Treaty** 1987 treaty that provided for the destruction of all U.S. and Soviet medium-range nuclear missiles and for verification with on-site inspections.

IN REAGAN'S SHADOW

☆ What constraints hampered Bush in developing a domestic agenda?

☆ What foreign-policy choices did Bush face in protecting American global interests?

Despite some concerns over the economy and the Iran-Contra revelations, most Republicans believed that the Reagan years had cemented a conservative ascendancy and that Vice President George Herbert

Walker Bush would be able to defeat any Democratic candidate. Although some in the New Right worried that he was not conservative enough, most Republicans believed that Bush had earned the nomination. He had served the party faithfully, holding important posts under Presidents Nixon and Ford, including chair of the Republican National Committee, ambassador to China, and director of the Central Intelligence Agency. He was expected to continue the Reagan revolution and defeat the Democratic candidate, Governor Michael Dukakis of Massachusetts.

Bush Assumes Office

The 1988 campaign followed a familiar pattern. Republicans labeled Dukakis too liberal, especially on fighting crime and drugs, while Bush emphasized his foreign policy experience and promised not to raise taxes: "Read my lips . . . no new taxes." Dukakis had no effective answer to the Republican attacks and Bush sailed to an easy victory. With 79.2 percent of the electoral vote and 54 percent of the popular vote, he became the first sitting vice president to be elected president since Martin Van Buren in 1836. Although Bush trounced Dukakis, the victory was not as sweet as he had hoped. Democrats maintained large majorities in the House and the Senate.

During the campaign, Bush had rested largely on Reagan's policies, saying that changes and "new directions" were not needed. As president, he kept many of Reagan's advisers and announced his goal was not "to remake society" but to "see that government doesn't get in the way." It was a realistic goal, given that he faced a Congress in which Democrats had a ten-vote majority in the Senate and an eighty-nine-vote majority in the House. By the end of his first year in office, Bush and his advisers believed they were managing well. Bush had used the veto extensively to block or modify Democratic-sponsored legislation, while also promoting a "kinder and gentler nation." His veto had blocked a Democratic effort to raise the minimum wage to $4.65 an hour and had forced Congress to accept his proposal of $4.25 an hour. Bush also supported passage of the **Americans with Disabilities Act** of 1990, giving it his administration's highest priority, despite opposition from many business groups and the high cost of the bill. He also credited his administration for protecting the environment and wilderness areas. The Clean Air Act of 1990 significantly reduced smokestack and auto emissions and created standards for a wide variety of pollutants in the air.

If Bush was pleased about his limited domestic agenda, he was concerned about the nation's economic condition. Facing a huge budget deficit, a recession, and an expensive bailout of the federal savings and loan system, Bush agreed that an increase in tax revenue was necessary—violating his election pledge not to raise taxes. His decision brought immediate condemnation from many Republicans and some Democrats. As the battle over the budget raged, Bush reluctantly agreed to the Omnibus Budget Reconciliation Act, which included a significant increase in the income tax, along with smaller increases on other taxes, like the gasoline tax. Bush's popularity dropped 25 percent and in the 1990 congressional elections, Democrats gained ten more Senate seats and twenty-five more seats in the House. Political gridlock followed.

While Bush's popularity recovered as he oversaw successes in foreign policy, the economy did not. Between 1990 and 1993 more than 1.9 million people lost their jobs, and 63 percent of American corporations cut their staffs. Families watched as average levels of income dropped below 1980 levels, to $37,300 from a 1980 high of $38,900. Consumers—caught between rising unemployment, falling wages, and nagging inflation—saw their savings shrink, and their confidence in the economy followed suit. "I don't see the United States regaining a substantial percentage of the jobs lost for five to ten years," said one chief executive.

Bush and a New International Order

Bush's own preferences and international events dictated that foreign affairs would consume most of his attention. The world was changing rapidly, and Bush considered the management of international relations as one of his strengths. As he assumed office, Gorbachev's reforms touched off a series of political changes that rocked the Soviet Union and its Eastern European satellites. Nationalism and the rejection of Communist rule resulted in new democratic governments in Poland, Hungary, and Czechoslovakia, as well as the unification of Germany and the fragmentation of Yugoslavia (see Map 28.3). By 1989, the **Berlin Wall** was torn down, and Gorbachev and Bush, meeting on the island of Malta in the Mediterranean Sea, had declared that the Cold War was over. In 1990, the Soviet Union began to disintegrate when the Baltic States—Latvia, Estonia, and Lithuania—declared

■ **Americans with Disabilities Act** 1990 act that prohibits private employers from discriminating against individuals with disabilities; it defines a disability as a physical or mental impairment that substantially limits one or more major life activities.

Berlin Wall Barrier that the Communist East German government built in 1961 to divide East and West Berlin; it was torn down in November 1989 as the Cold War was ending.

MAP 28.3 The End of the Cold War Changes the Map of Europe
As the Soviet Union collapsed and lost its control over the countries of Eastern Europe, the map of Eastern Europe and Central Asia changed. The Soviet Union disappeared into history, replaced by fifteen new national units. In Eastern Europe, West and East Germany merged, Czechoslovakia divided into two nations, and Yugoslavia broke into five feuding states. Copyright © Cengage Learning

their independence. Fearful that Gorbachev would allow the further fragmentation of the Soviet Union, in August 1991 conservatives staged a coup to replace him. The poorly planned coup failed when **Boris Yeltsin**, the president of the Russian Republic, called for a popular uprising against it. As Yeltsin emerged as the new leader of the reform movement, Gorbachev resigned, and by Christmas the Soviet Union ceased to exist. In its place was the **Commonwealth of Independent States** (CIS), a weak federation of once-Soviet republics, led by Yeltsin.

■ **Boris Yeltsin** Russian parliamentary leader who was elected president of the new Russian Republic in 1991 and provided increased democratic and economic reforms.

■ **Commonwealth of Independent States** (CIS) Weak federation of the former Soviet republics; it replaced the Soviet Union in 1992 and soon gave way to total independence of the member countries.

Central and Eastern Europe were not the only sites of democratic reform. In South Africa, the one-time apartheid (white supremacist) government freed opposition leader Nelson Mandela after twenty-seven years in prison, and in a 1992 election white voters officially ended apartheid and moved to allow non-whites to vote. The political changes in South Africa and much of Eastern Europe were relatively peaceful, but in parts of Yugoslavia religious and ethnic differences led to horrific violence.

In Yugoslavia, ethnic separatist movements demanded the dismantling of Yugoslavia and called for independence for the regions of Slovenia, Croatia, Bosnia-Herzegovina, and Macedonia. Representing a united Yugoslavia, Serbia fought to maintain its control, but by 1992 all but Bosnia-Herzegovina had achieved independence. In Bosnia-Herzegovina a religious and ethnic civil war continued until 1995 as Serb forces instituted a policy of "ethnic cleansing" to remove the Muslim population (as discussed further in the next chapter).

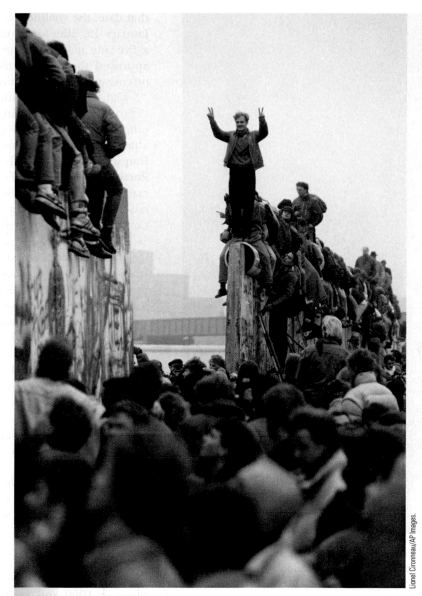

With the collapse of the Soviet Union and communism across Eastern Europe, the symbol of the iron curtain and the Cold War came tumbling down in Berlin. Jubilant Berliners sit atop the Berlin Wall, which had divided the city from 1962 to November 1989.

Democratic reformers were not always successful. In several Communist countries, like Cuba, Romania, and the People's Republic of China, the existing leadership maintained control. In China, thousands of people filled the massive expanse of Tiananmen Square in 1989 calling for political, social, and economic reforms, only to be attacked by Chinese troops who killed hundreds of protesters as the world watched on television. Bush condemned the attacks, but stuck to his policy of nonintervention and verbal support for the growth of democracy.

While some argued that the collapse of the Soviet Union created a "peace dividend," allowing the United States to reduce its global role and military budget, Bush insisted that the world was still a dangerous place and American power was still needed to promote national interests and world stability. His position seemed prudent when in 1990 American military force was needed to end an Iraqi invasion of neighboring Kuwait.

In August 1990, Iraq's forces overran the oil-rich sheikdom of Kuwait. Concerned that Iraqi leader

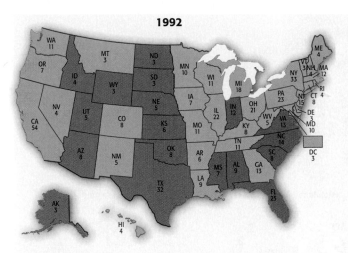

1992

Candidate (Party)	Electoral Vote		Popular Vote	
Clinton (Democrat)	370	68.8%	44,908,233	43.0%
Bush (Republican)	168	31.2%	39,102,282	37.4%
Perot (Independent)	0	0.0%	19,741,048	18.9%

MAP 28.5 Election of 1992, by State
Bill Clinton received almost 69 percent of the Electoral College votes—about double the electoral votes received by George Bush. Nevertheless, Clinton received only 43 percent of the popular vote—the lowest popular vote percentage since Woodrow Wilson's victory in 1912. Third-party candidate H. Ross Perot drew votes from both Democrats and Republicans in equal numbers and had no impact on the electoral vote. Copyright © Cengage Learning

had messed up the nation, Congress was ineffective, the deficit needed to be reduced, and his election would return control to the people. By June, Perot led in the polls but as the election neared Bush and Clinton passed Perot in the polling. For Clinton and his advisers there was one basic message, the economy. James Carvell, Clinton's chief political adviser, tacked reminders over his own desk reading, "It's the Economy, Stupid." Republicans had no answer to the economic issues and instead focused on their cultural agenda and Clinton's character. Bush had served gallantly in World War II, while Clinton had avoided the draft during the war in Vietnam. Bush had experience and family values. Clinton had used drugs and was a known womanizer.

The campaign culminated in the third televised debate, watched by an estimated 88 million people. Both Bush and Perot gained in the polls following the head-to-head encounter, but they could not overtake the front-running Clinton. In a three-way race, Clinton earned 43 percent of the popular vote, compared with Bush's 37 percent and Perot's 19 percent (see Map 28.5). Clinton swept to victory with 370 votes in the Electoral College, 100 more than he needed to win. While Democrats still held the majority in Congress, Republicans had gained nine seats in the House of Representatives. In both parties, a record number of women and minorities were elected to Congress.

Individual Voices

Diameng Pa Tells His Story

The 1965 Immigration Act changed the patterns of immigration, resulting in increasing numbers of Asians and Latin Americans migrating to the United States. Amid growing calls for limitations on immigration, in August 1977 a Senate subcommittee heard testimony from supporters of immigration. Among those speaking was Diameng Pa, a Cambodian refugee and a senior at Wakefield High School in Arlington, Virginia. Historians use testimony like that of Diameng Pa to discover not only how and why immigrants come to the United States but what their perceptions are of American society and its opportunities and freedoms.

I would like to thank the Committee on Immigration for giving me this opportunity to tell . . . my strong belief that America should continue to be a nation of immigrants. This institution is hope for those still seeking a new beginning similar to the one I received.

I was born in Batdambang, Cambodia, on November 23, 1978 . . . a rural village . . . several miles from the Thai border. . . . This period produced a Cambodian Communist faction known as the Khmer Rouge, who killed more than 400,000 Cambodians and forced many more to flee to refugee camps in Thailand, including my family.

To acquire a better life for their family, my parents fled to a refugee camp in Thailand, fortunately able to escape from the constant threat of guerrilla attacks by the Khmer Rouge . . . and then to escape to the United States. . . . By coming to the United States of America, we were traveling to a land that was foreign to us and whose language we did not speak. However, it would be a place that we would receive new identities and a new chance of a better life. It is a land that would take time to adapt to, however, it is a land of opportunity. ❶

My family initially settled in a minority neighborhood of South Arlington, Virginia, not far from Strayer College where my father, Mong Pa, pursued a degree in business administration. However, unfortunately, he abandoned his goals to support the family. My father would also mention the importance of education and its correlation with success. Though quite young, I realized that my father sacrificed his opportunity to pursue his business degree so that the family was financially stable. He encouraged me to reach out and to appreciate one of the many precious gifts that America offered—formal education.

Two years after I started school, I settled into the language thanks to my teachers and the miracle of TV. I remember adopting a few phrases here and there and soon enough I became accustomed to the English language and American culture. Bugs Bunny's "What's up, Doc" was my most favorite phrase during that time. . . . [W]hile attending Thomas Jefferson Middle School . . . I accelerated in my studies and took the most demanding courses possible. . . . I developed an interest in science activities. ❷

As a sophomore at Wakefield High School I was privileged to be the first student in Wakefield history to attend the international Science and Engineer Fair in . . . Canada and to win second place in the category of environmental science.

As an immigrant, valedictorian of my senior class and now a proud American citizen, I realize that becoming an American took time. I feel that pursuing a dream takes dedication and will to strive and succeed. Only in America are you given this generous privilege. A world-renowned . . . researcher by the name of David Da-i Ho states, "Success is a result of immigrant drive. People get in this new world, they want to carve out their place in it. . . . You always retain a bit of underdog mentality. And if they work assiduously and lie low long enough, even underdogs will have their day." ❸

❶ In what ways were Diameng Pa's experiences and goals similar to those of Franklin Chang-Diaz?

❷ What key obstacle did both Pa and Chang-Diaz have to overcome, and what was the role of education in their lives?

❸ Do you agree with the statement that immigrants are underdogs and have a special drive for success? In your opinion, are the success stories of Pa and Chang-Diaz proof that America is a land of opportunity, or are these two immigrants exceptions to the rule?

Study Tools

SUMMARY

The years between Carter's inauguration and Clinton's election witnessed changing expectations based in part on the health of the American economy. The economic growth that had characterized the postwar period was slowing, making the American dream harder to attain. During Carter's presidency the nation seemed beset by blows to its domestic prosperity and international status that neither Carter nor Congress seemed able to solve. These problems contributed to a conservative resurgence that blamed liberal policies for most of the nation's troubles.

During the 1980 campaign Reagan rejected Carter's view that the nation faced limits and argued that American greatness was constrained only by the government's excessive regulation and interference in society. He promised to reassert American power and renew the offensive in the Cold War. It was a popular message that elevated Reagan to the presidency. As president, Reagan fulfilled many conservative expectations by reducing support for some social programs, easing and eliminating some government regulations, and exerting American power around the world—altering the structure of Soviet-American relations. Supporters claimed that Reagan's choices had restored prosperity and pride and that the administration had worked to "change a nation, and instead . . . changed a world."

Bush used Reagan's legacy to ensure his election in 1988 but found that unlike Reagan, he was unable to project an image of strong and visionary leadership. Although he gained public approval for his handling of world affairs, those successes seemed only to highlight his inability to overcome a nagging recession that sapped the public's confidence in Republican leadership and the economy. Confident that his good intentions and foreign policy successes would propel him to another term, Bush lost to Clinton when the Democrat stressed the need for change, especially in the way the Republicans dealt with the economy.

CHRONOLOGY
New Directions, New Limits

1976	Jimmy Carter elected president
1977	Department of Energy created
	Panama Canal treaties
1978	Camp David Accords
1979	Ayatollah Khomeini assumes power in Iran
	United States recognizes People's Republic of China
	Nuclear accident at Three Mile Island, Pennsylvania
	Egyptian-Israeli peace treaty signed in Washington, D.C.
	Hostages seized in Iran
	Soviet Union invades Afghanistan
1980	Carter applies sanctions against Soviet Union
	Carter Doctrine
	Ronald Reagan elected president
1981	Iran releases American hostages
	Economic Recovery Tax Act
1983	Congress funds Strategic Defense Initiative
	United States invades Grenada
1984	Withdrawal of U.S. forces from Lebanon
	Boland Amendment
	Reagan reelected
	Newsweek's "Year of the Yuppie"
1985	Mikhail Gorbachev assumes power in Soviet Union
	Secret arms sales to Iran to obtain funds for the Contras
1986	U.S. bombing raid on Libya
	Gorbachev-Reagan summit in Reykjavik, Iceland
1987	Iran-Contra hearings
	Stock market crash
	Intermediate Nuclear Force Treaty
1988	George Bush elected president
1989	Berlin Wall pulled down
	United States invades Panama
1990	Recession begins
	Clean Air Act
	Iraq invades Kuwait
	Americans with Disabilities Act
1991	Breakup of the Soviet Union
	Gorbachev resigns
	First Iraqi War
1992	Clinton elected

Study Tools

FOCUS QUESTIONS

If you have mastered this chapter you should be able to answer these questions and to explain the terms that follow the questions.

1. ☆ *What problems did Carter face in implementing his domestic policies, and why were many Democrats unhappy with his approach?*

2. ☆ *What new directions in foreign policy did Carter take, especially in Central America and the Middle East?*

3. ☆ *What issues contributed to the emergence of the New Right, and how did the New Right help shape the 1980 election?*

4. ☆ *What is "Reaganomics," and what were the consequences of Reagan's economic policies?*

5. ☆ *How was the changing U.S. economy affecting Americans?*

6. ☆ *Who were the "new immigrants," and how were they received?*

7. ☆ *What did the Reagan administration view as the main issue in world affairs, and how did it try to implement a more assertive foreign policy?*

8. ☆ *How and why did Reagan shift U.S.-Soviet policy during his second term?*

9. ☆ *What constraints hampered Bush in developing a domestic agenda?*

10. ☆ *What foreign-policy choices did Bush face in protecting American global interests?*

KEY TERMS

Alan Bakke   *(p. 799)*

Equal Rights Amendment   *(p. 799)*

Phyllis Schlafly   *(p. 799)*

Roe v. Wade   *(p. 800)*

Right to Life movement   *(p. 800)*

Three Mile Island   *(p. 800)*

Carter Doctrine   *(p. 801)*

mujahedeen   *(p. 801)*

Camp David Accords   *(p. 802)*

Ayatollah Ruhollah Khomeini   *(p. 802)*

Moral Majority   *(p. 804)*

Proposition 13   *(p. 805)*

supply-side economics   *(p. 806)*

Reaganomics   *(p. 806)*

Aid to Families with Dependent Children   *(p. 806)*

Economic Recovery Tax Act   *(p. 806)*

postindustrial economy   *(p. 808)*

Rust Belt   *(p. 808)*

yuppie   *(p. 809)*

Immigration Reform and Control Act   *(p. 810)*

Strategic Defense Initiative   *(p. 811)*

Grenada   *(p. 811)*

Contras   *(p. 811)*

Boland Amendment   *(p. 811)*

Palestine Liberation Organization   *(p. 812)*

Muammar Qaddafi   *(p. 812)*

Iran-Contra Affair   *(p. 813)*

Mikhail Gorbachev   *(p. 814)*

Intermediate Nuclear Force Treaty   *(p. 814)*

Americans with Disabilities Act   *(p. 815)*

Boris Yeltsin   *(p. 816)*

Commonwealth of Independent States   *(p. 816)*

Persian Gulf War   *(p. 818)*

cultural war   *(p. 819)*

H. Ross Perot   *(p. 819)*

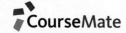 **CourseMate** Go to the History CourseMate website for primary source links, study tools, and review materials for this chapter. www.cengagebrain.com

29

Entering a New Century, 1992–2010

Behind the Stories

Over the preceding twenty-eight chapters of *Making America*, the patterns of American history have emerged as we, the authors, visualize them. We have tried not only to explain how and why events occurred, but also to emphasize that choices had to be made and that the outcomes often were not expected.

Over the centuries Americans have asked: "What are we doing, and where are we going?" This question still resonates across the country as we enter the second decade of the twenty-first century. Old familiar traditions seem to be changing, while their replacements seem less reliable. The nation's economic strength is no longer a certainty. Amid a worldwide economic crisis, many Americans continue to view globalization, the increasing size of the European Union, and the growth of the Pacific Rim economies, especially China, as evidence that the nation has lost its role as an economic leader. Politically, Americans have broken over two hundred years of tradition by choosing an African American president. Will new leadership open new paths in governance or will the conflicts between liberalism and conservatism continue to stifle cooperation and innovation? Similarly, what foreign-policy issues will replace the Cold War? Will the war on terror dominate or will a new form of diplomacy emerge to deal with such issues as global warming and pandemics? As in the past, change provides new opportunities and challenges even as it creates uncertainty and resistance.

Over the next years and generations, historians and others will try to explain the changes and events of the new century. They will attempt to provide historical perspective—but it will take years, if not decades, to define the new era—or to see how much the new era looks like the old. And historians will argue about broad currents and specific events—just as we have. History is about change, and as we confront the future there is comfort in knowing that our parents, grandparents, and those before them faced the same uncertainties.

—J.G.

Individual Choices
Evan Williams

For Evan Williams the choices were not difficult; he just allowed himself to follow his own interests. That included leaving the University of Nebraska halfway through his sophomore year when he concluded that college was not for him. He took jobs in Florida and Texas, becoming aware of his interests and opportunities in the emerging field of computer technology connected to the Internet. In 1994, he returned home to Nebraska and, with his father, formed a company that produced CD-ROMs and videos instructing people how to use the Internet. The company failed. Later, he admitted that he had no idea or real interest in running a company and that he was more interested in starting new projects than finishing old ones. Leaving angry employees behind, Williams moved to northern California where he worked for various computer-related industries, mostly in areas associated with Web development.

Evan Williams

Wanting to work on his own schedule and pursue his ideas, in 1999, he and Meg Houghton formed Prya Labs, which produced various marketing programs. Williams and his group tinkered with the process and developed a new application for general use on the Internet. He named the program the Blogger. It allowed people to create their own websites without knowing how to program. The blog allowed unlimited communications through the Internet with anyone wanting to log on to the site. Its use exploded, creating new forms of publishing and journalism. Some used it to keep not-so-personal diaries and journals, while others created specialized newsletters and information and opinion pieces. Many fully embrace the new technology and see the Internet, blogs, and texting as a positive, even liberating means of communication; but others, as shown in this chapter's Individual Voices feature, offer a different vision.

In 2003, with blogging reaching millions, Williams sold the company to Google, making him and his partners rich. They went to work for the corporate giant, but Williams found the corporate climate at Google stifled his curiosity and creativeness. After two years, he left Google to follow his own interests again. He needed freedom to scratch new "itches." One itch produced a new company, Obvious, and a brainstorming session brought a new variation of the blog—a mini blog—a Twitter. Although it limits text to only 140 characters and was designed to answer questions like "What are you doing now?" Twitter users have expanded its function, changing the nature of social networking and modern communications. By the spring of 2009, well over 15 million people were "twittering," "tweeting,"

Failing to resolve such inequalities, women and groups like the National Organization for Women initiated individual and class action lawsuits for sexual discrimination against a variety of companies, including the Publix chain of supermarkets and Wal-Mart. In 1993, the Supreme Court, in *Harris v. Forklift Systems*, found that sexual harassment involved not only "verbal and physical conduct" but also the creation of a "hostile environment."

The changing family and expanding roles of women also continued to fuel the culture wars. Conservatives and groups like Concerned Women of America claimed that liberalism and feminism endangered the traditional American family. They argued that even "mommy-friendly" workplaces were not a replacement for full-time mothers and an environment that respected moral values. As one antifeminist explained: "It all comes down to values. Traditional values work because they are the guidelines most consistent with human nature."

For many Americans, abortion remained one of the most divisive issues in the culture wars. Conservatives applauded the Supreme Court's 1992 decision in *Planned Parenthood of Southeastern Pennsylvania v. Casey,* which said that, in some cases, states could modify the right to an abortion. But many opponents of abortion were increasingly impatient with Congress's and the court's inability to reverse *Roe v. Wade.* Some within the Right to Life movement opted to take more direct and forceful tactics, targeting abortion clinic doctors, staff, and patients. By 1994, more than half of all abortion clinics reported varied cases of intimidation and violence, and a hundred clinics had been targets of arson or bombings. In response to these occurrences, in 1994 the Clinton administration supported the Freedom of Access to Clinic Entrances Act. It restricted the tactics of intimidation that pro-life supporters such as **Operation Rescue** could use.

■ **Operation Rescue** A militant anti-abortion group that advocates intimidation and physical confrontation as a means to stop abortion.

■ **Family and Medical Leave Act** Law that permits an employee to take job-protected unpaid leave owing to a serious health condition or to care for sick family members or a new child.

■ **North American Free Trade Agreement** (NAFTA) Agreement approved by the Senate in 1993 that eliminated most tariffs and other trade barriers between the United States, Mexico, and Canada.

■ **General Agreement on Tariffs and Trade** (GATT) First signed in 1947, the GATT sought to encourage free trade between member states by regulating and reducing tariffs and resolving trade disputes; in 1995 its functions were assumed by the World Trade Organization.

THE CLINTON YEARS

☆ *In what ways did President Clinton's centrist agenda and personal behavior shape his presidency?*

☆ *How did the Contract with America represent a conservative critique of liberalism and Democratic policies?*

☆ *What actions did Clinton take to expand trade and support global stability?*

Like many presidents entering office, Bill Clinton had an ambitious domestic agenda. "I want to get something done," he told a press conference. On his list of "to-dos" were parts of a liberal agenda, including providing national healthcare, signing the **Family and Medical Leave Act**, which had previously been vetoed by Bush, and supporting gay rights. But the economy was his first priority. As he assumed office, it appeared that the economy was beginning to recover, but Clinton understood that solving the problem of the deficit and putting the government on a firm financial foundation was a vital necessity. He told his economic team, "if we don't do this, we can't do anything else."

Clinton, the Economy, and Congress

The previous two administrations had quadrupled the national debt and piled up more debt in twelve years than the nation had in the previous two hundred. Clinton understood that he needed to take a bold step and implement a system that established fiscal discipline, supported critical social programs, and opened foreign markets to American producers. His economic plan crossed party lines and drew intense criticism from both Democrats and Republicans. Democrats protested his reduced spending, while Republicans vehemently opposed his increased taxes, which they claimed would harm the economy. The outcome was an August budget that passed the House by two votes and passed the Senate only when Vice President Al Gore cast the tie-breaking vote. For the first time since World War II, a bill had passed Congress when all members of the opposition party opposed it.

In an effort to improve the economy by increasing international trade, Clinton asked Congress to approve the **North American Free Trade Agreement** (NAFTA) and the **General Agreement on Tariffs and Trade** (GATT). Both initiatives were started by Bush but had encountered strong opposition, especially NAFTA, from many Democrats and from organized labor. Opponents claimed that both measures harmed the American economy by encouraging U.S. factories

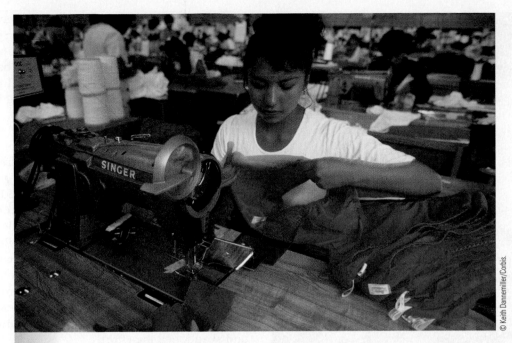

The North American Free Trade Agreement eliminated many trade barriers between the United States, Canada, and Mexico. Here, a Mexican worker sews garments to be shipped and sold north of the border. American supporters of the agreement argue that it has led to an overall increase in trade, while critics argue that it cost American jobs as American companies used Mexican plants and workers to produce what was once made in the United States.

to relocate to nations with lower costs and standards. Unable to convince many Democrats to support the bills, Clinton was forced to rely on Republican votes for their passage.

The Family and Medical Leave Act was less contentious, with several Republican supporters, and was signed by Clinton in February 1993. It allowed workers to take up to 12 months' unpaid leave because of illness or family needs and guaranteed they would be able to return to the same job. Clinton's efforts to expand gay rights by asking Congress to lift the ban against homosexuals in the military met irresistible opposition from both political parties, the military, and the public. Faced with such opposition, Clinton accepted a compromise that did not lift the ban but instead required the military not to ask recruits about their sexual preferences and expected gays and lesbians in the service to refrain from homosexual activities. The compromise, "Don't Ask, Don't Tell, Don't Pursue," failed to please either side but remains in force in the military. The future of the policy appeared in jeopardy when in 2010, the House of Representatives, with White House support, repealed the law and pressure mounted on the Senate to also vote to repeal the policy.

Clinton's efforts reflected growing support for efforts by gay-rights activists to gain antidiscriminatory sexual preference laws that would protect jobs, provide work-related benefits for partners, and allow

same-sex marriages. By the end of 2007, they could count some major victories as 19 states and the District of Columbia and over 140 cities and counties had passed legislation banning employment discrimination based on sexual orientation, and the Supreme Court in *Lawrence v. Texas* (2003) declared sodomy laws unconstitutional.

On a related issue, Clinton and Congress supported more funds to fight the AIDS epidemic. AIDS, or **acquired immune deficiency syndrome** (AIDS), began to be noticed in American cities in the early 1980s. Because the disease infected mostly gay men and drug users, and seemed confined to the inner cities, official and public response was at first largely apathetic. Linking AIDS to the "morality battle," some, like Pat Buchanan and Senator Jesse Helms (R.–North Carolina), even suggested that those with the disease were being punished for their unnatural perversions. Responding to conservative pressure, the Reagan administration did little to fight AIDS. However, as the number of victims climbed and the disease spread to

acquired immune deficiency syndrome (AIDS) Gradual and eventually fatal breakdown of the immune system caused by the human immunodeficiency virus (HIV); HIV/AIDS is transmitted by the exchange of body fluids through such means as sexual intercourse or needle sharing.

In 1987, the San Francisco-based Names Project started to make quilts in memory of those who had died of AIDS in the United States. In 1992, the quilts were displayed on the Mall in Washington, D.C., displaying the names of twenty-six thousand people.

Robert Giroux/AFP/Getty Images.

the heterosexual population, the public's fear of AIDS grew rapidly, and in the 1990s federal support became available for education and prevention programs and research. By 2007 AIDS had claimed more than half a million American lives and had killed over 20 million people worldwide. While significant advances have been made in research toward controlling AIDS, throughout many African countries AIDS remains at an epidemic stage.

■ **Contract with America** Pledge taken in 1994 by some three hundred Republican candidates for the House, who promised to reduce the size and scope of the federal government and to balance the federal budget by 2002.

■ **judicial restraint** Refraining from using the courts to interpret laws in ways that implement social change but instead deferring to Congress, the president, and the consensus of the people.

In addition to the budget, Clinton recorded several other political victories during his first two years in office, including the Brady Handgun Violence Prevention Act, which required federal background checks on those purchasing firearms and prohibited some individuals, like felons, from having handguns. But Clinton also suffered a glaring defeat in attempting to implement a national healthcare system. He had made it a campaign priority and after assuming office, he announced a task force, chaired by First Lady Hillary Rodham Clinton, to draft legislation. In September 1993, President Clinton asked Congress to write a "new chapter in the American story" and pass an extremely complicated plan—called Godzilla by one Democratic congressional leader. Republicans attacked the bill with gusto as an example of big government and bigger spending, saying that healthcare was too important to leave to the federal government. After a year of heated public and congressional hearings and debate, President Clinton admitted defeat and abandoned the effort.

The bitter fights over the budget, healthcare, and gays in the military, combined with allegations of various wrongdoings by the Clintons, boosted Republican popularity. In 1994, Republicans led by Newt Gingrich, a conservative representative from Georgia, seized the political initiative with a political agenda called the "**Contract with America**." It called for supporting family values, large cuts in federal spending, and a balanced budget by 2002. The public responded by giving the Republicans majorities in both houses of Congress for the first time in forty years. The new conservative majority was "going to change the world," predicted Gingrich, now the Republican Speaker of the House.

Judicial Restraint and the Rehnquist Court

Part of the Republican plan for a conservative restructuring of government and society rested with the Supreme Court under Chief Justice William Rehnquist. Reagan and Bush had appointed six justices who practiced **judicial restraint**, creating a narrow, but not always stable, conservative majority. Conservatives hoped the Court would reverse previous positions taken on desegregation and affirmative action programs while supporting gun-owners' rights and anti-abortion efforts.

But the results of the Rehnquist Court's decisions were mixed. Conservatives were disappointed when the Court upheld the right to an abortion, the ban on prayer in school, and the *Miranda* decision. But they hoped that Rehnquist's view that the Court had erred by "reflecting society's changing and expanding values" would produce desired decisions, and they applauded the Court's ruling in the *DeKalb County, Georgia* case (1992) that busing could not be used to integrate schools segregated by de facto housing patterns. Conservatives also approved the Court's position regarding affirmative action when, on several occasions, it ruled that government could not "set aside" positions for minorities and that age and disability discrimination did not always violate equal protection under the law. In addition, the Court earned Republican praise for its support of laws passed in California, Washington, and Florida that forbid special consideration for race, gender, or both in state hiring and in admissions to state colleges and universities.

The Rehnquist Court also chipped away at the federal government's power to make state and local governments comply with its directives. In several cases throughout the 1990s, the Court upheld state sovereignty by deciding that states and municipalities could resist implementing executive and congressional directives. In *Printz v. United States* (1997), the Court declared unconstitutional certain provisions in the so-called Brady Bill that required state police to do a background search of anyone wanting to buy a handgun. Continuing the pattern, in 2000 a divided Court invalidated provisions in the Violence Against Women Act that permitted suits in federal courts by victims of gender-motivated crimes. In writing for the majority, Chief Justice Rehnquist announced that distinctions must be made between "what is truly national and what is truly local."

Clinton's Comeback

The conservative resurgence in the 1994 election encouraged congressional Republicans to assume the political offensive and to reject compromises with the White House. They focused on the 1995 budget as a way to roll back social programs and worked on an economic plan that slashed spending on education, welfare, Medicare, Medicaid, and the environment. "You cannot sustain the old welfare state" with a balanced budget, Gingrich proclaimed.

Although he agreed that balancing the budget was the first priority, Clinton called the Republican cuts too extreme. He vowed to protect spending for education, Medicare, Social Security, and the environment. As the battle for the budget began, Clinton reasserted his leadership when, on April 19, 1995, an act of domestic terrorism destroyed the Murrah Federal Building in Oklahoma City, killing 168 people, including 19 children. The bombing was the work of Timothy McVeigh, an American extremist who believed that the federal government threatened the freedom of the American people. To many, his views and actions not only symbolized the dangers of extremism but also reflected what seemed deepening social and political divisions in the nation. Consequently, when Clinton asked that people reject such extremism and

stressed national unity, public opinion responded positively to the president's position.

Continuing to emphasize his centrism and to present Republicans as too extreme, Clinton gave a series of "common ground" speeches that committed his administration to passing anticrime legislation, finding methods to limit sex and violence on television, reforming welfare, and fixing affirmative action. This approach not only undercut Republican positions but, as in the case of welfare reform, made them appear hard-hearted. Conservatives argued that welfare programs created a class of welfare-dependent people—"welfare mothers" with little integrity and no work ethic who represented "spiritual and moral poverty." Clinton called such statements mean spirited and blind to the reality of those on welfare—especially considering the number of children on welfare. To replace relief with jobs, he said, it was vital to increase funds for daycare, job training, and educational programs.

When Republicans passed their budget bill, Clinton rejected it and sent it back to Congress. Overconfident, Republicans then refused to pass a temporary measure to keep the government operating unless their budget was accepted. Unmoved, Clinton shut down

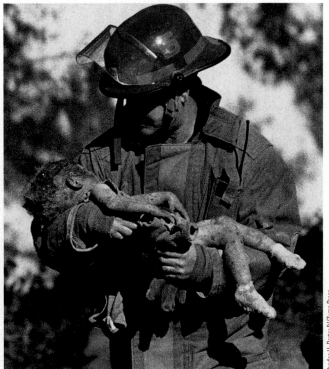

Charles H. Porter IV/Zuma Press.

On April 19, 1995, a terrorist truck bomb exploded in front of the Murrah Federal Building in Oklahoma City, killing 168 people. Here, a fireman carries the lifeless body of one of the 19 children who lost their lives in a daycare center housed in the building.

all nonessential functions of the government—first for six days in November, then for twenty-one days from December 16 to January 6, 1996. With the public blaming Republicans for the budget impasse, Clinton and Congress reached an agreement. Clinton accepted some Republican cuts, while congressional Republicans accepted most of the president's requests, including those for education, Medicare, and Medicaid. Having won the battle of the budget, Clinton committed himself to balancing the budget by 2002.

As the 1996 presidential election approached, Republicans chose to emphasize two issues: the culture war and Clinton's budget. They argued that the president's spending cuts were inadequate and that his "big spending" had "sucked the life out of the economy and eaten up the American workers' pay." The problem with the Republicans' rhetoric was that the economy was beginning to achieve the highs described in the first section of the chapter, allowing Clinton to boast that his administration had created 10 million new jobs and had reduced poverty.

Clinton's Second Term

Despite the improving economy and Clinton's shrewd political manuevering, Republicans remained confident they would regain the presidency in the 1996 election. Conservative Republicans dominated the convention, once again attacking Clinton's liberalism and personality. Amid battle cries of the "cultural war"

they nominated conservative Kansas Senator Robert Dole. Their expectations quickly faded as public opinion polls showed that over 60 percent of Americans gave Clinton's record good marks, even though 54 percent thought he was not necessarily "honest" or "trustworthy." Facing Clinton's popularity and a rebounding economy, Dole's campaign lacked energy. In an election marked by low voter turnout, Clinton became the first Democratic president to be reelected since Franklin D. Roosevelt. He captured 379 electoral votes and 49 percent of the popular vote.

In his 1997 State of the Union address, Clinton set a centrist agenda for his second term. The balanced budget, he stated, marked "an end to decades of deficits that have shackled our economy, paralyzed our policies, and held our people back." To undermine Republican calls for tax cuts, Clinton stressed that any surplus should be set aside to ensure the viability of Social Security. "Let's save Social Security first," he told Congress. Calling for an end to "bickering and extreme partisanship," he asked Congress to approve programs to improve education, daycare, Medicare, and Medicaid. Finding some common ground, Republicans and Democrats managed to approve the budget, pass the Balanced Budget Act of 1997, provide a small cut in taxes (the Taxpayer Relief Act of 1997), and make minor reforms to the healthcare system that helped limit growing costs. Beyond those agreements, however, Republicans and Democrats marched to different agendas and expressed bitter partisanship.

A Balanced Budget
That Protects Our Families, Invests in Our People and Cuts Taxes for Middle Class Families

On August 5, 1997, Bill Clinton signed the Balanced Budget Act. Applauding the president are Vice President Al Gore (*left*) and House Speaker Newt Gingrich (*right*). In the fall of 1998, Clinton announced a federal budget surplus of $70 billion, the first surplus since 1969.

In January 1998, Republicans seized on Clinton's sexual involvement with a White House intern, **Monica Lewinsky**, to try to remove him from office. At first Clinton denied the allegations, but an investigation confirmed the affair had gone on between 1995 and 1997. Clinton then admitted that he had had "inappropriate relations" with Lewinsky and had "misled" Congress and the public. His supporters argued that the affair was a private matter and in no way affected his running of the government. Even though the public seemed to agree with this assessment, Republicans—in a purely partisan action—cited two offenses, perjury and obstruction of justice, and in December 1997 voted to impeach Clinton. Clinton became the second president to face trial in the Senate to remove him from office (the first, Andrew Johnson, was acquitted in 1868, covered in Chapter 15).

The Republicans had a 55-to-45 majority in the Senate but needed a two-thirds majority for conviction. The trial lasted five weeks and confirmed to many that Republicans were more interested in destroying Clinton politically than in governing. On February 19, 1998, the Senate voted. On the issue of perjury, 10 Republicans voted with the Democrats to defeat the charge, 55 to 44. The vote on obstruction of justice was tied, 50 to 50, but nowhere near a two-thirds majority. The drama of impeachment was over. Clinton expressed his sorrow for the burden he had placed on the nation and the government returned to business.

Clinton's Foreign Policy

In foreign policy, Clinton proceeded cautiously and followed the general outline set by President Bush to expand trade. He oversaw passage of the NAFTA and GATT agreements, supported global economic efforts by the **G-8 nations** and the formation of the **World Trade Organization** (WTO), and improved trade with China. To promote global economic stability, the Clinton administration provided loans and encouraged the **International Monetary Fund** to do so to support the economies of several countries, including Mexico, Russia, and Indonesia.

Moving beyond economics, Clinton applied both direct diplomatic and military intervention to promote peace and resolve international issues. He actively supported the peace process in Northern Ireland that resulted in the Good Friday Agreements and ended thirty years of sectarian violence. Anxious to promote a solution to the "troubles" in Northern Ireland, Clinton in 1995 asked ex-Senator George J. Mitchell to help negotiate a settlement among the opposing political/religious factions and the Irish and British governments. After three years of negotiations and continued violence, Mitchell, with the aid of last-minute direct telephone calls from Clinton

to those negotiating a settlement, was able to bring about a peace accord.

To help stabilize the Middle East, Clinton sought to ease tensions between Israel and the Palestinians by brokering an accord that established Palestinian self-rule in some Israeli-occupied areas, as well as a treaty of cooperation between Jordan and Israel. In Haiti, following the failure of diplomatic and economic efforts, Clinton obtained UN support for an invasion to remove a military junta from power and restore democracy. Rather than face an invasion, in October 1994 the junta opened discussions that restored the presidency of Jean-Bertrand Aristide, who had been overthrown in a 1991 military coup, and established a time frame for free elections.

In the Balkan nation of Bosnia, Clinton faced a more difficult problem. Warring elements within Bosnia—Serbs, Christian and Muslim Bosnians, and Croats—fought each other with increasing intensity and brutality. Initially supporting UN peacekeeping and relief efforts there, Clinton sent American forces to join with the United Nations to establish and protect "safe areas" for refugees displaced by the fighting. In the fall of 1995, the United States sponsored peace talks resulting in the **Dayton Agreement**, which partitioned the country into a Bosnian-Croat federation and a Serb republic. It also called for UN forces, including twenty thousand Americans, to remain as peacekeepers. The last American forces were removed in 2004.

Clinton's commitment to promoting stablity in the Balkans was tested again in 1998 when President Slobodan Milosevic of Serbia sought to crush dissident and insurgent forces in the Serbian province of Kosovo. The conflict involved ancient hostilities between Serbian Orthodox Christians and Muslim

■ **Monica Lewinsky** White House intern who had a two-year sexual affair with President Clinton; Clinton's misleading testimony about the affair contributed to his impeachment by the House of Representatives.

■ **G-8 Nations** The leading industrial nations (Canada, China, France, Germany, Italy, Japan, the United Kingdom, and the United States), which meet annually to discuss economic and other global issues facing their countries and the international community.

■ **World Trade Organization** (WTO) Geneva-based organization that oversees world trading systems; founded in 1995 by 135 countries to replace the 1948 General Agreement on Tariffs and Trades (GATT).

■ **International Monetary Fund** UN agency established in 1945 to help promote the health of the world economy; among other efforts, it provides temporary loans for nations unable to maintain their balance of trade.

■ **Dayton Agreement** Agreement signed in Dayton, Ohio, in November 1995 by the three rival ethnic groups in Bosnia that pledged to end the four-year-old civil war there.

American forces played a key role in the United Nations (UN) and North Atlantic Treaty Organization (NATO) peacekeeping effort in Bosnia and Kosovo. In this picture, an American patrol greets Albanian children from a Kosovo village.

Alexander Zemlianichenko/AP Images.

ethnic Albanians, who made up 90 percent of Kosovo's population. When the Kosovo Liberation Army (KLA) began to fight for independence in 1998, Milosevic responded with force—instituting what many called a program of **ethnic cleansing** that targeted the Muslim population. Unable to halt the bloodshed, NATO leaders and Secretary of State Madeleine Albright called for "humanitarian intervention" and the establishment of autonomy for Kosovo within Serbia. Unwilling to use ground forces, NATO and U.S. forces began a bombing campaign in March 1999. When bombs fell on the Serbian capital of Belgrade, Milosevic, in June 1999, agreed to withdraw his troops, recognize Kosovo's autonomy, and allow UN peacekeeping forces into the area to ensure the peace. The war had cost the lives of more than ten thousand ethnic Albanian civilians. Milosevic, charged in May 1999 with crimes against humanity by the International War Crimes Tribunal at The Hague, was overthrown in

October 2000 in a popular uprising and in 2001 stood trial for his war crimes. He died in prison before the trial could be completed.

To explain his decisions to intervene, Clinton argued in what is called the Clinton Doctrine that the United States should act "where our values and our interests are at stake, and where we can make a difference" and that genocide necessitated a response. But Clinton did not apply his view evenly. In eastern Africa in 1994, he and most of the world ignored genocide in Rwanda; while in Somalia, after eighteen American UN peacekeeping troops were killed, Clinton withdrew American forces that President Bush had sent to the civil-war-torn nation in 1992 to provide humanitarian aid and keep the peace.

In other areas Clinton continued the previous administration's policies in supporting international efforts to control and eliminate biological and chemical weapons. In Iraq, he maintained Bush's efforts to pressure Saddam Hussein to allow UN inspection teams access to sites where he was suspected of manufacturing or stockpiling such weapons. Clinton, with the help of key Republican senators, also approved a Chemical Weapons Convention treaty that provided stronger sanctions against countries continuing to maintain and develop chemical weapons. The following year, however, without Republican support, Clinton failed to get Senate approval for the **Kyoto Protocol** to reduce global air pollution.

ethnic cleansing An effort to eradicate an ethnic or religious group from a country or region, often through mass killings.

■ **Kyoto Protocol** A set of international agreements, drafted by the United Nations in 1997, in which participating nations agreed to reduce their emissions rates of carbon dioxide and other industrial-produced gases that are linked to global climate change; the Senate failed to approve U.S. participation.

It Matters Today

Islamic Fundamentalism

When the shah of Iran was overthrown, most Americans were introduced to Islamic fundamentalism for the first time. It appeared to many Americans that Islamic fundamentalism was anti-American, antidemocratic, and militant, advocating violence, even the use of terrorism, to accomplish its goals. Since 1979, that belief has been hardened by terrorist attacks against the United States, including those against the World Trade Center and Pentagon. Some argue that fundamentalists' "objective is nothing less than the total destruction of the West" and there can be "no peaceful coexistence." Others respond that the extremists within the Islamic fundamentalist movement are a small minority and that most Muslims are neither antidemocratic nor anti-Western. Whether it is benign or hostile, it is clear that Islamic fundamentalism has become a powerful force in international politics and American politics.

- More Americans than ever before have negative views toward Islam and believe that it promotes violence more than other religions. Are these views based on their perceptions of terrorism, of fundamentalism, or of Islam?
- With Islam the fastest growing religion in the United States, should schools and institutions recognize Muslim religious holidays and dress codes?

THE TESTING OF PRESIDENT BUSH

☆ What issues contributed to Bush's election and how did his policies differ from those of the Clinton years?

☆ How did the events of September 11, 2001, affect politics, the public, and foreign policy?

Americans welcomed the twenty-first century with celebrations and optimism. With the economy expanding, it was an upbeat and popular President Clinton who told the American people: "We have restored the vital center, replacing outdated ideologies with a new vision anchored in basic enduring values: opportunity for all, responsibility from all, and a community for all Americans." Looking forward to the new year of 2000 and the upcoming presidential election, he called for a political agenda that included improving Social Security, healthcare, and the quality of education. It was an agenda that Vice President Al Gore could embrace as the expected Democratic candidate for the presidency. Republicans labeled the agenda as typically liberal and focused on the dangers of big government, "tax-and-spend" Democrats, and the need to cut taxes. They also stressed the need to restore integrity to the White House.

The 2000 Election

Leading the Republican hopefuls was George W. Bush, governor of Texas and son of the former president, who quickly outdistanced his rivals and won the nomination.

Running for the presidency, Bush announced a policy of "compassionate conservatism" that avoided the militancy of the cultural war and stressed the use of private sector initiatives to improve education, Social Security, and healthcare. At the heart of this campaign, however, was a promise to reduce taxes and restore dignity to the White House.

The campaign generated a lot of spending and almost no excitement, or heated rhetoric, or sharp debates. On the issues, the candidates' differences were largely matters of "how to," reflecting party ideologies. To improve education, Bush supported state initiatives and more stringent testing, whereas Gore wanted federal funds to hire more teachers and repair school facilities. On how to spend the budget surplus, Bush advocated a tax cut to give money back to the people. Gore called the tax cut dangerous and unfair—it favored the rich, he insisted—and said he would use the surplus to reduce the national debt and fund government programs.

The two candidates ran a dead heat, but the geography of support told a different story—of a confrontation between two Americas. Bush ran strong in the less populated states and was particularly popular with white males, who voted for him 5 to 3. Gore's strength was in urban areas (he received over 70 percent of the vote in large metropolitan areas), in the Northeast and Pacific Coast, and among Latinos and African Americans. On election day Gore received a minuscule majority of popular votes—half a million more out of the 10.5 million votes cast—but Bush won the Electoral College vote with 271 votes to 267, one vote more than necessary to win (see Map 29.1).

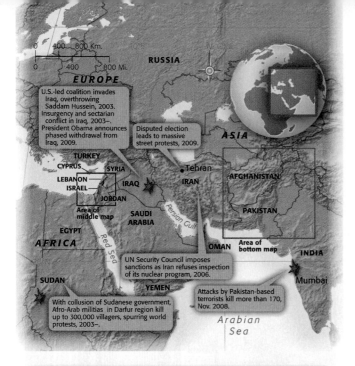

MAP 29.2 The Middle East and Afghanistan
These maps highlight events in the Middle East and southwestern Asia in the first decade of the twenty-first century. The bottom map shows Afghanistan, where Taliban leaders refused to turn over bin Laden and other Al Qaeda leaders, and the United States and its allies joined with anti-Taliban forces in a military action in 2001. Taliban and Al Qaeda leaders eluded capture. Copyright © Cengage Learning

Act for restricting civil liberties, most Americans supported actions that might prevent further acts of terrorism, including the Justice Department's detention of over 1,200 people, mostly Arab immigrants.

While Americans grappled with the enormity of the attacks, the Bush administration named **Al Qaeda**, a worldwide Islamic militant organization led by **Osama bin Laden**, as the organization responsible for the September 11 attacks. The son of a wealthy Saudi Arabian family, bin Laden had dedicated himself to freeing Muslim nations from outside control, especially American capitalist control. He announced in 1996 that it was the "duty of every Muslim" to "kill Americans and their allies." He and Al Qaeda were responsible for a series of attacks against American targets, including the 1996 bombing of a Saudi Arabian apartment complex that housed American servicemen and their families, and attacks on American embassies in Kenya and Tanzania in 1988.

President Bush quickly defined the new war on terrorism as a global effort, aimed not only against the "network of terrorists" but at any person or country that supported them. "Every nation in every region," he announced, had a choice to be "with us, or you are with the terrorists." Inside the White House, plans were being made for a military response against the **Taliban**, the Islamic fundamentalist government of Afghanistan, which supported bin Laden's operations. At the same time, Secretary of State Powell urged the president to first build an international coalition to support any American military action and to combat terrorism on a global basis. "We can't solve everything with one blow," stated a White House supporter of Powell's position.

Quickly, the Bush administration put in place a military campaign to remove the Taliban and worked to construct a global coalition against terrorism. While most nations agreed to eliminate and prevent terrorism in their own countries, several, including Britain, France, Germany, Australia, and Canada, agreed to join the campaign in Afghanistan. On October 7, 2001, the United States and its coalition began attacks on selected targets in Afghanistan. Accurate air and missile strikes effectively destroyed Taliban and Al Qaeda targets (see Map 29.2). They

In the war on terrorism, American forces joined with anti-Taliban forces in Afghanistan in attacking the government and Al Qaeda forces.

were followed by American ground forces, who joined existing anti-Taliban groups, especially the Northern Alliance, in an effort to remove the Taliban from power and kill or capture Osama bin Laden. Hundreds of Taliban and Al Qaeda fighters were captured and a new interim government headed by Hamid Kharzai was established, but Osama bin Laden and others had fled into the Tora Bora mountains bordering Pakistan and Afghanistan. To capture bin Laden, the military called for four thousand additional troops to search the mountains and pressured the Pakistani government to participate in the effort from their side of the border.

To defend against terrorism at home, Bush created a new cabinet department, Homeland Security, whose function would be to coordinate and direct various governmental agencies in preventing further acts of terrorism against the United States. He also asked Congress for large increases in spending for the military and for homeland defense. Bush accepted that the spending would create a deficit, maintaining that the price of freedom was "never too high."

The Bush administration, however, was shifting its focus away from Afghanistan toward Iraq. In November 2001, Bush rejected sending additional troops to hunt down bin Laden and had Secretary of Defense Donald Rumsfeld draw up secret plans to invade Iraq. In January, Bush defined what he termed an "axis of evil," saying that Iraq, Iran, and North Korea were threats to world peace. The administration also adopted a new strategy against terrorists and those

who threatened world peace, the **preemptive strike**, also referred to as the Bush Doctrine. It stated that in the war on terrorism, the nation could not wait until an attack came; it had to take positive steps to halt such attacks before they occurred. Clinton's policy had been "reflexive pullback," said Rumsfeld, but the Bush policy would be "forward leaning."

The first preemptive strike would be against Iraq. The reasons for the focus on Iraq were varied. In part, it was personal. Saddam Hussein represented unfinished business left over from the war to liberate Kuwait. He was also a vile dictator who had used chemical and biological weapons against his enemies, including citizens of his own country. Finally, the administration maintained that he supported terrorism and Al Qaeda and possessed **weapons of mass destruction**. By March 2002, Bush and his closest advisers, Vice President Richard Cheney and Secretary of Defense Rumsfeld, had concluded that the United States should use force, if necessary, to remove Saddam. The hawks in the administration, however, were faced with opposition from Secretary of State Powell and most of the international community. They favored tightening of UN economic sanctions to force Saddam to allow UN weapons inspectors into Iraq to determine if he did have weapons of mass destruction.

The pressure from the United Nations appeared to work. Saddam agreed to allow the weapons inspectors into Iraq, but then he hindered their inspections efforts. The result was that they found no weapons of mass destruction, but said they could not rule out the possibility that Iraq had them. Claiming that it had intelligence proof that Saddam had such weapons, the Bush administration insisted the UN demand that Iraq allow full access to the inspectors or face dire consequences. Speaking just before the first anniversary of 9/11, Vice President Cheney stated that Iraq was reviving its "nuclear weapons program," that it "directly threatened the United States," and that "time is not on our side." Condoleezza Rice admitted

■ **Al Qaeda** Terrorist network established by Saudi Osama bin Laden in 1989 to organize the activities of militant Islamic groups seeking to establish a global fundamentalist Islamic order; has orchestrated terrorist attacks against American targets and others.

■ **Osama bin Laden** Muslim fundamentalist who started and leads Al Qaeda.

■ **Taliban** An organization of Muslim fundamentalists that gained control over Afghanistan in 1996 after the Soviets withdrew and that established a strict Islamic government.

■ **preemptive strike** Policy adopted by the Bush administration allowing the United States to use force against suspected threats before the threats occurred.

weapons of mass destruction Nuclear, chemical, and biological weapons that have the potential to injure or kill large numbers of people—civilians as well as military personnel.

MAP 29.3 Second Iraq War
Saddam Hussein's regime collapsed within weeks of the beginning of the invasion north along the Tigris and Euphrates Rivers. Although the official hostilities ended, insurgents continued to resist the American occupation and the control of the interim Iraqi government, especially in the Sunni Triangle. Copyright © Cengage Learning

that the status of Saddam Hussein's nuclear weapons was unknown, but added: "We don't want the smoking gun to be a mushroom cloud." Based on the administration's statements, a majority of the public and Congress agreed with a congressional resolution permitting the use of force against Iraq (see Map 29.3).

By March 2003, American troop strength in the Persian Gulf reached about 250,000 and Bush was tired of playing "patty-cake" with the United Nations and Iraq. He gave Saddam Hussein notice to leave the country within forty-eight hours or face a military onslaught that would "shock and awe" those who witnessed it. Even before the forty-eight hours was up, on March 20, 2003, Bush launched an attack on Baghdad designed to kill Saddam and members of his government. It failed but following an aerial barrage, a land offensive began

advancing up the Tigris and Euphrates Rivers toward Baghdad, meeting only moderate resistance from regular and irregular Iraqi units. On April 9, Baghdad was in American hands. Saddam and his government fled into hiding. The official war ended without finding any weapons of mass destruction. Nonetheless, public opinion polls found that an overwhelming number of Americans considered the war a success and approved of Bush as president. But hostilities were not over, and the battle to remake Iraq would prove more difficult than toppling Saddam Hussein.

It quickly became apparent that the administration had made no plans for the occupation. The Department of State had proposed a complex plan to restore civil government and security forces, repair destroyed and damaged infrastructure, and provide food and other necessities for the Iraqis, but the White House had rejected the department's input. Consequently, there were not enough soldiers, equipment, or expertise to support a lengthy occupation. **Saboteurs** and looters attacked Iraqi infrastructure,

saboteurs Individuals who damage property or interfere with procedures to obstruct productivity and normal functions.

On March 20, 2003, U.S. and British forces crossed from Kuwait into Iraq in the second Iraq war. (*Left*) By May 1, on board the USS *Abraham Lincoln*, President Bush declared the war in Iraq over. But for thousands of American soldiers in Iraq, the conflict continued as insurgents fought on. (*Right*) An Iraqi armed with a rocket-propelled grenade (RPG) launcher stands by a burning vehicle in Basra. Between May 2003 and October 2004, more Americans had been killed in Iraq than during the "official" war.

already extensively damaged by the war. Although most Iraqis thanked the United States for Saddam's removal—he was found hiding in a small "spider hole" in the ground on December 14, 2003, and taken into custody—they quickly grew impatient and angry with the occupation. They complained about the slow restoration of electricity, water, and other necessities, and they criticized the ominous lack of security. Many disagreed with the U.S.-selected interim government and called for the formation of an Islamic-based state.

Iraq became a new kind of war zone as occupation forces faced rapidly expanding violence not only from those resisting the occupation, but also from those fighting a sectarian civil war between Sunni and Shiite religious factions and from Al Qaeda forces. As casualties increased, the Bush administration admitted that an extensive search for weapons of mass destruction had failed to find any. Over the next two years, various investigatory commissions established to evaluate the intelligence reports and decisions leading to the war determined that the information claiming Saddam possessed such weapons and links to Al Qaeda were wrong. As critics of the war blamed the Bush administration for manipulating the nation into war, it seemed as if the United States was trapped in an expensive war with no effective plans to end the conflict and withdraw American troops.

WAR AND POLITICS

★ How did the war in Iraq shape the issues Republicans wanted to highlight in the presidential elections of 2004 and 2008?

★ What major issues contributed to Barack Obama's election in 2008, and what constraints did he face in implementing his policies?

Amid growing questions about the justification and conduct of the war, Bush ran for reelection. Although he received positive public approval rates for combating terrorism, the public gave him lesser marks on conducting the Iraq war, dealing with the economy, and controlling the deficit. Accordingly, the Democratic presidential candidate, Senator John Kerry of Massachusetts, focused on the economy and the war. Bush attacked Kerry and the Democrats as too liberal and claimed that their opposition to the war in Iraq undermined the U.S. effort and encouraged terrorism. When critics pointed to the misinformation on weapons of mass destruction that had been used to justify the invasion, Bush now argued that his true motive was to end Saddam Hussein's brutal dictatorship. He stressed that he had met the need for decisive leadership. "We acted. We led," stated Bush.

Although the economy was improving by the summer of 2004, spurred by low interest rates, tax cuts, and military spending, Democrats argued that it was a selective recovery and that for most Americans jobs were being lost and real wages were dropping. "We've declared victory over the recession," said a Democratic representative, but "we're still laying off a couple of hundred thousand workers a month." Republicans, meanwhile, were dusting off the culture war of previous campaigns, exploiting the issue of gay marriage. In November 2003, the Massachusetts Supreme Court had ruled that banning same-sex marriage violated the state's constitution and gave the state legislature 180 days to act on the court's decision. The following April, the Massachusetts legislature approved a constitutional amendment that defined marriage as a union only between a man and a woman, although it would permit same-sex **civil unions**. However, the amendment could not be ratified until 2006, and meanwhile, Massachusetts became the first state to issue marriage licenses to same-sex couples.

The response across the nation was generally negative. In most states, laws against same-sex marriage already existed, based on the 1996 federal **Defense of Marriage Act**, which bans federal recognition of same-sex marriages and allows states to ignore such marriages performed in other states. Nonetheless, thirty-five states hurried to strengthen their prohibitions of same-sex marriage. In addition, many opponents of same-sex marriage believed that civil unions should also be banned. In February 2004, President Bush endorsed the idea of a constitutional amendment that would disallow same-sex marriage. When pressed for his view, Kerry opposed such an amendment and argued that the issue should be left to the states to legislate. He also said that he personally opposed same-sex marriages but approved of civil unions.

Targeting "battleground" swing states, both parties poured vast amounts of time and campaign money into a few states, along with venomous campaign ads.

Both also took new approaches to campaigning to woo supporters using the Internet. "Bloggers" created their own websites providing news, political analysis, and ads for and against the candidates. Days before the election, most polls showed the candidates tied in popular support.

On November 2, 2004, more Americans voted than ever before. They reelected Bush, giving him 51 percent of the vote. Bush had effectively mobilized his party's loyalists and won most of the battleground states. To the surprise of most observers, a majority of those supporting Bush stated that moral issues and family values were critical reasons for how they voted. Supporting this observation, in Ohio—which was critical to the president's reelection—and ten other states, voters affirmed their support for amendments to their state constitutions to prohibit same-sex marriages and civil unions. "Make no mistake—conservative Christians and 'value voters' won this election," stated one conservative observer.

Bush's Second Term

Referring to his victory as a public mandate for action and with Republican majorities in Congress, President Bush was eager to use his "political capital" to implement domestic goals that promoted an "ownership society," putting control in the hands of individuals regarding healthcare, Social Security retirement funds, and education. "Now comes the revolution," voiced some conservatives when the president announced that strengthening family values and reforming Social Security, tax codes, and education were agenda priorities. Bush's political capital fell apart within months when Congress and the public rejected his efforts to privatize Social Security and further reduce taxes. His leadership, which he had touted during the election campaign, suffered a serious blow following his lethargic response to the devastation caused by a category-four hurricane.

On August 29, 2005, **Hurricane Katrina** battered New Orleans, much of which is below sea level, and the levees protecting the city broke. Flood waters poured in and submerged some sectors of New Orleans under 20 feet of water. Earlier, as the storm approached, most upper- and middle-class residents had boarded up their homes and left the city, but those without resources and transportation had no way out. Unable to leave, thousands who were able to escape the flood waters took refuge in the Superdome, the covered downtown stadium. Sheer numbers quickly overwhelmed its facilities. Television crews broadcast worldwide the horrid conditions in the Superdome, the bodies floating in the flooded streets, and the widespread destruction.

As conditions worsened, it became clear that government agencies were periously slow to deal with the

civil union Term for a civil status similar to marriage, allowing same-sex partners access to legal, medical, and financial and other benefits enjoyed by married heterosexuals.

■ **Defense of Marriage Act** 1996 law that defines marriage as between a man and a woman for the purpose of federal law and prevents other jurisdictions (states, counties, cities) from being forced to accept any other definition of marriage.

■ **Hurricane Katrina** Formed in the Caribbean on August 23, 2005, it travelled over southern Florida as a weak hurricane before slamming into the coastline of Louisiana on August 29 as the sixth strongest Atlantic hurricane in history; from Florida to Texas it caused over 1,800 confirmed deaths and over $81 billion in damages; most of the damage and deaths occurred in Louisiana and the city of New Orleans, where over 80 percent of the city and surrounding areas were flooded.

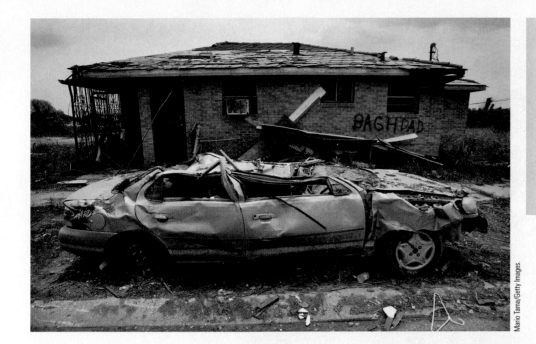

Among the areas most devastated by Hurricane Katrina when it struck the Gulf Coast in August 2005 was New Orleans' Ninth Ward, where waters from Lake Pontchartrain engulfed the area following the breach in the levees. One witness said, "It's like looking at a murder."

crisis. In fact, both President Bush and the Federal Emergency Management Administration (FEMA) appeared to ignore the stricken city and brush off the magnitude of the disaster. Four days passed before Bush took meaningful action. Only then, once Bush had belatedly ordered it, did FEMA begin to intensify its efforts in the region. The slow response caused many to question the administration's priorities and significantly damaged its aura of efficient management. "The rich escaped," conservative writer David Brooks editorialized, "while the poor were abandoned. . . . Leaving the poor in New Orleans was the moral equivalent of leaving the injured on the battlefield."

The inadequate response to Katrina was a huge blow to the public's confidence in Bush's leadership and policies. His popularity rating fell to under 50 percent, and criticism of the administration's war policies intensified. Despite the drafting of an Iraqi constitution and a large turnout to elect a parliamentary government in December 2005, conditions in Iraq failed to improve. The new government of Nouri al-Maliki was ineffective and unable even to limit the growing civil war between religious factions. Death tolls for both Americans and Iraqis soared—over three thousand American soldiers had died since the occupation started. For Iraqis, exact numbers are unknown, but estimates range from over half a million to less than 100,000. Bush's popularity ratings continued to fall, and polls disclosed that over 60 percent disapproved of his administration's handling of the war.

The 2006 congressional elections saw all 435 House seats and 33 Senate seats up for grabs. Democrats called for a "New Direction for America," and while they included the economy and protecting Social Security as important issues, nearly everyone considered the central issue to be Iraq. Democrats held that war policies needed to be changed and American troops withdrawn as soon as possible. They stressed that Bush and his advisers had lied about the reasons for going to war and had bungled the planning for a postwar Iraq, failing to establish a coherent policy to bring stability and security. The outcome was that American soldiers were being wounded and dying for no purpose. Bush and Republicans responded that they were better suited to protect the nation from terrorism and that to suggest withdrawing from Iraq would embolden the enemy and endanger American troops. Better, they argued, to increase the number of American troops in Iraq, especially in Baghdad, to enhance security and give the Iraqis time to take over their own battle.

Most observers believed that the Democrats would gain some congressional seats in the election, but that Republicans would maintain a slim majority. The results surprised nearly everyone. Democrats took a majority of 233 to 202 seats in the House of Representatives and a smaller majority of 51 to 49 in the Senate. Some saw the results as devastating for the Republican Party, sending a message to the administration to consider a timeline for the withdrawal of American forces in Iraq. With their majority confirmed, Democrats selected the first woman Speaker of the House, Congresswoman Nancy Pelosi from California. Upon taking office, she called her appointment "a historic moment" that women had been awaiting for more

In the congressional elections of 2006, Democrats regained control of both houses of Congress. Nancy Pelosi (D-California) became the first woman Speaker of the House of Representatives. In this picture, she is accompanied by her grandchildren and other members' children and grandchildren on the podium of the House.

than two hundred years. "The marble ceiling" had been broken, Pelosi said.

Denying that the election indicated a clear "call to change" policy toward Iraq, Bush in December announced a 21,500-troop "surge" to boost security, reduce the violence, and allow the Iraqi forces to complete the training they were receiving from U.S. troops. It was the way to win the war, according to the administration, and Vice President Cheney stressed that efforts to block the president's plan would "undermine" the troops. Democrats responded by passing nonbinding resolutions opposing the troop increase and, in April, passed a bill that linked funding for the war to establishing a time frame for the removal of American forces. Bush vetoed the bill, and Republicans accused Democrats of trying to manage the war. They pointed out that the surge was working and had reduced violence.

Economic Crisis and "Remaking America"

With the battle lines drawn over the war in Iraq, the 2008 presidential campaign started a year and a half before the election. The leading Democratic candidates, Senators Hillary Clinton of New York and Barack Obama of Illinois, were breaking historical traditions of gender and race, since neither a woman nor an African American had ever been nominated for the presidency by a major party. After a series of hard-fought primaries, Obama secured the nomination and selected Senator Joseph Biden of Delaware as his

running mate. In a less bruising series of primaries, Arizona Senator John McCain overcame his Republican challengers and captured the nomination. Hoping to consolidate his support from conservative Republicans and to attract women voters, McCain surprised everyone by naming Alaska Governor Sarah Palin as his running mate. Many expected the war in Iraq and Obama's lesser political experience to dominate the campaign issues.

The campaign began nearly as expected. McCain, who called himself a maverick to distance himself from Bush's unpopular policies, touted his decades of government service and attacked Obama as inexperienced, too liberal, and weak on foreign policy, and wrong in his position on the Iraq war. Obama countered by offering innovation and change, asking the nation if they wanted four more years of the same failed Bush policies. Obama argued that Bush had fought the wrong war. Instead of invading Iraq, he should have continued the effort in Afghanistan to destroy Al Qaeda. American forces should be withdrawn from Iraq as soon as possible, he said, and used to establish a stable Afghanistan and hunt down terrorists. But as the summer arrived, so too did a new and critical issue— the start of the worldwide "Great Recession."

The debate over what caused the recession and how best to deal with it reshaped the campaign. Signs of an unsteady economy were visible, for those choosing to see them, as early as 2006. At the center of the brewing economic storm were extremely low interest rates, a boom in the housing market, inattentive government regulators, and greed. Banks and other lending institutions made housing loans, including

subprime loans, to thousands of people who could normally not afford them. In many cases profit-seeking lenders actively marketed subprime and other special loan arrangements to high-risk borrowers with no concern for people's personal finances or the long-term consequences for the housing market. In one case a worker at McDonald's who earned $35,000 a year was able to get a half-million-dollar loan for a home.

Then housing values began to drop, leaving many owing more than the value of the house. A cascade of foreclosures began. Institutions that had either directly or indirectly invested in mortgages, once considered a safe investment, found themselves short of capital, unable to pay their investors, depositors, and creditors. As stock prices tumbled and banks and insurance and investment corporations tottered on the edge of bankruptcy, the fiscally conservative Bush administration concluded that a massive infusion of money was needed to prop up some of the nation's largest financial institutions. They were "too big" to fail, said one government official. Between July and December, the Bush administration asked Congress for financial bailouts to rescue the economy. In September, Federal Reserve Chairman Ben Bernanke (see page 626) and Treasury Secretary Henry M. Paulson Jr. asked Congress for $700 billion for the **Troubled Asset Relief Program** (TARP), saying that unless Congress acted immediately "we may not have an economy on Monday." Bush agreed, telling Congress to pass the rescue plan or see "this sucker [the economy] go down."

Congress approved the complex and controversial bill and Bush signed it on October 3. Responses to the TARP were mixed. Many people complained that it rewarded "Wall Street"—those who had caused the economic crisis—and did nothing for "Main Street," the hard-working Americans who were losing their jobs or homes, or both. Others voiced concerns about the TARP's effectiveness and cost and about the level of government intervention in buying the assets of private financial institutions. Even more controversial was the administration's request in December for more funds, $17.4 billion in loans to support failing American automobile manufacturers General Motors and Chrysler. Adding to the public's distrust and dissatisfaction with the behavior of CEOs and Wall Street financiers were revelations of elaborate illegal schemes by Bernard Madoff and R. Allen Stanford, whose actions epitomized the greedy quest for personal wealth that many believed was responsible for the nation's financial mess. Both used their role as financial advisers to steal millions of dollar from investors. Madoff, who bilked nearly $65 billion from investors in a massive **Ponzi scheme**, was found guilty and sentenced to 150 years in prison.

As the recession worsened, the central issue of the election campaign shifted away from McCain's comparative strength of experience and the war on terror. A mid-June Gallup Poll found that more than

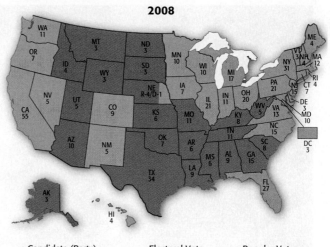

2008

Candidate (Party)	Electoral Vote		Popular Vote	
Obama (Democrat)	365	68%	69,498,459	52.9%
McCain (Republican)	173	32%	59,948,283	45.6%

MAP 29.4 Election of 2008, by State
In a spirited and historic election, Democrat Barack Obama more than doubled the electoral count of Republican John McCain (365 to 173) and earned nearly 53 percent of the popular vote. In a county–county analysis most counties showed larger Democratic votes than in 2004, except in Alaska, Arizona, Arkansas, Tennessee, Louisiana, and Kentucky. Copyright © Cengage Learning

56 percent of voters thought fixing the economy was more important than fighting terrorism; an almost equal number thought Obama was more qualified on economic issues than McCain. As Obama's popularity rose, Republicans intensified allegations that he lacked patriotism and was devoted to socialist-Marxist ideology. This time, their political attacks did not work. On Election Day more people voted than in any other presidential election, providing a decisive victory for Obama (see Map 29.4). While winning 53 percent of the popular vote, he received 365 electoral votes to

■ **subprime loan** A loan that carries a higher-than-normal interest rate, generally used to make a loan to someone with a history of bad credit and default; between 2005 and 2006 such loans represented 20 percent of all housing loans.

■ **Troubled Asset Relief Program** (TARP) 2008 act allowing the government to buy $700 billion of "troubled assets" from selected financial institutions to reduce their level of debt and to infuse capital into the system; the TARP's primary goal was to help deal with the economic crisis caused by subprime loans.

Ponzi scheme A fraudulent investment operation in which the operator keeps the majority of investment money, making small payouts to investors from their own money or money paid by other investors; Madoff's scheme was the largest financial investor fraud in history committed by a single person.

Having won the Democratic nomination for president, Barack Obama easily defeated the Republican candidate John McCain. Receiving news of his victory, President-elect Obama addressed his supporters gathered in Chicago's Grant Park. On stage with him was the new first family: his wife Michelle and their two daughters Sasha and Malia.

Over the next months, Obama unfolded an ambitious agenda that not only sought to reshape the economy, but to implement a national healthcare system and to change the direction of the wars in Iraq and Afghanistan. Many argued the agenda was too ambitious and that the administration should focus on fixing the economy before tackling other issues. In turn, Obama argued that nearly all the issues were intertwined and that it made sense to deal with the complexities rather than focus on a single aspect of the problem. It was also immediately clear that personal and partisan politics would dominate nearly every issue.

During the campaign Obama had argued it was necessary to reach out to international adversaries and work more closely with allies and for the United

McCain's 173. Democrats also added eight seats to their majority in the Senate and twenty-one to their margin in the House.

Around the world people waited to see what changes Obama would make in foreign and domestic policies. On January 20, 2009, President Obama gave his inaugural address to expectant listeners. Over a million people braved cold weather, descending on Washington, D.C., to watch the inauguration ceremonies, with many millions more watching television coverage around the world. Obama acknowledged the serious problems the nation confronted: "Our nation is at war against a far-reaching network of violence and hatred. Our economy is badly weakened, a consequence of greed and irresponsibility on the part of some but also our collective failure to make hard choices and prepare the nation for a new age." He added that meeting the challenges would not be easy or quickly accomplished, but that "starting today, we must pick ourselves up, dust ourselves off, and begin again the work of remaking America." He voiced the hope that the bitter polarization that had characterized politics would be laid aside for the common good.

States to regain its global moral authority. He also vowed to conduct the war on terrorism in a way that would ensure the safety of the American people and shift military priorities from Iraq to Afghanistan and Pakistan. In office, Obama and his foreign policy advisors established priorities based on the premise that American resources were limited and that the administration should focus on necessary problems. High on the list of those priorities were working with other industrial nations to confront the global economic crisis, improving trade relations with China, dealing with Afghanistan and Pakistan, and "resetting" the tone of American foreign policy.

By the end of the year, observers gave Obama mixed reviews. They gave him high marks for improving the image of American foreign policy and restoring the nation's moral authority. But on almost every other issue, there were serious objections and recognition that little had actually been accomplished. Both Democrats and Republicans objected to aspects of his conduct of the war on terrorism, to the failure to reduce the American military presence in Iraq, and to the deployment of nearly thirty thousand more American soldiers to Afghanistan. Some liberal critics

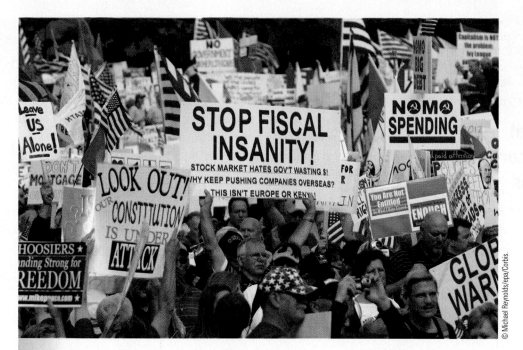

As 2009 primary and general elections neared, the Tea Party movement organized and sponsored rallies against Obama's programs and liberal policies, vowing to help elect those candidates holding similar conservative goals. In this picture thousands of people protest big government, federal spending, Obama's administration, and liberal policies in a September 2009 demonstration in Washington, D.C. As the November off-year election approached in 2010, Tea Partiers credited their movement for the expected success of several conservative Republican candidates running for state and national offices.

argued that apart from his rhetoric, his policies paralleled those of Bush, while some conservatives warned that he was too soft in protecting American interests and that his actions and speeches made the nation's enemies stronger. Obama, however, gained more domestic and international approval in early 2010, for restructuring the **Strategic Arms Limitation Treaty (START)** that reduced the number of American and Russian nuclear warheads from 6,000 to 1,500.

The Politics of Filibuster

With significant Democratic majorities in the House and Senate, Republicans called for solid opposition to many Democratic domestic programs, thereby possibly forcing the administration to overcome a filibuster. If Republicans maintained solidarity, Democrats would need to muster sixty votes, every Democratic vote, to pass a bill in the Senate. The politics of filibuster not only put great pressure on Senate Democrats, but gave every Senator tremendous political leverage

because one vote represented the margin of victory or defeat. Acting quickly to deal with the economic crisis, in February, with three Republicans in the Senate supporting the measure, Congress approved the **American Recovery and Reinvestment Act** to stimulate the economy. It provided $787 billion in federal spending and tax cuts to help the economy recover. Even as Obama watched his approval rating fall below

■ **Strategic Arms Limitation Treaty** (START) Modifying the original treaty signed in 1991 and expired in 2009, the new treaty reduced the number of nuclear war heads to 1,500 and the number of operationally deployed delivery systems to 700; other START agreements in 1993 and 1997 were never implemented.

■ **American Recovery and Reinvestment Act** 2009 act that increased federal spending for healthcare, infrastructure, education, various tax programs, and direct assistance to individuals to be spent over several years.

In the Wider World

National Healthcare Systems

All developed countries and many lesser-developed nations have national healthcare systems providing a form of government-mandated medical care for their citizens, with the majority of the cost covered through some sort of government-run or regulated program (see Map 29.5). Imperial Germany in 1883 was the first nation to develop such a program. Britain began a program in 1911 but did not cover all of its citizens until 1948. The goal of healthcare was incorporated in the United Nations Universal Declaration of Human Rights passed in 1948, which is the most widely translated document in the world. In Article 25 it states: "Everyone has the right to a standard of living adequate for the health and well-being of himself and his family," and "motherhood and childhood are entitled to special care and assistance." Today, on every continent but Africa, most nations have some form of national healthcare system. Iraq and Afghanistan are implementing a system paid for by the United States. In March 2010, amid significant opposition, the United States became the latest nation to begin implementing a form of national health coverage.

50 percent, Democrats pushed through bills creating national healthcare programs (see Map 29.5) in the face of solid Republican opposition. The House passed a bill without any Republican support, while in the Senate, in late December 2009, Democrats needed every Democratic and Independent vote to avoid a Republican filibuster. Because the Senate bill differed from the House's version, the two bills needed to be reconciled. On March 23, the House, without a single Republican vote, accepted the Senate's version (219 to 212), approving the **Patient Protection Affordable Care Act**, and sent to the Senate the **Health Care and Education Reconciliation Act** that incorporated changes the House wanted to the Patient Protection Affordable Care Act. Through a simple majority vote, Senate Democrats quickly approved the measure. By

■ **Patient Protection Affordable Care Act** and **Health Care and Education Reconciliation Act** Acts passed in 2010 that established a complex governmental and private system of national healthcare that will include nearly all Americans by 2014; it included provisions preventing health insurance companies from denying or cancelling coverage to those with pre-existing conditions; the latter act also modified the federal student loan system and provided more funds for Pell Grants.

■ **Tea Party movement** Arising in early 2009 in protest to the bailout and stimulus packages, the movement calls for limited government, a balanced budget, and a free market economy, attracting those who distrust Washington and seem most worried about the future. Polls taken in 2010 showed they represented about 18 percent of the electorate.

March 30, Obama had signed two acts establishing an American system of national healthcare. Republicans immediately denounced "Obamacare" and called for its repeal. At the same time, officials in eighteen states filed motions in federal court arguing the acts were unconstitutional and infringed on states' rights. "The Constitution," their motion read, "nowhere authorizes the United States to mandate, either directly or under threat of penalty, that all citizens and legal residents have qualifying healthcare coverage." Unfazed, President Obama dismissed the constitutional challenges as pure politics and argued that as the provisions of the national healthcare took effect and the "Armageddon" promised by opponents did not occur, public support for the system would increase. He also continued to focus on further reviving the economy, which by spring appeared to be recovering, In July 2010, the administration won another victory when in the Senate three Republicans broke party ranks and voted for a sweeping reform bill that placed new and increased regulations on financial and investment institutions. Responding to opposition statements that the legislation would expand an already bloated federal bureaucracy and harm the banking system, the president said that it was needed to prevent the actions that led to the recession and that only those financial institutions that depended "on cutting corners or bilking . . . customers" had anything to fear. Still, other Democratic and administrative programs and bills remained captive to filibuster politics and continuing divisions within the Democratic Party.

The debates over the economy and healthcare sparked a political wave called the **Tea Party movement**

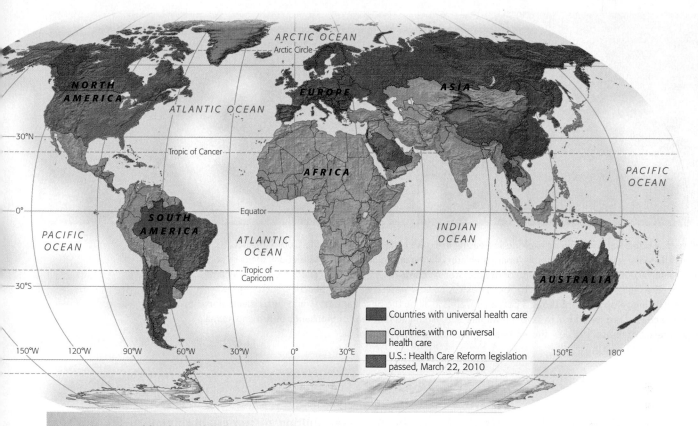

MAP 29.5 Worldwide Healthcare
As 2010 began, the United States remained the only industrial nation that did not have a national system for healthcare, even though most presidents since Theordore Roosevelt had supported a national healthcare program. Overcoming solid Republican opposition and divisions among themselves, Democrats in Congress passed and President Obama signed the Patient Protection and Affordable Care Act in March 2010. Copyright © Cengage Learning

that swept over the country. Focusing on taxes, the intrusive and "un-American" nature of big government and Obama programs, Tea Partiers leapt into state and congressional political races supporting the most conservative candidates, claiming victories in several state primaries. Buoyed by Obama's continued efforts to push programs that seemed to increase government spending and power and the surge of the Tea Party movement, Republicans projected significant political gains in the November congressional elections that would give them the ability to change the country's course.

Sharing the headlines with the Tea Party and partisan politics, on April 20, a BP deep-water drilling rig, the Deepwater Horizon, exploded in the Gulf of Mexico, killing eleven workers. Two days later the rig sank, releasing oil from its mile-deep well-head. Over the next few days, what was initially termed a small leak was recognized as a major oil spill, releasing thousands of gallons of oil into the Gulf each day. By June, after several efforts to stop the gushing oil had

failed, the spill became the largest in American history and a major ecological disaster that threatened not only the marine and wildlife habitats along the coastlines of Louisiana, Alabama, Mississippi, and Florida, but also the livelihoods of Gulf Coast residents working in the fishing and tourism industries. In mid-July, BP capped the gushing well, choking off further releases of oil, but still leaving millions of gallons of oil still threatening the gulf coast. Amid growing criticism of BP's drilling techniques and responses, the oil company accepted "full responsibility for the spill," vowing to pay for the costs of the clean-up and to financially compensate those affected by the disaster. Some also criticized Obama and the government for not taking effective control of the crisis and actually obstructing efforts to deal with the gushing oil and its ecological and financial consequences. The administration, in response, argued that it held BP fully responsible and was requiring the company to create a $20 billion fund to pay for the consequences of the spill. "Make no

In April 2010, a deep-water drilling rig exploded releasing millions of gallons of oil into the Gulf of Mexico, generating the worst ecological disaster in American history. In the image on the left, a work boat seeks to corral some of the surface oil floating near the site of the disaster. As containment of the oil failed, it eventually came ashore along the Gulf coast, from Florida to Texas, destroying Gulf waters, wetlands, beaches, and peoples' livelihoods. The image on the right shows a pelican covered in oil on the beach at East Grand Terre Island along the Louisiana coast. Despite efforts to save the wildlife, it is estimated that tens of thousands of fish and animals will die as a result of the spill. In July, the well was capped stopping the flow of oil.

mistake," President Obama stated, "we will fight this spill with everything we've got for as long as it takes." In 1974, Nixon said that the Santa Barbara oil spill (see page 788) "touched the conscience of the American people," helping awaken Americans to the ecological dangers facing the world and contributing to the establishment of the Environmental Protection Agency. Will the BP spill in the Gulf produce long- and short-term consequences having a similar role? How, as in earlier times, will disaster intersect with turbulent politics in the ongoing story of making America?"

Individual Voices

Nicholas Carr Asks, "Is Google Making Us Stupid?"

Historians are constantly reminded that some of the most important results of change are not always expected, or even beneficial. In this document a journalist comments on what he believes may be one of the most important and long-lasting outcomes of using new technologies to research and write.

❶ In what ways has the Internet changed the way in which people do research?

❷ How does the author believe technologies like the Internet have affected the brain and people's reading and comprehension skills?

❸ What evidence does Carr use to support his views? Is this really evidence? Should such evidence be accepted? Should historians rely on it?

Over the past few years, I've had an uncomfortable sense that someone, or something, has been tinkering with my brain, remapping the neural circuitry, reprogramming my memory. My mind isn't going—so far as I can tell—but it is changing. I'm not thinking the way I used to think. I can feel it most strongly when I'm reading. . . . Now my concentration often starts to drift after two or three pages. I get fidgety, lose the thread, begin to look for something else to do.

I think I know what's going on. . . . I've been spending a lot of time online, searching and surfing. . . . Research that once required days in . . . libraries can now be done in minutes. For me, as for others, the Net is becoming a universal medium, the conduit for most of the information that flows through my eyes and ears and into my mind. . . . And what the Net seems to be doing is chipping away my capacity for concentration and contemplation. My mind now expects to take in information the way the Net distributes it: in a swiftly moving stream of particles. Once I was a scuba diver in the sea of words. Now I zip along the surface like a guy on a Jet Ski. **❶**

Thanks to the ubiquity of text on the Internet, not to mention the popularity of text-messaging on cell phones, we may be reading more today than we did in the 1970s and 1980s. . . . But it's a different kind of reading, and behind it lies a different kind of thinking—perhaps even a new sense of self.

Reading . . . is not an instinctive skill. . . . We have to teach our mind how to translate the . . . characters we see . . . the media or other technologies we use in learning. . . . [R]eading plays an important part in shaping the . . . circuits inside our brain. **❷**

Maybe I'm just a worrywart. Just as there's a tendency to glorify technological progress, there's a countertendency to expect the worst of every new tool. . . . Socrates bemoaned the development of writing. He feared that, as people came to rely on the written word . . . they would "cease to exercise their memory and become forgetful" and would be "filled with the conceit of wisdom instead of real wisdom."

. . . [Y]ou should be skeptical of my skepticism. . . . Perhaps . . . [from] the Internet . . . will spring a golden age of intellectual discovery and universal wisdom. Then again the Net isn't the alphabet, and although it may replace the printing press, it produces something altogether different. **❸**

. . . [A]s we come to rely on computers to mediate our understanding of the world, it is our own intelligence that flattens into artificial intelligence.

Source: Nicholas Carr, "Is Google Making Us Stupid?" *The Atlantic* (July/August 2008).

Study Tools

SUMMARY

During the last two decades, the economy has significantly shaped political and social issues. The changing American economy provided new opportunities for some, but for many, including much of the middle class, it heightened worries about their and their children's future. Bill Clinton exploited those concerns to help win the 1992 election and assumed the presidency determined to place the nation on a firm financial footing. His economic plan, while divisive, worked, and although facing a Republican-controlled Congress, by the end of his two terms, Clinton had balanced the budget, reduced the national debt, and weathered a Republican effort to remove him from office through the impeachment process.

The 2000 close presidential election between Gore and Bush was finally decided by the Supreme Court, which awarded Florida's electoral votes to Bush. President Bush began by implementing a tax cut and educational reform, but before he could push other agenda items, the nation was overwhelmed by the events of September 11, 2001, when terrorists affiliated with Osama bin Laden attacked the World Trade Center and the Pentagon, killing over three thousand people. As the nation rallied around the administration, it established an Office of Homeland Security and created a global coalition to fight terrorist organizations and their supporters. In that effort, the United States joined forces with others to conduct a successful war that brought down the Taliban government and much of the Al Qaeda organization in Afghanistan—although Osama bin Laden escaped.

In 2003, the Bush administration shifted its attention to Iraq, claiming that Saddam Hussein possessed weapons of mass destruction and was linked to Al Qaeda. In March, an American-led invasion toppled Saddam Hussein's government in less than three weeks. However, the occupation and efforts to transform Iraq into a stable democracy proved more difficult. As violence continued and American casualties increased, some Americans began to question Bush's justification and his conduct of the war.

Growing dissatisfaction with Bush's Iraq policy paralleled frustration with his handling of the economy. Both of these developments raised Democratic hopes of regaining the presidency in 2004. In November, however, voters reelected Bush and returned more Republicans to the House and Senate. Claiming a political mandate, Bush unsuccessfully tried to implement a conservative agenda. With an administration weakened by increasing frustration over the war in Iraq and its weak response to

CHRONOLOGY
A New Century with New Challenges

1992	Bill Clinton elected president
1993	Congress ratifies North American Free Trade Agreement
	Clinton's national healthcare package fails
1994	U.S. troops sent to Haiti
	"Contract with America"
1995	Dayton Agreement
1996	Welfare reform passed
	Clinton reelected
1998	Terrorists attack U.S. embassies in Kenya and Tanzania
1999	NATO bombs Serbia over Kosovo crisis
	Effort to impeach Clinton fails
2000	George W. Bush elected president
2001	Terrorists associated with Al Qaeda attack World Trade towers and Pentagon
	Office of Homeland Security established
	U.S. launches operations in Afghanistan
	USA Patriot Act
2002	Taliban regime collapses; replaced by interim government
2003	U.S. invades Iraq, removes Saddam Hussein regime
	Massachusetts Supreme Court permits same-sex marriage
2004	George W. Bush reelected
2005	Hurricane Katrina strikes Gulf Coast
2006	Democrats regain majorities in Congress
2007	Nancy Pelosi becomes first woman Speaker of the House of Representatives
2008	Barack H. Obama elected
2009	Congress passes economic stimulus bill.
	Congress approves financial aid package for American automobile manufacturers, General Motors and Chrysler
2010	Congress passes a national healthcare bill
	Strategic Arms Limitation Treaty negotiated between United States and Russia
	Accident on a Gulf off-shore oil platform releases millions of barrels of oil, fouling wet-lands of many Gulf states
	Congress passes Wall Street financial regulation bill

Study Tools

Hurricane Katrina, Democrats in the congressional elections of 2006 regained a majority in Congress.

The 2008 presidential campaign pitted a young, African American Illinois senator, Barack Obama, against the more experienced senator from Arizona, John McCain. With the start of a major recession, the economy displaced Iraq as the most important factor for the majority of voters. Obama offered change and seemed more capable of dealing with the economic crisis. A war-weary public, worried about the economy, overwhelmingly chose to put Obama in the White House.

In office, President Obama not only faced an economic crisis and wars in Iraq and Afghanistan, but put forward an ambitious agenda he said would remake America that included changing the tone of American foreign and domestic priorities and implementing a comprehensive healthcare system that would cover nearly every American. He hoped for bipartisan support to deal with the issues, but found that on almost every occasion, Republicans opted to oppose his efforts. Conservative critics argued that Obama's recovery programs and national health programs were too expensive and expanded the size and role of the federal government. In response to Obama, the economic stresses, and expansive government programs, a "Tea Party" movement arose that stressed reducing the size and reach of government, cutting taxes, and electing true conservatives. By a year and a half into his presidency, although the economy was improving, many Americans appeared to be increasingly unhappy with his leadership and policies, and Republicans looked forward to reasserting their political power in the 2010 congressional elections.

FOCUS QUESTIONS

If you have mastered this chapter, you should be able to answer these questions and to explain the terms that follow the questions.

1. ☆ What changes were taking place in the American economy in the 1990s?
2. ☆ How did economic changes shape society and politics?
3. ☆ In what ways did President Clinton's centrist agenda and personal behavior shape his presidency?
4. ☆ How did the Contract with America represent a conservative critique of liberalism and Democratic policies?
5. ☆ What actions did Clinton take to expand trade and support global stability?
6. ☆ What issues contributed to Bush's election and how did his policies differ from those of the Clinton years?
7. ☆ How did the events of September 11, 2001, affect politics, the public, and foreign policy?
8. ☆ How did the war in Iraq shape the issues Republicans wanted to highlight in the presidential elections of 2004 and 2008?
9. ☆ What major issues contributed to Barack Obama's election in 2008, and what constraints did he face in implementing his policies?

KEY TERMS

Nasdaq *(p. 827)*
glass ceiling *(p. 829)*
Operation Rescue *(p. 830)*
Family and Medical Leave Act *(p. 830)*
North American Free Trade Agreement *(p. 830)*
General Agreement on Tariffs and Trade *(p. 830)*
Contract with America *(p. 832)*
judicial restraint *(p. 832)*
Monica Lewinsky *(p. 835)*
World Trade Organization *(p. 835)*
International Monetary Fund *(p. 835)*
Dayton Agreement *(p. 835)*
Kyoto Protocol *(p. 836)*
USA Patriot Act *(p. 839)*

Al Qaeda *(p. 840)*
Osama bin Laden *(p. 840)*
Taliban *(p. 840)*
preemptive strike *(p. 841)*
Defense of Marriage Act *(p. 844)*
Hurricane Katrina *(p. 844)*
subprime loans *(p. 847)*
Troubled Asset Relief Program *(p. 847)*
Strategic Arms Limitation Treaty *(p. 849)*
American Recovery and Reinvestment Act *(p. 849)*
Patient Protection Affordable Care Act *(p. 850)*
Health Care and Education
    Reconciliation Act *(p. 850)*
Tea Party movement *(p. 850)*

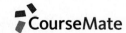
CourseMate

Go to the History CourseMate website for primary source links, study tools, and review materials for this chapter. www.cengagebrain.com

Suggested Readings

CHAPTER 1 Making a "New" World, to 1588

Marvin B. Becker. *Civility and Society in Western Europe, 1300–1600* (1988).
> A brief but comprehensive look at social conditions in Europe during the period leading up to and out of the exploration of the New World.

Alfred W. Crosby. *The Columbian Exchange: Biological and Cultural Consequences of 1492* (1972).
> The landmark book that brought the Columbian impact into focus for the first time. Parts of the book are technical, but the explanations are clear and exciting.

Roberta Hall, Diana Roy, and David Boling, "Pleistocene Migration Routes into the Americas: Human Biological Adaptations and Environmental Constraints," *Evolutionary Anthropology* 13, no. 4 (2004): 132–144.
> A recent overview of the scholarship concerning the migration of early Americans from Asia.

Alvin M. Josephy. *America in 1492: The World of the Indian Peoples Before the Arrival of Columbus* (1992).
> An overview of American civilizations prior to Columbus's and subsequent European intrusions. Nicely written, comprehensive, and engaging.

Roland Oliver and J. D. Fage. *A Short History of Africa* (1988).
> The most concise and understandably written comprehensive history of Africa available.

CHAPTER 2 A Continent on the Move, 1400–1725

Peter N. Moogk. *La Nouvelle France: The Making of French Canada—A Cultural History* (2000).
> An excellent overview of French activities in Canada during the colonial era.

Oliver A. Rink. *Holland on the Hudson: An Economic and Social History of Dutch New York* (1986).
> A comprehensive overview of Dutch colonial activities in New Netherland with an emphasis on both the activities of the Dutch West India Company and private traders in creating the culture of Dutch New York.

Daniel H. Usner, Jr. *Indians, Settlers, and Slaves in a Frontier Exchange Economy: The Lower Mississippi Valley before 1783* (1992).
> A highly acclaimed study of the complex world of colonial Louisiana.

David Weber. *The Spanish Frontier in North America* (1992).
> A broad synthesis of the history of New Spain by the foremost scholar in the field.

CHAPTER 3 Founding the English Mainland Colonies, 1585–1732

Francis Bremer. *The Puritan Experiment: New England Society from Bradford to Edwards* (1995).
> A concise and well-written account of the establishment and survival of the Puritan communities of New England.

David Cressy. *Coming Over: Migration and Communication between England and New England in the Seventeenth Century* (1987).
> An excellent introduction to the transatlantic community of England and the colonial world.

James Deetz and Patricia Scott Deetz. *The Times of Their Lives: Life, Love and Death in Plymouth Colony* (2001).
> A history of many aspects of life in the Pilgrim colony, from its relationship with local Indians to gender relations, to home life and the maintenance of law and order.

Mary Beth Norton. *In the Devil's Snare* (2003).
> This book places the events of 1692 in the context of European imperial rivalries, especially the intense struggles between England and France for control of North America.

Rusell Shorto. *The Island at the Center of the World: The Epic Story of Dutch Manhattan and the Forgotten Colony That Shaped America* (2005).
> This book traces the history of New Amsterdam, its highly diverse population, and its role in establishing many of the principles of self-government on which the United States was founded.

Benjamin Woolley. *Savage Kingdom: The True Story of Jamestown, 1607, and the Settlement of America* (2008).
> An engaging analysis of the economic, social, and cultural roots of the first permanent English colony in North America, with vivid portraits of major figures such as John Smith.

CHAPTER 4 The English Colonies in the Eighteenth Century, 1689–1763

Fred Anderson. *Crucible of War: The Seven Years' War and the Fate of Empire in British North America, 1754–1766* (2001).
> This study of what historians call "the great war for empire" sets the conflict in its global perspective and helps readers understand the context for British colonial policy in the postwar years.

Ira Berlin. *Generations of Captivity: A History of African American Slaves* (2004).
> An examination of the variety and complexities of slavery as an experience and as a legal and economic institution.

Jon Butler. *New World Faiths: Religion in Colonial America* (2007).
> A thorough and readable history of religious pluralism in colonial America.

Peter Hoffer. *The Great New York Conspiracy of 1741: Slavery, Crime and Colonial Law* (2003).
> A noted legal historian's account of the alleged conspiracy that reflected the undercurrent of racial tensions in New York City.

Marioleine Kars. *Breaking Loose Together: The Regulator Rebellion in Pre-Revolutionary North Carolina* (2001).

> A new examination of the struggle between backcountry farmers and the coastal planters who controlled the North Carolina government.

Kevin Kenny. *Peaceable Kingdom Lost: The Paxton Boys and the Destruction of William Penn's Holy Experiment* (2009).

> An account of one of the most violent frontier conflicts, pitting settlers against peaceful Indians and backcountry residents against Pennsylvania's government.

Jane T. Merritt. *At the Crossroads: Indians and Empires on a Mid-Atlantic Frontier, 1700–1763* (2003).

> Merritt takes a close look at the interaction between Indians and colonists in the backcountry of Pennsylvania and narrates the growing tensions between settlers and Native Americans.

CHAPTER 5   Deciding Where Loyalties Lie, 1763–1776

Carol Berkin. *Revolutionary Mothers: Women in the Struggle for America's Independence* (2005).

> This book recounts the role of European, African American, and Indian women in the years before and during the American Revolution.

Colin G. Calloway. *The American Revolution in Indian Country: Crisis and Diversity in Native American Communities* (1995).

> A well-written account of the variety of Indian experiences during the American revolutionary era.

David Hackett Fischer. *Paul Revere's Ride* (1994).

> This lively account details the circumstances and background of the efforts to rouse the countryside in response to the march of British troops toward Lexington.

Woody Holton. *Forced Founders: Indians, Debtors, Slaves and the Making of the American Revolution in Virginia* (1999).

> Holton provides a new interpretation of the factors that went into transforming wealthy planters into revolutionaries.

Liberty! PBS series on the American Revolution.

> Using the actual words of revolutionaries, loyalists, and British political leaders, this six-hour series follows events from the Stamp Act to the Constitution.

Pauline Maier. *American Scripture: Making the Declaration of Independence* (1998).

> This pathbreaking book points out that the ideas expressed in the Declaration of Independence were widely accepted by Americans, and proclaimed in state declarations of independence before Jefferson set them down in July 1776.

Edmund Morgan. *Benjamin Franklin* (2002).

> A distinguished historian of colonial America draws a compelling portrait of Benjamin Franklin, following the printer-writer-scientist-diplomat through major crises and turning points in his life and the life of his country.

Gordon Wood. *The American Revolution: A History* (2003).

> An excellent, brief account of the events leading up to and during the war for independence by a Pulitzer Prize–winning historian.

CHAPTER 6   Recreating America: Independence and a New Nation, 1775–1783

Sylvia Frey. *Water from a Rock: Black Resistance in a Revolutionary Age* (1991).

> This scholar of African American religion and culture examines the experiences of African Americans during the Revolution and the repression that followed in the southern states that continued to rely on slave labor.

Joseph Plumb Martin. *Ordinary Courage: The Revolutionary War Adventures of Joseph Plumb Martin*, ed. James Kirby Martin (1993).

> The military experiences of a Massachusetts soldier who served with the Continental Army during the American Revolution.

Charles Royster. *A Revolutionary People at War: The Continental Army and American Character, 1775–1783* (1996).

> Royster's in-depth account of military life during the Revolution provides insights into both the American character and the changing understanding of the political ideals of the war among the common soldiers.

Alfred Young. *The Shoemaker and the Tea Party: Memory and the American Revolution* (2000).

> Young looks at the memories of an aging shoemaker who witnessed the Boston Tea Party. These memories reveal the meaning of the Revolution to ordinary Americans.

CHAPTER 7   Competing Visions of the Virtuous Republic, 1770–1796

Carol Berkin. *A Brilliant Solution: Inventing the American Constitution* (2002).

> A highly readable account of the crises that led to the constitutional convention and the men who created a new national government.

Richard Bernstein. *The Founding Fathers Reconsidered* (2009).

> A concise and accessible overview of the men who drafted the constitution.

Ron Chernow. *Alexander Hamilton* (2005).

> A remarkable study of one of the most brilliant and influential of the founding fathers of the nation.

Saul Cornell. *The Other Founders: Anti-Federalism and the Dissenting Tradition in America, 1788–1828* (1999).

> A perceptive analysis of the ideology of dissent and its legacy in American political life.

Joseph Ellis. *Founding Brothers: The Revolutionary Generation* (2002).

> An award-winning study of the most notable leaders of the American Revolution, and an examination of their political ideas and actions.

Gordon Wood. *The Creation of the American Republic, 1776–1787* (1998).

> An award-winning examination of the ideals and political principles that form the basis of the American republic.

CHAPTER 8   The Early Republic, 1796–1804

Alexander DeConde. *This Affair of Louisiana* (1976).

> Dated, but still the best overview of the diplomacy surrounding the Louisiana Purchase.

Joseph J. Ellis. *American Sphinx: The Character of Thomas Jefferson* (1996).

> Winner of the National Book Award, this biography focuses on Jefferson's personality, seeking to expose his inner character; highly readable.

Joanne B. Freeman. *Affairs of Honor: National Politics in the New Republic* (2001).

Jeffrey L. Pasley. *"The Tyranny of Printers": Newspaper Politics in the Early American Republic* (2001).

> Taken together, these two groundbreaking studies of political culture in the early republic bring a whole set of new perspectives to the topic. Freeman concentrates on honor as a political force, while Pasley illustrates the power of an increasingly self-conscious press in shaping the political landscape.

Annette Gordon-Reed. *The Hemingses of Monticello: An American Family* (2008).
>   A masterful account of Jefferson's relationship with Sally Hemings and her family, which tells a much broader story about race, gender, and society during the Jeffersonian era.

David McCullough. *John Adams* (2001).
>   A highly acclaimed and extremely readable biography of one of America's true founding fathers.

Peter S. Onuf, ed. *Jeffersonian Legacies* (1993).
>   Assembled on the occasion of Jefferson's 250th birthday, this collection of essays by leading Jeffersonian scholars helps to put the often elusive founding father into perspective.

James Ronda. *Lewis and Clark Among the Indians* (1984).
>   A bold retelling of the expedition's story, showcasing the Indian role in both Lewis and Clark's and the nation's successful expansion into the Louisiana Territory and beyond.

CHAPTER 9   Increasing Conflict and War, 1805–1815

Gregory E. Dowd. *A Spirited Resistance: The North American Indian Struggle for Unity, 1745–1815* (1992).
>   Hailed by many as one of the best works on Native American history, this well-written study covers the efforts by Indians to unite in defense of their lands and heritages, culminating in the struggles during the War of 1812.

R. David Edmunds. *The Shawnee Prophet* (1983); *Tecumseh and the Quest for Indian Leadership* (1984).
>   Each of these biographies is a masterpiece, but taken together, they present the most complete recounting of the lives and accomplishments of these two fascinating Shawnee brothers and their historical world.

John Denis Haeger. *John Jacob Astor: Business and Finance in the Early Republic* (1991).

William E. Foley and C. David Rice. *The First Chouteaus: River Barons of Early St. Louis* (1983).
>   Taken together, these two books provide a comprehensive overview of the fur trade during its early years, showcasing the importance of business tycoons like Astor and the Chouteaus and demystifying this huge business enterprise.

Donald Hickey. *The War of 1812: A Forgotten Conflict* (1989).
>   Arguably the best single-volume history of the war, encyclopedic in content, but so colorfully written that it will hold anyone's attention.

Robert A. Rutland. *Madison's Alternatives: The Jeffersonian Republicans and the Coming of War, 1805–1812* (1975).
>   An interesting review of the events leading up to the outbreak of war in 1812 and the various alternatives Jefferson and Madison had to choose from in facing the evolving diplomatic and political crises.

CHAPTER 10   The Rise of a New Nation, 1815–1836

George Dangerfield. *The Era of Good Feelings* (1952).
>   An older book, but so well written and informative that it deserves its status as a classic. All students will enjoy this grand overview.

Angie Debo. *And Still the Waters Run: The Betrayal of the Five Civilized Tribes* (1940; reprint, 1972).
>   A classic work by one of America's most talented and sensitive historical writers, a truly engaging history of this tragic sequence of events.

Richard E. Ellis. *The Union at Risk: Jacksonian Democracy, States' Rights, and the Nullification Crisis* (1987).
>   An invigorating reconsideration of the nullification crisis set in context with the other problems that beset the Jackson administration, suggesting how close the nation came to civil war in the 1830s.

Jon Meacham. *American Lion: Andrew Jackson in the White House* (2008).
>   A lively new biography of the seventh U.S. president, focusing on his White House years and the political turmoil of that era.

Charles G. Sellers. *The Market Revolution: Jacksonian America, 1815–1846* (1991).
>   A far-reaching reassessment of economics and politics during this period, focusing on the rise of the market economy and the responses, both positive and negative, that led to the rise of Jacksonian democracy.

George Rogers Taylor. *The Transportation Revolution, 1815–1860* (1951).
>   The only comprehensive treatment of changes in transportation during the antebellum period and their economic impact. Nicely written.

John William Ward. *Andrew Jackson: Symbol for an Age* (1955).
>   More a study of American culture during the age of Jackson than a biography of the man himself. Ward seeks to explain Old Hickory's status as a living myth during his own time and as a continuing monument in American history.

CHAPTER 11   The Great Transformation: Growth and Expansion, 1828–1848

Ira Berlin. *Slaves Without Masters* (1975).
>   A masterful study of a forgotten population: free African Americans in the Old South. Lively and informative.

Ray Allen Billington. *America's Frontier Heritage* (1966).

Patricia Nelson Limerick. *The Legacy of Conquest* (1988).
>   Two classics in the field of American western history; Billington represents the classic Turnerian perspective while Limerick gives voice to the anti-Turnerian "new western history."

Stuart M. Blumin. *The Emergence of the Middle Class: Social Experience in the American City, 1760–1900* (1989).
>   Considered by many to be the most comprehensive overview of the emergence of the middle class in America during the nineteenth century.

Bill Cecil-Fronsman. *Common Whites: Class and Culture in Antebellum North Carolina* (1992).
>   A pioneering effort to describe the culture, lifestyle, and political economy shared by the antebellum South's majority population: nonslaveholding whites. Though confined in geographical scope, the study is suggestive of conditions that may have prevailed throughout the region.

Thomas Dublin. *Women at Work: The Transformation of Work and Community in Lowell, Massachusetts, 1826–1860* (1979).
>   An interesting look at the way in which the nature of work changed and the sorts of changes that were brought to one manufacturing community.

Elizabeth Fox-Genovese. *Within the Plantation Household* (1988).
>   A look at the lives of black and white women in the antebellum South. This study is quite long, but is well written and very informative.

Isabel Lehuu. *Carnival on the Page: Popular Print Media in Antebellum America* (2000).

> An overview of the explosion in print media during the early nineteenth century and its role in shaping national culture.

Donald W. Meinig. *Imperial Texas* (1969).

> A fascinating look at Texas history by a leading historical geographer.

Christopher L. Miller. *Prophetic Worlds* (2003).

> This new edition includes commentary that helps to define the debates that this book has sparked about the history of the Pacific Northwest during the pioneer era.

Kenneth N. Owens, ed. *Riches for All: The California Gold Rush and the World* (2002).

> A collection of essays by leading scholars about the California Gold Rush and its impact on both national and international life.

Wallace E. Stegner. *The Gathering of Zion* (1964).

> A masterfully written history of the Mormon Trail by one of the West's leading literary figures.

John David Unruh. *The Plains Across* (1979).

> Arguably the best one-volume account of the overland passage to Oregon. The many pages melt as the author captures the reader in the adventure of the Oregon Trail.

CHAPTER 12 Responses to the Great Transformation, 1828–1848

Eugene D. Genovese. *From Rebellion to Revolution: Afro-American Slave Revolts in the Making of the Modern World* (1979).

> Although it focuses somewhat narrowly on confrontation, as opposed to more subtle forms of resistance, this study traces the emergence of African American political organization from its roots in antebellum slave revolts.

Karen Haltunen. *Confidence Men and Painted Women: A Study of Middle-Class Culture in America, 1830–1870* (1982).

> A wonderfully well-researched study of an emerging class defining and shaping itself in the evolving world of early nineteenth-century urban space.

Edward Pessen. *Most Uncommon Jacksonians: The Radical Leaders of the Early Labor Movement* (1967).

> A look at early labor movements and reform by one of America's leading radical scholars.

Ronald G. Walters. *American Reformers, 1815–1860* (1978).

> The best overview of the reform movements and key personalities who guided them during this difficult period in American history.

Susan Zaeske. *Signatures of Citizenship: Petitioning, Antislavery, and Women's Political Identity* (2003).

> A fascinating study of how participation in reform campaigns helped lead early nineteenth-century women into a new sense of political identity.

CHAPTER 13 Sectional Conflict and Shattered Union, 1848–1860

Don E. Fehrenbacher. *Prelude to Greatness* (1962).
> A well-written and interesting account of Lincoln's early career.

Don E. Fehrenbacher. *Slavery, Law, and Politics: The* Dred Scott *Case in Historical Perspective* (1981).

> An excellent interpretive account of this landmark antebellum legal decision, placing it firmly into historical context.

William E. Gienapp, et al. *Essays in American Antebellum Politics, 1840–1860* (1982).

> A collection of essays by the rising generation of new political scholars. Exciting and challenging reading.

Thomas R. Hietala. *Manifest Design* (1985).

> An interesting and well-written interpretation of the Mexican War and the events leading up to it.

Michael F. Holt. *The Political Crisis of the 1850s* (1978).

> Arguably the best single-volume discussion of the political problems besetting the nation during this critical decade.

Stephen B. Oates. *To Purge This Land with Blood* (1984).

> The best biography to date on John Brown, focusing on his role in the emerging sectional crisis during the 1850s.

David Potter. *The Impending Crisis, 1848–1861* (1976).

> An extremely long and detailed work but beautifully written and informative.

James Rawley. *Race and Politics: "Bleeding Kansas" and the Coming of the Civil War* (1969).

> An interesting look at the conflicts in Kansas, centering upon racial attitudes in the West. Insightful and captivating reading.

Harriet Beecher Stowe. *Uncle Tom's Cabin* (1852; reprint, 1982).

> This edition includes notes and chronology by noted social historian Kathryn Kish Sklar, making it especially informative.

CHAPTER 14 A Violent Choice: Civil War, 1861–1865

Carol Berkin, *Civil War Wives: The Lives and Times of Angelina Grimké Weld, Varina Howell Davis, and Julia Dent Grant* (2009).

> In the life stories of three "accidental heroes"—women whose marriages provided them with position and perspective they would not otherwise have had—one of the nation's premier historians offers a unique understanding of the tumultuous social and political landscape of their time.

Bruce Catton. *This Hallowed Ground: The Story of the Union Side of the Civil War* (1956).

> Catton is probably the best in the huge company of popular writers on the Civil War. This is his most comprehensive single-volume work. More detailed but still very interesting titles by Catton include *Glory Road: The Bloody Route from Fredericksburg to Gettysburg* (1952), *Mr. Lincoln's Army* (1962), *A Stillness at Appomattox* (1953), and *Grant Moves South* (1960).

Paul D. Escott. *After Secession: Jefferson Davis and the Failure of Confederate Nationalism* (1978).

> An excellent overview of internal political problems in the Confederacy by a leading Civil War historian.

Ann Giesberg. *Civil War Sisterhood: The U.S. Sanitary Commission and Women's Politics in Transition* (2000).

> A study of how women's activism in forming the sanitary movement during the Civil War recast their view of themselves as political figures and helped shape an emerging women's movement.

Alvin M. Josephy. *The Civil War in the American West* (1991).

> A former editor for *American Heritage,* Josephy writes an interesting and readable story about this little-known chapter in Civil War history.

William Marvel. *The* Alabama *&* the Kearsarge: *The Sailor's Civil War* (1996).

> Military and social historians have compared this new study favorably with *The Life of Billy Yank* (1952) and

The Life of Johnny Reb (1943), Bell Irvin Willey's classic studies of life for the common soldier, calling it an insightful narrative of the Civil War experience for the common sailor.

James McPherson. *Battle Cry of Freedom: The Civil War Era* (1988).

Hailed by many as the best single-volume history of the Civil War era; comprehensive and very well written.

Emory M. Thomas. *The Confederate Nation* (1979).

A classic history of the Confederacy by an excellent southern historian.

Garry Wills. *Lincoln at Gettysburg: The Words That Remade America* (1992).

A prize-winning look at Lincoln's rhetoric and the ways in which his speeches, especially his Gettysburg Address, recast American ideas about equality, freedom, and democracy. Exquisitely written by a master biographer.

CHAPTER 15   Reconstruction: High Hopes and Shattered Dreams, 1865–1877

Philip Dray. *Capitol Men: The Epic Story of Reconstruction Through the Lives of the First Black Congressmen* (2008).

Dray views the events of Reconstruction through the experiences of the African Americans elected to the House of Representatives and the Senate.

W. E. B. Du Bois. *Black Reconstruction in America: An Essay Toward a History of the Part Which Black Folk Played in the Attempt to Reconstruct Democracy in America, 1860–1880* (1935; reprint edns., 1998, 2007).

Written more than seventy years ago, Du Bois's classic book is still useful for information and insights. Recent editions usually include useful introductions that place Du Bois's work into the context of work by subsequent historians.

Carol Faulkner. *Women's Radical Reconstruction: The Freedmen's Aid Movement* (2004).

A new study of the role of women in the Freedmen's Bureau and in federal Reconstruction policy more generally.

Eric Foner. *Reconstruction: America's Unfinished Revolution, 1863–1877* (1988; reprint, 2002).

A thorough treatment, incorporating insights from many historians who have written on the subject during the fifty years preceding its publication.

Leon F. Litwack. *Been in the Storm So Long: The Aftermath of Slavery* (1979).

Litwack focuses on the experience of the freed people.

William S. McFeely. *Frederick Douglass* (1991).

A highly readable biography of the most prominent black political leader of the nineteenth century.

Michael Perman. *Emancipation and Reconstruction*, 2nd ed. (2003).

A good, short, and well-written introduction to the topic.

Heather Cox Richardson. *West from Appomattox: The Reconstruction of America after the Civil War* (2008).

Richardson recasts the story of Reconstruction by viewing the years following the Civil War as a national story rather than an account of the South, and as the origin of many features of contemporary American poitics.

Hans L. Trefousse. *Thaddeus Stevens: Nineteenth-Century Egalitarian* (1997).

A recent study of perhaps the most important leader of the Radical Republicans.

C. Vann Woodward. *Reunion and Reaction: The Compromise of 1877 and the End of Reconstruction*, rev. ed. (1956; reprint, 2001).

The classic account of the Compromise of 1877 with an afterword by William S. McFeely.

CHAPTER 16   The Nation Industrializes, 1865–1900

Edward L. Ayers. *The Promise of the New South: Life After Reconstruction* (1992, 2007).

A comprehensive survey of developments in the South.

Alfred D. Chandler, Jr., with Takashi Hikino. *Scale and Scope: The Dynamics of Industrial Capitalism* (1990, 2004). Chandler, *The Visible Hand: The Managerial Revolution in American Business* (1993).

Alfred Chandler's writings changed historians' thinking about the emergence of industrial capitalism in the United States; these are two of his key works.

Ron Chernow. *The House of Morgan: An American Banking Dynasty and the Rise of Modern Finance* (1990, 2001).

An award-winning account of Morgan's bank and Morgan's role in the emergence of finance capitalism.

_____. *Titan: The Life of John D. Rockefeller, Sr.* (1998, 2004).

Well written and engaging, based on extensive research in Rockefeller family papers.

Norris Hundley, Jr. *The Great Thirst: Californians and Water, 1770s–1990s* (1992).

Among the best of the studies surveying the role of water in the West.

Patricia Nelson Limerick. *The Legacy of Conquest: The Unbroken Past of the American West* (1987).

A classic reinterpretation of the history of the West, stressing conquest of both the environment and the indigenous people, and the long-term consequences of those actions.

David Nasaw. *Andrew Carnegie* (2006).

A recent and highly readable reconsideration of Carnegie's career.

Richard J. Orsi. *Sunset Limited: The Southern Pacific Railroad and the Development of the American West, 1850–1930* (2005).

Based on extensive research in the company's archives, Orsi's book is about the development of the West as well as about one of the most powerful western companies.

Glenn Porter. *The Rise of Big Business, 1860–1910*, 3rd ed. (2006).

A brief and well-written introduction, surveying the role of the railroads, vertical and horizontal integration, and the merger movement.

Glenda Riley. *A Place to Grow: Women in the American West* (1992).

A short and lively survey of the subject by a leading historian on the topic.

Philip Weeks. *Farewell, My Nation: The American Indian and the United States in the Nineteenth Century*, 2nd ed. (2000).

An excellent overview of the experience of Native Americans when they confronted the expansion of U.S. settlement west of the Missouri River.

CHAPTER 17   Life in the Gilded Age, 1865–1900

Yong Chen. *Chinese San Francisco, 1850–1943: A Trans-Pacific Community* (2000).

A well-researched study of the largest Chinatown and its relations with China.

Melvyn Dubofsky. *Industrialism and the American Worker, 1865–1920,* 3rd ed. (1996).
> A brief introduction to the topic, organized chronologically.

Rebecca Edwards. *New Spirits: Americans in the "Gilded Age"* 2nd ed. (2011).
> A lively overview of the time period, focusing especially on new social and economic patterns.

Leon Fink. *Workingmen's Democracy: The Knights of Labor and American Politics* (1983).
> One of the best overall treatments of the Knights of Labor.

Juan Gómez-Quiñones. *Roots of Chicano Politics, 1600–1940* (1994).
> The political history of Mexican Americans from the first Spanish settlements in the Southwest up to the eve of World War II.

Louis R. Harlan. *Booker T. Washington: The Making of a Black Leader, 1856–1901* (1975).
> The standard biography of Washington, which includes a good account of the racial situation in the South in the 1890s.

John Higham. *Strangers in the Land: Patterns of American Nativism, 1860–1925* (1965, 1983).
> This classic book first defined the contours of American nativism and still provides an excellent introduction to the subject.

Rebecca J. Mead. *How the Vote Was Won: Woman Suffrage in the Western United States, 1868–1914* (2004).
> A recent study of the woman suffrage movement in the West.

Raymond A. Mohl. *The New City: Urban America in the Industrial Age, 1860–1920* (1985).
> An excellent introduction to nearly all aspects of the growth of the cities.

David Montgomery. *Workers' Control in America: Studies in the History of Work, Technology, and Labor Struggles* (1979).
> A classic work for understanding craft unions and labor more generally.

Frank Roney. *Frank Roney: Irish Rebel and California Labor Leader, an Autobiography,* edited by Ira B. Cross (1931).
> Roney's life as an iron molder and labor leader, in his own words.

David O. Stowell. *Streets, Railroads, and the Great Strike of 1877* (1999).
> An account of the great strike of 1877 that goes beyond the grievances of the railroad workers to look at the reasons so many others were receptive to supporting the strikers.

CHAPTER 18   Politics and Foreign Relations in a Rapidly Changing Nation, 1865–1902

Robert L. Beisner. *From the Old Diplomacy to the New, 1865–1900,* 2nd ed. (1986).
> A concise introduction to American foreign relations in this period, challenging some of LaFeber's conclusions.

Charles W. Calhoun. *Minority Victory: Gilded Age Politics and the Front Porch Campaign of 1888* (2008).
> A new and revealing study of politics before the upheaval of the 1890s.

Robert W. Cherny. *American Politics in the Gilded Age, 1868–1900* (1997).
> A brief survey of the politics of this period.

Lewis Gould. *The Presidency of William McKinley* (1980).
> A major contribution to historians' understanding of McKinley's presidency, including the war with Spain and the acquisition of the Philippines.

Ari Hoogenboom. *Rutherford B. Hayes: Warrior and President* (1995).
> An excellent biography that also includes important information on the politics of the era.

Walter LaFeber. *The New Empire: An Interpretation of American Expansion, 1860–1898* (1963).
> A classic account, the first to emphasize the notion of a commercial empire.

William S. McFeely. *Grant: A Biography* (1981, 2002).
> The standard biography of Grant, including his troubled presidency.

Robert C. McMath, Jr. *American Populism: A Social History, 1877–1898* (1993).
> A good, succinct introduction to Populism.

David Silbey. *A War of Frontier and Empire: The Philippine-American War, 1899–1902* (2007).
> The most recent treatment of the U.S. conquest of the Philippines.

CHAPTER 19   The Progressive Era, 1900–1917

Jane Addams. *Twenty Years at Hull House* (1910, reprint, 1999, 2006).
> Nothing conveys the complex world of Hull House and the striking personality of Jane Addams as well as her own account. The recent editions have useful introductions by current historians who help to establish the context. The original is available online.

Robert W. Cherny. *A Righteous Cause: The Life of William Jennings Bryan* (1985, 1994).
> Bryan remained the most significant figure in the Democratic Party from 1896 until 1912.

Kathleen Dalton. *Theodore Roosevelt: A Strenuous Life* (2002).
> Probably the best one-volume biography of the dominant figure of the age, who continues to fascinate both historians and the public more generally.

Maureen A. Flanagan. *America Reformed: Progressives and Progressivisms, 1890s–1920s* (2006).
> A lively overview of the progressive era, stressing the social origins of reform.

K. Austin Kerr. *Organized for Prohibition: A New History of the Anti-Saloon League* (1985).
> A well-written treatment of the organization that formed the prototype for many organized interest groups.

Lester D. Langley. *The Banana Wars: United States' Intervention in the Caribbean, 1898–1934,* 2nd ed. (2001).
> A sprightly and succinct account of the role of the United States in the Caribbean and Central America.

David Levering Lewis. *W. E. B. Du Bois: Biography of a Race, 1868–1919* (1993).
> A powerful biography of Du Bois that delivers on its promise to present the "biography of a race" during the Progressive Era.

Theodore Roosevelt. *An Autobiography* (1913; abridged ed. reprint, 1958).
> Roosevelt's account of his actions sometimes needs to be taken with a grain of salt but nevertheless provides insight into Roosevelt the person. Available online.

Upton Sinclair. *The Jungle* (1906).
> Several editions of this classic muckraking novel are in print. Those with introductions by James Barrett (1988) and Christopher Phelps (2005) offer useful perspectives by leading historians.

Shelton Stromquist. *Reinventing "The People": The Progressive Movement, the Class Problem, and the Origins of Modern Liberalism* (2006).

A leading historian provides an interpretation of progressivism with a focus on labor history.

CHAPTER 20   The United States in a World at War, 1913–1920

Kendrick A. Clements, Eric A. Cheezum. *Woodrow Wilson* (2003).

The best current one-volume treatment of Wilson's presidency.

Alfred W. Crosby. *America's Forgotten Pandemic: The Influenza of 1918* (2003).

A thorough study of the great flu epidemic of 1918 that killed 600,000 Americans.

Jeannette Keith. *Rich Man's War, Poor Man's Fight: Class and Power in the Rural South During the First World War* (2004).

A carefully researched study of opposition to the draft in the South.

David P. Kilroy. *For Race and Country: The Life and Career of Colonel Charles Young* (2003).

A carefully researched and well-written biography of Young, putting his struggles for racial equality into the context of the times.

Sinclair Lewis. *Main Street* (1920; reprint, 1999, 2003).

An absorbing novel about a woman's dissatisfaction with her life and her decision to work in Washington during the war. The recent reprints include useful introductions that help to understand the context. The original is available online.

Erich Maria Remarque. *All Quiet on the Western Front,* trans. A. W. Wheen (1930; reprint, 2005).

The classic and moving novel about World War I, seen through German eyes. Recent reprints include an introduction that helps to understand the context.

Richard Slotkin. *Lost Battalions: The Great War and the Crisis of American Nationality* (2005).

The wartime experiences of two New York state units, one of African Americans and the other largely of European immigrants.

Barbara W. Tuchman. *The Guns of August* (1962; reprint, 2004).

A popular and engaging account of the outbreak of the war, focusing on events in Europe.

Robert Zieger. *America's Great War: World War I and the American Experience* (2001).

An excellent and recent overview of the United States during World War I.

CHAPTER 21   Prosperity Decade, 1920–1928

Kareem Abdul-Jabbar with Raymond Obstfeld. *On the Shoulders of Giants: My Journey Through the Harlem Renaissance* (2007).

The former basketball superstar considers the long-term influence of the Harlem Renaissance, including its influence on his life and on basketball.

Frederick Lewis Allen. *Only Yesterday: An Informal History of the 1920s* (1931, 2000).

An anecdote-filled account that brings the decade to life.

Lynn Dumenil. *The Modern Temper: American Culture and Society in the 1920s* (1995).

A good examination of changing social and cultural patterns in the 1920s.

F. Scott Fitzgerald. *The Great Gatsby* (1925).

The most famous fictional portrayal of the fast cars, pleasure seeking, and empty lives of the wealthy in the early 1920s. Available online.

David E. Kyvig. *Daily Life in the United States, 1920–1940: How Americans Lived Through the Roaring Twenties and the Great Depression* (2004).

A detailed social history, exploring the ways that the lives of ordinary Americans were affected by economic and social changes.

The Smithsonian Collection of Classic Jazz. Five compact discs (1987).

An outstanding collection that reflects the development of American jazz, with annotations and biographies of performers.

David Stenn. *Clara Bow: Runnin' Wild* (1990).

The best and most carefully researched of the biographies of Bow.

Jules Tygiel. *The Great Los Angeles Swindle: Oil, Stocks, and Scandal During the Roaring Twenties* (1996).

An engagingly written account of Los Angeles in the 1920s.

CHAPTER 22   The Great Depression and the New Deal, 1929–1939

Julia Kirk Blackwelder. *Women of the Depression: Caste and Culture in San Antonio, 1929–1939* (1984).

A tightly focused study of Mexican American, African American, and Anglo women in the world of San Antonio during the Depression.

Lizabeth Cohen. *Making a New Deal: Industrial Workers in Chicago, 1919–1939* (1990).

A detailed examination of the inclusion of African American and immigrant workers in the CIO and in New Deal politics.

David Kennedy. *Freedom from Fear: The American People in Depression and War, 1929–1945* (1999).

A well-written and researched comprehensive examination of the era, including good coverage of social patterns as well as the economy and politics.

Maury Klein. *Rainbow's End: The Crash of 1929* (2001).

A compelling account of the stock market crash set within the framework of the many social, political, cultural, and economic events that surrounded it.

Alan Lawson. *A Commonwealth of Hope: The New Deal Response to Crisis* (2006).

A recent reassessment of the New Deal emphasizing links to previous reform efforts.

George McJimsey. *The Presidency of Franklin Delano Roosevelt* (2000).

An examination of Roosevelt's administration, including both the Depression years and the Second World War, with a well-presented annotated bibliography.

Amity Shaes. *The Forgotten Man: A New History of the Great Depression* (2007).

Develops the view that governmental actions contributed to the severity and length of the Great Depression.

Patricia Sullivan. *Days of Hope: Race and Democracy in the New Deal Era* (1996).

A positive view of the ways in which New Deal actions led to the shift in the African American vote from the Republican to the Democratic Party.

Studs Terkel. *Hard Times: An Oral History of the Great Depression* (1970).

A classic example of how oral histories can provide the human dimension to history.

Susan Ware. *Holding Their Own: American Women in the 1930s* (1982).

An examination of the impact of the Depression on the lives and lifestyles of women.

Joan Hoff Wilson. *Herbert Hoover: Forgotten Progressive* (1970).

A positive evaluation of the life of Herbert Hoover that stresses his accomplishments as well as his limitations.

CHAPTER 23 America's Rise to World Leadership, 1929–1945

Robert Dallek. *Franklin D. Roosevelt and American Foreign Policy, 1932–1945* (1979).

An excellent, balanced study of Franklin Roosevelt's foreign policy.

Sherna B. Gluck. *Rosie the Riveter Revisited: Women, the War, and Social Change* (1987).

An important work examining the changes that took place among women in society during the war.

William O'Neill. *A Democracy at War: America's Fight at Home and Abroad in World War II* (1993).

A good introduction to American society and politics during the war as well as an excellent view of the military campaigns against the Axis powers.

Maggie Rivas-Rodriquez, *Mexican Americans & World War II* (2005) and Richard Griswold del Castillo. *World War II and Mexican American Civil Rights* (2008).

Two important books that focus on the lives and hopes of Mexican Americans in a period that provided many their first experience of being included in American society, and their efforts to promote social, economic, and cultural equality.

Greg Robinson, *A Tragedy of Democracy* (2009).

A sweeping account of Japanese Americans prior to and after World War II that incorporates postinternment examination of Japanese Americans in civil rights efforts.

Andrew Rotter. *Hiroshima: The World's Bomb* (2008).

A readable, comprehensive view of the making and dropping of the first atomic bomb from an international perspective.

Ronald Takiaki. *Double Victory* (2002).

A wide-ranging look at American minorities' contribution to the war effort at home and abroad. Clearly demonstrates how these efforts set the foundation for the civil rights movements that followed.

David Wyman. *The Abandonment of the Jews* (1985).

A balanced account of the Holocaust.

CHAPTER 24 Truman and Cold War America, 1945–1952

Jim Cullen. *The American Dream: A Short History of an Idea that Shaped a Nation* (2003).

An introductory view of the multi-nature of the American Dream from colonial America with an emphasis on the postwar period.

John Gaddis. *The Cold War: A New History* (2005).

A concise, thoughtful analysis of the events, ideology, and people that characterized the Cold War from 1945 to 1991.

Max Hastings. *The Korean War* (1987).

A short, well-written study of the military dimension of the Korean War.

David McCullough. *Truman* (1992).

A highly acclaimed biography of Truman.

Ted Morgan. *Reds: McCarthyism in Twentieth-Century America* (2003).

An overview of anticommunism in the United States that places McCarthy as part of a widespread movement based on growing fears of Soviet communism and an uncertainty about the postwar world.

James Patterson. *Grand Expectations: The United States, 1945–1974* (1996).

A general, readable view of American society and politics in the postwar period.

Jason Sokol. *There Goes My Everything: White Southerners in the Age of Civil Rights, 1945–1975* (2006).

A needed look at the civil rights movement from the perspective of those who fought against it.

Marc Trachtenberg. *A Constructed Peace: The Making of the European Settlements, 1945–1963* (1999).

A well-researched study of the politics and issues that surrounded the origins of the Cold War from a multinational perspective.

Jules Tygiel. *Baseball's Great Experiment: Jackie Robinson and His Legacy* (1983).

Reflections on the life experiences and decisions that brought Jackie Robinson to break the color barrier in professional baseball.

Stephen J. Whitfield. *The Culture of the Cold War* (1991).

A critical account of the impact of the Cold War on the United States that argues that a consensus that equated "Americanism" with militant anticommunism dominated American life.

CHAPTER 25 Quest for Consensus, 1952–1960

Glenn C. Altschuyler. *All Shook Up: How Rock 'n' Roll Changed America* (2004).

A lively narrative that explains how musicians and their music, the media, politics, and society interacted to generate widespread cultural change.

Stephen E. Ambrose. *Eisenhower: The President* (1984).

A generally positive and well-balanced biography of Eisenhower as president by one of the most respected historians of the Eisenhower period.

Michael Bertrand. *Race, Rock, and Elvis* (2000).

Provides a view of how Elvis and his music not only shaped American music but altered views about class, race, and gender.

Taylor Branch. *Parting the Waters: America in the King Years, 1954–1963* (1988).

An interesting and useful description of the development of the civil rights movement that focuses on the role of Martin Luther King, Jr.

Elizabeth Cohen. *A Consumer's Republic: The Politics of Mass Consumption in Postwar America* (2003).

An important study of the connections between business, politics, and culture that have shaped American society following World War II to the mid-1960s.

David Halberstam. *The Fifties* (1993).

A positive interpretive view of the 1950s by a well-known journalist and author, especially recommended for its description of famous and not-so-famous people.

Peter Hahn. *Caught in the Middle East: U.S. Policy Toward the Arab-Israeli Conflict, 1945–1961* (2006).

An excellent examination of the United States' special relationship with Israel and the differences in approaches between Truman and Eisenhower.

Joanne J. Meyerowitz, ed. *Not June Cleaver: Women and Gender in Postwar America, 1945–1960* (1994).

An excellent collection of essays that explore the variety of views on women's roles in American culture, society, and politics.

Mark Newman. *The Civil Rights Movement* (2004).

A concise introduction to the civil rights movement with an emphasis on the activities of local communities and women.

James Patterson. Brown v. Board of Education: *A Civil Rights Milestone and Its Troubled Legacy* (2001).

A timely study of the events and decisions that led to the *Brown* case as well as an examination of the role the *Brown* decision has had on American politics, society, and race relations.

Harvard Sitkoff, *King: Pilgrimage to the Mountaintop* (2008).

A concise and excellent look at the civil rights and other movements of the 1960s through the actions and life of Martin Luther King, Jr.

CHAPTER 26   Great Promises, Bitter Disappointments, 1960–1968

Irving Bernstein. *Promises Kept: John F. Kennedy's New Frontier* (1991).

A brief and balanced account of Kennedy's presidency that presents a favorable report of the accomplishments and legacy of the New Frontier.

Peter Braunstein and Michael Doyle, eds. *Imagine Nation: The American Counterculture of the 1960s and 1970s* (2001).

A wide range of essays that provide useful evaluations of the many aspects of the counterculture.

Clayborne Carson. *In Struggle: SNCC and the Black Awakening of the 1960s* (1981).

A useful study that uses the development of SNCC to examine the changing patterns of the civil rights movement and the emergence of black nationalism.

Margaret Cruikshank. *The Gay and Lesbian Liberation Movement* (1992).

Provides a good introduction and insight into the gay and lesbian movement.

Robert Dallek. *Flawed Giant: Lyndon B. Johnson, 1960–1973* (1998).

An important biography that focuses on politics and foreign policy.

Michael Dobbs. *One Minute to Midnight: Kennedy, Khrushchev, and Castro on the Brink of Nuclear War* (2008).

Wonderfully written, detailed account of the events surrounding the Cuban missile crisis as the world faced the possibility of nuclear war.

David Horowitz. *Betty Friedan and the Making of the Feminist Movement* (1998).

Uses the central figure of the women's movement to examine the beginnings and development of the movement.

Michael Kazin and Maurice Isserman. *America Divided: The Civil War of the 1960s* (2000).

The social and cultural currents of the 1960s are skillfully woven into an overall picture of American society.

Sidney M. Milkis and Jerome M. Mileur. *The Great Society and the High Tide of Liberalism* (2005).

An excellent series of essays that examines Great Society liberalism and legislation.

Jeffrey Ogbar. *Black Power: Radical Politics and African American identity* (2005).

A well-written study of the varieties of the Black Power movement and the development of an American consciousness.

CHAPTER 27   America Under Stress, 1967–1976

Edward Berkowitz. *Something Happened: A Political and Cultural Overview of the Seventies* (2006).

An introduction to the seventies that shows that it was a period of activism with significant debate over the limits of the economy, culture, and foreign policy.

Larry Berman. *No Peace, No Honor: Nixon, Kissinger, and Betrayal in Vietnam* (2001).

A critical view of Vietnamization and the politics of ending the American presence in Vietnam.

Philip Caputo. *Rumor of War* (1986).

The author's account of his own changing perspectives on the war in Vietnam. Caputo served as a young marine officer in Vietnam and later covered the final days in Saigon as a journalist. His views frequently reflected those of the American public.

Ian F. Haney Lopez. *Racism on Trial: The Chicano Fight for Justice* (2003).

An interesting use of two trials to examine the development of Chicano identity and the idea of race and violence.

Burton Kaufman. *The Presidency of James Earl Carter, Jr.* (1993).

A well-balanced account and analysis of Carter's presidency and the changing political values of the 1970s.

Stanley Kutler. *The Wars of Watergate* (1990) and *Abuse of Power: The New Nixon Tapes* (1997).

The former work details the events surrounding the Watergate break-in and the hearings that led to Nixon's resignation. The latter provides transcripts of selected Nixon tapes.

Joanne Nagel. *American Indian Ethnic Revival: Red Power and the Resurgence of Identity and Culture* (1996).

A thorough analysis of the Red Power movement and how it helped to shape cultural and political change.

Rick Perlstein. *Nixonland: The Rise and Fall of a President and the Fracturing of America* (2008).

An excellent account of Nixon's role in the emergence of a resurgent conservatism and the growth of political partisanship.

David F. Schmitz. *The Tet Offensive: Politics, War, and Public Opinion* (2005).

An outstanding examination of the Tet offense and its ramifications for American policymakers and politics.

Marylin Young. *The Vietnam Wars, 1945–1990* (1991).

A brief, well-written, and carefully documented history of Vietnam's struggle for nationhood with a focus on American policy toward Vietnam since near the end of WWII.

CHAPTER 28   New Economic and Political Alignments, 1976–1992

A. J. Bacevich, et al. *The Gulf Conflict of 1991 Reconsidered* (2003).

A collection of essays that provide both insight and an excellent overview of the Gulf War.

Douglas Brinkley. *The Reagan Diaries* (2007).

An interesting personal view of Reagan's view of the events that shaped his administration and world affairs.

Roger Daniels. *Coming to America* (1990).

A solid analysis of the new immigrants seeking a place in American society; especially effective on Asian immigration.

John L. Gaddis. *The United States and the End of the Cold War* (1992).

An excellent narrative of events in the Soviet Union and the United States that led to the end of the Cold War, as well as a useful analysis of the problems facing the United States in the post–Cold War world.

David J. Garrow. *Liberty and Sexuality: The Right to Privacy and the Making of* Roe v. Wade (1994).

An in-depth and scholarly account of the origins and impact of *Roe v. Wade* and the legal and political issues dealing with privacy, gender, and abortion.

John R. Greene, *The Presidency of George Bush* (2000).

A balanced account of Bush's administration that provides valuable insight into the politics and administrative squabbles involved in making policy.

Lisa McGirr. *Suburban Warriors: The Origins of the New American Right* (2001).

A study of how the ideology and issues of the New Right found fertile soil within the American middle suburban class.

Bruce Schulman. *The Seventies: The Great Shift in American Culture, Society, and Politics* (2001).

A readable and comprehensive overview of the central issues that defined the decade.

Gil Troy and Vincent Cannato, eds. *Living in the Eighties* (2009).

A series of informative essays that cover the wide range of important topics from Reaganism to popular music to "Madonna Feminism."

Sean Wilentz. *The Age of Reagan: A History, 1974–2008* (2008).

A compelling look at Reagan and the politics of conservatism and how it changed American politics as well as policies.

CHAPTER 29 Entering a New Century, 1992–2010

Michael Bernstein and David A. Adler, eds. *Understanding American Economic Decline* (1994).

A collection of essays by economists and knowledgeable observers who analyze the slowing down of the American economy and its impact.

Douglas Brinkley. *The Great Deluge: Hurricane Katrina, New Orleans and the Mississippi Gulf Coast* (2007).

A narrative account of one of the greatest natural disasters to occur in the United States.

Congressional Quarterly's Research Reports.

A valuable monthly resource for information and views on issues facing the United States and the world.

Anthony Gidden. *Runaway World: How Globalization Is Reshaping Our World* (2002).

A readable and positive appraisal of globalization and its effects on a world society and its people.

David Halberstam. *War in Time of Peace: Bush, Clinton, and the Generals* (2001).

An understandable account of American foreign policy and policymakers coming to deal with a post–Cold War world where the major issues are terrorism, genocide, and nation-building.

John Heilemann and Mark Halperin. *Game Change: Obama and the Clintons, McCain and Palin and the Race of a Lifetime* (2010).

A fast-paced, popular account of the personalities and politics of the historic 2008 campaign as intrepreted by two nationally syndicated journalists.

John Keegan. *The Iraq War* (2004).

A military historian's examination of the Iraq war that provides valuable insight into the development of modern Iraq and the coming to power of Saddam Hussein.

James MacGregor Burns and Georgia J. Sorenson. *Dead Center: Clinton-Gore Leadership and the Perils of Moderation* (1999).

An interesting and readable view of the politics of the Clinton revival of the Democratic Party and the Clinton administration.

Ernest May, ed. *The 9/11 Commission Report with Related Documents* (2007).

Provides a background to the events preceding and after the 9/11 terrorist attacks with documents to examine the issues.

Henry Paulson, Jr. *On the Brink: Inside the Race to Stop the Collapse of the Global Financial System* (2010).

An insider's account of the events that led to the "Great Depression" and how the federal government took action to prevent a full-scale global depression.

Randy Shilts. *And the Band Played On: Politics, People and the AIDS Epidemic* (1987).

A compelling book on the AIDS epidemic and the early lack of action by society; written by a victim of AIDS.

Howard Wiarda and Ester M. Skelley. *The Crisis of American Foreign Policy: The Effects of a Divided America* (2006).

Links problems in implementing effective post–Cold War foreign policy to increasingly partisan domestic politics, arguing that American policy is in disarray.

Bob Woodward. *Plan of Attack* (2004).

Based on interviews, an account of the internal decisions the Bush administration made that led to the decision to go to war with Iraq.

Documents

Declaration of Independence in Congress, July 4, 1776

When, in the course of human events, it becomes necessary for one people to dissolve the political bonds which have connected them with another, and to assume, among the powers of the earth, the separate and equal station to which the laws of nature and of nature's God entitle them, a decent respect to the opinions of mankind requires that they should declare the causes which impel them to the separation.

We hold these truths to be self-evident: That all men are created equal; that they are endowed by their Creator with certain unalienable rights; that among these are life, liberty, and the pursuit of happiness; that, to secure these rights, governments are instituted among men, deriving their just powers from the consent of the governed; that whenever any form of government becomes destructive of these ends, it is the right of the people to alter or to abolish it, and to institute new government, laying its foundation on such principles, and organizing its powers in such form, as to them shall seem most likely to effect their safety and happiness. Prudence, indeed, will dictate that governments long established should not be changed for light and transient causes; and accordingly all experience hath shown that mankind are more disposed to suffer, while evils are sufferable, than to right themselves by abolishing the forms to which they are accustomed. But when a long train of abuses and usurpations, pursuing invariably the same object, evinces a design to reduce them under absolute despotism, it is their right, it is their duty, to throw off such government, and to provide new guards for their future security. Such has been the patient sufferance of these colonies; and such is now the necessity which constrains them to alter their former systems of government. The history of the present King of Great Britain is a history of repeated injuries and usurpations, all having in direct object the establishment of an absolute tyranny over these states. To prove this, let facts be submitted to a candid world.

He has refused his assent to laws, the most wholesome and necessary for the public good.

He has forbidden his governors to pass laws of immediate and pressing importance, unless suspended in their operation till his assent should be obtained; and, when so suspended, he has utterly neglected to attend to them.

He has refused to pass other laws for the accommodation of large districts of people, unless those people would relinquish the right of representation in the legislature, a right inestimable to them, and formidable to tyrants only.

He has called together legislative bodies at places unusual, uncomfortable, and distant from the depository of their public records, for the sole purpose of fatiguing them into compliance with his measures.

He has dissolved representative houses repeatedly, for opposing, with manly firmness, his invasions on the rights of the people.

He has refused for a long time, after such dissolutions, to cause others to be elected; whereby the legislative powers, incapable of annihilation, have returned to the people at large for their exercise; the state remaining, in the mean time, exposed to all the dangers of invasions from without and convulsions within.

He has endeavored to prevent the population of these states; for that purpose obstructing the laws for naturalization of foreigners; refusing to pass others to encourage their migration hither, and raising the conditions of new appropriations of lands.

He has obstructed the administration of justice, by refusing his assent to laws for establishing judiciary powers.

He has made judges dependent on his will alone, for the tenure of their offices, and the amount and payment of their salaries.

He has erected a multitude of new offices, and sent hither swarms of officers to harass our people and eat out their substance.

He has kept among us, in times of peace, standing armies, without the consent of our legislatures.

He has affected to render the military independent of, and superior to, the civil power.

He has combined with others to subject us to a jurisdiction foreign to our constitution, and unacknowledged by our laws, giving his assent to their acts of pretended legislation:

For quartering large bodies of armed troops among us;

For protecting them, by a mock trial, from punishment for any murders which they should commit on the inhabitants of these states;

For cutting off our trade with all parts of the world;

For imposing taxes on us without our consent;

For depriving us, in many cases, of the benefits of trial by jury;

For transporting us beyond seas, to be tried for pretended offenses;

For abolishing the free system of English laws in a neighboring province, establishing therein an arbitrary government, and enlarging its boundaries, so as to render it at once an example and fit instrument for introducing the same absolute rule into these colonies;

For taking away our charters, abolishing our most valuable laws, and altering fundamentally the forms of our governments;

For suspending our own legislatures, and declaring themselves invested with power to legislate for us in all cases whatsoever.

He has abdicated government here, by declaring us out of his protection and waging war against us.

He has plundered our seas, ravaged our coasts, burned our towns, and destroyed the lives of our people.

He is at this time transporting large armies of foreign mercenaries to complete the works of death, desolation, and tyranny already begun with circumstances of cruelty and perfidy scarcely paralleled in the most barbarous ages, and totally unworthy the head of a civilized nation.

He has constrained our fellow-citizens, taken captive on the high seas, to bear arms against their country, to become the executioners of their friends and brethren, or to fall themselves by their hands.

He has excited domestic insurrection among us, and has endeavored to bring on the inhabitants of our frontiers the merciless Indian savages, whose known rule of warfare is an undistinguished destruction of all ages, sexes, and conditions.

In every stage of these oppressions we have petitioned for redress in the most humble terms; our repeated petitions have been answered only by repeated injury. A prince, whose character is thus marked by every act which may define a tyrant, is unfit to be the ruler of a free people.

Nor have we been wanting in our attentions to our British brethren. We have warned them, from time to time, of attempts by their legislature to extend an unwarrantable jurisdiction over us. We have reminded them of the circumstances of our emigration and settlement here. We have appealed to their native justice and magnanimity; and we have conjured them, by the ties of our common kindred, to disavow these usurpations, which would inevitably interrupt our connections and correspondence. They, too, have been deaf to the voice of justice and of consanguinity. We must, therefore, acquiesce in the necessity which denounces our separation, and hold them, as we hold the rest of mankind, enemies in war, in peace friends.

We, therefore, the representatives of the United States of America, in General Congress assembled, appealing to the Supreme Judge of the world for the rectitude of our intentions, do, in the name and by the authority of the good people of these colonies, solemnly publish and declare, that these United Colonies are, and of right ought to be, FREE AND INDEPENDENT STATES; that they are absolved from all allegiance to the British crown, and that all political connection between them and the state of Great Britain is, and ought to be, totally dissolved; and that, as free and independent states, they have full power to levy war, conclude peace, contract alliances, establish commerce, and do all other acts and things which independent states may of right do. And for the support of this declaration, with a firm reliance on the protection of Divine Providence, we mutually pledge to each other our lives, our fortunes, and our sacred honor.

JOHN HANCOCK
and fifty-five others

Articles of Confederation

Whereas the Delegates of the United States of America in Congress assembled did on the fifteenth day of November in the Year of our Lord One Thousand Seven Hundred and Seventy seven, and in the Second Year of the Independence of America agree to certain articles of Confederation and perpetual Union between the States of Newhampshire, Massachusetts-bay, Rhodeisland and Providence Plantations, Connecticut, New-York, New-Jersey, Pennsylvania, Delaware, Maryland, Virginia, North-Carolina, South-Carolina and Georgia in the Words following, viz. "Articles of Confederation and perpetual Union between the states of Newhampshire, Massachusetts-bay, Rhodeisland and Providence Plantations, Connecticut, New-York, New-Jersey, Pennsylvania, Delaware, Maryland, Virginia, North-Carolina, South-Carolina and Georgia.

Article I The Stile of this confederacy shall be "The United States of America."

Article II Each state retains its sovereignty, freedom and independence, and every Power, Jurisdiction and right, which is not by this confederation expressly delegated to the United States, in Congress assembled.

Article III The said states hereby severally enter into a firm league of friendship with each other, for their common defence, the security of their Liberties, and their mutual and general welfare, binding themselves to assist each other, against all force offered to, or attacks made upon them, or any of them, on account of religion, sovereignty, trade, or any other pretence whatever.

Article IV The better to secure and perpetuate mutual friendship and intercourse among the people of the different states in this union, the free inhabitants of each of these states, paupers, vagabonds and fugitives from Justice excepted, shall be entitled to all privileges and immunities of free citizens in the several states; and the people of each state shall have free ingress and regress to and from any other state, and shall enjoy therein all the privileges of trade and commerce, subject to the same duties, impositions and restrictions as the inhabitants thereof respectively, provided that such restriction shall not extend so far as to prevent the removal of property imported into any state, to any other state of which the Owner is an inhabitant; provided also that no imposition, duties or restriction shall be laid by any state, on the property of the united states, or either of them.

If any Person guilty of, or charged with treason, felony, or other high misdemeanor in any state, shall flee from Justice, and be found in any of the united states, he shall upon demand of the Governor or executive power, of the state from which he fled, be delivered up and removed to the state having jurisdiction of his offence.

Full faith and credit shall be given in each of these states to the records, acts and judicial proceedings of the courts and magistrates of every other state.

Article V For the more convenient management of the general interests of the united states, delegates shall be annually appointed in such manner as the legislature of each state shall direct, to meet in Congress on the first Monday in November, in every year, with a power reserved to each state, to recall its delegates, or any of them, at any time within the year, and to send others in their stead, for the remainder of the Year.

No state shall be represented in Congress by less than two, nor by more than seven Members; and no person shall be capable of being a delegate for more than three years in any term of six years; nor shall any person, being a delegate, be capable of holding any office under the united states, for which he, or another for his benefit receives any salary, fees or emolument of any kind.

Each state shall maintain its own delegates in a meeting of the states, and while they act as members of the committee of the states.

In determining questions in the united states, in Congress assembled, each state shall have one vote.

Freedom of speech and debate in Congress shall not be impeached or questioned in any Court, or place out of Congress, and the members of congress shall be protected in their persons from arrests and imprisonments, during the time of their going to and from, and attendance on congress, except for treason, felony, or breach of the peace.

Article VI No state without the Consent of the united states in congress assembled, shall send any embassy to, or receive any embassy from, or enter into any conference, agreement, or alliance or treaty with any King, prince or state; nor shall any person holding any office of profit or trust under the united states, or any of them, accept of any present, emolument, office or title of any kind whatever from any king, prince or foreign state; nor shall the united states in congress assembled, or any of them, grant any title of nobility.

No two or more states shall enter into any treaty, confederation or alliance whatever between them, without the consent of the united states in congress assembled, specifying accurately the purposes for which the same is to be entered into, and how long it shall continue.

No state shall lay any imposts or duties, which may interfere with any stipulations in treaties, entered into by the united states in congress assembled, with any king, prince or state, in pursuance of any treaties already proposed by congress, to the courts of France and Spain.

No vessels of war shall be kept up in time of peace by any state, except such number only, as shall be deemed necessary by the united states in congress assembled, for the defence of such state, or its trade; nor shall any body of forces be kept up by any state, in time of peace, except such number only, as in the judgment of the united states, in congress assembled, shall be deemed requisite to garrison the forts necessary for the defence of such state; but every state shall always keep up a well regulated and disciplined militia, sufficiently armed and accoutred, and shall provide and constantly have ready for use, in public stores, a due number of field pieces and tents, and a proper quantity of arms, ammunition and camp equipage.

No state shall engage in any war without the consent of the united states in congress assembled, unless such state be actually invaded by enemies, or shall have received certain advice of a resolution being formed by some nation of Indians to invade such state, and the danger is so imminent as not to admit of a delay, till the united states in congress assembled can be consulted: nor shall any state grant commissions to any ships or vessels of war, nor letters of marque or reprisal, except it be after a declaration of war by the united states in congress assembled, and then only against the kingdom or state and the subjects thereof, against which war has been so declared, and under such regulations as shall be established by the united states in congress assembled, unless such state be infested by pirates, in which case vessels of war may be fitted out for that occasion, and kept so long as the danger shall continue, or until the united states in congress assembled shall determine otherwise.

Article VII When land-forces are raised by any state for the common defence, all officers of or under the rank of colonel, shall be appointed by the legislature of each state respectively by whom such forces shall be raised, or in such manner as such state shall direct, and all vacancies shall be filled up by the state which first made the appointment.

Article VIII All charges of war, and all other expences that shall be incurred for the common defence or general welfare, and allowed by the united states in congress assembled, shall be defrayed out of a common treasury, which shall be supplied by the several states, in proportion to the value of all land within each state, granted to or surveyed for any Person, as such land and the buildings and improvements thereon shall be estimated according to such mode as the united states in congress assembled, shall from time to time direct and appoint. The taxes for paying that proportion shall be laid and levied by the authority and direction of the legislatures of the several states within the time agreed upon by the united states in congress assembled.

Article IX The united states in congress assembled, shall have the sole and exclusive right and power of determining on peace and war, except in the cases mentioned in the sixth article—of sending and receiving ambassadors—entering into treaties and alliances, provided that no treaty of commerce shall be made whereby the legislative power of the respective states shall be restrained from imposing such imposts and duties on foreigners, as their own people are subjected to, or from prohibiting the exportation or importation of any species of goods or commodities whatsoever—of establishing rules for deciding in all cases, what captures on land or water shall be legal, and in what manner prizes taken by land or naval forces in the service of the united states shall be divided or appropriated.—of granting letters of marque and reprisal in times of peace—appointing courts for the trial of piracies and felonies committed on the high seas and establishing courts for receiving and determining finally appeals in all cases of captures, provided that no member of congress shall be appointed a judge of any of the said courts.

The united states in congress assembled shall also be the last resort on appeal in all disputes and differences now subsisting or that hereafter may arise between two or more states concerning boundary, jurisdiction or any other cause whatever; which authority shall always be exercised in the manner following. Whenever the legislative or executive authority or lawful agent of any state in controversy with another shall present a petition to congress, stating the matter in question and praying for a hearing, notice thereof shall be given by order of congress to the legislative or executive authority of the other state in controversy, and a day assigned for the appearance of the parties by their lawful agents, who shall then be directed to appoint by joint consent, commissioners or judges to constitute a court for hearing and determining the matter in question: but if they cannot agree, congress shall name three persons out of each of the united states, and from the list of such persons each party shall alternately strike out one, the petitioners beginning, until the number shall be reduced to thirteen; and from that number not less than seven, nor more than nine names as congress shall direct, shall in the presence of congress be drawn out by lot, and the persons whose names shall be so drawn or any five of them, shall be commissioners or judges, to hear and finally determine the controversy, so always as a major part of the judges who shall hear the cause shall agree in the determination: and if either party shall neglect to attend at the day appointed, without shewing reasons, which congress shall judge sufficient, or being present shall refuse to strike, the congress shall proceed to nominate three persons out of each state, and the secretary of congress shall strike in behalf of such party absent or refusing; and the judgment and sentence of the court to be appointed, in the manner before prescribed, shall be final and conclusive; and if any of the parties shall refuse to submit to the authority of such court, or to appear to defend their claim or cause, the court shall nevertheless proceed to pronounce sentence, or judgment, which shall in like manner be final and decisive, the judgment or sentence and other proceedings being in either case transmitted to congress, and lodged among the acts of congress for the security of the parties concerned: provided that every commissioner, before he sits in judgment, shall take an oath to be administered by one of the judges of the supreme or superior court of the state, where the cause shall be tried, "well and truly to hear and determine the matter in question, according to the best of his judgment, without favour, affection or hope of reward:" provided also that no state shall be deprived of territory for the benefit of the united states.

All controversies concerning the private right of soil claimed under different grants of two or more states, whose jurisdictions as they may respect such lands, and the states which passed such grants are adjusted, the said grants or either of them being at the same time claimed to have originated antecedent to such settlement of jurisdiction, shall on the petition of either party to the congress of the united states, be finally determined as near as may be in the same manner as is before prescribed for deciding disputes respecting territorial jurisdiction between different states.

The united states in congress assembled shall also have the sole and exclusive right and power of regulating the alloy and value of coin struck by their own authority, or by that of the respective states—fixing the standard of weights and measures throughout the united states.—regulating the trade and managing all affairs with the Indians, not members of any of the states, provided that the legislative right of any state within its own limits be not infringed or violated—establishing and regulating post-offices from one state to another, throughout all the united states, and exacting such postage on the papers passing thro' the same as may be requisite to defray the expences of the said office—appointing all officers of the land forces, in the service of the united states, excepting regimental officers.—appointing all the officers of the naval forces, and commissioning all officers whatever in the service of the united states—making rules for the government and regulation of the said land and naval forces, and directing their operations.

The united states in congress assembled shall have authority to appoint a committee, to sit in the recess of congress, to be denominated "A Committee of the States," and to consist of one delegate from each state; and to appoint such other committees and civil officers as may be necessary for managing the general affairs of the united states under their direction—to appoint one of their number to preside, provided that no person be allowed to serve in the office of president more than one year in any term of three years; to ascertain the necessary sums of Money to be raised for the service of the united states, and to appropriate and apply the same for defraying the public expences—to borrow money, or emit bills on the credit of the united states, transmitting every half year to the respective states an account of the sums of money so borrowed or emitted,—to build and equip a navy—to agree upon the number of land forces, and to make requisitions from each state for its quota, in proportion to the number of white inhabitants in such state; which requisition shall be binding, and thereupon the legislature of each state shall appoint the regimental officers, raise the men and cloath, arm and equip them in a soldier like manner, at the expence of the united states, and the officers and men so cloathed, armed and equipped shall march to the place appointed, and within the time agreed on by the united states in congress assembled: But if the united states in congress assembled shall, on consideration of circumstances judge proper that any state should not raise men, or should raise a smaller number than its quota, and that any other state should raise a greater number of men than the quota thereof, such extra number shall be raised, officered, cloathed, armed and equipped in the same manner as the quota of such state, unless the legislature of such state shall judge that such extra number cannot be safely spared out of the same, in which case they shall raise, officer, cloath, arm and equip as many of such extra number as they judge can be safely spared. And the officers and men so cloathed, armed and equipped, shall march to the place appointed, and within the time agreed on by the united states in congress assembled.

The united states in congress assembled shall never engage in a war, nor grant letters of marque and reprisal in time of peace, nor enter into any treaties or alliances, nor coin money, nor regulate the value thereof, nor ascertain the sums and expences necessary for the defence and welfare of the united states, or any of them, nor emit bills, nor borrow money on the credit of the united states, nor appropriate money, nor agree upon the number of vessels of war, to be built or purchased, or the number of land or sea forces to be raised, nor appoint a commander in chief of the army or navy, unless nine states assent to the same: nor shall a question on any other point, except for adjourning from day to day be determined, unless by the votes of a majority of the united states in congress assembled.

The congress of the united states shall have power to adjourn to any time within the year, and to any place within the united states, so that no period of adjournment be for a longer duration than the space of six Months, and shall publish the Journal of their proceedings monthly, except such parts thereof relating to treaties, alliances or military operations as in their judgment require secresy; and the yeas and nays of the delegates of each state on any question shall be entered on the Journal, when it is desired by any delegate; and the delegates of a state, or any of them, at his or their request shall be furnished with a transcript of the said Journal, except such parts as are above excepted, to lay before the legislatures of the several states.

Article X The committee of the states, or any nine of them, shall be authorised to execute, in the recess of congress, such of the powers of congress as the united states in congress assembled, by the consent of nine states, shall from time to time think expedient to vest them with; provided that no power be delegated to the said committee, for the exercise of which, by the articles of confederation, the voice of nine states in the congress of the united states assembled is requisite.

Article XI Canada acceding to this confederation, and joining in the measures of the united states, shall be admitted into, and entitled to all the advantages of this union: but no other colony shall be admitted into the same, unless such admission be agreed to by nine states.

Article XII All bills of credit emitted, monies borrowed and debts contracted by, or under the authority of congress, before the assembling of the united states, in pursuance of the present confederation, shall be deemed and considered as a charge against the united states, for payment and satisfaction whereof the said united states, and the public faith are hereby solemnly pledged.

Article XIII Every state shall abide by the determinations of the united states in congress assembled, on all questions which by this confederation are submitted to them. And the Articles of this confederation shall be inviolably observed by every state, and the union shall be perpetual; nor shall any alteration at any time hereafter be made in any of them; unless such alteration be agreed to in a congress of the united states, and be afterwards confirmed by the legislatures of every state.

AND WHEREAS it hath pleased the Great Governor of the World to incline the hearts of the legislatures we respectively represent in congress, to approve of, and to authorize us to ratify the said articles of confederation and perpetual union. Know Ye that we the undersigned delegates, by virtue of the power and authority to us given for that purpose, do by these presents, in the name and in behalf of our respective constituents, fully and entirely ratify and confirm each and every of the said articles of confederation and perpetual union, and all and singular the matters and things therein contained: And we do further solemnly plight and engage the faith of our respective constitutents, that they shall abide by the determinations of the united states in congress assembled, on all questions, which by the said confederation are submitted to them. And that the articles thereof shall be inviolably observed by the states we respectively represent, and that the union shall be perpetual. In Witness whereof we have hereunto set our hands in Congress. Done at Philadelphia in the state of Pennsylvania the ninth Day of July in the Year of our Lord one Thousand seven Hundred and Seventy-eight, and in the third year of the independence of America.

Constitution of the United States of America and Amendments*

Preamble

We the people of the United States, in order to form a more perfect union, establish justice, insure domestic tranquillity, provide for the common defense, promote the general welfare, and secure the blessings of liberty to ourselves and our posterity, do ordain and establish this Constitution for the United States of America.

Article I

Section 1 All legislative powers herein granted shall be vested in a Congress of the United States, which shall consist of a Senate and a House of Representatives.

Section 2 The House of Representatives shall be composed of members chosen every second year by the people of the several States, and the electors in each State shall have the qualifications requisite for electors of the most numerous branch of the State Legislature.

No person shall be a Representative who shall not have attained to the age of twenty-five years, and been seven years a citizen of the United States, and who shall not, when elected, be an inhabitant of that State in which he shall be chosen.

Representatives and direct taxes shall be apportioned among the several States which may be included within this Union, according to their respective numbers, *which shall be determined by adding to the whole number of free persons, including those bound to service for a term of years and excluding Indians not taxed, three-fifths of all other persons.* The actual enumeration shall be made within three years after the first meeting of the Congress of the United States, and within every subsequent term of ten years, in such manner as they shall by law direct. The number of Representatives shall not exceed one for every thirty thousand, but each State shall have at least one Representative; *and until such enumeration shall be made, the State of New Hampshire shall be entitled to choose three, Massachusetts eight, Rhode Island and Providence Plantations one, Connecticut five, New York six, New Jersey four, Pennsylvania eight, Delaware one, Maryland six, Virginia ten, North Carolina five, South Carolina five, and Georgia three.*

When vacancies happen in the representation from any State, the Executive authority thereof shall issue writs of election to fill such vacancies.

The House of Representatives shall choose their Speaker and other officers; and shall have the sole power of impeachment.

Section 3 The Senate of the United States shall be composed of two Senators from each State, *chosen by the legislature thereof,* for six years; and each Senator shall have one vote.

Immediately after they shall be assembled in consequence of the first election, they shall be divided as equally as may be into three classes. The seats of the Senators of the first class shall be vacated at the expiration of the second year, of the second class at the expiration of the fourth year, and of the third class at the expiration of the sixth year, so that one-third may be chosen every second year; *and if vacancies happen by resignation or otherwise, during the recess of the legislature of any State, the Executive thereof may make temporary appointments until the next meeting of the legislature, which shall then fill such vacancies.*

No person shall be a Senator who shall not have attained to the age of thirty years, and been nine years a citizen of the United States, and who shall not, when elected, be an inhabitant of that State for which he shall be chosen.

The Vice-President of the United States shall be President of the Senate, but shall have no vote, unless they be equally divided.

The Senate shall choose their other officers, and also a President *pro tempore,* in the absence of the Vice-President, or when he shall exercise the office of President of the United States.

The Senate shall have the sole power to try all impeachments. When sitting for that purpose, they shall be on oath or affirmation. When the President of the United States is tried, the Chief Justice shall preside: and no person shall be convicted with-out the concurrence of two thirds of the members present.

Judgment in cases of impeachment shall not extend further than to removal from the office, and disqualification to hold and enjoy any office of honor, trust or profit under the United States: but the party convicted shall nevertheless be liable and subject to indictment, trial, judgment and punishment, according to law.

Section 4 The times, places and manner of holding elections for Senators and Representatives shall be prescribed in each State by the legislature thereof; but the Congress may at any time by law make or alter such regulations, except as to the places of choosing Senators.

The Congress shall assemble at least once in every year, and such meeting *shall be on the first Monday in December, unless they shall by law appoint a different day.*

Section 5 Each house shall be the judge of the elections, returns and qualifications of its own members, and a majority of each shall constitute a quorum to do business; but a smaller number may adjourn from day to day, and may be authorized to compel the attendance of absent members, in such manner, and under such penalties, as each house may provide.

Each house may determine the rules of its proceedings, punish its members for disorderly behavior, and with the concurrence of two-thirds, expel a member. Each house shall keep a journal of its proceedings, and

---

* Passages no longer in effect are printed in italic type.

from time to time publish the same, excepting such parts as may in their judgment require secrecy; and the yeas and nays of the members of either house on any question shall, at the desire of one-fifth of those present, be entered on the journal.

Neither house, during the session of Congress, shall, without the consent of the other, adjourn for more than three days, nor to any other place than that in which the two houses shall be sitting.

Section 6 The Senators and Representatives shall receive a compensation for their services, to be ascertained by law and paid out of the treasury of the United States. They shall in all cases except treason, felony and breach of the peace, be privileged from arrest during their attendance at the session of their respective houses, and in going to and returning from the same; and for any speech or debate in either house, they shall not be questioned in any other place.

No Senator or Representative shall, during the time for which he was elected, be appointed to any civil office under the authority of the United States, which shall have been created, or the emoluments whereof shall have been increased, during such time; and no person holding any office under the United States shall be a member of either house during his continuance in office.

Section 7 All bills for raising revenue shall originate in the House of Representatives; but the Senate may propose or concur with amendments as on other bills.

Every bill which shall have passed the House of Representatives and the Senate, shall, before it become a law, be presented to the President of the United States; if he approve he shall sign it, but if not he shall return it with objections to that house in which it originated, who shall enter the objections at large on their journal, and proceed to reconsider it. If after such reconsideration two-thirds of that house shall agree to pass the bill, it shall be sent, together with the objections, to the other house, by which it shall likewise be reconsidered, and, if approved by two-thirds of that house, it shall become a law. But in all such cases the votes of both houses shall be determined by yeas and nays, and the names of the persons voting for and against the bill shall be entered on the journal of each house respectively. If any bill shall not be returned by the President within ten days (Sundays excepted) after it shall have been presented to him, the same shall be a law, in like manner as if he had signed it, unless the Congress by their adjournment prevent its return, in which case it shall not be a law.

Every order, resolution, or vote to which the concurrence of the Senate and House of Representatives may be necessary (except on a question of adjournment) shall be presented to the President of the United States; and before the same shall take effect, shall be approved by him, or being disapproved by him, shall be repassed by two-thirds of the Senate and House of Representatives, according to the rules and limitations prescribed in the case of a bill.

Section 8 The Congress shall have power

To lay and collect taxes, duties, imposts, and excises, to pay the debts and provide for the common defense and general welfare of the United States; but all duties, imposts and excises shall be uniform throughout the United States;

To borrow money on the credit of the United States;

To regulate commerce with foreign nations, and among the several States, and with the Indian tribes;

To establish an uniform rule of naturalization, and uniform laws on the subject of bankruptcies throughout the United States;

To coin money, regulate the value thereof, and of foreign coin, and fix the standard of weights and measures;

To provide for the punishment of counterfeiting the securities and current coin of the United States;

To establish post offices and post roads;

To promote the progress of science and useful arts by securing for limited times to authors and inventors the exclusive right to their respective writings and discoveries;

To constitute tribunals inferior to the Supreme Court;

To define and punish piracies and felonies committed on the high seas and offenses against the law of nations;

To declare war, grant letters of marque and reprisal, and make rules concerning captures on land and water;

To raise and support armies, but no appropriation of money to that use shall be for a longer term than two years;

To provide and maintain a navy;

To make rules for the government and regulation of the land and naval forces;

To provide for calling forth the militia to execute the laws of the Union, suppress insurrections, and repel invasions;

To provide for organizing, arming, and disciplining the militia, and for governing such part of them as may be employed in the service of the United States, reserving to the States respectively the appointment of the officers, and the authority of training the militia according to the discipline prescribed by Congress;

To exercise exclusive legislation in all cases whatsoever, over such district (not exceeding ten miles square) as may, by cession of particular States, and the acceptance of Congress, become the seat of government of the United States, and to exercise like authority over all places purchased by the consent of the legislature of the State, in which the same shall be, for erection of forts, magazines, arsenals, dockyards, and other needful buildings;—and

To make all laws which shall be necessary and proper for carrying into execution the foregoing powers, and all other powers vested by this Constitution in the government of the United States, or in any department or officer there of.

Section 9 *The migration or importation of such persons as any of the States now existing shall think proper to admit shall not be prohibited by the Congress prior to the year 1808; but a tax or duty may be imposed on such importation, not exceeding $10 for each person.*

The privilege of the writ of habeas corpus shall not be suspended, unless when in cases of rebellion or invasion the public safety may require it.

No bill of attainder or ex post facto law shall be passed.

No capitation, or other direct, tax shall be laid, unless in proportion to the census or enumeration herein before directed to be taken.

No tax or duty shall be laid on articles exported from any State.

No preference shall be given by any regulation of commerce or revenue to the ports of one State over those of another; nor shall vessels bound to, or from, one State, be obliged to enter, clear, or pay duties in another.

No money shall be drawn from the treasury, but in consequence of appropriations made by law; and a regular statement and account of the receipts and expenditures of all public money shall be published from time to time.

No title of nobility shall be granted by the United States: and no person holding any office of profit or trust under them, shall, without the consent of the Congress, accept of any present, emolument, office, or title, of any kind whatever, from any king, prince, or foreign state.

Section 10 No State shall enter into any treaty, alliance, or confederation; grant letters of marque and reprisal; coin money; emit bills of credit; make anything but gold and silver coin a tender in payment of debts; pass any bill of attainder, ex post facto law, or law impairing the obligation of contracts, or grant any title of nobility.

No State shall, without the consent of Congress, lay any imposts or duties on imports or exports, except what may be absolutely necessary for executing its inspection laws: and the net produce of all duties and imposts, laid by any State on imports or exports, shall be for the use of the treasury of the United States; and all such laws shall be subject to the revision and control of the Congress.

No State shall, without the consent of Congress, lay any duty of tonnage, keep troops or ships of war in time of peace, enter into any agreement or compact with another State, or with a foreign power, or engage in war, unless actually invaded, or in such imminent danger as will not admit of delay.

Article II

Section 1 The executive power shall be vested in a President of the United States of America. He shall hold his office during the term of four years, and, together with the Vice-President, chosen for the same term, be elected as follows:

Each State shall appoint, in such manner as the legislature thereof may direct, a number of electors, equal to the whole number of Senators and Representatives to which the State may be entitled in the Congress; but no Senator or Representative, or person holding an office of trust or profit under the United States, shall be appointed an elector.

The electors shall meet in their respective States, and vote by ballot for two persons, of whom one at least shall not be an inhabitant of the same State with themselves. And they shall make a list of all the persons voted for, and of the number of votes for each; which list they shall sign and certify, and transmit sealed to the seat of government of the United States, directed to the President of the Senate. The President of the Senate shall, in the presence of the Senate and House of Representatives, open all the certificates, and the votes shall then be counted. The person having the greatest number of votes shall be the President, if such number be a majority of the whole number of electors appointed; and if there be more than one who have such majority, and have an equal number of votes, then the House of Representatives shall immediately choose by ballot one of them for President; and if no person have a majority, then from the five highest on the list said house shall in like manner choose the President. But in choosing the President the votes shall be taken by States, the representation from each State having one vote; a quorum for this purpose shall consist of a member or members from two-thirds of the States, and a majority of all the States shall be necessary to a choice. In every case, after the choice of the President, the person having the greatest number of votes of the electors shall be the Vice-President. But if there should remain two or more who have equal votes, the Senate shall choose from them by ballot the Vice-President.

The Congress may determine the time of choosing the electors and the day on which they shall give their votes; which day shall be the same throughout the United States.

No person except a natural-born citizen, *or a citizen of the United States at the time of the adoption of this Constitution,* shall be eligible to the office of President; neither shall any person be eligible to that office who shall not have attained to the age of thirty-five years, and been fourteen years a resident within the United States.

In cases of the removal of the President from office or of his death, resignation, or inability to discharge the powers and duties of the said office, the same shall devolve on the Vice-President, and the Congress may by law provide for the case of removal, death, resignation, or inability, both of the President and Vice-President, declaring what officer shall then act as President, and such officer shall act accordingly, until the disability be removed, or a President shall be elected.

The President shall, at stated times, receive for his services a compensation, which shall neither be increased nor diminished during the period for which he shall have been elected, and he shall not receive within that period any other emolument from the United States, or any of them.

Before he enter on the execution of his office, he shall take the following oath or affirmation:—"I do solemnly swear (or affirm) that I will faithfully execute the office of the President of the United States, and will to the best of my ability preserve, protect and defend the Constitution of the United States."

Section 2 The President shall be commander in chief of the army and navy of the United States, and of the militia of the several States, when called into the actual service of the United States; he may require the opinion, in writing, of the principal officer in each of the executive departments, upon any subject relating to the duties of their respective offices, and he shall have power to grant reprieves and pardons for offenses against the United States, except in cases of impeachment.

He shall have power, by and with the advice and consent of the Senate, to make treaties, provided two-thirds of the Senators present concur; and he shall nominate, and by and with the advice and consent of the Senate, shall appoint ambassadors, other public ministers and consuls, judges of the Supreme Court, and all other officers of the United States, whose appointments are not herein otherwise provided for, and which shall be established by law: but Congress may by law vest the appointment of such inferior officers, as they think proper, in the President alone, in the courts of law, or in the heads of departments.

The President shall have power to fill up all vacancies that may happen during the recess of the Senate, by granting commissions which shall expire at the end of their next session.

Section 3 He shall from time to time give to the Congress information of the state of the Union, and recommend to their consideration such measures as he shall judge necessary and expedient; he may, on extraordinary occasions, convene both houses, or either of them, and in case of disagreement between them, with respect to the time of adjournment, he may adjourn them to such time as he shall think proper; he shall receive ambassadors and other public ministers; he shall take care that the laws be faithfully executed, and shall commission all the officers of the United States.

Section 4 The President, Vice-President and all civil officers of the United States shall be removed from office on impeachment for, and on conviction of, treason, bribery, or other high crimes and misdemeanors.

Article III

Section 1 The judicial power of the United States shall be vested in one Supreme Court, and in such inferior courts as the Congress may from time to time ordain and establish. The judges, both of the Supreme and inferior courts, shall hold their offices during good behavior, and shall, at stated times, receive for their services a compensation which shall not be diminished during their continuance in office.

Section 2 The judicial power shall extend to all cases, in law and equity, arising under this Constitution, the laws of the United States, and treaties made, or which shall be made, under their authority;—to all cases affecting ambassadors, other public ministers and consuls;—to

all cases of admiralty and maritime jurisdiction;—to controversies to which the United States shall be a party;—to controversies between two or more States;—*between a State and citizens of another State;*—between citizens of different States;—between citizens of the same State claiming lands under grants of different States, and between a State, or the citizens thereof, and foreign states, citizens or subjects.

In all cases affecting ambassadors, other public ministers and consuls, and those in which a State shall be party, the Supreme Court shall have original jurisdiction. In all the other cases before mentioned, the Supreme Court shall have appellate jurisdiction, both as to law and fact, with such exceptions, and under such regulations, as the Congress shall make.

The trial of all crimes, except in cases of impeachment, shall be by jury; and such trial shall be held in the State where said crimes shall have been committed; but when not committed within any State, the trial shall be at such place or places as the Congress may by law have directed.

Section 3 Treason against the United States shall consist only in levying war against them, or in adhering to their enemies, giving them aid and comfort. No person shall be convicted of treason unless on the testimony of two witnesses to the same overt act, or on confession in open court.

The Congress shall have power to declare the punishment of treason, but no attainder of treason shall work corruption of blood, or forfeiture except during the life of the person attainted.

Article IV

Section 1 Full faith and credit shall be given in each State to the public acts, records, and judicial proceedings of every other State. And the Congress may by general laws prescribe the manner in which such acts, records, and proceedings shall be proved, and the effect thereof.

Section 2 The citizens of each State shall be entitled to all privileges and immunities of citizens in the several States.

A person charged in any State with treason, felony, or other crime, who shall flee from justice, and be found in another State, shall on demand of the executive authority of the State from which he fled, be delivered up, to be removed to the State having jurisdiction of the crime.

No person held to service or labor in one State, under the laws thereof, escaping into another, shall, in consequence of any law or regulation therein, be discharged from such service or labor, but shall be delivered up on claim of the party to whom such service or labor may be due.

Section 3 New States may be admitted by the Congress into this Union; but no new State shall be formed or erected within the jurisdiction of any other State; nor any State be formed by the junction of two or more States, or parts of States, without the consent of the legislatures of the States concerned as well as of the Congress.

The Congress shall have power to dispose of and make all needful rules and regulations respecting the territory or other property belonging to the United States; and nothing in this Constitution shall be so construed as to prejudice any claims of the United States, or of any particular State.

Section 4 The United States shall guarantee to every State in this Union a republican form of government, and shall protect each of them against invasion; and on application of the legislature, or of the executive (when the legislature cannot be convened), against domestic violence.

Article V

The Congress, whenever two-thirds of both houses shall deem it necessary, shall propose amendments to this Constitution, or, on the application of the legislatures of two-thirds of the several States, shall call a convention for proposing amendments, which, in either case, shall be valid to all intents and purposes, as part of this Constitution, when ratified by the legislatures of three fourths of the several States, or by conventions in three-fourths thereof, as the one or the other mode of ratification may be proposed by the Congress; provided *that no amendments which may be made prior to the year one thousand eight hundred and eight shall in any manner affect the first and fourth clauses in the ninth section of the first article;* and that no State, without its consent, shall be deprived of its equal suffrage in the Senate.

Article VI

All debts contracted and engagements entered into, before the adoption of this Constitution, shall be as valid against the United States under this Constitution, as under the Confederation.

This Constitution, and the laws of the United States which shall be made in pursuance thereof; and all treaties made, or which shall be made, under the authority of the United States, shall be the supreme law of the land; and the judges in every State shall be bound thereby, anything in the Constitution or laws of any State to the contrary notwithstanding.

The Senators and Representatives before mentioned, and the members of the several State legislatures, and all executive and judicial officers, both of the United States and of the several States, shall be bound by oath or affirmation to support this Constitution; but no religious test shall ever be required as a qualification to any office or public trust under the United States.

Article VII

The ratification of the conventions of nine States shall be sufficient for the establishment of this Constitution between the States so ratifying the same.

Done in Convention by the unanimous consent of the States present, the seventeenth day of September in the year of our Lord one thousand seven hundred and eighty-seven and of the Independence of the United States of America the twelfth. In witness whereof we have hereunto subscribed our names.

GEORGE WASHINGTON
and thirty-seven others

Amendments to the Constitution*

Amendment I

Congress shall make no law respecting an establishment of religion, or prohibiting the free exercise thereof; or abridging the freedom of speech, or of the press; or the right of the people peaceably to assemble, and to petition the government for a redress of grievances.

Amendment II

A well-regulated militia being necessary to the security of a free State, the right of the people to keep and bear arms shall not be infringed.

Amendment III

No soldier shall, in time of peace, be quartered in any house without the consent of the owner, nor in time of war, but in a manner to be prescribed by law.

Amendment IV

The right of the people to be secure in their persons, houses, papers, and effects, against unreasonable searches and seizures, shall not be violated, and no warrants shall issue but upon probable cause, supported by oath or affirmation, and particularly describing the place to be searched, and the persons or things to be seized.

Amendment V

No person shall be held to answer for a capital, or otherwise infamous crime, unless on a presentment or indictment of a grand jury, except in cases arising in the land or naval forces, or in the militia, when in actual service in time of war or public danger; nor shall any person be subject for the same offense to be twice put in jeopardy of life or limb; nor shall be compelled in any criminal case to be a witness against himself, nor be deprived of life, liberty, or property, without due process of law; nor shall private property be taken for public use without just compensation.

---

* The first 10 amendments (the Bill of Rights) were adopted in 1791.

Amendment VI

In all criminal prosecutions, the accused shall enjoy the right to a speedy and public trial, by an impartial jury of the State and district wherein the crime shall have been committed, which district shall have been previously ascertained by law, and to be informed of the nature and cause of the accusation; to be confronted with the witnesses against him; to have compulsory process for obtaining witnesses in his favor, and to have the assistance of counsel for his defense.

Amendment VII

In suits at common law, where the value in controversy shall exceed twenty dollars, the right of trial by jury shall be preserved, and no fact tried by a jury shall be otherwise reexamined in any court of the United States, than according to the rules of the common law.

Amendment VIII

Excessive bail shall not be required, nor excessive fines imposed, nor cruel and unusual punishments inflicted.

Amendment IX

The enumeration in the Constitution, of certain rights, shall not be construed to deny or disparage others retained by the people.

Amendment X

The powers not delegated to the United States by the Constitution, nor prohibited by it to the States, are reserved to the States respectively, or to the people.

Amendment XI

[Adopted 1798]

The judicial power of the United States shall not be construed to extend to any suit in law or equity, commenced or prosecuted against one of the United States by citizens of another State, or by citizens or subjects of any foreign state.

Amendment XII

[Adopted 1804]

The electors shall meet in their respective States, and vote by ballot for President and Vice-President, one of whom, at least, shall not be an inhabitant of the same State with themselves; they shall name in their ballots the person voted for as President, and in distinct ballots the person voted for as Vice-President, and they shall make distinct lists of all persons voted for as President, and of all persons voted for as Vice-President, and of the number of votes for each, which lists they shall sign and certify, and transmit sealed to the seat of government of the United States, directed to the President of the Senate;—the President of the Senate shall, in the presence of the Senate and House of Representatives, open all the certificates and the votes shall then be counted;—the person having the greatest number of votes for President shall be the President, if such number be a majority of the whole number of electors appointed; and if no person have such majority, then from the persons having the highest numbers not exceeding three on the list of those voted for as President, the House of Representatives shall choose immediately, by ballot, the President. But in choosing the President, the votes shall be taken by States, the representation from each State having one vote; a quorum for this purpose shall consist of a member or members from two-thirds of the States, and a majority of all the States shall be necessary to a choice. And if the House of Representatives shall not choose a President whenever the right of choice shall devolve upon them, before the fourth day of March next following, then the Vice-President shall act as President, as in the case of the death or other constitutional disability of the President.

The person having the greatest number of votes as Vice-President shall be the Vice-President, if such number be a majority of the whole number of electors appointed; and if no person have a majority, then from the two highest numbers on the list the Senate shall choose the Vice-President; a quorum for the purpose shall consist of two-thirds of the whole number of Senators, and a majority of the whole number shall be necessary to a choice. But no person constitutionally ineligible to the office of President shall be eligible to that of Vice-President of the United States.

Amendment XIII

[Adopted 1865]

Section 1 Neither slavery nor involuntary servitude, except as a punishment for crime whereof the party shall have been duly convicted, shall exist within the United States, or any place subject to their jurisdiction.

Section 2 Congress shall have power to enforce this article by appropriate legislation.

Amendment XIV

[Adopted 1868]

Section 1 All persons born or naturalized in the United States, and subject to the jurisdiction thereof, are citizens of the United States and of the State wherein they reside. No State shall make or enforce any law which shall abridge the privileges or immunities of citizens of the United States; nor shall any State deprive any person of life, liberty, or property, without due process of law; nor deny to any person within its jurisdiction the equal protection of the laws.

Section 2 Representatives shall be apportioned among the several States according to their respective numbers, counting the whole number of persons in each State, excluding Indians not taxed. But when the right to vote at any election for the choice of Electors for President and Vice-President of the United States, Representatives in Congress, the executive and judicial officers of a State, or the members of the legislature thereof, is denied to any of the male inhabitants of such State, being twenty-one years of age and citizens of the United States, or in any way abridged, except for participation in rebellion, or other crime, the basis of representation therein shall be reduced in the proportion which the number of such male citizens shall bear to the whole number of male citizens twenty-one years of age in such State.

Section 3 No person shall be a Senator or Representative in Congress, or Elector of President and Vice-President, or hold any office, civil or military, under the United States, or under any State, who, having previously taken an oath, as a member of Congress, or as an officer of the United States, or as a member of any State legislature, or as an executive or judicial officer of any State, to support the Constitution of the United States, shall have engaged in insurrection or rebellion against the same, or given aid or comfort to the enemies thereof. Congress may, by a vote of two-thirds of each house, remove such disability.

Section 4 The validity of the public debt of the United States, authorized by law, including debts incurred for payment of pensions and bounties for services in suppressing insurrection or rebellion, shall not be questioned. But neither the United States nor any State shall assume or pay any debt or obligation incurred in aid of insurrection or rebellion against the United States, or any claim for the loss or emancipation of any slave; but all such debts, obligations, and claims shall be held illegal and void.

Section 5 The Congress shall have power to enforce, by appropriate legislation, the provisions of this article.

Amendment XV

[Adopted 1870]

Section 1 The right of citizens of the United States to vote shall not be denied or abridged by the United States or by any State on account of race, color, or previous condition of servitude.

Section 2 The Congress shall have power to enforce this article by appropriate legislation.

Amendment XVI

[Adopted 1913]

The Congress shall have power to lay and collect taxes on incomes, from whatever source derived, without apportionment among the several States, and without regard to any census or enumeration.

Amendment XVII

[Adopted 1913]

Section 1 The Senate of the United States shall be composed of two Senators from each State, elected by the people thereof, for six years; and each Senator shall have one vote. The electors in each State shall have the qualifications requisite for electors of [voters for] the most numerous branch of the State legislatures.

Section 2 When vacancies happen in the representation of any State in the Senate, the executive authority of such State shall issue writs of election to fill such vacancies: Provided, that the Legislature of any State may empower the executive thereof to make temporary appointments until the people fill the vacancies by election as the Legislature may direct.

Section 3 This amendment shall not be so construed as to affect the election or term of any Senator chosen before it becomes valid as part of the Constitution.

Amendment XVIII

[Adopted 1919; Repealed 1933]

Section 1 After one year from the ratification of this article the manufacture, sale, or transportation of intoxicating liquors within, the importation thereof into, or the exportation thereof from the United States and all territory subject to the jurisdiction thereof, for beverage purposes, is hereby prohibited.

Section 2 The Congress and the several States shall have concurrent power to enforce this article by appropriate legislation.

Section 3 This article shall be inoperative unless it shall have been ratified as an amendment to the Constitution by the legislatures of the several States, as provided by the Constitution, within seven years from the date of the submission thereof to the States by the Congress.

Amendment XIX

[Adopted 1920]

Section 1 The right of citizens of the United States to vote shall not be denied or abridged by the United States or by any State on account of sex.

Section 2 The Congress shall have power to enforce this article by appropriate legislation.

Amendment XX

[Adopted 1933]

Section 1 The terms of the President and Vice-President shall end at noon on the 20th day of January, and the terms of Senators and Representatives at noon on the 3rd day of January, of the years in which such terms would have ended if this article had not been ratified; and the terms of their successors shall then begin.

Section 2 The Congress shall assemble at least once in every year, and such meeting shall begin at noon on the 3d day of January, unless they shall by law appoint a different day.

Section 3 If, at the time fixed for the beginning of the term of the President, the President-elect shall have died, the Vice-President-elect shall become President. If a President shall not have been chosen before the time fixed for the beginning of his term, or if the President-elect shall have failed to qualify, then the Vice-President-elect shall act as President until a President shall have qualified; and the Congress may by law provide for the case wherein neither a President-elect nor a Vice-President-elect shall have qualified, declaring who shall then act as President, or the manner in which one who is to act shall be selected, and such persons shall act accordingly until a President or Vice-President shall have qualified.

Section 4 The Congress may by law provide for the case of the death of any of the persons from whom the House of Representatives may choose a President whenever the right of choice shall have devolved upon them, and for the case of the death of any of the persons from whom the Senate may choose a Vice-President whenever the right of choice shall have devolved upon them.

Section 5 Sections 1 and 2 shall take effect on the 15th day of October following the ratification of this article.

Section 6 This article shall be inoperative unless it shall have been ratified as an amendment to the Constitution by the Legislatures of three-fourths of the several States within seven years from the date of its submission.

Amendment XXI

[Adopted 1933]

Section 1 The eighteenth article of amendment to the Constitution of the United States is hereby repealed.

Section 2 The transportation or importation into any State, Territory, or Possession of the United States for delivery or use therein of intoxicating liquors, in violation of the laws thereof, is hereby prohibited.

Section 3 This article shall be inoperative unless it shall have been ratified as an amendment to the Constitution by conventions in the several States, as provided in the Constitution, within seven years from the date of submission thereof to the States by the Congress.

Amendment XXII

[Adopted 1951]

Section 1 No person shall be elected to the office of President more than twice, and no person who has held the office of President, or acted as President, for more than two years of a term to which some other person was elected President shall be elected to the office of President more than once. But this article shall not apply to any person holding the office of President when this article was proposed by the Congress, and shall not prevent any person who may be holding the office of President, or acting as President, during the term within which this article becomes operative from holding the office of President or acting as President during the remainder of such term.

Section 2 This article shall be inoperative unless it shall have been ratified as an amendment to the Constitution by the legislatures of three-fourths of the several States within seven years from the date of its submission to the States by the Congress.

Amendment XXIII

[Adopted 1961]

Section 1 The District constituting the seat of Government of the United States shall appoint in such manner as the Congress may direct:

A number of electors of President and Vice-President equal to the whole number of Senators and Representatives in Congress to which the District would be entitled if it were a State, but in no event more than the least populous State; they shall be in addition to those appointed by the States, but they shall be considered for the purposes of the election of President and Vice-President, to be electors appointed by a State; and they shall meet in the District and perform such duties as provided by the twelfth article of amendment.

Section 2 The Congress shall have the power to enforce this article by appropriate legislation.

Amendment XXIV

[Adopted 1964]

Section 1 The right of citizens of the United States to vote in any primary or other election for President or Vice-President, for electors for President or Vice-President, or for Senator or Representative in Congress, shall not be denied or abridged by the United States or any State by reason of failure to pay any poll tax or other tax.

Section 2 The Congress shall have the power to enforce this article by appropriate legislation.

Amendment XXV

[Adopted 1967]

Section 1 In case of the removal of the President from office or of his death or resignation, the Vice-President shall become President.

Section 2 Whenever there is a vacancy in the office of the Vice-President, the President shall nominate a Vice-President who shall take office upon confirmation by a majority vote of both Houses of Congress.

Section 3 Whenever the President transmits to the President pro tempore of the Senate and the Speaker of the House of Representatives his written declaration that he is unable to discharge the powers and duties of his office, and until he transmits to them a written declaration to the contrary, such powers and duties shall be discharged by the Vice-President as Acting President.

Section 4 Whenever the Vice-President and a majority of either the principal officers of the executive departments or of such other body as Congress may by law provide, transmit to the President pro tempore of the Senate and the Speaker of the House of Representatives their written declaration that the President is unable to discharge the powers and duties of his office, the Vice-President shall immediately assume the powers and duties of the office as Acting President.

Thereafter, when the President transmits to the President pro tempore of the Senate and the Speaker of the House of Representatives his written declaration that no inability exists, he shall resume the powers and duties of his office unless the Vice-President and a majority of either the principal officers of the executive department[s] or of such other body as Congress may by law provide, transmit within four days to the President pro tempore of the Senate and the Speaker of the House of Representatives their written declaration that the President is unable to discharge the powers and duties of his office. Thereupon Congress shall decide the issue, assembling within forty-eight hours for that purpose if not in session. If the Congress, within twenty-one days after receipt of the latter written declaration, or, if Congress is not in session, within twenty-one days after Congress is required to assemble, determines by two-thirds vote of both Houses that the President is unable to discharge the powers and duties of his office, the Vice-President shall continue to discharge the same as Acting President; otherwise, the President shall resume the powers and duties of his office.

Amendment XXVI

[Adopted 1971]

Section 1 The right of citizens of the United States, who are eighteen years of age or older, to vote shall not be denied or abridged by the United States or by any State on account of age.

Section 2 The Congress shall have power to enforce this article by appropriate legislation.

Amendment XXVII

[Adopted 1992]

No law, varying the compensation for the services of the Senators and Representatives, shall take effect, until an election of Representatives shall have intervened.

Presidential Elections

Year	Number of States	Candidates	Parties	Popular Vote	% of Popular Vote	Electoral Vote	% Voter Participation[a]
1789	11	**George Washington**	No party			69	
		John Adams	designations			34	
		Other candidates				35	
1792	15	**George Washington**	No party			132	
		John Adams	designations			77	
		George Clinton				50	
		Other candidates				5	
1796	16	**John Adams**	Federalist			71	
		Thomas Jefferson	Democratic Republican			68	
		Thomas Pinckney	Federalist			59	
		Aaron Burr	Democratic Republican			30	
		Other candidates				48	
1800	16	**Thomas Jefferson**	Democratic Republican			73	
		Aaron Burr	Democratic Republican			73	
		John Adams	Federalist			65	
		Charles C. Pinckney	Federalist			64	
		John Jay	Federalist			1	
1804	17	**Thomas Jefferson**	Democratic Republican			162	
		Charles C. Pinckney	Federalist			14	
1808	17	**James Madison**	Democratic Republican			122	
		Charles C. Pinckney	Federalist			47	
		George Clinton	Democratic Republican			6	
1812	18	**James Madison**	Democratic Republican			128	
		DeWitt Clinton	Federalist			89	
1816	19	**James Monroe**	Democratic Republican			183	
		Rufus King	Federalist			34	
1820	24	**James Monroe**	Democratic Republican			231	
		John Quincy Adams	Independent Republican			1	

Year	Number of States	Candidates	Parties	Popular Vote	% of Popular Vote	Electoral Vote	% Voter Participation[a]
1824	24	**John Quincy Adams**	Democratic Republican	108,740	30.5	84	26.9
		Andrew Jackson	Democratic Republican	153,544	43.1	99	
		Henry Clay	Democratic Republican	47,136	13.2	37	
		William H. Crawford	Democratic Republican	46,618	13.1	41	
1828	24	**Andrew Jackson**	Democratic Republican	647,286	56.0	178	57.6
		John Quincy Adams	National Republican	508,064	44.0	83	
1832	24	**Andrew Jackson**	Democratic Republican	688,242	54.5	219	55.4
		Henry Clay	National Republican	473,462	37.5	49	
		William Wirt	Anti-Masonic ⎫	101,051	8.0	7	
		John Floyd	Democratic ⎬			11	
1836	26	**Martin Van Buren**	Democratic	765,483	50.9	170	57.8
		William H. Harrison	Whig ⎫			73	
		Hugh L. White	Whig ⎬			26	
		Daniel Webster	Whig ⎬	739,795	49.1	14	
		W. P. Mangum	Whig ⎭			11	
1840	26	**William H. Harrison**	Whig	1,274,624	53.1	234	80.2
		Martin Van Buren	Democratic	1,127,781	46.9	60	
1844	26	**James K. Polk**	Democratic	1,338,464	49.6	170	78.9
		Henry Clay	Whig	1,300,097	48.1	105	
		James G. Birney	Liberty	62,300	2.3		
1848	30	**Zachary Taylor**	Whig	1,360,967	47.4	163	72.7
		Lewis Cass	Democratic	1,222,342	42.5	127	
		Martin Van Buren	Free-Soil	291,263	10.1		
1852	31	**Franklin Pierce**	Democratic	1,601,117	50.9	254	69.6
		Winfield Scott	Whig	1,385,453	44.1	42	
		John P. Hale	Free-Soil	155,825	5		
1856	31	**James Buchanan**	Democratic	1,832,955	45.3	174	78.9
		John C. Frémont	Republican	1,339,932	33.1	114	
		Millard Fillmore	American	871,731	21.6	8	
1860	33	**Abraham Lincoln**	Republican	1,865,593	39.8	180	81.2
		Stephen A. Douglas	Democratic	1,382,713	29.5	12	
		John C. Breckinridge	Democratic	848,356	18.1	72	
		John Bell	Constitutional Union	592,906	12.6	39	
1864	36	**Abraham Lincoln**	Republican	2,206,938	55.0	212	73.8
		George B. McClellan	Democratic	1,803,787	45.0	21	
1868	37	**Ulysses S. Grant**	Republican	3,013,421	52.7	214	78.1
		Horatio Seymour	Democratic	2,706,829	47.3	80	

Year	Number of States	Candidates	Parties	Popular Vote	% of Popular Vote	Electoral Vote	% Voter Participation[a]
1872	37	**Ulysses S. Grant**	Republican	3,596,745	55.6	286[b]	71.3
		Horace Greeley	Democratic	2,843,446	43.9		
1876	38	**Rutherford B. Hayes**	Republican	4,036,572	48.0	185	81.8
		Samuel J. Tilden	Democratic	4,284,020	51.0	184	
1880	38	**James A. Garfield**	Republican	4,453,295	48.5	214	79.4
		Winfield S. Hancock	Democratic	4,414,082	48.1	155	
		James B. Weaver	Greenback-Labor	308,578	3.4		
1884	38	**Grover Cleveland**	Democratic	4,879,507	48.5	219	77.5
		James G. Blaine	Republican	4,850,293	48.2	182	
		Benjamin F. Butler	Greenback-Labor	175,370	1.8		
		John P. St. John	Prohibition	150,369	1.5		
1888	38	**Benjamin Harrison**	Republican	5,477,129	47.9	233	79.3
		Grover Cleveland	Democratic	5,537,857	48.6	168	
		Clinton B. Fisk	Prohibition	249,506	2.2		
		Anson J. Streeter	Union Labor	146,935	1.3		
1892	44	**Grover Cleveland**	Democratic	5,555,426	46.1	277	74.7
		Benjamin Harrison	Republican	5,182,690	43.0	145	
		James B. Weaver	People's	1,029,846	8.5	22	
		John Bidwell	Prohibition	264,133	2.2		
1896	45	**William McKinley**	Republican	7,102,246	51.1	271	79.3
		William J. Bryan	Democratic	6,492,559	47.7	176	
1900	45	**William McKinley**	Republican	7,218,491	51.7	292	73.2
		William J. Bryan	Democratic; Populist	6,356,734	45.5	155	
		John C. Wooley	Prohibition	208,914	1.5		
1904	45	**Theodore Roosevelt**	Republican	7,628,461	57.4	336	65.2
		Alton B. Parker	Democratic	5,084,223	37.6	140	
		Eugene V. Debs	Socialist	402,283	3.0		
		Silas C. Swallow	Prohibition	258,536	1.9		
1908	46	**William H. Taft**	Republican	7,675,320	51.6	321	65.4
		William J. Bryan	Democratic	6,412,294	43.1	162	
		Eugene V. Debs	Socialist	420,793	2.8		
		Eugene W. Chafin	Prohibition	253,840	1.7		
1912	48	**Woodrow Wilson**	Democratic	6,296,547	41.9	435	58.8
		Theodore Roosevelt	Progressive	4,118,571	27.4	88	
		William H. Taft	Republican	3,486,720	23.2	8	
		Eugene V. Debs	Socialist	900,672	6.0		
		Eugene W. Chafin	Prohibition	206,275	1.4		
1916	48	**Woodrow Wilson**	Democratic	9,127,695	49.4	277	61.6
		Charles E. Hughes	Republican	8,533,507	46.2	254	
		A. L. Benson	Socialist	585,113	3.2		
		J. Frank Hanly	Prohibition	220,506	1.2		

Year	Number of States	Candidates	Parties	Popular Vote	% of Popular Vote	Electoral Vote	% Voter Participation[a]
1920	48	**Warren G. Harding**	Republican	16,143,407	60.4	404	49.2
		James M. Cox	Democratic	9,130,328	34.2	127	
		Eugene V. Debs	Socialist	919,799	3.4		
		P. P. Christensen	Farmer-Labor	265,411	1.0		
1924	48	**Calvin Coolidge**	Republican	15,718,211	54.0	382	48.9
		John W. Davis	Democratic	8,385,283	28.8	136	
		Robert M. La Follette	Progressive	4,831,289	16.6	13	
1928	48	**Herbert C. Hoover**	Republican	21,391,993	58.2	444	56.9
		Alfred E. Smith	Democratic	15,016,169	40.9	87	
1932	48	**Franklin D. Roosevelt**	Democratic	22,809,638	57.4	472	56.9
		Herbert C. Hoover	Republican	15,758,901	39.7	59	
		Norman Thomas	Socialist	881,951	2.2		
1936	48	**Franklin D. Roosevelt**	Democratic	27,752,869	60.8	523	61.0
		Alfred M. Landon	Republican	16,674,665	36.5	8	
		William Lemke	Union	882,479	1.9		
1940	48	**Franklin D. Roosevelt**	Democratic	27,307,819	54.8	449	62.5
		Wendell L. Wilkie	Republican	22,321,018	44.8	82	
1944	48	**Franklin D. Roosevelt**	Democratic	25,606,585	53.5	432	55.9
		Thomas E. Dewey	Republican	22,014,745	46.0	99	
1948	48	**Harry S. Truman**	Democratic	24,105,695	49.5	303	53.0
		Thomas E. Dewey	Republican	21,969,170	45.1	189	
		J. Strom Thurmond	States' Rights	1,169,021	2.4	39	
		Henry A. Wallace	Progressive	1,156,103	2.4		
1952	48	**Dwight D. Eisenhower**	Republican	33,936,234	55.1	442	63.3
		Adlai E. Stevenson	Democratic	27,314,992	44.4	89	
1956	48	**Dwight D. Eisenhower**	Republican	35,590,472	57.6	457	60.6
		Adlai E. Stevenson	Democratic	26,022,752	42.1	73	
1960	50	**John F. Kennedy**	Democratic	34,226,731	49.7	303	62.8
		Richard M. Nixon	Republican	34,108,157	49.5	219	
1964	50	**Lyndon B. Johnson**	Democratic	43,129,566	61.1	486	61.7
		Barry M. Goldwater	Republican	27,178,188	38.5	52	
1968	50	**Richard M. Nixon**	Republican	31,710,470	43.4	301	60.6
		Hubert H. Humphrey	Democratic	30,898,055	42.7	191	
		George C. Wallace	American Independent	9,446,167	13.5	46	
1972	50	**Richard M. Nixon**	Republican	47,169,911	60.7	520	55.2
		George S. McGovern	Democratic	29,170,383	37.5	17	
		John G. Schmitz	American	1,099,482	1.4		
1976	50	**Jimmy Carter**	Democratic	40,830,763	50.1	297	53.5
		Gerald R. Ford	Republican	39,147,793	48.0	240	

Year	Number of States	Candidates	Parties	Popular Vote	% of Popular Vote	Electoral Vote	% Voter Participation[a]
1980	50	**Ronald Reagan**	Republican	43,899,248	50.8	489	52.6
		Jimmy Carter	Democratic	35,481,432	41.0	49	
		John B. Anderson	Independent	5,719,437	6.6	0	
		Ed Clark	Libertarian	920,859	1.1	0	
1984	50	**Ronald Reagan**	Republican	54,455,075	58.8	525	53.1
		Walter Mondale	Democratic	37,577,185	40.6	13	
1988	50	**George Bush**	Republican	48,901,046	53.4	426	50.2
		Michael Dukakis	Democratic	41,809,030	45.6	111[c]	
1992	50	**Bill Clinton**	Democratic	44,908,233	43.0	370	55.0
		George Bush	Republican	39,102,282	37.4	168	
		Ross Perot	Independent	19,741,048	18.9	0	
1996	50	**Bill Clinton**	Democratic	47,401,054	49.2	379	49.0
		Robert Dole	Republican	39,197,350	40.7	159	
		Ross Perot	Independent	8,085,285	8.4	0	
		Ralph Nader	Green	684,871	0.7	0	
2000	50	**George W. Bush**	Republican	50,465,169	47.79	271	50.7
		Albert Gore, Jr.	Democratic	50,996,062	49.4	266[d]	
		Ralph Nader	Green	2,529,871	2.40	0	
2004	50	**George W. Bush**	Republican	62,040,610	51	286	60.7
		John F. Kerry	Democratic	59,028,109	48	252	
		Ralph Nader	Independent	463,653	1	0	
2008	50	**Barack Obama**	Democratic	69,498,459	52.9	365	61.7
		John McCain	Republican	59,948,283	45.7	173	

Candidates receiving less than 1 percent of the popular vote have been omitted. Thus the percentage of popular vote given for any election year may not total 100 percent.

Before the passage of the Twelfth Amendment in 1804, the Electoral College voted for two presidential candidates; the runner-up became vice president.

Before 1824, most presidential electors were chosen by state legislatures, not by popular vote.

[a]Percent of voting-age population casting ballots (eligible voters).
[b]Greeley died shortly after the election; the electors supporting him then divided their votes among minor candidates.
[c]One elector from West Virginia cast her Electoral College presidential ballot for Lloyd Bentsen, the Democratic Party's vice-presidential candidate.
[d]One elector from the District of Columbia abstained.

Index

Boldfaced terms indicate glossary terms that are defined on that page or spread.

Agrarian capitalism, 332

Agribusiness, in West, 442–443

Agricultural Adjustment Act (AAA): first, 630; second, 638, 641

Agricultural Adjustment Administration (AAA), 630

Agricultural Marketing Act (1929), 624

Agricultural revolution: in North America, 7–8

Agriculture: Indians and, 13, 43; in Africa, 14; in Dutch colonies, 36; Hamilton vs. Jefferson on, 175; depression in, 214; Civil War and, 367, 414; sharecropping and, 396–397, 397 (illus.); expansion of (1860–1900), 418–419, 418 (map); in New South, 432; rainfall and (1890), 441 (map); labor force in, 474–475; in 1920s, 594–595; in Great Depression, 624, 638; subsidies to, 720. See also Crops; Farms and farming; Farm workers; specific crops

Aguinaldo, Emilio, 518–519, 519 (illus.)

AIDS, See Acquired immune deficiency syndrome

Aid to Families with Dependent Children (AFDC), 806

Aircraft industry: women workers in, 709

Air force, in World War II, 659–661, 679

Airplane: as terrorist weapon, 839

Air pollution: Kyoto Protocol and, 836

Air Quality Act (1965), 758 (table)

Aix-la-Chapelle, Treaty of, 99 (table)

Alabama, 228, 343, 749–750

Alabama (ship), 508

Alamance, Battle at, 89, 90 (illus.)

Alamo, 313, 314

Alamogordo, New Mexico, atomic bomb tests at, 683

Alaska, 5; Russia and, 40; purchase of, 508; Eskimo lands in, 781

Albanians, ethnic, 836

Albany, New York, 36, 37 (illus.), 43, 139

Albany Argus (newspaper), 235, 236

Albany Plan of Union, 98

Albemarle Sound, 72

Albright, Madeleine, 152, 836

Albro, Maxine, 647 (illus.)

Alcatraz Island, Indian seizure of, 780

Alcohol and alcoholism: working class and, 297, 303; temperance movement and, 303, 530; prohibition of, 530, 583–584, 599, 600; in 1920s, 600. See also Prohibition

Alcott, Abigail and Bronson, 277

Alexander II (Russia), 508

Alexander v. Holmes, 789

Algiers, 166

Algonkian-speaking Indians, 3, 43, 57

Algonquin Indians, 42

Alien Act (1798), 188

Alien and Sedition Acts, 189, 192

Alienation, of 1920s intellectuals, 598

Alien Enemies Act (1798), 188

Alien Registration Act (1940), See Smith Act (1940)

Aliens, See Illegal immigrants; Immigrants and immigration

Alimony, 829

Allegories, of Hawthorne, 296

Allen, Ethan, 139

Allen, Richard, 203

Allende, Salvador, 786

Alliance for Progress, 753

Alliances: of Wahunsunacock, 25; among Indians, 42; Washington on, 181; World War I and, 563, 578; U.S. and, 616; Axis powers and, 662; in 1950s, 722. See also Confederacies; Farmers' Alliances; Populists; Treaties; specific alliances

Allies (American Revolution), 134

Allies (World War I), 563, 565 (map), 566; mandates and, 578; Paris Peace Conference and, 578. See also World War I

Allies (World War II): defeat of Germany, 678 (map); after war, 691–694. See also Cold War; World War II

Allotment checks, 671

"Aloha 'Oe" (Lili'uokalani), 512 (illus.)

Alphabet, Cherokee, 256

Al-Qaeda, 667, 840, 840 (map), 841, 843

Alsace-Lorraine, 578, 579 (map)

Alternating current (AC), 429

Alternative fuels, 800

Altgeld, John Peter, 480

Amendments: to Articles of Confederation, 162; as Bill of Rights, 174; Tallmadge, 245; for women's rights, 608; to Constitution, B11–B15. See also specific amendments

Amenities, 193

America(s), 5; Spain and, 18; as New World, 21–22; European empires in, 34–39; Russian frontier in, 40. See also Colonies and colonization; Expansion and expansionism; New World; specific countries and regions

American Academy of Arts and Sciences, 459

American and Foreign Anti-Slavery Society, 326

American Anti-Slavery Society, 304, 325

American Apparel, 428

American Bandstand, 734 (illus.), 735

American Bible Society, 276, 288

American Board of Commissioners for Foreign Missions, 263, 276, 289; manifest destiny and, 311

American Civil Liberties Union (ACLU): Scopes trial and, 602; in New Deal, 633; Korematsu v. United States and, 685

American Colonization Society, 303

American Dream: after World War II, 690

American Expeditionary Force (AEF), 574

American Federation of Labor (AFL), 480–481, 482, 637; unskilled and semiskilled workers and, 532; Congress and, 538; Homestead strike and, 582; in 1920s, 607, 610

American GI Forum, 711

American Indian Defense Association (AIDA), 605

American Indian Movement (AIM), 780

American Indians: origins of, 5–8; Anasazi, 11, 13 (illus.); culture areas of, 11, 12 (map); of Plains, 11; in Southwest, 11, 13, 13 (illus.); in Northeast, 18, 42–43; trade and, 18, 226; Europeans and, 19–20, 30; Columbian Exchange and, 20–21; in Spanish colonies, 29, 36; warfare and, 31; as slaves, 32, 40; settlements of, 35 (map); as serfs, 36; along frontier, 40–42, 45–46, 215, 255; economies in North America, 41 (map); in Southeast, 42; lifestyle before Europeans, 42 (illus.); in Louisiana, 48; Las Casas and, 49; in Jamestown, 57; lands of, 60, 209, 226–227, 471–472; in New England, 65–66, 68; conflicts with settlers, 66; backcountry violence and, 89; confederacies of, 96, 96 (map); wars with colonists, 96; French and Indian War and, 98, 107; Revolution and, 127–128, 138–139, 144, 144 (illus.), 149, 154; under Articles of Confederation, 165–166; in West, 165–166, 432–437; in Northwest, 165 (map), 179, 281; treaties with, 179–180, 255, 434–435, 436; Lewis and Clark expedition and, 197–198, 198 (map); citizenship for, 204, 605; reservations for, 204, 434–435, 435 (map); Prophet, The, and, 215; Tecumseh and, 216 (map); Jackson and, 221, 255–258; after War of 1812, 224; federal Indian policy and, 226–227; Indian agents and, 226–227; in Far West, 278; removal of, 281; in Oregon Country, 281–282; in California, 283; Mormons and, 284–285; Civil War and, 360, 360 (illus.); horses and, 432, 433, 433 (illus.); culture of, 432–433, 471–473;

buffalo and, 433, 435, 436; at Medicine Lodge Creek conference, 434–435; war of attrition against, 435; resistance by, 435–437; at Wounded Knee, 436–437, 437 (illus.); schools for, 471; forced assimilation of, 471–473, 472 (illus.); in World War I, 573 (illus.); in Great Depression, 643, 644; in New Deal, 646–647; in World War II, 671, 674; Navajo code talkers and, 674; in 1950s, 719–720, 720 (illus.); activism by, 780–782. *See also* Indian policy; Reservations; specific battles and treaties; specific groups and leaders

Americanization: in World War I, 570; phase of Vietnam War, 772–773

American Liberty League, 632

American Medical Association: birth control and, 608

American Mercury, The (magazine), 598

American Missionary Association, 405 (illus.)

American Plan, 606

American Prohibitory Act (1775), **124**

American Protective Association (APA), **469,** 506

American Psychiatric Association, homosexuality classified by, 764

American Railway Union (ARU), Debs and, 480–481

American Recovery and Reinvestment Act (2009), **849**

American Revenue Act (1764), *See* Sugar Act (1764)

American Revolution: events leading to, 122–126; loyalists and, 126, 128, 136, 146, 153–154; African Americans in, 126–127, 126 (illus.); Indians and, 127–128, 154; first years of, 134, 135–140; military camps in, 136; in South, 136, 144–146, 146 (illus.); in North, 136–140, 137 (map), 143–144; diplomacy during, 141–143; economy during, 142–143; in Carolinas, 144–146; rights after, 149–150; women after, 150–152; slavery and, 152–153; western land claims after, 162 (map)

"American Scholar, The" (Emerson), 295, 296

American Sugar Refining Company, 431

Americans with Disabilities Act (1990), **815**

American System (Clay), 236–238, **237,** 242, 246, 307, 308

American system of manufacturing, 270–271

American Tobacco Company, 431, 591

American Tract Society, 276, 288; "Moral Threat from Reading Fiction, The," 317

American Woman Suffrage Association (AWSA), **499,** 500

Ames, Adelbert, 408

Ames, Fisher, 192, 199

Amish, 71

Amnesty, 390; in American Revolution, **135;** Andrew Johnson and, 392

Amphibious assault, 679

Anaconda plan, 355, 356 (illus.), 361, 362

Anacosta Flats, Hooverville at, 627

Anarchists, 469, 582; Haymarket bombing and, 480

Anasazi Indians, 11, 13 (illus.)

Ancestors, fictive, 14

Anderson, Marian, 644 (illus.)

Anderson, Robert, 345, 346, 378

Andersonville prison camp, **371**

Andros, Edmund, 67

Anglicans, 91, 149. *See also* Church of England

Anglos: in California, 473; in Southwest, **473;** in New Mexico, 474; in Texas, 474; Mexicans and, 606, 674

Anglo Saxons: glorification of, 469; belief in superiority of, 511

Angola, 88; U.S. covert operations in, 811

Animals: migration of, 5. *See also* specific animals

Annapolis conference, 167

Anne of Austria, 38

Annexation: of New Mexico, **283;** of Texas, 314, 315, 316, 473; by cities, 456; of Hawai'i, 512, 515

Annuities, 217

Antebellum period: in South, **264**–269; immigration during, 272 (map); manifest destiny in, 311. *See also* South; specific issues

Anthony, Susan B., 399, 402, 499

Anthropologists, North American culture and, **11**

Antiballistic missile defense system, 839

Anti-Catholicism, 297 (illus.), 327, 469

Antidiscriminatory sexual preference laws, 831

Antietam Creek, battle of, 359 (map), **363**

Antifederalists, 160, **171**–173, 171 (map). *See also* Republicans

Antifeminists, 830

Anti-immigrant feelings, 297 (illus.), 327

Anti-imperialism, 517–518, 560

Anti-Imperialist League, 521

Anti-lynching laws, 604, 605 (illus.), 645, 703

Antimasonic Party, 248–249, 307–308, 327

Antimonopolism, 502–503

Anti-Saloon League, 530, 538, 584

Anti-Semitism, 469; of Henry Ford, 602; of Father Coughlin, 634; in United States, 659. *See also* Jews and Judaism

Antislavery movement, 153, 304; in states, 153; Kansas-Nebraska Act and, 335. *See also* Abolition; Slaves and slavery

Anti-Slavery Society (Britain), 246

Antitrust legislation, 540, 548

Antiwar movement: in Vietnam War, 773–775, 783

ANZUS treaty, *See* Australian–New Zealand–United States (ANZUS) treaty

Apache Indians, 13, 44, 46

Apartheid (South Africa), 466, 816

Apollo program, 748

Appalachian Mountains: settlement to west of, 195–196. *See also* Proclamation Line (1763)

Appalachian Regional Development Act (1965), 760

"Appeal of the Independent Democrats in Congress, . . . , The," 334

Appeasement, 659, 696

Apple Computer, 808

Appliances, 591, 731

"Application to Be a Missionary" (Elizabeth Yale Hancock), 289

Appomattox Courthouse, Lee's surrender at, 378

Apprentices, 87, 267, 269, 271

Aqueducts, 444; on Erie Canal, **239**

Arab Americans: after September 11 attacks, 839

Arabella (ship), 63

Arabian Peninsula, 4

Arab world: Muslims and, 8; slave trade and, 22 (illus.); partition of Palestine and, 697; nationalism in, 723–725; oil prices and, 788; Camp David Accords and, 802. *See also* Islam; Israel; Middle East; Muslims

Arapaho Indians, 43, 433

Arbenz, Jacobo, 725–726, 726 (illus.)

Arbitration: of British-U.S. Civil War claims, **508;** Venezuela boundary dispute and, 512–513; permanent court of, 545; under Wilson, 561

Architecture: skyscrapers and, 455, 455 (illus.); in New Deal, 650 (illus.)

Ardennes Forest, 679

Argentina, 467

Argus (newspaper), 235, 236

Aridity, 440, 441 (map)

Arikara Indians, 43, 433

Aristide, Jean Bertrand, 835

Aristocracy: of planters, 265, 266. *See also* Classes

Bill of Rights (U.S.), **174,** 399, 400; Antifederalists on, 172, 173

Bingham, George Caleb, 249 (illus.), 255 (illus.), 297

Bin Laden, Osama, 840, 841

Biological weapons, 836, 839

Bipartisanship, 629, 632

Birmingham, 463; iron industry in, 432; civil rights marches in, 751

Birney, James G., 326

Birth control, 275, 499, 608, 765

Birth of a Nation, The (film), 410, 603

Birth rate: in 1920s, 607–608; in 1950s, 710; 1930–2004, 711 (figure)

Bison, *See* Buffalo

Black, Hugo, 640; on *Korematsu v. United States,* 685

"Black Cabinet," of Franklin Roosevelt, **645**

Black codes, 397

Blackfeet Indians, 43, 433

Black Hills, Indians and, 436

Blacklisting: of union workers, **636**

Black market, during Revolution, **142**

Blackmun, Harry, 789

Black Muslims, 761

Black Nationalism, 762

Black Panthers, 761–762

Black Power, 761, 772

Black Reconstruction, 403–406, 408, 411

Black Reconstruction in America (Du Bois), 410

Blacks, *See* African Americans; Free blacks

Black separatism, 599–600, 761

"Black Thursday" (October 24, 1929), 622

"Black Tuesday," 622

Blackwell, Elizabeth, 460

Black women, 150. *See also* Women

Blaine, James G., 492, 493

Blake, George, 177

Bland-Allison Act (1878), **498**

Bleeding Kansas, 336–337

Blitzkrieg, 661 (illus.)

Blockade: by British and French, 212–213; in Civil War, 354, 355 (illus.), 357; in World War I, 566; of Berlin, 695, 696 (illus.)

Blogging: development of, 825; political campaigns and, 844

Blood supply: segregation by race, 673

Bloomingdale's, 430 (illus.)

Blue-collar workers, 731; lifestyle of, **274;** Nixon and, 789. *See also* Working class

B movies, 722

Boas, Franz, 471

Bobby pin, 591

Boer republics (South Africa), 466

Bohemia, immigrants from, **440**

Boland Amendment, 811–812

Bolsheviks (Russia), **576,** 577

Bombs and bombings: Red Scare and, 582; of Pearl Harbor, 654, 656, 663–665, 665 (illus.); of Hiroshima and Nagasaki, 656, 683–684, 683 (illus.); of Dresden, 679; in World War II, 682; of North Vietnam, 783, 784; of abortion clinics, 830; of Serbia, 836; by Al Qaeda, 840. *See also* Hydrogen bomb; Nuclear power

Bomb shelter, *See* Fallout shelter

Bonaparte, Napoleon, *See* Napoleon Bonaparte

Bonds: for War of 1812, **222;** railroad, **424.** *See also* War bonds

Bonus Army, 627

Book of Mormon, 285

Boom-and-bust economy, 445–448

Boone, Pat, 734

Booth, John Wilkes, 379

Bootlegging, 601

Borah, William E., 615, 616

Border Patrol, 810

Border ruffians, 336

Borders: in Revolution, 144; Oregon and, 312, 312 (map), 316; with Canada, 314; with Mexico, 314, 315, 322, 323 (map), 325; southwestern, 334; Texas/New Mexico dispute over, 538; between North and South Korea, 698, 699 (map). *See also* Boundaries

Border states: secession and, 344; Civil War and, 347–348, 360

Bosch, Juan, 772

Bosch loopers, 46–47

Bosnia, fighting in, 835

Bosnia-Herzegovina, 560, 816

Bosnians: Christian and Muslim, 835

Bosses (political), 490

Boston, 455, 456; Sons of Liberty in, 111–112; in Revolution, 135, 136

Boston Manufacturing Company, 225, 275

Boston Massacre, 117, 117 (illus.)

Boston Port Act, *See* Port Act (1774)

Boston Tea Party, 119–120, 119 (illus.)

Boukman, Dutty, 166

Boulder Dam, *See* Hoover Dam

Boundaries: Louisiana Territory/Canada, 241; Oregon and, 312, 312 (map), 316; Texas/Mexico, 314, 315, 322, 323 (map), 325; Venezuela/British Guiana dispute, 512–513; Europe and Middle East after World War I, 578, 579 (map). *See also* Borders; Frontier

Bourke-White, Margaret, 648, 649 (illus.)

Bouweries (Dutch farms), 46

Bow, Clara, 589–590, 589 (illus.), 596 (illus.), 597

"Bowery B'hoys" and "G'hals," 297

Boxcars, 447

Boxer Rebellion, 520

Boxing, 297, 597

Boycotts, 114; of English goods, 115, 121; labor, 482; in Montgomery, Alabama, 738–739; of grape growers, 779; of 1980 Olympics, 801

Boynton v. Virginia, 749

Bozeman Trail, 434

BP: deep-water drilling rig explosion and oil spill, 851–852

Braceros, **674**

Bracket creep, 805

Braddock, Edward, 97 (illus.), 98

Bradford, Dorothy, 62

Bradford, William, 62, 62 (illus.), 63

Brady, Mathew, 371 (illus.)

Brady Bill, 833

Brady Handgun Violence Prevention Act, 832

Bragg, Braxton, 373

Brain Trust, 629

Branches of government, 160–161, 168, 252

Brandeis, Louis, 528, **547,** 548, 549

Branding, 439

Brannan Plan, 704

Brant, Joseph, *See* Thayendanegea

Brazil: Indians from, 19 (illus.)

Breaux, John, 839

Breckinridge, John C., 336, 340, 341, 341 (illus.), 342

Breed's Hill, 135

Br'er Rabbit stories, 306

Brest-Litovsk: Treaty of, 564 (map), 576, 577

Brezhnev, Leonid, 786

Brezhnev Doctrine, 765

Briand, Aristide, 616

Bribery: by railroads, 406, 422; machine politics and, 490

Bridges, 456

Brigade, 354

Brinkmanship, 721

Bristow, Benjamin, 491, 492

Britain, *See* England (Britain)

British Empire: American colonies in 18th century, 78–102; after French and Indian War, 98–100; slavery in, 246. *See also* England (Britain)

British Guiana: boundary dispute with Venezuela, 512–513

Britton, Nan, 609

Broad constructionist, 176–177

Broadside (firing of guns), **213**

Broadside (public notice), **111**

Brodsky, Isaac, 576 (illus.)

Brook Farm, 299

Brookings Institution, 623

Brooklyn, 137
Brooklyn Dodgers: integration of, 689–690
Brooks, David, 845
Brooks, Preston, 336
Browder, Earl, 706
Brown, H. Rap, 761
Brown, Helen Gurley, 766
Brown, John, 336, 339–340, 339 (illus.)
Brown, Rita Mae, 764
Brownell, Herbert, 740
Brown Power, 761, 772, 779
Brown University, 92
Brown v. Board of Education, *Topeka,*
Kansas, **736,** 738
Bruce, Blanche K., 387–388, 387 (illus.),
389, 393, 403 (illus.); Black
Reconstruction and, 411
Bryan, William Jennings, 505; 1896
election and, 505–507, 505 (illus.),
507 (map); anti-imperialism of, 517;
1900 election and, 518; Philippines
and, 518; 1912 election and, 540; as
secretary of state, 548, 560–561; World
War I and, 563; Scopes trial and, 602
Brzezinski, Zbigniew, 801, 802
Buchanan, James, 341 (illus.), 346; 1852
election and, **333;** 1856 election and,
336–337; secession and, 345
Buchanan, Pat, 787, 819, 831
Buchenwald, 659, 673, 681
Buckley, William F., 756
Bucktail faction, **235,** 236, 248
Budget: under Articles of Confederation,
162; Jefferson and, 195; surplus and,
494–495, 494 (figure), 507, 510, 834
(illus.); military, 698; Eisenhower and,
719; Nixon and, 788; Clinton and,
826, 830, 833–834. *See also* Economy;
Federal deficit
Buena Vista, Battle of, 324 (illus.), **325**
Buffalo, 43; Plains Indians and, 43, 44,
433; hunting of, 44 (illus.), 434
(illus.), 435, 436
Buffon, Count de, 90
Bulganin, Nikolai, 727
Bulgaria, 579 (map), 679
Bulge, Battle of, *See* Bastogne, battle at
Bullish attitude, **594**
Bull Moose Party, 546
Bull Run: First Battle of, **358,** 358 (table),
359 (map); **Second Battle of, 363**
Bumppo, Natty (character), 296
Bunau-Varilla, Philippe, 542
Bunche, Ralph, 697
Bunker Hill, Battle of, 127 (illus.), **135**
Bunyan, John, 533
Bureaucracy: Spanish colonial, 36; under
Jackson, 251–252; in railroads, 420
Bureaucrats: colonial, **93–94**

Bureau of Indian Affairs, 781
Bureau of Labor Statistics, 476
Burger, Warren: and Burger Court, 789
Burghers, 37
Burgoyne, John ("Gentleman Johnny"),
137 (map) **138,** 139, 141
Burke-Wadsworth Act (1940), **662**
Burlington and Missouri Railroad, 468
(illus.)
Burma, 723, 727
Burnside, Ambrose E., 363, 372
Burr, Aaron, 186–187; Hamilton and,
164 (illus.), 211; 1796 election and,
186–187; 1800 election and, 191
(map); treason and, 211
Bus boycott: in Montgomery, Alabama,
738–739
Bush, George H. W., 798, 814–818; 1988
election and, 798, 811, 815; 1992
election and, 798, 815, 819–820, 820
(map); foreign policy of, 815–818
Bush, George W., 835, 836; 2000 election
and, 826, 837–838, 838 (map);
September 11, 2001, attacks and, 826,
839; Supreme Court and, 832; foreign
policy of, 838–839; war against
terrorism and, 840; Iraq and,
841–842, 843, 845; 2004 election and,
843–844; Hurricane Katrina and,
844–845; second term of, 844–846;
Great Recession and, 847
Bush Doctrine, 841
Bushmen, 14 (illus.)
Business: in 1920s, 609; politics of,
610–611; government and, 729; in
1990s, 827. *See also* Big business;
Economy; Panics (financial)
Business administration, 420
Busing, 789, 832–833
Butcher, Solomon, 442 (illus.)
Butler, Andrew, 336
Butler, Benjamin F., 367
Butler, Elizur, 256, 257
Butler, William, 326
***Butoku-kai,* 655**
Butte, Montana: gold in, 440
Byrd, William, slaves of, 85
Byrnes, James F., 669

Cabeza da Vaca, Álvar Núñez de, 32
Cabildo secular, 35–36
Cabinet (presidential), **174;** of
Washington, 174; of Monroe, 241;
Jackson's Kitchen Cabinet, 252; of
Tyler, 314, 315; of Lincoln, 345; of
Jefferson Davis, 346; of Grant, 491;
Roosevelt's Black Cabinet, 645; of
Lyndon Johnson, 758; by
administration, B23–B33

Cabot, John (Giovanni Caboto), 18
Caddoan languages, 11, **43,** 433
Caldwell, Erskine, 648
Calhoun, John C., 218, **237,** 315; War of
1812 and, 218; as secretary of war, 241;
economy and, 244; and tariffs, 247;
nullification and, 253–254; Clay and,
307; Jackson and, 308, 308 (illus.)
California: Indians in, 13, 283; Russian
exploration of, 40; gold in, 279, 328,
417; mission system in, 282–283, 283
(illus.); Mexico and, 283; Mexican
War and, 322, 324, 325; Bear Flag
Republic in, 324; slavery and, 328;
agribusiness in, 442, 443; growth of,
596–597; race riots in, 605; Mexican
Americans in, 605–606; in World War
II, 668; tract homes in, 708; farm
workers in, 779, 779 (illus.). *See also*
specific cities
California Agricultural Labor Relations
Act (1975), 771
Californios, 283, 473
Calles, Plutarco, 614, 614 (illus.)
Calley, William, 784
Calls for Reconciliation (Inglis), 129
Calvert family (Lords Baltimore):
George, 59 (illus.), 60; Cecilius, 60;
Benedict (fourth Lord Baltimore), 61
Cambodia, 727; Vietnam War and, 773,
783; immigrants from, 809, 821
Camden, battle at, 146
Camel, 14–15, 15 (illus.)
Cameron, Simon, 345, 347, 358–359
Campaigns (political), *See* Election(s);
Political campaigns
Campbell, John, 398 (illus.)
Camp David Accords, 802
Campo, Antonio, 710–711
Canada, 508; exploration of, 18; French,
38–39, 107–108, 120; colonies and, 96;
Catholicism in, 97, 108; British in, 98,
107; Iroquois relocation to, 144
(illus.); former slaves in, 153; loyalists
in, 153, 154; Indians and, 179, 215;
War of 1812 and, 219, 219 (map),
222–223, 223 (illus.), 224; borders
with, 241, 314; runaway slaves to, 329;
immigrants from, 467, 603; in World
War II, 679; Afghanistan and, 840
Canals, 237, 238–239, 285. *See also* Erie
Canal; Panama Canal; Suez Canal
Canary Islands, 15
Cane (Toomer), 598–599
Cane Ridge, Kentucky, 201–202
Cannon, Joseph, 541
Canvass, 170
Cape Cod, 62
Cape of Good Hope, 17

Spanish American War in, 515, 515 (illus.); U.S. intervention in, 517, 518, 612; Castro in, 726, 772; Soviets and, 746; communism in, 817

Cuba libre, 513

Cuban missile crisis, 753–**754,** 754 (illus.)

Cuffe, Paul, 203

Cult of domesticity, 277

Cultural war: Pat Buchanan on, 819

Culture(s): Indian, 8, 42, 432–433, 471–473; regional differences in, 82–88; of slaves, 84–85, 298–299; urban in Middle Colonies, 85–87; of immigrants, 273, 469; female, 293–294; genteel, 294–297; of workers, 297–298; consumer, 459; as evolutionary process, 471; in Southwest, 474; in early 1900s, 549–553; homogenized, 597; in Great Depression, 647–649; suburban, 731–732; of money, 808. *See also* Society; specific cultures

Culture areas: of American Indians, 11, 12 (map)

Culture wars: in 1990s, 830, 834; gay marriage and, 844

Cumberland Gap, 285

Cumberland River region: Civil War in, 361

Cumberland Road, 238, 239, 244, 285

Cummins, Albert B., 536

Cunard, Samuel, 285

Currency: "In God We Trust" on, 732. *See also* Bank of the United States; Federal Reserve System; Money

Currency Act, 110

Curriculum: public education and, 303; high school, 459; in universities, 459

Currier, Nathaniel, 329 (illus.)

Currier and Ives cartoon, 329 (illus.)

Custer, George A., 436

Customs: smuggling and, 110, 118. *See also* Taxation

Customs receivership, Nicaragua and, **543**

Cuyahoga River, 457

Czechoslovakia, 679; Nazi Germany and, 658 (illus.), 659, 661; coup in, 695; Prague Spring in, 765; democratic government in, 815; after Soviet Union, 816 (map)

Czolgosz, Leon, 469

Dachau, 659, 673, 681

Dakota: homesteads in, 440

Dakota, farming businesses in, 442–443

Dakota (Lakota) Indians, 43–44, 226

Dallas, Alexander, 178

Dallas, George M., 316 (illus.)

Dams: on Erie Canal, 239; in West, 636. *See also* Tennessee Valley Authority; specific dams

Dardanelles, 694

Darfur: Afro-Arab militias and killings in, 840 (map)

Dark horse, 246

Darrow, Clarence, 602

Dartmouth, 92

***Dartmouth College v. Woodward,* 240**

Darwin, Charles, 426

Daugherty, Harry, 584

Daughters of Bilitis, 735

Daughters of Liberty, 116

Daughters of the American Revolution: Marian Anderson and, 644

Davis, Alexander, 408

Davis, Benjamin O., Jr., 673, 674

Davis, Jefferson, 322, 344–345; as Secretary of War, **334;** as president of Confederacy, 345, 346, 357, 377; Civil War and, 346, 354, 358, 376, 380. *See also* Civil War (U.S.)

Davis, John W., 610, 610 (map)

Dawes, Charles G., 614–615

Dawes Plan, 615

Dawes Severalty Act (1887), **471**–472, 494

Daylight saving time, 568

Dayton Agreement, 835

D-Day, 679

DDT: banning of, 787

Dean, John, 791

Dearborn, Henry, 219

Death, *See* Mortality rates

Death squads: in El Salvador, 811

Debs, Eugene V., 480–481; Pullman strike and, 532; 1912 election and, 547; Sedition Act and, 571

Debt: after Revolution, 175, 176; national, 243, 670 (figure), 806; of farmers, 280, 396, 496

Debtors: in Georgia, 73–74

Decatur, Stephen, 196 (illus.), 220, 241, 242

Declaration of Independence (U.S.), 105, **125,** 126, 149; document, B1–B2

"Declaration of Indian Purpose," 780

Declaration of Principles, 499

Declaration of Rights (Virginia), 149

Declaration of Rights and Grievances, 121

Declaration of Sentiments, 305

"Declaration of the Causes and Necessity of Taking Up Arms," 124

"Declaration of the People, The" (Bacon), 75

Declaratory Act, 114

Deep South: 1860 election and, **341;** civil rights movement in, 749. *See also* Civil War (U.S.); South

"Deep Throat": in Watergate scandal, 790

Deere, John, 331

Deerfield, Massachusetts: raids on, 96

De facto segregation, **736,** 761

Defense industries: in World War II, 668, 669; decline in, 808

Defense of Marriage Act (1996), **844**

Defense spending, *See* Military spending

Deference, 94

Deficit, *See* Federal deficit

Deflation, 497–498

De Grasse, François-Joseph-Paul (Comte), 147, 148

Deism, 90, 201

De jure segregation, **736,** 760

DeKalb County, Georgia, case, 832–833

Delaware (state), 70, 173; in Civil War, 347

Delaware Indians, 43, 107, 154, 165, 180 (illus.)

Delaware River region, 43, 68, 70, 138

***Delgado v. Bastrop School District,* 711**

Delusions, 107

Demand, *See* Supply and demand

Demilitarization, 241

Demilitarized zone (DMZ), **722;** after World War I, 579 (map); in Korea, 722; in Vietnam, 776, 776 (illus.)

Demobilization, after World War I, 581

Democracy: in New Netherland, 37; in republic, 160–161; in Eastern Europe, 815

Democratic National Convention, in 1968, 777

Democratic Party, 249; 1826 elections and, 249; 1828 election and, 250, 250 (map); 1836 election and, 309; 1840 election and, 310–311, 310 (illus.), 311 (map); Young America Movement in, 333; 1860 election and, 340–342, 342 (map); in South, 403–405, 406–407, 466, 502, 507; New Departure strategy and, 406–407; 1876 election and, 408–409, 409 (map); after Civil War, 490–491; ethnicity, race, religion, and, 490–491; donkey as symbol of, 491 (illus.); 1892 election and, 503–504, 504 (map); divisions in, 504–505; Populists and, 506; Bryan and, 506–507; in 1924, 609, 609 (illus.); 1932 election and, 628; in Great Depression, 646; after World War II, 702–703; in 1972, 789–790; 2000 election and, 826, 837–838, 838 (map). *See also* Election(s); specific candidates and presidents

Democratic People's Republic of Korea, *See* North Korea

Democratic-Republicans, *See* Democratic Party

Democratic-Republican societies, 178, 179

Equality: before law, 410. *See also* Civil rights; Race and racism; specific rights and groups

Equal Pay Act (1963), **763**

Equal protection clause (Fourteenth Amendment), 465, 466

Equal rights: Reconstruction governments and, 405–406. *See also* Civil rights movement; specific rights

Equal Rights Amendment (ERA), **608;** in 1920s, 608; in 1960s–1970s, 763, **799**

Era of Good Feelings, 236, 241 (illus.), 244, 245–246

Erie, Lake, 221

Erie Canal, 239, 285

Erie Indians, 43

Erlichman, John, 782

Ervin, Sam, Jr., 790, 791

Escalation, 772

Escobedo v. Illinois, **756**

Eskimos: Alaskan lands of, 781

Espionage Act (1917), **571**

Esquire, 150

Essay Concerning Human Understanding (Locke), 90

Essex Junto, 210, 211, 236

Established church, 91

Estonia, 815–816

Ethiopia: Italian invasion of, 656, 658; U.S. covert operations in, 811

"Ethiopian Regiment": in Revolution, 127

Ethnic Albanians, 836

Ethnic cleansing, 836; in former Yugoslavia, 816

Ethnic groups, 469; of immigrants, 466–469, 467 (figure), 470–471; in 1920s, 602. *See also* Minorities; specific groups

Ethnic separatism: in former Yugoslavia, 816

Ethnology, 577

Eugenics, 603

Euler, Leonhard, 91

Euphrates River region, 842, 842 (map)

Europe: global contacts of, 8–9; Africa and, 15–17; Indians and, 18, 19–20, 19 (illus.); Columbian Exchange and, 20–21, 22; new world and, 22–24; slave trade and, 22 (illus.); warfare and, 31; American empires of, 34–39, 35 (map), 95–100, 95 (map); religious conflicts in, 60; civilization in Middle and North Atlantic colonies, 69 (map); immigrants from, 467–469; World War I in, 560, 562–563, 564 (map); economy in 1920s, 623–624; World War II and, 661–662, 675, 677–681; Cold War in, 693 (map);

postwar division of, 693 (map), 694–697. *See also* Empire(s); specific countries

Europe, James Reese, 575 (illus.)

European Union (EU), 824

Evangelicalism, 201–202, 300, 335; Whigs and, 308, 326; slavery and, 325; Know-Nothings and, 327; televangelists and, 804

Everett, Edward, 340

"Evil empire," Soviet Union as, 811

Evolution, 602, 603

Excise taxes, **178**

Executive branch, 168, 194; departments of, 173–174

Executive Order #9066, 666

Executive powers, 169

Exile's Return (Cowley), 598

Expansion (economic), **445**

Expansion and expansionism (territorial): Jefferson and, 195–198, 198 (map); William Henry Harrison and, 209, 314; under Monroe, 242; of railroads, 286 (map), 330–331, 330 (illus.), 420, 421 (map); to West, 311–312; manifest destiny and, 311–316, 322; Tyler and, 314–315; of Russia, 315; 1844 election and, 315–316; sectionalism and, 322–329; under Pierce, 334; American, 518–519; Japanese, 656, 664 (map); German and Italian (1933–1942), 660 (map). *See also* West; Westward movement

Expatriate intellectuals, in 1920s, **598**

Exploration: Portuguese, 15–16; European, 17, 18, 31–39; by Columbus, 18; of North America, 18; Spanish, 31–32; English, 32–34; French, 39; Russian, 40. *See also* specific explorers

Exports: under Jefferson, 211; agricultural, 213, 419; of cotton, 228; in 1920s, 614; in Great Depression, 623

Expositions, 552–553

Extermination camps: German, 660 (map)

External taxation, 111

Extinction: of animals, 6–7

Extractive industry, 278

Factionalism, 187

Factions, 175, 248. *See also* Political parties; specific groups

Factories, 417, 423; textile industry and, 230, 270, 270 (illus.); workers in, 263, 274, 303; in antebellum period, 269; company towns and, 271. *See also* Manufacturing

Factory system, 277

Fair Deal, 702

Fair Employment Practices Commission (FEPC), **673,** 701, 758

Fair Employment Practices Committee (FEPC), **755**

Fair Labor Standards Act (1938), 621, **641,** 645

Fait accompli, 173

Fall, Albert, 605, 609

Fallen Timbers, Battle of, 180, 180 (illus.), 209

Fallout shelter, 722

Falwell, Jerry, 804, 804 (illus.)

Families: in Africa, 14; in Massachusetts, 63; slave, 85, 265, 269, 298–299; in putting-out system, 270; in company towns, 271; of blue-collar workers, 274; middle class, 275, 458–459; pioneer, 280, 281; Mormon, 284 (illus.); in Civil War, 367; of freed people, 394; on Great Plains, 441, 442 (illus.); farm, 442; working class, 462; Indian, 472–473, 472 (illus.); in 1920s, 607–608; in Great Depression, 642–643; in World War II, 671; suburban culture and, 731–732; "togetherness" of, 731 (illus.), 733; abortion rights and, 800; in 1990s, 828–829, 830. *See also* Baby boom; Women

Family and Medical Leave Act, 830, 831

Family Assistance Plan, 787

Family values, 844

Famine, immigration and, **467**

Far East: water route to, 36

Farewell Address (Washington), 180–181

Farm Bloc, 609, 611

Farm Board, 624

Farm equipment industry, 419

Farmer, James, 673, 749, 750

Farmers' Alliances, 502

Farmers' Holiday Association, 626

Farms and farming: subsistence, 45; in Dutch settlements, 46; yeomen farmers and, 71; in New England, 81; Regulator movements and, 89, 90 (illus.); Shays's Rebellion and, 166–167; tariffs and, 244; in South, 266; in West, 280, 440–443; technology for, 331, 332 (illus.); sharecropping and, 396–397, 397 (illus.); after Civil War, 416, 496–497; increased output and, 419, 496; agribusiness and, 422–423; Indians and, 433, 471; railroads and, 440, 496; on Great Plains, 440–443; irrigation for, 441 (map), 442; methods of, 442; seasonal labor for, 443; mechanization of, 454, 475; by immigrants, 468; Grange and, 497,

Imperial wars, 95–100, 99 (table). *See also* Empire(s)

Implied power, 176

Import(s): protective tariffs and, 417, 507; in 1920s, 614. *See also* Taxation

Import duties, 110

Impressionism, 550

Impressment, 212, 212 (illus.)

Inauguration: of Washington, 173; of Jefferson, 192; of Obama, 949

Inchon, 698

Income: of farmers, 504–505; of Ford workers, 592; in Great Depression, 623; distribution of, 670; after World War II, 708 (map); of poor people, 735–736; educational level and, 809; in 1990s, 815; decline in, 828. *See also* Wages

Income gap: in 1990s, 828

Income tax, 505, 669, 670; graduated, 498

In Defense of the Indians: . . . (Las Casas), 49

Indemnity, after Boxer Rebellion, **520**

Indentured servants, 61, 83; in Lower South, 72. *See also* Slaves and slavery

Independence: movement toward, 104, 122–123; recognition of, 134, 140; diplomatic, 148–149; of Latin American colonies, 243; for Philippines, 518–519; in Eastern Europe, 815–816

Independent internationalism, 616

India: customer service centers in, 807 (illus.); immigrants from, 809; terrorism in, 840 (map)

Indiana, 164

Indian agents, 226–227

Indian Civil Rights Act (1968), 780

Indian New Deal, 646–647

Indian Ocean region, 17

Indian policy, 204; colonial, 89; of Harrison, 231; Tecumseh on, 231; of Jackson, 255–258, 256 (map); removal policy, 281; reservation, 434–435, 435 (map); Dawes Act, 471–472; forced assimilation as, 471–473; in 1920s, 605

Indian Removal Act (1830), **255,** 256 (map)

Indian Reorganization Act (1934), **646**

Indians, *See* American Indians

Indian Self-Determination and Education Assistance Act (1974), **781**

Indian Springs, Treaty of, 255

Indian Territory, 258, 334, 436, 439; Civil War and, 360, 360 (illus.)

Indict, 790

Indigenous peoples, 5–8; Hawaiians as, **510, 512.** *See also* American Indians

Indigo, 79, 80

Indirect taxation, 114–115

Individualism: transcendentalism and, 295

Indochina: U.S. aid to, **701;** "war of national liberation" in, 726–727. *See also* Cambodia; Laos; Vietnam

In Dubious Battle (Steinbeck), 648

Industrial accidents, 476

Industrial economy: expansion of, 416, 426–432; railroad expansion and, 421 (map)

Industrialization: workers and, 331, 417; resources, skills, capital, and, 416–418; interchangeable parts and, 417; steel and, 425–426. *See also* Factories; Industrial economy; Manufacturing

Industrial union, Debs and, **482**

Industrial Workers of the World (IWW, Wobblies), 532, 533 (illus.), 571

Industry, 416; mechanization of, 269–271, 270 (illus.), 273 (illus.); extractive, 278; in North, 329–330; in Civil War, 357, 366, 367; in Chicago, 423; consumer-goods, 431; in New South, 464; immigrant labor for, 468, 475; work force in, 474 (figure), 475–476; in Great Depression, 623; World War II and, 671; women in, 671–672; in Cold War, 698. *See also* Labor; Manufacturing; specific industries

Inequities, 176

Infant depravity, 277

Infant mortality: in Chesapeake, 61

Inflation, 34; in Revolution, 143; during Civil War, 365, 367, 380; Populist Party and, 503; after World War I, 581–582; after World War II, 701; Nixon and, 788; Carter and, 800; George H. W. Bush and, 815; Clinton and, 827

Influence of Sea Power upon History, The (Mahan), 510

Influence peddling, 248

Influenza epidemic (1918), **575**

Information: Twitter and, 825–826

Information technology: revolution in, 288; growth of, **827**

Infrastructure: urban, **456**

Ingalls, John J., 503

Inglis, Charles, 105, 105 (illus.), 106; "Calls for Reconciliation," 129

Inheritance: of slavery, 83

Initiative, 537

Injunction, against Pullman strikers, **482**

Injuries, workplace, 476

Inner light: of Quakers, 70

Inouye, Daniel Ken, 668

Insane asylums, 302

Installment plans, 243, 592, 623

Insular Cases, 518

Insull, Samuel, 594

Insurance: health, 828. *See also* Medicare

Insurgents: in Cuba, **513;** in Iraq, 842 (map)

Insurrection: slave, **127**

Integration: of schools, 389, 405, 736–737; of baseball teams, 689–690; of military, 703; of California schools, 712 (illus.); *Brown* decision and, 736, 738; Nixon and, 789. *See also* Desegregation

Intellectual thought: in colonies, 90–91; Romanticism and, 294–297; Social Darwinism and, 426; alienated intellectuals and, 598; in 1920s, 598–600

Interchangeable parts, 270–271, 329–330, **417**

Intercontinental ballistic missiles (ICBMs), 727, **752,** 786

Intercultural relations, in Southwest, 284

Interest groups, 526, 527, 537, 538

Interest rates, 798, 827; stock market and, 623

Interlocking directorates, 548

Intermarriage: Indian-European, 42, 46; Indian trading partnerships and, 226; interracial, 464

Intermediate Nuclear Force Treaty, 814

Intermediate-range ballistic missiles, 727

Intermountain Plateau: Indians of, 13

Internal improvements, 278; Jackson on, 254

Internal taxes, 195

International affairs, *See* Diplomacy; Foreign policy; International relations

International cooperation, 615–616

Internationalism: independent, 616; Eisenhower and, 725. *See also* Globalization

International Ladies' Garment Workers' Union, 607

International Monetary Fund, 691, **835**

International relations: Monroe Doctrine and, 242. *See also* Foreign policy

International Telephone and Telegraph, 729

International War Crimes Tribunal, 836

Internet, 825, 827; political campaigns on, 844

Internment camps, for Japanese Americans, 655–656, **666–668,** 667 (illus.)

Interposition, 189

Interstate commerce: federal role in, 240

Interstate Commerce Act (1887), 494

Interstate Commerce Commission (ICC), **494;** railroad rates and, 539

and, 153; after Revolution, 153–154; Indians as, 154
Loyalty affidavits, 702
Loyalty oaths: for Confederates, 379
Loyalty program: of Truman, 705
LSD, 765, 766
Lublin government, 679, 680
Lucas, Eliza, *See* Pinckney, Eliza Lucas
Luddites, 305
Ludwig, Mary, 150, 152
Luftwaffe, 662
Lumber mills, 443; in Pacific Northwest, 433 (map), 443–444
Lunch counter sit-ins, 749, 749 (illus.)
Lusitania (ship), **565,** 565 (map)
Lynch family, 72 (illus.)
Lynchings: of African Americans, 466, 531–532, 532 (illus.), 571; after World War I, 583; attacks on, 673
Lyon, Phyllis, 735

MacArthur, Douglas: Bonus Marchers and, 627; in World War II, **676,** 682; Korean War and, 700
Macdonough, Thomas, 223
Macedonia, 816
Macedonian (ship), 220 (illus.)
Machine politics, 308, 490
Machinery: in textile factories, 273 (illus.); farm, 419; for mining, 440. *See also* Factories; Mechanization
Macon's Bill No. 2, 216
Macy's, R. H. (store), 430
Maddox (ship), 773
Maddox, Lester, 756 (illus.)
Madero, Francisco, 561
Madison, James, 168; at constitutional convention, 169 (illus.), 181; *Federalist Papers* and, 172; tariffs and, 174; Hamilton's economic plan and, 175–176; national bank and, 176; national capital and, 176; 1808 election and, 214; 1812 election and, 220; War of 1812 and, 220, 221, 236; domestic policy of, 237; transportation bill and, 238
Madoff, Bernard, 847
Magazines, 430
Maggie: A Girl of the Streets (Crane), 550
Magnetic compass, 17
Mahan, Alfred Thayer, 510, 545
Mahone, William, 406 (illus.), 407
Mail-order sales, 423, 430
Maine, 56, 65; as free state, 245
Maine (ship), 511 (illus.), **514,** 514 (illus.)
Mainland colonies (English), 52–74, 73 (map), 92–94; government and politics in, 92–94. *See also* England (Britain); specific colonies

Maize, 7
Malaria, 787
Malay Peninsula, 727
Malaysia, 664
Malcolm X, 761
Malenkov, Georgii, 727
Male suffrage, *See* Suffrage; Voting and voting rights
Mali: manuscripts from, 17 (illus.)
al-Maliki, Nouri, 845
Mallory, Stephen, 357
Malnutrition: of slave children, 269
Malta: Gorbachev-Bush meeting on, 815
Malthus, Thomas, 87
Management: professionalization of, 431
Manassas, battle at, *See* Bull Run
Manchuria: Russo-Japanese War over, **543,** 544, 546; Japanese annexation of, 656
Mandan Indians, 11, 197, 433
Mandates, after World War I, **578**
Mandela, Nelson, 816
Mangum, W. P., 1836 election and, 309
Manhates Indians, 36
Manhattan: Dutch in, 36; in Revolution, 138, 147
Manhattan Project, 668, 683
Manifest destiny, 311–316, 322, 325
Manifesto, 194
"Manifesto Concerning the Troubles in Virginia, 1676" (Bacon), 75
"Manifesto of the People, The" (Bacon), 53
Manila Bay, Spanish-American War and, 515
Manioc, 21
Manliness, 460; Frank Roney on, 453, 483
Mann, Horace, 303
Mann, Thomas: Latin America and, 772
Mann Doctrine, 772
Man Nobody Knows, The (Barton), 593
Mansfield, Arabella, 460
Manufacturing: Hamilton on, 174–175; in textile industry, 225; in Northeast, 269–271; American System of, 270–271; immigrants in, 271–272; during Civil War, 366; urban growth and, 414, 455; skills and problem solving in, 417; vertical integration and, 425–426; decline in, 446 (figure), 447; mergers in, 448 (figure); in 1920s, 590; mass production and, 592; in Los Angeles, 596; Mexican workers in, 606; shift to service economy, 807; in postindustrial economy, 808. *See also* Factories
Manufacturing associations, 305
Manufacturing belt, 468

Manumission, 153. *See also* Emancipation
Manzanar internment camp, 667
Mao Zedong, 697, 786, 786 (illus.)
Maps: Powhatan's Mantle and, 25, 25 (illus.); of Louisiana Purchase, 197–198, 198 (m), 199 (illus.)
Marbury v. Madison, **194**–195
March on Washington: of 1894, 505; of 1948, 703; of 1963, **751**
March to the Sea, by Sherman, **377,** 377 (map)
Marcy, William, 489
Mariana Islands, 676, 682
Marina (Doña), 32
Marines: in Hawai'i, 512; in Beirut, 812. *See also* Armed forces; Intervention; Military
Marion, Francis ("Swamp Fox"), **146**
Market(s): loss of, 214; national debt and, 243; free, 244; for grain, 331. *See also* Stock market entries
Market economy, 180, 237
Marne River region, battles at, 574
Marr, Fort, 257 (illus.)
Marriage: Indian-European, 46; in Chesapeake, 61; in New England, 64; in planters society, 265; in middle class, 275; working-class, 298; Oneida Community and, 300 (illus.); same-sex, 462, 831, 844; after World War II, 710; counterculture and, 766
Married women: in work force, 608, 733–734
Marshall, George, 694
Marshall, John, 187, **191,** 192 (illus.), 211, 239, 257
Marshall, Thurgood, 736, 749, 758
Marshall Field (store), 430
Marshall Islands, 676
Marshall Plan, 694
Martial law: in Civil War, **347;** in South Carolina, 402
Martin, Del, 735
Martinique, 100
Marx, Groucho, 641
Marx Brothers, 648
Marxists: in Chile, 786. *See also* Communists and communism
Mary I (England), 24
Mary II (England), *See* William and Mary (England)
Maryland, 57 (map), 83; Catholics in, 60, 91; religion in, 60; government of, 60–61; free blacks in, 153; voting rights in, 160; constitution of, 161; Articles of Confederation and, 163; Civil War and, 347–348, 354, 363, 372
Masculinity: in Gilded Age, 460–461
Mason, George, 149, 169, 170

Mason, James Murray, 358
Mason-Dixon Line, 304
Masons, 248, 276, **460**
Massachusetts: religious conflicts in, 60, 64; government of, 64–65, 161; Maine and, 65; Puritan departures from, 65; witchcraft trials in, 67–68, 68 (illus.); revivalism in, 91–92; resistance to taxation in, 111–112, 115–116; battles in (1775), 122 (map); free education in, 152; antislavery campaign in, 153; Shays's Rebellion and, 166–167; ratification of Constitution in, 173; same-sex marriage and, 844. *See also* Boston; Massachusetts Bay Colony; Plymouth colony
Massachusetts Bay Colony, 63–64, 67
Massachusetts Government Act (1774), 120
Massacres, *See* specific massacres
Massasoit, 63
Mass entertainment, 551–552
Massive retaliation policy, **721**
Mass literacy, spread of, 295, 317
Mass production, 592; of clocks, 271
Matamoros, battle at, 323
Materialism, 115
Mathematics: Islamic, 91; teaching of, 720
Matisse, Henri, 550
Matrilineal society: Indian, 11
Matrilocal society: Indian, 11
Mattachine Society, 735
Mattoponi Indians, 57
Mawkish, 293
Maximilian (Austria), in Mexico, **508,** 509
Mayflower (ship), 62
Mayflower Compact, 62
McCain, John, 826, 846–848, 847 (map)
McCarran Internal Security Act (1950), **705**
McCarthy, Eugene, 776
McCarthy, Joseph, and McCarthyism, **706**–707, 720–721, 735
McClellan, George B.: in Civil War, **358,** 359, 359 (map); Peninsular Campaign and, 362–363; 1864 election and, 376, 377
McClure's Magazine, 533
McCormick, Cyrus, 331, 332 (illus.)
McCormick Harvest Works, 480
McCracken, Henry Joy, 166
McCulloch v. Maryland, **239**
McDonald's, 717, 730, 741, 808
"McDonald's Approach to Business" (Kroc), 741
McDowell, Irvin, 358
McGillivray, Alexander, 204
McGovern, George, 789
McHenry, Fort, 223
McHenry, James, 187

McIntosh, Ebenezer, 112
McKay, Claude, 598
McKinley, William, 495; assassination of, 469, 525; 1896 election and, 505–507, 505 (illus.), 507 (map); Spanish-American War and, 513–515; Philippines and, 516–517; 1900 election and, 518; Panama Canal and, 541–542
McKinley Tariff, 495; Democrats and, 503, 504; sugar industry and, 512, 513
McLane, Louis, 253
McNamara, Robert, 748, 775
McNary-Haugen bill, 611
McVeigh, Timothy, 833
Meade, George E., 364 (map), 372, 373, 374
Means, Russell, 780
Measles, 20
Meat Inspection Act (1906), 533, 539
Meatpacking industry, **423,** 534 (illus.); Swift and, 431; Sinclair and, 533
Mechanical reaper, 331
Mechanization, 225; of textile industry, 270–271, 270 (illus.); in farming, 454, 475
Medal of Honor: for Latinos, 674
Media: in 1920s, 597; in 1960s, 770. *See also* specific media
Mediation, with Spain, **514**
Medicaid, 758 (table), **760,** 833; Nixon and, 787; abortions and, 800
Medical Care Act (1965), 758 (table), 760
Medicare, 757 (illus.), 758 (table), **760,** 828, 833; Nixon and, 787
Medicine: women in, 460, 472; homosexuality classified by, 462, 608. *See also* Disease; Doctors; Health; Healthcare
Medicine Lodge Creek treaties, 434, 435, 436
Mediterranean region: Barbary pirates in, 195, 196 (illus.), 218, 241; terrorists in, 812
Meek, Joe, 278 (illus.)
Meigs, Fort, 220
Mellon, Andrew, 609, 615, 624
Melodrama, 551
Meltdown: of reactor core, **800**
Memphis: race riot in, 399
Men: Indian, 11, 433; in New England colonies, 63–64; property rights of, 149–150; slave, 269; in middle class, 275; changing gender roles of, 460–461; wages of, 475, 475 (figure); in Great Depression, 643; in 1950s, 728–729; in suburban families, 733. *See also* Gender; Women
Mencken, H. L., 598

Mendez v. Westminster, **711,** 712 (illus.), 736
Menéndez de Aviles, Pedro, 37
Mennonites, 71
Mental health: Dorothea Dix and, 302; immigration and, 603
Mental retardation: Special Olympics and, 745, 767
Mercantile theory, 110
Mercenaries: Hessian, 136
Merchant marine, 221
Meredith, James, 750–751
"Merger movement" (1898–1902), 447–448
Mergers, 430; in manufacturing and mining (1895–1905), 448 (figure); in 1920s, 593
Meridian, 440
Merit system: for civil service, 499
Merrimac (ship), 362 (illus.)
Mesa Verde, Colorado, 13 (illus.)
Mestizos, 473
Metacomet (King Philip), **66,** 66 (illus.)
Methodists, 92, 201, 299, 301; African American, 202 (illus.), 203; alcohol and, 530
Metropolis, San Francisco as, **444**–445, 444 (illus.)
Meuse-Argonne campaign, in World War I, 574–575
Mexican Americans, 605–606; as cowboys, 439, 439 (illus.); as ranchers, 439; in California, 473; in New Mexico, 473; in Southwest, 473–474; as farm workers, 606 (illus.), 779, 779 (illus.), 793; in Great Depression, 643–644, 645–646; repatriation of, 644; after World War II, 674, 710–711; *La Causa* and, 771, 778–779
Mexican Revolution: United States and, 561–562, 561 (map)
Mexican War, 322–325, 323 (map), 326, 333, 473; Polk and, 322, 323, 324; criticism of, 323; Treaty of Guadalupe Hidalgo and, 325
Mexico: maize from, 7; Southwest Indians and, 11; society of, 11–12; Indians from, 32; Texas and, 228; California and, 283; Texas Revolution and, 312–314, 314 (map); borders with, 314, 315, 322, 323 (map), 325; immigrants from, 474, 810; Maximilian of Austria in, 508, 509; France and, 508–509, 513; U.S. and, 567, 616; Zimmermann telegram and, 567; nationalization in, 614. *See also* Aztecs; Mexican Americans; Mexican War
Mexico City, Mexican War and, 324, 325
Miami Indians, 165, 179, 180 (illus.)

National healthcare, 701, 704, 748, 830, 850
National Housing Act, 632
National Indian Youth Council, 780
National Industrial Recovery Act (NIRA), **630**
National Irrigation Association, 444
Nationalism, 511; after War of 1812, 238; Monroe and, 240–241, 242; in 1830, 254; Arab, 723–725
Nationalist Chinese government, 697, 698, 701, 726. *See also* China
Nationalists, 167; at constitutional convention, 168, 170–171
Nationalized resources: in Mexico, **614**
National Labor Reform Party, 453, 477
National Labor Relations Act (NLRA), *See* Wagner Act (1935)
National Labor Relations Board (NLRB), 636
National Labor Union (NLU), 453, **477**
National Organization for Women (NOW), **763,** 800, 830
National Origins Act (1924), **602**–603, 606
National Recovery Administration (NRA), **630,** 633, 640
National Republicans, 249, 259
National Review, 756
National Road, 254, 285
National security: Truman and, 697; George W. Bush and, 839
National Security Council (NSC), **697,** 813; **NSC #68 of, 698**
National Trades' Union, 305
National treasury system, 309
National Union for Social Justice, 634
National War Labor Board, 568
National Woman's Party, 608
National Woman Suffrage Association (NWSA), **499,** 500
National Women's Political Caucus, 763 (illus.)
National Youth Administration (NYA), **636,** 670
Nation of Islam, *See* Black Muslims
Native American Church, 473
Native Americans, *See* American Indians
Native Son (Wright), 648
Nativism, 469; immigrants and, 469, 602–603; Democrats and, 506, 507
Nativity, 402
NATO, *See* North Atlantic Treaty Organization
Nat Turner's Rebellion, 307, 307 (illus.)
Naturalization Act (1798), 188. *See also* Immigration entries
Naturalized citizen, **188,** 605
Natural resources, 416–417; Pinchot and, 539. *See also* Raw materials

Nauvoo, Illinois, 280
Navajo Indians, 13, 44, 46, 646 (illus.); reservation for, 435; as code talkers, 674
Navigation: by Polynesians, 10; Portuguese, 15–16; European, 17; on Mississippi River, 179; to West, 200–201
Navy: English, 31, 124, 212–213, 615; French, 144, 615; in Revolution, 144, 145 (map); impressment into, 212; in War of 1812, 219–221, 220 (illus.), 222–223; Barbary pirates and, 241; in Civil War, 354, 357, 362, 362 (illus.); in East Asia, 509; Mahan and, 510; expansion of, 510–511; in Spanish-American War, 515; Pacific bases for, 519; in World War I, 565–566, 565 (map), 566 (illus.); Italian, 615; Japanese, 615; Washington Naval Conference and, 615; in World War II, 661
Nazi Germany: annexations by, 658 (map); Jews and, 659; expansion by, 660 (map); extermination and concentration camps of, 660 (map), 680–681, 681 (illus.); nonaggression pact with Soviet Union, 661; treaty with Japan and Italy, 664; in World War II, 675; bombing of, 679. *See also* Germany; World War II
Nebraska, 334
Necessary and proper clause, 177
Negro American Baseball League, 689
Negro Renaissance, *See* Harlem Renaissance
"Negro spiritual," 299
Neighborhoods, working-class, 456
Neoclassicism, 296–297
Netherlands, 33; U.S. independence recognized by, 142; Hitler's invasion of, 661–662. *See also* Dutch; Holland
Neutrality, 178; Washington and, 178; Jefferson and, 211–212, 213; of Britain during Civil War, 358; in World War I, **563;** before World War II, 657–658; in Western Hemisphere, 661
Neutrality Act: of 1935, 657; of 1937, 658, 659; **of 1939, 661,** 662
Neutral rights: in World War I, 565
Nevis, 80
New Amsterdam, 37, 37 (illus.). *See also* New York (city)
New Brunswick: loyalists in, 154
"New Day" for America: Hoover on, 622
New Deal, 622, 628, 649–650; Bank Holiday during, 629; First Hundred Days, 629–632; Second Hundred

Days, 634–636, 658; Social Security and, 635–636; major legislation of, 637 (table); Latinos in, 645–646; women in, 646; American Indians in, 646–647
New Departure Democrats, **406**–407
New Echota, Treaty of, 258
New economics: Kennedy and, **748**
New England, 69 (map), 80; English colonies in, 54, 62–71, 73 (map); Indians in, 65–66; Dominion of, 67; European civilization in, 69 (map); farming in, 81; imperial wars in, 96; after Revolution, 149; slavery in, 152 (illus.); Shays's Rebellion and, 167; embargo and, 214; economy in, 224–225; putting-out system in, 270; Mexican War and, 323; manufacturing systems in, 417
New England Anti-Slavery Society, 304
New England Emigrant Aid Society, 336
Newfoundland, 97, 98, 148
New France, 38, 39, 69 (map); surrender to British, 98
New Freedom program, of Wilson, **547**
New Frontier, 747, 748, 780
New Guinea, 10
New Hampshire, 65, 173; constitution of, 161; at constitutional convention, 168
New Harmony, 299
New Helvetia, California, 283
"New immigrants": vs. "old immigrants," **469**
New international order: of George H. W. Bush, 815–816
New Jersey, 68, 70, 86, 173; in Revolution, 138, 143–144; voting rights in, 151, 161, 161 (illus.); constitution of, 161
New Jersey Plan, 169
New Left, 765
New Light Congregationalists, 92
"New Look": in 1950s fashion, 710
New Look national security policy, 718, **721,** 726–727
"New man": in politics, 247–252
New Mexico, 42, 283, 322, 324, 325, 360; Catholic missionaries in, 40–41; Hispanos in, 474
New Nationalism, 546
New Netherland, 36, 37, 46–47, 68
New Orleans, 463; Spain and, 166; in War of 1812, 219 (map), 223–224; in Civil War, 362; race riot in, 399; Hurricane Katrina in, 844–845. *See also* Mississippi River region
New Orleans: Battle of, 224
New Orleans Delta, 342
New Orleans Tribune, 395
Newport, Rhode Island, 81; battle in, 144

proportional, 162, 168–169; in Congress, 168–169; of slaves, 169; of slave and free states, 245 (map); Texas and California acquisition and, 328 (map)

Republic, 125; women in, 150–151; United States as, 160; democracy within, 160–161

Republicanism: under Jefferson, 193–196

Republican Party: formation of (1856), **336;** 1860 election and, 340–342, 342 (map); during Civil War, 389–390, 490; after Civil War, 398, 401, 490–491; Reconstruction and, 398, 400–401, 407, 408; in South, 403–406, 407, 408, 492, 788–789; division in, 407; terrorism against, 408; 1872 election and, 408–409, 409 (map); Carl Schurz in, 487–488; ethnicity, race, religion, and, 490–491; elephant symbol of, 491 (illus.); fifty-first Congress and, 495, 503; elections between 1896 and 1932, 506; under Taft, 541, 546–547; in 1920s, 609; 1924 election and, 609–610, 610 (map); in 1950s, 707, 719; 2000 election and, 826, 837–838, 838 (map); Obama presidency and, 826; Clinton and, 830, 833, 834–835; Contract with America and, 832. *See also* Election(s); Liberal Republican movement; Radical Republicans; Republicans; specific candidates and presidents

Republican Party (of Jefferson), 307; 1832 election and, 308

Republicans, 175, 178, 185; Jefferson and, 175, 177; partisan press and, 189; 1800 election and, 190–192, 193; 1802 elections and, 198–199; 1804 election and, 198–199; Yazoo affair and, 211; 1808 election and, 214; Bucktail faction of, 235, 236, 248; Van Buren as, 235; market economy and, 237. *See also* Election(s); Republican Party; specific candidates

"Republican womanhood," 151–152

Republic of Haiti, 197

Republic of Korea (ROK), *See* South Korea

Republic of Vietnam, 727

Repudiate, 393, 512

Repudiation, 178

Requerimiento, 36

Requisition, 347

Research: scientific, 91; on contraception, 608

Research and development (R&D): of Edison, 429; for World War II, 668; in 1950s, 729

Reservations, 204, 434–435, 435 (map), 780, 781 (map); Cherokee, 256; Dawes Act and, 471, 472. *See also* American Indians; Bureau of Indian Affairs

Resettlement Administration (RA), 639

Resistance: colonial, 93, 111–114, 115–116; by French Canadians, 107–108; Indian, 107–108; to Tea Act, 119–120; slave, 305–307, 306 (map); by Indians, 435–437. *See also* Protest(s)

Resources, *See* Natural resources

Restoration (England), **56,** 67

Restrictive covenants, in housing, **469,** 602

Retailing: mail-order business and, 423, 430

Retaliatory tariff, 244

Retrenchment policy, of Jackson, **251**

Return: on capital, 265; on investment, **424,** 431

Reuben James (ship), 663

Revenue: sources of, 111. *See also* Taxation

Revenue cutters, 357

Revenue stamps, 239

Revere, Paul, 117, 117 (illus.), 123

Reverse discrimination, 799

Revivalism: Great Awakening and, 91–92; in West, 282; Second Great Awakening and, 301 (illus.)

Revolts and rebellions: Pueblo, 41–42; by Bacon, 53–54; by Leisler, 69; Stono Rebellion, 88; by slaves, 88–89; by Paxton Boys, 89; in Haiti, 166; in Ireland, 166; by Shays, 167; Whiskey Rebellion, 178–179; Fries's Rebellion, 190; by Gabriel, 203; by Denmark Vesey, 230; in Philippines, 518–519; Boxer Rebellion, 520. *See also* Protest(s); Resistance; Riots; Violence

Revolution(s): 1800 election as, 192–193; in Texas, 312–314, 314 (map); of 1848 (Germany), 487; in Hawai'i, 512. *See also* American Revolution; French Revolution

Revolutionary War, *See* American Revolution

Revolvers, 370

Reykjavik, Iceland: summit meeting in, 814

Reynolds, R.J. (company), 704

Rhapsody in Blue (Gershwin), 599

Rhee, Syngman, 698

Rhineland, 658

Rhine River region: in World War II, 679

Rhode Island, 65, 174; religion in, 60; *Gaspée* and, 118; in Revolution, 138; antislavery campaign in, 153; at constitutional convention, 168

Rhythm and blues (R&B), 734

Rice: in Carolina, 72; plantation society and, 80, 84

Rice, Condoleezza, 839, 841–842

Richelieu, Cardinal (Armand-Emmanuel du Plessis), 38

Richmond, Virginia: Confederate capital in, **347;** in Civil War, 362, 378

Richmond Examiner, 342

Rickey, Branch, 689

Ridgeway, Matthew, 700

Riesman, David, 735

Rifle clubs, Democratic, 408

Rifled muskets, **370**

Right (political), **622.** *See also* New Right

Rights: of women, 64, 79; colonial, 114–117; property, 149–150; after Revolution, 149–150; democratic, 160; in French Revolution, 177; of Indians, 204; of squatters, 255 (illus.); Eleanor Roosevelt and, 644–645; of criminals, 756. *See also* Civil rights; Equal rights; States' rights

Rights of the British Colonists Asserted and Proved (Otis), 113

Right to Life movement, 800, 830

Right-to-work laws, 702

Riis, Jacob, 462, 463 (illus.)

Rio Bravo region, **284**

Rio Grande region: Spanish exploration of, 40; as Texas-Mexico border, 314, 315, 322

Rio Pact, 697

Riots: land, 89; anti-Catholic/anti-immigrant, 297 (illus.); by immigrant weavers, 305; in Civil War, 348 (illus.); against draft laws, 365, 366 (illus.); anti-Chinese, 470–471; racial, 572, 737; Zoot Suit, 674. *See also* Race riots

Ripley, George, 299

Ripon, Wisconsin, 334

Rittenhouse, David, 178

Rivera, Diego, 647, 647 (illus.)

Rivers: transportation on, 200–201, 200 (illus.). *See also* Waterways; specific river regions

Rivington, James, 112 (illus.)

Roads and highways, 237, 238, 285; national road and, 254; urban, 457; Federal Highway Act (1956) and, 720; in 1950–1960, 730, 730 (map). *See also* Automobiles and automobile industry

Roanoke Island, 33–34, 55

Roaring Twenties, 590, 595–600

Robeson, Paul, 598

Robinson, Jackie, 689–690, 689 (illus.), 712

Rochambeau, Comte de (Jean-Baptiste-Donatien de Vimeur), 147

Rockefeller, John D., 414, 415 (illus.), 426; competition and, 415–416; Standard Oil and, 427–428; vertical and horizontal integration by, 427 (figure); on big business, 449; hookworm eradication and, 536 (illus.); bomb sent to, 582

Rockefeller Foundation, contraception research and, 608

"Rockefeller interests," 428

Rockefeller Sanitary Commission for the Eradication of Hookworm Disease, 536 (illus.)

Rocket-propelled grenade (RPG) launcher, 843 (illus.)

Rockingham, Lord (Charles Watson-Wentworth), 114

Rock 'n' roll, 734–735

Rock Springs, Wyoming: anti-Chinese violence in, 470–471

Rocky Mountains, 198

Roe v. Wade, 400, **800**, 830; opponents of, 829 (illus.)

Rogers, Edith Norse, 671

Rolfe, John, 58

Rolling Stones, 766

Roman Catholic Church, *See* Catholicism

Romania, 662, 679; communism in, 817

Romanticism, 294–297

Roney, Frank, 453, 453 (illus.), 476, 477, 483

Roosevelt, Eleanor, 636, 643 (illus.); New Deal and, 629, 644–645; civil rights and, 644 (illus.), 645

Roosevelt, Franklin D., 461; presidency and, 553; 1920 election and, 584; 1932 election and, 624 (map), 627–628, 628 (map); Bonus Army and, 627; New Deal and, 629–641; polio of, 629 (illus.); and Supreme Court, 635; 1936 election and, 640; 1933–1939, 656; death of, 656, 680; 1940 election and, 661, 662; 1944 election and, 670; at Tehran, 678; at Yalta, 679–680, 680 (illus.). *See also* New Deal; World War II

Roosevelt, Theodore, 515; Japanese immigration and, 471, 544; Rough Riders of, 515; Spanish-American War and, 515; 1900 election and, 518; coal mine strike and, 525; as mediator, 526, 544; meatpacking industry and, 533, 534 (illus.); muckrakers and, 533, 539; 1912 election and, 537 (illus.), 546–547; progressivism and, 538; anti-trust actions and, 538–539; presidency and, 538–539, 553; Square Deal of, 539; trustbusting by, 539; 1908 election and, 540, 541, 541

(illus.); foreign policy of, 541, 545; arbitration treaties and, 544; Great White Fleet and, 545, 545 (illus.); on presidential powers, 554

Roosevelt Corollary, 543, 544 (illus.)

Roosevelt's recession, 640

Root, Elihu, 525

Rose Bowl game: World War II and, 666

Rosecrans, William S., 367, 373

Rosenberg, Ethel and Julius, 705–706

Rosie the Riveter, 672, 672 (illus.)

Ross, John, 258

Rossiter, Thomas Pritchard, 169 (illus.)

Rotation system: under Jackson, 251

Rough Riders, 515, 516 (illus.)

Roundups, 439

Rousseau, Jean-Jacques, 79, 90

Route 66, 639 (map)

Royal Air Force (Britain), 662

Royal colonies: New France as, 39; Maryland as, 61; North and South Carolina as, 72

Royal navy, *See* Navy

Royal Society of London, 91

Rubenstein, Helena, 622

Ruby, Jack, 755

Rubyfruit Jungle (Brown), 764

Ruhr Valley, 614

Ruiz, Raul, 779

Rumsfeld, Donald, 839, 841

Runaway slaves, 329

Running away, as slave resistance, 306–307, 306 (map)

Runoff election, 246

Rural areas: workers from, 274, 275, 475; Second Great Awakening in, 301; urban growth and, 414, 453; mail-order business and, 430; population of (1860–1910), 454 (figure); education in, 459; poverty in, 828. *See also* Agriculture; Farms and farming

Rural Electrification Administration (REA), 639–640

Rush, Benjamin, 153

Rush-Bagot Agreement, 241

Russia: American frontier of, 40; Napoleon and, 213; expansionism of, 315; immigrants from, 440; World War I and, 576, 577–578; Communists in, 576 (illus.); after World War I, 578, 579 (map). *See also* Soviet Union

Russian-German immigrants, **442**

Russo-Japanese War, 546

Rust Belt, 808

Rutgers University, 92, 708–709

Ruth, Babe, 597

Rwanda: genocide in, 836

Ryswick, Treaty of, 96, 99 (table)

Sabbath: activities on, 64; observance of, 302–303

Saboteurs, 842

Sacajawea, 197–198

Sacco, Nicola, 582

Sadat, Anwar, 801 (illus.), 802

Saddam Hussein, 818, 819 (map), 826, 836, 841, 842, 843

Safe Drinking Water Act, 788

Sahara Desert, 14 (illus.), 15 (illus.). *See also* Sub-Saharan Africa

Saigon: in Vietnam War, 774 (map), 784, 785 (illus.), 792

Sailors: British impressment of, 212, 212 (illus.)

Saint Augustine, 37, 42

Saint-Domingue, 100, **196,** 197

Sainthood: in Puritan church, **64,** 67

St. Kitts, 80

St. Lawrence River region, 43, 201

St. Lawrence Seaway Act (1954), 720

St. Leger, Barry, 138, 139–140

Saint-Lô, 679

St. Louis, 283, 285, 455; Civil War and, 348; growth of, 454, 456

St. Mihiel salient, battle at, 574

Saipan, battle for, 682

Salem: Roger Williams and, 64–65

Salem, Peter, 127 (illus.)

Salem Village: witchcraft and, 67–68, 68 (illus.)

Salerno, 678

Sales: in automobile industry, 592–593

Salient, 574

Salinas Valley, 323

Salinger, J. D., 735

Salk, Jonas, 720

SALT agreements: SALT I, 786; SALT II, 801

Salutary neglect policy, **93**

Salvation, 64

Same-sex civil unions, 844

Same-sex marriage, 831, 844

Same-sex relations, 461, 608

Samoa, 10, **519**

San Antonio, 313

Sanchez, Juan, 809

San Diego, 282, 671

Sandinistas: in Nicaragua, 811, 818

Sandino, Augusto, 614

S&Ls, *See* Savings and loan industry

San Francisco: growth of, 444–445, 444 (illus.), 454; Chinese in, 470, 471; strike in, 633; Asians segregated in, 644

San Gabriel Mission, 283 (illus.)

Sanger, Margaret, 528, 532

Sanitation: in cities, 86; slaves and, 268; urban, 274, 457; in Civil War camps, 369–370

War in, 360–362, 361 (map); railroads in, 420, 433 (map), 437–438; Indians in, 432–437; cattle in, 433 (map), 438–440; in late nineteenth century, 433 (map); mining in, 433 (map), 440; reservations in, 435 (map); climate of, 440, 441 (map); farming in, 440–443; agribusiness in, 442–443; lumber industry in, 443–444; water in, 444, 596; San Francisco and, 444–445; Chinese in, 470–471; regional distribution of population by race (1900), 470 (figure); Japanese in, 471; Mexican Americans in, 473–474, 779; woman suffrage in, 499–500, 500 (illus.); race relations in, 604–605; dam construction in, 636; World War II and economic expansion in, 668; migration to, 671. *See also* Northwest Ordinances; Northwest Territory; Westward movement; specific cities and states

West Africa, 15, 17 (illus.); free black colony in, 153

West Berlin, 753. *See also* Berlin entries

Western bloc: NATO and, 693 (map)

Western Defense District: in World War II, 666

Western front, in World War I, **563**

Western Hemisphere, 4–5, 513; Monroe Doctrine and, 242; neutrality in, 661; Castro in, 772. *See also* Colonies and colonization; New World; specific locations

West Germany, 695 (map), 723, 728; German unification and, 816. *See also* Germany

West Indies: loyalists in, 153

Westmoreland, William, 773, 775, 776

West Point, 147, 347

West Virginia, 347

West Virginia (ship), 665 (illus.)

Westward movement, 180 (illus.), 227 (illus.), 730 (map); Jay's Treaty and, 180; under Jefferson, 195–198, 198 (map), 210; social stress and, 199–201; Tecumseh and, 216 (map); in 1830s and 1840s, 278–280; manifest destiny and, 311–316. *See also* American Indians; West

Wethersfield, 65

Weyl, Walter, 524

Weyler, Valeriano, 513

"What to the Slave Is the Fourth of July?" (Douglass), 349

Wheat, 81; prices of (1868–1900), 419 (figure); farms and, 442–443

Wheatley, Phillis, 153, 153 (illus.)

Wheeler, Burton K., 662

Wheelwright, 201

Whig Party, 326, 338; formation of, **308,** 308 (illus.); 1836 election and, 309; 1840 election and, 310–311, 310 (illus.), 311 (map); conscience Whigs, 333. *See also* Election(s)

Whiskey, 297; tax on, 178–179, 179 (illus.)

Whiskey Rebellion, 178–179, 179 (illus.)

Whiskey Ring, 492

White, Elijah, 315

White, Hugh Lawson, 309

White backlash, 762

White-collar reformers, 303

White-collar workers, 275, 430, 731

Whitefield, George, 92, 92 (illus.)

"White man's burden," 511

White Plains: battle at, 138

Whites: black slaves and, 83; population of, 87; in antebellum South, 264–267; in post–Civil War South, 395–396, 397–398; Alliances and, 502; school integration and, 737; southern voting rights and, 758–759. *See also* African Americans; American Indians

White supremacy, 303, 304, 388, **398,** 409, 410, 466

Whitman, Walt, 295

Whitney, Eli, 227

Whitney, William C., 510

Whyte, William H., 735

Wichita Indians, 43, 433

Wilburforce, William, 246

Wilderness, The, battle of, 374, 375 (map)

Wilderness Act (1964), 758 (table)

"Wilderness Zion," 64

Wildlife: BP oil spill and, 851, 852 (illus.)

Wild West Show, of Buffalo Bill, 472 (illus.)

Wilhelm (Germany), 577

Wilkinson, James, 211

Willard, Frances, 460, 500

William and Mary (England), 56, 67

Williams, Evan, 825–826

Williams, George Washington, 410

Williams, Roger, 64–65

Williamsburg, 59 (illus.)

Willkie, Wendell, 662

Wilmot, David, 324

Wilmot Proviso, 324, 327, 329 (illus.)

Wilson, Charles E., 721, 729

Wilson, Edith Bolling, 580

Wilson, Woodrow: Caribbean region and, 543; democratic progressivism and, 546; 1912 election and, 546–547, 549; presidency and, 548, 553; domestic issues and, 548–549; reform and, 548–549; 1916 election and, 549, 567; foreign policy of, 560–562; Mexican revolution and, 561–562, 561 (map); neutrality and, 563; World War I and, 567–568, 569–570; Allied Powers and, 577, 578; Fourteen Points and, 577, 585; Paris Peace Conference and, 578; illness of, 580

Windsor, Connecticut, 65

Winnebago Indians, 255, 278

"Winning Rights for Farm Workers" (Huerta), 793

Winthrop, John, 63, 65–66, 311

Wirt, William, 308

Wisconsin, 164; glaciation in, 5; reforms in, 535–536

Wisconsin Idea, 536

Witchcraft trials: in Salem Village, 67–68, 68 (illus.)

Wizard of Oz, The (Baum), 503 (illus.)

Wobblies, *See* Industrial Workers of the World

Wolcott, Oliver, 187

Wolf, Charlie, 573 (illus.)

Wolfe, James, 98

Wolf Meetings, 312, 315

Woman in the Nineteenth Century (Fuller), 296

Woman's Christian Temperance Union (WCTU), **460,** 461 (illus.)

Woman suffrage, 399, 402, 460, 499–500, 500 (illus.), 501 (table), 502, 503, 529, 530 (illus.); WCTU and, 460; Willard and, 500; around the world, 501 (table); Prohibition Party and, 502; Populists and, 503; ratification of, 583–584; Nineteenth Amendment and, 608. *See also* Voting and voting rights; Women

Women: American Indian, 11, 433; in New England colonies, 63–64; rights of, 64, 79; Quakers and, 71 (illus.); opportunities for, 82; as workers, 87, 87 (illus.), 275, 475, 568, 569 (illus.), 608, 643, 671–672, 671 (figure), 672 (illus.), 829; colonial resistance by, 116; fund-raising by, 133; property rights of, 149; after Revolution, 150–152; education for, 152; social roles of, 202; as missionaries, 262, 289; in plantation society, 265–266; African American, 267; free blacks in South, 267; slave, 267, 269, 298; in textile factories, 271, 305; in middle class, 275; genteel, 277; as pioneers, 280, 281, 281 (illus.); literature and, 293–294, 296; working-class, 298; Second Great Awakening and, 300; in anti-slavery movement, 304; Sojourner Truth, 325, 326 (illus.); during Civil

Yosemite National Park: water and, 444
Young, Brigham, 280
Young, Charles, 559–560
Young, Ellsworth, 570 (illus.)
Young America Movement, 333–334
Young Lords, 779
Young Men's Christian Association
    (YMCA), 460

Young people: in middle class,
    275–276; in 1920s, 600; in 1950s,
    734–735
Youth culture: youth movement of 1960s
    and, 764–765
Yugoslavia: German invasion of, 662;
    breakup of, 816 (map)
Yuppies, 809

Zahn, Barbara, 765
Zavala, Lorenzo de, 474
Zhou Enlai, 786, 786 (illus.)
Zimmermann, Arthur, 567
Zola, Émile, 550
Zones of occupation, *See* Occupation
    zones
Zoot suits, 674

GREENLAND
(DENMARK)

ICELAND

ALASKA
(U.S.)

60°N

CANADA

I
K
IRELAND

40°N

UNITED STATES

Azores
(Port.)

PORTUGAL

MOR

Bermuda
(U.K.)

ATLANTIC OCEAN

WESTERN
SAHARA
(MOROCCO)

Midway Is.
(U.S.)

BAHAMAS

DOMINICAN REP.

Hawaiian Is.
(U.S.)

MEXICO

CUBA
JAMAICA
BELIZE
HONDURAS

HAITI

Virgin Is.
(U.S.)

Puerto Rico
(U.S.)

ST. KITTS AND NEVIS
ANTIGUA AND BARBUDA
DOMINICA
BARBADOS
ST. LUCIA
GRENADA
ST. VINCENT AND
THE GRENADINES

20°N

MAURITAN

CAPE
VERDE

SENEGAL
GAMBIA

PACIFIC OCEAN

GUATEMALA
EL SALVADOR

NICARAGUA

GUINEA-BISSAU

GUINEA

COSTA RICA

TRINIDAD AND TOBAGO

SIERRA
LEONE

IV
CO

PANAMA

VENEZUELA

GUYANA

LIBERIA

G

FR. GUIANA
(FRANCE)

EQU

COLOMBIA

SURINAM

Equator

Galapagos Is.
(Ecuador)

ECUADOR

0°

SÃO TOMÉ

PERU

BRAZIL

SAMOA

French Polynesia
(France)

BOLIVIA

TONGA

20°S

PARAGUAY

Easter Is.
(Chile)

CHILE

0   1,000   2,000 Km.

URUGUAY

0   1,000   2,000 Mi.

ARGENTINA

40°S

Falkland Is.
(U.K.)

160°W   140°W   120°W   100°W   80°W   60°W   40°W   20°W

60°S